ANNUAL VOLUME
OF
STATUTORY INSTRUMENTS 1971
Please insert this correction slip in
Section 1 of Part I

On page v, in para. 1, in line 2, *for* 1968 *read* 1971

On page vi, in para. 6, in lines 4 and 8, *for* 1971/4 *read* 1971/1

December 1971

LONDON: Her Majesty's Stationery Office

(340294)

STATUTORY INSTRUMENTS

1971

PART I
(in two Sections)

SECTION 1

Published by Authority

LONDON
HER MAJESTY'S STATIONERY OFFICE
1971

© *Crown copyright* 1971

PRINTED AND PUBLISHED BY HER MAJESTY'S STATIONERY OFFICE

To be purchased from

49 High Holborn, LONDON, WC1V 6HB
13a Castle Street, EDINBURGH, EH2 3AR   109 St. Mary Street, CARDIFF, CF1 1JW
Brazennose Street, MANCHESTER, M60 8AS   50 Fairfax Street, BRISTOL, BS1 3DE
258 Broad Street, BIRMINGHAM, B1 2HE   80 Chichester Street, BELFAST, BT1 4JY

or through Booksellers

1971

Price for the two Sections: £12·20 net

PRINTED IN ENGLAND

SBN 11 840087 8*

Contents of the Volume

PART I, Section 1

PART I, Section 2

PART II

PART III

Preface

Scope and arrangement of the Volume

1. This volume gives the full text of the statutory instruments registered in the year 1978 which were classified as general, and gives particulars of those which were classified as local(**a**). Other instruments are contained in the Appendix (as to which see para. 3, below).

2. The general instruments are arranged according to their S.I. numbers(**b**), that is to say, in the order of their registration as statutory instruments. The volume is published in three Parts, containing the instruments registered between 1st January and 30th April, 1st May and 31st August, and 1st September and 31st December respectively.

Contents of the Volume

3. **Parts I and II.** At the beginning of each of these Parts is a list of the instruments whose text is contained in that Part, showing their S.I. numbers and titles. The list is followed by the text of the statutory instruments registered in the relevant period and an **Appendix of Instruments not registered as Statutory Instruments** issued in that period. This Appendix includes Orders in Council issued under the royal prerogative or otherwise outside the definition of a statutory instrument, Royal Proclamations which are of a legislative nature, and Letters Patent and Royal Instructions which relate to the constitutions, etc. of overseas territories.

At the end of each Part is a Table showing the modifications to legislation and an Index. Each Table is confined to the instruments in its own Part and gives particulars of those Acts and instruments which have been amended, extended, excluded, repealed or revoked by instruments in the Part. The Index to Part II will be cumulative to both Parts.

4. **Part III.** At the beginning is a list of the instruments in Part III similar to the lists in Parts I and II. It is followed by the text of the instruments comprising Part III, as in Parts I and II.

At the end of Part III are the features which are required by reg. 10 of the Statutory Instruments Regulations 1947 to be included in the Annual Volume of Statutory Instruments. They cover the instruments in all three Parts. In the order in which they occur in the Volume, they are as follows:—

The **Classified List of Local Instruments** gives particulars, including the S.I. numbers, of all local statutory instruments registered in the S.I. series of the year to which the Annual Volume relates. They are grouped in classes according to their subject-matter.

(**a**) *See* Statutory Instruments Regulations 1947 (S.I. 1948/1 (Rev. XXI, p. 498: 1948 I, p. 4002)), reg. 4 of which provides that S.I. which are in the nature of public general Acts of Parliament shall be classified as general and those which are in the nature of local and personal or private Acts shall be classified as local.

(**b**) Reg. 3 of the Statutory Instruments Regulations 1947 provides for instruments to be numbered in a separate series for each calendar year. Certain instruments bear a subsidiary number—

    C.   Commencement Orders (bringing an Act or part of an Act into operation).
    L.   Instruments relating to fees or procedure in courts in England or Wales.
    S.   Instruments made by a Scottish rule-making authority and applying to Scotland only.

The **Tables.** " Table A " gives particulars of the Acts of Parliament, and " Table B " particulars of statutory and other instruments, the operation of which was affected by the instruments appearing in the Volume. They include the information as to amendments, repeals, revocations, etc., already given in tables of " Modifications to Legislation " in Parts I and II and corresponding information with respect to the instruments in Part III, and also give particulars of Acts or instruments modified or restricted by general instruments throughout the Volume. In addition, Table B gives particulars of general instruments whose operation was affected expressly by Public General Acts of the year in question, or which ceased to operate through becoming spent during that year as a result of legislation of the year.

The **Numerical and Issue List** gives particulars of all statutory instruments which were printed and put on sale by the Queen's Printer of Acts of Parliament under the provisions of the Statutory Instruments Act 1946(a), during the year, with the date of first issue by Her Majesty's Stationery Office.

The **Index** will be cumulative to Parts I and II.

Definition of a statutory instrument

5. To determine whether or not any instrument is required to be a statutory instrument, reference must be made to s. 1 of the Statutory Instruments Act 1946, reg. 2 of the Statutory Instruments Regulations 1947, and arts. 1 and 2 of the Statutory Instruments (Confirmatory Powers) Order 1947(b).

The definition of what constitutes a statutory instrument, as respects instruments made under Acts passed before the commencement (1 Jan. 1948) of the 1946 Act, is governed by definitions contained in the Rules Publication Act 1893(c) (which was repealed and replaced by the 1946 Act); for those made under Acts passed after the commencement of the 1946 Act, the document is a statutory instrument if it is an Order in Council or if it is made by a Minister of the Crown and the Act provides that the power is to be exerciseable by statutory instrument.

Citation

6. For the purposes of citation, most statutory instruments are given a title. In addition, all statutory instruments may be identified by the year and number. The first instrument in Part I of this Volume would, by this method, be cited as " S.I. 1971/4 ". When a statutory instrument is referred to in another statutory instrument, a lettered footnote is provided in the latter, giving the identification of the first instrument as above, and also its Part and page reference in the Annual Volume. The footnote reference for the same instrument would therefore be " S.I. 1971/4 (1971 I, p. 1) ".

If the text of the instrument is set out in the current edition of *S.R. & O. and S.I. Revised* (Third Edition, as at 31st Dec., 1948) the footnote references give the volume reference in that edition as well as the page reference in the Annual Volume (see, for example, footnote (b) below). If a footnote contains the references of a number of instruments, they may in certain circumstances be run together, so as to give all the instrument numbers together and all the volume references together, e.g. " S.R. & O. 1946/157; S.I. 1948/1073, 1961/ 1942 (1946 II, p. 26; 1948 II, p. 13; 1961 III, p. 2650) ".

(a) 1946 c. 36.   (b) S.I. 1948/2 (Rev. XXI, p. 504: 1948 I, p. 4008).
(c) 1893 c. 66.

Production in Court

7. Under section 2 of the Documentary Evidence Act 1868**(a)**, read with section 2 of the Documentary Evidence Act 1882**(b)**, *prima facie* evidence of any proclamation, order or regulation made by certain rule-making authorities may be given in courts of justice by production of a copy purporting to be printed by the Government Printer or under the superintendence or authority of Her Majesty's Stationery Office. The Act of 1868 has since been extended by numerous Acts**(c)** to rules, etc., made thereunder by other rule-making authorities. The copies of proclamations, orders, regulations, etc., made by the authorities referred to above as printed in these volumes may therefore be produced as *prima facie* evidence.

Up to date information on statutory instruments

8. The *Index to Government Orders* contains, under subject headings, summaries of all powers to make subordinate legislation conferred by statute on H.M. in Council, the Privy Council, government departments and certain other public bodies. Below each summary appear particulars of any general instruments made in exercise of it which were in force at the date of publication of the *Index*. Details are also given of certain instruments made under prerogative powers. The work contains also a Table of Statutes showing the subject headings under which references to particular sections of enabling Acts appear. (The *Index* is published every two years by H.M.S.O.)

9. Information as to whether any instrument is still in operation, or whether anything has happened to it since it was made, can be obtained from the *Table of Government Orders*. This Table lists general statutory rules and orders and statutory instruments in numerical order, and gives the history of those which have been affected (i.e. revoked, amended, etc.) by subsequent legislation, whether statute or subordinate legislation, identifying the Act or instrument in question. Where any instrument has been amended, the Table gives particulars of the article, section, rule, etc., affected. A user who is interested in one particular provision only of the earlier instrument can thus ascertain whether or not he need consult the text of the amending enactment at all. The *Table of Government Orders* is published annually by H.M.S.O. and is cumulative. A Noter-Up is issued twice yearly.

Authority for Publication

10. The Annual Volumes of Statutory Instruments are published in pursuance of reg. 10 of the Statutory Instruments Regulations 1947 and are prepared under the direction of the Statute Law Committee. Any suggestion or communication relating to their contents should be addressed to the Editor, Statutory Publications Office, Queen Anne's Chambers, 41, Tothill Street, S.W.1.

(a) 1868 c. 37.   **(b)** 1882 c. 9.
(c) *See* the entries relating to extensions of the 1868 Act in the *Chronological Table of the Statutes*.

Abbreviations

Addnl. Instructions ...	Additional Instructions.
A.S.	Act of Sederunt.
am., amdg., amdt. ...	amended, amending, amendment.
appx.	appendix.
assocn.	association.
art(s).	article(s).
authy.	authority.
bd(s).	board(s).
c.	chapter(s).
cl(s).	clause(s).
Cmd., Cmnd.	Command Paper.
cont.	continued.
ctee.	committee.
ct(s).	court(s).
E.	England.
ext.	extended.
G.B.	Great Britain.
gen.	generally.
govt.	government.
H.C.	House of Commons Paper.
H.M.	Her Majesty, Her Majesty's.
incl.	included, including.
instrt.	instrument.
Is.	Island(s).
L.P.	Letter Patent.
Min(s).	Minister(s).
misc.	miscellaneous.
mod., mod(s).	modified, modification(s).
N.	North.
N.I.	Northern Ireland.
No.	number.
O.	Order(s).
O. in C., O. of C. ...	Order(s) in Council, Order(s) of Council.
p., pp.	page(s).
para(s).	paragraph(s).
prosp.	prospectively.
prov.	provisional, proviso.
pt.	part.
r.	revoked.
R.C.	Rules of the Court of Session.
R. Instructions	Royal Instructions.
R. Warrant	Royal Warrant.
reg(s).	regulation(s).
rep.	repealed.
retrosp.	retrospectively.
Rev.	Statutory Rules and Orders and Statutory Instruments Revised (Third Edition, 1948).
Rev. 1903	Statutory Rules and Orders Revised (Second Edition, 1903).
revn.	revocation.
S.	Scotland.
s., ss.	section(s).
sch(s).	schedule(s).

S.I. ...	...	...	...	Statutory Instrument(s).
S.R. & O. ...	...	...	Statutory Rule(s) and Order(s).
sch(s).	...	...	...	schedule(s).
Secy.	...	...	...	Secretary.
susp.	...	...	...	suspended.
temp.	...	...	...	temporarily.
transfd.	...	...	...	transferred.
Treas.	...	...	...	Treasury.
U.K.	...	...	...	United Kingdom of Great Britain and Northern Ireland.
vol.	...	...	...	volume.
W. ...	...	...	...	Wales.

Statutory Instruments in Part I

OTHER INSTRUMENTS IN PART I

STATUTORY INSTRUMENTS

1971 No. 1

THEATRES

The Theatres (Licence Application Fees) (Amendment) Order 1971

Made - - -	*1st January* 1971
Laid before Parliament	*11th January* 1971
Coming into Operation	*15th February* 1971

In exercise of the powers conferred on me by paragraph 3(1) and (2) of Schedule 1 to the Theatres Act 1968(a), I hereby make the following Order:—

1. This Order may be cited as the Theatres (Licence Application Fees) (Amendment) Order 1971 and shall come into operation on 15th February 1971.

2. In Articles 1(2)(*a*) and 3 of the Theatres (Licence Application Fees) Order 1968(b), for the sum "£1 5s. 0d.", in both places where it occurs, there shall be substituted the sum "£1·25".

3. In Articles 1(2)(*b*) and 2(1) of the said Order of 1968 for the sum "7s. 6d.", in both places where it occurs, there shall be substituted the sum "£0·35".

R. Maudling,
One of Her Majesty's Principal
Secretaries of State.

Home Office,
 Whitehall.
1st January 1971.

EXPLANATORY NOTE

(This Note is not part of the Order.)

This Order amends the Theatres (Licence Application Fees) Order 1968 and comes into operation on 15th February 1971.

The Order of 1968 provides for fees of £1 5s. 0d. and 7s. 6d. and of multiples of those sums. The present Order substitutes, for the first of these sums, the decimal equivalent and, for the second, the lesser sum of £0·35 (7s. 0d.).

(a) 1968 c. 54.   **(b)** S.I. 1968/1315 (1968 II, p. 3645).

STATUTORY INSTRUMENTS

1971 No. 2

CUSTOMS AND EXCISE

The Anti-Dumping Duty Order 1967 (Revocation) Order 1971

Made - - -	*5th January* 1971
Laid before the House of Commons - -	*11th January* 1971
Coming into Operation	*12th January* 1971

The Secretary of State, in exercise of his powers under sections 1, 2, 10(3), 15(4) and 18(2) of the Customs Duties (Dumping and Subsidies) Act 1969**(a)**, hereby orders as follows:—

1.—(1) This Order may be cited as the Anti-Dumping Duty Order 1967 (Revocation) Order 1971 and shall come into operation on 12th January 1971.

(2) The Interpretation Act 1889**(b)** shall apply to the interpretation of this Order as it applies to the interpretation of an Act of Parliament and as if this Order and the Orders hereby revoked were Acts of Parliament.

2. The Anti-Dumping Duty Order 1967**(c)** and the Anti-Dumping Duty (Temporary Suspension) Order 1970**(d)** are hereby revoked.

Anthony Grant,
Parliamentary Under Secretary of State,
Department of Trade and Industry.

5th January 1971.

EXPLANATORY NOTE

(*This Note is not part of the Order.*)

This Order removes the anti-dumping duties imposed by the Anti-Dumping Duty Order 1967 on stearine originating in Australia or Belgium. These duties have been suspended since 31st January 1970.

(a) 1969 c. 16.

(b) 1889 c. 63.

(c) S.I. 1967/553 (1967 I, p. 1767).

(d) S.I. 1970/98 (1970 I, p. 451).

STATUTORY INSTRUMENTS

1971 No. 7

AGRICULTURE

The Price Stability of Imported Products (Rates of Levy) (Eggs) (No. 1) Order 1971

Made - - - - *4th January* 1971

Coming into Operation *5th January* 1971

The Minister of Agriculture, Fisheries and Food, in exercise of the powers conferred upon him by section 1(2), (4), (5), (6) and (7) of the Agriculture and Horticulture Act 1964(**a**) and of all other powers enabling him in that behalf, hereby makes the following order:—

1. This order may be cited as the Price Stability of Imported Products (Rates of Levy) (Eggs) (No. 1) Order 1971, and shall come into operation on 5th January 1971.

2.—(1) In this order—

" the Principal Order " means the Price Stability of Imported Products (Levy Arrangements) (Eggs) Order 1970(**b**) as amended by any subsequent order, and if any such order is replaced by any subsequent order the expression shall be construed as a reference to such subsequent order;

AND other expressions have the same meaning as in the Principal Order.

(2) The Interpretation Act 1889(**c**) shall apply to the interpretation of this order as it applies to the interpretation of an Act of Parliament and as if this order and the order hereby revoked were Acts of Parliament.

3. In accordance with and subject to the provisions of the Principal Order (which provides for the charging of levies on imports of those eggs and egg products which are specified commodities for the purposes of the Agriculture and Horticulture Act 1964) the rate of general levy for such imports into the United Kingdom of any specified commodity as are described in column 2 of the Schedule to this order in relation to a tariff heading indicated·in column 1 of that Schedule shall be the rate set forth in relation thereto in column 3 of that Schedule.

4. The Price Stability of Imported Products (Rates of Levy) (Eggs) (No. 16) Order 1970(**d**) is hereby revoked.

In Witness whereof the Official Seal of the Minister of Agriculture, Fisheries and Food is hereunto affixed on 4th January 1971.

(L.S.)

G. P. Jupe,
Assistant Secretary.

(a) 1964 c. 28.   (b) S.I. 1970/359 (1970 I, p. 1277).   (c) 1889 c. 63.
(d) S.I. 1970/1993 (1970 III, p. 6501).

SCHEDULE

1. Tariff Heading	2. Description of Imports	3. Rate of General Levy
	Imports of:—	
04.05	*Birds' eggs (in shell or not in shell), fresh, dried or otherwise preserved, sweetened or not, other than egg yolks:*	(per 120 eggs) *s. d.*
	A. Eggs in shell:	
	1. Not exceeding 11 lb. in weight per 120 ..	2 6 [12½p]
	2. Over 11 lb. but not exceeding 12½ lb. in weight per 120	2 6 [12½p]
	3. Over 12¼ lb. but not exceeding 14 lb. in weight per 120	2 6 [12½p]
	4. Over 14 lb. but not exceeding 15½ lb. in weight per 120	3 0 [15p]
	5. Over 15½ lb. but not exceeding 17 lb. in weight per 120	4 6 [22½p]
	6. Over 17 lb. in weight per 120	3 6 [17½p]
	B. Eggs not in shell:	(per ton)
	Whole dried	£100

EXPLANATORY NOTE

(This Note is not part of the Order.)

This order, which comes into operation on 5th January 1971, supersedes the Price Stability of Imported Products (Rates of Levy) (Eggs) (No. 16) Order 1970. It—

(a) increases the rates of general levy on imports of eggs in shell in each of the weight grades which are numbered 1 to 5 in the Schedule to the order ;

(b) reimposes unchanged the rates of general levy to be charged on imports of eggs in the weight grade numbered 6 in the schedule and of whole dried eggs not in shell, which were in force immediately before the commencement of this order.

1971 No. 13

TELEGRAPHS

The Wireless Telegraphy (Broadcast Licence Charges & Exemption) Amendment (No. 1) Regulations 1971

Made - - -	*5th January* 1971
Laid before Parliament	18*th January* 1971
Coming into Operation	1*st February* 1971

The Minister of Posts and Telecommunications, with the consent of the Treasury, in the exercise of his powers under sections 1 and 2 of the Wireless Telegraphy Act 1949(**a**), by the said sections as extended to the Channel Islands by the Wireless Telegraphy (Channel Islands) Order 1952(**b**) and by the said sections as extended to the Isle of Man by the Wireless Telegraphy (Isle of Man) Order 1952(**c**), and of every other power enabling him in that behalf hereby makes the following Regulations :—

1.—(1) These Regulations shall come into operation on the 1st February 1971 and may be cited as the Wireless Telegraphy (Broadcast Licence Charges & Exemption) Amendment (No. 1) Regulations 1971.

(2) The Interpretation Act 1889(**d**) shall apply for the interpretation of these Regulations as it applies for the interpretation of an Act of Parliament.

2. The Wireless Telegraphy (Broadcast Licence Charges & Exemption) Regulations 1970(**e**) shall be amended as follows :—
   (*a*) by substituting in Regulation 3 thereof for the words "1st April 1971" the words "1st February 1971" ;
   (*b*) by substituting in paragraph (2) of Regulation 4 where the words "31st March 1971" appear the words "31st January 1971" ;
   (*c*) by deleting the last two entries in the third and fourth columns of item 1 of Schedule 2 thereof.

Dated 1st January 1971.

Christopher Chataway,
Minister of Posts and Telecommunications.

We consent to these Regulations.

V. H. Goodhew,
Bernard Weatherill,
Two of the Commissioners of
Her Majesty's Treasury.

5th January 1971.

(**a**) 1949 c. 54.   (**b**) S.I. 1952/1900 (1952 III, p. 3414).
(**c**) S.I. 1952/1899 (1952 III, p. 3418).   (**d**) 1889 c. 63.
(**e**) S.I. 1970/548 (1970 I, p. 1753).

EXPLANATORY NOTE

(This Note is not part of the Regulations.)

These Regulations amend the Wireless Telegraphy (Broadcast Licence Charges & Exemption) Regulations 1970 by bringing forward from the 1st April 1971 to the 1st February 1971 the date for the exemption of the requirement of a licence for the installation and use of apparatus for the reception of certain types of sound broadcasts and by making consequential amendments to the sliding scale of fees payable on the issue of such licences.

STATUTORY INSTRUMENTS

1971 No. 15

INDUSTRIAL TRAINING

The Industrial Training Levy (Iron and Steel) Order 1971

Made - - -	*6th January* 1971
Laid before Parliament	*15th January* 1971
Coming into Operation	*21st January* 1971

The Secretary of State after approving proposals submitted by the Iron and Steel Industry Training Board for the imposition of a further levy on employers in the iron and steel industry and in exercise of his powers under section 4 of the Industrial Training Act 1964(a) and of all other powers enabling him in that behalf hereby makes the following Order :—

Title and commencement

1. This Order may be cited as the Industrial Training Levy (Iron and Steel) Order 1971 and shall come into operation on 21st January 1971.

Interpretation

2.—(1) In this Order unless the context otherwise requires :—

(*a*) "agriculture" has the same meaning as in section 109(3) of the Agriculture Act 1947(b), or, in relation to Scotland, as in section 86(3) of the Agriculture Scotland Act 1948(c) ;

(*b*) "an appeal tribunal" means an industrial tribunal established under section 12 of the Industrial Training Act 1964 ;

(*c*) "assessment" means an assessment of an employer to the levy ;

(*d*) "average number" in relation to the persons employed at or from an iron and steel establishment of an employer means the number that is equal to the average (calculated to the lowest whole number) of the numbers of the persons employed, or deemed under the provisions of paragraph (3) of this Article to have been employed, at or from the establishment by the employer on 3rd April 1970 and on 2nd October 1970 ;

(*e*) "the Board" means the Iron and Steel Industry Training Board ;

(*f*) "business" means any activities of industry or commerce ;

(*g*) "charity" has the same meaning as in section 360 of the Income and Corporation Taxes Act 1970(d) ;

(*h*) "employer" means a person who is an employer in the iron and steel industry at any time in the sixth levy period ;

(*i*) "the industrial training order" means the Industrial Training (Iron and Steel Board) Order 1969(e) ;

(a) 1964 c. 16.　　　　　　　　　　(b) 1947 c. 48.
(c) 1948 c. 45.　　　　　　　　　　(d) 1970 c. 10.
(e) S.I. 1969/884 (1969 II, p. 2517).

(*j*) "iron and steel establishment" means an establishment in Great Britain engaged wholly or mainly in the iron and steel industry for a total of twenty-seven or more weeks in the period of twelve months that commenced on 4th October 1969 or, being an establishment that commenced to carry on business in the said period, for a total number of weeks exceeding one half of the number of weeks in the part of the said period commencing with the day on which business was commenced and ending on the last day thereof ;

(*k*) "the iron and steel industry" means any one or more of the activities which, subject to the provisions of paragraph 2 of the Schedule to the industrial training order, are specified in paragraph 1 of that Schedule as the activities of the iron and steel industry ;

(*l*) "the levy" means the levy imposed by the Board in respect of the sixth levy period ;

(*m*) "notice" means a notice in writing ;

(*n*) "the sixth levy period" means the period commencing with the day upon which this Order comes into operation and ending on 31st August 1971.

(2) For the purposes of this Order no regard shall be had to any person employed wholly in agriculture or in the supply of food or drink for immediate consumption.

(3) In the case where an iron and steel establishment is taken over (whether directly or indirectly) by an employer in succession to, or jointly with, another person, a person employed at or from the establishment on either or both of the days specified in paragraph (1)(*d*) of this Article by a person other than the employer carrying on the establishment on the day upon which this Order comes into operation shall be deemed for the purposes of this Order to have been employed by the last mentioned employer.

(4) Any reference in this Order to an establishment that commences to carry on business or that ceases to carry on business shall not be taken to apply where the location of the establishment is changed but its business is continued wholly or mainly at or from the new location, or where the suspension of activities is of a temporary or seasonal nature.

(5) The Interpretation Act 1889(**a**) shall apply to the interpretation of this Order as it applies to the interpretation of an Act of Parliament.

Imposition of the levy

3.—(1) The levy to be imposed by the Board on employers in respect of the sixth levy period shall be assessed in accordance with the provisions of this Article.

(2) The levy shall be assessed by the Board separately in respect of each iron and steel establishment of an employer (not being an employer who is exempt from the levy by virtue of paragraph (5) of this Article), but in agreement with the employer one assessment may be made in respect of any number of such establishments, in which case those establishments shall be deemed for the purposes of that assessment to constitute one establishment.

(3) Subject to the provisions of this Article, the levy in respect of an iron and steel establishment of an employer shall be assessed by reference to the

---

(**a**) 1889 c. 63.

average number of the persons employed at or from the establishment by the employer as follows—

    (*a*) where the said average number of persons did not exceed twenty, by multiplying the sum of £3 by that average number ; or

    (*b*) in any other case, by multiplying the sum of £6 by the said average number of persons less twenty and by adding to the amount so obtained the sum of £60.

(4) The amount of the levy imposed in respect of an iron and steel establishment that ceases to carry on business in the sixth levy period shall be in the same proportion to the amount that would otherwise be due under paragraph (3) of this Article as the number of days between the commencement of the said levy period and the date of cessation of business (both dates inclusive) bears to the number of days in the said levy period.

(5) There shall be exempt from the levy—

    (*a*) an employer in whose case the average number of all the persons employed by him at or from the iron and steel establishment or establishments of the employer was less than eleven ;

    (*b*) a charity.

Assessment Notices

4.—(1) The Board shall serve an assessment notice on every employer assessed to the levy, but one notice may comprise two or more assessments.

(2) An assessment notice shall state the Board's address for the service of a notice of appeal or of an application for an extension of time for appealing.

(3) An assessment notice may be served on the person assessed to the levy either by delivering it to him personally or by leaving it, or sending it to him by post, at his last known address or place of business in the United Kingdom or, if that person is a corporation, by leaving it, or sending it by post to the corporation, at such address or place of business or at its registered or principal office.

Payment of the Levy

5.—(1) Subject to the provisions of this Article and of Articles 6 and 7, the amount of each assessment appearing in an assessment notice served by the Board shall be payable to the Board in two equal instalments, and the said instalments shall be due respectively one month and seven months after the date of the notice.

(2) An instalment of an assessment shall not be recoverable by the Board until there has expired the time allowed for appealing against the assessment by Article 7(1) of this Order and any further period or periods of time that the Board or an appeal tribunal may have allowed for appealing under paragraph (2) or (3) of that Article or, where an appeal is brought, until the appeal is decided or withdrawn.

Withdrawal of Assessment

6.—(1) The Board may, by a notice served on the person assessed to the levy in the same manner as an assessment notice, withdraw an assessment if that person has appealed against that assessment under the provisions of Article 7 of this Order and the appeal has not been entered in the Register of Appeals kept under the appropriate Regulations specified in paragraph (5) of that Article.

(2) The withdrawal of an assessment shall be without prejudice to the power of the Board to serve a further assessment notice in respect of any establishment to which that assessment related and, where the withdrawal is made by reason of the fact that an establishment has ceased to carry on business in the sixth levy period, the said notice may provide that the whole amount payable thereunder in respect of the establishment shall be due one month after the date of the notice.

Appeals

7.—(1) A person assessed to the levy may appeal to an appeal tribunal against the assessment within one month from the date of the service of the assessment notice or within any further period or periods of time that may be allowed by the Board or an appeal tribunal under the following provisions of this Article.

(2) The Board by notice may for good cause allow a person assessed to the levy to appeal to an appeal tribunal against the assessment at any time within the period of four months from the date of the service of the assessment notice or within such further period or periods as the Board may allow before such time as may then be limited for appealing has expired.

(3) If the Board shall not allow an application for extension of time for appealing, an appeal tribunal shall upon application made to the tribunal by the person assessed to the levy have the like powers as the Board under the last foregoing paragraph.

(4) In the case of an establishment that ceases to carry on business in the sixth levy period on any day after the date of the service of the relevant assessment notice, the foregoing provisions of this Article shall have effect as if for the period of four months from the date of the service of the assessment notice mentioned in paragraph (2) of this Article there were substituted the period of six months from the date of the cessation of business.

(5) An appeal or an application to an appeal tribunal under this Article shall be made in accordance with the Industrial Tribunals (England and Wales) Regulations 1965(a) as amended by the Industrial Tribunals (England and Wales) (Amendment) Regulations 1967(b) except where the establishment to which the relevant assessment relates is wholly in Scotland in which case the appeal or application shall be made in accordance with the Industrial Tribunals (Scotland) Regulations 1965(c) as amended by the Industrial Tribunals (Scotland) (Amendment) Regulations 1967(d).

(6) The powers of an appeal tribunal under paragraph (3) of this Article may be exercised by the President of the Industrial Tribunals (England and Wales) or by the President of the Industrial Tribunals (Scotland) as the case may be.

Evidence

8.—(1) Upon the discharge by a person assessed to the levy of his liability under an assessment the Board shall if so requested issue to him a certificate to that effect.

(a) S.I. 1965/1101 (1965 II, p. 2805).   (b) S.I. 1967/301 (1967 I, p. 1040).
(c) S.I. 1965/1157 (1965 II, p. 3266).   (d) S.I. 1967/302 (1967 I, p. 1050).

(2) The production in any proceedings of a document purporting to be certified by the Director of the Board to be a true copy of an assessment or other notice issued by the Board or purporting to be a certificate such as is mentioned in the foregoing paragraph of this Article shall, unless the contrary is proved, be sufficient evidence of the document and of the facts stated therein.

Signed by order of the Secretary of State.
6th January 1971.

Paul Bryan,
Minister of State,
Department of Employment.

EXPLANATORY NOTE

(This Note is not part of the Order.)

This Order gives effect to proposals submitted by the Iron and Steel Industry Training Board to the Secretary of State for Employment for the imposition of a further levy on employers in the iron and steel industry for the purpose of raising money towards the expenses of the Board.

The levy is to be imposed in respect of the sixth levy period commencing with the day upon which this Order comes into operation and ending on 31st August 1971. The levy will be assessed by the Board and there will be a right of appeal against an assessment to an industrial tribunal.

STATUTORY INSTRUMENTS

1971 No. 20 (S.1)

EDUCATION, SCOTLAND

The Remuneration of Teachers (Scotland) Amendment Order 1971

Made - - - -	*6th January* 1971
Coming into Operation	*7th January* 1971

Whereas—

(1) under section 2(2) of the Remuneration of Teachers (Scotland) Act 1967(a) (hereinafter referred to as " the Act ") the Scottish Teachers Salaries Committee (hereinafter referred to as " the Committee "), constituted under section 1 of the Act for the purpose of considering the remuneration of (*a*) teachers employed whole-time by education authorities in the provision of school education under the Education (Scotland) Acts 1939 to 1969 and duly qualified for appointment other than temporary appointment in terms of regulations for the time being in force under the said Acts ; and (*b*) teachers employed whole-time by education authorities in the provision of further education under the said Acts, have transmitted to the Secretary of State recommendations agreed on by them with respect to the remuneration of teachers of the said descriptions ;

(2) there is in force an order made under section 2(4) of the Act with respect to the remuneration of such teachers, namely, the Remuneration of Teachers (Scotland) Order 1970(b) ;

(3) it appears to the Secretary of State that effect can more conveniently be given to the said recommendations by amending by virtue of section 2(5) of the Act the memorandum referred to in the said order namely, the memorandum published by Her Majesty's Stationery Office under the title " SCOTTISH TEACHERS' SALARIES MEMORANDUM 1970 " ;

(4) under section 2(5) of the Act the Secretary of State has prepared a draft order setting out the amendments to the said memorandum which, in his opinion, are requisite for giving effect to the said recommendations ; and

(5) the Secretary of State, as required by section 2(6) of the Act has consulted the Committee with respect to the draft order and the Committee have made no representations with respect thereto ;

Now therefore, the Secretary of State, in exercise of the powers conferred on him by section 2(6) and section 8(3) of the Act, and of all other powers enabling him in that behalf, hereby makes the following order—

Citation and commencement

1. This order may be cited as the Remuneration of Teachers (Scotland) Amendment Order 1971 and shall come into operation on 7th January 1971.

Interpretation

2. The Interpretation Act 1889(c) shall apply for the interpretation of this order as it applies for the interpretation of an Act of Parliament.

(a) 1967 c. 36.   (b) S.I. 1970/993 (1970 II, p. 3133).   (c) 1889 c. 63.

Amendment of memorandum

3. The provisions set out in the above-mentioned memorandum shall with effect from 1 April 1970 be amended in the following manner—

(*a*) In Part A of Appendix II :

(i) in sub-paragraph (1) of paragraph 3 the words " (4), (5) or (6) " shall be deleted and the words " (4A), (4B), (5), (6) or (7) " shall be substituted therefor ;

(ii) sub-paragraph (4) of paragraph 3 shall be deleted and the following sub-paragraphs shall be substituted therefor—

" (4A) A Teaching Qualification (Secondary Education) and a Teaching Qualification (Primary Education).

(4B) In the case of a man who is not a graduate of a university in the United Kingdom a Teaching Qualification (Primary Education) deemed to be held by a teacher with the Teacher's General Certificate awarded as a result of a course at a Scottish college of education commenced before 1 January 1964 and where the teacher is employed as described in sub-paragraph (2) of this paragraph."

(iii) at the end of paragraph 3 there shall be added the following sub-paragraph—

" (7) A Teaching Qualification (Secondary Education) held by virtue of the award of the Teacher's Technical Certificate under paragraph (*bb*) or paragraph (*c*) read in relation to the said paragraph (*bb*) of Article 47 of the Training Regulations of 1931 and where the teacher was, or would have been, eligible for payment of salary by reference to Scale 7 of Part B of Appendix II to the Scottish Teachers' Salaries Memorandum 1968."

(iv) in sub-paragraph (3) of paragraph 4 the words " paragraph 3(4)(*a*) or 5 " shall be deleted and the words " sub-paragraph (4A), (5) or (7) of paragraph 3 " shall be substituted therefor.

(*b*) In Part II of Appendix VI paragraph 10 shall be deleted and the following paragraph shall be substituted therefor—

" 10(*a*) Associate Membership by examination of the Institution of Structural Engineers, provided that the Associate Member passed the Associate Membership Examination after 1 April 1935 and before 1 January 1968 or an examination accepted during that period by the Institution as giving exemption from the Associate Membership Examination ; or

(*b*) Membership of the Institution, provided that the Member has fully satisfied the examination requirements for membership under the regulations in force from 1 January 1968."

Given under the seal of the Secretary of State for Scotland.

(L.S.)   *Norman W. Graham,*

Secretary.

Scottish Education Department,
St. Andrew's House,
Edinburgh.

6th January 1971

EXPLANATORY NOTE

(This Note is not part of the Order.)

This Order prescribes basic salary Scale 3 as the appropriate scale for certain teachers who were paid on Scale 7 under paragraph 7(5) of Appendix II to the Scottish Teachers' Salaries Memorandum 1968.

The Order also amends the descriptions of the qualifications required by certain other categories of teachers.

Article 3 has been given retrospective effect by virtue of the power in section 8(3) of the Remuneration of Teachers (Scotland) Act 1967.

STATUTORY INSTRUMENTS

1971 No. 21

INCOME TAX

The Income Tax (Employments) (No. 7) Regulations 1971

Made - - - - -	*8th January* 1971
Laid before the House of Commons	*15th January* 1971
Coming into Operation - -	*6th April* 1971

The Commissioners of Inland Revenue, in exercise of the powers conferred upon them by section 204 of the Income and Corporation Taxes Act 1970(**a**), hereby make the following Regulations:—

1.—(1) These Regulations shall come into operation on the 6th day of April 1971, and may be cited as the Income Tax (Employments) (No. 7) Regulations 1971.

(2) The Interpretation Act 1889(**b**) shall apply for the interpretation of these Regulations as it applies for the interpretation of an Act of Parliament.

(3) In these Regulations the expression "the Principal Regulations" means the Income Tax (Employments) Regulations 1965(**c**) as amended (**d**).

2. Paragraph (3)(*c*) of Regulation 17 of the principal Regulations shall have effect as if for the amount of £10 there were substituted the amount of £20.

By Order of the Commissioners of Inland Revenue.

Alan Lord,
Secretary.

8th January 1971.

EXPLANATORY NOTE

(This Note is not part of the Regulations.)

These Regulations increase from £10 to £20 the amount which an employer can repay to a new employee without authority from the Inspector of Taxes.

(**a**) 1970 c. 10.   (**b**) 52 & 53 Vict. c. 63.
(**c**) S.I. 1965/516 (1965 I, p. 1321).
(**d**) The amending Regulations are not relevant to the subject matter of these Regulations.

STATUTORY INSTRUMENTS

1971 No. 25

DECIMAL CURRENCY

The Decimal Currency (Amendment of Local Enactments etc.) Order 1971

Made - - -	*8th January* 1971
Laid before Parliament	*18th January* 1971
Coming into Operation—	
Articles 1, 2, 3, 5 *and* 6	*15th February* 1971
Remainder - -	*1st April* 1971

The Secretary of State for the Environment, in exercise of his powers under section 11 of the Decimal Currency Act 1969(**a**) and of all other powers enabling him in that behalf, with the consent of the Treasury, hereby makes the following order:—

Title and commencement

1. This order may be cited as the Decimal Currency (Amendment of Local Enactments etc.) Order 1971. Articles 1, 2, 3, 5 and 6 shall come into operation on 15th February 1971 and the remainder on 1st April 1971.

Interpretation

2. The Interpretation Act 1889(**b**) shall apply for the interpretation of this order as it applies for the interpretation of an Act of Parliament.

Amendment of local Acts

3. In section 59 (Officers and servants to contribute to pension fund) of the Manchester Corporation Act 1920(**c**), in subsection (2), for "fractions of one penny" there shall be substituted "fractions of 1p".

4. In section 112 (Provision of concerts, entertainments, etc.) of the Nottingham Corporation Act 1923(**d**), in subsection (6), for "one penny" there shall be substituted "0.4p".

5. In section 8 (Obligation of officers and servants to contribute to superannuation fund) of the City of London (Various Powers) Act 1931(**e**), for "fractions of one penny" there shall be substituted "fractions of 1p".

6. In section 191 (Charges for use of conservatories, etc.) of the Brighton Corporation Act 1931(**f**), for "one shilling", "threepence" and "twopence" there shall be substituted "5p", "1p" and "1p", respectively.

7. In section 129 (Power to establish information bureaux) of the Gloucester Corporation Act 1935(**g**), for "a rate of one halfpenny in the pound calculated according to the rules made pursuant to section 9 of the Rating and Valuation Act 1925" there shall be substituted "one-fifth of the product of a rate of one new penny in the pound as estimated or determined for the purpose of section 12(2) of the General Rate Act 1967".

(**a**) 1969 c. 19.   (**b**) 1889 c. 63.   (**c**) 10 & 11 Geo. 5. c. xcvii.
(**d**) 13 & 14 Geo. 5. c. c.   (**e**) 21 & 22 Geo. 5. c. xiv.   (**f**) 21 & 22 Geo. 5. c. cix.
(**g**) 25 & 26 Geo. 5. c. lxxxvii.

8. In section 41 (Renewal and repairs fund) of the Nottingham Corporation Act 1935(**a**), in subsection (2) as amended by section 44 of the Nottingham Corporation Act 1947(**b**), for "fourpence" there shall be substituted "1.7p".

9. In the Grimsby Corporation (Grimsby, Cleethorpes and District Water &c.) Act 1937(**c**), in section 181 (Power to establish information bureaux), in subsection (2), for "the amount which would be produced by a general rate of one halfpenny in the pound" there shall be substituted "one-fifth of the amount which would be produced by a general rate of one new penny in the pound".

10. In the Lancashire County Council (Rivers Board and General Powers) Act 1938(**d**)—

   (*a*) in section 106 (Power of county council to contribute towards expenses of sea defence works) for "one-eighth of a penny" there shall be substituted "0.05p"; and

   (*b*) in section 107 (Expenses in connection with ceremonies etc. and contributions to certain associations and societies), in subsection (3)(*b*) as amended by section 32 of the Lancashire County Council (General Powers) Act 1968(**e**), for "one-half of a penny" there shall be substituted "0.2p".

11. In section 78 (Art fund) of the Nottingham Corporation Act 1938(**f**), in subsection (1), for "one-fifth of a penny" there shall be substituted "0.1p".

12. In the Northampton Corporation Act 1943(**g**)—

   (*a*) in section 112 (Art fund), in subsection (1), for "one-fifth of a penny" there shall be substituted "0.1p"; and

   (*b*) in section 128 (Provision of lectures), for "one-third of a penny" there shall be substituted "0.14p".

13. In section 83 (Art fund) of the Beverley Corporation Act 1948(**h**), in subsection (1), for "one-fifth of the product of a rate of one penny in the pound as ascertained or estimated for the purpose of subsection (2) of section 9 (Provisions as to precepts) of the Rating and Valuation Act 1925" there shall be substituted "one-tenth of the product of a rate of one new penny in the pound as estimated or determined for the purpose of section 12(2) of the General Rate Act 1967".

14. In the West Riding County Council (General Powers) Act 1948(**i**)—

   (*a*) in section 48 (Capital fund), in subsection (1), for "four times the product of a penny rate as ascertained or estimated for the purpose of subsection (2) of section 9 of the Rating and Valuation Act 1925" there shall be substituted "seventeen-tenths of the product of a rate of one new penny in the pound as estimated or determined for the purpose of section 12(2) of the General Rate Act 1967"; and

   (*b*) in section 49 (Renewal and repairs fund), in subsection (1), for "six times the product of a penny rate as ascertained or estimated for the purpose of subsection (2) of section 9 of the Rating and Valuation Act 1925" there shall be substituted "ten-fourths of the product of a rate of one new penny in the pound as estimated or determined for the purpose of section 12(2) of the General Rate Act 1967".

(a) 25 & 26 Geo. 5. c. cxix.   (b) 10 & 11 Geo. 6. c. xxxvi.
(c) 1 Edw. 8 & 1 Geo. 6. c. xli.   (d) 1 & 2 Geo. 6. c. xciv.   (e) 1968 c. xxix.
(f) 1 & 2 Geo. 6. c. xcv.   (g) 6 & 7 Geo. 6. c. xv.   (h) 11 & 12 Geo. 6. c. li.
(i) 11 & 12 Geo. 6. c. lii.

15. In the Slough Corporation Act 1949(**a**)—

(*a*) in section 131 (Subscriptions to scientific bodies and other expenses), for "one-half of the product of a rate of one penny in the pound as ascertained or estimated for the purpose of subsection (2) of section 9 (Provisions as to precepts) of the Rating and Valuation Act 1925" there shall be substituted "one-fifth of the product of a rate of one new penny in the pound as estimated or determined for the purpose of section 12(2) of the General Rate Act 1967"; and

(*b*) in section 141 (Provision of lectures, etc.), for "one-third of the product of a rate of one penny in the pound as ascertained or estimated for the purpose of subsection (2) of section 9 (Provisions as to precepts) of the Rating and Valuation Act 1925" there shall be substituted "14/100ths of the product of a rate of one new penny in the pound as estimated or determined for the purpose of section 12(2) of the General Rate Act 1967".

16. In the Lancashire County Council (General Powers) Act 1951(**b**)—

(*a*) in section 21 (Capital fund), in subsection (1), for "three times the product of a penny rate as ascertained or estimated for the purpose of subsection (2) of section 9 of the Rating and Valuation Act 1925" there shall be substituted "thirteen-tenths of the product of a rate of one new penny in the pound as estimated or determined for the purpose of section 12(2) of the General Rate Act 1967"; and

(*b*) in section 23 (Capital funds of local authorities), in subsection (1), for "twice the product of a penny rate as ascertained or estimated for the purpose of section 9 of the Rating and Valuation Act 1925" there shall be substituted "four-fifths of the product of a rate of one new penny in the pound as estimated or determined for the purpose of section 12(2) of the General Rate Act 1967".

17. In the West Riding County Council (General Powers) Act 1951(**c**)—

(*a*) in section 104 (Capital fund), in subsection (1), for "twice the product of a penny rate as estimated for the purpose of subsection (2) of section 9 of the Rating and Valuation Act 1925" there shall be substituted "four-fifths of the product of a rate of one new penny in the pound as estimated or determined for the purpose of section 12(2) of the General Rate Act 1967";

(*b*) in section 107 (Art fund), in subsection (1), for "one-fifth of the product of a penny rate as estimated for the purpose of subsection (2) of section 9 of the Rating and Valuation Act 1925 or such larger fraction (not exceeding one-half)" there shall be substituted "one-tenth of the product of a rate of one new penny in the pound as estimated or determined for the purpose of section 12(2) of the General Rate Act 1967 or such larger fraction (not exceeding one-fifth)"; and

(*c*) in section 114 (Subscriptions to scientific bodies and other expenses), for "one-half of the product of a penny rate as estimated for the purposes of subsection (2) of section 9 of the Rating and Valuation Act 1925" there shall be substituted "one-fifth of the product of a rate of one new penny in the pound as estimated or determined for the purpose of section 12(2) of the General Rate Act 1967".

(a) 12 & 13 Geo. 6. c. xxxviii.   (b) 14 & 15 Geo. 6. c. xxxv.
(c) 14 & 15 Geo. 6. c. xliii.

18. In the Leamington Corporation Act 1952(a)—

   (a) in section 127 (Capital fund), in subsection (1), for "twice the product of a penny rate as ascertained or estimated for the purpose of section 9 of the Rating and Valuation Act 1925" there shall be substituted "four-fifths of the product of a rate of one new penny in the pound as estimated or determined for the purpose of section 12(2) of the General Rate Act 1967"; and

   (b) in section 131 (Art fund), in subsection (1), for "one-fifth of the product of a penny rate as ascertained or estimated for the purpose of section 9 of the Rating and Valuation Act 1925 or such greater fraction (not exceeding one-half)" there shall be substituted "one-tenth of the product of a rate of one new penny in the pound as estimated or determined for the purpose of section 12(2) of the General Rate Act 1967 or such greater fraction (not exceeding one-fifth)".

19. In the Birkenhead Corporation Act 1954(b)—

   (a) in section 149 (Art fund). in subsection (1), for "one-fifth of the product of a penny rate as ascertained or estimated for the purpose of subsection (2) of section 9 of the Rating and Valuation Act 1925 or such greater fraction (not exceeding one-half) of the product of a penny rate" there shall be substituted "one-tenth of the product of a rate of one new penny in the pound as estimated or determined for the purpose of section 12(2) of the General Rate Act 1967 or such greater fraction (not exceeding one-fifth) of such product";

   (b) in section 174 (Provision of lectures, exhibitions, etc.), in subsection (1), for "one-third of the product of a penny rate as ascertained or estimated for the purpose of subsection (2) of section 9 of the Rating and Valuation Act 1925" there shall be substituted "14/100ths of the product of a rate of one new penny in the pound as estimated or determined for the purpose of section 12(2) of the General Rate Act 1967"; and

   (c) in section 176 (Subscriptions to local government and scientific bodies and other expenses), for "one-half of the product of a penny rate as ascertained or estimated for the purpose of subsection (2) of section 9 of the Rating and Valuation Act 1925" there shall be substituted "one-fifth of the product of a rate of one new penny in the pound as estimated or determined for the purpose of section 12(2) of the General Rate Act 1967".

20. In the Leicester Corporation Act 1956(c)—

   (a) in section 221 (Art fund), in subsection (1), for "one-fifth of the product of a penny rate as estimated for the purpose of subsection (2) of section 9 of the Rating and Valuation Act 1925" there shall be substituted "one-tenth of the product of a rate of one new penny in the pound as estimated or determined for the purpose of section 12(2) of the General Rate Act 1967"; and

   (b) in section 235 (Power to advertise advantages of city), in subsection (1), for "the product of a penny rate levied in the city as estimated for the purpose of subsection (2) of section 9 of the Rating and Valuation Act 1925" there shall be substituted "two-fifths of the product of a rate of one new penny in the pound as estimated or determined for the purpose of section 12(2) of the General Rate Act 1967".

(a) 15 & 16 Geo. 6 & 1 Eliz. 2. c. xvi.   (b) 2 & 3 Eliz. 2. c. xlvii.
(c) 4 & 5 Eliz. 2. c. xlix.

21. In section 94 (Subscriptions to scientific bodies and other expenses) of the Gloucester Corporation Act 1958(a), for "one-tenth of the product of a penny rate as ascertained or estimated for the purpose of subsection (2) of section 9 of the Rating and Valuation Act 1925" there shall be substituted "4/100ths of the product of a rate of one new penny in the pound as estimated or determined for the purpose of section 12(2) of the General Rate Act 1967".

22. In the Kent County Council Act 1958(b)—
  (*a*) in section 66 (Provision of lectures, etc.), in subsection (1), for "one-third of the product of a penny rate as ascertained or estimated for the purpose of subsection (2) of section 9 of the Rating and Valuation Act 1925" there shall be substituted "14/100ths of the product of a rate of one new penny in the pound as estimated or determined for the purpose of section 12(2) of the General Rate Act 1967"; and
  (*b*) in section 68 (Subscriptions to scientific bodies and other expenses), for "one-tenth of the product of a penny rate for the county as ascertained or estimated for the purpose of subsection (2) of section 9 of the Rating and Valuation Act 1925" there shall be substituted "4/100ths of the product of a rate of one new penny in the pound for the county as estimated or determined for the purpose of section 12(2) of the General Rate Act 1967".

23. In the Durham County Council Act 1963(c)—
  (*a*) in section 55 (Provision of lectures, etc.), in subsection (1), for "one-third of the product of a penny rate as ascertained or estimated for the purpose of subsection (2) of section 9 of the Act of 1925" there shall be substituted "14/100ths of the product of a rate of one new penny in the pound as estimated or determined for the purpose of section 12(2) of the General Rate Act 1967";
  (*b*) in section 58 (Acquisition of pictures, etc.), in subsection (3), for "one-tenth of the product of a penny rate for the county as ascertained or estimated for the purpose of subsection (2) of section 9 of the Act of 1925" there shall be substituted "4/100ths of the product of a rate of one new penny in the pound for the county as estimated or determined for the purpose of section 12(2) of the General Rate Act 1967"; and
  (*c*) in section 105 (Power to advertise facilities), for "twice the product of a penny rate levied in the county as ascertained or estimated for the purpose of subsection (2) of section 9 of the Act of 1925" there shall be substituted "four-fifths of the product of a rate of one new penny in the pound for the county as estimated or determined for the purpose of section 12(2) of the General Rate Act 1967".

24. In section 19 (Provision of lectures, etc.), of the West Riding County Council (General Powers) Act 1964(d), in subsection (1), for "two-thirds of the product of a penny rate as ascertained or estimated for the purpose of subsection (2) of section 9 of the Rating and Valuation Act 1925" there shall be substituted "three-tenths of the product of a rate of one new penny in the pound as estimated or determined for the purpose of section 12(2) of the General Rate Act 1967".

25. In section 48 (Precepts) of the Lee Valley Regional Park Act 1966(e)—
  (*a*) in subsections (5) and (10), for "penny", wherever occurring, there shall be substituted "new penny";

(a) 6 & 7 Eliz. 2. c. xxxv.   (b) 7 Eliz. 2. c. vi.   (c) 1963 c. xxxvii.
(d) 1964 c. xxxix.   (e) 1966 c. xli.

(b) in subsection (8), for "the product of a penny rate" there shall be substituted "42/100ths of the product of a new penny rate"; and

(c) for subsection (11) there shall be substituted—

"(11) For the purposes of this section 'product of a new penny rate' means the product of a rate of one new penny in the pound as estimated or determined for the purpose of section 12(2) of the General Rate Act 1967.".

26. In section 103 of the Dudley Corporation Act 1969(a), in the definition of "gross rate income", for "penny" there shall be substituted "new penny".

Amendment of local subordinate instruments

27. In the scheme made by the rural district council of Sudbury under section 64 of the Rating and Valuation Act 1925(b) on 4th May 1927 for the purpose of securing the continued operation of certain privileges in respect of rating, in paragraph 1, for "two pence" there shall be substituted "0.8p".

28. In the Hereford (Sewer Rates) Scheme 1932 as amended by the Hereford (Sewer Rates) (Amendment) Scheme 1932, in paragraph 3, for "threepence" there shall be substituted "1.2p".

29. In section 9 (Art fund) of the Bedford (Amendment of Local Enactments) Order 1951(c), in subsection (1), for "one-fifth of the product of a penny rate as ascertained or estimated for the purpose of subsection (2) of section 9 of the Rating and Valuation Act 1925 or such greater fraction (not exceeding one-half) of the product of a penny rate" there shall be substituted "one-tenth of the product of a rate of one new penny in the pound as estimated or determined for the purpose of section 12(2) of the General Rate Act 1967 or such greater fraction (not exceeding one-fifth) of such product".

30. In section 4 (Capital fund) of the Leicester (Amendment of Local Enactments) Order 1953(d)—

(a) in subsection (1), for "four times the product of a penny rate as ascertained or estimated for the purpose of section 9 of the Rating and Valuation Act 1925" there shall be substituted "seventeen-tenths of the product of a rate of one new penny in the pound as estimated or determined for the purpose of section 12(2) of the General Rate Act 1967"; and

(b) in subsection (2) as amended by article 17 of the Leicester (Amendment of Local Enactments) Order 1959(e), for "five times the product of a penny rate as ascertained or estimated as aforesaid" there shall be substituted "twenty-one tenths of the product of a rate of one new penny in the pound as estimated or determined as aforesaid".

31. Article 48 (Differential rating) of the Sheffield Order 1967(f) shall have effect in relation to the parts of the parishes of Ecclesfield and Eckington transferred by article 5(1) of the said order to the city of Sheffield, and in respect of the year 1971-72, with the substitution for "6d" of "2.3p".

32. Article 43 (Differential rating) of the Grimsby Order 1967(g) shall have effect with the substitution for "6d" in respect of the year 1971-72—

(a) in relation to the parts of the parishes of Great Coates and Weelsby transferred by the said order to the county borough of Grimsby, of "2.6p"; and

(b) in relation to the parts of the parishes of New Waltham and Waltham so transferred, of "2.3p".

(a) 1969 c. liii.   (b) 1925 c. 90.   (c) S.I. 1951/2149.   (d) S.I. 1953/472.   (e) S.I. 1959/785.   (f) S.I. 1967/104.   (g) S.I. 1967/1820.

Peter Walker,
Secretary of State for the Environment.

6th January 1971.

We consent to this order.

V. H. Goodhew,
Bernard Weatherill,
Two of the Lords Commissioners of
Her Majesty's Treasury.

8th January 1971.

EXPLANATORY NOTE
(This Note is not part of the Order.)

This order amends a number of enactments etc. referring to shillings and pence by substituting decimal currency references.

STATUTORY INSTRUMENTS

1971 No. 29

WAGES COUNCILS

The Wages Regulation (Licensed Non-residential Establishment) (Amendment) Order 1971

Made - - -		11*th January* 1971
Coming into Operation		14*th February* 1971

Whereas the Secretary of State has received from the Licensed Non-residential Establishment Wages Council the wages regulation proposals set out in the Schedule hereto;

Now, therefore, the Secretary of State in exercise of his powers under section 11 of the Wages Councils Act 1959**(a)**, and of all other powers enabling him in that behalf, hereby makes the following Order:—

1. This Order may be cited as the Wages Regulation (Licensed Non-residential Establishment) (Amendment) Order 1971.

2.—(1) In this Order the expression "the specified date" means the 14th February 1971, provided that where, as respects any worker who is paid wages at intervals not exceeding seven days, that date does not correspond with the beginning of the period for which the wages are paid, the expression "the specified date" means, as respects that worker, the beginning of the next such period following that date.

(2) The Interpretation Act 1889**(b)** shall apply to the interpretation of this Order as it applies to the interpretation of an Act of Parliament.

3. The wages regulation proposals set out in the Schedule hereto shall have effect as from the specified date.

Signed by order of the Secretary of State.
11th January 1971.

R. R. D. *McIntosh*,
Deputy Secretary,
Department of Employment.

(a) 1959 c. 69.　　　　　(b) 1889 c. 63.

Article 3

SCHEDULE

The Wages Regulation (Licensed Non-residential Establishment) Order 1970(a) (Order L.N.R. (79)), shall have effect as if in the Schedule thereto for Part II there were substituted the following Part:—

"PART II
ANNUAL HOLIDAY AND HOLIDAY REMUNERATION
ANNUAL HOLIDAY

9. Subject to the provisions of this paragraph and of paragraph 11, an employer shall, between 1st March 1971 and 31st October 1971, and between 1st March and 31st October in each subsequent year, allow a holiday (hereinafter referred to as an 'annual holiday') to every worker in his employment to whom this Schedule applies who during the 12 months immediately preceding the commencement of the holiday season (hereinafter referred to as 'the qualifying period') was employed for any of the periods specified below, and the duration of the annual holiday shall be related to the period of the worker's employment during that 12 months as follows:—

Period of employment	Duration of holiday
At least 4 weeks	1 day
,, ,, 8 ,, ...	2 days
,, ,, 12 ,, ...	3 ,,
,, ,, 16 ,, ...	4 ,,
,, ,, 20 ,, ...	5 ,,
,, ,, 24 weeks	7 days
,, ,, 28 ,, ...	9 ,,
,, ,, 32 ,, ...	11 ,,
,, ,, 36 ,, ...	13 ,,
,, ,, 40 ,, ...	15 ,,
,, ,, 44 ,, ...	16 ,,
,, ,, 48 ,, ...	18 ,,

Provided that—

(1) the number of days of annual holiday which an employer is required to allow to a worker in respect of a period of employment during the 12 months immediately preceding 1st March 1971 and during the 12 months immediately preceding 1st March in any succeeding year shall not exceed *three times* the number constituting the worker's normal working week;

(2) in this Schedule the expression 'holiday season' means in relation to the year 1971 the period commencing on 1st March 1971 and ending on 31st October 1971, and in each succeeding year, the period commencing on 1st March and ending on 31st October of the same year.

10. An annual holiday shall be allowed on consecutive working days and days of holiday shall be treated as consecutive notwithstanding that the weekly day of rest or a public holiday or a day of holiday in lieu of a public holiday intervenes:

Provided that—

(a) where a worker is entitled to more days of annual holiday than the number of days constituting his normal working week *but not more than twice that number* his annual holiday may be allowed in two separate periods of which one shall consist of at least the number of days constituting his normal working week, and

(b) *where a worker is entitled to more days of annual holiday than twice the number of days constituting his normal working week his annual holiday may be allowed as follows:—*

   (i) *as to the period comprising twice the number of days constituting his normal working week in accordance with (a) of this paragraph; and*

   (ii) *as to any additional days, on working days which need not be consecutive, to be fixed by agreement between the employer and the worker or his representative on any working day or days in the holiday season or before the beginning of the next following holiday season.*

11. Notwithstanding the provisions of paragraph 9, the Council may vary the holiday season as there set out if they receive an application for that purpose from an employer

---

(a) S.I. 1970/1105 (1970 II, p. 3474).

and are satisfied that it is reasonable to do so to meet special circumstances. Such variation may provide for the commencement of the holiday season earlier than 1st March or its extension beyond 31st October. An application relating to the commencement of the holiday season shall be made to the Council not less than six weeks before the operative date and an application to extend the duration of the holiday season, before 1st July. Any such alteration in the holiday season shall not become effective until notice of the decision of the Council has been communicated to the employer concerned. In the case of any variation of the holiday season under this provision, the qualifying period in respect thereof shall be that stated in paragraph 9.

12. An employer shall give to a worker reasonable notice of the commencing date and duration of his annual holiday and such notice may be given individually to a worker or by the posting of a notice in the place where a worker is employed.

13. Where any day of annual holiday allowed to any worker under this Schedule falls upon a day of holiday or half-holiday to which the worker may be entitled under any enactment other than the Wages Councils Act 1959, that holiday or half-holiday shall be treated as part of the holiday allowed under this Schedule.

REMUNERATION FOR ANNUAL HOLIDAY

14. Holiday remuneration for annual holiday shall be paid on the last pay day preceding the holiday as follows:—
For each day of holiday a worker is allowed in accordance with the provisions of paragraph 9 not less than one-sixth of the amount he would be entitled to receive from his employer under the arrangement current immediately before the holiday if he worked his normal weekly hours of work, exclusive of overtime, with the addition in the case of a worker who is normally supplied with full board, meals or lodging of one-sixth of the following amounts for each day of holiday:—
(1) 47s. 6d. in the case of a worker normally supplied by his employer with full board and lodging;
(2) 38s. 6d. in the case of a worker normally supplied by his employer with 2 meals only a day and lodging;
(3) 28s. 6d. in the case of a worker normally supplied by his employer with 1 meal only a day and lodging;
(4) 29s. 6d. in the case of a worker normally supplied by his employer with full board but no lodging;
(5) 20s. 6d. in the case of a worker normally supplied by his employer with 2 meals only a day but no lodging;
(6) 10s. 6d. in the case of a worker normally supplied by his employer with 1 meal only a day but no lodging;
(7) 18s. 0d. in the case of a regular worker normally supplied by his employer with lodging but with no meals:
Provided that—
where under the provisions of paragraph 10 an annual holiday is taken in more than one period, the holiday remuneration shall be apportioned accordingly.

ACCRUED HOLIDAY REMUNERATION PAYABLE ON TERMINATION OF EMPLOYMENT

15. If a worker ceases to be employed by an employer, the employer shall, immediately on termination of his employment (hereinafter referred to as the 'termination date'), pay to the worker accrued holiday remuneration in accordance with the provisions of paragraphs 16 and 17.

16. *Subject to the provisions of this paragraph and of paragraph 17, accrued holiday remuneration shall be payable to a worker in respect of his employment with the employer in the 12 months immediately preceding the termination date. The amount of the accrued holiday remuneration shall be a sum equal to the holiday remuneration which would have been payable if that period of 12 months had been the qualifying period for an annual holiday and if the worker could have been allowed an annual holiday in respect of that employment at the time of leaving it.*
Provided that—
(1) no worker shall be entitled to the payment by his employer of accrued holiday remuneration if—
(a) he is dismissed on either of the following grounds, that is to say—
(i) dishonesty, or

(ii) misconduct involving contravention of the licensing laws,

and is so informed by the employer at the time of dismissal; or

(b) he leaves his employment without having notified his employer, not less than one week before terminating his employment, of his intention to do so;

(2) the amount of any accrued holiday remuneration payable at the termination date shall be reduced by the amount of any sum paid by the employer to the worker—

(a) as accrued holiday remuneration under the provisions of this Schedule or of Order L.N.R. (79) in so far as such sum is attributable to the period for which the accrued holiday remuneration is payable;

(b) in respect of any day or days of holiday for which the worker had not qualified under the provisions of this Schedule or of Order L.N.R. (79) and allowed during the period in respect of which the accrued holiday remuneration is payable;

(3) accrued holiday remuneration is not payable in respect of any period of employment for which a worker has been allowed or become entitled to be allowed an annual holiday under this Schedule.

17. Where a worker has been allowed in a holiday season part only of the annual holiday for which he has qualified under this Schedule and his employment is terminated before he becomes entitled to the rest of that holiday, the accrued holiday remuneration payable shall be the appropriate amount calculated in accordance with the provisions of paragraph 16:—

(1) in respect of his employment with the employer during the qualifying period, less the holiday remuneration received by the worker in respect of that part of the holiday which has been allowed, and

(2) in respect of the period of his employment since the end of the qualifying period immediately preceding the termination date.

18. Where under the provisions of this Schedule or of Order L.N.R. (79) any accrued holiday remuneration has been paid by the employer to the worker prior to the allowance of an annual holiday in accordance with the provisions of this Schedule, the amount of holiday remuneration payable by the employer in respect of the said annual holiday under the provisions of paragraph 14 shall be reduced by the amount of any previous payment of accrued holiday remuneration in so far as it is attributable to any part of the period of employment in respect of which the said holiday has been allowed.

CALCULATION OF EMPLOYMENT

19. For the purpose of calculating any period of employment entitling a worker to an annual holiday or to any accrued holiday remuneration under this Schedule the worker shall be treated as having been employed:—

(1) for a week in respect of any week in which he has worked for the employer for not less than 18 hours and has qualified for payment of statutory minimum remuneration;

(2) when absent from work in any of the following circumstances—

(a) during annual holiday, public holidays or days in lieu of public holidays;

(b) during proved sickness or accident up to and not exceeding 8 weeks in the aggregate during any such period as aforesaid;

(c) by leave of the employer."

EXPLANATORY NOTE
(*This Note is not part of the Order.*)

This Order, which has effect from 14th February 1971, amends the Wages Regulation (Licensed Non-residential Establishment) Order 1970 (L.N.R. (79)) by providing for a third week of annual holiday.

New provisions are printed in italics.

1971 No. 30

WAGES COUNCILS

The Wages Regulation (Licensed Non-residential Establishment) (Managers and Club Stewards) (Amendment) Order 1971

Made - - -	*11th January* 1971
Coming into Operation	*14th February* 1971

Whereas the Secretary of State has received from the Licensed Non-residential Establishment Wages Council the wages regulation proposals set out in the Schedule hereto;

Now, therefore, the Secretary of State in exercise of his powers under section 11 of the Wages Councils Act 1959(a), and of all other powers enabling him in that behalf, hereby makes the following Order:—

1. This Order may be cited as the Wages Regulation (Licensed Non-residential Establishment) (Managers and Club Stewards) (Amendment) Order 1971.

2.—(1) In this Order the expression "the specified date" means the 14th February 1971, provided that where, as respects any worker who is paid wages at intervals not exceeding seven days, that date does not correspond with the beginning of the period for which the wages are paid, the expression "the specified date" means, as respects that worker, the beginning of the next such period following that date.

(2) The Interpretation Act 1889(b) shall apply to the interpretation of this Order as it applies to the interpretation of an Act of Parliament.

3. The wages regulation proposals set out in the Schedule hereto shall have effect as from the specified date.

Signed by order of the Secretary of State.

11th January 1971.

R. R. D. McIntosh,
Deputy Secretary,
Department of Employment.

(a) 1959 c. 69.   (b) 1889 c. 63.

Article 3

SCHEDULE

The Wages Regulation (Licensed Non-residential Establishment) (Managers and Club Stewards) Order 1970(a) (Order L.N.R. (80)), shall have effect as if in the Schedule thereto:—

1. for paragraph 4 there were substituted the following paragraph:—

"4. Where the wife of a Manager, a Trainee Manager or of a Relief Manager is required by the employer to assist in the work of the licensed non-residential establishment (other than a club) she shall be paid not less than 72s. 6d. for any week in which she is employed and during any part of which she is capable of and available for work whether she performs any work for her employer in that week or not and irrespective of the number of hours she works:

Provided that the minimum remuneration payable under this paragraph shall be reduced in any week by the amount of any holiday remuneration paid to the worker in respect of any day or days of annual holiday allowed in that week to the worker under Part II of this Schedule."

2. for Part II there were substituted the following Part:—

"PART II

ANNUAL HOLIDAY AND HOLIDAY REMUNERATION
ANNUAL HOLIDAY

19. An employer shall, between the date on which the provisions of this Schedule become effective and 31st December 1971, and in each succeeding year between 1st January and 31st December (hereinafter referred to as the 'holiday season'), allow an annual holiday to every worker to whom this Schedule applies (other than a worker who is a Club Steward, a Club Stewardess or the wife of a Club Steward, and who ordinarily works for the employer for less than 18 hours a week). The dates between which the annual holiday is to be allowed shall be agreed between the employer and the worker, or if no agreement is reached, it shall be allowed so as to terminate not later than 31st December.

20. The duration of the annual holiday shall be determined by reference to the worker's period of employment during the 12 months immediately preceding the commencement of the holiday season (*hereinafter referred to as the 'qualifying period'*) in the following manner:—

Period of employment	Duration of holiday
At least 1 month	1 day
,, ,, 2 months	2 days
,, ,, 3 ,, ...	3 ,,
,, ,, 4 ,, ...	4 ,,
,, ,, 5 ,, ...	5 ,,
,, ,, 6 *months*	7 *days*
,, ,, 7 ,, ...	9 ,,
,, ,, 8 ,, ...	11 ,,
,, ,, 9 ,, ...	13 ,,
,, ,, 10 ,, ...	15 ,,
,, ,, 11 ,, ...	16 ,,
,, ,, 12 ,, ...	18 ,,

Provided that—

(1) the number of days of annual holiday to which a worker is entitled in any year shall not exceed *three times* the number of days constituting the worker's normal working week;

(2) the number of days of annual holiday which an employer is required to allow to a worker during the year 1971 under the provisions of this Schedule shall be reduced by the number of any days of paid annual holiday allowed to the worker under the provisions of Order L.N.R. (80) during 1971 prior to the date on which this Schedule becomes effective.

(a) S.I. 1970/1106 (1970 II, p. 3489).

21. An annual holiday shall be allowed on consecutive working days, being days upon which the worker is normally called upon to work, and days of holiday shall be treated as consecutive notwithstanding the intervention of a public holiday or a day of holiday in lieu of a public holiday:

Provided that where a worker is entitled to more days of annual holiday than the number of days constituting his normal working week, his annual holiday may be allowed in two or more separate periods of which one shall consist of at least the number of days constituting his normal working week.

REMUNERATION FOR ANNUAL HOLIDAY

22. Holiday remuneration for the annual holiday shall be paid on the last pay day preceding the holiday as follows:—

(1) Where a worker is not provided by the employer, for the duration of the holiday, with full board—for each day of holiday allowed in accordance with the provisions of paragraph 20—

   (a) in the case of Managers, Trainee Managers, Manageresses, Relief Managers, Relief Manageresses and the wives of Managers, Trainee Managers or Relief Managers where such wives are required by the employer to assist in the work of the licensed non-residential establishment (other than a club), not less than one-sixth of the statutory minimum remuneration to which the worker would be entitled at the date of the holiday for a week's work if he were not provided by the employer with full board;

   (b) in the case of Club Stewards, Club Stewardesses and the wives of Club Stewards where such wives are required by the employer to assist in the work of the club, not less than one-sixth of the statutory minimum remuneration to which the worker would be entitled at the date of the holiday for a week's work if he worked his normal weekly hours of work and if he were not provided by the employer with full board.

(2) Where a worker is provided by the employer, for the duration of the holiday, with full board—for each day of holiday allowed in accordance with paragraph 20—

   (a) in the case of Managers, Trainee Managers, Manageresses, Relief Managers, Relief Manageresses and the wives of Managers, Trainee Managers or Relief Managers where such wives are required by the employer to assist in the work of the licensed non-residential establishment (other than a club), not less than one-sixth of the statutory minimum remuneration to which the worker would be entitled in cash at the date of the holiday for a week's work if he were provided by the employer with full board;

   (b) in the case of Club Stewards, Club Stewardesses and the wives of Club Stewards where such wives are required by the employer to assist in the work of the club, not less than one-sixth of the statutory minimum remuneration to which the worker would be entitled in cash at the date of the holiday for a week's work if he worked his normal weekly hours of work and if he were provided by the employer with full board:

Provided that where under the provisions of paragraph 21 an annual holiday is taken in more than one period the holiday remuneration shall be apportioned accordingly.

ACCRUED HOLIDAY REMUNERATION PAYABLE ON TERMINATION OF EMPLOYMENT

23. If a worker (other than a worker who is a Club Steward, a Club Stewardess or the wife of a Club Steward, and who ordinarily works for the employer for less than 18 hours a week) ceases to be employed by an employer after the provisions of this Schedule become effective, the employer shall immediately on the termination of the employment (hereinafter referred to as 'the termination date') pay to the worker accrued holiday remuneration in accordance with the provisions of paragraph 24.

24.—(1) Subject to the provisions of this paragraph, accrued holiday remuneration shall be payable to a worker in respect of such period of his employment with the employer in the 12 months immediately preceding the termination date as has not already been counted as employment for the purpose of any day or days of annual holiday.

(2) *The amount of the accrued holiday remuneration shall be a sum equal to the holiday remuneration which would have been payable in accordance with paragraph 22(1) if the period of employment specified in sub-paragraph (1) of this paragraph had been the qualifying period for an annual holiday and if the worker could have been allowed an annual holiday in respect of that employment at the time of leaving it.*

Provided that—

(a) no worker shall be entitled to the payment by his employer of accrued holiday remuneration if—

(1) he is dismissed on either of the following grounds, that is to say—

(i) dishonesty, or

(ii) misconduct involving contravention of the licensing laws,

and is so informed by the employer at the time of dismissal; or

(2) he leaves his employment without having notified his employer, not less than one week before terminating his employment, of his intention to do so;

(b) the amount of any accrued holiday remuneration payable at the termination date shall be reduced by the amount of any sum paid by the employer to the worker—

(i) as accrued holiday remuneration under the provisions of this Schedule or of Order L.N.R. (80) in so far as such sum is attributable to the period for which the accrued holiday remuneration is payable;

(ii) in respect of any day or days of holiday for which the worker had not qualified under the provisions of this Schedule or of Order L.N.R. (80) and allowed during the period in respect of which the accrued holiday remuneration is payable;

(c) accrued holiday remuneration is not payable in respect of any period of employment for which the worker has become entitled to be allowed an annual holiday under the provisions of this Schedule or of Order L.N.R. (80).

25. Where under the provisions of this Schedule or of Order L.N.R. (80) any accrued holiday remuneration has been paid by the employer to a worker prior to the allowance of an annual holiday in accordance with the provisions of this Schedule, the amount of holiday remuneration payable by the employer in respect of the said annual holiday under the provisions of paragraph 22 shall be reduced by the amount of any previous payment of accrued holiday remuneration in so far as it is attributable to any part of the period of employment in respect of which the said holiday has been allowed.

CALCULATION OF EMPLOYMENT

26. For the purposes of calculating any period of employment qualifying a worker for an annual holiday or for any accrued holiday remuneration under this Schedule a worker shall be treated as having been employed:—

(1) for a month in respect of any month in which he has worked for the employer for not less than two weeks and has qualified for payment of statutory minimum remuneration;

(2) when absent from work in any of the following circumstances:—

(a) during annual holiday, public holidays or days in lieu of public holidays;

(b) during proved sickness or accident up to and not exceeding eight weeks in the aggregate during any such period as aforesaid;

(c) by leave of the employer."

EXPLANATORY NOTE

(This Note is not part of the Order.)

This Order, which has effect from 14th February 1971, amends the Wages Regulation (Licensed Non-residential Establishment) (Managers and Club Stewards) Order 1970 (L.N.R. (80)) by increasing the statutory minimum remuneration fixed by that Order for wives of managers, trainee managers and relief managers and by providing for a third week of annual holiday.

New provisions are printed in italics.

STATUTORY INSTRUMENTS

1971 No. 37

AGRICULTURE

The Price Stability of Imported Products (Rates of Levy) (Eggs) (No. 2) Order 1971

Made	-	-	-	11*th January* 1971
Coming into Operation				12*th January* 1971

The Minister of Agriculture, Fisheries and Food, in exercise of the powers conferred upon him by section 1(2), (4), (5), (6) and (7) of the Agriculture and Horticulture Act 1964(a) and of all other powers enabling him in that behalf, hereby makes the following order:—

1. This order may be cited as the Price Stability of Imported Products (Rates of Levy) (Eggs) (No. 2) Order 1971, and shall come into operation on 12th January 1971.

2.—(1) In this order—

" the Principal Order " means the Price Stability of Imported Products (Levy Arrangements) (Eggs) Order 1970(b) as amended by any subsequent order, and if any such order is replaced by any subsequent order the expression shall be construed as a reference to such subsequent order;

AND other expressions have the same meaning as in the Principal Order.

(2) The Interpretation Act 1889(c) shall apply to the interpretation of this order as it applies to the interpretation of an Act of Parliament and as if this order and the order hereby revoked were Acts of Parliament.

3. In accordance with and subject to the provisions of the Principal Order (which provides for the charging of levies on imports of those eggs and egg products which are specified commodities for the purposes of the Agriculture and Horticulture Act 1964) the rate of general levy for such imports into the United Kingdom of any specified commodity as are described in column 2 of the Schedule to this order in relation to a tariff heading indicated in column 1 of that Schedule shall be the rate set forth in relation thereto in column 3 of that Schedule.

4. The Price Stability of Imported Products (Rates of Levy) (Eggs) (No. 1) Order 1971(d) is hereby revoked.

In Witness whereof the Official Seal of the Minister of Agriculture, Fisheries and Food is hereunto affixed on 11th January 1971.

(L.S.)

G. P. Jupe,
Assistant Secretary.

(a) 1964 c. 28.　　(b) S.I. 1970/359 (1970 I, p. 1277).　　(c) 1889 c. 63.
(d) S.I. 1971/7 (1971 I, p. 3).

SCHEDULE

1. Tariff Heading	2. Description of Imports	3. Rate of General Levy
	Imports of:—	
04.05	*Birds' eggs (in shell or not in shell), fresh, dried or otherwise preserved, sweetened or not, other than egg yolks:*	(per 120 eggs)
	A. Eggs in shell:	s. d.
	1. Not exceeding 11 lb. in weight per 120 ..	5 0 [25p]
	2. Over 11 lb. but not exceeding 12½ lb. in weight per 120	5 0 [25p]
	3. Over 12½ lb. but not exceeding 14 lb. in weight per 120	5 0 [25p]
	4. Over 14 lb. but not exceeding 15½ lb. in weight per 120	5 0 [25p]
	5. Over 15½ lb. but not exceeding 17 lb. in weight per 120	5 0 [25p]
	6. Over 17 lb. in weight per 120	5 0 [25p]
	B. Eggs not in shell:	(per ton)
	Whole dried	£100

EXPLANATORY NOTE

(This Note is not part of the Order.)

This order, which comes into operation on 12th January 1971, supersedes the Price Stability of Imported Products (Rates of Levy) (Eggs) (No. 1) Order 1971. It—

(a) increases the rates of general levy on imports of eggs in shell in each of the weight grades which are numbered 1 to 6 in the Schedule to the order ;

(b) reimposes unchanged the rate of general levy to be charged on imports of whole dried eggs not in shell, which was in force immediately before the commencement of this order.

1971 No. 40

WEIGHTS AND MEASURES

The Weights (Amendment) Regulations 1971

Made - - -	*13th January* 1971
Laid before Parliament	*20th January* 1971
Coming into Operation	*21st January* 1971

The Secretary of State, in exercise of his powers under sections 11(3), 14(1)(a), (b) and (c) and 58 of the Weights and Measures Act 1963(a), and all other powers in that behalf enabling him, hereby makes the following Regulations:—

1.—(1) These Regulations may be cited as the Weights (Amendment) Regulations 1971 and shall come into operation on 21st January 1971.

(2) The Interpretation Act 1889(b) shall apply to the interpretation of these Regulations as it applies to the interpretation of an Act of Parliament.

2. The Weights Regulations 1970(c) shall have effect subject to the following amendments:—

(*a*) for Regulation 2(2) there shall be substituted:—

"(2) In the case of weights which are first passed as fit for use for trade before 1st January 1972, the provisions of Parts II and III of these Regulations shall have effect subject to the provisions of Schedule 4 hereto.";

(*b*) for Regulation 6(1) there shall be substituted:—

"(1) No metric weight of less than 20 grammes and no imperial weight of less than 1 ounce shall have an adjusting hole.";

(*c*) for Regulation 7(3) there shall be substituted:—

"(3) No weight shall bear any marking other than:—

(i) the markings hereinbefore mentioned;

(ii) the name or mark of the maker;

(iii) the stamp applied by an inspector of weights and measures; or

(iv) in the case of a weight in use for trade before 21st January 1971, the name of the owner or an indication of his name.";

(a) 1963 c. 31.   (b) 1889 c. 63.   (c) S.I. 1970/1370 (1970 III, p. 4584).

(*d*) in Schedule 2, paragraph 1(b), for "five per cent" there shall be substituted "ten per cent"; and

(*e*) in Schedule 4, paragraph 4 shall be omitted.

Nicholas Ridley,
Parliamentary Under Secretary of State,
Department of Trade and Industry.

13th January 1971.

EXPLANATORY NOTE

(*This Note is not part of the Regulations.*)

These Regulations amend the Weights Regulations 1970.

Provision is made for adjusting holes in 20 gramme and one ounce weights and the permitted amount of taper in the width of the rectangular metric weights described in Schedule 2 to the principal Regulations is increased from 5% to 10%.

Provision is also made for the continued use for trade of existing weights bearing the name of the owner or an indication of his name.

STATUTORY   INSTRUMENTS

1971 No. 43

CUSTOMS AND EXCISE

The Import Duties (Temporary Exemptions)
(No. 1) Order 1971

Made - - - -	13*th January* 1971
Laid before the	
House of Commons	14*th January* 1971
Coming into Operation	15*th January* 1971

The Lords Commissioners of Her Majesty's Treasury, by virtue of the powers conferred on them by sections 3(6) and 13 of the Import Duties Act 1958(a), and of all other powers enabling them in that behalf, on the recommendation of the Secretary of State, hereby make the following Order:—

1.—(1) This Order may be cited as the Import Duties (Temporary Exemptions) (No. 1) Order 1971.

(2) The Interpretation Act 1889(b) shall apply for the interpretation of this Order as it applies for the interpretation of an Act of Parliament.

(3) This Order shall come into operation on 15th January 1971.

2.—(1) Until the beginning of 4th May 1971 any import duty which is for the time being chargeable on goods of a heading of the Customs Tariff 1959 specified in the Schedule to this Order shall not be chargeable in respect of goods of any description there specified in relation to that heading.

(2) For the purposes of classification under the Customs Tariff 1959, in so far as that depends on the rate of duty, any goods to which paragraph (1) above applies shall be treated as chargeable with the same duty as if this Order had not been made.

V. H. Goodhew,

Bernard Weatherill,

Two of the Lords Commissioners
of Her Majesty's Treasury.

13th January 1971.

SCHEDULE

GOODS TEMPORARILY EXEMPT FROM IMPORT DUTY

Tariff heading   *Description*

25.19   Magnesite, dead-burned, containing (*a*) not less than 85 per cent. by weight of magnesium compounds expressed as MgO, (*b*) a total of not more than $8\cdot0$ per cent. by weight of aluminium compounds and iron compounds expressed as Al_2O_3 and Fe_2O_3, (*c*) a total of not less than $2\cdot5$ per cent. by weight and not more than $8\cdot5$ per cent. by weight of calcium compounds and silicon compounds expressed as CaO and SiO_2.

(a) 1958 c. 6.   (b) 1889 c. 63.

Tariff heading   *Description*

73.13   Steel plates containing not more than 0·35 per cent. by weight of silicon, of a width not less than 2,812 millimetres and not more than 2,825 millimetres, of a length of not less than 11,430 millimetres and not more than 12,395 millimetres and of a thickness of not less than 12 millimetres and not more than 14 millimetres.

73.19   Cold formed, longitudinally butt welded, circular steel pipes, of an outside diameter of not less than 35·875 inches and not more than 36·125 inches and of a wall thickness not less than 0·475 inches and not more than 0·550 inches, not painted or otherwise coated.

EXPLANATORY NOTE

(This Note is not part of the Order.)

This Order provides for the temporary exemption from import duty, until the 4th May 1971, of certain magnesite, steel plates and steel pipes, all as specified in the Schedule to the Order.

STATUTORY INSTRUMENTS

1971 No. 52

NATIONAL HEALTH SERVICE, ENGLAND AND WALES

LOCAL GOVERNMENT, ENGLAND AND WALES

LONDON GOVERNMENT

The National Health Service (Compensation) Regulations 1971

Made - - - -	*14th January* 1971
Laid before Parliament	*25th January* 1971
Coming into Operation	*28th January* 1971

ARRANGEMENT OF REGULATIONS

PART I
PRELIMINARY

PART II
ENTITLEMENT TO COMPENSATION

PART III
RESETTLEMENT COMPENSATION

PART IV
LONG-TERM COMPENSATION

Part V

Retirement Compensation and Payments on Death

Part VI

Adjustment, Review and Compounding of Compensation

Part VII

Procedure and Miscellaneous

The Secretary of State for Social Services to whom there were by the Secretary of State for Social Services Order 1968(a) transferred all functions of the Minister of Health (which Minister the Treasury had determined was the appropriate Minister for the purposes of section 60(2) of the Local Government Act 1958(b) and which Minister was the appropriate Minister for the purposes of section 85(4) of the London Government Act 1963(c)), in exercise of his powers under those sections and in exercise of his powers under section 35 of the Health Services and Public Health Act 1968(d) and all other powers enabling him in that behalf, hereby makes the following regulations:—

(a) S.I. 1968/1699 (1968 III, p. 4585).   (b) 1958 c. 55.
(c) 1963 c. 33.   (d) 1968 c. 46.

PART I

PRELIMINARY

Citation and commencement

1. These regulations may be cited as the National Health Service (Compensation) Regulations 1971, and shall come into operation on 28th January 1971.

Interpretation

2.—(1) In these regulations, unless the context otherwise requires, the following expressions have the meanings hereby respectively assigned to them, that is to say:—

"accrued pension", in relation to a pensionable officer who has suffered loss of employment, means the pension to which he would have become entitled under his last relevant pension scheme in respect of his pensionable service according to the method of calculation, modified where necessary for the purpose of giving effect to these regulations, prescribed by that scheme if, at the date on which he ceased to be subject to that scheme, he had attained normal retiring age and complied with any requirement of that scheme as to a minimum period of qualifying service or contribution and completed any additional contributory payments or payments in respect of added years which he was in the course of making;

"accrued retiring allowance", in relation to a pensionable officer who has suffered loss of employment, means any lump sum payment to which he would have become entitled under his last relevant pension scheme in respect of his pensionable service according to the method of calculation, modified where necessary for the purpose of giving effect to these regulations, prescribed by that scheme if, at the date on which he ceased to be subject to that scheme, he had attained normal retiring age and complied with any requirement of that scheme as to a minimum period of qualifying service or contribution and completed any additional contributory payments or payments in respect of added years which he was in the course of making;

"accrued incapacity pension" and "accrued incapacity retiring allowance" have the same respective meanings as "accrued pension" and "accrued retiring allowance" except that the reference to a person's attaining normal retiring age shall be construed as a reference to his becoming incapable of discharging efficiently the duties of his employment by reason of permanent ill-health or infirmity of mind or body;

"the Act of 1946" means the National Health Service Act 1946(a);

"additional contributory payment" has the same meaning as in the National Health Service (Superannuation) Regulations 1961(b);

"compensation question" means a question—

(*a*) as to a person's entitlement to compensation for loss of office or employment, or for loss or diminution of emoluments or

(*b*) as to the manner of a person's employment or the comparability of his duties;

"emoluments" means all salary, wages, fees and other payments paid or made to an officer as such for his own use, and also the money value of any apartments, rations or other allowances in kind appertaining to his employment, but does not include payments for overtime, other than payments which are a usual incident of his employment, or any allowance payable to him to

---

(a) 1946 c. 81.   (b) S.I. 1961/1441 (1961 II, p. 2824).

cover the cost of providing office accommodation or clerical or other assistance, or any travelling or subsistence allowance or other moneys to be spent, or to cover expenses incurred, by him for the purposes of his employment; and "net emoluments", in relation to any employment, means the annual rate of the emoluments of that employment less such part of those emoluments as the officer was or is liable to contribute under a pension scheme, except any periodical sum payable in respect of additional contributory payments, and in relation to any employment which has been lost or the emoluments of which have been diminished, the expression means the annual rate of emoluments as aforesaid immediately before the loss or diminution as the case may be:

Provided that where fees or other variable payments were paid to an officer as part of his emoluments during any period immediately preceding the loss or diminution the amount in respect of fees or other variable payments to be included in the annual rate of emoluments shall be the annual average of the fees or other payments paid to him during the period of 3 years immediately preceding the loss or diminution, or such shorter period as the Secretary of State may deem reasonable in the circumstances;

"enactment" means any Act or any instrument made under an Act;

"long-term compensation" means compensation payable in accordance with the provisions of part IV of these regulations for loss of employment or loss or diminution of emoluments;

"material date", in relation to any person who has suffered loss of employment or loss or diminution of emoluments which is attributable to any cause mentioned in regulation 4, means—

(a) in the case of loss or diminution which is attributable to an event mentioned in paragraphs (a) to (c) of section 11(9) of the Act of 1946, the date of operation of the order or scheme related to that event; and

(b) in any other case, the date of operation of the order or instrument to which the loss or diminution is attributable:

Provided that if the loss or diminution occurred before either of the said dates the expression shall mean the actual date of the loss or diminution;

"minimum pensionable age", in relation to a pensionable officer, means the earliest age at which, under his last relevant pension scheme, he could have become entitled to a pension, other than a pension payable in consequence of his redundancy or his incapacity to discharge efficiently the duties of his employment by reason of permanent ill-health or infirmity of mind or body or his retirement in the interests of the efficiency of the service;

"national service" means service which is relevant service within the meaning of the Reserve and Auxiliary Forces (Protection of Civil Interests) Act 1951(a), and includes service immediately following such service as aforesaid being service in any of Her Majesty's naval, military or air forces pursuant to a voluntary engagement entered into with the consent of the authority or person under whom an officer held his last relevant employment;

"normal retiring age" means the age of 65 years if the officer is a male, or 60 years if the officer is a female;

"officer" includes the holder of any place, situation or employment;

"payment in respect of added years" in relation to a pensionable officer means any payment made under regulation 32 of the National Health Service (Superannuation) Regulations 1961;

"pensionable officer", in relation to a person who has suffered loss of employment or loss or diminution of emoluments, means a person who immediately before such loss or diminution was subject to a pension scheme;

(a) 1951 c. 65.

"pension scheme", in relation to a pensionable officer, means any form of arrangement associated with his employment for the payment of superannuation benefits, whether subsisting by virtue of Act of Parliament, trust, contract or otherwise, other than benefits payable under any Act relating to National Insurance; and

"last relevant pension scheme", in relation to a pensionable officer, means the pension scheme to which he was last subject before suffering loss of employment or loss or diminution of emoluments;

"reckonable service", in relation to a person, means any period of wholetime or part-time employment in any relevant employment and includes any period of war service or national service undertaken on his ceasing to hold any such employment but does not include employment of which account has been taken, or is required to be taken, in calculating the amount of any superannuation benefit to which he has become entitled;

"relevant employment" means employment—

(a) under the Crown or in the service of an employing authority within the meaning of the regulations for the time being in force under section 67(1) of the Act of 1946, or

(b) preceding either of the foregoing employments which was reckonable for the purpose of any pension scheme associated with the employment which has been lost or in which the emoluments have been diminished, or

(c) in such other service as the Secretary of State may, in the case of any named officer, approve, but, except as provided in regulations 7(1)(c) and 13(1)(c), does not include service in the armed forces of the Crown;

"resettlement compensation" means compensation payable in accordance with part III of these regulations for loss of employment;

"retirement compensation" means compensation payable in accordance with the provisions of regulations 20, 21, 22 or 23;

"Secretary of State" means Secretary of State for Social Services;

"tribunal" means a tribunal established under section 12 of the Industrial Training Act 1964(a);

"war service" means war service within the meaning of the Local Government Staffs (War Service) Act 1939(b), the Teachers Superannuation (War Service) Act 1939(c), the Police and Firemen (War Service) Act 1939(d) or employment for war purposes within the meaning of the Superannuation Schemes (War Service) Act 1940(e) if such service immediately followed a period of relevant employment and was undertaken either compulsorily or with the permission of the employer in that employment.

(2) Unless the context otherwise requires, references in these regulations to the provisions of any enactment shall be construed as references to those provisions as amended, re-enacted or modified by any subsequent enactment.

(3) References in these regulations to a numbered regulation shall, unless the reference is to a regulation of specified regulations, be construed as references to the regulation bearing that number in these regulations.

(a) 1964 c. 16.   (b) 1939 c. 94.
(c) 1939 c. 95.   (d) 1939 c. 103.
(e) 1940 c. 26.

(4) References in any of these regulations to a numbered paragraph shall, unless the reference is to a paragraph of a specified regulation, be construed as references to the paragraph bearing that number in the first mentioned regulation.

(5) The Interpretation Act 1889(a) shall apply for the interpretation of these regulations as it applies for the interpretation of an Act of Parliament.

PART II

ENTITLEMENT TO COMPENSATION

Persons to whom the regulations apply

3. These regulations shall apply to any person who—

(a) was employed immediately before the material date for the whole or for part only of his time as an officer of—

(i) a regional hospital board or a board of governors of a teaching hospital,

(ii) an executive council or a joint committee of executive councils constituted for the purposes of part IV of the Act of 1946, or

(iii) a local medical committee, local pharmaceutical committee, local dental committee or local optical committee recognised by the Secretary of State under section 32 of that Act, or

(b) would have been so employed at that date but for any national service on which he was or had been engaged.

Grounds of entitlement to compensation

4. Subject to the provisions of these regulations, any person to whom these regulations apply and who suffers loss of employment or loss or diminution of emoluments which is attributable to—

(a) the provisions of any order made on or after the operative date of these regulations under part II of the Local Government Act 1958 or part VI of the Local Government Act 1933(b) or of any instrument made on or after the operative date of these regulations under the London Government Act 1963, or

(b) the occurrence on or after 9th September 1968 of any of the events mentioned in paragraphs (a) to (c) of section 11(9) of the Act of 1946, or

(c) the making on or after 9th September 1968 of an order under subsections (2), (3) or (4) of section 31 of the Act of 1946, or an order revoking an order made under any of those subsections,

shall be entitled to have his case considered for the payment of compensation under these regulations, and such compensation shall be determined in accordance with these regulations.

National Service

5.—(1) Where any person to whom these regulations apply would have been employed immediately before the material date as such an officer as is mentioned in regulation 3(a) but for any national service on which he was or had been engaged, then if before the expiry of 2 months after ceasing to be so engaged, or if prevented by sickness or other reasonable cause, as soon as practicable thereafter, he gives notice to the Secretary of State that he is available for employment, that person shall be entitled to have his case considered for the payment of compensation—

(a) 1889 c.63.   (b) 1933 c.51.

(a) if he is not given or offered re-employment in his former office or in any reasonably comparable office (whether in the same or in a different service), on the ground of loss of employment; or

(b) if he is so re-employed with diminished emoluments as compared with the emoluments which he would have enjoyed had he continued in his former employment, on the ground of diminution of emoluments.

(2) The loss of employment which is the cause of a claim for compensation under paragraph (1)(a) shall be treated as having occurred on the earlier of the 2 following dates, that is to say, the date of his being refused re-employment or a date one month after the date on which the person gave notice that he was available for employment: and the person shall be deemed to have been entitled to the emoluments which he would have enjoyed at such earlier date had he continued in his former employment.

PART III

RESETTLEMENT COMPENSATION

Resettlement compensation for loss of employment

6. The Secretary of State shall, subject to the provisions of these regulations, pay resettlement compensation to any person to whom these regulations apply and who satisfies the conditions set out in regulation 7.

Conditions for payment of resettlement compensation

7.—(1) Without prejudice to any other requirement of these regulations, the conditions for the payment of resettlement compensation to any person are that—

(a) he has suffered loss of employment attributable to any such provision, event or order as is mentioned in regulation 4 not later than 10 years after the material date;

(b) he had not at the date of the loss attained normal retiring age;

(c) he had been for a period of 3 years immediately before the material date continuously engaged (disregarding breaks not exceeding in the aggregate 6 months) for the whole or part of his time in relevant employment; and for this purpose the expression "relevant employment" includes any period of national service immediately following such employment;

(d) he has made a claim for such compensation in accordance with the provisions of part VII of these regulations not later than 13 weeks after the loss of employment which is the cause of his claim, or 13 weeks after the coming into operation of these regulations, whichever is the later or within such longer period as the Secretary of State may allow in any particular case where he is satisfied that the delay in making the claim was due to ill-health or other circumstances beyond the claimant's control;

(e) the loss of employment which is the cause of his claim has occurred for some reason other than misconduct or incapacity to perform such duties as, immediately before the loss, he was performing or might reasonably have been required to perform; and

(f) he has not, subject to paragraph (3), been offered any reasonably comparable employment under any body constituted under the Act of 1946.

(2) In ascertaining for the purposes of this regulation whether a person has been offered employment which is reasonably comparable with the employment which he has lost, no account shall be taken of the fact that the duties of the employment offered are in relation to a different service from that in connection with which his employment was held or are duties which involve a transfer of his employment from one place to another within England and Wales.

(3) No account shall be taken for the purposes of this regulation of an offer of employment where the Secretary of State is satisfied—

(a) that acceptance would have involved undue hardship to the person, or

(b) that he was prevented from accepting the offer by reason of ill-health or other circumstances beyond his control.

Amount of resettlement compensation

8.—(1) The amount of resettlement compensation which may be paid to a person shall, for each week for which such compensation is payable, be a sum ascertained by taking two thirds of the weekly rate of the net emoluments which that person has lost and deducting therefrom, in addition to the items mentioned in regulations 33(3) and (4), such of the following items as may be applicable—

(a) unemployment, sickness or injury benefit under any Act relating to National Insurance claimable by him in respect of such week (excluding any amount claimable by him in respect of a dependant); and

(b) two thirds of the net emoluments received by him in respect of such week from work or employment undertaken as a result of the loss of employment.

(2) For the purposes of this regulation the weekly rate of a person's net emoluments shall be deemed to be seven three hundred and sixty-fifths of those emoluments.

Period for payment of resettlement compensation

9. Subject to the provisions of these regulations, resettlement compensation shall be payable to a person only in respect of the period of 13 weeks next succeeding the week in which he lost the employment in respect of which his claim has been made or, in the case of a person who has attained the age of 45 years, the said 13 weeks and one additional week for every year of his age after attaining the age of 45 years and before the date of the loss of employment, subject to a maximum addition of 13 such weeks.

Additional provisions relating to resettlement compensation

10.—(1) Resettlement compensation shall be payable to a person at intervals equivalent to those at which the emoluments of his employment were previously paid or at such other intervals as may be agreed between the person and the Secretary of State.

(2) Resettlement compensation shall be terminated by the Secretary of State—

(a) if without reasonable cause the recipient fails to comply with any of the provisions of regulation 11, or

(b) if on being requested to do so, he fails to satisfy the Secretary of State that, so far as he is able, he is seeking suitable employment.

Claimant for resettlement compensation to furnish particulars of employment

11. Every person claiming or in receipt of resettlement compensation shall (after as well as before the compensation begins to be paid)—

(a) forthwith supply the Secretary of State in writing with particulars of any employment which the person obtains or of any change in his earnings from any such employment, and

(b) if the Secretary of State so requires, so long as the person is out of employment and is not receiving sickness or injury benefit, register with the Department of Employment.

Part IV

Long-Term Compensation

Long-term compensation for loss of employment or loss or diminution of emoluments

12. The Secretary of State shall, subject to the provisions of these regulations, pay long-term compensation to any person to whom these regulations apply and who satisfies the conditions set out in regulation 13.

Conditions for payment of long-term compensation

13.—(1) Without prejudice to any other requirement of these regulations, the conditions for the payment of long-term compensation to any person are that—

(a) he has suffered loss of employment or loss or diminution of emoluments attributable to any such provision, event or order as is mentioned in regulation 4 not later than 10 years after the material date;

(b) he had not, save as is provided in regulation 29, at the date of the loss or diminution attained normal retiring age;

(c) he had been, for a period of not less than 8 years immediately before the material date, continuously engaged (without a break of more than 12 months at any one time) for the whole or part of his time in relevant employment; and for this purpose the expression "relevant employment" includes any period of national service immediately following such employment;

(d) he has made a claim for such compensation in accordance with the provisions of part VII of these regulations not later than 2 years after the loss or diminution which is the cause of the claim or 2 years after the coming into operation of these regulations whichever is the later; and

(e) if the cause of the claim for compensation is loss of employment—

(i) the loss has occurred for some reason other than misconduct or incapacity to perform such duties as, immediately before the loss, he was performing or might reasonably have been required to perform; and

(ii) he has not been offered any reasonably comparable employment under any body constituted under the Act of 1946.

(2) Regulations 7(2) and (3) (which relate to offers of employment) shall apply for the purposes of this regulation in ascertaining whether a person has been offered reasonably comparable employment.

(3) Claims for long-term compensation for loss of employment shall in all respects be treated as claims for such compensation for the loss of emoluments occasioned thereby and the provisions of these regulations shall apply to all such claims accordingly.

Factors to be considered in determining payment of long-term compensation

14.—(1) For the purpose of determining whether long-term compensation should be paid to any person and, if so, the amount of the compensation (subject to the limits set out in these regulations), the Secretary of State shall have regard to such of the following factors as may be relevant, that is to say—

(*a*) the conditions upon which the person held the employment which he has lost, including in particular its security of tenure, whether by law or practice;

(*b*) the emoluments and other conditions, including security of tenure, whether by law or practice, of any work or employment undertaken by the person as a result of the loss of employment;

(*c*) the extent to which he has sought suitable employment and the emoluments which he might have acquired by accepting other suitable employment offered to him;

(*d*) all the other circumstances of his case.

(2) In ascertaining for the purposes of paragraph (1)(*c*) whether a person has been offered suitable employment, regulations 7(2) and (3) shall apply in like manner as they apply for the purpose of ascertaining whether employment is reasonably comparable with employment which has been lost.

Amount of long-term compensation payable for loss of emoluments

15.—(1) Long-term compensation for loss of emoluments shall, subject to the provisions of these regulations, be payable until the normal retiring age or death of a person to whom it is payable, whichever first occurs, and shall not exceed a maximum annual sum calculated in accordance with the provisions of paragraphs (2) to (4).

(2) The said maximum annual sum shall, subject as hereinafter provided, be the aggregate of the following sums, namely—

(*a*) for every year of the person's reckonable service, one sixtieth of the net emoluments which he has lost; and

(*b*) in the case of a person who has attained the age of 40 years at the date of the loss, a sum calculated in accordance with the provisions of paragraph (3) appropriate to his age at that date:

Provided that the said maximum annual sum shall in no case exceed two thirds of the net emoluments which the person has lost.

(3) The sum referred to in paragraph (2)(*b*) shall be—

(*a*) in the case of a person who has attained the age of 40 years but has not attained the age of 50 years at the date of the loss, the following fraction of the net emoluments which he has lost—

(i) where his reckonable service is less than 10 years, one sixtieth for each year of such service after attaining the age of 40 years; or

(ii) where his reckonable service amounts to 10 years but is less than 15 years, one sixtieth for each year of such service after attaining the age of 40 years and one additional sixtieth; or

(iii) where his reckonable service amounts to 15 years but is less than 20 years, one sixtieth for each year of such service after attaining the age of 40 years and 2 additional sixtieths; or

(iv) where his reckonable service amounts to 20 years or more, one sixtieth for each year of such service after attaining the age of 40 years and 3 additional sixtieths;

but the sum so calculated shall not in any case exceed one sixth of the said net emoluments;

(b) in the case of a person who has attained the age of 50 years but has not attained the age of 60 years at the date of the loss, one sixtieth of the said net emoluments for each year of his reckonable service after attaining the age of 40 years, up to a maximum of 15 such years; and

(c) in the case of a person who has attained the age of 60 years at the date of the loss, one sixtieth of the said net emoluments for each year of his reckonable service after attaining the age of 45 years.

(4) Where a person has become entitled (whether immediately or prospectively on attaining some greater age) to a superannuation benefit by way of annual amounts under his last relevant pension scheme, the maximum annual sum referred to in paragraph (1) shall be the maximum sum calculated under paragraphs (2) and (3) as if he had not become so entitled.

(5) Where long-term compensation is payable in respect of any period and resettlement compensation is also payable in respect of that period, the long-term compensation shall be limited to the amount (if any) by which it exceeds the resettlement compensation payable as aforesaid.

(6) Long-term compensation shall be payable to a person at intervals equivalent to those at which the emoluments of his employment were previously paid or at such other intervals as may be agreed between the person and the Secretary of State.

Long-term compensation for diminution of emoluments

16. Long-term compensation for diminution of emoluments in respect of any employment shall, subject to the provisions of these regulations, be awarded and paid in accordance with the following provisions:—

(a) the compensation shall consist of an annual sum which shall be payable to a person at intervals equivalent to those at which the emoluments of his employment are or were previously paid or at such other intervals as may be agreed between the person and the Secretary of State, and shall, subject to the provisions of these regulations, be payable until normal retiring age or death, whichever first occurs; and

(b) the said annual sum shall not exceed the maximum annual sum which could have been awarded under regulation 15 if the person had suffered loss of emoluments equivalent to the amount of the diminution:

Provided that no compensation shall be payable if the emoluments have been diminished by less than 2½ per cent.

Date from which long-term compensation is to be payable

17.—(1) Long-term compensation shall be payable with effect from the date of the claim or from any earlier date permitted by the succeeding provisions of this regulation.

(2) Where a claim for long-term compensation is duly made within 13 weeks of the occurrence of the loss or diminution which is the cause of the claim, the award shall be made retrospective to the date on which the loss or diminution occurred.

(3) Where a claim for long-term compensation is made after the expiry of the period mentioned in paragraph (2), the award may, at the discretion of the Secretary of State, be made retrospective to a date not earlier than 13 weeks prior to the date on which the claim was made:

Provided that if the Secretary of State is satisfied that the failure to make the claim within the period mentioned in paragraph (2) was due to ill-health or other circumstances beyond the claimant's control, the award may be made retrospective to a date not earlier than that on which the loss or diminution occurred.

PART V

RETIREMENT COMPENSATION AND PAYMENTS ON DEATH

Entitlement to retirement compensation and other payments

18.—(1) The Secretary of State shall, subject to the provisions of these regulations, pay retirement compensation to any person to whom this part of these regulations applies, and shall make the other payments for which provision is made in regulations 26 to 30.

(2) Save as is provided in regulation 29, this part of these regulations applies to a pensionable officer who satisfies the conditions set out in regulation 13.

(3) Regulation 14 shall apply in relation to retirement compensation as it applies in relation to long-term compensation.

Additional factors governing payment of retirement compensation

19.—(1) Where retirement compensation is payable under any one of regulations 20, 21, 22 and 23, such compensation shall not be payable under any other of those regulations.

(2) If a person has attained the age of 40 years at the date on which he lost his employment or suffered a diminution of his emoluments, the Secretary of State, in calculating the amount of the retirement compensation payable to that person, shall credit him with additional years of service or an additional period of contribution on the following basis, namely—

(a) 2 years, whether or not he has completed any years of service after attaining the age of 40 years, and

(b) 2 years for each of the first 4 completed years of his reckonable service between the date when he attained the age of 40 years and the date of the loss or diminution, and one year for each such year of service after the fourth,

but the additional years of service or period of contribution so credited shall not exceed the shortest of the following periods, namely—

(i) such number of years as, when added to his pensionable service, would amount to the maximum period of such service which would have been reckonable by him had he continued in his employment until attaining normal retiring age, or

(ii) the number of years of his reckonable service, or

(iii) 15 years;

and in calculating the amount of any retirement compensation payable to him any period so added shall be aggregated with any years of service or period of contribution entailing reduction of the relevant pension as a consequence of the provisions of section 30 of the National Insurance Act 1965(a).

(3) When retirement compensation is awarded, or when an award is reviewed under regulation 35, the additional compensation payable in consequence of any years of service or period of contribution credited to a person under paragraph (2) may be reduced or withheld to such extent as the Secretary of State may think reasonable having regard to the pension scheme (if any) associated with any further employment obtained by him.

(4) If under his last relevant pension scheme the amount of any benefit to which a person might have become entitled could have been increased or supplemented at the discretion of the authority administering the pension scheme or of any other body, the Secretary of State may increase, to an extent not exceeding that to which the person's accrued pension, accrued retiring allowance, accrued incapacity pension or accrued incapacity retiring allowance might have been increased or supplemented, the corresponding component of any retirement compensation payable to him.

(5) If under his last relevant pension scheme provision existed to enable a person to elect not to receive a lump sum payment on retirement or his widow to elect to receive a widow's pension at a higher rate, then—

(a) if on becoming entitled to such a payment in respect of the employment he has lost or the employment in which his emoluments were diminished or any subsequent employment he, or on his death his widow, so elects under the pension scheme; or

(b) if at the date on which compensation becomes payable to or in respect of the person under regulations 20, 21, 22, 23, 26 or 27 he, or as the case may be his widow, has not become entitled to so elect under the pension scheme, he or she may make the like election under this regulation in relation to his accrued retiring allowance or the annual sum payable to her under regulation 26 and, if he or she does so,

any retirement compensation shall be calculated by reference to the benefits that would have been payable under his last relevant pension scheme if such an election had been made and for the purpose of regulation 26 the "prescribed proportion" shall be determined accordingly.

(6) If under his last relevant pension scheme a person would have been entitled to surrender a proportion of any pension which might have become payable to him in favour of his spouse or any dependant, then, if he so desires and informs the Secretary of State by notice in writing accordingly within one month after becoming entitled to retirement compensation under these regulations, he may surrender a proportion of so much of the said compensation as is payable by way of an annual sum on the like terms and conditions and in consideration of the like payments by the Secretary of State as if the said annual sum were a pension to which he had become entitled under the said pension scheme.

(7) In calculating for the purposes of regulations 20, 21 or 22 the amount of the annual sum which is equal to a person's accrued pension, no account shall be taken of any reduction falling to be made in that pension by reason of the provisions of any Act relating to National Insurance until the person reaches the age at which under his last relevant pension scheme the pension would have been so reduced.

(a) 1965 c.51.

(8) In paragraph (2) the expression "reckonable service" includes any period of employment of which account has been taken or is required to be taken in calculating the amount of any superannuation benefit to which a person has become entitled under his last relevant pension scheme.

Retirement compensation for loss of emoluments payable to pensionable officer on attainment of normal retiring age

20.—(1) Subject to the provisions of these regulations, when a person to whom this part of these regulations applies reaches normal retiring age, the retirement compensation payable to him for loss of emoluments shall be—

(*a*) an annual sum equal to the amount of his accrued pension, and

(*b*) a lump sum equal to the amount of his accrued retiring allowance (if any).

(2) Where an annual sum is payable under this regulation in respect of any period and resettlement compensation is also payable in respect of that period, the said annual sum shall be limited to the amount (if any) by which it exceeds the resettlement compensation payable as aforesaid.

Retirement compensation payable to pensionable officer on his becoming incapacitated or reaching minimum pensionable age

21.—(1) Where a person to whom this part of these regulations applies and who has suffered loss of employment before attaining what would have been his normal retiring age—

(*a*) becomes incapacitated in circumstances in which, if he had continued in the employment which he has lost, he would have become entitled to a pension under his last relevant pension scheme; or

(*b*) attains the age which, had he continued to serve in the employment which he has lost, would have been his minimum pensionable age,

he shall be entitled on the happening of either event to claim, in lieu of any compensation to which he would otherwise be entitled under these regulations—

(i) in the case mentioned in head (*a*) of this paragraph, an annual sum equal to the amount of his accrued incapacity pension and a lump sum equal to the amount of his accrued incapacity retiring allowance (if any), and

(ii) in the case mentioned in head (*b*) of this paragraph, an annual sum equal to the amount of his accrued pension and a lump sum equal to the amount of his accrued retiring allowance (if any),

subject however to the conditions specified in paragraph (5).

(2) On receipt of a claim under paragraph (1) the Secretary of State shall consider whether the claimant is a person to whom that paragraph applies, and within 13 weeks after the date of the receipt of the claim—

(*a*) if satisfied that he is not such a person, shall notify him in writing accordingly; or

(*b*) if satisfied that he is such a person, shall assess the amount of compensation payable to him and notify him in writing accordingly,

and any such notification shall, for the purposes of these regulations, be deemed to be a notification by the Secretary of State of a decision on a claim for compensation.

(3) The Secretary of State may require any person who makes a claim under head (*a*) of paragraph (1) to submit himself to a medical examination by a registered medical practitioner selected by the Secretary of State, and in that event the Secretary of State shall also offer the person an opportunity of submitting a report from his own medical adviser as a result of an examination by him, and the Secretary of State shall take that report into consideration together with the report of the medical practitioner selected by him.

(4) If a person wishes to receive compensation under this regulation, he shall so inform the Secretary of State in writing within one month from the date of the receipt of a notification under paragraph (2) or, where the claim has been the subject of an appeal, from the date of the decision of the tribunal thereon; and the compensation shall be payable as from the date on which the Secretary of State received the claim.

(5) The calculation of compensation under this regulation shall be subject to the following conditions—

(*a*) where the Secretary of State, by virtue of regulation 19, has credited the person with additional years of service or an additional period of contribution, no account shall be taken of any additional years or period beyond the number of years which he could have served, had he not lost his employment, before the date on which the claim was received by the Secretary of State; and

(*b*) if, by reason of any provision of the relevant pension scheme for a minimum benefit, the amount of any such pension or retiring allowance is in excess of that attributable to the person's actual service, no account shall be taken of any such additional years or period except to the extent (if any) by which they exceed the number of years represented by the difference between his actual service and the period by reference to which the minimum benefit has been calculated; and

(*c*) if the number of years by reference to which an accrued incapacity pension or accrued incapacity retiring allowance is to be calculated is less than any minimum number of years of qualifying service prescribed by the relevant pension scheme, the amount of such pension or retiring allowance shall, notwithstanding any minimum benefit prescribed by the pension scheme, not exceed such proportion of such minimum benefit as the number of years of pensionable service bears to the minimum number of years of qualifying service.

Option to take retirement compensation prematurely

22.—(1) If a person to whom this part of these regulations applies has suffered loss of employment after attaining the age of 50 years and so requests the Secretary of State by notice in writing, he shall be entitled, as from the date on which the Secretary of State receives such notice, to an annual sum equal to the amount of his accrued pension and a lump sum equal to the amount of his accrued retiring allowance (if any), and in that event he shall not be entitled to receive any further payment of long-term compensation after that date:

Provided that—

(i) in calculating the amount of the compensation payable to a person who has given such notice as aforesaid no account shall be taken of any additional years of service or period of contribution credited to him under regulation 19; and

   (ii) where the person has claimed long-term compensation the said notice shall be given not later than 2 years after the decision on the claim has been notified or, where the decision has been reviewed under regulation 35(3), not later than 2 years after the review.

(2) Regulation 21(2) shall apply in relation to a notice given under paragraph (1) as it applies to a claim made under paragraph (1) of that regulation.

(3) Where an annual sum is payable under this regulation in respect of any period and resettlement compensation is also payable in respect of that period, the said annual sum shall be limited to the amount (if any) by which it exceeds the resettlement compensation payable as aforesaid.

Retirement compensation for diminution of emoluments

23.—(1) A person to whom this part of these regulations applies and who has suffered a diminution of his emoluments shall be entitled to receive retirement compensation in accordance with the provisions of this regulation.

(2) The provisions of regulations 20 and 21 shall apply to any such person as if he had suffered loss of employment immediately before the diminution occurred; but the amount of the retirement compensation payable shall be the amount which would have been payable in respect of loss of employment multiplied by a fraction of which—

   (*a*) the numerator is the amount by which his emoluments have been diminished, and

   (*b*) the denominator is the amount of his emoluments immediately before they were diminished.

For the purposes of this calculation no account shall be taken of any reduction which might otherwise fall to be made in the accrued pension or accrued incapacity pension as a consequence of the provisions of section 30 of the National Insurance Act 1965.

(3) No compensation shall be payable under this regulation—

   (*a*) if the person's emoluments have been diminished by less than $2\frac{1}{2}$ per cent or

   (*b*) if the person had continued to pay superannuation contributions as if his emoluments had not been diminished.

Superannuation contributions

24.—(1) A person entitled to retirement compensation under regulations 20, 21 or 22 shall pay to the Secretary of State an amount equal to any sum which was paid to him by way of return of superannuation contributions, including any interest, after ceasing to be employed, and the Secretary of State may at the person's request repay that amount to him at any time before he becomes entitled as aforesaid, but if that amount is not paid to the Secretary of State, or is repaid by him to the person, the compensation shall be reduced by an annual amount the capital value of which is equal to the amount of the said superannuation contributions.

(2) For the purposes of this regulation the expression "superannuation contributions" shall include payments made by the person in respect of added years and any additional contributory payments made by him.

Retirement compensation of a person who obtains further pensionable employment

25.—(1) Where a person to whom this part of these regulations applies, after suffering loss of employment or diminution of emoluments, enters employment in which he is subject to a pension scheme and thereafter becomes entitled to reckon for the purposes of that scheme any service or period of contribution which falls to be taken into account for the purpose of assessing the amount of any retirement compensation payable to him, his entitlement to retirement compensation shall be reviewed and no retirement compensation shall be payable in respect of such service or period unless the annual rate of the emoluments to which he was entitled immediately before such loss or diminution exceeds the annual rate on entry of the emoluments of the new employment by more than $2\frac{1}{2}$ per cent of such first mentioned emoluments, and any retirement compensation so payable to him shall, insofar as it is calculated by reference to remuneration, be calculated by reference to the difference between the said annual rates:

Provided that this paragraph shall not operate to increase the amount of any retirement compensation payable in respect of diminution of emoluments beyond the amount which would have been payable if the person had attained normal retiring age immediately before he ceased to hold the employment in which he suffered the diminution of emoluments.

(2) No retirement compensation shall be payable in the circumstances mentioned in paragraph (1) if the person has continued to pay superannuation contributions as if his emoluments had not been diminished.

Compensation payable to widow or dependants of a pensionable officer

26.—(1) Payments in accordance with this regulation and regulations 27 and 28 shall be made to or for the benefit of the widow, child or other dependant or to the personal representatives of a person to whom this part of these regulations applies.

(2) If the widow, child or other dependant of that person might have become entitled to a pension under his last relevant pension scheme, the widow, child or other dependant, as the case may be, shall be entitled to receive an annual sum equal to the prescribed proportion of any retirement compensation by way of annual amounts payable to the person under regulations 20, 21, 22 or 23 immediately before his death or, if he dies before becoming entitled to receive compensation under any of those regulations, the prescribed proportion of the compensation by way of annual amounts which he would have received under regulation 21 or 23 had he become entitled thereto in the circumstances mentioned in regulation 21(1)(*a*) immediately before his death:

Provided that—

    (i) where any retirement compensation has been surrendered under regulation 19(6) or compounded under regulation 36, any sum payable under this regulation shall be calculated as if such surrender or compounding had not taken place;

    (ii) where the pension scheme provides for payment of the pension to any person on behalf of a child or other dependant, any annual sum payable as aforesaid to a child or other dependant shall be paid to that person on behalf of the child or dependant in the like manner and for the like period as is provided in the pension scheme;

(iii) in calculating the sum payable as aforesaid, it shall be assumed that the retirement compensation payable, or which would have been payable, to a person under regulations 20, 21, 22 or 23 had been such sum as would have been payable if the accrued pension or accrued incapacity pension had not been reduced by reason of the provisions of any Act relating to National Insurance.

(3) Any annual sum payable to or for the benefit of a widow, child or other dependant under this regulation shall cease to be payable in any circumstances in which a corresponding pension under the pension scheme referred to in paragraph (2) would have ceased to be payable.

(4) Except where the compensation has been reduced under regulation 24, compensation payable under this regulation and regulation 27 shall in the aggregate be reduced by an amount the capital value whereof is equal to the amount of any superannuation contributions as defined in regulation 24(2) returned to the person in respect of whom the compensation is payable and either not paid to the Secretary of State or repaid by the Secretary of State to the person, the compensation under each such regulation being reduced in proportion to the capital value of each amount.

(5) In this regulation and regulation 19(5) "prescribed proportion" means the proportion which, under the last relevant pension scheme, the pension payable to the widow, child or other dependant of any person, as the case may be, bears to the person's pension.

Compensation where death gratuity would have been payable

27.—(1) If the widow or the personal representatives of a person to whom this part of these regulations applies might have become entitled to a death gratuity under his last relevant pension scheme, she or they, as the case may be, shall be entitled to receive a sum calculated in accordance with the provisions of regulation 26(4) and paragraph (2) of this regulation.

(2) The amount of the sum referred to in paragraph (1) shall be ascertained in accordance with the method of calculation prescribed by the last relevant pension scheme for the ascertainment of death gratuity as if the person had died immediately before losing his employment, subject to the following modifications—

(*a*) except where the person had been in receipt of retirement compensation under regulation 22, account shall be taken of any additional years of service or period of contribution credited to him under regulation 19(2)—

(i) in the case of a person who had been in receipt of retirement compensation under regulation 21, to the extent of the period between the loss of employment and the date of the claim made under that regulation; and

(ii) in any other case, to the extent of the period between the loss of employment and the person's death;

(*b*) if the number of years of the person's service or period of contribution is less than the minimum number of years of qualifying service or period prescribed by the pension scheme for the receipt of a death gratuity, the said sum shall not exceed such proportion of the death gratuity calculated as aforesaid as the number of years of the person's pensionable service or period of contribution bears to the minimum number of years of qualifying service or period prescribed by the pension scheme; and

(c) there shall be deducted from such sum the amount of any retirement compensation paid to the person under regulations 20, 21 or 22, or where any part of the compensation has been surrendered under regulation 19(6), the amount which would have been so paid but for any such surrender.

(3) In calculating such death gratuity for the purposes of these regulations, an annual sum payable to or for the benefit of a widow, child or other dependant under regulation 26 shall be deemed to be a pension payable to or for the benefit of the widow, child or dependant, as the case may be.

(4) In the case of a person who has suffered diminution of emoluments, the sum payable under this regulation to his widow or personal representatives shall be the sum which would have been payable if he had suffered loss of employment, multiplied by the fraction specified in regulation 23(2); but no sum shall be payable under this paragraph in the circumstances described in regulation 23(3)(a) or (b).

Balances payable to pensionable officer's widow or personal representatives

28.—(1) If no annual sum is payable to the widow, child or other dependant of any person under regulation 26 and no sum is payable under regulation 27 and the person dies before he has received in the aggregate by way of retirement compensation a sum equivalent to the amount of any contributions paid by him under regulation 24 and not repaid to him, together with compound interest thereon up to the date of his death calculated in accordance with the method prescribed by his last relevant pension scheme for the calculation of interest, there shall be paid to his personal representatives the difference between the aggregate amount received by way of retirement compensation as aforesaid and the said equivalent sum.

(2) If any annual sum which was payable to a widow under regulation 26 has ceased to be payable on her re-marriage or death, and any sum payable to a child or other dependant under the regulation has ceased to be payable, and if the aggregate amount of the payments which were made as aforesaid to her husband by way of retirement compensation and to the widow or personal representatives under regulation 27 is less than a sum equivalent to the amount which would have been payable to the personal representatives under that regulation if no annual sum had been payable under regulation 26, there shall be paid to or among such persons as the Secretary of State may determine the difference between such aggregate amount and the said equivalent sum.

(3) For the purposes of this regulation a person who has surrendered any part of his retirement compensation under regulation 19(6) shall be deemed to have received during any period the amount of compensation for that period which he would have received but for any such surrender.

Compensation payable to non-pensionable officer on reaching retiring age

29.—(1) Where a person who is not a pensionable officer is receiving long-term compensation for loss of employment and attains normal retiring age, the Secretary of State may, if satisfied that the person would, but for the loss, have continued in the employment he has lost for a substantial period beyond that age, continue to pay compensation to him for the remainder of his life at half its former rate.

(2) Where a person who is not a pensionable officer suffers loss of employment on or after attaining normal retiring age, the Secretary of State may, if satisfied that the person would in the normal course have continued in the employment he has lost for a further substantial period, pay compensation to him for the remainder of his life at half the rate to which he would have been entitled under regulation 15 had he not attained normal retiring age at the date on which he lost his employment.

Persons subject to policy schemes

30.—(1) Regulations 20, 21, 22, 23 and 27 shall not apply to a person (in this regulation referred to as a "policy scheme participant") who had been participating in a scheme associated with his employment for providing super-annuation benefits by means of contracts or policies of insurance, and who, after the loss of his employment or the diminution of his emoluments, continued to participate in that scheme, or became entitled to a benefit or prospective benefit thereunder other than a return of contributions.

(2) If a policy scheme participant has lost his employment, the Secretary of State may, if the relevant scheme so permits, make such payments to or in respect of him, whether by way of the payment of premiums or otherwise, as are actuarially equivalent to the amounts by which his retirement compensation might have been increased under regulation 19(2) or (4) had he been a person to whom regulations 20, 21 or 22 applied.

(3) If a policy scheme participant has suffered a diminution of his emoluments, the Secretary of State may, if the relevant scheme so permits, make such payments to or in respect of him, whether by way of the payment of premiums or otherwise, as will secure to him the like benefits as if his emoluments had not been diminished.

(4) If a policy scheme participant becomes entitled to a benefit under such a scheme as is mentioned in paragraph (1) before reaching normal retiring age, the Secretary of State may reduce any long-term compensation payable to him by the amount of such benefit.

Intervals for payment of compensation under part V

31. Any compensation awarded as an annual sum under this part of these regulations to or in respect of any person shall be payable at intervals equivalent to those at which the corresponding benefit would have been payable under the person's last relevant pension scheme or at such other intervals as may be agreed between the person entitled to receive the compensation and the Secretary of State.

Part VI

Adjustment, Review and Compounding of Compensation

Adjustment of compensation where superannuation benefit is also payable

32.—(1) Where any period of service of which account was taken in calculating the amount of any compensation payable under part IV or V of these regulations is subsequently taken into account for the purpose of calculating the amount of any superannuation benefit payable to or in respect of any person in accordance with a pension scheme associated with any employment undertaken subsequent to the loss of employment or diminution of emoluments which was the subject of the claim for compensation, the Secretary of State may in accordance with this regulation withhold or reduce the compensation payable in respect of any period for which such superannuation benefit is being received.

(2) If the part of any superannuation benefit by way of annual amounts which is attributable to a period of service mentioned in paragraph (1) equals or exceeds the part of any compensation by way of annual amounts which is attributable to the same period, that part of the compensation may be reduced or withheld, or if such part of the superannuation benefit is less than such part of the compensation, the compensation may be reduced by an amount not exceeding such part of the superannuation benefit.

(3) Where a death gratuity is payable in respect of any person, the sum payable under regulation 27 may be reduced by an amount not greater than the proportion of the death gratuity which the period of service mentioned in paragraph (1) bears to the total period of service of which account was taken in the calculation of the death gratuity.

(4) In addition to any reduction authorised by paragraphs (2) or (3), if, in the circumstances mentioned in paragraph (1), compensation by way of annual amounts is attributable in part to any provision of the relevant pension scheme for a minimum benefit, the compensation may be reduced by an amount not exceeding that part.

(5) Where any additional years of service or period of contribution have been credited to a person under regulation 19(2), if the number of such years or such period is equal to or less than the period spent in the subsequent employment mentioned in paragraph (1), the compensation by way of annual amounts may be reduced (in addition to any other reduction authorised by this regulation) by an amount not exceeding that attributable to the additional years or period so credited or, if the number of such years or such period is greater than the period spent in the subsequent employment, by such proportion of that amount as the period spent in the subsequent employment bears to the number of additional years or the period so credited.

(6) Where compensation has been calculated in accordance with regulation 25, the provisions of this regulation shall apply only in relation to such part (if any) of the superannuation benefit as is attributable to annual emoluments in excess of those to which the person was entitled on entering the new employment referred to in regulation 25.

(7) Where compensation is payable in respect of diminution of emoluments, the provisions of this regulation shall apply only in relation to such part (if any) of the superannuation benefit as is attributable to annual emoluments in excess of those to which the person was entitled immediately prior to the diminution.

Reduction of compensation in certain cases

33.—(1) If under a person's last relevant pension scheme any benefit for which the scheme provided would have been subject to reduction or suspension on his taking up other specified employment, any retirement compensation to which he is entitled shall, where such employment is taken up, be reduced or suspended in the like manner and to the like extent:

Provided that in calculating the amount of the reduction there shall be aggregated with the emoluments of the employment taken up the amount of any superannuation benefit payable to the person by way of annual amounts which is attributable to any period of service of which account was taken in calculating the retirement compensation and to so much of the emoluments as were so taken into account.

(2) There shall be deducted from the retirement compensation payable to any person any additional contributory payments remaining unpaid at the date when he suffered loss of employment; and any such payments not recovered at the date of his death shall be deducted from any compensation payable in respect of that person under regulations 26, 27 or 28(2).

(3) Where a person is entitled to compensation under these regulations and the circumstances are such that he is also entitled to—

(a) a redundancy payment under the Redundancy Payments Act 1965(a), or

(b) any similar payment in consequence of the loss of his employment under any contract or arrangement with the authority by whom he was employed (other than payments by way of a return of contributions under a pension scheme), or

(c) any payment under or by virtue of the provisions of any enactment relating to the reinstatement in civil employment of persons who have been in the service of the Crown,

the compensation which would, apart from this paragraph, become due to the person, whether by instalments or lump sum or both, shall in the aggregate be reduced by the amount of the payments referred to in this paragraph.

(4) Where compensation under these regulations is payable to or in respect of any person, and that person or his widow, child or other dependent or his or her personal representatives or any other person is or are also entitled (whether immediately or on the person's attaining some greater age) to a superannuation benefit under his last relevant pension scheme—

(a) any instalment of such compensation which is payable in respect of any period shall be reduced by so much of such superannuation benefit payable in respect of the same period as is attributable to any period of service of which account was taken in calculating the compensation and to so much of the emoluments as were so taken into account; and

(b) any such compensation which is payable as a lump sum shall be reduced by the amount of any lump sum superannuation benefit which is so attributable.

(5) For the purposes of paragraph (4) no account shall be taken of any sum payable in consequence of the surrender by any person of part of his superannuation benefit by way of annual amounts under any provision in that behalf in the relevant pension scheme with a view to obtaining or increasing allowances for his widow, child or other dependant; and the person shall be deemed to have received during any period the amount of superannuation benefit which he would have received but for any such surrender.

(6) Where in any week a person is entitled to long-term compensation and is also entitled to unemployment, sickness or injury benefit under any Act relating to National Insurance, other than a benefit claimable by him in respect of a dependant, there shall be deducted from the long-term compensation payable for that week a sum equal to the amount by which the aggregate of such National Insurance benefit claimable in respect of that week and the weekly rate at which the long-term compensation would be payable but for this regulation exceeds two thirds of the weekly rate of the net emoluments of the employment which he has lost or in which the emoluments have been diminished:

(a) 1965 c. 62.

Provided that this paragraph shall not apply in relation to any such sickness or injury benefit insofar as an equivalent sum is deducted from the emoluments of his current employment and such deduction from those emoluments has not occasioned an increase in his long-term compensation.

(7) In paragraph (6) the expression "weekly rate" means seven three hundred and sixty-fifths of the relevant annual rate.

Notification of change of circumstances

34. Where—

(*a*) a pensionable officer after suffering loss of employment or diminution of emoluments enters any employment referred to in regulation 25 or becomes entitled to any superannuation benefit on ceasing to hold such employment, or

(*b*) a person entitled to long-term compensation enters employment the remuneration whereof is payable out of public funds, or ceases to hold such employment, or receives any increase in his remuneration in such employment, or

(*c*) a person entitled to retirement compensation enters employment in which the compensation is subject to reduction or suspension under regulation 33, or ceases to hold such employment, or receives any increase in his remuneration in such employment, or

(*d*) a person entitled to long-term compensation starts to receive any benefit, any increase in benefit or any further benefit under any Act relating to National Insurance,

he shall forthwith inform the Secretary of State in writing of that fact.

Review of awards of long-term or retirement compensation

35.—(1) The Secretary of State shall, at intervals of not more than 6 months within a period of 2 years after the date on which any decision on a claim for long-term or retirement compensation for loss of employment (other than compensation payable under regulation 22) is notified to a claimant under regulation 37, or within such longer period as is specified in the subsequent provisions of this regulation, review his decision or, where the claim has been the subject of an appeal, the decision of the tribunal, and these regulations shall apply in relation to any such review as they apply in relation to the initial determination of the claim; and on such review, in the light of any material change in the circumstances of the case, compensation may be awarded, or compensation previously awarded may be increased, reduced or discontinued, subject to the limits set out in these regulations.

(2) The person to whom the decision relates may require the Secretary of State to carry out the review mentioned in paragraph (1) at any time within the period of 2 years mentioned in that paragraph if he considers that there has been a change in the circumstances of his case which is material for the purposes of these regulations.

(3) The Secretary of State shall carry out a review in accordance with paragraph (1), notwithstanding the expiration of the period mentioned in that paragraph, if—

(*a*) the emoluments of employment or work undertaken as a result of the loss of employment had been taken into account in determining the amount of any compensation awarded, and

(b) such employment or work has been lost or the emoluments thereof reduced, otherwise than by reason of misconduct or incapacity to perform such duties as the person might reasonably have been required to perform, and

(c) the Secretary of State is satisfied that such loss or reduction is causing the person hardship,

and where any decision is so reviewed, the decision shall be subject to further review in accordance with paragraph (1) as if the review carried out under this paragraph had been the initial determination of the claim.

(4) Paragraphs (1) and (2) shall apply in relation to any decision on a claim for long-term or retirement compensation in respect of diminution of emoluments as they apply in relation to any decision mentioned in the said paragraph (1):

Provided that—

(i) where the person to whom the decision relates ceases to hold the employment in which his emoluments were diminished, a review shall be held within 3 months after that date, but no further review shall be held after the expiry of that period, and

(ii) while that person continues to hold that employment, there shall be no limit to the period within which a review may take place.

(5) Notwithstanding anything contained in the foregoing provisions of this regulation, the Secretary of State shall review a decision (whether given by him or the tribunal) on a claim for long-term compensation after the expiration of any period within which a review is required to be made if at any time—

(a) the person to whom the decision relates becomes engaged in employment (hereinafter referred to as his "current employment") the remuneration whereof is payable out of public funds and which he has undertaken subsequent to the loss of employment or diminution of emoluments, and

(b) the aggregate of the net emoluments of his current employment, any superannuation benefit payable to the person by way of annual amounts which is attributable to any period of service of which account was taken in calculating the long-term compensation and to so much of the emoluments as were so taken into account and the long-term compensation payable to him exceeds the net emoluments of the employment which he has lost or, as the case may be, in which the emoluments were diminished.

(6) The Secretary of State shall further review any decision reviewed under paragraph (5) whenever the net emoluments of the person's current employment are increased.

(7) If on any review under paragraphs (5) or (6) the compensation is reduced, it shall not be reduced below the amount by which the net emoluments of the person's current employment, together with any superannuation benefit payable to him by way of annual amounts which is attributable to any period of service of which account was taken in calculating the long-term compensation and to so much of the emoluments as were so taken into account, falls short of the net emoluments of the employment which he has lost, or as the the case may be in which the emoluments were diminished.

(8) The Secretary of State shall give to a person to whom a decision relates not less than 14 days' notice of any review of that decision to be carried out under this regulation unless the review is carried out at the person's request.

(9) Nothing in this regulation shall preclude the making of any adjustment of compensation required by regulations 32 or 33.

Compounding of awards

36.—(1) In a case where an annual sum which has been or might be awarded under these regulations does not exceed £26, the Secretary of State may, at his discretion, compound his liability in respect thereof by paying a lump sum equivalent to the capital value of the annual sum and, if any lump sum payment has been or might be awarded in addition to such annual sum under regulations 20, 21, 22 or 23, the Secretary of State may likewise discharge his liability in respect thereof by an immediate payment.

(2) In any other case, if the person who has been awarded long-term or retirement compensation requests him to do so, the Secretary of State may, after having regard to the state of health of that person and the other circumstances of the case, compound up to one quarter of his liability to make payments under the award (other than payments to a widow, child or other dependant under regulation 26) by the payment of an equivalent amount as a lump sum or, where any compensation has been awarded as a lump sum, by increasing that compensation to such equivalent amount; and in calculating for this purpose the liability of the Secretary of State to make such payments, account shall be taken of the annual value of lump sum payments of compensation.

(3) The making of a composition under paragraph (2) in relation to an award of long-term or retirement compensation shall not prevent the subsequent making of a composition under paragraph (1) in relation to that award, but, subject as aforesaid, not more than one composition may be made in relation to any award.

PART VII

PROCEDURE AND MISCELLANEOUS

Procedure on making claims

37.—(1) Every claim for compensation under these regulations and every request for a review of an award of long-term or retirement compensation shall be made in accordance with this regulation.

(2) Every such claim and request shall be made to the Secretary of State in a form approved by him.

(3) Resettlement compensation shall be claimed separately from any other form of compensation claimable under these regulations.

(4) The Secretary of State shall consider any such claim or request in accordance with the relevant provisions of these regulations and shall notify the person making the claim or request in writing of his decision—

    (*a*) in the case of a claim for resettlement compensation, not later than one month after the receipt of the claim, and

    (*b*) in the case of a claim for, or request for the review of an award of, compensation under part IV or V of these regulations, not later than 13 weeks after the receipt of the claim or request, and

    (*c*) in any other case, as soon as possible after the decision;

but the decision of the Secretary of State shall not be invalidated by reason of the fact that notice of the decision is given after the expiry of the period mentioned in this paragraph.

(5) Every notification of a decision by the Secretary of State (whether granting or refusing compensation or reviewing an award, or otherwise affecting any compensation under these regulations) shall contain a statement—

(a) giving reasons for the decision;

(b) showing how any compensation has been calculated and, in particular, if the amount is less than the maximum which could have been awarded under these regulations, showing the factors taken into account in awarding that amount; and

(c) directing the attention of the claimant to his right under regulation 42, if he is aggrieved by the decision, to institute proceedings before a tribunal and giving him the address to which an application instituting such proceedings should be sent.

Claimants to furnish information

38.—(1) Any person claiming or receiving compensation or whose award of compensation is being reviewed shall furnish all such information as the Secretary of State may at any time reasonably require, and shall verify the same in such manner, including the production of books or of original documents in his possession or control, as may be reasonably so required.

(2) Any such person shall, on receipt of reasonable notice, present himself for interview at such place as the Secretary of State may reasonably require; and any person who attends for interview may, if he so desires, be represented by his adviser.

Procedure on death of claimant

39.—(1) In the event of the death of a claimant or of a person who, if he had survived, could have been a claimant, a claim for compensation under these regulations may be continued or made, as the case may be, by his personal representatives.

(2) Where any such claim is continued or made as aforesaid the personal representatives shall, as respects any steps to be taken or things to be done by them in order to continue or make the claim, be deemed for the purposes of these regulations to be the person entitled to claim, but, save as aforesaid, the person in whose right they continue or make the claim shall be deemed for the purposes of these regulations to be such person, and the relevant provisions of these regulations shall be construed accordingly:

Provided that the Secretary of State may in any such case extend the period within which, under regulation 7 or 13, a claim is required to be made.

Calculation of service

40.—(1) For the purpose of determining the amount of any compensation payable in respect of the loss of an employment to which, or of any 2 or more employments to which in the aggregate, a person devoted substantially the whole of his time, any previous period of part-time employment shall be treated as though it were whole-time employment for a proportionately reduced period.

(2) For the purpose of making any calculation under these regulations in respect of a person's reckonable service, all periods of such service shall be aggregated and, except where reference is made to completed years of service, if the aggregated service includes a fraction of a year, that fraction shall, if it exceeds 6 months, be treated as a year, and shall in any other case be disregarded.

Compensation not assignable

41. Subject to any statutory provision in that behalf, any compensation to which a person becomes entitled under these regulations shall be paid by the Secretary of State and shall be payable to, or in trust for, the person who is entitled to receive it, and shall not be assignable:

Provided that, without prejudice to any other right of recovery, any compensation paid in error may be recovered by the Secretary of State by deduction from any compensation payable under these regulations.

Right of appeal from decision of the Secretary of State

42.—(1) Every person who is aggrieved by any decision of the Secretary of State with respect to a compensation question or by any failure on the part of the Secretary of State to notify him of any such decision within the appropriate time prescribed by these regulations may, within 13 weeks of the notification to him of the decision or the expiry of the prescribed time as the case may be, institute proceedings for the determination of the question by a tribunal in accordance with the Industrial Tribunals (Employment and Compensation) Regulations 1967(a) and these regulations; and the tribunal shall determine the question accordingly.

(2) For the purpose of any such proceedings a person or persons may be appointed to sit with the tribunal as assessor or assessors.

(3) The Secretary of State shall give effect to the decision of a tribunal subject to any modifications that may be required in consequence of any appeal from that decision on a point of law.

Consequential provisions

43. The Local Government (Executive Councils) (Compensation) Regulations 1964(b) and the Local Government (Executive Councils) (Compensation) Amendment Regulations 1966(c) shall not apply to any person to whom these regulations apply by virtue of regulation 4(*a*).

Keith Joseph,
Secretary of State for Social Services.

14th January 1971.

EXPLANATORY NOTE

(This Note is not part of the Regulations.)

1. These Regulations are made under section 60(2) of the Local Government Act 1958, section 85(4) of the London Government Act 1963, and section 35 of the Health Services and Public Health Act 1968. They provide for the payment of compensation to or in respect of persons who suffer loss of employment or loss or diminution of emoluments which is attributable to a reorganisation in the National Health Service in England or in Wales as defined in regulation 4. The regulations can have retrospective effect in circumstances provided by regulation 4(*b*) and (*c*) by virtue of section 35(2) of the Health Services and Public Health Act 1968.

(a) S.I. 1967/361 (1967 I, p. 1205). (b) S.I. 1964/1177 (1964 II, p. 2696).
(c) S.I. 1966/254 (1966 I, p. 653).

2. Part I of the regulations contains definitions. Part II specifies the persons to whom the regulations apply and the grounds of entitlement to compensation. The regulations apply to persons employed whole-time or part-time by Regional Hospital Boards or Boards of Governors of teaching hospitals, by Executive Councils or joint committees of such Councils, or by local medical, pharmaceutical, dental or optical committees.

3. The compensation is payable by the Secretary of State for Social Services and is:—

(a) resettlement compensation for loss of employment (part III of the regulations);

(b) long-term compensation for loss of employment or loss or diminution of emoluments (part IV);

(c) retirement compensation for loss of employment or loss or diminution of emoluments (part V);

(d) compensation to the widow, child or other dependant or to the personal representative of a claimant who was a pensionable officer (part V).

4. Resettlement compensation is payable for a period not exceeding 26 weeks to officers with at least 3 years' service in the National Health Service and other relevant employments. The qualifying conditions and factors to be considered are set out in regulation 7 and the method of calculating the amount of compensation is contained in regulation 8.

5. Long-term compensation is payable to officers with at least 8 years' service in the National Health Service and other relevant employments. The qualifying and other conditions are set out in regulations 13 and 14. The method of calculating the maximum amount of long-term compensation is laid down in regulations 15 (loss or employment) and 16 (diminution of emoluments).

It is a proportion, not exceeding two-thirds, of the net emoluments lost or of the amount by which emoluments have been diminshed, as the case may be. This compensation is payable from a date determined under regulation 17 and can be payable up to normal retiring age.

6. Retirement compensation payable to a pensionable officer for loss of employment is based upon his accrued pension rights (regulation 20) supplemented in the case of persons aged 40 or over at the date of loss by the addition of notional years of service (regulation 19). Retirement compensation for diminution of emoluments is an appropriate proportion of that for loss of employment (regulation 23). In the case of a non-pensionable officer compensation not exceeding one half of the rate of long-term compensation may be paid (regulation 29) and special provision is made for any persons whose pension arrangements are by way of policies of insurance (regulation 30). Retirement compensation is ordinarily payable from normal retiring age but in certain circumstances may be put into payment earlier (regulations 21 and 22). The qualifying and other conditions for the payment of retirement compensation are the same as those for long-term compensation (regulation 18).

7. Compensation is payable to the widow, child or other dependant or to the personal representative of a claimant who dies, where such persons would have benefited under the relevant pension scheme (regulations 26 to 28).

8. Part VI of the regulations provides for long-term and retirement compensation to be reviewed and for awards to be varied in the light of changes in circumstances (regulation 35). It also contains provisions for the adjustment, suspension and compounding of compensation in certain circumstances.

9. Part VII contains provisions relating to the procedure for making claims and notifying decisions, and confers upon a claimant who is aggrieved by a decision on a compensation question or the failure of the Secretary of State for Social Services to notify his decision a right to refer the question for determination by a tribunal established under section 12 of the Industrial Training Act 1964.

STATUTORY INSTRUMENTS

1971 No. 60

COMMONWEALTH TELEGRAPHS

The Commonwealth Telegraphs (Pension Rights of Former Cable and Wireless Ltd. Staff) Regulations 1971

Made - - -		*8th January* 1971
Laid before Parliament		*21st January* 1971
Coming into Operation		*2nd March* 1971

The Minister of Posts and Telecommunications, with the consent of the Minister for the Civil Service, in the exercise of the powers conferred upon him by section 49 of the Post Office Act 1969(a), and of all other powers enabling him in that behalf, hereby makes the following Regulations:

Citation and commencement

1. These Regulations may be cited as the Commonwealth Telegraphs (Pension Rights of Former Cable and Wireless Ltd. Staff) Regulations 1971 and shall come into operation on the 2nd March 1971, but shall then have effect from the 30th September 1969, and shall be construed accordingly.

Interpretation

2.—(1) In these Regulations, unless the context otherwise requires, the following expressions have the meanings hereby respectively assigned to them:

"the Act" means the Post Office Act 1969;

"the Minister" means the Minister of Posts and Telecommunications, and "the Ministry" shall be construed accordingly;

"the pension schemes" means the schemes set out in the Schedule hereto, being the schemes referred to in section 49(1)(a) of the Act;

"a person to whom these Regulations apply" means a person who:

(a) on the passing of the Act was serving in the Department of the Postmaster General, and

(b) on 1st October 1969 (being the day appointed for the purposes of the Act) becomes employed by the Post Office or continues in the service of the Crown by virtue of employment in the Ministry or the Department for National Savings, and

(c) immediately before the 1st October 1969 is a member of any of the pension schemes.

"the Post Office" means the authority established under section 6 of the Post Office Act 1969.

(2) The Interpretation Act 1889(b), applies for the interpretation of these Regulations as it applies for the interpretation of an Act of Parliament.

(a) 1969 c. 48.　　　　　　　　(b) 1889 c. 63.

Right to remain in Cable and Wireless Ltd. pension schemes

3. Every person to whom these Regulations apply shall be entitled to remain a member of each of the pension schemes of which he was a member immediately before the appointed day, so long as :

(*a*) he remains employed by the Post Office or in the Ministry or the Department for National Savings, as the case may be, and

(*b*) the trustees or other persons administering the schemes receive the contributions (if any) which he is from time to time liable to make to the scheme, and such contributions as may be made in respect of him in accordance with Regulation 4.

Employers' contributions

4. The trustees or other persons administering the pension schemes shall accept as employers' contributions in respect of a person to whom these Regulations apply, in lieu of the employers' contributions falling to be made in respect of him by the Postmaster General under the scheme or under Regulation 5 of the Commonwealth Telegraphs (Pension Rights of Cable and Wireless Ltd. Staff) Regulations 1950(**a**), contributions made by the Post Office, the Minister or the Department for National Savings.

Pensionable service

5.—(1) The service of every person to whom these Regulations apply in such employment as is mentioned in Regulation 3 shall, so long as he remains a member of any of the pension schemes, be treated as pensionable service for the purposes of each of those schemes of which he remains a member and of any statutory provisions, trust deeds, rules, and other instruments relating thereto, but not for any other purpose.

(2) In relation to a person who by virtue of these Regulations remains a member of the Cable and Wireless Staff Dependants' Fund, any reference in any instrument relating thereto to that person's dying prior to or after his being retired from pensionable service in the Department of the Postmaster General (however described) shall be construed as including a reference to his dying prior to or after his being retired from pensionable service in the Post Office, the Ministry, or the Department for National Savings.

Regulations to be terms of pension schemes

6. The pension schemes and the said statutory provisions and instruments shall have effect as if the provisions of these Regulations were terms thereof notwithstanding anything to the contrary contained therein.

Dated 4th January 1971.

Christopher Chataway,
Minister of Posts and Telecommunications.

Given under the official seal of the Minister for the Civil Service on 8th January 1971.

(L.S.)   *K. H. McNeill,*
Authorised by the Minister for the Civil Service.

(**a**) S.I. 1950/356 (1950 I, p. 395).

THE SCHEDULE

Eastern and Associated Telegraph Companies' Pension Fund

Cable and Wireless Widows Fund

Pacific Cable Board Pension Fund

Pacific Cable Board Provident Fund

Eastern and Associated Telegraph Companies' Superannuation Fund

Post Office Transferees' Pension Fund

Communications Superannuation Fund

Indo-European Retirement Fund

Marconi Companies' Staff Superannuation Fund

Cable and Wireless Pension Fund

Cable and Wireless Staff Dependants' Fund

EXPLANATORY NOTE

(This Note is not part of the Regulations.)

These Regulations enable former employees of Cable and Wireless Ltd., who transferred to the Postmaster General's Department on terms that they remained in a pension scheme of the Company, to continue in such a pension scheme on their transfer to the new Post Office, the Ministry of Posts and Telecommunications, or the Department for National Savings, in consequence of the abolition of the Postmaster General's Department by the Post Office Act 1969.

The Regulations have retrospective effect under section 6(7) of the Commonwealth Telegraphs Act 1949 as applied by section 49(2) of the Post Office Act 1969.

STATUTORY INSTRUMENTS

1971 No. 61

COMMONWEALTH TELEGRAPHS

The Commonwealth Telegraphs (Cable and Wireless Ltd. Pension) Regulations 1971

Made - - -	*8th January* 1971
Laid before Parliament	*21st January* 1971
Coming into Operation	*2nd March* 1971

The Minister of Posts and Telecommunications, with the consent of the Minister for the Civil Service, in the exercise of the powers conferred upon him by section 49 of the Post Office Act 1969(a), and of all other powers enabling him in that behalf, hereby makes the following Regulations :

Citation and commencement

1. These Regulations may be cited as the Commonwealth Telegraphs (Cable and Wireless Ltd. Pension) Regulations 1971, and shall come into operation on 2nd March 1971, but shall then have effect from the 30th September 1969, and shall be construed accordingly.

Interpretation

2.—(1) These Regulations shall be read as one with the Commonwealth Telegraphs (Cable and Wireless Ltd. Pension) Regulations 1955(b) (hereinafter called "the principal Regulations").

(2) In these Regulations, unless the context otherwise requires, the following expressions have the meanings hereby respectively assigned to them :

"the appointed day" means the 1st October 1969, being the day appointed under section 1 of the Post Office Act 1969 for the purposes of that Act ;

"the Minister" means the Minister of Posts and Telecommunications, and "the Ministry" shall be construed accordingly ;

"the paying authority" in relation to a transferee who on the appointed day enters into the service of the Post Office means the Post Office, and in relation to one who remains in the employment of the civil service of the State means the Minister ;

"the Post Office" means the authority established under section 6 of the Post Office Act 1969 ;

"the Post Office Staff Superannuation Scheme" means the pension scheme established under Section 43(1) of the Post Office Act 1969.

(3) The Interpretation Act 1889(c), applies for the interpretation of these Regulations as it applies for the interpretation of an Act of Parliament.

(a) 1969 c. 48.
(c) 1889 c. 63.

(b) S.I. 1955/1893 (1955 I, p. 500).

Amendments to the principal Regulations

3. The principal Regulations shall be amended as specified in the Schedule hereto.

Dated 4th January 1971.

Christopher Chataway,
Minister of Posts and Telecommunications.

Given under the official seal of the Minister for the Civil Service on 8th January 1971.

(L.S.)

K. H. McNeill,
Authorised by the Minister for the Civil Service.

THE SCHEDULE

AMENDMENTS TO THE PRINCIPAL REGULATIONS

Item	Regulation	
1	2(1)	For "the Post Office" in each place where it occurs substitute "the Department of the Postmaster General".
2		In the definition of "the Superannuation Acts" delete "1950" and substitute "1965".
3		At the end of the definition of "transferee" add "being a person who on the appointed day enters into the service of the Post Office or remains in the employment of the civil service of the State, or who has previously retired from the service of the Department of the Postmaster General".
4	5	For "The Postmaster-General may" in line 1 substitute "The paying authority shall".
5		Delete "out of the Post Office Fund" (substituted for "out of moneys provided by Parliament" by section 1(5) of the Post Office Act 1961(**a**)).
6		After "or" in line 13 insert "the paying authority".
7		For "the Post Office" in line 14 substitute "the Department of the Postmaster General, the Post Office or the civil service of the State (as the case may be)".
8		For "the Postmaster-General" in the last line substitute "the Minister".
9	6(1)	For "The Postmaster-General may" in line 1 substitute "The paying authority shall".
10		Delete "out of the Post Office Fund" (substituted for "out of moneys provided by Parliament" by section 1(5) of the Post Office Act 1961).
11	6(2)	For "the Post Office" substitute "the Department of the Postmaster General".
12		At the end of the paragraph insert "and in the employment of the Post Office or the civil service of the State (as the case

(**a**) 1961 c. 15.

Item	Regulation	
		may be) into which the person concerned entered or in which he continued, respectively, on the appointed day.".
13	7	For "the Postmaster-General may" substitute "the paying authority shall".
14		Delete "out of the Post Office Fund" (substituted for "out of moneys provided by Parliament" by section 1(5) of the Post Office Act 1961).
15		After "employed" in line 10 insert "in the Post Office or".
16	8	After "Superannuation Acts" insert "or the Post Office Staff Superannuation Scheme".
17		After "civil service of the State" insert "or the Post Office".
18	10(3)	After "Superannuation Acts" insert "or the Post Office Staff Superannuation Scheme".
19	10(4)	After "serving" in line 2 insert "in the Post Office or".
20	10(4)(*b*)	For "the Postmaster-General" substitute "the paying authority".
21	10(5)	For the words from "shall be payable" to "total of", substitute "nor any Post Office Staff Superannuation Scheme benefits shall be payable but the paying authority shall pay to or in respect of the persons concerned a sum equal to the total of".
22	10(6)	Delete 'and "Superannuation Acts benefits" ' and substitute ' "Superannuation Acts benefits" and "Post Office Staff Superannuation Scheme benefits" '.
23	11(1)	After "the Post Office" insert "or the civil service of the State".
24		For "the Postmaster-General may" substitute "the paying authority shall".
25		Delete "out of the Post Office Fund" (substituted for "out of moneys provided by Parliament" by section 1(5) of the Post Office Act 1961).
26	11(2)	For "the Post Office" substitute "the Department of the Postmaster General".
27		At the end of the paragraph insert "and in the employment of the Post Office or the civil service of the State (as the case may be) into which the person concerned entered or in which he continued, respectively, on the appointed day.".
28	13(2)	After "Superannuation Acts" insert "or the Post Office Staff Superannuation Scheme".
29	14(1)	After "Superannuation Acts" insert "or the Post Office Staff Superannuation Scheme".
30	15	After "Superannuation Acts" insert "or the Post Office Staff Superannuation Scheme".
31	16(1)	Delete the definition of "Superannuation Acts benefits" and substitute ' "Superannuation Acts benefits" and "Post Office Staff Superannuation Scheme benefits" mean any pension

Item	Regulation	
		benefits (whether payable periodically or in a lump sum) which, apart from this regulation, would or might have been payable to or in respect of a person as an established civil servant or as an employee of the Post Office, except a return of periodical contributions under Part I or Part II of the Superannuation Act 1949(a) or Part III or Part IV of the Superannuation Act 1965(b) or in respect of pensions for widows, children and dependants under the Post Office Staff Superannuation Scheme.'.
32	16(2)	After "as an established civil servant" insert "or in the Post Office".
33		After "Superannuation Acts benefits" insert "or Post Office Staff Superannuation Scheme benefits".
34	16(2)(b)	For "the Postmaster-General" substitute "the paying authority".
35	16(3)	For the words from "shall be payable" to "total of" substitute "nor any Post Office Staff Superannuation Scheme benefits shall be payable but the paying authority shall pay to or in respect of the person concerned a sum equal to the total of".
36	16(5)	For "the Postmaster-General" in each place where it occurs substitute "the paying authority".
37	18(1)	For "The Postmaster-General may" in line 1 substitute "The paying authority shall".
38		Delete "out of the Post Office Fund" (substituted for "out of moneys provided by Parliament" by section 1(5) of the Post Office Act 1961).
39	18(2)	For "the Post Office" substitute "the Department of the Postmaster General".
40		At the end of the paragraph insert "and in the employment of the Post Office or the civil service of the State (as the case may be) into which the person concerned entered or in which he continued, respectively, on the appointed day.".
41	18(4)	After "Superannuation Acts" insert "or the Post Office Staff Superannuation Scheme".
42		After "civil service of the State" insert "or the Post Office".
43	19(2)	After "Superannuation Acts" in the second place where it occurs insert "or the Post Office Staff Superannuation Scheme".
44	19(3)	After "Superannuation Acts" insert "or the Post Office Staff Superannuation Scheme".
45		After "established civil servant" insert "or a pensionable employee of the Post Office, respectively".
46	20(2)	After "Superannuation Acts" insert "or the Post Office Staff Superannuation Scheme".

Item	Regulation	
47		After "unestablished civil servants" insert "or unpensionable employees of the Post Office, respectively".
48	20(3)	After "Superannuation Acts" in the second place where it occurs insert "or the Post Office Staff Superannuation Scheme".
49		After "established civil servant" in the second place where it occurs insert "or a pensionable employee of the Post Office, respectively".
50	26(1)-(4)	For "the Postmaster-General" in each place where it occurs substitute "the Minister".
51	26(5)	For "the Minister of Labour and National Service" substitute "the Secretary of State for Employment".
52	26(6)	For "the Postmaster-General" in line 2 substitute "the Minister".
53		For "the Postmaster-General" in the last line substitute "the paying authority concerned".
54	26(8)	For "the Treasury" in line 1 substitute "the Civil Service Department".

EXPLANATORY NOTE

(This Note is not part of the Regulations.)

These Regulations amend the Commonwealth Telegraphs (Cable and Wireless Ltd. Pension) Regulations 1955, in consequence of the abolition of the Postmaster General's Department by the Post Office Act 1969. The 1955 Regulations made provision with respect to the pensions of the Staff of Cable and Wireless Ltd. who became employed in that Department as a result of the transfer of the United Kingdom assets of the Company into public ownership on the 1st April 1950. The present Regulations extend these provisions to cover those persons who, on the 1st October 1969 (the appointed day under the Post Office Act 1969) transferred to the service of the new Post Office.

The Regulations have retrospective effect under section 6(7) of the Commonwealth Telegraphs Act 1949 as applied by section 49(2) of the Post Office Act 1969.

STATUTORY   INSTRUMENTS

1971 No. 62 (L.1)

LEGAL AID AND ADVICE, ENGLAND

The Legal Aid (General) Regulations 1971

Made - - - -	13th January 1971
Laid before Parliament	26th January 1971
Coming into Operation	1st February 1971

ARRANGEMENT OF REGULATIONS

The Lord Chancellor in exercise of the powers conferred on him by sections 1, 2, 3, 4, 5, 6 and 12 of, and the Third Schedule to, the Legal Aid and Advice Act 1949(**a**) as amended by the Legal Aid Act 1960(**b**) and with the concurrence of the Treasury, hereby makes the following Regulations:—

Title, commencement and interpretation

1.—(1) These Regulations may be cited as the Legal Aid (General) Regulations 1971 and shall come into operation on 1st February 1971.

(2) The Interpretation Act 1889(**c**) shall apply to the interpretation of these Regulations as it applies to the interpretation of an Act of Parliament.

(3) In these regulations, unless the context otherwise requires—

" the Act " means the Legal Aid and Advice Act 1949 ;

" area committee " means an area committee appointed by the Council of The Law Society under the provisions of a scheme ;

" appropriate area committee " means the area committee in whose area an application for a certificate has been granted or refused ;

" appropriate committee " means an area committee or local committee to which an application for a certificate has been made or transferred ;

" assisted person " means a person in respect of whom a certificate is in force ;

" authorised summary proceedings " means the following proceedings in a magistrates' court, namely—

> (*a*) proceedings for or relating to an order made under
>> (i) the Affiliation Proceedings Act 1957(**d**), or
>> (ii) the Matrimonial Proceedings (Magistrates' Courts) Act 1960(**e**), or
>> (iii) the Guardianship of Infants Acts 1886(**f**) and 1925(**g**), or
>> (iv) the Small Tenements Recovery Act 1838(**h**), and
> (*b*) proceedings for which legal aid is authorised by the schedule to the Legal Aid (Extension of Proceedings) Regulations 1969(**i**) ;

" certificate " means a civil aid certificate issued in accordance with these regulations entitling a person to legal aid and includes an amendment to a certificate issued under regulation 9(4)(*a*) and an emergency certificate issued under regulation 11 ;

" claim " means a claim which it is desired to assert or to dispute where the question of taking, defending or being a party to proceedings before a court does not arise or has not yet arisen ; but if it did arise the proceedings would or might properly be such that legal aid could be given in connection therewith under section 1 of the Act ;

" the Commission " means the Supplementary Benefits Commission ;

" the fund " means the legal aid fund ;

" legal aid " means legal aid under Part I of the Act ;

(**a**) 1949 c. 51.   (**b**) 1960 c. 28.   (**c**) 1889 c. 63.   (**d**) 1957 c. 55.
(**e**) 1960 c. 48.   (**f**) 1886 c. 27.   (**g**) 1925 c. 45.   (**h**) 1838 c. 74.
(**i**) S.I. 1969/921 (1969 II, p. 2800).

" Legal Aid (Assessment of Resources) Regulations " means the Legal Aid (Assessment of Resources) Regulations 1960(**a**), as amended(**b**) ;

" legal executive " means a fellow of the Institute of Legal Executives ;

" local committee " means a local committee appointed by an area committee and includes a certifying committee set up under the provisions of a scheme ;

" matrimonial proceedings " means any proceedings for divorce, nullity of marriage, judicial separation, jactitation of marriage, and includes ancillary proceedings arising therefrom ;

" patient " means a person who, by reason of mental disorder within the meaning of the Mental Health Act 1959(**c**), is incapable of managing and administering his property and affairs ;

" scheme " means a scheme made under section 8 of the Act ;

" secretary " means the secretary of an appropriate committee.

(4) Where a power to do any act or exercise any jurisdiction or discretion is conferred by any provision of these regulations on a court, it may, unless it is exercisable only during the trial or hearing of the action, cause or matter be exercised by—

(*a*) in the House of Lords, the Clerk of the Parliaments ; or

(*b*) a judge, master or district registrar ; or

(*c*) in the Probate, Divorce or Admiralty Division or in a county court, the registrar.

(5) Where an area committee or local committee are required or entitled to perform any function under these regulations, that function may be performed on behalf of the committee by the secretary :

Provided that he may not—

(i) approve or refuse an application for a certificate except under regulations 5(5) and (10), and 11(2) and (3) ;

(ii) determine an appeal under regulation 10 ; or

(iii) discharge or revoke a certificate except under regulation 12(2)(*a*), (*b*), (*c*)(i), (iii) and (iv) and (3)(*a*)(i).

(6) In these Regulations, unless the context otherwise requires, a regulation referred to by number means the regulation so numbered in these Regulations, and a reference to any enactment shall be construed as a reference to that enactment as amended by any subsequent enactment.

(7) In these Regulations a form referred to by number means the form so numbered in schedule 1 or a form substantially to the like effect, with such variations as the circumstances of the particular case may require.

Effect of certificates

2.—(1) Legal aid shall be available to any person to whom a certificate has been issued in accordance with these regulations.

(a) S.I. 1960/1471 (1960 II, p. 1749).
(b) The amending instruments are S.I. 1961/555, 1962/147, 1964/1907, 1966/1348, 1969/922, 1970/1162 (1961 I, p. 1220; 1962 I, p. 115; 1964 III, p. 4239; 1966 III, p. 3676; 1969 II, p. 2802; 1970 II, p. 3931).   (c) 1959 c. 72.

(2) Any document purporting to be a certificate issued in accordance with these regulations shall, until the contrary is proved, be deemed to be a valid certificate issued to the person named therein and for the purposes there set out.

Applications for certificates

3.—(1) Any person desiring legal aid in respect of proceedings in an appellate court (other than an interlocutory appeal from a court below) may apply for a certificate—

(a) if resident in the United Kingdom or in the Republic of Ireland, to any area committee ; and

(b) if resident elsewhere, to an area committee in London ;

(2) Any person desiring legal aid in respect of any other proceedings or in respect of any claim may apply for a certificate—

(a) if resident in the United Kingdom or in the Republic of Ireland, to any local committee ; and

(b) if resident elsewhere, to a local committee in London:

Provided that where a certificate is already in force in respect of a claim, any application in respect of proceedings relating to the claim shall be made to the appropriate area committee.

(3) Every application shall be made in writing on a form approved by The Law Society or in such other manner, being in writing, as the secretary may accept as sufficient in the circumstances of the case and shall be lodged with the secretary.

(4) An applicant for legal aid in connection with authorised summary proceedings may, with a view to expediting the issue to him of a certificate, lodge with the secretary, at the time of applying for the certificate or at any time prior to its being issued, an undertaking in a form approved by The Law Society to pay any contribution that may be assessed by the appropriate committee or its secretary in accordance with these Regulations.

(5) Every application shall state the name of the solicitor (being a member of the appropriate panel) selected by the applicant to act for him and shall also contain such other information and shall be accompanied by such documents as may be requisite to enable—

(a) the appropriate committee to determine—

(i) the nature of the proceedings or the nature of the claim in relation to which legal aid is sought and the circumstances in which legal aid is required ; and

(ii) whether it is reasonable that a certificate should be granted ; and

(b) the appropriate committee or the Commission to determine the disposable income, disposable capital and maximum contribution of the applicant ;

and the applicant, including a person to whom a certificate has been issued on a form of undertaking under paragraph (4) shall (for the purpose of providing additional information), if required by the appropriate committee or the Commission to do so, attend for an interview or supply such further information or documents as he or they may require.

(6) The appropriate committee shall, except as is provided by regulation 5(3) and regulation 6(10), unless they shall have previously refused the application, submit to the Commission so much of it as is relevant to the determination of the disposable income and disposable capital of the applicant.

(7) If it appears to the appropriate committee that the application could, without prejudice to the applicant, be more conveniently or appropriately considered by another committee, the papers relating to the application shall be transferred to that other committee.

(8) In the case of a person resident outside the United Kingdom and not able to be present there while his application is being considered, the application shall be in English and shall be sworn, if the person is resident within the Commonwealth or the Republic of Ireland, before any justice of the peace or magistrate or any person for the time being authorised by law in the place where he is to administer an oath for any judicial or other legal purpose, or, if he is resident elsewhere, before a consular officer in the service of Her Majesty's Government in the United Kingdom, or any other person for the time being authorised to exercise the functions of such consular officer or having authority to administer an oath in that place, and shall be accompanied by a statement in writing, signed by some responsible person who has knowledge of the facts, certifying that part of the application which relates to the applicant's income and capital:

Provided that these requirements may be waived by the secretary where compliance with them would cause serious difficulty, inconvenience or delay and the application satisfies the provisions of paragraphs (3) and (5).

Applications on behalf of minors and patients

4.—(1) Save as is hereinafter provided an application for legal aid for a minor or patient shall be made on his behalf by a person of full age and capacity and, where the application relates to proceedings which are required by rules of court to be brought or defended by a next friend or guardian *ad litem,* that person shall be the next friend or guardian *ad litem,* or, where the application relates to proceedings and they have not actually begun or to any claim, a person who, subject to any contrary order of the court, intends to act in either capacity when the proceedings begin or if the question of taking them were to arise.

(2) The appropriate committee shall not issue a certificate applied for by a person on behalf of a minor or patient unless that person has signed an undertaking to pay to The Law Society (if called upon to do so) any sum which, by virtue of any provision of the Act or these Regulations, the appropriate committee may require an assisted person of full age and capacity to pay upon the issue or during the currency or upon the discharge or revocation of the certificate.

(3) Any certificate issued by virtue of this Regulation shall be in the name of the minor or patient, stating the name of the person who has applied on his behalf.

(4) In any matter relating to the issue, amendment, revocation or discharge of a certificate issued by virtue of this Regulation and in any other matter which may arise as between an assisted person and an appropriate committee, the person who has applied on behalf of the minor or patient for a certificate shall be treated for all purposes (including the receipt of notices) as the agent of the minor or patient.

(5) The appropriate committee may, where the circumstances appear to make it desirable, waive all or any of the requirements of the preceding paragraphs of this Regulation.

Duties of committees receiving applications for certificates

5.—(1) An application for a certificate in respect of authorised summary proceedings shall be considered by the secretary, who, after having regard to the determination made by the Commission of the disposable income and disposable capital of the applicant and the maximum contribution payable by him or the terms of any undertaking lodged by him under regulation 3(4), may (save in the circumstances mentioned in paragraph (11)) approve the application on behalf of the appropriate committee ; and in every case in which he does not approve the application he shall refer it to the committee for their consideration and approval or refusal.

(2) An application for a certificate in respect of authorised summary proceedings which has been referred to an appropriate committee by the secretary shall be considered by that committee, and they may approve or refuse it after having regard to the determination by the Commission of the disposable income and disposable capital of the applicant and the maximum contribution payable by him or the terms of any undertaking lodged by him under the provisions of regulation 3(4).

(3) An application for a certificate in respect of a claim shall be considered by the secretary and if, after determination by him of the disposable income and disposable capital of the applicant and the maximum contribution payable by the applicant, it appears to the secretary—

(*a*) that the applicant has reasonable grounds for taking steps to assert or dispute a claim ; and

(*b*) that it is reasonable in the circumstances that he should receive legal aid ; and

(*c*) that the total cost of asserting or disputing the claim would not be likely to exceed one hundred pounds ; and

(*d*) that the question of taking, defending or being a party to proceedings before a court does not arise or has not yet arisen, but if it did arise the proceedings would or might properly be such that legal aid may be given in connection therewith under section 1 of the Act,

he shall (subject to paragraph (5)) approve the application on behalf of the appropriate committee ; and in every other case he shall refer the application to the appropriate committee for their consideration and approval or refusal.

(4) The determination of disposable income, disposable capital and maximum contribution for the purposes of paragraph(3) shall be made in accordance with schedule 2 save that, where the disposable income and disposable capital have been determined by the Commission in accordance with section 4(6) of the Act (which provides for the determination of an assisted person's disposable income and disposable capital and the maximum amount of his contribution by the Commission) and the Legal Aid (Assessment of Resources) Regulations, that determination shall be adopted.

(5) Where the appropriate committee are satisfied in accordance with paragraph 6 of schedule 2 that an applicant is not eligible for or should be refused legal aid in respect of a claim, they shall refuse the application.

(6) Where an application is made for a certificate relating to proceedings and the secretary considers that the question of taking, defending or being a party to proceedings does not arise or has not yet arisen, but that, if the

application had been for a certificate in respect of a claim, he would have approved it in accordance with paragraph (3), he may with the consent of the applicant so approve it.

(7) Where an application is made for a certificate relating to a claim and the appropriate committee consider that the applicant has reasonable grounds for taking, defending or being a party to proceedings and that it is reasonable in all the circumstances that he should receive legal aid in respect of proceedings, the committee may treat the application as relating to proceedings and, subject to paragraphs (9), (12) and (13) may approve the application.

(8) Where an application is made for a certificate relating to proceedings and refused on the ground that the applicant has not shown reasonable grounds for taking, defending or being a party to proceedings, or that it is not reasonable that he should receive it in the particular circumstances of the case, the appropriate committee may treat the application as relating to a claim and, subject to paragraph (5), if satisfied in accordance with paragraph (3) may approve the application.

(9) Subject to paragraphs (1) and (6), and regulations 6(5) and (10) and 11, an application for a certificate in respect of proceedings shall not be approved, except after determination by the Commission of the disposable income, disposable capital and maximum contribution of the applicant:

Provided that where an application is made by a person who is concerned in the proceedings or claim only in a representative, fiduciary or official capacity then for the purpose of determining whether legal aid is available or the amount of any contribution to be made to the fund, the Commission shall disregard the personal resources of the applicant.

(10) Where the Commission determine that an applicant having a disposable capital which renders him entitled to legal aid under the Act has, however, disposable income of an amount which makes him ineligible for legal aid, the appropriate committee shall refuse the application.

(11) Where the Commission determine that an applicant, having a disposable income of an amount which makes legal aid available for him, has a disposable capital of an amount which renders him liable to be refused legal aid, the appropriate committee shall refuse the application if it appears to them that the probable costs of the applicant, without legal aid in the proceedings in respect of which the application was made would not exceed the maximum contribution payable by the applicant under the Act.

(12) Without prejudice to the generality of section 1(6) and section 5(3) of the Act (which provide that a person shall not be given legal aid unless he has reasonable grounds for taking, defending or being a party to proceedings, or in the case of a claim, unless he has reasonable grounds for taking steps to assert or dispute it, and may also be refused legal aid if it appears unreasonable that he should receive it in the particular circumstances of the case), an application for a certificate shall not be approved except after consideration by the appropriate committee of all questions of fact or law arising out of the claim or the action, cause or matter to which the application relates and the circumstances in which it was made, including whether it is reasonable and proper for persons concerned jointly with or having the same interest as the applicant to defray so much of the costs as would be payable from the fund in respect of the proceedings if a certificate were issued.

(13) Without prejudice to paragraph 12, an application may be refused:—

(*a*) where it appears to the appropriate committee that only a trivial advantage would be gained by the applicant in asserting or disputing the claim, or from the proceedings, to which the application relates, or that on account of the simple nature of the claim or proceedings, a solicitor would not ordinarily be employed ; or

(*b*) where it is made in a representative, fiduciary or official capacity and the appropriate committee, having taken into account the value of the property or estate or the amount of the fund out of which the applicant is entitled to be indemnified and the resources of the persons, if any, who might benefit from the outcome of the proceedings, have concluded that such refusal will not cause hardship ; or

(*c*) where it is made by, or on behalf of, a person in connection with an action cause or matter in which numerous persons have the same interest and in accordance with rules of court, one or more persons may sue or be sued, or may be authorised by a court to defend any such action cause or matter on behalf of or for the benefit of all persons so interested and in the opinion of the appropriate committee the right of the applicant would not be seriously prejudiced by such refusal ; or

(*d*) where it appears to the appropriate committee that the applicant has available rights or facilities making it unnecessary for him to obtain legal aid or has a reasonable expectation of obtaining financial or other help from a body of which he is a member, and has failed, in the opinion of the committee, to take all reasonable steps to enforce or obtain such rights, facilities or help including permitting the appropriate committee to take those steps on his behalf :

Provided that, where it appears that the applicant has a right to be indemnified against expenses incurred in connection with any proceedings, it shall not, for the purposes of this paragraph, be deemed a failure to take reasonable steps, if he has not taken proceedings to enforce that right, whether for a declaration as to that right or otherwise.

Issue of certificates

6.—(1) A certificate may be issued in respect of—

(*a*) one or more steps to assert or dispute a claim ; or

(*b*) the whole or part of—

    (i) proceedings in a court of first instance, or

    (ii) proceedings in an appellate court ;

but no certificate shall relate to proceedings (other than interlocutory appeals) both in a court of first instance and in an appellate court or to proceedings in more than one appellate court.

(2) Unless a certificate otherwise provides it shall not without the authority of the appropriate committee given under regulation 15(1) extend to—

(*a*) the addition of any further parties except in matrimonial proceedings, or

(*b*) any steps having the same effect as a cross action or a reply thereto or to a cross-appeal ; or

(*c*) lodging an interlocutory appeal.

(3) A certificate shall not relate to more than one action, cause or matter except in the case of—

(*a*) authorised summary proceedings ; or

(*b*) matrimonial proceedings ; or

(*c*) an application for a grant of representation which is necessary to enable the action, which is the subject matter or purpose of the certificate, to be brought ; or

(*d*) proceedings which may be taken under section 1 of the Act (which deals with the scope and general conditions of legal aid for proceedings) to enforce or to give effect to any agreement made in asserting or disputing the claim, or any order, or agreement made in the proceedings to which the certificate relates ; and for the purposes of this paragraph proceedings to enforce or give effect to an agreement or order shall include proceedings in bankruptcy or to wind up a company.

(4) A certificate issued in respect of a claim—

(*a*) shall authorise the assisted person to incur expenditure of a sum not exceeding a specified amount ; and

(*b*) shall not relate to more than one claim except in the case of claims arising in connection with the same circumstances which can in the opinion of the appropriate committee conveniently be joined together in the same action, cause or matter, if proceeding were taken on them.

(5) Where an application is approved relating to—

(*a*) authorised summary proceedings where either an undertaking has been lodged in accordance with regulation 3(4) or where no contribution will be payable ; or

(*b*) a claim or proceedings, other than authorised summary proceedings, where no contribution will be payable,

the appropriate committee shall forthwith issue a certificate in Form 1 and shall send the certificate and one copy thereof to the solicitor selected by the applicant, and a copy of the certificate to the applicant and, where a certificate has been issued under paragraph (*b*) in respect of proceedings, draw the attention of the applicant to the provisions of section 2(2)(*e*) of the Act (which limits the liability of an assisted person under an order for costs made against him).

(6) The appropriate committee or the secretary when considering applications under regulation 5(1), (3) and (6) shall assess the amount of the contribution, if any, which is payable in respect of a certificate and, in so doing, the committee or the secretary shall have regard to the probable cost of taking the steps to assert or dispute the claim or of the proceedings, and, save as is provided by these Regulations, shall not assess an amount in excess of any maximum amount of contribution determined by them or by the Commission. Where the probable cost of taking the steps or of the proceedings exceeds the maximum amount of contribution determined, the committee or the secretary shall, save as aforesaid, assess the maximum amount as the amount of contribution payable in respect of the claim or proceedings.

(7) Where an application has been approved and the appropriate committee consider that it is reasonable that persons concerned jointly with or having the same interest as the applicant should contribute to the cost of the proceedings

they shall add the amount which should be payable by such persons to the contribution (if any) payable by the applicant and shall so notify him under paragraph (8)(*b*) provided that the appropriate committee may subsequently re-assess the amount of the contribution payable under this paragraph where they are satisfied that the applicant has, without success, taken all reasonable steps (including permitting the appropriate committee to take these steps on his behalf) to obtain such payment.

(8) Where an application is approved for any claim or proceedings other than those referred to in paragraph (5) the appropriate committee shall—

(*a*) require—

(i) any contribution payable out of capital to be paid forthwith if the sum is readily available or, if it is not, by such time as seems to them reasonable in all the circumstances ; and

(ii) any contribution payable out of income to be paid by instalments at a rate which would, if the maximum contribution from income was required, secure that it would be paid within the twelve months next ensuing, or within the period in relation to which the disposable income has been computed, whichever is the later ; and

(*b*) notify the applicant—

(i) of the maximum amount of his contribution, as determined by them or the secretary or the Commission ; and

(ii) of the terms upon which a certificate will be issued to him ; and

(iii) except in the case of authorised summary proceedings or a claim, of the provisions of section 2(2)(*e*) of the Act.

(9) An applicant who desires that a certificate should be issued to him on the terms notified to him by an appropriate committee shall, within 28 days of being so notified, or within such other period as the appropriate committee may allow—

(*a*) signify his acceptance of those terms on a form approved by The Law Society and lodge it with The Law Society ; and

(*b*) if those terms require a contribution to be paid, sign on a form approved by The Law Society an undertaking to pay the contribution by the method stated in the terms and, if the contribution or a part of it is required to be paid before the certificate is issued, make that payment accordingly.

(10) Where the appropriate committee approve an application relating to—

(*a*) proceedings (other than interlocutory proceedings) in an appellate court in any action, cause or matter, in which the applicant was an assisted person in the court below ; or

(*b*) proceedings by way of a new trial ordered by a court before whom the applicant was an assisted person,

they shall not require the Commission to redetermine the applicant's disposable income and disposable capital but if the maximum contribution has not been required in respect of the previous proceedings may increase the contribution to the maximum amount of contribution determined by the Commission in relation to such proceedings:

Provided that, if, since the last determination by the Commission of the disposable income and disposable capital of the applicant, his circumstances have altered otherwise than as a result of the payment of a contribution in respect of the previous proceedings, they may require the Commission to redetermine his disposable income and disposable capital and shall take into account any increase greater than £52 or any decrease greater than £26 in the amount of his disposable income and any increase greater than £75 in the amount of his disposable capital.

(11) Where the appropriate committee approve an application and the applicant appears to be a member of a body which might reasonably have been expected to give him financial help towards the cost of the proceedings, but does not appear to have any right to be indemnified by them against expenses incurred in connection therewith, the appropriate committee shall require the applicant to sign an undertaking to pay to The Law Society, in addition to his contribution, if any, any sum received from that body on account of the cost of the proceedings.

(12) When an applicant has complied with as much of paragraph (9) as is relevant to his case the appropriate committee shall issue a civil aid certificate in Form 1 and send it to the solicitor selected by the applicant.

(13) Where the appropriate committee or the secretary have assessed the amount of contribution payable at a sum less than the maximum amount determined or redetermined by them or the Commission and it appears that the costs incurred or likely to be incurred under the certificate are likely to exceed the contribution so assessed, the appropriate area committee shall increase the amount of contribution up to the amount or likely amount of those costs or to the maximum contribution determined or redetermined, where that amount is less.

(14) Whenever the circumstances upon which the Commission have determined the disposable income or disposable capital of an assisted person have altered so that he has reason to believe that his disposable income has increased by an amount greater than £52 or his disposable capital has increased by an amount greater than £75, he shall, if his certificate relates to proceedings, inform the appropriate area committee of that alteration in his circumstances and shall if required by the secretary, the appropriate area committee or the Commission attend for an interview or supply such further information or documents as may be required of him.

Refusal of certificates

7. If an appropriate committee refuse an application for a certificate, they shall notify the applicant, stating that the application has been refused on one or more of the following grounds—

(a) that the Commission have determined that the applicant's disposable income exceeds the amount which makes legal aid available ; or

(b) that the Commission have determined that the applicant, having a disposable income of an amount which makes legal aid available for him, has a disposable capital of an amount which renders him liable to be refused legal aid and it appears to the committee that, if the application were refused, the probable costs to the applicant, without legal aid, of the proceedings in respect of which the application was made, would not exceed the maximum contribution payable by the applicant under the Act ; or

(c) that the application relates to a claim and, having regard to paragraph 6 of schedule 2, the applicant is not eligible for legal aid in respect of a claim ; or (*d*) that the proceedings to which the application relates or, where the application relates to a claim, the proceedings which would have to be taken, defended or participated in, if the question of doing so were to arise, are not proceedings for which legal aid may be given ; or

(*e*) that the applicant has not shown that he has reasonable grounds for taking steps to assert or dispute the claim, or for taking, defending or being a party to proceedings ; or

(*f*) that it appears unreasonable that he should receive legal aid in the particular circumstances of the case (whether as a result of any discretion given to an appropriate committee under any provision of these regulations or otherwise) ;

and shall inform him of the provisions, if any, of these regulations which relate to the circumstances in which he may appeal to the appropriate area committee for the decision to be reviewed.

Repeated refusal of certificates

8.—(1) Where a person has applied for and has been refused a certificate on three occasions and it appears to any area or local committee to whom such person applies that his conduct may amount to an abuse of the facilities provided by the Act, then, if the last application has been made to a local committee, the committee may report thereon to the appropriate area committee.

(2) If the last application has been made to an area committee, or if a report under paragraph (1) has been made to them by a local committee, then the committee may—

(*a*) enquire whether any other local or area committee has received an application from the person referred to ;

(*b*) call for a report as to the circumstances of any such other application ; and

(*c*) if they consider that the person named in the report has abused the facilities provided by the Act, report thereon to The Law Society, making such recommendations as seem to the area committee to be just.

(3) The Law Society, on receipt of such report, shall give the person referred to therein an opportunity of making (either himself or by some other person acting on his behalf) representations in writing on the matter and shall make such other inquiries as seem to be necessary and, if they are satisfied that his conduct has amounted to an abuse of the facilities provided by the Act, may make a direction (hereinafter in this Regulation referred to as " a prohibitory direction ") that no consideration shall, for a period not exceeding five years, be given by any area or local committee either—

(*a*) to any future application by that person for a certificate with regard to any particular matter ; or

(*b*) in exceptional circumstances, to any future application by him whatsoever.

(4) The Law Society may in its discretion—

(*a*) include within the terms of any prohibitory direction any receiver, next friend or guardian *ad litem* applying for a certificate on behalf of the person referred to in the prohibitory direction ; and

(b) at any time vary or revoke any prohibitory direction in whole or in part.

(5) Where The Law Society make a prohibitory direction they shall inform the Lord Chancellor thereof and shall, if so requested, give him their reasons for making the same.

Amendment of certificates

9.—(1) The appropriate area committee may amend a certificate where in their opinion—

(a) there has been some mistake in the certificate ; or

(b) it has become desirable for the certificate to extend to—

(i) other claims arising in connection with the same circumstances, or

(ii) other steps to assert or dispute a claim, or

(iii) proceedings, or

(iv) other steps or proceedings, or

(v) proceedings which may be taken under section 1 of the Act to enforce or give effect to any order or agreement made in asserting or disputing the claim, or, as the case may be, in the proceedings, in respect of which it was issued ; or

(c) it has become desirable for the certificate not to extend to certain of the steps or certain of the proceedings in respect of which it was issued ; or

(d) a change of solicitor should be authorised ; or

(e) it is reasonable in all the circumstances that the amount of expenditure which is authorised by a certificate in respect of a claim should be increased ; or

(f) under regulation 15(1) a solicitor should be authorised to take any of the steps referred to in regulation 6(2)(a) or (b).

(2) Without prejudice to paragraph (1) the appropriate area committee may amend a certificate—

(a) where the certificate relates to proceedings and the circumstances upon which the Commision have determined an assisted person's disposable income or disposable capital have altered so that—

(i) his disposable income has increased by an amount greater than £52 or decreased by an amount greater than £26, or

(ii) his disposable capital has increased by an amount greater than £75 ; or

(b) where, under these Regulations, they alter the amount of an assisted person's contribution.

(3) Regulations 3, 4, 5 and 6 shall apply so far as appropriate, to applications for the amendment of certificates as they apply to applications for certificates, but with the substitution for references to an appropriate committee of references to the appropriate area committee.

(4) Where an area committee—

(a) amend a certificate, they shall issue an amendment to the certificate in Form 2, and shall send it to the assisted person's solicitor and a copy thereof to the assisted person ;

(*b*) refuse an application for the amendment of a certificate, they shall notify the assisted person's solicitor in writing.

(5) The decision of an area committee on any question relating to the amendment of a certificate shall be final.

Appeals against decisions of local committees

10.—(1) Where a local committee refuse an application for a certificate in respect of proceedings other than authorised summary proceedings or an applicant is dissatisfied with the terms upon which the local committee would be prepared to issue it, the applicant may appeal to the appropriate area committee:

Provided that no appeal shall lie to an area committee from—

(*a*) any determination of the Commission ; or

(*b*) any decision by a local committee as to the amount of any contribution or the method by which it shall be paid, unless such contribution has been assessed under regulation 6(7).

(2) Such appeal shall be by way of review of the general circumstances in which the application for a certificate was made.

(3) Every appeal shall be brought by giving to the appropriate area committee, within four days of the date of notice of refusal of a certificate or of the terms upon which a certificate would be issued (or such longer period as the local committee or area committee may allow), notice of appeal in writing on a form approved by The Law Society or in such other manner, being in writing, as the secretary of the area committee may accept as sufficient in the circumstances of the case.

(4) Upon an appeal the appellant may, at his own expense, furnish further statements, whether oral or in writing, in support of his application, conduct the appeal himself, be represented by counsel, solicitor or legal executive or be assisted by any other person whom he may appoint for the purpose.

(5) The area committee shall determine the appeal in such manner as seems to them to be just and, without prejudice to the generality of the foregoing, may—

(*a*) dismiss the appeal ; or

(*b*) direct the local committee to offer a certificate subject to such terms and conditions as the area committee think fit ; or

(*c*) instead of themselves settling such terms and conditions, direct the local committee to do so ; or

(*d*) refer the matter or any part of it back to the local committee for their determination or report.

(6) Any decision of an area committee with regard to an appeal shall be final, and they shall give notice of their decision, in a form approved by The Law Society, to the appellant and to any solicitor acting for him.

Emergency certificates

11.—(1) Any person who desires legal aid in relation to proceedings as a matter of urgency may apply for an emergency certificate on a form approved by The Law Society or in such other manner as the appropriate committee to whom the application is made may accept.

(2) The appropriate committee shall have power in accordance with the provisions of this Regulation to approve such application and—

> (a) issue an emergency certificate without reference to the Commission ; and

> (b) amend such a certificate in the circumstances set out in regulation 9(1)(a), (b)(iv) and (v), (c), (d) or (f).

(3) Where a certificate is already in force in respect of a claim and an application is made in accordance with the proviso to regulation 3(2) the appropriate area committee may issue an emergency certificate and may direct that no further steps be taken under the certificate relating to the claim and shall amend the certificate in respect of the claim accordingly.

(4) Subject to paragraph (3) an application for an emergency certificate shall be made to the local or area committee to whom application for legal aid in respect of the proceedings would have to be made in accordance with these regulations.

(5) An application for an emergency certificate shall contain such information and shall be accompanied by such documents as may be requisite to enable the appropriate committee to determine the nature of the proceedings for which legal aid is sought and the circumstances in which it is required and, whether—

> (a) the applicant is likely to fulfil the conditions under which legal aid may be granted under the Act and the regulations made thereunder ; and

> (b) it is in the interests of justice that the applicant should, as a matter of urgency, be granted legal aid ;

and shall furnish such additional information and documents (if any) as may be sufficient to constitute an application for a certificate under regulation 3 :

Provided that, if it appears to the appropriate committee that the applicant cannot at the time of the application reasonably furnish that information, or any part of it, that committee shall nevertheless have power to issue an emergency certificate subject to such conditions as to the furnishing of additional information as they think reasonable.

(6) An emergency certificate shall be in Form 3 and shall have the same effect in all respects as a certificate and any person holding an emergency certificate shall, while it is in force, be deemed for the purposes of Part I of the Act and these Regulations to have a disposable income and disposable capital of an amount which makes legal aid available for him.

(7) The emergency certificate and one copy thereof shall be sent to the solicitor selected by the applicant from the appropriate panel and one copy shall be sent to the applicant.

(8) Subject to paragraph (9) and regulation 12, an emergency certificate, including an emergency certificate which has been extended under paragraph (9), shall remain in force for such period as the appropriate committee may allow and on the expiration of such period shall be discharged or revoked :

Provided that where a certificate has been issued under paragraph (11) the emergency certificate may not be discharged or revoked.

(9) The secretary, whose decision shall be final, may extend the period referred to in paragraph (8), where—

> (a) the applicant is offered a certificate in respect of the proceedings to which the emergency certificate relates and either fails to signify his acceptance or appeals against the terms of such offer ; or

(b) the appropriate committee refuse an application for a certificate in respect of proceedings to which an emergency certificate relates and either notice of appeal has been given to the appropriate area committee within the time limits laid down by regulation 10(3) or the time limit for doing so has expired ; or

(c) there are exceptional circumstances ;

and thereafter, unless the certificate is further extended, it shall be discharged or revoked :

Provided that where the period is extended under sub-paragraph (a) or (b) no further work may be done or steps taken under the certificate.

(10) Upon an emergency certificate being extended, amended, discharged or revoked, the appropriate committee shall forthwith issue a notice to that effect and shall send the notice and one copy thereof to the solicitor acting for the person to whom the emergency certificate was issued and shall send a further copy to that person and it shall be the duty of the solicitor to notify forthwith any counsel whom he may have instructed that the certificate has been extended, amended, discharged or revoked.

(11) A certificate issued in respect of proceedings to which an emergency certificate relates shall take effect from the date upon which the emergency certificate was issued and shall state—

(a) the number and date of issue of the emergency certificate ; and

(b) that the emergency certificate has been continuously in force from that date until the date of the certificate.

(12) An emergency certificate shall not be issued in respect of authorised summary proceedings.

Discharge and revocation of certificates

12.—(1) A certificate may be either discharged or revoked in the circumstances specified in this Regulation or in regulation 11(8) or (9).

(2) The appropriate area committee may at any time discharge a certificate from such date as they consider appropriate—

(a) at the request of the assisted person ; or

(b) where an assisted person has been required to make a contribution and any payment in respect thereof is more than twenty-one days in arrear ; or

(c) on being satisfied by the report of an assisted person's solicitor or otherwise—

(i) that the assisted person has died ; or

(ii) that the assisted person has had a receiving order made against him ; or

(iii) that the claim or proceedings to which the certificate relates have been disposed of ; or

(iv) that the work authorised by the certificate has been completed ; or

(d) when the appropriate committee have offered to extend to proceedings a certificate relating to a claim and the offer has been refused or has not been accepted within the time limits provided by these regulations.

(3) The appropriate area committee shall discharge a certificate from such date as they consider appropriate if—

(*a*) as a result of a determination by the Commission it appears that—

(i) the disposable income of the assisted person exceeds the maximum amount which makes legal aid available to an applicant ;

(ii) the disposable capital of the assisted person is of an amount which renders him liable to be refused legal aid, and it appears to them that the probable cost to the assisted person without legal aid of continuing the proceedings, would not exceed the maximum contribution payable under the determination ; or

(*b*) as a result of information which has come to their knowledge or where the assisted person's solicitor or counsel has given up the case, they consider that—

(i) the assisted person no longer has reasonable grounds for asserting or disputing the claim or for taking, defending or being a party to the proceedings ; or

(ii) the assisted person has required the claim to be asserted or disputed or the proceedings to be conducted unreasonably so as to incur an unjustifiable expense to the fund ; or

(iii) it is unreasonable in the particular circumstances that the assisted person should continue to receive legal aid :

Provided that a certificate shall not be discharged under this subparagraph until notice has been served on the assisted person that the appropriate area committee may do so and that he may show cause why the certificate should not be discharged.

(4) Where the appropriate area committee have considered the discharge of a certificate in consequence of information brought to their knowledge by any person, they may, if they think fit, inform that person whether or not the certificate has been discharged.

(5) The court may make an order revoking a certificate or discharging it from such date as may be appropriate at any time during the hearing of any proceedings to which an assisted person is a party upon application by or on behalf of any other party to the proceedings or by The Law Society where it considers that the assisted person has—

(*a*) in relation to any application for a certificate, made an untrue statement as to his resources or has failed to disclose any material fact concerning them whether the statement was made or the failure occurred before or after the issue of the certificate and notwithstanding that it was made or occurred in relation to an application to another area or local committee in connection with the same proceedings ; or

(*b*) wilfully failed to comply with these Regulations by not furnishing to the appropriate committee any material information concerning anything other than his resources ; or

(*c*) knowingly made an untrue statement in furnishing such information :

Provided that no order shall be made under this paragraph—

(i) until the assisted person has been given an opportunity to show cause why the certificate should not be discharged or, as the case may be, revoked, and

(ii) by reason of any mis-statement or failure such as is referred to in subparagraph (*a*), if the assisted person satisfies the court that he used due care or diligence to avoid such mis-statement or failure.

(6) Where an application is made under paragraph (5) the decision of the court shall be final and where the application is made by The Law Society, the court may order The Law Society to be made a party to the proceedings for the purpose of the application.

(7) The appropriate committee may at any time revoke a certificate upon the grounds set out in and subject to the provisos of paragraph (5).

(8) The appropriate area committee may, after giving the assisted person an opportunity to show cause why the certificate should not be revoked, revoke a certificate if they are satisfied that the assisted person has failed to attend for an interview or provide information or documents when so required under these Regulations.

(9) Where an area committee discharge or revoke an assisted person's certificate they shall, unless the costs have already either been taxed under schedule 3 to the Act (which relates to the remuneration to be paid to counsel and solicitors giving legal aid under Part I of the Act) or assessed under regulation 21 or 22, forthwith issue a notice of discharge or a notice of revocation, as the case may be, and shall send the notice and one copy thereof to his solicitor, and shall send a further copy of the notice to the assisted person.

(10) When a court makes an order revoking or discharging an assisted person's certificate, his solicitor shall forthwith inform the appropriate area committee.

Effect of discharge and revocation of certificates

13.—(1) Subject to this Regulation, a person whose certificate is revoked shall be deemed never to have been an assisted person in relation to the claim or proceedings to which the certificate related, and a person whose certificate is discharged shall, from the date of discharge, cease to be an assisted person in the claim or proceedings.

(2) Upon receipt by him of notice of revocation or a notice of discharge of a certificate by an area or local committee or upon revocation or discharge of a certificate by the court, the retainer of any solicitor and counsel selected by or acting on behalf of the assisted person under the certificate shall forthwith determine:

Provided that, if an area committee revoke or discharge a certificate, or if a certificate has been revoked or discharged under regulation 11(8) or (9), and proceedings have commenced, whether ex parte or inter partes, the retainer of the solicitor shall not determine until he has sent to the appropriate court office or registry and, if the proceedings are inter partes, has served any notice required by regulation 17.

(3) Upon determination of a retainer under this Regulation—

(a) the costs of the claim or proceedings to which the certificate related, incurred by or on behalf of the person to whom it was issued, shall, as soon as practicable thereafter—

    (i) in the case of a claim be assessed in accordance with the provisions of the Act and these Regulations,

    (ii) in the case of proceedings be taxed or so assessed, as the case may be ;

(b) the fund shall remain liable for the payment of any costs so taxed or assessed.

(4) Where a certificate has been revoked or discharged, section 3(4) of the Act (which provides for a charge upon property recovered or preserved for an assisted person) shall apply to any property recovered or preserved as a result of the person whose certificate has been revoked or discharged continuing to assert or dispute the claim, whether by taking proceedings or otherwise, or continuing to take, defend or be a party to the proceedings to which the certificate related and, for the purpose of this paragraph, the reference to a person whose certificate has been discharged shall, where the certificate has been discharged under regulation 12(2)(c)(i) and (ii) include his personal representatives, or his trustee in bankruptcy or the Official Receiver, as the case may be.

(5) Where a certificate has been revoked—

(a) The Law Society shall have the right to recover from the person to whom the certificate was issued the costs paid or payable under paragraph (3)(b) less any amount received from him by way of contribution ; and

(b) the solicitor who has acted under the certificate shall have the right to recover from that person the difference between the amount paid or payable out of the fund and the full amount of his solicitor and own client costs.

(6) Where a certificate has been discharged, the person to whom the certificate was issued shall remain liable for the payment of his maximum contribution, if any, as determined by the appropriate committee or as determined or redetermined by the Commission up to the amount paid or payable by The Law Society under paragraph 3(b) and where he continues to assert or dispute the claim or to take, defend or be a party to the proceedings to which the certificate related, section 2(2)(e) of the Act shall apply in so far as the costs were incurred while he was an assisted person.

Legal aid granted after costs incurred

14.—(1) Where, after proceedings have been instituted in any court, any party becomes an assisted person in regard to those proceedings, the provisions of section 2(2)(e) of the Act shall apply only to so much of the costs of the proceedings as are incurred while a certificate is in force.

(2) Any solicitor who has acted on behalf of the assisted person in the claim or proceedings to which a certificate relates before the date of the certificate, and any solicitor who has by law a lien on any documents necessary for asserting or disputing the claim, or for the proceedings, and who has delivered them up subject to his lien, may give notice of the fact to the appropriate area committee.

(3) If moneys are recovered for the assisted person, The Law Society shall pay to such solicitor out of the sum so recovered the costs to which he would have been entitled following a taxation between solicitor and own client:

Provided that, in any case where the sums so recovered are insufficient to pay those costs in full in accordance with this paragraph and also to meet the sums paid out or payable out of the fund on the assisted person's account, the sums recovered in the proceedings shall be divided between the fund and the solicitor in the same proportion as those costs bear to the costs allowed on taxation as between party and party in respect of the period during which the certificate was in force, and the first charge for the benefit of the fund imposed by virtue of section 3(4) of the Act on property recovered or preserved in the proceedings shall take effect accordingly.

(4) In any case in which—

(*a*) the costs payable to the solicitors under this Regulation ; or

(*b*) the party and party costs incurred during the period in which the certificate was in force,

have not been ascertained by taxation they shall for the purpose of this Regulation be fixed by the appropriate area committee.

Duties of solicitors

15.—(1) Where it appears to the assisted person's solicitor necessary for the proper conduct of the proceedings to take any of the steps referred to in regulation 6(2) he shall, unless authority has been given in the certificate, apply to the appropriate area committee for such authority.

(2) Where it appears to an assisted person's solicitor that the proper conduct of proceedings requires counsel, such counsel shall be selected from the appropriate panel and every set of papers delivered to him shall include a copy of the certificate, be endorsed in the manner set out in schedule 3 with such variations as circumstances may require, and no fees shall be marked thereon.

(3) Where it appears to an assisted person's solicitor necessary for the proper conduct of the proceedings to instruct more than one counsel he shall, unless authority has been given in the certificate, apply to the appropriate area committee for such authority.

(4) Where it appears to an assisted person's solicitor necessary for the proper conduct of the proceedings to instruct counsel in authorised summary proceedings, he may, unless authority has been given in the certificate, apply to the appropriate area committee for such authority.

(5) The Law Society may give general authority to solicitors acting for assisted persons in any particular class of case—

(*a*) to obtain a report or opinion of one or more experts or to tender expert evidence ;

(*b*) to employ a person to provide a report or opinion (other than as an expert) ;

(*c*) to bespeak transcripts of shorthand notes or tape recordings of any proceedings ;

and if they do so they shall authorise the maximum fee payable for any such report, opinion, expert evidence or transcript.

(6) Where it appears to an assisted person's solicitor necessary for asserting or disputing the claim or for the proper conduct of the proceedings to do any of the following acts, namely—

(*a*) to obtain a report or opinion of an expert or to tender expert evidence in a case of a class not included in any general authority under paragraph (5) ; or

(*b*) to pay a person, not being an expert witness, a fee to prepare a report and give evidence if required in a case of a class not included in any general authority under paragraph (5) ; or

(*c*) in a case of a class included in any general authority under paragraph (5), to pay a higher fee than that authorised by The Law Society or to obtain more reports or opinions or to tender more evidence (expert or otherwise) than has been authorised ; or (*d*) to perform an act which is either unusual in its nature or involves unusually large expenditure ; or

(*e*) to bespeak any transcripts of shorthand notes or tape recordings of any proceedings not included in any general authority under the foregoing paragraph ;

he may, unless authority has been given in the certificate, apply to the appropriate area committee for such authority ; and if that committee give authority for any purposes mentioned in sub-paragraphs (*a*), (*b*), (*c*) and (*d*) they shall, if appropriate, state the number of reports or opinions that may be obtained or the number of persons who may be authorised to give expert evidence and the total fee to be paid.

(7) Where prior authority has been given under the provisions of paragraph (1) or (3) no question as to the propriety of any step or act shall be raised on a taxation in accordance with schedule 3 to the Act or on an assessment by an area committee in accordance with regulation 21 or 22 but where no such prior authority has been obtained, except in respect of an interlocutory appeal, no payment for the step or act shall be allowed on the taxation unless it is also allowed on a party and party taxation.

(8) Where prior authority or approval has been given under paragraph (4), (5) or (6) no question as to the propriety of the act shall be raised on a taxation in accordance with schedule 3 to the Act or on an assessment by an area committee in accordance with regulation 21 or 22 ; but where no such prior authority or approval has been obtained, or where an interlocutory appeal has been lodged without prior authority, payment for the act may still be allowed on taxation or assessment.

(9) Where a certificate has been issued in connection with any proceedings, the assisted person's solicitor or counsel shall not take any payment for work done in those proceedings during the currency of that certificate (whether within the scope of the certificate or otherwise) except such payments as may be made out of the fund.

Conduct of proceedings on behalf of assisted persons

16.—(1) Without prejudice to the right of a solicitor or counsel to give up a case for good reason, any solicitor or counsel may give up an assisted person's case if in his opinion, the assisted person has—

(*a*) required it to be conducted unreasonably so as to incur an unjustifiable expense to the fund or has required unreasonably that the case be continued ; or

(*b*) wilfully failed to comply with any regulation as to the information to be furnished by him or in furnishing such information has knowingly made a false statement or false representation.

(2) Where any solicitor or counsel exercises the right to give up an assisted person's case under paragraph (1) the solicitor shall make a report to the appropriate area committee of the circumstances in which that right was exercised.

(3) Where an area committee to whom such report is made do not discharge the assisted person's certificate under regulation 12, they shall require the assisted person to select another solicitor from the appropriate panel to act for him.

(4) No solicitor or counsel acting for an assisted person shall—

(*a*) receive or be party to any payment made in contravention of regulation 15(9) ; or

(b) entrust the conduct of any part of the case to any other person save to a solicitor or counsel who is a member of an appropriate panel:

Provided that nothing in this paragraph shall prevent a solicitor from entrusting the conduct of any part of the case to a person who is his partner or who is employed in his office.

(5) An assisted person's solicitor and his counsel (if any) shall give the appropriate area committee such information regarding the progress and disposal of the claim or proceedings to which the certificate relates as the area committee may from time to time require for the purpose of performing their functions under the scheme and, without prejudice to the generality of the preceding words, a solicitor who has acted or is acting for an assisted person shall on being satisfied that—

(a) the assisted person has died ; or

(b) has had a receiving order made against him,

report the facts to the appropriate area committee.

(6) Neither solicitor nor counsel shall be precluded, by reason of any privilege arising out of the relationship between counsel, solicitor and client, from disclosing to an area committee any information or from giving any opinion which may enable that committee to perform their functions under regulation 12(3)(b), and for the purpose of providing information under that paragraph any party may disclose to an area committee communications in relation to the proceedings sent to or by the assisted person's solicitor whether or not marked " without prejudice ".

(7) A solicitor shall, if required to do so, inform the appropriate area committee of his reasons for refusing to act or for giving up a case after being selected from the appropriate panel.

(8) Counsel, where he has been selected to act or is acting for an assisted person shall, if required to do so, inform the appropriate area committee of his reasons for refusing to accept instructions or for giving up the case or entrusting it to another.

(9) A solicitor shall report forthwith to the appropriate area committee either upon the completion of the case if he has completed the work authorised by the certificate or if for any reason he has been unable to do so.

Service of notices

17.—(1) Any notice required to be served under any provision of these Regulations shall be served either—

(a) personally ; or

(b) by sending it by prepaid post to the last known address of the person required to be served ; or

(c) if served together with any process of a court by any mode of service authorised by rules of court for service of that process.

(2) Whenever an assisted person becomes a party to proceedings, or a party to proceedings becomes an assisted person, his solicitor shall forthwith—

(a) serve all other parties with notice of the issue of a certificate in Form 4 ;

(b) if at any time thereafter any other person becomes a party to the proceedings, forthwith serve similar notice upon such person.

(3) Where an assisted person's solicitor—

(*a*) commences any proceedings for the assisted person in the county court ; or

(*b*) commences proceedings in accordance with Order 112, rule 3 or 4, of the Rules of the Supreme Court (**a**) or Rules 101 or 103 of the Matrimonial Causes Rules 1968(**b**) ;

and at the same time files a copy of the notice to be served in accordance with paragraph (2), the registrar shall annex a copy of the notice to the originating process for service.

(4) A solicitor who receives from an appropriate committee a certificate relating to proceedings shall, if proceedings have begun or otherwise upon their commencement, or thereafter, send it by prepaid post to the appropriate court office or registry.

(5) A solicitor who receives from an appropriate committee under the provisions of these regulations—

(*a*) a notice of revocation of certificate or a notice of discharge of certificate ;

(*b*) a certificate in respect of proceedings to which an emergency certificate related ; or

(*c*) an amendment to a certificate issued under regulation 9(1)(*a*)(*b*)(*c*)(*d*) or (*f*) or (2) ;

shall forthwith—

(i) send such notice, certificate or amendment to certificate by prepaid post to the appropriate court office or registry, and

(ii) except in the case of an amendment to a certificate issued under regulation 9(2), serve notice of the fact in Form 5 upon any other persons who are parties to the proceedings, and, if any other person becomes a party to the proceedings, serve similar notice upon such person.

(6) A solicitor who receives notice that an emergency certificate has been extended under regulation 11(9) hereof shall send a copy of such notice by prepaid post to the appropriate court office or registry.

(7) Copies of the notices referred to in paragraphs (2) and (5) shall form part of the papers for the use of the judge at the trial.

(8) Any person, not being himself an assisted person, who is a party to proceedings to which an assisted person is a party, may, at any time before the judgment, file in the appropriate court office or registry an affidavit exhibiting thereto a statement setting out the rate of his own income and amount of his own capital and any other facts relevant to the determination of his means in accordance with section 2(2)(*e*) of the Act.

(9) Any person filing an affidavit under paragraph (8) shall serve a copy thereof, together with the exhibit, upon the assisted person's solicitor, who shall forthwith serve him with a copy of the certificate but save as aforesaid, no document and no extract from a document sent to the court office or registry under paragraph (4), (5) or (6) or filed or exhibited under paragraph (8) shall be disclosed save by leave of the court.

(10) Any document sent to the court office or registry or filed or exhibited under the provisions of this regulation shall be bespoken or made available for the use of the court at the hearing or at any other stage of the proceedings.

(**a**) 1965/1776 (1965 III, p. 4995).   (**b**) 1968/219 (1968 I, p. 665).

(11) Save as is otherwise provided by these regulations, in any proceedings in any court to which an assisted person is a party the procedure shall be regulated by the rules of procedure for that court.

(12) Paragraphs (2) to (10) shall not apply to authorised summary proceedings and, where an assisted person is a party to such proceedings, his solicitor shall, before or at the first hearing that takes place after the certificate has been issued, file the certificate with the clerk to the justices.

Property recovered or preserved for and costs agreed to be paid to or awarded to an assisted person

18.—(1) For the purpose of this Regulation the expression "assisted person" includes a person in respect of whom a certificate has been, but is no longer, in force.

(2) Subject to paragraph (10) all moneys payable to an assisted person—

(*a*) by virtue of any agreement or order made in connection with the claim or action, cause or matter to which his certificate relates, whether such agreement was made before or after the proceedings were taken ; or

(*b*) being moneys payable in respect of the claim or the action, cause or matter to which his certificate relates upon the distribution of property of a person who had been adjudicated bankrupt or has entered into a deed of arrangement, or of a company in liquidation ; or

(*c*) being moneys which were paid into court by him or on his behalf in any proceedings to which his certificate relates and which have been ordered to be repaid to him ; or

(*d*) being moneys standing in court to the credit of any proceedings to which his certificate relates,

shall be paid or repaid, as the case may be, to the solicitor of the assisted person or, if he is no longer represented by a solicitor, to The Law Society, and only the solicitor, or, as the case may be, The Law Society, shall be capable of giving a good discharge for moneys so payable :

Provided that—

(i) the payment of any sum under an order for costs in favour of an assisted person in authorised summary proceedings shall be made to the clerk to the justices who shall pay it to The Law Society or as The Law Society shall direct and only the clerk to the justices shall be able to give a good discharge therefor ;

(ii) where moneys become payable to the solicitor of the assisted person or The Law Society out of property of a person who has been adjudicated bankrupt, or has entered into a deed of arrangement, or of a company in liquidation, as aforesaid, the solicitor or The Law Society as the case may be shall send to the trustee in bankruptcy, the trustee or assignee of the deed of arrangement, or the liquidator of the company in liquidation, a notice in accordance with Form 4 which shall thereupon operate as a request by the assisted person for payment of such moneys to the solicitor or The Law Society as the case may be and shall be a sufficient authority for that purpose ; and

(iii) where any moneys recovered or preserved for an assisted person in any proceedings have been paid into or remain in court and invested for the benefit of the assisted person, such part of those moneys as are not subject to the charge created by section 3(4) of the Act in accordance with paragraph (9) may be paid to the assisted person.

(3) An assisted person's solicitor shall—

(a) inform the appropriate area committee of any property recovered or preserved for the assisted person ; and

(b) pay all moneys received by him by virtue of an order or agreement made in the assisted person's favour to The Law Society :

Provided that where the appropriate area committee consider that the rights of the fund will thereby be safeguarded and so direct, he shall—

(i) pay only such sum which, in the opinion of the appropriate area committee, should be retained by The Law Society in order to safe-guard the rights of the fund under any provisions of the Act and these Regulations, and

(ii) pay any other moneys to the assisted person.

(4) Where in any proceedings to which an assisted person is a party—

(a) an order or agreement is made providing for the recovery or preservation of property for the benefit of the assisted person and, by virtue of the Act, there is a first charge on the property for the benefit of the fund ; or

(b) an order or agreement is made for the payment of costs to the assisted person,

The Law Society may take such proceedings in its own name as may be necessary to enforce or give effect to such an order or agreeement.

(5) An assisted person may take proceedings being proceedings which may be taken under section 1 of the Act to give effect to an order or agreement referred to in paragraph 2(a) with the consent of the appropriate committee.

(6) Where The Law Society takes proceedings it may authorise any person to swear an affidavit, file a proof, receive a dividend or take any other step in the proceedings in its name and the costs incurred by The Law Society in any such proceedings shall be a first charge on any sum so recovered.

(7) Upon receipt of moneys paid to them under this Regulation The Law Society shall retain—

(a) subject to regulation 14(3) any sum paid under an order or agreement for costs made in the assisted person's favour in respect of the period covered by his certificate ;

(b) a sum equal to the amount (if any) by which any property recovered or preserved is charged for the benefit of the fund by virtue of section 3(4) of the Act ; and

(c) any costs of proceedings taken by The Law Society under paragraph (4) ;

and shall pay the balance to the assisted person.

(8) The appropriate area committee may defer the payment to an assisted person's solicitor of his profit costs in connection with the proceedings until he has, in their opinion, given effect to any provisions of this Regulation.

(9) Where any moneys recovered or preserved for an assisted person in any proceedings are ordered to be paid into or remain in court and invested

for the benefit of the assisted person, the charge created by section 3(4) of the Act shall attach only to such parts of those moneys as, in the opinion of the appropriate area committee, as notified in writing to the court, will be sufficient to safeguard the rights of the fund under any provisions of the Act or these Regulations.

(10) The provisions of this Regulation shall not apply to—

(a) any payment of money in accordance with an order made or deemed to have been made under the provisions of—

(i) sections 3(2) and 5(4) of the Guardianship of Infants Act 1925, or

(ii) section 1 of the Inheritance (Family Provision) Act 1938(a), or

(iii) section 4 of the Affiliation Proceedings Act 1957, or

(iv) sections 15, 16, 19, 20(1), 21, 22, 26, 27, 31 and 34 of the Matrimonial Causes Act 1965(b), or

(v) sections 1, 2, 3, 6 and 9 of the Matrimonial Proceedings and Property Act 1970(c) ;

(b) periodical payments of money under the provisions of the Matrimonial Proceedings (Magistrates' Courts) Act 1960, in respect of the maintenance of a spouse or child ;

(c) any property affected by an order made or deemed to have been made under section 32 of the Matrimonial Causes Act 1965 or made under sections 4(a) and (b) and 16 of the Matrimonial Proceedings and Property Act 1970 ;

(d) moneys paid in lieu of or with respect to arrears of any payments referred to in sub-paragraphs (a) or (b) ;

(e) moneys payable, whether by way of arrears or otherwise, under an agreement in writing made between parties to a marriage for the purposes of their living separately and containing financial arrangements (whether made during the continuance or after the dissolution or annulment of the marriage) ;

(f) moneys payable under an affiliation agreement in writing or proceedings to enforce such an agreement ;

(g) any interim payment of damages in accordance with an order made under Order 29, rule 12, of the Rules of the Supreme Court ;

(h) payments of money under the provisions of any Act which provides for the enforcement of or giving effect to an order made under one of the sections set out in sub-paragraph (a) ;

(i) moneys paid as a result of proceedings taken in a court in England or Wales to enforce the order made by a court outside its jurisdiction in proceedings for relief comparable to that which may be given by a court in England and Wales under the provisions mentioned in this paragraph ;

and moneys so payable or property passing in lieu shall not be the subject of a charge within the terms of section 3(4) of the Act.

Charges upon property recovered or preserved

19.—(1) Any charge on property recovered or preserved for an assisted person arising under section 3(4) of the Act shall vest in The Law Society.

(a) 1938 c. 45.   (b) 1965 c. 72.   (c) 1970 c. 45.

(2) The Law Society may enforce any such charge in any manner which would be available if the charge had been given inter partes.

(3) Any such charge affecting land shall in the case of unregistered land be a land charge of Class B within the meaning of section 10 of the Land Charges Act 1925(a) and in the case of registered land shall be a registrable substantive charge.

(4) Subject to the provisions of the Land Charges Act 1925, all conveyances and acts done to defeat, or operating to defeat, such charge shall, except in the case of a conveyance to a bona fide purchaser for value without notice, be void as against The Law Society.

Costs awarded against an assisted person

20.—(1) Where proceedings have been concluded in which an assisted person (including, for the purpose of this Regulation, a person who was an assisted person in respect of those proceedings) is liable or would have been liable for costs if he had not been an assisted person, no costs attributable to the period during which his certificate was in force shall be recoverable from him until the court has determined the amount of his liability in accordance with section 2(2)(e) of the Act:

Provided that where the assisted person's certificate does not relate to or has been amended so that it no longer relates to the whole of the proceedings, the court shall nevertheless make a determination in respect of that part of the proceedings to which the certificate relates.

(2) The court may, if it thinks fit—

(a) postpone or adjourn the determination for such time and to such place, including chambers, as the court thinks fit, so however that the determination shall unless otherwise directed take place before the judge, official referee, master or registrar before whom the trial or hearing took place ; or

(b) refer to a master, registrar or the Clerk of the Parliaments or, in the case of an appeal from a decision of a county court or court of quarter sessions or court of summary jurisdiction, to the county court registrar, clerk of the peace or clerk to the justices respectively of the court from which the appeal is brought, for investigation in chambers or elsewhere, any question of fact relevant to the determination, requiring him to report his finding on that question to the court.

(3) In determining the amount of the assisted person's liability—

(a) his dwelling-house and household furniture and the tools and implements of his trade shall be left out of account to the like extent as they are left out of account by the Commission in determining his disposable income and disposable capital ; and

(b) any document which may have been sent to the court office or registry or filed or exhibited under regulation 17 shall be evidence of the facts stated therein :

Provided that the court may, if it thinks fit, order the assisted person and any party who has filed an affidavit pursuant to regulation 17(8) to attend for oral examination as to his means and as to any other facts (whether stated in any document before the court or otherwise) relevant to determine the amount of the assisted person's liability and may permit any party to give evidence and call witnesses thereon.

(a) 1925 c. 22.

(4) The court may direct—

(*a*) that payment under the order for costs shall be limited to such amount, payable in instalments or otherwise, including an amount to be determined on taxation, as the court thinks reasonable having regard to all the circumstances ; or

(*b*) where the court thinks it reasonable either for payment under sub-paragraph (*a*) not to be made immediately or for the assisted person to have no liability for payment, that payment under the order for costs be suspended either until such date as the court may determine or *sine die.*

(5) The party in whose favour the order is made may, within six years from the date thereof, apply to the court for the order to be varied on the ground that—

(*a*) material additional information as to the assisted person's means, being information which could not have been obtained by that party with reasonable diligence at the time the order was made, is available ; or

(*b*) there has been a change in the assisted person's circumstances since the date of the order ;

and on any such application the order may be varied as the court thinks fit ; but save as aforesaid the determination of the court shall be final.

(6) Where an order for costs is made against an assisted person who is concerned in the proceedings in a representative, fiduciary or official capacity, he shall have the benefit of section 2(2)(*e*) of the Act and his personal resources shall not (unless there is reason to the contrary) be taken into account for that purpose, but regard shall be had to the value of the property or estate, or the amount of the fund out of which he is entitled to be indemnified.

(7) Where a minor is an assisted person, his means for the purpose of determining his liability for costs under section 2(2)(*e*) of the Act shall be taken as including the means of any person whose disposable income and disposable capital has, by virtue of the Legal Aid (Assessment of Resources) Regulations, been included by the Commission in computing the minor's rate of income and amount of capital.

(8) Where an order for costs is made against a next friend or guardian *ad litem* of an assisted person who is a minor or patient, he shall have the benefit of section 2(2)(*e*) of the Act in like manner as it applies to an assisted person, and the means of the next friend or guardian *ad litem* shall be taken as being the means of the minor as defined in paragraph (7) or, as the case may be, of the patient.

Remuneration of counsel and solicitors in magistrates' courts

21.—(1) The sums allowed to counsel and solicitors in connection with authorised summary proceedings or proceedings in a court of quarter sessions shall be assessed by the appropriate area committee in accordance with the provisions of schedule 4.

(2) Any solicitor or counsel may, if he is dissatisfied with any decision on an assessment in accordance with the provisions of schedule 4, make written representations to the Council of The Law Society and the Council may allow such costs and fees in respect of the work to which the certificate relates as appears to it to represent fair remuneration according to the work actually and reasonably done.

(3) Regulations 22 to 25 inclusive shall not apply in respect of authorised summary proceedings or proceedings in a court of quarter sessions.

Miscellaneous provisions as to costs

22.—(1) Where—

(*a*) the work done by an assisted person's solicitor relates to a claim and the certificate has not been amended under regulation 9(1)(*b*)(iii) to include proceedings ; or

(*b*) the retainer of an assisted person's solicitor or counsel is determined before proceedings are actually begun and there has been no subsequent change of solicitor or counsel under the certificate,

the amount of the costs and counsel's fees (if any) shall be assessed by the appropriate area committee.

(2) Where proceedings have begun and—

(*a*) the solicitor is of opinion that the total amount which he and counsel (if any) would receive after a taxation in accordance with schedule 3 to the Act would not be more than £75 ; or

(*b*) the case of an assisted person (who is not such a person as is referred to in Order 62 rule 30 of the Rules of the Supreme Court) has been settled after the commencement of proceedings without any direction of the court as to costs on terms that include provision for an agreed sum in respect of costs to be paid to the assisted person which the solicitor and counsel (if any) is willing to accept in full satisfaction of the work done ; or

(*c*) there are special circumstances where a taxation would be against the interest of the assisted person or would increase the amount payable from the fund ; or

(*d*) after a direction or order that the assisted person's costs shall be taxed in accordance with schedule 3 to the Act, the solicitor incurs the costs for the purpose of recovering moneys payable to the fund,

the solicitor may apply to the appropriate area committee for an assessment of the amount of the costs and counsel's fees (if any) in respect of the work done.

(3) On any assessment under paragraphs (1) or (2) the appropriate area committee shall authorise the payment to the solicitor and counsel (if any) of such an amount as, in their opinion—

(*a*) in the case of work done in relation to a claim, or where the retainer of the assisted person's solicitor or counsel was determined before proceedings were actually begun, or where a settlement is reached within the terms of paragraph (2)(*b*), or where proceedings were conducted in the county court, is fair remuneration for work actually and reasonably done ; and

(*b*) in any other case, is the amount which would have been allowed to the solicitor or counsel had the costs been taxed under schedule 3 to the Act.

(4) Any solicitor or counsel if he is dissatisfied with any decision on an assessment in accordance with paragraphs (1) or (2) may make written representations to the Council of The Law Society and the Council may allow such costs and fees in respect of the work to which the certificate relates as appears to it to represent fair remuneration according to the work actually and reasonably done or, as the case may be, is the amount which would have been allowed to the solicitor or counsel had the costs been taxed under schedule 3 to the Act.

(5) Where in any proceedings to which an assisted person is a party—

(*a*) judgment is signed in default of appearance or defence, the judgment shall contain a direction that the costs of any assisted person shall be taxed in accordance with schedule 3 to the Act ;

(*b*) the court gives judgment or makes a final decree or order in the proceedings, the judgment, decree or order shall include a direction (in addition to any other direction as to taxation contained in the judgment, decree or order) that the costs of any assisted person shall be so taxed ;

(*c*) the plaintiff accepts money paid into court and judgment is signed for his taxed costs in accordance with Order 62, rule 10(2) of the Rules of the Supreme Court, the judgment shall contain a direction that the costs of any assisted person shall be taxed in accordance with schedule 3 to the Act.

(6) Where in any proceedings to which an assisted person or a former assisted person is a party and—

(*a*) the proceedings are, or have been, brought to an end without a direction having been given, whether under the foregoing paragraph or otherwise, as to the assisted person's costs being taxed in accordance with schedule 3 to the Act ; or

(*b*) a judgment or order in favour of an opposite party, which includes a direction that the assisted person's costs be so taxed, has not been drawn up or, as the case may be, entered by him ; or

(*c*) a retainer is determined under regulation 13(2) in such circumstances as to require a taxation in accordance with the provisions of the Act and these Regulations ;

the costs of that person shall be taxed in accordance with schedule 3 to the Act on production of a copy of the notice of discharge or revocation of the certificate at the appropriate taxing office.

(7) Where in any proceedings to which an assisted person, or a former assisted person, is a party and which have been brought to an end by judgment, decree or final order, there has been an agreement in respect of the costs to be paid by any other party to the assisted person, or former assisted person, which that person's solicitor and counsel (if any) is willing to accept in full satisfaction of the work done, the amount of the costs shall be submitted to the appropriate taxing officer who will, in accordance with schedule 3 to the Act, fix the amount of costs by assessment made without a taxation and for this purpose the solicitor for the assisted person, or former assisted person, shall supply the taxing officer with such documents and details as he may require.

(8) Where, in any proceedings to which a former assisted person was a party, an order or agreement has been made for the payment to him of costs and he has failed to ask for costs to be taxed or his certificate is discharged before taxation, The Law Society may authorise the making of the application for taxation on his behalf and the costs of the application and of taxation shall be deemed to be costs in the proceedings to which the certificate related.

(9) Costs incurred by reason of any application made under regulation 15 and of any report made by an assisted person's solicitor under regulation 12 or 16 shall be taxed in accordance with schedule 3 to the Act and costs incurred by reason of regulation 17 shall be costs in the cause.

(10) The sums allowed to counsel in connection with proceedings in the House of Lords or the Supreme Court, shall be ninety per cent of the amount allowed on taxation of the costs.

(11) The sums allowed to a solicitor in connection with proceedings in the House of Lords or the Supreme Court shall be the full amount allowed on taxation of the costs on account of disbursements and ninety per cent of the amount so allowed on account of profit costs.

Taxation of costs

23.—(1) Without prejudice to Order 62, rule 8 of the Rules of the Supreme Court and Order 47, rule 50 of the County Court Rules on any taxation of an assisted person's costs in connection with proceedings, except authorised summary proceedings and proceedings in a court of quarter sessions, any costs wasted by failure to conduct the proceedings with reasonable competence and expedition shall be disallowed or reduced:

Provided that no costs shall be disallowed or reduced under this Regulation until notice has been served by the taxing officer on the solicitor whose name appears on the assisted person's certificate and, in a case where those costs relate to counsel's fees, on the assisted person's counsel, requiring the solicitor or, as the case may be, counsel, to show cause orally or in writing why those costs should not be disallowed or reduced.

(2) The costs of proceedings to which an assisted person is a party shall be taxed in accordance with any direction or order given or made in the proceedings irrespective of the interest (if any) of the assisted person in the taxation, and for the purpose of these Regulations an order for the taxation of the costs of a review of taxation or of the costs of an appeal from a decision of the judge on such a review shall be deemed to be a final order.

(3) Any certificate or notice of revocation or discharge or a copy of any such certificate or notice shall be bespoken or made available upon taxation.

(4) It shall be the duty of an assisted person's solicitor to safeguard the interests of the fund on any taxation as between party and party pursuant to an order for costs made in favour of the assisted person where that person may himself have no interest in the result of the taxation and for this purpose take such steps as may appear to the solicitor to be necessary to obtain a review of taxation under the succeeding provisions of this Regulation.

(5) (*a*) Any proceedings under the succeeding provisions of this Regulation or under regulation 25 shall be deemed to be proceedings to which the assisted person's certificate relates, whether or not it has been discharged or revoked, and the costs of such proceedings shall be paid out of the fund.

(*b*) Where the assisted person has no interest in the taxation or would, save for this Regulation, have an interest adverse to that of his solicitor, he shall not be required to make any contribution to the fund on account of the costs of any proceedings arising under paragraphs (6) to (11) or regulation 25 or in consequence of any order made thereon nor shall any resulting increase in the net liability of the fund be a charge on any property recovered or preserved for the assisted person in the proceedings to which his certificate relates.

(6) Where—

(*a*) an assisted person is dissatisfied with any decision of a taxing officer in regard to the amount which he is entitled to recover by virtue of an order or agreement for costs made in his favour or for which he is liable by virtue of an order for costs made against him ; or

(*b*) the assisted person's solicitor is dissatisfied with any decision of the taxing officer—

   (i) on a taxation as between party and party pursuant to an order for costs made in favour of the assisted person, or

(ii) on a taxation in accordance with schedule 3 to the Act,

the solicitor shall apply to the appropriate area committee for authority to carry in objections to the taxation and if the area committee give authority the solicitor may thereupon carry in objections in accordance with rules of court ; and where the assisted person has no interest in the taxation or would, save for the provisions of this Regulation, have an interest adverse to that of his solicitor, it shall be the duty of the solicitor to place before the taxing officer all matters which are proper to be taken into account on the consideration of the objections and the taxing officer shall reconsider and review the taxation accordingly.

(7) Where the assisted person or his solicitor, as the case may be, is dissatisfied with the decision of the taxing officer on any matter to which objection has been taken as aforesaid, the solicitor shall apply to The Law Society for authority to have the taxation reviewed, and, if the Society give authority, the solicitor may thereupon apply to a judge either personally or by counsel to review the taxation in accordance with rules of court ; and where the assisted person has no interest in the taxation or would, save for the provisions of this Regulation, have an interest adverse to that of his solicitor, it shall be the duty of the solicitor to ensure that there are placed before the judge all matters which are proper to be taken into account on the review and the judge shall hear and determine the application accordingly.

(8) Where any party to a taxation is an assisted person, the certificate or allocatur shall not, save by consent, be signed within 21 days after the taxing officer's decision ; and where an assisted person's solicitor applies under either of the two foregoing paragraphs for authority to carry in objections or to have a taxation reviewed, he shall do so before the expiration of the time allowed by rules of court for applying to the taxing officer for a reconsideration or review of a taxation and shall thereupon give notice of his application to the taxing officer and to the opposite party and the time so allowed shall thereupon be extended by one month.

(9) Where counsel acting for an assisted person is dissatisfied with any decision on a taxation in accordance with schedule 3 to the Act, it shall be the duty of the assisted person's solicitor to report the matter to the appropriate area committee or to The Law Society, as the case may be, and, if the committee or the Society give authority in that behalf, to carry in objections to the taxation, to apply to a judge to review the taxation or to appeal from the decision of the judge, as the case may be, and paragraphs (5), (6) and (7) and regulation 25(1) shall apply as if the solicitor were the person dissatisfied.

(10) If, in proceedings to which an assisted person is a party, any other party carries in objections to a taxation as between party and party or applies to a judge to review the taxation, the assisted person's solicitor may be heard on the objection or review notwithstanding that the assisted person himself may have no interest in the taxation.

(11) The assisted person's solicitor shall forthwith inform counsel of any reduction of his fees on taxation.

Appointment of solicitor to intervene

24.—(1) The Lord Chancellor may appoint a solicitor to intervene for the purposes hereinafter mentioned in any review by a judge of a taxation of the costs of proceedings to which an assisted person is a party, and such appointment may be made in respect of a particular review or may extend to any review of taxation during the period for which the solicitor is appointed.

(2) Whenever The Law Society give authority to an assisted person's solicitor to apply to a judge to review a taxation, they shall notify the Lord Chancellor and inform him of the name and address of the assisted person's solicitor.

(3) If, in proceedings to which an assisted person is a party, any other party applies to a judge to review a taxation between party and party or the assisted person's solicitor applies to a judge to review any such taxation as is referred to in regulation 23(6), the assisted person's solicitor shall inform The Law Society of the fact and the Society shall notify the Lord Chancellor and inform him of the name and address of the assisted person's solicitor and, where the taxation to be reviewed is as between party and party, the name and address of the solicitor acting for the other party.

(4) The solicitor appointed by the Lord Chancellor to intervene in a review of taxation shall be entitled to production of all documents relevant to the matters in issue before the judge and to delivery of copies thereof and to appear by counsel and be heard on the review, with a view to ensuring that all considerations which are proper to be taken into account are placed before the court, whether they relate to the interests of the fund or of the assisted person or to the fair remuneration of solicitors and counsel acting for assisted persons.

(5) On any review in which the solicitor appointed by the Lord Chancellor has intervened the judge may make such order as may be just for the payment to or by that solicitor of the costs incurred by him or any other party, so however that any sum due to the solicitor by virtue of any such order shall be paid by him to The Law Society and any sum so payable by the solicitor shall be paid out of the fund ; and the solicitor shall be entitled to receive from the fund his costs of a review in which he has intervened.

Appeal from review of taxation

25.—(1) An assisted person's solicitor may, with the authority of The Law Society, appeal from the decision of the judge on a review of taxation under regulation 23(7) or (9) and shall be entitled to appear by counsel and be heard on an appeal by any other party notwithstanding that the assisted person may have no interest in the appeal or would, save for regulation 23, have an interest adverse to that of his solicitor:

Provided that nothing in this regulation shall be deemed to confer a right of appeal where there is no such right in proceedings to which an assisted person is not a party.

(2) Where an assisted person's solicitor applies for authority under paragraph (1) he shall do so before the expiration of the time allowed by rules of court for appeal from the decision of the judge and thereupon the time so allowed shall be extended by one month.

(3) The solicitor appointed by the Lord Chancellor under regulation 24(1) may appeal from the decision of the judge on a review of taxation under regulation 23(7) and (9) and regulation 24(2) to (5) shall apply to an appeal as it applies to a review.

The Lands Tribunal

26.—(1) In this regulation the expression "the tribunal" means the Lands Tribunal as established by section 1(1)(*b*) of the Lands Tribunal Act 1949(**a**) and the expression "the registrar" means the registrar of the tribunal.

(2) Except in so far as otherwise provided by this Regulation, these Regulations shall apply to applications for legal aid for proceedings in the tribunal and to the conduct of all proceedings in it for which a certificate is granted in like manner as they apply to applications for legal aid for, and the conduct of, proceedings in any court.

(3) Where any power to do any act or exercise any jurisdiction or discretion is conferred by these Regulations on a court it shall be exercised by the tribunal and may, unless it is exercisable only during the hearing of the proceedings, be exercised by the registrar.

(4) The provisions of schedule 3 to the Act shall apply to proceedings in the tribunal as they apply to proceedings in a county court.

(5) Notwithstanding anything in regulation 22, the following provisions shall have effect in relation to proceedings in the tribunal to which an assisted person is a party—

(*a*) where a final decision is given in writing by the tribunal, it shall, in addition to any direction as to costs, contain a direction that the costs of any assisted person shall be taxed in accordance with the provisions of schedule 3 to the Act and the costs shall be so taxed by the registrar ;

(*b*) where the proceedings are brought to an end without a direction having been given under the foregoing sub-paragraph of this regulation the costs of any assisted person shall be taxed by the registrar in accordance with schedule 3 to the Act ;

(*c*) in taxing the costs of any assisted person the registrar shall have power to determine the appropriate scale for the taxation, being a scale of costs prescribed by the Rules of the Supreme Court or by the County Court Rules.

Revocations

27. The regulations specified in schedule 5 are hereby revoked.

Dated 12th January 1971.

Hailsham of St. Marylebone, C.

We, the undersigned, two of the Lords Commissioners of Her Majesty's Treasury, do hereby concur in regulation 5 of and schedule 2 to the above Regulations.

Dated 13th January 1971.

V. H. Goodhew,
H. S. P. Monro.

(**a**) 1949 c. 42.

SCHEDULE 1

FORM 1

THE LAW SOCIETY

Legal Aid Acts 1949 to 1964
Civil Aid Certificate

Regulation 6(5)(12)

MR
MRS. MISS

Reference No.   Sols A/C No.   Case Code

Forenames

Surname

Address

Postal Code (if any)

This is to certify that the above named

has been granted legal aid as specified in paragraph 1 below subject to the above mentioned Acts and the Regulations and Schemes for the time being in force and made thereunder and subject also to the conditions and limitations (if any) specified below and the requirement as to contribution.

1. Description of Legal Aid

2. Conditions and Limitations (if any)

3. The Solicitor authorised to act in the case is
   of
4. Contribution to be paid. The Supplementary Benefits Commission have made the following determinations

Maximum
Disposable Income £   Disposable Capital £   Contribution £

The actual contribution towards the cost of the case has been assessed at   £

payable by monthly instalments as follows   of   £

then   of   £

Signed

Secretary to the   Local Committee in Legal Aid Area No.
Issued this   day of   19

Form 2

Regulation 9(4)

THE LAW SOCIETY
Legal Aid Acts 1949 to 1964
Amendment to Civil Aid Certificate

Reference No.

This is to certify that the Civil Aid Certificate issued

to

of

under the above reference has been amended as follows

Date

Area Secretary.

FORM 3   Regulation 11(6)

THE LAW SOCIETY

Legal Aid Acts 1949 to 1964

Emergency Certificate

For official use only

E/Cte Reference No.

Case Code

Forenames

Surname

Address

....

....

....

This is to certify that the above named
has been granted legal aid as specified in paragraph 1 below subject to the above mentioned Acts and the Regulations and Schemes for the time being in force and made thereunder and subject also to the conditions and limitations (if any) specified below.

1. Description of Legal Aid

2. Conditions and Limitations (if any)

Solrs. A/C No.

3. The solicitor is

of

4. This certificate, being an emergency certificate remains in force for a period of   weeks from the date hereof unless extended for such further period as the appropriate committee may allow or unless it is previously discharged revoked or replaced by a civil aid certificate.
Signed

Secretary to the   Area/Local Committee in Legal Aid Area No.   .

Day	Mth.	Year

Issued this   day of   19

Regulations 17(2) 18(2)

FORM 4

THE LAW SOCIETY

LEGAL AID ACTS 1949 TO 1964

NOTICE OF ISSUE OF CERTIFICATE

No.

In the

[Division]

Between   [Plaintiff] [Petitioner]

and

[Defendant] [Respondent]

TAKE notice that [an Emergency] [a Civil Aid] Certificate No.
dated the   day of   19   has been issued in Area No.
to
in connection with the following proceedings: —

TAKE further notice that, in consequence thereof, the   in
these proceedings is and has been from that date an assisted person.

Dated this   day of   19   .

(Signed)...

of

Solicitor for

To

FORM 5

THE LAW SOCIETY

LEGAL AID AND ADVICE ACTS 1949 AND 1960

NOTICE UNDER REGULATION 17(4)

In the

[Division]

Between   [Plaintiff] [Petitioner]

and

[Defendant] [Respondent]

TAKE notice that [a Civil Aid] [an Emergency] Certificate [dated the
day of   19 , issued in respect of the proceedings hitherto covered
by an Emergency Certificate] [dated the   day of   19 ,
issued to the above-named*   ] has, on
the   day of   19 , been [amended] [discharged] [revoked].
[The amendment provides:

                                        that the Certificate shall [not] extend to
the following proceedings:—

                                                                        ]
Dated this   day of   19 .

(Signed)..

of

Solicitor for

To

---

* Insert Plaintiff, Petitioner, Defendant, Respondent, etc., as the case may require.

SCHEDULE 2

Regulation 5(4)

ASSESSMENT OF RESOURCES OF APPLICANT FOR CERTIFICATE RELATING TO A CLAIM

1. In this schedule, unless the context otherwise requires—

" capital " means the amount or value of every resource of a capital nature ;

" income " means the total income from all sources which the applicant may reasonably expect to receive during the twelve months next ensuing from the date of the application ; that income in the absence of other means of ascertaining it being taken to be the income received during the preceding twelve months ;

" supplementary pension or allowance " means any supplementary pension or allowance payable under Part II of the Ministry of Social Security Act 1966(**a**) (including that part as modified for certain cases by paragraph 4 of schedule 7 to that Act).

2. Any question arising under this schedule shall be decided by the appropriate committee who, in deciding any such question, shall have regard to any guidance which may from time to time be given by The Law Society as to the application of this schedule.

3. The disposable capital and disposable income of an applicant shall be the capital and income as determined by the appropriate committee after deducting any sums which are to be left out of account or for which allowance is to be made under the provisions of this schedule.

4.—(1) Where an application is made on behalf of a minor, the capital and income of the minor shall, subject to the provisions of the next succeeding sub-paragraph, be treated as the capital and income of the applicant and the applicant's capital and income shall be left out of account.

(2) The resources of any person who, under section 22 of the Ministry of Social Security Act 1966, is liable to maintain the minor or who usually contributes substantially to the minor's maintenance, may be treated as the resources of the minor, if, having regard to all the circumstances, including the age and resources of the minor, it appears just and equitable to do so.

5. If it appears to the appropriate committee that any person whose capital and income falls to be computed under the provisions of this schedule has, with intent to reduce the disposable capital or disposable income or maximum contribution, directly or indirectly deprived himself of any resource or has converted any part of his resources into resources which are to be left out of account, the resources of which he has so deprived himself or which he has so converted shall be treated as part of his resources or as not so converted, as the case may be.

6. Subject to the provisions of this schedule, legal aid in respect of a claim shall be available to any person whose disposable capital does not exceed £125 and who either was in receipt of a supplementary pension or allowance at the date of his application or whose disposable income does not exceed £325:

Provided that legal aid may nevertheless be refused to a person who was in receipt of a supplementary pension or allowance at the date of his application if his disposable income exceeds £325 and it appears that the need for supplementary pension or allowance was or is likely to be temporary.

7. In computing the capital and income of an applicant—

(*a*) there shall be left out of account the value of the subject-matter of the claim in respect of which he is seeking legal aid ;

(*b*) the resources of any spouse of his shall be treated as his resources unless—

(i) the spouse has a contrary interest in the claim in respect of which he is seeking legal aid, or

   (ii) the applicant and his spouse are living separate and apart, or

   (iii) in all the circumstances of the case it would be inequitable or impracticable to do so.

8. In computing the capital of an applicant—

(a) the value of his dwelling house, household furniture and effects, articles of personal clothing and the tools and implements of his trade shall be left out of account ;

(b) where the applicant has living with him one or more of the following persons, namely, a spouse whose resources are required to be aggregated with his, a dependent child or a dependent relative wholly or substantially maintained by him, a deduction shall be made of £75 in respect of the first person, £50 in respect of the second person and £25 in respect of each further person ;

(c) where the disposable income of the applicant is less than £375, a deduction shall be made of a sum equal to the difference between the disposable income and £375.

9. In computing the income of an applicant—

(a) there shall be left out of account—

   (i) any income tax paid or payable on income treated under the provisions of this schedule as his income,

   (ii) the amount estimated to be payable in the twelve months next ensuing from the date of the application under National Health Service Contributions Act 1965(a) the National Insurance Act 1965(b) the National Insurance (Industrial Injuries) Act 1965(c) or any scheme made under either of the two last mentioned Acts by any person whose income is, under the provisions of this schedule, to be treated as the applicant's ;

(b) in respect of any one of the following, or for each of them if more than one, there shall be a deduction equivalent to the weekly amount by which that specified in paragraph 9(a) (requirements of husband and wife) of schedule 2 to the Ministry of Social Security Act 1966 exceeds that specified in paragraph 9(b) (normal requirements of single person) of that schedule—

   (i) the spouse of the applicant, if wholly or substantially maintained by him or if that spouse's capital and income are treated as resources of the applicant, and

   (ii) any person aged not less than 16 years being maintained by the applicant or, where the capital and income of the applicant's spouse are treated as resources of the applicant, being maintained by such spouse ;

(c) in respect of any of the following, or for each of them if more than one, there shall be a deduction equivalent to the weekly amount specified in paragraph 9(b) of the said schedule 2, viz., any child under the age of 16 years wholly or substantially maintained by the applicant or, where the capital and income of the applicant's spouse are treated as resources of the applicant, by the applicant's spouse ;

(d) regardless of their actual amount or cost, there shall be a deduction of £182 in respect of rent and on account of any other matters for which the person concerned must or reasonably may provide.

10. Where the disposable income of the applicant is or exceeds £303, he shall be required to pay a contribution to the fund in respect of sums payable thereout on his account of not more than £1 for each £3 in excess of £300.

11. Where it appears to the appropriate committee that there has been some error or mistake in the determination of the disposable income, disposable capital or maximum contribution of the applicant, they may redetermine the disposable income or disposable capital or maximum contribution or, as the case may be, amend the determination, and in the latter case the amended determination shall for all purposes be substituted for the original determination.

   (a) 1965 c. 54.   (b) 1965 c. 51.   (c) 1965 c. 52.

SCHEDULE 3

Regulation 15(2)

ENDORSEMENT OF PAPERS SENT TO COUNSEL

Every set of papers delivered to counsel shall be endorsed : —
" Legal Aid

Reference Number ...."

and in the case of authorised summary proceedings they shall where appropriate also be endorsed

" Authority for counsel to be instructed has been given by the certificate/the
....................................area committee."

SCHEDULE 4

Regulation 21

REMUNERATION OF SOLICITORS AND COUNSEL GIVING LEGAL AID IN PROCEEDINGS IN MAGISTRATES' COURTS AND COURTS OF QUARTER SESSIONS

1. Subject to paragraph 6—

(1) There shall be allowed to the solicitor acting under a certificate on behalf of an assisted person—

(a) where the hearing takes place in a magistrates' court, a fee of not less than £6 6s. 0d. and not exceeding £36 15s. 0d. and, in addition, a further fee not exceeding £12 12s. 0d. in respect of every day on which an adjourned hearing takes place ; or

(b) where the hearing takes place in a court of quarter sessions, a fee of not less than £8 8s. 0d. and not exceeding £36 15s. 0d. and, in addition, a further fee not exceeding £12 12s 0d. in respect of every day on which an adjourned hearing takes place or, if the court of quarter sessions is one in which a party may appear by a solicitor and counsel has not been instructed, a fee not exceeding £18 7s. 6d.

(2) In addition to any fee payable under sub-paragraph (1) of this paragraph, the solicitor shall be allowed—

(a) expenses actually and reasonably incurred by him or his clerk in travelling to and from the court in which the hearing takes place and to and from any place visited for the purpose of preparing or conducting the case ; and

(b) any other out-of-pocket expenses actually and reasonably incurred.

2. Subject to paragraph 6—

(1) There shall be allowed to counsel acting under a certificate on behalf of an assisted person a fee of not less than £6 11s. 0d. (except where the hearing takes place in a court of quarter sessions, where the fee shall not be less than £8 13s. 0d.) and not exceeding £37 15s. 0d.

(2) Where a hearing has not been concluded at the end of the first relevant period thereof, there shall be allowed to counsel in respect of each relevant period, or, in the case of an incomplete period, part thereof, after the first, a refresher fee.

(3) In this paragraph—

(a) " Relevant period " means, either, as The Law Society may determine generally, or as the appropriate area committee may determine in relation to any particular hearing, and day during any part of which the hearing continues or any period of five hours, whether continuous or not, during which the hearing continues ;

(b) " refresher fee " means such fee in addition to the fee allowed under the foregoing paragraph, not exceeding half the fee allowed as aforesaid, as appears to be proper in all the circumstances of the case.

(4) There shall be allowed to counsel in addition to any fees allowed under the foregoing paragraphs—

(a) in respect of any conference or consultation in chambers or elsewhere lasting not more than half-an-hour, a fee of £2 7s. 0d. ;

(b) in respect of any conference or consultation in chambers or elsewhere lasting more than half-an-hour, such fee as appears to be proper in all the circumstances of the case ;

(c) in respect of any application to the court for a case, which is in a list of cases to be heard on any particular day, not to be heard on that day, such fee as appears to be proper in all the circumstances of the case ;

(d) for advice in writing, if in the opinion of the appropriate area committee it was reasonably necessary to obtain counsel's advice in writing, a fee not exceeding £11 0s. 0d.

3. (1) Subject to the provisions of this schedule, the appropriate area committee in assessing the sums payable to a solicitor or counsel shall take into account all the relevant circumstances, including the nature, importance, complexity or difficulty of the work, and the time involved, including time spent at the court on any day waiting for the case to be heard, if the case was in that day's list, and shall allow such amounts as appear to them to represent fair remuneration for the work actually and reasonably done.

(2) In assessing as aforesaid, the appropriate area committee shall not allow any sum in respect of any conference, consultation, attendance or visit unless it is satisfied that such conference, consultation, attendance or visit was reasonably necessary—

(a) if, in assessing sums payable to a solicitor or counsel, they consider that the proper conduct of the proceedings required counsel, allow to the solicitor and counsel such fees as they shall assess in accordance with the preceding provisions of this schedule ; or

(b) if, in assessing such sums, they consider that the proper conduct of the proceedings did not require counsel, allow fees of such total amount as they would have considered proper to allow to the solicitor under paragraph 1 if counsel had not been instructed and the solicitor had conducted the case alone ; and in such case the committee shall determine the amount which they would have allowed to counsel under paragraph 2 had counsel been authorised, and such amount shall (to the extent that the total amount suffices) be paid to counsel and the balance, if any, of the total amount shall be paid to the solicitor.

4. If it appears to the appropriate area committee in assessing the sums payable to a solicitor or counsel that for any reason, including the exceptional length, difficulty or complexity of the case in respect of which the certificate was granted, the sums payable by virtue of this schedule would not provide fair remuneration according to the work actually and reasonably done, it shall certify accordingly, and where it so certifies, any limitation contained in this schedule on the amount of any fee payable shall not apply, and the appropriate area committee shall, after taking into account all the relevant circumstances of the case and having regard to the considerations mentioned in the preceding paragraph, allow such fees in respect of the work to which the certificate relates as appear to it to represent fair remuneration according to the work actually and reasonably done.

5. Where a solicitor acting on behalf of an assisted person under a certificate reasonably undertakes work in giving notice of appeal or in applying for a case to be stated and in matters preliminary thereto, being work done within the ordinary time for giving notice or making an application, there shall, in addition to the fees which may be paid to him under the foregoing provisions of this schedule and his disbursements on the said work, be allowed to him a fee not exceeding £10 10s. 0d. in respect of the said work and in any case where counsel's opinion is required, a fee not exceeding £11 0s. 0d. shall be allowed to counsel for his opinion.

6. Where a solicitor who is acting on behalf of an assisted person has instructed counsel without obtaining authority in accordance with these regulations, the area committee shall—

(a) if, in assessing sums payable to a solicitor or counsel, they consider that the proper conduct of the proceedings required counsel, allow to the solicitor and counsel such fees as they shall assess in accordance with the preceding provisions of this schedule ; or

(b) if, in assessing such sums, they consider that the proper conduct of the proceedings did not require counsel, allow fees of such total amount as they would have considered proper to allow to the solicitor under paragraph 1 if counsel had not been instructed and the solicitor had conducted the case alone ; and in such case the committee shall determine the amount which they would have allowed to counsel under paragraph 2 had counsel been authorised, and such amount shall (to the extent that the total amount suffices) be paid to counsel and the balance, if any, of the total amount shall be paid to the solicitor.

Regulation 27   SCHEDULE 5

REGULATIONS REVOKED

Title	Refence
The Legal Aid (General) Regulations 1962	S.I. 1962/148 (1962 I, p.117)
The Legal Aid (General) (Amendment) Regulations 1962	S.I. 1962/1714 (1962 II, p.2122)
The Legal Aid (General) (Amendment) Regulations 1964	S.I. 1964/1893 (1964 III, p.4218)
The Legal Aid (General) (Amendment) Regulations 1965	S.I. 1965/865 (1965 I, p.2340)
The Legal Aid (General) (Amendment) Regulations 1969	S.I. 1969/923 (1969 II, p.2804)
The Legal Aid (General) (Amendment No. 2) Regulations 1969	S.I. 1969/1346 (1969 III, p.4018)
The Legal Aid (General) (Amendment) Regulations 1970	S.I. 1970/690 (1970 II, p.2205)
The Legal Aid (General) (Amendment No. 2) Regulations 1970	S.I. 1970/787 (1970 II, p.2497)

EXPLANATORY NOTE

(This Note is not part of the Regulations.)

These Regulations consolidate with amendments the Legal Aid (General) Regulations 1962, the Legal Aid (General) (Amendment) Regulations 1962, the Legal Aid (General) (Amendment) Regulations 1964, the Legal Aid (General) (Amendment) Regulations 1965, the Legal Aid (General) (Amendment) Regulations 1969, the Legal Aid (General) (Amendment) Regulations 1970 and the Legal Aid (General) (Amendment No. 2) Regulations 1970.

The principal changes are as follows: —

(1) wider powers are given to committees to delegate certain of their functions (regulation 1(5)) ;

(2) an assisted person's contribution will be reassessed if his disposable income has increased by more than £52 (instead of £26) (regulation 6(10)) ;

(3) solicitors and counsel acting for assisted persons are prohibited from accepting payment for work done in the proceedings from any source other than the legal aid fund (regulation 15(9)) ;

(4) further categories of property recovered in assisted proceedings are exempted from the charge in favour of the legal aid fund (regulation 18(10)) ;

(5) costs may be disallowed on taxation where a solicitor or counsel incurs costs without reasonable cause or fails to conduct them with reasonable competence or expedition (regulation 23(1)) ;

(6) other amendments include provisions as to the service of notices (regulation 17), enforcement of orders, etc., on behalf of assisted persons (regulation 18(4)) and costs (regulations 20(1) and 22(7)).

1971 No. 63

LEGAL AID AND ADVICE, ENGLAND

The Legal Aid (Assessment of Resources) (Amendment) Regulations 1971

Made - - - -	13th January 1971
Laid before Parliament	26th January 1971
Coming into Operation	1st February 1971

The Lord Chancellor, in exercise of the powers conferred on him by sections 4 and 12 of the Legal Aid and Advice Act 1949(a), and with the concurrence of the Treasury, hereby makes the following Regulations :—

1.—(1) These Regulations may be cited as the Legal Aid (Assessment of Resources) (Amendment) Regulations 1971 and shall come into operation on 1st February 1971.

(2) The Interpretation Act 1889(b) shall apply to the interpretation of these Regulations as it applies to the interpretation of an Act of Parliament.

(3) In these Regulations a regulation referred to by number means a regulation so numbered in the Legal Aid (Assessment of Resources) Regulations 1960(c) as amended(d).

2. For regulation 9(a) there shall be substituted : —

" (a) his disposable income may have increased by an amount greater than £52 or decreased by an amount greater than £26 ; or ".

Dated 12th January 1971.

Hailsham of St. Marylebone, C.

We concur,

Dated 13th January 1971.

V. H. Goodhew,

H. S. P. Monro,

Two of the Lords Commissioners of Her Majesty's Treasury.

(a) 1949 c. 51.   (b) 1889 c. 63.   (c) S.I. 1960/1471 (1960 II, p. 1749).
(d) The relevant amending instrument is S.I. 1962/147 (1962 I, p. 115).

EXPLANATORY NOTE

(This Note is not part of the Regulations.)

These Regulations amend the Legal Aid (Assessment of Resources) Regulations 1960 so as to provide for the redetermination of an assisted person's disposable income and maximum contribution when his disposable income has increased by an amount greater than £52 (instead of £26).

STATUTORY INSTRUMENTS

1971 No. 64

ACQUISITION OF LAND
COMPENSATION

The Acquisition of Land (Rate of Interest after Entry) Regulations 1971

Made - - -	15*th January* 1971
Laid before Parliament	22*nd January* 1971
Coming into Operation	23*rd January* 1971

The Treasury, in exercise of the powers conferred upon them by section 32(1) of the Land Compensation Act 1961(a), and of all other powers enabling them in that behalf, hereby make the following Regulations:—

1. These Regulations may be cited as the Acquisition of Land (Rate of Interest after Entry) Regulations 1971, and shall come into operation on 23rd January 1971.

2. The Interpretation Act 1889(b) shall apply for the interpretation of these Regulations as it applies for the interpretation of an Act of Parliament.

3. The rate of interest on any compensation in respect of the compulsory acquisition of an interest in any land on which entry has been made before the payment of the compensation shall be 9 per cent. per annum.

4. The Acquisition of Land (Rate of Interest after Entry) (No. 2) Regulations 1970(c) are hereby revoked.

H. S. P. Monro,
Bernard Weatherill,
Two of the Lords Commissioners
15th January 1971.   of Her Majesty's Treasury.

EXPLANATORY NOTE
(*This Note is not part of the Regulations.*)

These Regulations increase from 8½ per cent. to 9 per cent. per annum, in respect of any period after the coming into operation of these Regulations, the rate of interest payable where entry is made, before payment of compensation, on land in England and Wales which is being purchased compulsorily, and revoke the Acquisition of Land (Rate of Interest after Entry) (No. 2) Regulations 1970.

(a) 1961 c. 33.   (b) 1889 c. 63.   (c) S.I. 1970/1390 (1970 III, p. 4632).

STATUTORY INSTRUMENTS

1971 No. 65

ACQUISITION OF LAND
COMPENSATION

The Acquisition of Land (Rate of Interest after Entry) (Scotland) Regulations 1971

Made - - -	*15th January* 1971
Laid before Parliament	*22nd January* 1971
Coming into Operation	*23rd January* 1971

The Treasury, in exercise of the powers conferred upon them by section 40(1) of the Land Compensation (Scotland) Act 1963(a), and of all other powers enabling them in that behalf, hereby make the following Regulations:—

1.—(1) These Regulations may be cited as the Acquisition of Land (Rate of Interest after Entry) (Scotland) Regulations 1971, and shall come into operation on 23rd January 1971.

(2) These Regulations shall extend to Scotland only.

2. The Interpretation Act 1889(b) shall apply for the interpretation of these Regulations as it applies for the interpretation of an Act of Parliament.

3. The rate of interest on any compensation in respect of the compulsory acquisition of an interest in any land on which entry has been made before the payment of the compensation shall be 9 per cent. per annum.

4. The Acquisition of Land (Rate of Interest after Entry) (Scotland) (No. 2) Regulations 1970(c) are hereby revoked.

Walter Clegg,

H. S. P. Monro,

Two of the Lords Commissioners
of Her Majesty's Treasury.

15th January 1971.

EXPLANATORY NOTE
(This Note is not part of the Regulations.)

These Regulations increase from $8\frac{1}{2}$ per cent. to 9 per cent. per annum, in respect of any period after the coming into operation of these Regulations, the rate of interest payable where entry is made, before payment of compensation, on land in Scotland which is being purchased compulsorily, and revoke the Acquisition of Land (Rate of Interest after Entry) (Scotland) (No. 2) Regulations 1970.

(a) 1963 c. 51.   (b) 1889 c. 63.   (c) S.I. 1970/1389 (1970 III p. 4631).

1971 No. 66 (S.3)

COURT OF SESSION, SCOTLAND

Act of Sederunt (Rules of Court Amendment No. 1) 1971

Made - - -		*12th January* 1971
Coming into Operation		*15th February* 1971

The Lords of Council and Session, under and by virtue of the powers conferred upon them by section 16 of the Administration of Justice (Scotland) Act 1933(a) and of all other powers competent to them in that behalf, do hereby enact and declare as follows :—

1. Chapter V of the Table of Fees continued in Rule 347 of the Rules of Court (b) as substituted by the Act of Sederunt (Rules of Court Amendment No. 5) 1970(c) shall be deleted and Chapter VI contained in the said Rule 347 shall be renumbered as Chapter V.

2. This Act of Sederunt may be cited as the Act of Sederunt (Rules of Court Amendment No. 1) 1971, and shall come into operation on 15th February 1971.

And the Lords appoint this Act of Sederunt to be inserted in the Books of Sederunt.

J. L. Clyde,
I.P.D.

Edinburgh.
12th January 1971.

EXPLANATORY NOTE

(*This Note is not part of the Act of Sederunt.*)

This Act of Sederunt abolishes the Table of Fees payable to Clerks of Counsel.

(a) 1933 c. 41.　　　　　　　　　(b) S.I. 1965/321 (1965 I, p. 803).
(c) S.I. 1970/1746 (1970 III, p. 5718).

STATUTORY INSTRUMENTS

1971 No. 67 (S.4)

COURT OF SESSION, SCOTLAND

Act of Sederunt (Fees in the Court of Teinds) 1971

Made   -   -   -   *12th January* 1971

Coming into Operation   *15th February* 1971

The Lords of Council and Session, under and by virtue of the powers conferred upon them by section 2 of the Courts of Law Fees (Scotland) Act 1895(**a**) and section 11(3) of the Church of Scotland (Property and Endowments) Act 1925(**b**) and of all other powers competent to them in that behalf, with the approval of the Treasury, do hereby enact and declare as follows :—

1. The Act of Sederunt dated 22nd July 1922(**c**) is hereby repealed.

2. The fees payable to the Clerk of Teinds shall be those prescribed in the Schedule hereto.

3. This Act of Sederunt may be cited as the Act of Sederunt (Fees in the Court of Teinds) 1971, and shall come into operation on 15th February 1971.

And the Lords appoint this Act of Sederunt to be inserted in the Books of Sederunt.

J. L. Clyde,
I.P.D.

Edinburgh.

12th January 1971.

SCHEDULE

1. Original petition	£4·00
2. Answers to original petition	£4·00
3. Certified copy interlocutors, each	£0·50
4. Reports by accountants, men of business, or persons of skill, under remits by the Court	£1·00
5. Copies of pleadings certified by clerk	£0·50
6. Searches in teind records for extracted processes...	£0·50

(**a**) 1895 c. 14.   (**b**) 1925 c. 33
(**c**) S.R. & O. 1922/846 (Rev. XXII, p. 306:1922 p. 988).

7. Framing teind rolls—

For first ten calculations	£2·10
For each calculation thereafter	£0·10
In addition for each sheet of writing	£0·30

NOTE:—The printing of the teind rolls will be undertaken by H.M. Stationery Office, and the cost (including the cost of copies for distribution), which will be additional to the above fees, will be payable therewith to the Clerk of Teinds, who shall collect same on behalf of H.M. Stationery Office.

8. Apportionment of expenses among heritors—
(Same charge as for framing teind rolls)

9. Amending teind rolls or making alterations under order from the Court—
(Same charge as for framing teind rolls)

10. Copy locality, small folio, per sheet, figs.	£0·50
Copy locality, large folio	£0·60
11. Certifying copy production, e.g. form of feu-charter	£1·00
12. Searching old register and examining decree	£0·50
13. Searching augmentation register and examining books other than extracts	£0·25

14. Making (and converting from Imperial to Standard) statutory list of fiars' prices and certifying same, *vide* Act, 1808, **(a).**

For each kind of grain	£0·25
15. Extract and record copy of ordinary copying, per sheet	£0·25
16. Certifying copy locality, one sheet	£0·25
If longer	£0·50
17. Certificates of Valuation	£4·00
18. Extract of decree *in foro*	£3·00

19. Notes for searches—(unextracted processes)

If under ten years from the date of the order, each search	£0·25
Ten years and under twenty-five	£0·75
Twenty-five years and upwards	£1·25
20. Every other step or pleading not here enumerated	£1·00

21. Making up from official returns of fiars' prices 1873-1922 an "average value" of victual, certifying and intimating same *vide* 2nd Schedule, 15 & 16 Geo. V c. 33. For each kind of victual ... ... £1·00

22. Making (and converting from Imperial to Standard) list of fiars' prices and certifying same *vide* 4th Schedule, 15 & 16 Geo. V c. 33. For each kind of victual ... ... £0·25

23. Entry in teind roll of redemption of standard charge	£0·50

24. Entry in teind roll of change of ownership of lands over which a standard charge has been constituted ... ... £0·50

25. Entry in teind roll of allocation of standard charge (£0·50 in respect of first five entries in an allocation and £0·10 in respect of each additional entry).

26. Excerpt from teind roll, per sheet, figs.	£0·50
27. Certifying excerpt, one sheet	£0·25
If longer	£0·50
28. Exhibitions and inspection of final teind roll, each search	£0·25

29. Valuation of Teinds—

Lodging valuer's certificate	£1·00
Note of Appeal to Lord Ordinary	£2·00
Objections, Defences, or Answers thereto, if first step by party	£2·00

Registration of Valuer's certificate, and issuing certificate of valuation (same charge as certificates of valuation No. 17).

(a) 48 Geo 3 c. 138.

30. Surrender of Teinds—
  (*a*) Where no process of teind roll—
    Minute of other document of surrender, for the teind surrendered
    of each item of a locality ... ... £2·00
      Objections thereto ... ... £2·00
  (*b*) Where process of teind roll—
    Minute of Surrender if first step by party in process ... ... £2·00
    Condescendence *re* extra judicial surrender in process ... ... £2·00

31. Certifying inventory of statutory properties and endowments of each
quoad sacra parish ... ... £1·00

32. Delivering to the General Trustees under any order of Scottish
Ecclesiastical Commissioners so far as in the custody of Clerk of Teinds—
  (*a*) titles to church and manse and any securities for the endowment of
    stipend of any parish contained in the 8th Schedule of the Act 15 & 16
    Geo. V c. 33,
  (*b*) title to church and manse contained in the 9th Schedule of the Act
    15 & 16 Geo. V c. 33,
  (*c*) title to church and manse contained in the 10th Schedule of the Act
    15 & 16 Geo. V c. 33,
  (*d*) any securities for investments representing the price or consideration
    received for any glebe or part thereof, sold under section 17th of the
    Glebe Lands (Scotland) Act, 1866**(a)**.
Fee for delivery under each order, and checking receipt therefor including
searching records ... ... £1·00

EXPLANATORY NOTE

(This Note is not part of the Act of Sederunt.)

This Act of Sederunt prescribes a new table of Fees in the Court of Teinds.

(a) 1866 c. 71.

STATUTORY   INSTRUMENTS

1971 No. 76

SOCIAL SECURITY

The National Insurance and Industrial Injuries (Collection of Contributions) Amendment Provisional Regulations 1971

Made - - - -	18*th January* 1971
Laid before Parliament	19*th January* 1971
Coming into Operation	20*th January* 1971

The Secretary of State for Social Services hereby certifies under section 108(4) of the National Insurance Act 1965(a) that on account of urgency the following regulations should come into operation without delay, and, in exercise of his powers under section 12(7) of the said Act and of all other powers enabling him in that behalf, hereby makes the following regulations as provisional regulations : —

Citation, interpretation and commencement

1. These regulations, which may be cited as the National Insurance and Industrial Injuries (Collection of Contributions) Amendment Provisional Regulations 1971, shall be read as one with the National Insurance and Industrial Injuries (Collection of Contributions) Regulations 1948(b) as amended(c) (hereinafter referred to as " the principal regulations ") and shall come into operation on 20th January 1971.

Addition to the principal regulations

2. After regulation 6 of the principal regulations there shall be added the following regulation—

" *Recovery by employer of insured person's contributions during period when sale of stamps is interrupted*

6A. If the Secretary of State for Social Services, in an announcement published in the London Gazette and the Edinburgh Gazette, states that he is satisfied that the sale of stamps to the public will be, or is likely to be, interrupted during any period specified in the announcement, the provisions of paragraph (b) of the proviso to section 12(2) of the National Insurance Act 1965 (recovery by employer of insured person's contribution) shall not apply in relation to a contribution payable for a contribution week which includes a day which falls within such specified period.".

Keith Joseph,
Secretary of State for
Social Services.

18th January 1971.

(a) 1965 c. 51.   (b) S.I. 1948/1274 (Rev. XVI, p. 148: 1948 I, p. 3037).
(c) The relevant amending instrument is the National Insurance Act 1965.

EXPLANATORY NOTE

(This Note is not part of the Regulations.)

These Provisional Regulations amend the National Insurance and Industrial Injuries (Collection of Contributions) Regulations 1948 so as to secure that, during a period when national insurance stamps are not available to the public, an employer may deduct from an employee's wages or remuneration the amount of any contribution the employer is liable to pay on the employee's behalf before the contribution is actually paid.

STATUTORY INSTRUMENTS

1971 No. 77

FOOD AND DRUGS

The Welfare Foods (Amendment) Order 1971

Made - - -	*19th January* 1971
Laid before Parliament	*28th January* 1971
Coming into Operation	*15th February* 1971

The Secretary of State for Social Services, the Secretary of State for Wales and the Secretary of State for Scotland acting jointly in exercise of their powers under sections 4 and 7 of the Emergency Laws (Re-enactments and Repeals) Act 1964**(a)** and of all other powers enabling them in that behalf, hereby order as follows:—

Citation, commencement and extent

1.—(1) This order may be cited as the Welfare Foods (Amendment) Order 1971 and shall come into operation on 15th February 1971.

(2) This order shall not extend to Northern Ireland.

Interpretation

2. In this order the expression "the principal order" means the Welfare Foods Order 1968**(b)**.

Amendment of the principal order

3. In article 4(1)(b) of the principal order (which relates to entitlement to dried milk) for the expression "of 2s. 4d." there shall be substituted the expression "of 11½p".

Keith Joseph,
Secretary of State for Social Services.

14th January 1971.

Given under my hand on 15th January 1971.

Peter Thomas,
Secretary of State for Wales.

Given under the seal of the Secretary of State for Scotland on 19th January 1971.

(L.S.)

Gordon Campbell,
Secretary of State for Scotland.

(a) 1964 c. 60.   (b) S.I. 1968/389 (1968 I, p. 1050).

EXPLANATORY NOTE

(This Note is not part of the Order.)

This Order adjusts the price of cheap national dried milk from 2 shillings and 4 pence to 11½ new pence as from the 15th February 1971.

STATUTORY INSTRUMENTS

1971 No. 78

SUGAR

The Sugar (Rates of Surcharge and Surcharge Repayments) Order 1971

Made - - -	18*th January* 1971
Laid before Parliament	20*th January* 1971
Coming into Operation	21*st January* 1971

The Minister of Agriculture, Fisheries and Food, in exercise of the powers conferred on him by sections 7(4), 8(6) and 33(4) of the Sugar Act 1956(a) having effect subject to the provisions of section 3 of, and Part II of Schedule 5 to, the Finance Act 1962(b), and section 58 of the Finance Act 1968(c) and of all other powers enabling him in that behalf, with the concurrence of the Treasury, on the advice of the Sugar Board, hereby makes the following order:—

1.—(1) This order may be cited as the Sugar (Rates of Surcharge and Surcharge Repayments) Order 1971; and shall come into operation on 21st January 1971.

(2) The Interpretation Act 1889(d) shall apply for the interpretation of this order as it applies for the interpretation of an Act of Parliament.

2. Notwithstanding the provisions of Article 2 of the Sugar (Rates of Surcharge and Surcharge Repayments) (No. 10) Order 1970(e), the rates of surcharge payable under and in accordance with the provisions of section 7 of the Sugar Act 1956, having effect as aforesaid, in respect of sugar and invert sugar imported or home produced or used in the manufacture of imported composite sugar products shall on and after 21st January 1971 be the appropriate rates specified in Schedule 1 to this order.

3. For the purpose of section 8(3)(*b*) of the Sugar Act 1956, having effect as aforesaid, the rates of surcharge repayments in respect of invert sugar produced in the United Kingdom from materials on which on or after 21st January 1971 sugar duty has been paid or, by virtue of paragraph 1 of Part II of Schedule 5 to the Finance Act 1962, is treated as having been paid shall, notwithstanding the provisions of Article 3 of the Sugar (Rates of Surcharge and Surcharge Repayments) (No. 10) Order 1970 be the appropriate rates specified in Schedule 2 to this order.

4. Unless the rates of surcharge specified in Schedule 1, Part II, and the rates of surcharge repayment specified in Schedule 2 to this order have been varied by a subsequent order which comes into operation before the 15th February 1971 (the appointed day for the purposes of the Decimal Currency Act 1969(*f*))

(a) 1956 c. 48.	(b) 1962 c. 44.
(c) 1968 c. 44.	(d) 1889 c. 63.
(e) S.I. 1970/2005 (1970 III, p. 6517).	(f) 1969 c. 19.

then in ascertaining the rates of surcharge chargeable, and the rates of surcharge repayable, in respect of invert sugar

(a) until the end of 14th February 1971 there shall be disregarded any entry in Schedule 1, Part II, and Schedule 2 to this order as consists in a sum of money shown in square brackets; and

(b) on and after 15th February 1971 there shall be disregarded any entry in Schedule 1, Part II, and Schedule 2 as consists in a sum of money not shown in square brackets.

In Witness whereof the Official Seal of the Minister of Agriculture, Fisheries and Food is hereunto affixed on 18th January 1971.

(L.S.)   *R. P. Fraser,*
Authorised by the Minister.

We concur.
18th January 1971.

Bernard Weatherill,
Walter Clegg,
Two of the Lords Commissioners of
Her Majesty's Treasury.

SCHEDULE 1

PART I

SURCHARGE RATES FOR SUGAR

Polarisation	Rate of Surcharge per ton
	£
Exceeding—	
99°	6·000
98° but not exceeding 99°	5·658
97° ,, ,, ,, 98°	5·520
96° ,, ,, ,, 97°	5·376
95° ,, ,, ,, 96°	5·232
94° ,, ,, ,, 95°	5·088
93° ,, ,, ,, 94°	4·944
92° ,, ,, ,, 93°	4·800
91° ,, ,, ,, 92°	4·656
90° ,, ,, ,, 91°	4·512
89° ,, ,, ,, 90°	4·368
88° ,, ,, ,, 89°	4·224
87° ,, ,, ,, 88°	4·104
86° ,, ,, ,, 87°	3·984
85° ,, ,, ,, 86°	3·876
84° ,, ,, ,, 85°	3·768
83° ,, ,, ,, 84°	3·660
82° ,, ,, ,, 83°	3·552
81° ,, ,, ,, 82°	3·456
80° ,, ,, ,, 81°	3·360
79° ,, ,, ,, 80°	3·264
78° ,, ,, ,, 79°	3·168
77° ,, ,, ,, 78°	3·072
76° ,, ,, ,, 77°	2·976
Not exceeding 76°	2·880

Part II

Surcharge Rates for Invert Sugar

Sweetening matter content by weight	Rate of Surcharge per cwt.	
	s. d.	£
70 per cent. or more	3 9	[0·19]
Less than 70 per cent. and more than 50 per cent.	2 9	[0·13]
Not more than 50 per cent...	1 4	[0·06]

SCHEDULE 2

Surcharge Repayment Rates for Invert Sugar

Sweetening matter content by weight	Rate of Surcharge Repayment per cwt.	
	s. d.	£
More than 80 per cent.	4 6	[0·22]
More than 70 per cent. but not more than 80 per cent.	3 9	[0·19]
More than 60 per cent. but not more than 70 per cent.	2 9	[0·13]
More than 50 per cent. but not more than 60 per cent.	2 1	[0·10]
Not more than 50 per cent. and the invert sugar not being less in weight than 14 lb. per gallon	1 4	[0·06]

EXPLANATORY NOTE

(*This Note is not part of the Order.*)

This order prescribes—

(*a*) reductions equivalent to 4s. 0d. per cwt. of refined sugar in the rates of surcharge payable on sugar and invert sugar which become chargeable with surcharge on or after 21st January 1971;

(*b*) correspondingly reduced rates of surcharge repayment in respect of invert sugar produced in the United Kingdom from materials on which surcharge has been paid.

This order also indicates decimal equivalents, effective from 15th February 1971, unless varied by a subsequent order, of the rates of surcharge and surcharge repayment on invert sugar specified in Schedule 1, Part II, and Schedule 2 respectively. Some of the rates have been rounded down.

STATUTORY INSTRUMENTS

1971 No. 79

SUGAR

The Composite Sugar Products (Surcharge and Surcharge Repayments—Average Rates) Order 1971

Made - - - -		18*th January* 1971
Laid before Parliament -		20*th January* 1971
Coming into Operation -		21*st January* 1971

Whereas the Minister of Agriculture, Fisheries and Food (hereinafter called " the Minister ") has on the recommendation of the Commissioners of Customs and Excise (hereinafter called " the Commissioners ") made an order(a) pursuant to the powers conferred upon him by sections 9(1) and 9(4) of the Sugar Act 1956(b), having effect subject to the provisions of section 3 of, and Part II of Schedule 5 to, the Finance Act 1962(c), to the provisions of section 52(2) of the Finance Act 1966(d), and to the provisions of section 58 of the Finance Act 1968(e), providing that in the case of certain descriptions of composite sugar products surcharge shall be calculated on the basis of an average quantity of sugar or invert sugar taken to have been used in the manufacture of the products, and that certain other descriptions of composite sugar products shall be treated as not containing any sugar or invert sugar, and that in the case of certain descriptions of goods in the manufacture of which sugar or invert sugar is used, surcharge repayments shall be calculated on the basis of an average quantity of sugar or invert sugar taken to have been so used:

Now, therefore, the Minister, on the recommendation of the Commissioners and in exercise of the powers conferred upon him by sections 9(1), 9(4) and 33(4) of the Sugar Act 1956, having effect as aforesaid, and of all other powers enabling him in that behalf, hereby makes the following order:—

1.—(1) This order may be cited as the Composite Sugar Products (Surcharge and Surcharge Repayments—Average Rates) Order 1971, and shall come into operation on 21st January 1971.

(2) The Interpretation Act 1889(f) shall apply for the interpretation of this order as it applies for the interpretation of an Act of Parliament.

2. Surcharge payable on or after 21st January 1971 under and in accordance with the Sugar Act 1956, having effect as aforesaid, in respect of sugar and invert sugar used in the manufacture of the descriptions of imported composite sugar products specified in the second column of Schedule 1 to this order shall, notwithstanding the provisions of the Sugar (Rates of Surcharge and Surcharge Repayments) Order 1971(g) and the Composite Sugar Products (Surcharge and Surcharge Repayments—Average Rates) (No. 11) Order 1970(a), be calculated by reference to the weight of the products at the appropriate rates specified in relation thereto in the third column of the said Schedule.

(a) S.I. 1970/2006 (1970 III, p. 6520).	(b) 1956 c. 48.	(c) 1962 c. 44.
(d) 1966 c. 18.	(e) 1968 c. 44.	(f) 1889 c. 63.
(g) S.I. 1971/78. (1971 I, p. 132).		

3. Imported composite sugar products other than those of a description specified in Schedules 1 and 2 to this order shall be treated as not containing any sugar or invert sugar for the purposes of surcharge payable on or after 21st January 1971.

4. Surcharge repayments payable on and after 21st January 1971 under and in accordance with the provisions of section 8 of the Sugar Act 1956, having effect as aforesaid, in respect of sugar and invert sugar used in the manufacture of the descriptions of goods specified in the first column of Schedule 3 to this order shall, notwithstanding the provisions of the Sugar (Rates of Surcharge and Surcharge Repayments) Order 1971(a) and the Composite Sugar Products (Surcharge and Surcharge Repayments—Average Rates) (No. 11) Order 1970(b), be calculated by reference to the quantity of the goods at the appropriate rates specified in relation thereto in the second column of the said Schedule.

5. Unless the rates of surcharge specified in Schedule 1, and the rates of surcharge repayment specified in Schedule 3, to this order have been varied by a subsequent order which comes into operation before the 15th February 1971 (the appointed day for the purposes of the Decimal Currency Act 1969(c)) then in ascertaining the rates of surcharge chargeable, and the rates of surcharge repayable, in respect of any goods

(a) until the end of 14th February 1971 there shall be disregarded any entry in Schedules 1 and 3 to this order as consists in a sum of money shown in square brackets; and

(b) on and after 15th February 1971 there shall be disregarded any entry in the said Schedules as consists in a sum of money not shown in square brackets.

In Witness whereof the Official Seal of the Minister of Agriculture, Fisheries and Food is hereunto affixed on 18th January 1971.

(L.S.)   *R. P. Fraser,*
                                          Authorised by the Minister.

SCHEDULE 1

In this Schedule:—

" Tariff heading " means a heading or, where the context so requires, a subheading of the Customs Tariff 1959 (see paragraph (1) of Article 2 of the Import Duties (General) (No. 7) Order 1970(d)).

Tariff heading	Description of Imported Composite Sugar Products	Rate of Surcharge	
		Per cwt. s. d.	Per cwt. £
04.02 ..	Milk and cream, preserved, concentrated or sweetened, containing more than 10 per cent. by weight of added sugar	2 7	[0·13]

(a) S.I. 1971/78 (1971 I, p. 132). (b) S.I. 1970/2006 (1970 III, p. 6520).   (c) 1969 c. 19.
(d) S.I. 1970/1522 (1970 III, p. 4935).

Tariff heading	Description of Imported Composite Sugar Products	Rate of Surcharge	
		Per cwt. s. d.	Per cwt. £
17.02 (B) (2) and 17.05 (B)	Syrups containing sucrose sugar, whether or not flavoured or coloured, but not including fruit juices containing added sugar in any proportion:—		
	containing 70 per cent. or more by weight of sweetening matter	3 9	[0·19]
	containing less than 70 per cent., and more than 50 per cent., by weight of sweetening matter	2 9	[0·13]
	containing not more than 50 per cent. by weight of sweetening matter	1 4	[0·06]
17.02 (F) ..	Caramel:—		
	Solid	6 0	[0·30]
	Liquid	4 2	[0·20]
17.04 ..	Sugar confectionery, not containing cocoa ..	4 10	[0·24]
18.06 ..	Chocolate and other food preparations containing cocoa and added sugar:—		
	Chocolate couverture not prepared for retail sale; chocolate milk crumb, liquid ..	2 7	[0·13]
	Chocolate milk crumb, solid	3 3	[0·16]
	Solid chocolate bars or blocks, milk or plain, with or without fruit or nuts; other chocolate confectionery consisting wholly of chocolate or of chocolate and other ingredients not containing added sugar, but not including such goods when packed together in retail packages with goods liable to surcharge at a higher rate	2 8	[0·13]
	Other	3 5	[0·17]
19.08 ..	Pastry, biscuits, cakes and other fine bakers' wares containing added sugar:—		
	Biscuits, wafers and rusks containing more than 12½ per cent. by weight of added sugar, and other biscuits, wafers and rusks included in retail packages with such goods	1 6	[0·07]
	Cakes with covering or filling containing added sugar; meringues	2 0	[0·09]
	Other	9	[0·03]
20.01 ..	Vegetables and fruit, prepared or preserved by vinegar or acetic acid, containing added sugar:—		
	Containing 10 per cent. or more by weight of added sugar	2 1	[0·10]
	Other	5	[0·02]
20.03 ..	Fruit preserved by freezing, containing added sugar	9	[0·03]
20.04 ..	Fruit, fruit-peel and parts of plants, preserved by sugar (drained, glacé or crystallised)	3 11	[0·19]
20.05 ..	Jams, fruit jellies, marmalades, fruit purée and fruit pastes, being cooked preparations, containing added sugar	3 9	[0·18]
20.06 ..	Fruit otherwise prepared or preserved, containing added sugar:—		
	Ginger	3 0	[0·15]
	Other	9	[0·03]

SCHEDULE 2

Tariff heading	Description of Imported Composite Sugar Products
17.05 (A) and (B)	Sugar and invert sugar, flavoured or coloured.

SCHEDULE 3

Description of goods	Rate of surcharge repayment per bulk barrel of 36 gallons
Lager	5·3d. [£0·022]
All beer other than lager	3·2d. [£0·013]

EXPLANATORY NOTE

(This Note is not part of the Order.)

This order provides for reductions on and after 21st January 1971 in the average rates of surcharge payable on imported composite sugar products of the descriptions specified in Schedule 1 and in the average rates of surcharge repayment in respect of exported goods of the descriptions specified in Schedule 3. These correspond to the reductions in surcharge rates effected by the Sugar (Rates of Surcharge and Surcharge Repayments) Order 1971 (S.I. 1971/78). Provision is also made for certain imported composite sugar products to be treated as not containing any sugar or invert sugar.

This order also indicates decimal equivalents, effective from 15th February 1971, unless varied by a subsequent order, of the average rates of surcharge on imported composite sugar products of the descriptions specified in Schedule 1 and the average rates of surcharge repayment in respect of exported goods of the descriptions specified in Schedule 3. Some of the rates have been rounded down.

STATUTORY INSTRUMENTS

1971 No. 82

MUSEUMS

The British Museum (Authorised Repositories) Order 1971

Made - - -	18*th January* 1971
Laid before Parliament	27*th January* 1971
Coming into Operation	1*st February* 1971

The Secretary of State for Education and Science with the agreement of the Trustees of the British Museum, in exercise of the powers conferred upon her by section 10(2) of the British Museum Act 1963(a), as amended by the Transfer of Functions (Cultural Institutions) Order 1965(b), hereby makes the following Order:—

1.—(1) This Order may be cited as the British Museum (Authorised Repositories) Order 1971 and shall come into operation on 1st February 1971.

(2) The Interpretation Act 1889(c) shall apply for the interpretation of this Order as it applies for the interpretation of an Act of Parliament.

2. Part I of the Third Schedule to the British Museum Act 1963 as amended **(d)** (authorised repositories for the collections of the British Museum) shall be amended by the addition of the following paragraph:—

"7. Nos. 9/13, Kean Street, London, W.C.2."

Given under the Official Seal of the Secretary of State for Education and Science on 18th January 1971.

(L.S.)

Margaret H. Thatcher,
Secretary of State
for Education and Science.

EXPLANATORY NOTE

(This Note is not part of the Order.)

This Order adds to the authorised repositories of the British Museum.

(a) 1963 c. 24.   **(b)** S.I. 1965/603 (1965 I, p. 1911).   **(c)** 1889 c. 63.
(d) S.I. 1966/99, 1968/1604, 1970/1956 (1966 I, p. 222; 1968 III, p. 4406; 1970 III, p. 6408).

STATUTORY INSTRUMENTS

1971 No. 86

NATIONAL HEALTH SERVICE, ENGLAND AND WALES

The Health and Welfare Services (Provision of Instruction) Regulations 1971

Made - - -	19*th January* 1971
Laid before Parliament	26*th January* 1971
Coming into Operation	29*th January* 1971

The Secretary of State for Social Services in exercise of his powers under section 63 of the Health Services and Public Health Act 1968(**a**) and of all other powers enabling him in that behalf, with the approval of the Treasury, hereby makes the following regulations : —

1. These Regulations may be cited as the Health and Welfare Services (Provision of Instruction) Regulations 1971 and shall come into operation on 29th January 1971.

2. The Interpretation Act 1889(**b**) shall apply to the interpretation of these regulations as it applies to the interpretation of an Act of Parliament.

3. The classes of person described in the schedule hereto are hereby specified as classes for the purposes of section 63(1)(*b*) of the Health Services and Public Health Act 1968 (under which the Secretary of State has power to provide instruction for persons of specified classes who are employed or contemplate employment in certain activities connected with health or welfare).

Revocation

4. The Health and Welfare Services (Provision of Instruction) Regulations 1968(**c**) are hereby revoked.

Regulation 3   SCHEDULE

SPECIFIED CLASSES

Ancillary staff in general medical practices
Architects
Chiropodists
Computer systems designers
Computer programmers
Dental auxiliaries
Dental hygienists
Dental technicians
Employees of
    (i) the Dental Estimates Board
    (ii) Executive Councils
    (iii) the Joint Pricing Committee for England
    (iv) the Welsh Joint Pricing Committee

(**a**) 1968 c. 46.   (**b**) 1889 c. 63.
(**c**) S.I. 1968/1406 (1968 II, p. 4052).

Engineers
Health Visitors
Managers
Midwives
Nurses
Occupational therapists
Opticians
Orthoptists
Pharmacists
Registered dentists
Registered medical practitioners
Social workers
Speech therapists
Supervisors
Surveyors
Teachers of mentally handicapped.

Keith Joseph,
Secretary of State for Social Services.

14th January 1971.

We approve these regulations.

Walter Clegg,

V. H. Goodhew,
Two of the Lords Commissioners of
Her Majesty's Treasury.

19th January 1971.

EXPLANATORY NOTE

(This Note is not part of the Regulations.)

The Secretary of State has powers under section 63(1) of the Health Services and Public Health Act 1968 to provide instruction for (*a*) persons employed or contemplating employment by hospital authorities and (*b*) classes of person, to be specified in Regulations, who are employed or contemplating employment in certain other health or welfare services. These Regulations add to the classes of person previously specified in the Health and Welfare Services (Provision of Instruction) Regulations 1968 which are now revoked. These classes include registered medical practitioners and dentists, nurses, midwives and health visitors, pharmacists, opticians, employees of Executive Councils and other bodies set up under Part IV of the National Health Service Act 1946 (1946 c. 81), ancillary staff in general medical practices, members of certain professions supplementary to medicine and certain administrative staff.

STATUTORY INSTRUMENTS

1971 No. 87

WAGES COUNCILS

The Wages Regulation (Dressmaking and Women's Light Clothing) (Scotland) Order 1971

Made - - -	*19th January* 1971
Coming into Operation	*10th February* 1971

Whereas the Secretary of State has received from the Dressmaking and Women's Light Clothing Wages Council (Scotland) the wages regulation proposals set out in the Schedule hereto ;

Now, therefore, the Secretary of State in exercise of his powers under section 11 of the Wages Councils Act 1959(a), and of all other powers enabling him in that behalf, hereby makes the following Order :—

1. This Order may be cited as the Wages Regulation (Dressmaking and Women's Light Clothing) (Scotland) Order 1971.

2.—(1) In this Order the expression "the specified date" means the 10th February 1971, provided that where, as respects any worker who is paid wages at intervals not exceeding seven days, that date does not correspond with the beginning of the period for which the wages are paid, the expression "the specified date" means, as respects that worker, the beginning of the next such period following that date.

(2) The Interpretation Act 1889(b) shall apply to the interpretation of this Order as it applies to the interpretation of an Act of Parliament and as if this Order and the Order hereby revoked were Acts of Parliament.

3. The wages regulation proposals set out in the Schedule hereto shall have effect as from the specified date and as from that date the Wages Regulation (Dressmaking and Women's Light Clothing) (Scotland) Order 1968(c) shall cease to have effect.

Signed by order of the Secretary of State.
19th January 1971.

R. R. D. McIntosh,
Deputy Secretary,
Department of Employment.

(a) 1959 c. 69. (b) 1889 c. 63.
(c) S.I. 1968/1609 (1968 III, p. 4414).

SCHEDULE

The following minimum remuneration shall be substituted for the statutory minimum remuneration fixed by the Wages Regulation (Dressmaking and Women's Light Clothing) (Scotland) Order 1968 (Order W.D.S. (91)).

STATUTORY MINIMUM REMUNERATION

PART I

GENERAL

1. The statutory minimum remuneration payable to a worker to whom this Schedule applies for all work except work to which a minimum overtime rate applies under Part V is:—

(1) in the case of a time worker, the general minimum time rate payable to the worker under Part II, Part III or Part IV of this Schedule;

(2) in the case of a worker employed on piece work, piece rates each of which would yield, in the circumstances of the case, to an ordinary worker at least the same amount of money as the piece work basis time rate applicable to the worker under Part III or Part IV of this Schedule, or, where no piece work basis time rate is applicable, at least the same amount of money as the general minimum time rate which would be payable under Part II of this Schedule if the worker were a time worker.

PART II

FEMALE WORKERS IN THE RETAIL BRANCH OF THE TRADE
GENERAL MINIMUM TIME RATES

2. The general minimum time rates payable to female workers employed in the retail branch in Area A or Area B are respectively as follows:—

	Area A		Area B	
	Up to and including 14th February 1971 per hour s. d.	*On and after 15th February 1971 per hour* p	*Up to and including 14th February 1971 per hour* s. d.	*On and after 15th February 1971 per hour* p
(1) BODICE, COAT, SKIRT, GOWN OR BLOUSE HANDS, aged 20 years or over, who:—				
(a) having worked for 4 years in the said branch in one or more of the occupations of learner, apprentice or improver and for at least 2 years in the said branch thereafter,				
(b) take bodices, coats, skirts, gowns or blouses direct from the fitter in an establishment in which a fitter is employed and make them up without supervision other than the general supervision of the fitter or the workroom foreman or forewoman	4 10	24	4 8	23½

	Area A		Area B	
	Up to and including 14th February 1971 per hour s. d.	*On and after 15th February 1971 per hour* p	*Up to and including 14th February 1971 per hour* s. d.	*On and after 15th February 1971 per hour* p
(2) LEARNERS during the following periods of employment in the retail branch:—				
First year	*2 0¼*	*10*	*1 10¾*	*9½*
Second,, ...	*2 5*	*12*	*2 3¼*	*11½*
Third „	*2 11¾*	*15*	*2 10¼*	*14½*
Fourth,, ...	*3 7¼*	*18*	*3 4¾*	*17*
Provided that a learner who enters, or has entered, the trade for the first time at or over the age of 18 years shall be treated for the purposes of this paragraph as though she had, at the date of her entry, completed her first year's employment as a learner in the said branch.				
(3) All other workers	*4 7*	*23*	*4 5¼*	*22*

RECKONING EMPLOYMENT IN THE WHOLESALE MANUFACTURING BRANCH

3. Where a worker has been employed in the wholesale manufacturing branch, one half of the period of such employment shall be treated for the purposes of this Part of this Schedule as employment in the retail branch.

DEFINITION OF AREAS

4. For the purposes of this Part of this Schedule:—

Area A comprises—

(1) all Burghs which, according to the Preliminary Report on the Sixteenth Census of Scotland 1961, had a population of 10,000 or more;

(2) the following Special Lighting Districts, the boundaries of which have been defined, namely, Vale of Leven and Renton in the County of Dunbarton; and Larbert and Airth in the County of Stirling;

(3) the following areas, the boundaries of which were defined as Special Lighting Districts prior to 10th March 1943, namely, Bellshill and Mossend, Blantyre, Cambuslang, Larkhall, Shotts and Dykehead, and Holytown, New Stevenston and Carfin, all in the County of Lanark; and

(4) the following Burghs—

ANGUS COUNTY	BUTE COUNTY	RENFREW COUNTY
Brechin	Rothesay	Gourock
ARGYLL COUNTY	DUNBARTON COUNTY	STIRLING COUNTY
Dunoon	Helensburgh	Kilsyth
AYR COUNTY	FIFE COUNTY	WEST LOTHIAN COUNTY
Troon	Leven	Armadale.
	Lochgelly	
	St. Andrews	

Area B comprises the whole of Scotland other than Area A.

PART III

FEMALE WORKERS IN THE WHOLESALE MANUFACTURING BRANCH OF THE TRADE
GENERAL MINIMUM TIME RATES

5. The general minimum time rates payable to female workers in the wholesale manufacturing branch are as follows:—

	Up to and including 14th February 1971 per hour s. d.	On and after 15th February 1971 per hour p
(1) CONVEYER BELT MACHINISTS (that is to say, female workers employed in machining any work conveyed directly to and from them on a mechanical conveyor belt), not being workers to whom (2) of this paragraph applies	4 11	24½
(2) LEARNERS during the following periods of employment in the wholesale manufacturing branch:—		
First six months	2 4¾	12
Second,, ,, ...	2 9½	14
Third ,, ,, ...	3 3	16½
Fourth,, ,, ...	3 5¾	17½
Fifth ,, ,, ...	3 8½	18½
Sixth ,, ,, ...	3 11½	20
Provided that a learner who enters, or has entered, the trade for the first time at or over the age of 18 years shall be treated for the purposes of this paragraph as though she had, at the date of her entry, completed her first year's employment as a learner in the said branch.		
(3) All other workers	4 9	24

RECKONING EMPLOYMENT IN THE RETAIL BRANCH

6. Where a worker has been employed in the retail branch, one half of the period of such employment shall be treated for the purposes of this Part of this Schedule as employment in the wholesale manufacturing branch.

	Up to and including 14th February 1971 per hour s. d.	On and after 15th February 1971 per hour p
PIECE WORK BASIS TIME RATE		
7. The piece work basis time rate applicable to female workers of any age employed in the wholesale manufacturing branch on piece work is...	5 0	25

Part IV

MALE WORKERS IN ANY BRANCH OF THE TRADE
GENERAL MINIMUM TIME RATES

8. The general minimum time rates payable to male workers in any branch of the trade are as follows:—

	Up to and including 14th February 1971 per hour s. d.	On and after 15th February 1971 per hour p
Aged 21 years or over...	6 1½	30½
„ 20 and under 21 years	5 1¼	25½
„ 19 „ „ 20 „	4 6¾	23
„ 18 „ „ 19 „	4 1	20½
„ 17 „ „ 18 „	3 7	18
„ 16 „ „ 17 „	2 11¾	15
„ under 16 years	2 5¼	12
Provided that the general minimum time rates payable during his first year's employment in the trade to a worker who enters, or has entered, the trade for the first time at or over the age of 19 years shall be—		
During the first six months of such employment ...	4 1¾	20¼
During the second six months of such employment...	4 5¼	22

PIECE WORK BASIS TIME RATE	Up to and including 14th February 1971 per hour s. d.	On and after 15th February 1971 per hour p
9. The piece work basis time rate applicable to male workers of any age employed in any branch of the trade on piece work is	6 6	32½

Part V

OVERTIME AND WAITING TIME

RETAIL BRANCH

OVERTIME

10. Subject to the provisions of this Part of this Schedule, the minimum overtime rates set out in paragraph 11 are payable to workers in the retail branch of the trade in respect of any time worked—

    (1) in excess of the hours following, that is to say—

        (a) in any week ... ...   40 hours

(b) on any day other than a Saturday, Sunday or customary
holiday...   ...   .   8 hours

(c) on a Saturday, not being a customary holiday, where the
worker normally attends on six days in the week...   ...   4 hours

(2) on a Sunday or a customary holiday or, where the worker normally attends on
five days only in the week, on a Saturday.

MINIMUM OVERTIME RATES

11.—(1) Subject to the provisions of this Part of this Schedule, minimum overtime
rates are payable to a worker in the retail branch of the trade as follows:—

(a) on any day other than a Saturday, Sunday or a
customary holiday—

(i) for the first two hours worked in excess of 8 hours...   time-and-a-quarter

(ii) thereafter   ...   .   time-and-a-half

(b) on a Saturday not being a customary holiday—

(i) where the worker normally attends on six days in
the week—
for all time worked in excess of 4 hours ...   ...   time-and-a-half

(ii) where the worker normally attends on five days
only in the week—
for the first two hours worked   ...   .   time-and-a-quarter
thereafter   ...   .   time-and-a-half

(c) on a Sunday or a customary holiday—
for all time worked   ...   .   double time

(d) in any week exclusive of any time in respect of which
a minimum overtime rate is payable under the foregoing
provisions of this paragraph—
for all time worked in excess of 40 hours   ...   ...   time-and-a-quarter

(2) Where the worker normally attends on Sunday and not on Saturday (except
where such attendance is unlawful) Saturday shall be treated as a Sunday and, subject
to the provisions of (3) of this paragraph, Sunday as a Saturday.

(3) For the purposes of sub-paragraph (1) of this paragraph, where by arrangement
an ordinary week day is substituted for Saturday (or where (2) applies, for Sunday)
that ordinary week day shall be treated as Saturday and Saturday (or where the case
requires Sunday) as an ordinary week day.

WHOLESALE MANUFACTURING BRANCH
OVERTIME

12. Subject to the provisions of this Part of this Schedule, the minimum overtime
rates set out in paragraph 13 are payable to workers in the wholesale manufacturing
branch of the trade in respect of any time worked—

(1) in excess of the hours following, that is to say,

(a) in any week   ...   .   40 hours

(b) on any day other than a Saturday, Sunday or customary
holiday—
where the normal working hours exceed $8\frac{1}{2}$ ...   ...   9 hours
or
where the normal working hours are more than 8 but
not more than $8\frac{1}{2}$ ...   . $8\frac{1}{2}$ hours
or
where the normal working hours are not more than 8   8 hours

(2) on a Saturday, Sunday or customary holiday.

MINIMUM OVERTIME RATES

13. Minimum overtime rates are payable to a worker in the wholesale manufacturing branch of the trade as follows:—

(1) on any day other than a Sunday or customary holiday—
    (a) for the first 2 hours of overtime worked ...   ... time-and-a-quarter
    (b) thereafter   ...   . time-and-a-half

(2) on a Sunday or customary holiday—
    for all time worked   ...   . double time
    Provided that where the worker normally attends on Sunday and not on Saturday (except where such attendance is unlawful) Saturday shall be treated as a Sunday and Sunday as a Saturday.

(3) in any week, exclusive of any time in respect of which any minimum overtime rate is payable under the foregoing provisions of this paragraph—
    for all time worked in excess of 40 hours   ...   ... time-and-a-quarter

14. In this Part of this Schedule—

(1) The expressions "time-and-a-quarter", "time-and-a-half" and "double time" mean respectively:—

    (a) in the case of a time worker, one and a quarter times, one and a half times, and twice the general minimum time rate otherwise payable to the worker;

    (b) in the case of a male worker employed on piece work in any branch or of a female worker employed on piece work in the wholesale manufacturing branch—
        (i) a time rate equal respectively to one quarter, one half and the whole of the piece work basis time rate otherwise applicable to the worker, and, in addition thereto,
        (ii) the piece rates otherwise payable to the worker under paragraph 1(2);

    (c) in the case of a female worker employed on piece work in the retail branch—
        (i) a time rate equal respectively to one quarter, one half and the whole of the general minimum time rate which would be payable to the worker under Part II of this Schedule if she were a time worker and a minimum overtime rate did not apply, and, in addition thereto,
        (ii) the piece rates otherwise payable to the worker under paragraph 1(2).

(2) The expression "customary holiday" means—

    (a) New Year's Day (or the following day if New Year's Day falls on a Sunday);
    The local Spring holiday;
    The local Autumn holiday; and
    Any day proclaimed as an additional bank holiday or a general holiday throughout Scotland:

    Provided that, where in any establishment it is not the custom or practice to observe all or any of such days as holidays, another day or days not fewer in number may, by agreement between the employer and the worker, be substituted therefor;

    (b) Four other days to be agreed between the employer and the worker.

WAITING TIME

15.—(1) A worker is entitled to payment of the minimum remuneration specified in this Schedule for all time during which he is present on the premises of his employer, unless he is present thereon in any of the following circumstances:—

    (a) without the employer's consent, express or implied;

(b) for some purpose unconnected with his work and other than that of waiting for work to be given to him to perform;

(c) by reason only of the fact that he is resident thereon;

(d) during normal meal times in a room or place in which no work is being done, and he is not waiting for work to be given to him to perform.

(2) The minimum remuneration payable under sub-paragraph (1) of this paragraph to a piece worker when not engaged on piece work is that which would be payable if he were a time worker.

PART VI

INTERPRETATION

16. In this Schedule—

(1) "the trade" means the trade of dressmaking and the making of women's light clothing, that is to say, those branches of the women's clothing trade which are specified in paragraph 17;

(2) "the retail branch" means that branch of the trade in which the employer supplies the garment direct to the individual wearer and employs the worker direct;

(3) "the wholesale manufacturing branch" means any branch of the trade other than the retail branch;

(4) "learner" means a female worker who is employed during the whole or a substantial part of her time in learning any branch or process of the trade by an employer who provides her with reasonable facilities for such learning.

PART VII

APPLICABILITY OF STATUTORY MINIMUM REMUNERATION

17. This Schedule applies to workers in relation to whom the Dressmaking and Women's Light Clothing Wages Council (Scotland) operates, that is to say, workers employed in Scotland in those branches of the Women's Clothing Trade which are specified in the Schedule to the Trade Boards (Dressmaking and Women's Light Clothing Trade, Scotland) (Constitution and Proceedings) Regulations 1933(a), excluding any processes or operations therein which may be included in the Appendix to the Trade Boards (Shirtmaking) Order 1920(b). The Schedule to the said Regulations is as follows:—

"Those Branches of the Women's Clothing Trade that are engaged in the making of Non-Tailored Garments, namely, the making from textile or knitted fabrics of (a) non-tailored wearing apparel (other than handkerchiefs) worn by women or girls, or by children without distinction of sex, or (b) boys' ready-made washing-suits or sailor suits, where carried out in association with or in conjunction with the making of garments to be worn by women or girls, or by children without distinction of sex;

INCLUDING—

1. All operations and processes of cutting, making or finishing by hand or machine of dresses, non-tailored skirts, wraps, blouses, blouse-robes, jumpers, sports-coats, neckwear, tea-gowns, dressing-gowns, dressing-jackets, pyjamas, under-clothing, underskirts, aprons, overalls, nurses' and servants' caps, juvenile clothing, baby-linen, or similar non-tailored articles;

2. The making of field bonnets, sun-bonnets, boudoir caps or infants' millinery where carried on in association with or in conjunction with the making of any of the articles mentioned in paragraph 1 above;

(a) S.R. & O. 1933/37 (1933 p. 2039).   (b) S.R. & O. 1920/711 (1920 II, p. 790).

3. (*a*) The altering, repairing, renovating or remaking of any of the above-mentioned articles;

    (*b*) The cleaning of any of the above-mentioned articles where carried on in association with or in conjunction with the altering, repairing, renovating or remaking of such garments;

4. All processes of embroidery or decorative needlework where carried on in association with or in conjunction with the making, altering, repairing, renovating or remaking of such articles other than hand embroidery or hand-drawn-thread work on articles made of linen or cotton or of mixed linen and cotton;

5. The following processes if done by machine:—thread-drawing, thread-clipping, top-sewing, scalloping, nickelling and paring;

6. Laundering, smoothing, folding, ornamenting, boxing, packing, ware-housing, or other operations incidental to or appertaining to the making, altering, repairing, renovating or remaking of any of the above-mentioned articles;

BUT EXCLUDING—

A. The making of knitted articles; the making of underclothing, socks and stockings, from knitted fabrics; and the making from knitted fabrics of articles mentioned in paragraphs 1 and 2 above, where carried on in association with or in conjunction with the manufacture of the knitted fabrics;

B. The making of gloves, spats, gaiters, boots, shoes and slippers;

C. The making of headgear, other than the articles mentioned in paragraph 2 above;

D. The branches of trade covered by the Trade Boards (Corset) Order 1919**(a)**;

E. The making of rubberised or oilskin garments;

F. The making of women's collars and cuffs and of nurses' stiff washing belts where carried on in association with or in conjunction with the making of men's or boys' shirts or collars;

G. Warehousing, packing and other similar operations carried on in shops mainly engaged in the retail distribution of articles of any description that are not made on the premises."

EXPLANATORY NOTE

(*This Note is not part of the Order.*)

This Order, which has effect from 10th February 1971, sets out the statutory minimum remuneration payable in substitution for that fixed by the Wages Regulation (Dressmaking and Women's Light Clothing) (Scotland) Order 1968 (Order W.D.S. (91)), which Order is revoked.

New provisions are printed in italics.

(a) S.R. & O. 1919/570 (1919 II, p. 509).

STATUTORY INSTRUMENTS

1971 No. 90 (S.5)
SHERIFF COURT, SCOTLAND
Act of Sederunt (Alteration of Sheriff Court Fees) 1971

Made - - -	14*th January* 1971
Laid before Parliament	27*th January* 1971
Coming into Operation	15*th February* 1971

The Lords of Council and Session, under and by virtue of the powers conferred upon them by section 40 of the Sheriff Courts (Scotland) Act 1907(a), as amended by section 39 of the Administration of Justice (Scotland) Act 1933(b), and of all other powers competent to them in that behalf, do hereby enact and declare as follows:—

1. None of the provisions referred to in Schedule 1 hereto shall apply to any work done or expenses incurred on or after 15th February 1971.

2. In the case of any work done or expenses incurred on or after 15th February 1971, the Regulations and Table of Fees contained in Schedule 2 hereto shall be applied in substitution for the relative provisions referred to in Schedule 1 hereto. The Regulations and Table of Fees contained in Schedule 2 hereto shall apply only to the said work or expenses.

3. This Act of Sederunt may be cited as the Act of Sederunt (Alteration of Sheriff Court Fees) 1971 and shall come into operation on 15th February 1971.

And the Lords appoint this Act of Sederunt to be inserted in the Books of Sederunt.

J. L. Clyde,
I.P.D.

Edinburgh,
14th January 1971.

SCHEDULE 1

PROVISIONS WHICH SHALL CEASE TO APPLY TO WORK DONE OR EXPENSES INCURRED ON OR AFTER 15TH FEBRUARY 1971

1. The Regulations, and Chapters I, III, V, VI, VII, IX and X of the Table of Fees, contained in the Schedule to the Act of Sederunt of 7th May 1935(c).

2. The Regulations and Table of Fees contained in the Schedule to the Act of Sederunt (Alteration of Sheriff Court Fees) 1965(d).

3. The Regulations and Table of Fees contained in the Schedule to the Act of Sederunt (Alteration of Sheriff Court Fees) 1967(e).

(a) 1907 c. 51.   (b) 1933 c. 41.
(c) S.R. & O. 1935/488 (Rev. XX, p. 880: 1935 p. 1588).
(d) S.I. 1965/1611 (1965 II, p. 4637).   (e) S.I. 1967/1294 (1967 II, p. 3744).

SCHEDULE 2
General Regulations

1. This Table of Fees shall regulate the taxation of accounts between (a) solicitor and client, client paying, (b) solicitor and client, third party paying, and (c) party and party; and shall be subject to the aftermentioned powers of the sheriff to increase or modify such fees.

2. The pursuer's solicitor's account as between party and party shall be taxed by reference to the sum decerned for unless the Sheriff otherwise directs.

3. Except where the Sheriff otherwise directs the fees in this table shall be reduced by 20 per cent. in actions where the value of the action, if ascertainable from the process, or the sum craved, does not exceed £250 and in removing and ejection actions where the annual rent or gross annual value does not exceed £250. Where a counterclaim is lodged the value of the action shall be the addition of the sum sued for and the sum in the counterclaim.

4. In the Small Debt Court expenses as between party and party shall be regulated in accordance with the scale set forth in Chapter IV of this Table. As between solicitor and client, a solicitor shall have the option of charging either under Chapter IV, or under Chapter III less twenty per cent.

5. Where the demand made does not exceed the value which may be competently concluded for in the Small Debt Court, Small Debt expenses only shall be allowed, unless the Sheriff shall otherwise appoint.

6. Fees for work done in terms of the Social Work (Scotland) Act 1968 shall be chargeable under Chapter III.

7. The Sheriff shall have the following discretionary powers in relation to this Table of Fees:—

    (i) in all cases the Sheriff may direct that expenses shall be subject to modification,

    (ii) in cases falling under Regulation 3 hereof the Sheriff may direct that the deduction of 20 per cent. shall not be made,

    (iii) in cases where the sum decerned for does not exceed £50 the Sheriff may allow Small Debt expenses only,

    (iv) in cases of importance or requiring special preparation the Sheriff hearing the case may, upon a motion made not later than seven days after the date of any interlocutor containing a finding for expenses, pronounce a further interlocutor regarding these expenses allowing a percentage increase not exceeding 50 per cent of the fees authorised by this Table to cover the responsibility undertaken by the Solicitor in the conduct of the litigation. Where such an increase is allowed a similar increase shall be chargeable by each solicitor in the cause against his own client. In fixing the amount of the percentage increase the following factors shall be taken into account:—

        (a) the complexity of the litigation and the number, difficulty or novelty of the questions involved;

        (b) the skill, specialised knowledge and responsibility required of and the time and labour expended by the solicitor;

        (c) the number and importance of the documents (however brief) prepared or perused;

        (d) the place and circumstances of the litigation or in which the solicitor's work of preparation for and conduct thereof has been carried out;

        (e) the importance of the litigation or the subject matter thereof to the client;

        (f) the amount or value of money or property involved;

        (g) any other fees and allowances payable to the solicitor in respect of other items in the same litigation and otherwise charged for in the account.

(v) Wherever a party or his solicitor on one side attends any Diet of Proof or Debate or any meeting ordered by the Sheriff and the other is absent or not prepared to proceed the Sheriff shall have power to decern against the latter party for payment of such expenses as the Sheriff may consider reasonable. If an Appeal be abandoned or any Debate or preliminary pleas or otherwise ordered by the Sheriff be departed from by any party and notice to that effect be given to the opposite party at least three lawful days before the date fixed for the Hearing no debate fee shall be allowed; but failing such notice a debate fee shall be allowed to the respondent's or other party's solicitor of one-half of the amount which would have been allowed had the debate proceeded.

8. The expenses to be charged against an opposite party shall be limited to proper expenses of process without any allowance (beyond that specified in the Table) for preliminary investigations, subject to this proviso, that precognitions, plans, analyses, reports, and the like (so far as relevant and necessary for proof of the matters in the record between the parties), although taken or made before the raising of an action or the preparation of defences, or before proof is allowed, and although the case may not proceed to trial or proof, may be allowed.

9. Save as otherwise provided in the Table it shall be in the option of the solicitor to charge an account either on the basis of the inclusive fees of Chapters I and II or on the basis of the detailed fees of Chapter III but in accounts as between party and party it shall not be competent to make charges partly on the one basis and partly on the other. In accounts as between solicitor and client, however, it shall be competent to charge an account partly on the basis of the inclusive fees of Chapters I and II and partly on the basis of the detailed fees of Chapter III but so, however, that if an inclusive fee is charged under Chapters I or II no work falling thereunder shall be charged again under Chapter III.

10. In order that the expenses of litigation may be kept within proper and reasonable limits only such expenses shall be allowed in the taxation of accounts between party and party as are necessary for conducting it in a proper manner with due regard to economy. And it shall be competent to the Auditor to disallow all charges for papers, parts of papers or particular procedure or agency which he shall judge irregular or unnecessary.

11. Notwithstanding that a party shall be found entitled to expenses generally yet if on the taxation of the account it shall appear that there is any particular part of the litigation in which such party has proved unsuccessful or that any part of the expenses has been occasioned through his own fault he shall not be allowed the expense of such parts of the proceedings.

12. When a Remit is made by the Court regarding matters in the Record between the parties to an accountant, engineer, or other reporter the solicitors shall not, without special agreement, be personally responsible to the reporter for his remuneration, the parties alone being liable therefor.

13. In all cases the solicitor's outlays reasonably incurred in the furtherance of the litigation shall be allowed. These outlays shall include a charge in respect of posts and sundries of 15 per cent. of the taxed amount of fees.

14. In the taxation of accounts as between party and party where Counsel is employed:—

(a) Counsel's fees and the fees for instruction of Counsel in Item 18 of Chapter II or in a detailed account charged under Chapter III are to be allowed only where the Sheriff has sanctioned the employment of Counsel,

(b) Except on cause shown fees to Counsel and Solicitor for only one consultation in the course of the case are to be allowed except where Counsel is employed both before the Sheriff-Substitute and the Sheriff Principal and there is a consultation prior to the debate on the appeal when fees for an additional consultation are to be allowed.

15. This Table of Fees shall apply to all work done or expenses incurred in any action or other litigation on or after 15th February 1971. References in any Statute or Act of Sederunt to the fees allowed in Acts of Sederunt of earlier date than these presents shall subject to Regulation 16 hereof be held as referring to the fees allowed in the like circumstances in the Table of Fees underwritten.

16. The general percentage increases in fees provided for in Tables or Acts of Sederunt prior to the date hereof shall have no application to this Table.

TABLE OF FEES
Chapter I—Undefended Actions

1. ACTIONS (other than those specified in paragraph 2 of this Chapter) IN WHICH DECREE IS GRANTED WITHOUT PROOF
Inclusive fee to cover all work from taking instructions up to and including obtaining Extract Decree   ...   . £12·00

In cases where settlement is effected after service of a Writ but before the expiry of the induciae ...   . £9·00

If the Pursuer's solicitor elects to charge this inclusive fee he shall endorse a Minute to that effect on the initial writ before ordering extract of the decree. Outlays such as Court dues for deliverance and posts shall be chargeable in addition and taxation shall be unnecessary.

2. ACTIONS OF SEPARATION AND ALIMENT, ADHERENCE AND ALIMENT AND CUSTODY AND ALIMENT WHERE PROOF TAKES PLACE

Inclusive fee to cover all work from taking instructions up to and including obtaining Extract Decree   ...   . £45·00

If the Pursuer's solicitor elects to charge this inclusive fee he shall endorse a Minute to that effect on the initial writ after the close of the proof and before extract of the decree is ordered and when the option is so exercised, decree for expenses shall be granted against the defender for said sum together with the shorthand writer's fee actually charged in terms of the Table of Shorthand Writers' Fees in force from time to time and of other outlays up to £7 without the necessity for taxation. If outlays in excess of £7, excluding the shorthand writer's fee aforesaid are claimed, an account of such outlays shall be remitted to the Auditor of Court for taxation and the sum allowed for outlays shall be the amount of the account as taxed.

Chapter II—Defended Actions

1. INSTRUCTION FEE

To cover all work (except as hereinafter otherwise specially provided for in this Chapter) to the lodging of Defences including copyings ...   ... £18·00

Where separate Statement of Facts and Counter claim and Answers lodged, additional fee of   ...   . £9·00

2. ADJUSTMENT FEE

To cover all work (except as hereinafter otherwise specially provided for in this Chapter) in connection with the adjustment of the Record including (when appropriate) closing thereof, making up and lodging Closed Record and copyings

  (a) Pursuer's Agent   ...   . £16·00

      Defender's Agent ...   . £12·50

  (b) If action settled before Record is closed or in Summary Causes before an Interlocutor allowing proof or debate is pronounced
      Each original party's Agent   ...   . £12·50

(c) If additional Defender brought in before closing of Record or in Summary Causes before an Interlocutor allowing proof or debate is pronounced
Additional fee to each original party's Agent ... ... £4·50

(d) If additional Defender brought in after closing of Record or in Summary Causes after an Interlocutor allowing proof or debate is pronounced
Additional fee to each original party's Agent ... ... £6·50

3. (a) DEBATE FEE
To include preparation for and conduct of any Hearing or Debate other than on evidence, enquiring for cause at avizandum and noting Interlocutor ...
When debate does not exceed 1 hour ... ... £12·00

For every half hour engaged after the first hour ... ... £2·00

(b) INTERIM INTERDICT HEARINGS
Pursuer's solicitor. The same fees as for debate fee above, but to include both the appearance at lodging of writ and the hearing at second diet.
Defender's solicitor's fee where the debate does not exceed 1 hour ... £6·00

4. APPLICATION FOR JURY TRIAL
To include application to have cause tried by Jury, including drawing, attending Court, drawing and discussing questions of fact to be submitted to Jury, and procuring Jury list ... ... £8·00

Fee to opposing Solicitor ... ... £5·50

5. PRECOGNITIONS
Drawing Precognitions. (To include instructions, attendances with witnesses, and all relative meetings and correspondence)

(i) Where cause concluded before Proof or Trial allowed, per sheet (250 words) ... ... £2·00

(ii) Where cause concluded after Proof or Trial allowed, per sheet ... £2·50

Note: Where a skilled witness prepares his own precognition or report, the solicitor shall be allowed half of above drawing fee for revising and adjusting it.

6. COMMISSIONS TO TAKE EVIDENCE
(a) On Interrogatories
Fee to Solicitor applying for commission to include drawing, intimating and lodging Motion, drawing and lodging Interrogatories, instructing Commissioner and all incidental work (except as otherwise specially provided for in this Chapter) but excluding attendance at execution of Commission ... ... £13·50

Fee to opposing Solicitor if cross-Interrogatories prepared and lodged £10·50

If no cross-Interrogatories lodged ... ... £3·00

Fee for attendance at execution of Commission—per hour including travelling time ... ... £3·00

(b) Open Commissions
Fee to Solicitor applying for Commission to include all work (except as otherwise specially provided for in this Chapter) up to lodging Report of Commission but excluding attendance thereat ... ... £8·00

Fee to Solicitor for opposing party ... ... £3·00

Fee for attendance at execution of Commission—per hour ... ... £3·00

Travelling time—per hour ... ... £3·00

7. SPECIFICATION OF DOCUMENTS
Fee to cover drawing, intimating and lodging Specification and relative Motion and attendance at Court debating Specification ... ... £5·00

Inclusive fee to opposing Solicitor ...   .   £4·50

Fee for citation of havers, preparation for and attendance before Commissioner at execution of Commission

Where attendance before Commissioner does not exceed 1 hour   ...   £7·00

For each additional half hour after the first hour ...   .   £3·00

If Commission not executed—Fee for serving each party with copy of Specification to include recovering and examining documents or productions referred to therein   ...   .   £2·50

8. AMENDMENT OF RECORD

Fee to cover drawing, intimating and lodging Minute of Amendment and relative Motion and relative attendances at Court.

(a) Where Answers lodged ...   .   £11·00

(b) Where no Answers lodged   ...   .   £7·00

Inclusive fee to opposing Solicitor

(a) Where Answers lodged ...   .   £9·00

(b) Where no Answers lodged   ...   .   £6·00

9. MOTIONS AND MINUTES

Fee to cover drawing, intimating and lodging any written Motion or Minute, including a Reponing Note, and relative attendances at Court (except as otherwise provided for in this Chapter)

(a) Where opposed   ...   .   £6·00

(b) Where unopposed (including for each party a Joint Minute other than under paragraph 14(b))   ...   .   £3·50

Fee to cover considering opponent's written Motion, Minute or Reponing Note and relative attendances at Court

(a) Where Motion, Minute or Reponing Note opposed ...   .   £5·00

(b) Where Motion, Minute or Reponing Note unopposed   ...   ...   £3·00

10. PROCEDURE PRELIMINARY TO PROOF

(a) Fee to cover fixing Diet of Proof, citation of witnesses, and generally preparing for Trial or Proof and if necessary instructing Shorthand Writer   ...   .   £12·00

(b) Fee to cover preparing for adjourned diet and all incidental work as in (a) if diet postponed for more than 6 days
For each adjourned diet   ...   .   £5·00

(c) Drawing and lodging an Inventory of Productions, lodging the productions specified therein and considering opponent's productions (to be charged once only in each process)   ...   .   £4·00

Where only one party lodges productions, opponent's charges for considering same ...   .   £2·00

11. CONDUCT OF PROOF OR TRIAL

Fee to cover conduct of Proof or Trial and Debate on Evidence if taken at close of Proof—per half hour   ...   .   £3·00

If Counsel Employed
Fee to Solicitor appearing with Counsel—per half hour   ...   ...   £2·50

12. DEBATE ON EVIDENCE

Where Debate on Evidence not taken at conclusion of Proof preparing for Debate   ...   .   £8·00

Fee for conduct of Debate—per half hour ...   .   £3·00

If Counsel employed—Fee to Solicitor appearing with Counsel—per half hour   ...   .   £2·50

13. APPEALS

    (*a*) To Sheriff Principal

        Fee to cover instructions, marking of Appeal or noting that Appeal marked, noting Diet of Hearing thereof and preparation for Hearing   £15·00

        Fee to cover conduct of Hearing—per half hour   ...   .   £3·00

        If Counsel employed—Fee to Solicitor appearing with Counsel—per half hour ...   .   £2·50

    (*b*) To Court of Session

        Fee to cover instructions, marking Appeal or noting that Appeal marked and instructing Edinburgh Correspondents ...   .   £7·50

14. SETTLEMENTS

    (*a*) Judicial Tender

        Fee for preparation and lodging or for consideration of Minute of Tender   ...   .   £6·00

        Fee on acceptance of Tender, to include preparation and lodging or consideration of Minute of Acceptance and attendance at Court when Decree granted in terms thereof   ...   .   £4·00

    (*b*) Extra-Judicial Settlements

        Fee to cover negotiations resulting in settlement, framing or revising Joint Minute and attendance at Court when authority interponed thereto   ...   .   £10·00

15. FINAL PROCEDURE

    Fee to cover settling with witnesses, enquiries for cause at avizandum, noting Final Interlocutor   ...   .   £3·00

    Fee to cover drawing Account of Expenses, arranging, intimating and attending Diet of Taxation and obtaining approval of Auditor's Report and adjusting Account with opponent where necessary, ordering, procuring and examining Extract Decree   ...   .   £6·00

    Fee to cover considering opponent's Account of Expenses and attending Diet of Taxation or adjusting account with opponent   ...   .   £3·00

16. COPYING FEES

    Copying all necessary papers by any means

    First copy—per sheet ...   .   £0·30

    Additional copies—per sheet   ...   .   £0·10

    A sheet shall be 250 words. When copied by photostatic or similar process, each page shall be charged as one sheet.

17. PROCESS FEE

    Fee to cover all consultations between Solicitor and client during the progress of the cause and all communications, written or verbal, passing between them.

    Ten per cent on total fees and copyings allowed on taxation.

18. FEE FOR INSTRUCTION OF COUNSEL ·

    Fee for instructing Counsel to revise Record   ...   .   £5·00

    Fee for instructing Counsel to conduct Debate, Proof or Trial ...   ...   £10·00

    Fee for instructing Counsel to conduct Appeal to Sheriff Principal   ...   £10·00

    In each case to cover all consultations, revisal of papers and all incidental work.

    Fee to Counsel to be allowed as outlay.

CHAPTER III—CHARGES FOR TIME, DRAWING OF PAPERS,
CORRESPONDENCE, ETC.

1. Attendance at Court conducting trial, proof or formal debate or hearing—
    per half hour ...   .   £3·00

2. Time occupied in the performance of all other work including attendances
    with client and others and attendances at Court in all circumstances, ex-
    cept as otherwise specifically provided.
    (a) Solicitor—per half hour ...   .   £2·50
    (b) Unqualified Assistant—per half hour ...   .   £1·50
    Note: Time necessarily occupied in travelling to such be chargeable at
    these rates.

3. Drawing all necessary papers (the sheet throughout this Chapter to consist
    of 250 words or numbers)—per sheet   ...   .   £1·00

4. Revising papers where revisal ordered—for each five sheets   ...   ...   £0·50

5. Copying all necessary papers by any means
    First copy—per sheet ...   .   £0·30
    Additional copies—per sheet   ...   .   £0·10
    When copied by photostatic or similar process each page shall be charged
    as one sheet.

6. Certifying or signing a document   ...   .   £0·50

7. Perusing any document (other than a letter) not exceeding 2 sheets in
    length ...   .   £1·00

8. Lodging in process
    Each necessary lodging in or uplifting from process, also for each neces-
    sary enquiry for documents due to be lodged   ...   .   £0·50

9. Borrowing process
    Each necessary borrowing of process to include return of same ...   ...   £0·50

10. Extracts
    Ordering, procuring and examining Extracts, interim or otherwise   ...   £2·00

11. Correspondence, Intimations, etc.
    (1) Formal letters and intimations ...   .   £0·20
    (2) Letters other than above—per page of 125 words   ...   .   £0·80
    (3) Telephone calls except under (4)   ...   .   £0·50
    (4) Telephone calls (lengthy) to be treated as attendances or long letters.

12. Citations
    Each citation of party or witness including execution thereof   ...   ...   £1·00

13. Instructions to Officers
    Instructing officer to serve, execute or intimate various kinds of writs or
    diligence including the examination of executions ...   .   £0·50
    For each party after the first on whom service or intimation is simulta-
    neously made ...   .   £0·50
    Agency accepting service of any writ   ...   .   £1·00
    Reporting diligence   ...   .   £1·00

14. Personal diligence
    (1) Recording execution of charge ...   .   £1·00
    (2) Procuring fiat   ...   .   £1·00
    (3) Instructing apprehension   ...   .   £1·00
    (4) Framing state of debt and attendance at settlement ...   .   £1·50

15. Sales
    (1) Obtaining Warrant to sell   ...   .   £1·00
    (2) Instructing auctioneer or officer to conduct sale   ...   .   £1·00
    (3) Perusing report of sale ...   .   £1·00
    (4) Reporting sales under poindings or sequestrations or any other
        judicial sales   ...   .   £0·75
    (5) Noting approval of roup roll   ...   .   £0·75
    (6) Obtaining warrant to pay   ...   .   £0·75

CHAPTER IV—SMALL DEBT CASES

1. Fee for either party to cover all work, other than under paragraph 8, from
   taking instructions up to and including attendance at first diet when
   necessary
   (a) where sum sued for is under £20   ...   .   £1.00
   (b) where sum sued for is £20 or over or the proceedings are taken under
       Section 3 of the Sheriff Court (Civil Jurisdiction and Procedure)
       (Scotland) Act 1963   ...   .   £4·20

2. Attendance at Court on each occasion subsequent to the first diet.
   For each hour or part thereof   ...   .   £1·00

3. Preparing for proof when proof allowed   ...   .   £3·00

4. Where a case is remitted under Section 48 of the Sheriff Courts (Scotland)
   Act 1907 to the Ordinary Court Roll, the fees to the date of the remit
   shall be chargeable under this Chapter and thereafter under Chapters II
   or III.

5. Where a case is remitted under Rule 61 of the Sheriff Courts (Scotland)
   Act 1907 to be dealt with under the provisions of the Small Debt Acts, the
   fees to the date of the remit shall be chargeable under Chapters II or III
   and thereafter under Sections 2 and 3 of this Chapter.

6. Necessary outlays, including fees for witnesses calculated in accordance
   with the provisions of the Act of Sederunt (Sheriff Court Witnesses Fees)
   1953 as amended or of any enactment which shall supersede that Act of
   Sederunt, shall be allowed in addition to the foregoing fees.

7. Fees for diligence in terms of Sections 13, 14 and 15 of Chapter III so
   far as applicable to diligence.

8. Fee in terms of the Citation Amendment (Scotland) Act 1882 to be
   allowed in addition.

CHAPTER V—MERCANTILE SEQUESTRATION
Charge according to Chapters III and VII of the Table

CHAPTER VI—SUMMARY SEQUESTRATION
Charge according to Chapter III of the Table—Less 20 per cent

CHAPTER VII—EXECUTRY BUSINESS—INTESTATE MOVEABLE SUCCESSION

1. Taking instructions to present petition for decree-dative, drawing petition and making necessary copies, lodging and directing publication, attendance at Court, moving for decree-dative, extracting decree where necessary and all matters incidental to petition.

   Inclusive fee ... ... £7·00

2. Preliminary Investigation and Confirmation of Executors.
   To be charged for according to General Table of Fees for Conveyancing and General Business in Testate Succession in force from time to time.

3. Bonds of Caution.

   Taking out Bond of Caution, getting it signed and lodged with Clerk of Court, and procuring attestation of cautioner's sufficiency ... ... £3·50

   Where caution is found through the medium of a Guarantee Company for all the work in connection therewith ... ... £3·00

4. Restriction of Caution.

   Taking Instructions to prepare petition for restriction of caution, drawing petition and making necessary copies, lodging, instructing advertisement, and all matters incidental to petition.

   Inclusive fee ... ... £7·00

EXPLANATORY NOTE

(This Note is not part of the Act of Sederunt.)

This Act of Sederunt prescribes new Regulations and a new Table of Fees for solicitors in the Sheriff Court in respect of work done and expenses incurred on or after 15th February, 1971.

STATUTORY INSTRUMENTS

1971 No. 91 (S.6)

LOCAL GOVERNMENT, SCOTLAND

CLERKS OF THE PEACE

Act of Sederunt (Fees of Town Clerks and Clerks of the Peace) 1971

Made	-	-	-	*14th January* 1971

Coming into Operation   *15th February* 1971

The Lords of Council and Session, under and by virtue of the powers conferred upon them by paragraph (c) of section 18 of the Moneylenders Act 1927(a) and section 29(1) of the Licensing (Scotland) Act 1959(b) and of all other powers competent to them in that behalf, on the application of the Lord Advocate, do hereby enact and declare as follows :—

1. The fees payable to a town-clerk for anything done under the Licensing (Scotland) Act 1959(b) the Licensing (Scotland) Act 1962(c) or the Moneylenders Act 1927(a) shall be those prescribed in Schedule 1 hereto.

2. The fees payable to a clerk of the peace for anything done under the Licensing (Scotland) Act 1959(b), the Licensing (Scotland) Act 1962(c) or the Moneylenders Act 1927(a) and in respect of certain other work specified in Schedule 2 hereto, shall be those prescribed in that Schedule.

3. The Act of Sederunt (Fees of Town Clerks and Clerks of the Peace) 1953(d), the Act of Sederunt (Fees of Town Clerks and Clerks of the Peace) 1962(e), and Sections 2, 3 and 4 of Book M Chapter V Schedule B to the Codifying Act of Sederunt 1913(f) are hereby repealed.

4. This Act of Sederunt may be cited as the Act of Sederunt (Fees of Town Clerks and Clerks of the Peace) 1971, and shall come into operation on 15th February 1971.

And the Lords appoint this Act of Sederunt to be inserted in the Books of Sederunt.

Edinburgh,

14th January 1971.

J. L. Clyde,
I.P.D.

(a) 1927 c. 21.   (b) 1959 c. 51.
(c) 1962 c. 51.   (d) S.I. 1953/1776 (1953 II, p. 2299).
(e) S.I. 1962/2334 (1962 III, p. 3231).
(f) S.R. & O. 1913/638 (Rev. XX, p. 776: 1913 III, p. 2013).

SCHEDULE 1

PART 1

TABLE OF FEES PAYABLE TO TOWN-CLERKS UNDER THE LICENSING (SCOTLAND) ACTS
1959 AND 1962

		Fee.
1.	Each printed copy of form of application for certificate of a public-house, inn, &c.	£0·10
2.	Lodging application for certificate or for renewal for inn, hotel, public-house, &c.	£0·85
3.	Lodging application by executors, representatives, or disponees of a deceased applicant, under section 33	£0·40
4.	Inspection of applications, or register of applications, for certificates, for each hour or part of an hour	£0·20
5.	Lodging application for transfer of certificate of inn, hotel, public-house, &c.	£0·85
6.	Lodging plans	£0·40
7.	Lodging objections	£0·85
	If proof led- each party before commencement of proof ...	£0·85
8.	Certificate of an inn, hotel, public-house, &c., or renewal	£0·50
9.	Transfer certificate	£0·50
10.	Duplicate certificate	£0·20
11.	Special permission	£0·85
12.	List for Inland Revenue of names of persons to whom certificates have been granted—	
	If not more than 25 names	£0·40
	For each name beyond 25	£0·02
13.	First application for insertion of conditions in certificate in respect of off-rate part of hotel or public-house	£0·85
14.	Insertion of such conditions (otherwise than where certificate is being granted, renewed or transferred)	£0·50
15.	Lodging application for declaration by court, under Rule 4 of the Licensing (Scotland) Rules 1962	£0·80
16.	Issue of declaration by court following application under Rule 4 of the Licensing (Scotland) Rules 1962	£0·50
17.	Lodging application for affirmation of provisional grant	£0·80
18.	Application for consent of court to reconstruction &c. of premises...	£0·50
19.	Lodging plan and description under section 12(1) of the Licensing (Scotland) Act 1962	£0·40

PART II

TABLE OF FEES PAYABLE TO TOWN-CLERKS UNDER THE MONEYLENDERS ACT, 1927

1.	Each printed copy of Application for certificate	£0·15
2.	Lodging application for certificate	£1·20
3.	Inspection of Applications of Register of Applications for certificates for each hour or part of an hour	£0·25
4.	Lodging objections	£1·20
	If proof led—each party before commencement of proof ...	£1·20
5.	Certificate, or renewal	£0·80
6.	Duplicate certificate	£0·25

SCHEDULE 2

TABLE OF FEES PAYABLE TO CLERKS OF THE PEACE FOR WORK DONE UNDER THE LICENSING (SCOTLAND) ACTS, 1959 AND 1962, THE MONEYLENDERS ACT, 1927, AND CERTAIN OTHER ENACTMENTS.

PART I.

FEES PAYABLE TO CLERKS OF THE PEACE BY APPLICANTS FOR LICENCES OR OTHERS.

Fee.

1. LICENCES

(a) Licensing (Scotland) Act, 1959

		Fee.
1.	Each printed copy of form of application for certificate of a public-house, inn, &c.	£0·10
2.	Lodging application for certificate, or for renewal for inn, hotel, public-house, &c.	£0·85
3.	Lodging application by executors, representatives, or disponees of a deceased applicant, under section 33	£0·40
4.	Inspection of applications, or Register of Applications, for certificates—for each hour or part of an hour	£0·20
5.	Lodging application for transfer of certificate of inn, hotel, public-house, &c.	£0·85
6.	Lodging plans	£0·40
7.	Lodging objections	£0·85
	If proof led, either in a Licensing Court or a Court of Appeal—each party before commencement of proof	£0·85
8.	Certificate of an inn, hotel, public-house, &c., or renewal	£0·50
9.	Transfer certificate	£0·50
10.	Duplicate certificate	£0·15
11.	Special permission	£0·85
12.	Lodging appeal to the Licensing Appeal Court or Quarter Sessions, and finding caution	£0·85
13.	Hearing and deciding appeal	£0·85
14.	Confirmation	£1·20
15.	Lists for Inland Revenue of names of persons to whom certificates have been granted:—	
	If not more than 25 names	£0·40
	For each name beyond 25	£0·02
16.	First application for insertion of conditions in certificate in respect of off-rate part of hotel or public-house	£0·85
17.	Insertion of such conditions (otherwise than where certificate is being granted, renewed or transferred	£0·50
18.	Lodging application for declaration by court, under Rule 4 of the Licensing (Scotland) Rules 1962	£0·80
19.	Issue of declaration by court following application under Rule 4 of the Licensing (Scotland) Rules 1962	£0·50
20.	Lodging application for affirmation of provisional grant	£0·80
21.	Application for consent of court to reconstruction &c. of premises	£0·50
22.	Lodging plan and description under section 12(1) of the Licensing (Scotland) Act 1962	£0·40

(b) Moneylenders Act, 1927

		Fee.
1.	Each printed copy of Form of Application for Certificate	£0·15
2.	Lodging application for certificate	£1·20
3.	Inspection of Application or Register of Applications for Certificates for each hour or part of an hour	£0·25
4.	Lodging objections	£1·20
	If proof led either in a Licensing Court or Court of Appeal— each party before commencement of proof	£1·20
5.	Certificate, or renewal	£0·80
6.	Duplicate certificate	£0·25
7.	Lodging appeal	£2·45

(c) Licences to Deal in Game

1.	Application for certificate or renewal	£0·40
2.	Certificate or renewal	£0·40
3.	Inspection of Register	£0·20

(d) Pawnbrokers' Licences

1.	Lodging application for certificate or renewal	£0·85
2.	Certificate or renewal	£0·50

2. PROCEEDINGS UNDER THE ARMY ACT

1.	Attestations of a recruit	£0·20
2.	Warrant for impressment of carriages	£0·20
3.	Descriptive return of a deserter	£0·35
4.	Warrant of committal	£0·20
5.	Certificate of conviction or acquittal	£0·50

3. PROCEEDINGS UNDER THE SMALL DEBT ACTS

1.	Complaint warrant to cite	£0·04
2.	Copy for service	£0·04
3.	Entering into procedure book	£0·04
4.	Decree and warrant of execution	£0·04
5.	Warrant de novo	£0·03
6.	Re-hearing	£0·10
7.	For inspection of book	£0·04
8.	Indorsing decree from other jurisdiction	£0·08

4. PROCEEDINGS UNDER THE SUMMARY JURISDICTION AND PROCESS ACTS.

1.	For each compliant	£0·25
2.	For whole procedure at trial:— ...	
	If proof led	£0·45
	If proof not led	£0·25
3.	Extract of any judgment, conviction or order	£0·10
4.	Separate search warrant or separate warrant to apprehend a witness ...	£0·25
5.	Separate warrant for citation of witnesses	£0·10
6.	Indorsing English warrant or decree	£0·25
7.	Certified copy of any proceedings or judgment, per sheet of 250 words	£0·20

5. PROCEEDINGS IN APPEALS

(a) Appeals Under Summary Jurisdiction (Scotland) Act, 1908.

		Fee.
1.	Lodging bond of caution or making consignation	£0·45
2.	Preparing and drawing case	£1·50
3.	Duplicate for respondent, per sheet	£0·15

(b) Appeals to Quarter Sessions or General Sessions.

1.	Lodging appeal and finding caution	£0·45
2.	Hearing and deciding appeal	£0·45

6. MISCELLANEOUS

1.	Order of detention in Approved School	£0·20
2.	Each Justice of the Peace on qualifying	£0·85
3.	Warrant for recovery of rates	£0·50
4.	Judicial or other bonds of caution not otherwise provided for ...	£0·85
5.	Affidavit—if printed form	£0·20
6.	Drawing affidavit, per sheet	£1·00
7.	Certifying foreign affidavits	£0·20

PART II

FEES PAYABLE TO CLERKS OF THE PEACE BY COUNTY COUNCILS AND TOWN COUNCILS

1. Framing circulars calling meetings of Quarter Sessions or Special General Sessions or Committees of Justices when the said committees are summoned for the despatch of administrative business, except the disposal of applications for licences, including instructing printer, addressing, and dispatching:—

For the first 50	£1·10
For each 50 after the first 50	£0·85

2. Attendance at any meeting of Quarter Sessions or Special General Sessions or any meeting of Committee of the Justices when met for the purpose of despatching administrative business, except the disposal of applications for licences ... ...   £5·00

3. Attendance at any meeting of a Licensing Court, under the Licensing (Scotland) Acts or any committee thereof, when met for the purpose of making bye-laws or regulations or despatching business other than the disposal of applications for licences ... ...   £5·00

4. Drawing and engrossing minutes of the meetings specified in Nos. 2 and 3, per sheet ... ...   £1·20

5. Drawing bye-laws and regulations under the Licensing (Scotland) Acts per sheet ... ...   £1·20

6. Advertisements and public notices:—

(1) Framing, per sheet	£0·85
(2) Ordering insertion in newspapers, each newspaper	£0·40

Fee.

7. Framing returns required by the Judicial Statistics Departments:—

    Small Debt Act, 1825, and Licensing (Scotland) Act, 1903:—

	Fee.
For the first 100 cases or licences	£1·65
For each 100 thereafter up to 500	£0·40
For each 100 after 500	£0·20
8. All other returns, per sheet	£1·00
9. Each necessary letter	£0·40
10. Copying, per sheet	£0·25

PART III

FEES PAYABLE TO CLERKS OF THE PEACE AS CLERKS OF THE COURTS OF APPEAL UNDER THE LICENSING (SCOTLAND) ACTS BY THE TOWN COUNCILS OF EVERY ROYAL, PARLIAMENTARY, OR POLICE BURGH CONTAINING A POPULATION OF OR EXCEEDING 20,000

	Fee.
1. Drawing regulations and engrossing in Minute Book, per sheet ...	£1·20
2. Each necessary letter	£0·40
3. Copying, per sheet	£0·25

EXPLANATORY NOTE

(This Note is not part of the Act of Sederunt.)

This Act of Sederunt re-enacts with approximate decimal equivalents the Tables of Fees payable to Town Clerks and Clerks of the Peace under the Licensing (Scotland) Acts 1959 and 1962 and the Moneylenders Act 1927 and to Clerks of the Peace for work under certain other enactments.

STATUTORY INSTRUMENTS

1971 No. 92 (S.7)

SHERIFF COURT, SCOTLAND

Act of Sederunt (Social Work) (Sheriff Court Procedure Rules) 1971

Made - - - -	15*th January* 1971
Coming into Operation	15*th February* 1971

ARRANGEMENT OF RULES

PART I

GENERAL

PART II

PROCEDURE IN APPLICATIONS UNDER SECTION 42 OF THE ACT

Procedure prior to hearing before sheriff

*Provisions applicable to all stages prior
to determination of application*

Conduct of hearing

Miscellaneous

Part III

Procedure in Appeals under Section 49 of the Act

Part IV

Citation and Intimation in Proceedings under Sections 42 and 49 of the Act

Part V

Miscellaneous and Supplemental

SCHEDULE 1

ARRANGEMENT OF FORMS

SCHEDULE 2

Part I

Exclusion of certain Enactments

Part II

Modification and Amendment of certain Enactments

The Lords of Council and Session, under and by virtue of the powers conferred on them by section 34 of the Administration of Justice (Scotland) Act 1933(a), and of all other powers enabling them in that behalf, do by this Act of Sederunt enact and declare the following Rules:—

Part I

General

Citation and commencement

1. These Rules may be cited as the Act of Sederunt (Social Work) (Sheriff Court Procedure Rules) 1971 and shall come into operation on 15th February 1971.

(a) 1933 c. 41.

Interpretation

2.—(1) In these Rules, unless the context otherwise requires—

"the Act" means the Social Work (Scotland) Act 1968**(a)**;

"appeal" means an appeal under section 49 of the Act;

"application" means an application under section 42 of the Act;

"child" has the meaning assigned to that term by section 30(1) of the Act;

"parent" has the meaning assigned to that term by section 94(1) as read with section 30(2), of the Act;

"reporter" includes deputy reporter;

"sheriff clerk" includes sheriff clerk depute.

(2) Unless the context otherwise requires, words and expressions used in these Rules and in Part III of the Act shall have the same meanings in these Rules as they have in the said Part III.

(3) In these Rules any reference, however expressed, to disputed grounds of referral shall be construed as a reference to grounds of referral which form the subject of an application under subsection (2)(*c*) or subsection (7) of section 42 of the Act.

(4) In these Rules any reference to any enactment shall be construed as a reference to that enactment as amended or extended, and as including a reference thereto as applied, by or under any other enactment.

(5) The Interpretation Act 1889**(b)**, shall apply for the interpretation of these Rules as it applies for the interpretation of an act of Parliament.

Schedule of Forms

3. The Forms in Schedule 1 to these Rules, or forms to the like effect, shall be used with such variations as circumstances may require and any reference to these Rules to a numbered Form shall, unless the context otherwise requires, be construed as a reference to the Form bearing that number set out in that Schedule.

PART II

PROCEDURE IN APPLICATION UNDER SECTION 42 OF THE ACT

Procedure prior to hearing before sheriff

Lodging of application, etc.

4.—(1) Within a period of seven days beginning with the date on which the reporter was directed to make the application, the reporter shall lodge it with the sheriff clerk.

(2) An application by the reporter to the sheriff shall be made in the form as nearly as may be of Form 1.

Form of warrant for diet in applications

5. As soon as practicable after the lodging of the application, the sheriff clerk shall assign a diet for the hearing of the application and shall issue a warrant in the form as nearly as may be of Form 2.

(a) 1968 c. 49.   (b) 1889 c. 63.

Citation of child and intimation to parent in applications

6.—(1) After the issue of the first warrant, the reporter shall forthwith cite the child by serving on him a copy of the application and the warant, together with a citation in the form as nearly as may be of Form 3.

(2) At the same time or as soon as possible thereafter, the reporter shall intimate the hearing of the application to any parent whose whereabouts are known to him by serving on him copies of the said application and warrant together with a citation in the form as nearly as may be of Form 4.

(3) An execution of citation or of intimation under this Rule shall be made in the form as nearly as may be of Form 5.

Provisions applicable to all stages prior to determination of application

Abandonment of application

7. At any stage of the proceedings before the application is determined the reporter may abandon the application, either in whole or insofar as it relates to any ground of referral in dispute, by lodging a minute to that effect or by motion at the hearing and by intimating the abandonment to the child and his parent and in that event the sheriff shall dismiss the application and discharge the referral in whole or, as the case may be, in respect of that ground.

Conduct of hearing

Hearing of evidence

8.—(1) In the case of any condition mentioned in section 32(2) of the Act, the sheriff shall, in relation to the grounds of referral which are in dispute, hear evidence tendered by or on behalf of the reporter.

(2) At the close of the case for the reporter the sheriff shall, unless he considers that a *prima facie* case has not been made out, tell the child and his parent or representative that they may give evidence or make a statement and call witnesses.

(3) Where the nature of the case or the evidence to be given is such that in the opinion of the sheriff it is in the interests of the child that the evidence should not be given in his presence, the sheriff may hear any such evidence in the absence of the child and in that event the parent or representative of the child shall be permitted to remain in court during the absence of the child.

(4) The sheriff may exclude the parent while the child is giving evidence or making a statement if the sheriff is satisfied that in the special circumstances it is proper so to do:

Provided that the sheriff shall inform the parent of the substance of any allegation made by the child and shall give the parent an opportunity of meeting the allegation by leading evidence or otherwise.

Adjournment for enquiry etc.

9. Subject to the provisions of section 42(4) of the Act (applications to be heard within twenty-eight days of lodging), in order to allow time for further inquiry into any case or for any other necessary cause, the sheriff on the motion of any party or on his own motion may continue the case for such reasonable time as he may in the circumstances consider necessary.

Miscellaneous

Power of sheriff in making findings as to offences

10. Where the grounds of referral are alleged to constitute an offence or offences or any attempt thereat the sheriff may find on the facts that any offence established by the facts has been committed.

Decision of sheriff

11. The sheriff shall give his decision orally at the conclusion of the Hearing, and a copy of the interlocutor embodying his decision shall be transmitted by the sheriff clerk to the child and his parents and, with any productions lodged, to the reporter.

PART III

PROCEDURE IN APPEALS UNDER SECTION 49 OF THE ACT

Form etc. of appeals under section 49 of the Act

12.—(1) An appeal to the sheriff under section 49 of the Act shall be made in the form as nearly as may be of Form 6A, 6B or 6C whichever is appropriate.

(2) The appeal shall be signed by the child or his parent.

(3) The reporter may lodge answers to the appeal and in that event shall serve a copy thereof on the child or his parent.

(4) The sheriff clerk shall endorse on the appeal and on any answers thereto the date on which they were lodged.

Warrant for first diet in appeals: intimation to reporter

13. As soon as practicable after the lodging of the appeal, the sheriff clerk shall—

(*a*) assign a diet for the hearing of the appeal;

(*b*) issue a warrant in the form as nearly as may be of Form 7; and

(*c*) send the reporter a copy of the appeal and that warrant.

Procedure at hearing of appeal

14.—(1) Before proceeding in accordance with section 49(3) of the Act to examine the reporter and the authors or compilers of any reports or statements, the sheriff shall hear the appellant or his representative.

(2) Where a ground of appeal is an alleged irregularity in the conduct of a case, the sheriff shall, except insofar as the facts stated in the appeal may be admitted by the reporter, hear evidence as to the irregularity tendered by or on behalf of the appellant and any evidence of the reporter relating to it and of any witnesses called by the parties.

(3) Where the nature of the appeal is such that in the opinion of the sheriff the child should not be present during the examination of an author or compiler of any report or at any other stage of the proceedings, the Sheriff may exclude the child from the court during that stage; and in that event his parent and any representative of the child shall be permitted to remain in court during the absence of the child.

(4) Paragraph (4) of Rule 8 above shall apply with any necessary modifications to the hearing of an appeal as it applies to the hearing of evidence in an application.

Adjournments in appeals

15.—(1) Subject to paragraph (2) below, the sheriff in order to allow time for the lodging of any further report which he may have called for under section 49(3) of the Act or for any other necessary cause, may on the motion of either party or on his own motion adjourn the hearing of the appeal for such reasonable time as may in the circumstances be necessary.

(2) If the child or his parent or a representative desires to lead evidence with regard to information disclosed to them in the course of an appeal, the sheriff may adjourn the diet to enable further evidence to be produced.

(3) The adjournment shall be made in the form as nearly as may be of Form 8.

Form and transmission of sheriff's decision in appeals

16.—(1) The sheriff shall give his decision orally either at the conclusion of the appeal or on such day as he shall appoint and where he has decided under section 49(5)(*b*) of the Act to remit the case to the children's hearing for reconsideration of their decision, he shall also issue a note of the reasons for his decision.

(2) The interlocutor containing the decision of the sheriff shall be in the form as nearly as may be of Form 9A, 9B or 9C whichever is appropriate.

(3) The sheriff clerk shall transmit a copy of the said interlocutor together with the said note to the reporter and to the appellant, and shall also return to the reporter any documents lodged by virtue of section 49(2) or (3) of the Act.

PART IV

CITATION AND INTIMATION IN PROCEEDINGS UNDER SECTIONS 42 AND 49 OF THE ACT

Period of notice in giving citation or intimation

17. Citation or intimation authorised or required by these Rules shall be made not later than forty-eight hours, or in the case of postal citation seventy-two hours, before the date of the diet to which the citation or intimation relates: Provided that this Rule shall not apply to the intimation of an appeal against a decision to issue a warrant for the detention of a child.

Warrants and form of citation of witnesses and havers

18.—(1) The following shall be warrants for citation of witnesses and havers, namely:—

    (*a*) the warrant for the first diet in an application;

    (*b*) a warrant fixing a diet for the continued hearing of an application;

    (*c*) any interlocutor certified by the sheriff clerk allowing a proof or for examination of witnesses in an appeal under section 49 of the Act concerned with an irregularity.

(2) In an application or an appeal under section 49 of the Act, witnesses or havers may be cited in the form as nearly as may be of Form 10.

(3) The execution of citation of witnesses and havers shall be in the form as nearly as may be of Form 11.

Modes of citation and intimation

19.—(1) Where a warrant in that behalf has been issued under these Rules, it shall be competent—

   (*a*) to cite a child to any diet in an application or an appeal under section 49 of the Act;

   (*b*) to cite witnesses to any diet in such an application or in an appeal under the said section 49 concerned with an irregularity in the conduct of a case;

   (*c*) to give intimation to a parent to any diet in an application,
by any mode specified in paragraph (2) below.

(2) It shall be deemed a legal citation of, or intimation to, a person mentioned in paragraph (1) above if the citation or, as the case may be, the intimation is—

   (*a*) delivered to him personally; or

   (*b*) left for him at his dwellinghouse or place of business with some person resident or employed therein; or

   (*c*) where it cannot be delivered to him personally and he has no known dwellinghouse or place of business, left for him at any other place at which he may at the time be resident; or

   (*d*) where he is the master of, or a seaman or person employed in, a vessel, left with a person on board thereof or connected therewith; or

   (*e*) sent by post in a registered or recorded delivery letter, to his dwelling-house or place of business, or if he has no known dwellinghouse or place of business to any other place in which he may at the time be resident:

Provided that in an application a copy of the application and warrant required to be sent under Rule 6 above shall be sent along with the citation to the child and, along with the intimation (if any) to the parent.

Persons who may execute citation and intimation under these Rules

20.—(1) Citation of witnesses on behalf of a child or parent shall be effected either—

   (*a*) by a sheriff officer of the jurisdiction in which the warrant was issued or, in the case of any mode of citation and intimation specified in paragraphs

   (*a*) to (*d*) of Rule 19(2) above, the jurisdiction in which the warrant is executed; or

   (*b*) in the case of postal citation, by a solicitor.

(2) The Sheriff clerk shall cite the reporter and the authors or compilers of any reports or statements whom the sheriff may wish to examine under section 49(2) of the Act.

Production of executions of citation and intimation

21.—(1) The production before the sheriff of—

(*a*) an execution of citation or intimation duly completed in the appropriate form prescribed by these Rules; and

(*b*) additionally, in the case of postal citation, the post office receipt of the registered or recorded delivery letter, shall be sufficient evidence that such citation or intimation, as the case may be, was duly given.

(2) It shall not be necessary to lodge with the sheriff clerk any execution of citation or intimation before a diet for the hearing of an application or appeal.

Endorsation of warrants of citation unnecessary

22. Any warrant of citation, intimation, or service under these Rules may be executed within the jurisdiction of any sheriff without endorsation by the sheriff clerk of that jurisdiction.

PART V

MISCELLANEOUS AND SUPPLEMENTAL

Signature of warrants

23. Warrants, other than warrants under section 42(3) of the Act, may be signed by the sheriff clerk but any warrant may, and a warrant under the said section 42(3) shall, be signed by the sheriff.

Expenses not exigible

24. No expenses shall be awarded in any proceedings to which these Rules apply.

Form of warrant under section 42(3) of the Act

25. A warrant for the apprehension and detention of a child under section 42(3) of the Act shall be in the form as nearly as may be of Form 12.

Record of proceedings

26. Proceedings under sections 42 and 49 of the Act shall be conducted summarily.

Exclusion, modification and amendment of certain enactments: Schedule 2

27.—(1) The enactments specified in column (1) of Part I of Schedule 2 to these Rules (being enactments relating to matters with respect to which these Rules are made) shall not, to the extent specified in column (3) of that Part, apply in relation to proceedings in the sheriff court under section 42 or section 49 of the Act.

(2) The provisions of the enactments specified in column (1) of Part II of the said Schedule 2 (being enactments which are specified in column (1) of Part I of that Schedule but which are not excluded from proceedings in the sheriff court under section 42 or section 49 of the Act by virtue of column (3) of that Part) shall have effect in relation to those proceedings subject to the amendments and modifications specified in relation thereto in column (3) of the said Part II.

And the Lords appoint this Act of Sederunt to be inserted in the Books of Sederunt.

J. L. Clyde,
I.P.D.

Edinburgh,

15th January 1971.

SCHEDULE 1 *Rule 3*

Number of Form	ARRANGEMENT OF FORMS	Number of Rule
1	Form of application to sheriff under section 42 of the Act ...	4(2)
2	Form of warrant for diet in application under section 42 of the Act	5
3	Form of schedule of citation of child in application under section 42 of the Act	6(1)
4	Form of intimation to parent in application under section 42 of the Act	6(2)
5	Form of execution of citation of child and intimation to parent ...	6(3)
6A, 6B, 6C	Forms of appeals to sheriff under section 49 of the Act	12(1)
7	Form of warrant (assignment of first diet and warrant of intimation) in appeal under section 49 of the Act	13
8	Form of interlocutor continuing hearing of appeal	15(3)
9A, 9B, 9C	Forms of interlocutors containing decisions of sheriff in appeals under section 49 of the Act	16(2)
10	Form of schedule of citation of witness or haver	18(2)
11	Form of execution of citation of witnesses and havers	18(3)
12	Form of warrant for apprehension and detention of child under section 42(3) of the Act	25

FORM 1 *Rule 4(2)*

FORM OF APPLICATION TO SHERIFF UNDER SECTION 42 OF THE ACT

Sheriff Court at (   )

Application
under
Section [42(2)(*c*)] [42(7)] of the
Social Work (Scotland) Act 1968
by
XY (address), Reporter of (local
authority)
in the case of
AB (address)

1. On (date) a children's hearing for (local authority area) gave a direction to the reporter of (local authority) under section [42(2)(c)] [42(7)] of the Social Work (Scotland) 1968 in respect of AB.

2. A copy of the statement by the reporter of the grounds for the referral of the case of the said AB to the children's hearing is appended hereto.

3. The said [AB or BB (address) the [father] [mother] [guardian] of the said AB] did not accept the grounds of referral so far as relating to conditions   to of the statement appended hereto.

OR

The children's hearing were satisfied that the said AB did not understand the explanation of the grounds of referral given under section 42(1) of the said statement of grounds of referral.   The reporter therefore craves the court to find whether or not the grounds of referral not accepted by the child or his parent (or not understood by the child) are established.

....

[Reporter]

Rule 5   FORM 2

FORM OF WARRANT FOR DIET IN APPLICATION UNDER SECTION 42 OF THE ACT

(Place and date)   The Court assigns

(date) at   (hour) within the (name Court) in chambers at (place) for the hearing of the application;

appoints the reporter forthwith to cite (name of child), and to intimate to his/her [parents] [guardian] whose whereabouts are known, by serving a copy of the application and relative statement of grounds of referral; and grants warrant to cite witnesses and havers.

....

Sheriff Clerk (depute)

Rule 6(1)   FORM 3

FORM OF SCHEDULE OF CITATION OF CHILD IN APPLICATION UNDER SECTION 42 OF THE ACT.

Under the Social Work (Scotland) Act 1968

(Place, date)

You are hereby served with the foregoing application and warrant. You are required to attend the hearing by the sheriff of the application [within (name Court) at (street address) on (date) at (hour)] or [at the time and place specified in the warrant].

....

NOTES

1. If you fail to attend the hearing by the court of the application you may be detained in a place of safety to ensure your attendance at a subsequent hearing.

2. You may ask witnesses to attend the hearing or arrange for their citation by a solicitor or sheriff officer.

FORM 4   *Rule* 6(2)

FORM OF INVITATION TO PARENT IN APPLICATION UNDER SECTION 42 OF THE ACT

Under the Social Work (Scotland) Act 1968

(Place, date)

(Name of parent)   Take notice that the reporter of (local authority) has lodged an application in the Sheriff Court at (   ) for a finding as to [a ground] [grounds] for the referral of the case of (name of child as in application) to a children's hearing.   You are hereby served with a copy of the application and warrant.   You may attend the hearing [within the said court at (street address) on (date) at (hour)] or [at the time and place specified in the warrant].

....

Reporter*
On behalf of Reporter*

NOTE

You may ask witnesses to attend the hearing or arrange for their citation by a solicitor or sheriff officer.

FORM 5   *Rule* 6(3)

FORM OF EXECUTION OF CITATION OF CHILD AND INTIMATION TO PARENT

I $\frac{\text{reporter*}}{\text{on behalf of the reporter*}}$ of (local authority)

lawfully $\frac{\text{cited*}}{\text{gave intimation to*}}$ (name of $\frac{\text{child as in citation*}}{\text{parent as in intimation*}}$) by [delivering a copy

of the foregoing application, warrant and $\frac{\text{citation*}}{\text{intimation*}}$ to him in person at (place) on

(date)].* [leaving a copy of the foregoing application, warrant and $\frac{\text{citation*}}{\text{intimation*}}$ for him

at his $\frac{\text{dwellinghouse*}}{\text{place of business*}}$ at (address) on (date)].*

[leaving a copy of the foregoing application, warrant and $\frac{\text{citation*}}{\text{intimation*}}$ for him on board

(name of vessel) at (place) on (date)].*

[posting on (date) between the hours of (   ) and (   ) at the (place)

Post Office a copy of the foregoing application, warrant and $\frac{\text{citation*}}{\text{intimation*}}$ to him in a

$\frac{\text{recorded delivery*}}{\text{registered*}}$ first class service letter and the post office receipt for the said letter

accompanies this certificate].*

....

*delete as appropriate

Rule 12(1)   FORM 6A

FORM OF APPEAL TO SHERIFF UNDER SECTION 49 OF THE ACT AGAINST DECISION OF
CHILDREN'S HEARING

Sheriff Court at (   )

> Appeal
> under
> section 49 of the Social Work
> (Scotland) Act 1968
> by
> AB (or/and CB, parent of the
> said AB) both residing at (
>   )
> against
> a decision of the children's hearing
> for (local authority area) at (
>   )

1. On (date) the said AB [along with the said CB, his parent] appeared before the children's hearing of (local authority area) at (   ).

2. The grounds for the referral of the case stated by the reporter [were accepted by the appellant(s)] [were established to the satisfaction of the sheriff] at (place) on (date). A copy of the statement of the grounds of referral is attached hereto. or [A supervision requirement, made on (date) in respect of the said AB, was under review by the children's hearing. The supervision requirement was to the effect that (state terms of requirement.]

3. The children's hearing decided that the said AB was in (continuing) need of compulsory measures of care and ordered (state the terms of the decision in the report of the proceedings of the children's hearing).

4. The measures prescribed by the supervision requirement are not appropriate in all the circumstances in respect that (state shortly the reasons for this view) (or if appeal is on a point of law or on grounds of irregularity state briefly that point or the facts which constitute the irregularity).

5. The said AB and/or CB appeals to the sheriff against the said decision.

(signed by appellant(s) or solicitor)

Rule 12(1)   FORM 6B

FORM OF APPEAL TO SHERIFF UNDER SECTION 49 OF THE ACT AGAINST ISSUE OF WARRANT
BY CHILDREN'S HEARING

Sheriff Court at (   )

> Appeal
> under
> section 49 of the Social Work
> (Scotland) Act 1968
> by
> AB (or/and CB, parent of the
> said AB) both residing at (
>   )
> against
> a decision by a children's hearing
> for (local authority area) at (
>   ) to issue a warrant
> for the detention of the said AB.

1. On (date) the said AB was apprehended and detained at (place) on a warrant issued by the children's hearing at (   ) [under section [   ] of the Social Work (Scotland) Act 1968].

2. The said warrant is unnecesary because (state reasons).

3. The said AB (or/and CB) appeals to the sheriff to recall the said warrant.

(signed by appellant(s) or solicitor)

FORM 6C   *Rule* 12(1)

FORM OF APPEAL TO SHERIFF UNDER SECTION 49 OF THE ACT AGAINST ISSUE OF WARRANT BY CHILDREN'S HEARING

Sheriff Court at (   )

Appeal
under
section 49 of the Social Work
(Scotland) act 1968
by
AB (or/and CB, parent of the
said AB) both residing at (
)
against
a decision by a children's hearing
for local authority area) at (
)
to issue a warrant for the detention
of the said AB.

1. On (date) a children's hearing for (local authority area) made a requirement under section 43(4) of the Social Work (Scotland) Act 1968. [A copy of] the said requirement is appended hereto.

2. The said requirement is unnecessary because (state reasons).

3. The said AB (or/and CB) appeals to the sheriff to [state remedy].

(signed by appellant(s) or solicitor).

FORM 7   *Rule* 13

FORM OF WARRANT (ASSIGNMENT OF FIRST DIET AND WARRANT OF INTIMATION) IN APPEAL UNDER SECTION 49 OF THE ACT

(Place and date)   The Court assigns (date) at (hour) within the (name Court) in chambers at (place) for the hearing of the appeal: appoints the appellant(s) forthwith to intimate the appeal and the diet to the reporter.

Sheriff Clerk (Depute)

FORM 8   *Rule* 15(3)

FORM OF INTERLOCUTOR CONTINUING HEARING OF APPEAL

(Place and date)   The Sheriff Substitute, having heard the appellant(s)' (solicitor) and the reporter on the appeal, and having considered the documents produced, adjourns the diet to (date) at (hour) to enable (eg. the parties to enable further reports to be obtained or the parties to lead (further) evidence).

....
Sheriff Clerk

FORMS 9A, 9B AND 9C   *Rule* 16(2)

FORMS OF INTERLOCUTORS CONTAINING DECISIONS OF SHERIFF IN APPEALS UNDER SECTION 49 OF THE ACT

FORM 9A

DECISION UNDER SECTION 49(4) AND (6)

(Place, date)   The Sheriff Substitute, being satisfied that the appeal has failed, confirms the decision of the children's hearing; [where necessary, add, being further satisfied that the appeal is frivolous, orders that no appeal against a decision by a children's hearing, to continue the supervision requirement, made on a subsequent review shall lie until the expiration of a period of twelve months beginning with this date].

(Signed by sheriff)
....

FORM 9B
DECISION UNDER SECTION 49(5)(*a*)

(place, date)   The Sheriff Substitute, being satisfied that the decision of the children's hearing to issue the warrant is not justified in all the circumstances of the case, allows the appeal and recalls the warrant.

(signed by sheriff)

....

FORM 9C
DECISION UNDER SECTION 49(5)(*b*)

(Place, date)   The Sheriff Substitute, being satisfied that the decision of the children's hearing is not justified in all the circumstances of the case [for the reasons given in the attached Note, remits the case to the children's hearing for reconsideration of their decision] or [discharges the child from any further hearing or other proceedings in relation to the grounds for the referral of the case.]

(signed by sheriff)

....

Rule 18(2)   FORM 10
FORM OF SCHEDULE OF CITATION OF WITNESS OR HAVER

Under the Social Work (Scotland) Act 1968
(Place, date, add if necessary hour)
(Name of witness), you are hereby required to attend at the Sheriff Court House at (street address) in chambers on (   ), the (   ) day of (   ) at   o'clock   noon, to give evidence in the hearing of [an application by the reporter of (local authority) to the sheriff for a finding as to grounds for the referral of the case of (name of child) to a children's hearing] OR [an appeal to the sheriff against a decision of a children's hearing in a case of (name of child)].
[if necessary, add—You are required to bring with you (specify documents.)]

....
Sheriff Officer*
Solicitor*

*delete as appropriate

Rule 18(3)   FORM 11
FORM OF EXECUTION OF CITATION OF WITNESSES AND HAVERS

reporter*   )
on behalf of reporter*)
I, (name of person who executed citation)   of (local authority)
sheriff officer*
solicitor*
lawfully cited (name of witness) by—
[delivering a copy of the foregoing citation to him in person at (place) on (date)].*

[leaving a copy of the foregoing citation for him at his $\frac{\text{dwellinghouse*}}{\text{place of business*}}$ at (address) on (date)].*

[Leaving a copy of the foregoing citation for him on board (name of vessel) at (place) on (date)].*

[sending a copy of the foregoing citation to him in a $\frac{\text{recorded delivery*}}{\text{registered*}}$ letter and the post office receipt for the said letter accompanies this certificate].*

to be signed by person who
executed the citation)
Sheriff Officer*
Solicitor*

*delete as appropriate

FORM 12   *Rule* 25

FORM OF WARRANT FOR APPREHENSION AND DETENTION OF CHILD UNDER SECTION 42(3) OF THE ACT

(Place, date)   The Sheriff, in respect that AB, a child in respect of whom an application has been made under section 42(3) of the Act, failed to attend at the hearing of the application, grants warrant to officers of law to apprehend the said AB, and to bring him before the sheriff, and to detain him in a place of safety until the sheriff can hear the application, or for a period of seven days or until the sheriff has disposed of the application, whichever first occurs.

....

(to be signed by the sheriff)

SCHEDULE 2   *Rule* 27(1)

PART I

(Exclusion of enactments relating to matters with respect to which these Rules are made)

Column (1) Enactment Excluded	Column (2) References	Column (3) Extent and exclusion
The Citation Act 1540	1540 c. 10	The whole Act
The Citation Act 1592	1592 c. 59	The whole Act
The Citation Act 1686	1686 c. 5	The whole Act
The Citation Act 1693	1693 c. 21	The whole Act
The Debtors (Scotland) Act 1838 section 32, (as explained by the Citation (Scotland) Act 1846 (a)	1838 c. 114	The words "and that, excepting in the case of poindings, more than one witness shall not be required for service or execution thereof."
The Citation Amendment (Scotland) Act 1882 as amended (b)	1882 c. 77	The whole Act except paragraph (4) of section 4.
The Sheriff Courts (Scotland) Act 1907 section 39 and Schedule 1	1907 c. 51	The whole section; the whole schedule except Rule 73 (second diligence against witness failing to attend).

(a) 1846 c. 67.   (b) 1926 c. 16. s. 4; 1933 c. 21 s. 49; 1962 c. 27 s. 1.

Rule 27(2)

PART II

(Modification and amendment of enactments in their application to proceedings under section 42 or section 49 of the act)

Column (1) Enactment modified or amended	Column (2) References	Column (3) Modifications and Amendments
The Citation Amendment (Scotland) Act 1882 section 4, paragraph (4) (which makes provision for letters containing citations etc. to be returned to the court by the post office and for connected purposes)	1882 c. 77	For the words "such registered letter" there shall be substituted the words "a letter containing a citation or intimation from a sheriff court in proceedings under section 42 or section 49 of the Social Work (Scotland) Act 1968"; [and for the words "in the case of a party" there shall be substituted the words "in the case of a child within the meaning of Part III of the said Act of 1968."]
The Sheriff Courts (Scotland) Act 1907, Schedule 1, Rule 73, (second diligence against witness failing to attend)	1907 c. 51	The word "further" shall be omitted; and for the words "said witness or haver" there shall be substituted the words "or witness or haver cited under the Act of Sederunt (Social Work) (Sheriff Court Procedure Rules 1971".

EXPLANATORY NOTE

(This Note is not part of the Act of Sederunt.)

This Act of Sederunt prescribes procedure for applications to the Sheriff under Section 42 of the Social Work (Scotland) Act 1968 and for appeals to the Sheriff under Section 49 of that Act, and makes miscellaneous provision in connection therewith.

STATUTORY INSTRUMENTS

1971 No. 93 (S.8)

COURT OF SESSION, SCOTLAND

Act of Sederunt (Sessions of Court) 1971

Made - - - -	*14th January* 1971
Coming into Operation	*1st January* 1972

The Lords of Council and Session, by virtue of the powers conferred upon them by section 2 of the Administration of Justice(Scotland) Act 1948(a) DO HEREBY ENACT and DECLARE that the ordinary sessions of the Court of Session during 1972 shall be as follows:—

From Thursday 6th January to Saturday 25th March;

From Tuesday 25th April to Thursday 13th July;

From Tuesday 26th September to Thursday 21st December.

This Act of Sederunt may be cited as the Act of Sederunt (Sessions of Court) 1971 and shall come into operation on 1st January 1972.

And the Lords appoint this Act of Sederunt to be inserted in the Books of Sederunt.

Edinburgh,

14th January 1971.

J. L. Clyde
I.P.D.

(a) 12, 13 & 14 Geo. 6. c. 10.

STATUTORY INSTRUMENTS

1971 No. 99 (S.9)

NATIONAL HEALTH SERVICE, SCOTLAND

The Health and Welfare Services (Provision of Instruction) (Scotland) Regulations 1971

Made - - -	*19th January* 1971
Laid before Parliament	*26th January* 1971
Coming into Operation	*29th January* 1971

In exercise of the powers conferred on me by section 63 of the Health Services and Public Health Act 1968(**a**) and of all other powers enabling me in that behalf, and with the approval of the Treasury, I hereby make the following regulations :—

1. These regulations may be cited as the Health and Welfare Services (Provision of Instruction) (Scotland) Regulations 1971 and shall come into operation on 29th January 1971.

2. The Interpretation Act 1889(**b**) shall apply for the interpretation of these regulations as it applies for the interpretation of an Act of Parliament.

3. The classes of person described in the schedule hereto are hereby specified as classes for the purposes of section 63(1)(*b*) of the Health Services and Public Health Act 1968 (which enables the Secretary of State to provide instruction for persons of specified classes who are employed or contemplate employment in certain activities connected with health and welfare).

Revocation

4. The Health and Welfare Services (Provision of Instruction) (Scotland) Regulations 1968(**c**) are hereby revoked.

St. Andrew's House,
Edinburgh.

7th January 1971.

Gordon Campbell,
One of Her Majesty's Principal
Secretaries of State.

We approve.

19th January 1971.

Walter Clegg,

V. H. Goodhew,
Two of the Lords Commissioners of
Her Majesty's Treasury.

(**a**) 1968 c. 46.　　　　　　　　(**b**) 1889 c. 63.
(**c**) S.I. 1968/1407 (1968 II, p. 4054).

SCHEDULE

SPECIFIED CLASSES

Ancillary staff in general medical practices
Architects
Chiropodists
Computer systems designers
Computer programmers
Dental auxiliaries
Dental hygienists
Dental technicians
Employees of
      (i) the Scottish Dental Estimates Board,
      (ii) Executive Councils,
      (iii) the Drug Accounts Committee.
Engineers
Health Visitors
Managers
Midwives
Nurses
Occupational therapists
Opticians
Orthoptists
Pharmacists
Registered dentists
Registered medical practitioners
Social workers
Speech therapists
Supervisors
Surveyors
Teachers of the mentally handicapped.

EXPLANATORY NOTE

(This Note is not part of the Regulations.)

Section 63(1) of the Health Services and Public Health Act 1968 enables the Secretary of State to provide instruction (*a*) for persons employed or contemplating employment under a hospital authority and (*b*) for classes of persons to be specified in Regulations who are employed or contemplating employment in certain other health and welfare services. These Regulations add to the classes of person previously specified in the Health and Welfare Services (Provision of Instruction) (Scotland) Regulations 1968 which are now revoked. These classes include registered medical practitioners, dentists, nurses, midwives and health visitors, pharmacists, opticians, employees of Executive Councils and other bodies set up under Part IV of the National Health Service (Scotland) Act 1947, ancillary staff in general medical practices, members of certain professions, supplementary to medicine and certain administrative staff.

STATUTORY INSTRUMENTS

1971 No. 100

DECIMAL CURRENCY

The Motor Vehicles (International Circulation) (Decimal Currency) Order 1971

Made - - -	*15th January* 1971
Laid before Parliament	*28th January* 1971
Coming into Operation	*15th February* 1971

The Secretary of State for the Environment in exercise of his powers under section 11(1) of the Decimal Currency Act 1969(a) and of all other enabling powers, and with the consent of the Treasury, hereby makes the following Order :—

1. This Order may be cited as the Motor Vehicles (International Circulation) (Decimal Currency) Order 1971 and shall come into operation on the 15th February 1971.

2. The Motor Vehicles (International Circulation) Order 1957(b), as amended (c), shall have effect as though in Schedule 2 for the amount of ten shillings and sixpence, in each place where it occurs, there were substituted an amount of 53 new pence and for the amount of seven shillings and sixpence there were substituted an amount of 37 new pence.

Signed by authority of the Secretary of State.

15th January 1971.

John Peyton,
Minister for Transport Industries,
Department of the Environment.

We consent to this Order.

Walter Clegg,
V. H. Goodhew,
Two of the Lords Commissioners
of Her Majesty's Treasury.

15th January 1971.

(a) 1969 c. 19. (b) S.I. 1957/1074 (1957 II, p. 2154).
(c) There is no relevant amending instrument.

EXPLANATORY NOTE

(This Note is not part of the Order.)

Schedule 2 to the Motor Vehicles (International Circulation) Order 1957 specifies the fees chargeable for certain documents mentioned in that Schedule. This Order amends that Schedule by specifying the fees in decimal currency.

STATUTORY INSTRUMENTS

1971 No. 101 (L.3)

COUNTY COURTS

FEES

The County Court Fees (Decimalisation) Order 1971

Made - - - -	18*th January* 1971
Laid before Parliament	27*th January* 1971
Coming into Operation	15*th February* 1971

The Lord Chancellor and the Treasury, in exercise of the powers conferred on them by section 177 of the County Courts Act 1959(**a**), section 2 of the Public Offices Fees Act 1879(**b**) and section 365(3) of the Companies Act 1948(**c**), hereby make, concur in and sanction the following Order:—

1.—(1) This Order may be cited as the County Court Fees (Decimalisation) Order 1971 and shall come into operation on 15th February 1971.

(2) The Interpretation Act 1889(**d**) shall apply to the interpretation of this Order as it applies to the interpretation of an Act of Parliament.

2. The County Court Fees Order 1959(**e**), as amended (**f**), shall have effect as further amended by this Order, and a fee referred to by number means the fee so numbered in the Table of Fees contained in the Schedule to that Order.

3. In Fees Nos. 4(ii), 12(ii), 26(iii), 32(ii), 36(i), 51 and 60(i) and (iii), for the words " 2s. 6d. " there shall in each case be substituted the words " 13p ".

4.—(1) In Fee No. 39(i), for the words " 6d. " there shall be substituted the words " 2½p " and for the words " 17s. 6d. " there shall be substituted the words " 87p ".

(2) At the end of Fee No. 39(i) there shall be inserted the following note:—

"*Any fraction of a penny in the total amount of the fee for the whole period of possession shall be disregarded.*"

5.—(1) In Fee No. 41, for the words " 6d. " there shall be substituted the words " 2½p ".

(2) At the end of Fee No. 41, there shall be inserted the following note:—

"*Any fraction of a penny in the total amount of the fee shall be disregarded.*"

(**a**) 1959 c. 22. (**b**) 1879 c. 58. (**c**) 1948 c. 38. (**d**) 1889 c. 63.
(**e**) S.I. 1959/1262 (1959 I, p. 803). (**f**) The relevant amending instruments are S.I. 1961/355, 1965/395, 1966/243 (1961 I, p. 565; 1965 I, p. 1099; 1966 I, p. 496).

6. In Fee No. 58, for the words " 17s. 6d. " there shall be substituted the words " 87p ".

Hailsham of St. Marylebone, C.

Dated 15th January 1971.

Walter Clegg,
V. H. Goodhew,
Two of the Lords Commissioners
of Her Majesty's Treasury.

Dated 18th January 1971.

EXPLANATORY NOTE

(This Note is not part of the Order.)

This Order amends the County Court Fees Order 1959 by altering all fees which would not otherwise be payable in a whole number of new pence. In the case of all but two of these, the Order substitutes decimal equivalents calculated in accordance with whole penny table prescribed by Schedule 1 to the Decimal Currency Act 1969 (c. 19). In the two cases, where the fees may include a new halfpenny, there is provision for any halfpenny in the total amount of the fee to be disregarded.

1971 No. 102 (L.4)

MATRIMONIAL CAUSES
SUPREME COURT OF JUDICATURE, ENGLAND
COUNTY COURTS
The Matrimonial Causes Fees Order 1971

Made - - - 18*th January* 1971

Coming into Operation 15*th February* 1971

The Lord Chancellor and the Treasury, in exercise of the powers conferred on them by section 8 of the Matrimonial Causes Act 1967(**a**) and sections 2 and 3 of the Public Offices Fees Act 1879(**b**), hereby make and concur in the following Order :—

1. This Order may be cited as the Matrimonial Causes Fees Order 1971 and shall come into operation on 15th February 1971.

2.—(1) In this Order—

(*a*) expressions used in the Matrimonial Causes Rules 1968(**c**), as amended (**d**), have the same meaning as in those rules ;

(*b*) a rule referred to by number means the rule so numbered in the Matrimonial Causes Rules 1968, as amended, and a form referred to by number means the form so numbered in Appendix II to those rules ;

(*c*) "the County Court Fees Order" means the County Court Fees Order 1959(**e**), as amended (**f**), and a fee referred to by a number prefixed by the letters "C.C." means the fee so numbered in the schedule to that Order ;

(*d*) "the Supreme Court Fees Order" means the Supreme Court Fees Order 1970(**g**), and a fee referred to by number prefixed by the letters "S.C." means the fee so numbered in the schedule to that Order.

(2) The Interpretation Act 1889(**h**) shall apply to the interpretation of this Order as it applies to the interpretation of an Act of Parliament.

3. The fees specified in Schedule 1 to this Order shall be taken in all matrimonial proceedings, whether in the High Court or a divorce county court.

4. In addition to the fees specified in Schedule 1, the fees specified in the first column of Schedule 2 to this Order (being fees prescribed by the County Court Fees Order and the Supreme Court Fees Order) shall be taken in the matrimonial proceedings specified opposite thereto in the second column, subject to the directions contained in the notes to that Schedule.

(**a**) 1967 c. 56. (**b**) 1879 c. 58.
(**c**) S.I. 1968/219 (1968 I, p. 665).
(**d**) S.I. 1969/763, 1970/29, 1161, 1349 (1969 II, p. 2176; 1970 I, p. 226; II, p. 3929;
III, p. 4514). (**e**) S.I. 1959/1262 (1959 I, p. 803).
(**f**) S.I. 1961/355, 1894, 1963/897, 1965/395, 1966/243, 1971/101 (1961 I, p. 565; III, p. 3554;
1963 II, p. 1508; 1965 I, p. 1099; 1966 I, p. 496).
(**g**) S.I. 1970/1870 (1970 III, p. 6135). (**h**) 1889 c. 63.

5. Any fee prescribed by this Order shall be taken in cash.

6. If any question arises with regard to the amount or payment of any fee prescribed by this Order, the registrar may report the matter to the Lord Chancellor and obtain his directions thereon.

7. Where it appears to the Lord Chancellor that the payment of any fee prescribed by this Order would, owing to the exceptional circumstances of the particular case, involve undue hardship, the Lord Chancellor may reduce or remit the fee in that case.

8. The Matrimonial Causes Fees Order 1968(**a**) and the Matrimonial Causes Fees (Amendment) Order 1970(**b**) are hereby revoked save as to any fee due or payable before the commencement of this Order.

Dated 15th January 1971.

Hailsham of St. Marylebone, C.

Dated 18th January 1971.

Walter Clegg,

V. H. Goodhew,

Two of the Lords Commissioners
of Her Majesty's Treasury.

SCHEDULE 1

FEES TO BE TAKEN IN ALL MATRIMONIAL PROCEEDINGS

Fee	Amount
	£
1. On filing an originating application or on sealing an originating summons	2·00
2. On presenting a petition except in a case to which rule 12(4) applies	12·00
3. On filing a notice in Form 8 or 9 except where the terms of any agreement as to the order which the court is to be asked to make are set out in the notice	2·00
4. On making a search in the index of decrees absolute kept under rule 66(2)	0·13
5. On a request for a photographic or office copy of a decree or of a certificate that a decree has been made absolute	0·25
6. On a certificate under the hand of a judge or registrar ...	0·25
7. On the issue of a notice under rule 55	2·00

(a) S.I. 1968/388 (1968 I, p. 1046).   (b) S.I. 1970/1840 (1970 III, p. 599f)

SCHEDULE 2

Fees to be taken in Specified Matrimonial Proceedings

Fee	Proceedings in which fee to be taken
C.C. Fees Nos. 4*, 20, 35, 37, 39 to 44, 46, 49, 54, 66†, 67, 70 and 71	Proceedings in a divorce county court
C.C. Fees Nos. 62 and 69	Proceedings in a divorce county court other than the divorce registry
C.C. Fees Nos. 50, 51 and 53	All proceedings, whether in the High Court or a divorce county court
S.C. Fees Nos. 9(*b*), 16, 22, 58, 59, 65†, 66†, 67, 68, 76, 77 and 90	Proceedings in the Supreme Court
S.C. Fees Nos. 69 to 72	Proceedings in the divorce registry, whether pending in the High Court or treated as pending in a divorce county court, and proceedings in a district registry

Notes
*This fee is payable only in respect of a document requiring personal service.
†This fee does not apply to a copy in respect of which Fee No. 5 in Schedule 1 above is payable.

EXPLANATORY NOTE
(*This Note is not part of the Order.*)

This Order consolidates the Matrimonial Causes Fees Order 1968 and the Matrimonial Causes Fees Amendment Order 1970, with minor alterations necessitated by the introduction of decimal currency and the coming into operation of the Matrimonial Causes (Amendment No. 3) Rules 1970 and the Supreme Court Fees Order 1970.

STATUTORY INSTRUMENTS

1971 No. 103

LEGAL AID AND ADVICE, ENGLAND

The Legal Aid (Assessment of Resources) (Decimalisation) Regulations 1971

Made - - - -	18*th January* 1971
Laid before Parliament	27*th January* 1971
Coming into Operation	15*th February* 1971

The Lord Chancellor, in exercise of the powers conferred on him by sections 4 and 12 of the Legal Aid and Advice Act 1949(**a**), and with the concurrence of the Treasury, hereby makes the following Regulations:—

1.—(1) These Regulations may be cited as the Legal Aid (Assessment of Resources) (Decimalisation) Regulations 1971 and shall come into operation on 15th February 1971 and shall apply to the computation of disposable income and disposable capital on or after that date.

(2) The Interpretation Act 1889(**b**) shall apply to the interpretation of these Regulations as it applies to the interpretation of an Act of Parliament.

(3) In these Regulations a rule referred to by number means a rule so numbered in Schedule 1 to the Legal Aid (Assessment of Resources) Regulations 1960(**c**) as amended(**d**).

2.—(*a*) for " 7s. 6d. " and " 5s. 6d. " in rule 5(1)(*f*) and (*g*) there shall be substituted " £0.38 " and " £0.28 " respectively ;

(*b*) for " 20s. " in rule 5(2) there shall be substituted " £1.00 " ;

(*c*) for " 40s. " in rule 5(1) and (3) there shall be substituted " £2.00 ".

Dated 14th January 1971.

Hailsham of St. Marylebone, C.

We concur,

Dated 18th January 1971.

Walter Clegg,
V. H. Goodhew,
Two of the Lords Commissioners
of Her Majesty's Treasury.

(**a**) 1949 c. 51.   (**b**) 1889 c. 63.   (**c**) S.I. 1960/1471 (1960 II, p. 1749).
  (**d**) The relevant amending instrument is S.I. 1966/1348 (1966 III, p. 3676).

EXPLANATORY NOTE

(This Note is not part of the Regulations.)

These Regulations provide for the decimalisation of amounts of money in connection with the assessment of resources of applicants for legal aid.

STATUTORY INSTRUMENTS

1971 No. 107

CRIMINAL PROCEDURE, ENGLAND AND WALES
COSTS AND EXPENSES
The Witnesses' Allowances Regulations 1971

Made - - - -	19*th January* 1971
Coming into Operation	15*th February* 1971

In pursuance of the powers conferred upon me by section 12 of the Costs in Criminal Cases Act 1952(a), as amended by section 52 of, and Schedule 5 to, the Criminal Appeal Act 1968(b), I hereby make the following Regulations:—

1. These Regulations may be cited as the Witnesses' Allowances Regulations 1971 and shall come into operation on 15th February 1971.

2.—(1) In these Regulations the expression "witness" means a person properly attending to give evidence, whether or not he gives evidence.

(2) The Interpretation Act 1889(c) shall apply to the interpretation of these Regulations as it applies to the interpretation of an Act of Parliament, and section 38(2) of that Act shall apply as if these Regulations were an Act of Parliament and the Regulations revoked by these Regulations were enactments repealed thereby.

3. The Regulations specified in the Schedule to these Regulations are hereby revoked.

4. These Regulations shall apply to costs payable out of local funds under the Costs in Criminal Cases Act 1952 or the Criminal Appeal Act 1968.

5. There may be allowed in respect of a witness practising as a member of the legal or medical profession or as a dentist or veterinary surgeon for attending to give professional evidence, whether in one or more cases, a professional witness allowance not exceeding £10 a day:

Provided that if the witness attends on any day to give evidence in one case only and the period during which he is necessarily absent from his place of residence or practice to attend as aforesaid does not exceed four hours, his professional witness allowance shall not exceed £5, unless he necessarily incurs expense in the provision of a person to take care of his practice during his absence.

6. There may be allowed in respect of an expert witness for attending to give expert evidence and for work in connection with its preparation an expert witness allowance of such amount as the court may consider reasonable having regard to the nature and difficulty of the case and the work necessarily involved.

7. There may be allowed in respect of a witness, who attends to give evidence (other than professional or expert evidence), whether in one or more cases, and thereby loses remuneration or necessarily incurs expense (other than expense on account of travelling, lodging or subsistence) to which he would not otherwise

---

(a) 1952 c. 48.   (b) 1968 c. 19.   (c) 1889 c. 63.

have been subject, a loss allowance not exceeding £4 a day in respect of that loss or expense:

Provided that if the period during which the witness is necessarily absent from his place of residence, business or employment to attend as aforesaid does not exceed four hours, his loss allowance shall not exceed £2 unless he necessarily loses more than half a day's remuneration or the expense necessarily incurred exceeds £2.

8.—(1) There may be allowed in respect of a witness (other than a witness who receives an allowance under Regulation 5 or 6 of these Regulations) who attends to give evidence, whether in one or more cases, a subsistence allowance not exceeding an amount calculated in accordance with paragraphs (2) and (3) of this Regulation.

(2) In respect of any period other than a period in respect of which a subsistence allowance is payable under paragraph (3) of this Regulation, the subsistence allowance shall not exceed—

> (a) if the period on any one day during which a witness is necessarily absent from his place of residence, business or employment for the purpose of attending to give evidence does not exceed four hours, 45p in respect of that day;
>
> (b) if the said period on any one day exceeds four hours but does not exceed eight hours, 95p in respect of that day;
>
> (c) if the said period on any one day exceeds eight hours but does not exceed twelve hours, £1·75 in respect of that day;
>
> (d) if the said period on any one day exceeds twelve hours but does not exceed sixteen hours, £2·50 in respect of that day;
>
> (e) if the said period on any one day exceeds sixteen hours, £2·95 in respect of that day.

(3) If a witness is necessarily absent from his place of residence overnight for the purpose of attending to give evidence, the subsistence allowance shall not exceed £5·50 in respect of each period of twenty-four hours or fraction thereof during which he is so absent overnight:

Provided that for such an absence overnight for the purpose of attending to give evidence in the City of London or an inner London borough there may be allowed a supplementary allowance not exceeding 50p a night.

9. There may be allowed in respect of a witness, who receives an allowance under Regulation 5 or 6 of these Regulations and is necessarily absent from his place of residence overnight for the purpose of attending as a witness, a night allowance not exceeding £3·75 a night:

Provided that for such an absence overnight for the purpose of attending to give evidence in the City of London or an inner London borough there may be allowed a supplementary allowance not exceeding 50p a night.

10.—(1) There may be allowed in respect of a seaman, who is detained on shore for the purpose of attending to give evidence and thereby misses his ship, for the time during which he is, and is likely to be, necessarily detained on shore—

> (a) an allowance not exceeding, unless for special reason the court allows a greater sum, £4 a day in respect of loss of wages, together with
>
> (b) an allowance not exceeding the sum actually and reasonably incurred for his maintenance.

(2) Nothing in the last five preceding Regulations shall apply to a person in respect of whom an allowance is made under this Regulation.

11.—(1) Where a witness travels to or from court by railway or other public conveyance there may be allowed in respect thereof the fare actually paid:

Provided that, unless for a special reason the court otherwise directs, only second class fare shall be allowed for travel by railway.

(2) Where a witness travels to or from court by a hired vehicle there may be allowed in respect thereof—

(a) in a case of urgency or where no public service is reasonably available, the amount of the fare and any reasonable gratuity paid; and

(b) in any other case, the amount of the fare for travel by the appropriate public services.

(3) Where a witness travels to or from court by a private conveyance there may be allowed in respect thereof—

(a) in any case where the witness travels by motor vehicle and the court is satisfied that the use of the vehicle results in a substantial saving of time or is otherwise reasonable, a sum not exceeding—

(i) in the case of a vehicle of engine capacity not exceeding 1000 c.c., $3\frac{1}{2}$p a mile each way;

(ii) in the case of a vehicle of engine capacity exceeding 1000 c.c. but not exceeding 1750 c.c., $4\frac{1}{2}$p a mile each way;

(iii) in the case of a vehicle of engine capacity exceeding 1750 c.c., 5p a mile each way; and

(b) in any other case, a sum not exceeding 2p a mile each way.

(4) There may be allowed—

(a) in respect of travelling expenses of a witness who, in the opinion of the court, is suffering from a serious illness, or

(b) in respect of the carriage of heavy exhibits,

such sums, in excess of the sums allowable under the preceding paragraphs of this Regulation, as appear to the court to have been reasonably incurred.

12. There may be allowed in respect of a person employed as an interpreter such allowances as the court may consider reasonable.

13. There may be allowed in respect of any prosecutor or other person who, in the opinion of the court, necessarily attends for the purpose of the prosecution otherwise than to give evidence, the same allowances as if he attended to give evidence other than professional or expert evidence.

14.—(1) Notwithstanding anything contained in the preceding Regulations no sum shall be allowed under these Regulations in respect of—

(a) a member of a police force attending court in his capacity as such;

(b) a whole-time officer of a prison attending court in his capacity as such;

(c) a prisoner produced in court in custody.

(2) In this Regulation "prison" means a prison, remand centre, detention centre or Borstal institution.

15.—(1) There may be allowed in respect of a written report made by a registered medical practitioner to a court, in pursuance of a request to which section 32(2) of the Criminal Justice Act 1967**(a)** applies, a medical report allowance as follows—

> (*a*) in the case of a request made by a court for the purpose of determining whether or not to make an order under section 4 of the Criminal Justice Act 1948**(b)** (probation orders requiring treatment for mental condition), section 60 of the Mental Health Act 1959**(c)** (hospital orders and guardianship orders), or section 12(4) of the Children and Young Persons Act 1969**(d)** (supervision order requiring treatment for mental condition), an allowance not exceeding £5 if the registered medical practitioner holds an appointment to a post in the consultant grade in the National Health Service or is for the time being approved by a local health authority for the purposes of section 28 of the Mental Health Act 1959 or £4·30 in the case of any other registered medical practitioner;

> (*b*) in the case of any other request made by a court, an allowance of not less than £5·20 and not exceeding £8 if the registered medical practitioner holds an appointment to a post in the consultant grade in the National Health Service or not exceeding £2·87 if he does not hold such an appointment.

(2) Where a registered medical practitioner who makes a written report to a court, in pursuance of a request to which the said section 32(2) applies, incurs travelling expenses in connection with the preparation of that report, there may be allowed in respect thereof a sum not exceeding 5p a mile each way for each journey, excluding that part of the journey which is within a radius of two miles from the place from which the practitioner practises.

(3) Nothing in this Regulation shall apply to a report by the medical officer of a prison, remand centre, detention centre or Borstal institution in his capacity as such.

R. Maudling,
One of Her Majesty's Principal
Secretaries of State.

Home Office,
  Whitehall.
19th January 1971.

(a) 1967 c. 80.   **(b)** 1948 c. 58.
(c) 1959 c. 72.   **(d)** 1969 c. 54.

SCHEDULE

REGULATIONS REVOKED

Regulations	References
The Witnesses' Allowances Regulations 1966	S.I. 1966/10 (1966 I, p. 5).
The Witnesses' Allowances Regulations 1967	S.I. 1967/39 (1967 I, p. 109).
The Witnesses' Allowances (Amendment) Regulations 1967	S.I. 1967/1776 (1967 III, p. 4754).
The Witnesses' Allowances (Amendment) Regulations 1969	S.I. 1969/214 (1969 I, p. 556).
The Witnesses' Allowances (Amendment) Regulations 1970	S.I. 1970/176 (1970 I, p. 757).

EXPLANATORY NOTE
(This Note is not part of the Regulations.)

These Regulations consolidate with amendments the Regulations specified in the Schedule. The only amendments of substance are the increases in the allowances (other than the London weighting) payable to witnesses under Regulation 8 (subsistence allowance), Regulation 9 (night allowance), and Regulation 11(3) (travelling allowance when private vehicle is used).

STATUTORY INSTRUMENTS

1971 No. 108

CORONERS

EXPENSES

The Coroners (Fees and Allowances) Rules 1971

Made - - - - 19*th January* 1971

Coming into Operation 15*th February* 1971

In pursuance of the powers conferred upon me by section 1(1) of the Coroners Act 1954**(a)**, I hereby make the following Rules:—

1. These Rules may be cited as the Coroners (Fees and Allowances) Rules 1971 and shall come into operation on 15th February 1971.

2.—(1) In these Rules any reference to a witness includes a reference to a person summoned as a witness.

(2) The Interpretation Act 1889**(b)** shall apply to the interpretation of these Rules as it applies to the interpretation of an Act of Parliament, and section 38(2) of that Act shall apply as if these Rules were an Act of Parliament and the Rules revoked by these Rules were enactments repealed thereby.

3. The Rules specified in the Schedule to these Rules are hereby revoked.

4.—(1) A medical practitioner who makes a post-mortem examination of a body by the coroner's direction or at the coroner's request and reports the result thereof to the coroner and who is not a witness at an inquest on that body shall be paid a fee of £6·25.

(2) A medical practitioner who makes a post-mortem examination of a body by the coroner's direction or at the coroner's request and reports the result thereof to the coroner and who is a witness at an inquest on that body shall be paid a fee of £10 in respect of the examination and of the first day on which he attends to give evidence at the inquest and in addition a further fee of £5 for each subsequent day on which he attends to give evidence at the inquest:

Provided that if he attends to give evidence at more than one inquest held on the same day on the bodies of persons whose deaths appear to have been caused by the same accident or occurrence, he shall be paid a fee of £6·25 in respect of the post-mortem examination of each such body made by him and in addition a fee of £5 in respect of each day on which he attends to give evidence at such inquests.

(3) A medical practitioner who travels to or from a place in connection with a post-mortem examination of a body made by the coroner's direction or at the coroner's request may, in addition to any fee paid to him under the preceding paragraphs of this Rule, be paid in respect of the journey—

(a) 1954 c. 31. (b) 1889 c. 63.

(a) if he travels by railway or other public conveyance and the journey to or from such place is in excess of two miles, the fare actually paid;

(b) if he travels by any other means, an allowance at the rate of 5p a mile for each mile, other than the first two miles, of the journey to or from such place:

Provided that no payment shall be made under this paragraph if in respect of such journey any payment may be made under Rule 10 of these Rules.

(4) A medical practitioner who is a witness at an inquest shall, for attending to give professional evidence otherwise than in connection with a post-mortem examination made by him by the coroner's direction or at the coroner's request, be paid a fee of £5 for each day on which he attends to give evidence at that inquest:

Provided that if he attends to give evidence at more than one inquest held on the same day, he shall be paid a fee of £3·10 in respect of his attendance at each inquest held on that day other than the first.

5. A witness practising as a member of the legal professions or as a dentist or veterinary surgeon may, for attending to give professional evidence whether at one or more inquests, be paid a professional witness allowance, not exceeding £10 a day:

Provided that if the witness attends on any day to give evidence at one inquest only and the period during which he is necessarily absent from his place of residence or practice to attend as aforesaid does not exceed four hours his professional witness allowance shall not exceed £5, unless he necessarily incurs expense in the provision for the occasion of a person to take care of his practice during his absence.

6. An expert witness at an inquest may, for attending to give expert evidence and for work in connection with its preparation, be paid an expert witness allowance of such amount as the coroner may consider reasonable having regard to the nature and difficulty of the case and the work necessarily involved.

7. A witness at an inquest to whom the preceding Rules do not apply, who attends to give evidence whether at one or more inquests and thereby loses remuneration or necessarily incurs expense (other than expense on account of travelling, lodging or subsistence) to which he would not otherwise have been subject, may be paid a loss allowance not exceeding £4 a day in respect of that loss or expense:

Provided that if the period during which the witness is necessarily absent from his place of residence, business or employment to attend as aforesaid does not exceed four hours, his loss allowance shall not exceed £2 unless he necessarily loses more than half a day's remuneration or the expense necessarily incurred exceeds £2.

8.—(1) A witness at an inquest (other than a witness who receives a fee or allowance under Rules 4 to 6 of these Rules) who attends to give evidence, whether at one or more inquests, may be paid a subsistence allowance not exceeding an amount calculated in accordance with paragraphs (2) and (3) of this Rule.

(2) In respect of any period other than a period in respect of which a subsistence allowance is payable under paragraph (3) of this Rule, the subsistence allowance shall not exceed—

(a) if the period on any one day during which a witness is necessarily absent from his place of residence, business or employment for the purpose of attending to give evidence does not exceed four hours, 45p in respect of that day;

(b) if the said period on any one day exceeds four hours but does not exceed eight hours, 95p in respect of that day;

(c) if the said period on any one day exceeds eight hours but does not exceed twelve hours, £1·75 in respect of that day;

(d) if the said period on any one day exceeds twelve hours but does not exceed sixteen hours, £2·50 in respect of that day;

(e) if the said period on any one day exceeds sixteen hours, £2·95 in respect of that day.

(3) If a witness is necessarily absent from his place of residence overnight for the purpose of attending to give evidence, the subsistence allowance shall not exceed £5·50 in respect of each period of twenty-four hours or fraction thereof during which he is so absent overnight:

Provided that for such an absence overnight for the purpose of attending to give evidence in the City of London or an inner London borough he may be paid a supplementary allowance not exceeding 50p a night.

9. A witness at an inquest, who receives a fee or allowance under Rules 4 to 6 of these Rules and is necessarily absent from his place of residence overnight for the purpose of attending as a witness may be paid a night allowance not exceeding £3·75 a night:

Provided that for such an absence overnight for the purpose of attending to give evidence in the City of London or an inner London borough he may be paid a supplementary allowance not exceeding 50p a night.

10.—(1) Where a witness travels to or from an inquest by railway or other public conveyance, he may be paid in respect thereof the fare actually paid:

Provided that, unless for a special reason the coroner otherwise directs, only second class fare shall be allowed for travel by railway.

(2) Where a witness at an inquest travels to or from the inquest by a hired vehicle, he may be paid in respect thereof—

(a) in a case of urgency or where no public service is available, the amount of the fare and any reasonable gratuity paid; and

(b) in any other case, the amount of the fare for travel by the appropriate public services.

(3) Where a witness at an inquest travels to or from the inquest by a private conveyance, he may be paid in respect thereof—

(a) in any case where the witness travels by motor vehicle and the coroner is satisfied that the use of the vehicle results in a substantial saving of time or is otherwise reasonable, a sum not exceeding—

(i) in the case of a vehicle of engine capacity not exceeding 1000 c.c., $3\frac{1}{2}$p a mile each way;

(ii) in the case of a vehicle of engine capacity exceeding 1000 c.c. but not exceeding 1750 c.c., $4\frac{1}{2}$p a mile each way;

(iii) in the case of a vehicle of engine capacity exceeding 1750 c.c., 5p a mile each way; and

(b) in any other case, a sum not exceeding 2p a mile each way.

(4) There may be paid—

    (*a*) in respect of his travelling expenses to a witness at an inquest who, in the opinion of the coroner, is suffering from a serious illness, or

    (*b*) in respect of the carriage of heavy exhibits,

such sums, in excess of the sums payable under the preceding paragraphs of this Rule, as appear to the coroner to have been reasonably incurred.

11.—(1) Notwithstanding anything contained in the preceding Rules no sum shall be paid under these Rules in respect of—

    (*a*) a member of a police force attending an inquest in his capacity as such;

    (*b*) a whole-time officer of a prison attending an inquest in his capacity as such;

    (*c*) a prisoner produced at an inquest in custody;

    (*d*) a coroner's officer attending an inquest in his capacity as such.

(2) In this Rule "prison" means a prison, remand centre, detention centre or Borstal institution.

R. Maudling,
One of Her Majesty's Principal
Secretaries of State.

Home Office,
  Whitehall.
19th January 1971.

SCHEDULE   Rule 3

RULES REVOKED

Rules	References
The Coroners (Fees and Allowances) Rules 1966.	S.I. 1966/11 (1966 I, p. 9).
The Coroners (Fees and Allowances) Rules 1967.	S.I. 1967/38 (1967 I, p. 107).
The Coroners (Fees and Allowances) (Amendment) Rules 1969.	S.I. 1969/213 (1969 I, p. 554).
The Coroners (Fees and Allowances) (Amendment) Rules 1970.	S.I. 1970/174 (1970 I, p. 754).

EXPLANATORY NOTE

(This Note is not part of the Rules.)

These Rules consolidate with amendments the Rules specified in the Schedule. The only amendments of substance are the increases in the allowances (other than the London weighting) payable to witnesses at inquests under Rule 8 (subsistence allowance), Rule 9 (night allowance), and Rule 10(3) (travelling allowance when private vehicle is used).

1971 No. 113

CUSTOMS AND EXCISE

The Export of Goods (Control) (Amendment) Order 1971

Made - - - -   *22nd January* 1971
Coming into Operation   *1st February* 1971

The Secretary of State, in exercise of his powers under section 1 of the Import, Export and Customs Powers (Defence) Act 1939(a), hereby orders as follows :—

1. This Order may be cited as the Export of Goods (Control) (Amendment) Order 1971 and shall come into operation on 1st February 1971.

2. The Interpretation Act 1889(b) shall apply to the interpretation of this Order as it applies to the interpretation of an Act of Parliament.

3. The Export of Goods (Control) Order 1970(c), as amended(d), shall have effect as if—

(i) in Article 5(1), (*k*), the words " or eggs, in shell, of domestic poultry," were omitted ; and

(ii) in Schedule 1, Group 8, the following entry was deleted, namely—

" Eggs, in shell, of domestic poultry . . . . A ".

N. E. Robins,
An Assistant Secretary,
22nd January 1971.   Department of Trade and Industry.

EXPLANATORY NOTE

(This Note is not part of the Order.)

The Order amends the Export of Goods (Control) Order 1970. It terminates export control on eggs.

(a) 1939 c. 69.   (b) 1889 c. 63.   (c) S.I. 1970/1288 (1970 III, p. 4270).
(d) The previous amending Order is not relevant to the subject matter of this Order.

STATUTORY INSTRUMENTS

1971 No. 114

PENSIONS

The Superannuation (Local Government and Approved Employment) Interchange (Amendment) Rules 1971

Made - - -	*22nd January* 1971
Laid before Parliament	*28th January* 1971
Coming into Operation	*15th February* 1971

The Secretary of State for the Environment, in exercise of his powers under sections 2 and 15 of the Superannuation (Miscellaneous Provisions) Act 1948(**a**), as amended by section 11(6) of the Superannuation (Miscellaneous Provisions) Act 1967(**b**), and of all other powers enabling him in that behalf, hereby makes the following rules:—

Title and commencement

1. These rules may be cited as the Superannuation (Local Government and Approved Employment) Interchange (Amendment) Rules 1971, and shall come into operation on 15th February 1971.

Interpretation

2.—(1) In these rules "the principal rules" means the Superannuation (Local Government and Approved Employment) Interchange Rules 1969(**c**); and words and expressions to which meanings are assigned by the principal rules shall bear the same respective meanings in these rules.

(2) The Interpretation Act 1889(**d**) shall apply for the interpretation of these rules as it applies for the interpretation of an Act of Parliament.

Amendment of principal rules

3.—(1) The principal rules, as amended (**e**), shall be further amended as provided in this rule.

(2) In paragraph (1) of rule 2 (interpretation), after the definition of "pension scheme trustees" there shall be inserted—

" "police employment" means employment in which a person is subject to the police pensions regulations;

"police pensions regulations" means the regulations from time to time in force under the Police Pensions Act 1948(**f**);".

(a) 1948 c. 33.   (b) 1967 c. 28   (c) S.I. 1969/997 (1969 II, p. 2906).   (d) 1889 c. 63.
(e) The amending rules are not relevant to the subject matter of these rules.   (f) 1948 c. 24.

(3) At the end of paragraph (2) of rule 2 there shall be inserted the following paragraph:—

"(2A) For the purposes of these rules—

    (*a*) references to a police authority shall be construed in the same manner as in the police pensions regulations;

    (*b*) a person in police employment shall be deemed to be in the employment of his police authority; and

    (*c*) a police authority shall be deemed to be pension scheme trustees.".

(4) Schedule 2 ("fractional" pension schemes) shall be amended by adding to the table, beneath the appropriate headings as repeated herein, the following entry:—

Approved body	*Approved pension scheme*	*Prescribed date for rule 5*	*Prescribed date for rule 9*	*Adjustment of service*
(1)	(2)	(3)	(4)	(5)
"Police authority	The scheme embodied in the police pensions regulations	4th February 1948	4th February 1948	Add $33\frac{1}{3}\%$"

(5) In paragraph 5 of schedule 2 (computation of transfer value), at the beginning there shall be inserted the words "(1) Except as subparagraph (2) below provides", and at the end there shall be added the following subparagraph:—

"(2) The transfer value receivable under these rules in respect of a person who leaves police employment shall be such transfer value as is payable in respect of him under the police pensions regulations; and any such transfer value which has not been reduced by reason of the provisions for flat-rate retirement pension in the National Insurance Act 1965(**a**) shall be treated as unreduced for the purposes of rule 14.".

(6) After paragraph 6 of schedule 2 there shall be added the following paragraph:—

"Police employment: returned contributions

7. In relation to a person leaving police employment, rule 10(a)(iii) shall have effect as if it provided as follows:—

"(iii) pay to the fund authority an amount equal to any award paid to him by way of return of contributions or gratuity on or after leaving that employment; but where under the police pensions regulations he had paid pension contributions at a rate related to $6\frac{1}{4}\%$ of his pensionable pay, or had paid additional contributions, within the meaning of those regulations, the payment shall be of an amount equal to so much of the award as would have been payable had he paid such pension contributions at a rate related to 5% of his pensionable pay and had not paid such additional contributions, and".".

(**a**) 1965 c. 51.

Adjustment of certain references to dates

4. In relation to any person who becomes eligible, subject to compliance with conditions, for the application of Part II or III of the principal rules by virtue of rule 3 above, the principal rules shall have effect as if—

> (*a*) any references therein to 18th August 1968 were references to 15th February 1970 and

> (*b*) any references therein, however expressed, to 18th August 1969 were references to 15th February 1971.

Peter Walker,

22nd January 1971. Secretary of State for the Environment.

EXPLANATORY NOTE

(This Note is not part of the Rules.)

These Rules amend the Superannuation (Local Government and Approved Employment) Interchange Rules 1969 so as to provide for the interchange of superannuation rights where a person transfers from employment in local government to service as a policeman and vice versa.

The Rules can have retrospective effect to a limited extent under the express powers of, and subject to the safeguards required by, section 2(5) of the Superannuation (Miscellaneous Provisions) Act 1948.

STATUTORY INSTRUMENTS

1971 No. 115

CUSTOMS AND EXCISE

The Import Duties (General) (No. 1) Order 1971

Made - - - -	*25th January* 1971
Laid before the House of Commons	*29th January* 1971
Coming into Operation -	*4th February* 1971

The Lords Commissioners of Her Majesty's Treasury, by virtue of the powers conferred on them by sections 1, 2 and 13 of the Import Duties Act 1958(a) and of all other powers enabling them in that behalf, on the recommendation of the Secretary of State hereby make the following Order:—

1.—(1) This Order may be cited as the Import Duties (General) (No. 1) Order 1971.

(2) The Interpretation Act 1889(b) shall apply for the interpretation of this Order as it applies for the interpretation of an Act of Parliament.

(3) This Order shall come into operation on 4th February 1971.

2. Apricot kernels, whole, shall cease to be included among the goods chargeable with import duty under heading 12.08 of the Customs Tariff 1959 (locust beans, fruit kernels etc.); and accordingly Schedule 1 to the Import Duties (General) (No. 7) Order 1970(c) (which by reference to the Tariff sets out the import duties chargeable under the Import Duties Act 1958) shall be amended by substituting for subheadings (A) and (B) of heading 12.08 the following:—

" (A) Locust bean kernels, whole and apricot kernels,   —   — whole

(B) Other   ...   .   10%   C — E 10% "

Bernard Weatherill,

H. S. P. Monro,

Two of the Lords Commissioners
of Her Majesty's Treasury.

25th January 1971.

EXPLANATORY NOTE

(This Note is not part of the Order.)

This Order removes the import duty on whole apricot kernels.

(a) 1958 c. 6.   (b) 1889 c. 63.   (c) S.I. 1970/1522 (1970 III, p. 4935).

STATUTORY INSTRUMENTS

1971 No. 116

TRANSPORT

PENSIONS AND COMPENSATION

The National Freight Corporation (Alteration of Pension Schemes) (No. 1) Order 1971

Made - - - -	25th January 1971
Laid before Parliament	29th January 1971
Coming into Operation	31st January 1971

The Secretary of State for the Environment, in exercise of his powers under section 74 of the Transport Act 1962(a) as read with section 136 of the Transport Act 1968(b) and of all other enabling powers, hereby makes the following Order:—

Commencement, citation and interpretation

1.—(1) This Order shall come into operation on the 31st January 1971, and may be cited as the National Freight Corporation (Alteration of Pension Schemes) (No. 1) Order 1971.

(2) In this Order, unless the context otherwise requires—

" the Corporation " means the National Freight Corporation ;

"funded scheme" means a pension scheme (not being an insurance scheme) where the pensions are payable out of a fund held by any person for the purposes of the scheme ;

"insurance scheme" means a pension scheme where the pensions are provided by means of contracts or policies made or effected with an insurance company carrying on life assurance business within the meaning of the Insurance Companies Act 1958(c) (including contracts or policies made or effected with such a company for the purpose of implementing any form of private superannuation fund) ;

"the Male Wages Grades Scheme" means the pension scheme established by the British Transport Commission (Male Wages Grades Pensions) Regulations 1954(d), as amended(e), (as that scheme now has effect subject to the provisions of any Order made under section 74 of the Transport Act 1962) ;

"the New Fund" means the National Freight Corporation (Wages Grades) Pension Fund which is a funded pension scheme established by the Corporation, with the consent of the Secretary of State, under the terms of an Interim Trust Deed executed by the Corporation and N.F.C. Trustees Limited on the 12th January 1971 ;

"the persons administering", in relation to a pension scheme, means the persons responsible for administering the scheme under the terms thereof, and includes the trustees (if any) of the scheme ;

"the service" means whole time employment with the Corporation or with a subsidiary of the Corporation ; and

---

(a) 1962 c. 46.   (b) 1968 c. 73.   (c) 1958 c. 72.   (d) S.I. 1954/898 (1954 I, p. 175).
(e) S.I. 1957/1455, 1960/784 (1957 I, p. 177; 1960 I, p. 430).

" term ", in relation to a pension scheme to which this Order applies, includes any rule or provision of the scheme, or of any statutory provision relating to the scheme, or of any deed or other instrument made for the purposes of the scheme.

(3) The Interpretation Act 1889(a) shall apply for the interpretation of this Order as it applies for the interpretation of an Act of Parliament.

Application of Order

2.—(1) This Order shall apply to the New Fund, the Male Wages Grades Scheme and the other pension schemes mentioned in this Order.

(2) A pension scheme to which this Order applies shall be construed and have effect as if the relevant provisions of this Order were terms of the scheme, any other term thereof, whether expressed or implied, to the contrary notwithstanding.

Application of interavailability provisions to New Fund

3. The provisions of the British Transport Reorganisation (Pensions of Employees) (No. 1) Order 1964(b) (so far as applicable) and of Articles 3 and 4 of the British Transport (Pensions of Employees) (No. 1) Order 1969(c) (which relate to the interavailability of pension schemes in the publicly owned transport industry) shall on and after the 1st February 1971 apply in relation to the New Fund as if that fund were an established scheme as defined in Article 2 of the said (No. 1) Order of 1969.

Alterations in the terms of the Male Wages Grades Scheme

4.—(1) This Article shall apply to the Male Wages Grades Scheme.

(2) Any person in the service who is a member of the Male Wages Grades Scheme and who becomes a member of the New Fund on or after the 1st February 1971 shall, on becoming such a member, cease to be a member of the Male Wages Grades Scheme.

(3) The terms of the Male Wages Grades Scheme which require persons to become members of Section B of that Scheme shall not apply to—

(*a*) any person referred to in paragraph (2) of this Article, or

(*b*) any other person who becomes a member of the New Fund on or after the 1st February 1971.

(4) A person who becomes a member of the New Fund on or after the 1st February 1971 shall at all times after becoming a member thereof be ineligible for membership of either Section A or Section B of the Male Wages Grades Scheme.

(5) Where a person ceases to be a member of the Male Wages Grades Scheme under the foregoing provisions of this Article, the New Fund shall be credited by the Corporation with a sum equal to the contributions paid by such person to the Male Wages Grades Scheme.

(6) Where under the foregoing provisions of this Article a person who has a right of re-admission to the Male Wages Grades Scheme becomes ineligible for membership thereof, that right of re-admission shall terminate.

Alterations in the terms of certain schemes for providing pensions and other benefits

5.—(1) This Article shall apply to the pension schemes listed in Schedule 1 to this Order.

(a) 1889 c. 63.　(b) S.I. 1964/1329 (1964 II, p. 3034).　(c) S.I. 1969/1824 (1969 III, p. 5668).

(2) A person who becomes a member of the New Fund on or after the 1st February 1971 shall, so long as he is a contributing member of the New Fund, be ineligible for membership of a pension scheme to which this Article applies.

(3) Where a member of a pension scheme to which this Article applies becomes a member of the New Fund on or after the 1st February 1971, the following provisions shall have effect:—

(a) upon the date of his admission to membership of the New Fund he shall cease to be a member of that pension scheme, his right to receive benefit from that scheme shall cease, and (except as hereinafter provided) his liability to pay contributions to that scheme (where the scheme is a contributory scheme) shall cease ; and

(b) as soon as may be after that date the persons administering that pension scheme shall pay to the New Fund an appropriate transfer value in respect of the accrued pension rights of that member in that scheme.

(4) Where under the foregoing provisions of this Article a person who has a right of re-admission to a pension scheme to which this Article applies becomes ineligible for membership thereof, that right of re-admission shall not be exercisable so long as the ineligibility continues.

Alterations in the terms of certain insurance schemes

6.—(1) This Article shall apply to the pension schemes listed in Schedule 2 to this Order.

(2) Where a member of a pension scheme to which this Article applies becomes a member of the New Fund on or after the 1st February 1971, the following provisions shall have effect:—

(a) upon the date of his admission to membership of the New Fund he shall (subject to this Order) cease to be liable to pay contributions to that scheme ; and

(b) as soon as may be after that date the Corporation shall make such arrangements as may be appropriate to secure to that member by means of insurance policies his accrued pension rights in that scheme.

(3) Any such insurance policy as is referred to in paragraph (2) of this Article may provide that the policy may be surrendered, by or at the request of the member in whose favour it is issued, upon condition that the sum payable as consideration for the surrender is paid to the New Fund, but in all other respects every such insurance policy shall be non-assignable and non-commutable.

Alteration as respects a part of a particular pension scheme

7.—(1) This Article shall apply to the pension scheme known as the London, Midland and Scottish Railway (London and North Western) Provident and Pension Society and Supplemental Pension Fund.

(2) Where a member of the pension scheme to which this Article applies becomes a member of the New Fund on or after the 1st February 1971, the following provisions shall have effect:—

(a) upon the date of his admission to membership of the New Fund he shall cease to be entitled to receive from that scheme any benefit payable on retirement or death and (subject to this Order) such adjustment as may be appropriate shall be made in respect of the liability of that member to pay contributions to that scheme after that date ; and (*b*) as soon as may be after that date the persons administering that pension scheme shall pay to the New Fund an appropriate transfer value in respect of the accrued pension rights of that member in that scheme to such benefits.

Ascertainment of transfer values

8.—(1) Where under any of the foregoing provisions of this Order there falls to be paid in relation to a member of a pension scheme to which this Order applies a transfer value in respect of his accrued pension rights in that scheme, then—

(*a*) if the scheme is a funded scheme, the amount to be paid shall be ascertained by first determining the portion of the funds of that scheme properly attributable to the accrued pension rights of that member in that scheme and then by deducting therefrom such sum as may be necessary to cover the cost actually incurred by the persons administering that scheme in making the apportionment and the payment and also an amount equal to any income tax which may then become payable by virtue of regulations made, or having effect as if made, under section 208 of the Income and Corporation Taxes Act 1970(a) ;

(*b*) if the scheme is not a funded scheme, the amount to be paid shall be ascertained by first determining a sum representing the value of the accrued pension rights of that member in that scheme and then by deducting therefrom such sum as may be necessary to cover the cost actually incurred by the persons administering that scheme in making the determination and the payment.

(2) Any payment of a transfer value under any provision of this Order may take the form of a transfer of securities, deposits or other assets, valued as at the date of the transfer, and any question whether a transfer value shall be paid in cash or in the form of such a transfer as aforesaid shall be determined in each case when the transfer value falls to be paid.

Consequential provisions

9.—(1) Where under the foregoing provisions of this Order a person ceases to be a member of a pension scheme to which this Order applies and which is a contributory scheme, or otherwise ceases to be liable to pay contributions to that scheme, or where under those provisions an adjustment falls to be made in respect of the liability of a member of such a pension scheme to pay contributions to that scheme, such cessation or adjustment (as the case may be) shall be without prejudice to the obligation of that person to pay any outstanding contributions to that scheme in respect of any period before such cessation or adjustment and at the rate appropriate to that period, or to the right of his employer to deduct such contributions from his emoluments.

(2) Where under the foregoing provisions of this Order a person ceases to be a member of a pension scheme to which this Order applies, his rights to benefit from that scheme shall, except as otherwise provided in this Order, terminate with the cessation of his membership of that scheme.

Determination of questions

10. Where under the foregoing provisions of this Order any matter or thing is to be determined in relation to a member of a pension scheme to which this Order applies who becomes a member of the New Fund, that matter or thing shall be determined by agreement between the persons

---

(a) 1970 c. 10.

administering that pension scheme on the one hand and the persons administering the New Fund on the other hand or, in default of such agreement, by the Secretary of State.

Safeguarding of existing rights

11. No person who is a member of, or has a right of re-admission to, a pension scheme to which this Order applies (other than the New Fund) shall be required by a term of his employment in the service to become a member of the New Fund.

Signed by authority of the Secretary of State 25th January 1971.

John Peyton,
Minister for Transport Industries
Department of the Environment.

SCHEDULE 1

SCHEMES FOR PROVIDING PENSIONS AND OTHER BENEFITS

British Railways (Wages Grades) Pension Fund.
British Road Services (Male Wages Grades) Group Pension Fund.
Great Eastern Railway New Pension Fund.
Great Eastern Railway New Pension Supplemental Fund.
Great Northern Railway Superannuation Fund.
London Brighton and South Coast Railway Pension Fund.
North Eastern Railway Servants' Pension Society (Tables A and B only).

SCHEDULE 2

INSURANCE SCHEMES

Colonial Mutual Life Assurance Society Ltd.: —
Barrack & Fenton Ltd.
Cowan & Co.
Crouchers Ltd.
D. West & Sons Ltd.
Direct Transport (Wellingbro.) Ltd.
Donaldson Wright.
F. Crowther & Son (Wakefield) Ltd.
Fisher Renwick Ltd.
G. H. Atkins & Sons.
Harding Bros. Transport Ltd.
H. & G. Dutfield Ltd.
Harold Wood & Sons Ltd.
H. W. Hawker Ltd.
J. & G. Barrack Ltd.
J. Gupwell Transport Ltd.
J. Keetch & Son.

Macks Hauliers.
Munro's Motor Transport Co.
P.X. Ltd.
R. Keetch & Son Ltd.
Robin Hood Transport Ltd.
S. Oatley & Sons Ltd.
Swindon Transport Ltd.
Tees-side Motor Transport Ltd.
Topham Bros.
Union Road Transport.
Wm. Clarke (Nottingham) Ltd.
W. Hesford Ltd.
W. Hill.
W. Wisely & Sons Ltd.
Youngs Express Deliveries.

Eagle Star Insurance Co. Ltd.: —
Fairclough Staff Pension Scheme.
T. M. Fairclough & Son Ltd. Group Life Assurance Scheme.

Equity & Law Life Assurance Society Ltd.: —
E. & E. J. Shaw Ltd. Pension & Life Assurance Scheme.

Legal & General Assurance Society Ltd.: —
Castle Bros. (Hauliers) Ltd. Staff Assurance Scheme.
C. Scott's Road Services Ltd. Life Assurance Scheme.

National Employer's Life Assurance Co. Ltd.: —
F. Crowther & Son (Wakefield) Ltd.

National Mutual Life Association of Australasia: —
Castleford Transport Ltd. Pension Scheme.

Northern Assurance Co. Ltd.: —
James Express Carriers Ltd.

Norwich Union Life Insurance Society Ltd.: —
Corringdon Ltd.
Tartan Arrow Service Ltd. Pension Fund.

Phoenix Assurance Co. Ltd.: —
Davies & Brownlow Ltd. Staff Pension Scheme.

Provident Mutual Life Assurance Association: —
Hay's Wharf Cartage Co. Ltd., Pickfords Ltd. & Carter Paterson & Co. Ltd. and Associated Cartage Companies Pension Scheme.

Prudential Assurance Co. Ltd.: —
J. Gerrard Transport Ltd. Scheme.

Scottish Widows' Fund and Life Assurance Society: —
C. H. Ward & Sons Ltd.

Sun Life Assurance Society Ltd.: —
R. J. Weeks & Co. Ltd. Staff Superannuation Scheme.
The Tayforth Group Operatives Pension Fund.

Sun Life of Canada:—

D. M. Smith Road Transport Staff Scheme.

H. & R. Duncan Ltd.

T. Brown Transport Pension Scheme.

Northern Motor Utilities Pension Scheme.

EXPLANATORY NOTE

(This Note is not part of the Order.)

This Order relates to the newly established National Freight Corporation (Wages Grades) Pension Fund, to the British Transport Commission (Male Wages Grades) Pension Scheme and to certain other pension schemes mentioned in the Order. It provides (Article 3) for the application of the inter-availability arrangements for pensions in the publicly owned transport industry to the newly established Wages Grades Pension Fund. It also regulates (Articles 4-7) the position of members of the British Transport Commission (Male Wages Grades) Pension Scheme or of the other pension schemes referred to above, who become members of the newly established Fund, so as to avoid duplication of membership. Provision is made (Articles 8-10) for the payment of transfer values, for certain consequential matters and for the determination of questions. Article 11 safeguards existing rights.

1971 No. 117

TRANSPORT

PENSIONS AND COMPENSATION

The National Freight Corporation
(Alteration of Pension Schemes) (No. 2) Order 1971

Made - - -	*25th January* 1971
Laid before Parliament	*29th January* 1971
Coming into Operation	*31st January* 1971

The Secretary of State for the Environment, in exercise of his powers under section 74 of the Transport Act 1962(a) as read with section 136 of the Transport Act 1968(b) and of all other enabling powers, hereby makes the following Order:—

Commencement, citation and interpretation

1.—(1) This Order shall come into operation on the 31st January 1971, and may be cited as the National Freight Corporation (Alteration of Pension Schemes) (No. 2) Order 1971.

(2) In this Order, unless the context otherwise requires—

"the Corporation" means the National Freight Corporation;

"funded scheme" means a pension scheme (not being an insurance scheme) where the pensions are payable out of a fund held by any person for the purposes of the scheme;

"insurance scheme" means a pension scheme where the pensions are provided by means of contracts or policies made or effected with an insurance company carrying on life assurance business within the meaning of the Insurance Companies Act 1958(c) (including contracts or policies made or effected with such a company for the purpose of implementing any form of private superannuation fund);

"the Male Wages Grades Scheme" means the pension scheme established by the British Transport Commission (Male Wages Grades Pensions) Regulations 1954 **(d),** as amended **(e),** (as that scheme now has effect subject to the provisions of any Order made under section 74 of the Transport Act 1962);

"the New Fund" means the National Freight Corporation (Salaried Staff) Pension Fund which is a funded pension scheme established by the Corporation, with the consent of the Secretary of State, under the terms of an Interim Trust Deed executed by the Corporation and N.F.C. Trustees Limited on the 12th January 1971;

"the persons administering", in relation to a pension scheme, means the persons responsible for administering the scheme under the terms thereof,

---

(a) 1962 c. 46.   (b) 1968 c. 73.   (c) 1958 c. 72.   (d) S.I. 1954/898 (1954 I, p. 175).
(e) S.I. 1957/1455, 1960/784 (1957 I, p. 177; 1960 I, p. 430).

and includes the trustees (if any) of the scheme;

"the service" means whole time employment with the Corporation or with a subsidiary of the Corporation; and

"term", in relation to a pension scheme to which this Order applies, includes any rule or provision of the scheme, or of any statutory provision relating to the scheme, or of any deed or other instrument made for the purposes of the scheme.

(3) The Interpretation Act 1889(a) shall apply for the interpretation of this Order as it applies for the interpretation of an Act of Parliament.

Application of Order

2.—(1) This Order shall apply to the New Fund, the Male Wages Grades Scheme and the other pension schemes mentioned in this Order.

(2) A pension scheme to which this Order applies shall be construed and have effect as if the relevant provisions of this Order were terms of the scheme, any other term thereof, whether expressed or implied, to the contrary notwithstanding.

Application of interavailability provisions to New Fund

3. The provisions of the British Transport Reorganisation (Pensions of Employees) (No. 1) Order 1964(b) (so far as applicable) and of Articles 3 and 4 of the British Transport (Pensions of Employees) (No. 1) Order 1969(c) (which relate to the interavailability of pension schemes in the publicly owned transport industry) shall on and after the 1st February 1971 apply in relation to the New Fund as if that fund were an established scheme as defined in Article 2 of the said (No. 1) Order of 1969.

Alterations in the terms of the Male Wages Grades Scheme

4.—(1) This Article shall apply to the Male Wages Grades Scheme.

(2) Any person in the service who is a member of the Male Wages Grades Scheme and who becomes a member of the New Fund on or after the 1st February 1971 shall, on becoming such a member, cease to be a member of the Male Wages Grades Scheme.

(3) The terms of the Male Wages Grades Scheme which require persons to become members of Section B of that Scheme shall not apply to—

(a) any person referred to in paragraph (2) of this Article, or

(b) any other person who becomes a member of the New Fund on or after the 1st February 1971.

(4) A person who becomes a member of the New Fund on or after the 1st February 1971 shall at all times after becoming a member thereof be ineligible for membership of either Section A or Section B of the Male Wages Grades Scheme.

(5) Where a person ceases to be a member of the Male Wages Grades Scheme under the foregoing provisions of this Article, the New Fund shall be credited by the Corporation with a sum equal to the contributions paid by such person to the Male Wages Grades Scheme.

(6) Where under the foregoing provisions of this Article a person who has a right of re-admission to the Male Wages Grades Scheme becomes ineligible for membership thereof, that right of re-admission shall terminate.

(a) 1889 c. 63.
(b) S.I. 1964/1329 (1964 II, p. 3034).   (c) S.I. 1969/1824 (1969 III, p. 5668).

Alterations in the terms of certain schemes for providing pensions and other benefits

5.—(1) This Article shall apply to the pension schemes listed in Schedule 1 to this Order.

(2) A person who becomes a member of the New Fund on or after the 1st February 1971 shall, so long as he is a contributing member of the New Fund, be ineligible for membership of a pension scheme to which this Article applies.

(3) Where a member of a pension scheme to which this Article applies becomes a member of the New Fund on or after the 1st February 1971, the following provisions shall have effect:—

   (a) upon the date of his admission to membership of the New Fund he shall cease to be a member of that pension scheme, his right to receive benefit from that scheme shall cease, and (except as hereinafter provided) his liability to pay contributions to that scheme (where the scheme is a contributory scheme) shall cease; and

   (b) as soon as may be after that date the persons administering that pension scheme shall pay to the New Fund an appropriate transfer value in respect of the accrued pension rights of that member in that scheme.

(4) Where under the foregoing provisions of this Article a person who has a right of re-admission to a pension scheme to which this Article applies becomes ineligible for membership thereof, that right of re-admission shall not be exercisable so long as the ineligibility continues.

Alterations in the terms of certain insurance schemes

6.—(1) This Article shall apply to the pension schemes listed in Schedule 2 to this Order.

(2) Where a member of a pension scheme to which this Article applies becomes a member of the New Fund on or after the 1st February 1971, the following provisions shall have effect:—

   (a) upon the date of his admission to membership of the New Fund he shall (subject to this Order) cease to be liable to pay contributions to that scheme; and

   (b) as soon as may be after that date the Corporation shall make such arrangements as may be appropriate to secure to that member by means of insurance policies his accrued pension rights in that scheme.

(3) Any such insurance policy as is referred to in paragraph (2) of this Article may provide that the policy may be surrendered, by or at the request of the member in whose favour it is issued, upon condition that the sum payable as consideration for the surrender is paid to the New Fund, but in all other respects every such insurance policy shall be non-assignable and non-commutable.

Ascertainment of transfer values

7.—(1) Where under any of the foregoing provisions of this Order there falls to be paid in relation to a member of a pension scheme to which this Order applies a transfer value in respect of his accrued pension rights in that scheme, then—

   (a) if the scheme is a funded scheme, the amount to be paid shall be ascertained by first determining the portion of the funds of that scheme properly attributable to the accrued pension rights of that member in that scheme and then by deducting therefrom such sum as may be necessary to cover the cost actually incurred by the persons administering that scheme in making the apportionment and the payment and also an amount equal to any income tax which may then become payable by virtue of regulations made, or having effect as if made, under section 208 of the Income and Corporation Taxes Act 1970**(a)**;

(b) if the scheme is not a funded scheme, the amount to be paid shall be ascertained by first determining a sum representing the value of the accrued pension rights of that member in that scheme and then by deducting therefrom such sum as may be necessary to cover the cost actually incurred by the persons administering that scheme in making the determination and the payment.

(2) Any payment of a transfer value under any provision of this Order may take the form of a transfer of securities, deposits or other assets, valued as at the date of the transfer, and any question whether a transfer value shall be paid in cash or in the form of such a transfer as aforesaid shall be determined in each case when the transfer value falls to be paid.

Consequential provisions

8.—(1) Where under the foregoing provisions of this Order a person ceases to be a member of a pension scheme to which this Order applies and which is a contributory scheme, or otherwise ceases to be liable to pay contributions to that scheme, such cessation shall be without prejudice to the obligation of that person to pay any outstanding contributions to that scheme in respect of any period before such cessation and at the rate appropriate to that period, or to the right of his employer to deduct such contributions from his emoluments.

(2) Where under the foregoing provisions of this Order a person ceases to be a member of a pension scheme to which this Order applies, his rights to benefit from that scheme shall, except as otherwise provided in this Order, terminate with the cessation of his membership of that scheme.

Determination of questions

9. Where under the foregoing provisions of this Order any matter or thing is to be determined in relation to a member of a pension scheme to which this Order applies who becomes a member of the New Fund, that matter or thing shall be determined by agreement between the persons administering that pension scheme on the one hand and the persons administering the New Fund on the other hand or, in default of such agreement, by the Secretary of State.

Safeguarding of existing rights

10. No person who is a member of, or has a right of re-admission to, a pension scheme to which this Order applies (other than the New Fund) shall be required by a term of his employment in the service to become a member of the New Fund.

Signed by authority of the Secretary of State 25th January 1971.

John Peyton,
Minister for Transport Industries
Department of the Environment.

(a) 1970 c. 10.

SCHEDULE 1

Schemes for providing pensions and other benefits

British Railways Superannuation Fund—L.N.E.R. Section
                                     G.W.R. Section
                                     S.R. Section
                                     L.M.S.R. Section
                                     New Section

British Railways (Wages Grades) Pension Fund
British Road Services (Male Wages Grades) Group Pension Fund
Coast Lines Superannuation Fund Association—Divided
Cooks Pension Fund
Foremen & Staff Mutual Benefit Society—Divided
Furness Withy Superannuation Scheme—Divided
Hay's Wharf Companies Superannuation Fund—Section A
Hay's Wharf Companies Superannuation Fund—Section B
London Transport (Administrative & Supervisory) Staff Superannuation Fund
National Freight Salaried Staff Pension Fund
Railway Clearing System Superannuation Fund
Superannuation Fund Association of Chaplins Ltd.
Thos. Bantock & Co. Superannuation Fund
Tillings Association Ltd. Endowment Fund.

SCHEDULE 2

Insurance Schemes

Colonial Mutual Life Assurance Society Ltd.:—
          Cowan & Co.
          Donaldson Wright
          Fisher Renwick Ltd.
          G.H. Atkins & Sons
          Harding Bros. Transport Ltd.
          Harold Wood & Sons Ltd.
          H.W. Hawker Ltd.
          Macks Hauliers
          P.X. Ltd.
          R. Keetch & Son Ltd.
          Robin Hood Transport Ltd.
          Robinson Transport (Beccles) Ltd.
          Swindon Transport Ltd.
          W. Wisely & Sons Ltd.
          Youngs Express Deliveries.

Eagle Star Insurance Co. Ltd.:—
          Fairclough Staff Pension Scheme
          Scribbans Kemp Pension Scheme.

Equity and Law Life Assurance Society Ltd.:—
          Morton's (Coventry) Ltd. Pension & Life Assurance Scheme
          Furness and Parker Ltd.

Friends' Provident & Century Life Office:—
          Southern Roadways Ltd. Endowment.

Legal & General Assurance Society Ltd.:—
          Castle Bros. (Hauliers) Ltd. Staff Assurance Scheme
          C. Scott's Road Services Ltd. Life Assurance Scheme
          S. J. Jeffrey Ltd. Staff Assurance Scheme.

London Assurance Group:—
          Eagle Transport Co. Ltd.

National Provident Institution:—
          N. Francis & Co. Ltd.

Northern Assurance Co. Ltd.:—
    James Express Carriers Ltd.
Norwich Union Life Insurance Society Ltd.:—
    Corringdon Ltd.
    Tartan Arrow Service Ltd. Pension Fund.
Provident Mutual Life Assurance Association:—
    Hay's Wharf Cartage Co. Ltd., Pickfords Ltd. & Carter Paterson & Co.
        Ltd. and Associated Cartage Companies Pension Scheme
    Joseph Nall & Co. Ltd.
Prudential Assurance Co. Ltd.:—
    J. Gerrard Transport Ltd. Scheme.
Scottish Provident Institution:—
    Lawther & Harvey Ltd. Pension & Life Assurance Scheme.
Scottish Widows' Fund & Life Assurance Society:—
    H. Viney & Co. Pension & Life Assurance Scheme.
Sun Life Assurance Society Ltd.:—
    George Read (Transport) Ltd.
    R. J. Weeks & Co. Ltd. Staff Superannuation Scheme
    Springfield Carriers Ltd. Staff Superannuation Scheme
    The Tayforth Group Staff Pension Fund
    The Tayforth Group Operatives Pension Fund.
Sun Life of Canada:—
    G. & B. Watson
    Northern Motor Utilities Pension Scheme
    W. A. Mitchell Road Transport.

EXPLANATORY NOTE

(This Note is not part of the Order.)

This Order relates to the newly established National Freight Corporation (Salaried Staff) Pension Fund, to the British Transport Commission (Male Wages Grades) Pension Scheme and to certain other pension schemes mentioned in the Order. It provides (Article 3) for the application of the inter availability arrangements for pensions in the publicly owned transport industry to the newly established Salaried Staff Pension Fund. It also regulates (Articles 4-6) the position of members of the British Transport Commission (Males Wages Grades) Pension Scheme or of the other pension schemes referred to above, who become members of the newly established Fund, so as to avoid duplication of membership. Provision is made (Articles 7-9) for the payment of transfer values, for certain consequential matters and for the determination of questions. Article 10 safeguards existing rights.

STATUTORY INSTRUMENTS

1971 No. 118

THERAPEUTIC SUBSTANCES

The Therapeutic Substances (Manufacture of Vaccines, Toxins and Antigens) Amendment Regulations 1971

Made - - - -	22nd January 1971
Laid before Parliament	2nd February 1971
Coming into Operation	1st March 1971

The Joint Committee constituted by section 4(1) of the Therapeutic Substances Act 1956(a), as amended by article 2(2) of and Schedule 1 to the Transfer of Functions (Wales) Order 1969(b), in exercise of the powers conferred on them by sections 1 and 5 of the said Act, after consultation with the Advisory Committee constituted under section 4(2) of the said Act, hereby make the following regulations:—

Citation, commencement and interpretation

1.—(1) These regulations may be cited as the Therapeutic Substances (Manufacture of Vaccines, Toxins and Antigens) Amendment Regulations 1971 and shall come into operation on 1st March 1971.

(2) The Therapeutic Substances (Manufacture of Vaccines, Toxins and Antigens) Regulations 1963 to 1967(c) and these regulations may be cited together as the Therapeutic Substances (Manufacture of Vaccines, Toxins and Antigens) Regulations 1963 to 1971.

(3) The Interpretation Act 1889(d) shall apply to the interpretation of these regulations as it applies to the interpretation of an Act of Parliament.

2. The Therapeutic Substances (Manufacture of Vaccines, Toxins and Antigens) Regulations 1963, as amended (e), shall be further amended as follows:—

(a) part XX (which relates to Poliomyelitis Vaccine (Oral)) shall be deleted, and after regulation 95 there shall be inserted the following regulations—

"PART XX

PROVISIONS RELATING TO POLIOMYELITIS VACCINE (ORAL)

Definition and proper name

96. Poliomyelitis vaccine (oral) is a preparation containing any one or more of types 1, 2 or 3 of live attenuated poliomyelitis virus. The proper name of any such preparation is "poliomyelitis vaccine (oral)" followed by words descriptive of the type or types of poliomyelitis virus contained therein.

(a) 1956 c. 25.   (b) S.I. 1969/388 (1969 I, p. 1070).
(c) S.I. 1963/1459, 1964/1434, 1965/1005, 1966/504, 1967/1196 (1963 II, p. 2561; 1964 III, p. 3324; 1965 I, p. 2454; 1966 I, p. 1046; 1967 II, p. 3502).
(d) 1889 c. 63.
(e) The relevant amending instruments are S.I. 1964/1434, 1965/1005, 1966/504, 1967/1196 (1964 III, p. 3324; 1965 I, p. 2454; 1966 I, p. 1046; 1967 II, p. 3502).

Buildings and Staff

97. Poliomyelitis vaccine (oral) shall be produced in a separate building or separate parts of a building to which, during production, only persons engaged in its production and testing have access. Procedures which potentially involve the presence of micro-organisms or the use of tissue culture cells other than those cell cultures in which it is proposed to produce the vaccine, shall not be carried out in the said separate building or parts of a building. If persons engaged in the production of the vaccine have been working with other infectious agents or with experimental animals, they shall not on the same day enter the areas where the vaccine is produced. The establishment for the production of the vaccine shall be under the complete control and direction of an expert in microbiology approved by the licensing authority.

Strains of poliomyelitis virus

98.—(1) The strains of poliomyelitis virus used for the production of poliomyelitis vaccine (oral) shall be approved by the licensing authority.

(2) Production of the vaccine shall be based on a virus seed system and the final vaccine shall not contain any virus which is more than 3 subcultures from the strain culture on which the original laboratory and clinical tests were made, if that strain culture is type 1 or type 2, or more than 2 subcultures from the strain culture if it is type 3.

(3) The working seed lot of each strain used shall conform to the same standards of purity as are required by these regulations to be applied to the final vaccine.

Information and samples required by the licensing authority

99. Protocols made and samples taken during stages of production and testing of each batch of vaccine shall be submitted to the licensing authority. Information shall also be submitted concerning the results of tests made on all cell cultures and virus suspensions intended for the preparation of poliomyelitis vaccine (oral) whether or not the cultures or the virus suspensions were used in preparing a finished batch.

Storage by manufacturer

100. Poliomyelitis vaccine (oral) during storage by the manufacturer shall be kept at a temperature not higher than $-20\,^\circ\text{C}$.

Labelling

101.—(1) In addition to the particulars required by regulation 6 of these regulations the following particulars shall be borne by the container of poliomyelitis vaccine (oral) or of preparations thereof:—

   (*a*) a statement that the vaccine shall not be administered by injection;

   (*b*) the virus titre of each type of poliomyelitis virus included in the vaccine;

   (*c*) a statement identifying the tissue used for preparing the cell cultures in which the poliomyelitis virus was grown.

(2) The label of the container and the package of the vaccine shall bear the particulars required by regulations 6(1)(*g*) and (*h*) of the general regulations.

SPECIAL PROVISIONS RELATING TO POLIOMYELITIS VACCINE (ORAL)
WHEN PREPARED IN MONKEY KIDNEY CELL CULTURES

Cells for vaccine production

102.—(1) Monkey kidney cell cultures used for the production of polio-myelitis vaccine (oral) shall be derived from a healthy stock of monkeys of suitable species free from *Mycobacterium tuberculosis*, B virus and from other adventitious pathogenic agents. Kidney tissue shall not be taken from a monkey that has been used previously for experimental purposes except with the approval of the licensing authority. The monkeys shall be kept in well constructed and ventilated animal rooms and shall be quarantined for an adequate period before being used. After they are killed, they shall be examined thoroughly by a qualified person experienced in the diagnosis of disease in monkeys, particularly for evidence of tuberculosis and B virus infection.

(2) If animal serum is added to initiate the cultures then, before virus propagation, the cultures shall be washed free from such serum. No extraneous protein shall be added to the tissue cultures during the course of virus propagation.

Testing of cell cultures

103.—(1) Twenty-five per cent of each batch of cell cultures intended for use for the propagation of virus shall be held as uninoculated control cultures and shall be incubated at the same temperature as the inoculated cultures. They shall be observed for 14 days from the time the production cultures are inoculated with virus, and shall show no evidence of the presence of adventitious agents. Not more than 20 per cent of the control cultures shall be discarded for accidental causes. At 7 and 14 days beyond the time of inoculation of the production cultures, two per cent of the fluids from the control cultures shall be inoculated into human, monkey and rabbit cell cultures, and the said cultures shall be incubated at the same temperature as the initial inoculated cultures and observed for 14 days during which time they shall show no evidence of the presence of adventitious agents.

(2) At the time of inoculation with virus all tissue cultures shall be examined for evidence of degeneration and if any show abnormal cytopathic change the whole batch concerned shall be discarded. The fluid removed from each culture bottle before inoculation with virus shall be tested for freedom from bacterial and mycotic contamination. The fluids from these cultures shall also be examined for freedom from adventitious agents by inoculating at least two per cent of the pooled cell culture fluid into a rabbit cell culture system and a further two per cent into human amnion cell cultures. Human amnion cell cultures may be substituted by any culture system shown to be as sensitive to measles virus as human amnion cell cultures. At the same time a further two per cent of pooled cell culture fluids shall be tested for freedom from adventitious agents on monkey tissue prepared from the same species but not the same animal as that used for the vaccine production. The cultures shall be maintained and observed over a period of at least 14 days. At the end of periods of 7 days and 14 days, sub-cultures shall be made from each of the inoculated tissues and examined over a further period of 14 days. No cultures shall show evidence of the presence of adventitious agents.

(3) At the time of virus harvest at least four per cent of the control cell cultures shall be examined for haemadsorption viruses using guinea-pig red

blood cells. Any remaining control tissue cultures shall be tested for hae-madsorption viruses at the end of the observation period. No cultures shall show evidence of the presence of haemadsorption viruses.

Production of virus suspensions

104.—(1) Virus for the preparation of poliomyelitis vaccine (oral) produced in monkey kidney cell cultures shall be grown by aseptic methods. The kidneys from each monkey shall be processed separately.

(2) During the course of virus propagation the cell culture vessels shall be incubated at a range of temperature which shall be approved by the licensing authority and which shall at no time rise above 35°C.

(3) Virus suspensions shall be harvested not later than 4 days after virus inoculation or at such time as the licensing authority may approve.

Testing of virus suspensions

105.—(1) Virus suspensions harvested from the cultures prepared from the kidneys of each monkey shall be kept separately during testing.

(2) Samples of the virus suspensions shall be taken immediately on harvest-ing and before clarification and shall be subjected to the tests described in paragraph (3) of this regulation. Between the time of harvesting and the time when the samples are tested they shall be kept under conditions that will preserve the agents that the tests are designed to detect.

(3) The samples shall be tested as follows:—

(a) for identification of the poliomyelitis virus type by a suitable serolog-ical test;

(b) for freedom from bacterial and mycotic contamination by methods approved by the licensing authority;

(c) for freedom from mycoplasmal contamination by tests made on solid and in liquid media that have been shown to be capable of growing mycoplasma;

(d) for freedom from B virus by the inoculation of rabbits or rabbit kidney cell cultures by a method approved by the licensing authority. If the presence of B virus is shown by this test, the manufacturer shall inform the licensing authority and the manufacture of all poliomyelitis vaccine shall be discontinued and shall be resumed only when a thorough investigation has been completed and the precautions necessary to prevent further contamination with B virus have been taken to the satisfaction of the licensing authority;

(e) for freedom from extraneous viruses. The poliomyelitis virus shall be neutralised by specific antisera prepared in animals other than monkeys. Such antisera shall be prepared using antigens grown in a non-simian cell line. The tests shall be made in monkey kidney cell cultures and in such other cell cultures as the licensing authority so requires. The monkey kidney cell cultures shall be prepared from the same species, but not from the same animal as that used for vaccine production.

(4) The samples shall also be tested as follows:—

(a) for freedom from other extraneous viruses by the inoculation of adult mice, new-born mice and guinea-pigs by methods approved by the licensing authority;

(b) for freedom from *Mycobacterium tuberculosis* by methods approved by the licensing authority.

The tests mentioned in this paragraph may if the licensing authority so allows, be carried out instead on samples taken from the bulk virus suspensions.

Preparation and testing of bulk virus suspensions

106.—(1) Bulk virus suspension shall be obtained by the combination of suitable virus suspensions. For the purpose of this regulation a batch of such bulk virus suspension is the quantity present in a bulk container from which final containers are to be filled. Samples of each such batch shall be taken immediately on pooling and before clarification. Between the time of taking and the time when the samples are tested the samples shall be kept under conditions suitable for the preservation of the agents that the tests are designed to detect.

(2) Samples of the bulk virus suspension shall be tested for freedom from B virus by the inoculation of rabbits by a method approved by the licensing authority. If the presence of B virus is shown by this test, the manufacture of all poliomyelitis vaccine shall be discontinued and shall be resumed only when a thorough investigation has been completed and the precautions necessary to prevent further contamination with B virus have been taken to the satisfaction of the licensing authority.

(3) If the contributory virus suspensions have not been tested individually in accordance with regulation 105(4), the samples of the bulk virus suspension shall be so tested.

(4) Bulk virus suspension shall be clarified by a method ensuring the removal of all cells and significant cell debris.

(5) Samples of the clarified bulk virus suspension shall be taken immediately after clarification and shall be kept frozen until tested as follows:—

(*a*) for identification of the poliomyelitis virus type by a suitable serological test;

(*b*) for concentration of live virus by titration by a method approved by the licensing authority;

(*c*) for genetic markers, if the licensing authority so requires, by tests made in parallel with similar tests on the virus seed used in preparing the vaccine, by methods approved by the licensing authority;

(*d*) for neurovirulence in monkeys by tests made in parallel with the virus seed used in preparing the vaccine, by methods approved by the licensing authority;

(*e*) for freedom from toxicity, if the licensing authority so requires, by tests made in both mice and guinea-pigs by methods approved by the licensing authority.

Further processing of bulk virus suspensions

107. Further processing, such as dilution and blending of types to form final vaccine, shall be done under aseptic conditions.

Tests of the final vaccine

108.—(1) Each batch of the final vaccine shall be subjected to the tests described in paragraph (3) of this regulation. The tests shall be carried out on the vaccine in the form in which it is to be issued for use.

(2) For the purposes of this regulation a batch of vaccine is the quantity filled into final containers in one continuous operation.

(3) Samples of each batch shall be tested as follows:—

    (a) for identification of the poliomyelitis virus type or types by suitable serological tests;

    (b) for the concentration of live virus by titration by a method approved by the licensing authority;

    (c) for freedom from bacterial and mycotic contamination by methods approved by the licensing authority;

    (d) for freedom from toxicity by tests made in both mice and guinea-pigs by methods approved by the licensing authority.

PART XXB

SPECIAL PROVISIONS RELATING TO POLIOMYELITIS VACCINE (ORAL) WHEN PREPARED IN HUMAN DIPLOID CELL CULTURES

Cells for vaccine production

109.—(1) Human diploid cell cultures used for the production of poliomyelitis vaccine (oral) shall satisfy the criteria for the acceptability of a passaged human diploid cell population as approved by the licensing authority.

(2) The production of the cell cultures shall be based on a cell seed culture system.

Testing of cell cultures

109A. The human diploid cell cultures used for vaccine production shall be tested for normal characteristics and for freedom from extraneous agents by methods approved by the licensing authority.

Production of virus suspensions

109B.—(1) During the course of virus propagation the cell culture vessels shall be incubated at a range of temperature which shall be approved by the licensing authority and which shall at no time rise above 35 °C.

(2) Virus suspensions shall be harvested not later than 4 days after virus inoculation or at such time as the licensing authority may approve.

Testing of virus suspensions

109C.—(1) Virus suspensions harvested from the cultures derived from a single ampoule of the cell seed shall be kept separately during testing.

(2) Samples of the virus suspensions shall be taken immediately on harvesting and before clarification and shall be subjected to the tests described in paragraph (3) of this regulation. Between the time of harvesting and the time when the samples are tested the samples shall be kept under conditions that will preserve the agents that the tests are designed to detect.

(3) The samples shall be tested as follows:—

    (a) for identification of the poliomyelitis virus type by a suitable serological test;

    (b) for freedom from bacterial and mycotic contamination by methods approved by the licensing authority;

    (c) for freedom from mycoplasmal contamination by tests made on solid and in liquid media that have been shown to be capable of growing mycoplasma;

(d) for freedom from B virus by the inoculation of rabbits or rabbit kidney cell cultures by a method approved by the licensing authority. If the presence of B virus is shown by this test, the manufacturer shall inform the licensing authority and the manufacture of all polio-myelitis vaccine shall be discontinued and shall be resumed only when a thorough investigation has been completed and the precautions necessary to prevent further contamination with B virus have been taken to the satisfaction of the licensing authority;

(e) for freedom from extraneous viruses. The poliomyelitis virus shall be neutralised by specific antisera prepared in animals other than humans or monkeys. Such antisera shall be prepared using antigens grown in human cells obtained from a different anatomical source from the cells used for vaccine production. At least 5 ml of each virus suspension, but not less than a total of 50 ml or 500 doses, whichever is the greater, from all the virus suspensions forming a single final batch of vaccine shall be tested in monkey kidney cell cultures. The cell cultures shall be examined for evidence of degeneration twice weekly for at least 14 days. At seven days, and at the end of the observation period, two per cent of the fluid from each culture bottle shall be sub-cultured into monkey kidney and human amnion cell cultures. These sub-cultures shall be observed for at least 14 days. Human amnion cell cultures may be substituted by any culture system shown to be as sensitive to measles virus as human amnion cell cultures.

(4) The samples shall also be tested as follows:—

(a) for freedom from other extraneous viruses by the inoculation of adult mice, new-born mice and guinea-pigs by methods approved by the licensing authority;

(b) for freedom from *Mycobacterium tuberculosis* by methods approved by the licensing authority.

The tests mentioned in this paragraph may, if the licensing authority so allow, be carried out instead on samples taken from the bulk virus suspensions.

Preparation and testing of bulk virus suspensions

109D.—(1) Suitable virus suspensions from the cell cultures prepared from each ampoule of the cell seed shall be pooled to form a bulk virus suspension, the volume of which shall not be less than 10 litres. Samples of the bulk virus suspension thus obtained shall be taken immediately on pooling and before clarification. Between the time of taking the samples and the time when the samples are tested the samples shall be kept under conditions suitable for the preservation of the agents that the tests are designed to detect.

(2) If the contributory virus suspensions have not been tested individually in accordance with regulation 109C(4) the samples of the bulk virus suspension shall be so tested.

(3) Bulk virus suspension shall be clarified by a method ensuring the removal of all cells and significant cell debris.

(4) Samples of the clarified bulk virus suspension shall be taken immediately after clarification and shall be kept frozen until tested as follows:—

(a) for identification of the poliomyelitis virus type by a suitable serolog-ical test;

(b) for concentration of live virus by titration by a method approved by the licensing authority;

(c) for genetic markers, if the licensing authority so requires, by tests made in parallel with similar tests on the virus seed used in preparing the vaccine, by methods approved by the licensing authority;

(d) for neurovirulence in monkeys by tests made in parallel with the virus seed used in preparing the vaccine, by methods approved by the licensing authority;

(e) for freedom from toxicity, if the licensing authority so require, by tests made in both mice and guinea-pigs by methods approved by the licensing authority.

Further processing of bulk virus suspensions

109E. Further processing, such as dilution and blending of types to form final vaccine, shall be done under aseptic conditions.

Tests of the final vaccine

109F.—(1) Each batch of the final vaccine shall be subjected to the tests described in paragraph (3) of this regulation. The tests shall be carried out on the vaccine in the form in which it is to be issued for use.

(2) For the purposes of this regulation a batch of vaccine is the quantity filled into final containers in one continuous operation.

(3) Samples of each batch shall be tested as follows:—

(a) for identification of the poliomyelitis virus type or types by suitable serological tests;

(b) for the concentration of live virus by titration by a method approved by the licensing authority;

(c) for freedom from bacterial and mycotic contamination by methods approved by the licensing authority;

(d) for freedom from toxicity by tests made in both mice and in guinea-pigs by methods approved by the licensing authority.";

(b) After regulation 172 there shall be inserted the following regulations—

"PART XXX

PROVISIONS RELATING TO RUBELLA VACCINE (LIVE ATTENUATED)

Definition and proper name

173.—(1) Rubella vaccine (live attenuated) is a freeze-dried preparation of a live attenuated rubella virus. The proper name of any such preparation is "rubella vaccine (live attenuated)".

Buildings and staff

174. Rubella vaccine (live attenuated) shall be produced in a separate building or separate parts of a building to which, during production, only persons engaged in its production and testing have access. Procedures which potentially involve the presence of micro-organisms or the use of tissue culture cells other than those cell cultures in which it is proposed to produce the vaccine shall not be carried out in the said separate building or parts of a building. If persons engaged in the production of the vaccine have been working with other infectious agents or with experimental animals, they shall not on the same day enter the areas where the vaccine is produced. The establishment for the production of the vaccine shall be under the complete control and direction of an expert in microbiology approved by the licensing authority.

Preparation and testing of vaccine in final containers

175. Bulk virus suspension shall be distributed into final containers and dried from the frozen state. For the purpose of this regulation a batch of the vaccine in final containers is the total number of the filled final sealed containers prepared by freeze-drying in a single operation. Samples of each such batch shall be tested as follows:—

(*a*) for concentration of live attenuated rubella virus by titration in comparison with a reference preparation of rubella virus kept as a standard preparation at the National Institute for Medical Research (Hampstead Laboratories) London;

(*b*) for freedom from bacterial and mycotic contamination by methods approved by the licensing authority;

(*c*) for freedom from toxicity by tests made in both mice and guinea-pigs by methods approved by the licensing authority.

Information and samples required by the licensing authority

176. Protocols made and samples taken during stages of production and testing of each batch of vaccine shall be submitted to the licensing authority. Information shall be submitted concerning the results of tests made on all cell cultures and virus suspensions intended for the preparation of rubella vaccine (live attenuated) whether or not the cultures or the virus suspensions were used in preparing a finished batch.

Storage by Manufacturer

177. Rubella vaccine (live attenuated) during storage by the manufacturer shall be kept at a temperature not higher than $-20\,^\circ$C.

Labelling

178.—(1) In addition to the particulars required by regulation 6 of these regulations the following particulars shall be borne by the container of rubella vaccine (live attenuated) or of preparations thereof:—

(*a*) a statement that the vaccine shall be reconstituted by using only the reconstituting fluid supplied by the manufacturers;

(*b*) a statement identifying the tissue used for preparing the cell cultures in which the rubella virus was grown;

(*c*) the strain type of the rubella virus included in the vaccine;

(*d*) the virus titre of the rubella virus included in the vaccine;

(*e*) a statement specifying the route of administration of the vaccine;

(*f*) a statement that the vaccine after reconstitution shall be used within the period of time approved by the licensing authority.

(2) the label of the container and the package of the vaccine shall bear the particulars required by regulations 6(1)(*g*) and (*h*) of the general regulations.

PART XXXA

SPECIAL PROVISIONS RELATING TO RUBELLA VACCINE
(LIVE ATTENUATED) WHEN PREPARED IN RABBIT KIDNEY CELL CULTURES

Cells for vaccine production

179.—(1) Rabbit kidney cell cultures used for the production of rubella vaccine (live attenuated) shall be derived from a healthy stock of rabbits free from *Mycobacterium tuberculosis*, myxomatosis, fibromatosis and rabbit pox viruses and from other adventitious pathogenic agents.

(2) If animal serum is added to initiate the cultures then, before virus propagation, the cultures shall be washed free from such serum. No extraneous protein shall be added to the cell cultures during the course of virus propagation.

Strain of rubella virus

180.—(1) The strain of rubella virus used for the production of rubella vaccine (live attenuated) shall be approved by the licensing authority.

(2) Production of the vaccine shall be based on a virus seed system and the final vaccine shall not contain any virus which is more than 5 subcultures from the strain culture on which the original laboratory and clinical tests were made.

(3) The working seed lot of the strain used shall conform to the same standards of purity as are required by these regulations to be applied to the final vaccine and it shall be shown to be free from neurovirulence.

Testing of cell cultures

181.—(1) Ten per cent of each batch of cultures intended for use for the propagation of rubella virus shall be held as uninoculated control cultures and shall be incubated at the same temperature as the inoculated cultures. They shall be observed for the time rubella virus is grown in the production tissue, or for 14 days beyond the time of inoculation of production tissue with rubella virus, whichever is the longer, and shall show no evidence of virus contamination.

(2) At the time of virus harvest from the production cultures the fluids from the control tissue cultures shall be examined for freedom from adventitious agents by inoculating at least two per cent of pooled control tissue culture fluids into each of a human and a simian tissue culture system. At the same time a further two per cent of pooled control tissue culture fluids shall be tested for freedom from adventitious virus agents on rabbit tissue prepared from the same species but not the same animal as that used for the vaccine production. The tests shall be done by methods approved by the licensing authority.

(3) If a multiple harvest production system is used, samples from the control tissue cultures shall be taken about midway between the first and last virus harvests and used for the tests described under paragraph (2) of this regulation.

(4) At the end of the period for which the control tissue is observed the above tests shall be repeated using two per cent of the pooled control tissue culture fluids on each tissue used in testing. Subcultures shall be made from the inoculated tissues at 14 days, and each sub culture observed for a further 14 days.

(5) At the time of virus harvest at least ten per cent of the control tissue cultures shall be examined for haemadsorption viruses using guinea-pig red blood cells. Any remaining control tissue cultures shall be tested for haemadsorption viruses at the end of the observation period.

(6) The tissue cultures for virus propagation are satisfactory only if at least 80 per cent of the remaining control tissue cultures survive the observation period and none of the tests show evidence of virus contamination.

Production of virus suspensions

182. Virus for the preparation of rubella vaccine (live attenuated) produced in primary rabbit kidney cell cultures shall be grown by aseptic methods.

Testing of virus suspensions

183.—(1) Samples of the virus suspensions shall be taken immediately on harvesting and before clarification or the addition of stabiliser and shall be subjected to the tests described in paragraphs (3), (4) and (5) of this regulation. Between the time of harvesting and the time when the samples are tested the samples shall be kept under conditions that will preserve the agents that the tests are designed to detect.

(2) Where multiple harvests have been made they shall be pooled for the purpose of the tests described in paragraphs (3), (4) and (5) of this regulation.

(3) The samples shall be tested as follows:—

    (*a*) for identification of rubella virus by a suitable serological test;

    (*b*) for freedom from bacterial and mycotic contamination by methods approved by the licensing authority;

    (*c*) for freedom from mycoplasmal contamination by tests made on solid and in liquid media that have been shown to be capable of growing mycoplasma.

(4) For the purpose of the tests described in this paragraph the rubella virus in the samples shall be neutralised by specific antiserum prepared in animals other than humans, monkeys or rabbits and the samples shall be tested as follows:—

    (*a*) for freedom from extraneous virus by the inoculation of at least 10 ml onto a suitable monkey kidney tissue culture known to be sensitive to SV40 virus. The culture shall be observed for at least 7 days and at the end of that period a sub culture shall be made from the inoculated tissue and observed for 7 days. A further sub culture shall then be made from this sub culture and observed for 7 days. Additional rubella virus antiserum prepared in animals other than humans, monkeys or rabbits may be added at the time of each sub-culture. At the end of each seven day observation period each sub-culture shall be challenged with a suitable virus to prove the absence of rubella virus;

    (*b*) by repeating the test described under paragraph 4(*a*) of this regulation using a human tissue culture system instead of monkey kidney tissue;

    (*c*) for freedom from other extraneous viruses by the inoculation of at least 5 ml in 0.5 ml quantities into each of the allantoic cavity and yolk sac in separate groups of embryonated eggs; and

    (*d*) by the inoculation of at least 5 ml in 0.1 ml quantities onto the chorioallantoic membrane of embryonated eggs.

(5) The samples shall also be tested as follows:—

    (*a*) for freedom from other extraneous viruses by the inoculation of adult mice, new-born mice, guinea-pigs and rabbits by methods approved by the licensing authority;

    (*b*) for freedom from *Mycobacterium tuberculosis* by methods approved by the licensing authority.

These tests described in this paragraph may, if the licensing authority so allows, be carried out instead on samples taken from the bulk virus suspension.

Preparation and testing of bulk virus suspension

184.—(1) Bulk virus suspension shall be obtained by the combination of suitable virus suspensions. For the purpose of this regulation a batch of such bulk virus suspension is the quantity present in a bulk container from which final containers are to be filled. Samples of each such batch shall be taken immediately on pooling and before clarification or addition of stabiliser. Between the time of taking and the time when the samples are tested the samples shall be kept under conditions suitable for the preservation of the agents that the tests are designed to detect.

(2) If the contributory virus suspensions have not been tested individually in accordance with regulation 183(5) the samples of the bulk virus suspension shall be so tested.

(3) Bulk virus suspension shall be clarified by a method ensuring the removal of all cells and significant cell debris.

(4) Any stabiliser or nutrient added at any stage in the production shall be approved by the licensing authority.

PART XXXB

SPECIAL PROVISIONS RELATING TO RUBELLA VACCINE
(LIVE ATTENUATED) WHEN PREPARED IN HUMAN DIPLOID CELL CULTURES

Cells for vaccine production

185.—(1) Human diploid cell cultures used for the production of rubella vaccine (live attenuated) shall satisfy the criteria for the acceptability of a passaged human diploid cell population as approved by the licensing authority.

(2) The production of the cell cultures shall be based on a cell seed culture system.

Strain of rubella virus

186.—(1) The strain of rubella virus used for the production of rubella vaccine (live attenuated) shall be approved by the licensing authority.

(2) Production of the vaccine shall be based on a virus seed system and the final vaccine shall not contain any virus which is more than 10 subcultures from the strain culture on which the original laboratory and clinical tests were made.

(3) The working seed lot of the strain used shall conform to the same standards of purity as are required by these regulations to be applied to the final vaccine, and it shall be shown to be free from neurovirulence.

Testing of cell cultures

187. The human diploid cell cultures used for vaccine production shall be tested for normal characteristics and for freedom from extraneous agents by methods approved by the licensing authority.

Production of virus suspensions

188.—(1) During the course of virus propagation the cell culture vessels shall be incubated at a range of temperature which shall be approved by the licensing authority.

(2) Virus suspensions shall be harvested not later than 28 days after virus inoculation or at such time as the licensing authority may approve.

Testing of virus suspensions

189.—(1) Virus suspensions harvested from the cultures derived from a single ampoule of the cell seed shall be kept separately during testing.

(2) Samples of the virus suspensions shall be taken immediately on harvesting and before clarification or the addition of stabiliser and shall be subjected to the tests described in paragraphs (4), (5) and (6) of this regulation. Between the time of harvesting and the time when the samples are tested the samples shall be kept under conditions that will preserve the agents that the tests are designed to detect.

(3) Where multiple harvests have been made they shall be pooled for the purpose of the tests described in paragraphs (4), (5) and (6) of this regulation.

(4) The samples shall be tested as follows:—

> (*a*) for identification of rubella virus by a suitable serological test;
>
> (*b*) for freedom from bacterial and mycotic contamination by methods approved by the licensing authority;
>
> (*c*) for freedom from mycoplasmal contamination by tests made on solid and in liquid media that have been shown to be capable of growing mycoplasma.

(5) For the purpose of the tests described in this paragraph the rubella virus in the samples shall be neutralised by specific antiserum prepared in animals other than humans or monkeys and the samples shall be tested as follows:—

> (*a*) for freedom from extraneous virus by the inoculation of at least 10 ml onto a suitable monkey kidney tissue culture known to be sensitive to SV40 virus. The cultures shall be observed for at least 7 days and at the end of that period a subculture shall be made from the inoculated tissue and observed for 7 days. A further subculture shall then be made from this subculture and observed for 7 days. Additional rubella virus antiserum prepared in animals other than humans and monkeys may be added at the time of each subculture. At the end of each 7 day observation period each subculture shall be challenged with a suitable virus to prove the absence of rubella virus;
>
> (*b*) by repeating the test described under paragraph (5)(*a*) of this regulation using a human tissue culture system instead of monkey kidney tissue.

(6) The samples shall also be tested as follows:—

> (*a*) for freedom from other extraneous viruses by the inoculation of adult mice, new-born mice and guinea-pigs by methods approved by the licensing authority;
>
> (*b*) for freedom from *Mycobacterium tuberculosis* by methods approved by the licensing authority.

The tests described in this paragraph may, if the licensing authority so allows, be carried out instead on samples taken from the bulk virus suspension.

Preparation and testing of bulk virus suspension

190.—(1) Suitable virus suspensions from the cell cultures from each ampoule of the cell seed shall be pooled to form a bulk virus suspension, the volume of which shall not be less than 3 litres. Samples of the bulk virus suspension thus obtained shall be taken immediately on pooling and before clarification or the addition of stabiliser. Between the time of taking and the time when the samples are tested the samples shall be kept under conditions suitable for the preservation of the agents that the tests are designed to detect.

(2) If the contributory virus suspensions have not been tested individually in accordance with regulation 189(6) the samples of the bulk virus suspension shall be so tested.

(3) Bulk virus suspensions shall be clarified by a method ensuring the removal of all cells and significant cell debris.

(4) Any stabiliser or nutrient added at any stage in the production shall be approved by the licensing authority.";

(c) In regulation 5 (which relates to tests on guinea-pigs) after the figure "XXIX" there shall be inserted the figures "XXA, XXB, XXXA and XXXB".

These regulations were made by the aforementioned Joint Committee on 22nd January 1971.

Keith Joseph,
Peter Thomas,
Gordon Campbell,
W. K. Fitzsimmons,

L. H. Hayward,   Members of the Joint Committee.
Clerk to the Joint Committee.

EXPLANATORY NOTE

(This Note is not part of the Regulations.)

These Regulations amend the provisions of the Therapeutic Substances (Manufacture of Vaccines, Toxins and Antigens) Regulations 1963 to 1967 by replacing Part XX (which made provisions for Poliomyelitis Vaccine (Oral)) by new special provisions and by extending the regulations to make special provisions for Rubella Vaccine (Live Attenuated).

STATUTORY INSTRUMENTS

1971 No. 124 (S.10)

EDUCATION, SCOTLAND

The Students' Allowances (Scotland) Regulations 1971

Made - - - -	18*th January* 1971
Laid before Parliament	29*th January* 1971
Coming into Operation	1*st February* 1971

In exercise of the powers conferred on me by paragraph (*f*) of section 75 of the Education (Scotland) Act 1962(**a**) as substituted by section 12(1) of the Education (Scotland) Act 1969(**b**) ; and by section 76(1) of said Act of 1962 and of all other powers enabling me in that behalf, I hereby make the following regulations : —

Citation and commencement

1. These regulations may be cited as the Students' Allowances (Scotland) Regulations 1971 and shall come into operation on 1st February 1971.

Interpretation

2.—(1) The Interpretation Act 1889(**c**) shall apply for the interpretation of these regulations as it applies for the interpretation of an Act of Parliament.

(2) In these regulations, unless the context otherwise requires, " allowance " means a scholarship, bursary or other allowance paid or to be paid under these regulations or the regulations revoked thereby.

Revocation

3.—(1) The Students' Allowances (Scotland) Regulations 1962(**d**) are hereby revoked.

(2) Section 38 of the Interpretation Act 1889 shall apply as if these regulations were an Act of Parliament and as if the regulations revoked by these regulations were an Act of Parliament repealed by an Act of Parliament.

Allowances

4.—(1) The amount of an allowance shall be determined by the Secretary of State and may include sums in respect of—

(*a*) tuition and other fees payable in respect of the holder of the allowance ;

(*b*) travelling expenses necessarily incurred or to be incurred by the holder in attending the course of study in respect of which the allowance is awarded ;

(*c*) the maintenance of the holder and of any persons dependent on him during periods of whole-time study and during vacations ;

(*d*) other expenses incurred or to be incurred by the holder in taking advantage of educational facilities.

(2) In determining the amount of an allowance, the Secretary of State shall take account of the sums, if any, which, in accordance with principles determined by him from time to time, the holder and his parents can reasonably be expected to contribute towards the holder's expenses.

(a) 1962 c. 47.   (b) 1969 c. 49.   (c) 1889 c. 63.   (d) S.I. 1962/2086 (1962 III, p. 2505).

(3) The amount of an allowance may be revised at any time if the Secretary of State thinks fit having regard to—

(a) the failure of the holder to comply with the conditions of tenure, or

(b) all the circumstances of the holder or his parents or both as the case may be,

and if the Secretary of State is satisfied that there has been an overpayment of an allowance, he may require the holder or his successors to repay the amount by which the allowance has been overpaid or he may take such other action as he may consider necessary to recover the amount by which the allowance has been overpaid or so much thereof as he may think fit.

Conditions of grant and tenure

5.—(1) Every allowance shall be held subject to the following conditions—

(a) the holder shall attend regularly the course of study in respect of which the allowance is awarded ;

(b) the Secretary of State shall be satisfied as to the conduct and progress of the holder ; and

(c) the holder shall provide the Secretary of State with such information and such documents as he may from time to time require to enable him to exercise his functions under these Regulations.

If the holder does not comply with these conditions or if the Secretary of State is not satisfied as to the conduct or progress of the holder or if the holder receives from any other source any sum which in the opinion of the Secretary of State makes it unnecessary for him to be assisted by means of an allowance, the Secretary of State may suspend payment of the allowance or terminate the allowance.

(2) It shall be a condition of the grant of an allowance that the applicant gives a written undertaking to repay the allowance or so much thereof as the Secretary of State may on demand require to be repaid if as a result of a revision of the amount of an allowance the Secretary of State is satisfied that an overpayment has been made.

(3) If the applicant is a minor paragraph (2) above shall have effect, with the necessary modifications, as if the reference to the applicant were a reference to the applicant and his parent.

Method of payment

6.—(1) The allowance may be paid to the holder or to another person for his behoof, or in part to the holder and in part to the said other person, and any sum in respect of fees payable to an educational institution which is included in the amount of the allowance may be paid on behalf of the holder to the institution.

(2) The allowance may be paid in a single payment or by instalments as the Secretary of State thinks fit: but no payment shall be made before the holder has been accepted for admission to the course of study in respect of which the allowance is awarded.

Gordon Campbell,
One of Her Majesty's Principal
Secretaries of State.

St. Andrew's House,
Edinburgh.
18th January 1971.

EXPLANATORY NOTE

(This Note is not part of the Regulations.)

These Regulations revoke and re-enact the Students' Allowances (Scotland) Regulations 1962 with minor alterations. They also prescribe further conditions of grant requiring students to undertake to repay allowances which have been overpaid.

STATUTORY INSTRUMENTS

1971 No. 126 (S. 11)

COURT OF SESSION, SCOTLAND

SHERIFF COURT, SCOTLAND

Act of Sederunt (Citation of Witnesses) 1971

Made - - -	*20th January* 1971
Coming into Operation	*21st January* 1971

The Lords of Council and Session, under and by virtue of the powers conferred upon them by section 16 and section 34 of the Administration of Justice (Scotland) Act 1933(a) and of the Act of the Parliaments of Scotland at Edinburgh on 14th March 1540 entitled "Ratificationne of the Institutionne of the "college of iustice"(b) and of all other powers competent to them in that behalf, do hereby enact and declare as follows:—

1. For so long only as there shall continue to be no postal delivery service provided by the Post Office, there shall, for the purpose of citing any witnesses in any Court of civil jurisdiction in Scotland where postal citation is competent, be deemed to be sufficient compliance with any statutory requirement for the citation of such witness by post if the solicitor to a party or any person authorised by him shall deliver the citation form to the witness; and a certificate recording such delivery signed by such solicitor or person authorised as aforesaid, who shall be designed in the certificate, shall be *prima facie* evidence of such citation.

2. This Act of Sederunt may be cited as the Act of Sederunt (Citation of Witnesses) 1971 and shall come into operation on 21st January 1971.

And the Lords appoint this Act of Sederunt to be inserted in the Books of Sederunt.

J. L. Clyde,

Edinburgh,
20th January 1971.   I.P.D.

EXPLANATORY NOTE

(*This Note is not part of the Act of Sederunt.*)

This Act of Sederunt, which applies to every Court of civil jurisdiction in Scotland, permits delivery of a witness citation by a solicitor or a person authorised by him in place of postal citation. The Act of Sederunt will remain in force only during the present Post Office strike.

(a) 1933 c.41.   (b) Act 12 ms Edition 1540, cap.93.

STATUTORY INSTRUMENTS

1971 No. 127 (S.12)

COURT OF SESSION, SCOTLAND

SHERIFF COURT, SCOTLAND

Act of Sederunt (Citation of Jurors) 1971

Made - - -		*22nd January* 1971
Coming into Operation		*25th January* 1971

The Lords of Council and Session, under and by virtue of the powers conferred upon them by section 16 and section 34 of the Administration of Justice (Scotland) Act 1933(a) and of all other powers competent to them in that behalf, do hereby enact and declare as follows :—

1. For so long only as there shall continue to be no postal delivery service provided by the Post Office,

(1) there shall, for the purpose of citing any juror for the trial of a civil cause in the Court of Session or in the Sheriff Court, be deemed to be sufficient compliance with the statutory requirements for the transmission of a citation to such juror by post if the sheriff clerk or his depute or any person authorised by the sheriff clerk or his depute shall deliver the citation to the juror or shall leave it at his residence ; and a certificate recording that the citation was so delivered or left, signed by the sheriff clerk or his depute or by such person authorised as aforesaid, shall have the like force and effect as a certificate in terms of section 47 of the Court of Session (Scotland) Act 1868(b) ;

(2) notwithstanding the provisions of section 7 of the Juries (Scotland) Act 1825(c) and of any other enactment or rule of law requiring the citation of jurors resident furth of Edinburgh for the trial of a cause in the Court of Session each of the thirty-six jurors to be cited to attend any jury trial in the Court of Session may be resident in Edinburgh.

2. This Act of Sederunt may be cited as the Act of Sederunt (Citation of Jurors) 1971 and shall come into operation on 25th January 1971.

And the Lords appoint this Act of Sederunt to be inserted in the Books of Sederunt.

Edinburgh,

22nd January 1971.

J. L. Clyde,
I.P.D.

(a) 1933 c. 41.　　　　　　　　　(b) 1868 c. 100.
(c) 1825 c. 22.

EXPLANATORY NOTE

(This Note is not part of the Act of Sederunt.)

This Act of Sederunt permits delivery of the citation of a juror for the trial of a civil cause, by the sheriff clerk or his depute or by a person authorised by one of them, in place of postal citation ; and permits the citation of a jury for the Court of Session composed entirely of residents of Edinburgh. The Act of Sederunt will remain in force only during the present Post Office strike.

STATUTORY INSTRUMENTS

1971 No. 128 (S.13)

NEW TOWNS

The New Towns Compulsory Purchase (Contemporaneous Procedure) (Scotland) Regulations 1971

Made - - -	*19th January* 1971	
Laid before Parliament	*29th January* 1971	
Coming into Operation	*1st February* 1971	

In exercise of the powers conferred upon me by paragraph 6 of Schedule 3 to the New Towns (Scotland) Act 1968(a) (hereinafter referred to as "the Act"), and of all other powers enabling me in that behalf, I hereby make the following regulations :—

1.—(1) These regulations may be cited as the New Towns Compulsory Purchase (Contemporaneous Procedure) (Scotland) Regulations 1971 and shall come into operation on 1st February 1971.

(2) The Interpretation Act 1889(b), shall apply for the interpretation of these regulations as it applies for the interpretation of an Act of Parliament.

(3) The New Towns Compulsory Purchase (Contemporaneous Procedure) (Scotland) Regulations 1947(c) are hereby revoked.

2. Where the Secretary of State has published in accordance with Schedule 1 to the Act a draft of an order which he proposes to make under section 1 of the Act designating an area as the site of a new town (hereinafter called "the designation order") and the designation order has not been made, a development corporation (acting under an order made in terms of section 5(1) of the Act) or a local highway authority may, pending the making of the designation order, take such proceedings under paragraphs 1, 2 and 4 of Schedule 3 to the Act, as are required to be taken by that authority in respect of the making of a Compulsory Purchase Order in respect of land in the said area.

3. Any proceedings taken by a development corporation or a local highway authority by virtue of the powers of regulation 2 of these regulations shall, for the purposes of Part I and Part III of Schedule 3 to the Act, be deemed to be proceedings taken after the date on which the Secretary of State makes the designation order.

4. Where, in respect of any new town (in this regulation referred to as "the new town") the Secretary of State has published in accordance with Schedule 1 to the Act a draft of an order which he proposes to make under sections 1 and 46 of the Act varying the designation order which designated the site of the new town so as to include therein an additional area of land (in this regulation referred to as "the additional area") and the said varying order has not yet been made, a development corporation or a local highway authority may, pending the making of the varying order, take such proceedings under para-

---

(a) 1968 c. 16.   (b) 1889 c. 63.
(c) S. R. & O. 1947/2243 (Rev. XXII p. 978: 1947 I, p. 2124).

graphs 1, 2 and 4 of Schedule 3 to the Act, as are required to be taken in respect of the making of a Compulsory Purchase Order in respect of land in the additional area.

5. Any proceedings taken by a development corporation or a local highway authority by virtue of the powers in regulation 4 of these regulations shall, for the purposes of Part I and Part III of Schedule 3 to the Act, be deemed to be proceedings taken after the date on which the Secretary of State makes the relevant varying order.

Gordon Campbell,
One of Her Majesty's Principal
Secretaries of State.

St. Andrew's House,
Edinburgh.
19th January 1971.

EXPLANATORY NOTE
(This Note is not part of the Regulations.)

These Regulations take account of the passing of the New Towns (Scotland) Act 1968 and supersede the New Towns Compulsory Purchase (Contemporaneous Procedure) (Scotland) Regulations 1947.

Regulations 2 and 3 provide that certain preliminary steps in the procedure for the compulsory purchase of land within the designated area of a new town may be taken by a development corporation or a local highway authority before the area has been designated formally but after the draft of such an order has been published, in accordance with the provisions of the New Towns (Scotland) Act 1968.

Regulations 4 and 5 provide that certain preliminary steps in the procedure for the compulsory purchase of land in an area proposed to be added to the site of a new town may be taken by a development corporation or a local highway authority, before the area has actually been added by an order under sections 1 and 46 of the New Towns (Scotland) Act 1968, but after the draft of such an order has been published in accordance with the provisions of the New Towns (Scotland) Act 1968.

STATUTORY INSTRUMENTS

1971 No. 129

REGISTRATION OF BIRTHS, DEATHS, MARRIAGES, ETC.

ENGLAND AND WALES

The Registration of Marriages (Welsh Language) Regulations 1971

Made - - - -	*25th January* 1971
Coming into Operation	1*st April* 1971

The Registrar General in exercise of the powers conferred on him by sections 27, 31, 32, 35, 55 and 74 of the Marriage Act 1949(a), section 20 of the Registration Service Act 1953(b), as extended by sections 2(2) and 3 of the Welsh Language Act 1967(c), and of all other powers enabling him in that behalf, with the approval of the Secretary of State for Wales, hereby makes the following regulations:—

Title and commencement

1. These regulations may be cited as the Registration of Marriages (Welsh Language) Regulations 1971 and shall come into operation on 1st April 1971.

Interpretation

2.—(1) The Interpretation Act 1889(d) shall apply to the interpretation of these regulations as it applies to the interpretation of an Act of Parliament.

(2) In these regulations, unless the context otherwise requires—"the principal regulations" means the Registration of Births, Deaths and Marriages Regulations 1968(e), as amended(f), and any expression in these regulations which is also used in the principal regulations has the same meaning as in those regulations.

Prescribed forms

3. In relation to a notice of marriage attested in Wales or Monmouthshire, regulations 63 and 64 of the principal regulations shall have effect as if they referred, instead of to forms 15 to 19 in schedule 1 to those regulations, to forms 1 to 5 respectively in schedule 1 to these regulations.

4. In relation to a certificate for marriage or certificate and licence for marriage issued in Wales or Monmouthshire, regulations 65 and 66 of the principal regulations shall have effect as if they referred, instead of to forms 20 to 22 in schedule 1 to those regulations, to forms 6 to 8 respectively in schedule 1 to these regulations.

(a) 1949 c. 76.　　　　　　　　　　(b) 1953 c. 37.
(c) 1967 c. 66.　　　　　　　　　　(d) 1889 c. 63.
(e) S.I. 1968/2049 (1968 III, p. 5522).　(f) The amending regulations are not
　relevant to the subject matter of these regulations.

5. In relation to any marriage solemnized in Wales or Monmouthshire, regulations 67 to 69 of the principal regulations shall have effect as if they referred, instead of to form 23 in schedule 1 to those regulations, to form 9 in schedule 1 to these regulations.

Completion of prescribed forms

6. Forms 1 to 7 and form 9 in schedule 1 to these regulations shall be completed in English and may be completed in Welsh as well as English if—

(a) in the case of forms 1 to 7 the party giving notice of marriage provides the required particulars in both languages and the officer by whom the notice is attested can understand and write Welsh;

(b) in the case of form 9 the parties to the marriage provide the required particulars in both languages and the person who registers the marriage can understand and write Welsh.

7. Where a form of words set out in column (1) of schedule 2 to these regulations is used in completing a prescribed form in English, the form of words set out opposite thereto in column (2) shall be used in any Welsh version.

Correction of errors

8. Where an error or omission is corrected in an entry in a marriage register book kept in Wales or Monmouthshire, the correction shall be made in English if the error or omission occurs in particulars entered in English and in Welsh if the error or omission occurs in particulars entered in Welsh.

Discrepancies

9. In case of any discrepancy between an English text and a Welsh text permitted by these regulations, the English text shall prevail.

Certified copies

10. When a certified copy of an entry either in a marriage register book or in a certified copy of such a book is made on a form containing words authorised by these regulations but differing in no other respect from that on which the original entry was made, it may nevertheless be treated as a true copy of that entry.

SCHEDULE 1

PRESCRIBED FORMS

CONTENTS

Form	Description	Statutory purpose	
1	Notice of marriage without licence	Marriage Act 1949,	Section 27(1)
2	Notice of marriage without licence	,,	,,
3	Notice of marriage with licence	,,	Section 27(2)
4	Notice of marriage with licence	,,	,,
5	Endorsement on notice of marriage	,,	Section 35(1)
6	Certificate for marriage	,,	Section 31
7	Certificate and licence for marriage	,,	Section 32
8	Form of instructions	,,	Sections 31 & 32
9	Form of marriage entry	,,	Section 55(1)

Notice of marriage without licence

FORM I

Marriage Act 1949, S.27(1)

PARTICULARS RELATING TO THE PARTIES TO BE MARRIED — MANYLION YNGLŶN Â'R PERSONAU A BRIODIR

Name and surname	Age	Marital status	Occupation	Place of residence	Period of residence	Church or other building in which the marriage is to be solemnized	District and county of residence
Enw a chyfenw	Oed	Cyflwr priodasol	Gwaith	Preswylfa	Cyfnod preswylio	Eglwys neu adeilad arall lle gweinyddir y briodas	Dosbarth a sir y breswylfa

To the Superintendent Registrar of the district of ....in the county..............
I'r Cofrestrydd Arolygol dosbarth {   yn sir ....

1. I the above-named } ....give you notice that I and the other person named above intend to be married by
   Yr wyf fi   a enwir uchod, yn eich hysbysu fy mod i a'r person arall a enwir uchod yn
certificate without licence within 3 months from the date of entry of this notice.
bwriadu priodi drwy dystysgrif heb drwydded o fewn 3 mis o ddyddiad cofnodi'r hysbysiad hwn.

2. I solemnly declare that I believe there is no impediment of kindred or alliance or other lawful hindrance to the marriage, and that I
and the other person named above have for the period of 7 days immediately preceding the giving of this notice had our usual places of residence within the above-named districts.

Datganaf yn ddifrifol fy mod i'n credu nad oes rhwystr o ran ach neu uniad neu unrhyw dramgwydd cyfreithiol arall i'r briodas ac i'm
preswylfa arferol i, a phreswylfa arferol y person arall a enwir uchod fod am gyfnod o 7 niwrnod yn union cyn cyflwyno'r hysbysiad hwn
o fewn y dosbarthau a enwir uchod.

3. And I further declare that I am not under the age of 18 years or, if under that age, am a widower or widow, and that the other person named above is not under the age of 18 years, or, if under that age, is a widower or widow.

A datganaf ymhellach nad wyf o dan 18 oed neu, os wyf o dan yr oed hwnnw fy mod yn ŵr gweddw neu'n wraig weddw ac nad yw'r person arall a enwyd uchod o dan 18 oed, neu, os yw o dan yr oed hwnnw ei fod yn ŵr gweddw neu'n wraig weddw.

4. I declare that to the best of my knowledge and belief the declarations which I have made above and the particulars relating to the persons to be married are true. I understand that if any of the declarations are false I MAY BE LIABLE TO PROSECUTION UNDER THE PERJURY ACT 1911.

Datganaf hyd y gwn ac y credaf fod y datganiadau a wnaed gennyf uchod a'r manylion ynglŷn â'r personau sydd i'w priodi yn gywir. Deallaf os oes unrhyw rai o'r datganiadau yn ffug FE ALL Y BYDDAF YN AGORED I ERLYNIAD O DAN PERJURY ACT 1911.

5. I also understand that if, in fact, there is an impediment of kindred or alliance or other lawful hindrance to the intended marriage the marriage may be invalid or void and the contracting of the marriage may render one or both of the parties GUILTY OF A CRIME AND LIABLE TO THE PENALTIES OF BIGAMY OR SUCH OTHER CRIME AS MAY HAVE BEEN COMMITTED.

Deallaf hefyd os oes, mewn gwirionedd, rwystr o ran ach neu uniad neu unrhyw dramgwydd cyfreithiol arall i'r briodas a arfaethir fe all y bydd y briodas yn ddi-rym ac y gall cyfamodi'r briodas wneud un neu'r ddau YN EUOG O DROSEDD AC YN AGORED I GOSBAU UN SY'N BRIOD Â RHAGOR NAG UN PERSON NEU GOSBAU UNRHYW DROSEDD ARALL Y GELLID BOD WEDI EI GYFLAWNI.

(Signed)   Date
(Llofnod)   Dyddiad

In the presence of   { (Signature of registration officer)
Ym mhresenoldeb   { (Llofnod y swyddog cofrestru)

Official designation
Disgrifiad swyddogol

Registration district of
Dosbarth cofrestru

Place of residence
Preswylfa

FORM 2

Marriage Act 1949, S.27(1)

Notice of marriage without licence

PARTICULARS RELATING TO THE PERSONS TO BE MARRIED

MANYLION YNGLŶN Â'R PERSONAU A BRIODIR

Name and surname Enw a chyfenw	Age Oed	Marital status Cyflwr priodasol	Occupation Gwaith	Place of residence Preswylfa	Period of residence Cyfnod preswylio	Church or other building in which the marriage is to be solemnized Eglwys neu adeilad arall lle gweinyddir y briodas	District and county of residence Dosbarth a sir y breswylfa

To the Superintendent Registrar of the district of .... in the county........................
I'r Cofrestrydd Arolygol dosbarth   yn sir ....

1. I the above-named }..give you notice that I and the other person named above intend to be
Yr wyf fi   a enwir uchod, yn eich hysbysu fy mod i a'r person arall a enwir uchod yn
married by certificate without licence within 3 months from the date of entry of this notice.
bwriadu priodi drwy dystysgrif heb drwydded o fewn 3 mis o ddyddiad cofnodi'r hysbysiad hwn.

2. I solemnly declare that I believe there is no impediment of kindred or alliance or other lawful hindrance to the said marriage, and that I and the other person named above have for the period of 7 days immediately preceding the giving of this notice, had our usual places of residence within the districts named above.

Datganaf yn ddifrifol fy mod i'n credu nad oes rhwystr o ran ach neu uniad neu unrhyw dramgwydd cyfreithiol arall i'r briodas a enwyd, ac i'm preswylfa arferol i a phreswylfa arferol y person arall a enwir uchod fod am gyfnod o 7 niwrnod yn union cyn cyflwyno'r hysbysiad hwn o fewn y dosbarthau a enwir uchod.

3. And I further declare that in respect of myself—   and in respect of the said‡ }........................
A datganaf ymhellach amdanaf fy hun—   ac am yr un a enwyd

*(i) the consent of
i mi gael caniatâd†
whose consent only is required by law has been obtained;
sef yr unig berson y mae'n ofynnol yn ôl y gyfraith i mi gael ei ganiatâd;

(ii) the necessity of obtaining the consent of†
i'r angenrheidrwydd am ganiatâd
has been dispensed with as provided by law;
gael ei ddileu yn ôl y gyfraith;

(iii) there is no person whose consent to my marriage is required by law;
nad oes unrhyw berson y mae'n ofynnol i mi yn ôl y gyfraith gael ei ganiatâd i briodi;

(iv) I am over the age of 18 years or if under that age am a widow/widower;
fy mod dros 18 oed neu os wyf o dan yr oed hwnnw fy mod yn wraig weddw/ŵr gweddw;

*(i) the consent of
iddo/iddi gael caniatâd†
whose consent only is required by law has been obtained;
sef yr unig berson y mae'n ofynnol yn ôl y gyfraith iddo/iddi gael ei ganiatâd;

(ii) the necessity of obtaining the consent of†
i'r angenrheidrwydd am ganiatâd
has been dispensed with as provided by law;
gael ei ddileu yn ôl y gyfraith;

(iii) there is no person whose consent to his/her marriage is required by law;
nad oes unrhyw berson y mae'n ofynnol iddo/iddi yn ôl y gyfraith gael ei ganiatâd i briodi;

(iv) he/she is over the age of 18 years or if under that age is a widow/widower;
ei fod ef/hi dros 18 oed neu os yw o dan yr oed hwnnw ei fod/ei bod yn wraig weddw/ŵr gweddw;

4. I declare that to the best of my knowledge and belief the declarations which I have made above and the particulars relating to the persons to be married are true. I understand that if any of the declarations are false I MAY BE LIABLE TO PROSECUTION UNDER THE PERJURY ACT 1911.

Datganaf fyd y gwn ac y credaf fod y datganiadau a wnaed gennyf uchod a'r manylion ynglŷn â'r personau sydd i'w priodi yn gywir. Deallaf os oes unrhyw rai o'r datganiadau yn ffug FE ALL Y BYDDAF YN AGORED I ERLYNIAD O DAN PERJURY ACT 1911.

5. I also understand that if, in fact, there is an impediment of kindred or alliance or other lawful hindrance to the intended marriage the marriage may be invalid or void and the contracting of the marriage may render one or both of the parties GUILTY OF A CRIME AND LIABLE TO THE PENALTIES OF BIGAMY OR SUCH OTHER CRIME AS MAY HAVE BEEN COMMITTED.

Deallaf hefyd os oes, mewn gwirionedd, rwystr o ran ach neu uniad neu unrhyw dramgwydd cyfreithiol arall i'r briodas a arfaethir fe ally bydd y briodas yn ddi-rym ac y gall cyfamodi'r briodas wneud un neu'r ddau YN EUOG O DROSEDD AC YN AGORED I GOSBAU UN SY'N BRIOD Â RHAGOR NAG UN PERSON NEU GOSBAU UNRHYW DROSEDD ARALL Y GELLID BOD WEDI EI GYFLAWNI.

(Signed)   Date
(Llofnod)   Dyddiad

In the presence of   (Signature of registration officer)
Ym mhresenoldeb   (Llofnod y swyddog cofrestru)

Official designation   Place of residence
Disgrifiad swyddogol   Preswylfa

Registration district of
Dosbarth cofrestru

*Delete the alternatives which do not apply, if none applies (e.g. the........Court has consented to the marriage) insert the appropriate declaration as to consent in the space provided.
Dilëer y rhai anghymwys, os nad oes un yn gymwys (e.e. mae Llys .... wedi rhoi caniatâd i'r briodas) rhowch y datganiad priodol am y caniatâd yn y gofod a geir i hynny.

†Insert the name(s) of the person(s) whose consent is/are required.
Rhowch enw(au)'r person(au) y mae'n ofynnol cael ei(eu) g/caniatâd.

‡Insert the name of the other party.
Rhowch enw'r parti arall.

FORM 3

Notice of marriage with licence

Marriage Act 1949, S.27(2)

PARTICULARS RELATING TO THE PARTIES TO BE MARRIED

MANYLION YNGLŶN Â'R PERSONAU A BRIODIR

Name and surname	Age	Marital status	Occupation	Place of residence	Period of residence	Church or other building in which the marriage is to be solemnized	District and county of residence
Enw a chyfenw	Oed	Cyflwr priodasol	Gwaith	Preswylfa	Cyfnod preswylio	Eglwys neu adeilad arall lle gweinyddir y briodas	Dosbarth a sir y breswylfa

To the Superintendent Registrar of the district of
I'r Cofrestrydd Arolygol dosbarth

1. I the above-named } ....give you notice that I and the other person named above intend to be
Yr wyf fi } .... a enwir uchod, yn eich hysbysu fy mod i a'r person arall a enwir uchod
married by certificate and licence within 3 months from the date of entry of this notice.
yn bwriadu priodi drwy dystysgrif a thrwydded o fewn 3 mis o ddyddiad cofnodi'r hysbysiad hwn.

2. I solemnly declare that I believe there is no impediment of kindred or alliance or other lawful hindrance to the said marriage and that
Datganaf yn ddifrifol fy mod i'n credu nad oes rhwystr o ran ach neu uniad neu unrhyw dramgwydd cyfreithiol arall i'r briodas, ac *i'm
*I have/the other person named above has for the period of 15 days immediately preceding the giving of this notice had*my/his/her usual place
preswylfa arferol i/i breswylfa arferol y person arall a enwir uchod fod am gyfnod o 15 niwrnod yn union cyn cyflwyno'r hysbysiad hwn o fewn
of residence within the above-mentioned district of } ....a enwir uchod
dosbarth

3. And I further declare that I am not under the age of 18 years or, if under that age, am a widower or widow, and that the other person
named above is not under the age of 18 years, or, if under that age, is a widower or widow.

..................................in the county..................
.................yn sir ....

A datganaf ymhellach nad wyf o dan 18 oed neu, os wyf o dan yr oed hwnnw fy mod yn ŵr gweddw neu'n wraig weddw ac nad yw'r person arall a enwyd uchod o dan 18 oed, neu, os yw o dan yr oed hwnnw ei fod yn ŵr gweddw neu'n wraig weddw.

4. I declare that to the best of my knowledge and belief the declarations which I have made above and the particulars relating to the persons to be married are true. I understand that if any of the declarations are false I MAY BE LIABLE TO PROSECUTION UNDER THE PERJURY ACT 1911.

Datganaf hyd y gwn ac y credaf fod y datganiadau a wnaed gennyf uchod a'r manylion ynglŷn â'r personau sydd i'w priodi yn gywir. Deallaf os oes unrhyw rai o'r datganiadau yn ffug FE ALL Y BYDDAF YN AGORED I ERLYNIAD O DAN PERJURY ACT 1911.

5. I also understand that if, in fact, there is an impediment of kindred or alliance or other lawful hindrance to the intended marriage the marriage may be invalid or void and the contracting of the marriage may render one or both of the parties GUILTY OF A CRIME AND LIABLE TO THE PENALTIES OF BIGAMY OR SUCH OTHER CRIME AS MAY HAVE BEEN COMMITTED.

Deallaf hefyd os oes, mewn gwirionedd, rwystr o ran ach neu uniad neu unrhyw dramgwydd cyfreithiol arall i'r briodas a arfaethir fe all y bydd y briodas yn ddi-rym ac y gall cyfamodi'r briodas wneud un neu'r ddau YN EUOG O DROSEDD AC YN AGORED I GOSBAU UN SY'N BRIOD Â RHAGOR NAG UN PERSON NEU GOSBAU UNRHYW DROSEDD ARALL Y GELLID BOD WEDI EI GYFLAWNI.

*Delete the alternatives which do not apply.
Dilëer y rhai anghymwys.

(Signed)
(Llofnod) } .... Date .... Dyddiad }

In the presence of } .... { (Signature of registration officer)
Ym mhresenoldeb } { (Llofnod y swyddog cofrestru)

Official designation }
Disgrifiad swyddogol }

Registration district of } ....
Dosbarth cofrestru }

Place of residence } ....
Preswylfa }

FORM 4

Marriage Act 1949, S.27(2)

Notice of marriage with licence

PARTICULARS RELATING TO THE PERSONS TO BE MARRIED

MANYLION YNGLŶN Â'R PERSONAU A BRIODIR

Name and surname Enw a chyfenw	Age Oed	Marital status Cyflwr priodasol	Occupation Gwaith	Place of residence Preswylfa	Period of residence Cyfnod preswylio	Church or other building in which the marriage is to be solemnized Eglwys neu adeilad arall lle gweinyddir y briodas	District and county of residence Dosbarth a sir y breswylfa

To the Superintendent Registrar of the district of }...........................in the county..................
I'r Cofrestrydd Arolygol dosbarth   yn sir

1. I the above-named }...................give you notice that I and the other person named above intend to be married by
   Yr wyf fi   a enwir uchod, yn eich hysbysu fy mod i a'r person arall a enwir uchod yn
certificate and licence within 3 months from the date of entry of this notice,
bwriadu priodi drwy dystysgrif a thrwydded o fewn 3 mis o ddyddiad cofnodi'r hysbysiad hwn.

2. I solemnly declare that I believe there is no impediment of kindred or alliance or other lawful hindrance to the said marriage, and that
   Datganaf yn ddifrifol fy mod i'n credu nad oes rhwystr o ran ach neu uniad neu unrhyw dramgwydd cyfreithiol arall i'r briodas a enwyd,
*I have/the other person named above has, for the period of 15 days immediately preceding the giving of this notice, had *my/his/her usual
ac *i'm preswylfa arferol i/i breswylfa arferol y person arall a enwir uchod fod am gyfnod o 15 niwrnod yn union cyn cyflwyno'r hysbysiad
place of residence within the above-mentioned district of }..................................a enwir uchod
hwn o fewn dosbarth

3. And I further declare that in respect of myself—   and in respect of the said‡ }.................
   A datganaf ymhellach amdanaf fy hun—   ac am yr un a enwyd

*(i) the consent of† ⎱
i mi gael caniatâd† ⎰
whose consent only is required by law has been obtained;
sef yr unig berson y mae'n ofynnol yn ôl y gyfraith i mi gael ei ganiatâd;

(ii) the necessity of obtaining the consent of† ⎱
i'r angenrheidrwydd am ganiatâd ⎰
has been dispensed with as provided by law;
gael ei ddileu yn ôl y gyfraith;

(iii) there is no person whose consent to my marriage is required by law;
nad oes unrhyw berson y mae'n ofynnol i mi yn ôl y gyfraith gael ei ganiatâd i briodi;

(iv) I am over the age of 18 years or if under that age am a widow/widower;
fy mod dros 18 oed neu os wyf o dan yr oed hwnnw fy mod yn wraig weddw/ŵr gweddw;

*(i) the consent of† ⎱
iddo/iddi gael caniatâd† ⎰
whose consent only is required by law has been obtained;
sef yr unig berson y mae'n ofynnol yn ôl y gyfraith iddo/iddi gael ei ganiatâd;

(ii) the necessity of obtaining the consent of† ⎱
i'r angenrheidrwydd am ganiatâd ⎰
has been dispensed with as provided by law;
gael ei ddileu yn ôl y gyfraith;

(iii) there is no person whose consent to his/her marriage is required by law;
nad oes unrhyw berson y mae'n ofynnol iddo/iddi yn ôl y gyfraith gael ei ganiatâd i briodi;

(iv) he/she is over the age of 18 years or if under that age is a widow/widower;
ei fod ef/hi dros 18 oed neu os yw o dan yr oed hwnnw ei fod/ei bod yn wraig weddw/ŵr gweddw;

4. I declare that to the best of my knowledge and belief the declarations which I have made above and the particulars relating to the persons to be married are true. I understand that if any of the declarations are false I MAY BE LIABLE TO PROSECUTION UNDER THE PERJURY ACT 1911.

Datganaf hyd y gwn ac y credaf fod y datganiadau a wnaed gennyf uchod a'r manylion ynglŷn â'r personau sydd i'w priodi yn gywir. Deallaf os oes unrhyw rai o'r datganiadau yn ffug FE ALL Y BYDDAF YN AGORED I ERLYNIAD O DAN PERJURY ACT 1911.

5. I also understand that if, in fact, there is an impediment of kindred or alliance or other lawful hindrance to the intended marriage the marriage may be invalid or void and the contracting of the marriage may render one or both of the parties GUILTY OF A CRIME AND LIABLE TO THE PENALTIES OF BIGAMY OR SUCH OTHER CRIME AS MAY HAVE BEEN COMMITTED.

Deallaf hefyd os oes, mewn gwirionedd, rwystr o ran ach neu uniad neu unrhyw dramgwydd cyfreithiol arall i'r briodas a arfaethir fe all y bydd y briodas yn ddi-rym ac y gall cyfamodi'r briodas wneud i neu'r ddau YN EUOG O DROSEDD AC YN AGORED I GOSBAU UN SY'N BRIOD Â RHAGOR NAG UN PERSON NEU GOSBAU UNRHYW DROSEDD ARALL Y GELLID BOD WEDI EI GYFLAWNI.

*Delete the alternatives which do not apply, if none applies (e.g. the............Court has consented to the marriage) insert the appropriate declaration as to consent in the space provided.
Dilëer y rhai anghymwys, os nad oes un yn gymwys (e.e. mae Llys............wedi rhoi caniatâd i'r briodas) rhowch y datganiad priodol am y caniatâd yn y gofod a geir i hynny.

†Insert the name(s) of the person(s) whose consent is/are required.
Rhowch enw(au)'r person(au) y mae'n ofynnol cael ei(eu) g/caniatâd

‡Insert the name of the other party.
Rhowch enw'r parti arall.

(Signed) ⎱
(Llofnod) ⎰ .... Date ....
Dyddiad

In the presence of ⎱
Ym mhresenoldeb ⎰ .... ⎱ (Signature of registration officer)
⎰ (Llofnod y swyddog cofrestru)

Official designation ⎱
Disgrifiad swyddogol ⎰ .... Place of residence ....
Preswylfa

Registration district of ⎱
Dosbarth cofrestru ⎰ ....

Form 5

Endorsement on notice of marriage   Marriage Act 1949, S.35(1)

I declare that I and the other person named in this notice desire our intended marriage to be solemnized according to the form, rite, or ceremony of the (i)........................
to which (ii)...........................belong(s); and that to the best of my belief there is not within the superintendent registrar's district in which (iii).............................
reside(s) any registered building in which marriage is solemnized according to that form, rite or ceremony; and that the nearest district to (iv) .... place of residence in which there is a registered building in which marriage may be so solemnized is the superintendent registrar's district of (v)..............................and that we intend to solemnize our marriage in the registered building described in this notice and which is situated within that district.

Signed.................................   Date...........................

Datganaf fy mod i a'r person arall a enwir yn yr hysbysiad hwn yn dymuno i'r briodas a fwriedir gennym gael ei gweinyddu yn ôl dull, defod neu seremoni'r (i).........
...............y perthyn(af) (ii)......................iddo; ac nad oes hyd y gwn i o fewn dosbarth y cofrestrydd arolygol lle yr wyf/y mae (iii)..yn byw unrhyw adeilad cofrestredig lle gellir gweinyddu priodas yn ôl y cyfryw ddull, defod neu seremoni; ac mai'r dosbarth agosaf at (iv).....................mhreswylfa/breswylfa/phreswylfa arferol lle mae adeilad cofrestredig y gweinyddir priodas felly yw dosbarth cofrestrydd arolygol (v).............................a'n bod yn bwriadu gweinyddu ein priodas yn yr adeilad cofrestredig a ddisgrifir yn yr hysbysiad hwn ac sydd o fewn y dosbarth hwnnw.

Llofnod.............................   Dyddiad....................

(i) Insert here the name of the body or denomination of Christians or other persons meeting for religious worship according to the form, rite or ceremony of which the parties desire the marriage to be solemnized.

Rhowch yma enw'r corff neu'r enwad o Gristnogion neu bersonau eraill sy'n cwrdd i gynnal addoliad crefyddol yn ôl y dull, defod neu seremoni y mae'r ddau yn dymuno i'w priodas gael ei gweinyddu.

(ii) Insert here "I" or "the said.................." (followed by the name of the other party) as the case may be.

Rhowch yma "Fi" neu "yr un a enwyd..............." (ac enw'r parti arall ar ei ôl) fel y bo'r achos.

(iii) Insert here "I" or "the other person named in this notice", as the case may be.

Rhowch yma "Fi" neu "y person arall a enwyd yn yr hysbysiad hwn", fel y bo'r achos.

(iv) Insert here "my", "his" or "her" according to the insertion in (iii).

Rhowch yma "fy", neu "ei" yn ôl y gosodiad yn (iii).

(v) Insert here the name of the district in which is situated the registered building in which the intended marriage is to take place.

Rhowch yma enw'r dosbarth lle saif yr adeilad cofrestredig lle cynhelir y briodas a fwriedir.

FORM 6

Certificate for marriage   Marriage Act 1949, S.31

I,
Yr wyf fi...

Superintendent Registrar of the district of
Cofrestrydd Arolygol dosbarth...

in the county/county borough of   hereby certify that on the
yn sir/bwrdeistref sirol...yn tystio drwy hyn i hysbysiad

day of
gael ei gofnodi'n briodol ar y..dydd o fis.................19......

notice was duly entered in the Marriage Notice Book of the said district of the marriage intended to be solemnized between the parties hereinafter named and described.

yn Llyfr Hysbysu Priodas y dosbarth hwnnw ynglŷn â'r briodas y bwriedir ei gweinyddu rhwng y ddau a enwir ac a ddisgrifir isod.

Name Enw (1)	Age Oed (2)	Marital status Cyflwr priodasol (3)	Occupation Gwaith (4)	Place of residence Preswylfa (5)	Period of residence Cyfnod preswylio (6)	Church or other building in which the marriage is to be solemnized Eglwys neu adeilad arall lle gweinyddir y briodas (7)	District and county of residence Dosbarth a sir y breswylfa (8)

I further certify that the issue of this certificate has not been forbidden by any person authorised to forbid the issue thereof.

Tystiaf ymhellach na wrthodwyd rhoi'r dystysgrif hon gan unrhyw berson ag awdurdod i wneud hynny.

Date   Signature
Dyddiad..   Llofnod   ....
                                             Superintendent Registrar
                                             Cofrestrydd Arolygol

NOTE: This certificate will be void if the marriage is not solemnized within 3 months from the date of entry of notice given above.

NODYN: Bydd y dystysgrif hon yn ddi-rym oni weinyddir y briodas o fewn 3 mis i ddyddiad cofnodi'r hysbysiad uchod.

FORM 7

Certificate and licence for marriage   Marriage Act 1949, S.32

I,   Superintendent Registrar of the district of
Yr wyf fi.. Cofrestrydd Arolygol dosbarth..

in the county/county borough of   hereby certify that on the
yn sir/bwrdeistref sirol...yn tystio drwy hyn i hysbysiad
                                               day of
gael ei gofnodi'n briodol ar y..dydd o fis....................................19......

notice was duly entered in the Marriage Notice Book of the said district of the marriage intended to be solemnized
between the parties hereinafter named and described.

yn Llyfr Hysbysu Priodas y dosbarth hwnnw ynglŷn â'r briodas y bwriedir ei gweinyddu rhwng y ddau a enwir
ac a ddisgrifir isod.

Name Enw (1)	Age Oed (2)	Marital status Cyflwr priodasol (3)	Occupation Gwaith (4)	Place of residence Preswylfa (5)	Period of residence Cyfnod preswylio (6)	Church or other building in which the marriage is to be solemnized Eglwys neu adeilad arall lle gweinyddir y briodas (7)	District and county of residence Dosbarth a sir y breswylfa (8)

I further certify that the issue of this certificate has not been forbidden by any person authorised to forbid the issue thereof.

Tystiaf ymhellach na wrthodwyd rhoi'r dystysgrif hon gan unrhyw berson ag awdurdod i wneud hynny.

Now therefore I, the said Superintendent Registrar, grant to the above-named parties licence to contract and solemnize their intended marriage.

Felly yr wyf fi y Cofrestrydd Arolygol a enwyd uchod yn rhoi trwydded yn awr i'r ddau a enwyd uchod i gyfamodi ac i weinyddu'r briodas a fwriedir ganddynt.

Date   Signature
Dyddiad...   Llofnod ....
                                               Superintendent Registrar
                                               Cofresttydd Arolygol

NOTE: This certificate and licence will be void if the marriage is not solemnized within 3 months from the date of entry of notice given above.

NODYN: Bydd y dystysgrif a'r drwydded hon yn di-rym oni weinyddir y briodas o fewn 3 mis i ddyddiad cofnodi'r hysbysiad uchod.

FORM 8

Form of instructions
Marriage Act 1949, Ss. 31 & 32

Instructions for the solemnization of a marriage in a registered building
without the presence of a registrar

1. This marriage must take place in the registered building named in the superintendent registrar's certificate or superintendent registrar's certificates for marriage, *and nowhere else.*

2. The authorised person duly appointed for the registered building named in the certificate or certificates, or an authorised person for some other registered building in the same registration district, must be present at the marriage.

3. At least two witnesses must also be present, and the doors of the registered building must be open. (The doors need not be actually open provided they are not so closed as to prevent persons from entering that part of the building in which the marriage is solemnized.)

4. Any certificate or certificates issued by the superintendent registrar as the legal authority for the marriage must be delivered to the authorised person in whose presence the marriage is to be solemnized. Unless this document (or these documents) are in his possession the authorised person must on no account allow the marriage to take place.

5. It is absolutely essential to the validity of the marriage that in some part of the ceremony each of the parties shall make the following declaration:—
"I do solemnly declare that I know not of any lawful impediment why I, A.B., may not be joined in matrimony to C.D."
and that each of them shall say to the other either—
"I call upon these persons here present to witness that I, A.B., do take thee C.D., to be my lawful wedded wife [or husband]"; or
"I, A.B., do take thee, C.D., to be my wedded wife [or husband]".

6. These declaratory and contracting words must be said in the presence of the authorised person acting on the occasion and of the witnesses to the marriage.

7. Immediately after the marriage is solemnized the authorised person must register all the particulars prescribed by law in the duplicate marriage register books of the registered building in which the marriage has taken place; the entry in both books must be signed by the parties married, by at least two witnesses and by the authorised person.

8. After the registration of the marriage a certified copy of the entry thereof may be obtained from the authorised person on payment of the prescribed fee.

Cyfarwyddiadau ar gyfer gweinyddu priodas mewn adeilad cofrestredig heb
gofrestrydd yn bresennol

1. Rhaid i'r briodas hon gael ei gweinyddu yn yr adeilad cofrestredig a enwyd yn nhystysgrif y cofrestrydd arolygol neu yn nhystysgrifau y cofrestrydd arolygol ar gyfer priodas; *ni ddylid ei gweinyddu yn unman arall.*

2. Rhaid i'r person awdurdodedig a benodwyd yn briodol dros yr adeilad cofrestredig a enwyd yn y dystysgrif neu'r tystysgrifau, neu berson awdurdodedig dros ryw adeilad cofrestredig arall o fewn yr un dosbarth fod yn bresennol yn y briodas.

3. Rhaid hefyd i ddau dyst fan lleiaf fod yn bresennol a rhaid i ddrysau'r adeilad cofrestredig fod yn agored. (Nid oes rhaid i'r drysau fod ar agor mewn gwirionedd cyn belled â'u bod heb eu cau fel ag i rwystro personau rhag cael mynediad i'r rhan honno o'r adeilad lle gweinyddir y briodas).

4. Rhaid trosglwyddo unrhyw dystysgrif neu dystysgrifau a roddwyd gan gofrestrydd arolygol fel awdurdod cyfreithiol y briodas i'r person awdurdodedig y gweinyddir y briodas yn ei ŵydd. Oni fydd y ddogfen hon (neu'r dogfennau hyn) yn ei feddiant ni ddylai'r person awdurdodedig ar unrhyw gyfrif adael i'r briodas gael ei gweinyddu.

5. Y mae'n hollol hanfodol ar gyfer dilysrwydd y briodas i'r ddau a briodir, wneud y datganiad canlynol rywbryd yn ystod y seremoni:—

"Yr wyf fi yn ddifrifol yn hysbysu na wn i am un rhwystr cyfreithlon, fel na ellir fy uno i, A.B., mewn priodas â C.D."

ac i bob un o'r ddau ddweud y naill wrth y llall, naill ai—

"Yr wyf fi yn galw ar y personau hyn sydd yma'n bresennol i dystiolaethu fy mod i A.B., yn dy gymryd di, C.D., yn wraig briod gyfreithlon [neu yn ŵr priod cyfreithlon] i mi; neu

"Yr wyf fi A.B., yn dy gymryd di C.D., yn wraig briod [neu yn ŵr priod] i mi."

6. Rhaid dweud geiriau'r datganiad a'r cyfamodi hwn yng ngŵydd y person awdurdodedig a fydd yn gweithredu ar yr achlysur, ynghyd â thystion y briodas.

7. Unwaith y gweinyddir y briodas rhaid i'r person awdurdodedig gofrestru ar unwaith yr holl fanylion a orchmynnir gan y gyfraith yn llyfrau deublyg cofrestru priodasau yr adeilad cofrestredig lle gweinyddwyd y briodas; rhaid i'r ddau a briodwyd, ynghyd â dau dyst fan lleiaf, a'r person awdurdodedig lofnodi'r gofnod ar y ddau lyfr.

8. Ar ôl cofrestru'r briodas gellir cael copi o'r gofnod a wnaed ohoni gan y person awdurdodedig am dâl penodedig.

FORM 9

Form of marriage entry   Marriage Act 1949, S.55(1)

PART I

Particulars of marriage

No. Rhif	Marriage solemnized at ⎤ Priodas a weinyddwyd yn ⎦			in the yn		in the yn	
1 When married Pryd y priodwyd	2 Name and surname Enw a chyfenw	3 Age Oed	4 Condition Cyflwr	5 Rank or profession Safle neu broffesiwn	6 Residence at the time of marriage Preswylfa adeg priodi	7 Father's name and surname Enw a chyfenw'r tad	8 Rank or profession of father Safle neu broffesiwn y tad
19......							

PART II

Particulars of attestation

(i) For marriage according to the rites and ceremonies of the Church in Wales

Married in the ⎤ Priodwyd yn ⎦ ....yn unol â defodau a seremoniau...........................drwy/ar ôl ......gennyf fi, by/after   by me, according to the rites and ceremonies of the

This marriage was solemnized between us, (..................) in the presence of us, (..................) Gweinyddwyd y yn ein ....
briodas hon rhyngom ni, (..................) presenoldeb ni, (..................)

(ii) For marriage in a superintendent registrar's office

Married in the ⎤ Priodwyd yn ⎦ ....drwy .... ger fy mron, by   before me,

This marriage was solemnized between us, (..................) in the presence of us, (..................) Gweinyddwyd y yn ein ....
briodas hon rhyngom ni, (..................) presenoldeb ni, (..................)

(iii) For marriage in a registered building in the presence of a registrar

Married in the ⎤ Priodwyd yn ⎦ ....yn unôl â defodau a seremoniau.. drwy... by
according to the rites and ceremonies of the

....gennyf fi, by me,

This marriage was solemnized between us, (..................) in the presence of us, (..................) Gweinyddwyd y yn ein
briodas hon rhyngom ni, (..................) presenoldeb ni, (..................)

(iv) For marriage in a registered building in the presence of an authorised person

Married in the ⎤ Priodwyd yn ⎦ ....yn unol â defodau a seremoniau..............................drwy .... by
according to the rites and ceremonies of the

This marriage was solemnized between us, (..................) in the presence of us, (..................) and in the presence of ac ym mhresenoldeb ....
Gwe inyddwyd y yn ein Authorised person for
briodas hon rhyngom ni, (..................) presenoldeb ni, (..................) Y Person Awdurdo— dedig dros ....

(v) For marriage according to the usages of the Society of Friends or the Jews

Married in the ⎤ Priodwyd yn ⎦ ....yn unol ag arferion..drwy .... by
according to the usages of the

This marriage was solemnized between us, (..................) in the presence of us, (..................) Gweinyddwyd y yn ein
briodas hon rhyngom ni, (..................) presenoldeb ni, (..................)

SCHEDULE 2

(1) Form of words required	(2) Welsh version
of full age	o gyflawn oed
minor	un o dan oed
Bachelor	Dyn di-briod
Spinster	Dynes ddi-briod
Widower	Gŵr gweddw
Widow	Gwraig weddw
Previous marriage dissolved	Priodas flaenorol wedi'i therfynu
Previously married at...............on......	Priodwyd o'r blaen yn.........ar y.........
Marriage dissolved on.........	Terfynwyd y briodas ar y.........
Previously went through a form of marriage at.........on.........	Aethpwyd o'r blaen drwy ddefod priodas yn.........ar y.........
Late of.........but now residing at.........	Gynt o.........ond yn preswylio yn awr yn.........
deceased	ymadawedig
certificate	tystysgrif
licence	trwydded
register office	swyddfa gofrestru
Registrar General's licence	trwydded y Cofrestrydd Cyffredinol

Given under my hand on 21st January 1971.

Michael Reed,
Registrar General.

I approve.

Peter Thomas,
Secretary of State for Wales.

25th January 1971.

EXPLANATORY NOTE

(This Note is not part of the Regulations.)

The Registration of Births, Still-births and Deaths (Welsh Language) Regulations 1969 (S.I. 1969/203) provide for Welsh as well as English to be used under certain conditions in the registration of births, still-births and deaths in Wales and Monmouthshire. The present regulations make complementary provision in respect of preliminaries to, and registration of, marriages.

Bilingual forms are prescribed (regulations 3-5 and schedule 1) for use in Wales and Monmouthshire in place of the existing forms printed in English only. The conditions under which these forms may be completed in both languages are set out (regulation 6) and Welsh wording to be used in those circumstances is specified (regulation 7 and schedule 2). Provision is also made for the correction of register entries to be made in Welsh where appropriate (regulation 8) and for certificates to be issued on bilingually printed forms whether or not the entry is in a bilingually printed register (regulation 10).

STATUTORY INSTRUMENTS

1971 No. 131 (S.14)

PUBLIC HEALTH, SCOTLAND

The Public Health (Aircraft) (Scotland) Regulations 1971

Made - - - -	*26th January* 1971
Laid before Parliament	*29th January* 1971
Coming into Operation	*1st February* 1971

In exercise of the powers conferred on me by section 1 of the Public Health (Scotland) Act 1945(a) and by that section as amended by section 69 of, and Schedule 11 to, the Civil Aviation Act 1949(b), and by section 13 of the Airports Authority Act 1965(c), and of all other powers enabling me in that behalf, I hereby make the following regulations:—

PART I

PRELIMINARY

Citation and commencement

1. These regulations may be cited as the Public Health (Aircraft) (Scotland) Regulations 1971, and shall come into operation on 1st February 1971.

Interpretation

2.—(1) In these regulations, unless the context otherwise requires—

"additional measures" means such of the additional measures specified in Schedule 2 with respect to the diseases subject to the International Health Regulations as are appropriate;

"aerodrome" means any area of land or water designed, equipped, set apart or commonly used for affording facilities for the take-off and landing of aircraft, not being an area the use of which for those purposes has been abandoned, and includes any area or space, whether on the ground, on the roof of a building or elsewhere, which is designed, equipped or set apart for affording facilities for the take-off and landing of aircraft capable of descending or climbing vertically;

"Aircraft Declaration of Health" means a declaration containing the information specified in Schedule 1, being either a separate document or a part of the Aircraft General Declaration delivered in accordance with Appendix 6 of the International Health Regulations 1969;

"authorised officer" means the medical officer or any other officer authorised by the responsible authority under regulation 4 to enforce and execute any of these regulations;

"baggage" means the personal effects of a traveller or of a member of the crew;

"commander" means the person for the time being in command of an aircraft;

(a) 9 & 10 Geo. 6 c. 15.   (b) 1949 c. 67.
(c) 1965 c. 16.

"crew" means the personnel of an aircraft who are employed for duties on board;

"customs airport" means an aerodrome designated by order of the Secretary of State for Trade and Industry under article 72 of the Air Navigation Order 1970(a), with the concurrence of the Commissioners of Customs and Excise, to be a place for the landing or departure of aircraft for the purposes of the enactments relating to customs;

"customs officer" means any officer as defined in the Customs and Excise Act 1952(b);

"day" means a period of twenty-four hours;

"disease subject to the International Health Regulations" means cholera, including cholera due to the El Tor vibrio, plague, smallpox, including variola minor (alastrim), or yellow fever;

"disinsecting" means the operation in which measures are taken to kill the insect vectors of human disease;

"enactment" includes any instrument having statutory effect;

"epidemic" means an extension of a disease subject to the International Health Regulations by a multiplication of cases in an area;

"excepted area" means all the territory of Belgium, Metropolitan France, Greece, the Republic of Ireland, Italy, Luxembourg, the Netherlands and the United Kingdom, the Channel Islands and the Isle of Man;

"excepted airport" means any airport in the excepted area;

"immigration officer" means any person appointed to act as an immigration officer under the Aliens Restriction Acts 1914(c) and 1919(d) or under the Commonwealth Immigrants Acts 1962(e), and 1968(f);

"infected aircraft" means—

(a) an aircraft which has on board on arrival a case of a disease subject to the International Health Regulations; or

(b) an aircraft on which a plague-infected rodent is found on arrival; or

(c) an aircraft which has had a case of smallpox on board during its voyage and which has not before arrival been subjected in respect of such case to appropriate measures equivalent to those provided in these regulations;

"infected area" means an area notified as such to health administrations by the World Health Organisation under Article 11 of the International Health Regulations and which has not been subsequently notified by that organisation as being free from infection;

"infected person" means a person who is suffering from a disease subject to the International Health Regulations or who is considered by the medical officer to be infected with such a disease;

"infectious disease" means a disease subject to the International Health Regulations or any other infectious or contagious disease other than venereal disease or tuberculosis;

"in flight" means the time elapsing between the closing of the doors of the aircraft before take-off and their opening on arrival;

"International Health Regulations" means the International Health Regulations as adopted by the World Health Assembly on 25th July 1969;

(a) S.I. 1970 954/(1970 II, p. 2964).   (b) 1952 c. 44.
(c) 1914 c. 12.   (d) 1919 c. 92.
(e) 1962 c. 21.   (f) 1968 c. 9.

"isolation", when applied to a person or group of persons, means the separation of that person or group of persons from other persons, except the health staff on duty, in such a manner as to prevent the spread of infection;

"local authority" means a local health authority for the purposes of the National Health Service (Scotland) Acts 1947 to 1968(a) and includes a port local authority or joint port local authority constituted under section 172 of the Public Health (Scotland) Act 1897(b);

"medical officer" means the medical officer of health of a responsible authority, or any other medical practitioner appointed by such authority under regulation 5;

"medical practitioner" means a registered medical practitioner;

"national airport" means an aerodrome for the time being vested in or under the control of the Secretary of State for Trade and Industry or owned or managed by the British Airports Authority;

"responsible authority", in relation to an aerodrome or other place, means the authority charged under regulation 4 with the duty of enforcing and executing these regulations;

"sanitary airport" means a customs airport which has been designated in accordance with article 19 of the International Health Regulations;

"suspect" means a person (not being an infected person) who is considered by the medical officer as having been exposed to infection by a disease subject to the International Health Regulations and is considered capable of spreading that disease;

"suspected aircraft" means an aircraft from which a case of cholera occurring on board during the voyage has been removed before the arrival of the aircraft, and which has not before arrival been subjected in respect of such case to appropriate measures equivalent to those provided for in these regulations;

"valid International Vaccination Certificate" means a certificate of vaccination or revaccination against smallpox or cholera which—

(a) being issued before the coming into operation of these regulations is in the form required by the Public Health (Aircraft) (Scotland) Regulations 1966(c) or a form substantially to the same effect, and conforms with the rules as to validity referred to in those regulations; or

(b) being issued on or after the coming into operation of these regulations is in the form laid down and conforms with the rules as to validity contained in Schedule 4 or 3 as the case may be;

"voyage", in relation to an aircraft, means the flight of the aircraft from its point of origin via any intermediate points to its point of termination.

(2) Any reference in these regulations to a numbered regulation or schedule shall, unless the reference is to a regulation or schedule of specified regulations, be construed as a reference to the regulation or schedule bearing that number in these regulations.

(3) In these regulations, unless the context otherwise requires, references to any enactment shall be construed as references to that enactment as amended or re-enacted by any subsequent enactment.

(4) The Interpretation Act 1889(a) shall apply for the interpretation of these regulations as it applies for the interpretation of an Act of Parliament.

(5) Any reference, however expressed, in these regulations to a person leaving an aircraft shall not be construed as a reference to that person leaving an aircraft and continuing his journey in that aircraft.

Regulations not to apply to aircraft of the armed forces

3. Without prejudice to any enactment or rule of law which applies in relation to Her Majesty's armed forces or to any of the other armed forces hereinafter mentioned as part thereof, nothing in these regulations shall apply to any aircraft forming part of Her Majesty's armed forces or of the armed forces of any country within the Commonwealth or of the armed forces of any other country for the time being designated for the purposes of all the provisions of the Visiting Forces Act 1952(b) following section 1(2) thereof, or to the officers and crew of such aircraft or to any aerodrome under the control of such forces.

PART II

GENERAL

Enforcement and execution of regulations

4.—(1) Subject to the provisions of these regulations, it shall be the duty of the following authorities to enforce and execute these regulations:—

(*a*) at a national airport, the Secretary of State, or if a local authority have undertaken duties at that aerodrome under section 18(2) of the Civil Aviation Act 1949(c) or section 13(2) of the Airports Authority Act 1965(d), that local authority;

(*b*) at an aerodrome maintained by a local authority that authority or, if so agreed, upon terms and conditions approved by the Secretary of State between the authority maintaining the aerodrome and any other authority within whose limits of jurisdiction any part of the aerodrome is situated, that other authority;

(*c*) at any other aerodrome if it is wholly within the limits of jurisdiction of a local authority, that authority; in any other case, such local authority within whose limits of jurisdiction any part of the aerodrome is situated as may be agreed upon terms and conditions approved by the Secretary of State among all such authorities or, in the absence of agreement, such authority as the Secretary of State may direct;

(*d*) at any place other than an aerodrome if the place is within the limits of jurisidiction of a local authority, that authority.

(2) The Secretary of State may attach such terms and conditions as he thinks fit to any direction given by him under this regulation.

(3) The Secretary of State shall exercise his functions as a responsible authority through such officers as may be designated for the purpose by him or (except in relation to aerodromes owned or managed by the British Airports Authority) by the Secretary of State for Trade and Industry.

(4) Every other responsible authority shall exercise their functions through the medical officer and such other officers as they may authorise in that behalf, and shall make such inquiries and take such other steps as may seem to them to be necessary for securing the proper exercise of those functions.

(a) 1889 c. 63.   (b) 1952 c. 67.
(c) 1949 c. 67.   (d) 1965 c. 16.

Appointment and duties of authorised officers and provision of services by responsible authorities

5. For the purposes of these regulations a responsible authority other than the Secretary of State may, and if so required by the Secretary of State shall—

(*a*) appoint such medical practitioners, in addition to their medical officer of health, as may be necessary for the proper enforcement and execution of these regulations;

(*b*) give directions from time to time as to the duties which are to be performed by any medical practitioner so appointed or any other officer authorised to enforce and execute these regulations;

(*c*) at or in connection with a customs airport, provide or arrange for the provision of—
  (i) premises or waiting rooms for the medical inspection and examination of persons;
  (ii) premises for the temporary isolation of persons in accordance with these regulations;

(*d*) at or in connection with a customs airport, arrange for the reception into a hospital of persons requiring to be removed thereto in accordance with these regulations;

(*e*) arrange for the provision of means of transport for the conveyance of persons to any premises referred to in paragraph (*c*) of this regulation, or to a hospital;

(*f*) at or in connection with a sanitary airport, provide or arrange for the provision of—
  (i) apparatus or other means for cleansing, disinfecting and disinsecting aircraft, persons or clothing and other articles and deratting aircraft;
  (ii) a laboratory for the examination of suspected material, or equipment for taking and despatching such material for examination in a laboratory;

(*g*) do all such other things as in their opinion or the opinion of the Secretary of State, as the case may be, are necessary to enable the provisions of these regulations to be complied with.

List of infected areas

6.—(1) The medical officer at a customs airport shall from time to time prepare and keep up to date a list of aerodromes and other areas which are infected or believed to be infected with a disease subject to the International Health Regulations or which may serve other places or areas so infected or believed to be so infected.

(2) The medical officer shall supply copies of every such list and any amendment thereof to the customs officer at the airport and to the person in charge of the airport.

(3) In preparing and amending such list the medical officer shall take into account all information sent to him from time to time by the Secretary of State or issued by the World Health Organisation.

PART III

INCOMING AIRCRAFT

Inspection of aircraft

7.—(1) The medical officer or other authorised officer may, for the purposes of these regulations, inspect any aircraft at a customs airport.

(2) The medical officer shall—

(a) inspect on arrival any aircraft in respect of which the commander has sent a message under regulation 12; and

(b) inspect any aircraft at the airport when he has reasonable grounds for believing that there is on board a case or suspected case of infectious disease.

(3) The medical officer may require any aircraft which he intends to inspect in accordance with this regulation to be taken to some safe and convenient part of the airport for such inspection if it cannot otherwise be carried out effectively.

Examination, etc., of persons on aircraft

8.—(1) The medical officer may, and if so requested by the commander or required by the Secretary of State shall, examine any person on board or leaving an aircraft at a customs airport, when there are reasonable grounds for suspecting that—

(a) the person is suffering from an infectious disease;

(b) the person has been exposed to infection from an infectious disease;

(c) the person is verminous.

(2) The medical officer may—

(a) detain any such person for such examination at a place appointed for the purpose;

(b) require the clothing and other articles belonging to any person so examined to be disinfected and, where necessary, disinsected and any person found to be verminous to be disinsected;

(c) except as provided in regulation 21, prohibit any person so examined from leaving the aircraft or airport, or permit him to leave it on such conditions and subject to the taking of such measures, in accordance with these regulations, as the medical officer considers reasonably necessary for preventing the spread of infection; and

(d) require the commander to take or assist in taking such steps as in the opinion of the medical officer are reasonably necessary for preventing the spread of infection, for disinsection and the destruction of vermin, and for the removal of conditions on the aircraft likely to convey infection, including conditions the existence of which might facilitate the harbouring of insects or vermin.

(3) The medical officer or other authorised officer or a customs officer may, and if so required by the Secretary of State shall, require any person on board or leaving an aircraft at a customs airport to produce a valid International Vaccination Certificate.

(4) A customs officer or other authorised officer may detain until the arrival of the medical officer or for three hours, whichever is the shorter period, any such person who has been required to produce such a certificate and is unable to do so.

(5) Where any such person fails to satisfy the medical officer that he possesses such a certificate, the medical officer may detain him for examination at a place appointed for that purpose, and may apply in his case the additional measures mentioned in Part II of Schedule 2 and in paragraphs (1) and (2) of Part IV of Schedule 2.

(6) The medical officer, customs officer or other authorised officer shall immediately notify the responsible authority of any directions given to him by the Secretary of State under this regulation.

Powers in respect of persons leaving aircraft

9.—(1) Where a person intending to leave an aircraft at a customs airport is suffering, or the medical officer suspects that he is suffering, from an infectious disease or tuberculosis, the medical officer may—

(*a*) in the case of an infectious disease, cause such person on leaving the aircraft to be isolated, or to be sent to a hospital or to some other suitable place approved for that purpose by the responsible authority, as may be appropriate; or, unless regulation 21 has been invoked, the medical officer may, by notice in writing to the commander, prohibit the person from leaving the aircraft without the consent in writing of the medical officer;

(*b*) in the case of tuberculosis, if the person leaves the aircraft, send information to that effect to the medical officer of health for the area in which the intended destination and address of the person is situated.

(2) If the Secretary of State is satisfied that a grave danger to public health exists by reason of infectious disease and notifies medical officers accordingly, the medical officer may, and if the Secretary of State so directs shall, require a person leaving an aircraft at a customs airport to state in writing his name and intended destination and address.

Notice to customs officer by medical officer

10. The medical officer at a customs airport shall inform the customs officer of any measure applied by him or at his direction, in accordance with these regulations, to an aircraft, any person thereon, or its stores, equipment or cargo.

Supply of information, etc., by commanders

11. The commander of an aircraft at a customs airport shall—

(*a*) answer all questions as to the health conditions on board which may be put to him by an authorised officer or a customs officer visiting the aircraft, and furnish any such officer with all such information and assistance as he may reasonably require for the purposes of these regulations;

(*b*) in addition to any message sent in accordance with regulation 12, notify immediately on arrival to the medical officer any death on the aircraft during its voyage caused otherwise than by accident, any case of infectious disease on the aircraft, or any circumstances on board which are likely to cause the spread of infectious disease, including in his notification particulars as to the presence of rodents on the aircraft;

(*c*) comply with these regulations, and with any directions or requirements of an authorised officer given or made for the purposes of these regulations.

Notification of infectious disease, etc., on board

12.—(1) When there is on board an aircraft during its voyage a person who is suffering from an infectious disease or who has symptoms which may indicate the presence of infectious disease, or when there are on board the aircraft any other similar circumstances requiring the attention of the medical officer, the commander shall, immediately he is aware of the presence of such disease, symptoms or other circumstances, send a radio message to that effect to the medical officer at the first customs airport at which the aircraft is due to arrive, or to the person in charge of such airport.

(2) If such radio message is sent to the medical officer, he shall immediately notify the customs officer of its contents.

(3) If such radio message is sent to the person in charge of the customs airport he shall immediately notify the medical officer and the customs officer of its contents.

Aircraft Declaration of Health

13.—(1) Except where the Secretary of State directs otherwise, on the arrival of an aircraft at a customs airport the commander or a member of the crew deputed to act on his behalf shall complete an Aircraft Declaration of Health in the form set out in Schedule 1 and deliver it to the customs officer or medical officer, whoever first boards the aircraft.

(2) If the customs officer detains the aircraft in accordance with these regulations and he requires a copy of the Declaration, the medical officer shall furnish him with such copy.

Detention of aircraft

14.—(1) When on the arrival of an aircraft at a customs airport the medical officer has reasonable grounds for believing that the aircraft may be an infected aircraft or a suspected aircraft, or an aircraft which although not falling within either of such categories, has had on board during the voyage a case of a disease subject to the International Health Regulations in respect of which the aircraft has not outside the United Kingdom been subjected to appropriate measures equivalent to those provided for in these regulations, he may cause the aircraft to be detained for medical inspection.

(2) If the medical officer has caused an aircraft to be so detained, he shall inform the person in charge of the customs airport of such detention and send a notice in writing of such detention to the customs officer.

15. If a customs officer receives in respect of an aircraft a notice in writing from the medical officer under regulation 14, he shall, if he visits the aircraft before the medical officer, deliver the notice to the commander and take all reasonable steps to secure compliance therewith.

16. Where on the arrival of an aircraft at a customs airport it appears to the customs officer, from information on the Aircraft Declaration of Health or otherwise, that during the voyage of the aircraft—

(a) there has been on the aircraft a death caused otherwise than by accident, or a case of illness which is or is suspected to be of an infectious nature; or

(b) the aircraft has been in an infected area; or

(c) death not attributable to poison or other measures for destruction has occurred amongst rodents on the aircraft,

he shall, unless the medical officer otherwise directs, give such directions as seem necessary to him to secure the detention of the aircraft, the persons carried thereon, and its stores, equipment and cargo.

17. The detention of an aircraft by a customs officer under these regulations shall cease as soon as the aircraft has been inspected by the medical officer or, if such inspection has not commenced within 3 hours after the aircraft has been so detained, on the expiration of that period:

Provided that nothing in this regulation shall affect the power of the medical officer to continue the detention of an aircraft in accordance with regulation 18.

18.—(1) The medical officer shall inspect any aircraft and persons carried thereon as soon as possible and in any case within 3 hours after it has been detained under these regulations.

(2) If the aircraft is one to which the medical officer is required by these regulations to apply any further or additional measure, or if after such inspection he considers it necessary to apply any further or additional measure under these regulations, he may continue the detention of the aircraft, if such continued detention is necessary for the application of that further or additional measure.

Release of aircraft

19. When the medical officer releases an aircraft from detention he shall give notice in writing to the customs officer, to the commander of the aircraft, and to the person in charge of the customs airport that, so far as control under these regulations is concerned, the aircraft is free to proceed at or after a date and time stated in the notice.

Persons from infected areas

20. On the arrival of an aircraft at a customs airport, the medical officer may place under surveillance for the appropriate period specified in regulation 30(1)—

(a) any person disembarking from the aircraft who has come from an infected area other than an area infected with yellow fever or plague, and

(b) any suspect disembarking from the aircraft who has come from an area infected with yellow fever or plague.

Removal of infected persons from aircraft when required by commander

21. The medical officer shall, if so required by the commander of an aircraft on arrival at a customs airport, cause any infected person to be removed from the aircraft.

Removal to sanitary airport

22. If the medical officer considers that there should be applied to an aircraft which alights elsewhere than at a sanitary airport or to any person carried thereon, measures in accordance with these regulations which can be applied only at a sanitary airport, he may direct that the aircraft or any such person shall proceed to a sanitary airport, and he shall give the commander notice in writing of the direction and of the reasons for the direction.

Additional measures

23. Without prejudice to any other provision in these regulations, the additional measures in Schedule 2 shall be applicable on the arrival at a customs airport of—

(a) any infected aircraft or suspected aircraft;

(b) any aircraft which has during its voyage been in an area infected with plague, cholera or yellow fever;

(c) any suspect for smallpox on an aircraft other than an infected aircraft;

(d) any other aircraft or person, when the medical officer is satisfied that, notwithstanding that measures equivalent to such additional measures have been applied to the aircraft or person previously during its voyage, there is on board or has been on board since such previous application an infected person or suspect and that it is necessary again to apply any such measure, or the medical officer has reasonable grounds for believing that such prevous application was not substantially effective.

Avoidance of delay

24. In applying any measures under these regulations, the medical officer shall have regard to the need for freeing aircraft from control under these regulations as quickly as possible.

Aircraft alighting elsewhere than at a customs airport

25.—(1) Where an aircraft alights elsewhere than at a customs airport—

(a) the commander shall forthwith give notice to that effect to the responsible authority or a customs officer or an immigration officer or a police officer and, if the aircraft has alighted at an aerodrome, to the person in charge thereof;

(b) except for the purpose of the preceding sub-paragraph, no person carried by the aircraft shall leave its vicinity unless authorised so to do by the medical officer, and any person so authorised shall inform such officer of his name and his intended destination and address, but this sub-paragraph shall not be construed as dispensing with the necessity to secure any consent arising under any other enactment;

(c) subject as aforesaid, these regulations shall apply, with any necessary modifications, in relation to the aircraft, the persons carried thereon, and its stores, equipment and cargo, to the extent to which they are not required by a police officer or customs officer to proceed or, as the case may be, to be taken to a customs airport, as if the aircraft had alighted at a customs airport and for the purposes of such application the list of infected areas kept in accordance with regulation 6 shall be any list so kept by the medical officer of the responsible authority or, if there is no such list, any list so kept by the medical officer for the customs airport nearest to the place where the aircraft has alighted.

(2) If any person who has informed an officer under this regulation of his intended destination and address arrives within fourteen days thereafter at some other address, he shall forthwith send particulars of that address to the medical officer of health of the responsible authority for the place at which he left the aircraft.

Saving for certain aircraft

26. In the case of an aircraft which has commenced its voyage at a place within the excepted area and has not during its voyage alighted at any place outside that area—

(a) the commander shall not be bound to comply with the provisions of regulation 11, 13(1) or 15(1)(a) unless he has been notified by the medical officer that compliance with those provisions is necessary because of danger to public health;

(b) no person carried by the aircraft shall be bound by the provisions of regulation 25(1)(b) or (c) unless he has been notified by the medical officer that those provisions apply to him because of danger to public health;

(c) the powers and duties conferred or imposed on the medical officer by regulations 7, 8(1) (2) (3) and (5), 9, 14(1), 18(2), 20, 21. 22 and 23 shall not be exercised or performed unless the medical officer is satisfied, or the Secretary of State has directed, that the exercise of the powers or the performance of the duties conferred or imposed by those provisions is necessary because of danger to public health;

(d) the powers and duties conferred on a customs officer or authorised officer by regulations 8(3) and (4) and 16 shall not be exercised or performed unless the Secretary of State has directed, or the medical officer is satisfied and has so informed the customs officer or authorised officer, that the exercise of the powers or the performance of the duties conferred or imposed by those provisions is necessary because of danger to public health.

PART IV

OUTGOING AIRCRAFT

Examination, etc., of persons proposing to embark

27. Where an aircraft is due to depart from an aerodrome for a destination outside the United Kingdom, the medical officer—

(a) may examine any person who proposes to embark thereon if he has reasonable grounds for believing him to be suffering from a disease subject to the International Health Regulations, and, if after examination the medical officer is of the opinion that he shows symptoms of such a disease, shall prohibit his embarkation and the time and place of this examination shall be arranged so as to take into account any other formalities and to avoid delay;

(b) shall prohibit any suspect from embarking thereon:

Provided that in the case of smallpox a person shall not be prohibited from embarking if he satisfies the medical officer that he is sufficiently protected by vaccination or by a previous attack of smallpox;

(c) shall notify by the most expeditious means the commander and the health authority for the place to which the person is proceeding of any person embarking or proposing to continue his voyage thereon who, in the opinion of the medical officer, should be placed under surveillance;

(d) may, notwithstanding the provisions of sub-paragraph (b) of this regulation, allow a person on an international voyage who, on arrival, was placed under surveillance, to continue his voyage; and the medical officer shall notify by the most expeditious means the health authority for the place to which the person is proceeding that such a person should, in the opinion of the medical officer, be placed under surveillance.

28. Where the Secretary of State has, by notice published in the Edinburgh Gazette, declared any place to be infected with a disease subject to the International Health Regulations or with any other disease which in his opinion constitutes a menace to other countries by reason of its spread or potential spread, then, until the notice is revoked by a subsequent notice published in the Edinburgh Gazette, every medical officer shall comply with any requirement which may be made, by the Secretary of State for preventing the spread of the disease, and in particular (but without prejudice to the generality of the foregoing provision) the following provisions of this regulation shall operate in relation to any aircraft departing from any aerodrome specified by the Secretary of State for a destination outside the United Kingdom—

    (*a*) an authorised officer, if so required by the Secretary of State, shall require a valid International Vaccination Certificate from departing travellers; and in the absence of such a certificate the medical officer may offer vaccination to any such traveller and apply the provisions of regulation 27(*c*);

    (*b*) the medical officer may, and within three hours after receiving a request from the commander so to do shall, medically examine any person who proposes to embark on or is on board the aircraft;

    (*c*) the medical officer may require any part of the aircraft which in his opinion may be infected to be cleansed and disinfected to his satisfaction;

    (*d*) an authorised officer shall inspect any clothing, bedding or other article which is on, or is intended to be taken by any person on, the aircraft and which, in the opinion of the officer, may have been exposed to infection and may require the disinfection or destruction of any such clothing, bedding or article, and the commander shall disclose to the authorised officer any relevant circumstances;

    (*e*) no person shall take or cause to be taken on board the aircraft any article which, in the opinion of an authorised officer, is capable of carrying infection, unless that officer is satisfied that it has been efficiently disinfected and, where necessary, disinsected;

    (*f*) if the aerodrome is situated in an area which is included in the said notice in the Edinburgh Gazette and is therein declared to be infected with plague, and if there is reason to believe that there are rodents on the aircraft, the medical officer may, and if so required by the Secretary of State shall, take steps to secure the deratting of the aircraft.

Part V

Miscellaneous

Compliance with directions, etc., under the regulations

29. Every person to whom these regulations apply shall comply with every direction, requirement or condition given, made or imposed by an authorised officer or customs officer in accordance with these regulations, and shall furnish all such information as that officer may reasonably require (including information as to his name and intended destination and address to which he is going on leaving an aerodrome) and every person who has for the time being the custody or charge of a child or other person who is under disability shall comply with any direction, requirement or condition so given, made or imposed, and shall furnish all such information as aforesaid, in respect of that child or other person.

Surveillance

30.—(1) Where these regulations permit a medical officer to place a person under surveillance, the period of such surveillance shall not exceed such of the following periods as may be appropriate:—

    (*a*) in respect of plague, six days;

    (*b*) in respect of cholera, five days;

    (*c*) in respect of yellow fever, six days;

    (*d*) in respect of smallpox, fourteen days;

(2) When a person has been so placed under surveillance for plague, cholera or smallpox in accordance with regulation 20 by reason of his having come from an infected area, the period shall be reckoned from the date of his leaving the infected area.

(3) When a person has been so placed under surveillance in accordance with the additional measures, the period shall be reckoned in the manner therein specified.

31. Every person who is placed under surveillance in accordance with these regulations shall—

(a) give facilities for any medical examination required by the medical officer or by the medical officer of health for any area in which he may be during the period of surveillance;

(b) furnish all such information as the medical officer or any such medical officer of health may reasonably require with a view to ascertaining the person's state of health;

(c) forthwith upon arrival during the period of surveillance at any address, other than the one stated as his intended address on leaving the aerodrome at which he arrived in Scotland, send particulars of that address to the medical officer;

(d) if so instructed by the medical officer report immediately to the medical officer of health for any area in which he may be during the period of surveillance, and thereafter during that period report to that officer at such intervals as he may require:

Provided that an instruction shall not be given under this sub-paragraph unless the Secretary of State has by direction (whether general or special) authorised the giving of instructions thereunder.

Charges for services

32.—(1) Where the commander of an aircraft is required by these regulations to carry out any measures with a view to reducing the danger or preventing the spread of infection, the responsible authority may themselves, at the request of the commander, cause any such requirement to be complied with at his cost instead of enforcing the requirement against the commander.

(2) The amount of the charge for any such measures or requirement undertaken by the responsible authority shall be such reasonable sum as represents the actual or estimated cost to be incurred in undertaking the work, excluding any charge or claim on the part of the authority in respect of profit, but shall not exceed the sum of one hundred pounds unless notice of the proposed charge has been given to the commander before the work is undertaken.

(3) Where, under this regulation, the responsible authority cause any requirement to be complied with at the cost of the commander they may require the amount of the charge for the work or a part thereof to be paid to, or deposited with, them before the work is undertaken.

(4) Where, under these regulations, any measures have been taken with regard to an aircraft, the responsible authority or the medical officer shall, on request by the commander, furnish him free of charge with particulars in writing of those measures and the reasons why they were taken.

(5) Where, under these regulations, any measures have been taken with regard to any person or to any articles in his possession, the medical officer shall, on the request of such a person, furnish him free of charge with particulars in writing of those measures, including the date on which they were taken.

Recovery of charges

33. Every charge authorised by regulation 32 shall be recoverable as a civil debt.

Expenses of responsible authorities

34. Subject to the provisions of regulation 32, any expenses incurred by a responsible authority in the enforcement and execution of these regulations shall be defrayed in the same manner as the expenses incurred by them in the execution and discharge of their other powers and duties.

Saving for mails

35. Except to the extent permitted by Part II-C of Schedule 2, nothing in these regulations shall render liable to detention, disinfection or destruction any article forming part of any mail conveyed under the authority of the Post Office or of the postal administration of any other Government, or shall prejudicially affect the receipt on board and delivery in due course at the place of destination of any such mail in accordance with the provisions of the Post Office Act 1953(a), as amended by Part II of Schedule 4 to the Post Office Act 1969(b).

Saving for aircraft unwilling to comply with these regulations

36.—(1) The commander of an aircraft on arrival, or already at an aerodrome, who is unwilling to comply with, or submit to, any provisions of, or requirement made under, these regulations which may be applicable, shall so notify the medical officer and the medical officer may then require the commander to remove the aircraft immediately from the aerodrome.

(2) If before leaving the aerodrome the commander wishes to discharge cargo or disembark passengers or to take on board fuel, water or stores, the medical officer shall permit him to do so but may impose such conditions under these regulations as the medical officer considers necessary.

(3) When the medical officer has required the removal of an aircraft from the aerodrome, it shall not during its voyage alight at any other place in Scotland.

Saving for existing enactments

37. Nothing in these regulations shall affect the Air Navigation Order 1970(c), the Aliens Order 1953(d), the Commonwealth Immigrants Acts 1962(e) and 1968(f), or the Immigration Appeals Act 1969(g).

(a) 1953 c. 36.
(c) S.I. 1970/954 (1970 II, p. 2964).
(e) 1962 c. 21.
(g) 1969 c. 21.

(b) 1969 c. 48.
(d) S.I. 1953/1671 (1953 I, p. 94).
(f) 1968 c. 9.

Revocation

38.—(1) The Public Health (Aircraft) (Scotland) Regulations 1966**(a)** are hereby revoked.

(2) Section 38 of the Interpretation Act 1889 shall apply as if these regulations were an Act of Parliament and as if the regulations revoked by these regulations were an Act of Parliament repealed by an Act of Parliament.

Gordon Campbell,
One of Her Majesty's Principal
Secretaries of State.

St. Andrew's House,
Edinburgh.
26th January 1971.

SCHEDULE 1   Regulation 13

PUBLIC HEALTH (AIRCRAFT) (SCOTLAND) REGULATIONS 1971

Aircraft Declaration of Health

Persons on board with illnesses other than air sickness or the effects of accidents (including persons with symptoms or signs of illness such as rash, fever, chills, diarrhoea) as well as those cases of illness disembarked during the flight............................

....

....

Any other conditions on board which may lead to the spread of disease..................

....

....

Details of each disinsecting or sanitary treatment (place, date, time, method) during the flight. If no disinsecting has been carried out during the flight, give details of most recent disinsecting ....

....

....

Signature, if required..

Date.............................

Crew member concerned.

(a) S.I. 1966/346 (1966 III, p. 794).

Regulations 2(1), 8(5) and 23   SCHEDULE 2

ADDITIONAL MEASURES WITH RESPECT TO DISEASES SUBJECT TO THE INTERNATIONAL HEALTH REGULATIONS

PART I—PLAGUE

A. *Infected aircraft*

(1) The medical officer may—

(a) require any suspect on board to be disinsected and place him under surveillance, the period of surveillance being reckoned from the date of arrival of the aircraft;

(b) require the disinsecting and, if necessary, disinfection of the baggage of any infected person or suspect, and of any other article on board and any part of the aircraft which the medical officer considers to be contaminated.

(2) When the presence of rodents is suspected on board an aircraft or if the aircraft is infected because a plague-infected rodent is found on board the medical officer shall require the aircraft to be deratted in a manner to be determined by him.

(3) On arrival of an aircraft having on board a person suffering from pulmonary plague the medical officer may—

(a) carry out the measures set out in paragraph 1 of Part I of this Schedule;

(b) require any person on board to be placed in isolation for six days reckoned from the date of the last exposure to infection.

B. *Aircraft which have been in infected areas*

(4) The medical officer may place under surveillance any suspect who disembarks, the period of surveillance being reckoned from the date of the departure of the aircraft from the infected area.

PART II—CHOLERA

A. *Infected aircraft and suspected aircraft*

(1) The medical officer may—

(a) place under surveillance any person who disembarks, the period of surveillance being reckoned from the date of arrival of the aircraft;

(b) require the disinfection of the baggage of any infected person or suspect, and of any other article on board and any part of the aircraft which the medical officer considers to be contaminated;

(c) require the disinfection and removal of any water on board which he considers to be contaminated, and the disinfection of the containers which have held such water.

(2) The medical officer shall prohibit the discharge or unloading from the aircraft of human dejecta and any other waste matter or water which may be contaminated and has not been disinfected.

B. *Aircraft which have been in infected areas*

(3) The medical officer may place under surveillance any person who disembarks, the period of surveillance being reckoned from the date of the departure of the aircraft from the infected area.

C. *Infected aircraft, suspected aircraft and aircraft which have been in infected areas*

(4) In addition to any measure permitted or required by the preceding provisions in this Part, the medical officer may prohibit the unloading of, or may remove from the aircraft, any fish, shellfish, fruit or vegetables to be eaten uncooked, or beverages, not forming part of cargo in a freight compartment of the aircraft, which he has reason to believe to be contaminated, and, if any such food or beverage is so removed, he shall arrange for its safe disposal in consultation with the customs officer.

(5) The medical officer may take samples of food (including fish, shellfish, fruit and vegetables) or beverages, for culture examination, unless such food and beverages are in sealed packages, and the responsible authority have no reason to believe that they are contaminated.

(6) If any of the said food or beverage forms part of cargo in a freight compartment of the aircraft and is so contaminated, the medical officer for the aerodrome at which such cargo is due to be discharged shall arrange for its safe disposal in consultation with the customs officer.

PART III—YELLOW FEVER

Infected aircraft and aircraft which have been in infected areas

The medical officer may require the aircraft to be disinsected.

Regulation 8(5)

PART IV—SMALLPOX

A. *Infected aircraft*

(1) The medical officer shall offer vaccination to any person on board or disembarking from the aircraft who does not show sufficient evidence of protection by a previous attack of smallpox or who does not satisfy the medical officer that he possesses a valid International Vaccination Certificate.

(2) The medical officer may either—
   (a) place under surveillance any person who disembarks, the period of surveillance being reckoned from the date on which the medical officer considers the person was last exposed to infection; or
   (b) if he considers any such person is not sufficiently protected against smallpox, isolate him for a similar period.

(3) The medical officer shall require the disinfection of the baggage of any infected person, and of any other article on board and any part of the aircraft which the medical officer considers to be contaminated.

B. *Suspects on other aircraft*

(4) The medical officer may also apply the provisions of paragraphs (1) and (2) of this Part to any suspect who disembarks from an aircraft which is not an infected aircraft.

Regulations 2(1) and 8(3)   **SCHEDULE 3**

International Certificate of Vaccination or Revaccination against Cholera
Certificat International de Vaccination ou de Revaccination contre le Choléra

Date	Signature and professional status of vaccinator *Signature et titre du vaccinateur*		Approved stamp *Cachet autorisé*
1	1	1	2
2	2		
3	3	3	4
4	4		
5	5	5	6
6	6		
7	7	7	8
8	8		

RULES

The vaccine used shall meet the requirements laid down by the World Health Organisation.

The validity of this certificate shall extend for a period of six months, beginning six days after one injection of the vaccine or, in the event of a revaccination within such period of six months, on the date of that revaccination.

The approved stamp mentioned overleaf must be in a form prescribed by the health administration of the territory in which the vaccination is performed.

This certificate must be signed by a medical practitioner in his own hand; his official stamp is not an accepted substitute for the signature.

Any amendment of this certificate, or erasure, or failure to complete any part of it, may render it invalid.

Le vaccin utilisé doit satisfaire aux normes formulées par l'Organisation Mondiale de la Santé.

La validité de ce certificat couvre une période de six mois commençant six jours après une injection de vaccin ou, dans le cas d'une revaccination au cours de cette période de six mois, le jour de cette revaccination.

Le cachet autorisé doit être conforme au modèle prescrit par l'administration sanitaire de territoire où la vaccination est effectuée.

Ce certificat doit être signé par un médecin de sa propre main, son cachet officiel ne pouvant être considéré comme tenant lieu de signature.

Toute correction ou rature sur le certificat ou l'omission d'une quelconque des mentions qu'il comporte peut affecter sa validité.

INTERNATIONAL CERTIFICATE OF VACCINATION OR REVACCINATION AGAINST CHOLERA

CERTIFICAT INTERNATIONAL DE VACCINATION OU DE REVACCINATION CONTRE LE CHOLÉRA

This is to certify that
Je soussigné(e) certifie que

name ....
nom

date of birth .... sex ....
né(e) le   sexe

whose signature follows
dont la signature suit

....

has on the date indicated overleaf been vaccinated or revaccinated against cholera.

a été vacciné(e) ou revacciné(e) contre le choléra à la date indiquée au verso.

SCHEDULE 4   Regulations 2(1) and 8(3)

INTERNATIONAL CERTIFICATE OF VACCINATION OR REVACCINATION AGAINST SMALLPOX
CERTIFICAT INTERNATIONAL DE VACCINATION OU DE REVACCINATION CONTRE LA VARIOLE

Date	Show by "x" whether *Indiquer par x s'il s'agit de:*	Signature and professional status of vaccinator *Signature et titre du vaccinateur*	Manufacturer and batch no. of vaccine *Fabricant du vaccin et numéro du lot*	Approved stamp *Cachet autorisé*
1a	Primary vaccination performed *Primo vaccination effectuée*		1a	
1b	Read as successful *Prise* Unsuccessful *Pas de prise*		1b	
2	Revaccination		2	
3	Revaccination		3	

RULES

The validity of this certificate shall extend for a period of three years beginning eight days after the date of a successful primary vaccination, or in the event of a revaccination, on the date of that revaccination.

The approved stamp mentioned overleaf must be in a form prescribed by the health administration of the territory in which the vaccination is performed.

This certificate must be signed by a medical practitioner in his own hand; his official stamp is not an accepted substitute for the signature.

Any amendment of this certificate, or erasure, or failure to complete any part of it, may render it invalid.

La validité de ce certificat couvre une période de trois ans commençant huit jours après la date de la primovaccination effectuée avec succès (prise) ou, dans le cas d'une revaccination, le jour de cette revaccination.

Le cachet autorisé doit être conforme au modèle prescrit par l'administration sanitaire du territoire où la vaccination est effectuée.

Ce certificat doit être signé par un médecin de sa propre main, son cachet officiel ne pouvant être considéré comme tenant lieu de signature.

Toute correction ou rature sur le certificat ou l'omission d'une quelconque des mentions qu'il comporte peut affecter sa validité.

INTERNATIONAL CERTIFICATE OF VACCINATION
OR REVACCINATION AGAINST SMALLPOX

*CERTIFICAT INTERNATIONAL DE VACCINATION
OU DE REVACCINATION CONTRE LA VARIOLE*

This is to certify that
Je soussigné(e) certifie que

name ....

nom

date of birth..................... sex ....

né(e) le   *sexe*

whose signature follows
dont la signature suit

....

has on the date indicated overleaf been vaccinated or revaccinated against smallpox, with a freeze-dried or liquid vaccine certified to fulfil the recommended requirements of the World Health Organisation.

a été vacciné(e) ou revacciné(e) contre la variole à la date indiquée au verso, avec un vaccin lyophilisé ou liquide certifié conforme aux normes recommandées par l'Organisation Mondiale de la Santé.

EXPLANATORY NOTE
(This Note is not part of the Regulations.)

These Regulations supersede the Public Health (Aircraft) (Scotland) Regulations 1966, which provide for public health control of aircraft arriving in or leaving Scotland. They also make amendments which ensure conformity, where required, with the current International Health Regulations of the World Health Assembly and the administrative arrangements for health control made by the Council of Europe's Public Health Committee (Partial Agreement).

Part I contains definitions of terms used in the Regulations. Provision is made for revised forms of International Vaccination Certificates against cholera (Schedule 3) and smallpox (Schedule 4).

Part II provides for the enforcement and execution of the Regulations by local authorities and, at a national airport, by the Secretary of State unless a local authority have assumed duties there (Regulations 4 and 5). Part II also provides for the preparation by medical officers at customs airports of lists of aerodromes and other areas infected or believed to be infected with specified diseases (Regulation 6).

Part III relates to incoming aircraft. It provides for the inspection of aircraft, the examination of persons suspected of suffering from, or of having been exposed to infection from, an infectious disease or suspected of being verminous; and in these and other similar circumstances authorises measures to be taken for preventing danger to public health (Regulations 7 to 9).

Part IV relates to outgoing aircraft. It provides for the examination, etc, in prescribed circumstances of persons proposing to travel to a destination outside the United Kingdom (Regulation 27) and, after publication by the Secretary of State in the Edinburgh Gazette of a notice declaring any place to be infected with diseases, the spread of which might endanger public health, special measures may be taken to prevent the disease spreading (Regulation 28).

Part V contains miscellaneous provisions concerning periods of surveillance, charges for services and expenses of responsible authorities. It also contains savings for mails carried by aircraft (Regulation 35) and for the removal of any aircraft whose commander is unwilling to comply with the Regulations (Regulation 36).

STATUTORY INSTRUMENTS

1971 No. 132 (S.15)

PUBLIC HEALTH, SCOTLAND

The Public Health (Ships) (Scotland) Regulations 1971

Made - - -	26*th January* 1971
Laid before Parliament	29*th January* 1971
Coming into Operation	1*st February* 1971

In exercise of the powers conferred on me by section 1 of the Public Health (Scotland) Act 1945(**a**), as extended by section 62 of the Health Services and Public Health Act 1968(**b**), and of all other powers enabling me in that behalf, I hereby make the following regulations :—

PART I

PRELIMINARY

Citation and commencement

1. These regulations may be cited as the Public Health (Ships) (Scotland) Regulations 1971, and shall come into operation on 1st February 1971.

Interpretation

2.—(1) In these regulations, unless the context otherwise requires—

"additional measures" means such of the additional measures specified in Schedule 4 with respect to the diseases subject to the International Health Regulations as are appropriate ;

"approved port" means a port approved by the Secretary of State in accordance with paragraph 1 of Article 17 of the International Health Regulations for the issue of Deratting Exemption Certificates only ;

"arrival", in relation to a ship, means the entry within the limits of jurisdiction of a district of a ship which has not during its voyage or since it last called at a port outside the United Kingdom, as the case may be, been subjected elsewhere in the United Kingdom to measures provided for in these regulations or any corresponding regulations in force in England and Wales or Northern Ireland, apart from any measure which may have been applied there to any person, baggage or cargo landed from the ship, and "arrives" shall be construed accordingly ;

"authorised officer" means the medical officer or any other officer authorised by the health authority under regulation 4 to enforce and execute any of these regulations ;

"baggage" means the personal effects of a traveller or of a member of the crew ;

(**a**) 9 &10 Geo. 6 c. 15.   (**b**) 1968 c. 46.

"crew" means the personnel of a ship who are employed for duties on board ;

"customs officer" means any officer as defined in the Customs and Excise Act 1952(a) ;

"day" means a period of twenty-four hours ;

"Deratting Certificate" means a certificate issued in accordance with paragraph 2 of Article 54 of the International Health Regulations ;

"Deratting Exemption Certificate" means a certificate issued in accordance with paragraph 4(b) of Article 54 of the International Health Regulations ;

"designated approved port" means an approved port designated by the Secretary of State in accordance with paragraph 2 of Article 17 of the International Health Regulations for the issue of both Deratting Certificates and Deratting Exemption Certificates ;

"disease subject to the International Health Regulations" means cholera, including cholera due to the El Tor vibrio, plague, smallpox, including variola minor (alastrim), or yellow fever ;

"disinsecting" means the operation in which measures are taken to kill the insect vectors of human disease ;

"district" means the area of a health authority which abuts on waters forming part of a port established for the purposes of the enactments relating to customs and includes the waters on which it so abuts ;

"enactment" includes any instrument having statutory effect ;

"epidemic" means an extension of a disease subject to the International Health Regulations by a multiplication of cases in an area ;

"excepted area" means all the territory of Belgium, Metropolitan France, Greece, the Republic of Ireland, Italy, Luxembourg, the Netherlands and the United Kingdom, the Channel Islands and the Isle of Man ;

"excepted port" means any port in the excepted area ;

"foreign port" means a port or other coastal place situated elsewhere than in the United Kingdom, the Channel Islands, the Isle of Man or the Republic of Ireland ;

"free pratique" means permission for a ship to disembark and commence operation ;

"health authority" means a local health authority for the purposes of the National Health Service (Scotland) Acts 1947 to 1968(b) and includes a port local authority or joint port local authority constituted under section 172 of the Public Health (Scotland) Act 1897(c) ;

"immigration officer" means any person appointed to act as an immigration officer under the Aliens Restriction Acts 1914(d) and 1919(e) or under the Commonwealth Immigrants Acts 1962(f) and 1968(g) ;

"infected area" means an area notified as such to health administrators by the World Health Organisation under Article 11 of the International

---

(a) 1952 c. 44.
(b) 1947 c. 27; 1949 c. 93; 1951 c. 31; 1952 c. 25; 1953 c. 41; 1961 c. 19; 1966 c. 8; 1968 c. 46.
(c) 1897 c. 38.   (d) 1914 c. 12.
(e) 1919 c. 92.   (f) 1962 c. 21.
(g) 1968 c. 9.

Health Regulations and which has not been subsequently notified by that organisation as being free from infection ;

"infected person" means a person who is suffering from a disease subject to the International Health Regulations or who is considered by the medical officer to be infected with such a disease ;

"infected ship" means—

(a) a ship which has on board on arrival a case of a disease subject to the International Health Regulations ; or

(b) a ship on which a plague-infected rodent is found on arrival ; or

(c) a ship which has had on board during its voyage—

(i) a case of human plague which developed more than six days after the embarkation of the person affected ; or

(ii) a case of cholera within five days before arrival ; or

(iii) a case of yellow fever or smallpox ;
and which has not before arrival been subjected in respect of such case to appropriate measures equivalent to those provided for in these regulations ;

"infectious disease" means a disease subject to the International Health Regulations or any other infectious or contagious disease other than venereal disease or tuberculosis ;

"International Health Regulations" means the International Health Regulations as adopted by the World Health Assembly on 25th July 1969 ;

"isolation", when applied to a person or group of persons, means the separation of that person or group of persons from other persons, except the health staff on duty, in such a manner as to prevent the spreading of infection ;

"Maritime Declaration of Health" means a declaration in the form set out in Schedule 2 ;

"master" means the person for the time being in charge of or in command of a ship ;

"medical officer" means the medical officer of health for a district, or any other medical practitioner appointed by the health authority in accordance with regulation 5 ;

"medical practitioner" means a registered medical practitioner ;

"mooring station" means a place, situated within the waters of a district, which is specified by the health authority, with the consent of the collector of customs for the area in which the district is situated and the harbour master, or in such other district as the Secretary of State may allow, for the mooring of ships for medical inspection so that they do not come into contact with other ships or the shore ;

"radio receiving port" means a district specified in a notice published in accordance with regulation 12(1)(a) ;

"radio transmitting port" means a district specified in a notice published in accordance with regulation 12(1)(b) ;

"ship" has the same meaning as the expression "vessel" bears for the purposes of the Public Health (Scotland) Act 1945 and accordingly includes—

(a) any ship or boat ;

(b) any other description of vessel used in navigation ;

(*c*) any hovercraft within the meaning of the Hovercraft Act 1968(**a**) ;

"suspect" means a person (not being an infected person) who is considered by the medical officer as having been exposed to infection by a disease subject to the International Health Regulations and is considered capable of spreading that disease ;

"suspected ship" means—

(*a*) a ship which, not having on board on arrival a case of human plague, has had on board during the voyage a case of that disease which developed within six days of the embarkation of the person affected ; or

(*b*) a ship on which there is evidence of abnormal mortality among rodents, the cause of which is unknown on arrival ; or

(*c*) a ship which has had on board during the voyage a case of cholera which developed more than five days before arrival ; or

(*d*) a ship which left within six days before arrival an area infected with yellow fever :

Provided that a ship to which the foregoing paragraph (*a*) or (*c*) applies shall not be deemed to be a suspected ship if in respect of such case of human plague or cholera, as the case may be, the ship has before arrival been subjected to appropriate measures equivalent to those provided for in these regulations ;

"valid" in relation to a Deratting Certificate or Deratting Exemption Certificate issued for a ship, means issued not more than six months before the production of the Certificate to the medical officer, or, if the ship is proceeding immediately to an approved port or a designated approved port, not more than seven months before such production ;

"valid International Vaccination Certificate" means a certificate of vaccination or revaccination against smallpox or cholera which—

(*a*) being issued before the coming into operation of these regulations, is in the form required by the Public Health (Ships) (Scotland) Regulations 1966(**b**) as amended (**c**) or a form substantially to the same effect, and conforms with the rules as to validity referred to in those regulations ;

or

(*b*) being issued on or after the coming into operation of these regulations, is in the form laid down and conforms with the rules as to validity contained in Schedule 5 or Schedule 6 as the case may be.

(2) Any reference in these regulations to a numbered regulation or schedule shall, unless the reference is to a regulation or schedule of specified regulations, be construed as a reference to the regulation or schedule bearing that number in these regulations.

(3) In these regulations, unless the context otherwise requires, references to any enactment shall be construed as references to that enactment as amended or re-enacted by any subsequent enactment.

(4) The Interpretation Act 1889(**d**) shall apply for the interpretation of these regulations as it applies for the interpretation of an Act of Parliament.

(**a**) 1968 c. 59.   (**b**) S.I. 1966/1570 (1966 III, p. 4822).
(**c**) The relevant amending instrument is S.I. 1968/1913 (1968 III, p. 5068).
(**d**) 1889 c. 63.

(5) For the purposes of these regulations a ship shall not be deemed to have been in an infected area if, without having itself been in contact with the shore, it has landed there only mail, passengers and baggage, or has taken on board there only mail, fuel, water or stores or passengers, with or without baggage, who have not themselves been in contact either with the shore or with any person from the shore.

Regulations not to apply to ships of the armed forces

3. Without prejudice to any enactment or rule of law which applies in relation to Her Majesty's armed forces or to any of the other armed forces hereinafter mentioned as part thereof, nothing in these regulations shall apply to any ship forming part of Her Majesty's armed forces or of the armed forces of any country within the Commonwealth or of the armed forces of any other country for the time being designated for the purposes of all the provisions of the Visiting Forces Act 1952(**a**) following section 1(2) thereof, or to the officers and crew of any such ship.

PART II

GENERAL

Enforcement and execution of regulations

4.—(1) Subject to the provisions of paragraph (2) of this regulation, every health authority shall enforce and execute these regulations and shall exercise their functions through the medical officer and such other officers as they may authorise in that behalf, and shall make such inquiries and take such other steps as seem to them to be necessary for securing the proper exercise of those functions.

(2) Any two health authorities may agree, upon terms and conditions approved by the Secretary of State, that one of them shall undertake the enforcement and execution of and arrange for their authorised officers to enforce and execute the whole or specified provisions of these regulations in the district and the other, and for this purpose the district in which any such provision is so enforced and executed shall be deemed to be the district of the authority who enforce and execute it ; and if their district is an approved port or a designated approved port and they so agree to enforce and execute in another district the provisions relating to Deratting Certificates and Deratting Exemption Certificates, the medical officer for the district shall have authority to grant such Certificates in such other district.

Appointment and duties of authorised officers and provision of services by health authorities

5. For the purpose of these regulations a health authority may, and if so required by the Secretary of State, shall—

(*a*) appoint such medical practitioners, in addition to their medical officer of health, as may be necessary for the proper enforcement and execution of these regulations ;

(*b*) give directions from time to time as to the duties which are to be performed by any medical practitioner so appointed or any other officer authorised to enforce and execute these regulations ;

(**a**) 1952 c. 67.

(c) provide or arrange for the provision of—

   (i) premises or waiting rooms for the medical inspection and examination of persons ;

   (ii) premises for the temporary isolation of persons pursuant to these regulations ;

   (iii) apparatus or other means for cleansing, disinfecting or disinsecting ships, persons or clothing and other articles ;

(d) arrange for the reception into a hospital of persons requiring to be removed thereto in accordance with these regulations ;

(e) arrange for the provision of means of transport for the conveyance of persons to any premises referred to in paragraph (c) of this regulation, or to a hospital ;

(f) do all such other things as in their opinion or the opinion of the Secretary of State, as the case may be, are necessary to enable the provisions of these regulations to be complied with.

List of infected areas

6.—(1) The medical officer of health for every district shall from time to time prepare and keep up to date a list of ports and other areas which are infected or believed to be infected with a disease subject to the International Health Regulations or which may serve other places or areas so infected or believed to be so infected.

(2) The medical officer of health shall supply copies of every such list and any amendment thereof to the pilots and customs officers employed in the district.

(3) In preparing and amending such list the medical officer of health shall take into account all information sent to him from time to time by the Secretary of State or issued by the World Health Organisation.

PART III

INCOMING SHIPS

Inspection of ships

7.—(1) The medical officer or other authorised officer may, for the purpose of these regulations, inspect any ship on arrival or already in the district.

(2) The medical officer shall—

(a) inspect on arrival any ship in respect of which the master has sent to the health authority a message or notification under regulation 14 ; and

(b) inspect any ship already in the district when he has reasonable grounds for believing that there is on board a case or suspected case of infectious disease.

Direction of ships

8. Any authorised officer may for the purposes of these regulations require a ship on arrival or already in the district to be brought to, and if necessary moored or anchored at, some safe and convenient place for the purpose of medical inspection.

Examination, etc., of persons on ships

9.—(1) The medical officer may, and if so requested by the master or required by the Secretary of State shall, examine any person on board a ship on arrival or already in the district, when there are reasonable grounds for suspecting that—

(a) the person is suffering from an infectious disease ;

(b) the person has been exposed to infection from an infectious disease ;

(c) the person is verminous.

(2) The medical officer may—

(a) detain any such person for such examination either upon the ship or at some place on shore appointed for the purpose ;

(b) require the clothing and other articles belonging to any person so examined to be disinfected and, where necessary, disinsected, and any person found to be verminous to be disinsected ;

(c) except as provided in regulation 32, prohibit any person so examined from leaving the ship, or permit him to leave it on such conditions and subject to the taking of such measures, in accordance with these regulations, as the medical officer considers reasonably necessary for preventing the spread of infection ; and

(d) require the master to take or assist in taking such steps as in the opinion of the medical officer are reasonably necessary for preventing the spread of infection, for disinsection and the destruction of vermin, and for the removal of conditions on the ship likely to convey infection, including conditions the existence of which might facilitate the harbouring of insects or vermin.

(3) On the arrival of any ship which during its voyage has been in a foreign port other than an excepted port the medical officer or other authorised officer, or at any port where their employment for this purpose is sanctioned by the Commissioners of Customs and Excise, a customs officer may, and if so required by the Secretary of State shall, require any person on board or disembarking from the ship to produce a valid International Vaccination Certificate.

(4) A customs officer or other authorised officer may detain until the arrival of the medical officer or for three hours, whichever is the shorter period, any such person who has been required to produce such a certificate and is unable to do so.

(5) Where any such person fails to satisfy the medical officer that he possesses such a certificate, the medical officer may detain him for examination at a place appointed for that purpose, and may apply in his case the additional measures specified in Part II of Schedule 4 and in paragraphs (1) and (2) of Part IV of Schedule 4.

(6) The powers conferred by paragraphs (3), (4) and (5) of this regulation shall not be exercised in respect of any person on board a ship arriving from an excepted port unless the Secretary of State has directed, or the medical officer is satisfied and has so informed the customs officer, that the exercise of this power is necessary on account of danger to public health.

(7) The medical officer or customs officer shall immediately notify the health authority of any directions given to him by the Secretary of State under this regulation.

(8) Nothing in this regulation shall be deemed to authorise the use of a ship for the isolation of a person who is suffering from, or has been exposed to infection from, an infectious disease unless such isolation can be effected without delaying or unduly interfering with the movements of the ship.

Powers in respect of certain persons on ships

10.—(1) Where there is, or the medical officer suspects that there is, on board a ship on arrival or already in the district a person suffering from an infectious disease or tuberculosis, the medical officer may—

(*a*) in the case of an infectious disease, cause such person to be removed from the ship and isolated or sent to a hospital or to some other suitable place approved for that purpose by the health authority, as may be appropriate; or, unless regulation 32 has been invoked, the medical officer may, by notice in writing to the master, prohibit the removal of the person or his disembarking from the ship without the consent in writing of the medical officer;

(*b*) in the case of tuberculosis, if the person disembarks, send information to that effect to the medical officer of health for the area in which the intended destination and address of the person is situated.

(2) If the Secretary of State is satisfied that a grave danger to public health exists by reason of infectious disease and notifies medical officers accordingly, the medical officer, if the Secretary of State so directs, shall require a person disembarking from a ship to state in writing his name and intended destination and address.

Supply of information, etc., by masters

11. The master of a ship on arrival or already in a district shall—

(*a*) answer all questions as to the health conditions on board which may be put to him by a customs officer or an authorised officer and furnish any such officer with all such information and assistance as he may reasonably require for the purposes of these regulations;

(*b*) notify the medical officer immediately of any circumstances on board which are likely to cause the spread of infectious disease, including in his notification particulars as to the sanitary condition of the ship and the presence of rodents, or mortality or sickness among rodents, on the ship;

(*c*) comply with these regulations, and with any directions or requirements of an authorised officer or customs officer given or made for the purposes of these regulations.

Designation of radio receiving ports and radio transmitting ports

12.—(1) The Secretary of State may, by notice published in the Edinburgh Gazette, declare that any district specified in such notice shall be—

(*a*) a district for the receipt from ships before arrival there of radio messages for the purposes of these regulations;

(*b*) a district for the transmission by radio to ships before arrival of the permission referred to in regulation 13.

(2) The Secretary of State may include in any such notice any variation of the requirement of regulation 14(2)(*b*) which he considers necessary.

Radio permission to enter a district

13. The medical officer for a radio transmitting port may, when he is satisfied by information received by radio from a ship from a foreign port before arrival in his district, or by any other information, that the arrival of the ship will not result in or contribute towards the spread of infectious disease, transmit to the master by radio permission, for the purposes of these regulations, for the ship to proceed direct to its intended place of mooring, discharge or loading.

Notification of infectious disease, etc., on board

14.—(1) When there is on board a ship before arrival a person who is suffering from an infectious disease or who has symptoms which may indicate the presence of infectious disease which require a positive answer to any question relating to health in the Maritime Declaration of Health set out in Schedule 2, or when there are on board a ship before arrival any other similar circumstances requiring the attention of the medical officer, the master shall—

(a) if the ship is equipped with a suitable radio transmitting apparatus and is due to arrive at a radio receiving port, send before arrival, either directly to the health authority or through an agent approved by them, a radio message complying with paragraph (2) of this regulation;

(b) if the ship is not so equipped or is due to arrive elsewhere than at a radio receiving port, notify the health authority, whenever practicable before arrival and otherwise immediately on arrival, of the presence on board of such infectious disease, symptoms or other similar circumstances.

(2) Any radio message sent for the purpose of this regulation shall—

(a) be sent so as to reach the health authority not more than twelve hours, and whenever practicable not less than four hours, before the expected arrival of the ship;

(b) if it is in code, conform with Part VIII of the International Code of Signals as reproduced in Schedule 1, unless the notice published in accordance with regulation 12 in respect of such radio receiving port otherwise provides.

Signals

15.—(1) The master of a ship which is due to arrive in a district from a foreign port, or of a ship which has proceeded from a port in the United Kingdom and which has met a ship which has proceeded from a foreign port other than an excepted port shall, when the ship comes within the district, show or give between sunrise and sunset the appropriate day signal set out in Part VIII of the International Code of Signals as reproduced in Schedule 1, and between sunset and sunrise the night signal set out in that Schedule:

Provided that the master of a ship engaged in regular packet-boat or excursion traffic with a port in France, Belgium or the Netherlands shall not be required to give or show any such signal unless it has met a ship which has proceeded from a foreign port other than an excepted port.

(2) The signal required by the foregoing paragraph of this regulation shall continue to be shown or given until the ship is granted free pratique in writing by an authorised officer or a customs officer.

Maritime Declaration of Health

16.—(1) Subject to the provisions of this regulation, on the arrival of a ship which during its voyage has been in a foreign port, or of a ship which has proceeded from an excepted port and which has met a ship which has proceeded from a foreign port other than an excepted port, the master shall complete a Maritime Declaration of Health in the form set out in Schedule 2, which shall be countersigned by the ship's surgeon if one is carried.

(2) The master shall deliver the Declaration to the customs officer or authorised officer, whoever first boards the ship, who shall forward it to the health authority.

(3) If the customs officer detains the ship in accordance with these regulations and he requires a copy of the Declaration, the health authority shall furnish him with a copy:

Provided that in the case of a ship which during its voyage has not been in a foreign port other than an excepted port, and has not during the voyage met a ship which has proceeded from a foreign port outside the excepted area, the master shall not be bound to comply with the provisions of this regulation unless he has been notified by the medical officer that compliance with those provisions is necessary on account of danger to public health.

17. If, within four weeks after the master of a ship has delivered a Maritime Declaration of Health in accordance with regulation 16 or a corresponding provision in force in England and Wales or Northern Ireland, the ship arrives in a district or calls at another district, as the case may be, the master shall report to the customs officer or authorised officer, whoever first boards the ship, any case or suspected case of infectious disease which has occurred on board since the Declaration was delivered and which has not already been reported.

Restriction on boarding or leaving ships

18.—(1) On the arrival of a ship from any foreign port or from any infected area, or of a ship which has proceeded from an excepted port and which has met a ship which has proceeded from a foreign port other than an excepted port, no person other than a pilot, a customs officer, an immigration officer or an authorised officer shall, without the permission of the medical officer, board or leave the ship until free pratique has been granted, and the master shall take all steps necessary to secure compliance with this provision.

(2) Before granting permission to a person to leave the ship, the medical officer may require him to state his name and his intended destination and address, and to give any other information which the medical officer may think necessary for transmission to the medical officer of health for the area in which the intended destination of the person is situated.

(3) If such a person cannot state his intended destination and address or arrives, within a period not exceeding fourteen days after landing, to be specified to him by the medical officer, at an address other than that which he has so stated, he shall immediately after his arrival at that address send particulars thereof to the medical officer of the port where he left the ship.

Deratting Certificates and Deratting Exemption Certificates

19.—(1) If the master of a ship which during its voyage has been in a foreign port cannot produce to the medical officer or other authorised officer for the district in which the ship arrives or for any district at which the ship calls a valid Deratting Certificate or Deratting Exemption Certificate in respect of the ship in the form set out in Schedule 3, the medical officer or other authorised officer shall—

(a) if the district is an approved port or a designated approved port, require the ship to be inspected to ascertain whether it is kept in such a condition that it is free of rodents and the plague vector; or

(b) if the district is not such a port, direct the ship to proceed at its own risk to the nearest approved port or designated approved port convenient to the ship at which a Deratting Certificate or Deratting Exemption Certificate, as the case may be, can be obtained.

(2) If, after the ship has been inspected, the medical officer or other authorised officer for the approved port or designated approved port is satisfied that the ship is free from rodents and the plague vector, he shall issue a Deratting Exemption Certificate.

(3) If, after the ship has been inspected, such medical officer or other authorised officer is not so satisfied, he shall—

(a) if the district is a designated approved port, require the ship to be deratted in a manner to be determined by him; or

(b) if the district is not a designated approved port, direct the ship to proceed at its own risk to the nearest designated approved port convenient to the ship for deratting.

(4) If the master produces a Deratting Certificate or a Deratting Exemption Certificate, but the medical officer or other authorised officer has evidence that the deratting was not satisfactorily completed, the medical officer or other authorised officer may, notwithstanding such Certificate, exercise in relation to the ship his powers under the last preceding paragraph.

(5) The master shall forthwith make arrangements for any deratting required by the medical officer or other authorised officer for the designated approved port.

(6) When deratting has been completed to the satisfaction of the medical officer or other authorised officer for the designated approved port, he shall issue a Deratting Certificate.

(7) Before the medical officer or other authorised officer directs under this regulation that a ship shall proceed to another port, he shall consult with a customs officer for the district.

20. Upon receipt of an application in writing from the owner of a ship in an approved port, or from the master acting for and on behalf of the owner, for a Deratting Certificate or a Deratting Exemption Certificate in respect of the ship, the medical officer or other authorised officer shall take any steps which he considers necessary to satisfy himself that the ship is kept in such a condition that it is free of rodents and the plague vector, or at a designated approved port give directions for the deratting of the ship, as the case may require, and, on being satisfied as to the condition of the ship or that the deratting has been properly carried out, he shall issue the appropriate Certificate.

21.—(1) Every Deratting Certificate and Deratting Exemption Certificate shall be in the form specified in Schedule 3.

(2) A copy of every such Certificate issued under regulation 19 or 20 shall be retained by the health authority.

(3) The owner or master of a ship shall pay to the health authority such charge as the Secretary of State may from time to time determine for the inspection of the ship for the purposes of regulation 19 or 20.

Detention of ships, and ships to be taken to mooring stations

22.—(1) On the arrival of an infected ship or a suspected ship, or any other ship on which there has been, during its current voyage and within the last four weeks before arrival, a case of a disease subject to the International Health Regulations in respect of which the ship has not, outside the United Kingdom, been subjected to appropriate measures equivalent to those provided for in these regulations, the master shall take it to a mooring station unless an authorised officer otherwise allows or directs.

(2) When the medical officer has reason to believe that a ship on arrival may be one to which paragraph (1) of this regulation applies, he may direct the master to take it to a mooring station or to such other place as he considers desirable.

23. The medical officer may for the purposes of these regulations direct that any ship from a foreign port shall on arrival be taken to a mooring station for medical inspection, and he may, if a customs officer is to be the first officer to board the ship, give a notice in writing of such direction to the customs officer, who shall deliver the notice to the master.

24. Where on the arrival of a ship from a foreign port it appears to a customs officer, from information in the Maritime Declaration of Health or otherwise, that the ship—

(*a*) has during its voyage been in an infected area; or

(*b*) is one to which regulation 22(1) applies,

he shall direct the master to take it to a mooring station for detention there unless an authorised officer otherwise allows or directs.

25. If after arrival of a ship a case of a disease subject to the International Health Regulations occurs on board, or plague-infected rodents are discovered or suspected on board, the medical officer may direct the master of the ship to take it to a mooring station.

26. A ship which has been taken to a mooring station or directed there by a medical officer shall remain there until it has been inspected by the medical officer.

27. A medical officer may detain, or give notice in writing to a customs officer to detain, any ship for medical inspection at its place of mooring (not being a mooring station) or at its place of discharge or loading.

28. The detention of a ship by a customs officer under these regulations shall cease as soon as the ship has been inspected by the medical officer, or, if such inspection has not commenced within twelve hours after the ship has been so detained, on the expiration of that period:

Provided that nothing in this regulation shall affect the power of the medical officer to continue the detention of a ship in accordance with regulation 29.

29.—(1) The medical officer shall inspect any ship and the persons on board as soon as possible after it has been taken or directed to a mooring station or after it has been detained under these regulations.

(2) If the ship is one to which the medical officer is required by these regulations to apply any further measure in accordance with these regulations or additional measure in Schedule 4, or if after such inspection he considers it necessary to apply any such further or additional measure, he may detain the ship at the mooring station or at such other place as he considers desirable, or continue the detention, as the case may be, if such detention or continued detention is necessary for the application of such further or additional measure.

30. The medical officer may require the master of a ship which has been taken or directed to a mooring station or detained because plague-infected rodents have been discovered, or there are reasonable grounds for suspecting that such rodents are on board, to take all practicable measures to prevent escape of rodents from the ship.

Persons from infected areas

31. On the arrival of a ship the medical officer may place under surveillance for the appropriate period specified in regulation 37(1)—

(a) any person disembarking from the ship who has come from an infected area other than an area infected with yellow fever or plague; and

(b) any suspect disembarking from the ship who has come from an area infected with yellow fever or plague.

Removal of infected persons from ships when required by master

32. The medical officer shall, if so required by the master of a ship on arrival, cause any infected person to be removed from the ship.

Additional measures

33. Without prejudice to any other provision in these regulations, the additional measures in Schedule 4 shall be applicable on the arrival of—

(a) any infected ship or suspected ship;

(b) any ship which has during its voyage been in an area infected with plague, cholera or yellow fever;

(c) any suspect for smallpox on a ship other than an infected ship;

(d) any other ship when the medical officer is satisfied that, notwithstanding that measures equivalent to such additional measures have been applied to the ship or any person on board at a previous port during its voyage, there is on board or has been on board since such previous application an infected person or suspect and that it is necessary again to apply any such measure, or the medical officer has evidence that such previous application was not effective.

PART IV

OUTGOING SHIPS

Examination, etc., of persons proposing to embark

34. Where a ship is due to depart for a destination, whether final or intermediate outside the United Kingdom, the medical officer—

(a) may examine any person who proposes to embark thereon if he has reasonable grounds for believing him to be suffering from a disease subject to the International Health Regulations, and, if after examination the medical officer is of the opinion that he shows symptoms of such a disease, shall prohibit his embarkation and the time and place of this examination shall be arranged to take into account any other formalities and to avoid delay;

(b) shall prohibit any suspect from embarking thereon:

Provided that in the case of smallpox a person shall not be prohibited from embarking if he satisfies the medical officer that he is sufficiently protected by vaccination or by a previous attack of smallpox;

(c) shall notify by the most expeditious means the master and, also, the health authority for the place to which the person is proceeding of any person embarking or proposing to continue his voyage thereon who, in the opinion of the medical officer, should be placed under surveillance;

(d) may, notwithstanding the provisions of sub-paragraph (b) of this regulation, allow a person on an international voyage who, on arrival, was placed under surveillance, to continue his voyage; and the medical officer shall notify by the most expeditious means the health authority for the place to which the person is proceeding that such a person should, in the opinion of the medical officer, be placed under surveillance.

Infected places in Scotland

35. Where the Secretary of State has, by notice published in the Edinburgh Gazette, declared any place to be infected with a disease subject to the International Health Regulations or with any other disease which in his opinion constitutes a menace to other countries by reason of its spread or potential spread, then, until the notice is revoked by a subsequent notice published in the Edinburgh Gazette, every medical officer shall comply with any requirement which may be made by the Secretary of State for preventing the spread of the disease, and in particular (but without prejudice to the generality of the foregoing provisions) the following provisions of this regulation shall operate in relation to any ship departing from any district specified by the Secretary of State for a destination, whether final or intermediate, outside the United Kingdom:—

(a) an authorised officer, if so required by the Secretary of State, shall require a valid International Vaccination Certificate from departing travellers; and in the absence of such a certificate the medical officer may offer vaccination to any such traveller and may apply the provisions of regulation 34(c);

(b) the medical officer may, and within three hours after receiving a request from the master so to do shall, medically examine any person who proposes to embark on or is on board the ship;

(c) the medical officer may require any part of the ship which in his opinion may be infected to be cleansed and disinfected to his satisfaction;

(d) an authorised officer shall inspect any clothing, bedding or other article which is on, or is intended to be taken by any person on, the ship and which, in the opinion of the officer, may have been exposed to infection and may require the disinfection or destruction of any such clothing, bedding or article, and the master shall disclose to the authorised officer any relevant circumstances;

(*e*) no person shall take or cause to be taken on board the ship any article which, in the opinion of an authorised officer, is capable of carrying infection unless that officer is satisfied that it has been efficiently disinfected and, where necessary, disinsected;

(*f*) if any part of the district is included in the said notice in the Edinburgh Gazette and is therein declared to be infected with plague, and if there is reason to believe that there are rodents on the ship, the medical officer may, and if so required by the Secretary of State shall, take steps to secure the deratting of the ship.

PART V

MISCELLANEOUS

Compliance with directions, etc., under the regulations

36. Every person to whom these regulations apply shall comply with every direction, requirement or condition given, made or imposed by an authorised officer or customs officer in accordance with these regulations, and shall furnish all such information as that officer may reasonably require (including information as to his name and intended destination and address to which he is going on leaving a ship), and every person who has for the time being the custody or charge of a child or other person who is under disability shall comply with any direction, requirement or condition so given made or imposed, and shall furnish all such information as aforesaid in respect of that child or other person.

Surveillance

37.—(1) Where these regulations permit a medical officer to place a person under surveillance, the period of such surveillance shall not exceed such of the following periods as may be appropriate:—

(*a*) in respect of plague, six days;

(*b*) in respect of cholera, five days;

(*c*) in respect of yellow fever, six days;

(*d*) in respect of smallpox, fourteen days;

(2) Where a person has been so placed under surveillance for plague, cholera or smallpox in accordance with regulation 31 by reason of his having come from an infected area, the period shall be reckoned from the date of his leaving the infected area.

(3) When a person has been so placed under surveillance in accordance with the additional measures in Schedule 4, the period shall be reckoned in the manner therein specified.

38. Every person who is placed under surveillance in accordance with these regulations shall—

(*a*) give facilities for any medical examination required by the medical officer or by the medical officer of health for any area in which he may be during the period of surveillance;

(*b*) furnish all such information as the medical officer or any such medical officer of health may reasonably require with a view to ascertaining the person's state of health;

(c) forthwith upon arrival during the period of surveillance at any address other than the one stated as his intended address when placed under surveillance, send particulars of that address to the medical officer;

(d) if so instructed by the medical officer, report immediately to the medical officer of health for any area in which he may be during the period of surveillance, and thereafter during that period report to that officer at such intervals as he may require:

Provided that an instruction shall not be given under this sub-paragraph unless the Secretary of State has by direction (whether general or special) authorised the giving of instructions thereunder.

Charges for services

39.—(1) Where the master of a ship in a district is required by these regulations to carry out any measures with a view to reducing the danger or preventing the spread of infection, the health authority may themselves, at the request of the master, cause any such requirement to be complied with at his cost instead of enforcing the requirement against the master.

(2) The amount of the charge for any such measures or requirement undertaken by the health authority shall be such reasonable sum as represents the actual or estimated cost to be incurred in undertaking the work, excluding any charge or claim on the part of the health authority in respect of profit, but shall not exceed the sum of one hundred pounds unless notice of the proposed charge has been given to the master before the work is undertaken.

(3) Where, under this regulation, the health authority cause any requirement to be complied with at the cost of the master they may require the amount of the charge for the work or a part thereof to be paid to or deposited with them before the work is undertaken.

(4) Where, under these regulations, any measures have been taken with regard to a ship, the health authority or the medical officer shall, on the request of the master, furnish him free of charge with particulars in writing of those measures and the reasons why they were taken.

(5) Where, under these regulations, any measures have been taken with regard to any person or to any articles in his possession, the medical officer shall, on request by such person, furnish him free of charge with particulars in writing of those measures, including the date on which they were taken.

Recovery of charges

40. Every charge authorised by regulation 21 or 39 shall be recoverable as a civil debt.

Expenses of health authorities

41. Subject to the provisions of regulation 39, any expenses incurred by a health authority in the enforcement and execution of these regulations shall be defrayed in the same manner as the expenses incurred by them in the execution and discharge of their other powers and duties.

Saving for mails

42. Except to the extent permitted by Part II-C of Schedule 4 with respect to fish, shellfish, fruit, vegetables and beverages, nothing in these regulations shall render liabile to detention, disinfection or destruction any article forming part of any mail conveyed under the authority of the Post Office or of the postal administration of any other Government, or shall prejudicially affect the receipt on board and delivery in due course at the place of destination of any such mail in accordance with the provisions of the Post Office Act 1953(a) as amended by Part II of Schedule 4 to the Post Office Act 1969(b).

Saving for ships unwilling to comply with these regulations

43.—(1) The master of a ship on arrival, or already in a district, who is unwilling to comply with, or submit to, any provision of, or requirement made under, these regulations which may be applicable shall so notify the medical officer, and the medical officer may then require the master to remove the ship immediately from the district.

(2) If before leaving the district the master wishes to discharge cargo or disembark passengers or to take on board fuel, water or stores, the medical officer shall permit him to do so, but may impose such conditions under these regulations as the medical officer considers necessary.

(3) When the medical officer has required the removal of a ship from the district, it shall not, during its voyage, call at any other district.

Saving for existing enactments

44. Nothing in these regulations shall affect the Aliens Order 1953(c) or the Commonwealth Immigrants Acts 1962(d) and 1968(e) and the Immigration Appeals Act 1969(f).

Revocations

45.—(1) The Public Health (Ships) (Scotland) Regulations 1966(g) and the Public Health (Ships) (Scotland) Amendment Regulations 1968(h) are hereby revoked.

(2) Section 38 of the Interpretation Act 1889 shall apply as if these regulations were an Act of Parliament and as if any regulations revoked by these regulations were Acts of Parliament repealed by an Act of Parliament.

Gordon Campbell,
One of Her Majesty's Principal
Secretaries of State.

St. Andrew's House,
Edinburgh.
26th January 1971.

(a) 1953 c. 36.
(c) S.I. 1953/1671 (1953 I, p. 94).
(e) 1968 c. 9.
(g) S.I. 1966/1570 (1966 III, p. 4822).
(b) 1969 c. 48.
(d) 1962 c. 21.
(f) 1969 c. 21.
(h) S.I. 1968/1913 (1968 III, p. 5068).

Regulation 15   SCHEDULE 1

INTERNATIONAL CODE OF SIGNALS

PART VIII

PRATIQUE MESSAGES

ZS   My vessel is "healthy" and I request free pratique.   Q
     *I require health clearance.   QQ

ZT   My Maritime Declaration of Health has negative answers to the six health
     questions.

ZU   My Maritime Declaration of Health has a positive answer to question(s).........
     (indicated by appropriate number(s)).

ZV   I believe I have been in an infected area during the last thirty days.

ZW   I require Port Medical Officer.
     ZW1 Port Medical Officer will be available (at time indicated).

ZX   You should make the appropriate pratique signal.

ZY   You have pratique.

ZZ   You should proceed to anchorage for health clearance (at place indicated).

     ZZ1 Where is the anchorage for health clearance?

     I have a doctor on board   AL

     Have you a doctor?   AM

---

   * By night a red light over a white light may be shown where it can best be seen by
vessels requiring health clearance.   These lights should *only* be about two metres (6 feet)
apart, should be exhibited within the precincts of a port, and should be visible all round the
horizon *as nearly as possible.*

Regulation 16

SCHEDULE 2

PUBLIC HEALTH (SHIPS) (SCOTLAND) REGULATIONS 1971
Maritime Declaration of Health

Port of Arrival...Date.........................

Name of Ship.............................From.................... To.......................

Nationality ....Master's Name............................

Net Registered Tonnage..................................

Deratting Certificate or ⎱ issued at.........................Dated.................
Deratting Exemption Certificate ⎰

Number of ⎧ Cabin...................................Number of crew.......................
Passengers ⎨
⎩ Deck...........................

List of ports of call from commencement of voyage with dates of departure...............
....
....

Health Questions	Answer Yes or No.
1. Has there been on board during the voyage* any case or suspected case of plague, cholera, yellow fever or smallpox? Give particulars in schedule	....
2. Has plague occurred or been suspected among the rats or mice on board during the voyage*, or has there been an abnormal mortality among them?	....
3. Has any person died on board during the voyage* otherwise than as a result of an accident? Give particulars in schedule	....
4. Is there on board or has there been during the voyage* any case of disease which you suspect to be of an infectious nature? Give particulars in schedule	....
5. Is there any sick person on board now? Give particulars in schedule	....
Note—In the absence of a surgeon, the Master should regard the following symptoms as ground for suspecting the existence of disease of an infectious nature: fever accompanied by prostration or persisting for several days, or attended with glandular swelling; or any acute skin rash or eruption with or without fever; severe diarrhoea with symptoms of collapse; jaundice accompanied by fever.	
6. Are you aware of any other condition on board which may lead to infection or the spread of disease?	....

I hereby declare that the particulars and answers to the questions given in this Declaration of Health (including the schedule) are true and correct to the best of my knowledge and belief.

Signed...
(*Master*)
Countersigned ....
Date.................................... (*Ship's Surgeon*)

* If more than four weeks have elapsed since the voyage began, it will suffice to give particulars for the last four weeks.

SCHEDULE TO THE DECLARATION

PARTICULARS OF EVERY CASE OF ILLNESS OR DEATH OCCURRING ON BOARD

Name	Class or rating	Age	Sex	Nationality	Port of embarkation	Date of embarkation	Nature of illness	Date of its onset	Results of illness*	Disposal of case†

*State whether recovered; still ill; died.

†State whether still on board; landed at (give name of port); buried at sea.

Regulation 19

SCHEDULE 3

DERATTING CERTIFICATE(a)—CERTIFICAT DE DÉRATISATION(*a*)

DERATTING EXEMPTION CERTIFICATE(a)—CERTIFICAT D'EXEMPTION DE LA DÉRATISATION(*a*)

issued in accordance with Article 54 of the International Health Regulations—délivré conformément à l'article 54 du Réglement Sanitaire
International

(*Not to be taken away by Port Authorities.*)—(Ce certificat ne doit pas être retiré par les authorités portuaires)

PORT OF   —   PORT DE

Date..................   Date..................

THIS CERTIFICATE records the inspection and $\left\{ \begin{array}{l} \textit{deratting} \\ \textit{exemption} \end{array} \right\}$ *(a) at this port and on the above date*

LE PRÉSENT CERTIFICAT atteste l'inspection et $\left\{ \begin{array}{l} \text{la dératisation} \\ \text{l'exemption} \end{array} \right\}$ *(a)* en ce port et à la date ci-dessus

of the $\left\{ \begin{array}{l} \textit{ship} \\ \textit{inland navigation vessel} \end{array} \right\}$ *(a)*   of $\left\{ \begin{array}{l} \textit{net tonnage for a sea-going vessel} \\ \textit{..........tonnage for an inland navigation vessel} \end{array} \right\}$ *(a)*(*f*)

du navire   de $\left\{ \begin{array}{l} \text{tonnage net dans le cas d'un navire de haute mer} \\ \text{tonnage..........dans le cas d'un navire de navigation intérieure} \end{array} \right\}$ *(a)*(*f*)

At the time of $\left\{ \begin{array}{l} \textit{inspection} \\ \textit{deratting} \end{array} \right\}$ *(a) the holds were laden with*   *tons of*   *cargo*

Au moment de $\left\{ \begin{array}{l} \text{l'inspection} \\ \text{le dératisation} \end{array} \right\}$ *(a)* les cales étaient chargées de   tonnes de   cargaison

COMPARTMENTS—(b)	RAT INDICATIONS / TRACES DE RATS (c)	RAT HARBOURAGE / REFUGES À RATS		DERATTING—DÉRATISATION					COMPARTMENTS—(b)
		discovered / trouvés (d)	treated / supprimés	by fumigation—par fumigation / Fumigant—Gaz utilisé ...... Hours exposure—Exposition (heures)			by catching, trapping or poisoning / par capture ou poison		
				Space (cubic feet) Espaces (mètres cubes)	Quantity used Quantités employées (e)	Rats found dead Rats trouvés morts	Traps set or poisons put out Pièges ou poisons mis	Rats caught or killed Rats pris ou tués	
Holds 1.									Cales 1.
2.									2.
3.									3.
4.									4.
5.									5.
6.									6.
7.									7.
Shelter deck space									Entrepont
Bunker space									Soute à charbon
Engineroom and shaft alley									Chaufferies, tunnel de l'arbre
Forepeak and storeroom									Peak avant et magasin
Afterpeak and storeroom									Peak arrière et magasin
Lifeboats									Canots de sauvetage
Charts and wireless rooms									Chambre des cartes T.S.F.
Galley									Cuisines
Pantry									Cambuses
Provision storerooms									Soute à vivres
Quarters (crew)									Postes (équipage)
Quarters (officers)									Chambres (officiers)
Quarters (cabin passengers)									Cabines (passagers)
Quarters (steerage)									Postes (émigrants)
Total									Total

(a) Strike out the unnecessary indications.—Rayer les mentions inutiles.

(b) In case any of the compartments enumerated do not exist on the ship or inland navigation vessel, this fact must be mentioned.—Lorsqu'un des compartiments énumérés n'existe pas sur le navire, on devra le mentionner expressément.

(c) Old or recent evidence of excreta, runs or gnawing.—Traces anciennes ou récentes d'excréments, de passages ou de rongements.

(d) None, small, moderate, or large.—Néant, peu, passablement ou beaucoup.

(e) State the weight of sulphur or of cyanide salts or quantity of HCN acid used.—Indiquer les poids de soufre ou de cyanure ou la proportion d'acide cyanhydrique.

(f) Specify whether applies to metric displacement or any other method of determining the tonnage.—Spécifier s'il s'agit de déplacement métrique ou, sinon, de quel autre tonnage il s'agit.

RECOMMANDATIONS MADE—OBSERVATIONS. In the case of exemption, state here the measures taken for maintaining the ship or inland navigation vessel in such a condition that they are free of rodents and the plague vector. Dans le cas d'exemption, indiquer ici les mesures prises pour que le navire soit maintenu dans des conditions telles qu'il n'y ait à bord ni rongeurs, ni vecteur de la peste.

Seal, name, qualification, and signature of the inspector.—Cachet, nom, qualité et signature de l'inspecteur.

SCHEDULE 4   Regulations 2(1), 9(5) and 33

ADDITIONAL MEASURES WITH RESPECT TO THE
DISEASES SUBJECT TO THE INTERNATIONAL HEALTH REGULATIONS

PART I—PLAGUE

A. *Infected ships and suspected ships*

(1) The medical officer may—

(*a*) require any suspect on board to be disinsected and may place him under surveillance, the period of surveillance being reckoned from the date of arrival of the ship;

(*b*) require the disinsecting and, if necessary, disinfection of the baggage of any infected person or suspect and of any other article on board and any part of the ship which the medical officer considers to be contaminated.

(2) If there is any rodent infected with plague on board, the medical officer or other authorised officer shall require the ship to be deratted in a manner to be determined by him, but without prejudice to the generality of this requirement the following special provisions shall apply to any such deratting:—

(*a*) the deratting shall be carried out as soon as the holds have been emptied or when they contain only ballast or other material, unattractive to rodents, of such a nature or so disposed as to make a thorough inspection of the holds possible; but a Deratting Exemption Certificate may be issued for an oil tanker with full holds;

(*b*) one or more preliminary derattings of a ship with the cargo in situ, or during its unloading, may be carried out to prevent the escape of infected rodents;

(*c*) if the complete destruction of rodents cannot be secured because only part of the cargo is due to be unloaded, a ship shall not be prevented from unloading that part, but the medical officer or other authorised officer may apply any measure which he considers necessary to prevent the escape of infected rodents, including placing the ship in quarantine.

(3) On arrival of a ship having on board a person suffering from pulmonary plague, or if there has been a case of pulmonary plague on board a ship within the period of six days before its arrival, the medical officer may—

(*a*) carry out the measures set out in paragraph 1 of Part I of this Schedule;

(*b*) require any person on board to be placed in isolation for six days reckoned from the date of the last exposure to infection.

B. *Ships which have been in infected areas*

(4) The medical officer may—

(*a*) place under surveillance any suspect who disembarks, the period of surveillance being reckoned from the date of the departure of the ship from the infected area;

(*b*) regard as suspect any person not isolated for 6 days before departure from an area with an epidemic of pulmonary plague;

(*c*) require, in exceptional circumstances and for well founded reasons, the destruction of rodents on the ship and disinsecting, but he shall give the master notice in writing of the reasons for the requirement.

Part II—Cholera

A. *Infected ships and suspected ships*

(1) The medical officer may—

> (*a*) place under surveillance any person who disembarks, the period of surveillance being reckoned from the date of arrival of the ship;

> (*b*) require the disinfection of the baggage of any infected person or suspect and of any other article on board and any part of the ship which the medical officer considers to be contaminated;

> (*c*) require the disinfection and removal of any water on board which he considers to be contaminated, and the disinfection of the water tanks.

(2) The medical officer shall prohibit the discharge or unloading from the ship of human dejecta, bilge water and any other waste matter or water which may be contaminated and has not been disinfected.

B. *Ships which have been in infected areas*

(3) The medical officer may place under surveillance any person who disembarks, the period of surveillance being reckoned from the date of the departure of the ship from the infected area.

C. *Infected ships, suspected ships and ships which have been in infected areas*

(4) On arrival of an infected or suspected ship in which a case of cholera has been discovered or a ship coming from an infected area, the health authority may take samples of food, including fish, shellfish, fruit, vegetables or beverages, for culture examination, unless such food and beverages are in sealed packages, and the health authority have no reason to believe that they are contaminated and may prohibit the unloading of, or may remove, any of these articles found to be contaminated.   If any such food or beverage is removed, arrangements shall be made for its safe disposal in consultation with the customs officer.

(5) If any of the said food or beverage forms part of a cargo in a hold of the ship or a container and is so contaminated, the medical officer for the district in which such cargo is due to be discharged shall arrange for its safe disposal in consultation with the customs officer.

(6) The master of a ship has the right to require the removal of any such food or beverage.

Part III—Yellow Fever

Infected ships, suspected ships, and ships which have been in infected areas

The medical officer may require the ship to be disinsected.

Regulation 9(5)

Part IV—Smallpox

A. *Infected ships*

(1) The medical officer shall offer vaccination to any person on board or disembarking from the ship who does not show sufficient evidence of protection by a previous attack of smallpox or who does not satisfy the medical officer that he possesses a valid International Vaccination Certificate.

(2) The medical officer may either—

    (*a*) place under surveillance any person who disembarks, the period of surveillance being reckoned from the date on which the medical officer considers the person was last exposed to infection; or

    (*b*) if he considers any such person is not sufficiently protected against smallpox, isolate him for a similar period.

(3) The medical officer shall require the disinfection of the baggage of any infected person, and of any other article on board and any part of the ship which the medical officer considers to be contaminated.

B.   *Suspects on other ships*

(4) The medical officer may also apply the provisions of paragraphs (1) and (2) of this Part to any suspect who disembarks from a ship which is not an infected ship.

Regulations 2(1) and 9(3)

SCHEDULE 5

INTERNATIONAL CERTIFICATE OF VACCINATION OR REVACCINATION AGAINST SMALLPOX

CERTIFICAT INTERNATIONAL DE VACCINATION OU DE REVACCINATION CONTRE LA VARIOLE

Date	Show by "x" whether Indiquer par x s'il s'agit de:	Signature and professional status of vaccinator Signature et titre du vaccinateur	Manufacturer and batch no. of vaccine Fabricant du vaccin et numéro du lot	Approved stamp Cachet autorisé
1a	Primary vaccination performed Primo vaccination effectuée		1a	
1b	Read as successful Prise Unsuccessful Pas de prise		1b	
2	Revaccination		2	
3	Revaccination		3	

RULES

The validity of this certificate shall extend for a period of three years, beginning eight days after the date of a successful primary vaccination or, in the event of a revaccination, on the date of that revaccination.

The approved stamp mentioned overleaf must be in a form prescribed by the health administration of the territory in which the vaccination is performed.

This certificate must be signed by a medical practitioner in his own hand; his official stamp is not an accepted substitute for the signature.

Any amendment of this certificate, or erasure, or failure to complete any part of it, may render it invalid.

La validité de ce certificat couvre une période de trois ans commençant huit jours après la date de la primovaccination effectuée avec succès (prise) ou, dans le cas d'une revaccination, le jour de cette revaccination.

Le cachet autorisé doit être conforme au modèle prescrit par l'administration sanitaire du territoire où la vaccination est effectuée.

Ce certificat doit être signé par un médecin de sa propre main, son cachet officiel ne pouvant être considéré comme tenant lieu de signature.

Toute correction ou rature sur le certificat ou l'omission d'une quelconque des mentions qu'il comporte peut affecter sa validité.

INTERNATIONAL CERTIFICATE OF VACCINATIO OR REVACCINATION AGAINST SMALLPOX
CERTIFICAT INTERNATIONAL DE VACCINATION OU DE REVACCINATION CONTRE LA VARIOLE

This is to certify that
Je soussigné(e) certifie que

name ....
nom

date of birth .... sex ....
né(e) le *sexe*

whose signature follows
dont la signature suit

....

has on the date indicated overleaf been vaccinated or revacc nated against smallpox, with a freeze-dried or liquid vacci certified to fulfil the recommended requirements of the Wor Health Organisation.

a été vacciné(e) ou revacciné(e) contre la variole à la date indiqu au verso, avec un vaccin lyophilisé ou liquide certifié conforn aux normes recommandées par l'Organisation Mondiale de Santé.

SCHEDULE 6 Regulations 2(1) and 9(3)

INTERNATIONAL CERTIFICATE OF VACCINATION OR REVACCINATION AGAINST CHOLERA

CERTIFICAT INTERNATIONAL DE VACCINATION OU DE REVACCINATION CONTRE LE CHOLÉRA

Date	Signature and professional status of vaccinator *Signature et titre du vaccinateur*		Approved stamp *Cachet autorisé*	
1	1	1		2
2	2			
3	3	3		4
4	4			
5	5	5		6
6	6			
7	7	7		8
8	8			

RULES

The vaccine used shall meet the requirements laid down by the World Health Organisation.

The validity of this certificate shall extend for a period of six months, beginning six days after one injection of the vaccine or, in the event of a revaccination within such period of six months, on the date of that revaccination.

The approved stamp mentioned overleaf must be in a form prescribed by the health administration of the territory in which the vaccination is performed.

This certificate must be signed by a medical practitioner in his own hand; his official stamp is not an accepted substitute for the signature.

Any amendment of this certificate, or erasure, or failure to complete any part of it, may render it invalid.

Le vaccin utilisé doit satisfaire aux normes formulées par l'Organisation Mondiale de la Santé

La validité de ce certificat couvre une période de six mois commençant six jours après une injection de vaccin ou, dans le cas d'une revaccination au cours de cette période de six mois, le jour de cette revaccination.

Le cachet autorisé doit être conforme au modèle prescrit par l'administration sanitaire du territoire où la vaccination est effectuée.

Ce certificat doit être signé par un médecin de sa propre main, un cachet officiel ne pouvant être considéré comme tenant lieu de signature.

Toute correction ou rature sur le certificat ou l'omission d'une quelconque des mentions qu'il comporte peut affecter sa validité.

INTERNATIONAL CERTIFICATE OF VACCINATION OR REVACCINATION AGAINST CHOLERA

CERTIFICAT INTERNATIONAL DE VACCINATION OU DE REVACCINATION CONTRE LE CHOLÉRA

This is to certify that
Je soussigné(e) certifie que

name ....
nom

date of birth.................... sex ....
né(e) le *sexe*

whose signature follows
dont la signature suit

has on the date indicated overleaf been vaccinated or revaccinated against cholera.
a été vacciné(e) ou revacciné(e) contre le choléra à la date indiquée au verso.

EXPLANATORY NOTE

(This Note is not part of the Regulations.)

These Regulations supersede the Public Health (Ships) (Scotland) Regulations 1966 and the Public Health (Ships) (Scotland) Amendment Regulations 1968 which provide for public health control of ships arriving at or leaving ports in Scotland. They also make amendments to conform with the current International Health Regulations of the World Health Assembly and the administrative arrangements for health control made by the Council of Europe's Public Health Committee (Partial Agreement).

Part I contains definitions of terms used in the Regulations. Provision is made for revised forms of International Vaccination Certificates against smallpox (Schedule 5) and cholera (Schedule 6).

Part II provides for the enforcement and execution of the Regulations by health authorities; it also provides for the preparation by Medical Officers of Health of lists of ports and other areas infected or believed to be infected with specified diseases (Regulation 6).

Part III relates to incoming ships. It provides for the inspection of ships, the examination of persons suspected of suffering from, or having been exposed to infection from, an infectious disease or suspected of being verminous;and in these and other similar circumstances authorises measures to be taken for preventing danger to public health (Regulations 7 to 10). Regulation 11 requires the master of a ship to give information about health conditions on board the ship and to notify circumstances likely to lead to the spread of infection. Provision is also made for radio messages to be sent and the signals to be used in given circumstances (Regulations 12 to 15) and for the completion of a Maritime Declaration of Health by the master of a ship arriving from a foreign port (i.e. a port outside the United Kingdom, the Channel Islands, the Isle of Man or the Republic of Ireland) unless it is an excepted port, as defined in Regulation 2. Regulation 16 imposes obligations upon the master of an incoming ship which has, during its voyage, been in a foreign port or has met a ship which has proceeded from a foreign port. Regulation 18 imposes restrictions on boarding or leaving ships from a foreign port, or from an infected area which is not a foreign port. Regulations 19 to 21 provide for deratting ships and for the grant of Deratting Certificates and Deratting Exemption Certificates. Regulations 22 to 33 provide for the detention and inspection of infected or suspected ships, the placing under surveillance of persons from infected areas, the removal of infected persons from ships and the application of such of the additional measures set out in Schedule 4 as are appropriate to specified diseases subject to the International Health Regulations of a kind particularly dangerous to the public health.

Part IV relates to outgoing ships. It provides for the examination, etc., in prescribed circumstances of persons proposing to embark for a destination outside the United Kingdom (Regulation 34) and, after publication by the Secretary of State in the Edinburgh Gazette of a notice declaring any place to be infected with diseases, the spread of which might endanger public health, special measures may be taken to prevent the disease spreading (Regulation 35).

Part V contains miscellaneous provisions concerning periods of surveillance, charges for services, and expenses of the health authorities enforcing the Regulations. It also contains savings for mails carried by a ship (Regulation 42) and for removal from a district of any ship whose master is unwilling to comply with the Regulations (Regulation 43).

STATUTORY INSTRUMENTS

1971 No. 133

POLICE

The Police (Discipline) (Amendment) Regulations 1971

Made - - -	*26th January* 1971
Laid before Parliament	*3rd February* 1971
Coming into Operation	*15th February* 1971

In exercise of the powers conferred on me by section 33 of the Police Act 1964(a), and after consulting the Police Council for the United Kingdom in accordance with section 4(4) of the Police Act 1969(b), I hereby make the following Regulations :—

1.—(1) These Regulations may be cited as the Police (Discipline) (Amendment) Regulations 1971.

(2) These Regulations shall come into operation on 15th February 1971 and shall have effect as from that date except that in the case of a member of a police force who is then suspended under Regulation 17 of the principal Regulations they shall have effect as from the date of his suspension.

2.—(1) In these Regulations any reference to the principal Regulations is a reference to the Police (Discipline) Regulations 1965(c), as amended (d).

(2) The Interpretation Act 1889(e) shall apply to the interpretation of these Regulations as it applies to the interpretation of an Act of Parliament.

3. For Regulation 17(2), (3) and (4) of the principal Regulations (pay and allowances in respect of a period of suspension) there shall be substituted the following provisions :—

"(2) Subject to paragraph (4), a member of a police force suspended under this Regulation shall not, by virtue of the Police Regulations, be entitled to any allowance, other than a rent allowance, supplementary rent allowance, compensatory grant or special area undermanning allowance, in respect of the period of suspension.

(3) Subject to paragraph (4), a member of a police force suspended under this Regulation who—

> (*a*) is detained in pursuance of a sentence of a court in a prison or other institution to which the Prison Act 1952(f) applies, or is in custody (whether in prison or elsewhere) between conviction by a court and sentence, or

---

(a) 1964 c. 48.
(c) S.I. 1965/543 (1965 I, p. 1678).
(e) 1889 c. 63.

(b) 1969 c. 63.
(d) S.I. 1967/185 (1967 I, p. 333).
(f) 1952 c. 52.

(*b*) has absented himself from duty and whose whereabouts are un-known to the chief constable concerned,

shall not, by virtue of the Police Regulations, be entitled to pay in respect of his period in detention or custody or, as the case may be, in respect of the period during which his whereabouts are unknown to the chief constable.

(4) Where a member of a police force returns to duty when the period of suspension comes to an end and—

(*a*) it has been decided that he shall not be charged with a disciplinary offence, or

(*b*) he has been so charged and all the charges have been dismissed, or

(*c*) he has been so charged and has been punished by a reduction in his rate of pay, fine, reprimand or caution,

he shall receive, as from the date of his suspension, the allowances to which, but for paragraph (2), and the pay to which, but for paragraph (3), he would have been entitled by virtue of the Police Regulations.".

R. Maudling,
One of Her Majesty's Principal
Secretaries of State.

Home Office,
Whitehall.

26th January 1971.

EXPLANATORY NOTE

(*This Note is not part of the Regulations.*)

These Regulations amend the Police (Discipline) Regulations 1965 and provide that a member of a police force who is suspended shall be entitled to full pay in circumstances in which, at present, he is, instead, paid a suspension allowance equal to two-thirds of his pay.

In so far as Regulation 1(2) provides that the Regulations shall have retrospective effect, it is made in exercise of the power conferred by section 33(4) of the Police Act 1964.

STATUTORY INSTRUMENTS

1971 No. 134

POLICE

The Police (Discipline) (Deputy Chief Constables, Assistant Chief Constables and Chief Constables) (Amendment) Regulations 1971

Made - - - -	*26th January* 1971
Laid before Parliament	*3rd February* 1971
Coming into Operation	*15th February* 1971

In exercise of the powers conferred on me by section 33 of the Police Act 1964(a), and after consulting the Police Council for the United Kingdom in accordance with section 4(4) of the Police Act 1969(b), I hereby make the following Regulations:—

1.—(1) These Regulations may be cited as the Police (Discipline) (Deputy Chief Constables, Assistant Chief Constables and Chief Constables) (Amendment) Regulations 1971.

(2) These Regulations shall come into operation on 15th February 1971 and shall have effect as from that date except that in the case of a member of a police force who is then suspended under Regulation 16 of the principal Regulations they shall have effect as from the date of his suspension.

2.—(1) In these Regulations any reference to the principal Regulations is a reference to the Police (Discipline) (Deputy Chief Constables, Assistant Chief Constables and Chief Constables) Regulations 1965(c), as amended(d).

(2) The Interpretation Act 1889(e) shall apply to the interpretation of these Regulations as it applies to the interpretation of an Act of Parliament.

3. For Regulation 16(3), (4) and (5) of the principal Regulations (pay and allowances in respect of a period of suspension) there shall be substituted the following provisions:—

"(3) Subject to paragraph (5), a senior officer suspended under this Regulation shall not, by virtue of the Police Regulations, be entitled to any allowance, other than a rent allowance, supplementary rent allowance or compensatory grant, in respect of the period of suspension.

(4) Subject to paragraph (5), a senior officer suspended under this Regulation who—

    (*a*) is detained in pursuance of a sentence of a court in a prison or other institution to which the Prison Act 1952(f) applies, or is in custody (whether in prison or elsewhere) between conviction by a court and sentence, or

---

(a) 1964 c. 48.   (b) 1969 c. 63.
(c) S.I. 1965/544 (1965 I, p. 1693).
(d) The amending instrument is not relevant to the subject matter of these Regulations.
(e) 1889 c. 63.   (f) 1952 c. 52.

(b) has absented himself from duty and whose whereabouts are unknown to the police authority,

shall not, by virtue of the Police Regulations, be entitled to pay in respect of his period in detention or custody or, as the case may be, in respect of the period during which his whereabouts are unknown to the police authority.

(5) Where a senior officer returns to duty when the period of suspension comes to an end and—

(a) it has been decided that he shall not be charged with a disciplinary offence, or

(b) he has been so charged and all the charges have been dismissed, or

(c) he has been so charged and has been punished by a reduction in his rate of pay, fine, reprimand or caution,

he shall receive, as from the date of his suspension, the allowances to which, but for paragraph (3), and the pay to which, but for paragraph (4), he would have been entitled by virtue of the Police Regulations.".

R. Maudling,
One of Her Majesty's Principal
Secretaries of State.

Home Office,
   Whitehall.
26th January 1971.

EXPLANATORY NOTE

(This Note is not part of the Regulations.)

These Regulations amend the Police (Discipline) (Deputy Chief Constables, Assistant Chief Constables and Chief Constables) Regulations 1965 and provide that a senior officer of a police force who is suspended shall be entitled to full pay in circumstances in which, at present, he is, instead, paid a suspension allowance equal to two-thirds of his pay.

In so far as Regulation 1(2) provides that the Regulations shall have retrospective effect, it is made in exercise of the power conferred by section 33(4) of the Police Act 1964.

STATUTORY INSTRUMENTS

1971 No. 136

JURIES

The Jurors' Allowances Regulations 1971

Made - - - -	*26th January* 1971
Coming into Operation	15*th February* 1971

In exercise of the powers conferred on me by section 1 of the Juries Act 1949(a), as amended by the Juries Act 1954(b), I hereby, with the consent of the Treasury, make the following Regulations:—

1. These Regulations may be cited as the Jurors' Allowances Regulations 1971 and shall come into operation on 15th February 1971.

2.—(1) In these Regulations any reference to a juror shall include a reference to a person who, in obedience to a summons to serve on a jury, attends for service as a juror notwithstanding that he is not subsequently sworn and any reference to service as a juror shall be construed accordingly.

(2) In these Regulations the expression "the Act" means the Juries Act 1949, as amended by the Juries Act 1954.

(3) The Interpretation Act 1889(c) shall apply to the interpretation of these Regulations as it applies to the interpretation of an Act of Parliament, and section 38(2) of that Act shall apply as if these Regulations were an Act of Parliament and the Regulations revoked by these Regulations were enactments repealed thereby.

3. The Jurors' Allowances Regulations 1967(d) and the Jurors' Allowances (Amendment) Regulations 1970(e) are hereby revoked.

4. The travelling allowance to which a juror is entitled under section 1 of the Act shall be in accordance with the rates set out in the Schedule hereto.

5.—(1) The subsistence allowance to which a juror is entitled under section 1 of the Act shall be calculated in accordance with paragraphs (2) and (3) of this Regulation.

(2) In respect of any period other than a period in respect of which a subsistence allowance is payable under paragraph (3) of this Regulation, the subsistence allowance shall be—

(*a*) if the period on any one day during which a juror is necessarily absent from his place of residence, business or employment for the purpose of serving as a juror does not exceed four hours, 45p in respect of that day;

(a) 1949 c. 27.　　　　　　　　　　(b) 1954 c. 41.
(c) 1889 c. 63.　　　　　　　　　　(d) S.I. 1967/72 (1967 I, p. 154).
(e) S.I. 1970/175 (1970 I, p. 755).

(*b*) if the said period on any one day exceeds four hours but does not exceed eight hours, 95p in respect of that day;

(*c*) if the said period on any one day exceeds eight hours, but does not exceed twelve hours, £1·75 in respect of that day;

(*d*) if the said period on any one day exceeds twelve hours but does not exceed sixteen hours, £2·50 in respect of that day;

(*e*) if the said period on any one day exceeds sixteen hours, £2·95 in respect of that day.

(3) If a juror is necessarily absent from his place of residence overnight for the purpose of serving as a juror, the subsistence allowance shall be £5·50 in respect of each period of twenty-four hours or fraction thereof during which he is so absent overnight.

6. The compensation for loss of earnings which a juror would otherwise have made or additional expense (other than expense on account of travelling or subsistence) to which he would not otherwise have been subject to which he is entitled under section 1 of the Act, shall be the amount of the said loss or additional expense:

Provided that the amount payable under this Regulation to a person in respect of his services as a juror on any one day shall not exceed—

(*a*) where the period of time over which the earnings are lost or additional expense is incurred does not exceed four hours, the sum of £2; or

(*b*) where the said period of time exceeds four hours, the sum of £4,

except that, where in obedience to a summons to serve on a jury he has served as a juror on more than ten days and the court so directs, the amount so payable in respect of his services as a juror in obedience to the same summons on any one day after the tenth such day may exceed the sum specified above but shall not exceed £8.

R. Maudling,
One of Her Majesty's Principal
Secretaries of State.

19th January 1971.

We consent,

H. S. P. Monro,
Bernard Weatherill,
Two of the Lords Commissioners
of Her Majesty's Treasury.

26th January 1971.

SCHEDULE   Regulation 4

TRAVELLING ALLOWANCE

1. Where a person travels by railway or other public conveyance, the allowance shall be the amount of the fare actually paid:

Provided that, unless for a special reason the court otherwise directs, only the amount of the second class fare shall be allowed for travel by railway.

2. Where a person travels by a hired vehicle, the allowance shall be—

    (*a*) in a case of urgency or where no public service is reasonably available, the amount of the fare and any reasonable gratuity paid; and

    (*b*) in any other case, the amount of the fare for travel by the appropriate public services.

3. Where a person travels by private conveyance, the allowance shall—

    (*a*) in any case where the use of a private conveyance results in a substantial saving of time or is otherwise reasonable, be at a rate not exceeding—

        (i) in the case of a vehicle of engine capacity not exceeding 1000 c.c., $3\frac{1}{2}$p a mile each way;

        (ii) in the case of a vehicle of engine capacity exceeding 1000 c.c. but not exceeding 1750 c.c., $4\frac{1}{2}$p a mile each way;

        (iii) in the case of a vehicle of engine capacity exceeding 1750 c.c., 5p a mile each way; and

    (*b*) in any other case, be at a rate not exceeding 2p a mile each way.

EXPLANATORY NOTE

(*This Note is not part of the Regulations.*)

These Regulations consolidate with amendments the Regulations specified in Regulation 3. The only amendments of substance are the increases in the allowances payable to jurors under Regulation 5 (subsistence allowance) and paragraph 3 of the Schedule (travelling allowance when a private vehicle is used).

STATUTORY INSTRUMENTS

1971 No. 144

NATIONAL HEALTH SERVICE, ENGLAND AND WALES

The National Health Service (Newcastle University Hospital Designation) Order 1971

Made - - -	*28th January* 1971
Laid before Parliament	*5th February* 1971
Coming into Operation	*1st October* 1971

The Secretary of State for Social Services, being satisfied that the group of hospitals specified in Schedule 1 to this order and vested in him provides for the University of Newcastle upon Tyne facilities for undergraduate and post-graduate clinical teaching and after consultation with that University, in exercise of his powers under section 5 of the Health Services and Public Health Act 1968(a) and of all other powers enabling him in that behalf, hereby makes the following order:—

1.—(1) This order may be cited as the National Health Service (Newcastle University Hospital Designation) Order 1971 and shall come into operation on 1st October 1971.

(2) The Interpretation Act 1889(b) applies to the interpretation of this order as it applies to the interpretation of an Act of Parliament.

2. The group of hospitals specified in Schedule 1 to this order (hereinafter in this order referred to as "the group") is hereby designated as a university hospital.

3. Part II of Schedule 3 to the National Health Service Act 1946(c) (constitution of Hospital Management Committees) shall have effect in relation to the Committee appointed to exercise functions with respect to the management and control of the group, as modified and set out in Schedule 2 to this order.

(a) 1968 c. 46.　　　　(b) 1889 c. 63.　　　　(c) 1946 c. 81.

SCHEDULE 1

List of Hospitals

1. Royal Victoria Infirmary, Newcastle upon Tyne.
2. Princess Mary Maternity Hospital, Newcastle upon Tyne.
3. Babies Hospital, Newcastle upon Tyne.
4. Dental Hospital, Newcastle upon Tyne.
5. Royal Victoria Infirmary, Country Branch, Wylam-on-Tyne.
6. Newcastle General Hospital, Newcastle upon Tyne.
7. Ethel Watson Convalescent Home and Hospital for Children, Rothbury.
8. Hunter's Moor Hospital, Newcastle upon Tyne.
9. Ponteland Hospital, Ponteland.
10. Walker Park Hospital, Newcastle upon Tyne.
11. Hospital for Sick Children (Fleming Memorial), Newcastle upon Tyne.
12. Rye Hill Hospital, Newcastle upon Tyne.
13. Wellburn Babies Hospital, Ovingham.
14. W. J. Sanderson Orthopaedic Hospital and School for Children, Gosforth.
15. Walker Gate Hospital, Newcastle upon Tyne.
16. Lemington Hospital, Lemington.
17. Newcastle (East) Chest Clinic, Newcastle upon Tyne.
18. Newcastle (West) Chest Clinic, Newcastle upon Tyne.
19. St. Nicholas Hospital, Gosforth.
20. Birney Hill Hospital, Throckley.
21. St. Thomas Clinic, Newcastle upon Tyne.

SCHEDULE 2

Constitution of the Newcastle University Hospital Management Committee

The provisions of Part II of Schedule 3 to the National Health Service Act 1946 shall have effect as modified and set out below:—

(1) subject to the following provisions of this Schedule, the Hospital Management Committee shall consist of a Chairman, appointed by the Newcastle Regional Hospital Board after consultation with the University of Newcastle upon Tyne, and 19 other members appointed by the Board; but of these 20 not more than 8 shall be medical or dental practitioners;

(2) of the 19 members other than the chairman:—

    (i) 4 shall be nominated by the University of Newcastle upon Tyne but of these 4 not more than 3 shall be medical or dental practitioners; and

    (ii) 4 shall be nominated by the senior medical and dental staff of the group after consultation with the Newcastle Regional Board and the University of Newcastle upon Tyne; and

    (iii) 11 shall be appointed after consultation with local health authorities, Executive Councils and such other bodies as appear to the Board to be concerned;

(3) before making appointments to fill vacancies, the Board shall consult the Committee.

Keith Joseph,
Secretary of State for Social Services.

28th January 1971.

EXPLANATORY NOTE

(This Note is not part of the Order.)

This Order designates the group of hospitals set out in Schedule 1 as a university hospital, associated with the University of Newcastle, and provides for a modified form of Hospital Management Committee (as set out in Schedule 2) to manage and control it.

STATUTORY INSTRUMENTS

1971 No. 145

FIRE SERVICES

The Firemen's Pension Scheme Order 1971

Made - - - -	*27th January* 1971
Laid before Parliament	*9th February* 1971
Coming into Operation	*15th February* 1971

In exercise of the powers conferred on me by section 26 of the Fire Services Act 1947(a), (read with Article 2(1) of the Minister for the Civil Service Order 1968(b)), as amended and extended by sections 1 and 2(1) of the Fire Services Act 1951(c), section 42 of the Reserve and Auxiliary Forces (Protection of Civil Interests) Act 1951(d) and section 8 of the Fire Services Act 1959(e), I hereby, with the approval of the Minister for the Civil Service and after consultation with the Central Fire Brigades Advisory Council and the Scottish Central Fire Brigades Advisory Council, make the following Order:—

1. This Order may be cited as the Firemen's Pension Scheme Order 1971 and shall come into operation on 15th February 1971.

2.—(1) The Firemen's Pension Scheme 1966 (set out in Appendix 2 to the Firemen's Pension Scheme Order 1966(f)) and the Orders set out in Appendix 1 to this Order shall cease to have effect save in relation to—

(*a*) any award or claim to an award on a person's retirement or dismissal or on his ceasing to serve in the armed forces of the Crown, before 15th February 1971;

(*b*) any award or claim to an award in respect of the death of a person before the said date;

(*c*) any pension or claim to a pension by the nominee of a fireman whose pension has been reduced before the said date as a result of his having given notice of intention to surrender a portion thereof, being a pension actuarially equivalent to that surrendered portion;

(*d*) any undertaking to make payments in accordance with Schedule 5 to the said Scheme, as amended(g); and

(*e*) any certificate of pensionable service or entitlement to such a certificate under Article 36 of the said Scheme.

(2) In the preceding paragraph the expression "award" includes a repayment of contributions.

(a) 1947 c. 41. (b) S.I. 1968/1656 (1968 III, p. 4485).
(c) 1951 c. 27. (d) 1951 c. 65.
(e) 1959 c. 44. (f) S.I. 1966/1045 (1966 II, p. 2504).
(g) The amending Orders are not relevant to the subject matter of sub-paragraphs (*d*) and (*e*).

(3) Section 38 of the Interpretation Act 1889**(a)** shall apply in relation to the Firemen's Pension Scheme 1966 and the Orders set out in Appendix 1 to this Order, to the extent that they cease to have effect under this Article, as if this Article were an Act of Parliament and the said Scheme and Orders were Acts of Parliament repealed by an Act of Parliament.

3. The Pension Scheme set out in Appendix 2 to this Order (hereinafter referred to as the Firemen's Pension Scheme 1971) is hereby brought into operation.

4.—(1) The Firemen's Pension Scheme 1964 (set out in the Appendix to the Firemen's Pension Scheme Order 1964**(b)**, as amended**(c)**, in so far as it continues to have effect under the Firemen's Pension Scheme Order 1966, shall do so as though any reference in Schedule 5 thereto to an award included a reference to an award under the Firemen's Pension Scheme 1971.

(2) The Firemen's Pension Scheme 1966, as amended**(d)**, in so far as it continues to have effect under this Order, shall do so as though any reference in Schedule 5 thereto to an award included a reference to an award under the Firemen's Pension Scheme 1971.

R. Maudling,
One of Her Majesty's Principal
Secretaries of State.

26th January 1971.

Approval of the Minister for the Civil Service given under his Official Seal on 27th January 1971.

(L.S.)   *K. H. McNeill,*
Authorised by the
Minister for the Civil Service.

(a) 1889 c. 63.   (b) S.I. 1964/1148 (1964 II, p. 2574).
(c) The amending Orders are not relevant to the subject matter of paragraph (1).
(d) The amending Orders are not relevant to the subject matter of paragraph (2).

Article 2   APPENDIX 1

ORDERS REVOKED WITH SAVINGS

The Firemen's Pension Scheme Order 1966   S.I. 1966/1045 (1966 II, p. 2504).

The Firemen's Pension Scheme (Amendment)
Order 1966   ...   .   S.I. 1966/1142 (1966 III, p. 2739).

The Firemen's Pension Scheme (Amendment)
Order 1967   ...   .   S.I. 1967/1230 (1967 II, p. 3586).

The Firemen's Pension Scheme (Amendment)
Order 1968   ...   .   S.I. 1968/157 (1968 I, p. 386).

The Firemen's Pension Scheme (Amendment)
(No. 2) Order 1968   ...   .   S.I. 1968/397 (1968 I, p. 1076).

The Firemen's Pension Scheme (Amendment)
Order 1969   ...   .   S.I. 1969/1001 (1969 II, p. 2945).

The Firemen's Pension Scheme (Amendment)
Order 1970   ...   .   S.I. 1970/250 (1970 I, p. 977).

APPENDIX 2　　　　　　　　　　　　　Article 3

THE FIREMEN'S PENSION SCHEME 1971

ARRANGEMENT OF ARTICLES

PART I

CITATION AND INTERPRETATION

PART II

AWARDS ON RETIREMENT OF REGULAR FIREMEN

PART III

AWARDS ON DEATH OF REGULAR FIREMEN

Widows

SCHEDULES

PART I

CITATION AND INTERPRETATION

Citation

1. This Scheme may be cited as the Firemen's Pension Scheme 1971.

Meaning of "regular fireman"

2. In this Scheme the expression "regular fireman" means—

(a) a whole-time member of a brigade who was appointed on terms under which he is or may be required to engage in fire-fighting, not being a person whose employment is temporary only; or

(b) a whole-time member of a brigade who—

(i) was, immediately before the appointed day, subject to the Fire Brigade Pensions Act 1925(a);

(ii) became, on that day, a whole-time member of a brigade serving the whole or any part of the area of the local authority by whom he was last employed as a member of a fire brigade before the appointed day; and

(iii) has not since the appointed day ceased to be a whole-time member of that brigade.

Meaning of "qualifying injury"

3. In this Scheme the expression "qualifying injury" means an injury received by a person without his own default in the execution of his duties—

(a) as a regular fireman;

(b) as a professional fireman within the meaning of the Fire Brigade Pensions Act 1925, whether or not a member of the London Fire Brigade, or as a member of a police force employed whole-time on fire brigade duties within the meaning of the Fire Brigades Act 1938(b); or

(c) as a whole-time member of the National Fire Service to whom the National Fire Service (Preservation of Pensions) (Act of 1925) Regulations 1941(c), the National Fire Service (Preservation of Pensions) (London and West Ham) Regulations 1941(d), the National Fire Service (Preservation of Pensions) (Birmingham and Leicester) Regulations 1941(e), the National Fire Service (Preservation of Pensions) (Bolton and Derby) Regulations 1941(f) or the National Fire Service (Preservation of Pensions) (Police Firemen) Regulations 1941(g) applied.

Meaning of infirmity or death occasioned by an injury

4.—(1) A person shall be deemed for the purposes of this Scheme to have died from the effects of a particular injury if it appears that if he had not suffered that injury he would not have died at the time he in fact died.

(2) Infirmity of mind or body shall be deemed for the purposes of this Scheme to be occasioned by a particular injury—

(a) where a person dies while serving as a fireman, if it appears that the injury has so substantially aggravated the infirmity of mind or body that if he had not received that injury he would not have died at the time he in fact died;

(b) where a person has ceased to be a fireman, if it appears that the injury has so substantially aggravated the infirmity of mind or body that if he had not received that injury he would not have had to retire at the time when he in fact retired.

(a) 1925 c. 47.	(b) 1938 c. 72.
(c) S.R. & O. 1941/1268 (1941 I, p. 320).	(d) S.R. & O. 1941/1272 (1941 I, p. 333).
(e) S.R. & O. 1941/1273 (1941 I, p. 337).	(f) S.R. & O. 1941/1274 (1941 I, p. 342).
(g) S.R. & O. 1941/1271 (1941 I, p. 328).	

Meaning of "aggregate contributions"

5.—(1) In this Scheme the expression "aggregate contributions" means in relation to a regular fireman—

    (*a*) all payments made by him to a fire authority under this Scheme, the Firemen's Pension Scheme 1966, the Firemen's Pension Scheme 1964, the Firemen's Pension Scheme 1956(**a**), the Firemen's Pension Scheme 1952(**b**) or the Firemen's Pension Scheme 1948(**c**) (including payments made by way of rateable deductions from pay, payments made by way of such additional pension contributions as are mentioned in Article 53 and payments made in pursuance of an undertaking) which relate to a period of service he is entitled to reckon as pensionable service for the purposes of this Scheme and have not been refunded to him; and

    (*b*) the amount of any award by way of return of contributions which would have been made to him at the end of any period of service or employment, otherwise than as a regular fireman, by virtue of which he was subject to superannuation arrangements, being a period which he is entitled to reckon as pensionable service for the purposes of this Scheme, had he then voluntarily retired in circumstances entitling him to such an award under those arrangements.

(2) In this Article the expression "award by way of return of contributions" shall include—

    (*a*) a payment under section 18 of the Fire Brigade Pensions Act 1925;

    (*b*) a payment under section 10 of the Local Government Superannuation Act 1937(**d**);

    (*c*) a payment under section 10 of the Local Government Superannuation (Scotland) Act 1937(**e**);

    (*d*) a payment under section 12 of the Teachers (Superannuation) Act 1925(**f**);

    (*e*) any analogous payment.

Meaning of reference to awards

6.—(1) Except where the context otherwise requires and subject to paragraph (2), any reference in this Scheme to a pension or other award is a reference to a pension or other award, as the case may be, under this Scheme.

(2) Any reference to a pension or other award to a regular fireman in Articles 21(1), 28(1), 35(1), 44, 45, 52(5), 60(6) or 65(1) includes a reference to a pension or other award, as the case may be, under the Firemen's Pension Scheme 1966, the Firemen's Pension Scheme 1964, the Firemen's Pension Scheme 1956, the Firemen's Pension Scheme 1952 or the Firemen's Pension Scheme 1948.

(3) Any reference in this Scheme to a widow's pension, however expressed, shall be construed as excluding a reference to a pension payable to a widow under Article 37.

Meaning of certain expressions related to the operation of the National Insurance Acts

7.—(1) In this Scheme the following expressions shall have the meanings respectively which they have for the purposes of the National Insurance Act 1965(**g**):—

    "employed contributor's employment";

    "graduated contribution";

    "graduated retirement benefit";

    "non-participating employment";

    "payment in lieu of contributions".

(**a**) *See* S.I. 1956/1022 (1956 I, p. 953).   (**b**) *See* S.I. 1952/944 (1952 I, p. 1003).
(**c**) *See* S.I. 1948/604 (Rev. VII, p. 776:   (**d**) 1937 c. 68.
    1948 I, p. 1091).
(**e**) 1937 c. 69.   (**f**) 1925 c. 59.
(**g**) 1965 c. 51.

(2) In this Scheme any reference to a participating period of relevant employment is a reference to a period of employed contributor's employment after 5th April 1961 and before insured pensionable age other than—

(a) relevant service in the armed forces; and

(b) non-participating employment at the end of which no payment in lieu of contributions falls to be made,

and for the purposes of this paragraph a period of employed contributor's employment or of non-participating employment shall be treated as continuing during periods of holiday, temporary incapacity for work and similar temporary interruptions.

(3) In this Scheme any reference to the secured portion of a pension is a reference to the portion of the pension which equals the graduated retirement benefit which would be payable to the pensioner, on the assumption that he retired from regular employment on attaining insured pensionable age, in return for a payment in lieu of contributions in respect of the whole of any period of non-participating employment by virtue of which he is entitled to reckon pensionable service for the purposes of the pension, being a period of non-participating employment at the end of which no payment in lieu of contributions in fact fell to be made; and any reference to the unsecured portion of a pension shall be construed accordingly.

For the purposes of this paragraph a period of non-participating employment shall be treated as continuing during periods of holiday, temporary incapacity for work and similar temporary interruptions.

(4) For the purposes of this Scheme, the annual rate of graduated retirement benefit shall be determined as if there were $52\frac{1}{8}$ weeks in each year.

(5) In the case of a person entitled to reckon a period of pensionable service by virtue of service or employment otherwise than as a regular fireman in respect of which he was subject to superannuation arrangements, being service or employment in Northern Ireland or the Isle of Man, this Scheme shall have effect as if any reference to the National Insurance Act 1946(a) or the National Insurance Act 1965 or any enactment contained therein included a reference to any enactment of the Parliament of Northern Ireland or, as the case may be, any enactment of Tynwald, making provision for corresponding purposes.

Meaning of certain expressions

8.—(1) In this Scheme, unless the context otherwise requires, the following expressions have the meanings hereby respectively assigned to them, that is to say:—

"appointed day" means, in relation to England, 1st April 1948, and in relation to Scotland, 16th May 1948;

"award" means a pension, allowance, gratuity or award by way of return of aggregate contributions;

"brigade" means a fire brigade maintained under the principal Act;

"child" includes, in relation to any person, a step-child, an illegitimate child and a child adopted by him in pursuance of an adoption order made under the Adoption of Children Act 1926(b), the Adoption of Children (Scotland) Act 1930(c), the Adoption Act 1950(d) or the Adoption Act 1958(e); and the expressions "father", "mother", "parent" and "grandparent" shall be construed accordingly;

"fireman" means, subject to paragraph (2), a member of a brigade including a regular fireman;

"former brigade" means the brigade in which a serviceman was serving immediately before undertaking relevant service in the armed forces;

"injury" includes disease;

"principal Act" means the Fire Services Act 1947;

(a) 1946 c. 67.   (b) 1926 c. 29.
(c) 1930 c. 37.   (d) 1950 c. 26.
(e) 1958 c. 5 (7 & 8 Eliz. 2).

"rank" includes the post of chief officer or, in Scotland, of firemaster;

"relative" means wife, widow, parent, grandparent or child, or any person who is a child of such a relative;

"relevant Pensions (Increase) Acts" means the Pensions (Increase) Acts 1944 and 1947(a), the Pensions (Increase) Act 1956(b), the Pensions (Increase) Act 1959(c), the Pensions (Increase) Act 1962(d), the Pensions (Increase) Act 1965(e) and the Pensions (Increase) Act 1969(f);

"relevant service in the armed forces" means—

(a) service specified in Schedule 1 to the Reserve and Auxiliary Forces (Protection of Civil Interests) Act 1951, other than service specified in sub-paragraph (b) of paragraph 5 thereof;

(b) part-time service under the National Service Act 1948(g), otherwise than pursuant to a training notice under that Act; and

(c) service for the purpose of training only performed by a person mentioned in paragraph 7 of Schedule 1 to the Reserve and Auxiliary Forces (Protection of Civil Interests) Act 1951 for a period shorter than 7 days;

"serviceman" means a person who immediately before undertaking relevant service in the armed forces was a regular fireman;

"service pension" means any armed forces pension or allowance payable in pursuance of any Royal Warrant or other instrument.

(2) Any reference in this Scheme to a member of a brigade or regular fireman shall, where appropriate, be construed as, or be construed as including, a reference to a person who has been a member of a brigade or, as the case may be, a regular fireman.

(3) Any reference in this Scheme to 1p or 6p a week less than a percentage of a person's pensionable pay shall, in relation to a period before 15th February 1971, be construed as a reference to 2d. or 1s. 2d. a week, as the case may be, less than that percentage.

Construction of references to provisions of Scheme

9. In this Scheme, unless the context otherwise requires, a reference to an Article shall be construed as a reference to an Article of this Scheme, a reference to a Schedule shall be construed as a reference to a Schedule to this Scheme, a reference to a paragraph shall be construed as a reference to a paragraph in the same Article or, as the case may be, the same Part of the same Schedule and a reference to a sub-paragraph shall be construed as a reference to a sub-paragraph in the same paragraph.

Construction of references to enactments and instruments

10. In this Scheme, unless the contrary intention appears, a reference to any enactment or instrument shall be construed as including a reference to that enactment or instrument as amended, extended or applied by any other enactment or instrument.

Application of the Interpretation Act 1889

11. The Interpretation Act 1889(h) shall apply for the purpose of the interpretation of this Scheme as it applies for the purpose of the interpretation of an Act of Parliament.

PART II

AWARDS ON RETIREMENT OF REGULAR FIREMEN

Fireman's ordinary pension

12.—(1) Every regular fireman who has attained the age of 50 years and retires, being entitled to reckon at least 25 years' pensionable service, shall be entitled to a fireman's ordinary pension of an amount calculated in accordance with Part I of Schedule 1, subject however to Parts III and IV of that Schedule.

(a) 1944 c. 21; 1947 c. 7.
(c) 1959 c. 50.
(e) 1965 c. 78.
(g) 1948 c. 64.

(b) 1956 c. 39.
(d) 1962 c. 2 (11 & 12 Eliz. 2).
(f) 1969 c. 7.
(h) 1889 c. 63.

(2) Notwithstanding anything in paragraph (1), a chief officer or in Scotland a firemaster who retires before attaining the age of 55 years shall not be entitled to a pension under this Article unless his notice of retirement was given with the permission of the fire authority.

Fireman's short service award

13.—(1) Every regular fireman who is required to retire on account of age, but is not entitled to an ordinary pension under Article 12 shall be entitled to a fireman's short service award as hereinafter provided.

(2) In the case of a fireman entitled to reckon at least 10 years' pensionable service, the award under paragraph (1) shall be a short service pension calculated in accordance with Part II of Schedule 1, subject however to Parts III and IV of that Schedule.

(3) In the case of any other fireman, the award under paragraph (1) shall be a short service gratuity calculated in accordance with Part V of Schedule 1, subject however to Part VI of that Schedule.

(4) Every regular fireman who retires at or over the age of 65 years and is entitled to reckon at least 10 years' pensionable service but is not entitled to a pension or gratuity under any other provision of this Part of this Scheme shall be entitled to a short service pension calculated in accordance with Part II of Schedule 1, subject however to Parts III and IV of that Schedule.

Fireman's ill-health award

14.—(1) Every regular fireman who is incapacitated for the performance of his duty by infirmity of mind or body and retires on that account shall, if it appears that the incapacity is likely to be permanent, be entitled to an ill-health award as hereinafter provided.

(2) In the case of a fireman—

    (*a*) who is entitled to reckon at least 10 years' pensionable service; or

    (*b*) whose infirmity of mind or body is occasioned by a qualifying injury,

the award under paragraph (1) shall be an ill-health pension calculated in accordance with Part II of Schedule 1, subject however to Parts III and IV of that Schedule.

(3) In the case of any other fireman the award under paragraph (1) shall be an ill-health gratuity calculated in accordance with Part V of Schedule 1, subject however to Part VI of that Schedule.

Fireman's special pension

15.—(1) Where—

    (*a*) an ill-health pension is payable to a regular fireman on the ground that he has been incapacitated for the performance of his duty by infirmity of mind or body occasioned by a qualifying injury; and

    (*b*) the amount of that pension, when aggregated with the amount of any additional benefit from time to time payable to him, is less than the minimum injury award calculated in accordance with Part VII of Schedule 1,

he shall be entitled to a special pension of an amount equal to the deficiency.

(2) In this Article the expression "additional benefit" means—

    (*a*) any injury benefit payable under the National Insurance (Industrial Injuries) Act 1965(a) which relates to the qualifying injury together with any supplement payable therewith under section 2 of the National Insurance Act 1966(b);

    (*b*) any disablement pension payable under section 12 of the National Insurance (Industrial Injuries) Act 1965 in respect of the qualifying injury at the rate mentioned in that section or so much of any such pension as relates to that injury, together with—

(a) 1965 c. 52.   (b) 1966 c. 6.

(i) any increase in such pension payable on account of unemployability or special hardship or in respect of children or adult dependants under section 13, 14, 17 or 18 of the said Act or, subject as hereinafter provided, so much of any such increase as is proportionate to that part of the said pension which relates to that injury,

(ii) so long as he is receiving treatment as an in-patient at a hospital as a result of that injury, any increase in such pension payable under section 16 of the said Act or in respect of children or adult dependants under section 17 or 18 of the said Act;

(c) any sickness benefit payable under the National Insurance Act 1965 until the first day after his retirement which is not, or is deemed not to be, a day of incapacity for work under section 20 of the said Act or regulations made thereunder, together with any supplement thereto payable under section 2 of the National Insurance Act 1966.

(3) Where a disablement gratuity is payable to a person under section 12 of the National Insurance (Industrial Injuries) Act 1965 in respect of the qualifying injury, this Article shall apply as if a disablement pension were so payable to him during the relevant period, of such amount as would be produced by converting the gratuity into an annuity for that period.

In this paragraph the expression "the relevant period" means the period taken into account, in accordance with section 12 of the said Act of 1965, for the purpose of making the assessment by reference to which the gratuity became payable.

(4) Where an ill-health pension payable to a person is reduced under Article 20 or 37, or in accordance with Part IV of Schedule 1, then, for the purposes of this Article, the pension shall be deemed not to have been so reduced.

Minimum aggregate amount of payments in respect of fireman's pension

16.—(1) Where a regular fireman dies while in receipt of an ordinary, short service or ill-health pension, then if the aggregate of—

(a) the sums paid in respect of the pension;

(b) any gratuity payable in respect of his death; and

(c) the actuarial value of any widow's pension or child's allowance payable in respect of his death,

is less than his aggregate contributions, there shall be paid to his estate the difference by way of adjustment of the amount of the pension.

(2) Where a regular fireman does not resume service in his brigade before the expiration of a month from the termination, under Article 17, of the unsecured portion of his ill-health pension, then if the aggregate of—

(a) the sums paid in respect of the pension; and

(b) the actuarial value of the secured portion of the pension (in so far as it is payable under Article 17(4)),

is less than his aggregate contributions, there shall be paid to him the difference by way of adjustment of the amount of the pension.

(3) For the purposes of this Article—

(a) where an ill-health pension is supplemented by a special pension in accordance with Article 15, any amount paid in respect of the special pension shall be treated as if it had been paid in respect of the ill-health pension;

(b) the actuarial value of a widow's pension, of a child's allowance or of the secured portion of an ill-health pension shall be calculated in accordance with the tables prepared from time to time by the Government Actuary;

(c) where a fireman's pension is reduced under Article 20 the lump sum paid to him under that Article shall be deemed to have been paid in respect of the pension; and

(d) where a fireman's pension is reduced under Article 37 any reference in this Article to the aggregate amount paid to him in respect of the pension shall be construed as a reference to the aggregate amount which would have been so paid had the pension not been so reduced.

Cancellation of fireman's ill-health and special pensions on recovery

17.—(1) As long as a person—

(a) is in receipt of an ill-health pension;

(b) would not, if he had continued to serve as a regular fireman instead of retiring with an ill-health pension, have become entitled to retire with an ordinary pension; and

(c) if he had continued so to serve, could not have been required to retire on account of age,

the fire authority may, if they wish to exercise the powers conferred by this Article, consider, at such intervals as they in their discretion think proper, whether he has become capable of performing the duties of a regular fireman.

(2) If on any such consideration it is found that he has become capable of performing the duties of a regular fireman, the fire authority may terminate the unsecured portion of the ill-health pension.

(3) Where the unsecured portion of a person's ill-health pension is terminated under this Article, the fire authority shall, if he presents himself for service in the brigade at any time before the expiration of a month from its termination, permit him to resume service in the brigade forthwith in a rank not lower than that which he held when he retired with the pension; and if the fire authority fail to comply with the requirements of this paragraph the termination shall be void and shall be deemed never to have taken effect.

(4) Where the unsecured portion of a person's ill-health pension is terminated under this Article—

(a) the secured portion of that pension shall not be payable in respect of any period before he attains the age of 65 years; and

(b) if the ill-health pension is supplemented by a special pension in accordance with Article 15, the special pension shall be terminated.

Reassessment of fireman's special pension

18. Where a person is in receipt of a fireman's special pension, the fire authority shall, at such intervals as they think fit, consider whether the extent of his disablement has substantially altered, and if they find that it has, the pension shall be reassessed accordingly:

Provided that this Article shall cease to have effect with respect to a pension if, at any time after the expiration of 5 years from the time when the pension first became payable, the fire authority so resolve.

Reduction of award to fireman who causes or aggravates his infirmity

19. Where a regular fireman retires on account of infirmity of mind or body, and he has brought about or contributed to the infirmity by his own default or his vicious habits, the fire authority may reduce the amount of any ill-health award or special pension payable to him on his retirement by an amount not exceeding one half of that to which he would otherwise be entitled.

Commutation of pension

20.—(1) A regular fireman may in accordance with the provisions of this Article commute for a lump sum a portion of any ordinary, ill-health or short service pension to which he is or may become entitled, provided in the case of an ordinary pension—

(a) that he retires when entitled to reckon at least 30 years' pensionable service; or (*b*) that he is required to retire on account of age; or

(*c*) that the notice of commutation referred to in paragraph (2) is given with the consent of the fire authority and that he retires when entitled to reckon at least 25 years' pensionable service and on or after attaining the age of 55 years.

(2) For the purpose of commuting a portion of his pension a person shall give notice in writing (in this Article called "notice of commutation") to the fire authority of his wish to commute for a lump sum such portion of his pension not exceeding a quarter thereof as (subject to the limitation contained in Article 38) he may specify.

(3) The notice of commutation shall be given by a person not earlier than 2 months before his intended retirement nor later than 6 months after his retirement.

(4) The notice of commutation given by a person shall become effective—

(*a*) as from the date on which it is received by the fire authority, or

(*b*) as from the date of his retirement,

whichever is the later:

Provided that the said notice shall not become effective if—

(i) it was given more than 2 months before his retirement, or

(ii) it relates to an ill-health pension and the unsecured portion of that pension has sooner been terminated under Article 17.

(5) Where a person retires or has retired and a notice of commutation given by him has become or becomes effective, the fire authority shall reduce the pension to which the notice relates in accordance with the notice as from the time from which the notice is effective and shall pay to him a lump sum of such amount as is the actuarial equivalent of the surrendered portion of the pension at the date of his retirement, calculated from tables prepared by the Government Actuary:

Provided that where the notice is effective as from the time mentioned in paragraph (4)(*a*), the lump sum shall be reduced by an amount equal to the difference between the aggregate payments made in respect of the pension and the aggregate payments which would have been so made had it been reduced from the date of the retirement.

(6) For the purposes of this Article no account shall be taken of any increase under Article 64(3) or 67 in an award to a serviceman.

(7) Where a regular fireman retires on or after 15th February 1971 any notice given or other thing done before that date for the purposes of Article 9 of the Firemen's Pension Scheme 1966 shall have effect as if it had been given or done for the purposes of this Article.

PART III

AWARDS ON DEATH OF REGULAR FIREMEN

Widows

Widow's ordinary award

21.—(1) Subject as hereinafter provided, where a regular fireman entitled to reckon at least 3 years' pensionable service—

(*a*) dies while serving as such a fireman;

(*b*) dies while in receipt of a pension granted in respect of service as such a fireman; or

(*c*) retires or has retired from service as such a fireman on account of any injury and subsequently (without any intervening period of service as such) dies in consequence of that injury,

his widow shall be entitled to a widow's ordinary pension as hereinafter provided:

Provided that she shall not be so entitled by reason only of the death of her husband while in receipt of the secured portion of an ill-health pension, the unsecured portion of which was terminated in the circumstances mentioned in Article 17(2).

(2) The amount of a widow's ordinary pension under paragraph (1) shall be calculated in accordance with—

(a) Part I of Schedule 2, where immediately before his death or retirement her husband was paying pension contributions at a rate related to 6 per cent. of his pensionable pay;

(b) Part II of Schedule 2, subject however to Schedule 4, in any other case.

(3) Subject as hereinafter provided, where a regular fireman entitled to reckon less than 3 years' pensionable service dies while serving as such a fireman his widow shall be entitled to a widow's ordinary gratuity of an amount calculated in accordance with Part III of Schedule 2.

Widow's special pension

22.—(1) Where a regular fireman dies from the effects of a qualifying injury or from the effects of infirmity of mind or body occasioned by such an injury, his widow shall be entitled to a widow's special pension.

(2) Without prejudice to Article 23, a widow's special pension shall be of an amount calculated in accordance with Part IV of Schedule 2, subject however to Schedule 4.

Widow's augmented award

23.—(1) This Article shall apply to a widow of a regular fireman who dies from the effects of a qualifying injury or from the effects of infirmity of mind or body occasioned by such an injury where one of the following conditions is satisfied, namely that—

(a) the injury was received in the execution of duties which were performed by the fireman—

(i) for the immediate purpose of saving the life of another person or of preventing loss of human life, and

(ii) in circumstances in which there was an intrinsic likelihood of his receiving a fatal injury, or

(b) the fire authority are of the opinion that the preceding condition may be satisfied, and that this Article should apply, or

(c) the fire authority are of the opinion that the injury was received otherwise than as aforesaid but in the course of duties performed in such circumstances that it would be inequitable if there were not payable in respect of him such an award as would have been payable had the condition specified in sub-paragraph (a) been satisfied.

(2) A widow's special pension payable to a widow to whom this Article applies shall be of an amount calculated in accordance with Part V of Schedule 2 in respect of any week for which the amount of the pension so calculated is greater than the amount calculated in accordance with Part IV of Schedule 2, subject however, in either case, to Schedule 4.

(3) A widow to whom this Article applies shall be entitled to a gratuity in addition to a widow's special pension.

(4) The gratuity under paragraph (3) shall be of an amount equal to twice the annual pensionable pay, at the date of the death of the person in respect of whom the gratuity is payable, of a regular fireman—

(a) holding the rank of fireman in the fire brigade maintained by the Greater London Council, and

(b) entitled to reckon 30 years' service for the purposes of pay.

Widow's gratuity by way of commuted pension

24.—(1) Where a widow is entitled to a pension and the fire authority are satisfied that there are sufficient reasons for granting her a gratuity in lieu of a pension they may, subject to the provisions of Article 36, in their discretion and with her consent commute the pension for a gratuity of an amount calculated in accordance with Part VI of Schedule 2.

(2) Where the fire authority are precluded by reason of the provisions of Article 36 from exercising their discretion under the preceding paragraph in the manner in which they would but for those provisions exercise it, they may, subject to those provisions, exercise that discretion in relation to part only of the pension.

Right to widow's pension dependent on date of marriage

25. A woman shall not be entitled to a widow's award if she married her husband after he last ceased to serve as a regular fireman.

Special provisions where widow was living apart from her husband

26.—(1) Where a woman was living apart from her husband at the time of his death, no widow's award shall be paid to her unless—

    (*a*) he was then making regular contributions for her support or to her for the support of her child;

    (*b*) he was then liable to make such contributions by virtue of an agreement or of the order or decree of a competent court; or

    (*c*) the fire authority determine that, in the circumstances of the case, the award should be payable.

(2) Where a pension is payable under paragraph (1)(*a*) or (*b*), it shall be payable at a rate not exceeding the rate at which the husband was making or was liable to make such contributions as are therein mentioned:

Provided that if the fire authority in the circumstances of the case so determine, the pension shall be payable for such period as they think fit, at such increased rate as they think fit not exceeding the rate at which it would be payable but for this Article.

(3) Where a gratuity is payable under paragraph (1)(*c*), it shall be payable in whole or in such part, as the fire authority think fit, and where a pension is so payable, it shall be payable for such period and at such rate as they think fit, not exceeding the rate at which it would be payable but for this Article.

Effect of remarriage

27.—(1) Where a widow's pension becomes payable to a woman, then, if she subsequently remarries, she shall not be entitled to receive any payment on account of the pension in respect of any period after her remarriage:

Provided that if at any time after her remarriage the woman again becomes a widow, or that marriage is dissolved, the fire authority may pay the whole or any part of the pension for such period after that time as they think fit.

(2) Where a widow's gratuity becomes payable to a woman, then, if she subsequently remarries, so much of the gratuity as has not been paid before her remarriage shall not be payable thereafter:

Provided that if at any time after her remarriage the woman again becomes a widow, or that marriage is dissolved, the fire authority may pay to her the whole or any part of the sums which they were actually or contingently liable to pay to her in respect of the gratuity immediately before her remarriage.

Children

Child's ordinary allowance

28.—(1) Where a regular fireman—

(a) dies while serving as such a fireman;

(b) dies while in receipt of a pension granted in respect of service as such a fireman; or

(c) retires or has retired from service as such a fireman on account of any injury and subsequently (without any intervening period of service as such) dies in consequence of that injury,

any child of his shall be entitled to a child's ordinary allowance for such period or periods, if any, that the mother is not in receipt of an ordinary pension payable in respect of the father's death and calculated in accordance with paragraph 1 of Part I of Schedule 2:

Provided that a child shall not be so entitled by reason only of the death of the father while in receipt of the secured portion of an ill-health pension, the unsecured portion of which was terminated in the circumstances mentioned in Article 17(2).

(2) The amount of a child's ordinary allowance shall be calculated in accordance with Part I of Schedule 3, subject however to Part III of that Schedule.

Child's special allowance

29. Where a regular fireman dies from the effects of a qualifying injury or from the effects of infirmity of mind or body occasioned by such an injury, any child of his shall be entitled to a child's special allowance of an amount calculated in accordance with Part II of Schedule 3, subject however to Part III of that Schedule and to Schedule 4.

Child's special gratuity

30.—(1) This Article shall apply to a child of a regular fireman who dies from the effects of a qualifying injury, or from the effects of infirmity of mind or body occasioned by such an injury, where one of the conditions set out in Article 23(1) is satisfied and the fireman does not leave a widow entitled to a gratuity under Article 23(3):

Provided that this Article shall apply to a child who at the date of the parent's death has attained the age of 16 years only if at that date the child has not attained the age of 19 years and either is receiving full-time education or is an apprentice.

(2) A child to whom this Article applies shall be entitled to a gratuity, as hereinafter provided, in addition to a child's special allowance.

(3) The gratuity under paragraph (2) shall be of the like amount as a widow's gratuity under Article 23(3) except that, where two or more gratuities are payable under paragraph (2) in respect of the death of the same person, each gratuity shall be of the said amount divided by the number of such gratuities.

Child's gratuity by way of commuted allowance

31.—(1) Where a child is entitled to an allowance, and the fire authority are satisfied that there are sufficient reasons for the grant of a gratuity in lieu of an allowance, they may, subject to the provisions of Article 36, in their discretion and with the consent of the child's guardian commute the allowance for a gratuity of an amount calculated in accordance with Part IV of Schedule 3.

(2) Where the fire authority are precluded by reason of the provisions of Article 36 from exercising their discretion under the preceding paragraph in the manner in which they would but for those provisions exercise it, they may, subject to those provisions exercise that discretion in relation to part only of the allowance.

Duration of child's allowance

32. A child's allowance shall only be payable if and so long as the child has not attained the age of 16 years or if and so long as he has not attained the age of 19 years and either is receiving full-time education or is an apprentice.

Right to child's award dependent on date of birth and other matters

33.—(1) A child's allowance shall not be granted—

(*a*) to a child born after the date the father last ceased to serve as a regular fireman, otherwise than of a marriage which took place before that date;

(*b*) by virtue of his being a step-child, to a child whose mother married his step-father after the said date;

(*c*) by virtue only of his being an adopted child, to a child adopted after the said date; or

(*d*) by virtue of his being a step-child, adopted child or illegitimate child, to a child who was not substantially dependent on his father at the date of his father's death.

(2) This Article shall apply in relation to a child's gratuity under Article 30 as it applies in relation to a child's special allowance.

Limitation on amount of child's special allowance

34. Where a widow is entitled to a pension and her children are entitled to children's special allowances the allowances shall be reduced by such fraction, if any, as is from time to time necessary to secure that the aggregate amount of these allowances, when added to the widow's pension, does not exceed 2 thirds of the fireman's average pensionable pay.

General

Gratuities for dependants other than widows and children

35.—(1) Where a person dies while serving as a regular fireman, or dies while in receipt of a pension granted in respect of such service, the fire authority may, if they think fit, grant a gratuity to any of his relatives who were substantially dependent on him at the time of his death, and who are not entitled to any pension, gratuity or allowance under any other provision of this Scheme.

(2) The aggregate of all gratuities paid under this Article in respect of the death of any one person shall not exceed the amount of his aggregate contributions.

Limitation on discretion to grant a gratuity in lieu of a pension or allowance

36.—(1) Where a person has died while in receipt of an ordinary, ill-health or short service pension (in this Article referred to as "the principal pension"), the fire authority shall not under Article 24 or 31 substitute for the whole or any part of a widow's pension or child's allowance payable in respect of him a gratuity the actuarial value of which, when added to that of—

(*a*) any other gratuity so substituted under Article 24 or 31, and

(*b*) any lump sum paid under Article 20 by reason that a portion of the principal pension was commuted,

exceeds a quarter of the actuarial value of the principal pension, any reduction therein under the said Article 20 being ignored.

(2) For the purposes of this Article the actuarial value of a gratuity, lump sum or pension shall be the actuarial value at the time of the husband's or father's retirement as calculated by the Government Actuary.

(3) For the purposes of this Article no account shall be taken of an increase under Article 64(3) or 67 in an award to a serviceman.

PART IV

ALLOCATION OF PENSIONS AND GENERAL PROVISIONS
AFFECTING RIGHTS TO AWARDS

Allocation of pension

37.—(1) Where a regular fireman who retires and is entitled to an ordinary, ill-health or short service pension has allocated that pension, that is to say—

(a) has given notice in writing (hereafter in this Article called "notice of surrender") to the fire authority of his wish to surrender such portion of his pension as (subject to the limitation contained in Article 38) he may specify and, in relation to such notice, has complied with the provisions of paragraphs (3) and (4);

(b) has specified in the said notice the person in whose favour the surrender is to take effect (hereafter in this Article called "the beneficiary"), being his wife or such other person as the fire authority are satisfied is substantially dependent on him; and

(c) has provided the fire authority with such evidence of his good health as they consider satisfactory,

then, subject to paragraph (5), his pension shall be reduced accordingly as from the date of his retirement.

(2) Notwithstanding that he has previously allocated his pension, a regular fireman who is entitled to retire with an ordinary pension may, in accordance with the preceding paragraph—

(a) further allocate that pension in favour of the beneficiary of the previous allocation; or

(b) where that beneficiary has died, further allocate that pension in favour of some other beneficiary.

(3) Except in the case of a fireman entitled to retire with an ordinary pension, the notice of surrender shall be given by the fireman not earlier than 2 months before his retirement.

(4) The total portion of a fireman's pension which he may surrender in accordance with paragraph (1) shall not exceed a third thereof and, except in the case of such a further allocation as is mentioned in paragraph (2)(a), shall be such as will produce for the beneficiary, in accordance with the following provisions of this Article, a pension of not less than £0·50 a week.

(5) Where the fire authority are satisfied that the fireman has complied with the provisions of paragraph (1)(a), (b) and (c), they shall forthwith send to the fireman a written notification that they have allowed the surrender, and the allocation shall take effect—

(a) in the case of a fireman who, when he gave the notice of surrender, was entitled to retire with an ordinary pension—

(i) at the time when the notification is received by him or, if sent by post, at the time when it would be delivered to him in the ordinary course of post, or

(ii) at the date of his retirement,

whichever is the earlier;

(b) in any other case, at the date of retirement;

and in a case to which sub-paragraph (a)(i) applies, the pension shall be reduced notwithstanding the death of the beneficiary specified in the notice of surrender before the date of retirement.

(6) Where a fireman retires having allocated his pension and the allocation has taken effect, the fire authority shall as from his death pay to the beneficiary specified in the notice of surrender, if that person survives the fireman, a pension of such amount as is the actuarial equivalent of the surrendered portion of the fireman's pension so specified.

The said actuarial equivalent shall be calculated from tables prepared by the Government Actuary at the time the allocation took effect, by reference to the ages of the fireman and the beneficiary at that time, and separate calculations shall be made in respect of separate allocations.

(7) Where a fireman has allocated an ordinary pension and the allocation has taken effect and he was entitled to retire with an ordinary pension when he gave the notice of surrender, then—

(a) if he dies before retiring, the fire authority shall pay to the beneficiary specified in the notice of surrender the like pension as they would have paid by virtue of that allocation if the fireman had retired immediately before he died;

(b) if he retires with an ill-health pension, the foregoing provisions of this Article shall apply as if the allocation related to such pension.

(8) In the case of a chief officer or in Scotland a firemaster, in determining for the purposes of this Article—

(a) whether he is entitled to retire with an ordinary pension; or

(b) where he dies before retiring, the pension which would have been paid if he had retired immediately before he died,

no account shall be taken of the restriction on entitlement to an ordinary pension contained in Article 12(2).

(9) For the purposes of this Article no account shall be taken of an increase under Article 64(3) or 67 in an award to a serviceman.

(10) Where a regular fireman retires on or after 15th February 1971 any notice given or other thing done before that date for the purposes of Article 13 of the Firemen's Pension Scheme 1952, as set out in Article 1 of the Firemen's Pension Scheme Order 1954**(a)**, of Article 23 of the Firemen's Pension Scheme 1956, of Article 24 of the Firemen's Pension Scheme 1964 or of Article 24 of the Firemen's Pension Scheme 1966**(b)** shall have effect as if it had been given or done for the purposes of this Article.

Limitation on right to commute or allocate part of a pension

38.—(1) A regular fireman shall not under Article 20 commute for a lump sum nor under Article 37 allocate in favour of his wife or other dependant such a portion of his pension that that pension becomes payable at a rate less than 2 thirds of the rate at which it would have been payable but for the provisions of the said Articles and of Part IV of Schedule 1.

(2) For the purposes of this Article no account shall be taken of an increase under Article 64(3) or 67 in an award to a serviceman.

Prevention of duplication

39. Where, apart from the provisions of this Article, a person would be entitled to receive two or more pensions or allowances under this Scheme in respect of any particular period, he shall be entitled in respect of that period to receive that one only of those pensions or allowances which is for the time being greater than the others, or, if for the time being they are all equal, one only of the said pensions or allowances shall be paid:

Provided that, for the purposes of this Article, where an ill-health pension is supplemented by a special pension in accordance with Article 15 those pensions shall be treated as one, and there shall be disregarded—

(a) a pension payable under Article 37(6) or (7);

(b) a pension payable under Part X of this Scheme;

(c) the secured portion of an ill-health pension the unsecured portion of which was terminated in the circumstances mentioned in Article 17(2), in so far as it is payable under Article 17(4).

(a) S.I. 1954/1365 (1954 I, p. 906).   **(b)** *See* S.I. 1966/1045 (1966 II, p. 2504).

Award not payable in case of transfer

40.—(1) Where a regular fireman retires from a brigade in pursuance of a written notice to the fire authority of his intention to retire for the purpose of joining another brigade, then, notwithstanding anything in Article 12(1) or Article 55(1), he shall not, on the occasion of that retirement, be entitled to an award under either of those provisions.

(2) Where paragraph (1) does not apply but a regular fireman retires or has retired from a brigade and after again becoming such a fireman in that or another brigade becomes entitled under Article 44(1) or (4) to reckon as pensionable service the period of pensionable service he was entitled to reckon on retiring, then, subject to paragraph (4), any award to which he has become entitled on the occasion of that retirement shall cease to be payable.

(3) Where a regular fireman retires or has retired from a brigade and enters other pensionable employment in such circumstances that a transfer value becomes payable by the fire authority in respect of him under rules made by virtue of section 9 of the Fire Services Act 1959(a) or regulations made under section 67 of the National Health Service Act 1946(b) or section 66 of the National Health Service (Scotland) Act 1947(c), then, subject to paragraph (4), any award to which he has become entitled on the occasion of that retirement shall cease to be payable.

(4) Where an award under Article 55(1) ceases to be payable under paragraph (2) or (3), there shall continue to be payable—

   (a) where the award ceases to be payable under paragraph (2) or (3), so much of the award as is unpaid and represents a return of such additional contributions as are mentioned in Article 53;

   (b) where the award ceases to be payable under paragraph (3), and the regular fireman concerned paid pension contributions at a rate related to 6% of his pensionable pay, so much of the award as is unpaid and would not have been payable had he paid such contributions at a rate related to 5% of his pensionable pay.

Withdrawal of pension or allowance for misconduct

41.—(1) Where any person to whom a pension or allowance is payable—

   (a) is sentenced for any offence to preventive detention or corrective training or to imprisonment for a term exceeding 12 months; or

   (b) becomes or continues to be engaged in any business, occupation or employment which is illegal,

the fire authority may, in relation to that pension or allowance, exercise the powers conferred by this Article.

(2) In the case of an ordinary, short-service or ill-health pension, the fire authority may—

   (a) withdraw the unsecured portion of the pension in whole or in part and either temporarily or permanently;

   (b) withdraw the secured portion of the pension in whole or in part for a period before the pensioner attains the age of 65 years or during his imprisonment or detention in legal custody.

(3) In the case of any other pension or of an allowance, the fire authority may withdraw the award in whole or in part and either temporarily or permanently.

(4) So much of any pension or allowance as is withdrawn under this Article may, to such extent as the fire authority at any time think fit—

   (a) be applied by that authority for the benefit of any dependant of the person to whom but for its withdrawal it would be payable;

   (b) be restored to that person.

(a) 1959 c. 44.   (b) 1946 c. 81.
(c) 1947 c. 27.

Withdrawal of pension during employment as a regular fireman

42. The fire authority by whom a pension is payable may, in their discretion, withdraw the whole or any part of the pension for any period during which the pensioner is employed as a regular fireman in any fire brigade.

PART V

PENSIONABLE SERVICE OF REGULAR FIREMEN

Current service in the brigade

43. A regular fireman shall be entitled to reckon as pensionable service—

(*a*) any period of service as such, in the brigade in which he is serving, on or after 15th February 1971; and

(*b*) where he was serving in that brigade both on and immediately before 15th February 1971, any period of pensionable service which he was entitled to reckon immediately before that date:

Provided that, subject as hereinafter provided, there shall not be reckonable as pensionable service—

(i) where he has left and rejoined the brigade on or after 15th February 1971, any period of service before he last rejoined the brigade;

(ii) any period of absence from duty as a fireman as a result of sickness or injury which is certified by a duly qualified medical practitioner to be due to his own misconduct or vicious habits; or

(iii) any period of absence from duty as a fireman without pay, including any period of suspension from duty terminating with the fireman having been found guilty of an offence against discipline or a criminal offence.

Previous service in a brigade

44.—(1) Subject to paragraph (2), where a regular fireman—

(*a*) retires or has retired from a brigade without a pension and without a transfer value becoming payable under rules made by virtue of section 9 of the Fire Services Act 1959 or regulations made under section 67 of the National Health Service Act 1946 or section 66 of the National Health Service (Scotland) Act 1947, and

(*b*) within twelve months of so retiring and without any intervening service as a regular fireman rejoins or has rejoined that brigade or joins or has joined another brigade,

he shall be entitled to reckon as pensionable service the period of pensionable service he was entitled to reckon on so retiring, but subject to his undertaking, within 6 months of rejoining or, as the case may be, joining the brigade or within such longer period as the fire authority may in his case allow, to pay in accordance with Schedule 5 the sum, if any, equal to the aggregate of—

(i) any sum paid to him by way of gratuity or return of aggregate contributions on retirement less so much of such sum, if any, as represents a return of such additional contributions as is mentioned in Article 53; and

(ii) the balance of any sum he had undertaken to pay in accordance with Schedule 5 to this Scheme, Schedule 5 to the Firemen's Pension Scheme 1966, Schedule 5 to the Firemen's Pension Scheme 1964 or Schedule 5 to the Firemen's Pension Scheme 1956 which was outstanding immediately before his retirement.

(2) In the case of a person who has completed less than 2 years' service as a regular fireman, paragraph (1) shall apply only where he retires or has retired from one brigade for the purpose of joining another brigade and joins that brigade with the written consent of the fire authority maintaining the first-mentioned brigade, and such consent may be given after he has left the first-mentioned brigade if he has applied to the fire authority for such consent while still a member of the brigade.

(3) Where a regular fireman—

    (a) retires or has retired from a brigade with an ill-health pension; and

    (b) resumes service in the brigade in the circumstances and within the period mentioned in Article 17(3),

he shall be entitled to reckon as pensionable service the period of pensionable service he was entitled to reckon on so retiring.

(4) Where a regular fireman—

    (a) retires or has retired from a brigade without a pension, other than an ill-health pension the unsecured portion of which has been terminated in the circumstances mentioned in Article 17(2);

    (b) without any intervening service as a regular fireman rejoins or has rejoined that brigade or joins or has joined another brigade; and

    (c) cannot under paragraph (1) or (3) reckon as pensionable service the period of pensionable service he was entitled to reckon on so retiring,

he shall be entitled to reckon that period as pensionable service, but subject to his undertaking, within 6 months of rejoining or, as the case may be, joining the brigade, or within such longer period as the fire authority may in his case allow, to pay in accordance with Schedule 5 a sum calculated in accordance with Schedule 6.

Period during which a special pension was payable

45.—(1) Where a regular fireman—

    (a) retires or has retired from a brigade with a special pension; and

    (b) resumes or has resumed service in the brigade in the circumstances and within the period mentioned in Article 17(3),

he shall be entitled to reckon as pensionable service the period for which that pension was payable, but subject to his undertaking, within 6 months of resuming service in the brigade or within such longer period as the fire authority may in his case allow, to pay in accordance with Schedule 5 a sum equal to the aggregate of the pension contributions (other than such additional contributions as are mentioned in Article 53) which would have been payable by him for that period had he continued to serve as a regular fireman in the brigade in the rank he held immediately before his retirement.

(2) In the case of a regular fireman who would have been entitled to a special pension but for the amount of additional benefit, within the meaning of Article 15(2), payable to him, paragraph (1) shall have effect as if he had been entitled to a special pension.

Absence from duty in the brigade without pay

46.—(1) Where a regular fireman is or has been absent from duty without pay, the fire authority may, at any time while he is such a fireman in their brigade, resolve that the whole or any part of the period of absence shall be reckoned as pensionable service for the purposes of this Scheme.

(2) Where by virtue of any such resolution as aforesaid any period is reckoned as pensionable service, the fireman shall become liable to pay to the fire authority the contributions (including such additional contributions as are mentioned in Article 53) which would have been payable by him for that period if he had been paid at the rate applicable to his case.

Previous local government service

47.—(1) This Article shall apply in the case of a person—

(*a*) who before becoming a regular fireman was in employment by virtue of which he was or was deemed to be a contributory employee or a local Act contributor within the meaning of the Local Government Superannuation Act 1937; and

(*b*) in respect of whom a transfer value relating to his former employment is paid to the fire authority under rules made under sections 2 and 15 of the Superannuation (Miscellaneous Provisions) Act 1948(a).

(2) Subject to paragraphs (3) and (4), such a person as is mentioned in the preceding paragraph shall be entitled to reckon as pensionable service the aggregate of—

(*a*) 3 quarters of the period of contributing service; and

(*b*) 3 eighths of the period of non-contributing service,

which he would have been entitled to reckon had he on becoming a regular fireman become a contributory employee within the meaning of the Local Government Superannuation Act 1937 entitled to the benefit of section 13 of that Act.

(3) Where he would have been entitled in the circumstances mentioned in the preceding paragraph to reckon a period as contributing service subject to his making certain payments by way of—

(*a*) additional contributory payments in discharge of a fixed sum; or

(*b*) additional contributions for added years,

whether on giving notice in that behalf or otherwise, then he shall and shall only be entitled to reckon 3 quarters of that period as pensionable service if within 3 months of his becoming a regular fireman or within such longer period as the fire authority may in his case allow, he undertakes to pay in accordance with Schedule 5 a sum equal to the capital value of those additional payments or contributions as the case may be, as determined by the fire authority.

(4) Where in the exercise of their discretion under rules made under the Superannuation (Miscellaneous Provisions) Act 1948 the authority by whom he was employed in his former employment increase his service for the purposes of those rules, then for the purposes of this Article the service reckonable by him immediately before ceasing to hold his former employment shall be deemed to have been correspondingly increased.

(5) Any reference in this Article to the Local Government Superannuation Act 1937 shall be construed as including a reference to the Local Government Superannuation (Scotland) Act 1937.

Previous service other than fire or local government service

48.—(1) This Article shall apply in the case of a person, other than a person to whom Article 47 applies—

(*a*) who before becoming a regular fireman was in service or employment otherwise than as a fireman by virtue of which he was subject to superannuation arrangements (hereafter in this Article referred to as "former service");

(*b*) in respect of whom a transfer value relating to his former service is paid to the fire authority under rules made under sections 2 and 15 of the Superannuation (Miscellaneous Provisions) Act 1948, under regulations made under section 67 of the National Health Service Act 1946, section 66 of the National Health Service (Scotland) Act 1947, or section 1 of the Police Pensions Act 1948(b) or under any such other provisions as may be approved for the purposes of this Article by the Secretary of State; and

(*c*) who within 3 months of his becoming a regular fireman or 6 months of the coming into operation of the Rules, Regulations or other provisions under which the transfer value is paid as aforesaid, whichever is the later, or within such longer

---

(a) 1948 c. 33.   (b) 1948 c. 24.

period as the fire authority may in his case allow, undertakes to pay in accordance with Schedule 5 a sum equal to the balance of any liability outstanding immediately before he ceased to be engaged in his former service in respect of payments or contributions he was then making as a condition of reckoning past service as contributing service or otherwise for the purposes of the said superannuation arrangements, being service of which account has been taken in the calculation of the said transfer value, together with a sum equal to any gratuity or award by way of return of contributions made under the said arrangements on his ceasing to be engaged as aforesaid, being a gratuity or return of contributions of which account has been taken in the calculation of the said transfer value.

(2) Where under the superannuation arrangements mentioned in paragraph (1)—

(a) a maximum pension is provided (otherwise than on retirement occasioned by injury or ill-health) for a person entitled to reckon 30 years' service for the purposes thereof, or

(b) after 20 years' service each year of service is reckonable as 2 years' service for the purposes thereof,

then such a person as is mentioned in paragraph (1) who was subject to those arrangements shall be entitled to reckon as pensionable service the whole of the period specified in paragraph (4), so, however, that, where under those arrangements such provision as is mentioned in sub-paragraph (a) or (b) is made in relation only to service or employment of a description designated therein (in this paragraph referred to as "designated service") and the former service included designated service, there shall be reckonable as aforesaid—

(i) the whole of that part of the period specified in paragraph (4) as is referable to designated service, and

(ii) 3 quarters of that part of that period as is not so referable.

(3) In any other case, such a person as is mentioned in paragraph (1) shall be entitled to reckon 3 quarters of the period specified in paragraph (4).

(4) The period referred to in paragraphs (2) and (3) is—

(a) the period of service which is or was reckonable for the purpose of calculating the transfer value; or

(b) where separate calculations are or were made in respect of contributing and non-contributing service reckonable for the purpose of calculating the said transfer value, the aggregate of the period of contributing service and a half of the period of non-contributing service which is so reckonable.

(5) In this Article the expression "award by way of return of contributions" has the meaning assigned thereto by Article 5(2).

Certificates of pensionable service

49.—(1) Where a regular fireman becomes entitled to reckon a period of service as pensionable service for the purposes of this Scheme by virtue of Article 44, 45, 47, 48 or 69, then the fire authority shall, within a period of 6 months, supply him with a certificate showing the pensionable service he was entitled to reckon on the date on which he became entitled to reckon the said period of service.

(2) Where a fireman is dissatisfied with a certificate supplied to him in accordance with the provisions of the preceding paragraph, he may, within 3 months of being supplied with it, appeal to the Secretary of State who shall either confirm or vary the said certificate.

(3) Where in accordance with the preceding provisions of this Article a certificate has been supplied to a fireman and he has not appealed to the Secretary of State within the period of 3 months aforesaid, or where a certificate has been confirmed or varied on such an appeal, then the certificate as supplied, confirmed or varied, as the case may be, shall be conclusive as to the pensionable service which the fireman was entitled to reckon on the date to which it refers.

(4) Where a fireman is entitled to a certificate under paragraph (1) but claims a pension or gratuity or dies—

(a) before the certificate has been supplied, then the obligation to supply a certificate shall cease;

(b) after the certificate has been supplied but before it has become conclusive, then the certificate shall cease to have effect and no further proceedings under paragraph (2) shall take place.

(5) For the purposes of this Article a fireman shall be treated as only becoming entitled to reckon service under Article 69 if and when he resumes service in his former brigade.

Prevention of double reckoning

50. A regular fireman who is entitled to reckon a period as pensionable service under any provision of this Part of this Scheme shall not be entitled also to reckon that period under some other such provision.

PART VI

PENSIONABLE PAY AND CONTRIBUTIONS OF REGULAR FIREMEN

Pensionable pay and average pensionable pay

51.—(1) In this Scheme the expression "pensionable pay" means the pay of a regular fireman as determined in relation to his rank or, in the case of a chief officer or an assistant chief officer or, in Scotland, a firemaster or an assistant firemaster, his pay as determined for the post.

(2) For the purpose of determining the benefits payable under this Scheme on the death or retirement of a regular fireman—

(a) the expression "average annual pensionable pay" means the aggregate of the pensionable pay of the fireman, ignoring any reduction of pay during sick leave and any stoppage of pay by way of punishment, during the 3 years immediately preceding his death or retirement or, in a case where he was not serving as a regular fireman when he died, the date on which he last ceased to serve as such, divided by 3:

Provided that where he was in receipt of pensionable pay for only part of the said period, the said aggregate shall be divided by the number of years and that fraction of a year for which he was in receipt of pensionable pay during the said period; and

(b) the expression "average pensionable pay" means the average annual pensionable pay of the fireman divided by 52¼.

(3) Notwithstanding anything in the preceding paragraph, for the purpose of determining the benefits payable under this Scheme in respect of a person who last ceased to serve as a regular fireman before 10th July 1956, the expressions "average annual pensionable pay" and "average pensionable pay" shall have the meanings assigned to "annual pensionable pay" and "pensionable pay" respectively by Article 46 of the Firemen's Pension Scheme 1952 for the purpose of determining the benefits payable under that Scheme.

Rate of payment of pension contributions

52.—(1) Subject to the provisions of this Scheme, a regular fireman shall pay pension contributions to the fire authority at the rate of 6p a week less than 6 per cent. of his pensionable pay.

(2) Where a man was on 26th August 1966—

(a) a regular fireman;

(b) a serviceman whose period of relevant service in the armed forces included that date; or

(c) in receipt of an ill-health pension,

then unless he elected in accordance with Article 39 of the Firemen's Pension Scheme 1966 to pay pension contributions at the rate specified in the preceding paragraph, he shall in respect of any period during which he is a regular fireman pay such contributions at the rate of 6p a week less than 5 per cent. of his pensionable pay.

(3) In the case of a person who—

(a) served before the appointed day in a fire brigade maintained by a local authority or in the National Fire Service;

(b) became a regular fireman on the appointed day or, where he was then a member of the armed forces of the Crown, after next ceasing to be such a member and without any intervening service in another capacity; and

(c) did not elect to pay pension contributions at the lower rate under Article 38 of the Firemen's Pension Scheme 1948,

this Article shall, subject to the proviso to paragraph (5), apply subject to the provisions of that paragraph.

(4) In the case of a person who—

(a) is entitled to reckon a period as pensionable service by virtue of service or employment otherwise than as a regular fireman in respect of which he was subject to superannuation arrangements; and

(b) has been excepted from the operation of any regulations made under section 69(4) of the National Insurance Act 1946(a) or section 110(1) of the National Insurance Act 1965(b) or of any other provisions modifying the said arrangements in connection with the passing of the said Act of 1946,

this Article shall, subject to the proviso to paragraph (5), apply subject to the provisions of that paragraph.

(5) In the case of a person such as is mentioned in paragraph (3) or (4), this Article shall apply as if for any reference to a rate of 6p a week less than a percentage of his pensionable pay there were substituted a reference to the rate of 1p a week less than that percentage of his pensionable pay:

(a) 1946 c. 67.   (b) 1965 c. 51.

Provided that in the case of a person who has previously retired from service as a regular fireman, otherwise than with an ill-health pension, and resumed service as such later than a year after that retirement this paragraph shall have effect only if he is such a person as is mentioned in paragraph (4) by reason of his being entitled to reckon pensionable service by virtue of such service or employment as is there mentioned which he entered after his previous retirement.

Rate of payment of additional contributions in certain cases

53. Where immediately before 15th February 1971 a person was liable to pay additional pension contributions in accordance with Article 40 of the Firemen's Pension Scheme 1966 he shall pay such contributions at a rate calculated in accordance with Schedule 7 until such time as he becomes entitled to reckon 25 years' pensionable service or retires otherwise than in pursuance of a written notice to the fire authority of his intention to retire for the purpose of joining another brigade.

Method of payment of pension contributions

54. The pension contributions (including additional contributions, if any) upon each instalment of pay shall fall due at the same time as that instalment and may, without prejudice to any other method of payment, be discharged by way of a deduction of an appropriate amount made by the fire authority from the said instalment.

Repayment of contributions on retirement or death

55.—(1) Where a regular fireman retires without a pension or gratuity he shall be entitled to an award by way of repayment of his aggregate contributions.

(2) Where a regular fireman dies while serving as such and either no pension, allowance or gratuity is payable in respect of his death or the aggregate of—

    (*a*) any gratuity so payable; and

    (*b*) the actuarial value of any widow's pension or child's allowance so payable (calculated in accordance with the tables prepared from time to time by the Government Actuary),

is less than his aggregate contributions, an award shall be made to his estate by way of repayment of his aggregate contributions or of so much thereof as represents the difference, as the case may be.

Repayment of contributions on dismissal

56.—(1) Where a regular fireman is dismissed from the brigade otherwise than for one of the offences mentioned in paragraph (3), the fire authority shall repay to him his aggregate contributions.

(2) Where a regular fireman is dismissed from the brigade for one of the offences mentioned in paragraph (3), the fire authority may in their discretion—

    (*a*) repay to him his aggregate contributions wholly or in part;

    (*b*) apply his aggregate contributions wholly or in part for the benefit of his dependants;

    (*c*) retain his aggregate contributions wholly or in part.

(3) The offences referred to in paragraphs (1) and (2) are the following disciplinary offences:—

    (*a*) by carelessness or neglect suffering any loss, damage or injury to occur to any person or property (which offence is specified in paragraph (4)(*b*) of the code of disciplinary offences set out in the Schedule to the Fire Services (Discipline) Regulations 1948**(a)** and in the Schedule to the Fire Services (Discipline) (Scotland) Regulations 1953**(b)**);

(a) S.I. 1948/545 (Rev. VII, p. 757: 1948 I, p. 1059).
(b) S.I. 1953/1086 (1953 I, p. 766).

(b) failing to account for, or to make a true return of, any money or property which comes into the fireman's possession in the course of his duties (which offence is specified in paragraph (7)(b) of the said code), and

(c) wilfully or negligently damaging any article of clothing or personal equipment with which the fireman has been provided or entrusted or failing to take proper care thereof (which offence is specified in paragraph (9)(a) of the said code).

PART VII

DETERMINATION OF QUESTIONS AND APPEALS

General functions of fire authority

57.—(1) Subject as hereinafter provided, the question whether a person is entitled to any and if so what awards shall be determined in the first instance by the fire authority.

(2) Subject to the provisions of this Scheme, the fire authority shall consider the medical evidence of at least one duly qualified medical practitioner selected by the authority before determining for the purposes of this Scheme—

(a) whether a person has been incapacitated for the performance of his duty as a fireman by infirmity of mind or body;

(b) whether any such incapacity is likely to be permanent;

(c) whether a person's incapacity has been occasioned by a qualifying injury;

(d) whether a person has become capable of performing the duties of a fireman;

(e) the extent to which a person has been disabled;

(f) any other question which ought to be determined in whole or in part on medical grounds:

Provided that where an authority are unable to obtain such evidence by reason of the refusal or the wilful or negligent failure of any person to submit to medical examination by a duly qualified medical practitioner selected by the authority, the authority may dispense with such evidence and may give such decision on the question at issue as they may in their discretion choose to give, either without medical evidence or upon such medical evidence as they think fit.

Appeal against opinion of fire authority's medical practitioner

58.—(1) Where for the purposes of any decision which falls to be made by a fire authority under this Scheme any person is medically examined by a medical practitioner selected by the authority, the opinion of the practitioner shall be given in writing to the authority.

(2) If within 14 days of being informed by the fire authority of the decision the said person applies to the authority for a copy of the opinion, the authority shall supply him with a copy thereof.

(3) If he is dissatisfied with the opinion of which a copy has been so supplied to him, he may, subject to and in accordance with the provisions of Schedule 8, appeal against the opinion to an independent person nominated by the Secretary of State (hereinafter referred to as a "medical referee").

(4) A fire authority shall be bound by any decision on a medical question duly given on any such appeal.

Appeal against decision of fire authority

59.—(1) Where any person claims that he is entitled to an award or to any payment on account of an award and the fire authority do not admit the claim at all, or do not admit the claim to the full extent thereof, the person aggrieved may apply to the fire authority for reconsideration of the case, and, if aggrieved by the decision on such reconsideration, may appeal to the next practicable court of quarter sessions for any county or borough which constitutes, or is wholly or partly included in, the area of the fire authority.

(2) Subject as hereinafter provided, a court of quarter sessions may, on an appeal under paragraph (1), make such order or declaration as appears to the court to be just.

(3) Nothing in this Article shall authorise a court of quarter sessions—

    (*a*) to make an order or declaration controlling or restricting the exercise of any discretion which by this Scheme is vested in a fire authority;

    (*b*) to reopen any decision on a medical question which has been given on an appeal under Article 58; or

    (*c*) to question any certificate of pensionable service which is deemed to be conclusive by Article 49 of this Scheme, by Article 36 of the Firemen's Pension Scheme 1966, by Article 36 of the Firemen's Pension Scheme 1964(a), by Article 34 of the Firemen's Pension Scheme 1956(b) or by Article 19D of the Firemen's Pension Scheme 1952(c), as set out in Article 3 of the Firemen's Pension Scheme Order 1953(d).

(4) Subject to and in accordance with rules of court, an appeal on a point of law from a decision of a court of quarter sessions under this Article shall lie to the High Court.

(5) In the application of this Article to Scotland, for any reference to a court of quarter sessions there shall be substituted a reference to the sheriff having jurisdiction in the place where the person concerned last served as a regular fireman, and for any reference to the High Court there shall be substituted a reference to the Court of Session.

Part VIII

Payment of Awards and Financial Provisions

Payment of awards generally

60.—(1) An award which is payable to or in respect of a person by reason of his having been employed as a regular fireman shall be payable by the fire authority by whom he was last employed as such.

(2) An award which is payable to or in respect of a person by reason of his having received an injury while employed as a member of a brigade otherwise than as a regular fireman, shall be payable by the fire authority by whom he was employed when he received the injury.

(3) Subject to the provisions of this Scheme, every pension or allowance shall be payable in respect of each week and shall, subject to such delay as may be necessary for the purpose of determining any question as to the liability of the fire authority in respect thereof, be discharged by payments in advance at such reasonable intervals as the fire authority may determine.

(4) Where a person dies after receiving a sum paid in advance on account of a pension or allowance, no claim for repayment shall be made on the ground that the said sum or any part thereof is referable to a period after his death.

(5) Where a widow remarries after receiving a sum paid in advance on account of a pension, no claim for repayment shall be made on the ground that the said sum or any part thereof is referable to a period after her remarriage.

(6) A pension or allowance payable to the widow, child or dependant of a fireman shall be payable as from his death, or, in the case of an allowance payable to a posthumous child as from the birth of the child, except—

    (*a*) where the fireman was in receipt of a pension and he died during a period in respect of which he had already received his pension, in which case the pension or allowance shall not be payable before the end of that period;

(a) *See* S.I. 1964/1148 (1964 II, p. 2574).   (b) *See* S.I. 1956/1022 (1956 I, p. 953).
(c) *See* S.I. 1952/944 (1952 I, p. 1003).   (d) S.I. 1953/1385 (1953 I, p. 778).

(b) where the fireman received an ill-health gratuity, in which case the pension or allowance shall be payable as from the first anniversary of his death or such earlier date as the fire authority, in the circumstances of the case, think fit.

(7) Subject to the provisions of this Scheme, every gratuity shall be paid in one sum:

Provided that where a fire authority are satisfied that it would be to the advantage of the beneficiary to pay a gratuity in instalments, they may pay it in instalments of such reasonable amounts and over such reasonable period as they think fit.

(8) Without prejudice to the provisions of any such regulations as are mentioned in section 60(5) of the National Insurance Act 1965 and for the time being in force, where a regular fireman is entitled under Article 55 to an award by way of repayment of his aggregate contributions the fire authority shall be under no obligation to make payment until the expiration of a year from the date of his retirement or until he requests payment, whichever first occurs.

Payment of awards in special cases

61.—(1) Where any sum is due on account of a pension, and any debt is due to the fire authority from the pensioner, so much of the said sum as does not exceed the debt may be applied by the authority in or towards the satisfaction of the debt:

Provided that where the pension is an ordinary, ill-health or short service pension, and the sum due is in respect of a period beyond the age of 65 years, only so much of the sum as is due on account of the unsecured portion of the pension may be applied as mentioned in this paragraph.

(2) If it appears to the fire authority that a pensioner is by reason of mental disorder or otherwise incapable of managing his affairs, the authority may in their discretion pay the pension or any part thereof to any person having the care of the pensioner, and, in so far as they do not dispose of the pension in that manner, may apply it in such manner as they think fit for the benefit of the pensioner or his dependants.

(3) On the death of a person to whom or to whose estate a sum not exceeding £500 is due on account of a pension, the fire authority may, without probate, confirmation or any other formality or proof of title, pay the said sum to the persons appearing to the authority to be beneficially entitled to the personal estate of the deceased, or, as the authority think fit, pay the said sum to one or more of those persons or distribute it among all or any of those persons in such proportions as the authority may determine.

(4) Where any sum is payable to a minor on account of a pension, the authority may, if they think fit, in lieu of paying the said sum to the minor, pay it to such other person as they may determine.

A person who receives any sum paid under this paragraph shall, subject to and in accordance with any directions of the fire authority, apply the said sum for the minor's benefit.

(5) Every assignment or charge on a pension shall be void to the extent that—

(a) it is in favour of a person other than a relative of the pensioner, or

(b) it relates to a sum due to an ordinary, ill-health or short service pensioner, in respect of a period beyond the age of 65 years, on account of the secured portion of the pension.

(6) A pension shall not pass to a trustee in bankruptcy or any other person acting on behalf of creditors of the pensioner.

(7) This Article shall apply with respect to awards other than pensions as it applies with respect to pensions, and accordingly any reference in this Article to a pension shall be construed as including a reference to any such award, and any reference therein to a pensioner shall be construed as including a reference to a person to whom any such award is payable.

(8) In the application of this Article to Scotland—

(a) the reference in paragraph (3) to the personal estate of the deceased shall be construed as a reference to his movable estate;

(b) any reference in paragraph (4) to a minor shall be construed as including a reference to a pupil.

Payment of transfer values

62. Where a regular fireman retires or has retired from a brigade and after again becoming such a fireman in another brigade becomes entitled under Article 44(1) to reckon as pensionable service the period of pensionable service he was entitled to reckon on retiring, the fire authority maintaining the first-mentioned brigade shall pay to the fire authority maintaining the other brigade a sum by way of transfer value calculated in accordance with Schedule 9.

Expenses and receipts of fire authorities

63.—(1) Every fire authority shall maintain an account showing all sums received or paid by the authority under, or for the purposes of, this Scheme, the Firemen's Pension Scheme 1966, the Firemen's Pension Scheme 1964, the Firemen's Pension Scheme 1956, the Firemen's Pension Scheme 1952 or the Firemen's Pension Scheme 1948(a).

(2) If and so long as the fire authority maintain a pension reserve account in accordance with paragraph (3) the account mentioned in paragraph (1) shall be separate from any account maintained by the fire authority which shows sums received or paid by the authority (not being such sums as are there mentioned) other than sums received or paid under rules made by virtue of section 9 of the Fire Services Act 1959, or payments in lieu of contributions made in respect of regular firemen.

(3) A fire authority which maintained a pension reserve account immediately before 15th February 1971 shall continue to maintain such an account on and after that day until it is exhausted in accordance with paragraph (4).

(4) Where in any year the payments debited to the account mentioned in paragraph (1) exceed the receipts credited thereto, and the fire authority maintain a pension reserve account, the balance shall be met out of the pension reserve account to the extent thereof.

(5) In this Article the expression "year" means a year beginning on the anniversary of the appointed day.

PART IX

SERVICEMEN

Awards to servicemen

64.—(1) This Article shall apply in the case of a serviceman who at the end of his period of relevant service in the armed forces is incapacitated by infirmity of mind or body for the performance of duty as a regular fireman if it appears that the incapacity is likely to be permanent.

(2) Such a person shall be entitled to the same award on the same conditions in all respects as if he had retired from his former brigade at the end of the said period on the ground that he had been so incapacitated.

(a) *See* S.I. 1948/604 (Rev. VII, p. 776: 1948 I, p. 1091).

(3) Where the infirmity of mind or body is occasioned by an injury received during the person's period of relevant service in the armed forces or by a qualifying injury, the fire authority may, in their discretion—

(a) pay him, in lieu of a gratuity, a pension at the rate of a twelfth of his average pensionable pay; and

(b) increase any pension payable under this Article, so however that the increased pension, when aggregated with any service pension other than an allowance for constant attendance, wear and tear of clothing, or comforts, shall not be payable at a rate exceeding that of the aggregate of the pensions to which he would have been entitled had the injury been treated, for the purposes of the preceding paragraph, as if it were a qualifying injury.

Awards on death of servicemen

65.—(1) This Article shall apply in the case of a serviceman who—

(a) dies during his period of relevant service in the armed forces; or

(b) having been incapacitated for duty as a regular fireman at the end of the said period and the incapacity having appeared likely to be permanent (without any intervening period of service as such a fireman) dies from the effects of the injury that resulted in his incapacity or while in receipt of a pension.

(2) Such a person's widow shall—

(a) if he was entitled to reckon 3 years' pensionable service, be entitled to a pension as though he were a person mentioned in Article 21(1); or

(b) if she is not so entitled to a pension and if her husband died during his period of relevant service in the armed forces, be entitled to a gratuity under Article 21(3) as though he died while serving as a regular fireman.

(3) Any child of such a person shall be entitled to an allowance as though he were mentioned in Article 28.

(4) Subject to paragraphs (5) and (6), where such a person dies from the effects of an injury received during his period of relevant service in the armed forces or of a qualifying injury, the fire authority may, in their discretion—

(a) pay to the widow, in lieu of a gratuity, a pension at the rate of £96 a year; and

(b) increase any pension or allowance payable under this Article, so however that the increased award, when aggregated with any service pension payable to or for the widow or child, as the case may be, in respect of the serviceman, shall not be payable at a rate exceeding that of the award to which the widow or child, as the case may be, would have been entitled had the serviceman died from the effects of a qualifying injury, ignoring any increase in accordance with the provisions of Schedule 4.

(5) In any case in which the rate of payment specified in paragraph (4)(a) falls to be increased under any of the relevant Pensions (Increase) Acts, otherwise than under section 2 of the Pensions (Increase) Act 1962(a), paragraph (4)(a) shall have effect as if for the rate of £96 a year there were substituted such lower rate as, together with the increase, yields a pension at the rate of £96 a year.

(6) Where an award is increased under paragraph (4)(b) the amount thereof shall be further increased in accordance with Schedule 4.

Gratuities for dependants other than widows and children

66. In relation to a serviceman who dies during his relevant service in the armed forces, Article 35 shall apply as though he died while serving as a regular fireman.

(a) 1962 c. 2.

Servicemen who resume service as regular firemen

67. If a serviceman who resumes service as a regular fireman—

(*a*) is incapacitated for the performance of his duties as such and 'the incapacity appears likely to be permanent; or

(*b*) dies (whether while serving as such a fireman or otherwise),

as a result of an injury received during his period of relevant service in the armed forces, the fire authority may, in relation to any award payable to or in respect of him, exercise the like discretions as are conferred on them by Article 64 or by Article 65.

Servicemen who do not resume service in their former brigade

68. If a serviceman within one month of the end of his period of relevant service in the armed forces does not resume service in his former brigade, he shall be treated for the purposes of Articles 25, 33, 40, 44, 51, 55 and 80 as having left his former brigade at the end of that period:

Provided that he may apply to the fire authority for the consent mɜntioned in Article 44(2) at any time within a month of the end of the said period.

Pensionable service, contributions and pay

69.—(1) A serviceman shall be entitled to reckon his period of relevant service in the armed forces as pensionable service in his former brigade for the purposes of this Scheme.

(2) A serviceman shall pay pension contributions (including additional contributions under Article 53) to the fire authority of his former brigade in respect of his period of relevant service in the armed forces as though he had remained a regular fireman in that brigade:

Provided that pension contributions shall not be payable by a serviceman in respect of any period during which he is in receipt of service pay which when aggregated with any payments under Part V of the Reserve and Auxiliary Forces (Protection of Civil Interests) Act 1951**(a)** is less than his pensionable pay.

(3) For the purpose of calculating pensionable pay, a serviceman shall be deemed to receive during his period of relevant service in the armed forces the pay which he would have received if he had continued to serve in his former brigade.

Servicemen deemed not to have retired

70. Except where the context otherwise requires, a reference in this Scheme to a regular fireman retiring or ceasing to be such does not include a reference to his so doing for the purpose of undertaking relevant service in the armed forces.

Application to regular firemen with war service

71.—(1) Articles 65 and 67 shall apply in the case of a regular fireman who received any injury during a period of war service at a time when section 1 of the Police and Firemen (War Service) Act 1939**(b)** applied to him as they apply in the case of a serviceman and as if any reference therein to a period of relevant service in the armed forces were a reference to a period of war service.

(2) In this Article any reference to "a period of war service" is a reference to a period of service in the armed forces of the Crown or to a period, beginning before 1st January 1948 and ending before 1st April 1948, of work which the Secretary of State directed should be treated as war work for the purpose of Regulation 60DA of the Defence (General) Regulations 1939, and the reference to the Police and Firemen (War Service) Act 1939 includes a reference to that Act as extended by the said Regulation 60DA.

(a) 1951 c. 65.   (b) 1939 c. 103.

Part X

Members of Brigades who are not Regular Firemen

Awards to and in respect of whole-time firemen

72.—(1) Where, while in attendance at a fire and without his own default, a whole-time member of a brigade who is not a regular fireman suffers or has suffered any injury in the execution of his duties as a member of the brigade, the provisions of this Article shall have effect in his case.

(2) If he retires in consequence of the injury, the fire authority may grant him such pension as they think fit, so however that the said pension, when aggregated with any additional benefit which may be payable to him, shall not exceed the minimum injury award which would have been appropriate in his case had he been a regular fireman of the rank of fireman and retired on account of a qualifying injury during his first year of service.

(3) If he dies from the effects of the injury, either before or after retiring from the brigade, the fire authority may grant his widow or child such pension or allowance, as the case may be, as they think fit, so however that the said pension or allowance, when aggregated with any additional benefit which may be payable to the recipient, shall not exceed the pension or allowance which would have been payable had he been a regular fireman of the rank of fireman who died or retired during his first year of service and died from the effects of a qualifying injury, any increase in accordance with Schedule 4 being ignored.

(4) The amount of a pension or allowance granted under the last foregoing paragraph shall be increased in accordance with Schedule 4.

(5) In this Article the expression "additional benefit" means any periodical payments of whatever nature which are made by the fire authority, otherwise than under this Article, by any other local authority or by a Minister of the Crown otherwise than by way of an increase in a disablement pension payable under section 15 of the National Insurance (Industrial Injuries) Act 1965(a) where constant attendance is needed, so however that in paragraph (3) the said expression does not include any benefit payable under that Act or the National Insurance Act 1965.

(6) Article 15(3) (which relates to disablement gratuities under the National Insurance (Industrial Injuries) Act 1965) shall apply for the purposes of this Article as it applies for the purposes of Article 15.

(7) This Article shall have effect in the case of a woman member of a brigade subject to Article 77(1).

Payment of contributions by retained firemen

73.—(1) Every part-time member of a brigade, being a retained fireman, shall pay an annual contribution to the fire authority which shall fall due at the same time as his annual retaining fee and may, without prejudice to any other method of payment, be discharged by way of a deduction made by the authority from the said fee.

(2) The annual contribution to be paid under paragraph (1) shall be—

    (*a*) £0·80 in the case of a man holding the rank of fireman;

    (*b*) £0·95 in the case of a man holding the rank of leading fireman;

    (*c*) £1·05 in the case of a man holding the rank of sub-officer;

    (*d*) £1·25 in the case of a man holding the rank of station officer;

    (*e*) £1·40 in the case of a man holding any higher rank;

    (*f*) £0·20 in the case of a woman.

(a) 1965 c. 52.

(3) In this Article any reference to a man's rank is a reference to his rank at the time the annual contribution falls due.

Part-time firemen: injury award

74.—(1) Where a part-time member of a brigade is incapacitated for the performance of his duty as such a member by infirmity of mind or body occasioned by an injury received without his own default in the execution of his duties as such a member and it appears that the incapacity is likely to be permanent, he shall on retiring on that account be entitled to an injury award as hereinafter provided.

(2) The award under paragraph (1) shall consist of an ill-health pension and a special pension which shall be payable at the like rates and be subject to the like conditions as they would have been if the part-time member concerned had been such a regular fireman as is mentioned in Article 77(2) and had retired on account of a qualifying injury; and, accordingly, Articles 14, 15, 17, 18, 19 and 87 shall have effect subject to any necessary modifications.

Widow of part-time fireman : injury pension

75.—(1) Where a part-time member of a brigade dies from the effects of an injury received without his own default in the execution of his duties as such a member or from the effects of infirmity of mind or body occasioned by such an injury, his widow shall be entitled to—

(a) a widow's injury pension as hereinafter provided, and

(b) where the part-time member last ceased to serve as such on or after 1st August 1964 and the injury was received in the circumstances mentioned in Article 23(1), a widow's injury gratuity, as hereinafter provided, in addition to a pension.

(2) Where the part-time member last ceased to serve as such on or after 1st August 1964, the injury pension or gratuity under paragraph (1) shall be a widow's special pension or gratuity of the like amount and payable subject to the like conditions as it would have been had he been such a regular fireman as is mentioned in Article 77(2) and had died from the effects of a qualifying injury received in the like circumstances; and, accordingly, Articles 22, 23, 24, 25, 26 and 27 shall have effect subject to any necessary modifications.

(3) Where the part-time member last ceased to serve as such before 1st August 1964, the injury pension under paragraph (1) shall, subject to Article 77(3), be payable—

(a) for such period as she is under the age of 40 years, at the rate of £1·56 a week;

(b) for such period as she is of the age of 40 years or over but under the age of 50 years, at the rate of £2·33 a week;

(c) for such period as she is of the age of 50 years or over or has a child in receipt of an injury allowance under Article 76, at the rate of £3·10 a week;

and in relation to the pension Articles 24, 25, 26 and 27 shall have effect subject to any necessary modifications:

Provided that the said pension shall not exceed that which would have been payable had it fallen to be calculated in accordance with paragraph (2).

Child of part-time fireman: injury allowance

76.—(1) Where a part-time member of a brigade dies as mentioned in Article 75(1) any child of his shall be entitled to, or, in the case of a woman member, any child of hers may be granted—

(a) a child's injury allowance as hereinafter provided, and

(b) where the part-time member last ceased to serve as such on or after 1st August 1964, the injury was received in the circumstances mentioned in Article 23(1), a child's injury gratuity, as hereinafter provided, in addition to an allowance.

(2) Where the part-time member last ceased to serve as such on or after 1st August 1964, the injury allowance or gratuity under paragraph (1) shall be a child's special allowance or gratuity of the like amount and payable subject to the like conditions as it would have been had he been such a regular fireman as is mentioned in Article 77(2) and had died from the effects of a qualifying injury received in the like circumstances; and, accordingly, Articles 29, 30, 31, 32, 33 and 34 shall have effect subject to any necessary modifications.

(3) Where the part-time member last ceased to serve as such before 1st August 1964, the injury allowance under paragraph (1) shall, subject to Article 77(3), be payable—

    (a) where the member is a man, at the rate of £0·83 a week;

    (b) where the member is a woman, at such rate as the fire authority from time to time think fit, not exceeding £0·63 a week if and so long as the child's father is living and not exceeding £0·83 a week if the child has no parent living;

and in relation to the allowance Articles 31, 32 and 33 shall have effect subject to the necessary modifications:

Provided that the said allowance shall not exceed that which would have been payable had it fallen to be calculated in accordance with paragraph (2).

(4) This Article shall have effect in the case of a woman member of a brigade subject to Article 77(1) and in such case an allowance which falls to be calculated in accordance with paragraph (2) shall be payable at such rate as the fire authority from time to time think fit, not exceeding the rate at which it would have been payable but for this paragraph.

Auxiliary provisions

77.—(1) In the case of a woman member of a brigade who is not a regular fireman this Part of this Scheme shall have effect—

    (a) as if for any reference in Article 72(2) or (3) to the rank of fireman there were substituted a reference to the rank of firewoman;

    (b) as if for any reference in Article 72(3) or 76(1) to a child there were substituted a reference to a child of the member substantially dependent upon her at the time of her death;

    (c) as if in Article 33—

        (i) for any reference to the father or step-father there were substituted a reference to the mother or step-mother as the case may be;

        (ii) for the reference to the mother there were substituted a reference to the father.

(2) For the purposes of the injury pension, allowance or gratuity payable to or in respect of a part-time member of a brigade, any reference in this Part of this Scheme to a regular fireman is a reference to such a fireman who—

    (a) held the same rank as the part-time member in fact held and had the same service in that rank,

    (b) was entitled to reckon as pensionable service a period equal to the part-time member's service as such, and

    (c) paid pension contributions at the rate of 6p a week less than 5 per cent. of his pensionable pay.

(3) In any case in which the rate of widow's injury pension or child's injury allowance specified in Article 75(3) or, as the case may be, Article 76(3) falls to be increased under any of the relevant Pensions (Increase) Acts, otherwise than under section 2 of the Pensions (Increase) Act 1962, the provision in question shall have effect as if for the rate specified there were substituted such lower rate as, together with the increase, yields a pension at the specified rate.

(4) The provisions of Article 41 and of Parts VII, VIII and XIII of this Scheme (in so far as they are applicable) shall apply to a member of a fire brigade who is not a regular fireman and to a pension, allowance or gratuity granted to or in respect of him, but, save as provided in this Part of this Scheme, the provisions of this Scheme shall not apply to such a member or to such a pension, allowance or gratuity.

PART XI
PERSONS WHO ARE NOT MEMBERS OF BRIGADES
Temporary employment in connection with the provision of fire services

78.—(1) This Article shall apply in the case of a person who ceases or has ceased to perform duties as a regular fireman in order to enter temporary employment on duties connected with the provision of fire services, being—

(a) employment as an instructor at the central training institution or any training centre maintained by the Secretary of State;

(b) employment as an inspector, assistant inspector or other officer appointed under section 24 of the principal Act;

(c) employment entered upon in pursuance of arrangements made by the Secretary of State in connection with the training in fire-fighting of members of the armed forces of the Crown; or

(d) employment entered upon in pursuance of arrangements made by the Secretary of State in connection with the training and organisation of fire-fighting forces in any country or territory outside the United Kingdom,

(hereafter in this Article referred to as "the relevant employment").

(2) In the case of a person to whom this Article applies the relevant employment shall be treated for the purposes of this Scheme as employment as a member of a fire brigade and, without prejudice to the following provisions of this Article, this Scheme shall apply in relation thereto as if—

(a) he were a regular fireman and his duties were his duties as such;

(b) his pay and rank were the same as they would have been had he not ceased to perform duties as such a fireman or, where section 10 of the Fire Services Act 1959 applies in his case, the same as his pay and rank as a member of a fire brigade;

(c) any reference to a brigade were a reference to the relevant employment;

(d) Articles 63, 85 and 86 were omitted; and

(e) any reference to a fire authority were a reference to the Secretary of State.

(3) Except where the relevant employment is such as is mentioned in paragraph (1)(d) and the person has served therein on or after 1st March 1970, this Scheme shall have effect as aforesaid as if—

(a) the reference to a court of quarter sessions in Article 59(1) were a reference to the court of quarter sessions for any county or borough which constitutes or is wholly or partly included in the area of the fire authority by whom he was employed immediately before entering the relevant employment, and

(b) the reference to the sheriff in Article 59(5) were a reference to the sheriff having jurisdiction in the place where he served as a fireman immediately before entering the relevant employment.

(4) Where the relevant employment is such as is mentioned in paragraph (1)(d) and the person has served therein on or after 1st March 1970, this Scheme shall have effect as aforesaid as if a reference in Article 59 to a court of quarter sessions were a reference to an appeal tribunal appointed by the Secretary of State and consisting of three persons including—

(a) a retired member of a fire brigade who before he retired held a rank not lower than that of Divisional Officer (Grade I), and

(b) a barrister or solicitor of seven years' standing or, where the person ceased to perform duties in a Scottish fire brigade in order to enter the relevant employment, an advocate or a solicitor of seven years' standing,

and paragraphs (4) and (5) were omitted from the said Article.

(5) In the case of an appeal to such a tribunal as is mentioned in paragraph (4)—

    (*a*) the time and place for the hearing, or the postponed or adjourned hearing, shall be determined by the tribunal, which shall give reasonable notice thereof to the appellant and to the Secretary of State (hereinafter described as "the parties");

    (*b*) either party may be represented before the tribunal by counsel or by solicitor or by some other person approved by the tribunal, adduce evidence and cross-examine witnesses;

    (*c*) the tribunal shall apply the rules of evidence applicable in the case of an appeal to quarter sessions under Article 59 or, where the person ceased to perform duties in a Scottish fire brigade in order to enter the relevant employment, in the case of such an appeal to the sheriff, and

    (*d*) subject to the preceding provisions of this paragraph, the tribunal shall determine its own procedure.

(6) Subject to and in accordance with rules of court, an appeal on a point of law from a decision of such a tribunal as is mentioned in paragraph (4) shall lie to the High Court or, where the person ceased to perform duties in a Scottish fire brigade in order to enter the relevant employment, to the Court of Session.

(7) For the purposes of paragraph (1)(*b*), any arrangements made by the Minister of Overseas Development on or after 1st April 1968 but before 15th November 1970 shall be treated as if they had been made by the Secretary of State.

Permanent employment as an instructor

79.—(1) This Article shall apply in the case of a person who ceases or has ceased to perform duties as a regular fireman in order to enter employment on duties connected with the provision of fire services, being permanent employment as an instructor at the central training institution or any training centre maintained by the Secretary of State.

(2) In the case of such a person as is mentioned in paragraph (1), the employment therein mentioned (hereafter in this paragraph referred to as "the relevant employment") shall be treated for the purposes of this Scheme as employment as a member of a brigade and this Scheme shall apply in relation to that employment as if—

    (*a*) he were a regular fireman and his duties were his duties as such;

    (*b*) any reference to a brigade were a reference to the relevant employment;

    (*c*) any reference to a fire authority were a reference to the Secretary of State;

    (*d*) the reference to a court of quarter sessions in Article 59(1) were a reference to the court of quarter sessions for any county or borough in which the central training institution or, as the case may be, training centre, is situate;

    (*e*) the reference to the sheriff in Article 59(5) were a reference to the sheriff having jurisdiction in the place where the central training institution is situate; and

    (*f*) Articles 63, 85 and 86 were omitted.

PART XII

PERSONS WHO WERE SERVING ON 10TH JULY 1956

Modification of Scheme

80.—(1) Subject to paragraph (3), this Article shall apply in the case of a person who—

(*a*) was, on 10th July 1956, a regular fireman or a serviceman performing relevant service in the armed forces; or

(*b*) was, on 10th July 1956, in receipt of an ill-health pension and subsequently, but before 1st August 1964, resumed service in his brigade in the circumstances and within the period mentioned in Article 17(3),

not being a person who exercised his right of election under Article 60 of the Firemen's Pension Scheme 1956 or to whom that Article, Article 66 of the Firemen's Pension Scheme 1964 or Article 68 of the Firemen's Pension Scheme 1966 ceased to apply.

(2) In the case of a person to whom this Article applies this Scheme shall have effect subject to the modification set out in Schedule 10.

(3) Where a person to whom this Article applies has ceased to serve as a regular fireman in any particular brigade, this Article shall not apply to him in relation to any subsequent period during which he serves as a regular fireman in the same or another brigade, beginning on or after 1st August 1964, unless in the circumstances mentioned in Article 44(1) or (3), he becomes or has become entitled to reckon as pensionable service the period so reckonable on his ceasing to serve.

PART XIII

MISCELLANEOUS PROVISIONS

Auxiliary firemen not subject to Scheme

81.—(1) This Scheme shall not apply in relation to a member of a brigade who is an auxiliary fireman.

(2) In this Article the expression "auxiliary fireman" means a member of a brigade who is enrolled for service therein which is restricted except in a war emergency to such duties as are desirable for training.

Exclusive application of Scheme in relation to regular firemen

82. Subject to the provisions of section 27 of the principal Act, the provisions of this Scheme and, in so far as they continue to have effect, of the Firemen's Pension Scheme 1966, the Firemen's Pension Scheme 1964, the Firemen's Pension Scheme 1956, the Firemen's Pension Scheme 1952 and the Firemen's Pension Scheme 1948 shall have effect in relation to regular firemen, their wives and dependants to the exclusion of any provision for pension allowance or gratuity in respect of a person's employment as such a fireman contained in or in force under any enactment:

Provided that nothing in this Article shall affect the operation of—

(*a*) any such provision in respect of a person's employment or service otherwise than as a member of a brigade which is treated for the purposes of this Scheme as employment as a regular fireman; or

(*b*) the National Insurance Act 1965 or the National Insurance (Industrial Injuries) Act 1965.

Application of Scheme to persons affected by local government reorganisation or a combination scheme

83.—(1) In relation to a member of a fire brigade who is or has been transferred to, or otherwise becomes or has become a member of, another fire brigade by virtue of an instrument mentioned in paragraph (4)—

(*a*) this Scheme shall apply as though the brigade of which he becomes a member and the authority maintaining that brigade were, respectively, the same brigade and authority as the brigade first mentioned in this paragraph and the authority maintaining that brigade;

(b) where he held the rank of assistant divisional officer or any higher rank in the brigade first mentioned in this paragraph but suffers or has suffered reduction in rank attributable to the provisions of such an instrument, Article 85 shall apply as though he had not suffered such reduction in rank, unless he elects otherwise by notice in writing to the fire authority.

(2) In relation to a member of a fire brigade who suffers or has suffered loss of employment as a regular fireman which is attributable to the provisions of an instrument mentioned in paragraph (4)—

(a) this Scheme shall apply as though he had retired from the brigade after having given due notice of retirement to the fire authority and, if the fire authority so agree, as though the notice of retirement had been given with their permission, and

(b) where he becomes a regular fireman in another brigade before the end of his resettlement period, Article 43 shall apply as though he had become a member of that other brigade immediately after ceasing to be a member of the brigade first mentioned in this paragraph.

(3) In relation to a member of a fire brigade who is or has been transferred to, or otherwise becomes or has become a member of, another fire brigade by virtue of the London Government Act 1963(a) or of any instrument mentioned in paragraph (4)—

(a) in whose case this Scheme has effect subject to the modifications set out in Schedule 10;

(b) whose last change of rank during the relevant period for the purposes of Article 51(3) (as modified by paragraph 4 of Schedule 10) was a reduction in rank attributable to the provisions of the said Act of 1963 or of any instrument mentioned in paragraph (4), and

(c) whose average pensionable pay during the said relevant period was less than his pensionable pay immediately before his death or retirement,

Article 51 (as modified as aforesaid) shall apply as though paragraph (3) were omitted therefrom.

(4) The reference in paragraphs (1), (2) and (3) to an instrument mentioned in this paragraph are references to—

(a) an order under Part VI of the Local Government Act 1933(b), Part II of the Local Government Act 1958(c) or section 85 of the London Government Act 1963, or

(b) a scheme under section 5, 6, or 9 of the principal Act or, in Scotland, an order under section 36(8) of that Act;

and the reference in paragraph (2) to a person's resettlement period is a reference to the period of 13 weeks next succeeding the week in which he ceased to be a member of the brigade first mentioned in that paragraph or, in the case of a person who has attained the age of 45 years, the said 13 weeks extended by an additional week for every year of his age after attaining the age of 45 years and before he ceased to be a member of that brigade, subject to a maximum extension of 13 such weeks.

Application of Scheme where modified by section 27 of principal Act

84.—(1) This Article shall apply in the case of a person in relation to whom this Scheme is modified as mentioned in section 27(3) of the principal Act.

(2) Where such a person as aforesaid is entitled to both an ill-health and a special pension, then, for the purposes of Articles 20, 36, 37 and 38, his entitlement to, and the amount of, the ill-health pension shall be deemed to be the same as they would have been had he not been entitled to a special pension.

(3) Where in relation to such a person as aforesaid this Scheme is modified by reference to regulations made under either the Metropolitan Fire Brigade Act 1865(d) or the West Ham Corporation Act 1925(e), Article 20(1) shall apply in relation to him as if for the reference to 30 years' pensionable service there were substituted a reference to 28 years' pensionable service.

(a) 1963 c. 33.   (b) 1933 c. 51.
(c) 1958 c. 55.   (d) 1865 c. 90.
(e) 1925 c. cxii.

Age of compulsory retirement

85.—(1) Subject to paragraphs (2) and (3), retirement shall be compulsory for a male whole-time member of a brigade appointed on terms under which he is or may be required to engage in fire-fighting—

(a) in the case of a member of the rank of assistant divisional officer or any higher rank, on attaining the age of 60 years; and

(b) in the case of a member of the rank of station officer or any lower rank, on attaining the age of 55 years,

except that in special cases the fire authority may extend any such member's service for a further period on being satisfied that such extension would be in the interests of efficiency.

(2) Without prejudice to the extension under paragraph (1) of the service of such a member of a brigade as is therein mentioned, in the case of a regular fireman of the rank of station officer or any lower rank, if the fireman so elects by notice in writing to the fire authority, that authority may extend his service by such period, if any, not exceeding 6 months from his attaining the age of 55 years as is requisite to enable him to reckon—

(a) an additional completed year of pensionable service, in the case of a member who will be entitled to reckon less than 20 years' pensionable service on attaining that age, or

(b) an additional completed half year of pensionable service, in any other case.

(3) Nothing in paragraph (1) shall apply to a member in whose case any regulations made for the purposes set out in paragraph 7 of the Schedule to the Fire Services (Emergency Provisions) Act 1941(a) had effect immediately before 1st April 1948 unless and until—

(a) he is entitled without a medical certificate to retire and receive a pension at the rate of 2 thirds of his average pensionable pay; or

(b) he elects that the provisions of paragraph (1) should apply to him, by notice in writing to the fire authority maintaining the brigade of which he is a member.

(4) Subject to paragraph (5), retirement shall also be compulsory for any male whole-time member of a brigade who has attained the age of 50 years and completed 25 years' pensionable service if he is required to retire by the fire authority on the grounds that his retention in the brigade would not be in the general interests of its efficiency.

(5) Nothing in paragraph (4) shall apply to a member of the brigade in whose case the National Fire Service (Preservation of Pensions) (Police Firemen) Regulations 1941(b), the National Fire Service (Preservation of Pensions) (Birmingham and Leicester) Regulations 1941(c) or the National Fire Service (Preservation of Pensions) (Bolton and Derby) Regulations 1941(d) had effect immediately before 1st April 1948, or to a member who, immediately before 18th August 1941, was a professional fireman within the meaning of the Fire Brigade Pensions Act 1925(e) as amended by the Fire Brigades Act 1938(f) and in whose case the National Fire Service (Preservation of Pensions) (General Pension Funds) Regulations 1941(g) had effect immediately before 1st April 1948.

(6) This Article shall apply to a member of a Scottish fire Brigade as if paragraphs (3) and (5) were omitted, but nothing in this Article shall apply to such a member in whose case any regulations made for the purposes set out in paragraph 7 of the Schedule to the Fire Services (Emergency Provisions) Act 1941 had effect immediately before 16th May 1948, unless and until—

(a) he could have been compelled to retire under the statutory provisions or regulations applicable to him immediately before 18th August 1941, or

(b) he elects that the provisions of paragraph (1) should apply to him, by notice in writing to the fire authority maintaining the brigade of which he is a member.

(a) 1941 c. 22.
(c) S.R. & O. 1941/1273 (1941 I, p. 337).
(e) 1925 c. 47.
(g) S.R. & O. 1941/1270 (1941 I, p. 325).

(b) S.R. & O. 1941/1271 (1941 I, p. 328).
(d) S.R. & O. 1941/1274 (1941 I, p. 342).
(f) 1938 c. 72.

Compulsory retirement on grounds of incapacity

86. A regular fireman may be required to retire on the date on which the fire authority determine he ought to retire on the ground that he is incapacitated for the performance of his duty by infirmity of mind or body and that the incapacity is likely to be permanent:

Provided that a retirement in accordance with this Article shall be void if after the said date, on an appeal against the medical opinion on which the fire authority acted in determining that he ought to retire, the medical referee decides that the appellant is not incapacitated as aforesaid.

Assessment of disablement

87.—(1) For the purposes of this Scheme the extent to which a person is disabled shall be determined by reference to the extent to which his earning capacity has been affected, and a person shall be deemed to be totally disabled if, and only if, he is incapable, by reason of infirmity of mind or body, of earning any money in any employment.

(2) For the purposes of this Article a person shall be treated as incapable of earning any money in any employment, notwithstanding that the infirmity of mind or body is not such as to prevent him being capable of work, if it is likely to prevent his earnings exceeding £104 in a year.

SCHEDULE 1

PART I   Article 12

FIREMAN'S ORDINARY PENSION

Subject as hereafter in this Schedule provided, an ordinary pension shall be of an amount of not more than 40 sixtieths of the fireman's average pensionable pay and, subject as aforesaid, shall be equal to 30 sixtieths of his average pensionable pay with the addition of a sixtieth for each completed half year by which his pensionable service exceeds 25 years.

PART II   Articles 13 and 14

FIREMAN'S SHORT SERVICE OR ILL-HEALTH PENSION

Subject as hereafter in this Schedule provided, a short service or ill-health pension shall be of an amount of not less than a sixtieth nor more than 40 sixtieths of the fireman's average pensionable pay and, subject as aforesaid, shall be equal to a sixtieth of his average pensionable pay for each completed year of pensionable service up to 20 years with the addition of a sixtieth for each completed half year by which his pensionable service exceeds 20 years.

PART III   Articles 12, 13 and 14

REDUCTION OF FIREMAN'S PENSION AT AGE 65

1.—(1) Subject as hereafter in this paragraph provided, the unsecured portion of an ordinary, ill-health or short service pension shall be reduced in respect of any period beyond the age of 65 years by an amount calculated at an annual rate obtained by multiplying £1·70 by the number of years specified in sub-paragraph (4).

. (2) In the case of a person who immediately before he retired and was granted a pension was paying pension contributions at a rate of 1p a week less than the appropriate percentage of his pensionable pay there shall not be any reduction in the pension under this paragraph.

Sch. 1 (*contd.*)

(3) Subject as hereafter in this paragraph provided, in the case of a person who immediately before he retired and was granted a pension was paying pension contributions at a rate of 6p a week less than the appropriate percentage of his pensionable pay by reason of his having elected so to do as mentioned in Article 52(3) the reduction under sub-paragraph (1) shall be calculated not as therein stated but at an annual rate obtained by multiplying the sum in the second column of the following Table set opposite to his age on the appointed day in the first column of the said Table by the number of years specified in sub-paragraph (4):—

TABLE

Age in years				Sum to be multiplied
				£
Under 23	...	...	...	1·700
23 but under 24	...	...	...	1·650
24 „ „ 25	...	...	...	1·600
25 „ „ 26	...	...	...	1·550
26 „ „ 27	...	...	...	1·525
27 „ „ 28	...	...	...	1·500
28 „ „ 29	...	...	...	1·475
29 „ „ 30	...	...	...	1·450
30 „ „ 31	...	...	...	1·425
31 „ „ 32	...	...	...	1·400
32 „ „ 33	...	...	...	1·375
33 „ „ 34	...	...	...	1·350
34 „ „ 35	...	...	...	1·325
35 „ „ 37	...	...	...	1·300
37 „ „ 38	...	...	...	1·275
38 „ „ 40	...	...	...	1·250
40 „ „ 42	...	...	...	1·225
42 „ „ 44	...	...	...	1·200
44 and over	...	...	...	1·175

(4) The number of years referred to in sub-paragraph (1) and in sub-paragraph (3), by which the sums therein respectively specified are to be multiplied for the purposes of those sub-paragraphs, is the number of complete years during which the person concerned has served as a regular fireman:

Provided that no account shall be taken of any service which is not reckonable as pensionable service.

(5) In the case of a person who is entitled to reckon a period as pensionable service for the purposes of the pension in question by virtue of service or employment otherwise than as a regular fireman in respect of which he was subject to superannuation arrangements—

(a) if he was subject to the operation of any regulations made under section 69(4) of the National Insurance Act 1946 or section 110(1) of the National Insurance Act 1965 or of other provisions modifying the said superannuation arrangements in connection with the passing of the said Act of 1946, otherwise than by virtue of an election made or notice given, then, for the purposes of sub-paragraph (1), sub-paragraph (4) shall apply as though the period he is so entitled to reckon as pensionable service were a period of service as a regular fireman;

(b) if he was subject to the operation of such regulations or other provisions by virtue of an election made or notice given, then sub-paragraph (3) shall apply in his case as if for the reference therein to his age on the appointed day there were substituted a reference to his age on the date on which the said election or notice became effective and, for the purposes of the said sub-paragraph, sub-paragraph (4) shall apply as though the period he is so entitled to reckon as pensionable service were a period of service as a regular fireman:

Provided that no account shall be taken of any period he is so entitled to reckon as pensionable service which is not attributable to service or employment which would have been taken into account for the purposes of the said regulations or provisions.

(6) The rate of reduction of a pension under this paragraph shall not in any case exceed £51 a year.

2.—(1) Where a person in receipt of an ordinary, ill-health or short service pension has been in service or employment otherwise than as a regular fireman—

(a) in respect of which he was subject to superannuation arrangements;

(b) by virtue of which he is entitled to reckon pensionable service for the purposes of the pension; and

(c) the period of which includes a participating period of relevant employment, then, for the purpose of abating the pension in relation to that participating period of relevant employment, any provision of the said arrangements in operation when he left the said service or employment the effect of which is that pensions payable thereunder are to be reduced in connection with the operation of the National Insurance Act 1959(a) or of any provision of the National Insurance Act 1965 relating to graduated contributions or graduated retirement benefit shall apply, subject to the necessary adaptations and modifications, as though the provision were contained in this paragraph and as if—

(i) the pension were payable under the said arrangements, and

(ii) any other period of service or employment by virtue of which he is entitled to reckon pensionable service for the purposes of the pension were a period of non-participating employment at the end of which no payment in lieu of contributions falls to be made.

(2) A fire authority, in determining any question arising under sub-paragraph (1) and relating to a particular service or employment, shall be entitled to treat as conclusive any relevant certificate issued, with the agreement of the person concerned, by his employer in that service or employment.

(3) Where for the purposes of the superannuation arrangements applicable to such service or employment as is mentioned in sub-paragraph (1) the person concerned was entitled to reckon service by virtue of some previous service or employment, that previous service or employment shall be treated for the purposes of this paragraph as if it were part of the service or employment first mentioned in this sub-paragraph.

3.—(1) Where a person in receipt of an ordinary, ill-health or short service pension is entitled to reckon as pensionable service for the purposes of the pension a period of employment as a regular fireman which is a participating period of relevant employment, then in relation to that period the unsecured portion of the pension shall be reduced in accordance with the provisions of sub-paragraph (2).

(2) Where the unsecured portion of a pension is reduced in accordance with the provisions of this sub-paragraph, the annual rate of that portion of the pension shall be reduced in respect of any period beyond the age of 65 years by the annual rate of the graduated retirement benefit which would be payable to the pensioner on the assumption that he retired from regular employment on attaining that age, in return for a payment in lieu of contributions in respect of the whole of the period referred to in sub-paragraph (1).

4.—(1) Where a person in receipt of the secured portion of an ill-health pension (granted under this Scheme, the Firemen's Pension Scheme 1966(b), the Firemen's Pension Scheme 1964 or the Firemen's Pension Scheme 1956), the unsecured portion of which has been terminated in the circumstances mentioned in Article 17, is also in receipt of some other pension (being an ordinary, ill-health or short service pension granted under this Scheme) and is entitled to reckon for the purposes of that other pension the period of pensionable service reckonable for the purposes of the ill-health pension, then the unsecured portion of that other pension shall be reduced in accordance with the provisions of sub-paragraph (2).

(a) 1959 c. 47. (b) *See* S.I. 1966/1045 (1966 II, p. 2504).

Sch. 1 (*contd*).

(2) Where the unsecured portion of an ordinary, ill-health or short service pension is reduced in accordance with the provisions of this sub-paragraph, the annual rate of that portion shall be reduced in respect of any period beyond the age of 65 years by the annual rate of the secured portion of the ill-health pension first mentioned in this paragraph.

Articles 12, 13 and 14   PART IV

REDUCTION OF PENSION PAYABLE TO PERSON PAYING PENSION CONTRIBUTION AT A RATE RELATED TO SIX PER CENT. OF PENSIONABLE PAY

1. The amount of an ordinary, ill-health or short-service pension payable to a man who was immediately before his retirement paying pension contributions at a rate related to 6 per cent. of his pensionable pay shall, subject to the provisions of this Part of this Schedule, be reduced by that percentage which is set out in the second column of the following Table opposite the number of completed years of pensionable service he is entitled to reckon—

    (a) by virtue of service before 26th August 1966;

    (b) by virtue of service on or after that date in respect of which he has not paid pension contributions at a rate related to 6 per cent. of his pensionable pay;

    (c) by virtue that he had been entitled to a special pension if, for the purposes of Article 29(3) of the Firemen's Pension Scheme 1956, of Article 32 of the Firemen's Pension Scheme 1964, of Article 32 of the Firemen's Pension Scheme 1966 or of Article 45 of this Scheme, as the case may be, he undertook to pay a sum calculated by reference to pension contributions at a rate related to 5 per cent. of pensionable pay;

    (d) subject to paragraph 2, by virtue of such service or employment as is mentioned in Article 47(1) or 48(1):—

TABLE

Completed years of pensionable service	Percentage reduction in pension
1	0·2
2	0·4
3	0·6
4	0·8
5	1·0
6	1·2
7	1·3
8	1·4
9	1·6
10	1·7
11	1·8
12	1·9
13	2·1
14	2·2
15	2·3
16	2·4
17	2·5
18	2·6
19	2·7
20	2·8
21	2·9
22	3·0
23	3·1
24	3·2
25	3·2
26	3·3
27	3·4
28	3·4
29	3·5
30 or more	3·5

2. In calculating the amount of the said reduction no account shall be taken of—

> (*a*) any period of pensionable service he became entitled to reckon before 1st September 1967 by virtue of such service or employment as is mentioned in Article 47(1) or 48(1);

> (*b*) any period of pensionable service he is entitled to reckon by virtue of service in the armed forces, on or after 26th August 1966, in respect of which pension contributions were not payable.

3. If he elected to pay additional pension contributions under Article 40 of the Firemen's Pension Scheme 1966 and paid such contributions until he became entitled to reckon 25 years' pensionable service or retired with a pension, in calculating the amount of the said reduction no account shall be taken of any pensionable service of which account was taken for the purpose of calculating the rate of his additional contributions.

4. In calculating the amount of the said reduction there shall be disregarded any reduction in the amount of the pension in accordance with the provisions of Article 20 or 37 or of Part III of this Schedule.

PART V   Articles 13 and 14

FIREMAN'S SHORT SERVICE OR ILL-HEALTH GRATUITY

1. Where the fireman is entitled to reckon at least a year's pensionable service, the short service or ill-health gratuity shall be whichever is the greater of the two following amounts:—

> (*a*) a twelfth of his average annual pensionable pay multiplied by the number of completed years of pensionable service which he is entitled to reckon; or

> (*b*) his aggregate contributions.

2. Where the fireman is not entitled to reckon at least a year's pensionable service, the gratuity shall be of an amount equal to his aggregate contributions.

PART VI   Articles 13 and 14

REDUCTION OF FIREMAN'S GRATUITY

1. Where a payment in lieu of contributions falls to be made by a fire authority in respect of a regular fireman and—

> (*a*) a short service gratuity is payable by that authority on his retirement, or

> (*b*) an ill-health gratuity is so payable and the fire authority determine that the provisions of this Part of this Schedule shall apply,

the gratuity in question shall be reduced by an amount equal to the amount which could be retained out of the gratuity by the fire authority under section 60(4) of the National Insurance Act 1965(a) if the gratuity were a refund of payments to which that subsection applies.

2. Where a payment in lieu of contributions may fall to be made by a fire authority in respect of a regular fireman and such a gratuity as is mentioned in paragraph 1 is payable as mentioned therein, the fire authority may reduce the amount of the gratuity in question by the amount by which it would be reduced under the said paragraph 1 if the payment in lieu of contributions in fact fell to be made, so however that, if the said payment does not fall to be made within the period of 78 weeks from the date when the person concerned ceases to be a regular fireman or within such shorter period as the fire authority may determine, then any reduction in the amount of the gratuity under this paragraph shall cease to have effect and the difference between the full and the reduced amounts thereof shall become payable.

(a) 1965 c. 51.

Sch. 1 (*contd.*)

Article 15   PART VII

MINIMUM INJURY AWARD

1. The minimum injury award shall be determined by reference to the number of completed years of pensionable service the fireman is entitled to reckon and by reference to his average pensionable pay.

2. Where the fireman is totally disabled, the minimum injury award shall be the amount specified in the second column of the following Table, and where the fireman is partly disabled, the minimum injury award shall be such proportion of the amount so specified as the extent of the actual disablement bears to total disablement, so however that it is not less than the lower limit specified in the third column of the said Table:—

TABLE

Fireman's completed years of pensionable service	Minimum injury award on total disablement expressed in 60ths of average pensionable pay	Lower limit of minimum injury award expressed in 60ths of average pensionable pay
Less than 11	40	15
11 but less than 12	40	16
12 „ „ „ 13	40	17
13 „ „ „ 14	40	18
14 „ „ „ 15	41	19
15 „ „ „ 16	41	20
16 „ „ „ 17	42	21
17 „ „ „ 18	42	22
18 „ „ „ 19	43	23
19 „ „ „ 20	43	24
20 „ „ „ 21	44	25
21 „ „ „ 22	44	27
22 „ „ „ 23	45	29
23 „ „ „ 24	45	31
24 „ „ „ 25	46	33
25 „ „ „ 26	46	35
26 „ „ „ 27	47	36
27 „ „ „ 28	47	37
28 „ „ „ 29	48	38
29 „ „ „ 30	49	39
30 or more	50	40

SCHEDULE 2

Article 21   PART I

WIDOW'S ORDINARY PENSION—STANDARD RATE

1. Subject to paragraph 2, the weekly amount of a widow's ordinary pension calculated in accordance with this Part of this Schedule shall be not more than 40 one-hundred-and-eightieths of her husband's average pensionable pay and, subject as aforesaid, shall be equal to a one-hundred-and-eightieth of his average pensionable pay for each completed year of pensionable service up to 20 years with the addition of a one-hundred-and-eightieth for each completed half year by which his pensionable service exceeded 20 years.

Sch. 2 (*contd*).

2.—(1) Subject to sub-paragraphs (2) and (3), where in respect of any period a widow so elects her ordinary pension in respect of that period shall be of such amount that the rate of payment is—

(*a*) where the husband's last rank was not higher than that of sub-officer £96 a year;

(*b*) where the husband's last rank was higher than that of sub-officer but not higher than that of divisional officer (Grade I), £126 a year;

(*c*) where the husband's last rank was higher than that of divisional officer (Grade I), £156 a year.

(2) Where the husband was entitled to reckon at least 10 years' pensionable service, the preceding sub-paragraph shall have effect as if for the rates of £96, £126 and £156 a year there were substituted, respectively, the rates of £101, £131 and £161 a year.

(3) In any case in which the rate of payment specified in sub-paragraph (1) (including that sub-paragraph as modified by sub-paragraph (2)) falls to be increased under the Pensions (Increase) Act 1969(a), this paragraph shall have effect as if for the rate so specified there were substituted such lower rate as, together with the increase, yields a pension at the rate so specified.

PART II   Article 21

WIDOW'S ORDINARY PENSION—PRESERVED RATE

The amount of a widow's ordinary pension in respect of each week shall be the amount calculated according to Scheme I set out below, or where the fireman was entitled to reckon at least 10 years' pensionable service, according to whichever of the two Schemes set out below would yield to the widow the higher pension, after taking into account the increase, if any, conferred by virtue of the relevant Pensions (Increase) Acts.

SCHEME I

1. Subject as hereinafter provided, the pension shall be of such amount that the rate of payment is—

(*a*) where the husband's last rank was not higher than that of sub-officer, £96 a year;

(*b*) where the husband's last rank was higher than that of sub-officer but not higher than that of divisional officer (Grade I), £126 a year; or

(*c*) where the husband's last rank was higher than that of divisional officer (Grade I), £156 a year.

2. In any case in which the rate of payment specified in the preceding paragraph falls to be increased under any of the relevant Pensions (Increase) Acts, otherwise than under section 2 of the Pensions (Increase) Act 1962, that paragraph shall have effect as if for the rate specified there were substituted such lower rate as, together with the increase, yields a pension at the specified rate.

SCHEME II

1. Subject as hereinafter provided, the pension shall be of such amount that, when it is added to any widow's benefit or retirement pension payable to the widow under the National Insurance Act 1965 in right of her husband's insurance, the total weekly rate of payment is equal to the percentage of his average pensionable pay specified in the second column of the following Table being the percentage set out opposite to the number of his completed years of pensionable service in the first column of the said Table:—

(a) 1969 c. 7.

Sch. 2 (*contd.*)

TABLE

Husband's completed years of pensionable service					Total weekly rate
10, 11, 12, 13 and 14	...	...	...	...	5·0 per cent.
15, 16, 17, 18 and 19	...	...	...	...	7·5 per cent.
20, 21, 22, 23 and 24	...	...	...	...	10·0 per cent.
25, 26, 27, 28 and 29	...	...	...	...	12·5 per cent.
30 or more ...	...	...	...	...	16·0 per cent.

2. The amount of the pension calculated in accordance with the preceding paragraph shall be increased in accordance with Schedule 4.

Article 21   PART III

WIDOW'S ORDINARY GRATUITY

1. Where the fireman was not entitled to reckon a year's pensionable service, the gratuity shall be an amount equal to his aggregate contributions.

2. Where the fireman was entitled to reckon at least a year's pensionable service, the gratuity shall be of such amount as the fire authority may determine, not being less than his aggregate contributions and not being more than a twelfth of his average annual pensionable pay multiplied by the number of his completed years of pensionable service.

Article 22   PART IV

WIDOW'S SPECIAL PENSION

1. Subject as hereinafter provided, a widow's special pension shall be of an amount not less than a fifth of her husband's average pensionable pay and, subject as aforesaid, shall be of such amount that, when it is added to—

(*a*) any pension payable to her under the National Insurance (Industrial Injuries) Act 1965 in consequence of the death of her husband; and

(*b*) any widow's benefit or retirement pension payable to her under the National Insurance Act 1965 in right of her husband's insurance,

the total weekly rate of payment is equal to a third of her husband's average pensionable pay.

2. The amount of the pension calculated in accordance with the preceding paragraph shall be increased in accordance with Schedule 4.

Article 23   PART V

WIDOW'S AUGMENTED SPECIAL PENSION

1. Subject as hereinafter provided, a widow's special pension calculated in accordance with this Part of this Schedule shall be of such an amount that, when it is added to—

(*a*) any pension payable to her under the National Insurance (Industrial Injuries) Act 1965 in consequence of the death of her husband; and

(*b*) any widow's benefit or retirement pension payable to her under the National Insurance Act 1965 in right of her husband's insurance,

the total weekly rate of payment is equal to a half of her husband's average pensionable pay.

2. The amount of the pension calculated in accordance with the preceding paragraph shall be increased in accordance with Schedule 4.

PART VI   Article 24

WIDOW'S GRATUITY BY WAY OF COMMUTED PENSION

A widow's gratuity by way of commuted pension shall be such sum as may be agreed between the fire authority and the widow, not exceeding the capitalised value of the pension or, as the case may be, of that part of the pension which is commuted, calculated in accordance with tables prepared from time to time by the Government Actuary.

SCHEDULE 3

PART I   Article 28

CHILD'S ORDINARY ALLOWANCE

1. Subject to paragraph 3 and Part III of this Schedule, where the mother of the child is alive the child's ordinary allowance shall be of such amount that the rate of payment is—

    (a) where the father's last rank was not higher than that of sub-officer, £34 a year;

    (b) where the father's last rank was higher than that of sub-officer but not higher than that of divisional officer (Grade I), £39 a year; or

    (c) where the father's last rank was higher than that of divisional officer (Grade I), £49 a year.

2. Subject to paragraph 3 and Part III of this Schedule, where the father was the child's only surviving parent or in respect of the period after the death of the mother, the child's ordinary allowance shall be of such amount that the rate of payment is—

    (a) where the father's last rank was not higher than that of sub-officer, £49 a year or such higher rate not exceeding £64 a year as the fire authority may from time to time determine;

    (b) where the father's last rank was higher than that of sub-officer but not higher than that of divisional officer (Grade I), £57 a year or such higher rate not exceeding £76 a year as the fire authority may from time to time determine; or

    (c) where the father's last rank was higher than that of divisional officer (Grade I), £72 a year or such higher rate not exceeding £96 a year as the fire authority may from time to time determine.

3. In any case in which the rate of payment specified in paragraph 1 or 2, as the case may be, falls to be increased under any of the relevant Pensions (Increase) Acts, the appropriate paragraph shall have effect as if for the rate specified there were substituted such lower rate as, together with the increase, yields an allowance at the specified rate.

PART II   Article 29

CHILD'S SPECIAL ALLOWANCE

1. Subject to the provisions of Part III of this Schedule, if and so long as the child has a parent living, the child's special allowance shall be payable at the rate of a fifteenth of the average pensionable pay of the parent in respect of whose death it is payable.

2. Subject to the provisions of Part III of this Schedule, a child's special allowance shall be payable, if the child has no parent living, at the rate of a tenth of the said parent's average pensionable pay or at such greater rate, not exceeding 2 fifteenths thereof, as the fire authority may from time to time determine.

Sch. 3 (*contd.*)

Articles 28 and 29   PART III

VARIATION OF CHILD'S ALLOWANCE

1.—(1) Subject as hereinafter provided, where under any enactment specified in the first column of the following Table a payment specified in the second column is made to the recipient mentioned in the third column thereof, a child's ordinary or special allowance shall be reduced by so much as is necessary to reduce the allowance or, in the case of a special allowance, the increased allowance, by the weekly amount specified in the fourth column, and where that reduction is greater than the allowance determined under Part I or II of this Schedule, that allowance shall not be payable.

In this sub-paragraph the expression "increased allowance" in relation to a child's special allowance means the amount which would be payable in respect thereof by virtue of this Scheme and the relevant Pensions (Increase) Acts, if this paragraph were not in force.

TABLE

1 Enactment	2 Type of Payment	3 Recipient	4 Weekly Reduction
National Insurance Act 1965, s. 27.	Widowed mother's allowance ...	Child's mother.	37p
National Insurance Act 1965, s. 29.	Guardian's allowance in respect of the child.	Child's guardian.	60p
National Insurance Act 1965, s. 40.	Increased widow's allowance ...	Child's mother.	37p
National Insurance Act 1965, s. 40.	Increased retirement pension ...	Child's mother.	37p
Family Allowances Act 1965.	Family allowance in respect of the child.	Any person	25p
National Insurance (Industrial Injuries) Act 1965, s. 21.	Death benefit in respect of the deceased's child at the higher weekly rate prescribed by that section.	Any person	37p

(2) Where a woman has 2 or more children who would apart from the provisions of this paragraph be entitled to a child's allowance, only the allowance of the elder or eldest of those children shall be reduced in respect of the payment to her of a widowed mother's allowance, increased widow's allowance or increased retirement pension.

(3) Where the child's allowance is an ordinary allowance, it shall not be reduced in respect of the payment of death benefit.

2. The amount of a child's special allowance calculated in accordance with the preceding provisions of this Schedule shall be increased in accordance with Schedule 4.

Article 31   PART IV

CHILD'S GRATUITY BY WAY OF COMMUTED ALLOWANCE

A child's gratuity by way of commuted allowance shall be such sum as may be agreed between the fire authority and the child's guardian, not exceeding the capitalised value of the allowance or, as the case may be, of that part of the allowance which is commuted, calculated in accordance with tables prepared from time to time by the Government Actuary.

SCHEDULE 4   Articles 21, 22, 29, 65 and 72

INCREASE IN WIDOW'S PENSION OR CHILD'S ALLOWANCE

Where it is provided in this Scheme that for the purpose of calculating a widow's pension or child's allowance an amount shall be increased in accordance with this Schedule, it shall be increased by the amount which, together with any increase relating to the last-mentioned amount under the Pensions (Increase) Acts 1944 and 1947(a), equals the amount, if any, by which the relevant widow's pension or child's allowance would from time to time be increased if—

(a) it were a pension specified in Part II of Schedule 1 to the Pensions (Increase) Act 1952(b) of the amount first mentioned in this paragraph; and

(b) any reference in Schedule 2 to that Act—

   (i) to a relevant pension included a reference to a pension or allowance under this Scheme of an amount which is increased in accordance with this Schedule;

   (ii) to the rate of a relevant pension included a reference to the rate of such a pension or allowance ignoring any increase in accordance with this Schedule; and

   (iii) to the authorised increase included a reference to the increase in the amount of such a pension or allowance in accordance with this Schedule.

SCHEDULE 5   Articles 44, 45, 47 and 48

PAYMENTS BY FIREMEN IN RESPECT OF PREVIOUS SERVICE

1. Where a fireman undertakes to make payments in accordance with this Schedule, he shall pay by regular instalments of such an amount that the payment will be completed within a period of 5 years and before he can be required to retire under Article 85:

Provided that—

(a) he may on giving the said undertaking or at any later date discharge his liability thereunder, in whole or in part by paying the whole or part of the sum, or balance of the sum then outstanding, as the case may be;

(b) if he retires and is not entitled to an award other than one of an amount equal to his aggregate contributions, or dies, all further liability under the said undertaking shall cease;

(c) if he retires before his liability under the said undertaking is discharged and his liability does not cease in accordance with the provisions of proviso (b) to this paragraph, the fire authority shall be empowered to deduct the balance of the sum then outstanding from payments of any award payable to him.

2. Where a fireman undertakes to make payments in accordance with this Schedule, he shall make payment to the authority by whom he is employed when he gives the undertaking and, without prejudice to any other method of payment, this liability may be discharged by way of a deduction by the said authority from his pay.

(a) 1944 c. 21; 1947 c. 7.   (b) 1952 c. 45.

Article 44 SCHEDULE 6

SUMS TO BE PAID BY FIREMEN IN RESPECT OF PREVIOUS SERVICE

1.—(1) Subject to the provisions of this Schedule, the sum to be paid by a regular fireman under an undertaking given under Article 44(4) of this Scheme shall be, in respect of each year of pensionable service reckonable under Article 44(4) and in respect of £100 of annual pensionable pay, the sum shown in the second column of the following Table in relation to an age which corresponds with that of the fireman, and the total sum to be paid as aforesaid shall be calculated proportionately by reference to the pensionable service so reckonable and to his annual pensionable pay:—

TABLE

Age in years	Amount for £100 of annual pensionable pay
	£
Under 38	9·50
38 but under 39	9·60
39 ,, ,, 40	9·70
40 ,, ,, 41	9·80
41 ,, ,, 42	9·90
42 ,, ,, 43	10·05
43 ,, ,, 44	10·20
44 ,, ,, 45	10·40
45 ,, ,, 46	10·55
46 ,, ,, 47	10·70
47 ,, ,, 48	10·90
48 ,, ,, 49	11·05
49 ,, ,, 50	11·25
50 ,, ,, 51	11·40
51 ,, ,, 52	11·60
52 ,, ,, 53	11·80
53 ,, ,, 54	12·00
54 ,, ,, 55	12·30
55 and over	12·60

(2) In this paragraph a reference to the age or annual pensionable pay of a fireman is a reference to his age or, as the case may be, the annual rate of his pensionable pay on joining or, as the case may be, rejoining the brigade, any retrospective increase in his pensionable pay granted after that time being ignored.

2. The sum to be paid by the fireman, calculated in accordance with the preceding provisions of this Schedule, shall be reduced by a half of the amount, if any, by which the sum which would have been payable in his case by way of transfer value under Article 62 would have been reduced under paragraphs 3, 4 and 5 of Schedule 9 had the pensionable service reckonable under Article 44(4) been reckonable under Article 44(1).

Article 53 SCHEDULE 7

ADDITIONAL PENSION CONTRIBUTIONS

1. Where a regular fireman has elected to pay additional pension contributions, he shall pay such contributions at a rate equal to that percentage of his pensionable pay which is set opposite in the following Table to the number of completed years

of pensionable service reckonable by him at the time he made his election, by virtue of a period of service, or period for which a special pension was payable, before 26th August 1966:—

TABLE

Completed years of pensionable service					Rate expressed as a percentage of pensionable pay
1	...	...	...	...	0·1
2	...	...	...	...	0·1
3	...	...	...	...	0·2
4	...	...	...	...	0·2
5	...	...	...	...	0·3
6	...	...	...	...	0·4
7	...	...	...	...	0·5
8	...	...	...	...	0·6
9	...	...	...	...	0·7
10	...	...	...	...	0·8
11	...	...	...	...	0·9
12	...	...	...	...	1·0
13	...	...	...	...	1·2
14	...	...	...	...	1·4
15	...	...	...	...	1·7
16	...	...	...	...	2·0
17	...	...	...	...	2·4
18	...	...	...	...	3·0
19	...	...	...	...	3·8
20	...	...	...	...	3·8

2. In calculating the rate at which additional pension contributions are payable by a person no account shall be taken of any period of pensionable service he is entitled to reckon by virtue of such service or employment as is mentioned in Article 47(1) or 48(1).

SCHEDULE 8

Article 58

APPEALS TO MEDICAL REFEREES

1. The person seeking to appeal must institute his appeal within 14 days from the date on which he is supplied by the fire authority with a copy of the opinion in pursuance of Article 58:

Provided that where the fire authority are of opinion that a person's failure to institute his appeal within the time allowed was not due to his own default, they may (notwithstanding that the said time has expired) extend it by so much as they think fit, but so that the appeal shall in any event be instituted before the expiration of 6 months from the aforesaid date.

2. He must institute his appeal by giving to the fire authority a notice in writing informing them of his intention to appeal and stating the grounds on which he proposes to appeal.

Any such notice shall state the appellant's name and his place of residence.

3.—(1) Upon receiving the said notice the fire authority shall supply the Secretary of State with 2 copies thereof and 2 copies of the opinion in question.

Sch. 8 (*contd.*)

(2) The Secretary of State shall supply a copy of the said notice and a copy of the said opinion to the medical referee nominated by the Secretary of State for the purposes of the appeal.

4.—(1) The medical referee so nominated shall forthwith after his nomination inform the appellant and the fire authority that he has been nominated to act as medical referee for the purposes of the appeal.

(2) It shall be the duty of the medical referee to secure that the appellant and the fire authority are at all material times aware of an address at which communications may be delivered to the referee for the purposes of the appeal.

5.—(1) Subject to the provisions of this Schedule, the medical referee shall interview the appellant at least once, and may interview him or cause him to be interviewed on such further occasions as the referee thinks necessary for the purpose of determining the appeal.

(2) The medical referee shall appoint a time and place for any such interview and shall give reasonable notice thereof to the appellant and to the fire authority.

(3) Where the medical referee is satisfied that the appellant is unable to travel, the place appointed for any such interview shall be the place where the appellant resides.

(4) It shall be the duty of the appellant to attend at the time and place appointed for any such interview and to submit himself at the interview to medical examination by the medical referee or by any person appointed by the referee for that purpose.

(5) If the appellant fails to comply with sub-paragraph (4), the medical referee may, unless satisfied that there was reasonable cause for the failure, dispense with the interview required by the preceding provisions of this Schedule, or, as the case may be, with any further interview, and give his decision upon such information as is then available.

(6) Any such interview may be attended by a person appointed for the purpose by the fire authority and by a person so appointed by the appellant.

6. At any time before the interview, or before the last interview if there is more than one, either party may submit to the medical referee a statement relating to the subject matter of the appeal, and the referee shall take account of any such statement and give to the other party such opportunity as he thinks necessary of replying thereto.

7. The decision of the medical referee shall take the form of an opinion on the medical questions which appear to him to be relevant, and the opinion shall be delivered in writing to both parties.

8.—(1) The medical referee shall be entitled to such fees and allowances as the Secretary of State may from time to time determine.

(2) The said fees and allowances shall be paid by the fire authority, and shall be treated as part of the fire authority's expenses for the purposes of the following provisions of this Schedule.

9.—(1) Save as hereinafter provided, the expenses of each party to the appeal shall be borne by that party.

(2) Where the medical referee decides in favour of the fire authority, the authority may, unless the referee otherwise directs, require the appellant to pay toward the cost of the appeal such sum not exceeding the referee's total fees and allowances as the authority think fit.

(3) Where the medical referee decides in favour of the appellant, the fire authority shall, unless the referee otherwise directs, refund to the appellant any personal expenses actually and reasonably incurred by the appellant in respect of any such interview as is mentioned in paragraph 5 and, if any duly qualified medical practitioner chosen by the appellant has attended any such interview, any fees and expenses reasonably paid by the appellant in respect of such attendance.

(4) If in connection with any payment claimed under this paragraph any question arises as to whether the decision of the medical referee is in favour of the fire authority or the appellant, that question shall be decided by the referee, or, in default of a decision by the referee, by the Secretary of State.

10. An appellant shall be deemed to have received any information, notice or document which he is entitled to receive for the purposes of this Schedule if that information, notice or document has been duly posted in a letter addressed to the appellant at his last known place of residence.

SCHEDULE 9   Article 62

Transfer Values

1.—(1) The sum to be paid by a fire authority under Article 62 shall be calculated in accordance with this paragraph.

(2) The amounts shown in the second and third columns of the following Table in relation to an age which corresponds with that of the fireman are to be multiplied respectively by the number of completed years and the number of completed months aggregating less than a year which the fireman is entitled to reckon as pensionable service immediately before he ceases to be employed by the said authority:

Provided that in calculating the number of completed years and completed months which he is entitled to reckon as pensionable service—

   (*a*) any period by which his pensionable service exceeds 20 years but does not exceed 30 years shall be counted twice;

   (*b*) any period by which his pensionable service exceeds 30 years shall be ignored.

(3) The sum of the products aforesaid is an amount appropriate in respect of £100 of annual pensionable pay.

(4) The total sum referred to in sub-paragraph (1) is to be calculated proportionately by reference to the annual pensionable pay of the fireman.

Sch. 9 (*contd.*)

(5) In this paragraph the expression "annual pensionable pay" means the annual value of the fireman's pensionable pay immediately before he ceases to be employed by the authority, any retrospective increase therein granted after that time being ignored.

TABLE

Age in years	Amount for £100 of annual pensionable pay in respect of each completed	
	Year	Month
	£	£
Under 35	18·20	1·50
35 but under 36	18·30	1·55
36 „ „ 37	18·45	1·55
37 „ „ 38	18·65	1·55
38 „ „ 39	18·90	1·60
39 „ „ 40	19·20	1·60
40 „ „ 41	19·45	1·60
41 „ „ 42	19·75	1·65
42 „ „ 43	20·05	1·65
43 „ „ 44	20·40	1·70
44 „ „ 45	20·75	1·75
45 „ „ 46	21·10	1·75
46 „ „ 47	21·45	1·80
47 „ „ 48	21·80	1·80
48 „ „ 49	22·15	1·85
49 „ „ 50	22·50	1·90
50 „ „ 51	22·85	1·90
51 „ „ 52	23·20	1·95
52 „ „ 53	23·60	1·95
53 „ „ 54	24·05	2·00
54 „ „ 55	24·60	2·05
55 and over	25·20	2·10

2. The sum to be paid by a fire authority under Article 62, calculated in accordance with the preceding provisions of this Schedule, shall be reduced by the amount he has, under Article 44(1), undertaken to pay in accordance with Schedule 5.

3. Except in the case of a fireman who is paying pension contributions at the rate of 1p a week less than the appropriate percentage of his pensionable pay, the sum to be paid by a fire authority under Article 62, calculated in accordance with the preceding provisions of this Schedule, shall be reduced by an amount calculated in accordance with paragraph 5.

4. In the case of a fireman entitled to reckon pensionable service, immediately before he ceases to be employed by a fire authority, by virtue of a participating period of relevant employment, the sum to be paid by that authority under Article 62, calculated in accordance with the preceding provisions of this Schedule, shall be reduced by an amount calculated in accordance with paragraph 5.

5.—(1) The amount shown in the second column of the following Table in relation to an age which corresponds with that of the fireman immediately before he ceases to be employed by the authority is the amount of the reduction referred to in paragraph 3 or, as the case may be, paragraph 4 in respect of each £1 by which the annual value of his pension would be reduced—

(*a*) under paragraph 1 of Part III of Schedule 1, in a case in which paragraph 3 applies;

(*b*) under paragraphs 2 and 3 of the said Part III, in a case in which paragraph 4 applies,

in respect of any period beyond the age of 65 years, if he had retired immediately before he ceased to be employed by the authority and had been entitled to a pension.

(2) The total reduction is to be calculated proportionately by reference to the amount by which the annual value of such a pension would be so reduced.

TABLE

Age in years	Amount of the reduction in respect of each £1 by which the annual value of a pension would be reduced
	£
Under 25	1·70
25 but under 26	1·80
26 ,, ,, 27	1·90
27 ,, ,, 28	2·00
28 ,, ,, 29	2·10
29 ,, ,, 30	2·20
30 ,, ,, 31	2·35
31 ,, ,, 32	2·45
32 ,, ,, 33	2·55
33 ,, ,, 34	2·65
34 ,, ,, 35	2·75
35 ,, ,, 36	2·90
36 ,, ,, 37	3·00
37 ,, ,, 38	3·10
38 ,, ,, 39	3·25
39 ,, ,, 40	3·35
40 ,, ,, 41	3·50
41 ,, ,, 42	3·65
42 ,, ,, 43	3·75
43 ,, ,, 44	3·90
44 ,, ,, 45	4·05
45 ,, ,, 46	4·20
46 ,, ,, 47	4·35
47 ,, ,, 48	4·50
48 ,, ,, 49	4·70
49 ,, ,, 50	4·90
50 ,, ,, 51	5·05
51 ,, ,, 52	5·25
52 ,, ,, 53	5·45
53 ,, ,, 54	5·65
54 ,, ,, 55	5·85
55 ,, ,, 56	6·10
56 ,, ,, 57	6·40
57 ,, ,, 58	6·70
58 ,, ,, 59	7·00
59 ,, ,, 60	7·30

Article 80   SCHEDULE 10

MODIFICATIONS TO SCHEME IN ITS APPLICATION TO FIREMEN
SERVING ON 10TH JULY 1956

1. For the words "average pensionable pay" wherever they occur, there shall be substituted the words "pensionable pay".

2. For the words "average annual pensionable pay" wherever they occur, there shall be substituted the words "annual pensionable pay".

3. In Article 12(1) the words "has attained the age of 50 years and" shall be omitted.

4. For Article 51(2) and (3) there shall be substituted the following provisions:—

"(2) For the purpose of determining the benefits payable under this Scheme on the death or retirement of a regular fireman—

(*a*) the expression "pensionable pay" means his pensionable pay immediately before the death or retirement or, in a case where he was not serving as such a fireman when he died, his pensionable pay immediately before he last ceased to serve as such; and

(*b*) the expression "annual pensionable pay" means the annual value of his said pensionable pay.

(3) Where during the relevant period before his death or retirement a regular fireman's rank has changed, paragraph (2) shall have effect in his case as if his pensionable pay immediately before the death or retirement were his average pensionable pay during that period:

Provided that where during the relevant period—

(*a*) he reverted to a rank from which he had been temporarily promoted (whether before or during that period), or

(*b*) the last change of rank was a promotion, and the said average is less than his pensionable pay would have been, immediately before his death or retirement, had he continued to hold the rank he held before the promotion until he reverted thereto or, as the case may be, until his death or retirement,

then paragraph (2) shall have effect in his case as though he had continued to hold that rank.

In this paragraph the expression "the relevant period" means the period of 3 years ending with the death or retirement.".

5. In Article 65—

(*a*) in paragraph (4)(*a*) for the words "£96 a year" there shall be substituted the words "£30 a year";

(*b*) for paragraph (5) there shall be substituted the following paragraph:—

"(5) Where an award is granted under paragraph (4)(*a*), the amount thereof shall be increased in accordance with Schedule 4 and for the purposes of the Pensions (Increase) Act 1952 as applied by that Schedule the pension shall be deemed to begin before 1st April 1948.".

6. In Article 85(2) for sub-paragraphs (*a*) and (*b*) there shall be substituted the words "an additional completed year of pensionable service".

7. For Part I of Schedule 1 there shall be substituted the following Part:—

"PART I

Subject as hereafter in this Schedule provided an ordinary pension shall be of an amount equal to 30 sixtieths of the fireman's pensionable pay with the addition of 2 sixtieths for each completed year by which his pensionable service exceeds 25 years up to the maximum set opposite his age at retirement in the following Table:—

TABLE

Years of age of fireman at retirement	Maximum pension expressed in 60ths of pensionable pay
Less than 51	30
Less than 52 but 51 or over	32
Less than 53 but 52 or over	34
Less than 54 but 53 or over	36
Less than 55 but 54 or over	38
55 or over	40"

8. For Part II of Schedule 1 there shall be substituted the following Part:—

"PART II

A short service or ill-health pension shall be of an amount of not less than a sixtieth nor more than 40 sixtieths of the fireman's pensionable pay and subject as aforesaid shall be equal to a sixtieth of his pensionable pay for each completed year of pensionable service up to 20 years, with the addition of 2 sixtieths for each completed year by which his pensionable service exceeds 20 years.".

9. For Scheme I of Part II of Schedule 2 there shall be substituted the following Scheme:—

"SCHEME I

1. The pension shall be of such amount that the rate of payment is—

(*a*) where the husband's last rank was not higher than that of sub-officer, £30 a year;

(*b*) where the husband's last rank was higher than that of sub-officer but not higher than that of divisional officer (Grade I), £40 a year; or

(*c*) where the husband's last rank was higher than that of divisional officer (Grade I), £50 a year:

Provided that the said amount shall be increased in accordance with Schedule 4 and, for the purposes of the Pensions (Increase) Act 1952, as applied by that Schedule, the pension shall be deemed to begin before 1st April 1948.".

10. For Part I of Schedule 3 there shall be substituted the following Part:—

Sch. 10 (*contd.*)

"PART I

1. Subject to paragraph 3 and Part III of this Schedule, where the mother of the child is alive the child's ordinary allowance shall be payable at the following rate:—

(*a*) where the father's last rank was not higher than that of sub-officer, £10 a year;

(*b*) where the father's last rank was higher than that of sub-officer but not higher than that of divisional officer (Grade I), £12 a year; or

(*c*) where the father's last rank was higher than that of divisional officer (Grade I), £15 a year.

2. Subject to paragraph 3 and Part III of this Schedule, where the father was the child's only surviving parent or in respect of the period after the death of the mother, the child's ordinary allowance shall be payable at the following rate:—

(*a*) where the father's last rank was not higher than that of sub-officer, £15 a year, or such higher rate not exceeding £20 a year as the fire authority may from time to time determine;

(*b*) where the father's last rank was higher than that of sub-officer but not higher than that of divisional officer (Grade I), £18 a year, or such higher rate not exceeding £24 a year as the fire authority may from time to time determine; or

(*c*) where the father's last rank was higher that that of divisional officer (Grade I), £22·50 a year, or such rate not exceeding £30 a year as the fire authority may from time to time determine.

3. A child's ordinary allowance, determined in accordance with paragraph 1 or, as the case may be, paragraph 2, shall be increased by the amount by which it would have been increased under the Pensions (Increase) Acts 1944 and 1947 had it been granted before the passing of the Pensions (Increase) Act 1956(a).".

11. In Part III of Schedule 3—

(*a*) in paragraph 1(1) the words "the allowance or, in the case of a special allowance" and the word "special", in the third place where it occurs, shall be omitted;

(*b*) after paragraph 2 there shall be added the following paragraph:—

"3. The amount of a child's ordinary allowance determined in accordance with the preceding provisions of this Schedule shall be increased in accordance with the provisions of Schedule 4 and, for the purposes of the Pensions (Increase) Act 1952 as applied by that Schedule, the allowance shall be deemed to begin before 1st April 1948.".

(a) 1956 c. 39.

EXPLANATORY NOTE

(This Note is not part of the Order.)

This Order consolidates, with amendments, the Firemen's Pension Scheme 1966 (set out in the Firemen's Pension Scheme Order 1966) and the amendments thereto contained in the other Orders specified in Appendix 1.

The main changes are mentioned below.

The Firemen's Pension Scheme 1971, which is brought into operation on 15th February 1971, takes account of the introduction of decimal currency on that date.

Article 23 (which corresponds to Article 11A of the Scheme of 1966, as amended) makes fresh provision as respects the circumstances in which a fireman's widow is entitled to an augmented award. Where the husband's death is the result of an injury received while saving life, the widow's entitlement is no longer dependent upon the opinion of the fire authority that this condition is fulfilled. Where this condition is not fulfilled but the fire authority are of opinion that it would be inequitable in the circumstances that she should not receive an augmented award, she is entitled to such an award. Article 30 (which corresponds to Article 17A of the Scheme of 1966, as amended) makes similar provision in relation to a child's special gratuity.

The rates at which flat rate awards are payable to widows and children are increased; the new rates correspond to the rates in the Scheme of 1966 as increased under the Pensions (Increase) Act 1969 but they do not attract any further increase thereunder.

STATUTORY INSTRUMENTS

1971 No. 146

PENSIONS

The Increase of Pensions (Fire Services) (Amendment) Regulations 1971

Made - - - -	*27th January* 1971
Laid before Parliament	*9th February* 1971
Coming into Operation	*15th February* 1971

In exercise of the powers conferred on me by paragraph 7 of Schedule 2 to the Pensions (Increase) Act 1956(a), subsection (2) of section 3 of the Pensions (Increase) Act 1959(b) (including that section as applied and modified by section 8(2) of the Pensions (Increase) Act 1962(c) and Part II of Schedule 1 thereto and by section 5(2) of the Pensions (Increase) Act 1965(d) and Part I of Schedule 2 thereto) and section 1(4) of the Pensions (Increase) Act 1969(e) and paragraph 12 of Schedule 2 thereto, I hereby, with the consent of the Minister for the Civil Service, make the following Regulations:—

Operation and citation

1. These Regulations may be cited as the Increase of Pensions (Fire Services) (Amendment) Regulations 1971 and shall come into operation on 15th February 1971.

Amendment of the Increase of Pensions (Modification) (No. 3) Regulations 1956

2. In Regulation 3(1) of the Increase of Pensions (Modification) (No. 3) Regulations 1956(f), as amended (g) (which provides that the Pensions (Increases Act 1956 shall apply in relation to a flat rate fire service pension, payable a) therein mentioned, as if the proviso to section 1(1) of that Act were omitted therefrom) after the words "Schedule 10 to the said Scheme" there shall be inserted the following provision:—

"or

(*f*) the Firemen's Pension Scheme 1971(h), where in relation to the pension that Scheme is subject to the modifications set out either in the said section 27(3) or in Schedule 10 to the said Scheme,".

(a) 1956 c. 39. (b) 1959 c. 50.
(c) 1962 c. 2. (d) 1965 c. 78.
(e) 1969 c. 7. (f) S.I. 1956/1239 (1956 II, p. 1736).
(g) S.I. 1964/1149, 1966/1046 (1964 II, p. 2628; 1966 II, p. 2564).
(h) *See* S.I. 1971/145 (1971 I, p. 320)

Amendment of the Increase of Pensions (Modification) (No. 2) Regulations 1959

3. In Regulation 2(1) of the Increase of Pensions (Modification) (No. 2) Regulations 1959**(a)**, as amended**(b)** (which provides that the Pensions (Increase) Act 1959 shall apply in relation to a flat rate fire service pension, payable as therein mentioned, as if it began for the purposes of the Act before 1st April 1952) after the words "Schedule 10 to the said Scheme" there shall be inserted the following provision:—

"or

(*f*) in accordance with the Firemen's Pension Scheme 1971, where in relation to the pension that Scheme is subject to the modifications set out either in the said section 27(3) or in Schedule 10 to the said Scheme,".

Amendment of the Increase of Pensions (Modification) (No. 4) Regulations 1963

4. In Regulation 3(2) of the Increase of Pensions (Modification) (No. 4) Regulations 1963**(c)**, as amended**(d)** (which provides that the Pensions (Increase) Act 1962 shall apply in relation to a flat rate fire service pension, payable as therein mentioned, as if it began for the purposes of the Act before 1st April 1956) after the words "the said section 27(3)", where they last occur, there shall be inserted the following provision:—

"or

(*e*) in accordance with the Firemen's Pension Scheme 1971 in respect of whole-time service, where that Scheme is subject to the modifications set out either in Schedule 10 thereto or in the said section 27(3),".

Amendment of the Increase of Pensions (Police and Fire Services) Regulations 1966

5. In Regulation 3(2) of the Increase of Pensions (Police and Fire Services) Regulations 1966**(e)** as amended**(f)** (which provides that the Pensions (Increase) Act 1965 shall apply in relation to a flat rate fire service pension, payable as therein mentioned, as if it began for the purposes of the Act before 1st April 1957) after the words "the said section 27(3)" there shall be inserted the following provision:—

"or

(*d*) in accordance with the Firemen's Pension Scheme 1971 in respect of whole-time service where that Scheme is subject to the modifications set out either in Schedule 10 thereto or in the said section 27(3),".

Amendment of the Increase of Pensions (Police and Fire Services) Regulations 1969

6. In paragraph (2) of Regulation 6 of the Increase of Pensions (Police and Fire Services) Regulations 1969**(g)** (which provides that the Pensions (Increase) Act 1969 shall apply in relation to a flat rate fire service pension, payable as mentioned in paragraph (2) or (3), as if it began for the purposes of the Act

---

(a) S.I. 1959/1831 (1959 II, p. 2064).
(b) S.I. 1964/1149, 1966/1046 (1964 II, p. 2628; 1966 II, p. 2564).
(c) S.I. 1963/1311 (1963 II, p. 2269).
(d) S.I. 1964/1149, 1966/1046 (1964 II, p. 2628; 1966 II, p. 2564).
(e) S.I. 1966/822 (1966 II, p. 1903).   (f) S.I. 1966/1046 (1966 II, p. 2564).
(g) S.I. 1969/567 (1969 I, p. 1526).

not later than 1st July 1955 or as if the definition for those purposes of the expression "adjusted rate" were modified) after the words "Firemen's Pension Scheme 1966" there shall be inserted the following provision:—

"or

(e) the Firemen's Pension Scheme 1971, where in relation to the pension that Scheme is subject to the modifications set out either in section 27(3) of the Fire Services Act 1947(a) or in Schedule 10 to the said Scheme;".

R. Maudling,

One of Her Majesty's Principal
Secretaries of State.

26th January 1971.

Consent of the Minister for the Civil Service given under his Official Seal on 27th January 1971.

(L.S.)   *K. H. McNeill*,

Authorised by the Minister
for the Civil Service.

EXPLANATORY NOTE

(*This Note is not part of the Regulations.*)

These Regulations amend the Increase of Pensions (Modification) (No. 3) Regulations 1956, the Increase of Pensions (Modification) (No. 2) Regulations 1959, the Increase of Pensions (Modification) (No. 4) Regulations 1963, the Increase of Pensions (Police and Fire Services) Regulations 1966 and the Increase of Pensions (Police and Fire Services) Regulations 1969, which modify respectively, the Pensions (Increase) Acts of 1956, 1959, 1962, 1965 and 1969 in their application to certain fire service pensions.

The amendments are consequential on the Firemen's Pension Scheme Order 1971 which brings the Firemen's Pension Scheme 1971 into operation on 15th February 1971. These Regulations come into operation on the same date.

(a) 1947 c. 41.

STATUTORY INSTRUMENTS

1971 No. 149

ROAD TRAFFIC
The Goods Vehicles (Operators' Licences) (Fees) Regulations 1971

Made	-	-	-	*27th January* 1971
Laid before Parliament			*5th February* 1971
Coming into Operation			*8th February* 1971

The Secretary of State for the Environment, in exercise of his powers under sections 89(1) and 91(1) of the Transport Act 1968(a), and of all other enabling powers, and after consultation with representative organisations in accordance with the provisions of section 91(8) of the said Act of 1968, hereby makes the following Regulations:—

Commencement, citation and revocation

1.—(1) These Regulations shall come into operation on 8th February 1971 and may be cited as the Goods Vehicles (Operators' Licences) (Fees) Regulations 1971.

(2) The Goods Vehicles (Carriers' and Operators' Licences) (Fees) Regulations 1969(b) are hereby revoked.

Interpretation

2.—(1) In these Regulations, unless the context otherwise requires—

"month" means a calendar month running from any date;

"operator's licence" means an operator's licence within the meaning of Part V of the Transport Act 1968;

"year" means a calendar year running from any date;

and any expression not defined above which is also used in the Goods Vehicles (Operators' Licences) Regulations 1969(c) has the same meaning as in those Regulations.

(2) The Interpretation Act 1889(d) shall apply for the interpretation of these Regulations as it applies for the interpretation of an Act of Parliament, and as if for the purposes of section 38 of that Act these Regulations were an Act of Parliament and the Regulations revoked by Regulation 1 above were an Act of Parliament thereby repealed.

Fees in respect of operators' licences

3.—(1) This Regulation applies in relation to an operator's licence other than such a licence granted under section 67(5) of the Transport Act 1968.

(2) Whenever a motor vehicle is specified in an operator's licence to which this Regulation applies the holder of the licence shall pay a fee at the rate of—

(a) £4 in respect of each motor vehicle so specified for each whole year of the unexpired term of the licence, calculated from the date when the vehicle is so specified; and

---

(a) 1968 c. 73.
(c) S.I. 1969/1636 (1969 III, p. 5141).
(b) S.I. 1969/1799 (1969 III, p. 5612).
(d) 1889 c. 63.

(b) one-twelfth of the said amount in respect of each motor vehicle so specified for each whole month (any part of a month counting as a whole month for this purpose) in any period less than a whole year which remains in the unexpired term of the licence when the whole years have been deducted.

(3) Whenever the number of motor vehicles specified in an operator's licence to which this Regulation applies is reduced the licensing authority shall, if an application in writing in that behalf is made to him by or on behalf of the holder of the licence within 3 months of the reduction, refund to the holder of the licence an amount at the rate specified in paragraph (2)(b) above in respect of each vehicle by which the total number of specified vehicles is reduced for each whole month of the unexpired term of the licence calculated from the date of the reduction:

Provided that:—
(i) no refund shall be made in respect of any period of less than 3 months, and

(ii) for the purposes of this paragraph any part of a month at the end of such term ending on the 24th March in any year, in the case of a licence which expires on the 24th March in that year, shall count as a whole month.

(4) (a) No identity disc shall be issued in respect of any vehicle until the applicant shall have paid to the licensing authority any fee payable by virtue of paragraph (2) above.

(b) No refund shall be paid under this Regulation in respect of any vehicle until the applicant shall have returned to the licensing authority the identity disc or any copy thereof issued in respect of that vehicle.

4. The fee payable in respect of an operator's licence granted under section 67(5) of the Transport Act 1968 shall be £1 in respect of each motor vehicle specified in the licence and shall become payable at the end of the period during which the licence continues in force.

5. On and after the day appointed for the beginning of the transitional period for the purposes of the Decimal Currency Act 1969(a) if any fee or refund payable under these Regulations is made in the new currency as defined in section 16(1) of that Act any remaining amount of such fee or refund of less than one new penny shall be disregarded.

Signed by authority of the
Secretary of State.
27th January 1971.

John Peyton,
Minister for Transport Industries,
Department of the Environment.

EXPLANATORY NOTE
(This Note is not part of the Regulations.)

These Regulations revoke the Goods Vehicles (Carriers' and Operators' Licences) (Fees) Regulations 1969 and re-enact their provisions so far as they prescribe the fees payable for the grant or variation of an operator's licence to use a goods vehicle for hire or reward or for business on own account under Part V of the Transport Act 1968, and for the refund of such fees in certain circumstances. Additional provision is made as to the fees payable in respect of an operator's licence which, on an application for such a licence, may be granted under section 67(5) of the 1968 Act pending determination of the application.

(a) 1969 c. 19.

STATUTORY INSTRUMENTS

1971 No. 150

WAGES COUNCILS

The Wages Regulation (Boot and Shoe Repairing) Order 1971

Made - - -		*28th January* 1971
Coming into Operation		*3rd March* 1971

Whereas the Secretary of State has received from the Boot and Shoe Repairing Wages Council (Great Britain) the wages regulation proposals set out in the Schedule hereto ;

Now, therefore, the Secretary of State in exercise of his powers under section 11 of the Wages Councils Act 1959(a), and of all other powers enabling him in that behalf, hereby makes the following Order :—

1. This Order may be cited as the Wages Regulation (Boot and Shoe Repairing) Order 1971.

2.—(1) In this Order the expression "the specified date" means the 3rd March 1971, provided that where, as respects any worker who is paid wages at intervals not exceeding seven days, that date does not correspond with the beginning of the period for which the wages are paid, the expression "the specified date" means, as respects that worker, the beginning of the next such period following that date.

(2) The Interpretation Act 1889(b) shall apply to the interpretation of this Order as it applies to the interpretation of an Act of Parliament and as if this Order and the Order hereby revoked were Acts of Parliament.

3. The wages regulation proposals set out in the Schedule hereto shall have effect as from the specified date and as from that date the Wages Regulation (Boot and Shoe Repairing) Order 1970(c) shall cease to have effect.

Signed by order of the Secretary of State.

28th January 1971.

R. R. D. McIntosh,
Deputy Secretary,
Department of Employment.

(a) 1959 c. 69. (b) 1889 c. 63.
(c) S.I. 1970/722 (1970 II, p. 2275).

ARRANGEMENT OF SCHEDULE

Article 3   SCHEDULE

The following minimum remuneration shall be substituted for the statutory minimum remuneration fixed by the Wages Regulation (Boot and Shoe Repairing) Order 1970 (Order D. (152)).

STATUTORY MINIMUM REMUNERATION

PART I

APPLICATION

1.--(1) Subject to the provisions of this Schedule, the minimum remuneration payable to a worker to whom this Schedule applies for all work except work to which a minimum overtime rate applies under Part VI of this Schedule is:—

(a) in the case of a time worker, the hourly general minimum time rate applicable to the worker under the provisions of this Schedule;

(b) in the case of a worker employed on piece work,

(i) where a general minimum piece rate applies under Part VIII of this Schedule, that piece rate;

(ii) where no general minimum piece rate applies, piece rates each of which would yield, in the circumstances of the case, to an ordinary worker at least the same amount of money as the hourly general minimum time rate which would be applicable if the worker were a time worker:

Provided that where a guaranteed time rate is applicable to the worker under paragraph 3 or 5 and the worker's minimum remuneration calculated on a time work basis at the hourly guaranteed time rate exceeds the minimum remuneration calculated under the provisions of (b) of this sub-paragraph, the worker shall be paid at not less than the hourly guaranteed time rate.

(2) In this Schedule, the expressions "hourly general minimum time rate" and "hourly guaranteed time rate" mean respectively the general minimum time rate and the guaranteed time rate applicable to the worker under Part II, Part III or Part IV of this Schedule divided by 41.

2.—(1) Subject to the provisions of sub-paragraph (2) of this paragraph, this Schedule applies to workers in relation to whom the Boot and Shoe Repairing Wages Council (Great Britain) operates, that is to say, workers employed in Great Britain in the circumstances specified in the Schedule to the Boot and Shoe Repairing Wages Council (Great Britain) (Variation) Order 1948(a), namely:—

(i) all workers employed in Great Britain in a boot and shoe repairing undertaking as defined in sub-paragraph (3) of this paragraph on any of the following work:—

(a) the repairing, altering or dyeing of boots, shoes, slippers and all other similar kinds of footwear;

(b) the making of bespoke footwear;

(c) work incidental or ancillary to any of the above-mentioned operations;

(d) shop duties in connection with the above operations, including attending to customers and sale by retail of boot and shoe laces and materials and articles used in connection with the cleaning or repair of boots or shoes;

(e) collection or despatch in connection with the operations in (a) and (b) above, and work ancillary thereto;

(f) canvassing for boot or shoe repairs and the collection of accounts in connection with the undertaking;

(g) clerical or other office work in connection with the undertaking, including costing and the work of a cashier;

(ii) all outworkers employed by way of trade in Great Britain on any of the operations specified in (a), (b) or (c) of (i) above.

(2) Notwithstanding the provisions of sub-paragraph (1) of this paragraph, this Schedule does not apply:—

(i) to workers employed in any shop or in any department in a shop, being a shop or department which is wholly or mainly engaged in the sale by retail of footwear (including operations in connection with such sale), in respect of their employment:—

(a) on retail sales at such shop and operations incidental thereto; or

(b) on transport or clerical work relating to such sales; or

(ii) to workers employed in or in connection with a factory which is wholly or mainly engaged on the manufacture of leather footwear on a large scale, in respect of their employment:—

(a) on the making of bespoke footwear and work incidental or ancillary thereto; or

(b) on transport or clerical work relating to bespoke footwear; or

(iii) to workers who are persons registered as handicapped by disablement in pursuance of the Disabled Persons (Employment) Acts 1944 and 1958(b), in respect of their employment by Remploy Limited.

(3) For the purpose of this Schedule a "boot and shoe repairing undertaking" means any undertaking or any part of an undertaking which is wholly or mainly engaged by way of trade on any of the following operations, including operations incidental or ancillary thereto, that is to say—

(i) the repairing of leather footwear;

(ii) the making of bespoke footwear:

Provided that as regards trainees who, under the Government Vocational Training Scheme for resettlement training, have been placed by the Department of Employment with, and are being trained by, an employer for a period of approved training, this Schedule shall not (subject to the condition that the requirements of the Training Scheme are complied with) apply during the period in respect of which the trainees are in receipt of allowances as provided under the Scheme.

(a) S.I. 1948/706 (Rev. XXIII, p. 453: 1948 I, p. 4398).
(b) 1944 c. 10; 1958 c. 33.

THE RATES IN PARTS II, III, AND IV ARE EXPRESSED AS WHOLE POUNDS AND DECIMAL PARTS THEREOF

PART II

MALE OR FEMALE WORKERS AGED 21 YEARS OR OVER

GENERAL MINIMUM TIME RATE AND GUARANTEED TIME RATE FOR FOREMEN OR MANAGERS

Per week of
41 hours

3.—(1) The general minimum time rate applicable to all male or female workers aged 21 years or over and employed as foremen or managers is...　**£13·80**

(2) The guaranteed time rate applicable to the workers specified in sub-paragraph (1) when employed on piece work is　...　...　...　...　**£13·80**

(3) For the purposes of this paragraph,

　(*a*) a foreman or manager is a male or female worker who either—

　　(i) exercises sole supervisory authority over all journeyworkers who must exceed three in number (excluding himself) working in the same shop or department, or

　　(ii) (whether working alone or with any other worker) under the terms of his employment and, in addition to any work which may be required of him as a journeyworker, fits up or supervises the fitting up of the work and has control of the repairing or making and the technical direction thereof;

　(*b*) a journeyworker is a male or female worker to whom there applies under this Schedule either a general minimum piece rate or a general minimum time rate of not less than £12·15 per week of 41 hours or to whom such a general minimum time rate would be applicable if he were a time worker.

GENERAL MINIMUM TIME RATES

4. The general minimum time rates applicable to all male or female workers aged 21 years or over, except (i) the foremen or managers specified in paragraph 3 and (ii) learners to whom the minimum rates specified in Part IV of this Schedule apply, are as follows:—

Per week of
41 hours
£

　(*a*) sewing or stitching machine operators employed in operating—

　　(i) power sole stitchers or both power sole stitchers and Blake or other sole sewing machines on the Blake principle...　...　*13·30*

　　(ii) Blake or other sole sewing machines on the Blake principle or edge trimming machines　...　...　...　...　...　...　*12·85*

Provided that where the worker, for the purpose of training thereon, is employed on such machines for one probationary period not exceeding four months, the general minimum time rate applicable during the said period shall be　...　...　...　...　...　...　...　...　...　*12·35*

　(*b*) (i) press cutters responsible for cutting and costing　...　...　*13·25*

　　(ii) press cutters other than those responsible for cutting and costing　*12·35*

　(*c*) workers employed—

　　(i) as makers of bespoke (which term includes surgical) footwear...　*14·00*

　　(ii) as repairers engaged in sewing down caps, re-welting, welt repairs, linking or any other hand stitching operation...　...　*12·65*

　　(iii) in clicking　...　...　...　...　...　...　...　...　*12·65*

　　(iv) in clicking and closing　...　...　...　...　...　...　*12·65*

	Male workers	Female workers
	Per week of 41 hours	
	£	£

(v) as closers (that is, in fitting and machining) in the making of uppers for bespoke (which term includes surgical) footwear and not employed in clicking   ...   .   *12·65*   *9·40*

All workers
Per week of 41 hours

(*d*) workers employed in altering footwear or on benching or finishing operations (whether performed by hand or machine) in repairing leather footwear   ...   £
12·30

	Male workers	Female workers
	Per week of 41 hours	
	£	£

(*e*) all other workers to whom this paragraph applies...   *12·15*   *9·10*

Part III

MALE OR FEMALE WORKERS AGED UNDER 21 YEARS

GENERAL MINIMUM TIME RATES AND GUARANTEED TIME RATE

5.—(1) The general minimum time rates applicable to all male or female workers aged under 21 years, being—

(*a*) foremen or managers as defined in paragraph 3(3),

(*b*) press cutters responsible for cutting and costing, or

(*c*) workers who have worked at least five years in the trade under a contract of apprenticeship,

are the general minimum time rates which would be applicable to those workers under paragraph 3 or 4 if they were aged 21 years or over.

Per week of 41 hours
£

(2) The guaranteed time rate applicable to the workers specified in sub-paragraph (1)(*a*) of this paragraph when employed on piece work is...   *13·80*

GENERAL MINIMUM TIME RATES

6.—(1) The general minimum time rates applicable to all male or female workers aged under 21 years except (i) the workers specified in paragraph 5 and (ii) learners or apprentices to whom the minimum rates specified in Part IV of this Schedule apply are those specified in the following Table.

	Column 1	Column 2	Column 3
	The workers specified in sub-para. (2) of this paragraph	Other male workers	Other female workers
	Per week of 41 hours		
	£	£	£
Aged 20 and under 21 years	9·90	9·90	8·05
„ 19 „ „ 20 „	8·90	8·90	7·25
„ 18 „ „ 19 „	8·20	8·20	6·70
„ 17 „ „ 18 „	6·85	6·85	5·70
„ 16 „ „ 17 „	6·40	6·40	5·30
Under 16 years	6·05	6·05	4·95

(2) The workers referred to in Column 1 of the foregoing Table are male or female workers who are—

(a) operators of sole stitching, sole sewing or edge trimming machines,

(b) press cutters not responsible for cutting and costing,

(c) employed as makers of bespoke (which term includes surgical) footwear,

(d) repairers engaged in sewing down caps, re-welting, welt repairs, linking or any other hand stitching operation,

(e) employed in clicking,

(f) employed in clicking and closing,

(g) employed in altering footwear or on benching operations (whether performed by hand or machine) in repairing leather footwear, or

(h) employed in finishing operations (whether performed by hand or machine) in repairing leather footwear.

PART IV

GENERAL MINIMUM TIME RATES FOR LEARNERS AND APPRENTICES
LEARNERS

7.—(1) The following general minimum time rates are applicable to male or female learners employed in accordance with the conditions set out in paragraph 9.

	Learners to bespoke hand sewn making	All others learners
	Per week of 41 hours	
	£	£
Aged 20 and under 21 years	9·60	9·55
„ 19 „ „ 20 „	8·60	8·55
„ 18 „ „ 19 „	7·90	7·85
„ 17 „ „ 18 „	6·55	6·50
„ 16 „ „ 17 „	6·05	6·00
„ under 16 years	5·75	5·70

(2) The general minimum time rate applicable to a learner to bespoke hand sewn making who is aged 21 years or over and who has not completed a period of five years in such learnership shall, until he attains the age of 22 years or until he completes the said period of learnership (whichever period is the less), be the rate applicable to a learner aged 20 and under 21 years, increased by 25p weekly.

APPRENTICES

8. The following general minimum time rates are applicable to male or female apprentices—

(a) who are employed under contracts of apprenticeship in writing to be taught one or more of the following sections of the trade—

(i) bespoke hand sewn making including hand finishing,

(ii) boot and shoe repairing in all its operations as performed in the establishment, including benching by hand and by such benching machines as are used in the establishment, hand sewing, re-stitching, re-welting, finishing by hand, by any finishing machine used in the establishment, by hand and such machine, patching by hand, by machine and by solution, and all other upper repairing,

(iii) clicking (including pattern cutting) and closing (including fitting and machining) of uppers for bespoke work or either of such operations, and

(b) in whose case the conditions specified in paragraph 10 are fulfilled.

	Per week of 41 hours
	£
Aged 20 and under 21 years	9·45
„ 19 „ „ 20 „	8·45
„ 18 „ „ 19 „	7·75
„ 17 „ „ 18 „	6·45
„ 16 „ „ 17 „	5·95
„ under 16 years	5·70

PART V

CONDITIONS AS TO LEARNERS AND APPRENTICES

LEARNERS

9.—(1) The general minimum time rates specified in paragraph 7 apply only to a male or female learner in whose case the conditions following are fulfilled—

(a) if he is a learner to bespoke hand sewn making, he shall be employed for not less than two-thirds of his time in learning the bespoke hand sewn making branch of the trade and shall, during the whole or a substantial part of such time, receive adequate instruction in either (i) bespoke hand sewn making, (ii) clicking, or (iii) clicking and closing of uppers for bespoke work;

(b) if he is a learner employed in a factory in which machinery driven by mechanical power is used for benching or finishing operations, he shall be employed, during the whole or a substantial part of his time, as a learner in the trade and shall receive, during such time, adequate instruction in a progressive manner in either—

(i) benching by hand and all operations of benching by machine which are carried out in the factory, or

(ii) benching by hand or machine and finishing by hand or machine, not less than one-third of the learner's time being spent in benching:

Provided that where the learner has been so employed for not less than three years he may be employed thereafter, in conjunction with a journeyworker finisher, as a learner to finishing by machine, and in such case the learner shall be employed for at least one-third of his time in learning the operations of edge trimming, edge setting and heel scouring;

(c) any other learner shall be employed during the whole or a substantial part of his time, as a learner in the trade and shall receive during such time adequate instruction in a progressive manner in either—

(i) benching by hand, throughout the whole period of his employment, or

(ii) benching by hand and finishing by hand or machine, not less than one-third of the learner's time being spent in benching;

(d) in the establishment in which the learner is employed the proportion of learners to journeyworkers shall not exceed that of one learner to two journeyworkers:

Provided that one learner of each of the classes specified at (a), (b) or (c) of this sub-paragraph may be employed in an establishment in which only one journeyworker is employed on the operation or group of operations in which the learner is receiving instruction.

(2) For the purposes of sub-paragraph (1) of this paragraph,

(a) the "bespoke hand sewn making branch of the trade" shall mean that branch in which workers are employed for not less than two-thirds of their time on bespoke hand sewn making, clicking or closing of uppers or on one or more of such operations for bespoke work;

(b) the expression "journeyworker" shall, save as is hereinafter provided in this sub-paragraph, have the same meaning as in paragraph 3(3);

(c) a worker aged under 21 years to whom a general minimum time rate specified in paragraph 6 applies shall not be reckoned as a learner, apprentice or journey worker;

(d) where an employer is wholly or mainly performing the work of a journey-worker he shall be reckoned as a journeyworker.

(3) For the purposes of determining the proportion of learners to journeyworkers in accordance with condition (d) of sub-paragraph (1) of this paragraph,

(a) a casual absence of a journeyworker or a casual vacancy for a short period in the number of journeyworkers employed shall not be treated as a failure to comply with the said condition;

(b) an apprentice shall be reckoned as a learner notwithstanding that the general minimum rates set out in paragraph 7 do not apply to him.

APPRENTICES

10.—(1) The general minimum time rates specified in paragraph 8 apply only to a male or female apprentice employed under a contract of apprenticeship in writing in whose case the conditions following are fulfilled:—

(a) The apprentice shall be employed under a written contract of apprenticeship which has been duly executed and which contains the following provisions (which the Wages Council considers necessary for the effective instruction of the apprentice) or provisions substantially to the like effect and no provisions contrary thereto:—

(i) A description of the section or sections of work in the trade to which the worker is apprenticed;

(ii) The date of the commencement of the apprenticeship and a provision for its continuance until the date on which the apprentice shall have completed five years' apprenticeship or reached his 21st birthday whichever is the earlier;

(iii) A term that during the period of apprenticeship the employer will pay to the apprentice not less than the appropriate statutory minimum re-muneration from time to time;

(iv) A covenant or agreement by the employer that, throughout the period of apprenticeship, he will keep the apprentice under his supervision and instruct the apprentice himself, or place him in the hands of one or more competent journeyworkers for instruction, so that in either case the apprentice shall receive throughout the period of apprenticeship and in a progressive manner effective instruction in the section or sections of work in the trade to which he is apprenticed;

(v) A covenant or agreement by the apprentice whereby, throughout the period of apprenticeship, he binds himself to the employer to learn the section or sections of work in the trade to which he is apprenticed;

(vi) A term, in the case of an apprentice who is apprenticed to the boot and shoe repairing section of work in the trade, that the employment of the apprentice on benching shall alternate regularly with his employment on finishing, so that not more than one-third of his time is spent on finishing operations;

(vii) A provision that, during the apprenticeship, the apprentice shall not be put on piece work and shall not be employed on any work to which any minimum overtime rate applies under Part VI of this Schedule.

(b) In the establishment in which the apprentice is employed the proportion of apprentices to journeyworkers in either branch of the trade shall not at any time exceed that of one apprentice to two journeyworkers:

Provided that—

(i) one apprentice may be employed in each branch of the trade if only one journeyworker is employed in the same branch;

(ii) where an employer who works personally at the trade and does not employ a journeyworker has one apprentice who has completed at least four years' apprenticeship, he may employ a second apprentice during the last year of the apprenticeship of the first apprentice, and for the purpose of calculating the proportion of apprentices to journeyworkers the first apprentice shall not be taken into account.

(c) The apprentice shall be the holder of a certificate of registration as an apprentice issued by, or on behalf of, the Wages Council or shall have made application for such a certificate which has been duly acknowledged and is still under consideration:

Provided that the certification of an apprentice may be cancelled by the Wages Council if the other conditions of apprenticeship are not complied with.

(2) For the purpose of determining the proportion of apprentices to journeyworkers in accordance with condition (b) of the last preceding sub-paragraph,

(a) one of the said branches of the trade shall be that branch in which workers are employed for not less than two-thirds of their time on one or more of the operations of (i) bespoke hand sewn making, (ii) hand sewn repairing, (iii) clicking (cutting), and (iv) the closing of uppers for bespoke work, and the other branch shall be any other section of the trade;

(b) a casual absence of a journeyworker or a casual vacancy for a short period in the number of journeyworkers employed shall not be treated as a failure to comply with the said condition;

(c) where an employer is wholly or mainly performing the work of a journeyworker he shall be reckoned as a journeyworker;

(d) a learner shall be reckoned as an apprentice notwithstanding that the general minimum time rates set out in paragraph 8 do not apply to him;

(e) a worker aged under 21 years to whom a general minimum time rate specified in paragraph 6 applies shall not be reckoned as a learner, apprentice or journeyworker;

(f) save as aforesaid, the expression "journeyworker" shall have the same meaning as in paragraph 3(3).

(3) Notwithstanding the foregoing provisions of this Schedule, where an employer employs a worker as a prospective apprentice for a probationary period not exceeding three months and the conditions of apprenticeship set out in sub-paragraph (1) of this paragraph, other than employment under a written contract of apprenticeship and certification by the Wages Council are fulfilled, the minimum remuneration payable to that worker during the said period shall be that applicable to an apprentice employed in accordance with the condition specified in sub-paragraph (1) of this paragraph, and, in the event of the worker being continued thereafter at his employment as an apprentice, the said probationary period shall, for the purposes of this Schedule, be treated as part of the period of apprenticeship, whether or not it is included therein:

Provided that where the employer does not, on or before the last day of the said probationary period, enter into with the worker such a contract of apprenticeship as is mentioned in sub-paragraph (1) of this paragraph, the employer shall pay to the worker a sum equal to the difference between the minimum remuneration payable to him as a prospective apprentice and the amount that would have been payable to him had the provisions of this sub-paragraph not applied.

PART VI
OVERTIME AND WAITING TIME
MINIMUM OVERTIME RATES

11. Minimum overtime rates are payable to a worker to whom this Schedule applies as follows:—

(1) on any day other than a Sunday or customary holiday or a day on which a rest period occurs,

     (a) for the first 2 hours worked in excess of 10 hours... time-and-a-quarter

     (b) thereafter   ...   .   time-and-a-half

(2) in any week for all time worked during rest periods,

     (a) for the first 2 hours worked   ...   .   time-and-a-quarter

     (b) thereafter   ...   .   time-and-a-half

(3) on a Sunday or customary holiday, for all time worked... double time

(4) in any week, for all time worked in excess of 41 hours, exclusive of any time for which a minimum rate is payable under the foregoing provisions of this paragraph,

     (a) for the first 3 hours so worked   ...   .   time-and-a-quarter

     (b) thereafter   ...   .   time-and-a-half.

12. In this Schedule

(1) the expressions "time-and-a-quarter", "time-and-a-half" and "double time" mean respectively—

     (a) in the case of a time worker, one and a quarter times, one and a half times and twice the hourly general minimum time rate otherwise applicable to the worker,

     (b) in the case of a worker employed on piece work

        (i) a time rate equal respectively to one quarter, one half and the whole of the hourly general minimum time rate which would be applicable to the worker if he were a time worker and a minimum overtime rate did not apply, and in addition thereto,

        (ii) the minimum remuneration otherwise applicable to the worker under paragraph 1(1)(b).

(2) the expression "customary holiday" means—

     (a) in England and Wales

        (i) Christmas Day, Boxing Day, Good Friday, Easter Monday, Whit Monday (or where another day is substituted therefor by national proclamation, that day), August Bank Holiday and any day proclaimed as a public holiday or additional bank holiday, or

        (ii) in the case of each of the named holidays, such other day (not being a day on which a rest period occurs) as may be substituted therefor by the employer by a notice posted in the factory throughout the three weeks immediately preceding the holiday for which it is substituted;

     (b) in Scotland

        (i) New Year's Day, Good Friday, the local Spring holiday, the day observed as Victoria Day or Queen's Birthday, the local Autumn holiday, Christmas Day and any day proclaimed as a public holiday or additional bank holiday, or

(ii) in the case of each of the named holidays, such other day (not being a day on which a rest period occurs) as may be substituted therefor by the employer by a notice posted in the factory throughout the three weeks immediately preceding the holiday for which it is substituted:

Provided that notification of days of holiday made by the employer for the purpose of Section 94 of the Factories Act 1961(a), shall be treated for the purposes of this sub-paragraph as effective notice of substitution.

(3) the expression "rest period" means—

    (a) a day (other than a Sunday or customary holiday) in each week of employment (or where one or more customary holidays fall in any such week either in that week or at the employer's option in the next succeeding week), appointed by the employer by giving at least three weeks' notice to the worker as the day upon which the worker will not normally be required to work, or

    (b) each of the periods during which a worker will not normally be required to work on two days (other than Sundays or customary holidays) in each week of employment (or where one or more customary holidays fall in any such week either in that week or at the employer's option in the next succeeding week) similarly appointed by the employer as days upon which the worker will not normally be required to work for more than 5 hours, or

    (c) in default of any such appointment by the employer as is mentioned in the preceding sub-paragraphs (a) and (b) hereof, Saturday or if Saturday is a customary holiday the last working day preceding it.

WAITING TIME

13.—(1) A worker is entitled to payment of the minimum remuneration specified in this Schedule for all time during which he is present on the premises of his employer, unless he is present thereon in any of the following circumstances:—

    (a) without the employer's consent, express or implied,

    (b) for some purpose unconnected with his work and other than that of waiting for work to be given to him to perform,

    (c) by reason only of the fact that he is resident thereon,

    (d) during normal meal times in a room or place in which no work is being done and he is not waiting for work to be given to him to perform.

(2) The minimum remuneration payable under sub-paragraph (1) of this paragraph to a piece worker when not engaged on piece work is that which would be applicable if he were a time worker.

PART VII
GUARANTEED REMUNERATION
GUARANTEED WEEKLY REMUNERATION

14.—(1) This paragraph applies to a worker (other than a casual worker) who ordinarily works for the employer for at least 36 hours weekly on work to which this Schedule applies.

(2) Notwithstanding anything contained in this Schedule, where in any week:—

    (a) no remuneration is payable to the worker under the foregoing provisions of this Schedule or by way of holiday remuneration under any wages regulation order made by the Secretary of State to give effect to the proposals of the Wages Council, or

    (b) the total amount of any such remuneration is less than the guaranteed weekly remuneration provided for by this paragraph,

the minimum remuneration payable to that worker for that week in lieu of any amount aforesaid shall, subject to the provisions of this paragraph, be the guaranteed weekly remuneration.

(a) 1961 c. 34.

(3) Subject to the provisions of the next following sub-paragraph the amount of the guaranteed weekly remuneration is as follows:—

(a) in the case of a worker who ordinarily works for the employer on work to which this Schedule applies for at least 41 hours weekly, 32 hours' pay calculated at the general minimum time rate ordinarily applicable to the worker, or

(b) in the case of a worker who ordinarily works for the employer for less than 41 but not less than 36 hours weekly on such work, 32/41sts of the amount payable at the said rate for the hours ordinarily worked by the worker in a week for the employer on such work.

(4) Payment of the guaranteed weekly remuneration in any week is subject to the condition that the worker throughout the period of his ordinary employment in that week, excluding any day allowed to him as a holiday, is (a) capable of and available for work and (b) willing to perform such duties outside his normal occupation as the employer may reasonably require if his normal work is not available to him in the establishment in which he is employed:

Provided that guaranteed weekly remuneration shall not cease to be payable to a worker in respect of any week by reason only of the fact that he is absent during any part of that week by reason of proved illness or with the consent of the employer but, in the case of any such absence (other than absence on a holiday with pay allowed under the provisions of a wages regulation order) the amount of the guaranteed weekly remuneration shall be reduced by the amount to which he would have been entitled under this Schedule as a time worker had he worked the number of hours ordinarily worked by him during the period of such absence in that week.

(5) If the employer is unable to provide the worker with work by reason of a strike, failure of supplies or any cause (other than shortage of work) outside the control of the employer, guaranteed weekly remuneration shall not be payable in respect of any week during which, or part of which, the employer is unable to provide work as aforesaid.

(6) The amount of the guaranteed weekly remuneration applicable to a piece worker shall be the sum to which he would be entitled if he were a time worker.

(7) In this paragraph the expression "week" means "pay week".

GUARANTEED DAILY REMUNERATION FOR CASUAL WORKERS

15.—(1) Notwithstanding anything contained in this Schedule, where the time worked by a casual worker on work to which this Schedule applies is less than 5 hours on a weekly short day (not being a customary holiday) or 8 hours on any other day, he shall be treated for the purposes of this Schedule (except Part VI) as if he had worked on such work 5 and 8 hours respectively.

(2) A casual worker who, in accordance with his employer's instructions, reports on any day for work to which this Schedule applies, but does not perform any such work, shall be treated as if the provisions of sub-paragraph (1) of this paragraph applied in respect of that day.

(3) For the purposes of this paragraph:—

(a) A casual worker is a worker who undertakes short engagements on an hourly or a day to day basis.

(b) A piece worker shall be treated as though he were a time worker.

PART VIII
GENERAL MINIMUM PIECE RATES FOR MALE OR FEMALE WORKERS

16.—(1) The general minimum piece rates applicable to male or female workers employed on repairing are the piece rates set out in Part IX of this Schedule increased by 3 per cent.

(2) The general minimum piece rates applicable to male or female workers employed on bespoke making are the piece rates set out in Parts X and XI of this Schedule increased by 3 per cent.

THE RATES IN PARTS IX, X AND XI ARE EXPRESSED AS NEW PENCE AND DECIMAL PARTS THEREOF, EXCEPT AMOUNTS OF OVER £1 IN PARAGRAPHS 70 AND 72

PART IX

PIECE RATES FOR MALE OR FEMALE WORKERS EMPLOYED ON REPAIRING

A.—SOLES—COMPLETED WORK

17.—(1) Subject to the provisions of paragraph 19 and the provisions as to extras and reductions specified in paragraphs 20 to 27 inclusive, the piece rates for male or female workers employed on repairing soles (completed work) are set out in the following Table.

(2) "Benching throughout" means the performance by a single worker of all the separate operations of benching, the appropriate rates for which, in paragraph 37, amount to the appropriate rate for benching throughout, and includes in the case of riveted work the operations of riveting round soles by machine when the riveting machine is operated by the benchman but does not include the sewing or stitching of the new soles where the work is sewn or stitched.

(3) The piece rates for "benching throughout" shall be increased by 1·667p per pair where nails have to be removed from full nailed or bradded work.

(4) The piece rates for "hand stitching (with square awl)" shall be increased by one-third when old stitches are taken out from welts before restitching.

	RIVETED WORK						SEWN OR STITCHED WORK					
	Men's	Ladies'	Youths'	Boys', Girls' and infants'			Men's	Ladies'	Youths'	Boys', Girls' and infants'		
Size	6-11	2-8	2-5½	11-1½	7-10½	Under 7	6-11	2-8	2-5½	11-1½	7-10½	Under 7
Column	1	2	3	4	5	6	7	8	9	10	11	12
	Per pair *p*	Per pair *p*	Per pair *p*	Per pair *p*	Per pair *p*	Per pair *p*	Per pair *p*	Per pair *p*	Per pair *p*	Per pair *p*	Per pair *p*	Per pair *p*
(a)(i) HALF SOLE (other than pumps):—												
Benching throughout	6·250	5·417	5·833	5·417	4·583	3·958	6·875	6·042	6·458	6·042	5·208	4·583
Hand sewing	—	—	—	—	—	—	10·625	8·542	9·375	8·542	6·667	6·667
Hand stitching (with square awl)	—	—	—	—	—	—	14·583	11·875	13·125	12·083	8·333	7·500
(ii) SOLE UNDER HEEL (other than pumps):—												
Benching throughout	11·667	10·833	11·250	10·833	8·750	7·500	12·500	11·667	12·083	11·667	9·583	8·125
Hand sewing	—	—	—	—	—	—	14·167	10·833	12·083	10·833	9·167	7·083
Hand stitching (with square awl)	—	—	—	—	—	—	19·167	14·583	16·250	14·583	11·667	9·167

PUMPS TURNED

	Men's	Ladies'	Youths'	Boys', girls' and infants'		
Size	6-11	2-8	2-5½	11-1½	7-10½	Under 7
Column	1	2	3	4	5	6
	Per pair	Per pair	Per pair	Per pair	Per pair	Per pair
	p	p	p	p	p	p
(b) HALF SOLE, PUMPS (other than slippers):— Benching and hand sewing of soles complete	20·833	17·500	18·333	17·500	15·833	14·167

PUMPS TURNED AND GRAFTED

	Men's	Ladies'	Youths'	Boys', girls' and infants'		
Size	6-11	2-8	2-5½	11-1½	7-10½	Under 7
Column	7	8	9	10	11	12
	Per pair	Per pair	Per pair	Per pair	Per pair	Per pair
	p	p	p	p	p	p
(b) HALF SOLE, PUMPS (other than slippers):— Benching and hand sewing of soles complete	24·167	20·833	21·667	20·833	18·333	16·667

(c) FITTING LADIES' BREASTED SOLES

(i) Where splitting and butting is completed by benchman by hand and cemented to heel breasts ...　...　...　...　...　10p per pair

(ii) Where splitting and butting is completed by benchman by machine and cemented to heel breasts　...　...　...　...　...　5p per pair

18. LEATHER SOLES CEMENTED ON

	MEN'S		LADIES'	
	By Hand	Machine only	By Hand	Machine only
	Per pair	Per pair	Per pair	Per pair
	p	p	p	p
(a) Stripping and levelling, including filling	2·292	2·292	1·875	1·875
(b) Skiving and securing old soles at waist ...	1·250	1·042	0·833	0·833
(c) Rolling and moulding soles	0·208	0·208	0·208	0·208
(d) Skiving new soles	0·208	0·208	0·208	0·208
(e) Roughing upper or welt...	1·042	1·042	1·042	1·042
(f) Roughing new soles	1·042	1·042	1·042	1·042
(g) Applying cement to upper or welt	0·625	0·625	0·625	0·625
(h) Applying cement to soles	0·625	0·625	0·625	0·625
(i) Attaching new soles and hammering down by hand...	1·042	—	1·042	—
(j) Fixing new soles in press (including use of activator)	—	0·625	—	0·417
(k) Securing with rivets at waist and toe as necessary ...	0·417	0·208	0·417	0·208
(l) Rounding	0·833	0·417	0·833	0·417
	9·584	8·334	8·750	7·083

19.—The piece rates for benching set out in paragraphs 17 and 18 do not include payment for:—

(a) Pegging the waists,

(b) Repairing insoles of welted work,

(c) In the case of sole under heel, the sewing or repairing of hand sewn or welted seats.

Where the benchman performs any of these operations, he shall be paid in respect of such work the piece rates specified in paragraph 1(1)(b)(ii).

20. SOLEING MATERIAL NOT CUT TO SHAPE

The piece rates for benching throughout set out in paragraphs 17 and 18 in respect of soles apply where the soleing material is cut into separate soles shaped rights and lefts. If the soleing material is not given out in this form, *0·833p* per pair extra is payable.

21. OUTSIZES

For men's work over size 11 the piece rates provided in paragraph 17 for soleing men's work sizes 6-11 and in paragraph 18 for men's work and for ladies' work over size 8 the piece rates provided in paragraph 17 for soleing ladies' work sizes 2-8 and in paragraph 18 for ladies' work shall be respectively payable, with the following additions:—

Per pair

(*a*) Hand sewn or hand stitched work where the benching and the sewing (or stitching) are done by the same worker ...   .   *1·250p*

(*b*) Benching of riveted work, machine sewn work or machine stitched work   ...   .   *0·417p*

(*c*) Hand sewing or hand stitching only...   ...   .   *0·833p*

22. LONG WORK

(*a*) Repairing men's or youths' Napoleon, jockey or riding boots, long Wellingtons, short Wellingtons, field boots or sea boots which reach to the knee or above—

(i) Sole only, men's (all sizes) and youths' (sizes 2-5½): *1·250p* per pair extra to the rates for benching;

(ii) Soleing and heeling (or half heeling) when done together, men's (all sizes) and youths' (sizes 2-5½): *2·083p* per pair extra to the rates for benching;

(*b*) Repairing ladies' long work—

(i) Sole only, or

(ii) Soleing and heeling (or half heeling) when done together: *0·625p* per pair extra to the rates for benching.

23. RIVETING SOLES ON WELTED BOOTS OR SHOES

Riveting soles by hand on welted boots or shoes, *0·833p* per pair extra to the rates for benching riveted work. This extra does not apply when the new sole is riveted on the top of the old sole or middle sole.

24. SEWING THROUGH (SOLES OR CLUMPS)

Soles or clumps, sewn through by hand on Blake principle, *4·167p* per pair extra to the rates for hand sewing.

25. SOLEING WITH LEATHER SUBSTITUTES

Soleing with leather substitutes, but excluding the work for which rates are provided in paragraphs 61 and 62:—

(*a*) Where the worker has to prepare or roughen or prepare and roughen both the new sole and the bottom and to apply an adhesive for the purpose of fixing the new sole before sewing or riveting   ...   .   *3·333p* per pair extra.

(*b*) Where the worker has no preparatory work to perform to the new sole but prepares or roughens or prepares and roughens the bottom and applies an adhesive for the purpose of fixing the new sole before sewing or riveting   ...   .   *1·667p* per pair extra.

26. SOLEING WITH WATERPROOF LEATHERS OTHER THAN CHROME

Benching throughout...   ...   .   *0·625p* per pair extra.

27. WOOD PEGGING BY HAND

Soleing, *4·375p* per pair extra to the rates for benching riveted work.

B.—HEELING, TOE BITS, SIDE BITS, UNDERLAYS AND CROSS PIECES

28.—Subject to the provisions of paragraph 29 and to the provisions as to addition and subtraction set out in paragraphs 30 to 36, the piece rates specified in the following Table apply to male or female workers employed on repairing.

	Men's	Ladies'	Youths'	Boys', Girls' and infants'		
				11–1½	7–10½	Under 7
Size	6–11	2–8	2–5½	4	5	6
Column	1	2	3	4	5	
	Per pair	Per pair	Per pair	Per pair	Per pair	Per pair
	p	p	p	p	p	p
(a) HEELING WITH LEATHER OR LEATHER SUBSTITUTES BENCHING—						
(i) Stripping top piece, removing old grindery, levelling and securing under lifts	1·667	1·042	1·458	1·458	1·458	1·042
(ii) Tacking on top pieces	0·208	0·208	0·208	0·208	0·208	0·208
(iii) Rounding by hand	0·208	0·208	0·208	0·208	0·208	0·208
(iv) Nailing round by hand	0·625	0·417	0·417	0·417	0·417	0·417
(v) Hammering down and filing nails	0·208	0·208	0·208	0·208	0·208	0·208

Benching for nailing round or slugging by machine when the nailing or slugging machine is not operated by the benchman.

The rates for benching set out above, subject to the following reductions:—

   (i) Boys' (size 11 and over), youths' (sizes 2 to 5½) and men's work   ...   0·625p per pair

   (ii) All other sizes   ...   .   0·417p ,, ,,

When the work is returned to the same benchman for hammering down and filing the heels after nailing round or slugging by machine the rates for benching shall be subject in respect of all sizes to a reduction of 0·208p per pair only.

HAND SEWN

	Men's	Ladies'	Youths'	Boys', Girls' and infants'		
Size ...	6-11	2-8	2-5½	11-1½	7-10½	Under 7
Column ...	1	2	3	4	5	6
(b) TOE BITS. SIDE BITS OR UNDER-LAYS	Per pair	Per pair	Per pair	Per pair	Per pair	Per pair
Benching, exclusive of hand sewing ...	p 2·917	p 2·083	p 2·500	p 2·500	p 2·083	p 1·250
Hand sewing	3·750	3·333	3·333	3·333	2·917	2·500

RIVETED

	Men's	Ladies'	Youths'	Boys', Girls' and infants'		
Size ...	6-11	2-8	2-5½	11-1½	7-10½	Under 7
Column ...	7	8	9	10	11	12
(b) TOE BITS. SIDE BITS OR UNDER-LAYS	Per pair	Per pair	Per pair	Per pair	Per pair	Per pair
Benching, exclusive of hand sewing ...	p 2·917	p 2·083	p 2·500	p 2·500	p 2·083	p 1·250
Hand sewing	—	—	—	—	—	—

(c) FIXING MOULDED RUBBER HEELS WHERE NO PARING RE-QUIRED ... ...   MEN'S, 2·500p per pair.   All other sizes, 1·667p per pair.

	HAND SEWN						RIVETED					
	Men's	Ladies'	Youths'	Boys', Girls' and infants'			Men's	Ladies'	Youths'	Boys', Girls' and infants'		
Size ...	6–11	2–8	2–5½	11–1½	7–10½	Under 7	6–11	2–8	2–5½	11–1½	7–10½	Under 7
Column ...	1	2	3	4	5	6	7	8	9	10	11	12
	Per pair p	Per pair p	Per pair p	Per pair p	Per pair p	Per pair p	Per pair p	Per pair p	Per pair p	Per pair p	Per pair p	Per pair p
(d) CROSS PIECES												
Benching, exclusive of hand sewing ...	4·583	3·333	4·167	2·917	2·500	2·083	4·583	3·333	4·167	2·917	2·500	2·083
Benching, cemented work ...	6·250	5·000	5·833	4·583	4·167	3·750	6·250	5·000	5·833	4·583	4·167	3·750
Hand sewing	5·833	5·000	5·417	4·583	4·167	3·333	—	—	—	—	—	—

29.—As respects the work specified in paragraph 28:—

(i) If benching (other than hand sewing) is not completed by one worker, the piece rates specified in paragraph 1(1)(b)(ii) apply.

(ii) The piece rates for benching are payable to the benchman whether his work includes or does not include the filing of heels, toe plates and metal tips.

(iii) The piece rates for benching heels do not apply to the removing of old heels and the fixing (including knifing up) of new ready made heels of pulp or leather. If the benchman performs these operations he shall be paid the piece rates specified in paragraph 1(1)(b)(ii).

30. OUTSIZES, HEEL OR HALF HEEL

For men's work over size 11, the piece rate provided in paragraph 28 for men's work sizes 6-11, and for ladies' work over size 8, the piece rate provided in paragraph 28 for ladies' work sizes 2-8 shall be payable respectively with the following additions:—

For benching (whether complete or in preparation for the
riveting or slugging machine)   ...   .   *0·208p* per pair.

31. NEW LIFTS AND PART LIFTS

(1) (*a*) New lifts—for each quarter of an inch or part thereof, *0·833p* per pair extra;

(*b*) Part lifts—where parts of heels have to be cut out to the depth of ½ inch or more for the purpose of levelling the heels, although complete new lifts may not be inserted, *0·833p* per pair extra.

(2) Where heels are stripped down to the seat piece, the piece rates for rebuilding heels and heeling (benching) set out in paragraph 58 shall apply.

32. QUARTER OR HALF-TIPS

(1) (*a*) Inserted iron quarter or half-tips ...   .   *0·833p* per pair extra.

(*b*) Inserted rubber tips:

(i) When solutioned...   ...   .   *1·667p* per pair extra.

(ii) When not solutioned   ...   .   *0·833p* per pair extra.

(*c*) Where the top piece has a quarter rubber tip already attached when the top piece is given out:

(i) For solutioning on the quarter rubber tip in the process of fixing the top piece to the heel...   *0·833p* per pair extra.

(ii) For attaching any additional leather to the top piece to make up the difference between the thickness of the quarter rubber tip and the top piece   ...   .   *0·417p* per pair extra.

(2) No extra is payable for affixing the top piece which has a quarter rubber tip already attached.

33. ELONGATED HEELS

Repairing elongated heels (where waists already filled in):

Men's (all sizes) and youths'

(sizes 2 to 5½)....   ...   ...   *1·458p* per pair extra to the rates for benching.

All other sizes   ...   .   *0·625p* per pair extra to the rates for benching.

34. LONG WORK—HEELING

(*a*) Repairing men's and youths' Napoleon, jockey, or riding boots, long Wellingtons, short Wellingtons, field boots or sea boots which reach to the knee or above—

(i) Heeling:

0·833p per pair extra to the rates for benching;

(ii) Toe bits, side bits, underlays, and cross pieces or any of them:

0·833p per pair extra to the rates for benching.

(*b*) Repairing ladies' long work—

   (i) Heeling:

      0·417p per pair extra to the rates for benching;

  (ii) Heeling when done together with toe bits, side bits, underlays, and cross pieces or any of them:

      0·625p per pair extra to the rates for benching;

 (iii) Toe bits, side bits, underlays, and cross pieces or any of them:

      0·417p per pair extra to the rates for benching.

35. TOE PIECES (SHAPED)

Shaped toe pieces:

  Hand sewn and benched, *2·917p* per pair extra;

  Riveted, *0·833p* per pair extra.

36. WOOD PEGGING BY HAND

Heeling, *1·458p* per pair extra to the rates for benching riveted work.

C.—PIECE RATES FOR SEPARATE OPERATIONS OF BENCHING SOLES

37.—(1) Subject to the provisions of paragraphs 38 and 39 and to the provisions as to extras set out in paragraphs 42 to 45, the piece rates for separate operations of benching soles set out in the following Table apply to male or female workers employed on repairing.

(2) If benching throughout is not performed by a single worker, the piece rates for any of the separate operations of benching specified in the said Table are the rates for the individual operations or, where more than one of these operations is performed by a single worker, the sum of the appropriate rates for the individual operations involved.

	RIVETED WORK						SEWN OR STITCHED WORK					
	Men's	Ladies'	Youths'	Boys', Girls' and infants'			Men's	Ladies'	Youths'	Boys', Girls' and infants'		
Size	6-11	2-8	2-5½	11-1½	7-10½	Under 7	6-11	2-8	2-5½	11-1½	7-10½	Under 7
Column	1	2	3	4	5	6	7	8	9	10	11	12
	Per pair p	Per pair p	Per pair p	Per pair p	Per pair p	Per pair p	Per pair p	Per pair p	Per pair p	Per pair p	Per pair p	Per pair p
(a) HALF SOLE (other than pumps):—												
1. Stripping and levelling, including filling	2·292	1·875	2·083	1·875	1·458	1·458	2·083	1·667	1·875	1·875	1·458	1·458
2. Skiving old soles at waist	0·833	0·417	0·625	0·417	0·417	0·417	0·833	0·417	0·625	0·417	0·417	0·417
3. Tacking on new soles	0·417	0·208	0·417	0·417	0·417	0·417	0·417	0·208	0·417	0·417	0·417	0·417
4. Rolling or moulding	0·208		0·208	0·208	0·208	0·208	0·208		0·208	0·208	0·208	0·208
5. Skiving new soles by hand or machine	0·208	0·208	0·208	0·208	0·208	0·208	0·208	0·208	0·208	0·208	0·208	0·208
6. Riveting across waist by hand	0·208	0·208	0·208	0·208	0·208	0·208	0·417	0·417	0·417	0·417	0·417	0·208
7. Rounding by hand	0·625	0·625	0·625	0·625		0·208	0·833	0·833	0·833	0·833	0·625	0·417
8. Riveting round soles by hand	1·042	1·042	1·042	1·042	0·833	0·625	—	—	—	—	—	—
9. Hammering down rivets	0·417	0·417	0·417	0·417	0·417	0·208	—	—	—	—	—	—
10. Cutting channels by hand	—	—	—	—	—	—	0·417	0·417	0·417	0·417	0·417	0·417
11. Opening channels by hand	—	—	—	—	—	—	0·417	0·417	0·417	0·417	0·417	0·417
12. Laying channels by hand	—	—	—	—	—	—	0·625	0·625	0·625	0·625	0·625	0·208
13. Hammering down bottoms	—	—	—	—	—	—	0·417	0·417	0·417	0·417	0·417	0·208

	RIVETED WORK						SEWN OR STITCHED WORK					
	Men's	Ladies'	Youths'	Boys', Girls' and infants'			Men's	Ladies'	Youths'	Boys', Girls' and infants'		
Size	6–11	2–8	2–5½	11–1½	7–10½	Under 7	6–11	2–8	2–5½	11–1½	7–10½	Under 7
Column	1	2	3	4	5	6	7	8	9	10	11	12
	Per pair	Per pair	Per pair	Per pair	Per pair	Per pair	Per pair	Per pair	Per pair	Per pair	Per pair	Per pair
	p	p	p	p	p	p	p	p	p	p	p	p
(b) SOLE UNDER HEEL (other than pumps):—												
1. Stripping and levelling, including filling	3·750	2·917	3·333	2·917	2·500	1·875	3·750	2·917	3·333	2·917	2·500	1·875
2. Tacking on	1·042	1·042	1·042	1·042	1·042	1·042	1·042	1·042	1·042	1·042	1·042	1·042
3. Removing old heels	1·458	1·458	1·458	1·458	1·042	1·042	1·458	1·458	1·458	1·458	1·042	1·042
4. Rolling or moulding	0·208	0·208	0·208	0·208	0·208	0·208	0·208	0·208	0·208	0·208	0·208	0·208
5. Fitting new sole to seat	0·208	0·208	0·208	0·208	0·208	0·208	0·208	0·208	0·208	0·208	0·208	0·208
6. Securing seat by hand riveting	0·208	0·208	0·208	0·208	0·208	0·208	0·208	0·208	0·208	0·208	0·208	0·208
7. Rounding by hand	1·250	1·250	1·250	1·250	0·833	0·625	1·458	1·458	1·458	1·458	1·042	1·042
8. Riveting round soles by hand	1·458	1·458	1·458	1·458	1·042	0·833	—	—	—	—	—	—
9. Hammering down rivets	0·625	0·625	0·625	0·625	0·625	0·417	1·458	1·458	1·458	1·458	1·042	1·042
10. Replacing old heels by hand	1·458	1·458	1·458	1·458	1·042	1·042	0·625	0·625	0·625	0·625	0·417	0·417
11. Cutting channels by hand	—	—	—	—	—	—	0·625	0·625	0·625	0·625	0·417	0·417
12. Opening channels by hand	—	—	—	—	—	—	0·833	0·833	0·833	0·833	0·833	0·625
13. Laying channels by hand	—	—	—	—	—	—	0·625	0·625	0·625	0·625	0·625	0·417
14. Hammering down bottoms	—	—	—	—	—	—						

38.—(1) The piece rates for stripping and levelling including filling set out at (a) and (b) of the last foregoing Table shall be increased by 0·833p per pair where nails have to be removed from full nailed or bradded work.

(2) Where new lifts are required, the piece rate for replacing old heels by hand set out at (b) of the said Table shall be increased as if paragraph 31 applied.

(3) Where piece rates for riveting round soles by hand, hammering down rivets, laying channels by hand and hammering down bottoms set out at (a) and (b) of the said Table are payable and:—

(a) the operation of riveting round soles is performed by hand, the worker shall also be paid the appropriate rate for hammering down rivets;

(b) the channels have not been laid by machine and hammering down bottoms is performed, the worker shall also be paid the appropriate rate for laying channels by hand.

39. The piece rates for benching set out in paragraphs 37 and 38 do not include payment for:—

(a) Pegging the waists,

(b) Repairing insoles of welted work,

(c) In the case of sole under heel, the sewing or repairing of hand sewn or welted seats,

Where the benchman performs any of these operations, he shall be paid in respect of such work the piece rates specified in paragraph 1 (1)(b) (ii).

(d) Fitting ladies' breasted through soles—see paragraph 40.

40. FITTING LADIES' BREASTED THROUGH SOLES

(a) Where splitting and butting is completed by benchman by hand and cemented to heel breasts ...   .   *10p* per pair.

(b) Where splitting and butting is completed by benchman by machine and cemented to heel breasts   ...   .   *5p* per pair.

41. LADIES' PLATFORM THROUGH SOLES

	By Hand Per pair p	Machine only Per pair p
1. Stripping and levelling, including securing and filling ...	3·958	3·958
2. Roughing uppers	1·875	1·042
3. Roughing new soles	1·667	1·042
4. Cementing uppers	1·250	0·833
5. Cementing soles	1·250	0·833
6. Attaching bottoms (including use of activator)	2·083	1·667
7. Rounding	1·250	0·625
	13·333	10·000

42. SOLEING MATERIAL NOT CUT TO SHAPE

The piece rates for stripping and levelling including filling set out in paragraph 37 apply where soleing material is cut into separate soles shaped rights and lefts.   If the soleing material is not given out in this form, an addition of *0·833p* per pair is payable.

43. OUTSIZES

For men's work over size 11, the piece rates provided in paragraph 37 for soleing men's work size 6-11 and for ladies' work over size 8 the piece rates provided in paragraph 37 for soleing ladies' work size 2-8 shall be payable respectively, with the following addition:—

Riveted work, machine sewn work or machine stitched work:
For stripping, levelling and tacking-on ...   .   *0·417p* per pair.

44. RIVETING SOLES ON WELTED BOOTS OR SHOES

Riveting soles by hand on welted boots or shoes—

0·833p per pair extra to the appropriate rate for riveting round soles.

This extra does not apply when the new sole is riveted on the top of the old sole or middle sole.

45. SOLEING WITH LEATHER SUBSTITUTES

Soleing with leather substitutes, but excluding the work for which rates are provided in paragraphs 61 and 62:—

(a) Where the worker has to prepare or roughen or prepare and roughen both the new sole and the bottom and to apply an adhesive for the purpose of fixing the new sole before sewing or riveting,

  3·333p per pair extra.

(b) Where the worker has no preparatory work to perform to the new sole but prepares or roughens or prepares and roughens the bottom and applies an adhesive for the purpose of fixing the new sole before sewing or riveting,

  1·667p per pair extra.

D.—PIECE RATES FOR OTHER REPAIRS TO SOLES

46.—(1) INSOLES OR HALF INSOLES—SHAPING AND SLIPPING IN (excluding welted insoles).

Men's (all sizes) and youths' (sizes 2 to 5½) ... ... *3·333p* per pair.

Ladies' ... ... *2·500p* per pair.

Boys' and girls' (up to size 1½) ... ... *1·667p* per pair.

(2) Where either the whole or half of the present insole has to be removed and a new insole (either whole or half) is fitted and the upper is lasted in, the above piece rates do not apply, and a piece worker doing such work shall be paid the piece rates specified in paragraph 1 (1)(b)(ii).

47. MIDDLES, (TOE TO JOINT) SECURELY ATTACHED BY EITHER GRINDERY OR SOLUTION, AND ROUNDING BY HAND

Men's (all sizes) and youths' (sizes 2 to 5½) ... ... *3·333p* per pair.

Ladies' ... ... *2·500p* per pair.

Boys' and girls' (up to size 1½) ... ... *1·667p* per pair.

Fitting of press cut slip middles, being a reinforcement and not separately attached or rounded, by hand ... ... *0·833p* per pair.

48. HALF MIDDLES (slotted and fitted)

Where half middles are slotted and fitted into the old middles... *1·667p* per pair.

49. TOE PLATES OR TOE TIPS (separate job)

Nailed on ... ... *0·833p* per pair.

Nailed on and sunk or inserted ... ... *2·917p* per pair.

Screwed on ... ... *1·667p* per pair.

Screwed on and sunk or inserted... ... ... *3·750p* per pair.

Provided that these rates shall not apply to toe plates or toe tips when combined with nailing to which the rates in paragraph 50 apply.

50. NAILS OR BRADS

(1) (a) Nailing or bradding foreparts (with or without toe plates or toe tips nailed on): the piece rates specified in the following Table:—

Column 1	Column 2	Column 3
—	Men's (all sizes) and Youths' (sizes 2 to 5½)	Ladies' (all sizes) and Children's (i.e., all under size 2)
	Per pair	Per pair
	p	*p*
NAILS:		
Full rows round, each row	1·458	1·042
Rows up middle, each row	0·625	0·417
Toe and joint :—One row ...	1·042	0·853
Two rows ...	1·667	1·458
BRADS:		
Full rows round, each row	1·667	1·250
Rows up middle, each row	0·833	0·625
Toe and joint :—One row ...	1·250	0·833
Two rows ...	2·083	1·667

If toe plates or toe tips screwed on, *0·833p* per pair extra.

If toe plates or toe tips sunk or inserted, *2·083p* per pair extra.

(b) Nailing waists:—*1·458p* per pair.

(2) The rates for nailing or bradding foreparts and for nailing waists set out in this paragraph do not include payments for fitters, clinkers, ice, climbing, cricket or golf nails, the removing of old nails or the filling up of old holes with wood pegs. If the benchman performs any of these operations, he shall be paid in respect thereof the piece rates specified in paragraph 1(1)(b)(ii).

51. RE-SEWING

(a) Re-sewing old soles or waists:—

Up to 4 inches, *2·500p*; *0·625p* per inch thereafter.

(b) Re-sewing old pumps:—

Joint to joint:—

Men's (all sizes) and youths' (sizes 2 to 5½), *15p* per pair.

Ladies' and other sizes, *11·667p* per pair.

Turning and re-turning, *5p* per pair extra.

Heel to heel:—

6·667p per pair additional to the rates for re-sewing from joint to joint set out above.

Part re-sewing only:—

Sewing, *1·667p* per inch with a minimum of *1·667p*.

Turning and re-turning, *5p* per pair extra.

52. LINK STITCHING OR LOOPING

1·250p per inch with a minimum of *2·500p*.

53. STIFFENERS (NEW)

New stiffeners (Blake or riveted work) lasted in:

Men's (all sizes) and youths' (sizes 2 to 5½), *15p* per pair.

Ladies', boys' and girls' *12·500p* per pair.

If welted:

With tingled or braced seats, *5p* per pair extra.

With sewn seats, *10p* per pair extra.

54. WELTS

(*a*) Re-welting (including taking out old welts):—

Heel to heel—

Men's (all sizes)	*30p* per pair.
Youths' (sizes 2 to 5½)	*25p* per pair.
Ladies' and other sizes	*20p* per pair.

Joint to joint—

Men's (all sizes)	*20p* per pair.
Youths' (sizes 2 to 5½)	*17·50p* per pair.
Ladies' and other sizes	*16·667p* per pair.

New pieces of welt on a job (that is on one boot or shoe or on a pair of boots or shoes) ... ... Up to one inch *2·708p*, with *1·042p* per inch thereafter.

(*b*) Re-sewing of old welts:—

Joint to joint—

Men's (all sizes)	*16·667p* per pair.
Youths' (sizes 2 to 5½)	*13·333p* per pair.
Ladies' and other sizes	*11·667p* per pair.

Re-sewing old welts whether of one boot or shoe or of a pair of boots or shoes ... ... Up to 2 inches *1·667p*, with *0·833p* per inch thereafter.

E.—PIECE RATES FOR OTHER REPAIRS TO HEELS

55. HEEL SUPPORTS

Metal or other ready made heel breast supports, *1·667p* per pair.

56. HEELING WITH LEATHER SUBSTITUTES

The piece rates appropriate under paragraphs 61 and 62.

57. NAILING HEELS

(1) Nailing heels when boots are not heeled or when performed as a job additional to complete heeling:

Less than two rows, *0·833p* per pair.

Two or more rows, *1·667p* per pair.

(2) The rates for nailing heels set out in this paragraph do not include payment for fitters, clinkers, ice, climbing, cricket or golf nails, the removing of old nails or the filling up of old holes with wood pegs. If the benchman performs any of these operations, he shall be paid in respect thereof the piece rates specified in paragraph 1(1)(*b*)(ii).

58.—(1) REBUILDING HEELS AND HEELING (BENCHING)

(i) Ladies' French	*11·667p* per pair up to 2 inches.
Ladies' Cuban	*8·750p* per pair up to 1½ inches.
Ladies' Square	*5·833p* per pair up to 1¼ inches.
Men's	*7·500p* per pair up to 1¼ inches.

The measurement of the height of the heel is to be taken from the upper at the breast of the heel.

(ii) For every quarter inch or part thereof higher, *0·833p* per pair extra.

(iii) When sole seat piece is required, *1·677p* per pair extra.

(2) The above rates do not apply to sewn seats.

59. REFASTENING HEELS

Refastening heels with pieced insoles and nailing through seat by hand, *2·5p* each.

60. WOOD HEELS

Turning back covers and lowering heels, *0·833p* per pair.
Replacing covers, *0·833p* per pair.

F.—PIECE RATES FOR FIXING STICK-ON SOLES (INCLUDING HAND TRIMMING WHERE REQUIRED)

61.—(1) *The piece rate for fixing stick-on soles (including hand trimming where required) is 6p per pair.*

(2) The rate set out in this paragraph does not apply to (a) other rubber soles for which the worker shall be paid the piece rates specified in paragraph 1(1)(b)(ii), or (b) rubber tips, the rates for which are set out in paragraph 32.

G.—PIECE RATES FOR CREPE WORK

62. The piece rates for crepe work are set out in the following Table:—

	Men's (all sizes)	Ladies' (all sizes) and Youths' (2 to 5½)	Boys' and Girls'
Column	1	2	3
	Per pair *p*	Per pair *p*	Per pair *p*
(1) THROUGH SOLE			
(a) Stripping, levelling and filling ...	4·583	3·750	2·708
(b) Preparing and solutioning bottoms ...	2·083	2·083	1·667
(c) Solutioning new middle soles ...	1·458	1·042	0·833
(d) Fixing and hammering down middles	2·292	1·458	1·042
(e) Solutioning outsoles and middles ...	2·083	1·875	1·250
(f) Fixing and hammering down outsoles	2·083	1·875	1·667
(g) Rounding both middles and outsoles	3·333	2·917	2·083
	17·915	15·000	11·250
(2) HALF-SOLE			
(a) Stripping, levelling, filling and skiving	3·750	2·917	2·292
(b) Preparing and solutioning bottoms ...	1·458	1·042	0·833
(c) Solutioning crepe middle soles ...	0·833	0·833	0·625
(d) Fixing and hammering down middles	1·458	1·042	1·042
(e) Solutioning outsoles and middles ...	1·875	1·458	1·042
(f) Fixing and hammering down outsoles	1·458	1·458	1·042
(g) Rounding outsoles and middles ...	2·500	2·500	2·083
	13·332	11·250	8·959

	Men's (all sizes)	Ladies' (all sizes) and Youths' (Sizes 2 to 5½)	Boys' and Girls'
Column	1	2	3
	Per pair	Per pair	Per pair
	p	*p*	*p*
(3) HEEL			
(a) Scouring and levelling old heel ...	*2·083*	*1·667*	*1·042*
(b) Solutioning old heels	*0·625*	*0·417*	*0·417*
(c) Solutioning new top pieces	*0·625*	*0·417*	*0·417*
(d) Fixing and hammering down top pieces	*0·417*	*0·417*	*0·417*
(e) Rounding by hand	*0·625*	*0·625*	*0·625*
	4·375	*3·543*	*2·918*
(4) TOE PIECES OR SIDE PIECES			
(a) Stripping, levelling and skiving old soles	*2·292*	*1·875*	*1·667*
(b) Fitting piece of new middle sole ...	*1·042*	*0·833*	*0·833*
(c) Attaching toe or side piece	*1·250*	*1·250*	*1·250*
(d) Rounding by hand	*0·625*	*0·625*	*0·417*
(e) Hammering down by hand	*0·625*	*0·625*	*0·417*
	5·834	*5·208*	*4·584*

Per pair

p

(5) EXTRAS ON CREPE WORK
(a) Rands, joint to joint, solutioned, fixed and pared to sole ... ... *5·833*
(b) Rands, joint to joint, frictioned, fixed and pared to sole ... ... *3·333*
(c) Rands, full, solutioned, fixed and pared to sole ... ... *8·750*
(d) Rands, full, frictioned, fixed and pared to sole ... ... *5·833*
(e) All round welts, solutioned, turned down and pared to sole ... ... *8·750*
(f) Building heels by single press cut lifts ... ... *1·667*
(g) Wedge shape lifts ... ... *1·667*
(h) Attaching ready-built heels (solutioned) ... ... *1·667*

H.—REPAIRS TO UPPERS

63. BACK STRAPS

(a) Completed work machined:

  (i) When not put under seat:

    Up to 4 inches, *2·083p* each.

    Over 4 inches, *0·833p* each per inch or part thereof extra.

  (ii) When put under seat:

    Up to 4 inches, *3·333p* each.

    Over 4 inches, *0·833p* each per inch or part thereof extra.

  (iii) When stabbed to seat:

    Up to 4 inches, *4·167p* each.

    Over 4 inches, *0·833p* each per inch or part thereof extra.

(b) Completed work solutioned:

    1·667p each additional to the rates for machined work set out in (a) of this paragraph.

64. The piece rates for PATCHES (other than seat patches) are set out in the following Table:—

	Each
	p
(a) Patches machined (when not soled):	
(i) If neither sewn to sole nor put under	3·333
(ii) If put under sole	5·000
(iii) If sewn down to sole or welt	5·833
(b) Patches machined (when to be soled):	
(i) If neither sewn to sole nor put under	3·333
(ii) If put under sole	3·750
(iii) If sewn down to sole or welt	5·833
(c) Patches solutioned: to be paid at the rates for machined work in (a) and	
(b) of this Table with the addition of	1·667
(d) Lasted in or put under (when to be soled)	0·833
(e) Put under (when not soled)	1·667
(f) Sewn down to sole or welt only	2·500

(g) Hand stabbed on, *2·083p* each extra to the rates for machined work set out in this Table.
(h) Saddle or cross patches to be paid for as two patches.

65. The piece rates for SEAT PATCHES are set out in the following Table:—

Column 1	Column 2	Column 3
—	Men's (all sizes) and Youths' (sizes 2 to 5½)	Ladies' and other sizes
Completed work:	Each	Each
	p	*p*
(a) Machined and lasted in:		
(i) Half way round heel or less	5·833	5·000
(ii) Over half way round heel	10·833	9·167
(b) Machined and sewn down to seat:		
(i) Half way round heel or less	7·500	5·833
(ii) Over half way round heel	13·333	10·833
(c) Solutioned on and lasted in:		
(i) Half way round heel or less	7·500	6·667
(ii) Over half way round heel	14·167	12·500
(d) Solutioned on and sewn down to seat:		
(i) Half way round heel or less	9·167	7·500
(ii) Over half way round heel	16·667	14·167
Separate operations: ...		
(e) Shaping, fitting and machining:		
(i) Half way round heel or less	2·917	2·917
(ii) Over half way round heel	5·000	5·000
(f) Shaping, fitting and solutioning:		
(i) Half way round heel or less	5·000	5·000
(ii) Over half way round heel	8·333	8·333
(g) Lasting-in:		
(i) Half way round heel or less	3·333	3·333
(ii) Over half way round heel	6·667	5·833
(h) Sewing down to seat:		
(i) Half way round heel or less	5·000	3·333
(ii) Over half way round heel	12·500	10·000

Hand stabbed on, *4·167p* each extra to the rates for machined work set out in this Table.

66. The piece rates for TOE CAPS are set out in the following Table:—

Column 1	Column 2	Column 3
—	Men's (all sizes) and Youths' (sizes 2 to 5½)	Ladies' and other sizes
	Per pair p	Per pair p
(a) Toe caps machined and lasted in:		
(i) When boots are soled	8·333	6·667
(ii) When boots are not soled	12·500	10·000
(iii) When boots are made longer (including piecing the insoles)	18·333	15·000
(b) Toe caps solutioned: to be paid at the rates for machined work in (a) of this Table with the addition of	1·667	1·667
(c) Lasted in only:		
(i) When boots are soled	5·000	3·750
(ii) When boots are not soled	11·667	7·500
(iii) When boots are made longer (including piecing the insoles)	15·000	10·000
(d) When sewn down to sole or welt, machined ...	10·000	8·333
(e) When sewn down to sole or welt, solutioned ...	14·167	11·667
(f) Sewn down only	7·500	5·000

(g) When caps are sewn in under welt, the appropriate rates specified in paragraph 54 are to be paid in addition to the rates in (a), (b) and (c) of this Table.

(h) Toe caps fitted and machined only, 2·917p per pair; if solutioned only, 4·583p per pair.

(i) All work when uppers are pulled up to joint for re-capping is to be paid for as lasting vamps with caps as set out in paragraph 68.

(j) Toe caps of waxed kips, waxed splits and heavy chrome leathers, 1·667p each extra.

67. TOE PUFFS

   (a) Toe puffs when not re-capped to be paid for as toe caps.

   (b) When toe puffs are put in and the material is not prepared for the worker, an extra of 1·667p per pair shall apply in addition to the rates for toe caps.

68. The piece rates for VAMPS (re-vamping) are set out in the following Table:—

Column 1	Column 2	Column 3	Column 4
—	Men's (all sizes) and Youths' (sizes 2 to 5½)	Ladies'	Other sizes
	Per pair p	Per pair p	Per pair p
(a) Vamps machined and fitted	9·167	7·500	5·833
If solutioned, extra	5·000	5·000	4·167
(b) Lasting	9·167	8·333	6·667
(c) Sewing down to sole or welt	13·333	11·667	10·000

(d) When vamps are sewn in under welt, the appropriate rates specified in paragraph 54 are to be paid in addition to the rates in (a), (b) and (c) of this Table.

(e) Toe capped vamps:

   Machined and fitted, 0·833p per pair   } extra to the rates in (a), (b) and (c) of this
   Lasted in, 0·833p per pair   } Table.
   Sewn down through welt 2·083p per pair }

(f) Lasting vamps of single soled boots, when being soled, 2·083p per pair less.

I.—SURGICAL REPAIRING AND EXTRAS

69. The piece rates for repairing set out in this Part of this Schedule apply to surgical repairing. The additional extras provided in paragraphs 71 and 72 for bespoke hand sewn surgical making apply also to bespoke hand sewn surgical repairing.

PART X

PIECE RATES FOR MALE OR FEMALE WORKERS EMPLOYED ON BESPOKE MAKING BESPOKE HAND SEWN WORK (INCLUDING BESPOKE HAND SEWN SURGICAL WORK)

70.—(1) Subject to the provisions of this Part of this Schedule, the piece rates applicable to male or female workers employed on the bespoke making of bespoke hand sewn work (including bespoke hand sewn surgical work) are set out in the following Table.

(2) Where surgical work is not hand stitched by the maker, the rates for completed work shall be reduced by an amount equal to the appropriate rate for "hand stitching" specified in Column 7 of the said Table.

(3) Where surgical work is not finished by the maker, the rates for completed work shall be reduced by an amount equal to the appropriate rate for "finishing by hand alone" specified in Column 8 of the said Table.

(4) In this Part of this Schedule, the expression "groundwork" includes the making of all boots and shoes of black leathers (other than patent) whether made with or without toe caps, puffs, or box, block or stiffened toes.

GROUND WORK

Column 1	Completed work	Work on sectional system					
		Lasting-up (tacking-on, rounding and holeing insoles including preparing stiffeners and toe puffs and trimming uppers out for sewer)	Hand sewing (including preparing and setting up of welts)	Rounding (fill up bottom, round sole, channel)	Heeling, closing channels, building heel, getting ready for finishing	Hand stitching	Finishing by hand alone
	Column 2	Column 3	Column 4	Column 5	Column 6	Column 7	Column 8
	Per pair	Per pair p	Per pair p	Per pair p	Per pair p	Per pair p	Per pair p
(a) MEN'S, LADIES' AND YOUTHS' LONG WORK: Napoleon, jockey or riding boots, long Wellingtons, short Wellingtons, field boots ...	£4·017	61·667	56·667	42·917	37·917	80·833	75·000
(b) MEN'S, LADIES' AND YOUTHS' SHORT WORK: Boots and Shoes ...	£3·333	48·333	48·333	30·000	32·500	65·000	75·000
(c) BOYS' AND GIRLS': Boots and Shoes ...	£2·308	34·583	32·917	20·833	24·167	40·417	50·833
(d) INFANTS': Boots and Shoes under size 9 ...	£2·013	28·333	28·333	15·833	22·500	35·833	48·333
(e) Chrome leather soles in hand stitched work, extra ...	20·000p	—	—	5·417	—	10·000	4·583
(f) Outsizes (i.e. men's size 11 and over, ladies' size 8 and over), extra ...	16·667p	2·500	2·500	2·500	2·500	2·500	2·500

EXTRAS TO GROUND WORK

71. The extras set out in the following Table apply to the piece rates specified in paragraph 70:—

Column 1	Completed work	Work on sectional system					
		Lasting	Hand sewing	Round-ing	Heeling	Hand stitching	Finishing by hand
	Column 2	Column 3	Column 4	Column 5	Column 6	Column 7	Column 8
	Per pair p	Per pair p	Per pair p	Per pair p	Per pair p	Per pair p	Per pair p
(a) MEN'S LONG WORK:							
(1) Ham or thigh boots ...	22·917	6·667	4·583	2·917	2·917	2·917	2·917
(2) Patent uppers or fronts:							
When patent calf used ...	35·000	21·250	7·500				6·250
When patent leathers · other than patent calf used ...	31·250	19·167	7·500				4·583
(3) Spur boxes	49·583				38·750		10·833
(4) Stabbing seats	23·333						
(5) Middles to field boots ...	17·083			4·583		10·833	1·667
(6) Stiff leg	19·583						—
(7) White, coloured or velvet finished leathers, whether covers are used or not (employer to find material for covers) ...	34·583	6·667	3·750	3·750	3·750	8·333	8·333
(8) Other extras as set out in paragraphs 72 and 75							
(b) MEN'S SHORT WORK:							
(1) Patent uppers: ...							
When patent calf used ...	29·583	8·333	4·583	2·083	2·083	6·250	6·250
When patent leathers other than patent calf used ...	25·417	7·500	4·583	1·667	1·667	5·417	4·583

Column 1	Completed work — Column 2 (Per pair, p)	Work on sectional system — Lasting — Column 3 (Per pair, p)	Hand sewing — Column 4 (Per pair, p)	Rounding — Column 5 (Per pair, p)	Heeling — Column 6 (Per pair, p)	Hand stitching — Column 7 (Per pair, p)	Finishing by hand — Column 8 (Per pair, p)
(2) Crupp uppers ...	10·000	2·083	1·667	0·833	0·833	2·917	1·667
(3) Patent golosh:							
When patent calf used	24·583	8·333	2·917	2·083	2·083	4·583	4·583
When patent leathers other than patent calf used	19·167	6·250	2·917	2·083	2·083	2·917	2·917
(4) Patent vamp:							
When patent calf used	13·333	7·500	2·917	—	—	2·917	—
When patent leathers other than patent calf used	12·083	6·250	2·917	—	—	2·917	—
(5) Patent toecap:							
When patent calf used	9·583	5·417	2·083	—	—	2·083	—
When patent leathers other than patent calf used	7·083	3·750	1·667	—	—	1·667	—
(6) Patent back golosh:							
When patent calf used	10·417	5·417	1·667	—	—	1·667	—
When patent leathers other than patent calf used	7·083	2·083	1·667	—	—	1·667	1·667
(7) Cloth leg ...	10·417	2·083	1·667	1·667	1·667	1·667	1·667
(8) Wing toecap ...	9·583	6·667	2·917	—	—	—	1·667
(9) Middle soles, through ...	23·333	—	—	7·500	—	11·250	4·583
(10) Middle soles to joint ...	13·750	—	—	4·583	—	7·500	1·667
(11) Welts from ¼ inch to ⅜ inch in width ...	10·000	—	3·750	1·657	—	1·667	2·917
(12) Welts over ⅜ inch in width ...	19·583	—	7·500	2·917	—	2·917	6·250
(13) Bevel clumps ...	29·583	—	—	19·583	—	—	10·000
(14) Square clumps ...	23·333	—	—	15·000	—	—	8·333
(15) Heels, for each ¼ inch over and above 1¼ inches per pair ...	5·417	—	—	—	3·750	—	1·667

Column 1	Completed work	Work on sectional system					
		Lasting	Hand sewing	Rounding	Heeling	Hand stitching	Finishing by hand
	Column 2	Column 3	Column 4	Column 5	Column 6	Column 7	Column 8
	Per pair	Per pair	Per pair	Per pair	Per pair	Per pair	Per pair
	p	p	p	p	p	p	p
(16) Seats welted or sewn ...	26·667	—	10·000	4·583	—	7·500	4·583
(17) Seats braced ...	5·000	—	5·000	—	—	—	—
(18) Heels seats sewn down ...	5·000	—	—	—	5·000	—	—
(19) Seats randed ...	26·667	—	10·000	4·583	—	7·500	4·583
(20) German seats ...	25·000	—	10·000	—	7·500	4·583	2·917
(21) Spur boxes ...	49·583	—	—	—	38·750	—	10·833
(22) Sock linings sewn in ...	23·750	12·917	10·833	—	—	—	—
(23) Arched insoles ...	20·000	20·000	—	—	—	—	—
(24) Inserted rubberettes or iron tips	5·417	—	—	—	3·750	6·250	1·667
(25) Stitching aloft and bunked ...	12·500	—	—	—	—	—	6·250
(26) French corks	69·167	60·000	9·167	—	—	—	—
(27) Mock corks	59·167	50·000	9·167	—	—	—	—
(28) Inside corks, not surgical ...	25·000	25·000	—	—	—	—	—
(29) White, coloured or velvet finished leathers whether covers are used or not (employer to find material for covers)	20·000	4·583	1·667	1·667	2·917	4·583	4·583
(30) Full bradding or nailing ...	12·083	—	—	—	—	—	—
(31) Bradding or nailing toe and joint	6·250	—	—	—	—	—	—
(32) Clinkered round	12·083	—	—	—	—	—	—
(33) Clinkered round toes	6·250	—	—	—	—	—	—
(34) Other extras as set out in paragraphs 72 and 75.							

Column 1	Completed work Column 2 Per pair p	Work on sectional system					
		Lasting Column 3 Per pair p	Hand sewing Column 4 Per pair p	Rounding Column 5 Per pair p	Heeling Column 6 Per pair p	Hand stitching Column 7 Per pair p	Finishing by hand Column 8 Per pair p
(c) LADIES' LONG WORK:							
(1) Patent uppers or fronts:							
When patent calf used ...	26·667	19·167	3·750				3·750
When patent leathers other than patent calf used ...	23·333	15·833	3·750				3·750
(2) Other extras the same as for "Men's long work" as set out in this paragraph and in paragraphs 72 and 75.							
(d) LADIES' SHORT WORK:							
(1) Cloth leg up to 7 inches ...	10·417	2·083	1·667	1·667	1·667	1·667	1·667
(2) Cloth leg over 7 inches ...	15·417	2·917	3·750	1·667	1·667	1·667	3·750
(3) Middle soles ...	10·000	—	—	2·917	—	5·417	1·667
(4) Welts above ¼ inch in width ...	10·000	—	3·750	1·667	—	1·667	2·917
(5) Heels above 1⅛ inches in height, for each ¼ inch or part of ¼ inch ...	5·417	—	—	—	3·750	—	1·667
(6) French corks ...	59·167	50·000	9·167	—	—	—	—
(7) Mock corks ...	46·667	40·417	6·250	—	—	—	—
(8) Inside corks, not surgical ...	19·583	19·583	—	—	—	—	—
(9) White, coloured or velvet finished leathers whether covers are used or not (employer to find material for covers) ...	13·750	2·917	1·667	1·667	1·667	2·917	2·917

72.—(1) Additional extras to ground work for bespoke hand sewn surgical work (including repairing) are set out in the following Table.

(2) For the purposes of (a) to (f) all measurements of the heights of corks are to be taken from the centre of the heel base or under the joint, whichever is the greater.

Column 1	Completed work	Work on sectional system				
		Preparing work ready for lasting (excluding covering)	Covering	Lasting	Sewing	Finishing by hand
	Column 2	Column 3	Column 4	Column 5	Column 6	Column 7
	Each	Each p	Each p	Each p	Each p	Each p
(a) Outside through cork (box randed):						
(1) Rising to 1 inch ...	£1·867	68·333	—	45·417	72·917	—
(2) For every additional half-inch or part thereof...	16·667p	10·833	—	2·917	2·917	—
(3) Bridge or arched waists, add ...	12·083p	—	—	—	9·167	2·917
(4) Steel bridge plate, fixing...	4·583p	—	—	—	—	—
(b) Outside through cork (randed other than box randed):						
(1) Rising to 1 inch ...	£1·458	48·750	—	29·167	67·917	—
(2) For every additional half-inch or part thereof...	16·667p	10·833	—	2·917	2·917	—
(3) Bridge or arched waists, add ...	12·083p	—	—	—	9·167	2·917
(4) Steel bridge plate, fixing...	4·583p	—	—	—	—	—
(c) Outside cork forepart:						
(1) Rising from joint to 1 inch ...	£1·050	32·083	—	21·250	51·667	—
(2) For every additional half-inch or part thereof...	10·000p	6·667	—	1·667	1·667	—
(d) Outside heel cork, cased:						
(1) Rising to 1 inch ...	35·000p	16·667	—	7·500	10·833	—
(2) For every additional half-inch or part thereof...	7·083p	3·750	—	1·667	1·667	—
(e) Through inside corks, covered:						
(1) Rising to 1 inch:						
(i) Loose ...	86·667p	54·583	9·167	18·333	4·583	—
(ii) Sewn ...	93·750p	38·750	9·167	27·500	18·333	—
(2) For every additional half-inch or part thereof...	22·917p	10·833	1·667	7·500	2·917	—

Column 1	Work on sectional system					
	Completed work	Preparing work ready for lasting (excluding covering)	Covering	Lasting	Sewing	Finishing by hand
	Column 2	Column 3	Column 4	Column 5	Column 6	Column 7
	Each p	Each p	Each p	Each p	Each p	Each p
(f) Inside heel cork, covered:						
(1) Rising to 1 inch:						
(i) Loose	59·167	32·083	7·500	16·667	2·917	—
(ii) Sewn in	68·750	32·500	7·500	19·583	9·167	—
(2) For every additional half-inch or part thereof	10·000	3·750	1·667	2·917	1·667	—
(g) Extra heel, loose cork fitted inside up to joint	35·000	—	—	—	—	—
(h) Cork fillers for Chopart's boots or false toe parts:						
(1) 2 inches long and over	30·000	22·500	7·500	—	—	—
(2) Under 2 inches long	14·167	7·500	6·667	—	—	—
(i) Fitting in brace or tack	25·000	—	—	15·000	10·000	—

	Each p
(j) Fitting heel round fixed iron heel stop (exclusive of riveting)...	10·000
(k) Stiffeners:	
(1) High stiffeners carried above ankle	12·083
(2) Double high stiffeners to cover each side of ankle ...	17·500
(3) Long stiffeners	4·483
(l) Completely filled in waist from heel to joint, completed job ...	35·000
(if not finished by maker, 5·833p each less)	
(m) (1) Meta bars (outside)	8·333
(2) ,, ,, (concealed)	12·083
(n) (1) Wedges or layers (either forepart or heel), sewn in... ...	4·583
(2) ,, ,, riveted on or sewn in made-up boot, on forepart, when not soled	8·333
(3) ,, ,, ,, in made-up boot, on heel, when not heeled ...	6·250
(4) Through wedges or layers from forepart to heel (including making up waist on stock boots)	26·667
(5) Where the wedge or layer sewn in is over ⅜ inch thick at the thickest point, 2·083p additional to above rates.	

	Each	Benching Each	Finishing Each	Each Side
	p	*p*	*p*	*p*
(o) (1) "T" straps ...	4·583			
(2) "T" straps if stabbed on to finished boot ...	8·333			
(p) "D" straps ...	4·583			
(q) Buckles ...	3·750			
(r) Sponge rubber insoles, cut, cemented to sock, inserted and, if required, cemented to leather insole ...	15·000			
(s) Valgus or Meta rubber pads with socks, fixing ...	8·333			
(t) Mechanical appliances:				
(1) Concealed ankle support springs (exclusive of riveting, see item (8) below) ...	17·500			
(2) Inserted metal arch supports (exclusive of riveting, see item (8) below) ...	17·500			
(3) Single or double sockets and fixed shoe pieces (exclusive of riveting, see item (8) below) ...	17·500			
(4) Sole or foot springs (exclusive of riveting, see item (8) below) ...	8·333			
(5) Fixing to heel and building round undetachable leg appliance ...	35·000			
(6) Riveting in socket, single or double ...	7·500			
(7) Taking down heel, fixing in socket by riveting, rebuilding heel and working over socket ...	25·000			

(8) For the work of riveting referred to in items (1) to (4) above, the worker must be paid the piece rates specified in paragraph 1(1)(*b*)(ii).

	Each	Benching Each	Finishing Each	Each Side
(u) Shaped oblique or elongated heels:				
(1) For an elongation up to and including ¼ inch ...	(No extra)			
(2) For an elongation exceeding ¼ inch but not exceeding 1 inch ...		3·750	1·667	
(3) For an elongation exceeding 1 inch but not extending more than half-way from the position of the ordinary heel to the joint ...		10·833	2·917	
(4) For an elongation extending more than half-way from the position of the ordinary heel to the joint ...		21·250	6·250	
(v) For any extra work involved in the building or re-building of a heel from the seat which is necessitated by the floating out of the heel above ¼ inch from the ordinary contour of the heel ...		3·750	1·667	

(w) Converting stock boot into surgical boot to be paid for on the basis of new work.

	Each Side
	p
(x) Sewing waist by hand where foreparts are stitched by machine ...	1·667

BESPOKE PEGGED WORK

73. The piece rates for all completed bespoke pegged work are *20p* per pair less than the rates for completed bespoke hand sewn work as set out in paragraph 70. The piece rates for extras to bespoke pegged work are the same as those set out in paragraphs 71 and 72 for the extras to hand sewn work.

BESPOKE RIVETED WORK

74. The piece rates for bespoke riveted work are set out in the following Table:—

—	Men's	Ladies' and Youths'	Boys' and Girls', sizes 11 to 1½	Boys' and Girls', sizes 7 to 10½
Column 1	Column 2	Column 3	Column 4	Column 5
	Per pair	Per pair	Per pair	Per pair
	p	*p*	*p*	*p*
(*a*) Benched (stuff cut by machinery)	*23·333*	*20·833*	*17·500*	*15·000*
(*b*) Finished by hand throughout ...	*13·333*	*8·333*	*5·833*	*5·000*
(*c*) Finished by hand (edges and heels only)	*8·333*	*5·833*	*4·167*	*3·750*
(*d*) Extras:—				
(i) Nailing or bradding soles by hand	*5·833*	*5·833*	*4·167*	*4·167*
(ii) Stuff not press cut... ...	*3·750*	*3·750*	*2·917*	*2·917*

(*e*) Light Bluchers (no cap):—

    (i) Putting-up ... ... *17·500p* per pair.
    (ii) Nailing or bradding ... ... *4·167p* per pair.
    (iii) Finishing by hand (edges and heels only) ... ... *7·917p* per pair.

Part XI

GENERAL

75.—(1) For each try on, or re-try on, outworkers shall be paid *13·333p* extra for one boot or shoe or pair of boots or shoes, and indoor workers, *6·667p* extra for one boot or shoe or pair of boots or shoes. These rates do not include bracing. Alterations (other than operations to which general minimum piece rates are applicable) are to be paid at the piece rates specified in paragraph 1(1)(*b*)(ii).

(2) Scafe or similar soles, *25p* per pair extra to the rates for completed work set out in paragraphs 70, 71 and 72.

(3) The minimum rates of wages specified in this Schedule do not include the cost of grindery.

76. Rates per pair—where a piece rate is specified in this Schedule as a rate per pair one-half of such rate shall be payable where only one boot or shoe is involved.

DEFINITIONS

77. (*a*) "German seat" is a piece of butt leather sewn round the heel.

(*b*) "Inside corks" are extra insoles of cork which are made with the boot.

(*c*) "Shaped toe piece" is a toe piece that is larger than the ordinary toe bit and extends along the side up to the joint.

(*d*) "Underlays" are inserted and slotted toe bits or side bits.

(*e*) "Grindery" is all material apart from tools used by the worker in the making or repairing of leather footwear.

(*f*) "Box randed"—a box rand is a rand which is made from a piece of bend, butt, fore-end, shoulder or belly leather.

EXPLANATORY NOTE

(*This Note is not part of the Order.*)

This Order, which has effect from 3rd March 1971, sets out the statutory minimum remuneration payable in substitution for that fixed by the Wages Regulation (Boot and Shoe Repairing) Order 1970 (Order D. (152)), which Order is revoked.

New provisions are printed in italics.

STATUTORY INSTRUMENTS

1971 No. 151

POLICE

The Police Cadets (Amendment) Regulations 1971

Made - - - -	*27th January* 1971
Laid before Parliament	*5th February* 1971
Coming into Operation	*15th February* 1971

In exercise of the powers conferred on me by section 35 of the Police Act 1964(a), and after consulting the Police Council for the United Kingdom in accordance with section 4(4) of the Police Act 1969(b), I hereby make the following Regulations:—

1. These Regulations may be cited as the Police Cadets (Amendment) Regulations 1971 and shall come into operation on 15th February 1971.

2. In these Regulations any reference to the principal Regulations is a reference to the Police Cadets Regulations 1968(c), as amended (d).

3. For Regulation 12(5) of the principal Regulations (calculation of pay and charges) there shall be substituted the following provision :—

"(5) In making any such payment as is referred to in paragraph (1) a fraction of a new penny shall be treated as a whole penny except that a fraction less than a half-penny shall be ignored.".

4. In Regulation 14(1) of the principal Regulations (travel allowances) for the sum "7s. 6d." there shall be substituted the sum "£0·40".

R. Maudling,
One of Her Majesty's Principal
Secretaries of State.

Home Office,
Whitehall.
27th January 1971.

EXPLANATORY NOTE
(This Note is not part of the Regulations.)

These Regulations amend Regulations 12 and 14 of the Police Cadets Regulations 1968. Regulation 12 relates to the calculation of pay and charges ; fresh provision is made as to the reckoning of fractions of a penny. Regulation 14 provides, in certain cases, for the payment of travel allowances in respect of return journeys costing more than 7s. 6d.; for this sum there is substituted the sum of £0·40.

(a) 1964 c. 48.
(c) S.I. 1968/25 (1968 I, p. 31).

(b) 1969 c. 63.
(d) The relevant amending instrument is S.I. 1969/408 (1969 I, p. 1150).

STATUTORY INSTRUMENTS

1971 No. 152

NATIONAL HEALTH SERVICE, ENGLAND AND WALES

HOSPITAL AND SPECIALIST SERVICES

The National Health Service (Designation of Teaching Hospitals) Amendment (No. 1) Order 1971

Made - - -	*28th January* 1971
Coming into Operation	*1st October* 1971

The Secretary of State for Social Services, in exercise of his powers under sections 11 and 75 of the National Health Service Act 1946(a) and of all other powers enabling him in that behalf, and after consultation with the University of Newcastle upon Tyne, for which University it appears to him that facilities for undergraduate or post-graduate clinical teaching are provided by the United Newcastle upon Tyne Hospitals, hereby orders as follows:—

1. This order may be cited as the National Health Service (Designation of Teaching Hospitals) Amendment (No. 1) Order 1971, and shall come into operation on 1st October 1971.

2.—(1) In this order—

"the Act" means the National Health Service Act 1946;

"the appointed day" means 1st October 1971;

"the Board of Governors" means the Board of Governors of the United Newcastle upon Tyne Hospitals;

"the Hospital Board" means the Newcastle Regional Hospital Board;

"the Management Committee" means the Newcastle University Hospital Management Committee.

(2) The Interpretation Act 1889(b) shall apply to the interpretation of this order as it applies to the interpretation of an Act of Parliament.

3. The National Health Service (Designation of Teaching Hospitals) Order 1959(c) as amended (d) shall be further amended by the deletion from Schedule 1 (list of teaching hospitals) of the words "The United Newcastle upon Tyne Hospitals" in column (1) and the words relating thereto in columns (2) and (3).

(a) 1946 c. 81.   (b) 1889 c. 63.   (c) S.I. 1959/748 (1951 I, p. 1813).

(d) There is no amendment which relates expressly to the subject matter of this Order.

4.—(1) The Board of Governors is hereby dissolved.

(2) In paragraph 6 of the National Health Service (Constitution of Boards of Governors of Teaching Hospitals) (No. 1) Order 1948 the words "The United Newcastle upon Tyne Hospitals" and the list of members with particulars of their appointment set out thereunder shall be deleted.

(3) In the Schedule to the said order the words "The United Newcastle upon Tyne Hospitals" in column 1 and the figures relating thereto in column 2 shall be deleted.

5.—(1) Any property held immediately before the appointed day under section 7 or under section 59 of the Act by the Board of Governors for purposes relating to hospital services or to the functions of the Board of Governors with respect to research shall on that day be transferred to and vest without further conveyance in the Management Committee.

(2) Any property held immediately before the appointed day under section 60 of the Act by the Board of Governors shall on that day be transferred to and vest without further conveyance in the Management Committee.

6. Any other property held immediately before the appointed day by the Board of Governors and all rights and liabilities to which the Board of Governors were entitled or subject immediately before the appointed day, other than rights and liabilities arising from any building or civil engineering works the estimated total cost of which exceeds £120,000, shall on that day be transferred to and vest in the Management Committee.

7. All rights and liabilities to which the Board of Governors were entitled or subject immediately before the appointed day arising from any building or civil engineering works the estimated cost of which exceeds £120,000, shall on that day be transferred to and vest in the Hospital Board.

8. All officers employed by the Board of Governors immediately before the appointed day shall on that day be transferred to and become officers of the Hospital Board.

9. The Management Committee shall be responsible for closing the accounts of the Board of Governors and with respect to these accounts references in regulation 13 of the National Health Service (Hospital Accounts and Financial Provisions) Regulations 1969**(a)** to "the chief financial officer" and "the hospital authority" shall be deemed respectively to be references to the chief financial officer of the Management Committee and to the Management Committee.

10. Any pending proceedings to which the Board of Governors are a party relating to any property, rights or liabilities transferred under the aforesaid provisions of this order and pending at the appointed day shall not be prejudicially affected by reason of such transfer, but any such proceedings shall be amended in such manner as may appear necessary or proper for enabling them

---

(a) S.I. 1969/1582 (1969 III, p. 5051).

to be prosecuted and enforced by or against the Hospital Board or the Management Committee to which the property, rights or liabilities were transferred.

Signed by authority of the Secretary of State for Social Services.

J. S. Orme,
Under Secretary,
Department of Health and Social Security.

28th January 1971.

EXPLANATORY NOTE

(This Note is not part of the Order.)

This Order revokes the designation of the group of hospitals known as the United Newcastle upon Tyne Hospitals as a teaching hospital by amending the National Health Service (Designation of Teaching Hospitals) Order 1959. The order dissolves the Board of Governors of the United Newcastle upon Tyne Hospitals and amends consequently the National Health Service (Constitution of Board of Governors of Teaching Hospitals (No. 1)) Order 1948. The order also provides for consequential matters relating to officers and property connected with the aforementioned group of hospitals.

STATUTORY INSTRUMENTS

1971 No. 154

CUSTOMS AND EXCISE

The Anti-Dumping Duty Order 1971

Made - - - -	*29th January* 1971
Laid before the House of Commons	*29th January* 1971
Coming into Operation	*31st January* 1971

The Secretary of State, in exercise of the powers conferred upon him by sections 1 and 2 of the Customs Duties (Dumping and Subsidies) Act 1969(a), hereby makes the following Order:—

1. This Order may be cited as the Anti-Dumping Duty Order 1971 and shall come into operation on 31st January 1971.

2. There shall be charged on the import into the United Kingdom of any goods of the description set out in the Schedule hereto (being goods classified in the Customs Tariff 1959(b) under the heading mentioned in the first column of that Schedule) a duty of customs at the rate mentioned in the third column.

3. Section 2 of the Customs Duties (Dumping and Subsidies) Act 1969 (which allows relief to be given where goods are shown not to have been dumped or where the margin of dumping is less than the amount of the duty) shall apply to the duty imposed by this Order.

Nicholas Ridley,
Parliamentary Under-Secretary of State,
Department of Trade and Industry.

29th January 1971.

SCHEDULE

Relevant Tariff Heading	Description of Goods	Rate of Duty
ex 97.02	Moving eyes for dolls, other than eyes made of glass, originating in the United States of America and being products of Jacoby-Bender Incorporated (trading as the Dollac Company of New York) or the Margon Corporation of New Jersey.	6d. [2½p] per pair.

(a) 1969 c. 16.   (b) See S.I. 1970/1522 (1970 III, p. 4935).

EXPLANATORY NOTE

(This Note is not part of the Order.)

This Order continues an anti-dumping duty on moving eyes for dolls made by Jacoby-Bender Incorporated (trading as the Dollac Company of New York) or by the Margon Corporation of New Jersey.

The Order applies section 2 of the Customs Duties (Dumping and Subsidies) Act 1969 to the duty. This section enables relief to be granted where particular goods have not been dumped or the margin of dumping is shown to be less than the amount of duty payable.

STATUTORY INSTRUMENTS

1971 No. 155

PURCHASE TAX
The Purchase Tax (No. 1) Order 1971

Made - - -	*29th January* 1971
Laid before the House of Commons	*29th January* 1971
Coming into Operation	*1st February* 1971

The Lords Commissioners of Her Majesty's Treasury, by virtue of the powers conferred on them by section 2(3) of the Purchase Tax Act 1963(a), and of all other powers enabling them in that behalf, hereby make the following Order :—

1.—(1) This Order may be cited as the Purchase Tax (No. 1) Order 1971.

(2) The Interpretation Act 1889(b) shall apply for the interpretation of this Order as it applies for the interpretation of an Act of Parliament.

(3) This Order shall come into operation on 1st February 1971.

2. In Group 9 of Part I of Schedule 1 to the Purchase Tax Act 1963, in paragraph (*a*)(ii), after the words "three-eighths of an inch" there shall be inserted the words "or, if ceramic, of less than one-quarter of an inch".

3. In Group 26 of Part I of Schedule 1 to the Purchase Tax Act 1963, after paragraph (1) of the heading "Exempt", there shall be inserted the following paragraph :—

(2) Envelopes, being more than $9\frac{1}{4}$ inches long and more than $4\frac{3}{4}$ inches wide.

P. L. Hawkins,

V. H. Goodhew,

Two of the Lords Commissioners
of Her Majesty's Treasury.

29th January 1971.

EXPLANATORY NOTE
(This Note is not part of the Order.)

This Order amends the Schedule of goods chargeable with purchase tax.
It excludes from the tax certain ceramic floor tiles.
It relieves from the tax certain large envelopes.

(a) 1963 c. 9. (b) 1889 c. 63.

STATUTORY INSTRUMENTS

1971 No. 156

POLICE

The Police Regulations 1971

Made - - - -	*28th January* 1971
Laid before Parliament	*10th February* 1971
Coming into Operation	*15th February* 1971

ARRANGEMENT OF REGULATIONS

PART I

CITATION, OPERATION, REVOCATIONS AND INTERPRETATION

PART II

GOVERNMENT

ORGANISATION

APPOINTMENT, PROMOTION AND RETIREMENT

Schedule 6—Detective duty and supplementary detective allowances.

Schedule 7—Subsistence, refreshment and lodging allowances.

Schedule 8—Motor vehicle allowances in respect of motor cars.

Schedule 9—Bicycle allowance.

Schedule 10—Typewriter allowance.

Schedule 11—Issue of uniform and equipment.

In exercise of the powers conferred on me by section 33 of the Police Act 1964(a), and after consulting the Police Council for the United Kingdom in accordance with section 4(4) of the Police Act 1969(b) and the Police Advisory Board for England and Wales in accordance with section 46(3) of the said Act of 1964 as amended by section 4(6) of the said Act of 1969, I hereby make the following Regulations:—

PART I

CITATION, OPERATION, REVOCATIONS AND INTERPRETATION

Citation and operation

1. These Regulations may be cited as the Police Regulations 1971 and shall come into operation on 15th February 1971.

Revocations and amendments

2.—(1) The Regulations set out in Part I of Schedule 1 are hereby revoked save for the purposes of regulating pay and allowances in respect of a period before the coming into operation of these Regulations; and for those purposes they shall have effect subject to the provisions of Part II of Schedule 1.

(2) Section 38 of the Interpretation Act 1889(c) shall apply as if these Regulations were an Act of Parliament and as if any Regulations revoked by these Regulations were Acts of Parliament repealed by an Act of Parliament.

References to transfers

3.—(1) Except where the context otherwise requires, a reference in these Regulations to a member of a police force voluntarily transferring from one force to another shall be construed as a reference to such a member leaving a force for the purpose of joining another force and joining that other force, where—

(*a*) he left the force first mentioned in this Regulation on or after 1st January 1963 for the purposes aforesaid with, in the case of the chief officer of police, the consent of the police authority;

(*b*) he left the force first mentioned in this Regulation before 1st January 1963 for the purposes aforesaid—

(i) in the case of the chief officer of police, with the consent of the police authority,

(ii) in any other case, with written consent of the chief officer of police.

(2) Except where the context otherwise requires, a reference in these Regulations to a member of a police force being statutorily transferred from one force to another shall be construed as a reference to such a member being transferred—

(a) 1964 c. 48.　　　　　　　　　　(b) 1969 c. 63.

(c) 1889 c. 63.

(*a*) by or under the Local Government Act 1933(**a**), the Police Act 1946(**b**), the Local Government Act 1958(**c**), the London Government Act 1963(**d**) or the Police Act 1964, or

(*b*) in the case of a person who was a member of the River Tyne police force, under the Harbours Act 1964(**e**).

(3) Except where the context otherwise requires, a reference in these Regulations to a member of a police force transferring from one force to another shall be construed as a reference to his either voluntarily so transferring or being statutorily so transferred.

References to provisions of these Regulations, to other instruments and to enactments

4.—(1) In these Regulations, unless the context otherwise requires, a reference to a Regulation shall be construed as a reference to a Regulation contained in these Regulations, a reference to a Schedule shall be construed as a reference to a Schedule to these Regulations, a reference to a paragraph shall be construed as a reference to a paragraph in the same Regulation or, as the case may be, the same Part of the same Schedule and a reference to a sub-paragraph shall be construed as a reference to a sub-paragraph contained in the same paragraph.

(2) In these Regulations, unless the context otherwise requires, a reference to any enactment or instrument shall be construed as including a reference to that enactment or instrument as amended, extended or applied by any other enactment or instrument.

Application of Interpretation Act 1889

5. The Interpretation Act 1889 shall apply for the interpretation of these Regulations as it applies for the interpretation of an Act of Parliament.

Meanings assigned to certain expressions

6.—(1) In these Regulations, unless the context otherwise requires, the following expressions have the meanings hereby respectively assigned to them, that is to say:—

"auxiliary policeman" means a member of the first class of the police reserve, a member of the Police War Reserve, or a member of the Women's Auxiliary Police Corps;

"central police officer" has the same meaning as in the Police Pensions Regulations;

"Discipline Regulations" means the regulations relating to discipline from time to time in force under section 33 of the Police Act 1964;

"inspector" includes chief inspector;

"overseas policeman" has the same meaning as in the Police Pensions Regulations;

"penny" means a new penny;

"pensionable service" has the same meaning as in the Police Pensions Regulations;

"Police Pensions Regulations" means the regulations from time to time in force under the Police Pensions Act 1948(**f**);

(a) 1933 c. 51.   (b) 1946 c. 46.
(c) 1958 c. 55.   (d) 1963 c. 33.
(e) 1964 c. 40.   (f) 1948 c. 24.

"Promotion **Regulations**" means the regulations relating to qualification and selection for promotion from time to time in force under section 4 of the Police Act 1919**(a)** or section 33 of the Police Act 1964;

"public holiday" means Christmas Day, Good Friday or a bank holiday;

"reversionary member of a home police force" has the same meaning as in the Police Pensions Regulations;

"sergeant" includes station sergeant and first class and second class sergeant (C.I.D.);

"superintendent" includes chief superintendent, superintendent (class I) and superintendent (class II);

"university scholar" and, in relation to such a scholar, "course" and "study" have the meanings respectively assigned to them in paragraph 1 of Schedule 4.

(2) In these Regulations, unless the context otherwise requires, a reference to a police force shall include a reference to a police force maintained under the Police (Scotland) Act 1967**(b)**, so however that nothing in these Regulations shall be construed as relating to the government, administration or conditions of service of such a force.

PART II
GOVERNMENT
ORGANISATION

Authorised establishment

7. The authorised establishment of the several ranks of a police force and any changes thereto shall be subject to the approval of the Secretary of State and shall be sufficient to provide for the carrying out of police duties under responsible supervision in each tour of duty.

Ranks

8.—(1) The ranks of a police force shall be known by the following designations:—

Chief Constable

Superintendent, Class I

Superintendent, Class II

Inspector

Sergeant

Constable:

Provided that in a police force where varying degrees of responsibility render intermediate ranks necessary, any of the following ranks may be adopted subject to the approval of the Secretary of State:—

Assistant Chief Constable or Commander

Chief Superintendent

Chief Inspector

Station Sergeant

First Class Sergeant (C.I.D.)

Second Class Sergeant (C.I.D.)

(a) 1919 c. 46.   (b) 1967 c. 77.

(2) Notwithstanding anything in paragraph (1), in the metropolitan police force ranks other than those specified in that paragraph may be adopted with the approval of the Secretary of State.

Beats, sections, sub-divisions and divisions

9. The area to which a constable is assigned for duty either generally or for a particular period of hours shall be known as a beat; a number of beats grouped for supervision by a sergeant or an inspector shall be known as a section; a number of sections grouped for supervision by an inspector shall be known as a sub-division; a number of sections or sub-divisions grouped for supervision by a superintendent or, in a borough police force by a member of the police force directly responsible to the chief officer of police, shall be known as a division.

Restrictions on the private life of members

10. The restrictions on private life contained in Schedule 2 shall apply to all members of a police force; and no restrictions other than those designed to secure the proper exercise of the functions of a constable shall be imposed by the police authority or the chief officer of police on the private life of members of a police force except such as may temporarily be necessary or such as may be approved by the Secretary of State after consultation with the Police Advisory Board for England and Wales, and any such restriction temporarily imposed shall be reported forthwith to the Secretary of State.

Business interests incompatible with membership of a police force

11.—(1) If a member of a police force or a relative included in his family proposes to have, or has, a business interest within the meaning of this Regulation, the member shall forthwith give written notice of that interest to the chief officer of police unless that business interest was disclosed to the chief officer of police at the time of his appointment as a member of the force.

(2) On receipt of a notice given under paragraph (1), the chief officer of police shall determine whether or not the interest in question is compatible with the member concerned remaining a member of the force and shall notify the member in writing of his decision.

(3) Within 10 days of being notified of the chief officer's decision as aforesaid, or within such longer period as the police authority may in all the circumstances allow, the member concerned may appeal to the police authority against that decision by sending written notice of his appeal to the police authority.

(4) Where a member of a police force, or a relative included in his family, has a business interest within the meaning of this Regulation which the chief officer of police has determined, under paragraph (2), to be incompatible with his remaining a member of the force and either the member has not appealed against that decision under paragraph (3) or, on such appeal, the police authority has upheld that decision, then, the chief officer of police may, subject to the approval of the police authority, dispense with the services of that member; and before giving such approval, the police authority shall give the member concerned an opportunity to make representations and shall consider any representations so made.

(5) For the purposes of this Regulation, a person or, as the case may be, a relative included in his family, shall have a business interest if—

(*a*) the person holds any office or employment for hire or gain (otherwise than as a member of a police force) or carries on any business;

(*b*) a shop is kept or a like business carried on by the person's spouse (not being separated from him) at any premises in the area of the police force in question or by any relative included in his family at the premises at which he resides, or

(*c*) the person, his spouse (not being separated from him) or any relative included in his family living with him holds, or possesses a pecuniary interest in, any such licence or permit as is mentioned in paragraph (6).

(6) The licence or permit referred to in paragraph (5)(*c*) is a licence or permit granted in pursuance of the law relating to liquor licensing or betting and gaming or regulating places of entertainment in the area of the police force in question.

(7) For the purposes of this Regulation, a reference to a relative included in a person's family shall include a reference to his spouse, parent, son, daughter, brother or sister.

(8) In its application to a chief constable, deputy chief constable or assistant chief constable, this Regulation shall have effect as if—

(*a*) for any reference in paragraph (1), (2), (3) or (4) to the chief officer of police, except in relation to such a disclosure as is mentioned in paragraph (1) made at the time of the person's appointment as a member of the force in a rank below that of assistant chief constable, there were substituted a reference to the police authority;

(*b*) for any reference in paragraph (3) or (4) to an appeal there were substituted a reference to a request for reconsideration, and

(*c*) the references in paragraph (4) to the approval of the police authority were omitted;

but a police authority shall not dispense with the services of a chief constable, deputy chief constable or assistant chief constable under this Regulation without giving him an opportunity of making representations and shall consider any representations so made.

APPOINTMENT, PROMOTION AND RETIREMENT

Business interests precluding appointment to a police force

12.—(1) Save in so far as the chief officer of police may allow at the request of the candidate concerned, a person shall not be eligible for appointment to a police force if he or a relative included in his family has a business interest within the meaning of Regulation 11, and paragraphs (5), (6) and (7) thereof shall apply for the purposes of the interpretation of this Regulation as they apply for the purposes of that Regulation.

(2) In its application to a candidate for appointment as chief officer of police or in the rank of assistant chief constable, paragraph (1) shall have effect as if for any reference to the chief officer of police there were substituted a reference to the police authority.

Qualifications for appointment to a police force

13.—(1) A candidate for appointment to a police force—

(*a*) must produce satisfactory references as to character, and, if he has served in any police force, in the armed forces, in the civil service or as a seaman, produce satisfactory proof of his good conduct while so serving;

(b) must have attained 19 years of age and not have attained, in the case of a man, 30 years of age or, in the case of a woman, 35 years of age:

Provided that a man or a woman who has attained 30 or 35 years of age, as the case may be, may be appointed—

(i) if he or she has had previous service in a police force otherwise than as an auxiliary policeman, or is otherwise entitled to reckon previous service as pensionable service,

(ii) if he or she has not attained 40 years of age and since attaining the age of 30 or 35 years of age, as the case may be, has performed whole-time service in the armed forces or served as a seaman, or

(iii) in other special circumstances approved by the Secretary of State upon the recommendation of the appointing authority, that is to say, the chief officer of police or the police authority, as the case may be;

(c) must be certified by a registered medical practitioner approved by the police authority to be in good health, of sound constitution and fitted both physically and mentally to perform the duties on which he will be employed after appointment;

(d) must, if a candidate for appointment in the rank of constable—

(i) unless the chief officer of police otherwise decides, be not less in height than, in the case of a man, 5 feet 8 inches, or in the case of a woman, 5 feet 4 inches, and

(ii) satisfy the chief officer of police that he is sufficiently educated by passing a written or oral examination in reading, writing and simple arithmetic, or an examination of a higher standard, as may be prescribed by the chief officer of police;

(e) must give such information as may be required as to his previous history or employment or any other matter relating to his appointment to the police force;

(f) shall be given a notice in terms approved by the Secretary of State drawing attention to the conditions of service contained therein.

(2) For the purposes of this Regulation—

(a) the expression "armed forces" means the naval, military or air forces of the Crown including any women's service administered by the Defence Council, and

(b) the expression "seaman" has the same meaning as in the Merchant Shipping Act 1894(a).

Appointment of chief constable

14. Every appointment to the office of chief constable shall be subject to the approval of the Secretary of State, and, without prejudice to Regulations 12 and 13, no person shall be appointed to such a post in a police force unless he has at least 2 years' experience in some other force in the rank of inspector or a higher rank.

Probationary service in the rank of constable

15.—(1) This Regulation shall apply to a member of a police force appointed

(a) 1894 c. 60.

in the rank of constable other than such a member who transferred to the force from another police force, having completed the required period of probation therein.

(2) A member of a police force to whom this Regulation applies shall, unless paragraph (3) applies in his case, be on probation for the first 2 years of his service as a constable in that police force following his last appointment thereto.

(3) A member of a police force to whom this Regulation applies who has served on probation for a period of not less than a year following a previous appointment to that or any other police force shall be on probation for the first year of his service as a constable in the police force first mentioned in this paragraph following his last appointment thereto:

Provided that the chief officer of police may at his discretion—

- (a) reduce the period of probation, so however that the reduced period, when aggregated with the previous period of probation, shall not be less than 2 years, or

- (b) dispense with the period of probation, if the member, following his previous appointment, completed the required period of probation in the force in question.

(4) Notwithstanding anything in paragraph (2) or (3), in the case of a member of a police force who has served as an auxiliary policeman for a period of not less than 2 years, the chief officer of police may dispense with the period of probation.

(5) For the purposes of this Regulation—

- (a) in the case of a woman, in reckoning service, any period of unpaid maternity leave shall be disregarded;

- (b) in the case of a university scholar whose course begins on or after 15th February 1971, in reckoning service his period of study shall be disregarded;

- (c) in the case of a member who has been statutorily transferred from one force to some other force, his service in those two forces shall be treated as if it were service in the same police force.

Discharge of probationer

16.—(1) Subject to the provisions of this Regulation, during his period of probation in the force the services of a constable may be dispensed with at any time if the chief officer of police considers that he is not fitted, physically or mentally, to perform the duties of his office, or that he is not likely to become an efficient or well conducted constable.

(2) A constable whose services are dispensed with under this Regulation shall be entitled to receive a month's notice or a month's pay in lieu thereof.

(3) A constable's services shall not be dispensed with in accordance with this Regulation and any notice given for the purposes thereof shall cease to have effect if he gives written notice to the police authority of his intention to retire and retires in pursuance of the said notice on or before the date on which his services would otherwise be dispensed with; and such a notice taking effect on that date shall be accepted by the police authority notwithstanding that less than a month's notice is given.

Retirement

17.—(1) Without prejudice to the provisions mentioned in paragraph (3), a member of a police force may retire only if he has given to the police authority a month's written notice of his intention to retire or such shorter notice as may have been accepted by that authority:

Provided that, while suspended under the Discipline Regulations, a member may not, without the consent of the chief officer of police, give notice for the purposes of this Regulation or retire in pursuance of a notice previously given.

(2) In the case of a chief officer of police, deputy chief constable or assistant chief constable, the preceding paragraph shall have effect as if for the reference to the chief officer of police there were substituted a reference to the police authority.

(3) The provisions referred to in paragraph (1) are—

    (*a*) the provisions of sections 5 and 6 of the Police Act 1964 relating to retirement in the interests of efficiency;

    (*b*) the provisions of section 58(3) of the Police Act 1964 relating to the retirement of chief constables affected by amalgamations or local government reorganisation;

    (*c*) the provisions of the Police Pensions Regulations relating to compulsory retirement, and

    (*d*) the provisions of the Discipline Regulations relating to resignation as an alternative to dismissal.

PERSONAL RECORDS

Contents of personal records

18.—(1) The chief officer of police shall cause a personal record of each member of the police force to be kept.

(2) The personal record shall contain—

    (*a*) a personal description of the member;

    (*b*) particulars of the member's place and date of birth;

    (*c*) particulars of his marriage (if any) and of his children (if any);

    (*d*) a record of his service (if any) in any branch of Her Majesty's naval, military or air forces or in the civil service;

    (*e*) a record of his service (if any) in any other police force (including service as an auxiliary policeman) and of his transfers (if any) from one police force to another;

    (*f*) a record of whether he passed or failed to pass any qualifying examination at which he was a candidate;

    (*g*) a record of his service in the police force including particulars of all promotions, postings, removals, injuries received, periods of illness, commendations, rewards, punishments other than cautions, and the date of his ceasing to be a member of the police force with the reason, cause or manner thereof:

Provided that, if the member so requests—

    (i) a punishment of a fine not exceeding 2 days' pay or of a reprimand shall be expunged after 3 years free from punishment, other than a caution;

(ii) any other punishment shall be expunged after 7 years free from punishment other than a caution.

(3) A member of a police force shall, if he so requests, be entitled to inspect his personal record.

Transfer of personal records

19. Where a member of a police force transfers to another police force his personal record shall be transferred to the chief officer of police of that other police force.

Personal record of member leaving force

20.—(1) Where a member of a police force ceases to be a member of that police force the member shall, unless he transfers to another police force, be given a certificate showing his rank and setting out the period of his service in that police force and in any other police force and the reason, cause or manner of his leaving the force, together with particulars of his personal description:

Provided that, where the member was required to resign or was dismissed, the certificate shall not contain any description of the circumstances in which he was required to resign or was dismissed.

(2) The chief officer of police may append to the certificate any recommendation which he feels justified in giving, such as that—

his conduct was exemplary;

his conduct was very good;

his conduct was good.

(3) Where a member of a police force ceases to be a member of that police force, otherwise than by transferring to another police force, his personal record shall be kept for such time as the chief officer of police may think fit and shall then be destroyed.

Fingerprints

21.—(1) Every member of a police force shall in accordance with the directions of the chief officer of police have his fingerprints taken.

(2) Fingerprints of members of a police force taken in accordance with paragraph (1) shall be kept separate from the fingerprints of persons whose fingerprints have been taken in pursuance of any enactment.

(3) The fingerprints of a member of a police force taken in accordance with paragraph (1) and all copies and records thereof shall be destroyed on his ceasing to be a member of that force, except that, where by reason of a statutory transfer he becomes a member of another force, his fingerprints and all copies and records thereof shall be transferred to the chief officer of police of that other police force.

Part III

Duty, Overtime and Leave

Duty to carry out lawful orders

22. Every member of a police force shall carry out all lawful orders and shall at all times punctually and promptly perform all appointed duties and attend to all matters within the scope of his office as a constable.

Limitations on duties to be assigned to members statutorily transferred

23.—(1) Where a member of a county or combined police force has been a member of a police force for a borough comprised in whole or in part in the county or combined area and he ceased to be a member of the borough force and became a member of the county or combined force by reason only of one or more statutory transfers, then, subject to paragraph (3), he shall while a member of the county or combined police force not be assigned to duties which, in the opinion of the Secretary of State, make it necessary for him to move his home to a place which is outside the area for which the borough force was maintained.

(2) Without prejudice to paragraph (1), where a member of a combined police force has been a member of a police force for an area, other than a borough, comprised in whole or in part in the combined area (hereafter in this paragraph referred to as "the former force") and he ceased to be a member of the former force and became a member of the combined force by reason only of the provisions of one or more amalgamation schemes under the Police Act 1964, then, subject to paragraph (3), he shall, while a member of the combined police force not be assigned to duties which, in the opinion of the Secretary of State, make it necessary for him to move his home to a place which is outside the area for which the former force was maintained.

(3) Paragraph (1) or, as the case may be, paragraph (2) shall not apply to such a member of a police force as is mentioned in the paragraph in question if, since he became a member of the borough police force or, as the case may be, of the county police force—

    (*a*) he has been a chief officer of police, or

    (*b*) he has given written notice to the chief officer of police of the police force of which he was at the time a member of his desire that paragraph (1) or, as the case may be, paragraph (2) should cease to apply to him,

and paragraph (2) shall not apply to such a member as is mentioned in that paragraph if before 1st February 1968 he was assigned to such duties as are there mentioned.

(4) Paragraph (1) or, as the case may be, paragraph (2) shall apply in the case of a member of a police force who ceased to be such and became a serviceman, a reversionary member of a home police force or a central police officer—

    (*a*) where on ceasing to be such, he resumed service in, or, as the case may be, exercised his right of reversion to, his former force, as if he had not ceased to be a member of that force, or

    (*b*) where on ceasing to be such, he resumed service in, or, as the case may be, exercised his right of reversion to some other force to which members of his former force had been transferred as mentioned in the paragraph in question, as if he had been so transferred from his former force to that other force.

Normal daily period of duty

24.—(1) This Regulation shall apply to every member of a police force below the rank of superintendent who is not assigned to duties which the Secretary of State has specially excepted from the provisions of this Regulation.

(2) The normal daily period of duty (including the period for refreshment referred to in paragraph (3)) of a member of a police force to whom this Regulation applies shall be 8 hours and, in addition, any time occupied in reporting at the appointed place for duty before a tour of duty begins:

Provided that in the case of a woman member, where the duty is wholly or mainly patrol duty, the police authority may substitute 7 hours or $7\frac{1}{2}$ hours for the said 8 hours.

(3) Where the normal daily period of duty is performed in one tour of duty an interval of 45 minutes shall normally be allowed for refreshment:

Provided that in the case of a woman member, where the duty is wholly or mainly patrol duty and the normal period of duty, other than the time occupied in reporting for duty, is $7\frac{1}{2}$ hours or more, the said interval shall normally be an hour.

Overtime

25.—(1) Subject to the provisions of this Regulation, where a member of a police force to whom Regulation 24 applies, other than a member who is paid a detective duty allowance, remains on duty after his tour of duty ends or is recalled to duty between 2 tours of duty, he shall be granted, if and as soon as the exigencies of duty in the opinion of the chief officer of police permit, in respect of each unit of time during which he so remains on duty after his tour of duty ends or after being so recalled (hereafter in these Regulations referred to as "overtime") an equal period of time off and in addition for each 3 units of overtime in any week an additional quarter of an hour of time off.

(2) If in respect of the overtime during any week time off is not granted within such time (not exceeding 3 months) after that week as the chief officer of police may fix, the member, if he is below the rank of inspector, shall be granted for each unit of overtime worked during that week for which time off has not been granted an allowance of a twenty-fourth of a day's pay, so, however, that in making any payment by way of such allowance a fraction of a penny shall be treated as a whole penny except that a fraction less than a half-penny shall be ignored; and after the time so fixed any right to time off in respect of that week shall cease.

(3) In computing any period of overtime for the purposes of this Regulation—

(*a*) where the member is engaged in casual escort duty, account shall be taken only of—

(i) the time during which he is in charge of the person under escort,

(ii) such other time as is necessarily spent in travelling to or from the place where the member is to take charge of, or hand over, the person under escort, as the case may be, and

(iii) any other time that may be allowed by the chief officer of police, so however that, if the member is so engaged overnight and has proper sleeping accommodation, whether in a train or otherwise, the chief officer of police may exclude such period, not exceeding 8 hours, during which the member is not in charge of the person under escort as he considers appropriate in the circumstances;

(*b*) where the tour or tours of duty does not or do not amount in the aggregate to more than the normal daily period of duty, no account shall be taken of any overtime except so much as together with the tour or tours of duty exceeds the normal daily period of duty;

(*c*) no account shall be taken of any overtime for which the member receives an allowance under Regulation 60 or 63;

(*d*) where a member is recalled to duty, the period of overtime shall include the time occupied by the member in going from and returning to his home not exceeding such reasonable limit as may be fixed by the chief officer of police;

(e) where a member has completed a full tour of night duty which ends at any time after 2 a.m. and before 10 a.m. and is recalled to duty before $9\frac{1}{2}$ hours have elapsed from the time when such tour of duty ended, he shall be deemed, if the period of overtime worked on that occasion amounts to less than 16 units of overtime to have worked in respect of that period a period of overtime equal to 16 units of overtime, and

(f) no account shall be taken of any casual overtime except as authorised by paragraph (4).

(4) A member shall for any period of not less than 2 units of casual overtime be granted, if and as soon as the exigencies of duty in the opinion of the chief officer of police permit, time off of 20 minutes for each such unit if in any fortnight the aggregate number of units of casual overtime, excluding any period of less than 2 units, is not less than 12.

(5) In respect of any overtime worked on any special occasion by an inspector, other than an inspector who is paid a detective duty allowance, paragraph (2) shall apply as it applies to overtime worked by members below the rank of inspector.

(6) Where on any special occasion a member below the rank of superintendent who is paid a detective duty allowance is required to do duty in connection with that special occasion, then, if he remains on such duty beyond the normal daily period of duty, he shall be entitled in respect of such overtime to time off in accordance with paragraph (1) or an allowance in lieu thereof in accordance with paragraph (2).

(7) For the purposes of this Regulation the following expressions shall have the meanings hereby respectively assigned to them, that is to say:—

"casual overtime" means a period of overtime of less than 4 units during which a member remains on duty after his tour of duty ends, other than a period in respect of which the member was informed at the commencement of his tour that he would be required to remain on duty after his tour ended;

"a day's pay" means a week's pay divided by 5;

"fortnight" means that period of 14 days beginning with such day as is fixed by the chief officer of police;

"member recalled to duty" does not include a member who is only warned to be in readiness for duty if required;

"special occasion" means an occasion designated as a special occasion for the purposes of this Regulation by the chief officer of police;

"unit" means a complete quarter of an hour;

"week" means that period of 7 days beginning with such day as is fixed by the chief officer of police.

Public holidays and rest days for lower ranks

26.—(1) This Regulation shall apply to every member of a police force below the rank of superintendent.

(2) Such a member shall, so far as the exigencies of duty permit, be allowed a day's leave on each public holiday and be granted rest days at the rate of two rest days in respect of each week.

(3) Such a member who is required to do duty on a public holiday or on a day which would otherwise have been a rest day shall be granted, if and as soon as the exigencies of duty permit, time off equal to $1\frac{1}{2}$ times the period of completed quarters of an hour of duty on each such day.

(4) If in the opinion of the chief officer of police the exigencies of duty do not permit the grant of time off under the last preceding paragraph within such time (not exceeding 3 months) as he may fix, the member shall be granted in lieu of time off an allowance at the rate of 3 sixty-fourths of a day's pay for each quarter of an hour of duty on each such day, so, however, that in making any payment by way of such allowance a fraction of a penny shall be treated as a whole penny except that a fraction less than a half-penny shall be ignored.

(5) For the purposes of this Regulation—

    (a) a member of a police force who is paid a detective duty allowance in respect of duty on a public holiday or on a day which would otherwise have been a rest day shall be deemed to be required to do duty on such day only if he has been specifically ordered to do duty;

    (b) a day's pay means a week's pay divided by 5;

    (c) a reference to a day which would otherwise have been a rest day is to be construed as a reference to a day which according to the roster of rest days was to have been a rest day for the member concerned, and for the purpose of determining what would have been such a day any alteration in the roster made less than 8 days before that day shall be ignored except where the alteration is made at the request of the member concerned;

    (d) in paragraph (2) the expression "week" means a period of 7 days beginning with such day as is fixed by the chief officer of police;

    (e) a period of less than 8 completed quarters of an hour of duty on a public holiday or on a day which would otherwise have been a rest day shall be treated as though it were a period of 8 completed quarters of an hour of duty;

    (f) where a member is recalled to duty after completing a tour of duty, his period of duty shall include the time occupied by him in going from and returning to his home on and after his recall, not exceeding such reasonable limit as may be fixed by the chief officer of police, and

    (g) where a member is required to do duty on a public holiday or on a day which would otherwise have been a rest day (otherwise than where he is recalled to duty after completing a tour of duty), his period of duty shall include the time occupied by him in going to and returning from his place of duty, not exceeding such reasonable limit as may be fixed by the chief officer of police, save that any period of time so occupied which together with the member's period of duty amounts to more than 4 hours shall be disregarded.

Public holidays and monthly leave days for higher ranks

27.—(1) This Regulation shall apply to every member of a police force of, or above, the rank of superintendent.

(2) Such a member shall, so far as the exigencies of duty permit, be allowed a day's leave on each public holiday and be granted in each month—

    (a) in the case of a superintendent, 4 monthly leave days;

    (b) in any other case, $1\frac{1}{2}$ monthly leave days.

(3) Such a member who is required to do duty on a public holiday shall be granted a day's leave in lieu of each such day unless the exigencies of duty do not permit such grant within 3 months.

(4) Where the exigencies of duty have precluded the grant to a superintendent, in any month, of 4 monthly leave days, then, during the next following month he shall, so far as the exigencies of duty permit, be granted the number of days not granted as additional monthly leave days.

Annual leave

28.—(1) Every member of a police force shall, so far as the exigencies of duty permit, be granted annual leave in accordance with Schedule 3.

(2) The annual leave of a member of a police force shall be additional to the days upon which he is not required to perform police duties in accordance with—

(*a*) Regulation 26, in the case of a member below the rank of superintendent, or

(*b*) Regulation 27, in the case of a member of, or above, the rank of superintendent;

and a member below the rank of superintendent shall, so far as the exigencies of duty permit, be allowed to take his annual leave in one period continuous with such days as aforesaid falling within the period in which he desires to take annual leave.

Sick leave

29.—(1) A member of a police force shall not be entitled to be absent from duty on account of injury or illness unless a registered medical practitioner has certified him to be unfit for duty:

Provided that—

(*a*) with the consent of the police authority, a member may be so absent, without such certificate of unfitness, for a period not exceeding 3 days on any occasion, excluding any day on which he would not have been required to perform police duty were he not absent;

(*b*) if, notwithstanding such certificate of unfitness for duty, a registered medical practitioner appointed or approved by the police authority has examined the member and certified him to be fit for duty he shall no longer be entitled to be absent from duty.

(2) This Regulation shall apply to a member who is in quarantine as it applies to a member who is ill and any reference to fitness or unfitness for duty shall be construed accordingly.

Maternity leave

30.—(1) During the maternity period a married woman member of a police force shall not be entitled to any sick leave in respect of any injury, illness or incapacity for duty which is solely or mainly due to pregnancy or childbirth or their after effects but shall be entitled to take maternity leave for the whole or any part or parts of the period.

(2) The maternity leave granted in respect of any particular maternity period shall be paid maternity leave, as respects 3 months thereof, and unpaid maternity leave, as respects the remainder:

Provided that a member shall not be entitled to more than 3 months' paid maternity leave during any period of 12 months or, in the case of a constable, to any paid maternity leave before the end of her period of probation in the force.

(3) In this Regulation the maternity period means, in relation to a married woman member of a police force who is certified by a registered medical practitioner approved by the police authority to be pregnant, the period beginning 6 months before the date which is estimated by the said medical practitioner as being the probable date of birth and ending 9 months after the birth of the child.

University scholars

31. This Part of these Regulations shall have effect in relation to a university scholar subject to the provisions of paragraph 2 of Schedule 4.

Part IV

Pay

Rate of pay

32.—(1) The rate of pay of a member of a police force shall be in accordance with the appropriate scale of pay mentioned in Schedule 5.

(2) Subject to Regulations 33, 34, 35 and 36 and Part III of Schedule 5, section 2(1) of the Police (Overseas Service) Act 1945**(a)** and section 43(1) of the Police Act 1964, in reckoning the service of a member of a police force in any rank for the purposes of any of the aforesaid scales of pay, account shall be taken only of service in the force in that rank since his last promotion thereto or, as the case may be, his last appointment to the force, together with any previous service in that or a higher rank on temporary promotion thereto, since his last appointment to the force:

Provided that in reckoning a member's service in any rank—

(a) that service shall be treated as unbroken by, and including, any period of service in a higher rank on temporary promotion thereto or any period of service in Her Majesty's forces which he is entitled to reckon as pensionable service;

(b) previous service in that or a higher rank, on temporary promotion thereto, shall be disregarded if, subsequent to that promotion, he has been reduced in rank as a punishment;

(c) any period of unpaid maternity leave shall be disregarded.

(3) Notwithstanding anything in paragraph (1), the pay of a member of a police force holding the office of deputy chief constable shall be increased by such amount as may be approved by the Secretary of State.

(4) Where a member of a combined police force has been a member of a police force for an area comprised in whole or in part in the combined area (hereafter in this paragraph referred to as "the former force") and—

(a) he ceased to be a member of the former force and became a member of the combined force by reason only of the provisions of one or more amalgamation schemes under the Police Act 1964, and

(b) immediately before he ceased to be a member of the former force he held the office of deputy chief constable,

---

(a) 1945 c. 17 (9 & 10 Geo. 6).

then, notwithstanding anything in paragraph (1), his pay may be increased by such amount as may be approved by the Secretary of State.

(5) Nothing in this Regulation shall affect the operation of any provision of the Discipline Regulations.

(6) Paragraph (1) and Schedule 5 shall have effect in relation to a university scholar subject to the provisions of paragraph 3 of Schedule 4.

Reckoning of previous service

33.—(1) A member of a police force of a rank higher than that of constable, who voluntarily transferred thereto from some other force in that higher rank, shall be entitled (subject to any contrary agreement) to reckon, for the purposes of the scale of pay for that rank, the service which was so reckonable immediately before he transferred.

(2) A member of a police force of the rank of constable who—

(a) voluntarily transferred thereto from some other force, or

(b) rejoined or joined that force after 10th May 1948, having previously resigned from that or some other force,

shall be entitled to reckon, for the purposes of the scale of pay for the rank of constable, the service which was so reckonable immediately before he transferred or previously resigned, as the case may be.

(3) For the purposes of the foregoing provisions of this Part of these Regulations, where a member of a police force has been statutorily transferred thereto from some other force, his service in those two forces shall be treated as if it were service in the same police force.

Reckoning of service in the Royal Ulster Constabulary

34.—(1) A member of a police force who joined or rejoined that force in a rank higher than that of constable—

(a) having left the Royal Ulster Constabulary, on or after 17th December 1969, for that purpose or on exercising the right of reversion conferred by section 2(1) of the Police Act 1969, and

(b) having held the corresponding or a higher rank immediately before he left the Royal Ulster Constabulary,

shall be entitled (subject to any contrary agreement) to reckon, for the purposes of the scale of pay for the rank in which he joined or rejoined the force, the service which he was entitled to reckon immediately before he left the Royal Ulster Constabulary for the purposes of the scale of pay for the corresponding rank or, where he then held a higher rank, would have been entitled so to reckon had he then held the corresponding rank.

(2) A member of a police force of the rank of constable shall be entitled to reckon, for the purposes of the scale of pay for that rank, any period of service in the Royal Ulster Constabulary.

(3) In this Regulation, any reference to a rank corresponding to a rank in a police force is a reference to a rank in the Royal Ulster Constabulary designated by the Secretary of State for the purposes hereof as the rank corresponding to the rank in question.

Reckoning by constables of auxiliary service

35.—(1) A member of a police force of the rank of constable shall be entitled to reckon for the purposes of the scale of pay for that rank any period of whole-time paid service after 3rd September 1939—

(*a*) as a police war reservist;

(*b*) as a special constable in receipt of pay under the Special Constables Order 1940**(a)**;

(*c*) as a member of the first class of the police reserve not in receipt of a pension in respect of service as a member of a police force;

(*d*) as a member of Class A of the Women's Auxiliary Police Corps;

(*e*) as a member of the Women's Auxiliary Police Corps, otherwise than of Class A thereof, assigned wholly or mainly to street patrol duties, motor patrol duties or outside detective duties, being a period of such service of not less than a complete month and ending before 1st April 1945.

(2) For the purposes of this Regulation, whole-time paid service includes all leave with full pay, any period of leave without full pay not exceeding 7 days in duration and any period of absence or suspension with full pay or the equivalent of full pay, and leave shall not be taken to be leave without full pay by reason only that there was deducted from pay the amount of benefits under the National Health Insurance Act 1936**(b)**, the National Insurance Act 1946**(c)** or the National Insurance Act 1965**(d)**, of payments under any scheme made by the Minister of Social Security under the Personal Injuries (Emergency Provisions) Act 1939**(e)**, or of weekly payments under the Workmen's Compensation Act 1925**(f)**; but save as aforesaid whole-time paid service does not include any period of leave or suspension.

Reckoning by constables of overseas police service

36.—(1) A member of a police force of the rank of constable shall be entitled to reckon for the purposes of the scale of pay for that rank the following periods of service, that is to say, any period of—

(*a*) service in the Palestine Police Force;

(*b*) certified overseas police service such as is mentioned in paragraph (2);

(*c*) certified service in the British South Africa Police such as is mentioned in paragraph (4),

notwithstanding that such service is not service in the rank of constable in a police force in Great Britain.

(2) The reference in paragraph (1) to certified overseas police service is a reference to—

(*a*) continuous service as a member of a police force in any territory or country outside the United Kingdom, being a colony, protectorate or protected state within the meaning of the British Nationality Act 1948**(g)**, or, where appropriate, the territory or country wherein the colony, protectorate or protected state was incorporated after the inception of the service, subject to it having been certified by or on behalf of the appropriate Minister that—

(a) S.R. & O. 1940/1193 (1940 I, p. 198); revoked by S.I. 1948/866 (Rev. XVIII, p. 180: 1948 I, p. 3480).

(b) 1936 c. 32.

(c) 1946 c. 67.

(d) 1965 c. 51.

(e) 1939 c. 82.

(f) 1925 c. 84.

(g) 1948 c. 56.

(i) the service was, at its inception, pensionable, and

(ii) in his opinion the person concerned ceased so to serve for reasons connected with constitutional developments in the territory or country in question, or

(b) continuous service for 6 years or more as a member of a police force outside the United Kingdom, subject to it having been certified by or on behalf of the appropriate Minister that—

(i) the person concerned so served under a contract of service,

(ii) immediately before he ceased so to serve, the person concerned was, for the purposes of section 1 of the Overseas Service Act 1961(a), a person designated in accordance with such an agreement as is therein mentioned, and

(iii) in his opinion the person concerned ceased so to serve for reasons connected with constitutional developments in the territory or country in question,

except that the said reference in paragraph (1) does not include a reference to service as a reversionary member of a home police force.

(3) In this Regulation the expression "the appropriate Minister" means—

(a) in relation to a certificate given before 27th November 1964, the Secretary for Technical Co-operation;

(b) in relation to a certificate given on or after 27th November 1964 but before 12th November 1970, the Minister of Overseas Development;

(c) in relation to a certificate given on or after 12th November 1970, the Secretary of State.

(4) The reference in paragraph (1) to certified service in the British South Africa Police is a reference to continuous service as a member thereof, for a period which included 11th November 1965, up to such time, on or after that date, as the person concerned ceased to perform duties therein, subject to it having been certified by or on behalf of the Secretary of State that in his opinion the person concerned so ceased to perform duties in circumstances which rendered him eligible for assistance as a loyal Rhodesian public servant under the scheme announced in the House of Commons on 22nd December 1965.

Deductions from pay of sickness or injury benefits

37.—(1) There shall be deducted from the pay of a member of a police force the amount of any sickness benefit or of any injury benefit to which he may be entitled.

(2) In this Regulation—

(a) the expression "sickness benefit" means sickness benefit under the National Insurance Act 1965 together with any supplement thereto payable under section 2 of the National Insurance Act 1966(b), and

(b) the expression "injury benefit" means injury benefit under the National Insurance (Industrial Injuries) Act 1965(c) together with any supplement payable therewith under the said section 2,

and, for the purposes thereof, a married policewoman who is excepted from liability to pay contributions under section 3 of the National Insurance Act

(a) 1961 c. 10.　　　　(b) 1966 c. 6.　　　　(c) 1965 c. 52.

1965 shall be deemed to be entitled to any sickness benefit, other than any supplement under section 2 of the National Insurance Act 1966, to which she would have been entitled had she not been so excepted.

Calculation of monthly, weekly and daily pay

38.—(1) A month's pay shall be calculated, for all purposes, at a monthly rate of pay determined by dividing by 12 the annual rate.

(2) A week's pay shall be calculated, for all purposes, at a weekly rate of pay determined by dividing by 52⅕ the annual rate.

(3) A day's pay shall be calculated, except for the purposes of Regulations 25 and 26, at a daily rate determined by dividing by 7 the weekly rate, determined as aforesaid.

(4) In making any payment by way of pay a fraction of a penny shall be treated as a whole penny except that a fraction less than a half-penny shall be ignored.

Pay day

39.—(1) Members of a police force shall be paid at such intervals as the police authority may fix and the police authority may fix different intervals for different classes of members.

(2) In fixing the interval for any class the police authority shall have regard to the wishes of the members of that class.

PART V

ALLOWANCES AND OTHER EMOLUMENTS

Restriction on payment of allowances

40.—(1) No allowances shall be paid to a member of a police force except as provided by these Regulations or approved by the Secretary of State, and the amounts and conditions of payment of such allowances shall be as so provided or approved.

(2) Nothing in this Regulation shall apply to the reimbursement of expenses incurred by a member of a police force in the execution of his duty, being expenses authorised either generally or specifically by the police authority in respect of which no allowance is payable under these Regulations.

Restriction on payments for private employment of police

41. Without prejudice to the generality of Regulation 40, a member of a police force who is engaged on duty at the request of any person who has agreed to pay the police authority or, in the case of a member of the metropolitan police force, the Receiver for the metropolitan police district for the member's services shall not be entitled to any payment for those services except as provided by these Regulations; and any payments made in pursuance of that agreement shall be made by that person to the police authority or to the Receiver for the metropolitan police district, as the case may be.

Rent allowance

42.—(1) A member of a police force who is not provided with a house or quarters free of rent and rates shall be paid a rent allowance which shall be either a maximum limit allowance or a flat-rate allowance:

Provided that—

 (a) a member to whom Regulation 43 applies who is provided with quarters shall be paid a rent allowance in addition;

 (b) a woman member of a police force shall not be paid a rent allowance if she is either married to a member of a police force and living with him or is on unpaid maternity leave.

(2) A maximum limit allowance—

 (a) shall be paid to a married man not separated from his wife;

 (b) shall be paid to a member, not being a married man (other than a man separated from his wife) or a married woman, who—

  (i) has attained the age of 30 years,

  (ii) has served for 5 years as a member of that or any other police force, and

  (iii) occupies as owner or tenant the accommodation in which he or she is living;

 (c) may, if the police authority think fit, be paid to a man, not being a man to whom sub-paragraph (a) or (b) applies who—

  (i) has a dependent relative living with him,

  (ii) is separated from, or has divorced or been divorced by, his wife, or

  (iii) is a widower;

 (d) may, if in special circumstances the police authority think fit, be paid to a woman member, not being a woman to whom sub-paragraph (b) applies;

and in all other cases a flat-rate allowance shall be paid.

(3)(a) A maximum limit allowance shall, subject to the maximum limit, be the aggregate of the amount paid in rates and—

  (i) where the member owns the house he occupies, the amount which in the opinion of the District Valuer would be paid in rent therefor if the house were let unfurnished,

  (ii) where the member is living in unfurnished accommodation, the amount paid in rent therefor, or

  (iii) subject to sub-paragraph (a)(i), where the member is living in furnished accommodation, an amount which in the opinion of the police authority would have been paid in rent therefor had the accommodation been unfurnished:

Provided that where part of the said house or part of the said accommodation is let to or occupied by a tenant or lodger, as the case may be, who is not a member of a police force, the police authority may make a deduction from the said aggregate in respect of such part.

 (b) The maximum limit shall be fixed by the police authority with the approval of the Secretary of State for each rank.

(4) A flat-rate allowance shall be an allowance equal to half the amount fixed as the maximum limit for members of the same rank.

(5) A member who is either a married man separated from his wife or a man who has divorced, or been divorced by, his wife and who regularly makes periodic payments to her or for her benefit may be granted—

(*a*) where he is in receipt of a rent allowance under paragraph (1), an addition to that rent allowance, or

(*b*) where he is provided with a house or quarters free of rent and rates, a rent allowance,

equal to whichever is the lesser of the two following amounts, namely, the amount by which his former allowance exceeds his present allowance or the amount paid by him to or for the benefit of his wife or former wife.

(6) In this Regulation—

(*a*) the expression "his former allowance" means—

(i) in relation to a man who, immediately before his wife commenced to live apart from him, was being provided with a house or quarters free of rent and rates, a sum fixed as the value for the time being of that house or those quarters;

(ii) in relation to any other man, the maximum limit allowance which would for the time being be payable to him if he were still entitled to such an allowance and the aggregate referred to in paragraph (3) (*a*) were unchanged since immediately before his wife commenced to live apart from him;

(*b*) the expression "his present allowance" means the rent allowance which is being paid to the man under paragraph (1) or, as the case may be, a sum fixed as the value for the time being of the house or quarters with which he is provided;

(*c*) the expression "rates" means—

(i) any rate as defined in section 68(1) of the Rating and Valuation Act 1925**(a)** and in addition any rate mentioned in paragraphs (*a*), (*b*) and (*c*) of that definition (which exclude from the definition drainage, tithe, common and other rates of a similar character), and

(ii) any rate or charge for a supply of water for domestic purposes.

Supplementary rent allowance

43.—(1) This Regulation shall apply to—

(*a*) a member of a police force, other than a woman member, who—

(i) is a widower with a child or children or a married man,

(ii) is not living with his family, and

(iii) satisfies the chief officer of police that the only reason why he is not so living is that he is unable to find suitable accommodation for his family at a reasonable cost within a reasonable distance of his place of duty;

(*b*) a member of a police force, other than such a member as is mentioned in sub-paragraph (*a*), who is temporarily assigned to duties which, in the opinion of the chief officer of police, require him to live otherwise than in his former accommodation,

except that this Regulation shall not apply to such a member as is mentioned in sub-paragraph (*b*) for a continuous period exceeding 30 months unless the

---

(a) 1925 c. 90.

police authority, in the circumstances of the case, so determine, or in respect of any period for which he has not retained, or has let or sub-let, his former accommodation.

(2) Notwithstanding the provisions of Regulation 42, the rent allowance to be paid to a member to whom this Regulation applies shall be that which would be payable under the said Regulation 42—

(a) in the case of such a member as is mentioned in paragraph (1)(a), if he were a member of the force of the police area in which his family are for the time being living and he were living with his family;

(b) in the case of such a member as is mentioned in paragraph (1)(b), if he had not been assigned to such duties as are there mentioned and had continued to occupy his former accommodation.

(3) A member to whom this Regulation applies shall be paid a supplementary rent allowance at the following rate:—

(a) if he is provided with quarters free of rent and rates, £2·35 a week;

(b) if he is not so provided, £3·35 a week.

(4) A supplementary rent allowance payable under paragraph (3) may be reduced or withdrawn by the police authority in respect of any period consisting of one or more complete weeks throughout which the member in question is absent from his usual or temporary normal place of duty and is either—

(a) on leave of absence; or

(b) provided with board and lodging free of charge or an allowance in lieu.

Application of Regulations 42 and 43 to members of regional crime squads and motorway patrol groups

44.—(1) This Regulation shall apply to a member of a police force who is assigned to duty with a regional crime squad or a motorway patrol group established in pursuance of a collaboration agreement made under section 13 of the Police Act 1964.

(2) Where a member of a police force to whom this Regulation applies moves his home and the removal is in the opinion of the appropriate committee of chief officers of police due to the exigencies of policy duty or is made at the request of that committee and is, in their opinion, in the interest of the efficiency of the crime squad concerned, then notwithstanding the provisions of Regulation 42, the rent allowance to be paid to him shall be that which would be payable to him under that Regulation if he was a member of the force of the police area in which his home is for the time being situate.

(3) Where a member of a police force to whom this Regulation applies does not move his home, then, Regulation 43 shall have effect in relation to him—

(a) as if for paragraph (1)(a)(iii) there were substituted the following provision:—

"(iii) in the opinion of the appropriate committee of chief officers of police, is not so living for the sole reason that he could not conveniently return daily to the family home;";

(b) as if in paragraph (1)(b) for the words "chief officer" there were substituted the words "appropriate committee of chief officers";

(c) as if in paragraph (1) for the words "30 months" there were substituted the words "24 months";

(*d*) as if for paragraph (2)(*a*) and (*b*) there were substituted the following provision:—

"if he were living with his family or, as the case may be, in his former accommodation";

(*e*) where he is a widower with a child or children or a married man and, if he were a member of the police force in which he is for the time being living and entitled to a flat-rate allowance under Regulation 42, that allowance would be payable at a higher rate than £3·35 a week, as if for the reference in paragraph (3)(*b*) to the rate of £3·35 a week there were substituted a reference to that higher rate.

(4) In this Regulation any reference to the appropriate committee of chief officers of police is a reference to the chief officers of police who are parties to the collaboration agreement referred to in paragraph (1) or such one or more of their number as they may have designated to act on their behalf for the purposes of this Regulation.

Compensatory grant

45.—(1) In each financial year, a member of a police force who has during the preceding financial year paid income tax in respect of a rent allowance or any compensatory grant paid or made to him in respect of his service in the force shall be paid a compensatory grant.

(2) The amount of the compensatory grant shall be equal to the amount by which the income tax in fact deducted during the preceding year, according to the tax tables prepared or prescribed by the Commissioners of Inland Revenue, from the member's emoluments in respect of his service in the force is increased by virtue of the inclusion in such emoluments of a rent allowance or any compensatory grant.

(3) The compensatory grant may, except in the circumstances described in paragraph (4), be paid by such instalments throughout the year in which it is payable as the police authority may determine.

(4) Where a member of a police force leaves the force or dies whilst serving in the force he or his personal representative, as the case may be, shall be paid the whole of the compensatory grant due to the member during that year and, in addition, shall be paid a further compensatory grant equal to the amount by which the income tax in fact deducted between the beginning of the year and the date on which he leaves the force or dies, according to the tax tables prepared or prescribed by the Commissioners of Inland Revenue, from the member's emoluments in respect of his service in the force during that period is increased by virtue of the inclusion in such emoluments of a rent allowance or any compensatory grant mentioned in this Regulation paid or made to him.

(5) For the purposes of this Regulation—

(*a*) the expression "year" or "financial year" means a year commencing on 6th April and ending on the following 5th April; and

(*b*) where a member of a police force has served more than once in the same force, references in this Regulation to service in the force shall be construed as references to his service therein since his last appointment thereto.

Discharge of tax liability in respect of police house or quarters

46. Where a member of a police force is provided with a house or quarters free of rent and rates and his liability to pay income tax is increased—

(*a*) in consequence thereof, by virtue of section 47 of the Finance Act 1963**(a)**; or

(*b*) in consequence of any payment required to be made by this Regulation,

that liability, to the extent that it is so increased, shall be discharged by the police authority.

Removal allowance

47.—(1) Where a member of the police force moves his home otherwise than on voluntary transfer from one force to another, and the removal is, in the opinion of the chief officer of police, due to the exigencies of police duty or is made at the request of the chief officer of police and is, in his opinion, in the interests of the efficiency of the force, the police authority—

(*a*) shall either reimburse the reasonably incurred cost of removal or carry out the removal;

(*b*) shall, where the member was the owner of his former home, reimburse expenses reasonably incurred by him in connection with the disposal thereof;

(*c*) shall, where the member is the owner of his new home, reimburse expenses reasonably incurred by him in connection with the acquisition thereof if—

(i) he was the owner of his former home, or

(ii) the police authority, after consulting the chief officer of police, are satisfied that he could neither have been provided with a suitable house or quarters nor have been reasonably expected to find suitable rented accommodation within a reasonable distance of his normal place of duty,

so, however, that where the police authority are of opinion that the member could have acquired a suitable home for a consideration less than that actually paid, they may restrict the reimbursement of expenses directly related to the consideration paid by him to expenses which would have been reasonably incurred had he paid that lesser consideration.

(2) Where a member of a police force moves his home on voluntary transfer from one force to another, the police authority of the force to which he transfers—

(*a*) may either reimburse the reasonable cost of removal or carry out the removal;

(*b*) may, in the circumstances mentioned in paragraph (1)(*b*), reimburse the expenses there mentioned;

(*c*) may, in the circumstances and subject to the conditions mentioned in paragraph (1)(*c*), reimburse the expenses there mentioned.

(3) Where the cost of removal is reimbursed or the removal is carried out by the police authority under paragraph (1) or (2), then, subject to paragraph (4), in respect of expenditure incidental to the move the police authority shall pay the member an allowance of the amount hereinafter provided.

(4) An allowance under paragraph (3)—

(*a*) shall not be payable, where a member who has never been married moves from furnished accommodation;

(*b*) shall only be payable if the chief officer of police so decides, where a member moves from unfurnished into furnished accommodation.

(a) 1963 c. 25.

(5) In the case of a member who—

(a) moves into furnished accommodation; or

(b) moves into unfurnished accommodation but has not previously, while a member of a police force, lived in such accommodation,

the amount of the allowance under paragraph (3) shall be £15.

(6) In the case of any other member the amount of the allowance under paragraph (3) shall be—

(a) where he holds, or is transferring to be appointed in, a rank higher than that of chief superintendent, such as may be determined by the police authority;

(b) where he holds, or is transferring to be appointed in, the rank of superintendent, £75;

(c) where he holds, or is transferring to be appointed in, the rank of inspector, £60;

(d) where he holds, or is transferring to be appointed in, any rank lower than that of inspector, £45.

(7) In this Regulation—

(a) any reference to an owner of any property is a reference to an occupier thereof whose interest therein is either a freehold interest or a leasehold interest which is neither a yearly or shorter tenancy nor a furnished tenancy, and

(b) any reference to expenses incurred in connection with the disposal or acquisition of any property shall be construed as including, in particular, estate agent's, auctioneer's and solicitor's fees and expenses in connection with the redemption, transfer or taking out of a mortgage.

Uniform allowance

48. A member of a police force of or above the rank of inspector who does duty in uniform but is not supplied with uniform by the police authority shall be paid in lieu a uniform allowance at a rate calculated to cover the cost of supplying and maintaining the required uniform.

Boot allowance

49. A member of a police force who is not supplied with boots or, in the case of a woman member, shoes, by the police authority shall be paid in lieu a boot allowance at the rate of £0·188 a week.

Plain clothes allowances

50.—(1) A member of a police force who is required for a continuous period of not less than a week to do duty in plain clothes shall be paid a plain clothes allowance.

(2) A plain clothes allowance payable under paragraph (1) shall be payable at the rate of—

(a) £57 a year, in the case of a superintendent;

(b) £54 a year, in the case of an inspector;

(c) £48 a year, in the case of a sergeant;

(d) £45 a year, in the case of a constable.

(3) An inspector, sergeant or constable required to perform duties in plain clothes for not less than 48 hours in the aggregate in any period of 6 months shall be paid a plain clothes allowance in respect of such duties:

Provided that for the purposes of calculating the said aggregate—

(a) where the duties were performed on an occasion falling within such a continuous period of plain clothes duty as is mentioned in paragraph (1), no account shall be taken of those duties;

(b) where the duties performed on any occasion lasted less than 4 completed hours, no account shall be taken of those duties;

(c) where the duties performed on any occasion lasted for a completed number of hours and a fraction of an hour, no account shall be taken of that fraction.

(4) A plain clothes allowance payable under paragraph (3) shall be payable at the rate of—

(a) £0·025 an hour, in the case of an inspector;

(b) £0·023 an hour, in the case of a sergeant;

(c) £0·021 an hour, in the case of a constable.

(5) Notwithstanding anything in paragraph (2) or (4), where a member of a police force is provided with overalls when doing duty in plain clothes or for any other reason is, in the opinion of the Secretary of State, put to substantially less or substantially more than the normal expense caused by wearing his own clothes, a plain clothes allowance payable to him under paragraph (1) or (3) shall be payable at such rate as may be approved by the Secretary of State.

Detective duty and detective expenses allowances

51.—(1) This Regulation shall apply in the case of a member of a police force below the rank of superintendent who is assigned, for a period of not less than a week, to detective duty and, while so assigned is, in the opinion of the chief officer of police, usually engaged in outside duty.

(2) Such a member shall be paid a detective duty allowance in accordance with Schedule 6 and a detective expenses allowance at the rate of £0·50 a week.

Supplementary detective allowances

52.—(1) A member of a police force to whom a detective duty allowance is payable in respect of any period falling within the quarter ending with 31st May 1971 or any subsequent quarter shall be paid a supplementary detective allowance, in accordance with Schedule 6 hereto, if the average qualifying overtime referred to in the next following paragraph, performed during the preceding quarter, is 8 hours a week or more.

(2) The qualifying overtime referred to in the preceding paragraph is, in the case of a constable, sergeant or inspector, overtime (within the meaning of, and computed in accordance with, Regulation 25) in respect of which an allowance is not payable under paragraph (6) of that Regulation, performed by members of the force of the rank of constable, sergeant or, as the case may be, inspector to whom a detective duty allowance is payable in respect of the period during which the overtime is performed; and the weekly average of such qualifying overtime shall be determined for the purposes of the preceding paragraph by reference to the average overtime performed each day by such members on duty on that day.

(3) Paragraph (1) of this Regulation shall have effect as respects the quarter in which a new police force is established, as if, in relation to a member of that force, any reference therein to the preceding quarter were a reference to the quarter in which the force is established.

(4) This Regulation shall have effect, where a member of a police force is assigned to duty with a regional crime squad or other body established in pursuance of a collaboration agreement made under section 13 of the Police Act 1964(a), as if so long as he is assigned to such a duty he were not a member of the police force in question, but in such case this Regulation shall apply as if a reference therein to a police force or member thereof were a reference to the regional crime squad or other body in question or a member assigned to duties therewith.

(5) In this Regulation the expression "quarter" means a period of 13 weeks.

Subsistence, refreshment and lodging allowances

53.—(1) A member of a police force of or below the rank of superintendent who, being retained on duty beyond his normal daily period of duty or being engaged on duty away from his usual place of duty, necessarily incurs additional expense to obtain food or lodging, shall—

(a) if the period for which he is so retained or engaged exceeds an hour but does not exceed 5 hours, be paid a refreshment allowance;

(b) if the period for which he is so retained or engaged exceeds 5 hours, be paid a subsistence allowance;

(c) if the said expense includes the expense of obtaining lodging, be paid a lodging allowance.

(2) A member of a police force of or below the rank of superintendent who satisfies the chief officer of police that during his normal daily period of duty he was, although not away from his usual place of duty, unable by reason of the exigencies of duty to obtain his meals in his usual way and that he necessarily incurred additional expense for the purpose may be paid a refreshment allowance.

(3) Where the place of duty of a member of a police force has been temporarily changed the expression in this Regulation "usual place of duty" shall, after such period from the date of change as the chief officer of police may determine, mean the temporary place of duty.

(4) A subsistence, refreshment or lodging allowance shall be of an amount determined in accordance with Schedule 7.

Advances to cover expenses when away on duty

54. Where a member of a police force of or below the rank of inspector is required to do duty away from his usual place of duty he shall be given an advance to cover, as far as practicable, any expenses which he will probably incur.

Motor vehicle allowances

55.—(1) Where the chief officer of police is of opinion that the duties normally performed by a member of a police force are of such a nature that it is—

(a) essential, or

(b) desirable,

(a) 1964 c. 48.

that the member in question should, at all material times, have a motor vehicle at his disposal, he may authorise that member to use (subject to his directions) a motor vehicle owned by the member for the purposes of duties performed by him and, subject as hereinafter provided, in respect of such use the member shall be paid a motor vehicle allowance.

(2) A motor vehicle allowance shall not be payable in respect of the authorised use of a motor vehicle unless there was in force in relation thereto a policy of insurance in terms approved by the police authority, in relation to the use in question, for the purposes hereof.

(3) A motor vehicle allowance shall not be payable in respect of the authorised use of a motor car of a cylinder capacity exceeding 500 c.c. unless the member concerned was willing to carry passengers for the purposes of the duties performed by him or, in the case of passengers being members of a police force, by those members.

(4) A motor vehicle allowance in respect of the authorised use of a motor car of a cylinder capacity exceeding 500 c.c. shall, subject as aforesaid, be payable—

(a) where the chief officer of police is of the opinion mentioned in paragraph (1)(a), at the essential user's rate;

(b) where the chief officer of police is of the opinion mentioned in paragraph (1)(b), at the casual user's rate,

as provided in Schedule 8:

Provided that where the member concerned holds the office of deputy chief constable or a rank above that of superintendent he may instead be paid a flat-rate motor vehicle allowance at such annual rate as is determined by the police authority with the approval of the Secretary of State.

(5) A motor vehicle allowance in respect of the authorised use of—

(a) a motor car of a cylinder capacity not exceeding 500 c.c., or

(b) a motor bicycle,

shall, subject as aforesaid, be payable on such conditions and at such rate as is approved by the Secretary of State.

(6) In its application to a chief officer of police this Regulation shall have effect as if any reference therein to that officer were a reference to the police authority.

(7) Paragraph 5 of Schedule 8 shall have effect for the purposes of the interpretation of this Regulation.

Bicycle allowance

56.—(1) Where a member of a police force is authorised by the chief officer of police to use a bicycle owned by him for the purposes of duties normally and from time to time performed by him, he shall in respect of such use be paid a bicycle allowance in accordance with Schedule 9.

(2) In this Regulation the expression "bicycle" does not include a motor bicycle, that is to say a mechanically propelled bicycle (including a motor scooter and a bicycle with an attachment for propelling it by mechanical power) and a reference to a bicycle owned by a member of a police force is a reference to a bicycle kept and used by him.

Typewriter allowance

57.—(1) Where a member of a police force is authorised by the chief officer of police to use a typewriter owned by him for the purposes of duties normally and from time to time performed by him, he shall, in respect of such use, be paid a typewriter allowance in accordance with Schedule 10, and the police authority shall supply him with typewriter ribbons free of charge.

(2) In this Regulation a reference to a typewriter owned by a member of a police force is a reference to a typewriter kept and used by him.

Allowance in respect of medical charges

58. A member of a police force shall be reimbursed any charges incurred in his case under section 38 of the National Health Service Act 1946**(a)**, under section 1 of the National Health Service Act 1951**(b)**, or under section 1 or 2 of the National Health Service Act 1952**(c)** (which sections relate to charges for certain drugs, medicines and appliances and for dental treatment).

Special area undermanning allowance

59.—(1) A member of a police force for a special area within the meaning of paragraph (3), being a member below the rank of superintendent, shall be paid an undermanning allowance—

(*a*) in the case of an inspector, at the rate of £45 a year;

(*b*) in the case of a sergeant, at the rate of £65 a year;

(*c*) in the case of a constable, at the rate of £30 a year or, if he has completed 3 years of service, at the rate of £65 a year.

(2) A constable shall be entitled to reckon for the purposes of this Regulation the service which he is entitled to reckon for the purposes of his scale of pay.

(3) The reference in paragraph (1) to a special area is a reference to the City of London police area, the metropolitan police district or any other police area which is for the time being designated by the Secretary of State a special area for the purposes of this Regulation.

Extra duty allowance

60.—(1) Where the police are required to undertake any of the following duties, a member of the police force below the rank of superintendent so engaged may receive an extra duty allowance of an amount approved by the Secretary of State, to be payable by the authority for which the duties are undertaken, if the police authority are satisfied that the performance of such extra duties causes, either regularly or on recurring occasions, a material addition to his normal hours of duty—

(*a*) duties of inspector under the Diseases of Animals Act 1950**(d)**, and making of returns in relation thereto;

(*b*) inspection of weights and measures;

(*c*) inspection and procuring samples under the Food and Drugs Act 1955**(e)** and the Fertilisers and Feeding Stuffs Act 1926**(f)**;

(*d*) inspection of premises for the purposes of the Explosives Acts 1875 and 1923**(g)**, and the Petroleum (Consolidation) Act 1928**(h)**;

(**a**) 1946 c. 81. (**b**) 1951 c. 31.
(**c**) 1952 c. 25. (**d**) 1950 c. 36.
(**e**) 1955 c. 16 (4 & 5 Eliz. 2). (**f**) 1926 c. 45.
(**g**) 1875 c. 17; 1923 c. 17. (**h**) 1928 c. 32.

(*e*) duties of inspector under the Shops Act 1950**(a)**;

(*f*) duties on behalf of the local authority in respect of local taxation licences.

(2) In respect of the following duties, no allowance shall be payable other than the allowance or payment (if any) to which the member of the police force would normally be entitled in respect of overtime as provided in these Regulations:—

(*a*) enforcement of the Cinematograph Act 1909**(b)**, and the Celluloid and Cinematograph Film Act 1922**(c)**;

(*b*) enforcement of borough byelaws;

(*c*) billeting;

(*d*) issue of pedlar's certificates;

nor in respect of any of the following duties where undertaken by the police:—

(*e*) inspection of domestic servants' registries;

(*f*) inspection of common lodging houses;

(*g*) inspection of hackney carriages;

(*h*) inspection of licensed boats;

(*i*) inspection of beach trading;

(*j*) inspection of markets;

(*k*) inspection of fire appliances;

(*l*) inspection of street lamps.

(3) The following are duties which the police shall not be required to perform:—

(*a*) collection and recovery of moneys due under affiliation orders;

(*b*) collection and recovery of moneys due under maintenance orders under the Matrimonial Proceedings (Magistrates' Courts) Act 1960**(d)**;

(*c*) collection of market tolls;

(*d*) Mayor's attendant;

(*e*) town crier;

(*f*) the regular duty of cleaning or any part of the cleaning of a particular police station which the Secretary of State has directed is not a duty which the police may be required to perform;

(*g*) any other work not connected with police duty which, in the opinion of the Secretary of State, the police may not properly be required to perform:

Provided that nothing in this Regulation shall preclude the receipt of moneys tendered at a police station, or shall affect the duties of the police in the execution of any warrant.

Temporary duty allowance

61.—(1) A member of a police force of the rank of superintendent, other than a member holding the office of deputy chief constable whose pay is for the time being increased under Regulation 32(3), who is required for a continuous period exceeding 7 days to perform duties normally performed by a member of the force of a higher rank than his own, otherwise than as the direct or indirect result of the absence of any member of the force on annual leave,

---

(a) 1950 c. 28. (b) 1909 c. 30.
(c) 1922 c. 35. (d) 1960 c. 48.

shall be granted in respect of that period, other than the first 7 days thereof, a temporary duty allowance at a rate equal to the difference between his rate of pay and the lowest rate of pay for that higher rank.

(2) A member of a police force below the rank of superintendent who, in any year, has been required to perform duties normally performed by a member of the force of a higher rank than his own for 14 complete days shall be granted, in respect of each further complete day in that year on which he is required to perform such duties, a temporary duty allowance at a rate equal to the difference between his rate of pay and the lowest rate of pay for the higher rank.

(3) For the purposes of this Regulation the expression "year" means a period of 12 months beginning on 1st April.

(4) For the purposes of this Regulation, the expression "day" means, in relation to a member of a police force below the rank of superintendent, his normal daily period of duty.

Promotion examination allowances

62.—(1) A constable who has taken an examination or paper in consequence of which he obtains a pass in the constables qualifying examination shall, subject to paragraph (3), be paid a constables promotion examination allowance of £30.

(2) A constable or sergeant who has taken an examination or paper in consequence of which he obtains a pass in the sergeants qualifying examination shall, subject to paragraph (3), be paid a sergeants promotion examination allowance of £30.

(3) A constables promotion examination allowance or a sergeants promotion examination allowance shall not be payable to a member of a police force who previously—

(a) has obtained, or been deemed to have obtained, a pass in the constables or, as the case may be, the sergeants qualifying examination held under any Promotion Regulations made on or after 17th September 1952, or

(b) while serving in a police force in Scotland or in such a constabulary as is mentioned in paragraph (4), has received a payment for passing the examination which qualified him, in that force or constabulary, for promotion from constable to sergeant or, as the case may be, from sergeant to inspector.

(4) The reference in paragraph (3) to a constabulary is a reference to any force of constables outside Great Britain previous service in which a member of a police force may reckon as pensionable service; and where the rank in such a constabulary which appears to the Secretary of State to correspond to that of constable, sergeant or, as the case may be, inspector is not so styled, paragraph (3)(b) shall have effect in relation to that constabulary as if for any reference therein to that rank there were substituted a reference to such rank as the Secretary of State determines to be the corresponding rank.

(5) Where an overseas policeman, a central police officer or a member of the Royal Ulster Constabulary enjoying a right of reversion to a home police force has, while serving as such, qualified for a promotion examination allowance under paragraph (1) or (2), he shall, subject to paragraph (3), be paid such an allowance on exercising his right of reversion to his police force under section 2(1) of the Police (Overseas Service) Act 1945, section 43(1) of the Police Act 1964 or, as the case may be, section 2(1) of the Police Act 1969(a).

(a) 1969 c. 63.

(6) An allowance payable under paragraph (1) or (2) shall be payable by the police authority maintaining the force of which the person concerned was a member when he took the examination or paper referred to in the paragraph in question, and an allowance payable under paragraph (5) shall be payable by the police authority maintaining the force to which the person concerned reverts.

(7) In this Regulation any reference to the constables qualifying examination or to the sergeants qualifying examination shall be construed as a reference to the qualifying examination or, in relation to a period before 1st June 1967, both the qualifying examinations, held under the Promotion Regulations, for promotion from constable to sergeant or, as the case may be, from sergeant to inspector.

Allowance for recurring escort duty, etc.

63. An allowance may be paid, of such amount and under such conditions as may be approved by the Secretary of State on the recommendation of the police authority, in respect of recurring escort duty or other specific duties involving recurring retention on duty beyond the normal daily period and not covered by any other payment.

Continuance of allowances when member ill

64. If a member of a police force who is regularly in receipt of a plain clothes allowance, detective duty allowance, detective expenses allowance, supplementary detective allowance, or any allowance to meet an expense which ceases during his or her absence from duty is placed upon the sick list or is on maternity leave, the allowance shall be payable during his or her absence from duty up to a period of a month, but thereafter, during the remainder of his or her absence from duty, payment may be suspended at the discretion of the chief officer of police:

Provided that a boot allowance shall not cease to be payable while the member is on the sick list.

University scholars

65. This Part of these Regulations shall have effect in relation to a university scholar subject to the provisions of paragraph 4 of Schedule 4.

Part VI

Housing, Uniform and Equipment

Provision of house or quarters

66. A member of a police force who is not paid a rent allowance under Regulation 42(1) shall be provided with a house or quarters free of rent and rates:

Provided that—

    (*a*) a member to whom Regulation 43 applies may be provided with quarters as aforesaid notwithstanding that he is paid a rent allowance under Regulation 42(1) as modified by Regulation 43(2);

    (*b*) a woman member shall not be provided with a house or quarters if she is either married to a member of a police force and living with him or is on unpaid maternity leave.

Issue of uniform and equipment

67.—(1) Uniform and equipment shall be issued by the police authority free of charge to sergeants and constables in accordance with the provisions of Schedule 11.

(2) Uniform and equipment may, if the police authority so determine, be issued as required to a member of the police force of or above the rank of inspector.

Ownership of uniform and equipment

68. Subject to Regulation 69 the uniform and equipment issued by the police authority shall not become the property of the member of the police force to whom they are issued and shall be handed back by him to the police authority on his leaving the force.

Replacement of uniform and equipment

69. On any article of uniform or equipment being replaced by the police authority the article shall be handed back to the police authority unless the member, with the consent of the police authority, buys such article at a price to be fixed by the police authority.

Re-issue of uniform and equipment

70. Uniform and equipment handed back to the police authority shall not be re-issued to another member of the police force until it has received any necessary cleaning or renovation and is in serviceable condition.

Boots

71. Where boots or, in the case of a woman member, shoes are not provided by the police authority for the purposes of duty, a member of the police force shall be in possession of two pairs of boots, or, in the case of a woman member, shoes, suitable for duty.

PART VII

MISCELLANEOUS AND TRANSITIONAL PROVISIONS

Meetings of Police Federation treated as police duty

72.—(1) The attendance of a member of a police force at one of the following meetings of the Police Federation, that is to say, a quarterly meeting of a branch board, an ordinary meeting of a central committee, the annual meeting of a central conference or a women's regional conference shall be treated as an occasion of police duty.

(2) Subject to the approval of the chief officer of police, the attendance of a member of a police force at an additional meeting of a branch board of the Police Federation or at a meeting of a committee of a branch board shall be treated as an occasion of police duty.

(3) Subject to the approval of the Secretary of State, the attendance of a member of a police force at a meeting of the Police Federation, other than such a meeting as is mentioned in paragraph (1) or (2), shall be treated as an occasion of police duty.

Payments by police authority for metropolitan police district

73. All payments required to be made under these Regulations by the Secretary of State as police authority for the metropolitan police district shall be paid out of the metropolitan police fund.

Regulations not to apply to auxiliary policemen

74. Nothing in these Regulations shall apply to the government, administration or conditions of service of auxiliary policemen.

Transitional provisions

75.—(1) Any appointment, deduction, payment, application, or election made, or approval, direction, consent, certificate or notice given, or any record or list kept, or any rank adopted, or any uniform or equipment issued, or any overtime worked or hours of duty worked on any public holiday or rest day, or any maximum limit fixed, or other thing done under any of the former Regulations or for the purposes thereof shall not be invalidated by the revocations effected by Regulation 2, but shall in so far as it could have been made, given, kept, adopted, issued, worked, fixed or done under a provision of these Regulations or for the purposes thereof have effect as if it had been made, given, kept, adopted, issued, worked, fixed or done under, or for the purposes of, that provision.

(2) Where immediately before the coming into operation of these Regulations a member of a police force was in receipt of a detective allowance by virtue of Regulation 67(2) of the Police Regulations 1968**(a)**, he shall continue to receive that allowance until—

(*a*) the chief officer of police is satisfied that he is no longer normally engaged in detective duty other than outside duty, or

(*b*) he is promoted otherwise than from second class to first class sergeant (C.I.D.) in the metropolitan police force;

and so long as a member continues to receive the said allowance he shall be treated for the purposes of these Regulations, other than Regulations 25 and 52, as if he were paid a detective duty allowance.

(3) In this Regulation the expression "the former Regulations" means the Regulations set out in Part I of Schedule 1 and any Regulations revoked by those Regulations.

> *R. Maudling,*
> One of Her Majesty's Principal
> Secretaries of State.

Home Office,
  Whitehall.
28th January 1971.

(**a**) S.I. 1968/26 (1968 I, p. 38).

Regulations 2 and 75 SCHEDULE 1

REVOCATIONS AND AMENDMENTS

PART I

REGULATIONS REVOKED WITH SAVINGS

Regulations	References
The Police Regulations 1968	S.I. 1968/26 (1968 I, p. 38).
The Police (Amendment) Regulations 1968 ...	S.I. 1968/552 (1968 I, p. 1294).
The Police (Amendment) (No. 2) Regulations 1968	S.I. 1968/766 (1968 II, p. 2142).
The Police (Amendment) (No. 3) Regulations 1968	S.I. 1968/1207 (1968 II, p. 3233).
The Police (Amendment) (No. 4) Regulations 1968	S.I. 1968/1761 (1968 III, p. 4774).
The Police (Amendment) Regulations 1969 ...	S.I. 1969/137 (1969 I, p. 369).
The Police (Amendment) (No. 2) Regulations 1969	S.I. 1969/911 (1969 I, p. 2724).
The Police (Amendment) Regulations 1970 ...	S.I. 1970/66 (1970 I, p. 375).
The Police (Amendment) (No. 2) Regulations 1970	S.I. 1970/417 (1970 I, p. 1446).
The Police (Amendment) (No. 3) Regulations 1970	S.I. 1970/601 (1970 I, p. 1923).
The Police (Amendment) (No. 4) Regulations 1970	S.I. 1970/1659 (1970 III, p. 5433).

PART II

TRANSITORY AMENDMENTS

1. For the purposes mentioned in Regulation 2(1) the Regulations thereby revoked with savings shall have effect as hereinafter provided.

2. Regulation 36 of the Police Regulations 1968(a), as amended(b), shall have effect as from 1st January 1971 as if in paragraph (1) after the words "a regional crime squad" there were inserted the words "or a motorway patrol group".

3. So far as a motor vehicle allowance payable under Regulation 48 of the said Regulations of 1968, as amended(c), falls to be calculated by reference to completed months of authorised use ending, or mileage of authorised use performed, on or after 1st October 1970, it shall be calculated as if for the provisions of paragraphs 1 and 2 of Schedule 6 to those Regulations there were substituted the provisions of paragraphs 1, 2 and 3 of Schedule 8 to these Regulations.

4. Nothing in this Part of this Schedule shall be construed as authorising allowances payable to any person to be reduced retrospectively.

(a) S.I. 1968/26 (1968 I, p. 38).
(b) The relevant amending instrument is S.I. 1970/1659 (1970 III, p. 5433).
(c) The relevant amending instruments are S.I. 1968/766, 1969/911 (1968 II, p. 2142; 1969 I, p. 2724).

SCHEDULE 2 Regulation 10

RESTRICTIONS ON THE PRIVATE LIFE OF MEMBERS OF POLICE FORCES

1. A member of a police force shall at all times abstain from any activity which is likely to interfere with the impartial discharge of his duties or which is likely to give rise to the impression amongst members of the public that it may so interfere; and in particular a member of a police force shall not take any active part in politics.

2. A member of a police force shall not reside at premises which are not for the time being approved by the chief officer of police.

3.—(1) A member of a police force shall not, without the previous consent of the chief officer of police, receive a lodger in a house or quarters with which he is provided by the police authority or sub-let any part of the house or quarters.

(2) A member of a police force shall not, unless he has previously given written notice to the chief officer of police, receive a lodger in a house in which he resides and in respect of which he receives a rent allowance or sub-let any part of such a house.

4. A member of a police force shall not wilfully refuse or neglect to discharge any lawful debt.

SCHEDULE 3 Regulation 28

ANNUAL LEAVE

1.—(1) Subject to Regulation 28 and the provisions of this Schedule, every member of a police force shall be granted in each leave year the period of annual leave set out opposite the rank he holds in the following Table:—

(a) where he has completed less than 10 years' relevant service, in the second column thereof;

(b) where he has completed 10 but has not completed 17 years' relevant service, in the third column thereof;

(c) where he has completed 17 or more years' relevant service, in the fourth column thereof.

TABLE

Rank	Annual leave		
	Under 10 years' relevant service	10 or more years' relevant service	17 or more years' relevant service
Constable	18 days	21 days	23 days
Sergeant (other than, in the metropolitan police force, station sergeant or first class sergeant (C.I.D.))	20 days	23 days	23 days
Station sergeant or first class sergeant (C.I.D.) in the metropolitan police force	22 days	25 days	25 days
Inspector	23 days	26 days	26 days
Chief inspector	26 days	29 days	29 days
Superintendent	42 days	48 days	48 days
Any rank higher than that of superintendent	Not less than 42 days	Not less than 48 days	Not less than 48 days

(2) In a leave year which began before 1st September 1970, this paragraph shall have effect in relation to a member of a police force holding a rank below that of superintendent as if each of the periods of annual leave set out in the above Table were decreased by a day.

2. In the leave year in which a member of a police force is appointed to, is promoted in, or retires from the force or completes 10 years' or, being of the rank of constable, completes 17 years' relevant service, his annual leave shall be calculated at the rate of a twelfth of the period of annual leave appropriate, under paragraph 1, to the rank held by him for each complete month of service in that rank in the leave year in question, a fraction of a day being reckoned as a day:

Provided that where a member of a police force is promoted or completes 10 years' or 17 years' relevant service while completing a month's service in the leave year in question, he shall be treated for the purposes of this paragraph as if he had been promoted or, as the case may be, completed 10 years' or 17 years' relevant service at the beginning of that month's service.

3. Notwithstanding anything in paragraphs 1 and 2, where the chief officer of police is satisfied that the exigencies of duty have prevented the grant in any leave year to a member of a police force below the rank of superintendent of the full period of annual leave specified in his case in those paragraphs, then the chief officer may, in his discretion and subject to the exigencies of duty, grant to the member, during the first 2 months of the following leave year, up to 6 days of the period not granted as additional days of annual leave.

4. For the purposes of this Schedule, the following expressions have the meanings hereby respectively assigned to them, that is to say:—

"leave year" means that period of 12 months beginning on such date as may from time to time be determined by the police authority;

"relevant service" means any service which the member concerned is entitled to reckon for the purposes of his scale of pay together with any service which he was previously so entitled to reckon—

(a) in the case of a member below the rank of superintendent, in any lower rank;

(b) in any other case, in the rank of superintendent or any higher rank,

except that relevant service shall not include any such service as is mentioned in Regulation 35 or 36.

Regulations 6, 31, 32 and 65   SCHEDULE 4

UNIVERSITY SCHOLARS

1.—(1) In this Schedule a reference to a university scholar is a reference to a member of a police force nominated for a course of university study by the Secretary of State or by the police authority maintaining the force of which he is a member in pursuance of arrangements in that behalf approved by the Secretary of State and, in relation to such a member, the expression "course" means the course for which he has been nominated and which he has undertaken and "study" means study for the purposes of that course.

(2) For the purposes of this paragraph a full-time course leading to a degree awarded by the Council for National Academic Awards shall be treated as a course of university study notwithstanding that the course is provided otherwise than at a university.

2. Regulations 24, 25 and 26 shall not apply to a university scholar for the duration of his course except for such period or periods, if any, as he is engaged otherwise than in study.

3.—(1) This paragraph shall apply to a university scholar, not being a member of the City of London or of the metropolitan police force, who has undertaken a course of study given wholly or mainly at an institution within the City of London or the metropolitan police district.

(2) Where such a university scholar takes up residence within the City of London or the metropolitan police district and the taking up of such residence is, in the opinion of the police authority, due to his having undertaken his course, then, for the duration of the course (whether or not he is so resident throughout that period), he shall be entitled to supplementary pay at the rate of £50 a year and his rate of pay, determined in accordance with Regulation 32(1) and Schedule 5, shall be increased accordingly.

4.—(1) Where a university scholar moves his home and the removal is in the opinion of the police authority due to his having undertaken his course, then, notwithstanding the provisions of Regulation 42, the rent allowance to be paid to him shall be that which would be payable to him under that Regulation if he was a member of the force of the police area in which his home is for the time being situate.

(2) Where a university scholar does not move his home, then, Regulation 43 shall have effect in relation to him for the duration of his course—

(a) as if for paragraph (1)(a)(iii) there were substituted the following provision:—

"(iii) satisfies the police authority that the only reason why he is not so living is that he could not, without detriment to his studies, return daily to the family home,";

(b) as if for paragraph (1)(b) there were substituted the following provision:—

"(b) a member of a police force, other than such a member as is mentioned in sub-paragraph (a), who satisfies the police authority that the only reason why he is not living in his former accommodation is that he could not, without detriment to his studies, return daily thereto,";

(c) as if for paragraph (2)(a) and (b) there were substituted the following provision:—

"if he were living with his family or, as the case may be, in his former accommodation.";

(d) where he is a widower with a child or children or a married man and, if he were a member of the force of the police area in which he is for the time being living and entitled to a flat-rate rent allowance under Regulation 42, that allowance would be payable at a higher rate than £3·35 a week, as if for the reference in paragraph (3)(b) to the rate of £3·35 a week there were substituted a reference to that higher rate.

(3) Where a university scholar moves his home and the removal is, in the opinion of the police authority, due to his having undertaken or completed his course of study and is, in their opinion, reasonable in all the circumstances of his case, Regulation 47 shall have effect in his case as if the removal were such as is mentioned in paragraph (1) thereof.

SCHEDULE 5   Regulation 32

PAY

PART I

SCALES OF PAY FOR MEN

1.—(1) The annual pay of a man holding—

(a) a rank in the City of London or metropolitan police force referred to in the following Table A; or

(b) a rank in any other police force referred to in the following Table B,

shall, subject to the next following sub-paragraph, be determined in accordance with the appropriate scale set out in the Table in question:—

TABLE A

MEMBERS OF CITY OF LONDON AND METROPOLITAN POLICE FORCES

Rank	Annual pay		
	Before completing 1 year of service in the rank	After 1 year of service in the rank	After 2 years of service in the rank
	£	£	£
Chief superintendent	3,075	3,180	3,295
Chief inspector in the City of London police force	2,350	2,430	2,525
Chief inspector in the metropolitan police force	2,050	2,115	2,185
Inspector	1,875	1,930	1,990
Station sergeant or first class sergeant (C.I.D.)	1,720	1,720	1,775
Sergeant or second class sergeant (C.I.D.)	1,555	1,605	1,660

TABLE B

MEMBERS OF OTHER POLICE FORCES

Rank	Annual pay		
	Before completing 1 year of service in the rank	After 1 year of service in the rank	After 2 years of service in the rank
	£	£	£
Chief superintendent	2,800	2,885	2,985
Superintendent, class I	2,590	2,675	2,770
Superintendent, class II	2,340	2,420	2,505
Chief inspector	1,980	2,045	2,110
Inspector	1,770	1,825	1,880
Sergeant	1,505	1,555	1,610

(2) Except in the case of a member of the City of London or metropolitan police force, the annual pay of a chief superintendent assigned to duties designated for the purposes hereof by the Secretary of State shall be—

(a) before completing 1 year of service in the performance of those duties, £3,075;

(b) after 1 year of such service, £3,180;

(c) after 2 years of such service, £3,295;

and, in the case of a member of the City of London police force, the scale of pay of a chief superintendent assigned to duties so designated shall be such as is determined by the Secretary of State.

2.—(1) The annual pay of a man holding the rank of constable who has not attained the age of 22 years shall, subject to sub-paragraph (3), be determined, by reference to his age in years, in accordance with the scale set out in the column of the following Table C appropriate to his police force:—

TABLE C

| Age | Annual pay | |
	City of London and metropolitan forces	Other forces
	£	£
19	950	900
20	990	940
21	1,030	980

(2) Save as provided in paragraph 3, the pay of a man holding the rank of constable who has attained the age of 22 years shall, subject to sub-paragraph (3), be determined, by reference to his service after attaining that age, in accordance with the scale set out in the column of the following Table D appropriate to his police force:—

TABLE D

| Service after attaining 22 years of age | Annual pay | |
	City of London and metropolitan forces	Other forces
	£	£
Before completing 1 year of service ...	1,075	1,025
After 1 year of service	1,120	1,070
After 2 years of service	1,200	1,150
After 3 years of service	1,245	1,195
After 4 years of service	1,290	1,240
After 5 years of service	1,340	1,290
After 6 years of service	1,390	1,340
After 14 years of service	1,430	1,380
After 19 years of service	1,470	1,420

(3) In the case of a man who has completed 2 years' service the scale set out in sub-paragraph (1) shall have effect as if it provided for supplementary pay of £45 a year and the scale set out in sub-paragraph (2) shall have effect—

(a) before completing a year's service after attaining the age of 22 years, as if it provided for supplementary pay of £45 a year, and

(b) after completing a year's service but before completing 2 years' service after attaining that age, as if it provided for supplementary pay of £40 a year.

3.—(1) The pay of a man holding the rank of constable whose period of service reckonable for the purposes of his scale of pay began on or before 1st March 1967 and who had attained the age of 22 years on or before that date shall be determined in accordance with sub-paragraphs (2) and (4) except that, in the case of a man who had completed a year of such service but not completed 4 years of such service on or before 1st March 1967, his pay shall be determined in accordance with sub-paragraphs (2) and (4) or in accordance with sub-paragraphs (3) and (4), whichever are for the time being the more favourable in his case.

(2) Where the pay of a man falls to be determined in accordance with this sub-paragraph, his annual pay shall be determined in accordance with the scale set out in the column of Table E in sub-paragraph (4) appropriate to his police force by reference to his relevant service for the purposes of this sub-paragraph, that is to say, by reference to his completed years of service reckonable for the purposes of his scale of pay reduced by the years of such service (if any) which he had completed on or before 1st March 1967, subject to a maximum reduction of 3 years:

Provided that—

(a) in the case of a man who, on or before 1st March 1967, had not completed 2 years' service reckonable for the purposes of his scale of pay, unless and until he has completed 2 years of such service, his annual pay, determined as aforesaid, shall be reduced as follows, that is to say—

(i) during his first year of relevant service, by £40, and

(ii) during his second year of relevant service, by £35,

(b) in the case of a man who, on or before 1st March 1967, had completed 2 years' but not 3 years' service so reckonable and had not attained the age of 24 years, unless and until he has completed 3 years of such service his annual pay, determined as aforesaid, shall be reduced by £40.

(3) Where the pay of a man falls to be determined in accordance with this sub-paragraph, his annual pay shall be determined in accordance with the scale set out in the column of Table E in sub-paragraph (4) appropriate to his police force, by reference to his relevant service for the purposes of this sub-paragraph, that is to say, by reference to his service after the commencement of the last anniversary of the day of his birth falling on or before 1st March 1967:

Provided that—

(a) in the case of a man who, on or before 1st March 1967, had not completed 2 years' service reckonable for the purposes of his scale of pay, unless and until he has completed 2 years of such service, his annual pay, determined as aforesaid, shall be reduced as follows, that is to say—

(i) during his first year of relevant service, by £40, and

(ii) during his second year of relevant service, by £35,

(b) in the case of a man who, on or before 1st March 1967, had completed 2 years' but not 3 years' service so reckonable and had not attained the age of 24 years, unless and until he has completed a year's relevant service his annual pay, determined as aforesaid, shall be reduced by £40.

(4) The Table E referred to in sub-paragraphs (2) and (3) is the following Table and, for the purposes thereof, the expression "relevant service" has the meaning assigned thereto by sub-paragraph (2) or, as the case may be, by sub-paragraph (3):—

TABLE E

Relevant service	Annual pay	
	City of London and metropolitan forces	Other forces
	£	£
Before completing 1 year of relevant service	1,120	1,070
After 1 year of relevant service	1,160	1,110
After 2 years of relevant service	1,200	1,150
After 3 years of relevant service	1,245	1,195
After 4 years of relevant service	1,290	1,240
After 5 years of relevant service	1,340	1,290
After 6 years of relevant service	1,390	1,340
After 14 years of relevant service	1,430	1,380
After 19 years of relevant service	1,470	1,420

4. The scale of pay of a man holding a rank above that of constable, not being a rank mentioned in Table A or, as the case may be, Table B in paragraph 1, shall be such as shall be determined by the Secretary of State.

5. For the purposes of paragraphs 2 and 3 a reference to service is a reference to service in the rank of constable.

PART II
SCALES OF PAY FOR WOMEN

1. The annual pay of a woman holding—

    (a) a rank in the City of London or metropolitan police force referred to in the following Table A; or

    (b) a rank in any other police force referred to in the following Table B,

shall be determined in accordance with the appropriate scale set out in the Table in question:—

TABLE A
MEMBERS OF CITY OF LONDON AND METROPOLITAN POLICE FORCES

Rank	Annual pay		
	Before completing 1 year of service in the rank	After 1 year of service in the rank	After 2 years of service in the rank
	£	£	£
Chief superintendent	2,770	2,860	2,965
Superintendent, class I	2,555	2,625	2,710
Chief inspector	1,850	1,910	1,975
Inspector	1,695	1,745	1,800
Sergeant	1,405	1,455	1,505

TABLE B
MEMBERS OF OTHER POLICE FORCES

Rank	Annual pay		
	Before completing 1 year of service in the rank	After 1 year of service in the rank	After 2 years of service in the rank
	£	£	£
Chief superintendent	2,520	2,600	2,685
Superintendent, class I	2,330	2,410	2,495
Superintendent, class II	2,105	2,180	2,255
Chief inspector	1,785	1,845	1,905
Inspector	1,595	1,645	1,695
Sergeant	1,355	1,405	1,455

2.—(1) The annual pay of a woman holding the rank of constable who has not attained the age of 22 years shall, subject to sub-paragraph (3), be determined, by reference to her age in years, in accordance with the scale set out in the column of the following Table C appropriate to her police force:—

TABLE C

Age	Annual pay	
	City of London and metropolitan forces	Other forces
	£	£
19	860	810
20	895	845
21	935	885

(2) Save as provided in paragraph 3, the pay of a woman holding the rank of constable who has attained the age of 22 years shall, subject to sub-paragraph (3), be determined, by reference to her service after attaining that age, in accordance with the scale set out in the column of the following Table D appropriate to her police force:—

TABLE D

Service after attaining 22 years of age	Annual pay	
	City of London and metropolitan forces	Other forces
	£	£
Before completing 1 year of service ...	975	925
After 1 year of service	1,015	965
After 2 years of service	1,085	1,035
After 3 years of service	1,125	1,075
After 4 years of service	1,165	1,115
After 5 years of service	1,210	1,160
After 6 years of service	1,255	1,205
After 14 years of service	1,290	1,240
After 19 years of service	1,330	1,280

(3) In the case of a woman who has completed 2 years' service the scale set out in sub-paragraph (1) shall have effect as if it provided for supplementary pay of £40 a year and the scale set out in sub-paragraph (2) shall have effect—

(a) before completing a year's service after attaining the age of 22 years, as if it provided for supplementary pay of £40 a year, and

(b) after completing a year's service but before completing 2 years' service after attaining that age, as if it provided for supplementary pay of £35 a year.

3.—(1) The pay of a woman holding the rank of constable whose period of service reckonable for the purposes of her scale of pay began on or before 1st March 1967 and who had attained the age of 22 years on or before that date shall be determined in accordance with sub-paragraphs (2) and (4) except that, in the case of a woman who had completed a year of such service but had not completed 4 years of such service on or before 1st March 1967, her pay shall be determined in accordance with sub-paragraphs (2) and (4) or in accordance with sub-paragraphs (3) and (4), whichever are for the time being the more favourable in her case.

(2) Where the pay of a woman falls to be determined in accordance with this sub-paragraph, her annual pay shall be determined in accordance with the scale set out in the column of Table E in sub-paragraph (4) appropriate to her police force by reference to her relevant service for the purposes of this sub-paragraph, that is to say, by reference to her completed years of service reckonable for the purposes of her scale of pay reduced by the years of such service (if any) which she had completed on or before 1st March 1967, subject to a maximum reduction of 3 years:

Provided that—

    (a) in the case of a woman who, on or before 1st March 1967, had not completed 2 years' service reckonable for the purposes of her scale of pay, unless and until she has completed 2 years of such service, her annual pay, determined as aforesaid, shall be reduced by £35;

    (b) in the case of a woman who, on or before 1st March 1967, had completed 2 years' but not 3 years' service so reckonable and had not attained the age of 24 years, unless and until she has completed 3 years of such service her annual pay, determined as aforesaid, shall be reduced by £35.

(3) Where the pay of a woman falls to be determined in accordance with this sub-paragraph, her annual pay shall be determined in accordance with the scale set out in the column of Table E in sub-paragraph (4) appropriate to her police force by reference to her relevant service for the purposes of this sub-paragraph, that is to say, by reference to her service after the commencement of the last anniversary of the day of her birth falling on or before 1st March 1967:

Provided that—

    (a) in the case of a woman who, on or before 1st March 1967, had not completed 2 years' service reckonable for the purposes of her scale of pay, unless and until she has completed 2 years of such service, her annual pay, determined as aforesaid, shall be reduced by £35;

    (b) in the case of a woman who, on or before 1st March 1967, had completed 2 years' but not 3 years' service so reckonable and had not attained the age of 24 years, unless and until she has completed a year's relevant service her annual pay, determined as aforesaid, shall be reduced by £35.

(4) The Table E referred to in sub-paragraphs (2) and (3) is the following Table and, for the purposes thereof, the expression "relevant service" has the meaning assigned thereto by sub-paragraph (2) or, as the case may be, by sub-paragraph (3).

TABLE E

Relevant Service	Annual pay	
	City of London and metropolitan forces	Other forces
	£	£
Before completing 1 year of relevant service	1,015	965
After 1 year of relevant service	1,050	1,000
After 2 years of relevant service	1,085	1,035
After 3 years of relevant service	1,125	1,075
After 4 years of relevant service	1,165	1,115
After 5 years of relevant service	1,210	1,160
After 6 years of relevant service	1,255	1,205
After 14 years of relevant service	1,290	1,240
After 19 years of relevant service	1,330	1,280

4. The scale of pay of a woman holding a rank above that of constable, not being a rank mentioned in Table A or, as the case may be, Table B in paragraph 1, shall be such as shall be determined by the Secretary of State.

5. For the purposes of paragraphs 2 and 3 a reference to service is a reference to service in the rank of constable.

PART III

TRANSITORY PROVISIONS RELATING TO THE PAY OF CERTAIN CHIEF
SUPERINTENDENTS

1. This Part shall have effect in respect of the period from 15th February until
3rd October 1971.

2. In relation to a period in respect of which this Part has effect, Regulation 32(2)
and Part I or, as the case may be, Part II of this Schedule shall have effect in the case of—

(a) a chief superintendent in the City of London police force promoted to that
rank on 3rd October 1969, or

(b) a chief superintendent in the metropolitan police force promoted to that rank
on 1st June 1969,

as if he had been so promoted on 1st April 1968 or on the date on which he was last
promoted to, or as the case may be appointed in, the rank of superintendent, class I,
whichever is the later.

Regulations 51 and 52   SCHEDULE 6

DETECTIVE DUTY AND SUPPLEMENTARY DETECTIVE ALLOWANCES

1. A detective duty allowance payable under Regulation 51 to a member of a police
force shall be paid at the annual rate set opposite the rank he holds in the second
column of the following Table A or, where the member is a woman, in the third
column thereof:—

TABLE A

Rank	Men	Women
	£	£
Chief inspector in the City of London police force	244	—
Chief inspector in the metropolitan police force	212	191
Chief inspector in any other police force	205	185
Inspector in the City of London and metropolitan police forces	193	175
Inspector in any other police force	183	165
First class sergeant (C.I.D.)	175	—
Sergeant in the City of London and metropolitan police forces or second class sergeant (C.I.D.)	161	146
Sergeant in any other police force	156	141
Constable in the City of London and metropolitan police forces	121	110
Constable in any other police force	116	105

2. A supplementary detective allowance payable under Regulation 52 to a member
of a police force shall be paid at the annual rate set opposite the rank he holds in the
following Table B:—

(a) where the average qualifying overtime mentioned in Regulation 52(1) is less
than 12 hours a week, in the second column or, where the member is a woman,
in the third column thereof;

(b) where the said overtime is 12 hours or more a week, in the fourth column or,
where the member is a woman, in the fifth column thereof:—

TABLE B

Rank	8 to 12 hours qualifying overtime		12 or more hours qualifying overtime	
	Men	Women	Men	Women
	£	£	£	£
Chief inspector in the City of London police force...	205	—	370	—
Chief inspector in the metropolitan police force...	175	160	315	290
Chief inspector in any other police force...	170	155	305	280
Inspector in the City of London and metropolitan police forces ...	160	145	290	260
Inspector in any other police force...	150	135	270	245
First class sergeant (C.I.D.)... ...	145	—	260	—
Sergeant in the City of London and metropolitan police forces or second class sergeant (C.I.D.) ...	135	120	245	215
Sergeant in any other police force ...	130	115	235	205
Constable in the City of London and metropolitan police forces ...	100	90	180	160
Constable in any other police force...	95	85	170	155

SCHEDULE 7   Regulation 53

SUBSISTENCE, REFRESHMENT AND LODGING ALLOWANCES

1. Subject as hereafter in this Schedule provided, the amount of a subsistence, refreshment or lodging allowance payable under Regulation 53 shall be in accordance with the scale set out in the following Table appropriate to the rank of the member of a police force concerned:—

TABLE

Description of Allowance	Superin-tendents	Inspectors, Sergeants and Constables
	£	£
Refreshment Allowance:		
(i) for one meal	0·410	0·375
(ii) for two meals	0·600	0·540
Subsistence Allowance:		
Period of retention or engagement on duty—		
(i) over 5 hours and not exceeding 8 hours	0·600	0·540
(ii) over 8 hours and not exceeding 12 hours	0·875	0·790
(iii) over 12 hours and not exceeding 24 hours	1·500	1·300
(iv) over 24 hours—at the rate under (iii) above for each complete period of 24 hours' retention or engagement, together with whichever is the appropriate amount under the preceding provisions of this Table for any excess over the aggregate of such complete periods.		
Lodging Allowance—for each night	2·700	2·100

2. If a lodging allowance is payable as well as a subsistence allowance in respect of a period of retention or engagement on duty of 16 hours or less, the subsistence allowance shall be of the amount appropriate to a retention or engagement for a period exceeding 8 hours and not exceeding 12 hours.

3. If the chief officer of police is satisfied in any particular case that the amount of the allowances calculated in accordance with paragraphs 1 and 2 is not sufficient to cover the actual expenses necessarily incurred, he may authorise payment of the difference.

4. If the chief officer of police is satisfied in any particular case that the amount of the allowances calculated in accordance with paragraphs 1 and 2 would be excessive having regard to the additional expenses necessarily incurred, he may direct that the amount of the allowances shall be reduced to such an amount as he determines, not being less than the amount of such expenses.

5. If in any particular case or class of cases the period of retention or engagement on duty exceeds a week and the chief officer of police is satisfied that the amount of the allowances calculated in accordance with paragraph 1 would be excessive, he may direct that there shall be granted in lieu thereof a weekly allowance at such lower rate as may be necessary to cover the reasonable expenses of the member concerned.

6. If a member of a police force below the rank of superintendent is required during any period to accompany a member of that or a higher rank, paragraph 1 shall apply to his case as respects that period as if he held the rank of superintendent.

Regulation 55   SCHEDULE 8

MOTOR VEHICLE ALLOWANCES IN RESPECT OF MOTOR CARS

1. Subject as hereinafter provided, the amount of a motor vehicle allowance shall be the standard amount calculated by reference to Table A or C of the following Tables except that it shall be the abated amount calculated by reference to Table B or D where it falls to be calculated by reference to completed months of authorised use beginning, or mileage of authorised use performed, at a time that the member of a police force concerned was—

    (a) provided with a garage free of rent and rates, or

    (b) in receipt of a maximum limit rent allowance which was less than the maximum limit applicable in his case and the house or accommodation occupied by him included a garage;

and references in paragraph 2 or 3 to the appropriate Table shall be construed accordingly.

2.—(1) Subject as hereinafter provided, the amount of a motor vehicle allowance payable at the essential user's rate shall in any year comprise—

    (a) a fixed element calculated, by reference to the number of completed months comprised in the period of authorised use in that year, at the annual rate set opposite the cylinder capacity of the motor car in question in the second column of the following Table A or B, as may be appropriate, or, in the case of a motor car of a cylinder capacity of 1,700 c.c. or more, at such annual rate as is approved by the Secretary of State, and

    (b) a mileage element calculated, in relation to the first 7,200 miles of authorised use in that year, at the basic rate so set out in the third column of the said Table and, in relation to any further authorised use in that year, at the reduced rate so set out in the fourth column of the said Table or, in the case of a motor car of a cylinder capacity of 1,700 c.c. or more, at such basic and reduced rates, respectively, as are approved by the Secretary of State:—

TABLE A

STANDARD AMOUNT

Cylinder capacity	Annual rate of fixed element	Mileage element	
		Basic rate per mile	Reduced rate per mile
	£	£	£
1,200 c.c. or more but less than 1,700 c.c.	102·000	0·036	0·022
1,000 c.c. or more but less than 1,200 c.c.	90·000	0·032	0·019
Less than 1,000 c.c. ...	81·000	0·028	0·017

TABLE B

ABATED AMOUNT

Cylinder capacity	Annual rate of fixed element	Mileage element	
		Basic rate per mile	Reduced rate per mile
	£	£	£
1,200 c.c. or more but less than 1,700 c.c.	87·000	0·034	0·022
1,000 c.c. or more but less than 1,200 c.c.	78·000	0·030	0·019
Less than 1,000 c.c. ...	69·000	0·026	0·017

(2) Where in any year a motor vehicle allowance is payable at the essential user's rate it shall be payable in such instalments, in advance or in arrears, as the police authority may determine; but when the amount of the allowance for that year is finally calculated, any overpayment shall be recoverable.

(3) Where in any year a motor vehicle allowance is payable at the essential user's rate to a member of a police force and he is on sick leave, or the motor car in question is out of order, for a continuous period of four or more weeks in that year the allowance shall be reduced by such amount as the police authority, with the approval of the Secretary of State, determines appropriate in all the circumstances.

(4) Where in any year a motor vehicle allowance is payable at the essential user's rate but the period of authorised use is a fraction only of that year, sub-paragraph (1)(b) shall have effect as if for the reference to 7,200 miles there were substituted a reference to the corresponding fraction of that mileage; and for the purposes of this paragraph the monthly rate of the fixed element of such an allowance so payable shall be taken to be a twelfth of the annual rate.

3. The amount of a motor vehicle allowance payable at the casual user's rate shall in any year be an amount calculated in relation to the mileage of authorised use in that year at the rate set out opposite the cylinder capacity of the motor car in question in the second column of the following Table C or D, as may be appropriate, or, in the case of a motor car of a cylinder capacity of 1,700 c.c. or more, at such rate as is approved

by the Secretary of State; except that, where the amount of the allowance would be less if it were payable at the essential user's rate it shall be of an amount calculated in accordance with paragraph 2:—

TABLE C
STANDARD AMOUNT

Cylinder capacity	Rate per mile
	£
1,200 c.c. or more but less than 1,700 c.c.	0·067
1,000 c.c. or more but less than 1,200 c.c.	0·059
Less than 1,000 c.c.	0·053

TABLE D
ABATED AMOUNT

Cylinder capacity	Rate per mile
	£
1,200 c.c. or more but less than 1,700 c.c.	0·061
1,000 c.c. or more but less than 1,200 c.c.	0·054
Less than 1,000 c.c.	0·048

4. The amount of a motor vehicle allowance payable to a member of a police force shall not exceed that which would be payable if the vehicle in question were of such a cylinder capacity as the chief officer of police, with the approval of the police authority, has determined appropriate for use for the purposes of the duties normally performed by the member concerned.

5. For the purposes of Regulation 55 and of this Schedule the following expressions have the meanings hereby respectively assigned to them:—

"authorised use" means the use, authorised under Regulation 55, of a motor vehicle owned by the member of a police force concerned for the purposes of his duties as a member of that force or, where he has been statutorily transferred from one force to another force, as a member of either of those forces, and

"period of authorised use" means the period during which such use is so authorised;

"cylinder capacity" means the cylinder capacity of the engine of a vehicle calculated in accordance with the regulations from time to time in force under the Vehicles (Excise) Act 1962 (a);

"motor bicycle" means a mechanically propelled bicycle (including a motor scooter, a bicycle with an attachment for propelling it by mechanical power and a mechanically propelled bicycle used for drawing a sidecar);

"motor car" means a mechanically propelled vehicle other than a motor bicycle and, accordingly, includes a mechanically propelled tricycle;

"year" means a period of 12 months beginning on 1st May;

and a reference to a motor vehicle owned by a member of a police force is a reference to such a vehicle kept and used by him.

(a) 1962 c. 13.

SCHEDULE 9   Regulation 56

BICYCLE ALLOWANCE

1. Subject as hereafter in this Schedule provided, the amount of a bicycle allowance shall be calculated by reference to the duration of the authority given for the purposes of Regulation 56 at the rate of £11 a year:

Provided that the amount of the allowance payable to a member of a police force in any year shall not be less than £2·75.

2. The allowance shall be payable quarterly or at such shorter intervals as the police authority may determine in advance or in arrears, as they may determine; but where payment is made in advance, any overpayment shall be recoverable.

SCHEDULE 10   Regulation 57

TYPEWRITER ALLOWANCE

1. The amount of a typewriter allowance shall be calculated by reference to the duration of the authority given for the purposes of Regulation 57 at a rate determined by the police authority not exceeding £4 a year.

2. The allowance shall be payable quarterly or at such shorter intervals as the police authority may determine in advance or in arrears, as they may determine; but where payment is made in advance, any overpayment shall be recoverable.

SCHEDULE 11   Regulation 67

ISSUE OF UNIFORM AND EQUIPMENT

1. The uniform specified in the following Tables for men and women respectively shall be issued in accordance with those Tables subject to any modifications approved by the Secretary of State:

Provided that where particular duties or the duties of a particular member of a police force entail greater or less wear than normal the issue of any article of uniform may be made as required:—

TABLES

MEN

Article	Issue	Period of wear	Number in possession
Jacket	One annually	Four years	Four
Trousers	Two pairs annually	Two years	Four pairs
Greatcoat	As required	—	One or two as may be determined by the police authority
Cape	As required	—	Two
Raincoat or mackintosh	As required	—	Two
Headdress	As required	—	Two
Shirts	Two annually, after an initial issue of not less than four nor more than six as may be determined by the police authority	—	—
Collars	Three for each shirt issued	—	—
Ties	Two annually	—	—

WOMEN

Article	Issue	Period of wear	Number in possession
Jacket	One annually	Four years	Four
Skirt	Two annually	Two years	Four
Greatcoat	As required	—	One or two as may be determined by the police authority
Raincoat or mackintosh	As required	—	Two
Headdress	As required	—	Two
Shirts	Two annually, after an initial issue of not less than four nor more than six as may be determined by the police authority	—	—
Collars	Three for each shirt issued	—	—
Ties	Two annually	—	—
Stockings	Twelve pairs annually	—	—

2. Uniform or equipment issued by the police authority which is lost or damaged otherwise than owing to the member's default or is faulty or is ill-fitting shall be replaced or repaired by the police authority free of charge:

Provided that this paragraph shall not apply to minor repairs or alterations which can be satisfactorily carried out by the member.

3. Clothing for particular duties such as mounted duty, cycling, driving of vehicles, or stable duty shall be issued as required.

4. Where boots or, in the case of women members, shoes are provided by the police authority for the purposes of duty the issue shall be at the rate of two pairs annually or as may be approved by the Secretary of State.

5. Issues of equipment shall be made as circumstances require and may include the issue of the following articles:—

Armlet and buckles
Button brushes and button stick
Cape strap and sling
Gloves
Handcuffs
Haversack or kit bag
Lamp
Overalls
Pocket note-book
Truncheon
Waist-belt
Warrant card
Waterproof cape
Waterproof leggings
Whistle and chain

EXPLANATORY NOTE

(*This Note is not part of the Regulations.*)

These Regulations consolidate, with amendments, the Police Regulations 1968 and the instruments amending those Regulations, namely the Regulations set out in Part I of Schedule 1.

The main changes are mentioned below.

The Regulations, which come into operation on 15th February 1971, take account of the introduction of decimal currency on that date.

Where a member of a police force holding the rank of constable is nominated for a course of university study before he has completed his probationary service, his period of study is to be disregarded in determining the period for which he is on probation (Regulation 15(5)(*b*)).

The special provisions as to rent allowances applicable to members of regional crime squads are extended to members of motorway patrol groups (Regulation 44(1)). By virtue of the amendment of the Regulations of 1968 contained in paragraph 2 of Part II of Schedule 1, this change has effect from 1st January 1971.

The rates of motor vehicle allowances are increased (Schedule 8). Provision is made for both standard and abated allowances. An abated allowance is payable where, for example, the recipient is provided with a garage free of rent and rates (paragraph 1 of Schedule 8). By virtue of the amendment of the Regulations of 1968 contained in paragraph 3 of Part II of schedule 1, these changes have effect from 1st October 1970.

The retrospective amendments made to the Regulations of 1968 by Part II of Schedule 1 are made in exercise of the power conferred by section 33(4) of the Police Act 1964.

STATUTORY INSTRUMENTS

1971 No. 157

POLICE

The Police (Promotion) (Amendment) Regulations 1971

Made	- - -	*28th January* 1971
Laid before Parliament		*10th February* 1971
Coming into Operation		*15th February* 1971

In exercise of the powers conferred on me by section 33 of the Police Act 1964(**a**), and after consulting the Police Advisory Board for England and Wales in accordance with section 46(3) of that Act as amended by section 4(6) of the Police Act 1969(**b**), I hereby make the following Regulations :—

1. These Regulations may be cited as the Police (Promotion) (Amendment) Regulations 1971 and shall come into operation on 15th February 1971.

2. In these Regulations any reference to the principal Regulations is a reference to the Police (Promotion) Regulations 1968(**c**).

3. Regulation 1(2)(*b*) of the principal Regulations (qualifications for promotion of sergeant to rank of inspector) is hereby revoked.

4.—(1) For paragraph (1)(*b*) of Regulation 8 of the principal Regulations (sergeant promoted inspector after Police College special course) there shall be substituted the following provision :—

"(*b*) who has completed a year's service in the rank of sergeant, otherwise than on temporary promotion under Regulation 7(1), to the satisfaction of the chief officer of police,".

(2) Paragraph (2) of the said Regulation 8 shall be omitted.

5.—(1) In paragraph (1) of Regulation 9 of the principal Regulations (interpretation)—

(*a*) the definition of the expression "ordinary outside police duty" shall be omitted, and

(*b*) the words "but does not include any period of unpaid maternity leave within the meaning of the Police Regulations 1968" shall be omitted from the definition of the expression "service".

(2) After paragraph (2) of the said Regulation 9 there shall be inserted the following paragraph :—

"(2A) In reckoning service or a period in any rank for the purposes of these Regulations there shall be disregarded—

(*a*) in the case of a woman, any period of unpaid maternity leave, and

---

(**a**) 1964 c. 48.   (**b**) 1969 c. 63.
(**c**) S.I. 1968/1074 (1968 II, p. 2893).

(*b*) in the case of a university scholar whose course begins on or after 15th February 1971, his period of study ;

and, for the purposes hereof, the expressions "unpaid maternity leave", "university scholar", "course" and "study" shall have the same meanings as in the Police Regulations 1971(**a**).".

R. Maudling,
One of Her Majesty's Principal
Secretaries of State.

Home Office,
Whitehall.

28th January 1971.

EXPLANATORY NOTE

(*This Note is not part of the Regulations.*)

These Regulations amend the Police (Promotion) Regulations 1968.

Regulation 3 makes it unnecessary for a sergeant to have performed a year's service as such in the performance of ordinary outside police duty before becoming qualified for promotion to the rank of inspector. Regulations 4 and 5(1)(*a*) make supplemental and consequential amendments.

Regulation 5 (apart from paragraph (1)(*a*)) relates to the reckoning of service for the purposes of the Regulations of 1968. It provides that, in the case of a member of a police force nominated for a course of university study, the period for which he is studying shall be disregarded.

(**a**) S.I. 1971/156(1971 I, p. 439).

STATUTORY INSTRUMENTS

1971 No. 161

CLEAN AIR

The Clean Air (Measurement of Grit and Dust from Furnaces) Regulations 1971

Made	-	-	-	*1st February* 1971
Laid before Parliament				*8th February* 1971
Coming into Operation				*1st March* 1971

The Secretary of State for the Environment, in exercise of his powers under section 7(2) of the Clean Air Act 1956(**a**) and of all other powers enabling him in that behalf, hereby makes the following regulations :—

Title and commencement

1. These regulations may be cited as the Clean Air (Measurement of Grit and Dust from Furnaces) Regulations 1971 and shall come into operation on 1st March 1971.

Interpretation

2. The Interpretation Act 1889(**b**) shall apply for the interpretation of these regulations as it applies for the interpretation of an Act of Parliament.

Measurement of grit and dust emitted from furnaces

3. Where, by virtue of a direction served by the local authority under section 7(1) of the Clean Air Act 1956 as amended by section 5(1) of the Clean Air Act 1968(**c**), the provisions of subsection (2) of the first-mentioned section apply to a furnace, the occupier of the building in which the furnace is situated shall comply with the requirements set out in the schedule hereto.

Revocation

4. The Clean Air (Measurement of Grit and Dust) Regulations 1968(**d**) are hereby revoked :

Provided that such revocation shall not affect any notice given, measurement made or recorded or any thing duly done under those regulations ; and every such notice given, measurement made or recorded or thing duly done shall have effect as if it had been given, made, recorded or done under these regulations.

(**a**) 1956 c. 52. (**b**) 1889 c. 63.
(**c**) 1968 c. 62. (**d**) S.I. 1968/431 (1968 I, p. 1139).

SCHEDULE

ADAPTATIONS TO CHIMNEYS AND PROVISION AND MAINTENANCE OF APPARATUS

1.—(1) Where the occupier receives not less than 6 weeks notice in writing from the local authority requiring adaptations to the chimney serving a furnace and the provision of apparatus for the purpose of making and recording the measurements of grit and dust emitted from the furnace, he shall, within the period specified in the notice, make such adaptations to the chimney as are necessary for the making and recording of such measurements by one of the procedures described in British Standard 3405, 1961, published by the British Standards Institution, and provide the apparatus therein mentioned.

(2) All apparatus provided for the purposes of this paragraph shall be maintained in good working order.

MAKING AND RECORDING MEASUREMENTS

2.—(1) When the requirements of paragraph 1 of this Schedule have been complied with the occupier, on receiving not less than 28 days notice in writing from the local authority requiring him to make and record measurements of grit and dust emitted from a furnace, shall within the period specified in the notice make and record such measurements in accordance with the procedure detailed in pages 13 to 26 of the publication "Measurement of Solids in Flue Gases" by P. G. W. Hawksley, S. Badzioch and J. H. Blackett, published in 1961 by the British Coal Utilisation Research Association.

(2) Before making any measurements the occupier shall give to the local authority not less than 48 hours notice in writing of the date on which and the time at which he proposes to commence to do so.

(3) The occupier shall, in relation to each chimney to which these regulations apply, keep a written record containing the following particulars—

(a) the date on which any measurements were made;

(b) the number of furnaces discharging into the chimney on that date;

(c) the measurements in terms of pounds per hour of grit and dust emitted and the percentage of grit contained in the solids emitted;

and shall transmit a copy of such particulars to the local authority within 14 days from the making of the measurements in respect of which the particulars are recorded.

(4) A notice served for the purpose of this paragraph may require the making of measurements from time to time or at stated intervals:

Provided that an occupier shall not be required to make measurements in respect of any one chimney more than once in any period of 3 months unless in the opinion of the local authority the true level of emission of grit and dust cannot be determined without the making of further measurements.

3. Anything required to be done by an occupier under the provisions of this schedule may be done on his behalf by any other person.

Peter Walker,

1st February 1971.   Secretary of State for the Environment.

EXPLANATORY NOTE

(This Note is not part of the Regulations.)

These Regulations re-enact the Clean Air (Measurement of Grit and Dust) Regulations 1968 which, under section 7 of the Clean Air Act 1956, prescribe the requirements to be observed in recording measurements of grit and dust emitted from certain furnaces. The provisions of that section have been considerably affected by the provisions of section 5 of the Clean Air Act 1968, and in particular the description of furnaces to which the Regulations can apply has been extended. (In some cases, however, the local authority can be asked to make and record the measurements.) The Regulations are now re-enacted so that they will apply to the extended description of furnaces ; and accordingly only minor amendments have been made in the text.

British Standard 3405, 1961 may be obtained from British Standards Institution, British Standards House, 2 Park Street, London, W.1, and "Measurements of Solids in Flue Gases" may be obtained from the British Coal Utilisation Research Association, Randalls Road, Leatherhead, Surrey.

STATUTORY INSTRUMENTS

1971 No. 162

CLEAN AIR

The Clean Air (Emission of Grit and Dust from Furnaces) Regulations 1971

Made - - -	*1st February* 1971
Laid before Parliament	*8th February* 1971
Coming into Operation	*1st November* 1971

The Secretary of State for the Environment, in exercise of his powers under section 2(1) of the Clean Air Act 1968(a), and of all other powers enabling him in that behalf, hereby makes the following regulations :—

Title and commencement

1. These regulations may be cited as the Clean Air (Emission of Grit and Dust from Furnaces) Regulations 1971 and shall come into operation on 1st November 1971.

Interpretation

2.—(1) In these regulations—

"indirect heating appliance" means a heating appliance in which the combustion gases are not in contact with the material being heated ;

"multiflue chimney" means a chimney structure which for the whole or the greater part of its vertical length carries separate flues from more than one furnace ; and

"schedule 1 furnace" and "schedule 2 furnace" mean respectively a furnace described in schedule 1 and a furnace described in schedule 2 to these regulations, being in either case a furnace to which section 2 of the Clean Air Act 1968 applies.

(2) The Interpretation Act 1889(b) shall apply for the interpretation of these regulations as it applies for the interpretation of an Act of Parliament.

Postponed application of regulations in certain cases

3. The provisions of these regulations shall not apply until 1st January 1978 to any furnace which has been installed, or the installation of which has been begun, or an agreement for the purchase or installation of which has been entered into, before the commencement of these regulations.

Limits on emission of grit and dust from certain furnaces

4.—(1) The quantities of grit and dust which may be emitted during any period from the chimney of a schedule 1 furnace or a schedule 2 furnace with a heat output or input which is within the highest and lowest values specified in column (1) of the relevant schedule shall not exceed the quantities prescribed by that schedule.

(a) 1968 c. 62. (b) 1889 c. 63.

(2) For the purposes of this regulation, where a chimney serves more than one furnace—

(a) if it is a multiflue chimney, each flue shall be taken as a separate chimney serving a separate furnace ; and

(b) in any other case, it shall be taken as a single chimney serving a single furnace with a heat output or input equivalent to the aggregate of the heat outputs or inputs of the furnaces concerned ;

and for these purposes any part of the emission which derives from a furnace to which these regulations do not apply shall be disregarded.

(3) The provisions of the next following paragraph shall have effect for applying the foregoing provisions to cases where the rating of a schedule 1 furnace or the heat input of a schedule 2 furnace is a value intermediate between two adjacent values in column (1) of the table in that schedule.

(4) In a case described in the preceding paragraph, the prescribed quantities in respect of the chimney of the furnace shall be arrived at as follows :—

(a) by interpolating the intermediate value into column (1) of the table between the two adjacent values (in this paragraph called "the two values") ;

(b) by calculating the interval between the lower of the two values and the intermediate value as a proportion of the interval between the two values, carried to two places of decimals ; and then

(c) by interpolating a figure, likewise carried to two places of decimals, into column (2) or (3), as the case may be, against the intermediate value at the same proportionate interval between the quantities prescribed in that column against the two values.

Circumstances in which the prescribed limits apply

5. These regulations shall apply to a furnace in respect of any period of standard operation, that is to say, any period during which the furnace is operating—

(a) at or close to the loading to which it is subject for the greater part of its working time or

(b) at any higher loading to which it is regularly subject for a limited time (whether or not that loading exceeds its Maximum Continuous Rating or designated heat input).

Regulations not to apply to incinerators

6. These regulations shall not apply to any incinerator, that is to say, to any appliance used to burn refuse or waste matter, whether solid or liquid, and whether or not the resulting heat is used for any purpose.

SCHEDULE 1

FURNACES RATED BY HEAT OUTPUT

Schedule 1 furnaces

1. The expression "schedule 1 furnace" means a furnace of—

(a) a boiler or

(b) an indirect heating appliance in which the material heated is a gas or liquid; and where any such furnace falls also within the definition of "schedule 2 furnace", it shall be treated for the purposes of these regulations as a schedule 1 furnace.

Heat output

2. The quantities of grit and dust which may be emitted from the chimney of a schedule 1 furnace shall be ascertained by reference to heat output, designated by Maximum Continuous Rating of the boiler or appliance in pounds of steam per hour (from and at 100 °C. (212 °F)) or in thousands of British thermal units per hour.

Quantities which may be emitted

3.—(1) Subject to the provisions of paragraph 4 below, the quantities of grit and dust, in pounds per hour, which may be emitted by the chimney of a schedule 1 furnace the heat output of which is within the highest and lowest values specified in column (1) of the following table shall not exceed—

(*a*) if the furnace burns solid matter, the quantities prescribed in column (2) against the value representing the output of that furnace or

(*b*) if the furnace burns liquid matter, the quantities prescribed in column (3) against that value.

Maximum Continuous Rating in pounds of steam per hour (from and at 100 °C. (212 °F.)) or in thousands of British thermal units per hour (1)	Maximum permitted quantities of grit and dust in pounds per hour	
	Furnaces burning solid matter (2)	Furnaces burning liquid matter (3)
825	1·10	0·25
1,000	1·33	0·28
2,000	2·67	0·56
3,000	4·00	0·84
4,000	5·33	1·12
5,000	6·67	1·4
7,500	8·50	2·1
10,000	10·00	2·8
15,000	13·33	4·2
20,000	16·67	5·6
25,000	20·0	7·0
30,000	23·4	8·4
40,000	30	11·2
50,000	37	12·5
100,000	66	18
150,000	94	24
200,000	122	29
250,000	149	36
300,000	172	41
350,000	195	45
400,000	217	50
450,000	239	54·5
475,000	250	57

Limitation on grit

4. In the case of a schedule 1 furnace which burns solid matter, the prescribed quantities may not contain more than the following proportion of particles exceeding 76 microns in diameter, that is to say—

(*a*) 33% where the Maximum Continuous Rating does not exceed 16,800 pounds per hour of steam or 16,800,000 British thermal units per hour or

(*b*) 20% in any other case.

SCHEDULE 2

Furnaces Rated by Heat Input

Schedule 2 furnaces

1. Subject to the provisions of paragraph 1 of schedule 1 above, the expression "schedule 2 furnace" means a furnace—

(*a*) of an indirect heating appliance or

(*b*) in which the combustion gases are in contact with the material being heated, but that material does not itself contribute to the grit and dust in the combustion gases.

Heat input

2. The quantities of grit and dust which may be emitted from the chimney of a schedule 2 furnace shall be ascertained by reference to the designated heat input, expressed as British thermal units per hour.

Quantities which may be emitted

3. Subject to the provisions of paragraph 4 below, the quantities of grit and dust, in pounds per hour, which may be emitted by the chimney of a schedule 2 furnace the heat input of which is within the highest and lowest values specified in column (1) of the following table shall not exceed—

(*a*) if the furnace burns solid matter, the quantities prescribed in column (2) against the value representing the heat input of that furnace or

(*b*) if the furnace burns liquid matter, the quantities prescribed in column (3) against that value.

Heat input in millions of British thermal units per hour	Maximum permitted quantities of grit and dust in pounds per hour	
	Furnaces burning solid matter	Furnaces burning liquid matter
(1)	(2)	(3)
1·25	1·1	0·28
2·5	2·1	0·55
5·0	4·3	1·1
7·5	6·8	1·7
10	7·6	2·2
15	9·7	3·3
20	11·9	4·4
25	14·1	5·5
30	16·3	6·6
35	18·4	7·7
40	20·6	8·8
45	22·8	9·8
50	25	10·9
100	45	16
200	90	26
300	132	35
400	175	44
500	218	54
575	250	57

Limitation on grit

4. In the case of a schedule 2 furnace which burns solid matter, the prescribed quantities may not contain more than the following proportion of particles exceeding 76 microns in diameter, that is to say—

> (*a*) 33% where the designed heat input of the furnace does not exceed 25 million British thermal units or
>
> (*b*) 20% in any other case.

Peter Walker,

1st February 1971.   Secretary of State for the Environment.

EXPLANATORY NOTE
(*This Note is not part of the Regulations.*)

Section 2 of the Clean Air Act 1968 contains provisions with respect to the emission of grit and dust from the chimneys of certain furnaces, and in particular empowers the making of regulations which prescribe specific limits on the quantities which may be emitted in particular cases. These Regulations prescribe limits applicable to certain furnaces, namely—

> (*a*) furnaces of steam boilers and of appliances for the indirect heating of gas or liquid with a Maximum Continuous Rating of between—
>
> > (i) 825 and 475,000 pounds of steam per hour (from and at 100°C. (212°F.)) or (the alternative being an equivalent)
> >
> > (ii) 825,000 and 475 million British thermal units per hour and
>
> (*b*) other furnaces of indirect heating appliances or in which the material being heated does not contribute to the emission, with a designated heat input of between 1·25 million and 575 million British thermal units per hour.

The section provides that emission of grit and dust at a higher rate will (subject to a statutory defence of "best practicable means") constitute an offence.

The Regulations will come into force on 1st November 1971; but their application to existing furnaces (as described in Regulation 3) is postponed until 1st January 1978.

STATUTORY INSTRUMENTS

1971 No. 163

SUGAR

The Sugar (Rates of Surcharge and Surcharge Repayments) (No. 2) Order 1971

Made	-	-	-	*2nd February* 1971
Laid before Parliament		-		*2nd February* 1971
Coming into Operation		-		*3rd February* 1971

The Minister of Agriculture, Fisheries and Food, in exercise of the powers conferred on him by sections 7(4), 8(6) and 33(4) of the Sugar Act 1956(a) having effect subject to the provisions of section 3 of, and Part II of Schedule 5 to, the Finance Act 1962(b), and section 58 of the Finance Act 1968(c) and of all other powers enabling him in that behalf, with the concurrence of the Treasury, on the advice of the Sugar Board, hereby makes the following order:—

1.—(1) This order may be cited as the Sugar (Rates of Surcharge and Surcharge Repayments) (No. 2) Order 1971; and shall come into operation on 3rd February 1971.

(2) The Interpretation Act 1889(d) shall apply for the interpretation of this order as it applies for the interpretation of an Act of Parliament.

2. Notwithstanding the provisions of Article 2 of the Sugar (Rates of Surcharge and Surcharge Repayments) Order 1971(e), the rates of surcharge payable under and in accordance with the provisions of section 7 of the Sugar Act 1956, having effect as aforesaid, in respect of sugar and invert sugar imported or home produced or used in the manufacture of imported composite sugar products shall on and after 3rd February 1971 be the appropriate rates specified in Schedule 1 to this order.

3. For the purpose of section 8(3)(b) of the Sugar Act 1956, having effect as aforesaid, the rates of surcharge repayments in respect of invert sugar produced in the United Kingdom from materials on which on or after 3rd February 1971 sugar duty has been paid or, by virtue of paragraph 1 of Part II of Schedule 5 to the Finance Act 1962, is treated as having been paid shall, notwithstanding the provisions of Article 3 of the Sugar (Rates of Surcharge and Surcharge Repayments) Order 1971 be the appropriate rates specified in Schedule 2 to this order.

4. Unless the rates of surcharge specified in Schedule 1, Part II, and the rates of surcharge repayment specified in Schedule 2 to this order have been varied by a subsequent order which comes into operation before the 15th February 1971 (the appointed day for the purposes of the Decimal Currency Act 1969(f))

(a) 1956 c. 48.
(c) 1968 c. 44.
(e) S.I. 1971/78 (1971 I, p. 132).

(b) 1962 c. 44.
(d) 1889 c. 63.
(f) 1969 c. 19.

then in ascertaining the rates of surcharge chargeable, and the rates of surcharge repayable, in respect of invert sugar

(a) until the end of 14th February 1971 there shall be disregarded any entry in Schedule 1, Part II, and Schedule 2 to this order as consists in a sum of money shown in square brackets; and

(b) on and after 15th February 1971 there shall be disregarded any entry in Schedule 1, Part II, and Schedule 2 as consists in a sum of money not shown in square brackets.

In Witness whereof the Official Seal of the Minister of Agriculture, Fisheries and Food is hereunto affixed on 29th January 1971.

(L.S.)   *R. P. Fraser,*
                                                      Authorised by the Minister.

We concur.
2nd February 1971.

Walter Clegg,
H. S. P. Monro,
Two of the Lords Commissioners of
Her Majesty's Treasury.

SCHEDULE 1

PART I

SURCHARGE RATES FOR SUGAR

Polarisation	Rate of Surcharge per ton
	£
Exceeding—	
99°	2·000
98° but not exceeding 99°	1·886
97° ,, ,, ,, 98°	1·840
96° ,, ,, ,, 97°	1·792
95° ,, ,, ,, 96°	1·744
94° ,, ,, ,, 95°	1·696
93° ,, ,, ,, 94°	1·648
92° ,, ,, ,, 93°	1·600
91° ,, ,, ,, 92°	1·552
90° ,, ,, ,, 91°	1·504
89° ,, ,, ,, 90°	1·456
88° ,, ,, ,, 89°	1·408
87° ,, ,, ,, 88°	1·368
86° ,, ,, ,, 87°	1·328
85° ,, ,, ,, 86°	1·292
84° ,, ,, ,, 85°	1·256
83° ,, ,, ,, 84°	1·220
82° ,, ,, ,, 83°	1·184
81° ,, ,, ,, 82°	1·152
80° ,, ,, ,, 81°	1·120
79° ,, ,, ,, 80°	1·088
78° ,, ,, ,, 79°	1·056
77° ,, ,, ,, 78°	1·024
76° ,, ,, ,, 77°	0·992
Not exceeding 76°	0·960

PART II

SURCHARGE RATES FOR INVERT SUGAR

Sweetening matter content by weight	Rate of Surcharge per cwt.	
	s. d.	£
70 per cent. or more	1 3	[0 ·06]
Less than 70 per cent. and more than 50 per cent.	11	[0 ·04]
Not more than 50 per cent.	5	[0 ·02]

SCHEDULE 2

SURCHARGE REPAYMENT RATES FOR INVERT SUGAR

Sweetening matter content by weight	Rate of Surcharge Repayment per cwt.	
	s. d.	£
More than 80 per cent.	1 6	[0 ·07]
More than 70 per cent. but not more than 80 per cent.	1 3	[0 ·06]
More than 60 per cent. but not more than 70 per cent.	11	[0 ·04]
More than 50 per cent. but not more than 60 per cent.	8	[0 ·03]
Not more than 50 per cent. and the invert sugar not being less in weight than 14 lb. per gallon	5	[0 ·02]

EXPLANATORY NOTE

(This Note is not part of the Order.)

This order prescribes—

(a) reductions equivalent to 4s. 0d. per cwt. of refined sugar in the rates of surcharge payable on sugar and invert sugar which become chargeable with surcharge on or after 3rd February 1971;

(b) correspondingly reduced rates of surcharge repayment in respect of invert sugar produced in the United Kingdom from materials on which surcharge has been paid.

This order also indicates decimal equivalents, effective from 15th February 1971, unless varied by a subsequent order, of the rates of surcharge and surcharge repayment on invert sugar specified in Schedule 1, Part II, and Schedule 2 respectively. Some of the rates have been rounded down.

STATUTORY INSTRUMENTS

1971 No. 164

SUGAR

The Composite Sugar Products (Surcharge and Surcharge Repayments—Average Rates) (No. 2) Order 1971

Made	-	-	-	*2nd February* 1971
Laid before Parliament		-		*2nd February* 1971
Coming into Operation		-		*3rd February* 1971

Whereas the Minister of Agriculture, Fisheries and Food (hereinafter called " the Minister ") has on the recommendation of the Commissioners of Customs and Excise (hereinafter called " the Commissioners ") made an order(a) pursuant to the powers conferred upon him by sections 9(1) and 9(4) of the Sugar Act 1956(b), having effect subject to the provisions of section 3 of, and Part II of Schedule 5 to, the Finance Act 1962(c), to the provisions of section 52(2) of the Finance Act 1966(d), and to the provisions of section 58 of the Finance Act 1968(e), providing that in the case of certain descriptions of composite sugar products surcharge shall be calculated on the basis of an average quantity of sugar or invert sugar taken to have been used in the manufacture of the products, and that certain other descriptions of composite sugar products shall be treated as not containing any sugar or invert sugar, and that in the case of certain descriptions of goods in the manufacture of which sugar or invert sugar is used, surcharge repayments shall be calculated on the basis of an average quantity of sugar or invert sugar taken to have been so used:

Now, therefore, the Minister, on the recommendation of the Commissioners and in exercise of the powers conferred upon him by sections 9(1), 9(4) and 33(4) of the Sugar Act 1956, having effect as aforesaid, and of all other powers enabling him in that behalf, hereby makes the following order:—

1.—(1) This order may be cited as the Composite Sugar Products (Surcharge and Surcharge Repayments—Average Rates) (No. 2) Order 1971, and shall come into operation on 3rd February 1971.

(2) The Interpretation Act 1889(f) shall apply for the interpretation of this order as it applies for the interpretation of an Act of Parliament.

2. Surcharge payable on or after 3rd February 1971 under and in accordance with the Sugar Act 1956, having effect as aforesaid, in respect of sugar and invert sugar used in the manufacture of the descriptions of imported composite sugar products specified in the second column of Schedule 1 to this order shall, notwithstanding the provisions of the Sugar (Rates of Surcharge and Surcharge Repayments) (No 2) Order 1971(g) and the Composite Sugar Products (Surcharge and Surcharge Repayments—Average Rates) Order 1971(a), be calculated by reference to the weight of the products at the appropriate rates specified in relation thereto in the third column of the said Schedule.

(a) S.I. 1971/79 (1971 I, p. 135).	(b) 1956 c. 48.	(c) 1962 c. 44.
(d) 1966 c. 18.	(e) 1968 c. 44.	(f) 1889 c. 63.
(g) S.I. 1971/163 (1971 I, p. 505).		

3. Imported composite sugar products other than those of a description specified in Schedules 1 and 2 to this order shall be treated as not containing any sugar or invert sugar for the purposes of surcharge payable on or after 3rd February 1971.

4. Surcharge repayments payable on and after 3rd February 1971 under and in accordance with the provisions of section 8 of the Sugar Act 1956, having effect as aforesaid, in respect of sugar and invert sugar used in the manufacture of the descriptions of goods specified in the first column of Schedule 3 to this order shall, notwithstanding the provisions of the Sugar (Rates of Surcharge and Surcharge Repayments) (No. 2) Order 1971(**a**) and the Composite Sugar Products (Surcharge and Surcharge Repayments—Average Rates) Order 1971(**b**), be calculated by reference to the quantity of the goods at the appropriate rates specified in relation thereto in the second column of the said Schedule.

5. Unless the rates of surcharge specified in Schedule 1, and the rates of surcharge repayment specified in Schedule 3, to this order have been varied by a subsequent order which comes into operation before the 15th February 1971 (the appointed day for the purposes of the Decimal Currency Act 1969(**c**)) then in ascertaining the rates of surcharge chargeable, and the rates of surcharge repayable, in respect of any goods

(*a*) until the end of 14th February 1971 there shall be disregarded any entry in Schedules 1 and 3 to this order as consists in a sum of money shown in square brackets; and

(*b*) on and after 15th February 1971 there shall be disregarded any entry in the said Schedules as consists in a sum of money not shown in square brackets.

In Witness whereof the Official Seal of the Minister of Agriculture, Fisheries and Food is hereunto affixed on 2nd February 1971.

(L.S.)   *R. P. Fraser,*
                                                         Authorised by the Minister.

SCHEDULE 1

In this Schedule:—

" Tariff heading " means a heading or, where the context so requires, a subheading of the Customs Tariff 1959 (see paragraph (1) of Article 2 of the Import Duties (General) (No. 7) Order 1970(**d**)).

Tariff heading	Description of Imported Composite Sugar Products	Rate of Surcharge	
		Per cwt. s. d.	Per cwt. £
04.02 ..	Milk and cream, preserved, concentrated or sweetened, containing more than 10 per cent. by weight of added sugar	10	[0 ·04]

(**a**) S.I. 1971/163(1971 I, p. 505).   (**b**) S.I. 1971/79(1971 I, p. 135).
(**c**) 1969 c. 19.   (**d**) S.I. 1970/1522 (1970 III, p. 4935).

Tariff heading	Description of Imported Composite Sugar Products	Rate of Surcharge	
		Per cwt. s. d.	Per cwt. £
17.02 (B) (2) and 17.05 (B)	Syrups containing sucrose sugar, whether or not flavoured or coloured, but not including fruit juices containing added sugar in any proportion:—		
	containing 70 per cent. or more by weight of sweetening matter	1　3	[0·06]
	containing less than 70 per cent., and more than 50 per cent., by weight of sweetening matter	11	[0·04]
	containing not more than 50 per cent. by weight of sweetening matter	5	[0·02]
17.02 (F) ..	Caramel:—		
	Solid	2　0	[0·10]
	Liquid	1　4	[0·06]
17.04 ..	Sugar confectionery, not containing cocoa ..	1　7	[0·08]
18.06 ..	Chocolate and other food preparations containing cocoa and added sugar:—		
	Chocolate couverture not prepared for retail sale; chocolate milk crumb, liquid ..	10	[0·04]
	Chocolate milk crumb, solid	1　1	[0·05]
	Solid chocolate bars or blocks, milk or plain, with or without fruit or nuts; other chocolate confectionery consisting wholly of chocolate or of chocolate and other ingredients not containing added sugar, but not including such goods when packed together in retail packages with goods liable to surcharge at a higher rate	10	[0·04]
	Other	1　1	[0·05]
19.08 ..	Pastry, biscuits, cakes and other fine bakers' wares containing added sugar:—		
	Biscuits, wafers and rusks containing more than 12½ per cent. by weight of added sugar, and other biscuits, wafers and rusks included in retail packages with such goods	6	[0·02]
	Cakes with covering or filling containing added sugar; meringues	8	[0·03]
	Other	3	[0·01]
20.01 ..	Vegetables and fruit, prepared or preserved by vinegar or acetic acid, containing added sugar:—		
	Containing 10 per cent. or more by weight of added sugar	8	[0·03]
	Other	1	[0·00½]
20.03 ..	Fruit preserved by freezing, containing added sugar	3	[0·01]
20.04 ..	Fruit, fruit-peel and parts of plants, preserved by sugar (drained, glacé or crystallised) ..	1　3	[0·06]
20.05 ..	Jams, fruit jellies, marmalades, fruit purée and fruit pastes, being cooked preparations, containing added sugar	1　3	[0·06]
20.06 ..	Fruit otherwise prepared or preserved, containing added sugar:—		
	Ginger	1　0	[0·05]
	Other	3	[0·01]

SCHEDULE 2

Tariff heading	Description of Imported Composite Sugar Products
17.05 (A) and (B)	Sugar and invert sugar, flavoured or coloured.

SCHEDULE 3

Description of goods	Rate of surcharge repayment per bulk barrel of 36 gallons
Lager	1 ·7d. [£0 ·007]
All beer other than lager	1 ·0d. [£0 ·004]

EXPLANATORY NOTE

(This Note is not part of the Order.)

This order provides for reductions on and after 3rd February 1971 in the average rates of surcharge payable on imported composite sugar products of the descriptions specified in Schedule 1 and in the average rates of surcharge repayment in respect of exported goods of the descriptions specified in Schedule 3. These correspond to the reductions in surcharge rates effected by the Sugar (Rates of Surcharge and Surcharge Repayments) (No. 2) Order 1971 (S.I. 1971/163). Provision is also made for certain imported composite sugar products to be treated as not containing any sugar or invert sugar.

This order also indicates decimal equivalents, effective from 15th February 1971, unless varied by a subsequent order, of the average rates of surcharge on imported composite sugar products of the descriptions specified in Schedule 1 and the average rates of surcharge repayment in respect of exported goods of the descriptions specified in Schedule 3. Some of the rates have been rounded down.

STATUTORY INSTRUMENTS

1971 No. 165

ROAD TRAFFIC

The Motor Vehicles (Tests) (Amendment) Regulations 1971

Made - - -	*1st February* 1971
Laid before Parliament	*10th February* 1971
Coming into Operation	*15th February* 1971

The Secretary of State for the Environment, in exercise of his powers under section 65(1) and (6) of the Road Traffic Act 1960(a) and of all other enabling powers, and after consultation with representative organisations in accordance with the provisions of section 260(2) of the said Act of 1960, hereby makes the following Regulations :—

1.—(1) These Regulations may be cited as the Motor Vehicles (Tests) (Amendment) Regulations 1971 and shall come into operation on the 15th February 1971.

(2) The Interpretation Act 1889(b) shall apply for the interpretation of these Regulations as it applies for the interpretation of an Act of Parliament.

2. The Motor Vehicles (Tests) Regulations 1968(c) as amended (d) shall have effect as though—

(1) in Regulation 19(1) for the fees shown as "seventeen shillings and six-pence" and "twenty-five shillings" there were substituted respectively the fees of "87 new pence" and "£1·25" ;

(2) in Regulation 23(2) for the fee shown as "two shillings and sixpence" there were substituted a fee of "13 new pence" ;

(3) in Regulation 25(2) for the words "of one shilling and threepence for each form of test certificate" there were substituted the words "at the rate of £6·25 for the supply of 100 forms of test certificate" ;

(4) for paragraph (3) of Regulation 27 there were substituted the following paragraph—

"(3) The Secretary of State may in respect of unissued forms of test certificate which are returned to him as having been cancelled because they have been spoilt or defaced make an appropriate refund to the authorised examiner or designated council by whom the forms are so returned." ;

(a) 8 & 9 Eliz. 2. c. 16.
(c) S.I. 1968/1714 (1968 III, p. 4607).
(b) 52 & 53 Vict. c. 63.
(d) S.I. 1969/1171 (1969 II, p. 3443).

(5) in Schedule 2, in paragraph (4) for the words "in sub-paragraphs (b)" there were substituted the words "in sub-paragraphs (a)" ;

(6) In Schedule 5—

(a) in Part I for the amounts shown in column 2 of the Table as "17s. 6d.", "25s. 0d.", "16s. 3d." and "23s. 9d." there were substituted respectively "87 new pence", "£1·25", "81 new pence" and £1·19" ;

(b) in Part II,

(i) in paragraph 2 for the definition of "earlier examination" there were substituted the following definition—

" 'earlier examination' means an examination of a motor vehicle in respect of which a fee of £1·19 or 81 new pence has been paid in accordance with the provisions of Parts I and III of this Schedule and includes such an examination in respect of which prior to 15th February 1971 a fee of 23s. 9d. or 16s. 3d. was paid in accordance with the said provisions as then applicable ;" ;

(ii) in proviso (a) to paragraph 4, for the words "four shillings" and "six shillings" there were substituted respectively the words "20 new pence" and "30 new pence" ;

(iii) in proviso (b) to paragraph 4, for the amounts of "4s. 0d." and "6s. 0d." there were substituted respectively the amounts of "20 new pence" and "30 new pence" ;

(iv) for the Table therein contained there were substituted the following Table :—

"TABLE

1	2
Description of examination	Amount of Fee
1. Examiner's re-test of a motor cycle not having a sidecar attached thereto, where a test certificate is issued where, after an earlier examination, no test certificate was issued because the prescribed statutory requirements were not complied with in respect of—	
(i) one of the relevant items	66 new pence*
(ii) two of the relevant items	46 new pence*
(iii) three of the relevant items...	26 new pence*
2. Examiner's re-test of any other motor vehicle to which these Regulations apply where a test certificate is issued where, after an earlier examination, no test certificate was issued because the prescribed statutory requirements were not complied with in respect of—	
(i) only the seat belt requirements	£1·25
(ii) one of the relevant items	96 new pence*
(iii) two of the relevant items	66 new pence*
(iv) three of the relevant items...	36 new pence*
3. Examiner's re-test of a motor cycle not having a sidecar attached thereto, where a test certificate is not issued where, after an earlier examination, no test certificate was issued because the prescribed statutory requirements were not complied with in respect of—	
(i) one of the relevant items	60 new pence*
(ii) two of the relevant items	40 new pence*
(iii) three of the relevant items...	20 new pence
4. Examiner's re-test of any other motor vehicle to which these Regulations apply where a test certificate is not issued where, after an earlier examination, no test certificate was issued because the prescribed statutory requirements were not complied with in respect of—	
(i) only the seat belt requirements	£1·19
(ii) one of the relevant items	90 new pence*
(iii) two of the relevant items	60 new pence*
(iv) three of the relevant items...	30 new pence
5. Examiner's special re-test of any motor vehicle to which these Regulations apply, where a test certificate is issued.	6 new pence."

Signed by authority of the Secretary of State.

John Peyton,
Minister for Transport Industries
1st February 1971.   Department of the Environment.

EXPLANATORY NOTE

(This Note is not part of the Regulations.)

These Regulations further amend the Motor Vehicles (Tests) Regulations 1968 by making minor amendments therein and expressing the various fees payable under those Regulations in decimal currency.

1971 No. 166

AGRICULTURE

The Price Stability of Imported Products (Rates of Levy) (Eggs) (No. 3) Order 1971

Made - - - - *1st February* 1971

Coming into Operation *2nd February* 1971

The Minister of Agriculture, Fisheries and Food, in exercise of the powers conferred upon him by section 1(2), (4), (5), (6) and (7) of the Agriculture and Horticulture Act 1964(a) and of all other powers enabling him in that behalf, hereby makes the following order:—

1. This order may be cited as the Price Stability of Imported Products (Rates of Levy) (Eggs) (No. 3) Order 1971, and shall come into operation on 2nd February 1971.

2.—(1) In this order—

" the Principal Order " means the Price Stability of Imported Products (Levy Arrangements) (Eggs) Order 1970(b) as amended by any subsequent order, and if any such order is replaced by any subsequent order the expression shall be construed as a reference to such subsequent order;

AND other expressions have the same meaning as in the Principal Order.

(2) The Interpretation Act 1889(c) shall apply to the interpretation of this order as it applies to the interpretation of an Act of Parliament and as if this order and the order hereby revoked were Acts of Parliament.

3. In accordance with and subject to the provisions of the Principal Order (which provides for the charging of levies on imports of those eggs and egg products which are specified commodities for the purposes of the Agriculture and Horticulture Act 1964) the rate of general levy for such imports into the United Kingdom of any specified commodity as are described in column 2 of the Schedule to this order in relation to a tariff heading indicated in column 1 of that Schedule shall be the rate set forth in relation thereto in column 3 of that Schedule.

4. The Price Stability of Imported Products (Rates of Levy) (Eggs) (No. 2) Order 1971(d) is hereby revoked.

In Witness whereof the Official Seal of the Minister of Agriculture, Fisheries and Food is hereunto affixed on 1st February 1971.

(L.S.)

G. P. Jupe,
Assistant Secretary.

(a) 1964 c. 28.   (b) S.I. 1970/359 (1970 I, p. 1277).   (c) 1889 c. 63.
(d) S.I. 1971/37 (1971 I, p. 32).

SCHEDULE

1. Tariff Heading	2. Description of Imports	3. Rate of General Levy
	Imports of:—	
04.05	*Birds' eggs (in shell or not in shell), fresh, dried or otherwise preserved, sweetened or not, other than egg yolks:*	(per 120 eggs)
	A. Eggs in shell:	s. d.
	1. Not exceeding 11 lb. in weight per 120 ..	3 6 [17½p]
	2. Over 11 lb. but not exceeding 12½ lb. in weight per 120	3 6 [17½p]
	3. Over 12½ lb. but not exceeding 14 lb. in weight per 120	3 6 [17½p]
	4. Over 14 lb. but not exceeding 15½ lb. in weight per 120	3 6 [17½p]
	5. Over 15½ lb. but not exceeding 17 lb. in weight per 120	3 6 [17½p]
	6. Over 17 lb. in weight per 120	3 6 [17½p]
	B. Eggs not in shell:	(per ton)
	Whole dried	£50

EXPLANATORY NOTE

(This Note is not part of the Order.)

This order, which comes into operation on 2nd February 1971, supersedes the Price Stability of Imported Products (Rates of Levy) (Eggs) (No. 2) Order 1971. It—

(a) reduces the rates of general levy on imports of eggs in shell in each of the weight grades which are numbered 1 to 6 in the Schedule to the order ;

(b) reduces the rate of general levy to be charged on imports of whole dried eggs not in shell.

STATUTORY INSTRUMENTS

1971 No. 167 (S.16)

SHERIFF COURT, SCOTLAND

Act of Sederunt (Citation of Defenders in the Sheriff Court) 1971

Made - - -	28*th January* 1971
Coming into Operation	29*th January* 1971

The Lords of Council and Session, under and by virtue of the powers conferred upon them by section 34 of the Administration of Justice (Scotland) Act 1933(**a**) and of all other powers competent to them in that behalf, do hereby enact and declare as follows :—

1. For so long only as there shall continue to be no postal delivery service provided by the Post Office, there shall, for the purpose of citing a defender in any civil proceedings in the Sheriff Court when postal citation is competent, be deemed to be sufficient compliance with any statutory requirement for the citation of such defender by post if the solicitor to a party or any person authorised by him shall deliver the citation form to the defender or shall leave it at his residence. The execution of citation in any such case shall be signed by such solicitor or person authorised as aforesaid, who shall be designed in the execution. Such execution shall set forth the mode of citation.

2. This Act of Sederunt may be cited as the Act of Sederunt (Citation of Defenders in the Sheriff Court) 1971 and shall come into operation on 29th January 1971.

And the Lords appoint this Act of Sederunt to be inserted in the Books of Sederunt.

J. L. Clyde,
I.P.D.

Edinburgh.
28th January 1971.

(**a**) 1933 c. 41.

EXPLANATORY NOTE

(This Note is not part of the Act of Sederunt.)

This Act of Sederunt, which applies only to the Sheriff Court, permits delivery of the citation of a defender by a solicitor or a person authorised by him in place of postal citation. The Act of Sederunt will remain in force only during the present Post Office strike.

STATUTORY INSTRUMENTS

1971 No. 169

EDUCATION, ENGLAND AND WALES

The Provision of Milk and Meals (Amendment) Regulations 1971

Made - - - -	*1st February* 1971
Laid before Parliament	*9th February* 1971
Coming into Operation	*15th February* 1971

The Secretary of State for Education and Science and the Secretary of State for Wales in joint exercise of their powers under section 49 of the Education Act 1944(**a**) as amended by section 3 of the Public Expenditure and Receipts Act 1968(**b**) and section 1 of the Education (School Milk) Act 1970(**c**) hereby make the following regulations:—

Citation, commencement and interpretation

1.—(1) These regulations may be cited as the Provision of Milk and Meals (Amendment) Regulations 1971 ; and the Provision of Milk and Meals Regulations 1969(**d**), the Provision of Milk and Meals (Amendment) Regulations 1970(**e**), the Provision of Milk and Meals (Amendment No. 2) Regulations 1970(**f**), the Provision of Milk and Meals (Amendment No. 3) Regulations 1970(**g**) and these regulations may be cited together as the Provision of Milk and Meals Regulations 1969 to 1971.

(2) These regulations shall come into operation on 15th February 1971.

(3) The Interpretation Act 1889(**h**) shall apply for the interpretation of these regulations as it applies for the interpretation of an Act of Parliament.

(4) References to regulations shall, unless the context otherwise requires, be construed as references to the Provision of Milk and Meals Regulations 1969 as amended.

(5) In the case of any school, " spring term " means the term ending last before the month of May and " summer term " means the term ending last before the month of September.

Charge for School Dinner

2.—(1) Subject to paragraphs (3) and (4) of regulation 10 (remission of charges), the charge for school dinners provided in a county or voluntary school under regulation 5(1) shall be—

(*a*) from 15th February 1971 until the end of the spring term 1971, 9p for every meal or 44p a week, as the parent may elect ;

(*b*) from the beginning of the summer term 1971, 12p for every meal—

and regulation 10(2)(a) (charge for school dinner) shall have effect accordingly.

(2) For the purposes of this regulation " week " means a period of five days beginning on Monday.

(**a**) 1944 c. 31. (**b**) 1968 c. 14. (**c**) 1970 c. 14.
(**d**) S.I. 1969/483 (1969 I, p. 1382). (**e**) S.I. 1970/339 (1970 I, p. 1225).
(**f**) S.I. 1970/511 (1970 I, p. 1715). (**g**) S.I. 1970/1417 (1970 III, p. 4667).
(**h**) 1889 c. 63.

Determination of financial hardship

3. Schedule 1 to the regulations (determination of financial hardship) shall, from the beginning of the summer term 1971, have effect subject to the substitution—

(*a*) for the table, of the table in the schedule to these regulations ; and

(*b*) for the references in the notes to that table to 52s and 9s, of references to £2·75 and £0·60 respectively.

SCHEDULE

| PART A | | | | | | | | | PART B | Regulation 3 |

Size of family	Net weekly income in £p									
	1	2	3	4	5	6	7	8	9	10
1	11·95									
2	14·70	14·10								
3	17·45	16·85	16·25							
4	20·20	19·60	19·00	18·40						
5	22·95	22·35	21·75	21·15	20·55					
6	25·70	25·10	24·50	23·90	23·30	22·70				
7	28·45	27·85	27·25	26·65	26·05	25·45	24·85			
8	31·20	30·60	30·00	29·40	28·80	28·20	27·60	27·00		
9	33·95	33·35	32·75	32·15	31·55	30·95	30·35	29·75	29·15	
10	36·70	36·10	35·50	34·90	34·30	33·70	33·10	32·50	31·90	31·30

Given under the Official Seal of the Secretary of State for Education and Science on 28th January 1971.

(L.S.)

Margaret Thatcher,
Secretary of State for Education
and Science.

Given under my hand on 1st February 1971.

Peter Thomas,
Secretary of State for Wales.

EXPLANATORY NOTE

(This Note is not part of the Regulations.)

These regulations convert the charge for school dinner in county and voluntary schools to decimal currency from 15th February and, as from the beginning of the summer term 1971, increase the charge to 12p and amend the provisions for the calculation of a parent's income for the purpose of determining his entitlement to remission of the charge.

STATUTORY INSTRUMENTS

1971 No. 170

GAS

The Gas (Meter) (Amendment) Regulations 1971

Made - - - -	*1st February* 1971
Laid before Parliament	*10th February* 1971
Coming into Operation	*15th February* 1971

The Secretary of State in exercise of his powers under section 54 of the Gas Act 1948(**a**) and all other powers him enabling hereby makes the following regulations: —

1. These regulations may be cited as the Gas (Meter) (Amendment) Regulations 1971 and shall come into operation on 15th February 1971.

2. The Interpretation Act 1889(**b**) shall apply to the interpretation of these regulations as it applies to the interpretation of an Act of Parliament.

3. The Gas (Meter) Regulations 1949(**c**), as amended by the Gas (Meter) (Amendment) Regulations 1961(**d**), shall have effect as though for the schedule there were substituted the schedule to these regulations.

Dated 1st February 1971.

John Davies,
Secretary of State
for Trade and Industry.

SCHEDULE
FEES

Column 1	Column 2
Meter examined	Fee
1. For examining, with or without stamping, or re-examining any meter (not being a prototype) with measuring capacity—	
(*a*) not exceeding 650 cubic feet per hour	£0·21
(*b*) exceeding 650 cubic feet, but not exceeding 1,850 cubic feet per hour	£0·75
(*c*) exceeding 1,850 cubic feet, but not exceeding 8,050 cubic feet per hour	£4
(*d*) exceeding 8,050 cubic feet, but not exceeding 15,050 cubic feet per hour	£10
(*e*) exceeding 15,050 cubic feet per hour	£20
In the case of the re-examination of a disputed meter under regulation 2 a surcharge of	£0·25
2. For examining the prototype of any meter with measuring capacity—	
(*a*) not exceeding 650 cubic feet per hour	£20
(*b*) exceeding 650 cubic feet per hour	£40

(a) 1948 c. 67.   (b) 1889 c. 63.   (c) S.I. 1949/790 (1949 I, p. 1985).
(d) S.I. 1961/714 (1961 I, p. 1453).

EXPLANATORY NOTE

(This Note is not part of the Regulations.)

These regulations modify the provisions of the Gas (Meter) Regulations 1949 as amended by the Gas (Meter) (Amendment) Regulations 1961 to take account of the introduction of decimal currency on 15th February 1971 the date on which these regulations also come into operation.

STATUTORY INSTRUMENTS

1971 No. 171

SEA FISHERIES

BOATS AND METHODS OF FISHING

The Salmon (Northwest Atlantic) Order 1971

Made - - -	*2nd February* 1971
Laid before Parliament	*10th February* 1971
Coming into Operation	*15th February* 1971

The Minister of Agriculture, Fisheries and Food and the Secretary of State for Scotland and the Secretary of State for the Home Department, being the Secretaries of State concerned with the sea-fishing industry in Scotland and Northern Ireland respectively, in exercise of the powers conferred on them by section 5 of the Sea Fish (Conservation) Act 1967(a) and of all other powers enabling them in that beha'f hereby make the following order :—

Citation and Commencement

1. This order may be cited as the Salmon (Northwest Atlantic) Order 1971 and shall come into operation on 15th February 1971.

Prohibition

2. Fishing for salmon in those waters of the Northwest Atlantic Ocean which are described in the Schedule to this order (being the waters to which the International Convention for the Northwest Atlantic Fisheries (**b**) applies) is hereby prohibited.

In witness whereof the Official Seal of the Minister of Agriculture, Fisheries ard Food is hereunto affixed on 28th January 1971.

(L.S.)   *J. M. L. Prior,*
Minister of Agriculture, Fisheries and Food.

Given under the Seal of the Secretary of State for Scotland on 29th January 1971.

(L.S.)   *Gordon Campbell,*
Secretary of State for Scotland.

Given under the hand of the Secretary of State for the Home Department on 2nd February 1971.

R. Maudling,
Secretary of State for the
Home Department.

(**a**) 1967 c. 84.   (**b**) Cmnd. 8071.

SCHEDULE

All waters, except territorial waters, bounded by a line beginning at a point on the coast of Rhode Island in 71° 40′ west longitude ; thence due south to 39° 00′ north latitude ; thence due east to 42° 00′ west longitude ; thence due north to 59° 00′ north latitude ; thence due west to 44° 00′ west longitude ; thence due north to the coast of Greenland ; thence along the west coast of Greenland to 78° 10′ north latitude ; thence southward to a point in 75° 00′ north latitude and 73° 30′ west longitude ; thence along a rhumb line to a point in 69° 00′ north latitude and 59° 00′ west longitude ; thence due south to 61° 00′ north latitude ; thence due west to 64° 30′ west longitude ; thence due south to the coast of Labrador ; thence in a southerly direction along the coast of Labrador to the southern terminus of its boundary with Quebec ; thence in a westerly direction along the coast of Quebec, and in an easterly and southerly direction along the coasts of New Brunswick, Nova Scotia, and Cape Breton Island to Cabot Strait ; thence along the coasts of Cape Breton Island, Nova Scotia, New Brunswick, Maine, New Hampshire, Massachusetts, and Rhode Island to the point of beginning.

EXPLANATORY NOTE

(*This Note is not part of the order.*)

This order, which is made under the powers contained in section 5 of the Sea Fish (Conservation) Act 1967, prohibits fishing for salmon in those parts of the North Atlantic Ocean to which the International Convention for the Northwest Atlantic Fisheries applies. By virtue of section 5(8) of the Act of 1967 the prohibition applies to all British fishing boats registered in the United Kingdom and to fishing boats which are British-owned but not registered under the Merchant Shipping Act 1894.

The order implements an agreement of the Commission established under the Convention.

STATUTORY INSTRUMENTS

1971 No. 172

SEA FISHERIES

LANDING AND SALE OF SEA FISH

The Salmon and Migratory Trout (Restrictions on Landing) Order 1971

Made - - -	*2nd February* 1971
Laid before Parliament	*10th February* 1971
Coming into Operation	*15th February* 1971

The Minister of Agriculture, Fisheries and Food, and the Secretary of State for Scotland and the Secretary of State for the Home Department, being the Secretaries of State concerned with the sea-fishing industry in Scotland and Northern Ireland respectively, in exercise of the powers conferred on them by section 6 of the Sea Fish (Conservation) Act 1967(a) and of all other powers enabling them in that behalf, after consultation with the Secretary of State for Trade and Industry (b), hereby make the following order :—

Citation and Commencement

1. This order may be cited as the Salmon and Migratory Trout (Restrictions on Landing) Order 1971 and shall come into operation on 15th February 1971.

Interpretation

2.—(1) In this order—

"drift-net" means any length of net allowed to float or drift being either attached to or released from a fishing boat and not being a length of net attached to or held on the shore ;

"the mouth of the River Tweed" means the area as defined by the Tweed Fisheries Amendment Act 1859(c) as amended by byelaw dated 10th August 1863 contained in Schedule A to the Salmon Fisheries (Scotland) Act 1868(d) ;

"the Northern part of British fishery limits" means the areas of sea described in Schedule 3 to this order ;

"North-East Atlantic waters" means the waters described in Schedule 2 to this order, being part of the waters to which the North-East Atlantic Fisheries Convention (e) applies ;

"North-West Atlantic waters" means the waters described in Schedule 1 to this order, being the waters to which the International Convention for the Northwest Atlantic Fisheries (f) applies ;

(a) 1967 c. 84.

(b) For transfer of functions from the Board of Trade to the Secretary of State for Trade and Industry see the Secretary of State for Trade and Industry Order 1970 (S.I. 1970/1537 (1970 III, p. 5293)).

(c) 1859 c. lxx.   (d) 1868 c. 123.   (e) Cmnd. 2190.   (f) Cmnd 8071.

"the Southern part of British fishery limits" means the area of sea described in Schedule 4 to this order ;

"specified method" means a method of fishing with drift-net, trawl net, seine net, troll or long-line, but does not include beach seining or fishing from the shore by net and coble.

(2) The Interpretation Act 1889(a) shall apply for the interpretation of this order as it applies for the interpretation of an Act of Parliament.

Prohibition of Landings

3. There is hereby prohibited the landing in Great Britain during the period from 15th February 1971 to 14th February 1973, both days inclusive, of :—

(*a*) salmon caught in North-West Atlantic waters ;

(*b*) salmon and migratory trout caught in North-East Atlantic waters ;

(*c*) salmon and migratory trout caught by a specified method in the Northern part of British fishery limits ;

(*d*) salmon and migratory trout caught in waters within the territorial waters of England and Wales and included in the Southern part of British fishery limits, and salmon and migratory trout caught in the course of fishing by way of trade or business in the remainder of that Southern part, subject nevertheless to the provisions of Article 4 of this order.

Exemption from prohibition of Landings

4. Notwithstanding the prohibition contained in Article 3 of this order, it shall be lawful to land in Great Britain salmon and migratory trout caught in the Southern part of British fishery limits provided that such catching was effected in the course of fishing under the authority of and in accordance with the conditions of a licence granted :—

(*a*) in respect of fishing for salmon and migratory trout in waters within the territorial waters of England and Wales and included in the Southern part of British fishery limits, by the River Authority having jurisdiction in those waters, or

(*b*) in respect of fishing for salmon and migratory trout in the remainder of the Southern part of British fishery limits, by the Minister of Agriculture, Fisheries and Food.

In witness whereof the Official Seal of the Minister of Agriculture, Fisheries and Food is hereunto affixed on 28th January 1971.

(L.S.)

J. M. L. Prior,
Minister of Agriculture, Fisheries and Food.

Given under the Seal of the Secretary of State for Scotland on 29th January 1971.

(L.S.)

Gordon Campbell,
Secretary of State for Scotland.

(a) 1889 c. 63.

Given under the hand of the Secretary of State for the Home Department on 2nd February 1971.

R. Maudling,
Secretary of State for the
Home Department.

SCHEDULE 1

NORTH-WEST ATLANTIC WATERS

All waters, except territorial waters, bounded by a line beginning at a point on the coast of Rhode Island in 71° 40′ west longitude ; thence due south to 39° 00′ north latitude ; thence due east to 42° 00′ west longitude ; thence due north to 59° 00′ north latitude ; thence due west to 44° 00′ west longitude ; thence due north to the coast of Greenland ; thence along the west coast of Greenland to 78° 10′ north latitude ; thence southward to a point in 75° 00′ north latitude and 73° 30′ west longitude ; thence along a rhumb line to a point in 69° 00′ north latitude and 59° 00′ west longitude ; thence due south to 61° 00′ north latitude ; thence due west to 64° 30′ west longitude ; thence due south to the coast of Labrador ; thence in a southerly direction along the coast of Labrador to the southern terminus of its boundary with Quebec ; thence in a westerly direction along the coast of Quebec, and in an easterly and southerly direction along the coasts of New Brunswick, Nova Scotia, and Cape Breton Island to Cabot Strait ; thence along the coasts of Cape Bretan Island, Nova Scotia, New Brunswick, Maine, New Hampshire, Massachusetts, and Rhode Island to the point of beginning.

SCHEDULE 2

NORTH-EAST ATLANTIC WATERS

Those areas of the Atlantic and Arctic Oceans and seas adjacent to those oceans which lie outside the fishery limits of the British Islands north of 36° north latitude, between 42° west longitude and 51° east longitude and north of 59° north latitude between 44° west longitude and 42° west longitude but excluding the Mediterranean and Baltic Seas and Belts lying to the south and east of lines drawn from Hasenore Head, Denmark, to Gniben Point, Denmark, from Kor-shage, Denmark, to Spodsbierg, Denmark and from Gilbierg Head, Denmark, to Kullen, Sweden.

SCHEDULE 3

NORTHERN PART OF BRITISH FISHERY LIMITS

Those areas of sea within the fishery limits of the British Islands lying north of 54° 30′ north latitude, excluding : —

(a) the territorial waters of England except in so far as they lie within the mouth of the River Tweed ;

(b) waters, other than the territorial waters mentioned in sub-paragraph (a) of this paragraph, lying on the east coast of England south of the southern boundary of the mouth of the River Tweed and of a line drawn due east from the eastmost point of that boundary ;

(c) waters within such part of the fishery limits of the British Islands as is mentioned in Section 4(2) of the Fishery Limits Act 1964(a).

(a) 1964 c. 72.

SCHEDULE 4

SOUTHERN PART OF BRITISH FISHERY LIMITS

The area of sea contained within a line drawn eastward from the coast of England along the southern boundary of the mouth of the River Tweed to the eastmost point of that boundary ; thence due east to the intersection with the boundary of the fishery limits of the British Islands ; thence along that boundary in a clockwise direction around the coasts of England and Wales to the intersection with the parallel of latitude 54° 30′ north in the Irish Sea ; thence eastwards along that parallel until it meets the coast of England.

EXPLANATORY NOTE

(This Note is not part of the Order.)

This order made under powers contained in section 6 of the Sea Fish (Conservation) Act 1967 prohibits the landing in Great Britain of salmon and migratory trout caught in certain specified waters.

STATUTORY INSTRUMENTS

1971 No. 174 (S.18)

LEGAL AID AND ADVICE, SCOTLAND

Act of Sederunt (Legal Aid Rules Amendment) 1971

Made - - - -	*29th January,* 1971
Coming into operation	*1st March,* 1971

The Lords of Council and Session, under and by virtue of the powers conferred upon them by section 16 of the Legal Aid (Scotland) Act 1967(a) and of all other powers competent to them in that behalf, do hereby enact and declare as follows: —

1. The Act of Sederunt (Legal Aid Rules) 1958(b) shall be amended as follows: —

(1) At the end of paragraph 1(2) there shall be added an additional clause in the following terms:
" ' court ' shall mean court or tribunal, unless the context otherwise requires."

(2) At the end of paragraph 2(1) there shall be added two new sections in the following terms:
" (*g*) proceedings in the Scottish Land Court ;
" (*h*) proceedings before the Lands Tribunal for Scotland."

(3) Paragraph 4(2) shall be deleted and there shall be substituted a new sub-paragraph (2) of paragraph 4 in the following terms:
" (2) Where a legal aid certificate has been issued to the other party to the proceedings in whose favour an award of expenses may fall to be made and where, as a result thereof, the Law Society of Scotland has an interest in the amount of expenses awarded to such other person, it shall be competent for the Law Society to be represented by counsel in the Court of Session, or by solicitor in the Scottish Land Court or the Sheriff Court or before the Lands Tribunal for Scotland, in order to make representations to the court as to the amount of the award of expenses to be made against the assisted person."

(4) Paragraph 5(2) shall be deleted and there shall be substituted a new sub-paragraph (2) of paragraph 5 in the following terms:
" (3) Where a court issues a direction under the foregoing paragraph, the Principal Clerk of Session, the Principal Clerk to the Scottish Land Court, the Sheriff Clerk, or the Clerk to the Lands Tribunal for Scotland, as the case may be, shall send a copy of the direction to the Committee by whom the certificate was issued, who shall forthwith discharge the certificate of the assisted person concerned in relation to the proceedings before that court."

(a) 1967 c. 43.   (b) S.I. 1958/1872 (1958 I, p. 389).

2. This Act of Sederunt may be cited as the Act of Sederunt (Legal Aid Rules Amendment) 1971, and shall come into operation on 1st March 1971.

And the Lords appoint this Act of Sederunt to be inserted in the Books of Sederunt.

J. L. Clyde,
I.P.D.

Edinburgh,
29th January 1971.

EXPLANATORY NOTE

(This Note is not part of the Act of Sederunt.)

This Act of Sederunt amends the Act of Sederunt (Legal Aid Rules) 1958 by making provision for proceedings in the Scottish Land Court and before the Lands Tribunal for Scotland to be treated as distinct proceedings for the purposes of legal aid.

STATUTORY INSTRUMENTS

1971 No. 175 (S.19)

THEATRES

The Theatres (Licence Application Fees) (Scotland) Amendment Order 1971

Made - - -	*28th January* 1971
Laid before Parliament	*9th February* 1971
Coming into Operation	*15th February* 1971

In exercise of the powers conferred on me by paragraph 3(1) and (2) of Schedule 1 to the Theatres Act 1968(a), I hereby make the following order :—

1. This order may be cited as the Theatres (Licence Application Fees) (Scotland) Amendment Order 1971 and shall come into operation on 15th February 1971.

2. In Articles 1(2)(*a*) and 3 of the Theatres (Licence Application Fees) (Scotland) Order 1968(b), for the sum "£1 5s. 0d.", in both places where it occurs, there shall be substituted the sum "£1·25".

3. In Articles 1(2)(*b*) and 2(1) of the said Order of 1968, for the sum "7s. 6d.", in both places where it occurs, there shall be substituted the sum "£0·35".

Gordon Campbell,
One of Her Majesty's Principal
Secretaries of State.

St. Andrew's House,
Edinburgh.
28th January 1971.

EXPLANATORY NOTE

(This Note is not part of the Order.)

This Order amends the Theatre (Licence Application Fees) (Scotland) Order 1968 and comes into operation on 15th February 1971. The Order of 1968 provides for fees of £1 5s. 0d. and 7s. 6d. and of multiples of those sums. The present Order substitutes, for the first of these sums, the decimal equivalent and, for the second, the lesser sum of £0·35 (7s. 0d.).

(a) 1968 c. 54. (b) S.I. 1968/1452 (1968 III, p. 4191).

STATUTORY INSTRUMENTS

1971 No. 176

CIVIL AVIATION

The Air Corporations (General Staff, Pilots and Officers Pensions) (Amendment) Regulations 1971

Made - - - *3rd February* 1971

Coming into Operation *16th February* 1971

The Secretary of State in exercise of his powers under section 24 of the Air Corporations Act 1967(a) and of all other powers enabling him in that behalf, after consulting with each of the Corporations and with such organisations representative of the employees to whom the Regulations will relate as appear to him to be appropriate, hereby makes the following Regulations :—

1.—(1) These Regulations shall come into operation on 16th February 1971 and may be cited as the Air Corporations (General Staff, Pilots and Officers Pensions) (Amendment) Regulations 1971.

(2) These Regulations—

(a) shall be construed as one with the Air Corporations (General Staff Pensions) Regulations 1948(b) ;

(b) may be cited together with the Air Corporations (Pensions) Regulations 1948 to 1970(c) as the Air Corporations (Pensions) Regulations 1948 to 1971.

(3) The Interpretation Act 1889(d) shall apply for the purpose of these Regulations as it applies for the purpose of the interpretation of an Act of Parliament.

2.—(1) The Joint Pension Scheme established and maintained by virtue of the Air Corporations (Pensions) Regulations 1948 to 1970 shall be in accordance with the provisions of the Trust Deed and Amending Deeds, copies of which are set out in the Schedules to those Regulations as further amended by a Deed dated 29th October 1970, a copy of which is set out in the Schedule to these Regulations.

(2) The said Deed dated 29th October 1970 is accordingly confirmed and shall come into operation on 16th February 1971.

3. British Air Services Ltd. (being a subsidiary of the British European Airways Corporation) whose employees are admitted to the Scheme by virtue of the said Deed dated 29th October 1970, and each of their employees who is a member of the Scheme shall, for the purpose of providing funds from which benefits under the said Scheme may be paid, pay contributions in accordance with the provisions of the said Trust Deeds.

(a) 1967 c. 33.
(b) S.I. 1948/2361 (Rev. I, p. 1275: 1948 I, p. 437).
(c) See S.I. 1948/2361 (Rev. I, p. 1275: 1948 I, p. 437) and amending instruments down to S.I. 1970/768 (1970 II, p. 2418).
(d) 1889 c. 63.

4. Contributions and benefits shall be paid in respect of the service of such an employee with British Air Services Ltd. before the coming into force of these Regulations in accordance with the provisions of the said Trust Deed.

P. A. R. Brown,
An Under Secretary,
Department of Trade and Industry.

3rd February 1971.

SCHEDULE

THIS DEED is made the twenty-ninth day of October One thousand nine hundred and seventy BETWEEN BRITISH OVERSEAS AIRWAYS CORPORATION whose principal office is situate at Speedbird House Heathrow Airport (London) Hounslow in the County of Middlesex and BRITISH EUROPEAN AIRWAYS CORPORATION whose principal office is situate at Bealine House Ruislip in the County of Middlesex BOAC RESTAURANTS LIMITED whose registered office is situate at Speedbird House aforesaid BEA HELICOPTERS LIMITED whose registered office is situate at Gatwick Airport (London) Horley in the County of Surrey BEA AIRTOURS LIMITED whose registered office is situate at Bealine House aforesaid (hereinafter called "the Employers") of the first part BRITISH AIR SERVICES LIMITED whose registered office is situate at Bealine House aforesaid (hereinafter called "Air Services") of the second part Rankin Lorimer Weir Derek Harding Glover Angus John Dore Betts Robert Gilchrist Cunningham Ralph Arthur Fuller Charles Victor Green Cyril Alfred Herring Oliver James Hinch Reginald Banwell Johnson Charles George Klimcke Thomas Nisbet and John Charles William Springbett the Management Trustees for the time being of The Airways Corporations Joint Pension Scheme (hereinafter called "the Management Trustees") of the third part and AIRWAYS CORPORATIONS JOINT PENSION FUND TRUSTEES LIMITED whose registered office is situate at Kershaw House Great West Road Hounslow in the County of Middlesex (hereinafter called "the Custodian Trustees" which expression shall include the Custodian Trustees for the time being) of the fourth part AND IS supplemental to the various Deeds set out in the Air Corporations Pensions Regulations 1948 to 1970.

WHEREAS

(1) Air Services is a subsidiary of British European Airways Corporation for the purposes of Section 24 of the Air Corporations Act 1967.

(2) The parties hereto are desirous of extending The Airways Corporations Joint Pension Scheme so as to enable employees of Air Services to be admitted to membership of the Scheme.

(3) At a meeting of the Management Trustees held on the eleventh day of March One thousand nine hundred and seventy the said Charles George Klimcke and the said John Charles William Springbett were appointed to execute this Deed in accordance with the provisions of Clause 18 of the said Trust Deed dated 8th October 1948 and set out in the schedule to the Airways Corporations (General Staff Pensions) Regulations 1948.

NOW IT IS HEREBY AGREED AND DECLARED BY AND BETWEEN THE PARTIES HERETO AS FOLLOWS:—

1. Air Services shall be deemed to be a party to the various Deeds set out in the Air Corporations Pensions Regulations 1948 to 1970.

2. Air Services shall enjoy all the rights and shall assume all the obligations of an Employer arising under the Trust Deed and Rules of the Scheme.

3. The Trust Deed shall be amended as follows:—

   (*a*) In Clause 1 of the Trust Deed for the definition of "Employer" there shall be substituted the following definition:—

      "Employer" means whichever of the following persons or bodies is the Employer of a Member for the time being:—

        (*a*) British Overseas Airways Corporation

        (*b*) British European Airways Corporation

        (*c*) BOAC Restaurants Limited

        (*d*) BEA Helicopters Limited

        (*e*) BEA Airtours Limited

        (*f*) British Air Services Limited

   (*b*) In Clauses 19A and 19A(*a*) the words "BRL, Helicopters or Airtours" shall be deleted and replaced by the words "BRL, Helicopters, Airtours or Air Services"

4. Save as expressly altered amended or varied hereby the Trust Deed and the Schedules thereto as heretofore amended shall continue and remain in force and shall have effect as if the alterations amendments or variations herein set out were where applicable inserted therein.

5. This Deed is conditional on its being confirmed by Regulations made by the Board of Trade under Section 24 of the Air Corporations Act 1967 and if so confirmed shall come into force on such date as may be specified in that behalf in such Regulations IN WITNESS WHEREOF the parties of the first and second and fourth parts have caused their respective Common Seals to be hereunto affixed and the Management Trustees have hereunto set their hands and seals the day and year first before written.

THE COMMON SEAL OF BRITISH OVERSEAS AIRWAYS
CORPORATION was hereunto affixed in the presence of:

                                                              (L.S.)

      D. H. GLOVER
        Member

      R. M. FORREST
        Secretary

THE COMMON SEAL OF BRITISH EUROPEAN AIRWAYS
CORPORATION was hereunto affixed in the presence of:

                                                              (L.S.)

      M. J. LESTER
        Secretary

THE COMMON SEAL OF BOAC RESTAURANTS LIMITED
was hereunto affixed in the presence of:

                                                              (L.S.)

      T. J. GLOVER
        Director

      D. G. DODSON
        Secretary

THE COMMON SEAL OF BEA HELICOPTERS LIMITED
was hereunto affixed in the presence of:

                                                                (L.S.)

      J. A. CAMERON
        Director

      R. D. KEEFE
        Secretary

THE COMMON SEAL OF BEA AIRTOURS LIMITED was
hereunto affixed in the presence of:

(L.S.)

    W. BAILLIE
      Managing Director

    T. M. ANKERS
      Secretary

THE COMMON SEAL OF BRITISH AIR SERVICES LIMITED
was hereunto affixed in the presence of:

(L.S.)

    H. E. MARKING
      Member

    M. J. LESTER
      Secretary

SIGNED SEALED AND DELIVERED by the said CHARLES
GEORGE KLIMCKE in the presence of:

                                    C. G. KLIMCKE

    M. C. SLATER (Secretary)
    1, Burlington Road,
    Isleworth, Middx.

SIGNED SEALED AND DELIVERED by the said JOHN
CHARLES WILLIAM SPRINGBETT in the presence of:

                                J. C. W. SPRINGBETT

    M. C. SLATER (Secretary)
    1, Burlington Road,
    Isleworth, Middx.

THE COMMON SEAL OF AIRWAYS CORPORATIONS JOINT
PENSION FUND TRUSTEES LIMITED was hereunto affixed
in the presence of:

(L.S.)

    R. L. WEIR
      Director

    H. BROMAGE
      Secretary

EXPLANATORY NOTE

(This Note is not part of the Regulations.)

These Regulations amend the Airways Corporations Joint Pension Scheme
so as to make provision whereby employees of British Air Services Ltd., a
subsidiary of BEA, can be admitted to the Scheme. Provision is also made
for the subsidiary to have the rights and obligations of an employer under the
Trust Deed and Rules of the Scheme and for payment of contributions by the
subsidiary and its employees.

STATUTORY INSTRUMENTS

1971 No. 178

MENTAL HEALTH

The Mental Health (Hospital and Guardianship) (Welsh Forms) Regulations 1971

Made - - -	*21st January* 1971
Laid before Parliament	*10th February* 1971
Coming into Operation	*1st April* 1971

The Secretary of State for Wales in exercise of his powers under section 56 of the Mental Health Act 1959(a) as extended by section 2(2) of the Welsh Language Act 1967(b) and of all other powers enabling him in that behalf, hereby makes the following regulations:—

1. These regulations may be cited as the Mental Health (Hospital and Guardianship) (Welsh Forms) Regulations 1971 and shall come into operation on 1st April, 1971.

2.—(1) In these regulations, unless the context otherwise requires, the following expressions have the meanings hereby assigned to them:—

"the Act" means the Mental Health Act 1959;

"hospital" has the meaning assigned to it by section 147(1) of the Act and includes a mental nursing home;

"mental nursing home" means a home in respect of which the particulars of registration are, for the time being, entered or treated as entered in the separate part of the register kept for the purposes of section 15(1) of the Act;

"principal regulations" means the Mental Health (Hospital and Guardianship) Regulations 1960(c).

(2) The Interpretation Act 1889(d) applies to the interpretation of these regulations as it applies to the interpretation of an Act of Parliament.

3.—(1) In relation to an application for admission to any hospital in Wales or Monmouthshire, regulation 4 of the principal regulations shall have effect as if it referred, instead of to the forms numbered 1, 2 and 4A in the Schedule to those regulations, to the forms numbered 1, 2 and 4A in the Schedule to these regulations.

(2) The forms numbered 1, 2 and 4A in the Schedule to these regulations may be completed in Welsh or in English or partly in Welsh and partly in English.

(a) 1959 c. 72. (b) 1967 c. 66. (c) S.I. 1960/1241 (1960 II, p. 1903). (d) 1889 c. 63.

SCHEDULE

FORM 1

FFURFLEN 1

APPLICATION FOR ADMISSION FOR OBSERVATION (SECTION 25)
CAIS AM GAEL MYNEDIAD I FOD O DAN WYLIADWRIAETH (ADRAN 25)

To the Managers of [name and address of hospital or mental nursing home]
At Reolwyr [enw a chyfeiriad yr ysbyty neu gartref nyrsio y meddwl]

1. I [name and address of applicant] hereby apply for the admission of [name and address of patient] to the above-named hospital for observation in accordance with Part IV of the Mental Health Act 1959.

1. Yr wyf fi [enw a chyfeiriad y sawl sy'n gwneud y cais] drwy hyn yn gwneud cais am i [enw a chyfeiriad y claf] gael mynediad i'r ysbyty a enwyd uchod er mwyn bod o dan wyliadwriaeth yn unol â Rhan IV, Mental Health Act 1959.

2.

(*a*) I am the patient's nearest relative within the meaning of the Act, being the patient's [state relationship].

2.

(*a*) Myfi yw perthynas agosaf y claf o fewn ystyr y Ddeddf, gan fy mod yn [noder y berthynas] iddo/iddi.

OR

Delete the two statements which do not apply.

(*b*) I have been authorised by $\dfrac{\text{a county court}}{\text{the patient's nearest relative}}$ to exercise the functions of the patient's nearest relative under the Act and a copy* of the authority is attached to this application.

NEU

Dilëer y ddau osodiad nad ydynt yn gymwys.

(*b*) Awdurdodwyd fi gan $\dfrac{\text{Lys Sirol}}{\text{berthynas agosaf y claf}}$ i gyflawni dyletswyddau perthynas agosaf y claf o dan y Ddeddf, a chysylltir copi* o'r awdurdod ynghlwm wrth y cais hwn.

OR

(*c*) I am an officer of [name of local health authority] appointed to act as a mental welfare officer for the purposes of the Act.

NEU

(*c*) Yr wyf yn swyddog dan [enw'r awdurdod iechyd lleol] wedi fy mhenodi i weithredu fel swyddog lles y meddwl at ddibenion y Ddeddf.

3. I last saw the patient on [date].

3. Gwelais y claf ddiwethaf ar [dyddiad].

4. This application is founded on the medical recommendations forwarded herewith.

4. Seilir y cais hwn ar yr argymhellion meddygol a ddanfonir yma gyda hwn.

5. †

Signed ....
Date ....

5. †

Llofnodwyd ....
Dyddiad ....

* Copy of the court order or of the authority signed by the nearest relative under Regulation 25 of the Mental Health (Hospital and Guardianship) Regulations 1960.

* Copi o'r gorchymyn llys neu o'r awdurdod wedi ei lofnodi gan y perthynas agosaf dan Reoliad 25, Mental Health (Hospital and Guardianship) Regulations 1960.

† If neither of the medical practitioners who have made the medical recommendations had previous acquaintance with the patient, the applicant should state here why it is not practicable to obtain a recommendation from a practitioner having such acquaintance.

† Os nad oedd yr un o'r meddygon a wnaeth yr argymhellion meddygol yn adnabod y claf o'r blaen, dylai'r sawl sy'n gwneud y cais nodi yma pam nad yw'n ymarferol cael argymhelliad gan feddyg a oedd yn ei adnabod.

RECORD OF ADMISSION
COFNOD AM Y MYNEDIAD

(This is not part of the application but is to be completed later at the hospital or mental nursing home.)

(Nid yw hwn yn rhan o'r cais ond dylid ei lenwi'n ddiweddarach yn yr ysbyty neu gartref nyrsio y meddwl.)

(*a*) [Name of patient] was admitted to [name of hospital or mental nursing home] in pursuance of this application on [date].

(*a*) Derbyniwyd [enw'r claf] i [enw'r ysbyty neu gartref nyrsio y meddwl] yn unol â'r cais hwn ar [dyddiad].

OR

(*b*) [Name of patient] was already an in-patient in [name of hospital or mental nursing home] on the date of this application and the application was received by me on behalf of the managers on [date].

NEU

(*b*) Yr oedd [enw'r claf] eisoes yn glaf preswyl yn [enw'r ysbyty neu gartref nyrsio y meddwl] ar y dyddiad y gwnaed y cais hwn, a derbyniais innau'r cais ar ran y rheolwyr ar [dyddiad].

Signed.............................
on behalf of the managers.

Date ....

Llofnodwyd ....
ar ran y rheolwyr.

Dyddiad ....

[Sections 49, 50 and 51 of the Act to be set out.]

[Gosoder allan adrannau 49, 50 a 51 o'r Ddeddf.]

FORM 2
FFURFLEN 2

EMERGENCY APPLICATION FOR ADMISSION FOR OBSERVATION (SECTION 29)
CAIS BRYS AM GAEL MYNEDIAD I FOD DAN WYLIADWRIAETH (ADRAN 29)

To the Managers of [name and address of hospital or mental nursing home]
At Reolwyr [enw a chyfeiriad yr ysbyty neu gartref nyrsio y meddwl]

1. I [name and address of applicant] hereby apply for the admission of [name and address of patient] to the above-named hospital for observation in accordance with Part IV of the Mental Health Act 1959.

1. Yr wyf fi (enw a chyfeiriad y sawl sy'n gwneud y cais) drwy hyn yn gwneud cais am i [enw a chyfeiriad y claf] gael mynediad i'r ysbyty a enwyd uchod i fod o dan wyliadwriaeth yn unol â Rhan IV, Mental Health Act 1959.

2.
(*a*) I am a relative of the patient within the meaning of the Act, being the patient's [state relationship].

2.
(*a*) Yr wyf yn berthynas i'r claf o fewn ystyr y Ddeddf, gan fy mod yn [noder y berthynas] iddo/iddi.

OR

Delete (*a*) or (*b*).

(*b*) I am an officer of [name of local health authority] appointed to act as a mental welfare officer for the purposes of the Act.

NEU

Dilëer (*a*) neu (*b*).

(*b*) Yr wyf yn swyddog dan [enw'r awdurdod iechyd lleol] wedi fy mhenodi i weithredu fel swyddog lles y meddwl at ddibenion y Ddeddf.

3. I last saw the patient on [date].
3. Gwelais y claf ddiwethaf ar [dyddiad].

4. In my opinion it is of urgent necessity for the patient to be admitted and detained under Section 25 of the Act, and compliance with the requirements of the Act relating to applications for admission other than emergency applications would involve undesirable delay.

4. Yn fy marn i, mae'n rheidrwydd brys i'r claf gael mynediad a'i gadw dan Adran 25 o'r Ddeddf, a byddai cydymffurfio â gofynion y Ddeddf ynglŷn â cheisiadau am fynediad, ar wahân i geisiadau brys, yn achosi oedi annymunol.

5. This application is founded on the medical recommendations forwarded herewith.
5. Seilir y cais hwn ar yr argymhellion meddygol a ddanfonir yma gyda hwn.

6. †

Signed ....

Date ....

6. †

Llofnodwyd ....

Dyddiad ....

† If the medical practitioner who has made the recommendation had no previous acquaintance with the patient, the applicant should state here why it is not practicable to obtain a recommendation from a practitioner having such acquaintance.

† Os nad oedd y meddyg a wnaeth yr argymhellion yn adnabod y claf o'r blaen, dylai'r sawl sy'n gwneud y cais nodi yma pam nad yw'n ymarferol cael argymhelliad gan feddyg a oedd yn ei adnabod o'r blaen.

RECORD OF ADMISSION

COFNOD AM Y MYNEDIAD

(This is not part of the application but is to be completed later at the hospital or mental nursing home.)

(Nid yw hwn yn rhan o'r cais, ond dylid ei lenwi'n ddiweddarach yn yr ysbyty neu gartref nyrsio y meddwl.)

(*a*) [Name of patient] was admitted to [name of hospital or mental nursing home] in pursuance of this application at [time] on [date].

(*a*) Derbyniwyd [enw'r claf] i [enw'r ysbyty neu gartref nyrsio y meddwl] yn unol â'r cais hwn am [amser] ar [dyddiad].

OR

(*b*) [Name of patient] was already an in-patient in [name of hospital or mental nursing home] on the date of this application and the application was received by me on behalf of the managers at [time] on [date]. Delete (*a*) or (*b*).

NEU

(*b*) Yr oedd [enw'r claf] eisoes yn glaf preswyl yn [enw'r ysbyty neu gartref nyrsio y meddwl] ar y dyddiad y gwnaed y cais hwn, a derbyniais innau'r cais ar ran y rheolwyr am [amser] ar [dyddiad]. Dilëer (*a*) neu (*b*).

Signed.............................

on behalf of the managers.

Date ....

Llofnodwyd ....

ar ran y rheolwyr.

Dyddiad ....

[Subsections (1), (2), (5) and (6) of Section 49 of the Act to be set out.]

[Gosoder allan Is-adrannau (1), (2), (5) a (6) Adran 49 o'r Ddeddf.]

FORM 4A

FFURFLEN 4A

APPLICATION BY NEAREST RELATIVE FOR ADMISSION FOR TREATMENT (SECTION 26)

CAIS GAN BERTHYNAS AGOSAF AM GAEL MYNEDIAD AM DRINIAETH (ADRAN 26)

To the Managers of [name and address of hospital or mental nursing home]
At Reolwyr [enw a chyfeiriad yr ysbyty neu gartref nyrsio y meddwl]

‡Insert mental illness, severe subnormality and/or psychopathic disorder.

1. I [name and address of applicant] hereby apply for the admission of [name and address of patient] to the above-named hospital for treatment in accordance with Part IV of the Mental Health Act 1959, as a patient suffering from‡.

1. Yr wyf fi [enw a chyfeiriad y sawl sy'n gwneud y cais] drwy hyn yn gwneud cais am i [enw a chyfeiriad y claf] gael mynediad i'r ysbyty a enwyd uchod am driniaeth yn unol â Rhan IV, Mental Health Act 1959, fel claf yn dioddef gan‡.

‡Ysgrifenner meddyliol salwch is-normaledd difrifol, is-normaledd ac/neu anhwyldeb seicopathig.

2.

(*a*) I am the patient's nearest relative within the meaning of the Act, being the patient's [state relationship].

2.

(*a*) Myfi yw perthynas agosaf y claf o fewn ystyr y Ddeddf, gan fy mod yn [noder y berthynas] iddo/iddi.

OR

Delete the statement that does not apply.

(*b*) I have been authorised by $\dfrac{\text{a county court}}{\text{the patient's nearest relative}}$ to exercise the functions of the patient's nearest relative under the Act and a copy* of the authority is attached to this application.

NEU

Dilëer y gosodiad nad yw'n gymwys.

(*b*) Awdurdodwyd fi gan $\dfrac{\text{lys sirol}}{\text{berthynas agosaf y claf}}$ i gyflawni dyletswyddau perthynas agosaf y claf dan y Ddeddf, a chysylltir copi* o'r awdurdod wrth y cais hwn.

3. I last saw the patient on [date].

3. Gwelais y claf ddiwethaf ar [dyddiad].

4. (This section is to be deleted if the patient is recorded above as suffering from mental illness or severe subnormality.)

4. (Dylid dileu'r adran hon os cofnodwyd uchod fod ·y claf yn dioddef gan salwch meddyliol neu is-normaledd difrifol.)

(*a*) The patient's date of birth is [   ].
(*a*) Ganwyd y claf ar [   ].

OR

Delete the statement that does not apply.

(if the exact age is not known)
(*b*) I believe the patient to be under twenty-one years.

NEU

Dilëer y gosodiad nad yw'n gymwys.

(os na wyddys yr oedran yn fanwl)
(*b*) Credaf fod y claf dan un ar hugain oed.

5. This application is founded on the medical recommendations forwarded herewith.

5. Seilir y cais ar yr argymhellion meddygol a ddanfonir yma gyda hwn.

6. †

Signed...............................

Date ....

6. †

Llofnodwyd ....

Dyddiad ....

* Copy of the court order or of the form of authority signed by the nearest relative under Regulation 25 of the Mental Health (Hospital and Guardianship) Regulations 1960.

* Copi o'r gorchymyn llys neu o'r ffurflen awdurdod wedi'i lofnodi gan y perthynas agosaf dan Reoliad 25, Mental Health (Hospital and Guardianship) Regulations 1960.

† If neither of the medical practitioners who have made the recommendations had previous acquaintance with the patient, the applicant should state here why it is not practicable to obtain a recommendation from a practitioner having such acquaintance.

† Os nad oedd un o'r meddygon a wnaeth yr argymhellion yn adnabod y claf, dylai'r sawl sy'n gwneud y cais nodi yma pam nad yw'n ymarferol cael argymhelliad oddi wrth feddyg a oedd yn ei adnabod o'r blaen.

RECORD OF ADMISSION

COFNOD AM Y MYNEDIAD

(*This is not part of the application, but is to be completed later at the hospital or mental nursing home.*)

(*Nid yw hwn yn rhan o'r cais, ond dylid ei lenwi'n ddiweddarach yn yr ysbyty neu gartref nyrsio y meddwl.*)

(*a*) [Name of patient] was admitted to [name of hospital or mental nursing home] in pursuance of this application on [date of admission].

(*a*) Derbyniwyd [enw'r claf] i [enw'r ysbyty neu gartref nyrsio y meddwl] yn unol â'r cais hwn ar [dyddiad mynediad].

OR

(*b*) [Name of patient] was already in [name of hospital or mental nursing home] on the date of this application, and the application was received by me on behalf of the managers on [date].   Delete (*a*) or (*b*) as appropriate.

NEU

(*b*) Yr oedd [enw'r claf] eisoes yn [enw'r ysbyty neu gartref nyrsio y meddwl] ar y dyddiad y gwnaed y cais hwn, a derbyniais innau'r cais ar ran y rheolwyr ar [dyddiad].   Dilëer (*a*) neu (*b*) fel y bo'n gymwys.

Signed ....
on behalf of the managers.

Date ....

Llofnodwyd ....
ar ran y rheolwyr.

Dyddiad ....

[Sections 49, 50 and 51 of the Act to be set out.]
[Gosoder allan Adrannau 49, 50 a 51 o'r Ddeddf.]

Peter Thomas,
Secretary of State for Wales.

21st January 1971.

EXPLANATORY NOTE

(*This Note is not part of the Regulations.*)

These regulations prescribe bilingual application forms to be used for the admission of patients into hospitals or mental nursing homes in Wales and Monmouthshire.

STATUTORY INSTRUMENTS

1971 No. 181

SEA FISHERIES

BOATS AND METHODS OF FISHING

The Salmon and Migratory Trout (Sea Fishing) Licensing Order 1971

Made - - -	*3rd February* 1971
Laid before Parliament	*10th February* 1971
Coming into Operation	*15th February* 1971

The Minister of Agriculture, Fisheries and Food, and the Secretary of State for Scotland and the Secretary of State for the Home Department, being the Secretaries of State concerned with the sea-fishing industry in Scotland and Northern Ireland respectively, in exercise of the powers conferred on them by section 4 of the Sea Fish (Conservation) Act 1967(**a**) and of all other powers enabling them in that behalf, with the consent of the Treasury, hereby make the following order :—

Citation and Commencement

1. This order may be cited as the Salmon and Migratory Trout (Sea Fishing) Licensing Order 1971 and shall come into operation on 15th February 1971.

Interpretation

2.—(1) In this order—

"the Act" means the Sea Fish (Conservation) Act 1967 ;

"mouth of the River Tweed" means the area as defined by the Tweed Fisheries Amendment Act 1859(**b**) as amended by byelaw dated 10th August 1863 contained in Schedule A to the Salmon Fisheries (Scotland) Act 1868(**c**).

(2) The Interpretation Act 1889(**d**) shall apply for the interpretation of this order as it applies for the interpretation of an Act of Parliament.

Appointed day

3. The appointed day for the purposes of section 4 of the Act in conjunction with this order is 15th February 1971.

(**a**) 1967 c. 84.	(**b**) 1859 c. lxx.
(**c**) 1868 c. 123.	(**d**) 1889 c. 63.

Area

4. This order applies only to fishing in the area of sea specified in the schedule to this order for salmon or migratory trout during the period 15th February 1971 until 14th February 1973 (both dates inclusive).

Licences

5. The Minister for the purpose of section 4(6) of the Act in relation to this order is the Minister of Agriculture, Fisheries and Food and he may make a charge of not more than £20 for the granting of a licence.

In witness whereof the Official Seal of the Minister of Agriculture, Fisheries and Food is hereunto affixed on 28th January 1971.

(L.S.)

J. M. L. Prior,
Minister of Agriculture, Fisheries and Food.

Given under the Seal of the Secretary of State for Scotland on 29th January 1971.

(L.S.)

Gordon Campbell,
Secretary of State for Scotland.

Given under the hand of the Secretary of State for the Home Department on 2nd February 1971.

R. Maudling,
Secretary of State for the
Home Department.

Approved on 3rd February 1971.

Walter Clegg,
Bernard Weatherill,
Two of the Lords Commissioners
of Her Majesty's Treasury.

SCHEDULE

The area of sea (excluding the territorial waters of England and Wales) contained within a line drawn from the coast of England along the southern boundary of the mouth of the River Tweed to the eastmost point of that boundary ; thence due east to the intersection with the boundary of the fishery limits of the British Islands ; thence along that boundary in a clockwise direction around the coasts of England and Wales to the intersection with the parallel of latitude 54° 30′ north in the Irish Sea ; thence eastwards along that parallel until it meets the coast of England.

EXPLANATORY NOTE

(This Note is not part of the Order.)

Section 4 of the Sea Fish (Conservation) Act 1967 provides that, from a day appointed by an order, no British-owned fishing boats shall fish, by way of trade or business, for specified kinds of fish in a specified area except under the authority of a licence issued by one of the fishery Ministers. This order appoints 15th February 1971 as the day from which no such fishing boats shall so fish for salmon and migratory trout in waters comprising almost all that part of the fishery limits of England and Wales which lies outside territorial waters except under the authority of a licence issued by the Minister of Agriculture, Fisheries and Food. The order will cease to have effect on 15th February 1973.

1971 No. 184 (C.1) (S.20)

SOCIAL WORK, SCOTLAND

The Social Work (Scotland) Act 1968 (Commencement No. 5) Order 1971

Made -   -   -   -   *1st February* 1971

In exercise of the powers conferred on me by section 98 of the Social Work (Scotland) Act 1968(**a**), as amended by paragraph 66 of Schedule 5 to the Children and Young Persons Act 1969(**b**), I hereby make the following order : —

1. This order may be cited as the Social Work (Scotland) Act 1968 (Commencement No. 5) Order 1971.

2. The provisions of the Social Work (Scotland) Act 1968 (hereinafter referred to as " the Act ") specified in Schedules 1 and 2 to this order shall come into operation on the dates and to the extent specified therein.

3. The transitional provisions contained in Schedule 3 to this order shall have effect in connection with the provisions brought into force by this order which are referred to in that Schedule.

Gordon Campbell,

One of Her Majesty's
Principal Secretaries of State.

St. Andrew's House,
Edinburgh.
1st February 1971.

(**a**) 1968 c. 49.   (**b**) 1969 c. 54.

SCHEDULE 1

PROVISIONS COMING INTO FORCE ON 1ST MARCH 1971

Provisions of the Act	Subject matter of provisions
Paragraph 4 of Schedule 7	Transitional provisions relating to certain court orders.

SCHEDULE 2

PROVISIONS COMING INTO FORCE ON 15TH APRIL 1971

Provisions of the Act	Subject matter of provisions
Section 1(5)	Transfer of functions from education authorities to local authorities.
Section 30	Definition of child and parent for Part III.
Section 31	Restriction on prosecution of children for offences.
Section 32	Children in need of compulsory measures of care.
Section 34(1) and (2) ...	Children's hearings.
Section 35(1) to (3) ...	Provisions as to privacy of children's hearings.
Section 37	Reports of cases of children who may require compulsory measures of care and the interim detention of such children in places of safety.
Section 38	Initial investigation of cases by reporter.
Section 39	Action on initial investigation by reporter.
Section 40	Attendance of child at children's hearing.
Section 41	Attendance of parent at children's hearing.
Section 42	Conduct of children's hearing and application to sheriff for findings.
Section 43	Discharge of referral and power of children's hearing to order further investigation after consideration of the facts.
Section 44	Disposal of case by children's hearing other than by discharge of referral.
Section 46	Children to whom Part IV of the Mental Health (Scotland) Act 1960(a) may apply.
Section 47	Duration of supervision requirements and their variation.
Section 48	Review of requirement of children's hearing.
Section 49	Appeal against decision of a children's hearing.
Section 50	Appeal to Court of Session.
Section 51	Reconsideration by hearing after appeal, and subsequent appeal.
Section 52	Power of Secretary of State to terminate a supervision requirement.
Section 53	Legal aid in proceedings before the sheriff and any appeals to the Court of Session.
Section 54	Transfer of case to another children's hearing.
Section 55	Presumption and determination of age.
Section 56	Reference and remit of children's cases by courts to children's hearings.
Section 57	Reference and remit of cases of certain young persons by courts to children's hearings.
Section 58	Prohibition of publication of proceedings.

(a) 1960 c. 61.

Provisions of the Act	Subject matter of provisions
Part V (Sections 69 to 77)	Return and removal of children within United Kingdom.
Part VI (Sections 78 to 83)	Contributions in respect of children in care, etc.
Section 97 insofar as not already brought into operation.	Extension of certain provisions to England and Wales, Northern Ireland and the Channel Islands.
Schedule 2	Amendment of Part IV of the Children and Young Persons (Scotland) Act 1937(a).
Schedule 4	Amendment of Legal Aid (Scotland) Act 1967(b).
Paragraphs 2, 5, 6 and 7 of Schedule 7.	Transitional provisions.
Schedule 8 to the extent set out in Appendix A hereto.	Minor and consequential amendments.
Schedule 9 to the extent set out in Appendix B hereto.	Enactments repealed.

APPENDIX A TO SCHEDULE 2

Provision of Schedule 8	Enactment amended
Paragraph 1	Section 9(4) of the Criminal Appeal (Scotland) Act 1926(c).
Paragraph 6	Section 38(3) of the Children and Young Persons (Scotland) Act 1937.
Paragraph 7	Section 87 of the Children and Young Persons (Scotland) Act 1937.
Paragraph 9	Section 103 of the Children and Young Persons (Scotland) Act 1937.
Paragraph 10	Section 110(1) of the Children and Young Persons (Scotland) Act 1937.
Paragraph 25	Section 8(1) of the Criminal Justice (Scotland) Act 1949(d).
Paragraph 26	Section 9(1) of the Criminal Justice (Scotland) Act 1949.
Paragraph 27 insofar as not already brought into operation.	Section 10 of the Criminal Justice (Scotland) Act 1949.
Paragraph 28	Section 28 of the Criminal Justice (Scotland) Act 1949.
Paragraph 29	Section 30(1) of the Criminal Justice (Scotland) Act 1949.
Paragraph 30 insofar as not already brought into operation.	Section 78(1) of the Criminal Justice (Scotland) Act 1949.
Paragraph 32	Section 8(1) of the Maintenance Orders Act 1950(e).
Paragraph 33	Section 9 of the Maintenance Orders Act 1950.
Paragraph 34	Section 16(2) of the Maintenance Orders Act 1950.
Paragraph 37 insofar as not already brought into operation.	Section 4(3) of the Adoption Act 1958(f).
Paragraph 39	Section 36(2) of the Adoption Act 1958.
Paragraph 55	Section 57(3) of the Mental Health (Scotland) Act 1960.
Paragraph 57	Section 66(7) of the Mental Health (Scotland) Act 1960.
Paragraph 58 insofar as not already brought into operation.	Section 72(1) of the Mental Health (Scotland) Act 1960.

(a) 1937 c. 37.   (b) 1967 c. 43.   (c) 1926 c. 15.   (d) 1949 c. 94.
(e) 1950 c. 37.   (f) 7 & 8 Eliz. 2. c. 5.

Provision of Schedule 8	Enactment amended
Paragraph 59A	Section 32(2) of the Criminal Justice Act 1961(**a**).
Paragraph 61	Section 36(3) of the Education (Scotland) Act 1962(**b**).
Paragraph 62	Section 44 of the Education (Scotland) Act 1962.
Paragraph 65	Section 85(5) of the Education (Scotland) Act 1962.
Paragraph 66	Section 141(2) of the Education (Scotland) Act 1962.
Paragraph 67	Section 145 of the Education (Scotland) Act 1962.
Paragraph 68 insofar as not already brought into operation.	Section 55 of the Children and Young Persons Act 1963(**c**).
Paragraph 69(1)	Section 57(2) of the Children and Young Persons Act 1963.
Paragraph 70	Section 1(4) of the Criminal Justice (Scotland) Act 1963(**d**).
Paragraph 71	Section 7(1) of the Criminal Justice (Scotland) Act 1963.
Paragraph 72	Section 29 of the Criminal Justice (Scotland) Act 1963.
Paragraph 74(1) and (3)...	Section 11 of the Family Allowances Act 1965(**e**).

APPENDIX B TO SCHEDULE 2

(*Provisions of Schedule 9 to the Act*)

PART I

Chapter	Short Title	Extent of Repeal
1 Edw. 8 & 1 Geo. 6. c. 37.	The Children and Young Persons (Scotland) Act 1937.	In section 21(2), the words from " may take " to the end of the subsection. In section 42(1), the words " or is for any other reason brought before a court " and in subsection (2) the words " or taken to a place of safety " and the words " or the person by whom he is taken to the place of safety, as the case may be ". In section 47(1) the words " until he can be brought before a juvenile court ", wherever occurring. In section 49(1) the words " either as being in need of care or protection or ", the words " or otherwise ", and the words " and for securing that proper provision is made for his education and training ". Section 49(2). Section 51. Section 53(2) and (3). Section 59(1) and in subsection (4), the words " under this section, or ". Sections 60 and 61. In section 63(3) the words " under the Probation of Offenders Act 1907 ". Sections 65 and 66.

(**a**) 1961 c. 39.   (**b**) 1962 c. 47.   (**c**) 1963 c. 37.   (**d**) 1963 c. 39.   (**e**) 1965 c. 53.

Chapter	Short Title	Extent of Repeal
		Sections 68 to 86.
		In section 87(2) and (4) the words " England or " wherever they occur, in subsection (5) the words " in relation to England, the Secretary of State, and " and subsection (6).
		Sections 88 to 95.
		Section 101(5) and (6).
		Section 107(1)(*a*), and (2).
		Section 109.
		In section 110(1)—
		the following definitions—
		" Approved school "
		" Approved school order ";
		" Headmaster ";
		" In need of care or protection ";
		in the definition of " Justice " the words " (except in section 51 of this Act) ";
		and the definition of " Managers ".
		In section 110, in subsection (3)(*a*)(ii) the words " and the juvenile court for any area " and subsection (3)(*a*)(iv).
		Section 111.
		Section 112.
		Schedule 2.
		Schedule 3.
11 & 12 Geo. 6. c. 43.	The Children Act 1948...	Sections 5 and 6(3) and (4) and Part III.
12, 13 & 14 Geo. 6. c. 94.	The Criminal Justice (Scotland) Act 1949.	Section 5(3).
		In section 28, subsection (2), and in subsection (3), the words " a remand home or " and the words " home or ".
		Sections 50 and 51.
		Sections 69 to 73.
		Section 75 to the extent specified in Schedule 9 insofar as not already brought into operation.
		Section 78(1) to the extent specified in Schedule 9 insofar as not already brought into operation.
14 Geo. 6. c. 37.	The Maintenance Orders Act 1950.	Schedule 1, insofar as relating to the modification of the Children and Young Persons (Scotland) Act 1937.
15 & 16 Geo. 6. & 1 Eliz. 2. c. 61.	The Prisons (Scotland) Act 1952.	In section 32, in subsection (3), the words " who is not less than seventeen years of age ", and subsection (4).
4 & 5 Eliz. 2. c. 24.	The Children and Young Persons Act 1956.	The whole Act.
4 & 5 Eliz. 2. c. 50.	The Family Allowances and National Insurance Act 1956.	The whole Act.
6 & 7 Eliz. 2. c. 65.	The Children Act 1958...	In section 2, in subsection (4) the words from " or by virtue of " to " of an approved school ".

Chapter	Short Title	Extent of Repeal
7 & 8 Eliz. 2. c. 5.	The Adoption Act 1958.	Section 4(3)(*b*). In section 11(1), the words " or juvenile court ". In section 15(3), the words from " fit person by " to " care of a " and the words " fit person order or " and " as the case may be ". In section 37(3), the words " in an approved school or ".
8 & 9 Eliz. 2. c. 61.	The Mental Health (Scotland) Act 1960.	In section 10, in subsection (1), in paragraph (*a*), head (i), and at the end of head (ii) the word " or ". Section 46(*a*). In section 55(10) the words from " including " to the word " school ". Section 56. In section 57, in subsection 3(*b*), the words " or young person "; and subsection (5). Section 69(1)(*b*). Section 71. In section 72, the definitions of " approved school " and " remand home " and in the definition of " place of safety " the words " or young person " first occurring.
10 & 11 Eliz. 2. c. 47.	The Education (Scotland) Act 1962.	Section 36(4) and (5). Section 44(3) and (4).
1963 c. 39. ...	The Criminal Justice (Scotland) Act 1963.	In section 11, in subsection (2), the words from " if the offender " to the words " detention centre ", and subsection (3) and (5). Part II. Schedule 2.

PART II

Chapter	Short Title	Extent of Repeal
6 & 7 Eliz. 2. c. 65.	The Children Act 1958.	In section 2(4) the words from " or of " to " 1937 ".
7 & 8 Eliz. 2. c. 72.	The Mental Health Act 1959.	In section 10(1), in sub-paragraph (*a*), head (ii). In section 50, sub-paragraph (*b*).
1963 c. 37 ...	The Children and Young Persons Act 1963.	Sections 51 and 52.
1965 c. 53 ...	The Family Allowances Act 1965.	In section 11(2), the words " or the said Act of 1937 ".

SCHEDULE 3

TRANSITIONAL PROVISIONS

1.—(1) Paragraph 4 of Schedule 7 to the Act shall have effect as if there was included among the classes of children specified in sub-paragraph (1) of that paragraph any child who immediately before the commencement of Part III of the Act was subject to—

(a) an order transferring him to an approved school made under subsection (1) or subsection (3) of section 87 of the Children and Young Persons (Scotland) Act 1937 (power to send children and young persons from England and Wales, Northern Ireland, Isle of Man and Channel Islands to approved schools in Scotland) ; or

(b) an order under paragraph 23 of Schedule 4 to the Children and Young Persons Act 1969 (interim power to send persons subject to care orders from England and Wales to approved schools in Scotland) ; or

(c) an order made either under section 51 of the Children and Young Persons Act 1963 (supervision of persons moving from England and Wales to Scotland) as originally enacted or under that section as amended by paragraphs 20 and 21 of Schedule 4 to the said Act of 1969,

and any reference in the said paragraph 4 to a child to whom that paragraph applies shall be construed accordingly.

(2) Sub-paragraph (2) of the said paragraph 4 shall have effect as if at the end of that sub-paragraph there were inserted the following words : —

" with the substitution for any reference to an approved school of a reference to an establishment which was immediately before the coming into operation of the said Part III an approved school, and with any other necessary modifications.".

2.—(1) Where by virtue of paragraph 5 of Schedule 7 to the Act a court exercises jurisdiction in respect of a child or young person charged with an offence before the commencement of Part III of the Act, the powers conferred on certain courts by sections 56 and 57 of the Act (which relate to the reference and remit of the cases of children and certain young persons by courts to children's hearings, being children and young persons charged with an offence after the said commencement) shall, subject to sub-paragraph (2) below, be available to and exercisable by the said court in relation to the said child or young person.

(2) In the case of any juvenile court constituted under section 51 of the Children and Young Persons (Scotland) Act 1937, the provisions of sub-paragraph (1) above shall apply until such time as the Secretary of State makes a direction in relation to that court under sub-paragraph (2) of the said paragraph 5, and on any such direction being made any question arising from any remit or reference by the said court under section 56 or section 57 of the Act shall be dealt with by the sheriff having jurisdiction in the former area of that court as if the said remit or, as the case may be, the said reference had been made by him.

3. Where by virtue of paragraph 5 of Schedule 7 to the Act a sheriff exercises jurisdiction in respect of a child or young person charged with an offence before the commencement of Part III of the Act, the powers conferred on the sheriff by section 58A of the Children and Young Persons (Scotland) Act 1937 set out in paragraph 16 of Schedule 2 to the Act (committal for residential training of children charged with an offence after the said commencement) shall be available to and exercisable by the said sheriff in relation to the said child or young person.

EXPLANATORY NOTE

(This Note is not part of the Order.)

This Order brings into force almost all the provisions of the Social Work (Scotland) Act 1968 not brought into force by earlier orders (other than those already obsolete and subject to the transitional provisions contained in Schedule 3 to the Order). The provisions brought into force include those relating to the establishment of the system of children's hearings for dealing with children who may need compulsory measures of care and those making consequential adjustments in the powers and duties of the courts and others.

STATUTORY INSTRUMENTS

1971 No. 185 (S.21)

POLICE

The Police Cadets (Scotland) Amendment Regulations 1971

Made - - -	*1st February* 1971
Laid before Parliament	*12th February* 1971
Coming into Operation	*15th February* 1971

In exercise of the powers conferred on me by section 27 of the Police (Scotland) Act 1967(**a**), and of all other powers enabling me in that behalf, and after consulting the Police Council for the United Kingdom in accordance with section 4(4) of the Police Act 1969(**b**), I hereby make the following regulations :—

Citation and operation

1. These regulations may be cited as the Police Cadets (Scotland) Amendment Regulations 1971 and shall come into operation on 15th February 1971.

Interpretation

2. In these regulations any reference to the principal regulations is a reference to the Police Cadets (Scotland) Regulations 1968(**c**), as amended (**d**).

Travel Allowances

3. In regulation 15(1) of the principal regulations (which relates to travel allowances) for the sum "7s. 6d." there shall be substituted "£0·400".

Calculation of Pay and Charges

4. For paragraph (5) of regulation 13 of the principal regulations (which relates to the calculation of pay and charges) there shall be substituted the following paragraph :—

"(5) In making any such payment as is referred to in paragraph (1) a fraction of a penny shall be treated as a whole penny except that a fraction less than a half-penny shall be ignored.".

Gordon Campbell,
One of Her Majesty's Principal
Secretaries of State.

St. Andrew's House,
Edinburgh.
1st February 1971.

(**a**) 1967 c. 77.   (**b**) 1969 c. 63.
(**c**) S.I. 1968/208 (1968 I, p. 557).
(**d**) The amending instruments are not relevant to the subject matter of these Regulations.

EXPLANATORY NOTE

(*This Note is not part of the Regulations.*)

These Regulations amend the Police Cadets (Scotland) Regulations 1968. Regulation 3 amends the provision for the payment, in certain cases, of travel allowances in respect of return journeys costing more than 7s. 6d. ; this sum is increased to £0·400.

STATUTORY INSTRUMENTS

1971 No. 187

EDUCATION, ENGLAND AND WALES

The Education (Handicapped Children) Act 1970
(Appointed Day) Order 1971

Made - - - *3rd February* 1971

The Secretary of State for Education and Science in relation to England and the Secretary of State for Wales in relation to Wales, in exercise of their powers under section 1(1) of the Education (Handicapped Children) Act 1970(a), hereby order as follows:—

1. This order may be cited as the Education (Handicapped Children) Act 1970 (Appointed Day) Order 1971.

2. The appointed day for the purposes of section 1(1) of the Education (Handicapped Children) Act 1970 shall be 1st April 1971.

Given under the Official Seal of the Secretary of State for Education and Science on 29th January 1971.

(L.S.)
Margaret Thatcher,
Secretary of State for
Education and Science.

Given under my hand on 3rd February 1971.

Peter Thomas,
Secretary of State for Wales.

EXPLANATORY NOTE
(This Note is not part of the Order.)
This Order appoints 1st April 1971 as the day for discontinuing the classification of handicapped children as unsuitable for education at school.

(a) 1970 c. 52.

STATUTORY INSTRUMENTS

1971 No. 188

MAGISTRATES' COURTS

FEES

The Magistrates' Courts Fees (Decimalisation) Order 1971

Laid before Parliament in draft

Made - - -		*4th February* 1971
Coming into Operation		*15th February* 1971

In pursuance of section 112(4) of the Magistrates' Courts Act 1952**(a)**, I hereby make the following Order:—

1. This Order may be cited as the Magistrates' Courts Fees (Decimalisation) Order 1971 and shall come into operation on 15th February 1971.

2. Part I of Schedule 4 to the Magistrates' Courts Act 1952 (fees chargeable by clerks of magistrates' courts) shall be varied by substituting for the sums specified in the second column of the Schedule to this Order the sums in new pence specified in the third column thereof.

R. Maudling,
One of Her Majesty's Principal
Secretaries of State.

Home Office,
Whitehall.
4th February 1971.

(a) 1952 c. 55.

SCHEDULE

1 Matter to which fee relates	2 Old fee	3 New fee
	s. d.	
ATTENDANCE:— On a justice, to view deserted premises in order to affix notice or to give possession thereof, to view a highway, bridge or nuisance	6 8	33p
CASE FOR THE OPINION OF HIGH COURT (s. 87 of the Magistrates' Courts Act 1952):— Every enlargement or renewal of recognizance required by s. 90 of the Magistrates' Courts Act 1952	2 6	13p
CIVIL DEBT (not including Rates):— Summons and copy	1 6	7p
COPY:— Of any document, per folio of 72 words	0 4	2p
LIST:— Every list not otherwise provided for which it is the duty of the clerk to the justices to make or transmit	2 6	13p
RATE:— If more than one rate is included in the summons, for each rate after the first	0 6	3p
When the form of warrant provided for by s. 3 of the Distress for Rates Act 1849(a) is used, for each name inserted in the schedule over and above eight	0 3	1p
SUMMONS:— Every copy	0 6	3p

(a) 1849 c. 14.

EXPLANATORY NOTE

(This Note is not part of the Order.)

The fees listed in the Schedule to this Order, being fees chargeable by magistrates' clerks under the Magistrates' Courts Act 1952, do not convert into whole numbers of new pence. This Order substitutes for these fees new fees expressed in whole numbers of new pence obtained by calculating the corresponding amounts in accordance with Schedule 1 to the Decimal Currency Act 1969 (c.19).

STATUTORY INSTRUMENTS

1971 No. 189

DECIMAL CURRENCY

The Transport Pension Schemes (Decimal Currency) Order 1971

Made - - - -	*4th February* 1971
Laid before Parliament	*12th February* 1971
Coming into Operation	*15th February* 1971

The Secretary of State for the Environment with the consent of the Treasury and in exercise of his powers under section 11(1) of the Decimal Currency Act 1969(a) (hereinafter called " the Act ") and of all other enabling powers hereby makes the following Order : —

1. This Order may be cited as the Transport Pension Schemes (Decimal Currency) Order 1971 and shall come into operation on the 15th February 1971.

2. The Interpretation Act 1889(b) shall apply for the interpretation of this Order as it applies for the interpretation of an Act of Parliament.

3. The Port of London Act 1968(c) and the subordinate instruments mentioned in the Schedule to this Order which contain references to amounts of money in the old currency of which the equivalent in the new currency is neither a new penny nor a multiple thereof shall have effect subject to the amendments provided for by that Schedule.

Signed by authority of the Secretary of State 4th February 1971.

John Peyton,
Minister for Transport Industries
Department of the Environment.

We consent to this Order.

P. L. Hawkins,
Bernard Weatherill,
Two of the Lords Commissioners of
Her Majesty's Treasury.

4th February 1971.

(a) 1969 c. 19.   (b) 52 & 53 Vict. c. 63.   (c) 1968 c. xxxii.

SCHEDULE

AMENDMENTS OF PROVISIONS REFERRING TO AMOUNTS IN SHILLINGS AND PENCE

The Port of London Act 1968

1. In Schedule 3 (Rules of the Port of London Authority Pension Fund) to the above-mentioned Act of 1968—

(a) in the proviso to rule 5(2), for the words " £3 0s. 8d." there shall be substituted the words " £3·03 " ;

(b) in rule 6—

(i) for the scale set out in the columns headed respectively " Fractional parts of a pound " and " Amount of deduction " there shall be substituted the following scale, that is to say—

" Fractional parts of a pound			Amount of deduction
p		p	
0	to	20	Nil
21	to	60	1p
61	to	100	2p ",

(ii) for the words " to the nearest penny ", in both places where they occur, there shall be substituted the words " to the nearest new penny ", and

(iii) for the words " an exact halfpenny " there shall be substituted the words " an exact new halfpenny " ; and

(c) in rule 17, where by virtue of section 10(1) of the Act, an amount of money in the old currency appearing in the Table set out at the end of the said rule is read as referring to the equivalent of that amount in the new currency and that equivalent is or includes a fraction of a new penny, then the annual reduction to be made in a pension calculated on the basis of the said amount in the old currency so read as aforesaid shall be adjusted—

(i) to the nearest multiple of a new penny if it includes a fraction of a new penny which is greater or less than one-half,

(ii) upwards to the nearest multiple of a new penny, if it is a fraction of a new penny which is exactly one-half or includes such a fraction following an even multiple of a new penny, and

(iii) downwards to the nearest multiple of a new penny if it includes a fraction of a new penny which is exactly one-half following an odd multiple of a new penny.

The British Transport Commission (Male Wages Grades Pensions) Regulations 1954(a) as amended(b)

2. In the Schedule (British Transport Commission (Male Wages Grades) Pension Scheme Rules) to the above-mentioned Regulations of 1954—

(a) where by virtue of section 10(1) of the Act an amount of money in the old currency appearing in Table II of those Rules is read as referring to the equivalent of that amount in the new currency and that equivalent is or includes a fraction of a new penny, then, subject to the next following sub-paragraph, the weekly contribution of a member of Section A to be deducted or paid under Rule 12 on the scale set out in the said Table II shall be adjusted in the same manner as provided in paragraph 1(c)(i) to (iii) of this Schedule ;

(a) S.I. 1954/898 (1954 I, p. 175).
(b) The relevant amending instrument is S.I. 1968/1249 (1968 II, p. 3379).

(*b*) where the weekly contributions of a person who is both a member of Section A and of Section B fall to be computed on the scales set out in Tables II and III of the said Rules, the equivalent in the new currency of the appropriate amount in the old currency as read in accordance with section 10(1) of the Act in each Table shall first be aggregated and thereafter the resulting sum adjusted in the same manner as provided in paragraph 1(*c*)(i) to (iii) of this Schedule ; and

(*c*) where any benefits payable to a person under the said Rules fall to be computed by reference to the pensions set out in any one or more of Tables I, IV or V thereof as those Tables are read in accordance with section 10(1) of the Act, the amount of benefit, after allowing for any reduction under Rule 31 and after adding any supplementary pension payable under Rule 17A(*b*), to be paid to that person under the said Rules in respect of any period specified in Rule 20 shall be a sum equal to the aggregate of the benefits to which he is entitled or of which he is in receipt thereunder, and if such a sum includes a fraction of a new penny, then that sum shall be adjusted in the same manner as provided in paragraph 1(*c*)(i) to (iii) of this Schedule.

The National Insurance (Modification of the London Transport and Railway Pension Schemes) Regulations 1956(**a**)

3. Where, in computing the reduction of any contribution to be made under Regulation 3(2), 4(2), 5(2), 9(2), 10(2) or 11(2) of the above-mentioned Regulations of 1956 or of any annual superannuation allowance to be made under Regulation 5(3) or 11(2) thereof, the computation involves application of any reference to an amount of money in the old currency contained in the relevant Table set out in Schedule 1, 2 or 3 to the said Regulations as that reference is read as referring to the equivalent of that amount in the new currency, being an amount which includes a fraction of a new penny, then, if the reduction of the contribution or allowance computed as aforesaid includes a fraction of a new penny, that reduction shall be adjusted in the same manner as provided in paragraph 1(*c*)(i) to (iii) of this Schedule.

The National Insurance (Modification of Transport Undertaking Superannuation Funds) Regulations 1961(**b**) *as amended*(**c**)

4. Where a member's retirement pension is reduced at the rate, construed in accordance with section 10(1) of the Act, of 6d. per week for each £7 10s. 0d. in the case of a man or £9 in the case of a woman paid as provided in Regulation 4(1) of the above-mentioned Regulations of 1961, and the amount of the reduction in the retirement pension falling due for payment to that member includes a fraction of a new penny, then the said amount shall be adjusted in the same manner as provided by paragraph 1(*c*)(i) to (iii) of this Schedule.

The London Transport (Male Wages Grades Pensions) Order 1966(**d**) *as amended*(**e**)

5. In the Schedule (London Transport (Male Wages Grades) Pension Scheme Rules) to the above-mentioned Order of 1966—

(*a*) the provisions of paragraph 2(*a*) of this Schedule shall have the same effect, subject to the next following sub-paragraph, in relation to Table I of the said Rules (in this paragraph called " the 1966 Scheme Rules ") as they have in relation to Table II of the British Transport Commission (Male Wages Grades) Pension Scheme Rules (in this paragraph called " the 1954 Scheme Rules "), the references in those provisions to " Section A " and to " Rule 12 " being treated for the purposes of this sub-paragraph as references respectively to the section of the scheme referred to as Section A in, and to Rule 11 of, the 1966 Scheme Rules ;

(**a**) S.I. 1956/732 (1956 I, p. 1645). (**b**) S.I. 1961/559 (1961 I, p. 1240).
(**c**) There is no relevant amending instrument.
(**d**) S.I. 1966/1164 (1966 III, p. 2789). (**e**) There is no relevant amending instrument.

(*b*) the provisions of paragraph 2(*b*) of this Schedule shall have the same effect in relation to Tables I and II of the 1966 Scheme Rules as they have in relation to Tables II and III of the 1954 Scheme Rules, the references in those provisions to " Section A " and to " Section B " being treated for the purposes of this sub-paragraph as references to Section A and Section B respectively of the scheme established by the above-mentioned Order of 1966 ; and

(*c*) the provisions of paragraph 2(*c*) of this Schedule shall have effect in relation to Tables III and IV of the 1966 Scheme Rules as though the expression " and after adding any supplementary pension payable under Rule 17A(*b*) " were omitted and for the references to the 1954 Scheme Rules, to the Tables and Rules 20 and 31 thereof there were substituted references respectively to the 1966 Scheme Rules, to Tables III or IV and Rules 19 and 31 thereof.

EXPLANATORY NOTE

(This Note is not part of the Order.)

The Order amends the Port of London Act 1968 and a number of subordinate instruments relating to pension schemes in the public sector of transport. Where that Act and those instruments contain references to amounts of money in the old currency of which the equivalent in decimal currency is neither a new penny nor a multiple of a new penny, the Order (*a*) substitutes for references to amounts in the old currency references to appropriate amounts in decimal currency ; and (*b*) provides, in cases where tables, scales or rates are applied for the purposes of calculations under the pension schemes, rules for the rounding up or down of fractions of a new penny to multiples of a new penny.

STATUTORY INSTRUMENTS

1971 No. 190 (C.2) (S.22)

LEGAL AID AND ADVICE, SCOTLAND

The Legal Aid (Scotland) Act 1967 (Commencement No. 1) Order 1971

Made - - - *4th February* 1971

In exercise of the powers conferred on me by section 22(3)(*b*) of the Legal Aid (Scotland) Act 1967(**a**), I hereby make the following order :—

1.—(1) This order may be cited as the Legal Aid (Scotland) Act 1967 (Commencement No. 1) Order 1971.

(2) In this order "the Act" means the Legal Aid (Scotland) Act 1967.

2. The provisions of the Act specified in column 1 of the Schedule to this order (which relate to the matters specified in column 2 thereof) shall come into operation on 1st March 1971 in so far as they provide for and relate to legal aid in connection with civil proceedings in the Scottish Land Court or before any person to whom a case is referred in whole or in part by that Court.

Gordon Campbell,
One of Her Majesty's Principal
Secretaries of State.

St. Andrew's House,
Edinburgh.

4th February 1971.

(**a**) 1967 c. 43.

SCHEDULE

Column 1 Provisions of the Act	Column 2 Subject matter of provisions
Section 1(1) to (6) and (8)	Scope and general conditions of legal aid.
Section 2(1) and (6) to (8)	Financial conditions of legal aid.
Section 3	Contributions from assisted persons and payments out of property recovered.
Section 4	Assessment of disposable capital and income and of maximum contribution.
Section 6	Solicitors and counsel.
Section 8	Functions of Law Society.
Section 9	Legal Aid (Scotland) Fund.
Section 10	Explanation of references to payments.
Section 11	Accounts and audit.
Section 13	Power to award expenses out of legal aid fund.
Section 14	Provisions supplementary to section 13.
Section 15	Regulations.
Section 16	Rules of Court.
Section 17(1) to (5)	Adaptation of rights to indemnity.
Section 18	Offences.
Section 19	Application to Crown.
Section 20	Interpretation and construction.
Schedule 1	Proceedings for which legal aid may be given.
Schedule 2	Remuneration of persons giving legal aid.

EXPLANATORY NOTE

(This Note is not part of the Order.)

This Order brings into operation on 1st March 1971, the provisions of the Legal Aid (Scotland) Act 1967 which are necessary to enable the operation as from that date of legal aid in connection with civil proceedings in the Scottish Land Court.

1971 No. 192

AGRICULTURE

The Price Stability of Imported Products (Rates of Levy) (Eggs) (No. 4) Order 1971

Made - ·· - - -	8th February 1971
Coming into Operation	9th February 1971

The Minister of Agriculture, Fisheries and Food, in exercise of the powers conferred upon him by section 1(2), (4), (5), (6) and (7) of the Agriculture and Horticulture Act 1964(a) and of all other powers enabling him in that behalf, hereby makes the following order:—

1. This order may be cited as the Price Stability of Imported Products (Rates of Levy) (Eggs) (No. 4) Order 1971, and shall come into operation on 9th February 1971.

2.—(1) In this order—

" the Principal Order " means the Price Stability of Imported Products (Levy Arrangements) (Eggs) Order 1970(b) as amended by any subsequent order, and if any such order is replaced by any subsequent order the expression shall be construed as a reference to such subsequent order;

AND other expressions have the same meaning as in the Principal Order.

(2) The Interpretation Act 1889(c) shall apply to the interpretation of this order as it applies to the interpretation of an Act of Parliament and as if this order and the order hereby revoked were Acts of Parliament.

3. In accordance with and subject to the provisions of the Principal Order (which provides for the charging of levies on imports of those eggs and egg products which are specified commodities for the purposes of the Agriculture and Horticulture Act 1964) the rate of general levy for such imports into the United Kingdom of any specified commodity as are described in column 2 of the Schedule to this order in relation to a tariff heading indicated in column 1 of that Schedule shall be the rate set forth in relation thereto in column 3 of that Schedule.

4. The Price Stability of Imported Products (Rates of Levy) (Eggs) (No. 3) Order 1971(d) is hereby revoked.

In Witness whereof the Official Seal of the Minister of Agriculture Fisheries and Food is hereunto affixed on 8th February 1971.

(L.S.)

G. P. Jupe,
Assistant Secretary.

(a) 1964 c. 28.　　(b) S.I. 1970/359 (1970 I, p. 1277).　　(c) 1889 c. 63.
(d) S.I. 1971/166 (1971 I, p.516).

SCHEDULE

1. Tariff Heading	2. Description of Imports	3. Rate of General Levy
	Imports of:—	
04.05	Birds' eggs (in shell or not in shell), fresh, dried or otherwise preserved, sweetened or not, other than egg yolks:	(per 120 eggs)
	A. Eggs in shell:	s. d.
	1. Not exceeding 11 lb. in weight per 120 ..	2 0 [10p]
	2. Over 11 lb. but not exceeding 12½ lb. in weight per 120	2 0 [10p]
	3. Over 12½ lb. but not exceeding 14 lb. in weight per 120	2 0 [10p]
	4. Over 14 lb. but not exceeding 15½ lb. in weight per 120	2 0 [10p]
	5. Over 15½ lb. but not exceeding 17 lb. in weight per 120	3 6 [17½p]
	6. Over 17 lb. in weight per 120	3 6 [17½p]
	B. Eggs not in shell:	(per ton)
	Whole dried	£50

EXPLANATORY NOTE

(*This Note is not part of the Order.*)

This order, which comes into operation on 9th February 1971, supersedes the Price Stability of Imported Products (Rates of Levy) (Eggs) (No. 3) Order 1971. It—

(a) reduces the rates of general levy on imports of eggs in shell in each of the weight grades which are numbered 1 to 4 in the Schedule to the order;

(b) reimposes unchanged the rate of general levy to be charged on imports of eggs in shell in the weight grades which are numbered 5 and 6 in the Schedule and of whole dried eggs not in shell.

STATUTORY INSTRUMENTS

1971 No. 193

AGRICULTURE

HORTICULTURE

The Agricultural and Horticultural Improvements (Standard Costs) (Amendment) Regulations 1971

Made - - - -	8th February 1971
Laid before Parliament	12th February 1971
Coming into Operation	13th February 1971

The Minister of Agriculture, Fisheries and Food, the Secretary of State for Scotland and the Secretary of State for Wales, acting jointly in exercise of the powers conferred on them by section 36 of the Agriculture Act 1967(a) (including the powers conferred on them by the said section 36 as applied by section 41(7) of the said Act), sections 3 and 6 of the Horticulture Act 1960(b) (including the powers conferred on them by the said section 3 as applied by section 3(2) of the Agriculture and Horticulture Act 1964(c), which latter section is by virtue of section 8 of that Act to be construed as one with Part I of the Horticulture Act 1960) and section 1 of the Agricultural Improvement Grants Act 1959(d), each of the aforesaid sections being read with the Transfer of Functions (Wales) Order 1969(e), and, as respects works for the supply of water, the Secretary of State for Scotland acting in exercise of the powers conferred on him by subsections (3) and (4) of section 1 of the said Act of 1959 and the Minister of Agriculture, Fisheries and Food and the Secretary of State for Wales acting jointly in exercise of the powers conferred on them by the said subsections as read with the Transfer of Functions (Wales) Order 1969, the said Ministers acting in exercise of the said sections 36 and 41(7) of the Agriculture Act 1967, section 3(2) of the Agriculture and Horticulture Act 1964 and section 1 of the Agricultural Improvement Grants Act 1959 to the extent that those sections continue in force by virtue of section 29(7) of the Agriculture Act 1970(f) and the Farm Capital Grant (Repeal of Enactments) (Savings) Order 1970(g) and the said Ministers also acting in exercise of all other powers enabling them in that behalf, with the consent and approval of the Treasury, hereby make the following regulations:—

Citation, commencement and interpretation

1.—(1) These regulations may be cited as the Agricultural and Horticultural Improvements (Standard Costs) (Amendment) Regulations 1971, and shall come into operation on 13th February 1971.

(2) The Interpretation Act 1889(h) shall apply to the interpretation of these regulations as it applies to the interpretation of an Act of Parliament.

(a) 1967 c. 22. (b) 1960 c. 22. (c) 1964 c. 28. (d) 1959 c. 31.
(e) S.I. 1969/388 (1969 I, p. 1070). (f) 1970 c. 40. (g) S.I. 1970/1758 (1970 III, p. 5736).
(h) 1889 c. 63.

Amendment of the principal regulations

2. The Agricultural and Horticultural Improvements (Standard Costs) Regulations 1968(**a**), as amended(**b**), shall be further amended as follows :—

   (*a*) by inserting in sub-paragraph (*a*) of regulation 2(5) thereof immediately after the words " after the commencement of these regulations " the words " and before 15th February 1971 " ;

   (*b*) by substituting in sub-paragraph (*b*) of the said regulation 2(5) for the words " while these regulations are in force " the words " after the commencement of these regulations and before 15th February 1971 ".

In Witness whereof the Official Seal of the Minister of Agriculture, Fisheries and Food is hereunto affixed on 3rd February 1971.

(L.S.)   *J. M. L. Prior,*

Minister of Agriculture,
Fisheries and Food.

Given under the Seal of the Secretary of State for Scotland on 8th February 1971.

(L.S.)   *Gordon Campbell,*

Secretary of State for Scotland.

Given under my hand on 5th February 1971.

Peter Thomas,
Secretary of State for Wales.

We consent and approve.

8th February 1971.

Bernard Weatherill,
Walter Clegg,
Two of the Lords Commissioners of
Her Majesty's Treasury.

EXPLANATORY NOTE

(This Note is not part of the Regulations.)

These regulations further amend the Agricultural and Horticultural Improvements (Standard Costs) Regulations 1968, as amended, so that those regulations apply only to works carried out in accordance with a written authority to start work given before 15th February 1971 and, in the case of certain horticultural grants, to works included in proposals approved before that date.

  (**a**) S.I. 1968/282 (1968 I, p. 822).   (**b**) S.I. 1969/1430 (1969 III, p. 4625).

STATUTORY INSTRUMENTS

1971 No. 194 (S.23)

LEGAL AID AND ADVICE, SCOTLAND

The Legal Aid (Scotland) (General) Amendment Regulations 1971

Made - - - -	8th February 1971
Laid before Parliament	16th February 1971
Coming into Operation	1st March 1971

In exercise of the powers conferred on me by section 15 of the Legal Aid (Scotland) Act 1967(a), and of all other powers enabling me in that behalf, and with the concurrence of the Treasury, I hereby make the following regulations:

1.—(1) These regulations may be cited as the Legal Aid (Scotland) (General) Amendment Regulations 1971 and shall come into operation on 1st March 1971.

(2) The Interpretation Act 1889(b) shall apply for the interpretation of these regulations as it applies for the interpretation of an Act of Parliament.

2.—(1) For regulation 8(2) of the Legal Aid (Scotland) (General) Regulations 1960(c) there shall be substituted the following:—

"(2) Where a legal aid certificate is suspended or discharged by a Committee acting under the powers given to them by these regulations or by paragraphs (5) or (6) of article 16 of the Legal Aid (Scotland) Scheme 1958, or by paragraphs (5) or (6) of article 8 of the Legal Aid (Scotland) (House of Lords) Scheme 1960, or by paragraphs (5) or (6) of article 8 of the Legal Aid (Scottish Land Court) Scheme 1971 or by paragraphs (5) or (6) of article 8 of the Legal Aid (Lands Tribunal for Scotland) Scheme 1971 or under a direction given by a court under rule 5 of the Act of Sederunt (Legal Aid Rules) 1958(d), or otherwise, the assisted person shall remain liable to pay to the Society so much of his contribution as is required to defray the expenses incurred up to the date of suspension or discharge:

Provided that where a certificate is discharged under paragraph 6 of article 16 of the Legal Aid (Scotland) Scheme 1958 or paragraph 6 of article 8 of the Legal Aid (Scotland) (House of Lords) Scheme 1960 or paragraph 6 of article 8 of the Legal Aid (Scottish Land Court) Scheme 1971 or paragraph 6 of article 8 of the Legal Aid (Lands Tribunal for Scotland) Scheme 1971 or the direction of a court requiring discharge of a certificate is given under sub-paragraph (c) of paragraph (1) of the said rule 5 or where, in any other case, a court so directs, the Society shall have the right to recover from the person by whom the certificate was held any sum over and above the amount of his contribution which may be required to meet the sums paid or payable by the Society on his account in respect of the proceedings to which the discharged certificate related."

(2) For regulation 10(5) of the Legal Aid (Scotland) (General) Regulations 1960 there shall be substituted the following:—

"(5) Where, at any stage in proceedings, a party who is an assisted person ceases to receive legal aid, he shall be deemed to be an assisted person for the

---

(a) 1967 c. 43.
(b) 1889 c. 63.
(c) S.I. 1960/2195 (1960 II, p. 1817).
(d) S.I. 1958/1872 (1958 I, p. 389).

purpose of any award of expenses made against him only to the extent that those expenses were incurred before he ceased to receive legal aid:

Provided that where an assisted person's legal aid certificate is discharged under paragraph (6) of article 16 of the Legal Aid (Scotland) Scheme 1958 or paragraph (6) of article 8 of the Legal Aid (Scotland) (House of Lords) Scheme 1960 or paragraph (6) of article 8 of the Legal Aid (Scottish Land Court) Scheme 1971 or paragraph (6) of article 8 of the Legal Aid (Lands Tribunal for Scotland) Scheme 1971, or the direction of a court requiring discharge of his certificate is given under sub-paragraph (c) of paragraph (1) of rule 5 of the Act of Sederunt (Legal Aid Rules) 1958, the provisions of paragraph (e) of sub-section (6) of section 2 of the Legal Aid (Scotland) Act 1967 shall not apply to him".

3.—There shall be substituted for the proviso to paragraph (2) of regulation 11 of the Legal Aid (Scotland) (General) Regulations 1960 the following:—

"Provided that the Committee shall not take into account any change of circumstances unless it appears that such change has increased the assisted person's disposable income by an amount greater than £52 or decreased the assisted person's disposable income by an amount greater than £26 or that his disposable capital has increased by an amount greater than £75."

4.—At the end of regulation 3 of the Legal Aid (Scotland) (General) Regulations 1960 there shall be added:—

"(e) an order for the payment of a capital sum or a periodical allowance or both under section 26 of the Succession (Scotland) Act 1964(**a**)".

Gordon Campbell,
One of Her Majesty's Principal
Secretaries of State.

St Andrew's House,
Edinburgh.
4th February 1971.

We concur.

Bernard Weatherill,
Walter Clegg,
Two of the Lord's Commissioners of
Her Majesty's Treasury.

8th February 1971.

EXPLANATORY NOTE

(This Note is not part of the Regulations.)

These Regulations make minor amendments in the Legal Aid (Scotland) (General) Regulations 1960 required by the extension of legal aid to proceedings in the Scottish Land Court and the Lands Tribunal for Scotland. They enable a Committee concerned with applications for legal aid to vary the amount of an assisted person's contribution or to discharge his legal aid certificate on account of a change in income where it appears that the change has increased his disposable income by more than £52, instead of by more than £26 as at present. They also exclude from the provisions of section 3(4) of the Legal Aid (Scotland) Act 1967 any moneys payable under an order for the payment of a capital sum or a periodical allowance or both under section 26 of the Succession (Scotland) Act 1964.

(**a**) 1964 c. 41.

STATUTORY INSTRUMENTS

1971 No. 195 (S.24)

AGRICULTURE

AGRICULTURAL GRANTS, GOODS AND SERVICES

HILL LANDS

The Agricultural Drainage (Standard Costs) (Scotland) Amendment Regulations 1971

Made - - -	*8th February* 1971
Laid before Parliament	*12th February* 1971
Coming into Operation	*15th February* 1971

In exercise of the powers conferred upon me by section 1 of the Agricultural Improvement Grants Act 1959(**a**) and by section 36 of the Agriculture Act 1967(**b**) as applied by section 41(7) of that Act (to the extent that all those sections continue in force by virtue of section 29(7) of the Agriculture Act 1970(**c**) and the Farm Capital Grant (Repeal of Enactments) (Savings) Order 1970(**d**)), and of all other powers enabling me in that behalf, and with the consent of the Treasury in accordance with section 1(3) of the said Act of 1959, I hereby make the following regulations :—

Citation, extent, commencement and interpretation

1.—(1) These regulations, which may be cited as the Agricultural Drainage (Standard Costs) (Scotland) Amendment Regulations 1971, shall apply to Scotland only and shall come into operation on 15th February 1971.

(2) The Interpretation Act 1889(**e**) shall apply for the interpretation of these regulations as it applies for the interpretation of an Act of Parliament.

Amendment of the principal regulations

2. Regulation 3 of the Agricultural Drainage (Standard Costs) (Scotland) Regulations 1968(**f**) shall be amended by inserting therein immediately after the words "any approved work" the words "not being work carried out in

---

(**a**) 1959 c. 31. (**b**) 1967 c. 22.
(**c**) 1970 c. 40. (**d**) S.I. 1970/1758 (1970 III, p. 5736).
(**e**) 1889 c. 63.
(**f**) S.I. 1968/71 (1968 I, p. 177).

accordance with a written authority to commence such work given by the Secretary of State on or after 15th February 1971."

Gordon Campbell,
One of Her Majesty's Principal
Secretaries of State.

St. Andrew's House,
Edinburgh.

5th February 1971.

We consent.

Bernard Weatherill,
Walter Clegg,
Two of the Lords Commissioners
of Her Majesty's Treasury.

8th February 1971.

EXPLANATORY NOTE

(This Note is not part of the Regulations.)

The Agricultural Drainage (Standard Costs) (Scotland) Regulations 1968 provide that where a person eligible for grant in respect of the drainage of agricultural land under section 16 of the Agriculture Act 1937 or for a grant under the Hill Land Improvement (Scotland) Scheme 1967 by way of supplement to such a grant under the said section 16, so elects, the cost of specified cases shall be of a standard amount calculated in accordance with the regulations. These Regulations disapply the said regulations of 1968 to work carried out in accordance with a written authority to start the work given on or after 15th February 1971.

STATUTORY INSTRUMENTS

1971 No. 196 (S.25)

POLICE

The Police (Scotland) Amendment Regulations 1971

Made - - -	*5th February* 1971
Laid before Parliament	*12th February* 1971
Coming into Operation	*15th February* 1971

In exercise of the powers conferred on me by section 26 of the Police (Scotland) Act 1967(a), and of all other powers enabling me in that behalf, and after consulting (i) the Police Advisory Board for Scotland in accordance with section 26(9) of the said Act, and (ii) the Police Council for the United Kingdom in accordance with section 4(4) of the Police Act 1969(b), I hereby make the following regulations :—

PART I

CITATION, COMMENCEMENT AND INTERPRETATION

1. These regulations may be cited as the Police (Scotland) Amendment Regulations 1971.

2. These regulations shall come into operation on 15th February 1971, and shall have effect as follows, that is to say—

(*a*) for the purposes of Part II thereof, as from that date ;

(*b*) for the purposes of Part III thereof, as from 1st July 1970 ;

(*c*) for the purposes of Part IV thereof, as from 1st June 1970 ; and

(*d*) for the purposes of Part V thereof, as from 15th February 1971.

3. In these regulations any reference to the principal regulations is a reference to the Police (Scotland) Regulations 1968(c), as amended(d).

4. The Interpretation Act 1889(e) shall apply for the interpretation of these regulations as it applies for the interpretation of an Act of Parliament.

PART II

PROVISIONS TAKING EFFECT AS FROM 15TH FEBRUARY 1971

5. For regulation 6(*a*)(iii) of the principal regulations (which relates to qualifications for appointment of constables) there shall be substituted the following provision :—

"(iii) There are other special circumstances approved by the chief constable ;".

(a) 1967 c. 77.   (b) 1969 c. 63.
(c) S.I. 1968/716 (1968 II, p. 2024).
(d) The relevant amending instruments are S.I. 1969/168, 927, 1586, 1970/425, 1463 (1969 I, p. 429; II, p. 2805; III, p. 5060; 1970 I, p. 1462; III, p. 4796).
(e) 1889 c. 63.

6. For regulation 14(2)(*h*) of the principal regulations (which relates to contents of personal records) there shall be substituted the following provision :—

"(*h*) a record of his service in the police force, including particulars of all promotions, changes of pay, postings, transfers, removals, injuries received, periods of illness, attendances at training courses, commendations, rewards, punishments other than cautions, and the date of his ceasing to be a constable of the police force with the reason, cause or manner thereof :

Provided that punishments shall be expunged after three years free from punishment, other than a caution."

7. For regulation 29(1) of the principal regulations (which relates to the reckoning of previous service) there shall be substituted the following provision :—

"(1) A constable of a police force of a rank higher than that of constable, who voluntarily transferred thereto from some other force in that higher rank, shall be entitled (subject to any contrary agreement) to reckon, for the purposes of the scale of pay for that rank, the service which was so reckonable immediately before he transferred."

8.—(1) For the Table in paragraph 1 of Schedule 2 of the principal regulations (which relates to annual leave) there shall be substituted the following Table :—

"TABLE

Rank	Annual Leave		
	Under 10 years' relevant service	10 or more years' relevant service	17 or more years' relevant service
	Days	Days	Days
Constable	18	21	23
Sergeant	20	23	23
Inspector	23	26	26
Chief Inspector	26	29	29
Superintendent	42	48	48
Any rank higher than that of Superintendent	Not less than 42	Not less than 48	Not less than 48"

(2) For sub-paragraph (2) of the said paragraph 1 there shall be substituted the following provision :—

"(2) In a leave year which began before 1st September 1970, this paragraph shall have effect in relation to a constable holding a rank below that of superintendent as if each of the periods of annual leave set out in the above Table were decreased by a day."

Part III

Provisions Taking Effect as from 1st July 1970

9. For regulation 39(3) of the principal regulations (which relates to the application of regulation 38 to constables assigned to duty with the Scottish Crime Squad) there shall be substituted the following provision :—

"(3) Where a constable to whom this regulation applies does not move his home, then, regulation 38 shall have effect in relation to him—

(*a*) as if for paragraph (1)(*a*)(iii) there were substituted the following provision :—

"(iii) in the opinion of the Scottish Crime Squad Committee of Chief Constables, is not so living for the sole reason that he could not conveniently return daily to the family home ;"

(*b*) as if in paragraph (1)(*b*) for the words "chief constable" there were substituted the words "Scottish Crime Squad Committee of Chief Constables" ;

(*c*) as if in paragraph (1) for the words "30 months" there were substituted the words "24 months" ;

(*d*) as if for paragraph (2)(*a*) and (*b*) there were substituted the following provision :—

"if he were living with his family or, as the case may be, in his former accommodation." ;

(*e*) where he is a widower with a child or children or a married man and, if he were a constable of the force of the police area in which he is for the time being living and entitled to a flat rate allowance under regulation 37, that allowance would be payable at a higher rate than 67s. 0d. a week, as if for the reference in regulation 38(3)(*b*) to the rate of 67s. 0d. a week there were substituted a reference to that higher rate."

10.—(1) For paragraphs (1) and (2) of regulation 42 of the principal regulations (which relates to removal allowance) there shall be substituted the following provisions :—

"(1) Where a constable moves his home otherwise than on voluntary transfer from one force to another, and the removal is, in the opinion of the chief constable, due to the exigencies of police duty or is made at the request of the chief constable and is, in his opinion, in the interests of the efficiency of the force, the police authority—

(*a*) shall either reimburse the reasonably incurred cost of removal or carry out the removal ;

(*b*) shall, where the constable was the owner of his former home, reimburse expenses reasonably incurred by him in connection with the disposal thereof ;

(*c*) shall, where the constable is the owner of his new home, reimburse expenses reasonably incurred by him in connection with the acquisition thereof if—

(i) he was the owner of his former home, or

(ii) the police authority, after consulting the chief constable, are satisfied that he could neither have been provided with a suitable house or quarters nor have been reasonably expected to find suitable rented accommodation within a reasonable distance of his normal place of duty,

so, however, that where the police authority are of opinion that the constable could have acquired a suitable home for a consideration less than that actually paid, they may restrict the reimbursement of expenses directly related to the consideration paid by him to expenses which would have been reasonably incurred had he paid that lesser consideration.

(2) Where a constable moves his home on voluntary transfer from one force to another, the police authority of the force to which he transfers—

(a) may either reimburse the reasonable cost of removal or carry out the removal ;

(b) may, in the circumstances mentioned in paragraph (1)(b), reimburse the expenses there mentioned ;

(c) may, in the circumstances and subject to the conditions mentioned in paragraph (1)(c), reimburse the expenses there mentioned."

(2) At the end of the said regulation 42 there shall be added the following provision :—

"(7) In this regulation—

(a) any reference to an owner, being an owner of property mentioned in this regulation, is a reference to an occupier thereof whose interest therein is either (i) that of proprietor of the *dominium utile* or, in the case of property not held on feudal tenure, that of proprietor thereof or (ii) a leasehold interest which is neither an interest under a lease (which term includes sublease) from year to year or for a lesser period, or any other lease the unexpired period of which does not exceed a year, nor a furnished tenancy :

Provided that, in the case of property subect to a heritable security constituted by *ex facie* absolute disposition or assignation, the person who, if the debt were discharged, would be entitled to be vested in that property shall, for the purposes of this regulation, be treated as the proprietor or, as the case may be, as the tenant ;

(b) any reference to expenses incurred in connection with the disposal or acquisition of any property shall be construed as including, in particular, estate agent's, auctioneer's and solicitor's fees and expenses in connection with the discharge, redemption, transfer or taking out of a heritable security."

PART IV

PROVISIONS TAKING EFFECT AS FROM 1ST JUNE 1970

11. In regulation 38(3) of the principal regulations (which relates to supplementary rent allowance)—

(a) for the rate "35s." there shall be substituted the rate "47s. 0d.", and

(b) for the rate "50s." there shall be substituted the rate "67s. 0d."

12. Regulation 39(3)(*c*) of the principal regulations (which relates to the application of regulation 38 to constables who are assigned to duty with the Scottish Crime Squad) shall have effect as respects the period ending immediately before 1st July 1970 (from which date regulation 9 of these regulations has effect) as if for the reference to the rate of 50s. a week, in both places where it occurs, there were substituted a reference to the rate of 67s. 0d. a week.

13.—(1) For paragraph (2) of regulation 45 of the principal regulations (which relates to plain clothes allowance) there shall be substituted the following provision :—

"(2) A plain clothes allowance payable under paragraph (1) shall be payable at the rate of—

(*a*) £57 a year, in the case of a superintendent ;

(*b*) £54 a year, in the case of an inspector ;

(*c*) £48 a year, in the case of a sergeant ;

(*d*) £45 a year, in the case of a constable of the rank of constable."

(2) For paragraph (4) of the said regulation 45 there shall be substituted the following provision :—

"(4) A plain clothes allowance payable under paragraph (3) shall be payable at the rate of—

(*a*) 6d. an hour, in the case of an inspector ;

(*b*) 5½d. an hour, in the case of a sergeant ;

(*c*) 5d. an hour, in the case of a constable of the rank of constable."

14. In paragraph 4(2)(*d*) of Schedule 11 to the principal regulations (which relates to the application of regulation 38 to university scholars) for the rate "50s. 0d.", in both places where it occurs, there shall be substituted the rate "67s. 0d."

PART V

PROVISIONS TAKING EFFECT AS FROM 15TH FEBRUARY 1971

15.—(1) In paragraph (2) of regulation 22 of the principal regulations (which relates to overtime) for the words "fractions of a penny being ignored" there shall be substituted the words "so, however, that in making any payment by way of such allowance a fraction of a penny shall be treated as a whole penny except that a fraction less than a half-penny shall be ignored,".

(2) In paragraph (7)(*a*) of the said regulation 22 the words "fractions of a penny being ignored" shall be omitted.

16.—(1) In paragraph (4) of regulation 23 of the principal regulations (which relates to public holidays and rest days for lower ranks) for the words "fractions of a penny being ignored" there shall be substituted the words "so, however, that in making any payment by way of such allowance a fraction of a penny shall be treated as a whole penny except that a fraction less than a half-penny shall be ignored."

(2) In paragraph (5)(*b*) of the said regulation 23 the words "fractions of a penny being ignored" shall be omitted.

17. For paragraph (4) of regulation 33 of the principal regulations (which relates to calculation of monthly, weekly and daily pay) there shall be substituted the following paragraph :—

"(4) In making any payment by way of pay a fraction of a penny shall be treated as a whole penny except that a fraction less than a half-penny shall be ignored."

18. In regulation 38(3) of the principal regulations, as amended by regulation 11 of these regulations, (which relates to supplementary rent allowance)—

(*a*) for the sum "47s. 0d." there shall be substituted "£2·350", and

(*b*) for the sum "67s. 0d." there shall be substituted "£3·350".

19. In regulation 39(3)(*e*) of the principal regulations, as amended by regulation 9 of these regulations, (which relates to the application of regulation 38 to constables who are assigned to duty with the Scottish Crime Squad for the sum "67s. 0d.", in both places where it occurs, there shall be substituted "£3·350".

20. In regulation 44 of the principal regulations (which relates to footwear allowance) for the sum "3s. 9d." there shall be substituted "£0·188".

21. For paragraph (4) of regulation 45 of the principal regulations, as amended by regulation 13(2) of these regulations, (which relates to plain clothes allowance) there shall be substituted the following paragraph :—

"(4) A plain clothes allowance payable under paragraph (3) shall be payable at the rate of—

(*a*) £0·025 an hour, in the case of an inspector ;

(*b*) £0·023 an hour, in the case of a sergeant ;

(*c*) £0·021 an hour, in the case of a constable of the rank of constable."

22. In regulation 46(2) of the principal regulations (which relates to detective duty and detective expenses allowances) for the sum "10s." there shall be substituted "£0·500".

23. In Schedule 5 of the principal regulations (which relates to refreshment, subsistence and lodging allowances) for the Table in paragraph 1 there shall be substituted the following Table :—

"Table

Description of Allowance	Superin-tendents	Inspectors, Sergeants and Constables
	£	£
Refreshment Allowance:		
(i) for one meal	0·410	0·375
(ii) for two meals	0·600	0·540
Subsistence Allowance:		
Period of retention or engagement on duty—		
(i) over 5 hours and not exceeding 8 hours ...	0·600	0·540
(ii) over 8 hours and not exceeding 12 hours ...	0·875	0·790
(iii) over 12 hours and not exceeding 24 hours ...	1·500	1·300
(iv) over 24 hours—at the rate under (iii) above for each complete period of 24 hours' retention or engagement, together with whichever is the appropriate amount under the preceding provisions of this Table for any excess over the aggregate of such complete periods.		
Lodging Allowance—for each night	2·700	2·100"

24. In Schedule 6 of the principal regulations (which relates to motor vehicle allowances :—

(*a*) for the Table in sub-paragraph (1) of paragraph 1 there shall be substituted the following Table :—

"Table

Cylinder capacity	Annual rate of fixed element	Mileage element	
		Basic rate per mile	Reduced rate per mile
	£	£	£
1,200 c.c. or more but less than 1,700 c.c.	86·000	0·033	0·021
1,000 c.c. or more but less than 1,200 c.c.	77·000	0·029	0·019
Less than 1,000 c.c.	69·000	0·026	0·017"

(*b*) for the Table in paragraph 2 there shall be substituted the following Table :—

"TABLE

Cylinder capacity	Rate per mile
	£
1,200 c.c. or more but less than 1,700 c.c.	0·059
1,000 c.c. or more but less than 1,200 c.c.	0·053
Less than 1,000 c.c.	0·047"

25. In paragraph 1 of Schedule 7 of the principal regulations (which relates to bicycle allowance)—

(*a*) for the sum "£11" there shall be substituted "£11·000", and

(*b*) for the sum "£2 15s. 0d." there shall be substituted "£2·750".

26. In paragraph 4(2)(*d*) of Schedule 11 of the principal regulations, as amended by regulation 14 of these regulations, (which relates to the application of regulation 38 to university scholars) for the sum "67s. 0d.", in both places where it occurs, there shall be substituted "£3·350".

Gordon Campbell,
One of Her Majesty's Principal
Secretaries of State.

St. Andrew's House,
Edinburgh.
5th February 1971.

EXPLANATORY NOTE

(This Note is not part of the Regulations.)

These Regulations amend the Police (Scotland) Regulations 1968.

Part II relates to the appointment as constables of persons over 30 years of age, the expungement of punishments from personal records and annual leave. It revokes the requirement for chief constables to obtain the approval of the Secretary of State to the appointment of persons over 30 years of age. It provides that all punishments will be expunged from a constable's personal record after three years free from punishment other than a caution. Subject to transitional provision applicable to the current leave year where that began before 1st September 1970, it increases by three days the period of annual leave of a constable who holds a rank below that of superintendent. Regulation 7 amends Regulation 29(1) of the 1968 Regulations relating to the reckoning of previous service for pay purposes by dropping the proviso as otiose.

Part III relates to rent allowances and removal allowances and has effect from 1st July 1970. Regulation 9 amends the provisions of Regulation 39 of the 1968 Regulations relating to the payment of supplementary rent allowances to constables assigned for duty with the Scottish Crime Squad and applies these provisions to unmarried constables. Regulation 10 amends the provisions of Regulation 42 of the 1968 Regulations relating to constables who move home and under which a police authority are in some circumstances required, and in other circumstances have a discretion, to carry out removals or reimburse removal expenses. Where a constable owns his own home, they are required or empowered, in the like circumstances, to reimburse the constable for expenses reasonably incurred by him in disposing of his old home or, where certain conditions are fulfilled, in acquiring his new home.

Part IV, which has effect from 1st June 1970, increases the rates of supplementary rent and plain clothes allowances.

Part V, which has effect from 15th February 1971, provides for the conversion of money rates into decimal terms.

The provision that Parts III and IV shall have retrospective effect is contained in Regulation 2 (made in exercise of the power conferred by section 26(3) of the Police (Scotland) Act 1967).

STATUTORY INSTRUMENTS

1971 No. 197 (S. 26)

SHERIFF COURT, SCOTLAND

Act of Sederunt (Alteration of Fees of Shorthand Writers in the Sheriff Courts) 1971

Made - - -	*4th February* 1971
Laid before Parliament	*17th February* 1971
Coming into Operation	*4th March* 1971

The Lords of Council and Session, under and by virtue of the powers conferred upon them by section 40 of the Sheriff Courts (Scotland) Act 1907(a) and of all other powers competent to them in that behalf, do hereby enact and declare as follows:—

1. The schedule annexed to the Act of Sederunt of 7th May 1935(b) as amended by the Act of Sederunt (Increase of Fees of Shorthand Writers in the Sheriff Courts) 1970(c) shall be further amended by deleting Chapter II thereof, being the chapter relating to Shorthand Writers' Fees, and by substitution therefor the following:—

"Chapter II—Shorthand Writers' Fees

1. Attending trials, proofs and commissions per hour ... ... £1·70

With a minimum fee of £5 per day if the Court is at a town where the shorthand writer carries on business or has a branch office, or £6·65 per day if the shorthand writer's place of business is at a distance exceeding 5 miles from the Court, and subsistence allowance appropriate to Civil Servants entitled to Class B rates.

No fee will be paid where intimation of postponement or settlement is made by 4 p.m. on the previous day.

2. Extending Notes, per sheet of 250 words ... ... £0·33

Note—An extra allowance will be payable when notes are extended overnight.

3. Carbon copies, per sheet (1st copy) ... ... £0·06
   Other copies ... ... £0·05"

2. This Act of Sederunt may be cited as the Act of Sederunt (Alteration of Fees of Shorthand Writers in the Sheriff Courts) 1971, and shall come into operation on 4th March 1971.

And the Lords appoint this Act of Sederunt to be inserted in the Books of Sederunt.

J. L. Clyde,
I.P.D.

Edinburgh.
4th February 1971.

(a) 1907 c. 51.   (b) S.R. & O. 1935/488 (Rev. XX, p. 880: 1935, p. 1588).
(c) S.I. 1970/177 (1970 I, p. 758).

EXPLANATORY NOTE

(This Note is not part of the Act of Sederunt.)

This Act of Sederunt re-enacts the table of fees payable to shorthand writers for attendance in the Sheriff Court and for extension of Notes, showing the decimal equivalent calculated in terms of Schedule 1 to the Decimal Currency Act 1969.

STATUTORY INSTRUMENTS

1971 No. 198 (S.27)

COURT OF SESSION, SCOTLAND

Act of Sederunt (Rules of Court Amendment No. 5 1970) (Alteration of Fees to Shorthand Writers) 1971

Made - - -	*5th February* 1971	
Coming into Operation	*9th February* 1971	

The Lords of Council and Session, under and by virtue of the powers conferred upon them by section 16 of the Administration of Justice (Scotland) Act 1933(a) and of all other powers competent to them in that behalf, do hereby enact and declare as follows :—

1. The Act of Sederunt (Rules of Court Amendment No. 5) 1970(b), which comes into operation on 15th February 1971, shall come into operation with the substitution of a new Chapter IV in the following terms in place of Chapter IV of the Schedule thereto, and the said Schedule is hereby amended by the substitution of the new Chapter IV accordingly :

"Chapter IV

Table of Fees to Shorthand Writers

"1. Attending trials, proofs and commissions, per hour, with a minimum fee of £5 per day ... ... £1·70

The above fees will be paid by the Exchequer.

No fee will be paid where intimation of postponement or settlement is made by 4 p.m. on the previous day.

2. Extending Notes, except when these are transcribed daily, per sheet of 250 words ... ... £0·36

Extending Notes, when these are transcribed daily but not on stencils, per sheet of 250 words ... ... £0·46

Extending Notes, when these are transcribed daily on stencils, per sheet of 250 words ... ... £0·55

3. Transcripts of Notes of Evidence will only be made on directions from the Court, and the cost thereof in defended cases will in the first instance be payable by the solicitors for the parties in equal shares. The daily transcript of Notes of Evidence shall be made only if all compearing parties shall consent thereto, and the daily transcript of Notes of Evidence on stencils shall be made only if all compearing parties shall consent to such transcript stencils. Where an undefended case is continued, or where for other reasons the Court considers it necessary that the Notes should be extended for the use of the Court and so directs, the cost will be borne by the pursuer's solicitor in the first instance. In any case where the

---

(a) 1933 c. 41.　　　　　　　　(b) S.I. 1970/1746 (1970 III, p. 5718).

Notes of Evidence have not been extended, but are required for a reclaiming motion, the solicitor for the reclaimer may request the shorthand writer to extend the Notes, and the transcript thereof will thereupon be lodged in process, the cost being payable in the first instance by the reclaimer's solicitor.

4. In any case where the Court on a motion enrolled for that purpose certifies that there is reasonable ground for reclaiming and that the reclaimer is unable, for financial reasons, to meet the cost of the necessary transcript from which copies for the use of the Inner House are made, the cost of such transcript will be paid out of public funds.

5. Carbon Copies—

Where Notes of Evidence have been directed to be supplied for the use of the Court, carbon or duplicate copies may be made available to parties at a cost of £0·06 per sheet payable to the shorthand writer by the solicitor for the parties obtaining the said copies."

2. This Act of Sederunt may be cited as the Act of Sederunt (Rules of Court Amendment No. 5 1970) (Alteration of Fees to Shorthand Writers) 1971, and shall come into operation on 9th February 1971.

And the Lords appoint this Act of Sederunt to be inserted in the Books of Sederunt.

J. L. Clyde,
I.P.D.

Edinburgh,
5th February 1971.

EXPLANATORY NOTE

(This Note is not part of the Act of Sederunt.)

This Act of Sederunt amends the Act of Sederunt (Rules of Court Amendment No. 5) 1970, which comes into operation on 15th February 1971 and which prescribed new tables of fees for work done or expenses incurred in the Court of Session. It alters the Chapter of the tables of fees which prescribes fees payable to Shorthand Writers, to the effect that the fees now in force shall continue to be applicable after 15th February 1971 subject only to their conversion to new pence on the scale set forth in Schedule 1 to the Decimal Currency Act 1969.

STATUTORY INSTRUMENTS

1971 No. 199 (C.3) (S.29)

LANDS TRIBUNAL

The Conveyancing and Feudal Reform (Scotland) Act 1970 (Commencement) Order 1971

Made - - - - *4th February* 1971

In exercise of the powers conferred on me by section 54(2) of the Conveyancing and Feudal Reform (Scotland) Act 1970(a), and of all other powers enabling me in that behalf, I hereby make the following order:—

1. Sections 1 to 6 of the Conveyancing and Feudal Reform (Scotland) Act 1970 and sections 51 to 53 thereof in so far as they relate to those sections shall come into operation on 1st March 1971.

2. This order may be cited as the Conveyancing and Feudal Reform (Scotland) Act 1970 (Commencement) Order 1971.

Gordon Campbell,
One of Her Majesty's Principal
Secretaries of State.

St. Andrew's House,
  Edinburgh.
4th February 1971.

EXPLANATORY NOTE

(This Note is not part of the Order.)

This Order brings into force on 1st March 1971 those provisions of the Conveyancing and Feudal Reform (Scotland) Act 1970 not yet in operation. The provisions relate to the variation and discharge of land obligations by the Lands Tribunal for Scotland and the allocation of unallocated feuduties and ground annuals.

(a) 1970 c. 35.

STATUTORY INSTRUMENTS

1971 No. 200 (S. 28)

FEU, SCOTLAND

The Allocation of Feuduty etc. (Form of Notice) Regulations 1971

Made - - -	*4th February* 1971
Coming into Operation	*1st March* 1971

In exercise of the powers conferred on me by section 3(4) of the Conveyancing and Feudal Reform (Scotland) Act 1970(a), and of all other powers enabling me in that behalf, I hereby make the following regulations:—

1.—(1) These regulations may be cited as the Allocation of Feuduty etc. (Form of Notice) Regulations 1971 and shall come into operation on 1st March 1971.

(2) The Interpretation Act 1889(b) shall apply for the interpretation of these regulations as it applies for the interpretation of an Act of Parliament.

2. A notice of allocation shall be in, or as nearly as may be in, the form set out in the Schedule hereto.

Gordon Campbell,
One of Her Majesty's Principal
Secretaries of State.

St. Andrew's House,
Edinburgh.
4th February 1971.

(a) 1970 c. 35.   (b) 1889 c. 63.

SCHEDULE

CONVEYANCING AND FEUDAL REFORM (SCOTLAND) ACT 1970

NOTICE OF ALLOCATION

To ....
Name and address of Superior [Creditor in Ground Annual] or his agent.

Take notice that the sum of £...

which is the portion of a *cumulo*
feuduty/ground annual* which
has been apportioned on..
Distinguish the property (including, where appropriate, the postal address) so that it can be clearly identified.

....

....

of which ....
Name and address of proprietor.

is the proprietor, is to be allocated on the
said subjects under the Conveyancing and
Feudal Reform (Scotland) Act 1970

*The said portion of *cumulo* feuduty/ground annual* is
*Name and address of the person to whom the portion of *cumulo* feuduty [ground annual] is paid.*

paid to...

....

or

*The *cumulo* feuduty/ground annual* of which the said portion
forms part is paid by the proprietor to the superior.
To be signed by the proprietor or his agent. An agent should state his designation and add the words "Agent of ....

Date....................... Signed...
(name of proprietor)"

....

NOTES:

1. If the Superior [Creditor in Ground Annual] wishes to object to the amount of the portion of feuduty [ground annual] specified in this Notice he *must* apply to the Lands Tribunal for Scotland within 28 days.

2. Unless an application is made to the Lands Tribunal for Scotland by the Superior [Creditor in Ground Annual] the allocation of feuduty [ground annual] specified in this Notice shall take effect in respect of any feuduty [ground annual] so allocated which becomes due at any term occurring not less than 3 months after service of this Notice.

*Delete whichever is not applicable.

EXPLANATORY NOTE

(*This Note is not part of the Regulations.*)

These Regulations prescribe the form of the notice of allocation to be used to allocate a *cumulo* feuduty/ground annual in terms of the Conveyancing and Feudal Reform (Scotland) Act 1970.

STATUTORY INSTRUMENTS

1971 No. 201 (S. 30)

COURT OF SESSION, SCOTLAND

Act of Sederunt (Rules of Court Amendment No. 1) (Alteration of Operative Date) 1971

Made - - -		*4th February* 1971
Coming into Operation		*5th February* 1971

The Lords of Council and Session, under and by virtue of the powers conferred upon them by section 16 of the Administration of Justice (Scotland) Act 1933(a) and of all other powers competent to them in that behalf, do hereby enact and declare as follows:—

1. The Act of Sederunt (Rules of Court Amendment No. 1) 1971(b) shall not come into operation on 15th February 1971 but shall come into operation on 1st March 1971.

2. During the period from 15th February 1971 until 1st March 1971 Chapter V of the Schedule to the Act of Sederunt (Rules of Court Amendment No. 5) 1970(c) shall operate as the Table of Fees to Clerks of Counsel.

3. This Act of Sederunt may be cited as the Act of Sederunt (Rules of Court Amendment No. 1) (Alteration of Operative Date) 1971 and shall come into operation on 5th February 1971.

And the Lords appoint this Act of Sederunt to be inserted in the Books of Sederunt.

J. L. Clyde

Edinburgh,
4th February 1971.   I.P.D.

EXPLANATORY NOTE

(This Note is not part of the Act of Sederunt.)

This Act of Sederunt postpones from 15th February 1971 to 1st March 1971 the coming into operation of the Act of Sederunt (Rules of Court Amendment No. 1) 1971 which abolishes the Table of Fees payable to Clerks of Counsel.

(a) 1933 c. 41.   (b) S.I. 1971/66 (1971 I, p. 124)..   (c) S.I. 1970/1746 (1970 III, p. 5718).

STATUTORY INSTRUMENTS

1971 No. 202 (S. 31)

COURT OF SESSION, SCOTLAND
Act of Sederunt (Rules of Court Amendment No. 2) 1971

Made - - -		*4th February* 1971
Coming into Operation		*4th March* 1971

The Lords of Council and Session, under and by virtue of the powers conferred upon them by section 16 of the Administration of Justice (Scotland) Act 1933**(a)** and of all other powers competent to them in that behalf, do hereby enact and declare as follows:—

1. Rule 168 of The Rules of Court **(b)** is hereby amended by redesignating paragraphs (*b*), (*c*) and (*d*) as (*c*), (*d*) and (*e*) respectively and by adding a new paragraph (*b*) as follows:—

"(*b*) In any action for divorce, nullity of marriage or separation in which the Court may make provision for the custody, maintenance and education of any child of the marriage or of any such child as is mentioned in section 7 of the Act of 1958 intimation shall be made to any local authority having the formal care of any such child, and such local authority may apply to the Court to be heard with respect to the care and maintenance of such child. Any such application shall be made by minute craving leave to be sisted as a party to the action and setting forth any relevant averments with respect to the care and maintenance of the child".

2. This Act of Sederunt may be cited as the Act of Sederunt (Rules of Court Amendment No. 2) 1971, and shall come into operation on 4th March 1971.

And the Lords appoint this Act of Sederunt to be inserted in the Books of Sederunt.

J. L. Clyde

Edinburgh,
4th February 1971.   I.P.D.

EXPLANATORY NOTE
(This Note is not part of the Act of Sederunt.)

This Act of Sederunt amends the Rules of Court by requiring intimation to be made in an action for divorce, nullity of marriage or separation to a local authority having care of a child of the marriage. It permits such authority to be sisted as a party and to make averments as to the care and maintenance of such child.

(a) 1933 c. 41.   (b) S.I. 1965/321 (1965 I, p. 803).

STATUTORY INSTRUMENTS

1971 No. 203 (S.32)

COURT OF SESSION, SCOTLAND

Act of Sederunt (Rules of Court Amendment No. 3) 1971

Made - - - -	*4th February* 1971
Coming into Operation	*4th March* 1971

The Lords of Council and Session, under and by virtue of the powers conferred upon them by sections 16 and 34 of the Administration of Justice (Scotland) Act 1933(a) and of all other powers competent to them in that behalf, do hereby enact and declare as follows:—

Citation and commencement

1. This Act of Sederunt may be cited as the Act of Sederunt (Rules of Court Amendment No. 3) 1971 and shall come into operation on 4th March 1971.

Appeals under section 50 of the Social Work (Scotland) Act 1968

2. The Rules of Court **(b)** shall be amended as follows:—

After Rule 289 there shall be inserted the following Rule:—

"289A. *Appeals under section 50 of the Social Work (Scotland) Act 1968*

(1) Where within the period mentioned in section 50(2) of the Social Work (Scotland) Act 1968(c) an application is made to the sheriff to state a case under subsection (1) of that section, the sheriff shall, within fourteen days after the date on which the application is made, prepare a draft stated case and shall cause a copy thereof to be sent forthwith to the applicant and the other parties including the reporter in the case if he is not the applicant.

(2) Where on an application being made to him as aforesaid it appears to the sheriff that any report or statement lodged with the sheriff clerk by the reporter in accordance with section 49(2) or 49(3) of the said Act of 1968 in the appeal to the sheriff is relevant to any issue which is likely to arise in the proceedings upon the stated case and the report or statement has been returned to the reporter in accordance with Rule 16(3) of the Act of Sederunt (Social Work) (Sheriff Court Procedure) Rules 1971**(d)**, the sheriff may require the reporter to lodge again the report or statement with the sheriff clerk.

(3) If the applicant or any of the other parties including the reporter in the case if he is not the applicant desires to have any adjustments made on the draft case he shall, within fourteen days after the date on which a copy of the draft was sent to him as aforesaid, return that copy to the sheriff showing thereon the said adjustments.

(a) 1933 c. 41.	(b) S.I. 1965/321 (1965 I, p. 803).
(c) 1968 c. 49.	(d) S.I. 1971/92 (1971 I, p. 167).

(4) As soon as possible after the return of the said copies of the draft case or, in the event of default in the return thereof, upon the expiry of the period of fourteen days mentioned in the last foregoing paragraph, the sheriff shall state and sign the case for the opinion of the court and the sheriff clerk shall deliver the case to the party who applied for it or, as the case may be, who first applied for it and at the same time shall return to the reporter any report or statement lodged with him under paragraph (2) above.

(5) Subject to the next following paragraphs the provisions of paragraphs (h), (j) and (k) of Rule 277 shall apply to the procedure thereafter as if any reference in those paragraphs to a party included a reference to the reporter and as if in paragraphs (h)(ii) and (k)(iii) there were omitted the words "and it may, if one party only has applied for a stated case, find him liable for payment to the other party of the sum of £5.5s. of expenses" and with any other necessary modifications.

(6) The reporter shall, within seven days after the date on which the case is, in accordance with Rule 277(k), lodged in the general department, deliver to the deputy principal clerk, the principal and ten copies of every report or statement which he was required by the sheriff to lodge again with the sheriff clerk under paragraph (2) above but no copy of any such report or statement shall be made available to any of the other parties except on the order of the court.

(7) The court may direct that all or any of the proceedings upon the stated case shall be heard in chambers.

(8) Subject to any order in that behalf made by the court, any reports or statements delivered to the deputy principal clerk under paragraph (6) of this Rule shall remain in his custody until the appeal is determined or abandoned and thereupon he shall return the said copies to the reporter.

(9) No expenses shall be awarded to or against any party in respect of any of the proceedings upon the stated case."

And the Lords appoint this Act of Sederunt to be inserted in the Books of Sederunt.

Edinburgh,   *J. L. Clyde*
4th February, 1971.   I.P.D.

EXPLANATORY NOTE

(This Note is not part of the Act of Sederunt.)

This Act of Sederunt amends the Rules of the Court of Session. It prescribes procedure for appeals by stated case under section 50 of the Social Work (Scotland) Act 1968 and makes provision for connected purposes.

1971 No. 207

WAGES COUNCILS

The Wages Regulation (Sack and Bag) Order 1971

Made - - - *9th February* 1971

Coming into Operation *9th March* 1971

Whereas the Secretary of State has received from the Sack and Bag Wages Council (Great Britain) the wages regulation proposals set out in the Schedule hereto ;

Now, therefore, the Secretary of State in exercise of his powers under section 11 of the Wages Councils Act 1959(a), and of all other powers enabling him in that behalf, hereby makes the following Order :—

1. This Order may be cited as the Wages Regulation (Sack and Bag) Order 1971.

2.—(1) In this Order the expression "the specified date" means the 9th March 1971, provided that where, as respects any worker who is paid wages at intervals not exceeding seven days, that date does not correspond with the beginning of the period for which the wages are paid, the expression "the specified date" means, as respects that worker, the beginning of the next such period following that date.

(2) The Interpretation Act 1889(b) shall apply to the interpretation of this Order as it applies to the interpretation of an Act of Parliament and as if this Order and the Order hereby revoked were Acts of Parliament.

3. The wages regulation proposals set out in the Schedule hereto shall have effect as from the specified date and as from that date the Wages Regulation (Sack and Bag) Order 1969(c) shall cease to have effect.

Signed by Order of the Secretary of State.
9th February 1971.

R. R. D. McIntosh,
Deputy Secretary,
Department of Employment.

(a) 1959 c. 69.   (b) 1889 c. 63.
(c) S.I. 1969/1739 (1969 III, p. 5457).

SCHEDULE   Article 3

The following minimum remuneration shall be substituted for the statutory minimum remuneration fixed by the Wages Regulation (Sack and Bag) Order 1969 (Order S.B. (68)).

STATUTORY MINIMUM REMUNERATION

PART I

GENERAL

1. The minimum remuneration payable to a worker to whom this Schedule applies for all work except work to which a minimum overtime rate applies under Part IV of this Schedule is:—

(1) in the case of a time worker, the general minimum time rate payable to the worker under Part II or Part III of this Schedule;

(2) in the case of a male worker employed on piece work, piece rates each of which would yield, in the circumstances of the case, to an ordinary worker at least the same amount of money as the general minimum time rate which would be payable under Part II of this Schedule if he were a time worker;

(3) in the case of a female worker employed on piece work, piece rates each of which would yield, in the circumstances of the case, to an ordinary worker at least the same amount of money as the piece work basis time rate applicable to the worker under Part III of this Schedule.

PART II

MALE WORKERS

GENERAL MINIMUM TIME RATES

2. The general minimum time rates payable to male workers are as follows:—

	Per hour
	p

(1) Workers aged 21 years or over and employed during the whole or part of their time:—

    (a) as superintendents of packing presses (hand or machine) or as press foremen (hand or machine), or

    (b) in setting up or minding, or in setting up and minding, branding or printing machines or both such machines   ...   ...   *30·3*

Provided that the general minimum time rate payable during his first six months' employment in the trade to a worker who enters, or who has entered, the trade for the first time at or over the age of 21 years shall be   ...   .   *30·0*

(2) All other workers aged—

	p
21 years or over	*29·2*
20 and under 21 years	*26·3*
19 „ „ 20 „	*25·0*
18 „ „ 19 „	*24·2*
17 „ „ 18 „	*19·8*
16 „ „ 17 „	*17·5*
under 16 years...	*16·1*

Provided that the general minimum time rate payable during his first two months' employment in the trade to a worker who enters, or who has entered, the trade for the first time at or over the age of 18 years shall be *0·2p* per hour less than the minimum rate otherwise payable under this sub-paragraph.

PART III

FEMALE WORKERS

GENERAL MINIMUM TIME RATES

3. The general minimum time rates payable to female workers are as follows:—

Per hour
p

(1) Workers aged 18 years or over and employed as examiners of mended work, allocators, forewomen, hand sewers of heavy twill sacks and bags of 10 porter and upwards, selectors or graders of mixed loads or setters-up on branding machines ... ...   24·9

    Provided that the general minimum time rate payable during her first six months' employment in the trade to a worker who enters, or who has entered, the trade for the first time at or over the age of 18 years shall be ... ...   24·4

(2) All other workers aged—

18 years or over	24·2
17 and under 18 years	19·8
16 „ „ 17 „	17·5
under 16 years...	16·1

    Provided that the general minimum time rate payable during her first two months' employment in the trade to a worker who enters, or who has entered, the trade for the first time at or over the age of 16 years shall be *0·2p* per hour less than the minimum rate otherwise payable under this sub-paragraph.

PIECE WORK BASIS TIME RATES

4. The piece work basis time rates applicable to female workers of any age employed on piece work are as follows:—

Per hour
p

(1) Workers employed as examiners of mended work, allocators, forewomen, hand sewers of heavy twill sacks and bags of 10 porter and upwards, selectors or graders of mixed loads or setters-up on branding machines ... ...   25·6

(2) All other workers ... ...   25·0

PART IV

OVERTIME AND WAITING TIME

MINIMUM OVERTIME RATES

5. Minimum overtime rates are payable to any worker, not being a male worker employed on piece work, as follows:—

(1) on any day other than a Saturday, Sunday or customary holiday—

    (*a*) for the first two hours worked in excess of 8½ hours   time-and-a-quarter

    (*b*) thereafter ... ...   time-and-a-half

Provided that, where the employer normally requires the worker's attendance on five days only in the week, the foregoing minimum overtime rates of time-and-a-quarter and time-and-a-half shall be payable after 9 and 11 hours' work respectively.

(2) on a Saturday, not being a customary holiday—

    (*a*) where the worker is normally required to attend on six days in the week—
    for the first 2 hours worked in excess of 4 hours ...   time-and-a-quarter
    thereafter ... ...   time-and-a-half

    (*b*) where the worker is normally required to attend on five days only in the week—
    for the first 2 hours worked ... ...   time-and-a-quarter.
    thereafter ... ...   time-and-a-half

(3) on a Sunday or a customary holiday—

for all time worked ... ... double time

(4) in any week exclusive of any time for which a minimum overtime rate is payable under the foregoing provisions of this paragraph—

for all time worked in excess of 40 hours ... ... time-and-a-quarter.

6. In this Part of this Schedule—

(1) the expressions "time-and-a-quarter", "time-and-a-half" and "double time" mean respectively—

(a) in the case of a time worker, one and a quarter times, one and a half times and twice the general minimum time rate otherwise payable to the worker;

(b) in the case of a female worker employed on piece work—

(i) a time rate equal respectively to one-quarter, one-half and the whole of the piece work basis time rate otherwise applicable to the worker under Part III of this Schedule and, in addition thereto—

(ii) the piece rates otherwise applicable to the worker under paragraph 1(3).

(2) the expression "customary holiday" means

(a) (i) in England and Wales—

Christmas Day (or, if Christmas Day falls on a Sunday, such weekday as may be appointed by national proclamation, or, if none is so appointed, the next following Tuesday), Boxing Day, Good Friday, Easter Monday, Whit Monday (or where another day is substituted therefor by national proclamation, that day), and August Bank Holiday;

(ii) in Scotland—

New Year's Day and the following day:

Provided that if New Year's Day falls on a Sunday the holidays shall be the following Monday and Tuesday, and if New Year's Day falls on a Saturday the holidays shall be New Year's Day and the following Monday;

the local Spring holiday;

the local Autumn holiday; and

two other days (being days on which the worker would normally work) in the course of a calendar year, to be fixed by the employer and notified to the worker not less than three weeks before the holiday;

or (b) in the case of each of the said days (other than a day fixed by the employer in Scotland and notified to the worker as aforesaid) such weekday as may be substituted therefor by the employer being either—

(i) a day which is by local custom recognised as a day of holiday, or

(ii) a day (being a day on which the worker would normally work) which falls within three weeks of the day for which it is substituted and is mutually agreed between the employer and the worker.

WAITING TIME

7.—(1) A worker is entitled to payment of the minimum remuneration specified in this Schedule for all time during which he is present on the premises of his employer unless he is present thereon in any of the following circumstances:—

(a) without the employer's consent, express or implied;

(b) for some purpose unconnected with his work and other than that of waiting for work to be given to him to perform;

(c) by reason only of the fact that he is resident thereon;

(*d*) during normal meal times in a room or place in which no work is being done and he is not waiting for work to be given to him to perform.

(2) The minimum remuneration payable under sub-paragraph (1) of this paragraph to a piece worker when not engaged on piece work is that which would be payable if he were a time worker.

PART V

APPLICATION

8. This Schedule applies to workers in relation to whom the Sack and Bag Wages Council (Great Britain) operates, namely, workers employed in Great Britain in the trade specified in the Schedule to the Trade Boards (Sack and Bag Trade, Great Britain) (Constitution and Proceedings) Regulations 1933(a), that is to say:—

The making from woven fabrics of corn sacks, flour sacks, coal sacks, sugar sacks, cement bags, sand bags, nail bags, potato bags, seed bags and similar sacks or bags, or the repairing thereof:

including:—

(*a*) the following and similar operations (whether performed by hand or machine) known in the trade as:—

(i) Folding (or hooking), cutting, machining, turning;

(ii) Brushing, selecting, mending;

(iii) Branding, tarring, bundling;

(*b*) the warehousing of, the packing of, and similar operations in regard to sacks or bags of the kind mentioned above when carried on in association with or in conjunction with the making or repairing thereof;

(*c*) the warehousing of, the packing of, and similar operations in regard to any other articles when carried on in or in association with or in conjunction with any business, establishment, branch or department mainly engaged in any of the operations mentioned in paragraph (*b*) above;

excluding:—

(i) any of the operations mentioned above when carried on in association with or in conjunction with the weaving of jute, flax or hemp, or the dyeing, bleaching or finishing of jute, flax or hemp yarn or cloth;

(ii) any of the operations mentioned above when carried on in or in association with or in conjunction with any business, establishment, branch or department mainly engaged in a business in which the sacks or bags are used as containers for other articles the production or sale of which forms part of the business;

(iii) the making of rope-bound coal or coke sacks when carried on in association with or in conjunction with any business, establishment, branch or department engaged in the making of made-up textile articles other than sacks or bags, whether rope-bound or not, of the kind mentioned;

(iv) any of the operations mentioned in paragraph (*b*) above when carried on in or in association with or in conjunction with any business, establishment, branch or department mainly engaged in the warehousing of, the packing of, and similar operations in regard to made-up textile articles other than sacks or bags, whether rope-bound or not, of the kind mentioned;

(v) operations included in the Trade Boards (Waste Materials Reclamation) Order 1920(b).

(a) S.R. & O. 1933/1157 (1933, p. 2052).   (b) S.R. & O. 1920/305 (1920 II, p. 794).

EXPLANATORY NOTE

(This Note is not part of the Order.)

This Order, which has effect from 9th March 1971, sets out the statutory minimum remuneration payable in substitution for that fixed by the Wages Regulation (Sack and Bag) Order 1969 (Order S.B. (68)), which Order is revoked.

New provisions are printed in italics.

STATUTORY INSTRUMENTS

1971 No. 209

LANDS TRIBUNAL

The Lands Tribunal (Temporary Provisions) Rules 1971

Made	-	-	-	*9th February* 1971
Coming into Operation			*10th February* 1971

The Lord Chancellor, in exercise of the powers conferred on him by section 3 of the Lands Tribunal Act 1949(**a**) after consultation with the Council on Tribunals in accordance with section 8 of the Tribunals and Inquiries Act 1958(**b**), hereby makes the following Rules :—

1. These Rules may be cited as the Lands Tribunal (Temporary Provisions) Rules 1971 and shall come into operation on 10th February 1971.

2.—(1) The Interpretation Act 1889(**c**) shall apply to the interpretation of these Rules as it applies to the interpretation of an Act of Parliament.

(2) In these Rules a Rule referred to by number means the Rule so numbered in the Lands Tribunal Rules 1963(**d**) as amended by the Lands Tribunal (Amendment) Rules 1968(**e**) and 1970(**f**).

3. The registrar shall for the time being have power (notwithstanding the provision to the contrary effect in paragraph (1) of Rule 55) to accept a notice of appeal against the decision of a local valuation court outside the time appointed by paragraph (1) of Rule 9 if he is satisfied that the delay in lodging the appeal arises out of the present postal strike :

Provided that the time within which a late notice of appeal may be accepted by virtue of this Rule shall not extend beyond 28 days after the end of the present postal strike.

Dated 9th February 1971.

Hailsham of St. Marylebone, C.

EXPLANATORY NOTE

(This Note is not part of the Rules.)

These Rules enable the Lands Tribunal to accept a late notice of appeal from the decision of a local valuation court for reasons arising out of the postal strike. This provision is temporary and does not extend beyond 28 days from the end of the strike.

(**a**) 1949 c. 42.	(**b**) 1958 c. 66.
(**c**) 1889 c. 63.	(**d**) S.I. 1963/483 (1963 I, p. 532).
(**e**) S.I. 1968/1700 (1968 III, p. 4592).	(**f**) S.I. 1970/858 (1970 II, p.2724).

STATUTORY INSTRUMENTS

1971 No. 211

DIPLOMATIC SERVICE

The Consular Fees Order 1971

Made -   -   -   -   10*th February* 1971
Coming into Operation   1*st April* 1971

At the Court at Buckingham Palace, the 10th day of February 1971

Present,

The Queen's Most Excellent Majesty in Council

Her Majesty, by virtue and in exercise of the powers in that behalf by section 2(1) of the Consular Salaries and Fees Act 1891(**a**) and section 8(1) of the Fees (Increase) Act 1923(**b**) or otherwise in Her Majesty vested, is pleased, by and with the advice of Her Privy Council, to order, and it is hereby ordered, as follows :—

1. This Order shall come into operation on 1st April 1971 and may be cited as the Consular Fees Order 1971.

2.—(1) The Interpretation Act 1889(**c**) shall apply for the interpretation of this Order as it applies for the interpretation of an Act of Parliament and as if this Order and the Orders hereby revoked were Acts of Parliament.

(2) In this Order " consular officer " has the same meaning as in section 3 of the Consular Salaries and Fees Act 1891, read with section 13(4) of the Consular Relations Act 1968(**d**).

(3) In this Order " consular employee " and " consular premises " have the same meanings as in Article 1 of Schedule 1 to the Consular Relations Act 1968.

3. The several fees set forth in the table in the Schedule annexed to this Order are hereby established to be levied by consular officers, by public officers in Great Britain acting under the authority of a Secretary of State, and by marriage officers under the Foreign Marriage Act 1892(**e**) and the Marriage with Foreigners Act 1906(**f**) in the execution of their duties, and the said table shall be construed as part of the Order.

4. The following Orders in Council are hereby revoked :—

The Consular Fees Order 1968(**g**)

The Consular Fees (Amendment) Order 1970(**h**).

W. G. Agnew.

(**a**) 1891 c. 36.   (**b**) 1923 c. 4.   (**c**) 1889 c. 63.   (**d**) 1968 c. 18.   (**e**) 1892 c. 23.
(**f**) 1906 c. 40.   (**g**) S.I. 1968/114 (1968 I, p. 328).   (**h**) S.I. 1970/1683 (1970 III, p. 5568).

SCHEDULE

TABLE OF CONSULAR FEES

PART I

NOTARIAL AND KINDRED MATTERS

Fee		£
1	Preparing any certificate, declaration or document not otherwise provided for—	
	(*a*) in standard form, per copy	2·00
	(*b*) not in standard form, per 100 words:	
	(i) in English	2·00
	(ii) in any other language	3·00
2	Preparing or signing, or both, a declaration of existence ... except in connexion with pay or pensions payable by a department of the Government of the United Kingdom or of any other Government within the Commonwealth	1·00
3	Administering an oath or receiving a declaration or affirmation or attesting or legalising a signature or seal ... ... except where—	1·50
	(*a*) the oath, declaration or affirmation is made under the Merchant Shipping Acts or in connexion with the loss of a passport, or	
	(*b*) fee 20, 25, 26, 28, 37 or 38 is to be taken, or	
	(*c*) the signature or seal is on a certificate of survey of foreign passenger ships running to or from the United Kingdom, or	
	(*d*) the signature or seal is on a document required for the deposit or withdrawal of money in or from any British Post Office or other Government Savings Bank, or	
	(*e*) the signature or seal is in connexion with stocks or bonds on the registers of the Post Office, with Savings Bank Annuities or with annuities granted direct by the National Debt Commissioners	

when an oath of allegiance is taken on the form set out in the Second Schedule to the British Nationality Regulations 1965(a) at the same time as the declaration set out therein is made the fee shall be charged once only

4	Supplying witnesses, for each witness	0·50
5	Initialling alterations in any document not prepared by the consular officer or marking exhibits, for each initialling or marking	0·25
6	Making or verifying (including certifying where necessary) a copy of a document—	
	(*a*) in typescript or made by photographic process outside the consular premises, for every 100 words	1·50
	(*b*) by photographic process, if the copy is made in the consular premises, for each page (with a minimum charge of £1)...	0·25
7	Uniting documents and sealing the fastening ... ... except where fee 38 is to be taken	0·75
8	Obtaining a legalisation or other certification from another authority upon any document ... ... in addition to costs, if any	1·00

(a) S.I. 1965/1753 (1965 III, p. 4956).

Fee £

9   Supplying certified copies of documents forming part of the records of a court which is, or was formerly, established under the Foreign Jurisdiction Acts 1890(a) and 1913(b)—
for every folio of 72 words or less   ...   .   0·50

10   Making or verifying (including certifying where necessary) a translation in writing of a document or part of document, for each 100 words or characters (or part thereof) in the foreign language—

     (*a*) from or into Amharic, Chinese, Japanese or Korean (three Japanese *Kana* being counted as one character when used independently) ...   .   5·00

     (*b*) from or into any other language   ...   .   2·50
     except where fee 28 or 40 is to be taken

11   Translating and interpreting *viva voce* (except when necessary for the performance of official duties)—
for every 15 minutes   ...   .   1·00

PART II

Passports, Visas and Kindred Matters

12   Issuing a passport   ...   .   5·00
     except where fee 13 is to be taken

13   Issuing an additional passport of restricted validity   ...   ...   2·50
     except in replacement of a passport lost or temporarily unavailable

14   Issuing a British Visitors' passport ...   .   1·50

15   Issuing a collective passport   ...   .   5·00

16   Renewing a passport issued before 7th February 1968, a certificate of identity, or other travel document   ...   .   2·00
     except where fee 17, 23 or 24 is to be taken

17   Extending for the first time the validity of an additional passport   2·50
     except of one in replacement of a passport lost or temporarily unavailable

18   Amending an existing passport in one of the following ways—

     (*a*) adding the particulars of a child or children

     (*b*) amending the holder's name at the request of the holder

     (*c*) adding a fresh photograph or amending the holder's description, except where the holder is under 21 years of age   1·00

19   Making or forwarding, or both, a request or recommendation to an authority of Her Majesty's Government in the United Kingdom, or of a foreign State or Commonwealth country, Colony, Protectorate, Protected State or Trust Territory for the issue or renewal of—

     (*a*) a visa or entry permit (except a visa or entry certificate for the United Kingdom) ...   .   0·50

     (*b*) any certificate or document (except a Home Office travel document) or any application for registration or naturalization   ...   .   1·00

     in addition to costs, if any

       (a) 1890 c. 37.   (b) 1913 c. 16.

Fee		£
20	Issuing and, where required, preparing an Emergency Passport or other document not otherwise provided for in lieu of a passport, or accepting a Declaration of Identity on which a visa is to be granted and ssuing a certificate on such declaration describing the applicant	1·00
21	Granting a visa or entry permit—	
	for an ordinary visa or entry permit	2·00
	for a transit visa or permit	0·50
	or for any visa or entry permit such sums, being the equivalents of fees charged by the authorities of any State for granting a visa or entry permit to a citizen of the United Kingdom and Colonies, as the Secretary of State, with the consent of the Treasury, directs to be taken for granting a visa or entry permit to a national or citizen of that State	
	except where a United Kingdom visa is issued on a foreign passport held by a British subject	
22	Issuing a Travel Certificate on behalf of Nigeria, Ghana, or The Gambia	1·50
23	Renewing a Travel Certificate, certificate of identity or other travel document on behalf of—	
	(*a*) Nigeria, Ghana or The Gambia	1·00
	(*b*) Hong Kong	2·00
	except where fee 24 is to be taken	
24	Revalidating or renewing a Seaman's Certificate of Nationality and Identity or a Seaman's Identity Book	0·50
	in addition to fee 19 where applicable	

PART III

MARRIAGES, BIRTHS AND DEATHS

25	Receiving notice of an intended marriage	2·00
26	Solemnising or attending a marriage under the Foreign Marriage Acts 1892 to 1947(**a**), administering oaths to the parties and registering the marriage	8·00
27	Issuing in English or in the local language a certificate that no impediment to an intended marriage has been shown to exist	2·00
28	Transmitting a record of a marriage under the local law to the appropriate Registrar General in accordance with Article 7(1) of the Foreign Marriage Order 1970(**b**), including the provision of any necessary certification	3·00
29	Issuing a " certificat de coutume " for an intended marriage in accordance with the local law	3·00
30	Registering a birth or death or making an addition to or correction in the register at the request of the parties concerned ...	1·50
31	Referring an application for registration of a birth (or births) where the permission of the Secretary of State is required ...	2·50
	in addition to fees 30 and 32 where applicable	
32	Furnishing a certified copy of an entry in the consular register of births, deaths or marriages—	
	(*a*) at the time of registration	0·50
	(*b*) subsequently	1·00
	in addition to fee 33 where applicable	

(**a**) 1892 c. 23; 1934 c. 13; 1947 c. 33.   (**b**) S.I. 1970/1539 (1970 III, p. 5299).

Fee　　　　　　　　　　　　　　　　　　　　　　　　　　£

Part IV

Searches

33　Making a search in

(*a*) the consular registers of births, deaths or marriages
where the number or date of entry is not provided　...　0·50

(*b*) any other records or archives of Her Majesty's Government　1·50
in addition to fee 32 where applicable

34　Having a search made for, or obtaining copies of, or both, entries
in the local registers or records not kept by a consular officer—

for an entry in a local register of births, deaths or marriages　3·50

for any other document ...　...　...　...　...　...　4·00
in addition to costs exceeding £0·50

Part V

Estates

35　Administering in full or in part, safeguarding, or arranging the
transmission of all or part of the personal effects and other
estate of a deceased person or proceeds thereof, other than
the wages and personal effects of a seaman—

on the amount up to £1,000, if over £30, of the gross current　2% rounded
market value　　　　　　　　　　　　　　　　　　　upwards to
the nearest
£0·25

on the amount over £1,000　...　...　...　...　... 1% rounded
upwards to
the nearest
£0·25

with a minimum, to be taken also where a local lawyer is
employed and the matters or things to be done by the
consular officer are nominal, of　...　...　...　...　£5·00

Part VI

Attendances

36　Attending (except in connexion with commercial enquiries) for
each hour or lesser period, including the time taken in proceeding from a reasonable point of departure and in returning to
a reasonable point—

　　　　　　　　　　　　　　　　　　　　　　　　　　£

during customary business hours but elsewhere than at the
consular premises　...　...　...　...　...　...　5·00

outside customary business hours—
at the consular residence　　　...　...　...　...　6·00

elsewhere　...　...　...　...　...　...　...　10·00

with—

(*a*) a maximum in any period of 24 hours of　...　...　30·00

(*b*) an increase of one-half where the consular officer is
accompanied away from the consular premises or
residence by another consular officer or a consular
employee with a maximum in this event of...　...　45·00

Fee   £

Part VII

Matters Relating to Legal Proceedings

37 Presiding at the taking of evidence under a commission or order from a Court, including any matter or thing done by the consular officer as examiner—

    (a) for the first two hours or less on the first day   ...   ...   15·00

    (b) for the first two hours or less on each subsequent day   ...   10·00

    (c) for each additional hour on any day   ...   .   5·00

38 Providing evidence of service or attempted service   ...   ...   3·00
    in addition to fee 36 or 39.

39 Providing the services of a consular officer or consular employee—

    (a) to assist the consular officer in the taking of evidence under a commission or order from a Court, for each such person—

        for each sitting of two hours or less   ...   .   3·00

        for each additional hour at each sitting ...   .   1·00

    (b) to effect or endeavour to effect service of a document, for each hour or shorter period elsewhere than at the consular premises—

        during customary business hours ...   .   3·00

        outside customary business hours   ...   .   5·00

40 Forwarding a request to a local authority for the taking of evidence or the service of a document and, where necessary, certifying the accuracy of a translation accompanying the document   ...   .   3·00

Part VIII

Repatriation

41 Arranging the repatriation of a person or a group of persons of the same family and travelling together   ...   .   6·00

Part IX

Shipping, Seamen and Kindred Matters

42 Receiving or recording a declaration under Part I of the Merchant Shipping Act 1894(a) with a view to the registry, transfer and transmission of ships, interests in ships, or mortgages of ships...   4·00

43 Endorsing a memorandum of change of master upon the certificate of registry and initialling, where required, the new master's signature on the agreement with the crew   ...   .   2·00

44 Granting a provisional certificate of registry   ...   .   10·50
    in addition to fee 42 where applicable

45 Recording a mortgage of a ship or of shares in a ship   ...   ...   10·50

46 Recording the transfer of a mortgage of a ship or of shares in a ship ...   .   10·50

47 Recording the discharge of a mortgage of a ship or of shares in a ship ...   .   10·50

48 Making an interposition in the sale of a ship or of shares in a ship ...   .   10·50

(a) 1894 c. 60.

Fee	£

49 Sanctioning the engagement of seamen—

for each seaman ... ...   1·00

with—

   (*a*) a maximum where a crew or part of a crew transfer from one British ship to another, or

   (*b*) a maximum in respect of each ship where crews or parts of crews transfer between British ships,

of ... ...   20·00

in addition to fee 62 or 69 where applicable

50 Attesting alterations in the agreement with the crew—

foɪ each alteration in respect of each seaman concerned ...   1·00

with a maximum on each separate occasion of ... ...   20·00

51 Sanctioning the discharge of seamen or leaving behind of seamen and apprentices—

for each seaman or apprentice ... ...   1·00

with—

   (*a*) a maximum where a crew or part of a crew transfer from one British ship to another, or

   (*b*) a maximum in respect of each ship where crews or parts of crews transfer between British ships,

of ... ...   20·00

except where an apprentice—

   (*a*) is transferred whilst overseas from one ship to another, or

   (*b*) having come to the end of his indentures, signs on as a seaman

in addition to fee 69 where applicable

52 Certifying desertions of seamen and apprentices—

for each seaman or apprentice ... ...   1·00

53 Receiving a return of the birth or death of any person on board a ship and endorsing the agreement with the crew accordingly   1·00

54 Certifying a form of claim for wages and other matters, if any, of a deceased seaman or apprentice ... ...   1·50

55 Examining or arranging for the examination of provisions or water, payable by the party who proves to be in default ...   5·00

in addition to the cost, if any, of survey

56 Preparing and attesting a salvage bond executed in pursuance of section 560(1) of the Merchant Shipping Act 1894, payable by the master or owner of the property salved ... ...   20·00

57 Taking custody of a ship's papers, making any necessary endorsements thereon, and giving the certificate required by section 257(2) of the Merchant Shipping Act 1894 ... ...   2·00

58 Noting a marine protest and furnishing one certified copy if required ... ...   4·00

for every further copy ... ...   2·00

59 Extending a marine protest, filing the original and furnishing one certified copy if required—

for any number of words up to 200, excluding the declaratory clause ... ...   10·50

for every subsequent 100 words or less ... ...   2·00

in addition to fees 1 and 3 where applicable

60 Filing a request for survey and issuing an order of survey ...   5·00

61 Receiving a report of a survey, filing the original and furnishing one certified copy, if required, of the request, order and report of survey—

for any number of words up to 200, excluding the words in the consular certificate ... ...   10·50

for every subsequent 100 words or less ... ...   2·00

Fee		£

62 Preparing a fresh agreement with the crew when a new agreement is opened at a foreign port and furnishing the copy which must be made accessible to the crew—

    for each seaman ... ...   1·00

    with a minimum of ... ...   10·00

    and a maximum of ... ...   20·00

    in addition to fee 49

63 Issuing a bill of health ... ...   4·00

64 Addressing at the request of the master an application to local authorities for the arrest, imprisonment or release of seamen or apprentices—

    for each seaman or apprentice ... ...   2·50

65 Granting such certificates as to the number of the crew and other matters as may be required by local authorities for the clearance inwards and outwards of a ship ... ...   3·00

    in addition to fee 57 or 69 where applicable

66 Drawing up, in the form and language required by local authorities, a muster-roll or detailed list giving the names and other details of each member of the crew ... ...   2·00

    in addition to fee 65 unless a certificate in the form of a muster-roll or list is required for the clearance of the vessel

67 Signing and, if required, sealing the original of a ship's manifest and signing any copies on the same occasion ... ...   2·50

68 Signing and, if required, sealing any entry in the official log-book of a ship where such entry is not required under the Merchant Shipping Acts ... ...   1·50

69 Inspecting a ship's papers when required to enable a consular officer to do any matter or thing in respect of a ship ...   2·00

    except where—

    (*a*) the papers are already in the custody of the consular officer and fee 57 has been taken, or

    (*b*) the master opens a new agreement at the consular premises

70 Inspecting the marking of a ship, irrespective of the number of visits ... ...   2·00

    in addition to fee 36

71 Making a request for survey and arranging for the issue of a certificate in accordance with the International Convention for the Safety of Life at Sea 1960(a) ... ...   2·00

EXPLANATORY NOTE

(*This Note is not part of the Order.*)

The present Order revokes all previous Consular Fees Orders. Various alterations have been made to the fees, most of which have been increased. Some anachronistic fees have been abolished and the number of fees has been further reduced by consolidation.

(a) Cmnd. 2812.

STATUTORY INSTRUMENTS

1971 No. 212

CROWN PROCEEDINGS

The Northern Ireland (Crown Proceedings) (Amendment) Order 1971

Made - - - -	10*th February* 1971
Laid before Parliament	12*th February* 1971
Coming into Operation	15*th February* 1971

At the Court at Buckingham Palace, the 10th day of February 1971

Present,

The Queen's Most Excellent Majesty in Council

Her Majesty, in exercise of the powers conferred on Her by section 53 of the Crown Proceedings Act 1947(a), and of all other powers enabling Her in that behalf, is pleased, by and with the advice of Her Privy Council, to order, and it is hereby ordered, as follows :—

PART I

GENERAL

1.—(1) This Order may be cited as the Northern Ireland (Crown Proceedings) (Amendment) Order 1971 and shall come into operation on 15th February 1971.

(2) In this Order " the Act " means the Crown Proceedings Act 1947 and " the principal Order " means the Northern Ireland (Crown Proceedings) Order 1949(b).

(3) This Order shall be construed as one with the principal Order and that Order and this Order may be cited together as the Northern Ireland (Crown Proceedings) Orders 1949 and 1971.

PART II

AMENDMENT OF PART III OF THE PRINCIPAL ORDER

2. In Article 3 of the principal Order—

(*a*) in paragraph (2), the words from " and for any reference " onwards shall be revoked ; and

(*b*) in paragraph (3), for the words from " shall mean county court rules " to " section four of that Act " there shall be substituted the words " shall have the same meaning as in section 21(5) of the Interpretation Act (Northern Ireland) 1954(c) ".

(a) 1947 c. 44. (b) S.I. 1949/1836 (1949 I, p. 1261).
(c) 1954 c. 33 (N.I.).

1u

3. After Article 8 of the principal Order there shall be inserted the following Article : —

" 8A. For section 16 there shall be substituted the following section : —

"Interpleader. 16. The Crown may obtain relief by way of interpleader proceedings, and may be made a party to such proceedings, in the same manner in which a subject may obtain relief by way of such proceedings or be made a party thereto ; and the provisions of section 43 of the Judgments (Enforcement) Act (Northern Ireland) 1969(a) relating to interpleader proceedings shall, subject to the provisions of this Act, have effect accordingly." "

4. For Article 14 of the principal Order there shall be substituted the following Article : —

" 14.—(1) For section 24(1) there shall be substituted the following subsection :—

" (1) Section 106 of the Judgments (Enforcement) Act (Northern Ireland) 1969 (which provides that a money judgment shall, subject to an exception and to any contrary provision in the judgment, carry interest) shall apply to money judgments given against or in favour of the Crown."

(2) Section 24(2) shall be excepted.

(3) In section 24(3) for the reference to section 3 of the Law Reform (Miscellaneous Provisions) Act 1934(b) there shall be substituted a reference to section 17 of the Law Reform (Miscellaneous Provisions) Act (Northern Ireland 1937(c)."

5. For Article 15 of the principal Order there shall be substituted the following Articles : —

" 15. For section 26(2) there shall be substituted the following subsections :—

" (2) Without prejudice to the generality of subsection (1) above, the Judgments (Enforcement) Act (Northern Ireland) 1969 and any rules of court, rules or regulations made thereunder shall, save as otherwise provided by any statutory provision within the meaning of that Act, apply to judgments given in favour of the Crown.

(2A) Sections 87 and 88 of the said Act of 1969 (which relate respectively to limitation on arrest and imprisonment of debtors and to committal for default) shall apply to sums of money payable and debts due to the Crown.

(2B) Sections 96 and 104 of the said Act of 1969 (which relate respectively to committal for contempt in certain cases of default and to the effect of imprisonment under section 88 or 96) shall—

(*a*) have effect in relation to sums of money payable and debts due to the Crown ; and

(*b*) have effect as if those provisions in terms applied to default in payment of any sum payable in respect of death duties or purchase tax."

(a) 1969 c. 30 (N.I.).   **(b)** 1934 c. 41.   (c) 1937 c. 9 (N.I.).

15A. For section 27 there shall be substituted the following section : —

"Attachment of moneys payable by the Crown.

27.—(1) Where any money is payable by the Crown to some person who, under any order of any court, is liable to pay any money to any other person, and that other person would, if the money so payable by the Crown were money payable by a subject, be entitled under the Judgments (Enforcement) Act (Northern Ireland) 1969 to obtain an order for the attachment thereof as a debt due or accruing due, or an order for the appointment of a receiver to receive the money on his behalf, the Enforcement of Judgments Office may, subject to the provisions of this Act and in accordance with the said Act of 1969, make an order restraining the first-mentioned person from receiving that money and directing payment thereof to that other person or to the receiver :

Provided that no such order shall be made in respect of—

(*a*) any wages or salary payable to any officer of the Crown as such ;

(*b*) any money which is subject to the provisions of any enactment prohibiting or restricting assignment or charging or taking in execution ; or

(*c*) any money payable by the Crown to any person on account of a deposit in the National Savings Bank.

(2) Subsection (1) above shall apply to the appointment of, and directing the payment of money to, a sequestrator as it applies to the appointment of, and directing the payment of money to, a receiver, subject to the following modifications : —

(*a*) for the words " the Judgments (Enforcement) Act (Northern Ireland) 1969 " and " the said Act of 1969 " there shall be substituted the words " rules of court or, as the case may require, county court rules " ;

(*b*) for the words " the Enforcement of Judgments Office " there shall be substituted the words " a judge of the High Court or, as the case may require, the county court which made the original order "." "

6. For Article 17 of the principal Order there shall be substituted the following Article : —

" 17. Section 31(2) shall be excepted."

W. G. Agnew.

EXPLANATORY NOTE

(This Note is not part of the Order.)

The Judgments (Enforcement) Act (Northern Ireland) 1969 amended the law in Northern Ireland relating to the enforcement of judgments, including the enforcement of judgments in favour of the Crown in right of the Government of Northern Ireland, and to interest on money judgments against, as well as in favour of, the Crown in right of the Government of Northern Ireland.

This Order amends the Northern Ireland (Crown Proceedings) Order 1949 in relation to the Crown in right of the Government of the United Kingdom so as to make the position of the Crown in right of the Government of the United Kingdom the same in Northern Ireland, as regards those matters, as that of the Crown in right of the Government of Northern Ireland.

1971 No. 213

JUDICIAL COMMITTEE

PROCEDURE

The Judicial Committee (Fees) Rules 1971

Made	- - -		10*th February* 1971
Coming into Operation			15*th February* 1971

At the Court at Buckingham Palace, the 10th day of February 1971

Present,

The Queen's Most Excellent Majesty in Council

Whereas there was this day read at the Board a representation from the Judicial Committee of the Privy Council recommending that the Fees set out in Part II of Schedule B to the Judicial Committee Rules 1957(a) and the Fees set out in Part I of Schedule B contained in the Schedule to the Judicial Committee (Fees) Rules 1963(b) ought to be revoked and that the Fees set out in the Schedule thereunto annexed ought to be substituted therefor:

Now, therefore, Her Majesty, having taken the said representation into consideration, and in exercise of the powers conferred on Her by section 24 of the Judicial Committee Act 1833(c) or otherwise in Her vested, is pleased, by and with the advice of Her Privy Council, to approve thereof and to order, as it is hereby ordered, as follows:—

1. The Fees set out in Part II of Schedule B to the Judicial Committee Rules 1957 and the Fees set out in Part I of Schedule B contained in the Schedule to the Judicial Committee (Fees) Rules 1963 are hereby revoked and the Fees set out in the Schedule annexed to the said representation are substituted therefor, as set out in the Schedule to these Rules.

2. These Rules may be cited as the Judicial Committee (Fees) Rules 1971 and shall come into operation on 15th February 1971.

W. G. Agnew.

(a) S.I. 1957/2224 (1957 I, p. 1205).   (b) S.I. 1963/372 (1963 I, p. 333).   (c) 1833 c. 41.

SCHEDULE

PART I

Fees Allowed in Appeals or Other Matters Before The Judicial Committee of the Privy Council

Agents are required to adhere as far as possible to the items shown in the Scale, but it is within the discretion of the Taxing Officer to allow further charges:—

(a) in relation to items not mentioned in the Scale;
   or
(b) of an amount higher than that prescribed by the Scale.

A

Appellant's Costs of Petition for Special Leave to Appeal(a)

	£
Instructions for Petition	1·50
Perusing papers sent from abroad in support of Petition, according to length(b)	
Drawing Petition, per page	1·25
(Extracts or copied matter, if any, at £0·25 per page)	
Making copies of all necessary papers for Counsel, per page(c)...	0·25
Attending Counsel with papers	1·00
Paid fee to Counsel to settle Petition	
Six copies Petition to lodge, at per page for each copy	0·25
Six copies Judgment to lodge, at per page for each copy	0·25
Drawing affidavit in support of Petition, per page	1·00
Copying same, per page	0·25
Attending to be sworn	1·00
Paid oath (unless sworn at the Privy Council Office) as paid	
Attending lodging Petition and necessary documents	1·00
Copying Petition and affidavit for Respondent, per page	0·25
Attending serving Respondent's Solicitors	1·00
Instructions to Counsel to support Petition	1·50
Copying same, per page	0·25
Copy Petition for Counsel, per page	0·25
Copy affidavit(s) for Counsel, per page	0·25
Attending Counsel with papers, if fee under 30 pounds	1·00
if 30 pounds or more	3·00
Paid fee to Counsel(d)	
Copy summons for hearing, for Counsel	0·25
Attending Counsel therewith	1·00
	3·00
Attending Council Chamber when Petition heard...	to
	5·00
Attending paying Office fees	1·00
Paid fees (as paid)	
Approving draft order	1·00
Attending lodging order approved	1·00
Writing Appellant's Agent with order and copy for use	1·00
Letters, etc.	2·25

(a) These fees are applicable mutatis mutandis to an application for stay of execution and other matters of a similar character. The costs of obtaining special leave to appeal form part of the bill of costs of the Appeal, and are usually taxed at the conclusion of the matter.

(b) If leave to appeal is granted, this amount is taken into consideration in connection with the fee allowed for perusing the Record, as most of the documents sent over for the application for special leave to appeal ultimately form part of the Record. At this preliminary stage an entire perusal of the Record is unnecessary.

(c) Only those strictly necessary for the purpose of settling the petition—not the whole Record.

(d) One Counsel only is allowed. Retainer fee not allowed.

B

RESPONDENT'S COSTS OF OPPOSING PETITION FOR SPECIAL LEAVE TO APPEAL(a)

	£
Instructions to oppose Petition for special leave to appeal	1·50
Preparing and copy Caveat	0·50
Attending at Privy Council Office lodging same	1·00
Paid fee...	1·25
Notice of lodging Caveat, copy and service (if Petition already lodged) ...	0·50
Perusing documents sent by Respondent's Agent, according to length	
Perusing Petition for special leave to appeal and affidavit, according to length...	
Instructions to Counsel to oppose Petition	1·50
Copying same per page	0·25
Copy Petition and affidavit for Counsel, per page	0·25
Attending Counsel with papers, if fee under 30 pounds	1·00
if 30 pounds or more	3·00
Paid his fee(b)	
Copy summons for hearing	0·25
Attending Counsel therewith	1·00
Attending Council Chamber when Petition heard...	3·00 to 5·00
Drawing Bill of Costs and copy, per page	1·00
Attending lodging same	1·00
Copy order to tax for Appellant	0·50
Copy Bill of Costs for Appellant, per page	0·25
Attending him therewith and with order to tax	1·00
Attending taxing	3·00
Attending paying Council Office fees	1·00
Paid fees (as paid)	
Approving draft order	1·00
Attending lodging order approved	1·00
Writing agent therewith	1·00
Letters, etc.	2·25

C

APPELLANT'S COSTS OF APPEAL

	£
Retainer fee	3·00
Attending at Privy Council Office lodging Security for Respondent's Costs, special leave to appeal having been granted	1·00

Appearance

	£
Attending at Privy Council Office to enquire if Record had arrived, filing enquiry card if it had not	1·00
On receiving notice that it had, attending taking particulars for the purpose of entering Appearance	1·00
Drawing Appearance	0·50
Attending at the Council Office to enter same	1·00
Notice to Respondent's Solicitor if he has entered appearance	0·50

Record

Printed Abroad

	£
Attending at Privy Council Office, obtaining six prints of Record	1·00
Perusing printed Record, per each 8 full pages	2·25
If there are maps or plans, a further small fee may be allowed for examining.	

(a) When special leave to appeal is granted, these costs form part of a successful Respondent's costs of Appeal, and are taxed at the conclusion of the matter. This contemplates the Petition being dismissed with costs.

(b) One Counsel only is allowed. Retainer fee not allowed.

£

Printed or duplicated in England

Attending bespeaking official copy of Record, and signing undertaking to pay costs of copying and printing or duplicating**(a)**	1·00
Attending obtaining same	1·00
Paid Privy Council stationer's charges for same (as paid)	
Perusing manuscript Record, for each 5 pages**(b)**	0·75
Drawing Index, per page**(c)**	1·00
Copy for printer, per page	0·25
Drawing marginal notes, per document	0·05
Attending Respondent with official copy of Record, and arranging as to order or omission of documents**(d)**	1·00
On receipt of copy Record from Respondent, attending at Privy Council Office therewith for printing or duplicating	1·00
Attending at Privy Council Office lodging cheque to cover cost of printing or duplicating	1·00
Attending at Privy Council Office examining proof with certified copy**(e)**,	
each day	6·50
each half day	3·25
Correcting revised print of Record, per sheet of 8 pages	1·00
Correcting revised duplicated copy of Record, per sheet of 10 pages	1·00
Attending Respondent with revise to compare corrections and obtaining consent to its being struck off	1·00
Attending lodging same at Privy Council Office	1·00
Paid printer's bill (as paid).	
Attending at Privy Council Office to pay same and to obtain prints of Record...	1·00

Revivor

Instructions for petition to revive	1·00
Perusing Supplemental Record or Certificate as to parties from Court appealed from, same scale as Record.	
Drawing Petition, per page	1·25
Copy, per page	0·25
Attending serving Respondent and obtaining his consent to prayer	1·00
Attending lodging Petition	1·00
Copy for Respondent, per page	0·25
Approving draft order	1·00
Attending lodging same at Privy Council Office	1·00
Writing to agent abroad with order...	1·00

Consolidation

Instructions for Petition to consolidate	1·00

The remaining charges are mutatis mutandis similar to those on a Petition to revive.

Retainer

Instructions for and preparing retainer to Counsel**(f)**	1·25
Attending Counsel therewith	1·00
Paid his fee	3·50

(a) If the Appellant has a duplicate Record in his possession, this should be used instead of obtaining a copy, after checking same against certified copy.

(b) If the Record is in a confused state and requires re-arrangement, a further fee may be allowed.

(c) No copy allowed for Respondent, who sees the draft.

(d) Attention is directed to Rules 17 and 18 of the Judicial Committee Rules 1957 as to the disallowance of the costs of including unnecessary documents.

(e) Appointments for this are made by the Privy Council Office.

(f) Retainer allowed to one Counsel only. If Counsel retained dies or is promoted to the Bench no second retainer is allowed, and this also applies to the Brief fee.

£

Petition of Appeal

	£
Instructions for Petition of Appeal	1·00
Drawing same, per page	1·25
Attending Counsel therewith to settle(a)	1·00
Paid his fee	6·00
Copying Petition, per page	0·25
Copy Petition for Respondent, per page	0·25
Attending him therewith	1·00
Attending lodging Petition	1·00

Case

	£
Instructions for Appellant's case	
Drawing same, per page	1·25
When two Counsel instructed:—	
Two copies Petition of Appeal for Counsel, each, per page	0·25
Attending Junior Counsel with papers to settle case,	
if fee under 30 pounds	1·00
if 30 pounds or more	3·00
Paid his fee	
Two fair copies Case as settled by Junior Counsel to settle in consultation, per	
page, each	0·25
Attending Senior Counsel therewith, if fee under 30 pounds	1·00
if 30 pounds or more	3·00
Paid his fee	
Attending both Counsel arranging consultation	2·50
Paid consultation fee to Senior Counsel	11·00
Paid consultation fee to Junior Counsel	7·50
Attending consultation	2·50
Copy case for printer, per page	0·25
Attending him therewith	1·00
Correcting proofs of printed case, per sheet of 8 pages	1·00
Correcting proofs of duplicated copy of case, per sheet of 10 pages	1·00
Attending printer, instructing him to strike off fifty copies	1·00
Paid printer's bill. (Charge to be in accordance with current agreement with	
Printers' Association.)	
Attending paying	1·00
Attending at Privy Council Office lodging thirty copies	1·00
Writing Respondent with appointment to exchange Cases	0·50
Attending exchanging ten copies	1·00
Perusing Respondent's case, per printed sheet of 8 pages	2·25
Perusing Respondent's case, per duplicated sheet of 10 pages	2·25

Case Notice

(Where Respondent makes default in lodging case)

	£
Drawing and copy Case Notice	1·00
Service upon Respondent	1·00
Attending at Council Office to see if Case lodged...	1·00
Drawing affidavit of service of Case Notice	1·00
Copying	0·50
Attending to be sworn	1·00
Paid (unless sworn at the Privy Council Office) as paid.	
Lodging affidavit	1·00

(a) The Petition of Appeal is not now usually settled by Counsel.

Binding Record and Cases

	£
Attending at Privy Council Office, obtaining seven copies of Record and Cases to bind for the use of the Board(a)	1·00
Drawing instructions to bind and endorse	1·00
Attending binder	1·00
Paid him	
Attending paying	1·00
Attending lodging bound copies	1·00

Briefs

Instructions to Senior Counsel to argue(b)	2·50
Attending him with papers, if fee under 30 pounds	1·00
if 30 pounds or more	3·00
Paid his fee	
Instructions to Junior Counsel to argue	2·50
Attending him with papers, if fee under 30 pounds	1·00
if 30 pounds or more	3·00
Paid his fee	

Hearing

Copy for each Counsel of summons for hearing	0·25
Attending both Counsel therewith	2·00
Preparing list of authorities to be cited at hearing and lodging same	1·00
Estimating length of hearing and lodging same	1·00
Attending Council Chamber, but Appeal not reached, each day	7·50
Attending Council Chamber, when Appeal heard(c) each day	10·00
Paid refresher fee to Senior Counsel	
Attending him	1·00 or 2·00
Paid refresher fee to Junior Counsel	
Attending him	1·00 or 2·00

Judgment

On receiving summons for Judgment:—

Copy for Counsel	0·25
Attending Junior Counsel therewith	1·00
Paid fee to hear Judgment	11·00
Attending to hear Judgment	3·00

Taxation and Concluding Charges

Drawing Bill of Costs and copy, per page	1·00
Attending lodging same	1·00
Copy order to tax for Respondent	0·50
Copy Bill of Costs for Respondent, per page	0·25
Attending him therewith	1·00
Attending taxing	4·50
Attending paying Office fees	1·00
Paid fees (as paid)	
Approving draft order	1·00
Attending lodging same at Privy Council Office	1·00
Writing agent with order	1·00
Sessions fee (for each year or part of a year from the date of Appearance) ...	6·50
Letters, etc. for the first year	4·50
And for each following year	2·25

(a) No charge for binding must appear in the Respondent's Bill, as this is entirely a matter for the Appellant.

(b) Two Counsel only allowed.

(c) Cost of shorthand notes are not allowed.

D

RESPONDENT'S COSTS OF APPEAL

With the exception of the following items the charges are, mutatis mutandis, similar
to those in Appellant's bill.

Record	£
(When Record printed or duplicated in England)	
Attending Appellant on his calling with copy of the manuscript proceedings and arranging as to order or omission of documents	1·00
Perusing manuscript proceedings, for each 5 pages	0·75
If there are maps or plans, a further small fee may be allowed for examining.	
Attending at Privy Council Office examining proof with official copy, each day...	6·50
Correcting revised print of record, per sheet of 8 pages	1·00
Correcting revised duplicated copy of record, per sheet of 10 pages	1·00
Attending Appellant therewith	1·00
Attending at Privy Council Office for copies	1·00

Petition of Appeal

Perusing Petition	2·25

Revivor

Perusing Supplemental Record or Certificate as to parties from Court appealed
from, same scale as Record.

Perusing Petition to revive	2·25
Attending Appellant giving consent to prayer	1·00

Consolidation

Perusing Petition to consolidate	2·25
Attending Appellant giving consent to prayer	1·00

PART II

COUNCIL OFFICE FEES

	£
Entering Appearance	1·25
Amending Appearance	0·60
Examining proof of Record with the certified record at the Registry (chargeable to Appellant only) ... ... per day	2·50
per half-day	1·25
Lodging Petition of Appeal	3·75
Lodging Petition for special leave to appeal	2·50
Lodging any other Petition or Motion	1·25
Lodging Case or Notice under Rule 60	2·50
Setting down Appeal (chargeable to Appellant only)	6·25
Setting down Petition for special leave to appeal (chargeable to Petitioner only)	2·50
Setting down any other Petition (chargeable to Petitioner only)	1·25
Summons	1·25
Committee Report on Petition	2·50
Committee Report on Appeal	3·75
Original Order of Her Majesty in Council determining an Appeal	6·25
Any other original Order of Her Majesty in Council	3·75
Plain copy of an Order of Her Majesty in Council	0·35
Original Order of the Judicial Committee	2·50
Plain copy of Committee Order	0·35
Lodging Affidavit	0·60
Certificate delivered to parties	0·60
Lodging Caveat	1·25

Taxing Fee $2\frac{1}{2}\%$ of the sum allowed.

EXPLANATORY NOTE

(This Note is not part of the Rules.)

These Rules express in decimal currency the Fees allowed in Appeals before the Judicial Committee of the Privy Council and also the Council Office Fees. They also substitute a page rate for computing charges in place of the previous folio rate.

STATUTORY INSTRUMENTS

1971 No. 214

JUDICIAL COMMITTEE
PROCEDURE

The Judicial Committee (Medical Rules) Order 1971

Made - - -	10*th February* 1971
Laid before Parliament	16*th February* 1971
Coming into Operation	1*st March* 1971

At the Court at Buckingham Palace, the 10th day of February 1971

Present,

The Queen's Most Excellent Majesty in Council

Her Majesty, in exercise of the powers conferred upon Her by section 36(3) of the Medical Act 1956(**a**), and of all other powers enabling Her in that behalf, is pleased, by and with the advice of Her Privy Council, to order, as it is hereby ordered, as follows :—

1.—(1) This Order shall come into operation on 1st March 1971, and may be cited as the Judicial Committee (Medical Rules) Order 1971.

(2) The Judicial Committee (Medical Rules) Order 1958(**b**) is hereby revoked.

2. The Rules set out in the Schedule to this Order shall take effect for the purpose of appeals to Her Majesty in Council by virtue of the Medical Acts 1956 to 1969(**c**).

W. G. Agnew.

SCHEDULE

RULES

1. In these Rules, unless the context otherwise requires:—

"The Act" means the Medical Act 1956 as amended.

"The Council" means the General Medical Council.

"The Committee" means the Disciplinary Committee constituted under section 32 of the Act.

"The Registry" and "the Registrar" mean the Registry and the Registrar respectively of the Privy Council.

"Typewritten" includes reproduction by type, lithography, stencil, duplicating or photography.

(**a**) 1956 c. 76.   (**b**) S.I. 1958/765 (1958 I, p. 1330).
(**c**) 1956 c. 76; 1958 c. 58; 1969 c. 40.

Appeals against a direction given under section 33(1) *or an order made under section* 35 *of the Act.*

2. A person who desires to appeal to Her Majesty in Council against a direction given under section 33(1) or an order made under section 35 of the Act shall, within 28 days of the service upon him of a notification under section 36 of the Act, enter an Appearance in the Registry and at the same time lodge therein a Petition of Appeal and serve a copy thereof upon the Council.

3. The Petition of Appeal shall recite succinctly the principal steps in the proceedings leading up to the Appeal but shall not contain argumentative matter or travel into the merits of the case.

4. Upon receipt of a copy of the Petition of Appeal the Council shall with all convenient speed deliver to the Appellant an authenticated typewritten Record of the proceedings before the Committee and shall notify the Registrar of the date of such delivery and shall, if they desire to be heard as Respondents before the Judicial Committee, enter an Appearance forthwith in the Registry and give notice thereof to the Appellant.

5. Within 21 days of the receipt by the Appellant of the authenticated Record referred to in Rule 4 the Appellant shall lodge in the Registry the said authenticated Record together with eight copies thereof and shall also transmit three copies thereof to the Council.

6. Such copies and all copies of cases shall be typewritten or, if the Appellant or Council so desire, printed on foolscap paper with a quarter margin.

7. Within 28 days from the lodging in the Registry of the said authenticated Record as provided by Rule 5 there shall be lodged in the Registry eight copies of the Appellant's case in the Appeal signed by at least one of the Counsel who attends the hearing of the Appeal or by the Appellant himself if he conducts his Appeal in person.

8. Within 28 days of the transmission to the Council of the three copies of the said authenticated Record as provided by Rule 5 the Council shall likewise lodge eight copies of their Case in the Appeal signed by at least one of the Counsel who attends at the hearing of the Appeal.

9. The Cases shall consist of paragraphs numbered consecutively and shall state, as concisely as possible, the circumstances out of which the Appeal arises, the contentions to be urged by the parties lodging the same respectively, and the reasons of appeal.

10. The Appeal shall be set down *ipso facto* as soon as the Cases on both sides are lodged and the parties shall thereupon exchange cases by delivering each to the other three copies of their respective Cases.

11. If the Council do not enter an Appearance or do not lodge their Case within the period prescribed by Rule 8, or within such further period as may be allowed by the Registrar, the Appeal shall be set down for hearing *ex parte* provided that the Appellant has already lodged his Case.

Appeals against a direction given under section 33(1A) *of the Act.*

12. A person who desires to appeal to Her Majesty in Council against a direction given under section 33(1A) of the Act shall, within 28 days of the service upon him of a notification under section 36 of the Act, enter an appearance in the Registry, lodge therein six copies of a Petition of Appeal and serve one copy thereof on the Council.

13. Such Petition of Appeal shall recite succinctly the grounds of appeal. It shall consist of paragraphs numbered consecutively and shall be typewritten on foolscap paper with a quarter margin.

14. Within 14 days of the service on them of a copy of the Petition of Appeal (or within such further time as the Registrar may allow) the Council shall lodge in the Registry an authenticated typewritten Record of the proceedings before the Committee at which was given the direction appealed against and six copies thereof and shall serve

one copy thereof on the Appellant; such copies shall be typewritten on foolscap paper with a quarter margin. If the Council desire to be heard as Respondents to such Appeal they shall at the same time enter an Appearance in the Registry.

15. The Appeal shall be set down *ipso facto* when the copies of the Record are lodged.

16. At the hearing of such Appeal not more than one Counsel shall be admitted to be heard on a side.

17. The provisions of Rules 60 and 72 of the Judicial Committee Rules 1957 shall not apply to such Appeal.

General Provisions

18. Where an Appellant who has lodged his Petition of Appeal desires to withdraw his Appeal he shall present a Petition to that effect to Her Majesty in Council. On the hearing of any such Petition the Council shall be entitled to apply to the Judicial Committee for their costs.

19. Where the Appellant, who has lodged his Petition of Appeal, fails to take any further step in prosecution of his Appeal within the period prescribed by these Rules, or within such further period as may be allowed by the Registrar, the Council may lodge a Petition to Her Majesty in Council praying that the Appeal be dismissed for non-prosecution.

20. All bills of costs under any Order of the Judicial Committee made on the Appeal, shall stand referred to the Registrar, or such other person as the Judicial Committee may appoint, for taxation, and all such taxations shall be regulated by the Schedule of Fees annexed to these Rules.

21. Rules 77 to 81, inclusive, of the Judicial Committee Rules, 1957(a), shall apply, as nearly as may be, to the taxation of all such bills of costs as aforesaid.

22. Where a person desiring to appeal *in forma pauperis* proves by Affidavit to the satisfaction of the Registrar that he is not worth £100 in the world excepting his wearing apparel and that he is unable to provide sureties and also lodges a certificate of Counsel that he has reasonable grounds of appeal, the Appeal shall proceed *in forma pauperis*, and the Appellant shall not be required to pay any Council Office fees.

23. Rule 83 of the Judicial Committee Rules, 1957, shall apply as if the reference to "these Rules" therein contained wherever those words appear was a reference to the Judicial Committee (Medical Rules) Order 1971.

24. Rules 42, 60, 71, 72, 74, 84, 85 and 86 of the Judicial Committee Rules 1957 shall, so far as applicable and subject to the provisions of Rule 17 hereof and of any Statute or of any Statutory Instrument to the contrary, apply to Appeals under the Act. Save as aforesaid and as stated in Rules 21 and 23 of these Rules, the Judicial Committee Rules 1957 shall not apply to such Appeals.

(a) S.I. 1957/2224 (1957 I, p. 1205).

SCHEDULE OF FEES ALLOWED IN APPEALS OR OTHER MATTERS BEFORE THE JUDICIAL
COMMITTEE OF THE PRIVY COUNCIL

Agents are required to adhere as far as possible to the items shown in the Scale, but it
is within the discretion of the Taxing Officer to allow further charges:—

(a) in relation to items not mentioned in the Scale; or

(b) of an amount higher than that prescribed by the Scale.

A.

Appellant's Costs of Appeal	£
Retainer Fee	3·00
Drawing Appearance	·50
Attending to enter same	1·00
Instructions for Petition of Appeal under Rule 2	1·00
Instructions for Petition of Appeal under Rule 12	—
Drawing same per foolscap page	1·25
Two copies thereof per foolscap page	·25
Attending Council Office lodging the same	1·00
Attending Respondent serving the same	1·00
Perusing Record per 6 foolscap pages	2·25
Attending stationer instructing him to make copies	1·00
Paid stationer	—
Attending paying	1·00
Attending lodging copies at Council Office	1·00
Attending Respondent with copies	1·00
Instructions for Case	—
Drawing Case per foolscap page	1·25
Copy Petition of Appeal for Counsel per foolscap page	·25
Attending Counsel with papers to settle Case	3·00
Paid his fee	—
Attending appointing conference	1·00
Paid his fee	7·50
Attending conference	2·50
Copy Case for printer per foolscap page	·25
Attending him herewith	1·00
Correcting proof of case per 8 foolscap pages	1·00
Attending stationer instructing him to strike off copies	1·00
Paid stationer	—
Attending paying him	1·00
Attending Registry lodging Case	1·00
Writing Respondent with appointment to exchange Cases	·50
Attending exchanging Cases	1·00
Perusing Respondent's Case per 6 pages	2·25
Instructions to Counsel to argue	2·50
Attending him with papers	3·00
Paid his fee	—
Copy for Counsel of Summons for hearing	·25
Attending Counsel therewith	2·00
Preparing list of authorities and lodging same	1·00

	£
Estimating length of hearing and lodging same	1·00
Attending hearing per day	10·00
Paid refresher fee to Counsel	—
Attending paying him	1·00
Copy Summons for judgment for Counsel	·25
Attending Counsel therewith	1·00
Paid Counsel to hear judgment	11·00
Attending to hear judgment	3·00
Drawing petition or motion per foolscap page	1·25
Copy petition or motion per foolscap page	·25
Perusing petition or motion per foolscap page	·50
Drawing bill of costs and copy, per page	1·00
Attending lodging same	1·00
Copy Order to tax for Respondent	·50
Copy bill of costs for Respondent per page	·25
Attending him therewith	1·00
Attending taxing...	4·50
Attending paying Office Fees	1·00
Paid fees	—
Approving draft Order	1·00
Attending lodging same	1·00
Sessions fee	6·50
Letters etc.	4·50

B.

Respondent's Costs of Appeal

With the exception of the following items, the charges are, *mutatis mutandis*, similar to those in the Appellant's Bill.

Perusing Petition of Appeal, per foolscap page	·50
Notice of entry of appearance	1·00
Attending Committee bespeaking authenticated record	1·00
Paid Committee's Shorthand Writer for transcript	—
Attending paying him	1·00
Copy Exhibits per page	·25
Drawing Index per foolscap page	1·00
Attending Appellant with authenticated record	1·00
Attending Registry notifying them thereof	1·00

SCHEDULE OF COUNCIL OFFICE FEES

Entering Appearance	1·25
Amending Appearance	0·63
Examining proof print of Record with the certified record at the Registry (chargeable to Appellant only) per day	2·50
per half day	1·25
Lodging Petition of Appeal	3·75
Lodging any other Petition or Motion	1·25
Lodging Case	2·50

Setting down Appeal (chargeable to Appellant only) ... ... 6·25
Setting down any other Petition (chargeable to Petitioner only) ... ... 1·25
Summons ... ... 1·25
Committee Report on Petition ... ... 2·50
Committee Report on Appeal ... ... 3·75
Original Order of Her Majesty in Council determining an Appeal ... 6·25
Any other original Order of Her Majesty in Council ... ... 3·75
Plain copy of an Order of Her Majesty in Council ... ... 0·33
Original Order of the Judicial Committee ... ... 2·50
Plain copy of Committee order ... ... 0·33
Lodging Affidavit ... ... 0·63
Certificate delivered to parties ... ... 0·63
Taxing fee £0·025 for each pound allowed, or a fraction thereof.

EXPLANATORY NOTE

(This Note is not part of the Order.)

This Order enacts Rules to revoke and replace the Rules contained in the Judicial Committee (Medical Rules) Order 1958. The procedure in most appeals is substantially unchanged but a new procedure is provided for appeals against directions for extensions of periods of suspension from registration.

The Rules also contain a new Scale of Fees.

STATUTORY INSTRUMENTS

1971 No. 215 (C. 4)

LANDS TRIBUNAL

The Lands Tribunal Act 1949 (Appointed Day) (Scotland) Order 1971

Made - - - *10th February* 1971

At the Court at Buckingham Palace, the 10th day of February 1971
Present,
The Queen's Most Excellent Majesty in Council

Whereas it is provided by section 10(2) of the Lands Tribunal Act 1949(a), that sections 1 to 4 of that Act shall come into force on such day as Her Majesty may by Order in Council appoint, and that different days may be appointed for Scotland and for the remainder of the United Kingdom:

Now, therefore, Her Majesty, in pursuance of section 10(2) of the said Act, is pleased, by and with the advice of Her Privy Council, to order, and it is hereby ordered, as follows:—

1. Sections 1 to 4 of the Lands Tribunal Act 1949 shall come into force in Scotland on 1st March 1971.

2.—(1) This Order may be cited as the Lands Tribunal Act 1949 (Appointed Day) (Scotland) Order 1971.

(2) The Interpretation Act 1889(b) shall apply for the interpretation of this Order as it applies for the interpretation of an Act of Parliament.

W. G. Agnew.

EXPLANATORY NOTE
(*This Note is not part of the Order.*)

This Order brings into force for Scotland on 1st March 1971 those provisions of the Lands Tribunal Act 1949 which are not already in operation. This enables the Lands Tribunal for Scotland to be established.

(a) 1949 c. 42.   (b) 1889 c. 63.

STATUTORY INSTRUMENTS

1971 No. 216

MERCHANT SHIPPING

The Merchant Shipping (Load Lines Convention) (Various Countries) Order 1971

Made - - -	10*th February* 1971
Laid before Parliament	16*th February* 1971
Coming into Operation	22*nd February* 1971

At the Court at Buckingham Palace, the 10th day of February 1971

Present,

The Queen's Most Excellent Majesty in Council

Whereas by section 31(1) of the Merchant Shipping (Load Lines) Act 1967(a) it is enacted that Her Majesty may, if satisfied that the Government of any country has accepted or acceded to the International Convention on Load Lines 1966, by Order in Council make a declaration to that effect :

And whereas Her Majesty is satisfied that the Governments of the countries specified in the Schedule hereto have accepted or acceded to the said Convention :

Now, therefore, Her Majesty in pursuance of the powers conferred upon Her by the said section 31(1) and of all other powers enabling Her in that behalf is pleased, by and with the advice of Her Privy Council, to order, and it is hereby ordered, as follows :—

1. This Order may be cited as the Merchant Shipping (Load Lines Convention) (Various Countries) Order 1971, and shall come into operation on 22nd February 1971.

2. It is hereby declared that the Governments of the countries specified in the Schedule to this Order have accepted or acceded to the International Convention on Load Lines 1966.

W. G. Agnew.

SCHEDULE

Canada	Principality of Monaco
Republic of Iceland	New Zealand
Lebanese Republic	Republic of Portugal
United States of Mexico	Republic of Zambia

(a) 1967 c. 27.

STATUTORY INSTRUMENTS

1971 No. 217

MERCHANT SHIPPING

The Merchant Shipping (Safety Convention) (Various Countries) Order 1971

Made - - -	10*th February* 1971
Laid before Parliament	16*th February* 1971
Coming into Operation	22*nd February* 1971

At the Court at Buckingham Palace, the 10th day of February 1971

Present,

The Queen's Most Excellent Majesty in Council

Whereas by section 31 of the Merchant Shipping (Safety Convention) Act 1949(a) as amended by section 1 of the Merchant Shipping Act 1964(b) it is enacted that Her Majesty, if satisfied that the Government of any country has accepted the International Convention for the Safety of Life at Sea 1960 (hereinafter referred to as "the 1960 Convention"), may by Order in Council make a declaration to that effect:

And whereas Her Majesty is satisfied that the Governments of the countries specified in the Schedule to this Order have accepted the 1960 Convention:

Now, therefore, Her Majesty, in pursuance of the powers conferred upon Her by the aforesaid sections and of all other powers enabling Her in that behalf is pleased, by and with the advice of Her Privy Council, to order, and it is hereby ordered, as follows:—

1. This Order may be cited as the Merchant Shipping (Safety Convention) (Various Countries) Order 1971, and shall come into operation on 22nd February 1971.

2. It is hereby declared that the Governments of the countries specified in the Schedule to this Order have accepted the 1960 Convention.

W. G. Agnew.

SCHEDULE

Hungarian People's Republic.
Principality of Monaco.
Republic of Nauru.
Republic of Senegal.
Republic of Zambia.

(a) 1949 c. 43.   (b) 1964 c. 47.

STATUTORY INSTRUMENTS

1971 No. 218 (S.35)

LANDS TRIBUNAL

The Lands Tribunal for Scotland Rules 1971

Made - - -	*8th February* 1971
Coming into Operation	*1st March* 1971

ARRANGEMENT OF RULES

In exercise of the powers conferred upon me by section 3 of the Lands Tribunal Act 1949(a) as amended by section 50 of the Conveyancing and Feudal Reform (Scotland) Act 1970(b), and of all other powers enabling me in that behalf, and after consultation with the Council on Tribunals, and with the approval of the Treasury in regard to the fees prescribed by these rules in respect of proceedings before the Tribunal, I hereby make the following rules :—

PRELIMINARY

Citation and commencement

1. These rules may be cited as the Lands Tribunal for Scotland Rules 1971 and shall come into operation on 1st March 1971.

Interpretation

2.—(1) In these rules, unless the context otherwise requires—

"the Act of 1949" means the Lands Tribunal Act 1949 ;

"the Act of 1963" means the Land Compensation (Scotland) Act 1963(c) ;

"the Act of 1970" means the Conveyancing and Feudal Reform (Scotland) Act 1970 ;

"benefited proprietor", "burdened proprietor", "interest in land" and "land obligation" have the meanings assigned to them by section 2(6) of the Act of 1970 ;

"*cumulo* feuduty" and "feu" have the meanings assigned to them by section 3(2) of the Act of 1970 ;

"General Commissioners" have the same meaning as in the Taxes Management Act 1970(d) ;

"notice of allocation", "proprietor", and "superior" have the meanings assigned to them by section 5(7) of the Act of 1970 ;

"the President" means the President of the Lands Tribunal for Scotland, or the member appointed under the provisions of the Act of 1949 to act for the time being as deputy for the President ;

"Special Commissioners" have the same meaning as in the Taxes Management Act 1970 ;

"the Tribunal" means the Lands Tribunal for Scotland.

(2) A form referred to by number means the form so numbered in Schedule 1 to these rules.

(3) In these rules any reference to any enactment shall be construed as a reference to that enactment as amended by or under any other enactment.

(4) The Interpretation Act 1889(e) shall apply for the interpretation of these rules as it applies for the interpretation of an Act of Parliament.

(a) 1949 c. 42.   (b) 1970 c. 35.
(c) 1963 c.51.   (d) 1970 c.9.
(e) 1889 c.63.

Part I

Applications under Section 1 of the Conveyancing and Feudal Reform (Scotland) Act 1970

Method of making Application

3. Any burdened proprietor who wishes to make an application under section 1 of the Act of 1970 (variation and discharge of land obligations) shall send to the Tribunal an application in or as nearly as may be in accordance with Form 1.

Giving of Notices

4.—(1) On receipt of an application the Tribunal shall—

(*a*) give notice thereof in writing to the persons who appear to it to be either benefited or burdened proprietors having an interest in the subject of the application ; and

(*b*) give notice in writing or by advertisement or by such other method as the Tribunal thinks fit to any other persons whom it considers should receive notice.

(2) The notice shall require those benefited and burdened proprietors who wish to oppose or to make representations in relation to the application to send intimation thereof in writing to the Tribunal and to the applicant within such time, not being less than 14 days from the date of the notice, as may be specified. Such intimation shall contain a concise statement of the facts and contentions on which it is intended to rely. The Tribunal shall send copies of any such intimations to those other persons whom at that stage it considers should receive a copy.

(3) The notice shall also intimate that subject to the Tribunal's discretion other persons to whom notice has been given under paragraph (1) of this rule may be heard in relation to the application.

Provisions as to orders

5.—(1) Subject to the provisions of paragraphs (2) and (3) of this rule, an order made by the Tribunal varying or discharging a land obligation shall take effect on the date it is made by the Tribunal.

(2) Where a land obligation is varied or discharged subject to the payment of any compensation awarded by the Tribunal, the order of the Tribunal shall not, so far as it affects such variation or discharge, take effect until the Tribunal has endorsed the order to the effect either that the compensation has been paid or that all persons to whom any compensation has been awarded but who have not received payment of it have agreed to the order taking effect.

(3) The Tribunal may direct that the compensation shall be paid or satisfied within a specified time and that, unless it is so paid or satisfied, the order shall be void on the expiration of the time so specified.

Part II

Applications under Section 4 of the Conveyancing and Feudal Reform (Scotland) Act 1970

Method of making Application

6. A superior who wishes to make an application under section 4 of the Act of 1970 (applications to Tribunal regarding allocation of feuduties) shall, within 28 days of the receipt by him of the notice of allocation, send to the Tribunal an application in or as nearly as may be in accordance with Form 2 and he shall enclose with his application a copy of the notice of allocation.

Giving of Notices

7.—(1) On receipt of an application the Tribunal shall—

(a) give notice thereof in writing to the persons who appear to it to be proprietors of parts of the feu in respect of which the *cumulo* feuduty is exigible ; and

(b) give notice in writing or by advertisement or by such other method as the Tribunal thinks fit to any other persons whom it considers should receive notice.

(2) The notice shall contain a statement of the Tribunal's intention to allocate the *cumulo* feuduty on each part of the feu which is held by a separate proprietor and shall require those proprietors of parts of the feu and other persons having an interest who wish to make representations to send intimation thereof in writing to the Tribunal within such time, not being less than 14 days from the date of the notice, as may be specified. Any written statement of such representations must be sent to the Tribunal and to the applicant within the said time. The Tribunal shall send copies of any such written statements to those persons to whom written notice has been given under paragraph (1) of this rule.

Decision of Tribunal

8. Without prejudice to the provisions of rule 32 the Tribunal shall send a copy of its decision to those persons to whom written notice has been given under rule 7(1) and to the superior.

Ground Annuals

9. In accordance with section 6 of the Act of 1970 the provisions of rules 6, 7 and 8 shall apply in relation to a ground annual as they apply in relation to a feuduty.

PART III

DETERMINATION OF QUESTIONS OF DISPUTED COMPENSATION

General

10. Subject to the provisions of Part II of the Act of 1963 and of Part VI of these rules the procedure regulating the determination of questions of disputed compensation shall be as set out in this Part of these rules.

Method of making Application

11.—(1) Proceedings for the determination of any question or dispute to which this Part of these rules applies may be instituted by any party who requires to have the question or dispute determined sending to the Tribunal an application in or as nearly as may be in accordance with Form 3 and the

Tribunal shall send copies of such application to the other parties to the question or dispute and to any other persons whom it considers should receive a copy.

(2) There shall be sent with the application—

(a) if the compensation is payable on the compulsory acquisition of land, a copy of the notice to treat (if such notice has been served) and of any notice of claim and any amendment thereof delivered to the acquiring authority in pursuance of section 5 of the Act of 1963 ; or

(b) in any other case, a copy of the order, direction, notice, decision, authorisation or other document which is evidence of the proceedings giving rise to compensation.

(3) An application shall not be made before the expiry of 30 days from the date of service or constructive service of notice to treat or (where no notice to treat is served or is deemed to be served) of notice of claim.

PART IV

APPEALS AGAINST DETERMINATIONS BY COMMISSIONERS OF INLAND REVENUE UNDER THE FINANCE (1909-10) ACT 1910

Notice of appeal

12. Any person who wishes to appeal against any determination by the Commissioners of Inland Revenue in respect of which, but for the provisions of the Act of 1949, there would be a right of appeal to one of the panel of referees appointed under Part I of the Finance (1909-10) Act 1910(**a**) may institute proceedings by sending to the Tribunal in duplicate a notice of appeal. In the case of an appeal against a decision of the Commissioners under section 60 of that Act, the notice shall be in or as nearly as may be in accordance with Form 4.

Time for giving notice

13. A notice of appeal under rule 12 shall not be valid unless it is sent to the Tribunal within 30 days from the date on which notice of the determination was served upon the appellant, or within such other time as may be prescribed by the enactment by virtue of which an appeal against the determination lies to the Tribunal.

Giving of Notices

14.—(1) On receipt of a notice of appeal, the Tribunal shall forthwith send the duplicate notice to the Commissioners of Inland Revenue.

(2) On receipt of the duplicate notice of appeal the Commissioners of Inland Revenue shall forthwith send to the Tribunal a copy of the determination referred to therein.

Appearance by persons other than appellants

15. In any proceedings under this Part of the rules the Tribunal shall on the application of any person who appears to it to be interested in the land in respect of which the appeal was made or to be otherwise interested in the

(**a**) 1910 c.8.

matter of the appeal allow him to make written representations, copies of which shall be sent by him to the other parties to the proceedings within such time as may be specified, and the Tribunal shall allow him to be heard in relation to the proceedings.

PART V

REFERENCES UNDER THE FINANCE ACT 1965 AND THE TAXES MANAGEMENT ACT 1970

General

16. Subject to the provisions of Part VI of these rules the procedure regulating the determination by the Tribunal of any question of the value of any land or of a lease of land under section 44(6) and (7) of the Finance Act 1965(a) and section 47(1) and (2) of the Taxes Management Act 1970 shall be as set out in this Part of these rules.

Notice of Reference

17. Proceedings for the determination of any question or dispute to which this Part of these rules applies may be instituted by General or Special Commissioners or an Inspector of Taxes sending to the Tribunal a notice of reference in or as nearly as may be in accordance with Form 5 together with sufficient copies thereof to enable the Tribunal to send copies to all the other parties to the proceedings.

Giving of Notices

18. On receipt of a notice of reference, the Tribunal shall forthwith send a copy of the notice to all the parties to the proceedings (other than the party or parties by whom the notice of reference is signed).

PART VI

GENERAL

Method of making Application

19. Except where these rules otherwise provide any question which is to be determined by or referred to the Tribunal shall be brought before it by way of written application and a copy of the application shall be sent by the Tribunal to each of the other parties to the proceedings and to such other persons whom it considers should receive a copy. In a case in which the Tribunal is acting as arbiter under a reference by consent the notice of reference shall be in or as nearly as may be in accordance with Form 3.

Procedure

20. Subject to the provisions of these rules and to any direction given by the President the Tribunal may—

    (*a*) regulate its procedure as it thinks fit ; and

    (*b*) amend in such way as it thinks fit any of the forms in Schedule 1 to these rules.

(a) 1965 c.25.

Sittings of Tribunal

21.—(1) Sittings of the Tribunal shall be on such dates and at such times and places as the President may from time to time determine and, not less than 21 days or such shorter period as the parties agree to before the date of a hearing, the Tribunal shall—

(a) give notice in writing to the parties to the proceedings and

(b) give notice by such method as it may determine (whether by way of advertisement or otherwise) to any other persons whom it considers have an interest in the proceedings

of the date, time and place of the hearing.

(2) The Tribunal shall sit in public except that when it is acting as arbiter under a reference by consent the proceedings shall be heard in private if the parties to the reference so request.

Representation

22. In any proceedings before the Tribunal any party to the proceedings may appear and may be heard in person or be represented by counsel or solicitor or, with the leave of the Tribunal, by any other person.

Administration of Oaths

23. The Tribunal may administer oaths to witnesses in due form.

Default of Appearance

24. If, after due notice of a hearing has been given to a party, that party or his representative fails to appear at the hearing, the Tribunal may dispose of the application in the absence of that party or his representative or may adjourn the hearing :

Provided that where the Tribunal has so disposed of the application, the Tribunal, on an application made by that party within seven days of the disposal, may if it is satisfied that there was sufficient reason for such absence, set aside its decision on such terms as to expenses or otherwise as it thinks fit.

Power to require further particulars and attendance of witnesses and to order recovery of documents

25.—(1) The Tribunal may on the motion of any party to the proceedings or *ex proprio motu*—

(a) require a party to furnish in writing further particulars of his case ;

(b) order a record to be made up ;

(c) grant to a party such recovery of documents as might be granted by the Court of Session ; and

(d) require the attendance of any person as a witness or require the production of any document relating to the question to be determined ;

and may appoint the time at or within which or the place at which any act required in pursuance of this rule is to be done :

Provided that—

(i) No person shall be required in obedience to such a requirement to attend at any place which is more than 10 miles from the place where he resides unless the necessary expenses are paid or tendered to him by the party at whose instance his attendance has been required or by the Tribunal as the case may be ; and

(ii) nothing in this provision shall empower the Tribunal to require any person to produce any book or document or to answer any question which he would be entitled, on the ground of privilege or confidentiality, to refuse to produce or to answer if the proceedings were proceedings in a Court of Law.

(2) Every notice containing a requirement under paragraph (1) of this rule shall contain a reference to the fact that under section 3(12)(c) of the Act of 1949, any person who without reasonable excuse fails to comply with any such requirement is liable on summary conviction to a fine not exceeding £50 or imprisonment for a term not exceeding three months or both.

Provision for other Parties

26. Subject to the provisions of these rules the Tribunal, on the application of any person who appears to it to have an interest in the proceedings, may allow that person to become a party to the proceedings.

Withdrawal of Party

27. The Tribunal may, on such terms as to expenses or otherwise as it thinks fit, consent to any party withdrawing from the proceedings.

Extension of Time and Adjournment of Hearing

28. The Tribunal may on such terms as to expenses or otherwise as it thinks fit—

(a) extend any time appointed by, or specified by it in terms of, these rules notwithstanding that that time may have expired ;

(b) postpone, or adjourn, any hearing.

Assessors

29.—(1) If it appears to the President that any case before the Tribunal calls for special knowledge and that it would be desirable for the Tribunal to sit with an Assessor or Assessors, he may direct that the Tribunal shall hear the case with the aid of such Assessor or Assessors as the President may, after consulting such persons, if any, as he may think fit, appoint.

(2) The remuneration to be paid to any Assessor appointed under this rule shall be such as the President may, with the approval of the Treasury determine.

Notices

30. Any notice or other document required or authorised to be given to any person for the purpose of these rules shall be deemed to have been duly given if sent by post by means of the recorded delivery service or registered post or delivered to that person at his ordinary address or to the address specified by him for intimation under these rules :

Provided that, when difficulty is experienced in effecting such intimation for any reason, the Tribunal, on being satisfied that all practicable steps have been taken in an effort to intimate, may dispense with intimation upon such person or may take such other steps as it thinks fit.

Power to Dispose of Case Without a Hearing

31. Notwithstanding the provisions of these rules the Tribunal, with the consent of all parties whom it considers to have an interest in the application, may dispose of any application before it without a hearing.

Decision of Tribunal

32.—(1) The decision of the Tribunal in any proceedings shall be given in writing, and shall include a statement of the Tribunal's reasons for its decision.

(2) Where an amount awarded or value determined by the Tribunal is dependent upon the decision of the Tribunal on a question of law which is in dispute in the proceedings, the Tribunal shall ascertain, and shall state in its decision the alternative amount or value (if any) which it would have awarded or determined if it had decided otherwise on the question of law.

(3) The Tribunal shall send a copy of the decision to all parties to the proceedings.

Expenses

33.—(1) Except in cases to which the provisions of section 11 of the Act of 1963 apply, the Tribunal shall deal in such manner with expenses as in its discretion it thinks fit.

(2) The Tribunal may order that a party shall pay to another party either a specific sum in respect of the expenses incurred by that other party or such proportion of these expenses as the Tribunal thinks fit.

(3) In default of agreement between the parties as to the amount of the expenses, the expenses shall be taxed, in the discretion of the Tribunal, either by the Auditor of the Court of Session according to the fees payable in the Court of Session or by the Auditor of the Sheriff Court specified by the Tribunal according to the Sheriff Court Table of Fees.

(4) Counsel's fees and the fees for instruction of Counsel shall be allowed as an item of a party's expenses only where the Tribunal has sanctioned the employment of Counsel.

(5) Additional expenses at such rate as the Auditor taxing the expenses considers fair and reasonable shall be allowed for the employment of expert witnesses only where the Tribunal has certified the employment of such expert witnesses.

Fees

34.—(1) The fees specified in Schedule 2 to these rules shall be payable to the Tribunal in respect of the matters mentioned in the said Schedule :

Provided that the Tribunal may waive the whole or part of the fees payable by a party in connection with proceedings under Part I of these rules where it considers that the financial circumstances of the party are such that undue hardship would be caused by payment of the said fees.

(2) The hearing fee shall, unless the Tribunal otherwise directs, be payable by the party by whom the proceedings were instituted (without prejudice to his right to recover the amount of the fee from any other party by virtue of any order as to expenses).

Transitional provisions

35. Where, before the date on which sections 1 to 4 of the Act of 1949 come into operation in Scotland, proceedings have been commenced for the determination of any question, dispute or other matter which, by virtue of the coming into operation in Scotland of the said sections, is required to be referred to and determined by the Tribunal then—

(*a*) where the hearing has not begun at that date, anything done for the purpose of determining such question, dispute or other matter shall be treated, so far as practicable, as if it had been done for the purpose of an application under these rules and shall be dealt with by the Tribunal in accordance with the provisions of these rules ; and

(*b*) where the hearing has begun the hearing, unless the parties agree otherwise, shall proceed in accordance with the procedure in force immediately before the coming into operation in Scotland of the said sections.

Revocations

36.—(1) The rules specified in Schedule 3 to these rules are hereby revoked as from the date when sections 1 to 4 of the Act of 1949 come into operation in Scotland.

(2) Section 38 of the Interpretation Act 1889 shall apply as if these rules were an Act of Parliament and as if the rules revoked by these rules were Acts of Parliament repealed by an Act of Parliament.

Gordon Campbell,
One of Her Majesty's Principal
Secretaries of State.

St. Andrew's House,
Edinburgh.
4th February 1971.

We approve the fees prescribed by these rules in respect of proceedings before the Lands Tribunal for Scotland.

Bernard Weatherill,
Walter Clegg,
Two of the Lords Commissioners
of Her Majesty's Treasury.

8th February 1971.

SCHEDULE 1

FORM 1   Rule 3

*Application under Section 1 of the Conveyancing
and Feudal Reform (Scotland) Act 1970*

To: The Lands Tribunal for Scotland
    (*address*)

1. I/We, AB (*name and address of applicant*), proprietor of the subjects known as†
which subjects are under burden of the land obligation of which particulars
are set out in paragraph 2 below, hereby apply for the land obligation*[to be discharged
wholly] [to be discharged to the extent of (*here specify*)] [to be varied by (*here specify*)].
The circumstances rendering necessary the application are set out in paragraph 3 below.
The statutory basis of the application is set out in paragraph 4 below.

2. Particulars of Land Obligation—

    (*a*) Nature of land obligation

    (*b*) Land burdened by land obligation

    (*c*) Manner and date of creation of land obligation

    (*d*) Persons entitled to benefit of the land obligation (*here state names and addessses
        of benefited proprietors*)

3. Details of Application (*here give a concise statement of the circumstances which
have led to the application*)

4. Statutory basis of application (*here specify which of the circumstances referred
to in section 1(3) of the Conveyancing and Feudal Reform (Scotland) Act 1970 is/are
considered relevant*)

Signed...

Date ....
(*To be signed by the burdened proprietor or by
his Solicitor, who will add his designation and
the words Agent of the said AB*)

*Strike out words not applicable
†Here distinguish the subjects sufficiently precisely to enable them to be identified.

NOTES FOR THE INFORMATION OF APPLICANTS

1. It will be in the applicant's own interest to enclose with this application a copy of the conveyance, deed, instrument or writing under which the land obligation was created

2. At any hearing relating to this application you will be required to adhere to the case set out
above unless the Tribunal considers that the introduction of new material would not prejudice
the interests of other parties.

3. Section 1(3) of the Conveyancing and Feudal Reform (Scotland) Act 1970 reads as follows:—

"Subject to the provisions of this section and of section 2 of this Act, the Lands Tribunal, on the application of any person who, in relation to a land obligation, is a burdened proprietor, may from time to time by order vary or discharge the obligation wholly or partially in relation to the interest in land in respect of which the application is made, on being satisfied that in all the circumstances,

(a) by reason of changes in the character of the land affected by the obligation or of the neighbourhood thereof or other circumstances which the Tribunal may deem material, the obligation is or has become unreasonable or inappropriate; or

(b) the obligation is unduly burdensome compared with any benefit resulting or which would result from its performance; or

(c) the existence of the obligation impedes some reasonable use of the land."

FORM 2

Rule 6

Application under Section 4 of the Conveyancing and
Feudal Reform (Scotland) Act 1970

To: The Lands Tribunal for Scotland
    (*address*)

1. I/We AB (*name and address of the superior/creditor in ground annual*)* proprietor of the superiority of/creditor in the ground annual payable out of †
in respect of which there is exigible a *cumulo feuduty/ground annual of £X object to the amount of the portion of *feuduty/ground annual specified in Notice of Allocation dated   , a copy of which is enclosed herewith, which relates to the subjects known as†   of which CD (*address*) is the proprietor.

2. The reason(s) for this objection *is/are as follows:— (*here give brief note of the reason(s)*)

Signed ....

Date ....
(*To be signed by the superior/creditor in ground annual, or his Solicitor, who will add his designation and the words Agent of the said AB*)

**Strike out words not applicable*

†*Here distinguish the subjects sufficiently precisely to enable them to be identified.*

NOTE FOR THE INFORMATION OF APPLICANTS

At any hearing relating to this application you will be required to adhere to the case set out above unless the Tribunal considers that the introduction of new material would not prejudice the interests of other parties.

Rules 11, 19   FORM 3

Application for Determination of Question of
Disputed Compensation

To:— The Lands Tribunal for Scotland
        (*address*)

I/We A B (*name and address of the applicant*) hereby apply for the determination by the Lands Tribunal for Scotland of the question of which particulars are set out below.

Particulars

1. (*Here distinguish the subjects to which the application relates sufficiently precisely to enable them to be identified.   Where appropriate give Ordnance Survey Grid Reference for the subjects*)

2. (*Give names and addresses of the parties to the dispute*)

3. (*Give a concise statement of the nature of the dispute, and of the grounds on which compensation is claimed*)

4. Where compensation is claimed for compulsory purchase, state whether the acquiring authority has entered upon the land or possession has been given and if so, on what date.

Signed ....

Date ....

(*To be signed by the applicant, or his Solicitor, who will add his designation and the words Agent of the said A B*)

NOTES FOR THE INFORMATION OF APPLICANTS

1. Where the application relates to the compensation payable on a compulsory acquisition of land a copy of the notice to treat (if such notice has been served) and of any notice of claim or amended notice of claim delivered to the acquiring authority *must* be sent with this notice.

2. In any other case a copy of the order, direction, notice, decision, authorisation or other document which is evidence of the proceedings giving rise to compensation *must* be sent to the Tribunal with this notice.   Where a reference is made in pursuance of an agreement to refer any matter to arbitration a copy of the agreement should be sent with this notice.

3. At any hearing relating to this application you will be required to adhere to the case set out above unless the Tribunal considers that the introduction of new material would not prejudice the interests of other parties.

FORM 4   Rule 12

ESTATE DUTY

FINANCE (1909—10) ACT 1910 SECTION 60

Notice of Appeal under Part IV of the Lands Tribunal for Scotland Rules 1971

To: The Lands Tribunal for Scotland
   (*address*)

County   Parish   No. of Property

I, AB (*name and address of the applicant*) being a person aggrieved by the determination dated   of the Commissioners of Inland Revenue for purposes of estate duty in connection with the death on
of   as to the value of the following heritable property viz:—

hereby give notice of appeal.   I claim that the value of the said property should be
£

The grounds of appeal are as follows:—

I *do/do not propose to call an expert witness to give evidence in support of my valuation.

Signed ....

Date ....
(*To be signed by the applicant, or his Solicitor, who will add his designation and the words Agent of the said AB*)

*Strike out words not applicable

Rule 17   FORM 5

FINANCE ACT 1965 AND TAXES MANAGEMENT ACT 1970

Notice of Reference under Part V of the Lands Tribunal for Scotland Rules 1971

To : The Lands Tribunal for Scotland
      (*address*)

Description of Land or Lease of Land to which this reference relates

I/We *[Inspector of Taxes   District (*address*)] [Special
Commissioners of Income Tax, Turnstile House, 94-99 High Holborn, London,
WC1] [General Commissioners for the   Division (*address*)]
in accordance with the provisions of section 44(6) and (7) of the Finance Act 1965
and section 47(1) and (2) of the Taxes Management Act 1970 hereby apply for the
determination by the Lands Tribunal for Scotland of the question of which particulars
are set out below.

All communications regarding this reference should be addressed to *[me] [the Clerk to
the Special Commissioners for Income Tax] [the Clerk to the General Commissioners]
at the address shown above.

Particulars

I/We *do/do not propose to call an expert witness to give evidence in support of any
valuations.

                                        Signed...

                                        Date...

*Strike out words not applicable

SCHEDULE 2   Rule 34

FEES

Item	Fee
Applications etc.	
1. On an application under section 1 of the Conveyancing and Feudal Reform (Scotland) Act 1970	£5·00
2. On an application under section 4 of the Conveyancing and Feudal Reform (Scotland) Act 1970 and in respect of all subsequent proceedings	£2·00
3. On an application under Part III of these rules or in relation to any dispute relating to the assessment of betterment levy referred to the Tribunal under section 47 of the Land Commission Act 1967(a) or where the Tribunal is acting under a reference by consent	£2·00
4. On any other application (not being an appeal under Part IV or a reference under Part V of these rules)	50p
Hearing Fees	
5. On the hearing of an application under section 1 of the Conveyancing and Feudal Reform (Scotland) Act 1970	£15·00
6. On the hearing of an application under Part III of these rules or in relation to any dispute relating to the assessment of betterment levy referred to the Tribunal under section 47 of the Land Commission Act 1967 or where the Tribunal is acting under a reference by consent:—	
(*a*) Where the amount determined (in terms of a lump sum)	
(i) does not exceed £250·00 ...	£5·00
(ii) exceeds £250·00 but does not exceed £500·00	£5·00 with an addition of £1·00 in respect of every £50·00 or part of £50·00 by which the amount determined exceeds £250·00.
(iii) exceeds £500·00 but does not exceed £5,000·00	£10·00 with an addition of £1·00 in respect of every £100·00 or part of £100·00 by which the amount determined exceeds £500·00.
(iv) exceeds £5,000·00	£55·00 with an addition of £1·00 in respect of every £200·00 or part of £200·00 by which the amount determined exceeds £5,000·00 but not exceeding in any case £250·00.

(a) 1967 c.1.

Item	Fee
(*b*) Where the amount determined (in terms of rent or other annual payment)	
(i) does not exceed £10·00 per annum	£5·00
(ii) exceeds £10·00 per annum but does not exceed £25·00 per annum	£5·00 with an addition of £1·00 in respect of every £2·50 or part of £2·50 by which the rent etc. determined exceeds £10·00 per annum.
(iii) exceeds £25·00 per annum but does not exceed £250·00 per annum	£11·00 with an addition of £1.00 in respect of every £5·00 or part of £5·00 by which the rent etc. determined exceeds £25·00 per annum.
(iv) exceeds £250·00 per annum ...	£56·00 with an addition of £1·00 in respect of every £10·00 or part of £10·00 by which the rent etc. determined exceeds £250·00 but not exceeding in any case £250·00.
7. On the hearing of any other appeal or reference (not being an appeal under Part IV or a reference under Part V of these rules) in which no fee is payable by reference to an amount determined	£5·00
Miscellaneous Fees	
8. On supplying and certifying a copy of an order or determination of the Tribunal.	50p
9. For a copy of all or part of any document (other than a copy to which item 8 applies)—for each sheet	20p
10. On a case for the decision of the Court of Session—on application for appeal by way of stated case (to include drafting of case and any necessary copies)	£2·25

SCHEDULE 3   Rule 36

Column 1 Rules revoked	Column 2 References
The Land Values (Referee) (Scotland) Rules 1911	S.R. & O. 1911/433 (Rev. XII, p. 187: 1911, p. 188).
The Land Values (Referee) (Scotland) —Additional Rule 1912	S.R. & O. 1912/861 (Rev. XII, p. 187: 1912, p. 254).
The Land Values (Referee) (Scotland) —Additional Rule 1913	S.R. & O. 1913/1275 (Rev. XII, p.187: 1913, p. 346).
The Acquisition of Land (Assessment of Compensation) (Scotland) Act 1919, —Rules.	S.R. & O. 1934/581 (Rev. XI, p. 792: 1934 I, p. 919).
The Acquisition of Land (Assessment of Compensation) (Fees) Rules 1931.	S.R. & O. 1931/157 (Rev. XI, p. 797: 1931, p. 558).
The Atomic Energy (Assessment of Compensation for Work done in Searching for Minerals) (Scotland) Rules 1948.	S.I. 1948/35 (Rev. II, p. 1020: 1948 I, p. 244).

EXPLANATORY NOTE

(This Note is not part of the Rules.)

These Rules prescribe the procedure to be followed in proceedings before the Lands Tribunal for Scotland.

Part I of the Rules deals with applications to the Tribunal under section 1 of the Conveyancing and Feudal Reform (Scotland) Act 1970 for the variation or discharge of land obligations. Part II is concerned with applications to the Tribunal under section 4 of the Act where a superior objects to the amount of feuduty which is to be allocated in terms of a notice of allocation served on him under section 3 of the Act. Part II also applies to ground annuals.

Part III deals with the determination by the Tribunal of questions of disputed compensation. Such questions include questions arising on the compulsory acquisition of land by a public authority.

Part IV deals with appeals to the Tribunal under the Finance (1909-10) Act 1910 against determinations of property value made by the Commissioners of Inland Revenue. Part V is concerned with references to the Tribunal by the Inland Revenue or by Special or General Commissioners in connection with the valuation of land for tax purposes under the Finance Act 1965 and the Taxes Management Act 1970.

Part VI provides for the Tribunal acting as arbiter in references by consent and also contains general procedural and other provisions.

Schedule 1 sets out forms to be used in connection with applications to the Tribunal. Schedule 2 prescribes fees to be charged by the Tribunal. Schedule 3 lists rules which are revoked with effect from the coming into existence of the Tribunal.

1971 No. 219 (S.17)

LEGAL AID AND ADVICE, SCOTLAND

Act of Sederunt (Legal Aid Fees) 1971

| Made | - | - | - | 29th January 1971 |
| Coming into Operation | | | | 1st March 1971 |

The Lords of Council and Session, under and by virtue of the powers conferred upon them by section 16(2) of the Legal Aid (Scotland) Act 1967(**a**) and of all other powers competent to them in that behalf, do hereby enact and declare as follows :—

1. The fees to be paid to a solicitor out of the Legal Aid Fund in respect of the representation of a person receiving legal aid in connection with proceedings in the Scottish Land Court shall be ninety per cent of the corresponding amount of fees calculated on the basis of the Table from time to time applicable in terms of Rule 109 of the Rules of the Scottish Land Court (**b**) as amended (**c**).

2.—(1) Subject to sub-paragraph (2) hereof and to any direction made in terms of the proviso hereto, the fees to be paid to a solicitor out of the Legal Aid Fund in respect of the representation of a person receiving legal aid in connection with proceedings in the Lands Tribunal for Scotland shall be ninety per cent of the corresponding amount of fees calculated on the basis of the Table from time to time regulating the taxation of accounts in the Sheriff Court : Provided that the Law Society of Scotland may, where circumstances warrant it, direct that the fees shall be ninety per cent of the corresponding amount of fees calculated on the basis of the Table from time to time regulating the taxation of accounts in the Court of Session.

(2) In any proceedings where the Land Tribunal for Scotland have, in terms of Rule 33(3) of the Lands Tribunal for Scotland Rules 1971(**d**), made an order as to the taxation of expenses the fees to be paid to a solicitor out of the Legal Aid Fund in respect of the representation of a person receiving legal aid in connection with such proceedings shall be ninety per cent of the corresponding amount of fees calculated on the basis of the Table of fees to which the order relates.

3. The fees to be paid to counsel out of the Legal Aid Fund in respect of the representation of a person receiving legal aid in connection with proceedings in the Scottish Land Court shall be ninety per cent of the corresponding amount which would have been allowed on taxation if such representation had not been subject to the benefit of legal aid.

(**a**) 1967 c. 43.   (**b**) S.R. & O. 1912/1750 (Rev. XII, p. 235).

(**c**) S.R. & O. 1932/439 (Rev. XII, p. 235: 1932, p. 714); S.I. 1949/144, 1957/1955, 1963/1518, 1970/1763, 1970/1764 (1949 I, p. 2418; 1957 II, p. 2260; 1963 III, p. 2799; 1970 III, pp. 5751, 5753).

(**d**) S.I. 1971/218 (**1971 I, p. 629**).

4. The fees to be paid to counsel out of the Legal Aid Fund in respect of the representation of a person receiving legal aid in connection with proceedings before the Lands Tribunal for Scotland shall be ninety per cent of the corresponding amount which would have been allowed on taxation if such representation had not been subject to the benefit of legal aid.

5.—(1) If any question or dispute arises as to the amount payable to any Solicitor or counsel in respect of any remuneration for the representation of a person receiving legal aid in connection with proceedings in the Scottish Land Court, the matter shall be referred for taxation to the Auditor of the Scottish Land Court, and the fees to be paid to the Auditor for such taxation shall be on the scale from time to time in force for taxations in the Scottish Land Court.

(2) A reference to the Auditor under sub-paragraph (1) hereof need not be joint but may be made at the instance either of the solicitor concerned or of the Law Society of Scotland, and the Auditor shall give reasonable notice to both of the diet of taxation.

(3) The Law Society of Scotland and any other party to a reference to the Auditor under sub-paragraph (1) hereof shall have the right to state written objections to the Chairman of the Scottish Land Court in relation to the Auditor's report within seven days of the date of issue of such report, and the Law Society of Scotland and any such other party may be heard in chambers thereon.

6.—(1) If any question or dispute arises as to the amount payable to any solicitor or counsel in respect of any remuneration for the representation of a person receiving legal aid in connection with proceedings in the lands Tribunal for Scotland, the matter shall be referred for taxation

(*a*) where the fees are to be taxed according to the Sheriff Court Table of Fees to the Auditor of a Sheriff Court to be specified, failing agreement by the tribunal, and

(*b*) where the fees are to be taxed according to the fees payable in the Court of Session by the Auditor of the Court of Session and,

the fees to be paid to the Auditor for such taxation shall be on the scale from time to time in force for taxation in either the Sheriff Court or the Court of Session as appropriate.

(2) A reference to an Auditor under sub-paragraph (1) hereof need not be joint but may be at the instance either of the solicitor concerned or of the Law Society of Scotland, and the Auditor concerned shall give reasonable notice to both of the diet of taxation.

(3) The Law Society of Scotland and any other party to a reference to an Auditor under sub-paragraph (1)(*a*) hereof shall have the right to state written objections to the Sheriff in relation to the Auditor's report within seven days of the date of issue of such report, and the Law Society of Scotland and any such other party may be heard in chambers thereon.

(4) The Law Society of Scotland and any other party to a reference to the Auditor under sub-paragraph 1(*b*) hereof shall have the right to state written objections to the Court of Session in relation to the Auditor's report within

seven days of the date of issue of such report, and the Law Society of Scotland and any such other party may be heard by a Lord Ordinary in Chambers thereon. Rule 349 of the Rules of the Court of Session (a) shall apply to the determination of any such objections and hearing.

7. This Act of Sederunt may be cited as the Act of Sederunt (Legal Aid Fees) 1971 and shall come into operation on 1st March 1971.

And the Lords appoint this Act of Sederunt to be inserted in the Books of Sederunt.

J. L. Clyde,

I.P.D.

Edinburgh.
29th January 1971.

EXPLANATORY NOTE

(This Note is not part of the Act of Sederunt.)

This Act of Sederunt prescribes the fees payable out of the legal aid fund to solicitors and counsel in respect of representation of assisted persons in the Scottish Land Court and before the Lands Tribunal for Scotland.

(a) S.I. 1965/321 (1965 I, p. 803).

STATUTORY INSTRUMENTS

1971 No. 220 (S.34)

JURIES

The Jurors' Allowances (Scotland) Regulations 1971

Made - - - -	*8th February* 1971
Coming into Operation	*15th February* 1971

In exercise of the powers conferred on me by sections 24(1) and 32(1) of the Juries Act 1949**(a)**, as amended by the Juries Act 1954**(b)**, and of all other powers enabling me in that behalf, I hereby, with the consent of the Treasury, make the following regulations:—

Citation, commencement and revocation

1.—(1) These regulations may be cited as the Jurors' Allowances (Scotland) Regulations 1971 and shall come into operation on 15th February 1971.

(2) The Jurors' Allowances (Scotland) Regulations 1967**(c)** and the Jurors' Allowances (Scotland) Amendment Regulations 1970**(d)** are hereby revoked.

Interpretation

2.—(1) In these regulations any reference to a juror shall include a reference to a person who, in obedience to a citation to serve on a jury, attends for service as a juror notwithstanding that he is not subsequently impanelled, and any reference to service as a juror shall be construed accordingly.

(2) In these regulations, unless the context otherwise requires:—

"the Act" means the Juries Act 1949 as amended by the Juries Act 1954; and

"public service" means any service provided for travel by the public by railway, ship, vessel, omnibus, trolley vehicle or tramway.

(3) The Interpretation Act 1889**(e)** shall apply for the interpretation of these regulations as it applies for the interpretation of an Act of Parliament and section 38(2) of that Act shall apply as if these regulations were an Act of Parliament and the regulations revoked by these regulations were enactments repealed thereby.

Travelling Allowance

3. The travelling allowance to which a juror is entitled under section 24 of the Act shall be in accordance with the rates set out in the Schedule hereto.

(a) 1949 c. 27.
(c) S.I. 1967/144 (1967 I, p. 231).
(e) 1889 c. 63.
(b) 2 & 3 Eliz. 2. c. 41.
(d) S.I. 1970/262 (1970 I, p. 1011).

Subsistence Allowance

4.—(1) The subsistence allowance to which a juror is entitled under section 24 of the Act shall be calculated in accordance with paragraphs (2) and (3) of this regulation.

(2) In respect of any period other than a period in respect of which a subsistence allowance is payable under paragraph (3) of this regulation, or during which meals are provided for him, the subsistence allowance shall be—

   (a) if the period on any one day during which a juror is necessarily absent from his place of residence, business or employment for the purpose of serving as a juror does not exceed four hours, 45p in respect of that day;

   (b) if the said period on any one day exceeds four hours but does not exceed eight hours, 95p in respect of that day;

   (c) if the said period on any one day exceeds eight hours but does not exceed twelve hours, £1·75 in respect of that day;

   (d) if the said period on any one day exceeds twelve hours but does not exceed sixteen hours, £2·50 in respect of that day;

   (e) if the said period on any one day exceeds sixteen hours, £2·95 in respect of that day.

(3) If a juror is necessarily absent overnight from his place of residence, business or employment for the purpose of serving as a juror, and board and lodging is not provided for him, the subsistence allowance shall be £5·50 in respect of each period of twenty-four hours or fraction thereof during which he is so absent overnight.

Financial Loss Allowance

5. The compensation for loss of earnings which a juror would otherwise have made or additional expense (other than expense on account of travelling or subsistence) to which he would not otherwise have been subject, to which he is entitled under section 24 of the Act, shall be the amount of the said loss or additional expense:

Provided that the amount payable under this regulation to a person in respect of his services as a juror on any one day shall not exceed—

   (a) where the period of time over which the earnings are lost or additional expense is incurred does not exceed four hours, the sum of £2·00; or

   (b) where the said period of time exceeds four hours, the sum of £4·00,

except that, where in obedience to a citation to serve on a jury he has served as a juror on more than ten days and the court so directs, the amount so payable in respect of his services as a juror in obedience to the same citation on any one day after the tenth such day may exceed the sum specified above but shall not exceed £8·00.

Gordon Campbell,
One of Her Majesty's Principal
Secretaries of State.

St Andrew's House,
Edinburgh.

4th February 1971.

We consent,

Bernard Weatherill,

Walter Clegg,

Two of the Lords Commissioners
of Her Majesty's Treasury.

8th February 1971.

SCHEDULE   Regulation 3

TRAVELLING ALLOWANCE

1. The rate for travel by public service shall not exceed the amount of the fare actually paid:

Provided that—

(a) unless for a special reason the court otherwise directs, only the amount of the second class fare shall be allowed for travel by railway;

(b) if the journey is by steamer and a cabin is occupied, cabin fare shall be allowed.

2. The rate for travel by a hired vehicle—

(a) in cases of urgency or where no public service is reasonably available, shall not exceed the amount of the actual fare and any reasonable gratuity paid, and

(b) in any other case, shall not exceed the amount of the fare for travel by an appropriate public service.

3. Where the use of a private motor vehicle results in a substantial saving of time or is otherwise reasonable, the rate shall not exceed—

(a) for the use of a vehicle of cylinder capacity of 1,000 c.c. or less, 3½p a mile;

(b) for the use of a vehicle of cylinder capacity from 1,001 c.c. to 1,750 c.c., 4½p a mile;

(c) for the use of a vehicle of cylinder capacity over 1,751 c.c. 5p a mile;

for each mile necessarily travelled to and from court. In any other case the rate shall not exceed 2p a mile for each mile necessarily travelled as aforesaid.

EXPLANATORY NOTE

(This Note is not Part of the Regulations.)

These Regulations consolidate with amendments the Jurors' Allowances (Scotland) Regulations 1967 and the Jurors' Allowances (Scotland) Amendment Regulations 1970. The regulations now consolidated laid down the rates of travelling allowance for jurors, the rates of day and night subsistence allowance and the rates for compensation for loss of earnings or additional expenses (other than travelling or subsistence expenses). The principal amendments increase the rates for mileage allowances for travel by private motor vehicle which allowances now depend on the cylinder capacity of the vehicle (Regulation 3) and also the subsistence allowances payable to a juror where he is necessarily absent from his place of residence, business or employment (Regulation 4(1)).

STATUTORY INSTRUMENTS

1971 No. 221

CIVIL DEFENCE

The Civil Defence (Posts and Telecommunications) Regulations 1971

Laid before Parliament in draft

| Made | - | - | - | *9th February* 1971 |

Coming into Operation   1st *March* 1971

Whereas by the Civil Defence (Designation of the Minister of Posts and Telecommunications) Order 1969(**a**), the Minister of Posts and Telecommunications is the designated Minister in relation to the provision and maintenance of postal and telecommunication services for purposes which include the making of regulations under section 6 of the Civil Defence Act 1948(**b**) :

Now, therefore, the Minister of Posts and Telecommunications, in exercise of the powers conferred upon him by section 6 of the Civil Defence Act 1948, and of all other powers him enabling, with the consent of the Treasury, hereby makes the following regulations in the terms of a draft duly approved by resolution of each House of Parliament :—

1. These regulations may be cited as the Civil Defence (Posts and Telecommunications) Regulations 1971 and shall come into operation on the 1st March 1971.

2.—(1) In these regulations, except where the context otherwise requires—

"the Minister" means the Minister of Posts and Telecommunications ;

"the Post Office" has the meaning assigned to it in section 6 of the Post Office Act 1969(**c**)

"the Act of 1939" means the Civil Defence Act 1939(**d**)

(2) The Interpretation Act 1889(**e**), applies for the interpretation of these regulations as it applies for the interpretation of an Act of Parliament.

3. Sections 36, 37 and 39 of the Act of 1939 are brought again into force (with amendments) to the extent provided in the next two following regulations.

4. The Minister may serve a notice in writing on the Post Office requiring it within the time specified in the notice—

(*a*) to make a report stating what measures it has taken or is taking or proposing to take to secure the due functioning of its undertaking in the event of hostile attack, or

(*b*) to take such measures as may be specified in the notice to secure the due functioning of its undertaking in the event of hostile attack.

(**a**) S.I. 1969/1072 (1969 II, p. 3143).   (**b**) 12, 13 & 14 Geo. 6. c. 5.
(**c**) 1969 c. 48.   (**d**) 2 & 3 Geo. 6. c. 31.   (**e**) 52 & 53 Vict. c. 63.

5.—(1) The Minister may pay out of monies provided by Parliament towards the approved expenses of the Post Office in taking measures, whether before or after the coming into operation of these regulations, to secure the due functioning of its undertaking in the event of hostile attack grants not exceeding fifty-two and three quarters per centum of those expenses.

(2) In this regulation the expression "approved expenses" means such expenses of a capital nature incurred on such measures as the Minister acting in accordance with general directions of the Treasury may approve for the purposes of this regulation.

6.—(1) Section 79 and section 91(28) of the Act of 1939, are brought again into force in relation to notices, reports or other action under these regulations.

(2) Section 80 and subsections (3) and (4) of section 83 of the Act of 1939 shall apply in relation to notices, reports or other action under these regulations but as if references in those sections to the Minister were references to the Minister of Posts and Telecommunications.

Dated 3rd February 1971.

Christopher Chataway,
Minister of Posts and Telecommunications.

We consent.

V. H. Goodhew,
Bernard Weatherill,
Two of the Lords Commissioners of
Her Majesty's Treasury.

9th February 1971.

EXPLANATORY NOTE

(This Note is not part of the Regulations.)

These Regulations, made under section 6 of the Civil Defence Act 1948, empower the Minister of Posts and Telecommunications to make grants to the Post Office towards approved expenses incurred in securing the due functioning of its undertaking in the event of hostile attack.

They also provide that the Post Office shall furnish the Minister with such information as he may require as to the measures it has taken, and shall take such measures as the Minister may specify, to secure the due functioning of its undertaking in the event of hostile attack.

STATUTORY INSTRUMENTS

1971 No. 222

CHILDREN AND YOUNG PERSONS

The Approved Schools and Classifying Centres (Contributions by Local Authorities) Regulations 1971

Made - - -		10*th February* 1971
Coming into Operation		1*st April* 1971

The Secretary of State for Social Services, in exercise of his powers under paragraph 8(2) of Schedule 3 to the Children and Young Persons Act 1969(a) and of all other powers enabling him in that behalf, hereby makes the following regulations:—

1. These Regulations may be cited as the Approved Schools and Classifying Centres (Contributions by Local Authorities) Regulations 1971 and shall come into operation on 1st April 1971.

2. The Interpretation Act 1889(b) shall apply to the interpretation of these Regulations as it applies to the interpretation of an Act of Parliament.

3. The contributions which, under paragraph 8(1) of Schedule 3 to the Children and Young Persons Act 1969 (financial provisions in respect of approved schools and certain classifying centres), are payable by local authorities in respect of children in their care who are accommodated and maintained in the premises of an approved school or in a classifying centre falling within paragraph 4(3)(*a*) of the said Schedule 3 to the managers of the school or, as the case may be, to the local authority providing the centre, shall be at the rate of £18.55 a week.

4. The Approved Schools and Classifying Centres (Contributions by Local Authorities) Regulations 1970(c) are hereby revoked.

Keith Joseph,
Secretary of State for Social Services.

10th February 1971.

(a) 1969 c. 54.　　　(b) 1889 c. 63.　　　(c) S.I. 1970/1959 (1970 III, p. 6413).

EXPLANATORY NOTE

(This Note is not part of the Regulations.)

These Regulations prescribe a rate of £18.55 a week as the rate of contributions payable under paragraph 8 of Schedule 3 to the Children and Young Persons Act 1969 to the managers of an approved school or the local authority providing a remand home designated as a classifying centre in respect of which the Secretary of State has directed that the whole or part of its expenses shall be treated for certain purposes as if they were the expenses of an approved school, by local authorities in respect of children in their care who are accommodated and maintained in the school or classifying centre.

STATUTORY INSTRUMENTS

1971 No. 224

AGRICULTURE

HILL LANDS

The Northern Pennines Rural Development Board (Dissolution) Order 1971

Made - - -	*10th February* 1971
Laid before Parliament	*18th February* 1971
Coming into Operation	*31st March* 1971

The Minister of Agriculture, Fisheries and Food in exercise of the power conferred on him by subparagraphs (1)(*b*) and (3) of paragraph 6 of Part I of Schedule 5 to the Agriculture Act 1967(a) (as having effect under section 45(5) of that Act), and of all other powers enabling him in that behalf, hereby orders as follows :—

Citation and commencement

1. This order may be cited as the Northern Pennines Rural Development Board (Dissolution) Order 1971 and shall come into operation on 31st March 1971.

Interpretation

2.—(1) In this Order—

"the Act" means the Agriculture Act 1967 ;

"the Board" means the Northern Pennines Rural Development Board established by the Northern Pennines Rural Development Board Order 1969(b), and "the Board area" has the meaning assigned to it in article 2(1) of that Order ;

"the Minister" means the Minister of Agriculture, Fisheries and Food.

(2) The Interpretation Act 1889(c) shall apply to the interpretation of this order as it applies to the interpretation of an Act of Parliament.

Dissolution of the Board

3.—(1) On the coming into operation of this order the Board shall be dissolved, and accordingly the Board area shall thereupon cease to be a Rural Development Board area for the purposes of the Act or any other enactment.

(2) The provisions contained in the Schedule to this order, being provisions which appear to the Minister expedient in consequence of and incidental to the dissolution of the Board, shall have effect.

In Witness whereof the Official Seal of the Minister of Agriculture, Fisheries and Food is hereunto affixed on 10th February 1971.

(L.S.)

J. M. L. Prior,
Minister of Agriculture, Fisheries and Food.

(a) 1967 c. 22.
(c) 1889 c. 63.

(b) S.I. 1969/1095 (1969 III, p. 3184).

SCHEDULE

Consequential and incidental provisions

Transfer of assets and liabilities

1.—(1) On the coming into operation of this order the property, rights, obligations and liabilities of the Board shall, by virtue of this order and without further assurance, be transferred to the Minister.

(2) Without prejudice to the generality of the foregoing, where an applicant has served notice on the Board under subsection (6) of section 49 of the Act requiring the Board to purchase an estate or interest in respect of which consent to its transfer has been previously refused by the Board under that section, subsections (7) and (8) thereof shall have effect as if for each reference therein to the Board there were substituted a reference to the Minister.

Matters pending under sections 49 and 52 of the Act

2.—(1) Any application pending for consent to the transfer of land in the Board area made under section 49 of the Act, and any application pending for a licence to plant trees in the Board area made under section 52 of the Act, shall lapse.

(2) Any refusal of such consent under section 49 of the Act, and any refusal of such a licence under section 52 of the Act, made before the coming into operation of this order shall, subject to paragraph 1(2) above, cease to have effect ; and insofar as any licence under the last-mentioned section was granted subject to conditions the conditions shall cease to have effect.

(3) Any appeal pending to the Minister against refusal of consent under section 49 of the Act, and any appeal pending to the Minister against refusal, or against the conditions, of a licence under section 52 of the Act, shall lapse.

(4) The lapse, in consequence of the dissolution of the Board by virtue of this order, of any consent under section 49 of the Act, and any licence under section 52 of the Act, shall not render unlawful any action which would but for this order be unlawful under either of those sections without such a consent or licence.

Cancellation of local land charges

3. On the dissolution of the Board by virtue of this order any entry registered by any local authority within the Board area pursuant to section 45(6) of the Act, controlling sales of land and controlling afforestation within that area, shall be cancelled by the proper officer of that authority.

Board's annual report and accounts

4. The Board's financial year current on the date of the dissolution of the Board by virtue of this order shall be deemed to end on that date, and section 53 of the Act (Board's annual reports and accounts) shall have effect accordingly.

EXPLANATORY NOTE

(This Note is not part of the Order.)

This Order dissolves the Northern Pennines Rural Development Board established under Part III of the Agriculture Act 1967, and contains consequential and incidental provisions.

STATUTORY INSTRUMENTS

1971 No. 225 (C.5)

SOCIAL SECURITY

The Family Income Supplements Act 1970 (Commencement) Order 1971

Made - - - -	*11th February* 1971
Laid before Parliament	*22nd February* 1971
Coming into Operation	*3rd May* 1971

The Secretary of State for Social Services, in exercise of the powers conferred on him by section 16(1) of the Family Income Supplements Act 1970(a) and of all other powers enabling him in that behalf, hereby makes the following order: —

Citation and commencement

1. This order may be cited as the Family Income Supplements Act 1970 (Commencement) Order 1971 and shall come into operation on 3rd May 1971.

Appointed day

2. The day appointed for the purposes of section 16 of the Family Income Supplements Act 1970 (commencement of family income supplement) shall be 3rd August 1971.

Keith Joseph,
Secretary of State for
Social Services.

11th February 1971.

(a) 1970 c. 55.

STATUTORY INSTRUMENTS

1971 No. 226

SOCIAL SECURITY

The Family Income Supplements (General) Regulations 1971

Made - - - -	*11th February* 1971
Laid before Parliament	*22nd February* 1971
Coming into Operation	*3rd May* 1971

The Secretary of State for Social Services, in exercise of powers conferred upon him by sections 4(2), 5(2), 6(2), 8(2) and (3) and 10(2) of the Family Income Supplements Act 1970(**a**), and of all other powers enabling him in that behalf, hereby makes the following regulations: —

Citation, commencement and interpretation

1.—(1) These regulations may be cited as the Family Income Supplements (General) Regulations 1971, and shall come into operation on 3rd May 1971.

(2) In these regulations, unless the context otherwise requires—

" the Act " means the Family Income Supplements Act 1970 ;

" the Appeal Tribunal" has the same meaning as in section 7(3) of the Act ;

" the appointed day " means the day appointed by the Secretary of State under section 16 of the Act ;

" attendance allowance " means an attendance allowance under the National Insurance Acts 1965 to 1970 ; an increase of disablement pension under section 15 of the National Insurance (Industrial Injuries) Act 1965(**b**) ; a payment under regulations made in exercise of the power in section 81(2)(*b*) of that Act ; an increase of allowance under Article 8 of the Pneumoconiosis, Byssinosis and Miscellaneous Diseases Benefit Scheme 1966(**c**) ; and an allowance in respect of constant attendance on account of disablement for which a person is in receipt of a war disablement pension, including an allowance in respect of exceptionally severe disablement ;

" benefit " means a family income supplement under the Act ;

" beneficiary " means a person by whom benefit is or was receivable and any person authorised or appointed to act for such a person ;

" claim " means a claim for benefit ;

" the Commission " means the Supplementary Benefits Commission ;

" war disablement pension " means—

(*a*) retired pay, pension or allowance granted under powers conferred by or under the Ministry of Pensions Act 1916(**d**), the Air Force (Constitution) Act 1917(**e**), the Pensions (Navy, Army, Air Force and Mercantile Marine) Act 1939(**f**), the Personal Injuries

---

(**a**) 1970 c. 55.　　(**b**) 1965 c. 52.　　(**c**) S.I. 1966/164 (1966 I, p. 303).　　(**d**) 1916 c. 65.
(**e**) 1917 c. 51.　　(**f**) 1939 c. 83.

(Emergency Provisions) Act 1939(a), the Polish Resettlement Act 1947(b), the Home Guard Act 1951(c) or the Ulster Defence Regiment Act 1969(d) ; and

(b) injury or disablement pension payable under any scheme made under the Injuries in War Compensation Act 1914(e) and the Injuries in War Compensation Act 1915(f), or under any War Risks Compensation Scheme for the Mercantile Marine ;

and other expressions have the same meanings as in the Act.

(3) References in these regulations to any enactment or regulation shall, except in so far as the context otherwise requires, include references to such enactment or regulation as amended or extended by or under any other enactment, order or regulation and as including references to any enactment or regulation thereby consolidated.

(4) The rules for the construction of Acts of Parliament contained in the Interpretation Act 1889(g) shall apply for the purposes of the interpretation of these regulations (including any regulations read as one therewith) as they apply for the purposes of the interpretation of an Act of Parliament.

Computation of normal gross income of members of a family

2.—(1) For the purposes of the Act, a person's normal gross income and the weekly amount thereof shall be calculated or estimated in the manner provided in the following provisions of this regulation.

(2) In so far as a person's normal gross income consists of earnings from a gainful occupation, the weekly amount of that person's normal gross income therefrom shall be calculated or estimated by reference to the average of his earnings from that occupation over the period of the five weeks (being pay-weeks if in respect of that occupation he is paid weekly) or the two pay-months (if in respect of that occupation he is paid monthly) immediately preceding the date on which the claim is made, so, however, that in any case, and in particular in a case where a person has been working abnormally long or short hours in a gainful occupation, or has commenced working in a gainful occupation shortly before the claim is made, or is following a gainful occupation from which his earnings normally fluctuate at approximately the same time or times each year, or is following a gainful occupation otherwise than under a contract of service, the Commission or the Appeal Tribunal may have regard to the average of a person's earnings from a gainful occupation over such other period or periods as may appear to them to be appropriate in order properly to determine what is that person's normal weekly income therefrom.

(3) In so far as a person's earnings from any gainful occupation comprise salary, wages or fees related to a fixed period, the gross amount thereof shall be taken into account ; and in so far as a person's earnings from any gainful occupation do not comprise salary, wages or fees related to a fixed period, the net profit derived from that occupation shall be taken into account.

(4) In so far as a person's normal gross income does not consist of earnings from a gainful occupation, the weekly amount thereof shall be calculated or estimated on such basis as appears to the Commission or the Appeal Tribunal to be appropriate in the circumstances of the particular case.

(a) 1939 c. 82.   (b) 1947 c. 19.   (c) 1951 c. 8 (15 & 16 Geo. 6 & 1 Eliz. 2.).
(d) 1969 c. 65.   (e) 1914 c. 30.   (f) 1915 c. 24.   (g) 1889 c. 63.

(5) In calculating or estimating a person's normal gross income and the weekly amount thereof, there shall be disregarded—

(*a*) the whole of any sums by way of attendance allowance ;

(*b*) the whole of any payments made in respect of a child who is boarded out for the purposes of the Boarding-Out of Children Regulations 1955(**a**) or the Boarding-Out of Children (Scotland) Regulations 1959(**b**) ;

(*c*) the whole of any sums by way of benefit under the Act ;

(*d*) the whole of any sums by way of benefit under the Ministry of Social Security Act 1966(**c**) ; and

(*e*) up to £2·00 a week of any war disablement pension payable.

Circumstances in which benefit may be made payable otherwise than for twenty-six weeks beginning with the date of the claim therefor

3.—(1) Benefit may be made payable otherwise than for a period of twenty-six weeks beginning with the date of the claim therefor in the circumstances set out in the following paragraphs of this regulation.

(2) Subject to paragraph (4) of this regulation, where the available evidence leaves the Commission or the Appeal Tribunal in doubt as to the rate at which benefit should be payable, but satisfies them that benefit should be payable at not less than a certain weekly rate, they may determine that benefit shall be payable at the latter rate for a period of less than twenty-six weeks, but not less than four weeks.

(3) Where a beneficiary makes a claim not more than four weeks before or after the expiration of a period for which benefit is payable (hereinafter in this paragraph referred to as a " renewal claim "), any benefit payable on the basis of the renewal claim shall be payable for a period commencing immediately after the expiration of the period for which benefit was previously payable.

(4) Where the Commission or the Appeal Tribunal determine that benefit is payable in relation to a claim made during the transitional period, that is to say a claim made on or after the date on which these regulations come into operation but before the appointed day, benefit shall be payable for such period beginning on the appointed day, being a period of not more than thirty-nine weeks or less than four weeks, as the Secretary of State shall in any case decide.

Circumstances in which payment of supplementary benefit is to make benefit under the Act not payable for a family or not receivable by a person

4.—(1) Subject to the provisions of paragraph (2) of this regulation, no benefit shall be paid for any family during any period during which, due to the refusal or neglect of a person by whom the benefit is receivable to maintain any other person included in the family, the requirements of that other person are taken into account for the purposes of any benefit under the Ministry of Social Security Act 1966(**c**).

(2) Where a family includes both a man and a woman and benefit is receivable by either of them, paragraph (1) of this regulation shall not apply if it is due to the refusal or neglect of one only of them to maintain any other person included in the family that the requirements of that other person have been taken into account for the purposes of any benefit under

(**a**) S.I. 1955/1377 (1955 I, p. 286).   (**b**) S.I. 1959/835 (1959 I, p. 579).   (**c**) 1966 c. 20.

the said Act of 1966, but benefit shall cease to be receivable by that one of them due to whose refusal or neglect to maintain any other person included in the family the requirements of that other person are taken into account for the purposes of any benefit under the said Act of 1966.

Circumstances in which a person is to be treated as being or as not being engaged and normally engaged in remunerative full-time work

5. A person shall be treated as being engaged and normally engaged in remunerative full-time work if he is and is normally engaged in remunerative work for not less than thirty hours a week, and shall be treated as not being engaged and normally engaged in remunerative full-time work unless he is and is normally engaged in remunerative work for not less than thirty hours a week.

Circumstances in which a person is to be treated as not providing in whole or in part for the requirements of a child

6. A person shall be treated as not providing in whole or in part for the requirements of any child who is boarded-out for the purposes of the Boarding-Out of Children Regulations 1955 or the Boarding-Out of Children (Scotland) Regulations 1959.

Claims for a child who could be included in more than one family for the purposes of the Act

7. Where, apart from the provisions of this regulation, a child could be included in more than one family for the purposes of the Act, it shall be included in such family as the persons claiming benefit agree, or, in default of agreement, in such family as the Commission or the Appeal Tribunal shall, in its discretion, determine.

Circumstances in which a family is to be treated as being or as not being in Great Britain

8. A family shall be treated as being in Great Britain if, and shall be treated as not being in Great Britain unless, at the date when benefit is claimed it is ordinarily resident in the United Kingdom and at least one member of the family who is not a child is resident in Great Britain, so, however, that if the Parliament of Northern Ireland enacts provisions for purposes similar to the purposes of the Act, a family shall in any event be treated as not being in Great Britain where that date falls within a period during which any member of it is a member of a family for which benefit in respect of that period is payable or has been paid under such provisions.

Circumstances in which a person of or over the age of sixteen is to be treated as a child

9. A person of or over the age of sixteen shall be treated as a child for the purposes of the Act while he continues to receive full-time instruction in a school or to receive full-time instruction of a kind given in a school ; and for the purposes of this regulation " school " has the same meaning as in the Education Act 1944(a) or, in Scotland, the Education (Scotland) Act 1962(b).

(a) 1944 c. 31.   (b) 1962 c. 47.

Recovery of overpayments of benefit

10. Where it is found by the Commission or the Appeal Tribunal that sums paid by way of benefit were not due and the persons by whom the sums were receivable cannot satisfy the Commission or the Appeal Tribunal that they had disclosed all material facts, the Secretary of State shall be entitled to recover the sums from the persons by whom they were receivable.

Review of determinations made by the Commission and the Appeal Tribunal

11.—(1) A determination made by the Commission may be reviewed by the Commission if it is satisfied that it was based on a mistake as to the law ; and a determination made by the Commission or by the Appeal Tribunal may be reviewed by the Commission if—

(a) the Commission is satisfied that the determination was made in ignorance of, or was based on a mistake as to, some material fact ; or

(b) the Commission is satisfied that benefit should not be paid for any family or should not be receivable by any person by reason of the provisions of regulation 4 of these regulations.

(2) Any determination made by the Commission on a review and any determination made by the Commission refusing to review a determination under paragraph (1) of this regulation shall be subject to appeal in like manner as an original determination by the Commission.

Notice of determinations by the Commission

12. A person whose right to benefit is affected by a determination made by the Commission shall be given notice in writing of that determination, of the reasons therefor and of his right of appeal therefrom ; and where such a person is a member of a family which includes both a man and a woman the foregoing requirement as to the giving of notice shall, unless in any case or class of cases the Secretary of State otherwise directs, be deemed to have been complied with in relation to both that man and that woman if one of them is given notice as aforesaid.

Keith Joseph,
Secretary of State for
Social Services.

11th February 1971.

EXPLANATORY NOTE

(This Note is not part of the Regulations.)

These Regulations contain miscellaneous provisions relating to the Family Income Supplements Act 1970 (hereafter called " the Act ").

Regulation 1 contains various definitions for the purposes of the Regulations ; Regulation 2 relates to the computation of the normal gross income of members of a family ; Regulation 3 relates to the circumstances in which benefit may be awarded for a period other than one of twenty-six weeks beginning with the date of the claim ; Regulation 4 relates to the circumstances in which payment of benefit under the Ministry of Social Security Act 1966 may make benefit under the Act not payable for a family or receivable by a person ; Regulation 5 relates to the circumstances in which a person is to be treated as being or as not being engaged and normally engaged in remunerative full-time work ; Regulation 6 relates to the circumstances in which a person is to be treated as not providing in whole or in part for the requirements of a child ; Regulation 7 makes provision for the situation where a child could be included in more than one family for the purposes of the Act ; Regulation 8 relates to the circumstances in which a family is to be treated as being or as not being in Great Britain ; Regulation 9 relates to the circumstances in which a person of or over the age of 16 is to be treated as a child for the purposes of the Act ; Regulation 10 relates to the recovery of overpayments of benefit under the Act ; Regulation 11 relates to the review of determinations by the Supplementary Benefits Commission and the Appeal Tribunal ; and Regulation 12 relates to notifying persons of determinations made by the Supplementary Benefits Commission.

STATUTORY INSTRUMENTS

1971 No. 227

SOCIAL SECURITY

The Family Income Supplements (Claims and Payments) Regulations 1971

Made - - - -	11*th February* 1971
Laid before Parliament	22*nd February* 1971
Coming into Operation	3*rd May* 1971

The Secretary of State for Social Services, in exercise of the powers conferred upon him by sections 5(2) and 10(2) of the Family Income Supplements Act 1970(**a**), and of all other powers enabling him in that behalf, hereby makes the following regulations: —

PART I

General

Citation, commencement and interpretation

1.—(1) These regulations may be cited as the Family Income Supplements (Claims and Payments) Regulations 1971, and shall come into operation on 3rd May 1971.

(2) In these regulations, unless the context otherwise requires—

" the Act " means the Family Income Supplements Act 1970 ;

" benefit " means a family income supplement under the Act ;

" beneficiary " means a person by whom benefit is or has been receivable and any person authorised or appointed to act for such a person ;

" claim " means a claim for benefit ;

" the Department " means the Department of Health and Social Security ;

" determining authority " means, as the case may require, the Appeal Tribunal as defined in section 7(3) of the Act or the Supplementary Benefits Commission ;

" the Secretary of State " means the Secretary of State for Social Services ;

" instrument of payment " means a serial order and any other instrument whatsoever which is intended to enable a person to obtain payment of benefit ;

" serial order " means one of a series of orders for the payment of sums on account of benefit which is or has been contained in a book of such orders ;

" approved place " means a place approved by the Secretary of State for the purpose of obtaining payment of benefit ;

and other expressions have the same meanings as in the Act.

(**a**) 1970 c. 55.

(3) References in these regulations to any enactment or regulation shall, except in so far as the context otherwise requires, include references to such enactment or regulation as amended or extended by or under any other enactment, order or regulation and as including references to any enactment or regulation thereby consolidated.

(4) The rules for the construction of Acts of Parliament contained in the Interpretation Act 1889(a) shall apply for the purposes of the interpretation of these regulations (including any regulations read as one therewith) as they apply for the purposes of the interpretation of an Act of Parliament.

PART II

Claims

Manner in which claims are to be made

2.—(1) Every claim shall be made in writing and delivered or sent to an office of the Department on a form approved by the Secretary of State, or in such other manner, being in writing, as the Secretary of State may accept as sufficient in the circumstances of any particular case or class of cases.

(2) Forms of claim shall be supplied without charge by such persons as the Secretary of State may appoint or authorise for that purpose.

(3) If a claim is defective at the date when it is received at an office of the Department, or has been made otherwise than on the form approved for the time being, the Secretary of State may, in his discretion, refer the claim to the person making it, or, as the case may be, supply him with the approved form, and if the form is returned properly completed within one month from the date on which it is so referred or supplied, the Secretary of State shall treat the claim as if it had been duly made in the first instance.

(4) A person who has made a claim may withdraw it at any time before a determination has been made on it by a notice in writing delivered or sent to an office of the Department.

(5) Any reference in the Act or in regulations to the date on which a claim is made shall, in the case of a claim which is treated as if it had been duly made in the first instance under paragraph (3) of this regulation, be construed as a reference to the date on which such claim is so treated as having been duly made.

(6) Where for the purposes of the Act a family includes both a man and a woman, the Secretary of State may, if he is satisfied that it would be unreasonable to require a joint claim, accept as a valid claim a claim made by the man alone or by the woman alone.

(7) No claim made by or on behalf of a person who was included in a family for which benefit is payable shall be entertained if it is made more than four weeks before the expiration of the period for which benefit is payable for that family.

Information to be given in connection with a claim

3. Every person who makes a claim shall furnish such certificates, documents, information and evidence in connection with the claim as may be required by the Secretary of State and, if reasonably so required, shall for that purpose attend at such office of the Department or other place as the Secretary of State may direct.

(a) 1889 c. 63.

PART III

Payments

Time and manner of payment of benefit

4.—(1) Payment of benefit shall be made in such manner and at such times as the Secretary of State in any particular case or class of cases may determine.

(2) Instruments of payment and books of serial orders issued by the Secretary of State shall remain his property ; and any person having such an instrument of payment or book of serial orders shall, on ceasing to be entitled to the benefit to which such instrument or book relates, or when so required by the Secretary of State, deliver the said instrument or book to the Secretary of State or to such other person as he may direct.

(3) Where, by reason of any provision of the Act or of regulations, the date as from which benefit would commence, or as from which a change in the rate of benefit would take effect, is not a Tuesday, benefit shall commence only, or the change in the rate of benefit shall take effect only, as from the next Tuesday ; and where the date on which benefit would cease to be payable is not a Monday, benefit shall continue to be payable in respect of the days of the week up to but not including the next Tuesday.

Extinguishment of right to payment of sums on account of benefit

5.—(1) The right to payment of any sum by way of benefit shall, subject to paragraph (2) of this regulation, be extinguished where payment thereof is not obtained within the period of twelve months from the date on which the right is to be treated as having arisen ; and for the purposes of this regulation the right shall be treated as having arisen—

(*a*) in relation to any such sum contained in an instrument of payment which has been given or sent, for the purpose of making payment thereof, to the beneficiary or to an approved place for collection by him (whether or not received or collected as the case may be) and notwithstanding that that sum is greater or less than the sum to which the beneficiary has the right to payment—

　(i) on the date on the said instrument of payment ; or

　(ii) if a further instrument of payment has been so given or sent as a replacement for an instrument of payment previously given or sent, on the date on the last such instrument of payment ;

(*b*) in relation to any such sum to which sub-paragraph (*a*) of this paragraph does not apply, but where notice is given (whether orally or in writing) or is sent that the sum contained in the notice is available for collection and notwithstanding that that sum is greater or less than the sum to which the beneficiary has the right to payment—

　(i) if written notice is sent through the post, on the date on which it would be delivered in the ordinary course of post ; and

　(ii) in any other case, on the date of the notice ;

and if more than one such notice is given or sent, on the date determined by reference to the first such notice ;

(*c*) in relation to any such sum to which neither sub-paragraph (*a*) nor sub-paragraph (*b*) of this paragraph applies, on such date as the Secretary of State determines.

(2) Where a question arises whether the right to payment of any sum by way of benefit has been extinguished by the operation of this regulation and the determining authority is satisfied that—

(a) after the expiration of the said period of twelve months the Secretary of State has received written notice requesting payment of that sum ; and

(b) throughout the period commencing within the said period of twelve months and continuing up to the date on which the said notice was given there was good cause for not giving that notice ;

the said period of twelve months shall be extended to the date on which the determining authority decides that question and for the purposes of the operation of this regulation thereafter the right to payment of that sum shall, notwithstanding the provisions of paragraph (1) of this regulation, be treated as having arisen on that date.

PART IV

Miscellaneous provisions

Persons unable to act

6.—(1) Where a person by whom benefit is receivable or is alleged to be receivable is or becomes unable for the time being to act, the Secretary of State may, upon written application being made to him, appoint any person who has attained the age of eighteen, whom he may consider suitable and who is prepared to be so appointed, to exercise on behalf of the person unable to act any right to which that person may be entitled under the Act and to receive and deal with any sums payable on behalf of that person ; and the receipt of any person appointed under this regulation shall be a good discharge to the Secretary of State for any sum paid.

(2) The Secretary of State may at any time in his discretion revoke any appointment made under paragraph (1) of this regulation and any person appointed under the said paragraph (1) may, on giving the Secretary of State not less than one month's notice in writing of his intention so to do, terminate his appointment.

Effect of death on claims and payments

7.—(1) A claim shall be treated as having lapsed if—

(a) in a case where a man and a woman were included in the family in respect of which the claim was made, that man and that woman have both died before any determination making benefit payable on the claim has been made ;

(b) in any other case, where the man or the single woman included in the family in respect of which the claim was made has died before any determination making benefit payable on the claim has been made.

(2) On the death of a person by whom benefit is receivable, the Secretary of State may, upon written application being made to him, appoint such person who has attained the age of eighteen as he may consider suitable, and who is prepared to be so appointed, to exercise the rights that the deceased would have had under the Act in relation to the claim in respect of which benefit was receivable by the deceased and may pay sums on account of benefit determined to be due under such claim to any person who has attained the age of eighteen and who satisfies him that he will apply them for the benefit of any surviving member of the family for which benefit was determined to be payable.

(3) Where the right to payment of any sum on account of benefit receivable by a deceased person was not extinguished at the date of his death, the period of twelve months referred to in regulation 5 of these regulations shall be calculated from the date on which the right to payment of that sum is treated as having arisen in relation to any such person as is referred to in paragraph (2) of this regulation, so, however, that this paragraph shall not apply to any sum on account of benefit for the payment of which written application has not been made to the Secretary of State within twelve months after the date of death or within such longer period as the Secretary of State may allow in any particular case.

(4) The receipt of any person to whom benefit is paid under paragraph (2) of this regulation shall be a good discharge to the Secretary of State.

Suspension of payment of benefit

8. Where it appears to the Secretary of State that a question has arisen whether a determination by a determining authority awarding benefit ought to be revised in accordance with regulation 11 of the Family Income Supplements (General) Regulations 1971(**a**), he may direct that payment of the benefit shall be suspended in whole or in part until that question has been decided.

Keith Joseph,
Secretary of State for
Social Services.
11th February 1971.

EXPLANATORY NOTE

(This Note is not part of the Regulations.)

These Regulations provide for the manner in which claims for, and payments of, family income supplements under the Family Income Supplements Act 1970 are to be made.

Part I of the Regulations contains various definitions which are relevant for the succeeding Parts of the Regulations ; Part II of the Regulations contains provisions relating to the manner in which claims for supplements are to be made and to the information to be given in connection with such claims ; Part III of the Regulations contains provisions relating to the time and manner of payment of supplements and to the extinguishment of the right to receive sums on account of supplements where payment is not obtained in time ; and Part IV of the Regulations contains miscellaneous provisions relating to claimants who are unable to act or have died and to suspension of payment of supplements pending review decisions by the Supplementary Benefits Commission or the Appeal Tribunal.

(a) S.I. 1971/226 (1971 I, p. 652).

STATUTORY INSTRUMENTS

1971 No. 228

LONDON GOVERNMENT

The London Authorities (Parks and Open Spaces) Order 1971

Made - - - 11*th February* 1971

Whereas section 58(2) of the London Government Act 1963(**a**) required the Greater London Council to prepare and submit to the Minister of Housing and Local Government a scheme with respect to the retention or transfer of the land (being parks and open spaces) referred to in the said subsection ;

And whereas article 8 of the London Authorities (Property etc.) Order 1964(**b**) and article 5(2) of the London Government Order 1966(**c**) required the inclusion of certain further lands in the said scheme ;

And whereas certain schemes made under article 9 of the said order of 1964 and confirmed by the said Minister made the like requirement in respect of certain lands referred to therein ;

And whereas the Greater London Council submitted the said scheme to the said Minister on 8th October 1969 ;

And whereas the functions of the said Minister were transferred to the Secretary of State by the Secretary of State for the Environment Order 1970(**d**) ;

And whereas, under the said section 58(2), the Secretary of State for the Environment is empowered by order, after such consultation as is there specified, to give effect to the said scheme without modification or with such modifications as he thinks fit or to make such other provision for the retention by the Greater London Council, or the transfer to one, or to two or more jointly, of the London borough councils, of any of the land comprised in the scheme as appears to him appropriate ;

And whereas the said section 58(2) provides that any reference therein to a London borough council shall be construed as including a reference to the Common Council of the City of London and, in relation to any land outside Greater London, as including a reference to the council of any county or county district in whose area any of the land is situated :

Now therefore the Secretary of State for the Environment, after consultation with the Greater London Council and the other local authorities referred to in section 58(2) of the London Government Act 1963, in exercise of his powers under the said section 58(2) as extended as aforesaid, hereby makes the following order :—

(**a**) 1963 c. 33. (**b**) S.I. 1964/1464 (1964 III, p. 3392).
(**c**) S.I. 1966/1305 (1966 III, p. 3627). (**d**) S.I. 1970/1681 (1970 III, p. 5551).

Title, commencement and interpretation

1. This order may be cited as the London Authorities (Parks and Open Spaces) Order 1971, and shall come into operation with the London Authorities (Parks and Open Spaces) (Staff) Order 1971(**a**) and the London Authorities (Parks and Open Spaces) (Miscellaneous Property) Order 1971(**b**).

2.—(1) The Interpretation Act 1889(**c**) shall apply for the interpretation of this order as it applies for the interpretation of an Act of Parliament.

(2) In this order—

"article 4" means article 4 of this order ;

"land" includes land covered by water and any interest or right in, to or over land ; and

"transferee authority", in respect of any land transferred by article 4, means the authority to whom that land is so transferred.

(3) In this order, unless the context otherwise requires, references to any enactment shall be construed as references to that enactment as amended, extended or applied by or under any other enactment or by this order.

Retention of lands by Greater London Council

3. The Greater London Council shall retain the lands described in Schedule 1 to this order, freed henceforth from any obligations created by or in respect of section 58(2) of the London Government Act 1963.

Transfer of lands

4. Any land described in column (1) of Schedule 2 to this order and all liabilities attaching to the Greater London Council in respect of any such land shall by virtue of this order be transferred to and vest in or attach to the authority described in relation to such land in column (2), and—

> (*a*) all contracts, deeds, bonds, agreements and other instruments subsisting in favour of, or against, and all notices in force which were given (or have effect as if they had been given) by, or to, the Greater London Council in respect of such land and liabilities shall be of full force and effect in favour of, or against, the authority described as aforesaid ; and

> (*b*) any action or proceeding or any cause of action or proceeding, pending or existing at 1st April 1971, by, or against, the Greater London Council in respect of such land and liabilities shall not be prejudicially affected by reason of this order, and may be continued, prosecuted and enforced by, or against, the authority described as aforesaid.

5. Any land or liability transferred by article 4 to the authority for any area shall be held or discharged by them in respect of the area.

6. Unless the context otherwise requires, in the application of any enactment to land transferred by article 4, for any reference to the Greater London Council there shall be substituted a reference to the transferee authority.

(**a**) 1971/229(1971 I, p. 681).   (**b**) 1971/230(1971 I, p. 685).
(**c**) 1889 c. 63.

7. Any byelaws in force for the regulation of any land transferred by article 4 shall have effect as if they had been made by the transferee authority.

8. Any legal proceedings pending on 1st April 1971 may be amended in such manner as may be necessary or proper in consequence of this order.

9. Where under this order or any adjustment made in consequence hereof any liability or part of a liability charged indifferently on all the revenues of a public body or on any particular revenues or fund of such body is transferred to another public body, the liability or part of the liability shall be charged indifferently on all the revenues of the public body to whom it is transferred and shall cease to be a charge on any revenues or fund of the public body from whom it is transferred.

In this article, 'public body' and 'revenues' have the same meanings as in the Local Government Act 1933(**a**).

10. Where by virtue of this order any matter in respect of which, if this order had not been made, sums would have become due and owing to a consolidated loans fund is transferred to an authority other than the authority by whom such fund is maintained on and after 1st April 1971, such sums shall be paid by the first-mentioned authority to the authority by whom the fund is maintained.

Covenants affecting land

11. Unless the Greater London Council and the transferee authority otherwise agree, section 62 of the Law of Property Act 1925(**b**) (which implies certain words in conveyances of land, subject to the terms of the conveyance and the provisions therein contained) shall have effect—

 (a) in respect of any land transferred by article 4 ; and

 (b) in respect of any land, being land vested in the Greater London Council, which is affected by the said transfer,

as if the land described in (a) and (b) respectively had been the subject of a conveyance on 1st April 1971.

Arbitration

12. Any dispute arising under this order or in consequence thereof shall be determined by an arbitrator appointed by agreement between the parties in dispute or, in default of agreement, by the Secretary of State for the Environment and, subject as aforesaid, the provisions of the Arbitration Act 1950(**c**) shall apply to any arbitration under this article.

SCHEDULE 1   Article 3

LANDS RETAINED BY THE GREATER LONDON COUNCIL

PARKS AND OPEN SPACES

Abbey Wood Park

Avery Hill Park and Nursery

Battersea Park

Bostall Heath together with the extension thereof comprising land south of Bostall Heath adjoining Old Park Road

Bostall Woods

(**a**) 1933 c. 51.   (**b**) 1925 c. 20.
(**c**) 1950 c. 27.

Brickfield Gardens together with the extension thereof comprising 240 Burdett Road and 58 Turner's Road

Land at the junction of Brockley Hill and Wood Lane in the London borough of Harrow

Burdett Gardens together with the extension thereof comprising 290 Roman Road

Castlewood

Clinton Road Open Space in the London borough of Tower Hamlets comprising—
37, 39 and 99 Clinton Road
22 Longfellow's Road
19 Whitman Road

Cutty Sark Gardens together with the extension thereof comprising 2 to 6 (even) Wood Wharf and other land at Wood Wharf

Daubeney Road Recreation Ground in the London borough of Hackney

Dulwich Park

Eltham Common

Eltham Park North

Eltham Park South

Falconwood Field

Finsbury Park together with the Training Centre therein

Geffrye's Garden together with the extension thereof comprising 63 to 81 (odd) Geffrye Street and 34 Cremer Street

Golders Hill

Grims Dyke Golf Course (part only)

Grims Dyke Mansion and outbuildings

Hackney Marsh

Hainault Forest

Hampstead Heath

Hampstead Heath Extension

The Hill, Hampstead

Holland Park and Holland Park House

Jackwood

Kenwood

King George's Field, Eltham

King George's Fields in the London borough of Tower Hamlets together with the extension thereof comprising—
6 Burdett Road
13, 15, 29 to 33 (odd) and 41 to 49 (odd) Canal Road
1, 3 and 11 to 21 (odd) Ewing Street
2 to 4 (consecutive) 9, 14 and 15 Forester Street
548 to 552 (even) and 558 Mile End Road
5 to 11 (consecutive) and 25 to 27 (consecutive) Maidman Street
2 Rhodeswell Road
5 to 11 (odd) St Paul's Way
57, 59, 59A and 61 to 73 (odd) Solebay Street
123 Timothy Road
Paul's House (Flats 1 to 10) Timothy Road
2 to 20 (even), 1 to 7 (odd) and 11 to 13 (odd) Venour Road

King's Stairs Gardens in the London borough of Southwark together with the extension thereof comprising 43 to 63 (odd), 53A Rotherhithe Street and Yardley's Wharf

Lesnes Abbey Woods

Mabley Green

Marble Hill House and Park

Newdigate Estate, Harefield, in the London borough of Hillingdon

North Camberwell Open Space together with the extension thereof comprising—
3 to 13 (odd) Aboukir Street
27, 36 and part of 25 Addington Square
23, 27, 53 to 61 (odd), 81, 109 to 129 (odd), 195 to 199 (odd), 289 to 315 (odd), 399 and 409 Albany Road
Land at the rear of 385 to 399 (odd) Albany Road and Canal Towpath
52 to 56 (even) and 1 to 39 (odd) Caldew Street
2 to 8 (even), 20 to 38 (even) Calmington Road, and Addington Wharf, Camberwell Road
Land comprising the forecourt of 109 Camberwell Road
39 Chumleigh Street and adjoining stable
18 to 58 (even), 35 to 45 (odd) and 127 Cobourg Road
30 to 42 (even) and 43 to 49 (odd) Cowan Street
9 to 15 (odd) Dartnell Road
9 to 11 (consecutive) Glengall Terrace
59 to 65 (odd) Goldie Street
Land comprising former towpath of Grand Surrey Canal
Land on the north side of Grand Surrey Canal, and west of St George's Bridge
13 to 21 (odd) Herring Street
1 to 7 (odd), 11 to 25 (odd) and 35 Jardin Street
15 Loncroft Road
143 to 177 (odd), 178A to D and 205 to 215 (odd) Neate Street
67 to 81 (odd) New Church Road
Land adjoining 125 to 131 (odd) New Church Road
41 and 43 Odell Street
332 and 334 Old Kent Road
Land lying to the east of St George's Bridge
69, 145 and 171 to 175 (odd) St George's Way
The site of All Saints Church Hall and land adjoining at junction of St George's Way and Trafalgar Avenue
6 and 8 Sumner Road
73 Trafalgar Avenue
Land lying at the junction of Trafalgar Avenue and Canal Place
9 to 13 (odd) Villette Place
Port of London Authority factory on the south side of Willowbrook Grove adjoining the Towpath

Old Oak Common

Part of Oxhey Lane Farm, Hatch End

Oxleas Wood together with the extension thereof comprising—
162 (Flats 1 to 4), 176 and 178 Shooters Hill
Summerscourt
Warren Wood

Parliament Hill Field

The riverside open space between Westminster Bridge and the National Theatre site, known as South Bank, in the London borough of Lambeth

Stanmore Golf Course

Tower Hill Precinct extension comprising part of 93 The Minories and other land in The Minories and Vine Street together with part of the site of a private roadway, Trinity Place

Transport Farm, Stanmore

Warnham Court Nursery, Horsham, Sussex

Warren House Estate, Harrow

Wormwood Scrubs, other than an area of 10 acres or thereabouts on the southern boundary thereof

Part of Youngwood Farm, Northwood

MISCELLANEOUS LANDS

London borough of Bexley
Land comprising that part of the open space development at Thamesmead which is
  included in phases I and II of stage I of the said development

London borough of Brent
Approximately 0·1 acre of land fronting the former Harlesden Lane, forming part of
  Roundwood Park, Brent

London borough of Camden
Land surrounding Cranley Buildings forming part of Brookes Market

London borough of Greenwich
Land on the north side of Hyde Vale facing 38A to 54 Hyde Vale

London borough of Hackney
Land forming part of Clapton Pond Gardens
Land formerly the site of St Augustine's Church

London borough of Hammersmith
Land to the north of Australia Road forming part of the White City Estate
Land at the junction of Edith Road and North End Road

London borough of Hillingdon
Pelham Clinton Estate

London borough of Hounslow
Approximately one acre of land fronting Sunbury Way, forming part of Rectory
  Meadow, Hounslow

London borough of Islington
92 and 94 Pembroke Street
Land at the rear of 86 to 110 (even) Pembroke Street
119 Bemerton Street
45 to 51 (odd) St John's Way

London borough of Lambeth
1 Royal Street
16 to 28 (even) and 36 to 50 (even) Carlisle Lane
Land adjoining 22 Carlisle Lane
Land fronting Lambeth Palace Road

London borough of Lewisham
Land comprising Sectors F and G of the former Crystal Palace High Level Branch
  Railway
Boundary wall encroachment at 57 Westwood Park
Land bounded by London Road, Sydenham Hill and Sydenham Rise
75 Horniman Drive
3 and 4 Hill Rise
Land to the east of Hill Rise
Land to the south of 75 Horniman Drive
Land near Downderry Road, forming part of Woodland Walk

London borough of Southwark
Land adjoining Gray Street, forming part of Short Street Open Space
The fitted playground, Nelson Recreation Ground
The site of 1 to 15 (odd) Longville Road, Southwark
106 to 110 (consecutive) Snowsfields
Land forming units 9 to 14 (consecutive) at 32 Tyers Gate
Land adjoining the east side of unit 14 Leathermarket Gardens

London borough of Tower Hamlets
Land forming part of and held for extension to Commemoration Park
Land forming part of Island Gardens Extension
Prince's Square (otherwise known as Swedenborg Square)

City of Westminster
47 to 51 (odd), part of 39 and part of 41 Hampden Crescent
56 and 58 Torquay Street, Westbourne Green

London boroughs of Bromley and Lewisham
Land at the western end of Lower Marvel's Wood

SCHEDULE 2 Article 4

LANDS TRANSFERRED BY ARTICLE 4

(1)	(2)
Lands transferred	*Transferee authority*
Kennington Park	The corporation of the London borough of Lambeth
Little Wormwood Scrubs	The corporation of the London borough of Hammersmith
Pepys Park and part of the former Royal Victoria Yard	The corporation of the London borough of Lewisham
Land for addition to Dante Road Open Space comprising— 134 Brook Drive 1A to 1F and 2 to 46 (even) Dante Road 1 to 19 (odd), 8 to 72 (even), 76 and 77 Holyoak Road 106 to 118 (even) Newington Butts	The corporation of the London borough of Southwark
Clapham Common	The corporation of the London borough of Lambeth
Tooting Common	The corporation of the London borough of Wandsworth
Beckenham Place Park	The corporation of the London borough of Lewisham
Dumsey Meadows, Staines Laleham House, Staines Land adjoining the towpath near Laleham House, Staines River Park Estate, Staines	The county council of the administrative county of Surrey
Any other land within section 58(2) of the London Government Act 1963 as extended as described in the second and third recitals to this order situated in—	
(a) the City of London	The corporation of the City of London
(b) a London borough	The corporation of the London borough
(c) a county district	The corporation or the council, as may by appropriate, of the county district

Peter Walker,
Secretary of State for the Environment.

11th February 1971.

EXPLANATORY NOTE

(This Note is not part of the Order.)

This Order gives effect, with minor modifications, to the scheme made by the Greater London Council for the redistribution between local authorities in and near Greater London of the ownership and management of certain parks and open spaces vested in that Council.

This Order is to come into operation with the London Authorities (Parks and Open Spaces) (Staff) Order 1971 and the London Authorities (Parks and Open Spaces) (Miscellaneous Property) Order 1971 for which the operative date is 1st April 1971.

STATUTORY   INSTRUMENTS

1971 No. 229

LONDON GOVERNMENT

The London Authorities (Parks and Open Spaces) (Staff) Order 1971

Made - - - -	11*th February* 1971
Laid before Parliament	19*th February* 1971
Coming into Operation	1*st April* 1971

The Secretary of State for the Environment, in exercise of his powers under sections 84 and 85 of the London Government Act 1963(**a**) and of all other powers enabling him in that behalf, hereby makes the following order: —

Title, commencement and interpretation

1. This order may be cited as the London Authorities (Parks and Open Spaces) (Staff) Order 1971, and shall come into operation on 1st April 1971.

2.—(1) The Interpretation Act 1889(**b**) shall apply for the interpretation of this order as it applies for the interpretation of an Act of Parliament.

(2) In this order—

" officer " includes the holder of any place, situation or employment ;

" Parks order " means the London Authorities (Parks and Open Spaces) Order 1971(**c**) ;

" transferred park " means a park or open space transferred by article 4 of the Parks order ; and

"transferee authority " has the same meaning as in the Parks order.

Transfer of staff

3.—(1) Any officer of the Greater London Council who is employed wholly or mainly in or in connection with a park or parks transferred to a transferee authority shall be transferred to the employment of that transferee authority.

(2) (*a*) Where, immediately before 1st April 1971, any officer has not taken up the duties of his employment he shall be deemed, in the application of paragraph (1), to be discharging such duties, and to be employed in the transferred park in which he would be employed if he had taken up such duties.

(*b*) Where any officer is, immediately before 1st April 1971, absent from his normal duties for the purpose of undergoing training, paragraph (1) shall apply—

(i) if it was part of the arrangements under which he is so absent that at the completion of such training he should be employed in a place, situation or employment different from the place, situation or employ-

---

(a) 1963 c. 33.   (b) 1889 c. 63.   (c) S.I. 1971/228(1971 I, p. 673).

ment which he occupied prior to the commencement of the training, as if he was, immediately before 1st April 1971, occupying such different place, situation or employment ;

(ii) otherwise, as if he was, immediately before 1st April 1971, occupying the place, situation or employment which he occupied immediately prior to the commencement of such training.

(c) Where any officer is, immediately before 1st April 1971, absent from his normal duties otherwise than for the purpose of undergoing training he shall be deemed, in the application of paragraph (1), to be discharging such duties, and to be discharging them in the transferred park in which he normally discharges them.

(3) (a) Any question whether an officer is employed in the manner described in paragraph (1) shall be determined by a tribunal established under section 12 of the Industrial Training Act 1964(a). References to such tribunal may be made as soon as may be and in any case not later than 30th April 1971.

(b) Where any question that an officer is not, or is, employed in the manner described in paragraph (1) is outstanding on 1st April 1971 the officer shall not be transferred until the expiration of the second week following that in which the decision of the tribunal is notified.

Officers appointed before 1st April 1971

4. Where a transferee authority, before 1st April 1971, with the consent of the Greater London Council, appoint to hold any place, situation or employment before or as from that day any person (hereinafter referred to as " the officer ") who, but for that appointment, would fall to be transferred under article 3(1), the officer in that appointment shall be deemed to have been transferred by article 3(1).

Saving for certain staff

5. Subject to article 4, nothing in article 3 applies—

(a) to any person who will, by virtue of any agreement entered into between him and any authority before 1st April 1971, enter into the employment of that authority on that date ; or

(b) to any person as regards any employment which is to be terminated on 31st March 1971.

Secondary transfers

6. Any officer transferred by article 3(1) to a transferee authority may, before 1st July 1971, be transferred by the said authority with the agreement of any other such authority and of the officer to the employment of that authority, and this order shall continue to apply to him.

Protection of staff

7.—(1)(a) Every officer transferred (or deemed to have been transferred) by article 3(1) to the employment of a transferee authority shall, so long as he continues in that employment by virtue of the transfer or appointment and until he is served with a statement in writing of new terms and conditions of

---

(a) 1964 c. 16.

employment, enjoy terms and conditions of employment not less favourable than those he enjoyed immediately before 1st April 1971. The said new terms and conditions shall be such that—-

(i) so long as the officer is engaged in duties reasonably comparable to those in which he was engaged immediately before 1st April 1971, the scale of his salary or remuneration, and

(ii) the other terms and conditions of his employment,

are not less favourable than those he enjoyed immediately before 1st April 1971, and any question whether duties are reasonably comparable as aforesaid shall be determined by a tribunal established under section 12 of the Industrial Training Act 1964. The statement of new terms and conditions shall contain information that any question shall be so determined and as to the person and address to whom any question should be referred.

(*b*) A statement of new terms and conditions of employment shall not be served in respect of any officer in relation to whom a question has been referred under article 3(3)(*a*) until the decision of the tribunal has been notified.

(*c*) If after service of a statement of new terms and conditions of employment upon him a question is referred in respect of an officer under article 3(3)(*a*), the statement shall cease to have effect, sub-paragraph (*a*) of this paragraph shall have effect as if the statement had not been served, and no new statement shall be served until the decision on the question has been notified.

(2) A written statement given in accordance with section 4(1) of the Contracts of Employment Act 1963(a) shall not be regarded as a statement of new terms and conditions of employment for the purposes of paragraph (1) unless the statement so indicates.

Saving for dispensations

8. Any dispensation from the requirements of any regulation granted to the Greater London Council shall have effect, in relation to any officer transferred (or deemed to have been transferred) by article 3(1), as if it had been granted to the authority to whose employment he has been transferred (or is deemed to have been transferred).

Saving for extensions of service

9. Any extension of service under section 7(1) of the Local Government Superannuation Act 1937(b) effective on 1st April 1971 in relation to an officer transferred (or deemed to have been transferred) by article 3(1) shall continue to have effect as if it had been made by the authority to whose employment he has been transferred (or is deemed to have been transferred).

Appointment of assessor

10. On any reference under article 3(3)(*a*) or 7 the tribunal may, if they think fit, appoint a person having special knowledge or experience in relation to the subject matter of the reference to sit with them as assessor.

(a) 1963 c. 49.   (b) 1937 c. 68.

Superannuation

11.—(1) Where an officer who, immediately before his transfer (or deemed transfer) to an authority by article 3(1)—

(*a*) was subject to an election in consequence of which he did not participate in the benefits of the superannuation fund maintained by the Greater London Council under Part I of the Local Government Superannuation Act 1937 ; and

(*b*) had an expectation of a gratuity payable according to years of service,

that election shall remain in effect and such a gratuity shall, subject to terms and conditions which are not less beneficial, be payable by that authority in respect of his previous service and of any service rendered to that authority.

(2) Section 35 of the Local Government Superannuation Act 1937 shall apply to an expectation under this article as it applies to a right under that Act.

Protection of housing accommodation

12. Where, immediately before 1st April 1971, an officer of the Greater London Council occupied a dwelling (whether as a tenant or otherwise) provided by that Council in connection with, or as a term of, his employment and—

(*a*) he is transferred (or deemed to have been transferred) by this order but the dwelling is not transferred by the Parks order ; or

(*b*) he is so transferred (or deemed to have been transferred) to any authority but the dwelling is transferred by the Parks order to another authority ; or

(*c*) he is not so transferred (or deemed to have been transferred) but the dwelling is transferred by the Parks order,

nothing in this order shall prejudice that occupation and for the purposes of that occupation the authority in whom the dwelling is vested shall permit the authority by whom the officer is employed to deal with the dwelling as if it were vested in that authority, and that authority shall make any necessary payment to the authority in whom the dwelling is vested to take account of the occupation of the dwelling by the officer.

Peter Walker,

11th February 1971.   Secretary of State for the Environment.

EXPLANATORY NOTE

(This Note is not part of the Order.)

The London Authorities (Parks and Open Spaces) Order 1971 redistributes the ownership and management of certain parks and open spaces vested in the Greater London Council between local authorities in and near Greater London. This Order makes consequential provision as to the transfer and protection of staff.

STATUTORY INSTRUMENTS

1971 No. 230

LONDON GOVERNMENT

The London Authorities (Parks and Open Spaces)
(Miscellaneous Property) Order 1971

Made - - - -	11*th February* 1971
Laid before Parliament	19*th February* 1971
Coming into Operation	1*st April* 1971

The Secretary of State for the Environment, in exercise of his powers under section 84 of the London Government Act 1963(a) and of all other powers enabling him in that behalf, hereby makes the following order:—

Title, commencement and interpretation

1. This order may be cited as the London Authorities (Parks and Open Spaces) (Miscellaneous Property) Order 1971, and shall come into operation on 1st April 1971.

2.—(1) The Interpretation Act 1889(b) shall apply for the interpretation of this order as it applies for the interpretation of an Act of Parliament.

(2) In this order—

"Parks order" means the London Authorities (Parks and Open Spaces) Order 1971(c);

"transferred park" means a park or open space transferred by article 4 of the Parks order; and

"transferee authority" has the same meaning as in the Parks order.

Transfer of certain property

3.—(1) Any property described in column (1) of the schedule to this order and all liabilities attaching to the Greater London Council in respect of any such property shall by virtue of this order be transferred to and vest in or attach to the authority described in relation to such property in column (2), and—

(*a*) all contracts, deeds, bonds, agreements and other instruments subsisting in favour of, or against, and all notices in force which were given (or having effect as if they had been given) by, or to, the Greater London

---

(a) 1963 c. 33.   (b) 1889 c. 63.
(c) S.I. 1971/228 (1971 I, p. 673).

Council in respect of such property and liabilities shall be of full force and effect in favour of, or against, the authority described as aforesaid; and

(b) any action or proceeding or any cause of action or proceeding, pending or existing at 1st April 1971, by, or against, the Greater London Council in respect of such property and liabilities shall not be prejudicially affected by reason of this order, and may be continued, prosecuted and enforced by, or against, the authority described as aforesaid.

(2) Articles 5 to 12 of the Parks order shall apply as if paragraph (1) were contained in the said order.

Compulsory purchase orders

4. Any order authorising the compulsory acquisition of land by the Greater London Council for the purpose of providing or extending a park or open space (whether confirmed before the coming into operation of this order or submitted for confirmation before or after such coming into operation) may be amended by the Secretary of State by the substitution, as the authority to be authorised to acquire the land comprised therein, of one or more of the following councils, namely the London borough councils, the Common Council of the City of London and, in relation to any land outside Greater London, the councils of counties and county districts in whose area any of the land is situated, and thereafter the order shall have effect, or be considered and if confirmed have effect, accordingly.

Article 3

SCHEDULE

PROPERTY TRANSFERRED BY ARTICLE 3

(1) Property transferred	(2) Transferee authority
Land acquired or appropriated by the Greater London Council for the extension of St. Luke's Churchyard Open Space 12 Barnsbury Road, Islington	The corporation of the London borough of Islington
12, 26 and 77 St Agnes Place, Kennington Land appropriated by the Greater London Council for the extension of Kennington Park 55 Millbrook Road, Lambeth	The corporation of the London borough of Lambeth
35 Drakefell Road, Lewisham	The corporation of the London borough of Lewisham
2 Manthorpe Road, Greenwich	The corporation of the London borough of Greenwich
66 and 72 St. Rule Street, Wandsworth	The corporation of the London borough of Wandsworth

Land appropriated by the Greater London Council for the provision of the Barley Mow Open Space	The corporation of the London borough of Tower Hamlets
Land appropriated by the Greater London Council for the extension of the Bartlett Park Open Space	

Any moveable buildings, structures, fittings, furniture, equipment, plant, stores or materials sited on or held for the purposes of—

any transferred park or other land transferred by article 4 of the Parks order	The transferee authority
any land included in this Schedule	The corporation or council to whom such land is transferred

11th February 1971.

Peter Walker,
Secretary of State for the Environment.

EXPLANATORY NOTE

(This Note is not part of the Order.)

The London Authorities (Parks and Open Spaces) Order 1971 redistributes the ownership and management of certain parks and open spaces vested in the Greater London Council between local authorities in and near Greater London. This Order makes consequential provision as to the transfer of certain additional property.

STATUTORY INSTRUMENTS

1971 No. 231

LONDON GOVERNMENT

The London Authorities (Transfer of Housing Estates etc.) Order 1971

Made - - - -	11*th February* 1971
Laid before Parliament	19*th February* 1971
Coming into Operation	22*nd February* 1971

Whereas the Greater London Council and the councils of certain London boroughs have requested the Secretary of State for the Environment to provide by an order under section 23(3) of the London Government Act 1963(a) for the transfer of certain housing accommodation for the time being vested in the Greater London Council;

And whereas the said councils have agreed the terms of such transfer;

And whereas the Secretary of State is required by the said section 23(3) to give effect to those terms;

And whereas certain further matters appear to the Secretary of State necessary and proper for the purposes of or in consequence of that transfer:

Now therefore the Secretary of State for the Environment, in exercise of his powers under sections 23(3), 84 and 85 of the London Government Act 1963 and all other powers enabling him in that behalf, hereby makes the following order:—

Title, commencement and interpretation

1. This order may be cited as the London Authorities (Transfer of Housing Estates etc.) Order 1971, and shall come into operation on 22nd February 1971.

2.—(1) The Interpretation Act 1889(b) shall apply for the interpretation of this order as it applies for the interpretation of an Act of Parliament.

(2) In this order—

"the deposited Schedule" means the Schedule "Properties transferred by article 3 of the London Authorities (Transfer of Housing Estates etc.) Order 1971" prepared in duplicate and signed by an Assistant Secretary in the Department of the Environment and as to which further provision is made in article 3(2);

"officer" includes the holder of any place, situation or employment;

"the Secretary of State" means the Secretary of State for the Environment; and

"transferee authority", in relation to housing accommodation transferred by article 3, means the London borough council to whom that accommodation is so transferred.

(a) 1963 c. 33.   (b) 1889 c. 63.

(3) In the articles of this order, unless the context otherwise requires, any reference to housing accommodation shall include—

    (*a*) a reference to garages, parking spaces and estate amenities; and

    (*b*) a reference to shops where any such shop gives such access to a dwelling transferred by article 3 as to render the said shop and dwelling suitable for occupation by a single occupier;

and references to an area of housing accommodation shall be construed accordingly.

(4) In this order, unless the context otherwise requires, references to any enactment shall be construed as references to that enactment as amended, extended or applied by or under any other enactment or by this order.

(5) Any reference in this order to a numbered article shall, unless the reference is to an article of a specified order, be construed as a reference to the article bearing that number in this order.

(6) Any reference in any article of this order to a numbered paragraph shall, unless the reference is to a paragraph of a specified article, be construed as a reference to the paragraph bearing that number in the first-mentioned article.

Transfer of property

3.—(1) Subject to the provisions of article 13(3) and of Part III of Schedule 1 to this order, on 1st April 1971 any property described in any Part of the deposited Schedule and all liabilities (other than liabilities in respect of money borrowed) attaching to the Greater London Council in respect of any such property shall by virtue of this order be transferred to and vest in or attach to the authority named in the description of such Part, and—

    (*a*) all contracts, deeds, bonds, agreements and other instruments subsisting in favour of, or against, and all notices in force which were given (or having effect as if they had been given) by, or to, the Greater London Council in respect of such property and liabilities shall be of full force and effect in favour of, or against, the authority named as aforesaid; and

    (*b*) any action or proceeding or any cause of action or proceeding, pending or existing at 1st April 1971, by, or against, the Greater London Council in respect of such property and liabilities shall not be prejudicially affected by reason of this order, and may be continued, prosecuted and enforced by, or against, the authority named as aforesaid.

(2) One duplicate of the deposited Schedule is deposited in the offices of the Secretary of State and the other in the offices of the Greater London Council. Copies of the deposited Schedule have been deposited with the transferee authorities and shall be open to inspection at all reasonable times.

(3) Nothing in paragraph (1) shall affect any grant or subsidy receivable by the Greater London Council in respect of housing accommodation transferred by that paragraph.

4. Any property or liability transferred by article 3 to the authority for any area shall be held or discharged by them in respect of the area.

5. Any byelaws in force for the regulation of any property transferred by the said article shall have effect as if they had been made by the authority to whom such property is transferred.

6. Any legal proceedings pending at 1st April 1971 may be amended in such manner as may be necessary or proper in consequence of this order.

7. Where under this order or any adjustment made in consequence hereof any liability or part of a liability charged indifferently on all the revenues of a public body or on any particular revenues or fund of such body is transferred to another public body, the liability or part of the liability shall be charged indifferently on all the revenues of the public body to whom it is transferred and shall cease to be a charge on any revenues or fund of the public body from whom it is transferred.

In this article, 'public body' and 'revenues' have the same meanings as in the Local Government Act 1933(a).

8. Where by virtue of this order any matter in respect of which, if this order had not been made, sums would have become due and owing to a consolidated loans fund is transferred to an authority other than the authority by whom such fund is maintained on and after 1st April 1971, such sums shall be paid by the first-mentioned authority to the authority by whom the fund is maintained.

Covenants affecting property

9. Unless the Greater London Council and the transferee authority otherwise agree, section 62 of the Law of Property Act 1925(b) (which implies certain words in conveyances of land, subject to the terms of the conveyance and the provisions therein contained) shall have effect—

  (*a*) in respect of any property transferred by article 3; and

  (*b*) in respect of any property, being property vested in the Greater London Council, which is affected by the said transfer,

as if the property described in (*a*) and (*b*) respectively had been the subject of a conveyance on 1st April 1971.

10.—(1) This article applies to any land within the extent of an area of housing accommodation transferred by article 3, being land in respect of which the Greater London Council have powers under section 151 of the Housing Act 1957(c) to enforce covenants entered into on the sale or exchange of land.

  (2) In respect of any land to which this article applies—

  (*a*) the Greater London Council shall consult with the transferee authority before exercising their powers under the said section 151;

  (*b*) the transferee authority may require the Greater London Council to exercise the said powers in any case where such exercise is requisite in the interests of the area of housing accommodation within the extent of which the land is situated.

  (3) The Greater London Council shall notify the transferee authority of any land to which this article applies and provide sufficient particulars of the covenants to which the said section 151 relates.

11. Any covenant (not being a covenant affected by article 10) which would be enforceable by the Greater London Council immediately before 1st April 1971 in respect of land within the extent of an area of housing accommodation

---

    (a) 1933 c. 51.   (b) 1925 c. 20.
    (c) 1957 c. 56.

transferred by article 3, being land which was sold or exchanged by the Greater London Council or by the London County Council and, immediately before such sale or exchange, was held by them for the purposes of the Housing Act 1957 or of any Act re-enacted by that Act, shall be of full force and effect in favour of the transferee authority.

Rent books

12. Until a new rent book is issued by a transferee authority in respect of any housing accommodation transferred by article 3, notification to the tenant of the said accommodation of that transfer shall be deemed to be a compliance by the said authority as landlord with the requirements of section 2(1)(*a*) of the Landlord and Tenant Act 1962**(a)**.

Terms of transfer of housing accommodation

13.—(1) A transferee authority shall make payments to the Greater London Council in accordance with the provisions of Part I of Schedule 1 to this order.

(2) The Greater London Council shall pay to a transferee authority sums calculated in accordance with the provisions of Part II of the said Schedule.

(3) The Greater London Council shall discharge the liabilities described in Part III of the said Schedule.

Housing Revenue Account

14. Notwithstanding the provisions of paragraphs 1 and 2 of Schedule 5 to the Housing (Financial Provisions) Act 1958**(b)**, the Greater London Council and each transferee authority shall enter in their Housing Revenue Account any sums receivable or payable under or by virtue of this order, being sums which relate to matters which would have been so entered if this order had not been made.

Nomination rights

15.—(1) Until 1st April 1983 the Greater London Council may, without payment, nominate tenants to such proportion of the vacancies in the dwellings transferred by article 3 to a transferee authority, not exceeding 65 per centum of such vacancies, as they may determine from time to time.

(2) Without prejudice to paragraph (1), the Greater London Council may agree with a transferee authority, before 1st April 1983 in respect of nominations in excess of the said 65 per centum, or after that date as to any nominations, and any such agreement may include such terms (whether as to payment or otherwise) as may be agreed between the parties or, in default of agreement, as may be determined by the Secretary of State or by an arbitrator appointed by him.

(3) Nothing in this article shall affect any agreement as to nominations subsisting between the Greater London Council and a London borough council at the coming into operation of this order.

(a) 1962 c. 50.   **(b)** 1958 c. 42.

Notices to be given

16. To enable the Greater London Council to provide the Secretary of State with such information as he may require from time to time in order to determine any question relating to a grant or subsidy or the amount thereof, a transferee authority shall notify the Greater London Council of any action taken in respect of any housing accommodation transferred by article 3, being such action as may affect the payment of such a grant or subsidy or the amount thereof.

17.—(1) This article applies to each financial year until 1st April 1974.

(2) Where the Greater London Council—

(*a*) have, as from 1st April or any later date in any year, applied a general increase to the rents payable on housing accommodation provided by them; or

(*b*) have resolved to apply (whether or not they have authority to apply) any such general increase as from 31st March next following, or any earlier date,

they shall give notice to that effect to each transferee authority not later than 31st December in the said year.

(3) A notice given under paragraph (2) shall include sufficient details of how the increase would have applied to the housing accommodation transferred under article 3 to the transferee authority concerned if the transfer had not been effected.

(4) The Greater London Council shall provide to each transferee authority sufficient information from time to time of the cost and functioning of the rent rebate scheme operated by them under section 113 of the Housing Act 1957.

(5) The Greater London Council shall notify each transferee authority by 30th September in each year of their estimate of the average cost of maintenance and management of each dwelling owned by them in the year concerned, such notice including separate particulars as to flats and other housing accommodation so owned.

Transfer of staff

18.—(1) Any officer of the Greater London Council described in column (1) of Part I of Schedule 2 to this order shall, on 1st April 1971, be transferred to the employment of the authority specified opposite that description in column (2).

(2) In Part I of Schedule 2, references to employment or to a place of employment are references to such employment or place on 31st March 1971.

19.—(1) The Greater London Council shall notify to each transferee authority the number of officers employed on maintenance operations within each class described in Part II of Schedule 2 to this order who are available for transfer to that authority.

(2) On receipt of a notification under paragraph (1), the transferee authority shall inform the Greater London Council of the number in each such class (not exceeding that notified) acceptable to the authority for such transfer.

(3) In respect of each transferee authority, the Greater London Council shall notify the accepted number of officers of each class described as aforesaid of their intended transfer to that authority.

(4) Any officer notified by the Greater London Council under the last fore-going paragraph shall, on 1st April 1971, be transferred to the employment of the transferee authority.

(5) Where, before the transfer of any officer under this article, that officer resigns from the service of the Greater London Council, that Council shall notify another officer of the like description, and paragraph (4) shall apply to such officer as it applied to the first-mentioned officer:

Provided that nothing in this paragraph shall apply where there is no such officer of the Greater London Council who would be surplus to the requirements of the Council after the date of transfer.

20. Any officer of the Greater London Council in the grade of clerical officer 1, clerical officer 2 or housing officer 1 who applies to that Council to be transferred to the employment of a transferee authority shall, if that Council and that authority so agree, be transferred, on 1st April 1971, to the employment of the last-mentioned authority.

21.—(1) Where, immediately before 1st April 1971, any officer has not taken up the duties of his employment he shall be deemed, in the application of article 18 or 19, to be discharging such duties, and to be employed in connection with the area of housing accommodation at which he would be employed if he had taken up such duties.

(2) Where any officer is, immediately before 1st April 1971, absent from his normal duties for the purpose of undergoing training, article 18 or 19 shall apply—

    (i) if it was part of the arrangements under which he is so absent that at the completion of such training he should be employed in a place, situation or employment different from the place, situation or employment which he occupied prior to the commencement of the training, as if he was, immediately before 1st April 1971, occupying such different place, situation or employment;

    (ii) otherwise, as if he was, immediately before 1st April 1971, occupying the place, situation or employment which he occupied immediately prior to the commencement of such training.

(3) Where any officer is, immediately before 1st April 1971, absent from his normal duties otherwise than for the purpose of undergoing training he shall be deemed, in the application of article 18 or 19, to be discharging such duties, and to be discharging them in connection with the area of housing accommodation at which he normally discharges them.

22.—(1) Any question whether an officer is employed in the manner described in article 18 or 19 shall be determined by a tribunal established under section 12 of the Industrial Training Act 1964(a). References to such tribunal may be made as soon as may be and in any case not later than 30th April 1971.

(2) Where any question that an officer is not, or is, employed in the manner described as aforesaid is outstanding on 1st April 1971 the officer shall not be transferred until the expiration of the second week following that in which the decision of the tribunal is notified.

(a) 1964 c. 16.

Officers appointed before 1*st April* 1971

23. Where a transferee authority, before 1st April 1971, with the consent of the Greater London Council, appoint to hold any place, situation or employment before or as from that day any person (hereinafter referred to as "the officer") who, but for that appointment, would fall within a description of officers in Part I or II of Schedule 2 to this order, the officer in that appointment shall be deemed to have been transferred by article 18 or 19 as appropriate and, in a case falling within article 19, he shall be included within the number of officers mentioned in paragraph (2) of that article in respect of the transferee authority.

Saving for certain staff

24. Subject to articles 20 and 23, nothing in article 18 or 19 (other than article 19(5)) applies—

(*a*) to any person who will, by virtue of any agreement entered into between him and any authority before 1st April 1971, enter into the employment of that authority on that date; or

(*b*) to any person as regards any employment which is to be terminated on 31st March 1971.

Secondary transfers

25. Any officer transferred by article 18 or 19 to a transferee authority may, before 1st July 1971, be transferred by the said authority with the agreement of any other such authority and of the officer to the employment of that authority, and this order shall continue to apply to him.

Protection of staff

26.—(1) (*a*) Every officer transferred (or deemed to have been transferred) by article 18, 19 or 20 to the employment of a transferee authority shall, so long as he continues in that employment by virtue of the transfer or appointment and until he is served with a statement in writing of new terms and conditions of employment, enjoy terms and conditions of employment not less favourable than those he enjoyed immediately before 1st April 1971. The said new terms and conditions shall be such that—

(i) so long as the officer is engaged in duties reasonably comparable to those in which he was engaged immediately before 1st April 1971, the scale of his salary or remuneration, and

(ii) the other terms and conditions of his employment,

are not less favourable than those he enjoyed immediately before 1st April 1971, and any question whether duties are reasonably comparable as aforesaid shall be determined by a tribunal established under section 12 of the Industrial Training Act 1964. The statement of new terms and conditions shall contain information that any question shall be so determined and as to the person and address to whom any question should be referred.

(*b*) A statement of new terms and conditions of employment shall not be served in respect of any officer in relation to whom a question has been referred under article 22(1) until the decision of the tribunal has been notified.

(*c*) If after service of a statement of new terms and conditions of employment upon him a question is referred in respect of an officer under article 22(1), the statement shall cease to have effect, sub-paragraph (*a*) of this paragraph shall have effect as if the statement had not been served, and no new statement shall be served until the decision on the question has been notified.

(2) A written statement given in accordance with section 4(1) of the Contracts of Employment Act 1963(**a**) shall not be regarded as a statement of new terms and conditions of employment for the purposes of paragraph (1) unless the statement so indicates.

Saving for dispensations

27. Any dispensation from the requirements of any regulation granted to the Greater London Council shall have effect, in relation to any officer transferred (or deemed to have been transferred) by article 18, 19 or 20, as if it had been granted to the authority to whose employment he has been transferred (or is deemed to have been transferred).

Saving for extensions of service

28. Any extension of service under section 7(1) of the Local Government Superannuation Act 1937(**b**) effective on 1st April 1971 in relation to an officer tranferred (or deemed to have been transferred) by article 18, 19 or 20 shall continue to have effect as if it had been made by the authority to whose employment he has been transferred (or is deemed to have been transferred).

Appointment of assessor

29. On any reference under article 22(1) or 26 the tribunal may, if they think fit, appoint a person having special knowledge or experience in relation to the subject matter of the reference to sit with them as assessor.

Superannuation

30.—(1) Where an officer who, immediately before his transfer (or deemed transfer) to an authority by article 18, 19 or 20—

(*a*) was subject to an election in consequence of which he did not participate in the benefits of the superannuation fund maintained by the Greater London Council under Part I of the Local Government Superannuation Act 1937; and

(*b*) had an expectation of a gratuity payable according to years of service,

that election shall remain in effect and such a gratuity shall, subject to terms and conditions which are not less beneficial, by payable by that authority in respect of his previous service and of any service rendered to that authority.

(2) Section 35 of the Local Government Superannuation Act 1937 shall apply to an expectation under this article as it applies to a right under that Act.

Protection of housing accommodation

31. Where, immediately before 1st April 1971, an officer of the Greater London Council occupied a dwelling (whether as a tenant or otherwise) provided by that Council in connection with, or as a term of, his employment and

---

(**a**) 1963 c. 49.　　　　　　　　　(**b**) 1937 c. 68.

(*a*) he is transferred (or deemed to have been transferred) by this order but the dwelling is not transferred by article 3; or

(*b*) he is so transferred (or deemed to have been transferred) to any authority but the dwelling is transferred by article 3 to another authority; or

(*c*) he is not so transferred (or deemed to have been transferred) but the dwelling is transferred by article 3,

nothing in this order shall prejudice that occupation and for the purposes of that occupation the authority in whom the dwelling is vested shall permit the authority by whom the officer is employed to deal with the dwelling as if it were vested in that authority, and that authority shall make any necessary payment to the authority in whom the dwelling is vested to take account of the occupation of the dwelling by the officer.

Payment in lieu of transfer

32. In the case of a transferee authority where the accepted number of officers for the purposes of article 19(2) is less than the notified number of such officers for the purposes of paragraph (1) of the said article, the Greater London Council may require payment from the transferee authority until 1st April 1973 of sums equal to not more than one half of the basic remuneration of each such officer who has not been so accepted:

Provided that nothing in this article shall apply to the remuneration of an officer for the time being required for the normal establishment of the Greater London Council.

Arbitration

33. Subject to any provision of this order, any dispute arising under this order or in consequence thereof shall be determined by an arbitrator appointed by agreement between the parties in dispute or, in default of agreement, by the Secretary of State and, subject as aforesaid, the provisions of the Arbitration Act 1950(**a**) shall apply to any arbitration under this article.

SCHEDULE 1   Article 13

TERMS OF TRANSFER OF HOUSING ACCOMMODATION

PART I—PAYMENTS TO THE GREATER LONDON COUNCIL

1. In the year ending on 31st March 1972, a transferee authority shall pay to the Greater London Council by quarterly instalments in arrears a sum being the amount of the rents which were receivable by the latter authority on 31st March 1971 less the amount of—

(*a*) the estimated value of rent rebates in the said year based on the said rents calculated as if the housing accommodation had not been transferred; and

(*b*) the costs of management and costs of maintenance which were met in the year ending on 31st March 1971.

2. In each of the years ending on 31st March 1973, 31st March 1974 and 31st March 1975, a transferee authority shall pay to the Greater London Council by quarterly instalments in arrears a sum being the amount of the rents which would have been receivable by the latter authority on 31st March 1972, 31st March 1973 or 31st March 1974, as the case may be, if the housing accommodation had not been transferred, less the amount of—

(*a*) the estimated value of rent rebates in the said year on the basis of the said rents; and

(*b*) the costs of management and costs of maintenance which would have been met in the year ending on 31st March 1972, 31st March 1973 or 31st March 1974 as the case may be if the housing accommodation had not been transferred.

(a) 1950 c. 27.

3. In each subsequent year until 31st March 1983, a transferee authority shall make the like payments to the Greater London Council as those mentioned in the last preceding paragraph with reference to the year ending on 31st March 1975.

4. In this Schedule, references to rents receivable on 31st March in a year are references to the amount of those rents on that basis for the year immediately after the said date.

5. In this Schedule, references to rents, rent rebates, costs of management and costs of maintenance are references to the rents, rebates or costs in respect of the housing accommodation transferred by article 3 to the transferee authority.

6. In the calculation of the amount of payments for the purposes of this Schedule, no regard shall be taken of any improvement carried out wholly or partly at the expense of a transferee authority or of any disposal or demolition of housing accommodation transferred.

7. In the calculation of rent rebates for the purposes of this Schedule, no regard shall be had to any change of tenancy after 31st March 1971.

8.—(1) In the calculation of the costs of management and costs of maintenance for the purposes of this Schedule, the Greater London Council shall assess such costs in respect of separate classes, namely flats and other housing accommodation transferred by article 3, and, in the calculation of costs of maintenance, each such class shall be divided into housing accommodation first occupied before 1st January 1940 and on or after the said date.

(2) The Treasurer of the Greater London Council shall certify—

(a) the average cost of management and the average cost of maintenance of each class and division of housing accommodation assessed under this paragraph; and

(b) the number of units transferred in each such class and division;

and the costs of management and the costs of maintenance shall be the total sum of the average costs in (a) multiplied by the relevant number in (b).

9. Where a transferee authority takes any action in respect of housing accommodation transferred by article 3 which results in the reduction or withdrawal of any grant or subsidy payable, that authority shall pay to the Greater London Council such sum (whether annually or as a single amount) as may be agreed to represent the value of the grant or subsidy which would have been paid.

10. After 31st March 1983, a transferee authority shall pay to the Greater London Council such sum as may be agreed to meet the liabilities of the latter authority with respect to the housing accommodation transferred by article 3 to the transferee authority, and any such agreement may include terms as to payment over a period and as to the allocation of any grant or subsidy receivable by the Greater London Council.

PART II—SUMS PAYABLE BY THE GREATER LONDON COUNCIL

1. By 30th September 1971 the Greater London Council shall pay to each transferee authority the two sums calculated under this Part of this Schedule.

2. The first sum is $\frac{x}{y}$ of the amount of the total balance of the Housing Repairs Account of the Greater London Council on 31st March 1971, where—

x   is that number of dwellings to which the said account relates which are transferred by article 3 to the transferee authority; and

y   is the total number of dwellings to which the said account relates on 31st March 1971.

3. The second sum is $\frac{p}{q}$ of the amount of the total balance of the Key Deposit Account of the Greater London Council on 31st March 1971, where—

p   is that number of dwellings to which the said account relates which are transferred by article 3 to the transferee authority; and

q   is the total number of dwellings to which the Housing Revenue Account of the Greater London Council relates on 31st March 1971.

Part III—Liabilities of the Greater London Council

1. The Greater London Council shall meet the costs of works of modernisation or major improvement, being costs incurred in respect of a period before 1st April 1971.

2. The Greater London Council shall meet all costs of repair and minor improvement started or contracted for before 1st April 1971.

SCHEDULE 2

Transfer of Officers

Part I   Article 18

Staff employed in connection with property transferred by Article 3

Description of officers	Authority
(1)	(2)
1. The Area Officer, Deputy Area Officer, Area Clerk and other clerical staff employed—	
(a) at the Bellingham Area Office in the Mottingham District of the Housing Department of the Greater London Council	The council of the London borough of Lewisham
(b) at the Woodward Road Area Office in the Becontree District of that Department	The council of the London borough of Barking
2. The sector foreman, sector chargehand, storekeeper and driver employed—	
(a) at the Bellingham Sector in the said Mottingham District	The council of the London borough of Lewisham
(b) at the Woodward Road Sector in the said Beacontree District	The council of the London borough of Barking
3. The following officers, being officers employed for not less than one half of their time on duties of the specified class in connection with property transferred by article 3,—	
(a) officers engaged on the collection of rents being— (i) estate officers; or (ii) temporary rent collectors;	
(b) resident estate officers;	The transferee authority
(c) old peoples' wardens; or	
(d) other officers being— (i) resident caretakers and assistant caretakers; (ii) resident stoker/plant attendants; (iii) non-resident porters; (iv) temporary relief porters; or (v) cleaners	
4. Any other officers specified by the Greater London Council with the approval of the transferee authority as being officers affected by the transfer of property by article 3.	The transferee authority

PART II

Article 19

MAINTENANCE STAFF

Assistant Gardener   Gardener chargehand
Bricklayer   Labourer
Bricklayer chargehand   Painter
Carpenter   Painter chargehand
Carpenter chargehand   Plumber
Electrician   Plumber chargehand
Gardener

Any other officers specified by the Greater London Council with the approval of the transferee authority as being officers affected by the transfer of property by article 3.

11th February 1971.

Peter Walker,
Secretary of State for the Environment.

EXPLANATORY NOTE

(This Note is not part of the Order.)

This Order gives effect to the terms agreed between the Greater London Council and the councils of certain London boroughs for the transfer of housing accommodation to the latter councils, and makes consequential provision as to the transfer and protection of staff and other matters.

STATUTORY INSTRUMENTS

1971 No. 232

POLICE

The Police Pensions Regulations 1971

Laid before Parliament in draft

Made - - - -	*11th February* 1971
Coming into Operation	*15th February* 1971

ARRANGEMENT OF REGULATIONS

PART I

CITATION, COMMENCEMENT, REVOCATIONS ETC.

PART II

INTERPRETATION

Part III

Awards on Retirement and Disablement

Part IV

Awards on Death

Widows

Children

General

Part V

Pensionable Service

Part VI

Pensionable Pay and Contributions

Part VII

Cancellation, Revision, Reduction and Withdrawal of Awards

Part VIII

Determination of Questions

Part IX

Payment of Awards and Transfer Values

Part X

Compulsory Retirement

Part XI

Servicemen

Part XII

Supplemental Provisions in Special Cases

Part XIII

Application of Pensions (Increase) Acts

Part XIV

Miscellaneous

SCHEDULES

SCHEDULE 6—INTERCHANGE ARRANGEMENTS

SCHEDULE 7

Additional pension contributions.

SCHEDULE 8

Medical appeals.

SCHEDULE 9

Transfer values.

SCHEDULE 10

Limits in respect of awards to or in respect of servicemen.

SCHEDULE 11

Preserved pensionable pay.

In exercise of the powers conferred on me by sections 1, 3 and 5(4) of the Police Pensions Act 1948(a) (read with Article 2(1) of the Minister for the Civil Service Order 1968(b)), as extended and amended by section 43 of the Reserve and Auxiliary Forces (Protection of Civil Interests) Act 1951(c), section 5(3) of the Overseas Service Act 1958(d) and Schedule 2 thereto, section 1(1) of the Police Pensions Act 1961(e), sections 40, 43(4), 45(4) and 63 of the Police Act 1964(f) and Schedules 6 and 9 thereto, section 11(7) of the Superannuation (Miscellaneous Provisions) Act 1967(g), sections 35 and 38(4) of the Police (Scotland) Act 1967(h) and section 4(5) of the Police Act 1969(i), and after consultation with the Police Council for the United Kingdom, and, so far as Regulation 74 is concerned, with the Council on Tribunals, I hereby, with the consent of the Minister for the Civil Service, make the following Regulations, a draft of which has been laid before Parliament and has been approved by resolution of each House of Parliament:—

PART I

CITATION, COMMENCEMENT, REVOCATIONS ETC.

Citation and commencement

1. These Regulations may be cited as the Police Pensions Regulations 1971 and shall come into operation on 15th February 1971.

Revocations

2. The former Regulations, that is to say the Regulations made under the Act before the making of these Regulations, are hereby revoked to the extent that they have not heretofore been revoked by Regulations so made and, accordingly, the Regulations set out in Schedule 1 are hereby revoked.

(a) 1948 c. 24.	(b) S.I. 1968/1656 (1968 III, p. 4485).
(c) 1951 c. 65.	(d) 1958 c. 14.
(e) 1961 c. 35.	(f) 1964 c. 48.
(g) 1967 c. 28.	(h) 1967 c. 77.
(i) 1969 c. 63.	

Transitional provisions

3.—(1) These Regulations shall have effect as if—

(*a*) anything done under or for the purposes of any provision of the former Regulations had been done under or for the purposes of the corresponding provision of these Regulations; and

(*b*) anything done in relation to an award which was granted, or the entitlement to which was continued, under any provision of the former Regulations had applied to the like award under the corresponding provision of these Regulations.

(2) Without prejudice to the generality of paragraph (1), references therein to anything done shall include—

(*a*) the determination of a question;

(*b*) the exercise of a discretion;

(*c*) the selection of an award;

(*d*) the making of a payment;

(*e*) the giving of a notice;

(*f*) the making of an election; and

(*g*) the cancellation, forfeiture, revision or withdrawal of an award, in whole or in part.

(3) No payment shall be made under these Regulations on account of—

(*a*) any widow's pension or child's allowance for a period before 15th February 1971; or

(*b*) any award, other than a pension or allowance, payable on a person's death or on his ceasing to be a member of a police force before the said date,

save in so far as the said payment would have been made under the former Regulations had these Regulations not been made.

Part II

Interpretation

Meanings assigned to certain expressions

4.—(1) In these Regulations, unless the context otherwise requires, the following expressions have the meanings hereby respectively assigned to them, that is to say:—

"the Act" means the Police Pensions Act 1948;

"approved service" has the same meaning as in the former Acts;

"armed forces" means the naval, military or air forces of the Crown, including any women's service administered by the Defence Council or formerly administered by the Admiralty, Army Council or Air Council;

"auxiliary policeman" means a member of the first class of the police reserve, a member of the Police War Reserve and a member of Class A of the Women's Auxiliary Police Corps;

"average pensionable pay" has the meaning assigned to it by Regulation 60;

"central police officer" means a member of a home police force engaged on central service who enjoys a right of reversion under section 43(1) of the Police Act 1964 or section 38(1) of the Police (Scotland) Act 1967, as the case may be;

"central service" means temporary service under the Crown performed on or after 1st August 1964, being such service as is mentioned in section 43(5) of the Police Act 1964 or section 38(5) of the Police (Scotland) Act 1967;

"chief officer of police" in relation to an overseas corps means the senior member of that corps;

"child" includes step-child, illegitimate child and adopted child and the expressions "father", "mother" and "parent" shall be construed accordingly;

"former Acts" means the Police Pensions Acts 1921 and 1926(a), including those Acts as applied and extended by or under any enactment, and any Act repealed by those Acts;

"former force" means the police force in which a serviceman was serving immediately before undertaking a period of relevant service in the armed forces;

"former Regulations" means the Regulations made under the Act before the making of these Regulations;

"home police force" means any police force within the meaning of the Police Act 1964 or the Police (Scotland) Act 1967;

"injury" includes any injury or disease, whether of body or mind;

"inspector" includes chief inspector, sub-divisional inspector, first class inspector, C.I.D., station inspector and sub-inspector;

"medical referee" has the meaning assigned to it by Regulation 71(2);

"member of a police force" includes—

(a) the commissioner and assistant commissioners of police of the metropolis;

(b) the commissioner of police for the City of London and any person who, on 5th July 1948, was either the surgeon of the City of London police force or a clerk or other person employed in, or in connection with, that force;

(c) an overseas policeman;

(d) an inspector or assistant inspector of constabulary appointed on or after 1st August 1964; and

(e) a central police officer;

"member of the first class of the police reserve" includes any member of a home police force appointed temporarily other than a member of the Police War Reserve or the Women's Auxiliary Police Corps or a re-engaged pensioner who was serving in a police force on 1st September 1918;

"overseas corps" means any body in which persons such as are mentioned in section 1(1) of the Police (Overseas Service) Act 1945(b) are serving and in relation to which regulations made under section 1(2) of that Act have been made;

"overseas policeman" means a member of an overseas corps, or an officer to whom the Overseas Service Act 1958 applies and whose service as such an officer is for the time being service in respect of which the provisions of section 5 of that Act have effect;

(a) 1921 c. 31; 1926 c. 34.   (b) 1945 c. 17 (9 & 10 Geo. 6).

"overseas service" means service as an overseas policeman;

"pensionable pay" has the meaning assigned to it by Regulation 60;

"police authority" has the same meaning as in the Act, and accordingly in relation to a Scottish police force has the same meaning as in the Police (Scotland) Act 1967;

"police force" means a home police force or an overseas corps;

"regular policeman" means—

(a) a member of a home police force who is not an auxiliary policeman;

(b) an overseas policeman who is a reversionary member of a home police force;

(c) an inspector or assistant inspector of constabulary appointed on or after 1st August 1964; and

(d) a central police officer;

"reversionary member of a home police force" means an overseas policeman who has been a member of a home police force and has not lost his right of reversion under section 2(1) of the Police (Overseas Service) Act 1945, and includes a person who has transferred to an overseas corps from being either a civil servant within the meaning of the Superannuation Act 1887**(a)** or a member of the metropolitan civil staffs within the meaning of section 15 of the Superannuation (Miscellaneous Provisions) Act 1967;

"sergeant" includes station sergeant, first class sergeant (C.I.D.), second class sergeant (C.I.D.) and the former rank of acting sergeant;

"serviceman" means a person who immediately before undertaking a period of relevant service in the armed forces was a regular policeman and includes a serviceman (1939-1945);

"serviceman (1939-1945)" means a person who ceased to serve as a regular policeman in such circumstances that he became a person to whom section 1 of the Police and Firemen (War Service) Act 1939**(b)** applied;

"superintendent" includes chief superintendent;

"tour of central service" means the period of central service for which a central police officer has engaged with the consent of the appropriate authority for the purposes of section 43 of the Police Act 1964 or section 38 of the Police (Scotland) Act 1967, as the case may be, and, if such a period has been varied, means the period as so varied, so however that where the officer engaged for an indefinite period of central service the said expression means his actual period of such service;

"tour of overseas service" means the period of overseas service for which an overseas policeman has engaged with the consent, in the case of a reversionary member of a home police force, of the appropriate authority for the purposes of the Police (Overseas Service) Act 1945 and of the Secretary of State, and, if such a period has been varied under regulations made under section 1 of that Act, means the period as so varied, so however that where the overseas policeman has engaged for an indefinite period of overseas service the said expression means his actual period of such service.

(2) In these Regulations any reference to 1p or 6p a week less than a percentage of a person's pensionable pay includes, in relation to a period before 15th February 1971, a reference to 2d. or 1s. 2d. a week, as the case may be, less than that percentage.

(a) 1887 c. 67.   (b) 1939 c. 103.

(3) In these Regulations any reference to the Police Authority for Northern Ireland includes in relation to a period before 15th February 1971, a reference to the Ministry of Home Affairs for Northern Ireland.

Meaning of certain expressions related to the operation of the National Insurance Acts

5.—(1) In these Regulations the following expressions shall have the meanings respectively which they have for the purposes of the National Insurance Act 1965**(a)**:—

"employed contributor's employment";

"graduated contribution";

"graduated retirement benefit";

"non-participating employment";

"payment in lieu of contributions".

(2) In these Regulations any reference to insured pensionable age is a reference to the age of 65 years in the case of a man, or 60 years in the case of a woman.

(3) In these Regulations any reference to a participating period of relevant employment is a reference to a period of employed contributor's employment after 5th April 1961 and before insured pensionable age other than—

(*a*) service in the armed forces; and

(*b*) non-participating employment at the end of which no payment in lieu of contributions falls to be made;

and for the purposes of this paragraph a period of employed contributor's employment or of non-participating employment shall be treated as continuing during periods of holiday, temporary incapacity for work and similar temporary interruptions.

(4) In these Regulations any reference to the secured portion of a pension is a reference to the portion of the pension which equals the graduated retirement benefit which would be payable to the pensioner, on the assumption that he retired from regular employment on attaining insured pensionable age, in return for a payment in lieu of contributions in respect of the whole of any period of non-participating employment by virtue of which he is entitled to reckon pensionable service for the purposes of the pension, being a period of non-participating employment at the end of which no payment in lieu of contributions in fact fell to be made; and any reference to the unsecured portion of a pension shall be construed accordingly.

For the purposes of this paragraph a period of non-participating employment shall be treated as continuing during periods of holiday, temporary incapacity for work and similar temporary interruptions.

(5) For the purposes of these Regulations the annual rate of graduated retirement benefit shall be calculated as if there were $52\frac{1}{6}$ weeks in each year.

(6) Any provision of these Regulations which refers to the Family Allowances Act 1945**(b)** or the National Insurance Act 1946**(c)** either as originally enacted or as amended by any subsequent enactment shall be construed as if the Statute Law Revision (Consequential Repeals) Act 1965**(d)** had not been passed.

(**a**) 1965 c. 51. (**b**) 1945 c. 41.
(**c**) 1946 c. 67. (**d**) 1965 c. 55.

Meaning of certain expressions in relation to persons who are not members of a home police force

6.—(1) A reference in these Regulations to a rank, being a rank in a home police force, shall, in relation to a member of an overseas corps, be construed as a reference to such rank in that corps as the Secretary of State may from time to time direct.

(2) For the purposes of these Regulations—

(*a*) an overseas policeman who is not a member of an overseas corps; or

(*b*) a central police officer,

shall be deemed to hold the rank in which he is entitled to revert to his home police force at the end of his tour of overseas service or, as the case may be, of central service.

(3) For the purposes of these Regulations—

(*a*) an inspector of constabulary shall be deemed to hold the rank and office of chief constable;

(*b*) an assistant inspector of constabulary shall be deemed to hold the rank of chief superintendent.

(4) Except where the context otherwise requires, for the purposes of these Regulations—

(*a*) an overseas policeman who is not a member of an overseas corps shall be deemed to be a member of such a corps;

(*b*) an inspector or assistant inspector of constabulary or a central police officer shall be deemed to be a member of a home police force;

and any reference to such a person joining or leaving a police force or transferring from one force to another, however expressed, shall be construed accordingly.

(5) Subject to paragraph (6), in relation to an overseas policeman, an inspector or assistant inspector of constabulary or a central police officer, any reference in these Regulations to the police authority shall be construed as a reference to the Secretary of State.

(6) As respects anything done on or after 1st April 1968 but before 12th November 1970 in relation to an overseas policeman—

(*a*) any reference in these Regulations to the police authority, and

(*b*) any reference in paragraph (1) or in Regulation 21(1)(*c*), 71(2) or 74 or in paragraph 2 or 7 of Schedule 8 to the Secretary of State,

shall be construed as including a reference to the Minister of Overseas Development.

Persons who have been members of a police force

7. In these Regulations, unless the context otherwise requires, a reference to a member of a police force, however expressed, shall include a reference to a person who has been such a member.

Transfers

8. A reference in these Regulations to a regular policeman transferring from one force to another shall be construed as a reference to a regular policeman—

(*a*) leaving a home police force for the purpose of joining another home police force as a regular policeman and joining that other force in that capacity, where—

    (i) not being the chief officer of police of, or a constable on probation in, the force first mentioned in this sub-paragraph, he leaves or left that force on or after 1st January 1963 for the purpose aforesaid, after giving a month's notice in writing of his intention to do so to the police authority of that force or such shorter period of notice as may have been accepted by that authority on or after 15th February 1971, or

    (ii) he left the said force before 1st January 1963 or, being the chief officer of police of, or a constable on probation in, the said force, he leaves or left that force on or after that date, in either case for the purpose aforesaid and with the written consent of the chief officer of police or, in the case of the chief officer of police, of the police authority of that force;

(b) leaving a home police force with the consent of the Secretary of State and with the written consent of the chief officer of police of that force acting with the consent of the police authority or, if he is the chief officer of police of that force, of the police authority, for the purpose of engaging for a tour of overseas service as a reversionary member of a home police force and engaging in such a tour of service;

(c) transferring or being transferred from one overseas corps to another;

(d) exercising his right of reversion to a home police force, under section 2(1) of the Police (Overseas Service) Act 1945, at the end of a tour of overseas service; or

(e) at the end of a tour of overseas service joining another home police force as a regular policeman subject, in the cases hereinafter mentioned, to his doing so with the consent so mentioned, namely—

    (i) in the case of a person who was, at the time he left the home police force to which he had the right of reversion referred to in sub-paragraph (d), the chief officer of that force, the written consent of the police authority of that force;

    (ii) in the case of any other person whose tour of overseas service ended before 15th February 1971, the written consent of the chief officer of police of the home police force to which he had such right of reversion, acting with the consent of the police authority of that force.

Retirement

9.—(1) A reference in these Regulations to retirement includes a reference to the services of a member of a police force being dispensed with under regulations for the time being in force under section 33 of the Police Act 1964 or section 26 of the Police (Scotland) Act 1967 (other than regulations relating to the maintenance of discipline), to an auxiliary policeman ceasing to be called up for active service and to the termination of a tour of overseas service otherwise than by dismissal or transfer, but does not include a reference to leaving a force on transferring from one force to another, or on joining the Royal Ulster Constabulary with such consent as is mentioned in paragraph (2) and a reference to a continuous period of service is a reference to a period of service uninterrupted by any such retirement.

(2) The consent referred to in paragraph (1) is—

(a) in the case of a member of a police force who left his force before 17th December 1969 or was a chief officer of police, an assistant chief constable or a deputy chief constable and left his force on or after that date, the consent of the police authority;

(b) in any other case, the consent of the chief officer of police acting with the consent of the police authority.

Persons treated as being in receipt of a pension

10. For the purposes of these Regulations a person shall be treated as being in receipt of an ordinary or, as the case may be, supplemental pension if he would be in receipt of such a pension—

(a) in the case of an ordinary pension, had he attained the age of 50 years; or

(b) in the case of a supplemental pension, had the aggregate of any of the payments described in Regulation 22(4) been less than the standard amount appropriate to his case.

Aggregate pension contributions

11.—(1) For the purpose of calculating the amount of an award by reference to the aggregate pension contributions of a person in respect of the relevant period of service, the relevant period of service shall be taken to be the period ending in the retirement, dismissal or death on which the award is payable and beginning, where the person—

(a) was a regular policeman, with the date on which he became a regular policeman in the force from which he retired or was dismissed or in which he died or, if he has more than once been a regular policeman in that force, the date on which he last joined that force otherwise than as a serviceman resuming service in his former force within a month of the end of his period of relevant service in the armed forces;

(b) was an auxiliary policeman, with the date of the commencement of his last continuous period of active service as such;

(c) was a member of an overseas corps but not a reversionary member of a home police force, with the date of the commencement of his tour of overseas service.

(2) For the purpose aforesaid the aggregate pension contributions in respect of the relevant period of service shall be taken to be the sum of the following amounts—

(a) the aggregate of the pension contributions (including such additional contributions as are mentioned in Regulation 62) made in respect of that period by that person to the police authority by whom the award is payable and any rateable deductions made in respect of that period by that authority from his pay under the former Acts and, where that person has made no pension contributions but has had rateable deductions made in respect of that period from his pay by that authority, those rateable deductions;

(b) the amount of any sums paid by the person concerned to the said police authority (including sums paid in pursuance of an undertaking) as a condition of being entitled to reckon pensionable service or, as the case may be, approved service, by virtue of service before the said period;

(c) where the person concerned has transferred to the force of the police authority by whom the award is payable, any sum which had he retired instead of transferring would have been calculable under this paragraph as aggregate pension contributions at the time of transfer, and (*d*) where the person concerned, while a member of the force of the said police authority, became entitled, in the circumstances mentioned in Regulation 52(*d*) or (*e*) or Regulation 55, to reckon pensionable service by virtue of a period of previous service or employment otherwise than as a member of a police force, the amount of any award by way of return of contributions or of any analogous payment which would have been made to him at the end of that period of previous service or employment had he voluntarily retired therefrom in circumstances entitling him to such an award or payment under the superannuation arrangements applicable thereto.

Injury received in the execution of duty

12.—(1) A reference in these Regulations to an injury received in the execution of duty by a member of a police force—

(*a*) means an injury received in the execution of that person's duty as a constable and, where the person concerned is an auxiliary policeman, during a period of active service as such; and

(*b*) where the person concerned is treated as a member of a police force by virtue of the definition of "member of a police force" in Regulation 4(1) but is not a constable, means an injury received in the execution of his duty in the appropriate capacity mentioned in the said definition,

and includes any injury received while on duty or while on a journey necessary to enable him to report for duty or to return home after duty.

(2) Notwithstanding anything in these Regulations relating to a period of service in the armed forces, an injury received in the execution of duty as a member of the armed forces shall not be deemed to be an injury received in the execution of duty as a member of a police force.

(3) In the case of a regular policeman who has served as a police cadet in relation to whom the Police Cadets (Pensions) Regulations had taken effect, a qualifying injury within the meaning of those Regulations shall be treated for the purposes of these Regulations as if it had been received by him as mentioned in paragraph (1); and, where such a qualifying injury is so treated, any reference to duties in Regulation 32(1) shall be construed as including a reference to duties as a police cadet.

In this paragraph the reference to the Police Cadets (Pensions) Regulations is a reference to the Regulations from time to time in force under section 35 of the Police Act 1964, as extended by section 13 of the Superannuation (Miscellaneous Provisions) Act 1967, or under section 27 of the Police (Scotland) Act 1967, read with the said section 13.

Disablement

13.—(1) A reference in these Regulations to a person being permanently disabled is to be taken as a reference to that person being disabled at the time when the question arises for decision or arose for decision under the former Regulations and to that disablement being at that time likely to be permanent.

(2) Disablement, where the person concerned is a member of a police force, means inability to perform the ordinary duties of a male or of a female member of the force, as the case may be.

(3) Where it is necessary to determine the degree of a person's disablement, it shall be determined by reference to the degree to which his earning capacity has been affected as a result of an injury received without his own default in

the execution of his duty as a member of a police force or, where he ceased to be such a member before 1st January 1967, of the injury in respect of which the award is made:

Provided that a person shall be deemed to be totally disabled if, and only if, as a result of a relevant injury, either he is incapable by reason of the disablement of earning any money in any employment or is receiving treatment as an in-patient at a hospital.

(4) Where a person has retired before becoming disabled and the date on which he becomes disabled cannot be ascertained, it shall be taken to be the date on which the claim that he is disabled is first made known to the police authority.

Disablement or death the result of an injury

14. For the purposes of these Regulations disablement or death or treatment at a hospital shall be deemed to be the result of an injury if the injury has caused or substantially contributed to the disablement or death or the condition for which treatment is being received.

Relevant service in the armed forces

15. A reference in these Regulations to relevant service in the armed forces shall be construed as a reference to—

(a) service specified in Schedule 1 to the Reserve and Auxiliary Forces (Protection of Civil Interests) Act 1951, other than service specified in paragraph 5(b) thereof;

(b) part-time service under the National Service Act 1948**(a)**, otherwise than pursuant to a training notice under that Act;

(c) service for the purposes of training only performed by a person mentioned in paragraph 7 of Schedule 1 to the Reserve and Auxiliary Forces (Protection of Civil Interests) Act 1951, for a period shorter than 7 days;

(d) in relation to a serviceman other than a serviceman (1939-1945), whole-time service in the armed forces under the National Service Acts 1939 to 1946, the National Service Act 1947**(b)** or, without prejudice to sub-paragraph (a), the National Service Act 1948;

(e) in relation to a serviceman (1939-1945), service in the armed forces up to such date as the Secretary of State on the application of the police authority of his former force may in his case have fixed.

References to awards

16. In these Regulations, unless the context otherwise requires, a reference to an award shall be construed as a reference to an award under these Regulations.

References to provisions

17.—(1) In these Regulations, unless the context otherwise requires, a reference to a Regulation shall be construed as a reference to a Regulation contained in these Regulations, a reference to a Schedule shall be construed as a reference to a Schedule to these Regulations, a reference to a paragraph shall be construed as a reference to a paragraph in the same Regulation or, as the case may be, the same Part of the same Schedule and a reference to a sub-paragraph shall be construed as a reference to a sub-paragraph contained in the same paragraph.

(a) 1948 c. 64. (b) 1947 c. 31.

(2) In these Regulations, unless the context otherwise requires, a reference to any enactment or instrument shall be construed as including a reference to that enactment or instrument as amended, extended or applied by any other enactment or instrument.

Application of Interpretation Act 1889

18. The Interpretation Act 1889(a), shall apply for the interpretation of these Regulations as it applies for the interpretation of an Act of Parliament.

PART III

AWARDS ON RETIREMENT AND DISABLEMENT

Policeman's ordinary pension

19.—(1) Subject to paragraphs (2) and (4), this Regulation shall apply to a regular policeman who retires or has retired on or after 5th July 1948 when entitled to reckon at least 25 years' pensionable service.

(2) Except in the circumstances mentioned in paragraph (3), this Regulation shall not apply to a member of a home police force where—

    (a) he retires or retired without having given to the police authority a month's written notice of his intention to retire or such shorter notice as may have been accepted by the police authority; or

    (b) being a chief officer of police, assistant commissioner of police of the metropolis, assistant commissioner of police for the City of London, assistant chief constable, a commander, or a deputy assistant commissioner or deputy commander in the metropolitan police, he retires or retired before attaining the age of 60 years.

(3) The circumstances referred to in paragraph (2) are that—

    (a) the police authority decide or have decided that this Regulation or the corresponding provision of any of the former Regulations should apply in his case; or

    (b) he is or was required to retire on account of age, or on the ground that his retention in the force would not be in the general interests of efficiency, or as an alternative to dismissal, or

    (c) he is or was required to retire under section 6(3)(d) of the Police (Scotland) Act 1956(b) or section 4(4)(d) of the Police (Scotland) Act 1967 or, as the case may be, under section 5(4) of the Police Act 1964.

(4) This Regulation shall not apply to an overseas policeman or central police officer who retires or retired before the completion of the tour of overseas service or, as the case may be, of central service, if any, applicable in his case.

(5) Subject to the provisions of these Regulations, a regular policeman to whom this Regulation applies shall be entitled to an ordinary pension of an amount calculated in accordance with Part I of Schedule 2, subject however to Parts III and IV of that Schedule; but, in the case of a person entitled to reckon less than 30 years' pensionable service who retires or retired after 7th August 1961, no payments shall be made on account of the pension in respect of the period, if any, after his retirement and before he has attained the age of 50 years.

(a) 1889 c. 63.   (b) 1956 c. 26.

(6) In the case of a person who was serving as a regular policeman on 15th February 1971 the limitation imposed by paragraph (2) on the application of this Regulation shall not apply to his first retirement on or after that date by reason of his being a commander in a police force other than the metropolitan police force.

(7) In the case of a person who—

(*a*) was serving as a regular policeman on 7th August 1961; or

(*b*) is entitled under Regulation 52(*c*) or under Regulation 94 to reckon as pensionable service a period which includes that date,

the limitation imposed by paragraph (5) on the making of payments in respect of a period before a person has attained the age of 50 years shall not apply to his first retirement on or after that date; and any person who has retired with an ill-health pension and subsequently rejoins the force in the circumstances, and within the period, mentioned in Regulation 65(2) shall be treated for the purposes of this paragraph as if he had not retired but had served as a regular policeman throughout the period for which he was in receipt of that pension.

Policeman's ill-health award

20.—(1) This Regulation shall apply to a regular policeman who retires or has retired on or after 5th July 1948 on the ground that he is or was permanently disabled.

(2) A regular policeman to whom this Regulation applies shall be entitled to an ill-health award as hereinafter provided.

(3) In the case of a policeman who is or was at the time of his retirement—

(*a*) entitled to reckon at least 10 years' pensionable service; or

(*b*) disabled as the result of an injury received in the execution of duty,

the award under paragraph (2) shall be an ill-health pension calculated in accordance with Part II of Schedule 2, subject however to Parts III and IV of that Schedule.

(4) In the case of any other policeman the award under paragraph (2) shall be an ill-health gratuity calculated in accordance with Part II of Schedule 2, subject however to Part V of that Schedule.

Policeman's short service award

21.—(1) This Regulation shall apply to a regular policeman entitled at the time of his retirement to reckon less than 25 years' pensionable service who—

(*a*) is or was required to retire on account of age on or after 5th July 1948;

(*b*) is treated for the purposes of these Regulations, by virtue of Regulation 98(2), as having retired on or after the said date;

(*c*) being a reversionary member of a home police force, in pursuance of a notice in that behalf given to the Secretary of State and having attained the age of 60 years, retires or retired on or after 5th July 1948 on the termination of the tour of overseas service, if any, applicable in his case;

(*d*) is or was required to retire under section 6(3)(*d*) of the Police (Scotland) Act 1956 or section 4(4)(*d*) of the Police (Scotland) Act 1967 or, as the case may be, under section 5(4) of the Police Act 1964; or

(*e*) was serving as a chief constable on 1st July 1964 and is treated for the purposes of these Regulations, by virtue of Regulation 99(2), as having retired.

(2) A regular policeman to whom this Regulation applies shall be entitled to a short service award as hereinafter provided.

(3) In the case of a policeman entitled at the time of his retirement to reckon at least 10 years' pensionable service, the award under paragraph (2) shall be a short service pension calculated in accordance with Part II of Schedule 2, subject however to Parts III and IV of that Schedule.

(4) In the case of any other policeman, the award under paragraph (2) shall be a short service gratuity calculated in accordance with Part II of Schedule 2, subject however to Part V of that Schedule.

Policeman's supplemental pension

22.—(1) This Regulation shall apply to a person who ceases or has ceased to be a member of a police force on or after 5th July 1948, and is permanently disabled as a result of an injury received without his own default in the execution of his duty (hereafter in this Regulation referred to as the "relevant injury").

(2) A person to whom this Regulation applies shall be entitled to a supplemental pension in respect of any week in respect of which—

(*a*) none of the payments described in paragraph (4) is payable to him; or

(*b*) if one or more of the said payments is payable, that payment or the aggregate of those payments, as the case may be, is less than the standard amount appropriate to his case calculated in accordance with Part VI of Schedule 2.

(3) The amount of the supplemental pension in respect of any week shall—

(*a*) if none of the said payments is payable in respect of that week, be equal to the said appropriate standard amount;

(*b*) if one or more of the said payments is payable in respect of that week, be equal to the difference between that payment or, as the case may be, the aggregate of those payments and the said appropriate standard amount.

(4) The payments referred to in paragraph (2) are—

(*a*) any injury benefit payable under the National Insurance (Industrial Injuries) Act 1965**(a)** which relates to the relevant injury together with, where he ceases to be a member of a police force on or after 6th October 1966, any supplement payable therewith under section 2 of the National Insurance Act 1966**(b)**;

(*b*) any disablement pension payable under section 12 of the National Insurance (Industrial Injuries) Act 1965 in respect of the relevant injury or so much of any such pension as relates to that injury, together with—

(i) any increase in such pension payable under section 13, 14, 17 or 18 of the said Act or so much of any such increase as is proportionate to that part of the said pension which relates to that injury, and

(ii) so long as he is receiving treatment as an in-patient at a hospital as a result of that injury, any increase in such pension payable under section 16, 17 or 18 of the said Act;

(*c*) any sickness benefit payable under the National Insurance Act 1965, until the first day after his retirement which is not or is deemed not to be a day of incapacity for work under section 20 of that Act or regulations

---

(a) 1965 c. 52.   **(b)** 1966 c. 6.

made thereunder, together with, where he ceases to be a member of a police force on or after 6th October 1966, any supplement thereto payable under section 2 of the National Insurance Act 1966; and

(*d*) where the person concerned received the relevant injury while serving as a regular policeman, any pension (payable otherwise than under this Regulation) which first becomes or became payable after the time when he received the relevant injury by the police authority of the force in which he was serving at that time;

and for the purposes of paragraphs (2) and (3), any such pension as is mentioned in sub-paragraph (*d*) which is reduced in accordance with the provisions of Regulation 23, 24 or 26 or of Part IV of Schedule 2 shall be deemed not to have been so reduced.

(5) Where a person has received a disablement gratuity under the National Insurance (Industrial Injuries) Act 1965 or under the National Insurance (Industrial Injuries) Act 1946**(a)**, this Regulation shall apply as if he were entitled during the relevant period to a disablement pension under the said Act of 1965 of such amount as would be produced by converting the gratuity into an annuity for that period.

In this paragraph the expression "the relevant period" means the period taken into account, in accordance with section 12 of the Act in question, for the purpose of making the assessment by reference to which the gratuity became payable.

(6) Where a member of a police force is entitled to both a supplemental pension and some other such pension as is mentioned in paragraph (4)(*d*), then, except where the context otherwise requires, those pensions shall, for the purposes of these Regulations, constitute a single award.

Former provisions as to commutation of part of pension

23.—(1) This Regulation shall apply to a regular policeman who retired on or after 14th April 1958 but before 1st August 1964 and, in accordance with this Regulation, commutes or has commuted for a lump sum a portion of any pension, other than a supplemental pension, to which he is entitled, provided, in the case of an ordinary pension, that he retired either when entitled to reckon at least 30 years' pensionable service or in the circumstances mentioned in sub-paragraph (*a*) or (*b*) of Regulation 21(1).

(2) For the purpose of commuting a portion of his pension in accordance with this Regulation a person shall—

(*a*) give notice in writing (in this Regulation called "notice of commutation") to the police authority of his wish to surrender and commute for a lump sum such portion of his pension, not exceeding a sixth of the pension which would be payable but for the provisions of Regulation 26 and of Part IV of Schedule 2, as (subject to the limitation contained in Regulation 27) he may specify; and

(*b*) satisfy the police authority of his good health and for that purpose submit himself to such medical examination as they may require.

(3) The notice of commutation shall be given by a person—

(*a*) not earlier than 2 months before his retirement nor later than 6 months after his retirement; or

---

(a) 1946 c. 62.

(b) in the case of a person who retired with an ill-health pension and was entitled to reckon less than 25 years' pensionable service, not earlier than 2 months before his retirement nor later than 6 months after he would, if he had continued to serve as a regular policeman instead of retiring with an ill-health pension, have been either entitled to reckon 25 years' pensionable service or liable to be required to retire on account of age;

and, in the case of such a person as is mentioned in sub-paragraph (b), the notice of commutation shall be given only with the written consent of the police authority unless, at the time when the notice is given, he would, if he had continued to serve as aforesaid, have been either entitled to reckon 25 years' pensionable service or liable to be required to retire as aforesaid.

(4) Where a person has complied with the provisions of paragraph (2), the police authority shall forthwith send to him a written notification that they have accepted the notice of commutation, which shall become effective—

(a) as from the time when the notification is received by him or, if sent by post, as from the time when it would be delivered to him in the ordinary course of post; or

(b) as from the date of his retirement,

whichever is the later.

(5) Where a person has retired and a notice of commutation given by him becomes or has become effective, the police authority shall reduce the pension to which the notice relates in accordance with the notice as from the time from which the notice is effective and shall pay to him a lump sum of such amount as is the actuarial equivalent of the surrendered portion of the pension at the date of his retirement, calculated from tables prepared by the Government Actuary:

Provided that—

(a) where the notice is effective as from the time mentioned in paragraph (4)(a), the lump sum shall be reduced by an amount equal to the difference between the aggregate payments made in respect of the pension and the aggregate payments which would have been so made had it been reduced from the date of the retirement;

(b) in relation to such a person as is mentioned in paragraph (3)(b), the preceding provisions of this paragraph shall have effect as if any reference therein to the date of retirement were a reference to the time as from which the notice is effective.

Current provisions as to commutation of part of pension

24.—(1) This Regulation shall apply to a regular policeman who retires or has retired on or after 1st August 1964.

(2) A regular policeman to whom this Regulation applies may, in accordance therewith, commute for a lump sum a portion of any pension, other than a supplemental pension, to which he is or may become entitled, provided, in the case of an ordinary pension, that he retires or retired either when entitled to reckon at least 30 years' pensionable service or in the circumstances mentioned in sub-paragraph (a), (b), (d) or (e) of Regulation 21(1).

(3) For the purpose of commuting a portion of his pension in accordance with this Regulation a person shall give notice in writing (in this Regulation called "notice of commutation") to the police authority of his wish to surrender and

commute for a lump sum such portion of his pension, not exceeding a quarter of the pension which would be payable but for the provisions of Regulation 26, as (subject to the limitation contained in Regulation 27) he may specify.

(4) The notice of commutation shall be given by a person not earlier than 2 months before his intended retirement nor later than 6 months after his retirement.

(5) The notice of commutation given by a person shall become effective—

(a) as from the date of his retirement; or

(b) as from the date on which the notice is received by the police authority, whichever is the later:

Provided that the notice of commutation shall not become effective if—

(i) it was given more than 2 months before his retirement, or

(ii) it relates to an ill-health pension and the unsecured portion of that pension has sooner been terminated under Regulation 65.

(6) Where a person retires or has retired and a notice of commutation given by him becomes or has become effective, the police authority shall reduce the pension to which the notice relates in accordance with the notice as from the time from which the notice is effective and shall pay to him a lump sum of such amount as is the actuarial equivalent of the surrendered portion of the pension at the date of his retirement, calculated from tables prepared by the Government Actuary:

Provided that where the notice is effective as from the date mentioned in paragraph (5)(b), the lump sum shall be reduced by an amount equal to the difference between the aggregate payments made in respect of the pension and the aggregate payments which would have been so made had it been reduced from the date of the retirement.

(7) Where the unsecured portion of an ill-health pension is terminated under Regulation 65, after a notice of commutation in relation to the pension has become effective—

(a) no reduction shall be made under paragraph (6) in the secured portion of the pension, in so far as it is payable under Regulation 65;

(b) if thereafter the person concerned becomes entitled to a pension, other than a supplemental pension, and is entitled to reckon for the purposes thereof the period of pensionable service reckonable for the purposes of the ill-health pension first mentioned in this paragraph, the unsecured portion of the other pension shall be reduced by the amount by which the ill-health pension would have been reduced if it had not been terminated as aforesaid.

(8) Where a person wishes to surrender and commute for a lump sum a portion of a pension which falls to be reduced under paragraph (7)(b), he shall not specify in the notice of commutation a portion of the pension which, when aggregated with the said reduction, exceeds a quarter of the pension which would be payable but for the provisions of paragraph (7)(b) and of Regulation 26.

(9) A notice of commutation for the purposes of Regulation 23, given before 1st August 1964, shall have effect for the purposes of this Regulation as if it had been given hereunder unless the person elected, by notice in writing given to the police authority before the date of his retirement, that it should not have effect for the purposes of the corresponding provision of the former regulations; and, where he so elected, a subsequent notice of commutation given by him may have effect for the purposes of this Regulation.

Former provisions as to allocation of part of pension

25.—(1) This Regulation shall apply to a regular policeman who retired on or after 5th July 1948, but before 14th April 1958.

(2) If before retiring with an ordinary or short service pension a regular policeman to whom this Regulation applies—

(*a*) gave notice to the police authority by whom the pension was payable of his intention to surrender a portion of the pension not exceeding a third thereof;

(*b*) nominated the person in whose favour the surrender was to take effect, being his spouse or some other person who the police authority were satisfied was substantially dependent on him; and

(*c*) provided the police authority with such evidence of his good health as the authority considered satisfactory,

the pension shall be reduced accordingly, and after his death the police authority shall pay to the person so nominated, if that person survives him, a pension of such amount as, according to tables from time to time prepared by the Government Actuary, is actuarially equivalent, as at the time when the ordinary or short service pension first became payable, to that part of the pension which he has surrendered.

Current provisions as to allocation of part of pension

26.—(1) This Regulation shall apply to a regular policeman who retires or retired on or after 14th April 1958.

(2) A regular policeman to whom this Regulation applies and who is entitled to reckon not less than 25 years' pensionable service may, in accordance with the provisions thereof, allocate a portion of any pension, other than a supplemental pension, to which he may become entitled and, notwithstanding that he has already allocated a portion of such a pension, he may—

(*a*) allocate a further portion of that pension in favour of the beneficiary of the previous allocation; or

(*b*) where that beneficiary has died, allocate a further portion of that pension in favour of some other beneficiary.

(3) A regular policeman to whom this Regulation applies may, in accordance with the provisions thereof, allocate a portion of a short service pension.

(4) For the purpose of allocating a portion of his pension a person shall—

(*a*) give notice in writing (in this Regulation called "notice of allocation") to the police authority of the force in which he is serving stating—

(i) his wish to surrender such portion of his pension as, subject to the limitations contained in paragraph (5) and in Regulation 27, he may specify,

(ii) the person in whose favour the surrender is to take effect (in this Regulation called "the beneficiary"), being his wife or some other person who the police authority are satisfied is substantially dependent on him,

(iii) in the case of an allocation by a person entitled to reckon not less than 25 years' pensionable service, whether the notice of allocation is to become effective in accordance with sub-paragraph (*a*) or (*b*) of paragraph (6); and

(b) satisfy the police authority of his good health and for that purpose submit himself to such medical examination as they may require.

Except where, in such case as is mentioned in sub-paragraph (a)(iii), the notice of allocation is to become effective in accordance with paragraph (6)(a), the notice shall be given not earlier than 2 months before the person's intended retirement.

(5) The total portion of a pension which may be surrendered by a person under this Regulation shall not exceed a third of the pension which would be payable in his case but for the provisions of this Regulation, of Regulation 23, of Regulation 24 and of Part IV of Schedule 2.

(6) Where a person has complied with the provisions of sub-paragraphs (a) and (b) of paragraph (4), the police authority shall forthwith send to him a written notification that they have accepted the notice of allocation, which shall become effective—

(a) in the case of an allocation by a person who was entitled to reckon not less than 25 years' pensionable service when he gave the notice of allocation and stated therein that the notice should become effective in accordance with this sub-paragraph—

(i) as from the time when the notification is received by him or, if sent by post, as from the time when it would be delivered to him in the ordinary course of post, or

(ii) as from the date of his retirement,

whichever is the earlier;

(b) in any other case, if, and only if, he retires within 2 months of giving the notice of allocation and in such case as from the date of retirement.

(7) Where a person retires or has retired and a notice of allocation given by him becomes or has become effective—

(a) the pension to which the notice relates shall be reduced in accordance with the notice as from the date from which it is payable (notwithstanding the death before that date of the beneficiary specified in the notice); and

(b) the police authority shall, as from the person's death, pay to the beneficiary specified in the notice, if that person survives him, a pension of such amount as is the actuarial equivalent of the surrendered portion of the pension so specified.

(8) For the purposes of paragraph (7)(b) the actuarial equivalent of the surrendered portion of the pension shall be calculated from tables prepared by the Government Actuary and in force at the time when the notice of allocation became effective, which tables shall—

(a) take account of the age of the regular policeman and of the age of the beneficiary at that time; and

(b) make different provision according to whether the notice of allocation became effective in accordance with sub-paragraph (a) or (b) of paragraph (6),

and separate calculations shall be made in respect of separate allocations.

(9) Where a person was entitled to reckon at least 25 years' pensionable service when he gave the notice of allocation and stated therein that it should become effective in accordance with paragraph (6)(a), then, if he dies or died before retiring, the police authority shall pay to the beneficiary the like pension as they would have paid by virtue of that notice if he had retired immediately before he died.

(10) Without prejudice to the generality of Regulation 3, the allocation of a portion of a pension, the giving of a notice or any other thing done under any provision of the former Regulations corresponding to this Regulation shall have effect for the purposes of this Regulation as if it had been done hereunder.

(11) Any reference in these Regulations to a widow's pension, however expressed, shall be construed as excluding a reference to a pension payable to a widow under this Regulation.

Limitation on right to commute or allocate part of pension

27. A regular policeman shall not under Regulation 23 or 24 commute for a lump sum, nor under Regulation 26 allocate in favour of his wife or other dependant, such a portion of his pension that that pension becomes payable at a rate less than 2 thirds of the rate at which it would have been payable but for the provisions of the said Regulations and Part IV of Schedule 2.

Award where no other award payable

28 —(1) This Regulation shall apply to a person who ceases or has ceased to be a member of a police force on or after 5th July 1948 in circumstances in which no transfer value is payable in respect of him and which do not entitle him to any award other than such as is mentioned in this Regulation.

(2) Subject to the provisions of Part V of Schedule 2, a person to whom this Regulation applies shall, on retirement, be entitled to an award of an amount equal to the amount of his aggregate pension contributions in respect of the relevant period of service.

(3) Subject to the provisions of Part V of Schedule 2, if a person to whom this Regulation applies is dismissed the police authority shall grant an award of an amount equal to the amount of his aggregate pension contributions in respect of the relevant period of service to such one of those persons hereinafter described as, in their discretion, they may think fit or, if in their discretion they think fit, shall distribute that award among such of those persons in such shares and in such manner as in their discretion they may think fit.

The persons above referred to are the said person and all his dependants.

PART IV

AWARDS ON DEATH

Widows

Widow's ordinary pension

29.—(1) This Regulation shall apply to a widow of a regular policeman—

(a) who, being entitled to reckon at least 3 years' pensionable service, dies or has died on or after 5th July 1948 while serving as such; or

(b) who, being entitled to reckon at least 3 years' pensionable service, retires or retired on or after 5th July 1948, and—

  (i) having so retired because he was disabled, dies or has died as a result of the same injury as resulted in his disablement, or

  (ii) having so retired with a pension, dies or has died while still in receipt of the pension; or (*c*) who, being entitled to reckon at least 3 years' approved service, retired between 1st September 1918 and 5th July 1948, and—

   (i) having so retired on account of an injury, dies or has died on or after 5th July 1948 in consequence of the injury, or

   (ii) having so retired with a pension, dies or has died on or after the said date while in receipt of the pension, or

   (iii) having so retired after being granted a pension by a police authority in respect of previous service as a regular policeman, dies or has died on or after the said date while in receipt of the pension; or

(*d*) who either was serving as a regular policeman on 1st September 1918 or was a person who, having while serving as a regular policeman been called out as a reservist or entered or re-entered, enlisted or re-enlisted in any of the armed forces for the purposes of the war in progress on that date, was on the said date serving in the armed forces, and—

   (i) would have been such a regular policeman as is referred to in subparagraph (*c*) if he had been entitled to reckon 3 years' approved service, or

   (ii) dies or has died on or after 5th July 1948 while entitled to a pension granted under the Police Reservists (Allowances) Act 1914**(a)**, whether or not he was in receipt of payments in respect of the said pension at the date of his death; or

(*e*) who died between 1st September 1918 and 5th July 1948 and whose widow would have been entitled to a pension if in paragraph (*a*) of section 3 of the Police Pensions Act 1921**(b)** the words "three years' approved service" had been substituted for the words "five years' approved service"; or

(*f*) who died before 1st September 1918 while serving as a regular policeman; or

(*g*) who retired on or before 1st September 1918 and has not been a regular policeman since that date and—

   (i) so retired on account of an injury or else with a pension and dies or has died either in consequence of the injury or else while in receipt of the pension, or

   (ii) dies or has died while entitled to a pension granted under the Police Reservists (Allowances) Act 1914, whether or not he was in receipt of payments in respect of the said pension at the date of his death; or

(*h*) who, having while serving as a regular policeman been called out as a reservist or entered or re-entered, enlisted or re-enlisted in any of the armed forces for the purposes of the war in progress on 1st September 1918, died while so serving in the armed forces.

(2) A widow of a regular policeman to whom this Regulation applies shall be entitled to a widow's ordinary pension of an amount calculated in accordance with—

(*a*) Part I of Schedule 3, where immediately before his death or retirement her husband was paying pension contributions at a rate related to 6.25% of his pensionable pay;

(*b*) Part II of Schedule 3 in any other case, subject however to Part V of that Schedule, so however that the amount of the pension of the widow

---

(a) 1914 c. 34.   **(b)** 1921 c. 31.

of such a regular policeman as is mentioned in sub-paragraph (*e*), (*f*), (*g*) or (*h*) of paragraph (1), including any increase therein under Regulation 30, shall be reduced by the amount of any other pension which is also payable to her by the police authority in respect of her husband's death.

Discretionary increase in widow's ordinary pension

30.—(1) Where a widow who is in receipt of an ordinary pension calculated in accordance with Part II of Schedule 3 would have been entitled to receive widow's benefit or a retirement pension under the National Insurance Act 1965 or under the National Insurance Act 1946, either as originally enacted or as amended by any subsequent enactment, had her husband satisfied the contribution conditions therefor, the police authority may, in their discretion and in accordance with the provisions of this Regulation, increase that ordinary pension.

(2) The increase shall be payable only in respect of any week during which the widow is not receiving—

(*a*) a retirement pension under the National Insurance Act 1965;

(*b*) a pension under the Old Age Pensions Act 1936**(a)**;

(*c*) any armed forces pension or award payable in respect of her husband in pursuance of any Royal Warrant or other instrument; or

(*d*) any payment made in respect of the death of her husband under any scheme made under the Personal Injuries (Emergency Provisions) Act 1939**(b)**.

(3) A pension increased under this Regulation shall be payable at a rate increased by £7·00 a week for the first 26 weeks that the pension is payable and thereafter during the periods and in the conditions set out in Part VI of Schedule 3 at a rate increased by £5·00 a week:

Provided that where a pension calculated in accordance with Scheme II of Part II of Schedule 3 is increased under this Regulation, the increased pension shall not be at a higher rate than it would have been if it had been calculated in accordance with Scheme I of the said Part II and increased in accordance with the provisions of this Regulation.

(4) In this Regulation a reference to widow's benefit or a retirement pension under the National Insurance Act 1965 does not include a reference to such a benefit or pension payable by virtue of section 1 of the National Insurance (Old persons' and widows' pensions and attendance allowance) Act 1970**(c)**; but the amount of any increase in a widow's pension under this Regulation in respect of any week shall be abated by the amount of any retirement pension received by the widow in respect of that week by virtue of the said section 1:

Provided that where the retirement pension so received is increased by virtue of section 40 of the National Insurance Act 1965, it shall be deemed not to have been so increased.

Widow's special pension

31.—(1) This Regulation shall apply to a widow of a member of a police force who dies or has died on or after 5th July 1948 as the result of an injury received without his own default in the execution of his duty.

(a) 1936 c. 31. **(b)** 1939 c. 82.
(c) 1970 c. 51.

(2) A widow to whom this Regulation applies shall be entitled to a widow's special pension.

(3) Without prejudice to Regulation 32, a widow's special pension shall be calculated in accordance with Part III of Schedule 3, subject however to Part V of that Schedule.

Widow's augmented award

32.—(1) This Regulation shall apply to a widow of a member of a police force whose death is the result of an injury received without his own default in the execution of his duty where, subject to paragraph (5), one of the following conditions is satisfied, namely that—

(*a*) he was attacked by a person or persons in a manner which was intrinsically likely to cause death and death ensued, on or after 5th July 1948, as a result of the attack, or

(*b*) the injury was received in the course of duties performed for the immediate purpose of effecting an arrest or of preventing an escape or rescue from legal custody and death ensued on or after 1st August 1964, or

(*c*) the injury was received in the course of duties performed—

(i) for the immediate purpose of saving the life of another person or of preventing loss of human life, and

(ii) in circumstances in which there was an intrinsic likelihood of his receiving a fatal injury,

and death ensued on or after 1st January 1970, or

(*d*) the police authority are of the opinion that one of the preceding conditions may be satisfied, and that this Regulation should apply, or

(*e*) the police authority are of the opinion that the injury was received otherwise than as aforesaid but in the course of duties performed in such circumstances that it would be inequitable if there were not payable in respect of him such an award as would have been payable had one of the conditions specified in sub-paragraphs (*a*), (*b*) and (*c*) been satisfied, and death ensued on or after 15th February 1971.

(2) A widow's special pension payable to a widow to whom this Regulation applies shall be calculated in accordance with Part IV of Schedule 3 in respect of any week for which the amount of the pension so calculated is greater than the amount calculated in accordance with Part III of Schedule 3, subject however, in either case, to Part V of that Schedule.

(3) A widow to whom this Regulation applies whose husband dies or died on or after 1st August 1964 shall be entitled to a gratuity, as hereinafter provided, in addition to a widow's special pension.

(4) The gratuity under paragraph (3) shall be of an amount equal to twice the annual pensionable pay, at the date of the death of the person in respect of whom the gratuity is payable, of a man—

(*a*) holding the rank of constable in the metropolitan police force or, where the death occurred before 1st April 1968, in the police force of which that person was a member, and

(*b*) entitled to reckon 30 years' service for the purposes of pay.

(5) Without prejudice to the application of this Regulation by virtue of paragraph (1) in the case of a widow of a member of a police force who died before 15th February 1971, this Regulation shall apply to such a widow if it would have applied by virtue of paragraph (1) had the words "in the opinion of the police authority" been inserted—

(a) in sub-paragraph (a) thereof, after the word "which",

(b) in sub-paragraph (b) thereof, after the word "performed", and

(c) in sub-paragraph (c) thereof, after the word "performed",

and had sub-paragraph (d) thereof been omitted.

Discretionary increase in widow's special pension

33.—(1) Where a widow who is entitled to a special pension under Regulation 31 of these Regulations would have been entitled to receive widow's benefit or a retirement pension under the National Insurance Act 1965 or under the National Insurance Act 1946, either as originally enacted or as amended by any subsequent enactment, had her husband satisfied the contribution conditions therefor, the police authority may, in their discretion and in accordance with the provisions of this Regulation, from time to time increase that special pension.

(2) The increase shall be payable only in respect of any week during which the widow is not receiving—

(a) a retirement pension under the National Insurance Act 1965;

(b) a pension under the Old Age Pensions Act 1936;

(c) any armed forces pension or award payable in respect of her husband in pursuance of any Royal Warrant or other instrument;

(d) any payment made in respect of the death of her husband under any scheme made under the Personal Injuries (Emergency Provisions) Act 1939; or

(e) a pension under section 19 of the National Insurance (Industrial Injuries) Act 1965.

(3) The weekly amount up to which the pension may be increased shall be a sixth of her husband's average pensionable pay for a week, increased in accordance with Part XIII of these Regulations, together with, for the first 26 weeks that the pension is payable, £7·00 a week and thereafter, during the periods and in the conditions set out in Part VI of Schedule 3, £5·00 a week.

(4) In this Regulation a reference to widow's benefit or a retirement pension under the National Insurance Act 1965 does not include a reference to such a benefit or pension payable by virtue of section 1 of the National Insurance (Old persons' and widows' pensions and attendance allowance) Act 1970; but the amount of any increase in a widow's pension under this Regulation in respect of any week shall be abated by the amount of any retirement pension received by the widow in respect of that week by virtue of the said section 1:

Provided that where the retirement pension so received is increased by virtue of section 40 of the National Insurance Act 1965, it shall be deemed not to have been so increased.

Widow's award under former Acts

34.—(1) This Regulation shall apply to a widow of a member of a police force who died before 5th July 1948.

(2) Where a widow to whom this Regulation applies was immediately before 5th July 1948 entitled to an award under the former Acts, she shall continue to be entitled to the award in all respects in the same manner as if no regulations under the Act had come into force, so however that in the case of a pension it shall be calculated in accordance with the provisions of this Regulation.

(3) Subject to the provisions of paragraph (4)—

(a) where the former Acts provided that the pension should be calculated otherwise than by reference to annual pay, it shall be of an amount calculated in accordance with Scheme I of Part II of Schedule 3;

(b) where the former Acts provided that it should be calculated by reference to annual pay, it shall be of an amount calculated in accordance with those Acts (without taking into account any increase under the Pensions (Increase) Acts 1944 and 1947(a)) increased either in accordance with Part XIII of these Regulations or by such amount as will secure that it is not less than it would have been had it fallen to be calculated in accordance with sub-paragraph (a), whichever increase is from time to time the more favourable to the widow.

(4) Where a widow is entitled under this Regulation to a pension and her husband acting in the execution of his duty as a member of a police force was attacked by a person or persons in a manner which in the opinion of the police authority was intrinsically likely to cause death and death ensued as a result of the attack, then the pension shall be of an amount calculated in accordance with Part IV of Schedule 3, subject however to Part V of that Schedule, in respect of any week for which that amount is greater than the amount calculated in accordance with paragraph (3) together with any increase therein under Regulation 35.

Discretionary increase in widow's award under former Acts

35.—(1) Where a widow is entitled to a pension calculated in accordance with Regulation 34(3), the police authority may, in their discretion and in accordance with the provisions of this Regulation, increase that pension.

(2) The increase shall be payable only in respect of any week during which the widow is not receiving—

(a) widow's benefit under the National Insurance Act 1965(b);

(b) a retirement pension under that Act;

(c) a pension under the Old Age Pensions Act 1936;

(d) any armed forces pension or award payable in respect of her husband in pursuance of any Royal Warrant or other instrument; or

(e) any payment made in respect of the death of her husband under any scheme made under the Personal Injuries (Emergency Provisions) Act 1939.

(3) A pension increased under this Regulation shall be payable during the periods and in the conditions set out in Part VI of Schedule 3 at a rate increased by £5·00 a week:

Provided that where a pension calculated in accordance with Regulation 34(3)(b), otherwise than by reference to the non-accidental rate specified in paragraph 7 of Part II of Schedule 1 to the Police Pensions Act 1921, is increased under this Regulation, the increased pension shall not be at a higher rate than it would have been if it had been calculated in accordance with Regulation 34(3)(a) and increased in accordance with the provisions of this Regulation.

(4) In this Regulation a reference to widow's benefit or a retirement pension under the National Insurance Act 1965 does not include a reference to such a benefit or pension payable by virtue of section 1 of the National Insurance (Old persons' and widows' pensions and attendance allowance) Act 1970; but the amount of any increase in a widow's pension under this Regulation in respect of any week shall be abated by the amount of any retirement pension received by the widow in respect of that week by virtue of the said section 1:

Provided that where the retirement pension so received is increased by virtue of section 40 of the National Insurance Act 1965, it shall be deemed not to have been so increased.

Gratuity in lieu of pension

36.—(1) Where a widow is entitled to a pension and the police authority are satisfied that there is sufficient reason for granting her a gratuity in lieu thereof, they may, subject to the provisions of Regulation 48, in their discretion and with her consent substitute for the pension a gratuity calculated in accordance with Part VII of Schedule 3.

(2) Where the police authority are precluded by reason of the provisions of Regulation 48 from exercising their discretion under the preceding paragraph in the manner in which they would, but for those provisions, exercise it, they may, subject to those provisions, exercise that discretion in relation to part only of the pension.

Widow's ordinary gratuity

37.—(1) This Regulation shall apply to a widow of a member of a police force who—

(a) dies or has died on or after 5th July 1948, while serving as a regular policeman; or

(b) dies or has died on or after 3rd January 1949, while called up for service as an auxiliary policeman; or

(c) dies or has died on or after 1st January 1963, while serving as a member of an overseas corps otherwise than as a regular policeman.

(2) The widow of a regular policeman to whom this Regulation applies by virtue of sub-paragraph (a) of paragraph (1) shall, if she is not entitled to a pension, be entitled to a widow's ordinary gratuity calculated in accordance with Part VIII of Schedule 3.

(3) The widow of an auxiliary policeman or member of an overseas corps to whom this Regulation applies by virtue of sub-paragraph (b) or (c) of paragraph (1) shall, if she is not entitled to a special pension, be entitled to a gratuity of an amount equal to that of his aggregate pension contributions in respect of the relevant period of service.

Limitation on award to widow with reference to date of marriage

38.—(1) A widow shall not be entitled to a widow's ordinary pension unless she was married to her husband before he last ceased to be a regular policeman.

(2) A widow shall not be entitled to a widow's special pension or gratuity under Regulation 32(3) unless she was married to her husband—

(*a*) before he last ceased to be a regular policeman, if he received the injury while serving as a regular policeman;

(*b*) before the end of the continuous period of service during which he received the injury, in any other case.

Limitation on award to widow living apart from husband

39.—(1) Subject to paragraph (2), a widow shall not be entitled to an award under any provision of this Part of these Regulations, other than Regulation 34, if at the time of her husband's death—

(*a*) she was separated from him by an order or decree of a competent court; and

(*b*) he was not required by an order or decree of a competent court to contribute to her support and was not in fact regularly contributing to her support.

(2) Nothing in paragraph (1) shall apply to an award to a widow if she became entitled to the like award under the corresponding provision of the former Regulations before 1st April 1956, but in such a case, where the widow was living apart from her husband at the time of his death, the award shall not be payable unless either—

(*a*) at the time of his death her husband was regularly contributing to her support, or was liable to contribute to her support by virtue of any agreement or any order of a competent court; or

(*b*) she was living apart from him because he had deserted her:

Provided that where the preceding provisions of this paragraph would prevent the payment of an award, the police authority may, in their descretion, if they consider that the application of those provisions would cause substantial hardship in that case, pay the award.

(3) For the purposes of this Regulation contributions to a woman for the support of her child shall be treated as contributions to her support.

Termination of widow's pension on remarriage

40.—(1) Where a widow entitled to a pension under any provision of this Part of these Regulations, other than Regulation 34, remarries or has remarried, she shall not be entitled to receive any payment on account of the pension in respect of any period after her remarriage:

Provided that if at any time after her remarriage she has again become a widow or that marriage has been dissolved, the police authority may, in their discretion, bring the pension into payment.

(2) Where a widow entitled to a gratuity under this Part of these Regulations remarries or has remarried, so much of the gratuity as has not been paid before her remarriage shall not be payable thereafter:

Provided that if at any time after her remarriage the woman has again become a widow or that marriage has been dissolved, the police authority may, in their discretion, pay to her the sums which they were actually or contingently liable to pay to her in respect of the gratuity immediately before her remarriage.

(3) Where after her husband's death a woman has cohabited with another man, this Regulation shall apply as if for the period of such cohabitation she were married to him and any reference in this Regulation to her remarriage, her again becoming a widow or the marriage being dissolved shall be construed accordingly.

Children

Child's ordinary allowance

41.—(1) This Regulation shall apply to a child of a regular policeman who dies or has died on or after 5th July 1948—

(a) while serving as such; or

(b) having retired with a pension, while still in receipt of the pension; or

(c) having retired with a gratuity when entitled to reckon at least 3 years' pensionable service.

(2) A child to whom this Regulation applies shall be entitled to a child's ordinary allowance for such period or periods, if any, as the mother is not in receipt of an ordinary pension payable in respect of the father's death and calculated in accordance with paragraph 1 of Part I of Schedule 3.

(3) A child's ordinary allowance shall be calculated in accordance with Part I of Schedule 4, subject however to Part IV of that Schedule.

Child's special allowance

42.—(1) This Regulation shall apply to a child of a member of a police force who dies or has died on or after 5th July 1948 as the result of an injury received without his own default in the execution of his duty.

(2) A child to whom this Regulation applies shall be entitled to a child's special allowance calculated in accordance with Part II of Schedule 4, subject however to Part IV of that Schedule.

Child's special gratuity

43.—(1) This Regulation shall apply to a child of a member of a police force who dies or has died on or after 1st August 1964 as the result of an injury received in the execution of his duty where, subject to paragraph (4), one of the conditions set out in Regulation 32(1) is satisfied and—

(a) in the case of a man, does not leave a widow entitled to a gratuity under Regulation 32(3), or

(b) in the case of a woman, was the child's only surviving parent:

Provided that this Regulation shall apply to a child who at the date of the parent's death has attained the age of 16 years only if at that date the child has not attained the age of 19 years and either is undergoing full-time education or is an apprentice.

(2) A child to whom this Regulation applies shall be entitled to a gratuity, as hereinafter provided, in addition to a child's special allowance.

(3) The gratuity under paragraph (2) shall be of the like amount as a widow's gratuity under Regulation 32(3) except that, where two or more gratuities are payable under paragraph (2) in respect of the death of the same person, each gratuity shall be of the said amount divided by the number of such gratuities.

(4) Without prejudice to the application of this Regulation by virtue of paragraph (1) in the case of a child of a member of a police force who died before 15th February 1971, this Regulation shall apply to such a child if it would have applied by virtue of paragraph (1) had Regulation 32(1) been modified as provided in Regulation 32(5).

Discretionary increase in child's ordinary or special allowance

44. Subject to the provisions of these Regulations, a child's ordinary or special allowance may, if the police authority in their discretion from time to time think fit, be increased in accordance with Part III of Schedule 4, subject however to Part IV of that Schedule.

Gratuity in lieu of allowance

45.—(1) Where a child is entitled to an ordinary or special allowance and the police authority are satisfied that there are sufficient reasons for the grant of a gratuity in lieu thereof, they may, subject to the provisions of Regulation 48, in their discretion and with the consent of the child's surviving parent (if any) or guardian, substitute for the allowance a gratuity calculated in accordance with Part V of Schedule 4.

(2) Where the police authority are precluded by reason of the provisions of Regulation 48 from exercising their discretion under the preceding paragraph in the manner in which they would but for those provisions exercise it, they may, subject to those provisions, exercise that discretion in relation to part only of the allowance.

Limitation on right to child's allowance

46.—(1) A child's ordinary or special allowance shall not be payable under these Regulations—

(*a*) to a child born on or after the relevant date otherwise than of a marriage which took place before the relevant date;

(*b*) by virtue of his being a step-child, to the child of a spouse whose marriage to the parent in respect of whose death the allowance is payable took place on or after the relevant date;

(*c*) by virtue only of his being an adopted child, to a child adopted on or after the relevant date; or

(*d*) by virtue of his being a step-child, adopted child or illegitimate child, to a child who was not substantially dependent on the parent in respect of whose death the allowance is payable at the time of that parent's death.

(2) The relevant date, in the case of a child's ordinary allowance, is the date on which the person in respect of whose death the allowance is payable last ceased to be a regular policeman.

(3) The relevant date, in the case of a child's special allowance—

(*a*) if the person in respect of whose death the allowance is payable received the injury while he was a regular policeman, is the date on which he last ceased to be a regular policeman;

(*b*) if the said person received the injury while serving as an auxiliary policeman, is the end of the continuous period of active service during which he received the injury;

(*c*) if the said person received the injury while serving as a member of an overseas corps and he was not a reversionary member of a home police force, is the date of the end of the tour of overseas service during which he received the injury.

(4) This Regulation shall apply in relation to a child's gratuity under Regulation 43(2) as it applies in relation to a child's special allowance.

General

Awards to dependent relatives or estate

47.—(1) Where a member of a police force dies while serving as such and no other award is payable under these Regulations, the police authority—

(a) may, if in their discretion they think fit, grant a gratuity to any of his relatives who were dependent on him to any degree at the time of his death; and

(b) if either no gratuity is paid under sub-paragraph (a) or any gratuities so paid do not exhaust the maximum amount provided for in paragraph (3), shall pay his legal personal representatives a gratuity sufficient to exhaust the said maximum amount.

(2) Where a member of a police force dies while in receipt of a pension and death—

(a) results from an injury received in the execution of his duty; or

(b) takes place within 2 years of the grant of his pension,

the police authority may, in their discretion, grant a gratuity to any relative who was at the time of his death dependent on him to any degree.

(3) The aggregate of all gratuities paid under this Regulation shall not exceed the aggregate pension contributions in respect of the relevant period of service of the member of the police force concerned.

Limitation on discretion to grant a gratuity in lieu of a pension or allowance

48.—(1) Where a person has died while in receipt of a pension other than a supplemental pension (in this Regulation referred to as "the principal pension"), the police authority shall not under Regulation 36 or 45 substitute for the whole or any part of a widow's pension or child's allowance payable in respect of him a gratuity the actuarial value of which, when added to that of—

(a) any other gratuity so substituted under Regulation 36 or 45; and

(b) any lump sum paid under Regulation 23 or 24 by reason that a portion of the principal pension was commuted,

exceeds a quarter of the actuarial value of the principal pension, any reduction therein under Regulation 23 or 24 being ignored.

(2) For the purposes of this Regulation the actuarial value of a gratuity, lump sum or pension shall be the actuarial value at the time of the husband's or parent's retirement as calculated by the Government Actuary.

Prevention of duplication

49.—(1) A person who, but for this Regulation, would be entitled to receive two awards under this Part of these Regulations in respect of any particular period shall be entitled to receive one only of those awards in respect of that period; and the award payable shall be that from time to time selected by the person or, in default of such selection, where one award is for the time being greater than the other, the award which is for the time being the greater.

(2) For the purposes of this Regulation a gratuity granted under Regulation 32(3), 37(3) or 43(2) or substituted for part of a widow's pension or child's allowance under Regulation 36 or 45, as the case may be, shall be ignored.

Part V

Pensionable Service

Reckoning of pensionable service

50. The pensionable service reckonable by a member of a police force at any date (hereafter referred to in this Part of these Regulations as the "relevant date") shall be determined in accordance with the succeeding provisions of these Regulations:

Provided that the following periods shall not be reckonable by a regular policeman as pensionable service in the cases and for the purposes hereinafter mentioned:—

(*a*) in the case of a woman, any period of unpaid maternity leave;

(*b*) if the police authority so direct, in the case of a person who before 15th February 1971 has been suspended under regulations from time to time in operation under section 4 of the Police Act 1919(a), section 11 of the Police (Scotland) Act 1956, section 33 of the Police Act 1964(b) or section 26 of the Police (Scotland) Act 1967(c), not being a person who returned to duty at the end of the period of suspension without having been found guilty of any offence under such regulations, the whole or such part of the period of suspension as may be directed;

(*c*) for the purposes of any award granted on the death or retirement, before 1st July 1949, of a person who was not permanently disabled as the result of an injury received in the execution of his duty as a regular policeman without his own default, any period of service before attaining the age of 20 years.

Current service

51.—(1) Subject to the provisions of these Regulations, there shall be reckonable by a regular policeman in respect of his service as such in the force in which he is or was serving on the relevant date, being service since he last joined or rejoined that force before that date—

(*a*) all such service on or after 5th July 1948; and

(*b*) where he last joined or rejoined the force before 5th July 1948, any period of approved service which he was entitled to reckon immediately before that date under the former Acts.

(2) There shall be reckonable by an auxiliary policeman as pensionable service, in respect of his service in the force in which he is or was serving on the relevant date, all his active service as such since he was last called up for active service before that date.

(3) There shall be reckonable as pensionable service by a member of an overseas corps who is not, or was not, on the relevant date a reversionary member of a home police force all his service as a member of an overseas corps, while not being such a reversionary member, since he last became a member of an overseas corps before the relevant date.

Previous service reckonable without payment

52. There shall be reckonable by a regular policeman as pensionable service—

(*a*) where from being a regular policeman in another force he transferred on or after 5th July 1948 to the force in which he is or was serving on the

---

(a) 1919 c. 46. **(b)** 1964 c. 48.

(c) 1967 c. 77.

relevant date, any period of pensionable service reckonable by him immediately before the transfer;

(*b*) where he previously retired with an ill-health pension or a pension under the former Acts from the force in which he is or was serving on the relevant date, that pension was terminated in whole or in part under Regulation 65 or any corresponding provision of the former Regulations or former Acts, and he rejoined the force on or after 5th July 1948, any period of pensionable service or of approved service under the former Acts, as the case may be, reckonable by him at the time he retired;

(*c*) where he previously retired with a pension under the former Acts in respect of a non-accidental injury from the force in which he is or was serving on the relevant date, and the approved service under the former Acts reckonable by him at the time he retired is reckonable as pensionable service under sub-paragraph (*b*), the period during which he was in receipt of the pension;

(*d*) where the relevant date is 15th May 1950 or any later date and he left the Royal Ulster Constabulary with the consent of the chief officer of that force and the approval of the Police Authority for Northern Ireland for the purpose of becoming a regular policeman in a home police force, any period of approved or pensionable service which was reckonable by him, immediately before he so left, for the purposes of any legislation for the time being in force in Northern Ireland relating to the superannuation of members of the Royal Ulster Constabulary;

(*e*) where he previously engaged for a period of service in the Royal Ulster Constabulary as mentioned in section 2(1) of the Police Act 1969(a) and he exercises the right of reversion to a home police force conferred by the said section 2(1) or, on that right arising, does not exercise it but joins another home police force, any period of pensionable service which was reckonable by him, for the purposes mentioned in sub-paragraph (*d*), immediately before he left the Royal Ulster Constabulary.

Previous service reckonable on payment

53.—(1) There shall be reckonable by a regular policeman as pensionable service, in the circumstances specified in this Regulation, the periods so specified before he last entered the force before the relevant date, subject to his having made to the police authority the appropriate payment.

(2) Where before the relevant date he retired without a pension (including a pension under the former Acts) from the same force as that in which he is, or was, serving on the relevant date—

(*a*) the period shall be any period of pensionable service, or approved service under the former Acts, reckonable by him at the time he retired, not being a period reckonable by virtue of Regulation 51(1)(*b*);

(*b*) the appropriate payment shall be an amount equal to any gratuity or return of pension contributions or rateable deductions, as the case may be, which he may have received on his retirement together with the balance outstanding immediately before his retirement of any sum he had undertaken to pay in accordance with Schedule 5, so however, that, where immediately before his retirement he was paying additional pension contributions under Regulation 62 or any corresponding provision of the former Regulations, the payment shall be reduced by the amount he had paid by way of such contributions.

(a) 1969 c. 63.

(3) Where he previously served as a member of the first class of the police reserve, of the Police War Reserve or of Class A of the Women's Auxiliary Police Corps or, subject to paragraph (5), as a special constable—

(*a*) the period shall be half the period of active service as a member of the first class of the police reserve during which he was not in receipt of a pension (including a pension under the former Acts), half the period of active service as a member of the Police War Reserve, half the period of active service as a member of the Women's Auxiliary Police Corps, whether in Class A of that Corps or otherwise, or half the period of service as a special constable while serving as such in a whole-time capacity and in receipt of pay in respect of such service, as the case may be;

(*b*) the appropriate payment shall be 5 % of, in the case of a man, £4·50, and in the case of a woman, £3·95, in respect of each week which he is entitled under this paragraph to reckon as pensionable service.

(4) Where he was a person to whom section 1 of the Police and Firemen (War Service) Act 1939(a), as extended by Regulation 60DA of the Defence (General) Regulations 1939, applied—

(*a*) the period shall be the period during which he was engaged in war work within the meaning of the said Defence Regulation during the year 1947;

(*b*) the appropriate payment shall be the aggregate of the payments that he would have been required to make under the said Act as so extended in respect of the said period if the emergency that was the occasion of the passing of that Act had not come to an end.

(5) Except where the appropriate payment has been made before 1st January 1963, the references in paragraph (3) to a special constable shall be construed as references only to a special constable appointed—

(*a*) in England or Wales, under the Special Constables Act 1831(b) or section 196 of the Municipal Corporations Act 1882(c);

(*b*) in Scotland, under section 96 of the Burgh Police (Scotland) Act 1892(d) or the corresponding provisions of any local enactment.

Previous service reckonable at discretion of police authority

54.—(1) If the appropriate police authority in their discretion have so decided, there shall be reckonable by a regular policeman as pensionable service, in the circumstances specified in this Regulation, the periods before he last entered the force before the relevant date so specified, subject, in the case of such a period as is mentioned in paragraph (2), to his having made to that police authority the appropriate payment.

(2) Where he previously retired without a pension (including a pension under the former Acts) from a force other than that in which he is or was serving on the relevant date—

(*a*) the period shall be the whole of any period of pensionable service, or approved service under the former Acts, reckonable by him at the time he retired, not being a period reckonable by virtue of Regulation 51(1)(*b*), or so much of that period as the appropriate police authority in their discretion think fit;

(a) 1939 c. 103.
(c) 1882 c. 50.

(b) 1831 c. 41.
(d) 1892 c. 55.

(b) the appropriate police authority shall be the authority of the force in which he is or was serving on the relevant date;

(c) the appropriate payment shall be the whole or the proportionate part of an amount equal to any gratuity or return of pension contributions or rateable deductions, as the case may be, which he may have received on his retirement together with the balance outstanding immediately before he retired of any sum he had undertaken to pay in accordance with Schedule 5, so however that, where immediately before his retirement he was paying additional pension contributions under Regulation 62 or any corresponding provision of the former Regulations, the payment shall be reduced by the whole or the proportionate part of the amount he had paid by way of such contributions.

(3) Where he previously ceased to serve as a regular policeman in order to enter or enlist in any of the armed forces for the purposes of the war in progress on 18th September 1914—

(a) the period shall be his period of service in the armed forces immediately following that enlistment or entry;

(b) the appropriate police authority shall be the authority of the force in which he ceased to serve as aforesaid.

(4) Where a serviceman (1939-1945), after receiving a pension under the Police and Firemen (War Service) Acts 1939 and 1944(a), rejoins or has rejoined the force in which he is or was serving on the relevant date, being the force of the police authority by whom the pension was payable—

(a) the period shall be the whole of the period for which he was in receipt of the said pension or such part thereof as the said police authority have, in their discretion, decided shall be reckonable;

(b) the appropriate police authority shall be the police authority of the force in which he is or was serving on the relevant date.

Previous service reckonable under interchange arrangements

55.—(1) Subject to paragraph 5 of Part I of Schedule 6, this Regulation shall apply to a regular policeman—

(a) who before he last became a regular policeman before the relevant date was in such service or employment as is mentioned in Schedule 6 by virtue of which he was subject to superannuation arrangements (hereafter in this Regulation referred to, respectively, as "former service" and "former superannuation arrangements");

(b) who has served as a regular policeman on or after the date specified in Schedule 6 in relation to the former service;

(c) who last became a regular policeman before the relevant date within 12 months of the termination of his former service or within such longer period as may be agreed, in the circumstances of his case, between the police authority and the authority specified in Schedule 6 in relation to his former service;

(d) in respect of whom such a transfer value relating to his former service as is mentioned in Schedule 6 is paid to the police authority of the force in which he is or was serving on the relevant date, and

---

(a) 1939 c. 103; 1944 c. 22.

(*e*) who, within 6 months of the date specified in Schedule 6 in relation to the former service or 3 months of last becoming a regular policeman before the relevant date, whichever is the later, or within such longer period as the police authority may allow in his case—

  (i) pays, or undertakes to pay in accordance with Schedule 5, a sum equal to the balance of any liability outstanding, immediately before he ceased to be engaged in his former service, in respect of payments or contributions he was then making as a condition of reckoning past service as contributing service or otherwise for the purposes of the former superannuation arrangements, being service taken into account for the purpose of calculating the transfer value referred to in sub-paragraph (*d*), and

  (ii) pays to the police authority a sum equal to the amount, if any, by which the transfer value referred to in sub-paragraph (*d*) falls to be reduced on account of any sum paid to him under the former superannuation arrangements by way of return of contributions.

(2) Subject to paragraph (3), there shall be reckonable by a regular policeman to whom this Regulation applies, as pensionable service in respect of his former service, 3 quarters of the period specified in paragraph (4).

(3) Where under the former superannuation arrangements—

  (*a*) the maximum pension payable (otherwise than on retirement occasioned by injury or ill-health) is payable where the person concerned has been engaged for a period of 30 years in service which counts in full for the purposes of those arrangements, or

  (*b*) after 20 years of such service, each year of service counts as 2 years service for the said purposes,

paragraph (2) shall not apply but there shall be reckonable as therein mentioned the whole of the period specified in paragraph (4) so, however, that, where under the former superannuation arrangements such provision as is mentioned in sub-paragraph (*a*) or (*b*) is made in relation only to service or employment of a description designated therein (in this paragraph referred to as "designated service") and the regular policeman's former service included designated service, there shall be reckonable as aforesaid—

  (i) the whole of that part of the period specified in paragraph (4) as is referable to designated service, and

  (ii) 3 quarters of that part of that period as is not so referable.

(4) The period referred to in paragraphs (2) and (3) shall be—

  (*a*) the period of service which is reckonable for the purpose of calculating the transfer value referred to in paragraph (1)(*d*); or

  (*b*) where separate calculations are made in respect of contributing and non-contributing service reckonable for the purpose of calculating the said transfer value, the aggregate of the period of contributing service and half the period of non-contributing service which is so reckonable.

Added years in case of chief constable displaced under Police Act 1946

56.—(1) Where a police area has been amalgamated with another police area by a scheme made under the Police Act 1946(**a**) and the chief constable of the force of an area so amalgamated is deemed to have retired under section 11(3) of that Act—

___

(**a**) 1946 c. 46.

(a) if during the period of 3 months referred to in the said provision he joins or joined the combined force, he shall be entitled to treat the period during which he was in receipt of a salary under the said provision as service in the combined force for the purpose of reckoning pensionable service;

(b) if during the said period he does not, or did not, join the combined force, at the expiration of the said 3 months there shall be reckonable by him as pensionable service the pensionable service which he was entitled to reckon at the date when he was so deemed to retire, with the addition of the said period of 3 months and also of the shortest of the following periods, namely:—

   (i) a period of 10 years,

   (ii) the period between the date on which he was so deemed to retire and the date on which he would, if he had continued to serve in the force from which he was so deemed to retire, have been entitled to reckon 30 years' pensionable service, and

   (iii) the period between the date when he was so deemed to retire and the date on which he would, if he were to live so long, attain the age of 65 years.

(2) The reference in paragraph (1) to the chief constable of the force of an amalgamated area includes a reference to a person who engaged for a tour of overseas service and, immediately before he so engaged, was the chief constable of the force of an area which, while he was so engaged, was amalgamated with another police area, and the reference to section 11(3) of the Police Act 1946 includes a reference to that provision as applied by section 14(3)(a) of that Act.

(3) In the application of this Regulation to Scotland, references to the Police Act 1946, section 11(3) and section 14(3)(a) thereof shall be construed as references to—

(a) the Police (Scotland) Act 1946(**a**), section 7(2) and section 9(3)(a) thereof, respectively; or

(b) the Police (Scotland) Act 1956, section 22(2) and section 23(2) thereof, respectively; or

(c) the Police (Scotland) Act 1967, section 23(2) and section 24(2) thereof, respectively.

Added years in case of displaced reversionary member of home police force

57. A reversionary member of a home police force—

(a) who was a member of the Special Police Corps of the Control Commission for Germany (British Element) or the Public Safety Branch of the Allied Commission for Austria (British Element); and

(b) who, after notice had been given to him that for the purpose of reducing the numbers of the corps it was desired to vary the tour of overseas service applicable in his case by advancing the date of its termination from a date at which he would have been entitled to retire and receive an ordinary pension, has had his tour of overseas service varied in accordance with the said notice; and

(c) who gave written notice to the Secretary of State of his intention to receive the benefit of any provision of the former Regulations corresponding to this Regulation, and of the date of the end of the period which he

(**a**) 1946 c. 71.

desired to reckon as a period of pensionable service thereunder, not being later than the date on which his tour of overseas service would have terminated if it had not been so varied,

shall on retirement at the end of his tour of overseas service from the overseas corps of which he was a member, otherwise than on being disabled, be entitled to reckon the pensionable service which he was then entitled to reckon, with the addition of the period between the time when he retired and such date as he may have specified in the aforesaid notice.

Certain service in the Glasgow, Orkney and Zetland police forces

58.—(1) In the case of a woman serving as a regular policewoman in the Glasgow police force on the relevant date who was attested as such a policewoman in that force at any time in the year 1924, there shall be reckonable as pensionable service the period of her service as an unattested policewoman in that force prior to the time at which she was attested as aforesaid, subject to her having paid to the police authority a contribution equal to 2·5% of her pay in respect of each week of her said service as an unattested policewoman.

(2) In the case of a person serving as a regular policeman in the Orkney or Zetland police force on the relevant date, there shall be reckonable as pensionable service the period of his non-contributing service, subject to his having paid to the police authority the appropriate pension contribution.

(3) For the purpose of paragraph (2)—

    (a) non-contributing service means, in the case of a member of the Orkney police force, whole-time service in that force before 15th January 1938, or, in the case of a member of the Zetland police force, whole-time service in that force or in the Lerwick Burgh police force before 29th May 1940;

    (b) the appropriate pension contribution means a contribution equal to 2·5% of his pay in respect of each week of his non-contributing service, within the meaning of sub-paragraph (a), during any period before 22nd November 1926, together with 5% of his pay in respect of each week of such service on or after that date.

Approved service reckonable under former Acts

59.—(1) Any reference in this Part of these Regulations to approved service reckonable under the former Acts shall include—

    (a) subject to paragraph (2), a reference to approved service which would have been so reckonable if there had been omitted from section 7(1) of the Police Pensions Act 1921 the words "but shall not include" to the end;

    (b) subject to paragraph (3), a reference to approved service which would have been so reckonable if there had been omitted from section 8(1) of the said Act the words "in which he has completed not less than one year's approved service, and".

(2) Paragraph (1)(a) shall not apply for the purposes of an award granted on a person's death or retirement before 1st July 1949 or on the disablement of a person who has not been a member of a police force since that date.

(3) Paragraph (1)(b) shall not apply for the purposes of an award granted on a person's death, retirement or disablement before 1st January 1952, except in the case of a reversionary member of a home police force who had served as an overseas policeman for a year or less.

PART VI

PENSIONABLE PAY AND CONTRIBUTIONS

Pensionable pay

60.—(1) The pensionable pay of a member of a police force at any time means his pay at the rate to which he is or was at that time entitled.

(2) The average pensionable pay of a member of a police force means the aggregate of his pensionable pay during the 3 years immediately preceding the relevant date, ignoring any temporary reduction in rate of pay by way of punishment, divided by 3:

Provided that where he was in receipt of pensionable pay for only part of the said period, the said aggregate shall be divided by the number of years and that fraction of a year for which he was in receipt of pensionable pay during the said period.

(3) The relevant date for the purposes of calculating average pensionable pay shall be—

(a) where an award is made to or in respect of a regular policeman, the date when he last ceased to be such in the force of the police authority by whom the award is payable;

(b) where an award is made to or in respect of an auxiliary policeman, the date of the end of the continuous period of active service as such during which he received the injury which resulted in disablement;

(c) where an award is made to or in respect of an overseas policeman who is not a reversionary member of a home police force, the date of the end of the tour of overseas service during which he received the injury which resulted in disablement.

(4) Where, for the purpose of calculating an award to a widow or a child, it is necessary to determine average pensionable pay for a period of a week, it shall be taken to be average pensionable pay divided by $52\frac{1}{8}$.

(5) A serviceman shall, for the purposes of these Regulations, be deemed to receive, during his period of relevant service in the armed forces, the amount of pay he would have received if he had continued to serve in his former force.

(6) For the purpose of calculating the pension of the chief constable of the force of an area which has been amalgamated with another police area by a scheme made under the Police Act 1946, the Police (Scotland) Act 1946, the Police (Scotland) Act 1956(a) or the Police (Scotland) Act 1967, being a pension payable by virtue of Regulation 98(2), his average pensionable pay shall include—

(a) where he was immediately before the date on which the area was amalgamated in receipt of a rent allowance, the annual amount of that rent allowance;

(b) where he was immediately before the said date provided with a house or quarters free of rent and rates, the annual worth of the house or quarters as determined in their discretion and with the approval of the Secretary of State by the police authority of the force of which he was chief constable.

(a) 1956 c. 26.

(7) The average pensionable pay of a reversionary member of a home police force who gave such notice as is referred to in Regulation 57 shall be deemed to be a third of the aggregate of his pensionable pay and the pay to which he would have been entitled, if he had continued to serve in the overseas corps without alteration in the amount of his pay, during the 3 years immediately preceding the date specified in the said notice.

(8) Where a member of a home police force—

(a) has been a member of the Special Police Corps of the Control Commission for Germany (British Element) or the Public Safety Branch of the Allied Commission for Austria (British Element) and a reversionary member of a home police force;

(b) has had his tour of overseas service as a member of one of the aforesaid overseas corps varied by way of advancement of the date of its termination; and

(c) on or after 1st October 1949 has ceased to be such a member and has exercised his right of reversion to a home police force,

then his average pensionable pay shall be deemed to be not less than it would have been had he been entitled, until the date when his tour of overseas service would have terminated if it had not been so varied, to a rate of pay equal to the rate of pay to which he was entitled immediately before he ceased to be a member of one of the aforesaid overseas corps.

(9) Where a regular policeman has served as a member of the Royal Ulster Constabulary on or after 1st May 1970 and so served during part of the period of 3 years referred to in paragraph (2), then, that paragraph shall have effect in his case as if any reference therein to pensionable pay included a reference to such pay within the meaning of the legislation for the time being in force in Northern Ireland relating to the superannuation of members of the Royal Ulster Constabulary.

Rate of payment of pension contributions

61.—(1) Subject to the provisions of these Regulations, a member of a police force shall pay pension contributions to the police authority, in the case of a man, at the rate of 6p a week less than 6·25% of his pensionable pay or, in the case of a woman, less than 4·5% of her pensionable pay.

(2) Where a man was on 1st April 1956—

(a) a regular policeman in a home police force;

(b) a reversionary member of a home police force; or

(c) a serviceman whose period of relevant service in the armed forces included that day,

then, unless he elected in accordance with the relevant provisions of the former Regulations to pay pension contributions at the rate specified in the preceding paragraph, he shall pay pension contributions at the rate of 6p a week less than 5% of his pensionable pay.

(3) Where a man was on 1st April 1956 an auxiliary policeman, he shall in respect of any period during which he is such a policeman pay pension contributions at the rate of 6p a week less than 5% of his pensionable pay.

(4) Where a man who was on 1st April 1956 an auxiliary policeman becomes or has become a regular policeman, then, unless before the day appropriate to his case specified in paragraph (5), by written notice to the police authority he elects or has elected to pay pension contributions at the rate specified in para-

graph (1), he shall in respect of any period on or after the appropriate day during which he is a member of a police force pay such contributions at the rate of 6p a week less than 5% of his pensionable pay and there shall be refunded to him by the police authority to whom he has paid pension contributions the difference between 5% and 6·25% of his pensionable pay in respect of the period between his becoming a regular policeman and the day appropriate to his case.

(5) For the purposes of the preceding paragraph the appropriate day means—

    (a) the day following the expiration of 3 months from his first becoming a regular policeman after 1st April 1956; or

    (b) where he retires or has retired before the expiration of that period, the day immediately preceding his retirement,

except that in the case of a person who gives or has given written notice to the police authority of his intention not to elect as mentioned in the preceding paragraph, the appropriate day means the day of the giving of such notice.

(6) This Regulation shall apply, in the case of a regular policeman who was on 5th July 1948 a member of a police force or a serviceman (1939-1945) and did not give notice in accordance with the relevant provisions of the former Regulations, as if for any reference to a rate of 6p a week less than a percentage of his pensionable pay there were substituted a reference to a rate of 1p a week less than that percentage of his pensionable pay.

(7) In this Regulation a reference to the relevant provisions of the former Regulations is a reference—

    (a) for the purposes of paragraph (2), to the provisions of Regulation 35(2) of the Police Pensions Regulations 1955(a), as set out in Regulation 13 of the Police Pensions Regulations 1956(b), or of Regulation 37(2) of the Police Pensions (Scotland) Regulations 1955(c), as set out in Regulation 13 of the Police Pensions (Scotland) Regulations 1956(d);

    (b) for the purposes of paragraph (6), to the provisions of Regulation 41(3) of the Police Pensions Regulations 1948(e) or of Regulation 43(3) of the Police Pensions (Scotland) Regulations 1948(f).

Rate of payment of additional contributions in certain cases

62.—(1) Where a man elected, in accordance with the relevant provisions of the former Regulations, to pay additional pension contributions and has not since he so elected become entitled to reckon 25 years' pensionabie service or retired, he shall pay such contributions at a rate calculated in accordance with Schedule 7 until such time as he becomes entitled to reckon 25 years' pensionable service or retires, whichever is the earlier.

(2) In this Regulation the reference to the relevant provisions of the former Regulations is a reference to the provisions of Regulation 35A of the Police Pensions Regulations 1955, as set out in Regulation 13 of the Police Pensions Regulations 1956, or of Regulation 37A of the Police Pensions (Scotland) Regulations 1955, as set out in Regulation 13 of the Police Pensions (Scotland) Regulations 1956.

(a) S.I. 1955/480 (1955 II, p. 1903).   (b) S.I. 1956/385 (1956 II, p. 1808).
(c) S.I. 1955/485 (1955 II, p. 1959).   (d) S.I. 1956/434 (1956 II, p. 1842).
(e) S.I. 1948/1531 (1948 I, p. 3429).   (f) S.I. 1948/1530 (1948 I, p. 3503).

Application of Regulations 61 *and* 62 *to persons with service otherwise than in a police force*

63.—(1) This Regulation shall apply to a member of a police force who—

(*a*) first became a regular policeman on or after 1st January 1963 and is entitled to reckon pensionable service by virtue of service or employment (otherwise than as a member of a police force or of the Royal Ulster Constabulary) in respect of which he was subject to superannuation arrangements; or

(*b*) has been a member of the Royal Ulster Constabulary.

(2) In the case of a person to whom this Regulation applies by virtue of paragraph (1)(*a*) and who was excepted from the operation of any regulations made under section 110(1) of the National Insurance Act 1965 or under section 69(4) of the National Insurance Act 1946**(a)** or other provisions modifying the said superannuation arrangements in connection with the passing of the said Act of 1946, Regulation 61 shall apply as if he were such a person as is mentioned in paragraph (6) thereof.

(3) In the case of a person to whom this Regulation applies by virtue of paragraph (1)(*b*)—

(*a*) Regulation 61(2) shall apply as if a member of the Royal Ulster Constabulary were a regular policeman and the reference therein to the relevant provisions of the former Regulations included a reference to paragraph 36(6) of the Schedule to the Royal Ulster Constabulary Pensions Order 1949, as amended by the Royal Ulster Constabulary Pensions (Amending) Order 1956;

(*b*) Regulation 61(6) shall apply as if such a member were a regular policeman and the reference therein to the relevant provisions of the former Regulations included a reference to paragraph 36(3) of the Schedule to the said Order of 1949; and

(*c*) Regulation 62 shall apply as if the reference therein to the relevant provisions of the former Regulations included a reference to paragraph 36A of the Schedule to the said Order of 1949.

Method of payment of pension contributions

64. The pension contributions (including additional pension contributions, if any) upon each instalment of pay shall fall due at the same time as that instalment and may, without prejudice to any other method of payment, be discharged by way of a deduction of an appropriate amount made by the police authority from the said instalment.

PART VII

CANCELLATION, REVISION, REDUCTION AND WITHDRAWAL OF AWARDS

Cancellation of ill-health and supplemental pensions

65.—(1) As long as a person—

(*a*) is in receipt of an ill-health pension;

(*b*) would not, if he had continued to serve as a regular policeman instead of retiring with an ill-health pension, have been entitled to reckon 25 years' pensionable service; and

---

(a) 1946 c. 67.

(c) if he had continued so to serve, could not have been required to retire on account of age,

the police authority may, if they wish to exercise the powers conferred by this Regulation, consider, at such intervals as they in their discretion think proper, whether his disability has ceased.

(2) If on any such consideration it is found that his disability has ceased, the police authority may give the person concerned notice that if he wishes to rejoin the force as a regular policeman within a period of not less than 3 months from the date on which he has been given such notice he will be permitted to do so.

(3) If the person concerned within the period referred to in paragraph (2) offers to rejoin the force as a regular policeman, he shall be permitted to do so in a rank not lower than that he held immediately before he retired with the ill-health pension.

(4) On the person concerned rejoining the force as mentioned in paragraph (3) or, where he does not offer to rejoin within the period referred to in paragraph (2), at the end of that period, there shall be terminated—

(a) his ill-health pension or, where he retired on or after 3rd April 1961, the unsecured portion of that pension; and

(b) subject to paragraph (5), any supplemental pension to which he is entitled.

(5) Paragraph (4)(b) shall not apply to a supplemental pension payable to a person who last ceased to be a member of a police force before 1st July 1949.

(6) Where the unsecured portion of an ill-health pension is terminated under paragraph (4), the secured portion of that pension shall not be payable in respect of any period before insured pensionable age.

Reassessment of supplemental pension

66.—(1) Subject as hereinafter provided, where a supplemental pension is payable under these Regulations, the police authority shall, at such intervals as may be suitable, consider whether the degree of the pensioner's disablement has altered; and if after such consideration the police authority find that the degree of the pensioner's disablement has substantially altered, the pension shall be revised accordingly.

(2) Subject to paragraph (3), if on any such reconsideration it is found that his disability has ceased, his supplemental pension shall be terminated.

(3) Paragraph (2) shall not apply—

(a) where the person concerned has been a regular policeman and is also in receipt of an ordinary, ill-health or short service pension;

(b) where the person concerned last ceased to serve as a member of a police force on or after 1st July 1949, but before 25th April 1955, and the pension is payable in respect of an injury received while serving as a regular policeman; or

(c) where the person concerned last ceased to serve as a member of a police force before 1st July 1949.

Reduction of pension in case of default

67. Where a member of a police force or a person who has been a member of a police force becomes permanently disabled and has brought about or sub-stantially contributed to the disablement by his own default, the police authority may reduce the amount of any ill-health award or supplemental pension payable to him by them by an amount not exceeding a half of that to which he would otherwise be entitled:

Provided that this Regulation shall not apply where the person concerned has been a regular policeman and is in receipt of an ill-health pension and would, if he had continued to serve instead of retiring with that pension, have been entitled to reckon 25 years' pensionable service.

Withdrawal of pension during employment as a regular policeman

68.—(1) Subject to paragraph (2), a police authority by whom a pension is payable may, in their discretion, withdraw the whole or any part of the pension for any period during which the pensioner is employed as a regular policeman in any police force.

(2) This Regulation shall not apply to a widow's pension or pension under Regulation 25 or 26 payable in respect of the death of a member of a police force on or after 1st January 1963.

Discharge of liability of police authority on withdrawal of pension

69. To the extent to which a pension or allowance is withdrawn under any power conferred by the preceding provisions of these Regulations, the police authority shall be discharged from all actual or contingent liability in respect thereof.

PART VIII

DETERMINATION OF QUESTIONS

Reference of medical questions

70.—(1) Subject as hereinafter provided, the question whether a person is entitled to any and, if so, what awards under these Regulations shall be determined in the first instance by the police authority.

(2) Where the police authority are considering whether a person is permanently disabled, they shall refer for decision to a duly qualified medical practitioner selected by them the following questions:—

    (*a*) whether the person concerned is disabled;

    (*b*) whether the disablement is likely to be permanent;

and, if they are further considering whether to grant a supplemental pension, shall so refer the following questions:—

    (*c*) whether the disablement is the result of an injury received in the execution of duty; and

    (*d*) the degree of the person's disablement;

and, if they are considering whether to revise a supplemental pension, shall so refer question (*d*) above.

(3) A police authority, if they are considering the exercise of their powers under Regulation 67, shall refer the question whether the person concerned has brought about or substantially contributed to the disablement by his own default to a duly qualified medical practitioner selected by them for decision.

(4) The decision of the selected medical practitioner on the questions referred to him under this Regulation shall be expressed in the form of a certificate and shall, subject to Regulations 71 and 72, be final.

Appeal to medical referee

71.—(1) Where a person has been informed of the determination of the police authority on any question which involves the reference of questions under Regulation 70 to a selected medical practitioner, he shall, if, within 14 days after being so informed or such further period as the police authority may allow, he applies to the police authority for a copy of the certificate of the selected medical practitioner, be supplied with such a copy.

(2) If the person concerned is dissatisfied with the decision of the selected medical practitioner as set out in his certificate, he may, within 14 days after being supplied with the certificate or such longer period as the police authority may allow, and subject to and in accordance with the provisions of Schedule 8, give notice to the police authority that he appeals against the said decision, and the police authority shall notify the Secretary of State accordingly, and the Secretary of State shall appoint an independent person or persons (hereafter in these Regulations referred to as the "medical referee") to decide the appeal.

(3) The decision of the medical referee shall, if he disagrees with any part of the certificate of the selected medical practitioner, be expressed in the form of a certificate of his decision on any of the questions referred to the selected medical practitioner on which he disagrees with the latter's decision, and the decision of the medical referee shall, subject to the provisions of Regulation 72, be final.

Further reference to medical referee

72.—(1) A court hearing an appeal under section 5 of the Act or a tribunal hearing an appeal under Regulation 74 may, if they consider that the evidence before the medical authority who has given the final decision was inaccurate or inadequate, refer the decision of that authority to him for reconsideration in the light of such facts as the court or the tribunal may direct, and the medical authority shall accordingly reconsider his decision and, if necessary, issue a fresh certificate which, subject to any further reconsideration under this paragraph, shall be final.

(2) The police authority and the claimant may, by agreement, refer any final decision of a medical authority who has given such a decision to him for reconsideration on fresh evidence, and he shall accordingly reconsider his decision and, if necessary, issue a fresh certificate, which, subject to any further reconsideration under this paragraph or paragraph (1), shall be final.

(3) If a court or tribunal decide, or a claimant and the police authority agree, to refer a decision to the medical authority for reconsideration under this Regulation and that medical authority is unable or unwilling to act, the decision may be referred to a duly qualified medical practitioner selected by the court or tribunal or, as the case may be, agreed upon by the claimant and the police authority, and his decision shall have effect as if it were that of the medical authority who gave the decision which is to be reconsidered.

(4) In this Regulation a medical authority who has given a final decision means the selected medical practitioner, if the time for appeal from his decision has expired without an appeal to a medical referee being made, and the medical referee, if there has been such an appeal.

Refusal to be medically examined

73. If a question is referred to a medical authority under Regulation 70, 71 or 72 and the person concerned wilfully or negligently fails to submit himself to such medical examination or to attend such interviews as the medical authority may consider necessary in order to enable him to make his decision, then—

> (*a*) if the question arises otherwise than on an appeal to a medical referee, the police authority may make their determination on such evidence and medical advice as they in their discretion think necessary;

> (*b*) if the question arises on an appeal to a medical referee, the appeal shall be deemed to be withdrawn.

Appeal by overseas policeman, inspector of constabulary or central police officer

74.—(1) This Regulation shall apply in relation to—

> (*a*) an overseas policeman;

> (*b*) an inspector or assistant inspector of constabulary, or

> (*c*) a central police officer,

and any such person is hereafter in this Regulation referred to as an officer to whom this Regulation applies.

(2) Where an officer to whom this Regulation applies or person claiming an award in respect of such an officer is aggrieved by the refusal of the Secretary of State as police authority to admit a claim to receive as of right an award or a larger award than that granted, or by the forfeiture under the Act, by the Secretary of State as police authority, of any award granted to or in respect of such an officer, he may, subject to the proviso to subsection (1) and subsection (4) of section 5 of the Act, give notice of appeal to the Secretary of State.

(3) The Secretary of State, on receiving such notice of appeal, shall appoint an appeal tribunal (hereafter in this Regulation referred to as the tribunal) consisting of 3 persons, including a barrister or solicitor of not less than 7 years' standing and a retired member of a police force who, before he retired, held a rank not lower than that of superintendent.

(4) The time and place for the hearing, or any postponed or adjourned hearing, of the appeal shall be determined by the tribunal, which shall give reasonable notice thereof to the appellant and to the Secretary of State as police authority (hereafter in this Regulation described as the parties).

(5) Either party may be represented before the tribunal by counsel or by a solicitor, or by some other person approved by the tribunal, adduce evidence and cross-examine witnesses.

(6) The rules of evidence applicable in the case of an appeal to quarter sessions under section 5(1) of the Act shall apply in the case of an appeal under this Regulation.

(7) Subject to the preceding provisions of this Regulation, the tribunal shall determine its own procedure.

(8) The tribunal, after enquiring into the case, may make such order in the matter as appears to it to be just.

(9) The provisions of section 5(3) of the Act (which relates to appeals to the High Court) shall have effect in relation to any decision of a tribunal with the substitution for references to quarter sessions of references to the tribunal.

(10) In the case of an officer to whom this Regulation applies who has served as such on or after 15th February 1971 and who—

(*a*) in the case of an overseas policeman or a central police officer, immediately before becoming such, was a member of a Scottish police force, or

(*b*) in the case of an inspector or assistant inspector of constabulary, was appointed (or treated as appointed) under section 33 or 34 of the Police (Scotland) Act 1967;

this Regulation shall have effect as if—

(i) any reference to section 5 of the Act were a reference to that section in its application to Scotland;

(ii) any reference to a barrister were a reference to an advocate; and

(iii) any reference to quarter sessions or the High Court were a reference to the sheriff or, as the case may be, the Court of Session.

Part IX

Payment of Awards and Transfer Values

Authorities responsible for payment of awards

75.—(1) An award which is payable to or in respect of a person by reason of his having served as a regular policeman shall be payable by the police authority of the force in which he last served as such.

(2) An award which is payable to or in respect of a person by reason of his having been injured while serving as a member of a police force other than a regular policeman shall be payable by the police authority of the force in which he was serving when he received the injury.

Funds out of which and into which payments are to be made

76.—(1) Subject to the provisions of this Regulation, all payments by or to a police authority under these Regulations shall be paid out of or into the police fund.

(2) All payments by or to the Secretary of State as police authority for the metropolitan police district shall be paid out of or into the metropolitan police fund, save that there shall be paid out of moneys provided by Parliament or, as the case may be, into the Consolidated Fund—

(*a*) to such extent as in any particular case the Secretary of State may determine to be appropriate, any award to or in respect of a person who has been commissioner of police of the metropolis and any transfer value received or payable in respect of a person who is or has been commissioner of police of the metropolis;

(*b*) the whole of the pension contributions of the commissioner of police of the metropolis.

(3) All payments by or to the Secretary of State, by reason that he is treated as the police authority in relation to—

(*a*) an overseas policeman;

(*b*) an inspector or assistant inspector of constabulary; or (*c*) a central police officer,

shall be paid out of moneys provided by Parliament or, as the case may be, into the Consolidated Fund.

(4) Paragraph (1) shall not extend to Scotland.

Payment and duration of awards

77.—(1) Subject to the provisions of these Regulations, the pension of a member of a police force shall be payable in respect of each year as from the date of his retirement, except—

- (*a*) where the pension is an ordinary pension and the limitation imposed by Regulation 19(5) on the making of payments in respect of the period before he has attained the age of 50 years applies, in which case the pension shall be so payable as from the date he attains that age;
- (*b*) where the pension is a supplemental pension and he retired before becoming disabled, in which case the pension shall be so payable as from the date he becomes disabled.

(2) Subject to the provisions of these Regulations, a widow's pension or child's allowance shall be payable in respect of each week as from the death of the husband or, as the case may be, the parent or, in the case of an allowance payable to a posthumous child, as from the birth of the child, except—

- (*a*) where the husband or parent was in receipt of a pension and dies during a period in respect of which he has already received his pension, in which case the pension or allowance shall not be payable before the end of that period;
- (*b*) where the husband or parent has received a gratuity, in which case the pension or allowance shall be payable as from such time as the police authority may, in their discretion, determine to be reasonable, not being more than a year after his death, having regard to all the circumstances, including the amount of the gratuity;
- (*c*) where the entitlement to the pension or allowance arises, or arose under the former Regulations, at a date subsequent to the death of the husband or parent, in which case the pension or allowance shall, subject to sub-paragraphs (*a*) and (*b*), be payable as from that date.

(3) Subject to the provisions of these Regulations and of section 4 of the Act (which relates to forfeiture), a pension or allowance shall be payable as hereinafter provided, that is to say—

- (*a*) a pension payable to a member of a police force or a widow's pension shall be payable for life;
- (*b*) a child's allowance shall be payable up to the time when the child attains the age of 19 years:

Provided that a child's allowance shall not be payable for any period after the child has attained the age of 16 years during which he is neither undergoing full-time education nor is an apprentice.

(4) Subject to the provisions of these Regulations, every pension or allowance shall, subject to such delay as may be necessary for the purpose of determining any question as to the liability of the police authority in respect thereof, be discharged by payments in advance at such reasonable intervals as the police authority may, in their discretion, determine.

(5) Where a person dies after receiving a sum paid in advance on account of a pension or allowance, neither the said sum nor any part thereof shall be recoverable although referable to a period after his death.

(6) Where a widow remarries after receiving a sum paid in advance on account of a pension, neither the said sum nor any part thereof shall be recoverable although referable to a period after her remarriage.

(7) Subject to the provisions of these Regulations, a gratuity shall become payable as soon as the entitlement thereto arises and shall be payable in one sum:

Provided that where a police authority are satisfied that it would be for the advantage of the beneficiary to pay a gratuity in instalments, they may pay it in instalments of such reasonable amounts and over such reasonable period as they think fit.

Payment of awards otherwise than to person entitled

78.—(1) Where any sum is due on account of a pension, and any debt is due to the police authority or, where the police authority is the police authority for the metropolitan police district, to the Receiver for that district, from the pensioner, so much of the said sum as does not exceed the debt may be applied by the authority or, as the case may be, the Receiver in or towards the satisfaction of the debt:

Provided that where the pension is an ordinary, ill-health or short service pension granted on retirement on or after 3rd April 1961, and the sum due on account thereof is in respect of a period beyond insured pensionable age, only so much of the sum as is due on account of the unsecured portion of the pension may be applied as mentioned in this paragraph.

(2) If it appears to the police authority that a pensioner is by reason of mental disorder or otherwise incapable of managing his affairs, the authority may in their discretion pay the pension or any part thereof to any person having the care of the pensioner, and, in so far as they do not dispose of the pension in that manner, may apply it in such manner as they think fit for the benefit of the pensioner or his dependants.

(3) On the death of a pensioner to whom a sum not exceeding £500 is due on account of a pension, the police authority may, without probate, confirmation or any other formality or proof of title, pay the said sum to the persons appearing to the authority to be beneficially entitled to the personal estate of the deceased or, as the authority think fit, pay the said sum to one or more of those persons or distribute it among all or any of those persons in such proportions as the authority may determine.

(4) Where any sum is payable to a minor on account of a pension, the authority may, if they think fit, in lieu of paying the said sum to the minor, pay it to such other person as they may determine.

A person who receives any sum paid under this paragraph shall, subject to and in accordance with any directions of the police authority, apply the said sum for the benefit of the minor.

(5) This Regulation shall apply with respect to awards other than pensions as it applies with respect to pensions, and accordingly any reference in this Regulation to a pension shall be construed as including a reference to any other award, and any reference therein to a pensioner shall be construed as including a reference to a person to whom any award is payable.

(6) A police authority shall obtain a good discharge by applying or paying any sum in the manner provided by this Regulation.

(7) In the application of this Regulation to Scotland—

(*a*) the reference in paragraph (3) to the personal estate of the deceased shall be construed as a reference to his movable estate;

(*b*) any reference in paragraph (4) to a minor shall be construed as including a reference to a pupil.

Transfer values payable on transfer between police forces

79.—(1) This Regulation shall apply where a regular policeman who has served as such on or after 1st January 1967 is entitled to reckon previous service as pensionable service by reason of the fact that he has at any time transferred from one police force to another police force, except where the transfer was before 1st January 1967 and, by reason of his having retired after so transferring, the previous service would not be reckonable but for the provisions of Regulation 54(1) and (2) or of section 9(2) of the Police Pensions Act 1921**(a)**.

(2) Where this Regulation applies the police authority of the force first mentioned in paragraph (1) shall pay to the police authority of the other police force a transfer value calculated in accordance with Schedule 9.

Contributions between police authorities where no transfer value is payable

80.—(1) This Regulation shall apply where a regular policeman has at any time transferred from one police force to another police force and a transfer value is not payable in respect of that transfer under Regulation 79 by reason of the fact that he has not served as a regular policeman on or after 1st January 1967.

(2) Subject to the provisions of this Regulation, the police authority of the force to which the policeman has transferred shall be entitled, if they are liable to pay or contribute towards any award to or in respect of him, to a contribution of a proportionate part of such award or contribution from the police authority of the force from which he transferred, reckoned according to his service and pay and the pension contributions paid by him while a member of that force, of an amount agreed between the authorities or, in default of agreement, of an amount settled by arbitration.

(3) Where a regular policeman who has transferred from an overseas corps to a home police force is entitled to a supplemental pension, or the widow or any child of such a man is entitled to a widow's special pension or, as the case may be, a child's special allowance by reason of an injury received by the policeman while he was a member of the overseas corps, the police authority of the home police force shall be entitled to a contribution from the Secretary of State as police authority of the overseas corps of an amount equal to—

(*a*) the amount of any supplemental pension and the difference between any widow's special pension and the widow's ordinary pension that would otherwise have been payable and between any child's special allowance and the child's ordinary allowance that would otherwise have been payable, and

---

(a) 1921 c. 31.

(*b*) the amount which the Secretary of State as police authority of the overseas corps would have been liable to contribute if the policeman had received the injury otherwise than in the execution of his duty.

(4) Where a reversionary member of a home police force has given the notice referred to in Regulation 57, the Secretary of State as the said police authority shall not be entitled to a contribution from the police authority of any home police force in respect of the period between the date when the member retired and the date on which he would have completed 25 years' pensionable service if his tour of overseas service had not been varied as mentioned in the said Regulation.

(5) The police authority of the force to which the policeman has transferreid if they are empowered to pay or contribute towards a transfer value payable in respect of him under Regulation 82, may be paid a contribution of a proportionate part of such transfer value by the police authority of the force from which he transferred; and a contribution payable under this paragraph shall be reckoned in like manner as a contribution under paragraph (2).

Payments on transfer to the Royal Ulster Constabulary

81.—(1) This Regulation shall apply to a regular polceman who has left, a police force and joined the Royal Ulster Constabulary with the consent mentioned in Regulation 9(2) if the Government of Northern Ireland is liable, or contingently liable, to make payments to or in respect of him under any legislation for the time being in force in Northern Ireland relating to the superannuation of members of the Royal Ulster Constabulary.

(2) Where the policeman left his police force on or after 1st January 1967 and the Government of Northern Ireland is contingently liable to make such payments as aforesaid, the said Government shall be entitled to a transfer value from the police authority of that force calculated in accordance with Schedule 9.

(3) Where the policeman left his police force before 1st January 1967, then, if the Government of Northern Ireland becomes liable to make such payments as aforesaid, the said Government shall be entitled to a contribution from the police authority of that force of an amount agreed between the said Government and the said police authority or, in default of agreement, of an amount settled by arbitration, and the arbitrator shall take into consideration the amount of the contribution that would have been payable if it had been payable under Regulation 80.

Transfer values payable under interchange arrangements

82.—(1) Subject to paragraph 5 of Part I of Schedule 6, this Regulation shall apply to a regular policeman—

(*a*) who retires or has retired and subsequently enters or entered such service or employment as is mentioned in Schedule 6 (hereafter in this Regulation referred to as "new service");

(*b*) who was—

(i) not entitled to a pension on so retiring, or

(ii) if so entitled, has not received any payment in respect of the pension;

(*c*) who enters or entered the new service within 12 months of so retiring or within such longer period as may be agreed, in the circumstances of his case, between the police authority and the authority specified in Schedule 6 in relation to his new service;

(*d*) who, within 6 months of the date specified in Schedule 6 in relation to the new service or 3 months of his entering the new service, whichever is the later, or within such longer period as may be agreed as aforesaid in the circumstances of his case, notifies the police authority that he desires this Regulation to apply in his case,

where in the new service he is, or subject to the payment of a transfer value would be, entitled to reckon service for superannuation purposes by virtue of his service as a member of a police force.

(2) Subject to paragraph 5 of Part I, and paragraph 5 of Part III of Schedule 6, in the case of a regular policeman to whom this Regulation applies the police authority shall, where he ceased to serve as such on or after the date specified in Schedule 6 in relation to the new service, and may, where he ceased so to serve before that date, pay a transfer value calculated in accordance with Schedule 9 to the authority specified in Schedule 6 in relation to his new service.

(3) Where a regular policeman to whom this Regulation applies was entitled to an award on retiring but has received no payment in respect thereof, the award shall cease to be payable.

(4) Where a regular policeman to whom this Regulation applies—

(*a*) was paying pension contributions at a rate related to 6·25% of his pensionable pay, and

(*b*) has not received any award,

he shall be entitled to an award of an amount equal to the difference between his aggregate contributions in respect of the relevant period of service and what that aggregate would have been had he paid pension contributions at a rate related to 5% of his pensionable pay and had paid no additional contributions under Regulation 62 or any corresponding provision of the former Regulations; and nothing in paragraph (3) shall apply in relation to such an award.

PART X

COMPULSORY RETIREMENT

Compulsory retirement on account of age

83.—(1) Subject to paragraph (2), every regular policeman—

(*a*) who is not a member of the metropolitan police or an overseas policeman shall be required to retire—

(i) if he is the commissioner or assistant commissioner of police for the City of London or is a chief constable or assistant chief constable, on attaining the age of 65 years,

(ii) if he is a superintendent or inspector, on attaining the age of 60 years,

(iii) if he is a sergeant or constable, on attaining the age of 55 years;

(*b*) who is a member of the metropolitan police shall be required to retire—

(i) if he is an assistant commissioner, on attaining the age of 60 years,

(ii) if he is a deputy assistant commissioner, commander or deputy commander, on attaining the age of 57 years,

(iii) if he holds any lower rank, on attaining the age of 55 years:

Provided that where a regular policeman was serving in any force immediately before 5th July 1948, the time at which he shall be required to retire shall, unless at any time he elects or has elected by notice in writing to the police authority of the force in which he is or was serving that this proviso, or the relevant provisions of the former Regulations, shall not apply to him, be the time at which he would have been required to retire on the ground of age if no Regulations under the Act had come into force.

(2) The time at which, under paragraph (1), a person shall be required to retire may be postponed, if the person concerned holds a rank above that of superintendent, by the police authority, and, if he holds the rank of superintendent or any lower rank, by the chief officer of police with the approval of the police authority in a borough force in England or Wales, and by the chief officer of police in any other force:

Provided that no such postponement or postponements shall extend beyond 5 years from the time at which, under paragraph (1), he would have been required to retire.

(3) In this Regulation the reference to the relevant provisions of the former Regulations is—

> (a) in its application to England and Wales or to Scotland, a reference to the proviso to—
>> (i) Regulation 66(1) of the Police Pensions Regulations 1966(a), or
>> (ii) Regulation 59(1) of the Police Pensions Regulations 1962(b);
>
> (b) in its application to England and Wales, a reference to the proviso to—
>> (i) Regulation 51(1) of the Police Pensions Regulations 1955,
>> (ii) Regulation 50(1) of the Police Pensions Regulations 1949(c), or
>> (iii) Regulation 54(1) of the Police Pensions Regulations 1948;
>
> (c) in its application to Scotland, a reference to the proviso to—
>> (i) Regulation 51(1) of the Police Pensions (Scotland) Regulations 1955,
>> (ii) Regulation 51(1) of the Police Pensions (Scotland) Regulations 1949(d), or
>> (iii) Regulation 55(1) of the Police Pensions (Scotland) Regulations 1948.

Compulsory retirement on grounds of efficiency of the force

84.—(1) This Regulation shall apply to a regular policeman, other than a chief officer of police, deputy chief constable or assistant chief constable, who if required to retire would be entitled to receive a pension of an amount not less than 2 thirds of his average pensionable pay.

(2) If a police authority determine that the retention in the force of a regular policeman to whom this Regulation applies would not be in the general interests of efficiency, he may be required to retire on such date as the police authority determine.

Compulsory retirement of regular policeman whose pension is reduced

85. For the purposes of the preceding provisions of this Part of these Regulations, a regular policeman shall be deemed, if required to retire, to be entitled to the pension to which he would be entitled but for the provisions of Part IV of Schedule 2.

(a) S.I. 1966/1582 (1966 III, p. 4894).   (b) S.I. 1962/2756 (1962 III, p. 3785).
(c) S.I. 1949/1241 (1949 I, p. 3331).   (d) S.I. 1949/1240 (1949 I, p. 3401).

Compulsory retirement on grounds of disablement

86. Every regular policeman may be required to retire on the date on which the police authority determine that he ought so to retire on the ground that he is permanently disabled for the performance of his duty:

Provided that a retirement under this Regulation shall be void if, after the said date, on an appeal against the medical opinion on which the police authority acted in determining that he ought to retire, the medical referee decides that the appellant is not permanently disabled.

Effect of requirement to retire

87. Where a person is required to retire under this Part of these Regulations, he shall be deemed to retire on the date on which he is so required to retire.

PART XI

SERVICEMEN

Servicemen to whom Part XI applies

88. This Part of these Regulations shall, subject to Regulation 95, have effect in the case of a serviceman whose period of relevant service in the armed forces ends or has ended, or who dies or has died, or who, having resumed service as a regular policeman, retires or has retired, as the case may be, on or after 5th July 1948:

Provided that, in the case of a serviceman other than a serviceman (1939-1945) whose period of relevant service in the armed forces ended, or who died, as the case may be, on or after the said date but before 15th July 1950—

(a) only the following provisions of this Part shall have effect, that is to say, Regulations 89(1) and (2), 90(1), (2), (3) and (7), 91, 93, and 94; and

(b) the said provisions shall have effect only where he was called up for service in the armed forces under the National Service Acts 1939 to 1946, the National Service Act 1947(a) or the National Service Act 1948(b), or required for training or called into actual service or called out for training or for permanent service in the armed forces in pursuance of his obligations as a member of the territorial army or any reserve of the armed forces.

Awards to servicemen

89.—(1) This Regulation shall apply to a serviceman who at the end of his period of relevant service in the armed forces is or was permanently disabled for the performance of duty as a regular policeman.

(2) A serviceman to whom this Regulation applies shall be entitled to the same award on the same conditions in all respects as if he had retired from his former force at the end of the said period on the ground of disablement.

(3) Where the disablement is the result of an injury received during the serviceman's period of relevant service in the armed forces, the police authority may, in their discretion—

(a) 1947 c. 31.   (b) 1948 c. 64.

(a) pay in lieu of a gratuity under this Regulation a pension at the rate of a twelfth of his average pensionable pay; and

(b) subject to and in accordance with paragraph 1 of Schedule 10, increase any pension payable under this Regulation.

(4) In the case of a serviceman whose period of relevant service in the armed forces ends or has ended on or after 1st January 1963 and whose pension is increased under paragraph (3)(b), no account of the increase shall be taken for the purposes of Regulations 23, 24 and 26 and of Part IV of Schedule 2.

(5) In the case of a serviceman (1939-1945) whose period of relevant service in the armed forces ended before 1st January 1952, paragraph (3)(a) shall have effect as if it referred to a rate of not less than a twelfth of his average pensionable pay increased in accordance with Regulation 106, and the police authority may exercise their discretion under paragraph (3) notwithstanding that the disablement arose otherwise than as therein mentioned.

Awards on death of servicemen

90.—(1) If a serviceman entitled to reckon 3 years' pensionable service—

(a) dies or has died during his period of relevant service in the armed forces; or

(b) having been permanently disabled for duty as a regular policeman at the end of the said period (without any intervening period of service as such) dies or has died as a result of the same injury as resulted in his disablement or while in receipt of a pension,

his widow shall be entitled to the same pension on the same conditions in all respects as if he were such a regular policeman as is described in Regulation 29(1).

(2) If a serviceman dies or has died during his period of relevant service in the armed forces and his widow is not entitled to a pension, she shall be entitled to a gratuity under Regulation 37 on the same conditions in all respects as if he were a regular policeman.

(3) If a serviceman—

(a) dies or has died during his period of relevant service in the armed forces; or

(b) having been permanently disabled for duty as a regular policeman at the end of the said period (without any intervening period of service as such) dies or has died while in receipt of a pension, or, being a person entitled to reckon not less than 3 years' pensionable service, dies or has died having received a gratuity,

then each of his children shall be entitled to the same allowance on the same conditions in all respects as if he were such a member of a police force as is mentioned in Regulation 41(1).

(4) Where a serviceman dies or has died as a result of an injury received during his period of relevant service in the armed forces, the police authority may, in their discretion—

(a) pay to the widow, in lieu of a gratuity under this Regulation, a pension; and

(b) subject to and in accordance with paragraphs 2 and 3 of Schedule 10, from time to time increase any pension or allowance payable in respect of him under this Regulation.

(5) The weekly amount of any pension payable under paragraph (4)(*a*) shall be £1·97 increased in accordance with Regulation 110(2) and (4).

(6) Where a serviceman (1939-1945) died before 1st January 1952, the police authority may exercise their discretion under paragraph (4) notwithstanding that he died otherwise than as therein mentioned.

(7) Regulations 40 and 49 shall apply to an award under this Regulation as though this Regulation were included in Part IV of these Regulations.

Application of Regulation 47

91. In relation to a serviceman, Regulation 47 shall apply—

(*a*) where he dies during his relevant period of service in the armed forces, as if he died while serving as a member of a police force; and

(*b*) where he dies as a result of an injury received during the said period, as if he died as a result of an injury received in the execution of his duty as a member of a police force.

Servicemen who resume service as regular policemen

92.—(1) If a serviceman who resumes or has resumed service as a regular policeman is permanently disabled or dies or has died as a result of an injury received during his period of relevant service in the armed forces, the police authority may, in relation to any award payable to or in respect of him (other than an award under Regulation 28), exercise the same discretions as are conferred by Regulation 89 or by Regulation 90.

(2) In the case of a regular policeman who retires or has retired on or after 1st January 1963 and whose pension is increased under Regulation 89(3)(*b*) as applied by this Regulation, no account of the increase shall be taken for the purposes of Regulations 23, 24 and 26 and of Part IV of Schedule 2.

Servicemen who do not resume service in their former force

93. If a serviceman within 1 month of the end of his period of relevant service in the armed forces does not or did not resume service in his former force, he shall be treated for the purposes of Regulations 8, 11, 28, 52, 53, 54, 96 and 97 as having left his former force at the end of his period of relevant service in the armed forces.

Pensionable service

94.—(1) A serviceman shall be entitled to reckon as pensionable service in his former force his period of relevant service in the armed forces on and after 5th July 1948.

(2) A serviceman (1939-1945) shall also be entitled so to reckon as pensionable service—

(*a*) such further period as the Secretary of State may fix or has fixed, not exceeding 3 months after the end of his period of relevant service in the armed forces and before becoming a member of a police force or becoming entitled to an award; and

(*b*) any period of approved service under the former Acts reckonable by him immediately before 5th July 1948.

(3) Regulation 59 shall apply for the purposes of the interpretation of this Regulation as it applies for the purposes of the interpretation of Part V.

Pension contributions

95.—(1) This Part of these Regulations shall have effect only in the case of a serviceman who pays or has paid pension contributions (other than additional pension contributions) to the police authority of his former force, as though he had remained a regular policeman in that force, in respect of his period of relevant service in the armed forces and, in the case of a serviceman (1939-1945), such further period as the Secretary of State may have fixed which is reckonable as pensionable service:

Provided that this Part shall have effect notwithstanding that pension contributions are not or have not been paid as aforesaid—

(a) by a serviceman other than a serviceman (1939-1945) in respect of—

    (i) any period during which his service pay when aggregated with any payments under Part V of the Reserve and Auxiliary Forces (Protection of Civil Interests) Act 1951**(a)** is less than his pensionable pay, or

    (ii) any period before 1st January 1952 for which he has been required to serve in the armed forces as mentioned in proviso (b) to Regulation 88 and in respect of which no payments under Part V of the Reserve and Auxiliary Forces (Protection of Civil Interests) Act 1951 have been made;

(b) by a serviceman (1939-1945) in respect of any periods in respect of which he would not have been compelled to pay sums equal to rateable deductions if the Act had not been passed.

(2) Where this Part has effect in the case of a serviceman by virtue of proviso (a) to paragraph (1), he shall be deemed, for the purposes of Regulation 29(2) and of paragraph 1 of Part IV of Schedule 2, to have paid pension contributions in respect of any period beginning on or after 1st April 1956 at the rate at which he last paid such contributions or, where he was on that day performing relevant service in the armed forces and did not give the notice referred to in the relevant provisions of the former Regulations, at a rate related to 6·25% of his pensionable pay.

(3) In this Regulation the reference to the relevant provisions of the former Regulations is a reference to the provisions of the proviso to Regulation 35(2) of the Police Pensions Regulations 1955, as set out in Regulation 13 of the Police Pensions Regulations 1956, or of the proviso to Regulation 37(2) of the Police Pensions (Scotland) Regulations 1955, as set out in Regulation 13 of the Police Pensions (Scotland) Regulations 1956.

PART XII

SUPPLEMENTAL PROVISIONS IN SPECIAL CASES

Persons who ceased to serve before 1st July 1949

96. Notwithstanding anything in these Regulations, for the purpose of calculating an award to or in respect of a person and relating to a period of service—

(a) which ended in his death, retirement or dismissal before 5th July 1948, references in these Regulations to average pensionable pay and pensionable service shall be construed respectively as references to annual pay and approved service within the meaning of the former Acts;

(a) 1951 c. 65.

(b) which ended in his death, retirement or dismissal on or after 5th July 1948, but before 1st July 1949, any reference in these Regulations to average pensionable pay shall be construed as a reference to preserved pensionable pay within the meaning of Schedule 11.

Certain persons serving on 1st July 1949

97.—(1) Notwithstanding anything in these Regulations, in the case of a person who was on 1st July 1949—

(a) a member of a police force; or

(b) a serviceman entitled under the relevant provisions of the former Regulations to reckon as pensionable service a period including that date,

and who died or retired within the period of 3 years beginning with that date, any award payable to or in respect of him shall not be less than it would have been if it had been calculated in accordance with the provisions of these Regulations applicable to persons who died or retired immediately before the said date and if he had been entitled during the said period to a rate of pay in accordance with the scales in force immediately before the said date.

(2) Notwithstanding anything in these Regulations, where a person who was serving as a member of a police force on 1st July 1949—

(a) was so serving on 28th August 1921 and is or has been compelled to retire on account of age, paragraph (3) shall apply for the purposes of calculating the ordinary pension payable to him on such retirement and any widow's ordinary pension payable in respect of him and calculated in accordance with paragraph 1 of Part I of Schedule 3;

(b) does not elect or has not elected otherwise, paragraph (3) shall apply for the purposes of calculating any award subsequently granted to or in respect of him.

(3) Any award to which this paragraph applies and which but for this Regulation would take into account the person's average pensionable pay shall in lieu thereof take into account his preserved pensionable pay within the meaning of Schedule 11.

(4) Any election under paragraph (2) shall be made by giving notice in writing to the police authority of the force in which the person making the election is serving at the time of giving the notice.

(5) In this Regulation the reference to the relevant provisions of the former Regulations is—

(a) in its application to England and Wales, a reference to the provisions of Regulation 29(2) or 69 of the Police Pensions Regulations 1949, as originally made;

(b) in its application to Scotland, a reference to Regulation 30(2) or Regulation 66 of the Police Pensions (Scotland) Regulations 1949, as originally made.

Chief constables affected by an amalgamation scheme under the Police Act 1946

98.—(1) Where the chief constable of an area that has been amalgamated with another area by a scheme made under the Police Act 1946(a) has been transferred to the combined police force in pursuance of an agreement made

---

(a) 1946 c. 46.

by him before the date of transfer, or joined that force within the period of 3 months beginning with the date of transfer, in any capacity other than that of chief constable or assistant chief constable, then, subject to any agreement to the contrary made between him and the police authority for the combined area, he shall be treated for the purposes of Regulations 19 and 83 as if, while serving in that force, he were a chief constable.

(2) Where the chief constable of an area that has been amalgamated with another area by a scheme made under the Police Act 1946 was not transferred to the combined force by the scheme and did not, during the period of 3 months referred to in section 11(3) of that Act or, as the case may be, that provision as applied by section 14(3)(a) of that Act, join the combined force, he shall be treated for the purposes of these Regulations as if he had retired at the end of the said period from the force of which he was chief constable, and Regulation 19 shall have effect in relation to him as if—

(a) paragraph (2) thereof were omitted; and

(b) the limitation imposed by paragraph (5) thereof on the making of payments in respect of a period before a person has attained the age of 50 years did not apply to him.

(3) In the application of this Regulation to Scotland, references to the Police Act 1946 and to sections 11(3) and 14(3)(a) thereof shall be construed as references to—

(a) the Police (Scotland) Act 1946**(a)** and to sections 7(2) and 9(3)(a) thereof, respectively; or

(b) the Police (Scotland) Act 1956**(b)** and to sections 22(2) and 23(2) thereof, respectively;

(c) the Police (Scotland) Act 1967**(c)** and to sections 23(2) and 24(2) thereof, respectively,

and the reference to the police authority for the combined area shall be construed as a reference to the joint police committee for the combined area and references to things done in the past shall include references to things done in the future.

Chief constables affected by local government reorganisation or an amalgamation scheme under the Police Act 1964

99.—(1) This Regulation shall apply to a chief constable of a police force who becomes a member of another force by virtue of an order mentioned in paragraph (4) and section 58(1) of the Police Act 1964**(d)**.

(2) In relation to such a member of a police force as is mentioned in paragraph (1) who suffers loss of office as such which is attributable to the provisions of an order mentioned in paragraph (4)—

(a) these Regulations shall apply as though he had retired from the police force, having given to the police authority a month's written notice of his intention to retire;

(b) where he becomes a member of another police force at or before the end of his resettlement period, Regulation 51 shall apply as though he had become a member of that other force immediately after ceasing to be a member of the force first mentioned in this paragraph, and

---

(a) 1946 c. 71. (b) 1956 c. 26.
(c) 1967 c. 77. (d) 1964 c. 48.

(c) where he was serving as a chief constable on 1st July 1964, Regulation 19 shall apply as though paragraph (2)(b) thereof were omitted.

(3) In relation to such a member of a police force as is mentioned in paragraph (1) who suffers reduction in rank attributable to the provisions of an order mentioned in paragraph (4), Regulation 83 shall apply as though he had not suffered such reduction in rank, unless he elects otherwise by notice in writing to the police authority.

(4) Any reference in this Regulation to an order mentioned in this paragraph is a reference to an order under Part I of the Police Act 1964 or Part II of the Local Government Act 1958(a); and the reference in paragraph (2) to a person's resettlement period is a reference to the period of 13 weeks next succeeding the week in which he ceased to be a member of the police force first mentioned in that paragraph or, in the case of a person who has attained the age of 45 years, the said 13 weeks extended by an additional week for every year of his age after attaining the age of 45 years and before he ceased to be a member of that force, subject to a maximum extension of 13 such weeks.

Chief constables who joined or were transferred to a county police force

100. Where the chief constable of an area consisting of a non-county borough that was treated as part of the police area of the county under section 1 of the Police Act 1946 transferred to the county police force, in pursuance of an agreement made by him before 1st April 1947, or joined that force within the period of 3 months beginning with that date, in any capacity other than that of chief constable or assistant chief constable, then, subject to any agreement to the contrary made between him and the police authority for the county, he shall, while serving in the county police force on and after 1st January 1952, be treated for the purposes of Regulation 83 as if he were a chief constable.

Commissioner of police of the metropolis

101. Notwithstanding anything in these Regulations, any such special arrangements as to the rates and conditions of awards payable in respect of a commissioner of police of the metropolis as had effect immediately before 15th February 1971 by virtue of Regulation 84 of the Police Pensions Regulations 1966 shall have effect, on and after that date, as if authorised by these Regulations.

Certain ex-reversionary members of home police forces

102. Notwithstanding anything in these Regulations, where a person who has been a reversionary member of a home police force becomes or has become a regular policeman in a home police force and an award is payable to or in respect of him by reason of his having received an injury in the execution of his duty as an overseas policeman without his own default, the award shall not be less than it would have been if he had not after being a reversionary member of a home police force become such a regular policeman.

Members of an overseas corps with previous service outside Great Britain

103. Notwithstanding anything in these Regulations, where the Secretary of State is satisfied that a member of an overseas corps before becoming such had been engaged in the performance of police duties in any country or territory outside Great Britain, and that under legislation in force in that country or territory grants were, at the time he became such a member, payable to or in respect of persons similarly engaged on their retirement or, as the case may be,

---

(a) 1958 c. 55.

death, the Secretary of State may in accordance with any agreement made with that person in consideration of his becoming a member of an overseas corps, pay awards, in addition to any award payable under these Regulations, to or in respect of that person, to such persons, on such conditions and of such a nature and amount as will ensure that the awards and any grants under the said legislation taken together are on the whole not less favourable to the person concerned than they would have been if the said police duties had been performed as a regular member of a home police force and the member of the overseas corps had been a reversionary member of a home police force.

Former lieutenants in Scottish police forces

104. Where a member of a Scottish police force—

(a) retired before 5th July 1948 and at the time of his retirement held the rank of lieutenant; or

(b) immediately before the said date held the rank of lieutenant and on ceasing to be a member of a police force held the rank of chief inspector,

his widow and any child of his shall be entitled to receive the like awards as if, on ceasing to be a member of a police force, he had held the rank of superintendent.

Regular policemen dismissed after 25 years' service

105.—(1) This Regulation shall apply in the case of a regular policeman entitled to reckon at least 25 years' pensionable service and dismissed—

(a) on or after 1st January 1963; or

(b) on or after 5th July 1948 but before 1st July 1949,

otherwise than for a cause for which a pension granted to him could have been forfeited under the Act.

(2) If a regular policeman in whose case this Regulation applies would have been entitled to an ordinary pension if he had retired on the date of his dismissal, having given a month's notice to the police authority of his intention to retire, then these Regulations shall apply in his case as if he had so retired.

Part XIII

Application of Pensions (Increase) Acts

Application of Pensions (Increase) Acts 1944 and 1947

106.—(1) Where it is provided in these Regulations that an amount shall be increased in accordance with this Regulation or this Part of these Regulations, it shall be increased by the amount, if any, by which a pension of the amount first mentioned would be increased if the person concerned were in receipt of such a pension and paragraph 2 of Part II of Schedule 1 to the Pensions (Increase) Act 1944**(a)** and section 2(3) of the Pensions (Increase) Act 1947**(b)** had not been included in Part I of Schedule 1 to the Act.

(2) Where it is provided in these Regulations that an amount shall be increased in accordance with this Part of these Regulations, any increase in accordance with this Regulation shall be additional to any increase in accordance with any other provision of this Part of these Regulations.

(a) 1944 c. 21.   **(b)** 1947 c. 7.

Application of Pensions (Increase) Act 1952

107.—(1) Where it is provided in these Regulations that an amount shall be increased in accordance with this Part of these Regulations, it shall be increased by the amount, if any, by which a pension of the amount first mentioned would be increased under the Pensions (Increase) Act 1952(a) if—

(a) the person concerned were in receipt of such a pension;

(b) that pension were specified in Part II of Schedule 1 to that Act; and

(c) any increase in the first-mentioned amount in accordance with Regulation 106 were an increase granted under the Pensions (Increase) Acts 1944 and 1947.

(2) For the purposes of this Regulation any reference in Schedule 2 to the Pensions (Increase) Act 1952 to—

(a) a relevant pension shall be construed as including a reference to an award of an amount which these Regulations provide shall be increased in accordance with this Part of these Regulations;

(b) the rate of the relevant pension shall be construed as including a reference to the rate of such an award, ignoring any increase in accordance with this Regulation;

(c) the authorised increase shall be construed as including a reference to the increase in accordance with this Regulation.

(3) Any increase in accordance with this Regulation shall be additional to any increase in accordance with any other provision of this Part of these Regulations.

Application of Pensions (Increase) Act 1956

108.—(1) Where it is provided in these Regulations that an amount shall be increased in accordance with this Part of these Regulations, it shall be increased by the amount, if any, by which a pension of the amount first mentioned would be increased under the Pensions (Increase) Act 1956(b) if—

(a) the person concerned were in receipt of such a pension; and

(b) that pension were specified in Part II of Schedule I to that Act.

(2) For the purposes of this Regulation any reference in section 1(1) of the Pensions (Increase) Act 1956 or Schedule 2 thereto to 31st December 1947 shall be construed as a reference to 1st July 1949, and any reference in the said Schedule 2—

(a) to a relevant pension shall be construed as including a reference to an award of an amount which these Regulations provide shall be increased in accordance with this Part of these Regulations;

(b) to the basic rate of the relevant pension shall be construed as including a reference to the annual rate of such an award, ignoring any increase in accordance with this Regulation; and

(c) to the authorised increase shall be construed as including a reference to the increase in accordance with this Regulation.

(3) Any increase in accordance with this Regulation shall be additional to any increase in accordance with any other provision of this Part of these Regulations.

(a) 1952 c. 45.   (b) 1956 c. 39.

Application of Pensions (Increase) Act 1959

109.—(1) Where it is provided in these Regulations that an amount shall be increased in accordance with this Part of these Regulations, it shall be increased by the amount, if any, by which a pension of the amount first mentioned would be increased under the Pensions (Increase) Act 1959(a) if—

(*a*) the person concerned were in receipt of such a pension; and

(*b*) that pension were specified in the Schedule to that Act.

(2) For the purposes of this Regulation any reference in section 1(1) of the Pensions (Increase) Act 1959 to an annual rate or an aggregate annual rate shall be construed, in relation to an amount which these Regulations provide shall be increased in accordance with this Part of these Regulations, as a reference to that amount expressed as an annual rate or, as the case may be, to that amount after any increase thereof in accordance with Regulation 106, 107 or 108, expressed as an annual rate.

(3) Any increase in accordance with this Regulation shall be additional to any increase in accordance with any other provision of this Part of these Regulations.

Application of Pensions (Increase) Act 1962

110.—(1) Where it is provided in these Regulations that an amount shall be increased in accordance with this Part of these Regulations, it shall be increased by the amount, if any, by which a pension of the amount first mentioned would be increased under sections 1 and 2 of the Pensions (Increase) Act 1962(b) if—

(*a*) the person concerned were in receipt of such a pension; and

(*b*) that pension were specified in the Schedule to the Pensions (Increase) Act 1959, and so might be increased under sections 1 and 2 of the said Act of 1962.

(2) Where it is provided in these Regulations that an amount calculated otherwise than by reference to a rate, or an average rate, of emoluments shall be increased in accordance with this paragraph, then, subject to paragraph (4), it shall be increased by the amount, if any, by which a pension of the appropriate amount specified in paragraph (3) would be increased under section 2 of the Pensions (Increase) Act 1962 if—

(*a*) the person concerned were in receipt of such a pension;

(*b*) that pension were specified in the Schedule to the Pensions (Increase) Act 1959, and so might be increased under section 2 of the said Act of 1962; and

(*c*) that pension were one which began for the purposes of the said Act of 1962 before 1st April 1956.

(3) The appropriate amount mentioned in paragraph (2) shall be the weekly amount of—

(*a*) £2·12 where the weekly amount which falls to be increased under that paragraph is £3·26;

(*b*) £1·70, where the weekly amount which falls to be so increased is £2·62;

(*c*) £1·28, where the weekly amount which falls to be so increased is £1·97.

(a) 1959 c. 50.　　　　　(b) 1962 c. 2 (11 & 12 Eliz. 2).

(4) Where such an amount as is mentioned in paragraph (2) is increased in accordance with that paragraph—

(a) the amount of the increase under paragraph (2) shall be increased in accordance with Regulation 111 and for the purposes thereof shall be treated as if it were a pension which began for the purposes of the Pensions (Increase) Act 1965(a) before 1st April 1957, and

(b) the amount of the increase under paragraph (2) (increased as aforesaid) shall be further increased in accordance with Regulation 112 and for the purposes thereof shall be treated as if it were a pension which began for the purposes of the Pensions (Increase) Act 1969(b) before 1st July 1955.

(5) For the purposes of this Regulation—

(a) in relation to an increase under paragraph (1), the reference in section 1(1) of the Pensions (Increase) Act 1962 to an annual rate and the reference in section 10(1) of that Act to an aggregate annual rate shall be construed, respectively, as a reference to the amount which falls to be increased expressed as an annual rate and as a reference to that amount, after any increase thereof in accordance with Regulations 106, 107, 108 and 109, expressed as an annual rate;

(b) in relation to an increase under paragraph (2), the reference in section 10(1) of that Act to an aggregate annual rate shall be construed as a reference to the appropriate amount specified in paragraph (3) expressed as an annual rate.

(6) Where it is provided in these Regulations that an amount shall be increased in accordance with this Part of these Regulations, any increase in accordance with this Regulation shall be additional to any increase in accordance with any other provision of this Part of these Regulations.

Application of Pensions (Increase) Act 1965

111.—(1) Where it is provided in these Regulations that an amount shall be increased in accordance with this Regulation or this Part of these Regulations, it shall be increased by the amount, if any, by which a pension of the amount first mentioned would be increased under the Pensions (Increase) Act 1965 if—

(a) the person concerned were in receipt of such a pension; and

(b) that pension were specified in Schedule 1 to that Act.

(2) For the purposes of this Regulation the reference in section 1(1) of the Pensions (Increase) Act 1965 to an annual rate and the reference in section 1(3) of that Act to an aggregate annual rate shall be construed, respectively, as a reference to the amount which falls to be increased expressed as an annual rate and as a reference to that amount, after any increase thereof in accordance with Regulations 106, 107, 108, 109 and 110, expressed as an annual rate.

(3) Where it is provided in these Regulations that an amount shall be increased in accordance with this Part of these Regulations, any increase in accordance with this Regulation shall be additional to any increase in accordance with any other provision of this Part of these Regulations.

(a) 1965 c. 78.   (b) 1969 c. 7.

Application of Pensions (Increase) Act 1969

112.—(1) Where it is provided in these Regulations that an amount shall be increased in accordance with this Regulation or this Part of these Regulations, it shall be increased by the amount, if any, by which a pension of the amount first mentioned would be increased under the Pensions (Increase) Act 1969 if—

(a) the person concerned were in receipt of such a pension; and

(b) that pension were specified in Part I or II of Schedule 1 to that Act.

(2) For the purposes of this Regulation the reference in section 1(1) of the Pensions (Increase) Act 1969 to an annual rate and the reference in paragraph 2 of Schedule 2 to that Act to an aggregate annual rate shall be construed, respectively, as a reference to the amount which falls to be increased expressed as an annual rate and as a reference to that amount, after any increase thereof in accordance with Regulations 106, 107, 108, 109, 110 and 111, expressed as an annual rate.

(3) Where it is provided in these Regulations that an amount shall be increased in accordance with this Part of these Regulations, any increase in accordance with this Regulation shall be additional to any increase in accordance with any other provision of this Part of these Regulations.

Duration of increase in child's allowance

113. Where it is provided in these Regulations that for the purpose of calculating a child's allowance an amount shall be increased in accordance with this Part of these Regulations, then that amount shall be so increased so long as the allowance is payable, and accordingly this Part of these Regulations shall have effect for the said purpose as if—

(a) section 1(3) were omitted from the Pensions (Increase) Act 1944 (which provision governs the increase, under the Pensions (Increase) Acts of 1944 and 1947, of 1952 and of 1956, of pensions payable to dependants other than widows), and

(b) section 1(3) were omitted from the Pensions (Increase) Act 1959 (which provision governs the increase, under the Pensions (Increase) Acts of 1959, of 1962, of 1965 and of 1969 of such pensions).

PART XIV

MISCELLANEOUS

Lincolnshire

114. Notwithstanding anything in these Regulations, the police forces maintained before 1st April 1967 for the three divisions of Lincolnshire shall be treated for the purposes of these Regulations as having been one force and Regulation 116 shall have effect accordingly.

River Tyne police force

115. In relation to a person who served as a member of the River Tyne police force, which was dissolved on 1st July 1968 by the Port of Tyne Reorganisation Scheme 1967(a), whether he ceased so to serve before that date or was transferred by that Scheme, the police force, police authority and police fund for the Durham police area shall for the purposes of these Regulations, be deemed to be the same force, authority and fund as the force, authority and fund for the River Tyne police area.

(a) S.I. 1968/942.

Alterations in police areas

116.—(1) Where a police area is or has been combined with another police area, the police force, police authority and police fund for the combined police area of which the first-named area for the time being forms part shall, for the purposes of these Regulations, be deemed to be the same force, authority and fund as the force, authority and fund for the first-named area.

(2) Where a police area is or has been divided, in relation to any person—

    (*a*) who is transferred by the instrument effecting the division from the force for the divided area to another force, the other force and the police authority and police fund for the area thereof shall, for the purposes of these Regulations, be deemed to be the same force, authority and fund as the force, authority and fund for the divided area;

    (*b*) who ceased to be a member of the force for the divided area before the division thereof, if the instrument effecting the division makes provision in that behalf, the force, authority and fund designated for the purpose thereby shall, for the purposes of these Regulations, be deemed to be the same force, authority and fund as the force, authority and fund for the divided area.

(3) In this Regulation—

    (*a*) a reference to the combination or division of a police area includes a reference to an agreement under section 14 of the County Police Act 1840**(a)** or, as the case may be, the termination of such an agreement, and a reference to the force, authority or fund for a combined area shall be construed accordingly;

    (*b*) a reference to the division of a police area includes a reference to the transfer of part of a police area, on or after 1st April 1966, on the date on which an order affecting the area, made under section 140 of the Local Government Act 1933**(b)** or under Part II of the Local Government Act 1958, comes into force, and

    (*c*) a reference to the combination of a police area with another police area includes a reference to the inclusion of a police area in a county or county borough police area, on or after 1st April 1968, on a date on which an order affecting the area, made under Part II of the Local Government Act 1958, comes into force and, in such case, a reference to the combined police area shall be construed as a reference to the county or, as the case may be, the county borough police area.

(4) In its application to Scotland, this Regulation shall have effect as if—

    (*a*) any reference to a police fund were omitted;

    (*b*) any reference to the police authority for a combined area or to a combined authority were a reference to the joint police committee for a combined area; and

---

(a) 1840 c. 88.   **(b)** 1933 c. 51.

(*c*) the reference to section 14 of the County Police Act 1840 were a reference to section 61 of the Police (Scotland) Act 1857**(a)**.

R. Maudling,
One of Her Majesty's Principal
Secretaries of State.

11th February 1971.

Consent of the Minister for the Civil Service given under his Official Seal on 11th February 1971.

(L.S.)

K. H. McNeill,
Authorised by the
Minister for the Civil Service.

SCHEDULE 1   Regulation 2

FORMER REGULATIONS REVOKED

The Police Pensions Regulations 1966	S.I. 1966/1582 (1966 III, p. 4894).
The Police Pensions (Amendment) Regulations 1967	S.I. 1967/453 (1967 I, p. 1395).
The Police Pensions (Amendment) (No. 2) Regulations 1967	S.I. 1967/1500 (1967 III, p. 4204).
The Police Pensions (Amendment) Regulations 1968	S.I. 1968/530 (1968 I, p. 1269).
The Police Pensions (Amendment) Regulations 1969	S.I. 1969/723 (1969 II, p. 1952).
The Police Pensions (Amendment) (No. 2) Regulations 1969	S.I. 1969/1484 (1969 III, p. 4745).
The Police Pensions (Amendment) (No. 3) Regulations 1969	S.I. 1969/1849 (1969 III, p. 5788).
The Police Pensions (Amendment) Regulations 1970	S.I. 1970/587 (1970 I, p. 1849).
The Police Pensions (Amendment) (No. 2) Regulations 1970	S.I. 1970/1570 (1970 III, p. 5320).

SCHEDULE 2

POLICEMEN

PART I   Regulation 19

POLICEMAN'S ORDINARY PENSION

1. Subject as hereafter in this Schedule provided, the pension shall be of an amount equal to 30 sixtieths of the policeman's average pensionable pay with the addition, subject to a maximum of 40 sixtieths—

    (*a*) of a sixtieth for each completed half year by which his pensionable service exceeds 25 years, in the case of a person who retires or retired on or after 1st July 1949; or

---

(a) 1857 c. 72.   1z

Sch. 2 (contd.)

(b) of 2 sixtieths for each completed year by which his pensionable service exceeds 25 years, in the case of a person who retired before that date.

2. In the case of a person who retired before 25th April 1955, and to whom, immediately before 5th July 1948—

(a) the scale of ordinary pension applicable immediately before the commencement of the Police Pensions Act 1921 applied by virtue of section 29(1)(a) of that Act (which relates to persons serving on 28th August 1921); or

(b) a scale of ordinary pension different from that under the Police Pensions Act 1921 applied by virtue of section 26(4) of that Act (which relates to members of the City of London police force),

the scale which so applied shall be substituted for that contained in paragraph 1, so however as though for any reference in those provisions to annual pay there were substituted a reference to average pensionable pay.

3. In the case of a person who retires or retired—

(a) on or after 1st January 1963; or

(b) before 1st July 1949,

if the amount of the pension calculated in accordance with the preceding provisions of this Schedule would be less than the amount it would have been had the person in question become entitled to receive an ordinary pension by retiring after due notice from the same police force at an earlier date, then, subject as hereafter in this Schedule provided, the pension shall be of the last-mentioned amount.

4. In the case of a person who retired before 1st July 1949, the amount of the pension calculated in accordance with the preceding provisions of this Schedule shall be increased in accordance with Regulation 106.

Regulations 20 and 21   **PART II**

POLICEMAN'S ILL-HEALTH OR SHORT SERVICE AWARD

1. Subject as hereafter in this Schedule provided, where the award is a gratuity and the policeman has completed at least a year's pensionable service, the gratuity shall be whichever is the greater of the two following amounts:—

(a) a twelfth of the policeman's average pensionable pay multiplied by the number of completed years of pensionable service which he is entitled to count; or

(b) the policeman's aggregate pension contributions in respect of the relevant period of service.

2. Subject as hereafter in this Schedule provided, where the award is a gratuity and the policeman has not completed a year's pensionable service, the gratuity shall be an amount equal to the policeman's aggregate pension contributions in respect of the relevant period of service.

3. Subject as hereafter in this Schedule provided, where the award is a pension, the amount thereof shall not be less than a sixtieth of the policeman's average pensionable pay and subject as aforesaid shall be equal to a sixtieth of his average pensionable pay for each completed year of pensionable service up to 20 years, with the addition, subject to a maximum of 40 sixtieths—

(a) of a sixtieth for each completed half year by which his pensionable service exceeds 20 years, in the case of a person who retires or retired on or after 1st July 1949; or

(b) of 2 sixtieths for each completed year by which his pensionable service exceeds 20 years, in the case of a person who retired before that date.

Sch. 2 (contd.)

4. Where an ill-health pension or the unsecured portion thereof is terminated under Regulation 65(4) on the policeman not offering to rejoin the force within the period mentioned in Regulation 65(2), then if the aggregate of—

(a) the sums paid in respect of the pension; and

(b) where only the unsecured portion of the pension is terminated, the actuarial value of the secured portion of the pension (in so far as it is payable under Regulation 65(6)) determined in accordance with tables prepared by the Government Actuary,

is less than his aggregate pension contributions in respect of the relevant period of service, the police authority shall pay to the pensioner the difference.

5. In the case of a person who retired before 1st July 1949, the amount of a pension calculated in accordance with the preceding provisions of this Part of this Schedule shall be increased in accordance with Regulation 106.

PART III   Regulations 19, 20 and 21

REDUCTION OF PENSION AT INSURED PENSIONABLE AGE

1.—(1) Subject as hereafter in this paragraph provided, an ordinary, ill-health or short service pension or, in the case of such a pension granted on retirement on or after 3rd April 1961, the unsecured portion thereof shall be reduced in respect of any period beyond insured pensionable age by an amount calculated at an annual rate obtained by multiplying £1·70 by the number of years specified in sub-paragraph (4).

(2) In the case of a person who immediately before he retired and was granted a pension was paying pension contributions at a rate 1p a week less than the appropriate percentage of his pensionable pay there shall not be any reduction in the pension or the unsecured part thereof, as the case may be, under this paragraph.

(3) Subject as hereafter in this paragraph provided, in the case of a person who immediately before he retired and was granted a pension was paying pension contributions at a rate of 6p a week less than the appropriate percentage of his pensionable pay by reason of the giving of such a notice as is mentioned in Regulation 61(6) as extended by Regulation 63(3)(b) the reduction under sub-paragraph (1) shall be calculated not as therein stated but at an annual rate obtained by multiplying the sum in the second column of the following Table set opposite to the age in the first column of the said Table which he had attained at the appropriate date by the number of years specified in sub-paragraph (4):—

TABLE

Age at appropriate date	Sums to be multiplied
	£
Less than 23 ...	1·70
23	1·65
24	1·60
25	1·55
26	1·525
27	1·50
28	1·475
29	1·45
30	1·425

Sch. 2 (contd.)

TABLE—*continued*

Age at appropriate date	Sums to be multiplied
	£
31	1·40
32	1·375
33	1·35
34	1·325
35	1·30
36	1·30
37	1·275
38	1·25
39	1·25
40	1·225
41	1·225
42	1·20
43	1·20
44 or more ...	1·175

In this sub-paragraph the expression "appropriate date" means 5th July 1948, or, in the case of a person who was then an auxiliary policeman, the date on which he first thereafter became a regular policeman.

(4) The number of years referred to in sub-paragraph (1) and in sub-paragraph (3) by which the sums therein respectively specified are to be multiplied for the purposes of those sub-paragraphs is the highest whole number of years in the aggregate period during which the person concerned has paid contributions as a regular policeman or as a member of the Royal Ulster Constabulary at a rate of 6p less than the appropriate percentage of his pensionable pay:

Provided that in arriving at the said aggregate there shall be disregarded any period or periods—

(*a*) in respect of which the person concerned was not entitled to reckon any pensionable service for the purposes of the pension in question; or

(*b*) which fell after the date on which the person concerned would have been entitled, if he had retired, to a pension equal to 2 thirds of his average pensionable pay.

(5) When a person in receipt of a pension by virtue of Regulation 98(2) attains the age of 65 years, the pension or, when he is treated as having retired on or after 3rd April 1961, the unsecured portion thereof shall, in addition to any other reduction under this Part of this Schedule, be reduced by any amount by which it was increased by the operation of Regulation 60(6).

(6) In the case of a person who first became a regular policeman on or after 1st January 1963 and is entitled to reckon pensionable service for the purposes of the pension in question by virtue of service or employment (otherwise than as a member of a police force or of the Royal Ulster Constabulary) in respect of which he was subject to superannuation arrangements—

(*a*) if he was subject to the operation of any regulations made under section 69(4) of the National Insurance Act 1946(a), or section 110(1) of the National Insurance Act 1965(b) or of other provisions modifying the said superannuation arrangements in connection with the passing of the said Act of 1946, other-

---

(a) 1946 c. 67.   (b) 1965 c. 51.

Sch. 2 (contd.)

wise than by virtue of an election made or notice given, then, for the purposes of sub-paragraph (1), there shall be included in the aggregate period specified in sub-paragraph (4) the period he is so entitled to reckon as pensionable service;

(b) if he was subject to the operation of such regulations or other provisions by virtue of an election made or notice given, then, for the purposes of sub-paragraph (3), the appropriate date shall mean the date on which the said election or notice became effective and there shall be included in the aggregate period specified in sub-paragraph (4) the period he is so entitled to reckon as pensionable service:

Provided that no account shall be taken of any period he is so entitled to reckon as pensionable service which is not attributable to service or employment which would have been taken into account for the purposes of the said regulations or provisions.

2.—(1) Where a person in receipt of an ordinary, ill-health or short service pension granted on retirement on or after 3rd April 1961 has been in service or employment otherwise than as a regular policeman—

(a) in respect of which he was subject to superannuation arrangements;

(b) by virtue of which he is entitled to reckon pensionable service for the purposes of the pension; and

(c) the period of which includes a participating period of relevant employment,

then, for the purpose of abating the pension in relation to that participating period of relevant employment, any provision of the said arrangements in operation when he left the said service or employment the effect of which is that pensions payable thereunder are to be reduced in connection with the operation of the National Insurance Act 1959(a) or of any provision of the National Insurance Act 1965 relating to graduated contributions or graduated retirement benefit shall apply, subject to the necessary adaptations and modifications, as though the provision were contained in this paragraph and as if—

(i) the pension were payable under the said arrangements, and

(ii) any other period of service or employment by virtue of which he is entitled to reckon pensionable service for the purposes of the pension were a period of non-participating employment at the end of which no payment in lieu of contributions falls to be made.

(2) A police authority, in determining any question arising under sub-paragraph (1) and relating to a particular service or employment, shall be entitled to treat as conclusive any relevant certificate issued, with the agreement of the person concerned, by his employer in that service or employment.

(3) Where for the purposes of the superannuation arrangements applicable to such service or employment as is mentioned in sub-paragraph (1) the person concerned was entitled to reckon service by virtue of some previous service or employment, that previous service or employment shall be treated for the purposes of this paragraph as if it were part of the service or employment first mentioned in this sub-paragraph.

3.—(1) Where a person in receipt of an ordinary, ill-health or short service pension granted on retirement on or after 3rd April 1961 is entitled to reckon as pensionable service for the purposes of the pension a period of employment as a regular policeman which is a participating period of relevant employment, then in relation to that period the unsecured portion of the pension shall be reduced in accordance with the provisions of sub-paragraph (2).

(a) 1959 c. 47.

Sch. 2 (contd.)

(2) Where the unsecured portion of a pension is reduced in accordance with the provisions of this sub-paragraph, the annual rate of that portion of the pension shall be reduced in respect of any period beyond insured pensionable age by the annual rate of the graduated retirement benefit which would be payable to the pensioner, on the assumption that he retired from regular employment on attaining insured pensionable age, in return for a payment in lieu of contributions in respect of the whole of the period referred to in sub-paragraph (1).

4.—(1) Where a person in receipt of the secured portion of an ill-health pension the unsecured portion of which has been terminated in the circumstances mentioned in Regulation 65(4) is also in receipt of some other pension, being an ordinary, ill-health or short service pension granted on retirement on or after 3rd April 1961, and is entitled to reckon for the purposes of that other pension the period of pensionable service reckonable for the purposes of the ill-health pension, then the unsecured portion of that other pension shall be reduced in accordance with the provisions of sub-paragraph (2).

(2) Where the unsecured portion of an ordinary, ill-health or short service pension is reduced in accordance with the provisions of this sub-paragraph, the annual rate of that portion shall be reduced in respect of any period beyond insured pensionable age by the annual rate of the secured portion of the ill-health pension first mentioned in this paragraph.

Regulations 19, 20 and 21   PART IV

REDUCTION OF PENSION PAYABLE TO PERSON PAYING PENSION CONTRIBUTIONS AT A RATE RELATED TO 6·25% OF PENSIONABLE PAY

1. The amount of an ordinary, ill-health or short service pension payable to a man who was immediately before his retirement paying pension contributions at a rate related to 6·25% of his pensionable pay shall, subject to the provisions of this Part, be reduced by that percentage which is set out in the second column of the following Table opposite the number of completed years of pensionable service he is entitled to reckon—

   (a) by virtue of service before 1st April 1956; and

   (b) by virtue of service on or after that date, not being service as a member of a police force or of the Royal Ulster Constabulary in respect of which he has paid pension contributions at a rate related to 6·25% of his pensionable pay:—

TABLE

Completed years of pensionable service	Percentage reduction in pension
1	0·2
2	0·4
3	0·5
4	0·6
5	0·8
6	0·9
7	1·0
8	1·2
9	1·3
10	1·5
11	1·6

Sch. 2 (contd.)

Completed years of pensionable service	Percentage reduction in pension
12	1·7
13	1·8
14	1·9
15	2·0
16	2·1
17	2·2
18	2·3
19	2·4
20	2·5
21	2·6
22	2·7
23	2·8
24	2·9
25	2·9
26	3·0
27	3·1
28	3·1
29	3·2
30 or more ...	3·3

2. In calculating the amount of the said reduction no account shall be taken—

(a) of any service he is entitled to reckon as pensionable service by virtue of section 10 of the Police Pensions Act 1921 or of section 14 of the Police Act 1890(a); or

(b) of any service on or after 1st April 1956 which he is entitled to reckon as pensionable service by virtue of Regulation 94 and the proviso to Regulation 95(1).

3. If he elected to pay additional pension contributions as mentioned in Regulation 62 as extended by Regulation 63(3)(c) and paid such contributions until he became entitled to reckon 25 years' pensionable service or retired with a pension, in calculating the amount of the said reduction no account shall be taken of any service before 1st April 1956 which he was entitled to reckon as pensionable service when he made the said election.

4. In calculating the amount of the said reduction there shall be disregarded any reduction in the amount of the pension in accordance with the provisions of Part III of this Schedule.

PART V   Regulations 20, 21 and 28

REDUCTION OF AWARDS OTHER THAN PENSIONS

1. Where a payment in lieu of contributions falls to be made by a police authority in respect of a regular policeman and—

(a) a short service gratuity is payable by that authority on his retirement; or

(b) an ill-health gratuity is so payable and the police authority determine that the provisions of this Part of this Schedule shall apply; or

(c) an amount equal to his aggregate pension contributions in respect of the relevant period of service is payable by the police authority to him or his dependants on his retirement or dismissal,

the award in question shall be reduced by an amount equal to the amount which could be retained out of the award by the police authority under section 60(4) of the

---

(a) 1890 c. 45.

Sch. 2 (contd.)

National Insurance Act 1965 if the award were a refund of payments to which that provision applies.

2. Where a payment in lieu of contributions may fall to be made by a police authority in respect of a regular policeman and such an award as is mentioned in paragraph 1 is payable as mentioned therein, the police authority may reduce the amount of the award in question by the amount by which it would be reduced under the said paragraph 1 if the payment in lieu of contributions in fact fell to be made, so however that, if the said payment does not fall to be made within the period of 78 weeks from the date when the person concerned ceases to be a regular policeman or within such shorter period as the police authority may determine, then any reduction in the amount of the award under this paragraph shall cease to have effect and the difference between the full and the reduced amounts thereof shall become payable.

Regulation 22   PART VI

POLICEMAN'S SUPPLEMENTAL PENSION

1. The standard amount referred to in Regulation 22 shall be calculated by reference to the number of the policeman's completed years of pensionable service and by reference to his average pensionable pay.

2. Subject as provided in this Part of this Schedule, where the policeman is totally disabled, the standard amount shall be the amount specified in the second column of the following Table, and where the policeman is partly disabled, the standard amount shall be such proportion of the amount so specified as the degree of actual disablement bears to total disablement, subject to its not being less than the proportion of the average pensionable pay specified in the third column of the said Table:—

TABLE

Policeman's completed years of pensionable service	Standard amount on total disablement expressed in 60ths of average pensionable pay	Lower limit of standard amount expressed in 60ths of average pensionable pay
Less than 11	40	15
11	41	16
12	41	17
13	42	18
14	42	19
15	43	20
16	43	21
17	44	22
18	44	23
19	45	24
20	45	25
21	46	27
22	46	29
23	47	31
24	47	33
25	48	35
26	48	36
27	49	37
28	49	38
29	50	39
30 or more	50	40

Sch. 2 (contd.)

3. In the case of a person who retired before 1st July 1949, the standard amount appropriate in his case and the lower limit of the standard amount shall, respectively, be increased in accordance with Regulation 106.

4. In the case of a member of the police force of the City of London who was serving as such on 28th July 1921, the standard amount appropriate in his case shall, whatever the degree of his disablement, be the amount of the pension that could have been granted to him had the first proviso to section 4 of the City of London Police Superannuation Act 1889(a) been still in force.

SCHEDULE 3

WIDOWS

PART I   Regulation 29

WIDOW'S ORDINARY PENSION—STANDARD RATE

1. Subject to paragraphs 2 and 3, the weekly amount of a widow's ordinary pension calculated in accordance with this Part of this Schedule shall be not more than 40 one-hundred-and-eightieths of her husband's average pensionable pay for a week and, subject as aforesaid, shall be equal to a one-hundred-and-eightieth of his average pensionable pay for a week for each completed year of pensionable service up to 20 years with the addition of a one-hundred-and-eightieth for each completed half year by which his pensionable service exceeded 20 years.

2. The amount of a widow's ordinary pension calculated in accordance with paragraph 1 shall be increased in accordance with Part XIII of these Regulations.

3.—(1) Where in respect of any period a widow so elects, then, subject to paragraph 4, the weekly amount of her ordinary pension in respect of that period shall be, if her husband at the time when he ceased to be a regular policeman—

    (a) held a rank higher than that of inspector, £3·26;

    (b) held the rank of inspector, £2·62;

    (c) held a rank lower than that of inspector, £1·97.

(2) Where the husband held the rank of chief inspector in the City of London police force, the preceding sub-paragraph shall apply as though he had held a rank higher than that of inspector.

4. The weekly amount of a widow's ordinary pension calculated in accordance with paragraph 3 shall be increased—

    (a) in accordance with Regulation 110(2) and (4), and

    (b) where the husband was entitled to reckon at least 10 years' pensionable service, by 10p.

PART II   Regulation 29

WIDOW'S ORDINARY PENSION—PRESERVED RATE

The amount of a widow's ordinary pension calculated in accordance with this Part of this Schedule shall be, in respect of each week, the amount calculated according to Scheme I set out below or, where the husband was entitled to reckon at least 10 years' pensionable service, according to whichever of the Schemes set out below would yield to the widow the higher pension in respect of that week.

(a) 1889 c. cxxvii.

Sch. 3 (contd.)

Scheme I

1. Subject to paragraphs 2, 3 and 4 of this Scheme, the weekly amount of a widow's ordinary pension shall be, if her husband at the time when he ceased to be a regular policeman—

(*a*) held a rank higher than that of inspector, £3·26;

(*b*) held the rank of inspector, £2·62;

(*c*) held a rank lower than that of inspector, £1·97.

2. Where the husband—

(*a*) held the rank of chief inspector in the City of London police force and died on or after 1st July 1949;

(*b*) held the rank of chief inspector in the metropolitan police force and—

(i) died on or after 1st July 1949 but before 25th April 1955, or

(ii) ceased to be a regular policeman before 4th January 1954 and died on or after 25th April 1955; or

(*c*) held the rank of inspector in the City of London police force or the rank of sub-divisional inspector or first class inspector, C.I.D., in the metropolitan police force, ceased to be a regular policeman before 1st July 1949, and died on or after that date,

then paragraph 1 shall apply as though he had held a rank higher than that of inspector.

3. Where the husband was a member of a home police force who—

(*a*) had been a member of the Special Police Corps of the Control Commission for Germany (British Element) or the Public Safety Branch of the Allied Commission for Austria (British Element) and a reversionary member of a home police force;

(*b*) had had the tour of overseas service applicable in his case as a member of one of the aforesaid overseas corps varied by way of advancement of the date of its termination;

(*c*) on or after 1st October 1949 had ceased to be such a member and had exercised his right of reversion to a home police force; and

(*d*) ceased to be a regular policeman before the date when his tour of overseas service would have terminated if it had not been so varied,

then the widow's ordinary pension shall not be less than it would have been under the preceding paragraphs had he ceased to be a regular policeman when he ceased to be a member of one of the aforesaid overseas corps.

4. The weekly amount specified in paragraph 1 of this Scheme shall be increased in accordance with Regulation 110(2) and (4).

Scheme II

1. Subject to paragraphs 2 and 3 of this Scheme, the weekly amount of a widow's ordinary pension shall be equal to that percentage of her husband's average pensionable pay for a week set out in the second column of the following Table opposite to the number of his completed years of pensionable service:—

TABLE

Number of completed years of pensionable service	Percentage of average pensionable pay for a week
10, 11, 12, 13 and 14	4
15, 16, 17, 18 and 19	6
20, 21, 22, 23 and 24	8
25, 26, 27, 28 and 29	10
30 or more	12·5

Sch. 3 (contd.)

2. The weekly amount specified in the Table to the preceding paragraph shall be increased in accordance with Part XIII of these Regulations.

3. The weekly amount calculated in accordance with the preceding provisions of this Scheme shall be reduced in accordance with Part V of this Schedule.

PART III Regulation 31

WIDOW'S SPECIAL PENSION

1. Subject to paragraphs 2 and 3, the weekly amount of a widow's special pension calculated in accordance with this Part of this Schedule shall be equal to a third of her husband's average pensionable pay for a week.

2. The weekly amount calculated in accordance with paragraphs 1 and 3 shall be reduced in accordance with Part V of this Schedule:

Provided that it shall not be reduced below the minimum weekly amount of, subject to paragraph 3, a sixth of her husband's average pensionable pay for a week.

3. The weekly amount calculated in accordance with paragraph 1 and the minimum weekly amount calculated in accordance with paragraph 2 shall, respectively, be increased in accordance with Part XIII of these Regulations.

PART IV Regulation 32

WIDOW'S AUGMENTED SPECIAL PENSION

1. Subject to paragraphs 2 and 3, the weekly amount of a widow's special pension calculated in accordance with this Part of this Schedule shall be equal to a half of her husband's average pensionable pay for a week.

2. The weekly amount calculated in accordance with paragraph 1 shall be increased in accordance with the provisions of Part XIII of these Regulations, other than those contained in Regulation 106 or 107.

3. The weekly amount calculated in accordance with paragraphs 1 and 2 shall be reduced in accordance with Part V of this Schedule.

PART V Regulations 29, 31 and 32

REDUCTION OF WIDOW'S PENSION IN RESPECT OF NATIONAL INSURANCE BENEFIT

1. A widow's ordinary pension calculated in accordance with Scheme II of Part II of this Schedule or a widow's special pension shall be reduced by the amount of any widow's benefit or retirement pension received by her under the National Insurance Act 1965 by virtue of her husband's insurance:

Provided that—

(a) where the widow is entitled under the said Act of 1965 to a widow's allowance or a retirement pension which is increased by virtue of section 40 of that Act, the allowance or pension shall be deemed not to have been so increased;

(b) where the widow is entitled under the said Act of 1965 to a widowed mother's allowance or a retirement pension which is increased by virtue of section 37 of that Act, the allowance or pension shall be deemed not to have been so increased;

(c) where the widow is entitled under the said Act of 1965 to a widowed mother's allowance which is increased by virtue of section 40 of that Act, the allowance shall be deemed not to have been so increased.

Sch. 3 (contd.)

2.—(1) A widow's ordinary pension calculated in accordance with Scheme II of Part II of this Schedule or a widow's special pension shall be reduced in accordance with the provisions of sub-paragraph (2) where—

(*a*) she is entitled to a widowed mother's allowance or a retirement pension under the National Insurance Act 1965 (whether by virtue of her husband's insurance or otherwise) which is increased by virtue of section 37 of that Act;

(*b*) her husband ceased to be a regular policeman on or after 3rd April 1961 and was entitled to reckon pensionable service by virtue of a period of service or employment which was a participating period of relevant employment; and

(*c*) her husband dies on or after 1st January 1963.

(2) Where a widow's pension is reduced in accordance with the provisions of this sub-paragraph, the rate of the reduction shall be half the rate at which the husband's pension fell to be abated or reduced in respect of any period beyond insured pensionable age under paragraphs 2 and 3 of Part III of Schedule 2.

(3) Where the husband was not entitled to an ordinary, ill-health or short service pension, the preceding sub-paragraph shall apply as if he had become entitled to an ill-health pension on ceasing to be a regular policeman or, where he died while serving as such a policeman, immediately before his death.

3. A widow's special pension shall be reduced by the amount of any pension payable to her under section 19 of the National Insurance (Industrial Injuries) Act 1965(**a**) in consequence of the death of her husband.

4. In this Part of this Schedule a reference to widow's benefit or a retirement pension under the National Insurance Act 1965 does not include a reference to such a benefit or pension payable by virtue of section 1 of the National Insurance (Old persons' and widows' pensions and attendance allowance) Act 1970(**b**).

Regulations 30, 33 and 35   PART VI

DISCRETIONARY INCREASE IN WIDOW'S PENSION

1. The periods referred to in Regulations 30, 33 and 35 are as follows:—

(*a*) where the husband died before 5th July 1948, the period after the widow has attained the age of 60 years;

(*b*) where the husband died on or after the said date, the rest of the widow's life if, at the date of the husband's death, either she had attained the age of 60 years or he and the widow had been married for not less than 3 years and she had attained the age of 50 years;

(*c*) any period during which the widow—

(i) is pregnant by her late husband,

(ii) has a child resident with her who is entitled to an allowance under these Regulations, or

(iii) has a family within the meaning of the Family Allowances Act 1965(**c**) or of the Family Allowances Act 1945(**d**), either as originally enacted or as amended by any subsequent enactment, which includes a child not resident with her who is entitled to an allowance under these Regulations and (in a case where the child is not included in the family within the meaning of the said Act of 1945 as originally enacted) to the cost of providing for whom the widow is contributing at the rate of 82p a week or more;

(*d*) any period during which the widow is incapable of self-support within the meaning of section 34(6)(*a*) of the National Insurance (Industrial Injuries)

(a) 1965 c. 52.	(b) 1970 c. 51.
(c) 1965 c. 53.	(d) 1945 c. 41.

Sch. 3 (contd.)

Act 1965, by reason of any infirmity which rendered her so incapable at the expiry of the period specified in sub-paragraph (c) or—

(i) where the husband died before 5th July 1948, on that date;

(ii) where the husband died on or after 5th July 1948 but before 6th July 1966, at the expiry of the first 13 weeks that the pension is payable; or

(iii) where the husband died on or after 6th July 1966, at the expiry of the first 26 weeks that the pension is payable;

(e) if the conditions specified in sub-paragraph (c) have been fulfilled in respect of a widow, the period of the rest of the widow's life after the expiry of the period mentioned in sub-paragraph (c) if at the expiry of that period either the widow has attained the age of 60 years or 3 years have elapsed since the date of the marriage and the widow has attained the age of 40 years;

(f) if the conditions specified in sub-paragraph (d) have been fulfilled in respect of a widow, the period of the rest of the widow's life after the expiry of any period of incapability of self-support within the meaning of sub-paragraph (d) which expires at a date when either the widow has attained the age of 60 years or 3 years have elapsed since the date of the marriage and the widow has attained the age of 50 years.

2. In this Part of this Schedule any reference to a child being entitled to an allowance shall be construed as including a reference to a child who would be in receipt of an allowance but for the provisions of the proviso to Regulation 77(3)(b) or of Part IV of Schedule 4.

3. For the purposes of sub-paragraph (e) of paragraph 1 the conditions specified in sub-paragraph (c) thereof shall be treated as having been fulfilled if, on any day in the period between the passing of the Family Allowances and National Insurance Act 1964(a) and the coming into operation of section 1 of that Act, those conditions would have been fulfilled had that section and these Regulations come into operation at the passing of the said Act, and the reference in the said sub-paragraph (e) to the period mentioned in sub-paragraph (c) shall be construed accordingly.

PART VII   Regulation 36

WIDOW'S GRATUITY IN LIEU OF PENSION

The gratuity referred to in Regulation 36 shall be such sum as may be agreed between the police authority and the widow, not exceeding the capitalised value of the pension, or of that part thereof to which the gratuity is an alternative, calculated in accordance with tables prepared from time to time for that purpose by the Government Actuary.

PART VIII   Regulation 37

WIDOW'S ORDINARY GRATUITY

The widow's gratuity referred to in Regulation 37 shall be equal to whichever is the greater of the two following amounts:—

(a) a twelfth of her husband's average pensionable pay multiplied by the number of his completed years of pensionable service;

(b) the aggregate of the husband's pension contributions in respect of the relevant period of service.

(a) 1964 c. 10.

SCHEDULE 4

CHILDREN

Regulation 41

PART I

CHILD'S ORDINARY ALLOWANCE

1. Subject to this Part and to Parts III and IV of this Schedule, where one of a child's parents is alive, the child's ordinary allowance shall be the weekly amount in the second column of the following Table set opposite to the rank in the first column of the said Table which the parent in respect of whose death the allowance is payable held at the time when he ceased to be a regular policeman:—

TABLE

Parent's Rank	Weekly Amount
Higher than Inspector	99p
Inspector	80p
Lower than Inspector	67p

2. Subject to this Part and to Parts III and IV of this Schedule, where the parent in respect of whose death the allowance is payable was the child's only surviving parent, or in respect of the period after the death of the child's other parent, the child's ordinary allowance shall be the weekly amount in the second column of the following Table set opposite to the rank in the first column of the said Table which the parent in respect of whose death the allowance is payable held at the time when he ceased to be a regular policeman:—

TABLE

Parent's Rank	Weekly Amount
Higher than Inspector	£1·48
Inspector	£1·19
Lower than Inspector	£1·00

3. Where the parent in respect of whose death the allowance is payable—

    (a) held the rank of chief inspector in the City of London police force and died on or after 1st July 1949;

    (b) held the rank of chief inspector in the metropolitan police force, and—

        (i) died on or after 1st July 1949 but before 25th April 1955, or

        (ii) ceased to be a regular policeman before 4th January 1954 and died on or after 25th April 1955; or

    (c) held the rank of inspector in the City of London police force or the rank of sub-divisional inspector or first class inspector, C.I.D., in the metropolitan police force, ceased to be a regular policeman before 1st July 1949, and died on or after that date,

this Part shall apply as though he had held a rank higher than that of inspector.

4. Where the parent in respect of whose death the allowance is payable was a member of a home police force who—

    (a) had been a member of the Special Police Corps of the Control Commission for Germany (British Element) or the Public Safety Branch of the Allied Commission for Austria (British Element) and a reversionary member of a home police force;

Sch. 4 (contd.)

(b) had had the tour of overseas service applicable in his case as a member of one of the aforesaid overseas corps varied by way of advancement of the date of its termination;

(c) on or after 1st October 1949 had ceased to be such a member and had exercised his right of reversion to a home police force; and

(d) ceased to be a regular policeman before the date when his tour of overseas service would have terminated if it had not been so varied,

then the child's ordinary allowance shall not be less than it would have been under the preceding paragraphs had he ceased to be a regular policeman when he ceased to be a member of one of the aforesaid overseas corps.

<table>
<tr><td align="center">PART II</td><td align="right">Regulation 42</td></tr>
</table>

CHILD'S SPECIAL ALLOWANCE

1. Subject to this Part and to Parts III and IV of this Schedule, where one of a child's parents is alive the child's special allowance shall be an amount equal to a fifteenth of the average pensionable pay for a week of the parent in respect of whose death the allowance is payable.

2. Subject to this Part and to Parts III and IV of this Schedule, where the parent in respect of whose death the allowance is payable was the child's only surviving parent or in respect of the period after the death of the child's other parent, the child's special allowance shall be an amount equal to a tenth of the average pensionable pay for a week of the parent in respect of whose death the allowance is payable.

3. The amount of the allowance calculated in accordance with the preceding provisions of this Part shall be increased in accordance with Part XIII of these Regulations.

<table>
<tr><td align="center">PART III</td><td align="right">Regulation 44</td></tr>
</table>

DISCRETIONARY INCREASE IN CHILD'S ALLOWANCE

1.—(1) Where both parents of the child are dead—

(a) subject to the provisions of the following sub-paragraphs and of Part IV of this Schedule, the weekly amount of a child's ordinary allowance may be increased to an amount not exceeding the amount in the second column of the following Table set opposite to the rank in the first column of the said Table which the parent in respect of whose death the allowance is payable held at the time when he ceased to be a regular policeman:—

TABLE

Parent's Rank	Increased Amount
Higher than Inspector	£1·97
Inspector	£1·58
Lower than Inspector	£1·32

(b) subject to sub-paragraph (4) and to Part IV of this Schedule, the weekly amount of a child's special allowance may be increased to an amount equal to the amount, increased in accordance with Part XIII of these Regulations, of 2 fifteenths of the average pensionable pay for a week of the parent in respect of whose death the allowance is payable.

Sch. 4 (contd.)

(2) Where both parents of the child are dead and the parent in respect of whose death an ordinary allowance is payable—

(a) held the rank of chief inspector in the City of London police force and died on or after 1st July 1949;

(b) held the rank of chief inspector in the metropolitan police force, and—

    (i) died on or after 1st July 1949 but before 25th April 1955, or

    (ii) ceased to be a regular policeman before 4th January 1954 and died on or after 25th April 1955; or

(c) held the rank of inspector in the City of London police force or the rank of sub-divisional inspector or first class inspector, C.I.D., in the metropolitan police force, ceased to be a regular policeman before 1st July 1949, and died on or after that date,

sub-paragraph (1) shall apply as though he had held a rank higher than that of inspector.

(3) Where both parents of the child are dead and the parent in respect of whose death an ordinary allowance is payable was a member of a home police force who—

(a) had been a member of the Special Police Corps of the Control Commission for Germany (British Element) or the Public Safety Branch of the Allied Commission for Austria (British Element) and a reversionary member of a home police force;

(b) had had the tour of overseas service applicable in his case as a member of one of the aforesaid overseas corps varied by way of advancement of the date of its termination;

(c) on or after 1st October 1949 had ceased to be such a member and had exercised his right of reversion to a home police force; and

(d) ceased to be a regular policeman before the date when his tour of overseas service would have terminated if it had not been so varied,

the weekly amount of the allowance may be increased under sub-paragraph (1) to an amount not exceeding that to which it might have been increased had he ceased to be a regular policeman when he ceased to be a member of one of the aforesaid overseas corps.

(4) Where both parents of the child are dead and the parent in respect of whose death an ordinary or special allowance is payable was the child's father and he had attained the age of 65 years on 5th July 1948, then in respect of any week during which—

(a) no person is receiving a guardian's allowance under the National Insurance Act 1965 in respect of the child;

(b) the child is included in a family within the meaning of the Family Allowances Act 1965 or of the Family Allowances Act 1945, either as originally enacted or as amended by any subsequent enactment;

(c) where the allowance is a special allowance, no allowance is payable under section 21 of the National Insurance (Industrial Injuries) Act 1965 in respect of the child;

(d) no armed forces pension or award is payable to or for the child in pursuance of any Royal Warrant or other instrument; and

(e) no grant is payable to or in respect of the child under any scheme made under the Personal Injuries (Emergency Provisions) Act 1939(a),

the amount of the allowance may, without prejudice to the provisions of the preceding sub-paragraphs but subject to Part IV of this Schedule, be increased under sub-paragraph (1) to an amount not exceeding £2·45.

(a) 1939 c. 82.

Sch. 4 (contd.)

2.—(1) Where the mother of a child is alive and would have been entitled to receive widow's benefit or a retirement pension under the National Insurance Act 1965 or under the National Insurance Act 1946, either as originally enacted or as amended by any subsequent enactments, had her husband satisfied the contribution conditions therefor, then in respect of any week during which—

(a) the mother is not receiving a retirement pension under the said Act of 1965;

(b) the child is included in a family within the meaning of the Family Allowances Act 1965 or of the Family Allowances Act 1945, either as originally enacted or as amended by any subsequent enactment;

(c) where the allowance is a special allowance, no allowance is payable under section 21 of the National Insurance (Industrial Injuries) Act 1965 in respect of the child;

(d) no armed forces pension or award is payable to or for the child in pursuance of any Royal Warrant or other instrument; and

(e) no grant is payable to or in respect of the child under any scheme made under the Personal Injuries (Emergency Provisions) Act 1939,

the amount of the child's ordinary or special allowances may, subject to Part IV of this Schedule, be increased to an amount not exceeding the appropriate amount set out in sub-paragraph (2).

(2) The appropriate amount referred to in the preceding sub-paragraph shall be—

(a) irrespective of the date of the father's death, £2·45 in the case of the only or eldest child included in a family within the meaning of the Family Allowances Act 1965 or of the Family Allowances Act 1945, either as originally enacted or as amended by any subsequent enactment;

(b) where the father died on or after 9th April 1968—

(i) £1·80 in the case of the second child so included, and

(ii) £1·70 in the case of each subsequent child so included;

(c) where the father died before 9th April 1968—

(i) £1·98 in the case of the second child so included;

(ii) £1·88 in the case of the third child so included, and

(iii) £1·75 in the case of each subsequent child so included.

PART IV   Regulations 41, 42 and 44

REDUCTION OF CHILD'S ALLOWANCE

1. In the circumstances hereinafter set out the amount of an allowance calculated in accordance with Part I or, as the case may be, Part II of this Schedule, or, if a police authority decide in their discretion to increase such an allowance in accordance with Regulation 44 and Part III of this Schedule, the maximum to which that allowance may be increased under the said Part III, shall be reduced by the appropriate amount or amounts hereinafter set out.

2. Where a child who is entitled to an allowance is the only or eldest child in that family so entitled and the child's mother is in receipt under the National Insurance Act 1965 of a widow's allowance, a retirement pension or a widowed mother's allowance, which allowance or pension is increased under section 40 of the said Act, then the appropriate reduction shall be 37p a week.

3. Where an allowance is payable in respect of a child under section 21(1) of the National Insurance (Industrial Injuries) Act 1965 at the higher weekly rate prescribed by the said section 21(1), and a child's special allowance is also payable to that child, then the appropriate reduction shall be 37p a week.

Sch. 4 (contd.)

4. Where an allowance is payable in respect of a child under the Family Allowances Act 1965, then the appropriate reduction shall be 25p a week.

5. Where a guardian's allowance is payable in respect of a child under the National Insurance Act 1965, then the appropriate reduction shall be 60p a week.

Regulation 45   PART V

CHILD'S GRATUITY IN LIEU OF ALLOWANCE

The gratuity referred to in Regulation 45 shall be such sum as may be agreed between the police authority and the father, mother or guardian, as the case may be, not exceeding the capitalised value of the allowance or of that part thereof to which the gratuity is an alternative calculated in accordance with tables prepared from time to time by the Government Actuary.

Regulations 53, 54 and 55   SCHEDULE 5

PAYMENT BY POLICEMAN IN RESPECT OF PREVIOUS SERVICE OTHER THAN POLICE SERVICE

1.—(1) Where a regular policeman undertakes to pay a sum in accordance with this Schedule he shall, subject as hereafter in the Schedule provided, pay by regular instalments of such amount that the payment of the sum will be completed within a period of 5 years and before he becomes liable to be required to retire on account of age:

Provided that he may at any time discharge his liability under the undertaking, in whole or in part, by paying the whole or part of the balance of the sum then outstanding.

(2) Any payment in accordance with this paragraph shall be made by the policeman to the police authority of the force in which he is serving when the payment falls to be made and, without prejudice to any other method of payment, the liability to make any such payment may be discharged by way of a deduction by the said authority from his pay.

2. If, before he has discharged his liability under the undertaking, a regular policeman—

(a) retires without an award other than one of the amount of his aggregate pension contributions in respect of the relevant period of service;

(b) leaves his police force on joining the Royal Ulster Constabulary with the consent of the police authority;

(c) dies, or

(d) is dismissed,

all further liability under that undertaking shall cease.

3. If before he has discharged his liability under the undertaking, a regular policeman retires with an award and his liability does not cease under paragraph 2(a), the police authority by whom the award is payable shall be empowered to deduct the balance of the sum then outstanding from payments on account of the award:

Provided that where a payment is made on account of an ordinary or ill-health pension and in respect of a period beyond insured pensionable age no deduction shall be made from so much of the payment as is on account of the secured portion of the pension.

SCHEDULE 6 Regulations 55 and 82

INTERCHANGE ARRANGEMENTS

PART I

CIVIL SERVICE AND METROPOLITAN CIVIL STAFFS SERVICE

1. This Part shall apply in relation to service or employment—

(*a*) as an established civil servant, or

(*b*) in the metropolitan civil staffs within the meaning of section 15 of the Super-annuation (Miscellaneous Provisions) Act 1967**(a)**.

2. In relation to the said service or employment the specified date for the purposes of Regulations 55 and 82 shall be 1st January 1967.

3. In relation to the said service or employment the transfer value for the purposes of Regulation 55 shall be one payable under Rules made under sections 2 and 15 of the Superannuation (Miscellaneous Provisions) Act 1948**(b)**, including such Rules as they have effect by virtue of section 15(2) of the Superannuation (Miscellaneous Provisions) Act 1967.

4. The specified authority for the purposes of Regulations 55 and 82 shall be—

(*a*) in relation to service or employment as an established civil servant, the Minister for the Civil Service;

(*b*) in relation to service or employment in the metropolitan civil staffs, the Secretary of State.

5. In relation to the said service or employment—

(*a*) Regulation 55(1) shall have effect as if sub-paragraph (*c*) were omitted and, where the relevant date was before 15th February 1971, as if sub-paragraph (*e*)(ii) were omitted;

(*b*) Regulation 82(1) shall have effect as if sub-paragraphs (*b*)(ii), (*c*) and (*d*) were omitted;

(*c*) Regulation 82(2) shall have effect as if the words "where he ceased to serve as such on or after the date specified in Schedule 6 in relation to the new service, and may, where he ceased so to serve before that date," were omitted.

PART II

LOCAL GOVERNMENT, FIRE, EDUCATION AND HEALTH SERVICE

1. This Part shall apply in relation to service or employment—

(*a*) such as is mentioned in section 2(2)(*c*), (*d*), (*e*) or (*ee*) of the Superannuation (Miscellaneous Provisions) Act 1948,

(*b*) in respect of which awards may be made under the Firemen's Pension Scheme, that is to say, under the Scheme for the time being in force under section 26 of the Fire Services Act 1947**(c)**, or

(*c*) in respect of which awards may be made under Regulations for the time being in force under section 67 of the National Health Service Act 1946**(d)** or section 66 of the National Health Service (Scotland) Act 1947**(e)**.

2.—(1) Subject to sub-paragraphs (2) and (3), in relation to the said service or employment the specified date for the purposes of Regulations 55 and 82 shall be 15th February 1971.

(**a**) 1967 c. 28.   (**b**) 1948 c. 33.
(**c**) 1947 c. 41.   (**d**) 1946 c. 81.
(**e**) 1947 c. 27.

Sch. 6 (contd.)

(2) Where in relation to a particular service or employment no provisions are in operation on 15th February 1971 for the payment of a transfer value to the police authority, as mentioned in Regulation 55(1)(*d*), then in relation thereto the specified date for the purposes of Regulation 55 shall be the date on which such provisions first thereafter come into operation.

(3) Where in relation to a particular service or employment no provisions are in operation on 15th February 1971 for the reckoning of service for superannuation purposes by virtue of service as a regular policeman, as mentioned in Regulation 82(1), then in relation thereto the specified date for the purposes of Regulation 82 shall be the date on which such provisions first thereafter come into operation.

3. In relation to the said service or employment the transfer value for the purposes of Regulation 55 shall be one payable under Rules made under sections 2 and 15 of the Superannuation (Miscellaneous Provisions) Act 1948 or under Regulations made under section 67 of the National Health Service Act 1946 or section 66 of the National Health Service (Scotland) Act 1947.

4. The specified authority for the purposes of Regulations 55 and 82 shall be—

(*a*) in relation to such employment as is mentioned in section 2(2)(*c*) or (*d*) of the Superannuation (Miscellaneous Provisions) Act 1948, the local authority maintaining the superannuation fund in the benefits of which the person concerned is or was entitled to participate;

(*b*) in relation to service in a fire brigade maintained by a local authority and in respect of which awards may be made under the Firemen's Pension Scheme, the fire authority concerned;

(*c*) in relation to any other service or employment, the Secretary of State.

Part III

Other Service or Employment

1. This Part shall apply in relation to service or employment in which a person is subject to any superannuation arrangements specified in the second column of the following Table.

2. In relation to any such service or employment the specified date for the purposes of Regulations 55 and 82 shall be 15th February 1971.

3.—(1) In relation to any such service or employment the transfer value for the purposes of Regulation 55 shall, subject to sub-paragraphs (2) and (3), be one of the like amount, and calculated in the like manner, as the transfer value which would have been receivable under Part III of the Superannuation (Local Government and Approved Employment) Interchange Rules 1969(a) had the person concerned entered local government employment, within the meaning of those Rules, on the date on which he became a regular policeman and in circumstances in which the said Part III applied.

(2) For the purposes of sub-paragraph (1)—

(*a*) to the extent that the Table in Schedule 1 to the said Rules of 1969 does not contain entries in columns (1) and (2) thereof corresponding to the entries in the following Table, it shall be deemed to do so, and

(*b*) paragraph 6 of Schedule 1 to the said Rules of 1969 shall have effect as if any references therein to 18th August 1968 and to 18th August 1969 were, respectively, references to 15th February 1970 and to 15th February 1971 and sub-paragraphs (1)(*a*) and (*b*) and (3) were omitted.

(a) S.I. 1969/997 (1969 II, p. 2906).

Sch. 6 (contd.)

(3) In relation to service in which a person is subject to the Isle of Man Police Pensions Regulations, that is to say, the Regulations for the time being in operation under section 16 of the Police (Isle of Man) Act 1962 (an Act of Tynwald), the transfer value shall be one payable under those Regulations.

4. In relation to any such service or employment the specified authority for the purposes of Regulations 55 and 82 shall be the persons having the general control and management of the relevant superannuation arrangements specified in the second column of the following Table.

5. Where the person concerned is subject to any superannuation arrangements specified in the second column of the following Table (other than the Isle of Man Police Pensions Regulations) but is not employed by a body specified opposite thereto in the first column thereof, Regulation 82(2) shall have effect as if the words "shall, where he ceased to serve as such on or after the date specified in Schedule 6 in relation to the new service, and" and the woi ds"where he ceased so to serve before that date," were omitted.

TABLE

Employing body	Superannuation arrangements
Agricultural Research Council	Industrial Superannuation Scheme
,,	Agricultural Research Council Superannuation Scheme 1951
Area Electricity Board	British Electricity Authority Superannuation (Protected. Persons) Scheme
,,	Electricity Boards' Superannuation (Protected Persons) Schemes
,,	Electricity Supply (Manual Workers) Superannuation Scheme
,,	Electricity Supply (Staff) Superannuation Scheme
British Airports Authority	The British Airports Authority Superannuation Scheme
British Broadcasting Corporation	The B.B.C. New Pension Scheme
British Council	British Council Superannuation Scheme
British European Airways Corporation	The Airways Corporations Joint Pension Scheme for General Staff members
British Overseas Airways Corporation	The Airways Corporations Joint Pension Scheme for General Staff members
British Waterways Board	Cheshire County Council Superannuation Fund—Divided
,,	Grand Union Canal Company Superannuation Fund
,,	Nottingham Corporation Superannuation Fund—Divided
,,	Scheme embodied in section 23 of and Schedule 4 to the Regent Canal and Dock Company (Grand Junction Canal Purchase) Act 1928(a)

(a) 1928 c. xcviii.

Sch. 6 (contd.)

Employing body	Superannuation arrangements
British Waterways Board (*continued*)	Scheme embodied in the Superannuation Act 1965(a) (as applied to former staff of the Lee Conservancy Board)
Central Electricity Generating Board	British Electricity Authority Superannuation (Protected Persons) Scheme
,,	Electricity Boards' Superannuation (Protected Persons) Schemes
,,	Electricity Supply (Manual Workers) Superannuation Scheme
,,	Electricity Supply (Staff) Superannuation Scheme
Commonwealth War Graves Commission	The Commonwealth War Graves Commission Superannuation Scheme (1952)
Corporation of Trinity House	Trinity House Service Superannuation Scheme
Crown Agents for Oversea Governments and Administrations	Crown Agents' Pension Scheme
Crown Estate Commissioners	Crown Estate Commissioners Superannuation Scheme
Development Commission	The Development Commission Superannuation Scheme 1940
Electricity Council	British Electricity Authority Superannuation (Protected Persons) Scheme
,,	Electricity Boards' Superannuation (Protected Persons) Schemes
,,	Electricity Supply (Manual Workers) Superannuation Scheme
,,	Electricity Supply (Staff) Superannuation Scheme
Forestry Commission	The Forestry Commission Superannuation Scheme
General Lighthouse Authority	General Lighthouse Fund Superannuation Scheme
Horserace Betting Levy Board	Horserace Betting Levy Board Pension Schemes A and B
Industrial Training Boards	The Joint Pension and Retirement Benefits Funds for the Industrial Training Boards
—	The Isle of Man Police Pensions Regulations
Metropolitan Water Board	Metropolitan Water Board Superannuation and Provident Fund Scheme
National Coal Board	National Coal Board Staff Superannuation Scheme

---

(a) 1965 c. 74.

Sch. 6 (contd.)

Employing body	Superannuation arrangements
National Industrial Fuel Efficiency Service	National Industrial Fuel Efficiency Service Superannuation Scheme
National Institute of Agricultural Botany	Industrial Superannuation Scheme
Natural Environment Research Council	Natural Environment Research Council Superannuation Arrangements
North of Scotland Hydro-Electric Board	Hydroboard Superannuation Fund
Port of London Authority	Port of London Authority Pension Fund
Post Office	Post Office Staff Superannuation Scheme
Scottish Agricultural Colleges and Research Institutes	Industrial Superannuation Scheme
Science Research Council	Science Research Council Superannuation Scheme
"	Principal Non-Industrial Superannuation Scheme of the United Kingdom Atomic Energy Authority
"	The United Kingdom Atomic Energy Authority's Industrial Superannuation Scheme
South of Scotland Electricity Board	The South of Scotland Electricity Board's Superannuation Scheme
United Kingdom Atomic Energy Authority	The Principal Non-Industrial Superannuation Scheme of the United Kingdom Atomic Energy Authority
"	Protected Persons Superannuation Scheme of the United Kingdom Atomic Energy Authority
"	United Kingdom Atomic Energy Authority's Industrial Superannuation Scheme

SCHEDULE 7   Regulation 62

ADDITIONAL PENSION CONTRIBUTIONS

1. Where a man has elected to pay additional pension contributions, he shall pay such contributions at the rate specified in the second column of the following Table set opposite to the number of completed years of pensionable service reckonable by him, at the time he made his election, by virtue of service before 1st April 1956:—

Sch. 7 (contd.)

TABLE

Completed years of pensionable service				Rate expressed as a percentage of pen-sionable pay
1	...	...	...	0·1
2	...	...	...	0·1
3	...	...	...	0·2
4	...	...	...	0·2
5	...	...	...	0·3
6	...	...	...	0·4
7	...	...	...	0·5
8	...	...	...	0·6
9	...	...	...	0·7
10	...	...	...	0·8
11	...	...	...	0·9
12	...	...	...	1·1
13	...	...	...	1·3
14	...	...	...	1·6
15	...	...	...	1·9
16	...	...	...	2·3
17	...	...	...	2·7
18	...	...	...	3·3
19	...	...	...	4·1
20	...	...	...	4·1

2. In calculating the rate at which additional pension contributions are payable no account shall be taken of any service reckonable by him as pensionable service by virtue of section 10 of the Police Pensions Act 1921(a), of section 14 of the Police Act 1890 or of section 14 of the Police (Scotland) Act 1890(b).

Regulation 71   SCHEDULE 8

MEDICAL APPEALS

1. Every notice of appeal under Regulation 71(2) shall be in writing.

2. On receipt of the appeal the police authority shall forward to the Secretary of State 2 copies thereof and of the certificate appealed against, with the name and address of the appellant.

3. A medical referee shall appoint a time and place for interviewing the appellant and for any such further interviews or examinations as he may consider necessary and shall give reasonable notice thereof to the appellant and the police authority.

4. At any time before any interview with the medical referee the appellant or the police authority may submit to the medical referee a statement relating to the subject matter of the appeal, and if they so submit a statement they shall send a copy thereof to the other party.

5. Any interview or examination may be attended by—

    (a) the selected medical practitioner; and

    (b) any duly qualified medical practitioner appointed for the purpose by either party.

   (a) 1921 c. 31.   (b) 1890 c. 67.

Sch. 8 (contd.)

6. The medical referee shall give written notice to the police authority and appellant of his decision and, if that decision is that he disagrees with any part of the certificate of the selected medical practitioner, shall send a copy of his certificate to the police authority and the appellant.

7.—(1) The medical referee shall be entitled to such fees and allowances as the Secretary of State may from time to time determine.

(2) The said fees and allowances shall be paid by the police authority and shall be treated as part of the police authority's expenses for the purposes of this Schedule.

8.—(1) Save as hereinafter provided, the expenses of each party to the appeal shall be borne by that party.

(2) Where the medical referee decides in favour of the police authority, the authority may require the appellant to pay towards the cost of the appeal such sum not exceeding the referee's total fees and allowances as the authority think fit.

(3) Where the medical referee decides in favour of the appellant, the police authority shall refund to the appellant any expenses actually and reasonably incurred by the appellant in respect of any such interview or examination as is mentioned in paragraph 3.

SCHEDULE 9   Regulations 79, 81 and 82

TRANSFER VALUES

1.—(1) The transfer value payable by a police authority under Regulation 79, 81 or 82 shall, subject as hereafter in this Schedule provided, be calculated in accordance with this paragraph.

(2) The amounts shown in the second and third columns of the appropriate Table or, where the transfer value is payable under Regulation 79 or 81 in respect of a woman, in the fourth and fifth columns thereof, in relation to an age which corresponds with that of the policeman are to be multiplied respectively by the number of completed years and the number of completed months aggregating less than a year, which the policeman was entitled to reckon as pensionable service immediately before he ceased to be a member of his former force:

Provided that in calculating the number of completed years and completed months which he was entitled to reckon as aforesaid, any period by which his pensionable service exceeded 30 years shall be ignored, and—

(a) where the transfer value is payable under Regulation 79 or 81 or is payable to a fire authority or to the Government of the Isle of Man under Regulation 82, any period by which his pensionable service exceeded 20 years but did not exceed 30 years shall be counted twice;

(b) where the transfer value is payable under Regulation 82 otherwise than as aforesaid, the period of his pensionable service not exceeding 30 years shall be increased by a third.

(3) The sum of the products aforesaid is the transfer value appropriate in respect of £100 of annual pensionable pay.

(4) The total transfer value referred to in sub-paragraph (1) is to be calculated proportionately by reference to the annual pensionable pay of the policeman.

Sch. 9 (contd.)

(5) In this paragraph a reference to the appropriate Table is—

(a) in the case of a transfer value payable under Regulation 79 or 81 or payable to a fire authority or to the Government of the Isle of Man under Regulation 82, a reference to the following Table A;

(b) in the case of a transfer value payable under Regulation 82 otherwise than as aforesaid, a reference to the following Table B.

TABLE A

Age in Years	Sum in respect of £100 of annual pensionable pay			
	In the case of a man, for each completed		In the case of a woman, for each completed	
	Year	Month	Year	Month
	£	£	£	£
Less than 24	19·70	1·65	12·50	1·05
24	19·70	1·65	12·60	1·05
25	19·70	1·65	12·85	1·05
26	19·70	1·65	13·30	1·10
27	19·70	1·65	13·90	1·15
28	19·70	1·65	14·60	1·20
29	19·70	1·65	15·40	1·30
30	19·75	1·65	16·25	1·35
31	19·85	1·65	17·15	1·45
32	20·05	1·65	18·05	1·50
33	20·30	1·70	18·90	1·55
34	20·60	1·70	19·75	1·65
35	21·00	1·75	20·55	1·70
36	21·45	1·80	21·25	1·75
37	21·95	1·85	21·85	1·80
38	22·45	1·85	22·40	1·85
39	22·95	1·90	22·90	1·90
40	23·45	1·95	23·40	1·95
41	23·90	2·00	23·90	2·00
42	24·35	2·05	24·40	2·05
43	24·80	2·05	24·90	2·05
44	25·25	2·10	25·40	2·10
45	25·65	2·15	25·90	2·15
46	25·95	2·15	26·40	2·20
47	26·20	2·20	26·85	2·25
48	26·40	2·20	27·25	2·25
49	26·55	2·20	27·55	2·30
50	26·65	2·20	27·80	2·30
51	26·70	2·20	28·05	2·35
52	26·75	2·25	28·30	2·35
53	26·80	2·25	28·50	2·40
54	26·85	2·25	28·70	2·40
55 or more	26·90	2·25	28·85	2·40

Sch. 9 (contd.)

TABLE B

Age in years				Sum in respect of £100 of annual pensionable pay for each completed	
				Year	Month
				£	£
Less than 36	...	...	...	9·00	0·75
36	...	...	...	9·05	0·75
37	...	...	...	9·10	0·75
38	...	...	...	9·15	0·75
39	...	...	...	9·30	0·75
40	...	...	...	9·45	0·80
41	...	...	...	9·60	0·80
42	...	...	...	9·80	0·80
43	...	...	...	10·00	0·85
44	...	...	...	10·20	0·85
45	...	...	...	10·45	0·85
46	...	...	...	10·65	0·90
47	...	...	...	10·85	0·90
48	...	...	...	11·10	0·90
49	...	...	...	11·35	0·95
50	...	...	...	11·60	0·95
51	...	...	...	11·85	1·00
52	...	...	...	12·15	1·00
53	...	...	...	12·45	1·05
54	...	...	...	12·80	1·05
55	...	...	...	13·20	1·10
56	...	...	...	13·65	1·15
57	...	...	...	14·10	1·15
58	...	...	...	14·55	1·20
59	...	...	...	15·05	1·25

2.—(1) A transfer value calculated as aforesaid shall be reduced in accordance with sub-paragraphs (2) and (3)—

(a) in the case of a policeman other than a policeman who, immediately before he ceased to be a member of his former force, was paying pension contributions at the rate of 1p a week less than the appropriate percentage of his pensionable pay;

(b) in the case of a policeman entitled to reckon pensionable service, immediately before he ceased to be a member of his former force, by virtue of a participating period of relevant employment.

(2) The amount shown in the second column of the following Table or, in the case of a woman, in the third column thereof, in relation to an age which corresponds with that of the policeman is the amount of the reduction in respect of each £1 by which the annual value of his pension would be reduced—

(a) under paragraph 1 of Part III of Schedule 2, in a case in which sub-paragraph (1)(a) applies, and

(b) under paragraphs 2 and 3 of the said Part III, in a case in which sub-paragraph (1)(b) applies,

in respect of any period beyond insured pensionable age, if he had become entitled to a pension on ceasing to be a member of his former force.

Sch. 9 (contd.)

(3) The total reduction is to be calculated proportionately by reference to the amount by which the annual value of such a pension would be so reduced.

(4) For the purposes of sub-paragraph (1)(*b*) and of the provisions applied by sub-paragraph (2)(*b*) a period shall be treated as a participating period of relevant employment notwithstanding that a payment in lieu of contributions only fell to be made after the policeman ceased to be a member of his former force.

TABLE

REDUCTION OF TRANSFER VALUE

Age in years				Reduction for each £1 by which annual value of pension would be reduced	
				In the case of a man	In the case of a woman
				£	£
Less than 24	...	...	...	1·80	1·40
24	...	...	...	1·95	1·65
25	...	...	...	2·10	1·90
26	...	...	...	2·25	2·20
27	...	...	...	2·35	2·55
28	...	...	...	2·45	2·90
29	...	...	...	2·60	3·30
30	...	...	...	2·70	3·75
31	...	...	...	2·80	4·25
32	...	...	...	2·95	4·70
33	...	...	...	3·05	5·10
34	...	...	...	3·20	5·45
35	...	...	...	3·30	5·75
36	...	...	...	3·45	6·05
37	...	...	...	3·60	6·35
38	...	...	...	3·70	6·65
39	...	...	...	3·85	6·95
40	...	...	...	4·00	7·25
41	...	...	...	4·15	7·55
42	...	...	...	4·30	7·80
43	...	...	...	4·45	8·05
44	...	...	...	4·60	8·30
45	...	...	...	4·75	8·60
46	...	...	...	4·95	8·95
47	...	...	...	5·15	9·30
48	...	...	...	5·35	9·65
49	...	...	...	5·55	10·00
50	...	...	...	5·75	10·35
51	...	...	...	5·95	10·70
52	...	...	...	6·20	11·10
53	...	...	...	6·45	11·50
54	...	...	...	6·70	11·90
55	...	...	...	7·00	12·35
56	...	...	...	7·30	12·80
57	...	...	...	7·60	13·30
58	...	...	...	7·95	13·85
59	...	...	...	8·30	14·45
60	...	...	...	8·70	
61	...	...	...	9·15	
62	...	...	...	9·60	
63	...	...	...	10·10	
64	...	...	...	10·60	

Sch. 9 (contd.)

3. A transfer value calculated as aforesaid shall be reduced, in the case of a policeman who had undertaken to make payments in accordance with Schedule 5, by the balance outstanding, immediately before he ceased to be a member of his former force, of the sum he had undertaken to pay or so much thereof as has not been deducted under paragraph 3 of that Schedule from a gratuity payable to him.

4. Where a transfer value is payable by a police authority under Regulation 79 in respect of the transfer before 1st January 1967 of a member of a police force who—

(a) after transferring but before 1st January 1967 retired with an ill-health pension or a pension under the former Acts which has at any time been terminated in whole or in part under Regulation 65 or any corresponding provision of the former Regulations or former Acts, and

(b) is entitled to reckon his previous service as pensionable service by virtue of Regulation 52(b) or any corresponding provision of the former Acts,

the transfer value, calculated in accordance with paragraphs 1 and 2, shall be reduced by the aggregate of the payments or contributions made by the police authority towards the pension before it was terminated as aforesaid.

5.—(1) Where a transfer value is payable by a police authority under Regulation 82 the transfer value, calculated as aforesaid, shall be reduced by an amount, subject to sub-paragraph (2), equal to that of any award payable on the policeman ceasing to be a member of his former force so, however, that where he had paid pension contributions at a rate related to 6·25% of his pensionable pay or had paid additional contributions under Regulation 62 or any corresponding provision of the former Regulations the reduction shall be limited to so much of the award as would have been payable had he paid contributions at a rate related to 5% of his pensionable pay and had not paid such additional contributions.

(2) Where the new service (within the meaning of Regulation 82) is such as is mentioned in Part II or III of Schedule 6 and the time limit mentioned in Regulation 82(1)(c) is extended thereunder the amount to be deducted under sub-paragraph (1) may be increased by an amount equal to compound interest thereon at the rate of 3% per annum, with half-yearly rests, in respect of the period beginning with whichever is the later of the two following dates, that is to say—

(a) the first anniversary of the policeman's ceasing to be a member of his former force, or

(b) the date on which he was paid his award,

and ending with the date on which he notifies the police authority as mentioned in Regulation 82(1)(d):

Provided that the amount to be deducted shall not exceed a half of the difference between the transfer value which would be payable but for this sub-paragraph and that which would be so payable if paragraph 6(2)(a) applied.

6.—(1) For the purpose of calculating a transfer value payable under Regulation 79 or 81 or, where the new service (within the meaning of that Regulation) is such as is mentioned in Part I of Schedule 6, under Regulation 82, any reference to the age of the policeman shall be construed as a reference to his age—

(a) at the time he ceased to be a member of his former force, where he so ceased on or after 1st January 1967, or

(b) at 1st January 1967 where he so ceased before that date.

(2) For the purpose of calculating a transfer value payable under Regulation 82 where the new service (within the meaning of that Regulation) is such as is mentioned in Part II or III of Schedule 6, any reference to the age of the policeman shall be construed as a reference to his age—

(a) at the time he ceased to be a member of his former force, where he enters or entered the new service within 12 months therefrom, or

(b) at the time he enters or entered the new service where the preceding sub-paragraph does not apply,

Sch. 9 (contd.)

except that, where he ceased to be a member of his former force more than 12 months before the date specified in Schedule 6 for the purposes of Regulation 82, any such reference shall be construed as a reference to his age at that date.

(3) Any reference in this Schedule to the annual pensionable pay of a policeman is a reference to the annual value of his pensionable pay immediately before he ceased to be a member of his former force, any retrospective increase therein granted after that time being ignored.

(4) Where a policeman ceased to be a member of his former force before 5th July 1948, any references in this Schedule to pensionable service and annual pensionable pay shall be construed, respectively, as references to approved service and annual pay within the meaning of the former Acts.

(5) Any reference in this Schedule to a policeman's former force is a reference to the police force maintained by the police authority by whom the transfer value is payable.

Regulations 89 and 90   SCHEDULE 10

LIMITS IN RESPECT OF AWARDS TO OR IN RESPECT OF SERVICEMEN

1.—(1) The amount of the pension payable to a serviceman for any period shall not, when aggregated with the amount of any armed forces pension or award which is also payable to or in respect of him for that period in pursuance of any Royal Warrant or other instrument, exceed—

(a) in the case of a serviceman other than a serviceman (1939-1945), the amount of the award which would have been payable for that period if the injury as a result of which he is permanently disabled had been treated as if it were an injury received without his own default in the execution of his duty as a member of a police force;

(b) in the case of a serviceman (1939-1945), the amount calculated according to the following Table:—

Completed years of pensionable service	Amount expressed in 60ths of average pensionable pay
Less than 11	45
11 or more but less than 16	48
16 or more but less than 21	51
21 or more but less than 26	54
26 or more but less than 30	57
30 or more	60

(2) The reference in the preceding sub-paragraph to an armed forces pension or award shall not include an allowance for constant attendance, wear and tear of clothing or comforts, except in the case of a serviceman (1939-1945) whose period of relevant service in the armed forces ended before 1st January 1952.

2. The amount of the pension payable to the widow of a serviceman for any period shall not, when aggregated with the amount of any armed forces pension or award which is also so payable for that period in respect of her husband in pursuance of any Royal Warrant or other instrument, exceed—

(a) in the case of the widow of a serviceman other than a serviceman (1939-1945), the amount of the pension which would have been payable for that period if the injury as a result of which her husband died had been treated as if it were an injury received without his own default in the execution of his duty as a member of a police force;

Sch. 10 (contd.)

(b) in the case of the widow of a serviceman (1939-1945), an amount, which shall be increased in accordance with Part XIII of these Regulations, equal to a third of his average pensionable pay for a week.

3. The amount of the allowance payable to a child of a serviceman for any period shall not, when aggregated with the amount of any armed forces pension or award payable to or for the child for that period in respect of the father in pursuance of any Royal Warrant or other instrument, exceed—

(a) in the case of a child of a serviceman other than a serviceman (1939-1945), the amount of the allowance which would have been payable for that period if the injury as a result of which the father died had been treated as if it were an injury received without his own default in the execution of his duty as a member of a police force;

(b) in the case of a child of a serviceman (1939-1945), an amount, which shall be increased in accordance with Part XIII of these Regulations, equal to a fifteenth of his average pensionable pay for a week.

4. Where the armed forces award the amount whereof for any period is to be aggregated for the purpose of this Schedule with the amount of any pension or allowance payable to any person for that period is a gratuity, the amount of the armed forces award for the period shall be taken to be the amount which would be payable for that period under Part I of the Government Annuities Act 1929(a) if the gratuity had been laid out at the date when it became payable in the purchase of an annuity dependent on the life of that person.

SCHEDULE 11   Regulations 96 and 97

PRESERVED PENSIONABLE PAY

1.—(1) Subject to paragraph 2, the preserved pensionable pay of a member of a police force shall be his annual pensionable pay immediately before the relevant date for the purposes of calculating the award.

(2) For the purposes of this paragraph the relevant date shall be—

(a) where the award is made to or in respect of a regular policeman, the date when he last ceased to be such in the force of the police authority by whom the award is payable;

(b) where the award is made to or in respect of an auxiliary policeman, the date of the end of the continuous period of active service as such in which he received the injury which resulted in disablement;

(c) where the award is made to or in respect of an overseas policeman who is not a reversionary member of a home police force, the date of the end of the tour of overseas service in which he received the injury which resulted in disablement.

2. Where a member of a police force at the date of his death or retirement held a rank to which he had been promoted within the 3 preceding years, his preserved pensionable pay shall be the average of the annual pensionable pay to which he had been entitled during those 3 years:

Provided that—

(a) promotion within any of the following 3 groups of ranks in a home police force shall, for the purposes of this paragraph, be deemed not to be a promotion:—

(a) 1929 c. 29.

Sch. 11 (contd.)

Group 1
Chief Superintendent
Superintendent

Group 2
Chief Inspector
Sub-Divisional Inspector
Inspector
Station Inspector
Sub-Inspector

Group 3
Station Sergeant
Sergeant
Acting Sergeant

and promotion within such groups of ranks in an overseas corps as have from time to time been specified in a direction of the Secretary of State for the purposes of Regulation 68 of the Police Pensions Regulations 1948(a) or Regulation 65 of the Police Pensions (Scotland) Regulations 1948(b) shall be deemed not to be a promotion;

(b) in the case of a reversionary member of a home police force his appointment to an overseas corps otherwise than by way of transfer from another overseas corps shall be deemed to be a promotion for the purposes of this paragraph, and where he gave the notice referred to in Regulation 57 the average of his annual pensionable pay shall be deemed to be the average of the annual pensionable pay to which he would have been entitled if he had continued to serve in the corps without alteration in the amount of his pay till the date when his tour of overseas service would have terminated if it had not been varied as mentioned in that Regulation;

(c) this paragraph shall not apply in the case of a member of the City of London police force who was serving as such on 28th July 1921 and was still so serving on 5th July 1948;

(d) the effect of this paragraph shall not reduce the amount of any award below what it would have been if the promotion had not occurred.

3. For the purposes of this Schedule any temporary reduction in rate of pay imposed by way of punishment shall be ignored.

4. For the purposes of this Schedule the annual pay of a person who was in receipt of weekly pay shall be calculated as if there were $52\frac{1}{8}$ weeks in each year.

(a) S.I. 1948/1531 (1948 I, p. 3429).   (b) S.I. 1948/1530 (1948 I, p. 3503).

EXPLANATORY NOTE

(This Note is not part of the Regulations.)

These Regulations consolidate, with amendments, the Police Pensions Regulations 1966 and the instruments amending those Regulations, namely, the Regulations set out in Schedule 1.

The main changes are mentioned below.

The Regulations, which come into operation on 15th February 1971, take account of the introduction of decimal currency on that date.

Regulation 32 (which corresponds to Regulation 14 of the Regulations of 1966) makes fresh provision as respects the circumstances in which a policeman's widow is entitled to an augmented award. Where the husband's death is the result of an attack upon him or of an injury received while effecting an arrest or saving human life, the widow's entitlement is no longer dependent upon the opinion of the police authority that the appropriate condition is fulfilled. Where none of these conditions is fulfilled but the police authority are of opinion that it would be inequitable in the circumstances that she should not receive an augmented award, she is entitled to such an award. Regulation 43 (which corresponds to Regulation 25 of the Regulations of 1966) makes similar provision in relation to a child's special gratuity.

Regulations 55 and 82 (which correspond to Regulations 38 and 65 of the Regulations of 1966) extend the provisions for the reckoning of previous service or the payment of transfer values, in the case of persons with mixed service, to cover persons who, before or after being members of police forces, have been in local government, fire, education or health service or in such other service or employment as is mentioned in Part III of Schedule 6.

STATUTORY INSTRUMENTS

1971 No. 233

POLICE

The Special Constables (Pensions) Regulations 1971

Made - - -	*11th February* 1971
Laid before Parliament	*12th February* 1971
Coming into Operation	*15th February* 1971

In exercise of the powers conferred on me by section 34 of the Police Act 1964(**a**) (read with section 1(2) of the Police Pensions Act 1961(**b**)), I hereby make the following Regulations :—

Citation and commencement

1. These Regulations may be cited as the Special Constables (Pensions) Regulations 1971 and shall come into operation on 15th February 1971.

Revocations

2. The former pension provisions are hereby revoked to the extent that they have not heretofore been revoked and, accordingly, the Regulations set out in Schedule 1 to these Regulations are hereby revoked.

Interpretation

3.—(1) In these Regulations the expression "the principal Regulations" means the Police Pensions Regulations 1971(**c**).

(2) Regulations 4, 5(6), 10, 13(1), (3) and (4), 14, 17(2) and 18 of the principal Regulations shall apply for the purposes of these Regulations as they apply for the purposes of the said Regulations.

(3) For the purposes of these Regulations a reference to an injury received by a person in the execution of his duty as a special constable shall include a reference to any injury received while on duty or while on a journey necessary to enable him to report for duty or to return home after duty.

(4) (*a*) Where a police area is or has been combined with another police area, the combined police area of which the first named area for the time being forms part and the police authority and police fund therefor shall, for the purposes of these Regulations, be deemed to be the same area, authority and fund as the first named area and the authority and fund therefor.

(**a**) 1964 c. 48.   (**b**) 1961 c. 35.   (**c**) S.I. 1971/232.(1971 I, p. 700).

(b) Where a police area is or has been divided, in relation to any special constable who is transferred by the instrument effecting the division from the divided area to another police area, the other area and the police authority and police fund therefor shall, for the purposes of these Regulations, be deemed to be the same area, authority and fund as the divided area and the authority and fund therefor.

(c) Where a police area is or has been combined or divided as aforesaid, any special constable who is transferred, by the instrument effecting the combination or division, from that police area to another police area shall, for the purposes of these Regulations, be deemed to have been appointed a special constable for the area to which he is transferred on the day on which he was last appointed a special constable for the police area first mentioned in this sub-paragraph.

(d) In relation to a special constable who has served as such on or after 23rd May 1966, a reference in this paragraph to the division of a police area includes a reference to the transfer of part of a police area, on or after 1st April 1966, on the date on which an order affecting the area, made under section 140 of the Local Government Act 1933(a) or under Part II of the Local Government Act 1958(b), comes into force.

(5) For the purposes of these Regulations a reference in the principal Regulations to a continuous period of service shall be construed as a reference to a period during which a special constable holds or held that office in the police area for which he is or was appointed ; and any reference in the said Regulations to retirement, or to ceasing to be a member of a police force, shall be construed as a reference to the termination of such a period.

(6) For the purposes of these Regulations a reference to the former pension provisions is a reference to the provisions of the Special Constables (Pensions) Orders and Regulations set out in Schedule 1 to these Regulations, in Schedule 2 to the Special Constables (Pensions) Regulations 1966(c) and in Schedule 2 to the Special Constables (Pensions) Order 1962(d) (that is to say the instruments made before the making of these Regulations which applied to special constables provisions of regulations made under the Police Pensions Act 1948(e)), except that a reference to the former pension provisions of 1923 or 1945 shall be construed as a reference to—

(a) paragraph 11 of the Special Constables Order 1923(f) as originally made or as from time to time amended (g) ; or

(b) paragraphs 1 and 2 of the Special Constables Order 1945(h).

(7) For the purposes of these Regulations a reference to a special constable is a reference to a special constable appointed under the Special Constables Act 1831(i), section 196 of the Municipal Corporations Act 1882(j) or section 16 of the Police Act 1964 and, except where the context otherwise requires, includes a reference to a person who has been a special constable.

(a) 1933 c. 51.   (b) 1958 c. 55.
(c) S.I. 1966/1590 (1966 III, p. 5008); revoked by these Regulations.
(d) S.I. 1962/2786 (1962 III, p. 3977); revoked by S.I. 1966/1590 (1966 III, p. 5008).
(e) 1948 c. 24.
(f) S.R. & O. 1923/905 (Rev. XVIII, p. 180: 1923, p. 147); revoked as respects paragraph 11 by S.I. 1949/589 (1949 I, p. 3379).
(g) The relevant amending instruments are S.R. & O. 1942/1904, 1945/323, 1640, 1947/1010 (Rev. XVIII, pp. 180, 185; 1942 I, p. 76; 1945 I, pp. 125, 126; 1947 I, p. 353).
(h) S.R. & O. 1945/323 (1945 I, p. 125); revoked by S.I. 1948/866 (1948 XVIII, p. 180; 1948 I, p. 3480).
(i) 1831 c. 41; repealed by 1964 c. 48.
(j) 1882 c. 50; repealed as respects section 196 by 1964 c. 48.

Special constable's supplemental pension

4.—(1) This Regulation shall apply to a person who ceases or has ceased to hold the office of special constable on or after 11th April 1949 and is permanently disabled from following his ordinary employment as a result of an injury received without his own default in the execution of his duty as a special constable.

(2) Subject to the provisions of these Regulations, a person to whom this Regulation applies shall be entitled to a supplemental pension and Regulations 22, 66(1) and (2), 67 and 106 of the principal Regulations shall apply as if he had been an auxiliary policeman at the time that he received the injury.

(3) Regulation 66(2) of the principal Regulations shall not apply where the person concerned last ceased to hold the office of special constable before 16th May 1950.

Widow's special pension

5.—(1) This Regulation shall apply to a widow of a special constable who dies or has died on or after 11th April 1949 as the result of an injury received without his own default in the execution of his duty as a special constable.

(2) Subject to the provisions of these Regulations, a widow to whom this Regulation applies shall be entitled to a special pension and Regulations 31, 33, 36(1), 38(2), 39(1) and (3) and 40 of the principal Regulations and Part XIII thereof shall apply as if her husband had been an auxiliary policeman at the time that he received the injury.

(3) Nothing in Regulation 39(1) of the principal Regulations shall apply to a widow's special pension if she became entitled to the like pension before 6th May 1957 under the former pension provisions, but in such a case, Regulation 39(2) of the principal Regulations shall apply as if the pension were an award mentioned in that provision.

Widow's augmented award

6.—(1) This Regulation shall apply to a widow of a special constable whose death is the result of an injury received without his own default in the execution of his duty where, subject to paragraph (4) of this Regulation, one of the following conditions is satisfied, namely that—

(*a*) he was attacked by a person or persons in a manner which was intrinsically likely to cause death and death ensued, on or after 11th April 1949, as a result of the attack, or

(*b*) the injury was received in the course of duties performed for the immediate purpose of effecting an arrest or of preventing an escape or rescue from legal custody and death ensued on or after 1st August 1964, or

(*c*) the injury was received in the course of duties performed—

(i) for the immediate purpose of saving the life of another person or of preventing loss of human life, and

(ii) in circumstances in which there was an intrinsic likelihood of his receiving a fatal injury,

and death ensued on or after 1st January 1970, or

(*d*) the police authority are of the opinion that one of the preceding conditions may be satisfied. and that this Regulation should apply. or

(*e*) the police authority are of the opinion that the injury was received
otherwise than as aforesaid but in the course of duties performed in
such circumstances that it would be inequitable if there were not payable in respect of him such an award as would have been payable
had one of the conditions specified in sub-paragraphs (*a*), (*b*) and (*c*)
been satisfied, and death ensued on or after 15th February 1971.

(2) For the purpose of calculating a widow's special pension payable to
a widow to whom this Regulation applies. Regulation 31 of the principal
Regulations (as applied by Regulation 5 of these Regulations) shall have effect
subject to the provisions of Regulation 32(1), (2) and (5) of the principal
Regulations.

(3) Subject to the provisions of these Regulations, a widow to whom this
Regulation applies whose husband dies on or after 1st August 1964 shall be
entitled to a gratuity in addition to a special pension and Regulations 32(1),
(3), (4) and (5), 38(2), 39(1) and (3) and 40 of the principal Regulations shall
apply as if her husband, at the time that he received the injury, had been
serving as an auxiliary policeman in the police force for the police area for
which he was appointed.

(4) Without prejudice to the application of this Regulation by virtue of
paragraph (1) thereof in the case of a widow of a special constable who died
before 15th February 1971, this Regulation shall apply to such a widow if it
would have applied by virtue of paragraph (1) had the words "in the opinion
of the police authority" been inserted—

(*a*) in sub-paragraph (*a*) thereof, after the word "which",

(*b*) in sub-paragraph (*b*) thereof, after the word "performed", and

(*c*) in sub-paragraph (*c*) thereof, after the word "performed",

and had sub-paragraph (*d*) thereof been omitted.

Widow's pension under the pension provisions of 1923 or 1945

7.—(1) This Regulation shall apply to a widow of a special constable who
died before 11th April 1949.

(2) Where a widow to whom this Regulation applies was immediately before
11th April 1949 entitled to a pension under the former pension provisions
of 1923 or 1945 (which applied to special constables certain provisions of the
Police Pensions Act 1921(**a**)), she shall continue to be entitled to the pension
in all respects in the same manner as if the said provisions had not been
revoked, so however that it shall be calculated in accordance with this Regulation.

(3) For the purposes of calculating the pension Regulations 34(3) and (4)
and 35 of the principal Regulations and Part XIII thereof shall apply as if—

(*a*) the pension was one to which the widow continued to be entitled under
Regulation 34(2) of the principal Regulations, and

(*b*) her husband had been an auxiliary policeman at the time that he
received the injury as a result of which he died.

(**a**) 1921 c. 31.

Child's special allowance

8.—(1) This Regulation shall apply to a child of a special constable who dies or has died on or after 11th April 1949 as the result of an injury received without his own default in the execution of his duty as a special constable.

(2) Subject to the provisions of these Regulations, a child to whom this Regulation applies shall be entitled to a child's special allowance and Regulations 42, 44, 45(1) and 46 of the principal Regulations and Part XIII thereof shall apply as if the parent had been an auxiliary policeman at the time that he received the injury.

Child's special gratuity

9.—(1) This Regulation shall apply to a child of a special constable who dies or has died on or after 1st August 1964 as the result of an injury received without his own default in the execution of his duty where, subject to paragraph (3) of this Regulation, one of the conditions set out in paragraph (1) of Regulation 6 of these Regulations is satisfied and—

> (*a*) in the case of a man, does not leave a widow entitled to a gratuity under paragraph (3) of the said Regulation 6, or

> (*b*) in the case of a woman, was the child's only surviving parent:

Provided that this Regulation shall apply to a child who at the date of the parent's death has attained the age of 16 years only if at that date the child has not attained the age of 19 years and either is undergoing full-time education or is an apprentice.

(2) Subject to the provisions of these Regulations, a child to whom this Regulation applies shall be entitled to a gratuity in addition to a special allowance and Regulations 43 and 46 of the principal Regulations shall apply as if the parent, at the time that he received the injury, had been serving as an auxiliary policeman in the police force for the police area for which he was appointed.

(3) Without prejudice to the application of this Regulation by virtue of paragraph (1) thereof in the case of a child of a special constable who died before 15th February 1971, this Regulation shall apply to such a child if it would have applied by virtue of paragraph (1) had Regulation 6(1) been modified as provided in Regulation 6(4) of these Regulations.

Increase in award to widow of special constable who both ceased to serve and died between 1st July 1949 and 16th May 1950

10.—(1) This Regulation shall apply to a widow entitled to an award under Regulation 5 of these Regulations where the husband—

> (*a*) first ceased to hold the office of special constable, after receiving the injury as a result of which he died, on or after 1st July 1949, and

> (*b*) died before 16th May 1950.

(2) The police authority may increase the award to a widow to whom this Regulation applies by such amount as they may from time to time think fit, not exceeding £0·50 a week.

Average pensionable pay and pensionable service

11. For the purpose of calculating an award under these Regulations to or in respect of a special constable—

(*a*) his average pensionable pay or average pensionable pay for a period of a week, as the case may be, shall be calculated in accordance with Schedule 2 to these Regulations ;

(*b*) he shall be deemed to have completed less than 11 years' pensionable service.

Limitation on application of Regulation 106 *of the principal Regulations*

12. Where, for the purpose of calculating an award to or in respect of a special constable, it is provided in the principal Regulations, as applied by these Regulations, that an amount shall be increased in accordance with Regulation 106 of the principal Regulations or with Part XIII thereof (which includes Regulation 106), the said amount shall be increased in accordance with the said Regulation 106 only if the injury by virtue of which the award is payable was received by the special constable—

(*a*) during a period for which he held the office of special constable which ended before 1st April 1947, or

(*b*) after 31st March 1945 and during a continuous period of whole-time service for which he was granted pay under the Special Constables Order 1940(**a**).

Application of certain provisions of the principal Regulations

13. Regulations 3, 69, 70, 71, 72, 73, 76, 77 and 78 of the principal Regulations shall apply for the purposes of these Regulations as if a special constable were a member of a police force and as if any reference in the said Regulation 3 to the former Regulations (that is to say, the Regulations made under the Police Pensions Act 1948 before the making of the principal Regulations)—

(*a*) were a reference to those Regulations as applied to special constables by the former pension provisions, and

(*b*) included a reference to Regulations 2(2) and 4(2) of the Special Constables (Pensions) Order 1949(**b**), as set out in the Schedule to the Special Constables (Pensions) Order 1950(**c**), to Regulation 6 of the Special Constables (Pensions) Order 1962 and to Regulation 8 of the Special Constables (Pensions) Regulations 1966.

Application of certain provisions of the Police Pensions Act 1948

14.—(1) Section 4 of the Police Pensions Act 1948 (which relates to the forfeiture of pensions) shall apply to—

(*a*) an award under these Regulations as though it were a pension mentioned in subsection (1) of that section ;

(*b*) an award under the former pension provisions of 1923 or 1945 as though those provisions were included in the rules and regulations referred to in subsection (4) of that section.

(**a**) S.R. & O. 1940/1193 (1940 I, p. 198); revoked by S.I. 1948/866 (Rev. XVIII, p. 180: 1948 I, p. 3480).
(**b**) S.I. 1949/589 (1949 I, p. 3379); revoked by S.I. 1962/2786 (1962 III, p. 3977).
(**c**) S.I. 1950/673 (1950 II, p. 341); revoked by S.I. 1962/2786 (1962 III, p. 3977).

(2) Section 5 of the said Act of 1948 (which relates to appeals against forfeiture or refusal of a pension) shall apply to—

(a) an award under these Regulations as though it were a pension mentioned in subsections (1)(a) and (1)(b) of that section ;

(b) an award under the former pension provisions of 1923 or 1945 as though it were a pension mentioned in subsection (1)(b) of that section,

and, in either case, as though a special constable served in the police force for the police area for which he is appointed.

(3) Section 7 of the said Act of 1948 (which relates to assignments of, or charges on, a pension and to fraudulent conduct in obtaining a pension) shall apply to an award under these Regulations as though such an award were a pension mentioned in that section.

Limitation on application of Regulations to constables to whom the Police and Firemen (War Service) Act 1939 applied

15.—(1) This Regulation shall apply to a person who—

(a) ceased to serve as a member of a police force in such circumstances that section 1 of the Police and Firemen (War Service) Act 1939(a), as extended by Regulation 60DA of the Defence (General) Regulations 1939, applied in his case, and

(b) was appointed a special constable during the period which was treated, in his case, as a period of approved service in a police force, by virtue of section 2(1) of that Act as so extended (hereafter in this Regulation referred to as his period of war service).

(2) No award shall be payable to or in respect of a person to whom this Regulation applies by virtue of an injury received by him during his period of war service.

(3) If a person to whom this Regulation applies continued to hold the office of special constable after the end of his period of war service, by virtue of his appointment during that period, then, for the purposes of Schedule 2 to these Regulations, the date of his appointment as a special constable shall be deemed to be the date of the end of his period of war service.

Authority by whom payments are to be made

16. An award under these Regulations shall be payable by the police authority for the police area for which the special constable was appointed at the time when he received the injury by virtue of which the award is payable.

R. Maudling,
One of Her Majesty's
Principal Secretaries of State.

Home Office,
    Whitehall.
11th February 1971.

(a) 1939 c. 103.

Regulation 2

SCHEDULE 1

FORMER PENSION PROVISIONS REVOKED

The Special Constables (Pensions) Regulations 1966	S.I. 1966/1590 (1966 III, p. 5008).
The Special Constables (Pensions) (Amendment) Regulations 1967	S.I. 1967/1546 (1967 III, p. 4311).
The Special Constables (Pensions) (Amendment) Regulations 1968	S.I. 1968/1989 (1968 III, p. 5420).
The Special Constables (Pensions) (Amendment) Regulations 1969	S.I. 1969/724 (1969 II, p. 1958).
The Special Constables (Pensions) (Amendment) (No. 2) Regulations 1969	S.I. 1969/1514 (1969 III, p. 4920).
The Special Constables (Pensions) (Amendment) (No. 3) Regulations 1969	S.I. 1969/1850 (1969 III, p. 5790).
The Special Constables (Pensions) (Amendment) Regulations 1970.	S.I. 1970/1571 (1970 III, p. 5323).

Regulation 11

SCHEDULE 2

AVERAGE PENSIONABLE PAY

1.—(1) Subject to the provisions of this Schedule, for the purpose of calculating an award under these Regulations to or in respect of a special constable his average pensionable pay or average pensionable pay for a period of a week—

(a) in the case of a special constable last appointed such on or after 1st March 1967, shall be of an amount determined in accordance with sub-paragraph (2) of this paragraph ;

(b) in the case of a special constable last appointed such before 1st March 1967 who ceased to hold that office on or after that date, shall be of an amount determined in accordance with sub-paragraph (2) of this paragraph or with sub-paragraph (3) thereof if the amount so calculated is higher ;

(c) in the case of a special constable who ceased to hold that office before 1st March 1967, shall be determined in accordance with sub-paragraph (3) of this paragraph.

(2) In a case in which this sub-paragraph applies, the average pensionable pay or average pensionable pay for a period of a week of a special constable shall be deemed to be of the like amount as his average pensionable pay or, as the case may be, his average pensionable pay for a week (within the meaning of the principal Regulations) would have been, at the date at which he ceased to hold that office, had his appointment and service at any time as a special constable for any police area been appointment and service in the rank of a constable as a regular policeman in the police force for that area.

(3) In a case in which this sub-paragraph applies, the average pensionable pay or average pensionable pay for a period of a week of a special constable shall be deemed to be the sum set out, opposite to the period during which he ceased to hold that office, in the second column of the appropriate Table in this Schedule with the addition of the sum so set out in the third column of that Table for each completed year of service as a special constable from the date of his appointment as such, subject to the maximum, if any, so set out in the fourth column of that Table.

2. Where a special constable ceased to hold that office on or after 20th December 1945 but before 8th September 1955, then for the purpose of paragraph 1(3) of this Schedule no account shall be taken of his first two completed years of service as such.

3. Where a special constable appointed for the City of London or for the Metropolitan Police District ceased to hold that office on or after 1st January 1966, his average pensionable pay determined in accordance with paragraph 1(3) of this Schedule shall be increased by £50 00 a year.

4. Where an award is payable under any provision of these Regulations to or in respect of a special constable, and the like award first became payable to or in respect of him under the former pension provisions—

    (a) on or after 1st July 1949, but before 16th May 1950 ;

    (b) on or after 3rd August 1951, but before 3rd March 1952 ;

    (c) on or after 14th January 1954, but before 19th April 1954 ;

    (d) on or after 8th September 1955, but before 6th May 1957 ;

    (e) on or after 22nd April 1958, but before 6th April 1959 ;

    (f) on or after 1st September 1960, but before 1st July 1961 ; or

    (g) on or after 1st September 1962, but before 1st January 1963,

then, for the purpose of calculating the award under these Regulations, the appropriate Table shall have effect as if for any reference therein to the first date mentioned in the applicable sub-paragraph of this paragraph there were substituted a reference to the second date so mentioned.

5. Where an award under these Regulations to or in respect of a special constable is payable by virtue of an injury received by him after 31st March 1945 and during a continuous period of whole-time service for which he was granted pay under the Special Constables Order 1940, then paragraph 1 of this Schedule shall not apply for the purpose of calculating the award but his average pensionable pay for a period of a week shall be deemed to be his pay for a week at the rate to which he was entitled immediately before the end of that continuous period of service.

6. For the purpose of calculating an award under these Regulations to or in respect of a special constable, his average pensionable pay for a period of a week shall be taken to be his average pensionable pay divided by $52\frac{1}{6}$.

7. In this Schedule a reference to a person's appointment as a special constable, otherwise than in paragraph 1(2) thereof, is a reference to his last appointment as such before he received the injury by virtue of which the award is payable and a reference to his ceasing to hold that office is a reference to his first ceasing to hold that office after he received that injury.

TABLE 1

AVERAGE PENSIONABLE PAY (MEN)

Period during which office ceased to be held	Average pensionable pay or average pensionable pay for period of a week	Increment	Maximum
Before 20th December 1945	£3·50 a week	£0·05	—
On or after 20th December 1945, but before 21st May 1947	£4·50 a week	£0·075	£5·85 a week
On or after 21st May 1947, but before 1st July 1949	£5·25 a week	£0·075	£6·60 a week
On or after 1st July 1949, but before 3rd August 1951	£330·00 a year	£5·00	£420·00 a year
On or after 3rd August 1951, but before 14th January 1954	£400·00 a year	£5·00	£505·00 a year
On or after 14th January 1954, but before 8th September 1955	£445·00 a year	£5·00	£550·00 a year
On or after 8th September 1955, but before 1st February 1957	£475·00 a year	£7·50	£640·00 a year
On or after 1st February 1957, but before 22nd April 1958	£490·00 a year	£7·50	£660·00 a year
On or after 22nd April 1958, but before 1st September 1960	£510·00 a year	£8·25	£695·00 a year
On or after 1st September 1960, but before 1st September 1962	£600·00 a year	£17·00	£970·00 a year
On or after 1st September 1962, but before 1st February 1963	£620·00 a year	£18·00	£1,005·00 a year
On or after 1st February 1963, but before 1st September 1964	£635·00 a year	£18·00	£1,030·00 a year
On or after 1st September 1964	£800·00 a year	£14·00	£1,105·00 a year

TABLE II

Average Pensionable Pay (Women)

Period during which office ceased to be held	Average pensionable pay or average pensionable pay for period of a week	Increment	Maximum
Before 20th December 1945　...　...	£3·50 a week	£0·05	—
On or after 20th December 1945, but before 21st May 1947　...　...	£4·50 a week	£0·075	£5·85 a week
On or after 21st May 1947, but before 1st July 1949　...　...　...　...	£5·25 a week	£0·075	£6·60 a week
On or after 1st July 1949, but before 3rd August 1951　...　...　...　...	£290·00 a year	£5·00	£380·00 a year
On or after 3rd August 1951, but before 14th January 1954　...　...　...	£355·00 a year	£5·00	£455·00 a year
On or after 14th January 1954, but before 8th September 1955　...　...	£395·00 a year	£5·00	£495·00 a year
On or after 8th September 1955, but before 1st February 1957　...　...	£425·00 a year	£7·50	£575·00 a year
On or after 1st February 1957, but before 22nd April 1958　...　...	£440·00 a year	£7·50	£595·00 a year
On or after 22nd April 1958, but before 1st September 1960　...　...　...	£460·00 a year	£8·25	£625·00 a year
On or after 1st September 1960, but before 1st September 1962　...　...	£540·00 a year	£17·00	£875·00 a year
On or after 1st September 1962, but before 1st February 1963　...　...	£560·00 a year	£18·00	£905·00 a year
On or after 1st February 1963, but before 1st September 1964　...　...	£570·00 a year	£18·00	£930·00 a year
On or after 1st September 1964 ...　...	£720·00 a year	£14·00	£995·00 a year

EXPLANATORY NOTE

(This Note is not part of the Regulations.)

These Regulations (which come into force on 15th February 1971 and apply to special constables appointed in England and Wales) consolidate, subject to amendments, the Regulations set out in Schedule 1, that is to say the Special Constables (Pensions) Regulations 1966 and the instruments amending those Regulations.

The instruments revoked gave to special constables and their dependants certain pension benefits for which members of police forces and their dependants were eligible by applying, with modifications, certain provisions of the Police Pensions Regulations 1966. The present Regulations make fresh provision for this purpose by similarly applying the Police Pensions Regulations 1971, which consolidated (subject to amendments) the earlier Police Pensions Regulations.

STATUTORY INSTRUMENTS

1971 No. 234 (S.37)

POLICE

The Special Constables (Pensions) (Scotland) Regulations 1971

Made - - - -	12*th February* 1971
Laid before Parliament	13*th February* 1971
Coming into Operation	15*th February* 1971

In exercise of the powers conferred on me by section 26 of the Police (Scotland) Act 1967(a) (as read with section 1(2) of the Police Pensions Act 1961(b)), and of all other powers enabling me in that behalf, and after consultation with the Joint Central Committee and such bodies and associations as are mentioned in section 26(9)(b) of the said Act of 1967, I hereby make the following regulations:—

Citation and commencement

1. These regulations may be cited as the Special Constables (Pensions) (Scotland) Regulations 1971 and shall come into operation on 15th February 1971.

Revocations

2. The regulations set out in Schedule 1 to these regulations are hereby revoked.

Interpretation

3.—(1) In these regulations the expression "the principal regulations" means the Police Pensions Regulations 1971(c).

(2) Regulations 4, 5(6), 10, 13(1), (3) and (4), 14, 17(2) and 18 of the principal regulations shall apply for the purposes of these regulations as they apply for the purposes of the said regulations.

(3) For the purposes of these regulations a reference to an injury received by a person in the execution of his duty as a special constable shall include a reference to any injury received while on duty or while on a journey necessary to enable him to report for duty or to return home after duty.

(4) (*a*) Where an amalgamation scheme is or has been made or approved by the Secretary of State under section 1, 2 or 4 of the Police (Scotland) Act 1946(d); section 17, 18 or 20 of the Police (Scotland) Act 1956(e) or section 19, 20 or 21 of

---

(a) 1967 c. 77.
(c) S.I. 1971/232.(1971 I, p. 700).
(e) 1956 c. 26.

(b) 1961 c. 35.
(d) 1946 c. 71.

the Police (Scotland) Act 1967 (which relate to the amalgamation of police areas) the joint police committee for the combined area shall be deemed, for the purposes of these regulations, to be the same authority as the police authority or joint police committee for an area which ceases to be a separate police area by virtue of such a scheme.

(*b*) For the purposes of this paragraph "combined area" shall have the meaning assigned to it in the said Act of 1967.

(5) For the purposes of these regulations a reference in the principal regulations to a continuous period of service shall be construed as a reference to a period during which a special constable holds or held that office in the police area for which he is or was appointed; and any reference in the said regulations to retirement, or to ceasing to be a member of a police force, shall be construed as a reference to the termination of such a period.

(6) For the purposes of these regulations a reference to the former pension provisions is a reference to the provisions of the Orders and Regulations set out in Schedule 1 to these Regulations, in Schedule 2 to the Special Constables (Pensions) (Scotland) Regulations 1966(**a**) and in Schedule 2 to the Special Constables (Pensions) (Scotland) Regulations 1962(**b**) (that is to say the instruments made before the making of these regulations which applied to special constables provisions of regulations made under the Police Pensions Act 1948(**c**)), except that a reference to the former pension provisions of 1923 or 1945 shall be construed as a reference to—

(*a*) paragraph 6 of the Special Constables (Scotland) Order 1923(**d**) as originally made or as from time to time amended; or

(*b*) paragraphs 1 and 2 of the Special Constables (Scotland) Order 1945(**e**).

(7) For the purposes of these regulations a reference to a special constable is a reference to a special constable appointed under the Burgh Police (Scotland) Act 1892(**f**) or any local Act or the Special Constables (Scotland) Act 1914(**g**) or the Police (Scotland) Act 1956 or the Police (Scotland) Act 1967 and, except where the context otherwise requires, includes a reference to a person who has been a special constable.

Special constable's supplemental pension

4.—(1) This regulation shall apply to a person who ceases or has ceased to hold the office of special constable on or after 2nd June 1949 and is permanently disabled from following his ordinary employment as a result of an injury received without his own default in the execution of his duty as a special constable.

(2) Subject to the provisions of these regulations, a person to whom this regulation applies shall be entitled to a supplemental pension and regulations 22, 66(1) and (2), 67 and 106 of the principal regulations shall apply as if he had been an auxiliary policeman at the time that he received the injury.

(3) Regulation 66(2) of the principal regulations shall not apply where the person concerned last ceased to hold the office of special constable before 16th May 1950.

(**a**) S.I. 1966/1625 (1966 III, p. 5066).   (**b**) S.I. 1962/2808 (1962 III, p. 4041).
(**c**) 1948 c. 24.
(**d**) S.R. & O. 1923/1232 (Rev. XVIII, p. 254: 1923, p. 152).
(**e**) S.R. & O. 1945/324 (1945 I, p. 127).   (**f**) 1892 c. 55.
(**g**) 4 & 5 Geo. 5. c. 53.

Widow's special pension

5.—(1) This regulation shall apply to a widow of a special constable who dies or has died on or after 2nd June 1949 as the result of an injury received without his own default in the execution of his duty as a special constable.

(2) Subject to the provisions of these regulations, a widow to whom this regulation applies shall be entitled to a special pension and regulations 31, 33, 36(1), 38(2), 39(1) and (3) and 40 of the principal regulations and Part XIII thereof shall apply as if her husband had been an auxiliary policeman at the time that he received the injury.

(3) Nothing in regulation 39(1) of the principal regulations shall apply to a widow's special pension if she became entitled to the like pension before 6th May 1957 under the former pension provisions, but in such a case, regulation 39(2) of the principal regulations shall apply as if the pension were an award mentioned in that provision.

Widow's augmented award

6.—(1) This regulation shall apply to a widow of a special constable whose death is the result of an injury received without his own default in the execution of his duty where, subject to paragraph (4) of this regulation, one of the following conditions is satisfied, namely that—

(*a*) he was attacked by a person or persons in a manner which was intrinsically likely to cause death and death ensued, on or after 2nd June 1949, as a result of the attack, or

(*b*) the injury was received in the course of duties performed for the immediate purpose of effecting an arrest or of preventing an escape or rescue from legal custody and death ensued on or after 1st August 1964, or

(*c*) the injury was received in the course of duties performed—

(i) for the immediate purpose of saving the life of another person or of preventing loss of human life, and

(ii) in circumstances in which there was an intrinsic likelihood of his receiving a fatal injury,

and death ensued on or after 1st January 1970, or

(*d*) the police authority are of the opinion that one of the preceding conditions may be satisfied, and that this regulation should apply, or

(*e*) the police authority are of the opinion that the injury was received otherwise than as aforesaid but in the course of duties performed in such circumstances that it would be inequitable if there were not payable in respect of him such an award as would have been payable had one of the conditions specified in sub-paragraphs (*a*), (*b*) and (*c*) been satisfied, and death ensued on or after 15th February 1971.

(2) For the purpose of calculating a widow's special pension payable to a widow to whom this regulation applies, regulation 31 of the principal regulations (as applied by regulation 5 of these regulations) shall have effect subject to the provisions of regulation 32(1), (2) and (5) of the principal regulations.

(3) Subject to the provisions of these regulations, a widow to whom this regulation applies whose husband dies on or after 1st August 1964 shall be

entitled to a gratuity in addition to a special pension and regulations 32(1), (3), (4) and (5), 38(2), 39(1) and (3) and 40 of the principal regulations shall apply as if her husband, at the time that he received the injury, had been serving as an auxiliary policeman in the police force for the police area for which he was appointed.

(4) Without prejudice to the application of this regulation by virtue of paragraph (1) thereof in the case of a widow of a special constable who died before 15th February 1971, this regulation shall apply to such a widow if it would have applied by virtue of paragraph (1) had the words "in the opinion of the police authority" been inserted—

(a) in sub-paragraph (a) thereof, after the word "which",

(b) in sub-paragraph (b) thereof, after the word "performed", and

(c) in sub-paragraph (c) thereof, after the word "performed",

and had sub-paragraph (d) thereof been omitted.

Widow's pension under the pension provisions of 1923 or 1945

7.—(1) This regulation shall apply to a widow of a special constable who died before 2nd June 1949.

(2) Where a widow to whom this regulation applies was immediately before 2nd June 1949 entitled to a pension under the former pension provisions of 1923 or 1945 (which applied to special constables certain provisions of the Police Pensions Act 1921(a)), she shall continue to be entitled to the pension in all respects in the same manner as if the said provisions had not been revoked, so however that it shall be calculated in accordance with this regulation.

(3) For the purposes of calculating the pension, regulations 34(3) and (4) and 35 of the principal regulations and Part XIII thereof shall apply as if—

(a) the pension was one to which the widow continued to be entitled under regulation 34(2) of the principal regulations, and

(b) her husband had been an auxiliary policeman at the time that he received the injury as a result of which he died.

Child's special allowance

8.—(1) This regulation shall apply to a child of a special constable who dies or has died on or after 2nd June 1949 as the result of an injury received without his own default in the execution of his duty as a special constable.

(2) Subject to the provisions of these regulations, a child to whom this regulation applies shall be entitled to a child's special allowance and regulations 42, 44, 45(1) and 46 of the principal regulations and Part XIII thereof shall apply as if the parent had been an auxiliary policeman at the time that he received the injury.

Child's special gratuity

9.—(1) This regulation shall apply to a child of a special constable who dies or has died on or after 1st August 1964 as the result of an injury received

---

(a) 1921 c. 31.

without his own default in the execution of his duty where, subject to paragraph (3) of this regulation, one of the conditions set out in paragraph (1) of regulation 6 of these regulations is satisfied and—

(*a*) in the case of a man, does not leave a widow entitled to a gratuity under paragraph (3) of the said regulation 6, or

(*b*) in the case of a woman, was the child's only surviving parent:

Provided that this regulation shall apply to a child who at the date of the parent's death has attained the age of 16 years only if at that date the child has not attained the age of 19 years and either is undergoing full-time education or is an apprentice.

(2) Subject to the provisions of these regulations, a child to whom this regulation applies shall be entitled to a gratuity in addition to a special allowance and regulations 43 and 46 of the principal regulations shall apply as if the parent, at the time that he received the injury, had been serving as an auxiliary policeman in the police force for the police area for which he was appointed.

(3) Without prejudice to the application of this regulation by virtue of paragraph (1) thereof in the case of a child of a special constable who died before 15th February 1971, this regulation shall apply to such a child if it would have applied by virtue of paragraph (1) had regulation 6(1) been modified as provided in regulation 6(4) of these regulations.

Increase in award to widow of special constable who both ceased to serve and died between 1st July 1949 and 16th May 1950

10.—(1) This regulation shall apply to a widow entitled to an award under regulation 5 of these regulations where the husband—

(*a*) first ceased to hold the office of special constable, after receiving the injury as a result of which he died, on or after 1st July 1949, and

(*b*) died before 16th May 1950.

(2) The police authority may increase the award to a widow to whom this regulation applies by such amount as they may from time to time think fit, not exceeding £0·50 a week.

Average pensionable pay and pensionable service

11. For the purpose of calculating an award under these regulations to or in respect of a special constable—

(*a*) his average pensionable pay or average pensionable pay for a period of a week, as the case may be, shall be calculated in accordance with Schedule 2 to these regulations;

(*b*) he shall be deemed to have completed less than 11 years' pensionable service.

Limitation on application of regulation 106 of the principal regulations

12. Where, for the purpose of calculating an award to or in respect of a special constable, it is provided in the principal regulations, as applied by these regulations, that an amount shall be increased in accordance with regulation 106 of the principal regulations or with Part XIII thereof (which includes regulation 106), the said amount shall be increased in accordance with the said regulation 106 only if the injury by virtue of which the award is payable was received by the special constable—

(a) during a period for which he held the office of special constable which ended before 1st April 1947, or

(b) after 31st March 1945 and during a continuous period of whole-time service for which he was granted pay under the Special Constables (Scotland) Order No. 2 1940(a).

Application of certain provisions of the principal regulations

13. Regulations 3, 69, 70, 71, 72, 73, 76, 77 and 78 of the principal regulations shall apply for the purposes of these regulations as if any reference in the said regulation 3 to the former regulations (that is to say, the regulations made under the Police Pensions Act 1948 before the making of the principal regulations)—

(a) were a reference to those regulations as applied to special constables by the former pension provisions, and

(b) included a reference to regulations 2(2) and 4(2) of the Special Constables (Pensions) (Scotland) Order 1949(b), as set out in the Schedule to the Special Constables (Pensions) (Scotland) Order 1950(c), to regulation 8 of the Special Constables (Pensions) (Scotland) Regulations 1962 and to regulation 10 of the Special Constables (Pensions) (Scotland) Regulations 1966.

Application of certain provisions of the Police Pensions Act 1948

14.—(1) Section 4 of the Police Pensions Act 1948 (which relates to the forfeiture of pensions) shall apply to—

(a) an award under these regulations as though it were a pension mentioned in subsection (1) of that section;

(b) an award under the former pension provisions of 1923 or 1945 as though those provisions were included in the rules and regulations referred to in subsection (4) of that section.

(2) Section 5 of the said Act of 1948 (which relates to appeals against forfeiture or refusal of a pension) shall apply to—

(a) an award under these regulations as though it were a pension mentioned in subsections (1)(a) and (1)(b) of that section;

(b) an award under the former pension provisions of 1923 or 1945 as though it were a pension mentioned in subsection (1)(b) of that section,

and, in either case, as though a special constable served in the police force for the police area for which he is appointed.

(3) Section 7 of the said Act of 1948 (which relates to assignments of, or charges on, a pension and to fraudulent conduct in obtaining a pension) shall apply to an award under these regulations as though such an award were a pension mentioned in that section.

(a) S.R. & O. 1940/1275 (1940 I, p. 200).   (b) S.I. 1949/1056 (1949 I, p. 3444).
(c) S.I. 1950/674 (1950 II, p. 362).

Limitation on application of regulations to constables to whom the Police and Firemen (War Service) Act 1939 applied

15.—(1) This regulation shall apply to a person who—

(*a*) ceased to serve as a member of a police force in such circumstances that section 1 of the Police and Firemen (War Service) Act 1939**(a)**, as extended by regulation 60DA of the Defence (General) Regulations 1939, applied in his case, and

(*b*) was appointed a special constable during the period which was treated, in his case, as a period of approved service in a police force, by virtue of section 2(1) of that Act as so extended (hereafter in this regulation referred to as "his period of war service").

(2) No award shall be payable to or in respect of a person to whom this regulation applies by virtue of an injury received by him during his period of war service.

(3) If a person to whom this regulation applies continued to hold the office of special constable after the end of his period of war service by virtue of his appointment during that period, then, for the purposes of Schedule 2 to these regulations, the date of his appointment as a special constable shall be deemed to be the date of the end of his period of war service.

Authority by whom payments are to be made

16. An award under these regulations shall be payable by the police authority for the police area for which the special constable was appointed at the time when he received the injury by virtue of which the award is payable.

Gordon Campbell,
One of Her Majesty's
Principal Secretaries of State.

St. Andrew's House,
Edinburgh.

12th February 1971.

(a) 1939 c. 103.

SCHEDULE 1   Regulation 2

SPECIAL CONSTABLES (PENSIONS) (SCOTLAND) REGULATIONS REVOKED

The Special Constables (Pensions) (Scotland) Regulations 1966	S.I. 1966/1625 (1966 III, p. 5066).
The Special Constables (Pensions) (Scotland) Amendments Regulations 1967	S.I. 1967/1553 (1967 III, p. 4315).
The Special Constables (Pensions) (Scotland) Amendment Regulations 1968	S.I. 1968/1995 (1968 III, p. 5425).
The Special Constables (Pensions) (Scotland) Amendment Regulations 1969	S.I. 1969/989 (1969 II, p. 2903).
The Special Constables (Pensions) (Scotland) Amendment (No. 2) Regulations 1969 ...	S.I. 1969/1529 (1969 III, p. 4960).
The Special Constables (Pensions) (Scotland) Amendment (No. 3) Regulations 1969 ...	S.I. 1969/1880 (1969 III, p. 5821).
The Special Constables (Pensions) (Scotland) Amendment Regulations 1970	S.I. 1970/1583 (1970 III, p. 5335).

SCHEDULE 2   Regulation 11

AVERAGE PENSIONABLE PAY

1.—(1) Subject to the provisions of this Schedule, for the purpose of calculating an award under these regulations to or in respect of a special constable his average pensionable pay or average pensionable pay for a period of a week—

(a) in the case of a special constable last appointed such on or after 1st March 1967, shall be of an amount determined in accordance with sub-paragraph (2) of this paragraph;

(b) in the case of a special constable last appointed such before 1st March 1967 who ceased to hold that office on or after that date, shall be of an amount determined in accordance with sub-paragraph (2) of this paragraph or with sub-paragraph (3) thereof if the amount so calculated is higher;

(c) in the case of a special constable who ceased to hold that office before 1st March 1967, shall be of an amount determined in accordance with sub-paragraph (3) of this paragraph.

(2) In a case in which this sub-paragraph applies, the average pensionable pay or average pensionable pay for a period of a week of a special constable shall be deemed to be of the like amount as his average pensionable pay or, as the case may be, his average pensionable pay for a week (within the meaning of the principal regulations) would have been, at the date at which he ceased to hold that office, had his appointment and service at any time as a special constable for any police area been appointment and service in the rank of a constable as a regular policeman in the police force for that area.

(3) In a case in which this sub-paragraph applies, the average pensionable pay or average pensionable pay for a period of a week of a special constable shall be deemed to be the sum set out, opposite to the period during which he ceased to hold that office, in the second column of the appropriate Table in this Schedule with the addition of the sum so set out in the third column of that Table for each completed year of service as a special constable from the date of his appointment as such, subject to the maximum, if any, so set out in the fourth column of that Table.

2. Where a special constable ceased to hold that office on or after 20th December 1945 but before 8th September 1955, then for the purpose of paragraph 1(3) of this Schedule no account shall be taken of his first two completed years of service as such.

3. Where an award is payable under any provision of these regulations to or in respect of a special constable, and the like award first became payable to or in respect of him under the former pension provisions—

(*a*) on or after 1st July 1949, but before 16th May 1950;

(*b*) on or after 3rd August 1951, but before 12th March 1952;

(*c*) on or after 14th January 1954, but before 19th April 1954;

(*d*) on or after 8th September 1955, but before 6th May 1957;

(*e*) on or after 22nd April 1958, but before 7th April 1959;

(*f*) on or after 1st September 1960, but before 3rd April 1961; or

(*g*) on or after 1st September 1962, but before 1st January 1963,

then, for the purpose of calculating the award under these regulations, the appropriate Table shall have effect as if for any reference therein to the first date mentioned in the applicable sub-paragraph of this paragraph there were substituted a reference to the second date so mentioned.

4. Where an award under these regulations to or in respect of a special constable is payable by virtue of an injury received by him after 31st March 1945 and during a continuous period of whole-time service for which he was granted pay under the Special Constables (Scotland) Order No. 2 1940, then paragraph 1 of this Schedule shall not apply for the purpose of calculating the award but his average pensionable pay for a period of a week shall be deemed to be his pay for a week at the rate to which he was entitled immediately before the end of that continuous period of service.

5. For the purpose of calculating an award under these regulations to or in respect of a special constable, his average pensionable pay for a period of a week shall be taken to be his average pensionable pay divided by $52\frac{1}{8}$.

6. In this Schedule a reference to a person's appointment as a special constable, otherwise than in paragraph 1(2) thereof, is a reference to his last appointment as such before he received the injury by virtue of which the award is payable and a reference to his ceasing to hold that office is a reference to his first ceasing to hold that office after he received that injury.

TABLE I

Average Pensionable Pay (Men)

Period during which office ceased to be held	Average pensionable pay or average pensionable pay for period of a week	Increment	Maximum
Before 20th December 1945	£3·50 a week	£0·05	—
On or after 20th December 1945, but before 21st May 1947	£4·50 a week	£0·075	£5·85 a week
On or after 21st May 1947, but before 1st July 1949	£5·25 a week	£0·075	£6·60 a week
On or after 1st July 1949, but before 3rd August 1951	£330·00 a year	£5·00	£420·00 a year
On or after 3rd August 1951, but before 14th January 1954	£400·00 a year	£5·00	£505·00 a year
On or after 14th January 1954, but before 8th September 1955	£445·00 a year	£5·00	£550·00 a year
On or after 8th September 1955, but before 1st February 1957	£475·00 a year	£7·50	£640·00 a year
On or after 1st February 1957, but before 22nd April 1958	£490·00 a year	£7·50	£660·00 a year
On or after 22nd April 1958, but before 1st September 1960	£510·00 a year	£8·25	£695·00 a year
On or after 1st September 1960, but before 1st September 1962	£600·00 a year	£17·00	£970·00 a year
On or after 1st September 1962, but before 1st February 1963	£620·00 a year	£18·00	£1,005·00 a year
On or after 1st February 1963, but before 1st September 1964	£635·00 a year	£18·00	£1,030·00 a year
On or after 1st September 1964	£800·00 a year	£14·00	£1,105·00 a year

POLICE

TABLE II

AVERAGE PENSIONABLE PAY (WOMEN)

Period during which office ceased to be held	Average pensionable pay or average pensionable pay for period of a week	Increment	Maximum
Before 20th December 1945	£3·50 a week	£0·05	—
On or after 20th December 1945, but before 21st May 1947	£4·50 a week	£0·075	£5·85 a week
On or after 21st May 1947, but before 1st July 1949	£5·25 a week	£0·075	£6·60 a week
On or after 1st July 1949, but before 3rd August 1951	£290·00 a year	£5·00	£380·00 a year
On or after 3rd August 1951, but before 14th January 1954	£355·00 a year	£5·00	£455·00 a year
On or after 14th January 1954, but before 8th September 1955	£395·00 a year	£5·00	£495·00 a year
On or after 8th September 1955, but before 1st February 1957	£425·00 a year	£7·50	£575·00 a year
On or after 1st February 1957, but before 22nd April 1958	£440·00 a year	£7·50	£595·00 a year
On or after 22nd April 1958, but before 1st September 1960	£460·00 a year	£8·25	£625·00 a year
On or after 1st September 1960, but before 1st September 1962	£540·00 a year	£17·00	£875·00 a year
On or after 1st September 1962, but before 1st February 1963	£560·00 a year	£18·00	£905·00 a year
On or after 1st February 1963, but before 1st September 1964	£570·00 a year	£18·00	£995·00 a year
On or after 1st September 1964	£720·00 a year	£14·00	£995·00 a year

EXPLANATORY NOTE

(This Note is not part of the Regulations.)

These Regulations (which come into force on 15th February 1971 and apply to special constables appointed in Scotland) consolidate, subject to amendments, the Regulations set out in Schedule 1, that is to say the Special Constables (Pensions) (Scotland) Regulations 1966 and the instruments amending those Regulations.

The instruments revoked gave to special constables and their dependants certain pension benefits for which regular policemen and their dependants were eligible by applying, with modifications, certain provisions of the Police Pensions Regulations 1966 S.I. 1966/1582. The present Regulations make fresh provision for this purpose by similarly applying the Police Pensions Regulations 1971, which consolidated (subject to amendments) the earlier Police Pensions Regulations.

STATUTORY INSTRUMENTS

1971 No. 239

POLICE

The Police Cadets (Pensions) Regulations 1971

Made - - -	*11th February* 1971	
Laid before Parliament	*19th February* 1971	
Coming into Operation—		
for the purposes of		
Regulation 3(2)	*22nd February* 1971	
for all other purposes	*1st April* 1971	

In exercise of the powers conferred on me by section 35 of the Police Act 1964(**a**), as extended by section 13 of the Superannuation (Miscellaneous Provisions) Act 1967(**b**), and after consulting the Police Council for the United Kingdom in accordance with section 4(5) of the Police Act 1969(**c**), I hereby make the following Regulations :—

Citation and commencement

1. These Regulations may be cited as the Police Cadets (Pensions) Regulations 1971 and shall come into operation—

(*a*) for the purposes of Regulation 3(2), on 22nd February 1971 :

(*b*) for all other purposes, on 1st April 1971.

Interpretation

2.—(1) In these Regulations the expression "the principal Regulations" means the Police Pensions Regulations 1971(**d**).

(2) Regulations 4, 5, 10, 13(1) and (4), 14, 17, 18 and 116 of the principal Regulations shall apply for the purposes of these Regulations as they apply for the purposes of the said Regulations, in the case of the said Regulation 116, as if a police cadet were a member of the police force to which he is attached.

(3) For the purposes of these Regulations a reference to a qualifying injury is a reference to an injury received by a person, without his own default—

(*a*) while on duty as a police cadet or while on a journey necessary to enable him to report for duty or to return to his usual place of abode after duty, or

(*b*) while taking action which, in the opinion of the police authority, it was appropriate that he should have taken by reason of his being a police cadet :

and, in the case of a police cadet in relation to whom these Regulations have taken effect, includes a reference to an injury so received before these Regulations took effect in relation to him.

(**a**) 1964 c. 48.
(**c**) 1969 c. 63.

(**b**) 1967 c. 28.
(**d**) S.I. 1971/232.(1971 I, p. 700).

(4) For the purposes of these Regulations, disablement means inability to perform the ordinary duties of a male or of a female member of a police force, as the case may be, but where it is necessary to determine the degree of a person's disablement it shall be determined by reference to the degree to which his earning capacity has been affected as a result of a qualifying injury :

Provided that a person shall be deemed to be totally disabled if, and only if, as a result of a qualifying injury, either he is incapable by reason of the disablement of earning any money in any employment or is receiving treatment as an in-patient at a hospital.

(5) For the purposes of these Regulations, a reference in the principal Regulations to a person serving as a regular policeman or member of a police force shall be construed as a reference to a person serving as a police cadet attached to a particular police force ; and any reference in the said Regulations to retirement, or to ceasing to be a member of a police force, shall be construed as a reference to the termination of a period of such service.

(6) For the purposes of these Regulations, a reference to a police cadet is a reference to a police cadet appointed under section 17 of the Police Act 1964 and, except where the context otherwise requires, includes a reference to a person who has been a police cadet ; and references to the police force to which a police cadet is attached, to the chief officer of police and to the police authority are, respectively, references to the police force with a view to becoming a member of which the cadet is undergoing training, the chief officer of that force and the police authority maintaining that force.

Effect of Regulations

3.—(1) These Regulations shall have effect in relation to a police cadet who serves as such on or after 1st April 1971 and, in relation to such a cadet—

  (*a*) who on appointment has not attained the age of 18 years, only as from his attaining that age ;

  (*b*) who on appointment has attained that age, as from his appointment ;

and, except where the context otherwise requires, any reference in these Regulations to a police cadet is a reference to a cadet who has so served and has attained that age.

(2) Notwithstanding anything in paragraph (1), these Regulations shall have effect as from 1st April 1971 in relation to a police cadet who on that date—

  (*a*) is serving as such by virtue of his appointment before that date, and

  (*b*) has attained the age of 18 years,

except that these Regulations shall not have effect in relation to such a police cadet if, before that date, he has so elected by notice in writing given to the police authority.

(3) Where these Regulations have effect in relation to a police cadet they shall have effect to the exclusion of any other provision for pension, allowance or gratuity in respect of his service as such contained in or in force under any enactment ; and on these Regulations taking effect in relation to a police cadet attached to a police force other than the metropolitan police force (otherwise than as mentioned in paragraph (1)(*b*)), he shall be deemed for the purpose of a return of any contributions made by him under any such other provision to have ceased to serve as a police cadet ; and, accordingly, to have ceased to be treated as employed by his police authority :

Provided that nothing in this paragraph shall affect the operation of the National Insurance Act 1965(**a**) or the National Insurance (Industrial Injuries) Act 1965(**b**).

Police cadet's ill-health and supplemental pensions

4.—(1) This Regulation shall apply to a police cadet who ceases to serve as such and is permanently disabled as a result of a qualifying injury.

(2) Subject to the provisions of these Regulations, a police cadet to whom this Regulation applies shall be entitled to a supplemental pension together with, where he ceases to serve as such on the ground that he is disabled, an ill-health pension ; and, subject to paragraphs (3), (4) and (5), Regulations 20, 22, 24(1) to (6), 66(1) and (2), 67 and 68 of the principal Regulations shall apply as if he were such a regular policeman as is mentioned in paragraphs (1) and (3)(*b*) of the said Regulation 20 or, as the case may be, in paragraph (1) of the said Regulation 22.

(3) Regulation 20 of the principal Regulations, as so applied, shall have effect as if the references to Parts III and IV of Schedule 2 were omitted therefrom ; but an ill-health pension payable hereunder shall be reduced in respect of any period beyond insured pensionable age—

(*a*) by an amount calculated at an annual rate obtained by multiplying £1·70 by the number of completed years of pensionable service which the person concerned is entitled to reckon, and

(*b*) by an amount calculated at the annual rate of the graduated retirement benefit which would be payable to the person concerned, on the assumption that he retired from regular employment on attaining insured pensionable age, in return for the payment in respect of his period of pensionable service of graduated contributions at the rate specified in section 4(1)(*c*) of the National Insurance Act 1965, as originally enacted.

(4) Regulation 66(2) of the principal Regulations, as so applied, shall have effect as if the reference to Regulation 66(3) were omitted therefrom and the reference to a supplemental pension included a reference to an ill-health pension.

(5) Regulation 67 of the principal Regulations, as so applied, shall have effect as if the proviso were omitted therefrom.

Widow's special pension

5.—(1) This Regulation shall apply to a widow of a police cadet who dies as the result of a qualifying injury.

(2) Subject to the provisions of these Regulations, a widow to whom this Regulation applies shall be entitled to a special pension and Regulations 31, 36, 38(2), 39(1) and (3), 40 and 48 of the principal Regulations shall apply as if her husband had been a regular policeman at the time that he received the injury.

(**a**) 1965 c. 51.   (**b**) 1965 c. 52.

Widow's augmented award

6.—(1) This Regulation shall apply to a widow of a police cadet who dies as the result of a qualifying injury where one of the following conditions is satisfied, namely that—

(*a*) he was attacked by a person or persons in a manner which was intrinsically likely to cause death and death ensued as a result of the attack, or

(*b*) the injury was received in the course of duties performed for the immediate purpose of effecting an arrest or of preventing an escape or rescue from legal custody, whether in the course of assisting a constable or otherwise, or

(*c*) the injury was received in the course of duties performed—

(i) for the immediate purpose of saving the life of another person or of preventing loss of human life, and

(ii) in circumstances in which there was an intrinsic likelihood of his receiving a fatal injury, or

(*d*) the police authority are of the opinion that one of the preceding conditions may be satisfied, and that this Regulation should apply, or

(*e*) the police authority are of the opinion that the injury was received otherwise than as aforesaid but in the course of duties performed in such circumstances that it would be inequitable if there were not payable in respect of him such an award as would have been payable had one of the conditions specified in sub-paragraphs (*a*), (*b*) and (*c*) been satisfied.

(2) For the purpose of calculating a widow's special pension payable to a widow to whom this Regulation applies, Regulation 31 of the principal Regulations (as applied by Regulation 5 of these Regulations) shall have effect subject to the provisions of Regulation 32(1) and (2) of the principal Regulations.

(3) Subject to the provisions of these Regulations, a widow to whom this Regulation applies shall be entitled to a gratuity in addition to a special pension and Regulations 32(1), (3) and (4), 38(2), 39(1) and (3) and 40 of the principal Regulations shall apply as if her husband had been a regular policeman at the time that he received the injury and as if the reference in the said Regulation 32(4) to annual pensionable pay were a reference to the annual pensionable pay of a police cadet attached to the metropolitan police force who has attained the age of 19 years.

Child's special allowance

7.—(1) This Regulation shall apply to a child of a police cadet who dies as the result of a qualifying injury.

(2) Subject to the provisions of these Regulations, a child to whom this Regulation applies shall be entitled to a child's special allowance and Regulations 42, 44, 45, 46 and 48 of the principal Regulations shall apply as if the parent had been a regular policeman at the time that he received the injury.

Child's special gratuity

8.—(1) This Regulation shall apply to a child of a police cadet who dies as a result of a qualifying injury where one of the conditions set out in Regulation 6(1) is satisfied and—

(*a*) in the case of a man, does not leave a widow entitled to a gratuity under Regulation 6(3), or

(*b*) in the case of a woman, was the child's only surviving parent.

(2) Subject to the provisions of these Regulations, a child to whom this Regulation applies shall be entitled to a gratuity in addition to a special allowance and Regulations 43 and 46 of the principal Regulations shall apply as if the parent had been serving as a regular policeman at the time that he received the injury and as if any reference in the said Regulation 43 to Regulation 32 of the principal Regulations were a reference to that Regulation as applied by Regulation 6 of these Regulations.

Prevention of duplication

9.—(1) This Regulation shall apply to a police cadet who becomes a member of a police force.

(2) Where a person to whom this Regulation applies is permanently disabled or dies as a result of a qualifying injury and in consequence thereof an award is payable under the principal Regulations to him, his widow or child, then, he or, as the case may be, his widow or child shall not be entitled to an award under these Regulations.

10. For the purpose of calculating an award under these Regulations to or in respect of a police cadet—

(*a*) his period of pensionable service shall be his period of service as a police cadet on and after the date on which these Regulations have effect in relation to him ;

(*b*) his average pensionable pay shall be the aggregate of the pay to which he has been entitled in respect of his period of pensionable service divided by the number of years and fraction of a year comprised in that period, and

(*c*) his average pensionable pay for a period of a week shall be taken to be his average pensionable pay divided by $52\frac{1}{6}$.

Application of certain provisions of the principal Regulations

11. Regulations 69, 70, 71, 72, 73, 76, 77 and 78 of the principal Regulations shall apply for the purposes of these Regulations as if a police cadet were a member of a police force.

Application of certain provisions of the Police Pensions Act 1948

12.—(1) Section 4 of the Police Pensions Act 1948(**a**) (which relates to the forfeiture of pensions) shall apply to an award under these Regulations as though it were a pension mentioned in subsection (1) of that section.

(**a**) 1948 c. 24.

(2) Section 5 of the said Act of 1948 (which relates to appeals against forfeiture or refusal of a pension) shall apply to an award under these Regulations as though it were a pension mentioned in subsections (1)(*a*) and (1)(*b*) of that section, and, in either case, as though a police cadet served in the police force to which he was attached.

(3) Section 7 of the said Act of 1948 (which relates to assignments of, or charges on, a pension and to unlawful conduct in obtaining a pension) shall apply to an award under these Regulations as though such an award were a pension mentioned in that section.

Authority by whom payments are to be made

13. An award under these Regulations shall be payable by the police authority maintaining the police force to which the police cadet was attached at the time when he received the injury by virtue of which the award is payable.

> *R. Maudling,*
> One of Her Majesty's Principal
> Secretaries of State.

Home Office,
Whitehall.

11th February 1971.

EXPLANATORY NOTE

(This Note is not part of the Regulations.)

These Regulations (which become fully operative on 1st April 1971) have effect in relation to police cadets in England and Wales who have attained the age of 18 years (Regulation 3(1)) except that such a cadet appointed before 1st April 1971 may elect that they shall not have effect in his case (Regulation 3(2)).

The Regulations give to police cadets and their dependants certain pension benefits for which members of police forces and their dependants are eligible by applying, with modifications, certain provisions of the Police Pensions Regulations 1971.

Where the Regulations have effect in relation to a police cadet, they do so to the exclusion of other statutory provisions for pension (e.g. the Local Government Superannuation Act 1937) (c. 68) subject, however, to savings for the National Insurance Act 1965 and the National Insurance (Industrial Injuries) Act 1965 (Regulation 3(3)).

STATUTORY INSTRUMENTS

1971 No. 240

SUGAR

The Sugar (Rates of Surcharge and Surcharge Repayments) (No. 3) Order 1971

Made - - -	*12th February* 1971
Laid before Parliament	*16th February* 1971
Coming into Operation	*17th February* 1971

The Minister of Agriculture, Fisheries and Food, in exercise of the powers conferred on him by sections 7(4), 8(6) and 33(4) of the Sugar Act 1956(**a**) having effect subject to the provisions of section 3 of, and Part II of Schedule 5 to, the Finance Act 1962(**b**), and section 58 of the Finance Act 1968(**c**) and of all other powers enabling him in that behalf, with the concurrence of the Treasury, on the advice of the Sugar Board, hereby makes the following order:—

1.—(1) This order may be cited as the Sugar (Rates of Surcharge and Surcharge Repayments) (No. 3) Order 1971; and shall come into operation on 17th February 1971.

(2) The Interpretation Act 1889(**d**) shall apply for the interpretation of this order as it applies for the interpretation of an Act of Parliament.

2. Notwithstanding the provisions of Article 2 of the Sugar (Rates of Surcharge and Surcharge Repayments) (No. 2) Order 1971(**e**), the rates of surcharge payable under and in accordance with the provisions of section 7 of the Sugar Act 1956, having effect as aforesaid, in respect of sugar and invert sugar imported or home produced or used in the manufacture of imported composite sugar products shall on and after 17th February 1971 be the appropriate rates specified in Schedule 1 to this order.

3. For the purpose of section 8(3)(*b*) of the Sugar Act 1956, having effect as aforesaid, the rates of surcharge repayments in respect of invert sugar produced in the United Kingdom from materials on which on or after 17th February 1971 sugar duty has been paid or, by virtue of paragraph 1 of Part II of Schedule 5 to the Finance Act 1962, is treated as having been paid shall, notwithstanding the provisions of Article 3 of the Sugar (Rates of Surcharge and Surcharge Repayments) (No. 2) Order 1971 be the appropriate rates specified in Schedule 2 to this order.

(**a**) 1956 c. 48.	(**b**) 1962 c. 44.
(**c**) 1968 c. 44.	(**d**) 1889 c. 63.
(**e**) S.I. 1971/163. (1971 I, p. 505).	

In Witness whereof the Official Seal of the Minister of Agriculture, Fisheries and Food is hereunto affixed on 11th February 1971.

(L.S.)

R. P. Fraser,
Authorised by the Minister.

We concur.
12th February 1971.

V. H. Goodhew,
P. L. Hawkins,
Two of the Lords Commissioners of
Her Majesty's Treasury.

SCHEDULE 1

PART I

SURCHARGE RATES FOR SUGAR

Polarisation	Rate of Surcharge per ton
	£
Exceeding—	
99°	6·000
98° but not exceeding 99°	5·658
97° ,, ,, ,, 98°	5·520
96° ,, ,, ,, 97°	5·376
95° ,, ,, ,, 96°	5·232
94° ,, ,, ,, 95°	5·088
93° ,, ,, ,, 94°	4·944
92° ,, ,, ,, 93°	4·800
91° ,, ,, ,, 92°	4·656
90° ,, ,, ,, 91°	4·512
89° ,, ,, ,, 90°	4·368
88° ,, ,, ,, 89°	4·224
87° ,, ,, ,, 88°	4·104
86° ,, ,, ,, 87°	3·984
85° ,, ,, ,, 86°	3·876
84° ,, ,, ,, 85°	3·768
83° ,, ,, ,, 84°	3·660
82° ,, ,, ,, 83°	3·552
81° ,, ,, ,, 82°	3·456
80° ,, ,, ,, 81°	3·360
79° ,, ,, ,, 80°	3·264
78° ,, ,, ,, 79°	3·168
77° ,, ,, ,, 78°	3·072
76° ,, ,, ,, 77°	2·976
Not exceeding 76°	2·880

PART II

SURCHARGE RATES FOR INVERT SUGAR

Sweetening matter content by weight	Rate of Surcharge per cwt.
	£
70 per cent. or more	0·19
Less than 70 per cent. and more than 50 per cent.	0·13
Not more than 50 per cent.	0·06

SCHEDULE 2

SURCHARGE REPAYMENT RATES FOR INVERT SUGAR

Sweetening matter content by weight	Rate of Surcharge Repayment per cwt.
	£
More than 80 per cent.	0·22
More than 70 per cent. but not more than 80 per cent.	0·19
More than 60 per cent. but not more than 70 per cent.	0·13
More than 50 per cent. but not more than 60 per cent.	0·10
Not more than 50 per cent. and the invert sugar not being less in weight than 14 lb. per gallon	0·06

EXPLANATORY NOTE

(This Note is not part of the Order.)

This order prescribes—

(a) increases equivalent to 20p per cwt. of refined sugar in the rates of surcharge payable on sugar and invert sugar which become chargeable with surcharge on or after 17th February 1971;

(b) correspondingly increased rates of surcharge repayment in respect of invert sugar produced in the United Kingdom from materials on which surcharge has been paid.

STATUTORY   INSTRUMENTS

1971 No. 241

SUGAR

The Composite Sugar Products (Surcharge and Surcharge Repayments—Average Rates) (No. 3) Order 1971

Made - - -	*12th February* 1971
Laid before Parliament	*16th February* 1971
Coming into Operation	*17th February* 1971

Whereas the Minister of Agriculture, Fisheries and Food (hereinafter called " the Minister ") has on the recommendation of the Commissioners of Customs and Excise (hereinafter called " the Commissioners ") made an order(a) pursuant to the powers conferred upon him by sections 9(1) and 9(4) of the Sugar Act 1956(b), having effect subject to the provisions of section 3 of, and Part II of Schedule 5 to, the Finance Act 1962(c), to the provisions of section 52(2) of the Finance Act 1966(d), and to the provisions of section 58 of the Finance Act 1968(e), providing that in the case of certain descriptions of composite sugar products surcharge shall be calculated on the basis of an average quantity of sugar or invert sugar taken to have been used in the manufacture of the products, and that certain other descriptions of composite sugar products shall be treated as not containing any sugar or invert sugar, and that in the case of certain descriptions of goods in the manufacture of which sugar or invert sugar is used, surcharge repayments shall be calculated on the basis of an average quantity of sugar or invert sugar taken to have been so used:

Now, therefore, the Minister, on the recommendation of the Commissioners and in exercise of the powers conferred upon him by sections 9(1), 9(4) and 33(4) of the Sugar Act 1956, having effect as aforesaid, and of all other powers enabling him in that behalf, hereby makes the following order:—

1.—(1) This order may be cited as the Composite Sugar Products (Surcharge and Surcharge Repayments—Average Rates) (No. 3) Order 1971, and shall come into operation on 17th February 1971.

(2) The Interpretation Act 1889(f) shall apply for the interpretation of this order as it applies for the interpretation of an Act of Parliament.

2. Surcharge payable on or after 17th February 1971 under and in accordance with the Sugar Act 1956, having effect as aforesaid, in respect of sugar and invert sugar used in the manufacture of the descriptions of imported composite sugar products specified in the second column of Schedule 1 to this order shall, notwithstanding the provisions of the Sugar (Rates of Surcharge and Surcharge Repayments) (No 3) Order 1971(g) and the Composite Sugar Products (Surcharge and Surcharge Repayments—Average Rates) (No. 2) Order 1971(a), be calculated by reference to the weight of the products at the appropriate rates specified in relation thereto in the third column of the said Schedule.

(a) S.I. 1971/164. (1971 I, p. 508).	(b) 1956 c. 48.	(c) 1962 c. 44.
(d) 1966 c. 18.	(e) 1968 c. 44.	(f) 1889 c. 63.
(g) S.I. 1971/240. (1971 I, p. 832).		

3. Imported composite sugar products other than those of a description specified in Schedules 1 and 2 to this order shall be treated as not containing any sugar or invert sugar for the purposes of surcharge payable on or after 17th February 1971.

4. Surcharge repayments payable on and after 17th February 1971 under and in accordance with the provisions of section 8 of the Sugar Act 1956, having effect as aforesaid, in respect of sugar and invert sugar used in the manufacture of the descriptions of goods specified in the first column of Schedule 3 to this order shall, notwithstanding the provisions of the Sugar (Rates of Surcharge and Surcharge Repayments) (No. 3) Order 1971(a) and the Composite Sugar Products (Surcharge and Surcharge Repayments—Average Rates) (No. 2) Order 1971(b), be calculated by reference to the quantity of the goods at the appropriate rates specified in relation thereto in the second column of the said Schedule.

In Witness whereof the Official Seal of the Minister of Agriculture, Fisheries and Food is hereunto affixed on 12th February 1971.

(L.S.)   *R. P. Fraser,*
                                    Authorised by the Minister.

SCHEDULE 1

In this Schedule:—

" Tariff heading " means a heading or, where the context so requires, a subheading of the Customs Tariff 1959 (see paragraph (1) of Article 2 of the Import Duties (General) (No. 7) Order 1970(c)).

Tariff heading	Description of Imported Composite Sugar Products	Rate of Surcharge
		Per cwt. £
04.02 ..	Milk and cream, preserved, concentrated or sweetened, containing more than 10 per cent. by weight of added sugar	0·13

(a) S.I. 1971/240 (1971 I, p. 832).   (b) S.I. 1971/164 (1971 I, p. 508).
(c) S.I. 1970/1522 (1970 III, p. 4935).

Tariff heading	Description of Imported Composite Sugar Products	Rate of Surcharge
		Per cwt. £
17.02 (B) (2) and 17.05 (B)	Syrups containing sucrose sugar, whether or not flavoured or coloured, but not including fruit juices containing added sugar in any proportion:—	
	containing 70 per cent. or more by weight of sweetening matter	0·19
	containing less than 70 per cent., and more than 50 per cent., by weight of sweetening matter	0·13
	containing not more than 50 per cent. by weight of sweetening matter	0·06
17.02 (F) ..	Caramel:—	
	Solid	0·30
	Liquid	0·20
17.04 ..	Sugar confectionery, not containing cocoa ..	0·24
18.06 ..	Chocolate and other food preparations containing cocoa and added sugar:—	
	Chocolate couverture not prepared for retail sale; chocolate milk crumb, liquid ..	0·13
	Chocolate milk crumb, solid	0·16
	Solid chocolate bars or blocks, milk or plain, with or without fruit or nuts; other chocolate confectionery consisting wholly of chocolate or of chocolate and other ingredients not containing added sugar, but not including such goods when packed together in retail packages with goods liable to surcharge at a higher rate	0·13
	Other	0·17
19.08 ..	Pastry, biscuits, cakes and other fine bakers' wares containing added sugar:—	
	Biscuits, wafers and rusks containing more than 12½ per cent. by weight of added sugar, and other biscuits, wafers and rusks included in retail packages with such goods	0·07
	Cakes with covering or filling containing added sugar; meringues	0·09
	Other	0·03
20.01 ..	Vegetables and fruit, prepared or preserved by vinegar or acetic acid, containing added sugar:—	
	Containing 10 per cent. or more by weight of added sugar	0·10
	Other	0·02
20.03 ..	Fruit preserved by freezing, containing added sugar	0·03
20.04 ..	Fruit, fruit-peel and parts of plants, preserved by sugar (drained, glacé or crystallised)	0·19
20.05 ..	Jams, fruit jellies, marmalades, fruit purée and fruit pastes, being cooked preparations, containing added sugar	0·18
20.06 ..	Fruit otherwise prepared or preserved, containing added sugar:—	
	Ginger	0·15
	Other	0·03

SCHEDULE 2

Tariff heading	Description of Imported Composite Sugar Products
17.05 (A) and (B)	Sugar and invert sugar, flavoured or coloured.

SCHEDULE 3

Description of goods	Rate of surcharge repayment per bulk barrel of 36 gallons
Lager	£0·022
All beer other than lager	£0·013

EXPLANATORY NOTE

(This Note is not part of the Order.)

This order provides for increases on and after 17th February 1971 in the average rates of surcharge payable on imported composite sugar products of the descriptions specified in Schedule 1 and in the average rates of surcharge repayment in respect of exported goods of the descriptions specified in Schedule 3. These correspond to the increases in surcharge rates effected by the Sugar (Rates of Surcharge and Surcharge Repayments) (No. 3) Order 1971 (S.I. 1971/240). Provision is also made for certain imported composite sugar products to be treated as not containing any sugar or invert sugar.

STATUTORY INSTRUMENTS

1971 No. 242

SEA FISHERIES

BOATS AND METHODS OF FISHING

The Salmon and Migratory Trout (Prohibition of Fishing) Order 1971

Made - - - -	*21st January* 1971
Laid before Parliament	*28th January* 1971
Coming into Operation	*15th February* 1971

The Minister of Agriculture, Fisheries and Food, and the Secretary of State for Scotland and the Secretary of State for the Home Department, being the Secretaries of State concerned with the sea-fishing industry in Scotland and Northern Ireland respectively, in exercise of the powers conferred on them by section 5(1) and (2) of the Sea Fish (Conservation) Act 1967(a) and of all other powers enabling them in that behalf, hereby make the following order: —

Citation and Commencement

1. This order may be cited as the Salmon and Migratory Trout (Prohibition of Fishing) Order 1971 and shall come into operation on 15th February 1971.

Interpretation

2.—(1) In this order—

" mouth of the River Tweed " means the area as defined by the Tweed Fisheries Amendment Act 1859(b) as amended by byelaw dated 10th August 1863 contained in Schedule A to the Salmon Fisheries (Scotland) Act 1868(c).

(2) The Interpretation Act 1889(d) shall apply for the interpretation of this order as it applies for the interpretation of an Act of Parliament.

3. During the period 15th February 1971 to 14th February 1973, both days inclusive, fishing for salmon or migratory trout within the area of sea specified in Part I of the Schedule to this Order (being part of the area to which the North-East Atlantic Fisheries Convention(e) applies) is hereby prohibited.

4.—(1) During the period from 15th February 1971 to 14th February 1973, both days inclusive, fishing for salmon or migratory trout by a specified method within the area of sea specified in Part II of the said Schedule is hereby prohibited.

(a) 1967 c. 84.   (b) 1859 c. lxx.   (c) 1868 c. 123.   (d) 1889 c. 63.   (e) Cmnd. 2190.

(2) In this Article—

" specified method " means a method of fishing with drift-net, trawl net, seine net, troll or long-line, but does not include beach seining or fishing from the shore by net and coble ;

" drift-net " means any length of net allowed to float or drift being either attached to or released from a fishing boat and not being a length of net attached to or held on the shore.

5. In accordance with the provisions of section 5(3) of the Sea Fish (Conservation) Act 1967 it is hereby declared that this order is not made for the sole purpose of giving effect to such a convention or agreement as is mentioned in section 5(1) of that Act.

In witness whereof the Official Seal of the Minister of Agriculture, Fisheries and Food is hereunto affixed on 21st January 1971.

(L.S.) *J. M. L. Prior,*
Minister of Agriculture, Fisheries and Food.

Given under the Seal of the Secretary of State for Scotland on 20th January 1971.

· (L.S.) *Gordon Campbell,*
Secretary of State for Scotland.

Given under the hand of the Secretary of State for the Home Department on 21st January 1971.

R. Maudling,
Secretary of State for the Home Department

SCHEDULE

PART I

Those areas of the Atlantic and Arctic Oceans and seas adjacent to those oceans which lie outside the fishery limits of the British Islands, north of 36° north latitude, between 42° west longitude and 51° east longitude and north of 59° north latitude between 44° west longitude and 42° west longitude, but excluding the Mediterranean and Baltic Seas and Belts lying to the south and east of lines drawn from Hasenore Head, Denmark, to Gniben Point, Denmark, from Korshage, Denmark, to Spodsbierg, Denmark and from Gilbierg Head, Denmark, to Kullen, Sweden.

PART II

Those areas of sea within the fishery limits of the British Islands lying north of 54° 30′ north latitude excluding—

(a) the territorial waters of England except in so far as they lie within the mouth of the River Tweed ;

(b) waters, other than territorial waters mentioned in sub-paragraph (a) of this paragraph, lying on the east coast of England south of the southern boundary of the mouth of the River Tweed and of a line drawn due east from the eastmost point of that boundary ;

(c) waters within such part of the fishery limits of the British Islands as is mentioned in section 4(2) of the Fishery Limits Act 1964(a).

(a) 1964 c. 72.

EXPLANATORY NOTE

(This Note is not part of the Order.)

This Order, which is made under the powers contained in Section 5 of the Sea Fish (Conservation) Act 1967—

- (i) prohibits fishing for salmon or migratory trout in the whole of the North-East Atlantic Fisheries Convention area, outside the fishery limits of the British Islands ; and
- (ii) prohibits fishing for salmon or migratory trout by drift-net, trawl net, seine net, troll or long-line, but not beach seining or fishing from the shore by net and coble, in a specified area off the coast of Scotland and the Tweed, inside the fishery limits of the British Islands.

In each case the period of prohibition extends from 15th February 1971 to 14th February 1973, both days inclusive.

By virtue of section 5(8) of the Act, the prohibition referred to at (i) above applies to all British fishing boats registered in the United Kingdom and to fishing boats which are British owned but not registered under the Merchant Shipping Act 1894 ; the prohibition at (ii) applies to all fishing boats, including foreign vessels.

STATUTORY INSTRUMENTS

1971 No. 244 (C.6)

ROAD TRAFFIC

The Vehicle and Driving Licences Act 1969 (Commencement No. 7) Order 1971

Made - - -	*12th February* 1971
Laid before Parliament	*19th February* 1971
Coming into Operation	*22nd February* 1971

The Secretary of State for the Environment hereby makes this Order in exercise of his powers under section 38(2) of the Vehicle and Driving Licences Act 1969(a) and of all other enabling powers.

1. This Order shall come into operation on 22nd February 1971 and may be cited as the Vehicle and Driving Licences Act 1969 (Commencement No. 7) Order 1971.

2. Section 1, section 2(1), (2), (5), (6) and (7) and section 3 of the Vehicle and Driving Licences Act 1969 shall come into operation on 22nd February 1971.

Signed by authority of the Secretary of State 12th February 1971.

John Peyton,
Minister for Transport Industries,
Department of the Environment.

EXPLANATORY NOTE
(This Note is not part of the Order.)

This Order brings into operation, on 22nd February 1971, sections 1, 2(1), (2), (5), (6) and (7) and 3 of the Vehicle and Driving Licences Act 1969 (which provide for the transfer to the Secretary of State for the Environment, on a date to be appointed under section 1(2) of that Act, of the functions conferred on local authorities by the Vehicles (Excise) Act 1962 and Part II of the Road Traffic Act 1960 of levying excise duty on vehicles, licensing and registration of vehicles and licensing of drivers).

(a) 1969 c. 27.

STATUTORY INSTRUMENTS

1971 No. 245

INDUSTRIAL TRAINING

The Industrial Training Levy (Agricultural, Horticultural and Forestry) Order 1971

Made - - -	*12th February* 1971
Laid before Parliament	*22nd February* 1971
Coming into Operation	*3rd March* 1971

The Secretary of State after approving proposals submitted by the Agricultural, Horticultural and Forestry Industry Training Board for the imposition of a further levy on certain employers in the agricultural, horticultural and forestry industry and in exercise of his powers under section 4 of the Industrial Training Act 1964(**a**) and of all other powers enabling him in that behalf hereby makes the following Order :—

Title and Commencement

1. This Order may be cited as the Industrial Training Levy (Agricultural, Horticultural and Forestry) Order 1971 and shall come into operation on 3rd March 1971.

Interpretation

2.—(1) In this Order unless the context otherwise requires—

 (*a*) "agriculture" has the same meaning as in section 109(3) of the Agriculture Act 1947(**b**) or, in relation to Scotland, as in section 86(3) of the Agriculture (Scotland) Act 1948(**c**) ;

 (*b*) "an appeal tribunal" means an industrial tribunal established under section 12 of the Industrial Training Act 1964 ;

 (*c*) "assessment" means an assessment of an employer to the levy ;

 (*d*) "the base period" means the period of twelve months that commenced on 6th April 1969 ;

 (*e*) "the Board" means the Agricultural, Horticultural and Forestry Industry Training Board ;

 (*f*) "business" means any activities of industry or commerce ;

 (*g*) "charity" has the same meaning as in section 360 of the Income and Corporation Taxes Act 1970(**d**) ;

 (*h*) "emoluments" means all emoluments assessable to income tax under Schedule E (other than pensions), being emoluments from which tax under that Schedule is deductible, whether or not tax in fact falls to be deducted from any particular payment thereof ;

(**a**) 1964 c. 16.	(**b**) 1947 c. 48.
(**c**) 1948 c. 45.	(**d**) 1970 c. 10.

(*i*) "employer" means a person who at any time in the third levy period is an employer in forestry or arboriculture activities ;

(*j*) "establishment" (except in sub-paragraphs (*k*) and (*m*) of this paragraph) means an establishment comprising forestry or arboriculture activities or a forestry or arboriculture establishment ;

(*k*) "establishment comprising forestry or arboriculture activities" means an establishment in Great Britain engaged in the base period mainly in agriculture for a total of twenty-seven or more weeks or, being an establishment that commenced to carry on business in the said period, for a total number of weeks exceeding one half of the number of weeks in the part of the said period commencing with the day on which business was commenced and ending on the last day thereof, at or from which persons were employed in the base period in forestry or arboriculture activities but does not include a forestry or arboriculture establishment ;

(*l*) "forestry or arboriculture activities" means any activities which, subject to the provisions of paragraph 2 of the Schedule to the industrial training order, are included amongst the activities of the agricultural, horticultural and forestry industry by virtue of sub-paragraph (*b*) or (*c*) of paragraph 1 of that Schedule ;

(*m*) "forestry or arboriculture establishment" means an establishment in Great Britain engaged in the base period wholly or mainly in forestry or arboriculture activities for a total of twenty-seven or more weeks or, being an establishment that commenced to carry on business in the said period, for a total number of weeks exceeding one half of the number of weeks in the part of the said period commencing with the day on which business was commenced and ending on the last day thereof ;

(*n*) "the industrial training order" means the Industrial Training (Agricultural, Horticultural and Forestry Board) Order 1970(**a**) ;

(*o*) "the levy" means the levy imposed by the Board in respect of the third levy period ;

(*p*) "notice" means a notice in writing ;

(*q*) "the third levy period" means the period commencing with the day upon which this Order comes into operation and ending on 31st March 1971.

(2) Any reference in this Order to an establishment that commences to carry on business or that ceases to carry on business shall not be taken to apply where the location of the establishment is changed but its business is continued wholly or mainly at or from the new location, or where the suspension of activities is of a temporary or seasonal nature.

(3) The Interpretation Act 1889(**b**) shall apply to the interpretation of this Order as it applies to the interpretation of an Act of Parliament.

Imposition of the levy

3.—(1) Subject to the provisions of this Order, the levy to be imposed by the Board on employers in respect of the third levy period shall be assessed in accordance with the provisions of this Article.

(**a**) S.I. 1970/1886 (1970 III, p. 6227). (**b**) 1889 c. 63.

(2) The levy shall be assessed by the Board separately in respect of each establishment of an employer (not being an employer who is exempt from the levy by virtue of paragraph (8) of this Article), but in agreement with the employer one assessment may be made in respect of any number of establishments of the same kind that is to say either forestry or arboriculture establishments, or, as the case may be, establishments comprising forestry or arboriculture activities and where a levy is so assessed such establishments shall be deemed for the purposes of the assessment to constitute one establishment.

(3) The levy assessed in respect of an establishment shall be an amount equal to 1·6 per cent. of the sum of the reckonable emoluments (calculated as the case may require in accordance with the provisions of paragraph (4) or paragraph (5) of this Article).

(4) The reckonable emoluments in the case of a forestry or arboriculture establishment shall not include the emoluments of any person employed wholly in agriculture or wholly in the supply of food or drink to persons for immediate consumption or any part of the emoluments of any person who is employed partly in agriculture which is attributable to that part of his employment, but save as aforesaid the reckonable emoluments shall be the sum of the emoluments of all persons employed by the employer at or from the establishment in the base period.

(5) The reckonable emoluments in the case of an establishment comprising forestry or arboriculture activities shall be such part of the sum of the emoluments of persons employed by the employer at or from the establishment in the base period wholly or partly in forestry or arboriculture activities as is attributable to their employment in the said activities.

(6) In the case where the business of an establishment is carried on by an employer (either solely or jointly with another person or persons) in succession to another person or persons, a person employed at any time in the base period at or from the establishment by a person other than the employer carrying on the said business on the day upon which this Order comes into operation shall be deemed, for the purposes of this Article, to have been employed by the last mentioned employer.

(7) The amount of the levy imposed in respect of an establishment that ceases to carry on business in the third levy period shall be in the same proportion to the amount that would otherwise be due under the preceding provisions of this Article as the number of days between the commencement of the said levy period and the date of cessation of business (both dates inclusive) bears to the number of days in the said levy period.

(8) There shall be exempt from the levy—

(a) an employer in whose case the sum of reckonable emoluments in respect of the establishment or establishments of the employer is less than £500 ;

(b) a charity.

Assessment Notices

4.—(1) The Board shall serve an assessment notice on every employer assessed to the levy, but one notice may comprise two or more assessments.

(2) The amount of any assessment payable under an assessment notice shall be rounded down to the nearest fifty new pence.

(3) An assessment notice shall state the Board's address for the service of a notice of appeal or of an application for an extension of time for appealing.

(4) An assessment notice may be served on the person assessed to the levy either by delivering it to him personally or by leaving it, or sending it to him by post, at his last known address or place of business in the United Kingdom or, if that person is a corporation, by leaving it, or sending it by post to the corporation, at such address or place of business or at its registered or principal office.

Payment of the Levy

5.—(1) Subject to the provisions of this Article and of Articles 6 and 7, the amount of each assessment appearing in an assessment notice served by the Board shall be due and payable to the Board one month after the date of the notice.

(2) The amount of an assessment shall not be recoverable by the Board until there has expired the time allowed for appealing against the assessment by Article 7(1) of this Order and any further period or periods of time that the Board or an appeal tribunal may have allowed for appealing under paragraph (2) or (3) of that Article or, where an appeal is brought, until the appeal is decided or withdrawn.

Withdrawal of Assessment

6.—(1) The Board may, by a notice served on the person assessed to the levy in the same manner as an assessment notice, withdraw an assessment if that person has appealed against that assessment under the provisions of Article 7 of this Order and the appeal has not been entered in the Register of Appeals kept under the appropriate Regulations specified in paragraph (5) of that Article.

(2) The withdrawal of an assessment shall be without prejudice to the power of the Board to serve a further assessment notice in respect of any establishment to which that assessment related.

Appeals

7.—(1) A person assessed to the levy may appeal to an appeal tribunal against the assessment within one month from the date of the service of the assessment notice or within any further period or periods of time that may be allowed by the Board or an appeal tribunal under the following provisions of this Article.

(2) The Board by notice may for good cause allow a person assessed to the levy to appeal to an appeal tribunal against the assessment at any time within the period of four months from the date of the service of the assessment notice or within such further period or periods as the Board may allow before such time as may then be limited for appealing has expired.

(3) If the Board shall not allow an application for extension of time for appealing, an appeal tribunal shall upon application made to the tribunal by the person assessed to the levy have the like powers as the Board under the last foregoing paragraph.

(4) In the case of an establishment that ceases to carry on business in the third levy period on any day after the date of the service of the relevant assessment notice, the foregoing provisions of this Article shall have effect as if for the period of four months from the date of the service of the assessment notice mentioned in paragraph (2) of this Article there were substituted the period of six months from the date of the cessation of business.

(5) An appeal or an application to an appeal tribunal under this Article shall be made in accordance with the Industrial Tribunals (England and Wales) Regulations 1965(a) as amended by the Industrial Tribunals (England and Wales) (Amendment) Regulations 1967(b) except where the establishment to which the relevant assessment relates is wholly in Scotland in which case the appeal or application shall be made in accordance with the Industrial Tribunals (Scotland) Regulations 1965(c) as amended by the Industrial Tribunals (Scotland) (Amendment) Regulations 1967(d).

(6) The powers of an appeal tribunal under paragraph (3) of this Article may be exercised by the President of the Industrial Tribunals (England and Wales) or by the President of the Industrial Tribunals (Scotland) as the case may be.

Evidence

8.—(1) Upon the discharge by a person assessed to the levy of his liability under an assessment the Board shall if so requested issue to him a certificate to that effect.

(2) The production in any proceedings of a document purporting to be certified by the Secretary of the Board or any other person, being a member, officer or servant of the Board authorised to act in that behalf, to be a true copy of an assessment or other notice issued by the Board or purporting to be a certificate such as is mentioned in the foregoing paragraph of this Article shall, unless the contrary is proved, be sufficient evidence of the document and of the facts stated therein.

Signed by order of the Secretary of State.

12th February 1971.

> *Paul Bryan,*
> Minister of State,
> Department of Employment.

(a) S.I. 1965/1101 (1965 II, p. 2805).   (b) S.I. 1967/301 (1967 I, p. 1040).
(c) S.I. 1965/1157 (1965 II, p. 3266).   (d) S.I. 1967/302 (1967 I, p. 1050).

EXPLANATORY NOTE

(This Note is not part of the Order.)

This Order gives effect to proposals submitted by the Agricultural, Horticultural and Forestry Industry Training Board to the Secretary of State for Employment for the imposition of a further levy upon certain employers in the industry for the purpose of raising money towards the expenses of the Board.

The levy is to be imposed in respect of the third levy period commencing on the day upon which this Order comes into operation and ending on 31st March 1971. Section 104 of the Agriculture Act 1970 provides that the Board's expenses attributable to the exercise of its functions in relation to activities in agriculture shall not be raised by levy. Accordingly agricultural activities are not taken into account. There will be a right of appeal against an assessment to an industrial tribunal.

S T A T U T O R Y   I N S T R U M E N T S

1971 No. 246 (S.38)

POLICE

The Police Cadets (Pensions) (Scotland) Regulations 1971

Made - - -	*12th February* 1971
Laid before Parliament	*19th February* 1971
Coming into Operation—	
for all purposes of regulation 3(2)	*22nd February* 1971
for all other purposes	*1st April* 1971

In exercise of the powers conferred on me by section 27 of the Police (Scotland) Act 1967(a), as read with section 13 of the Superannuation (Miscellaneous Provisions) Act 1967(b), and of all other powers enabling me in that behalf, and after consultation with the Police Council for the United Kingdom in accordance with section 4(5) of the Police Act 1969(c), I hereby make the following regulations:—

Citation and commencement

1. These regulations may be cited as the Police Cadets (Pensions) (Scotland) Regulations 1971 and shall come into operation—

(*a*) for all purposes of regulation 3(2), on 22nd February 1971;

(*b*) for all other purposes, on 1st April 1971.

Interpretation

2.—(1) In these regulations the expression "the principal regulations" means the Police Pensions Regulations 1971(d).

(2) Regulations 4, 5, 10, 13(1) and (4), 14, 17, 18 and 116 of the principal regulations shall apply for the purposes of these regulations as they apply for the purposes of the said regulations, in the case of the said regulation 116, as if a police cadet were a member of the police force to which he is attached.

(3) For the purposes of these regulations a reference to a qualifying injury is a reference to an injury received by a person, without his own default—

(*a*) while on duty as a police cadet or while on a journey necessary to enable him to report for duty or to return to his usual place of abode after duty, or

(*b*) while taking action which, in the opinion of the police authority, it was appropriate that he should have taken by reason of his being a police cadet;

and, in the case of a police cadet in relation to whom these regulations have taken effect, includes a reference to an injury so received before these regulations took effect in relation to him.

(a) 1967 c. 77.　　　　(b) 1967 c. 28.
(c) 1969 c. 63.　　　　(d) S.I. 1971/232. 1971 I, p. 700).

(4) For the purposes of these regulations, disablement means inability to perform the ordinary duties of a male or of a female member of a police force, as the case may be, but where it is necessary to determine the degree of a person's disablement it shall be determined by reference to the degree to which his earning capacity has been affected as a result of a qualifying injury:

Provided that a person shall be deemed to be totally disabled if, and only if, as a result of a qualifying injury, either he is incapable by reason of the disablement of earning any money in any employment or is receiving treatment as an in-patient at a hospital.

(5) For the purposes of these regulations, a reference in the principal regulations to a person serving as a regular policeman or member of a police force shall be construed as a reference to a person serving as a police cadet attached to a particular police force; and any reference in the said regulations to retirement, or to ceasing to be a member of a police force, shall be construed as a reference to the termination of a period of such service.

(6) For the purposes of these regulations, a reference to a police cadet is a reference to a police cadet appointed under section 8 of the Police (Scotland) Act 1967 and, except where the context otherwise requires, includes a reference to a person who has been a police cadet; and references to the police force to which a police cadet is attached, to the chief constable and to the police authority are, respectively, references to the police force with a view to becoming a member of which the cadet is undergoing training, the chief constable of that force and the police authority maintaining that force.

Effect of regulations

3.—(1) These regulations shall have effect in relation to a police cadet who serves as such on or after 1st April 1971 and, in relation to such a cadet—

(*a*) who on appointment has not attained the age of 18 years, only as from his attaining that age;

(*b*) who on appointment has attained that age, as from his appointment;

and, except where the context otherwise requires, any reference in these regulations to a police cadet is a reference to a cadet who has so served and has attained that age.

(2) Notwithstanding anything in paragraph (1), these regulations shall have effect as from 1st April 1971 in relation to a police cadet who on that date—

(*a*) is serving as such by virtue of his appointment before that date, and

(*b*) has attained the age of 18 years,

except that these regulations shall not have effect in relation to such a police cadet if, before that date, he has so elected by notice in writing given to the police authority.

(3) Where these regulations have effect in relation to a police cadet they shall have effect to the exclusion of any other provision for pension, allowance or gratuity in respect of his service as such contained in or in force under any enactment; and on these regulations taking effect in relation to him (otherwise than as mentioned in paragraph (1)(*b*)), he shall be deemed for the purpose of a return of any contributions made by him under any such other provision to have ceased to serve as a police cadet, and, accordingly, to have ceased to be treated as employed by his police authority.

Provided that nothing in this paragraph shall affect the operation of the National Insurance Act 1965(**a**) or the National Insurance (Industrial Injuries) Act 1965(**b**).

(**a**) 1965 c. 51.   (**b**) 1965 c. 52.

Police cadet's ill-health and supplemental pensions

4.—(1) This regulation shall apply to a police cadet who ceases to serve as such and is permanently disabled as a result of a qualifying injury.

(2) Subject to the provisions of these regulations, a police cadet to whom this regulation applies shall be entitled to a supplemental pension together with, where he ceases to serve as such on the ground that he is disabled, an ill-health pension; and, subject to paragraphs (3), (4) and (5) of this regulation, regulations 20, 22, 24(1) to (6), 66(1) and (2), 67 and 68 of the principal regulations shall apply as if he were such a regular policeman as is mentioned in paragraphs (1) and (3)(*b*) of the said regulation 20 or, as the case may be, in paragraph (1) of the said regulation 22.

(3) Regulation 20 of the principal regulations, as so applied, shall have effect as if the references to Parts III and IV of Schedule 2 were omitted therefrom; but an ill-health pension payable hereunder shall be reduced in respect of any period beyond insured pensionable age—

    (*a*) by an amount calculated at an annual rate obtained by multiplying £1·70 by the number of completed years of pensionable service which the person concerned is entitled to reckon, and

    (*b*) by an amount calculated at the annual rate of the graduated retirement benefit which would be payable to the person concerned, on the assumption that he retired from regular employment on attaining insured pensionable age, in return for the payment in respect of his period of pensionable service of graduated contributions at the rate specified in section 4(1)(*c*) of the National Insurance Act 1965, as originally enacted.

(4) Regulation 66(2) of the principal regulations, as so applied, shall have effect as if the reference to regulation 66(3) were omitted therefrom and the reference to a supplemental pension included a reference to an ill-health pension.

(5) Regulation 67 of the principal regulations, as so applied, shall have effect as if the proviso were omitted therefrom.

Widow's special pension

5.—(1) This regulation shall apply to a widow of a police cadet who dies as the result of a qualifying injury.

(2) Subject to the provisions of these regulations, a widow to whom this regulation applies shall be entitled to a special pension and regulations 31, 36, 38(2), 39(1) and (3), 40 and 48 of the principal regulations shall apply as if her husband had been a regular policeman at the time that he received the injury.

Widow's augmented award

6.—(1) This regulation shall apply to a widow of a police cadet who dies as the result of a qualifying injury where one of the following conditions is satisfied, namely that—

    (*a*) he was attacked by a person or persons in a manner which was intrinsically likely to cause death and death ensued as a result of the attack, or

    (*b*) the injury was received in the course of duties performed for the immediate purpose of effecting an arrest or of preventing an escape or rescue from legal custody, whether in the course of assisting a constable or otherwise, or

(c) the injury was received in the course of duties performed—

(i) for the immediate purpose of saving the life of another person or of preventing loss of human life, and

(ii) in circumstances in which there was an intrinsic likelihood of his receiving a fatal injury, or

(d) the police authority are of the opinion that one of the preceding conditions may be satisfied, and that this regulation should apply, or

(e) the police authority are of the opinion that the injury was received otherwise than as aforesaid but in the course of duties performed in such circumstances that it would be inequitable if there were not payable in respect of him such an award as would have been payable had one of the conditions specified in sub-paragraphs (a), (b) and (c) been satisfied.

(2) For the purpose of calculating a widow's special pension payable to a widow to whom this regulation applies, regulation 31 of the principal regulations (as applied by regulation 5 of these regulations) shall have effect subject to the provisions of regulation 32(1) and (2) of the principal regulations.

(3) Subject to the provisions of these regulations, a widow to whom this regulation applies shall be entitled to a gratuity in addition to a special pension and regulations 32(1), (3) and (4), 38(2), 39(1) and (3) and 40 of the principal regulations shall apply as if her husband had been a regular policeman at the time that he received the injury and as if the reference in the said regulation 32(4) to annual pensionable pay were a reference to the annual pensionable pay of a police cadet attached to the metropolitan police force who has attained the age of 19 years.

Child's special allowance

7.—(1) This regulation shall apply to a child of a police cadet who dies as the result of a qualifying injury.

(2) Subject to the provisions of these regulations, a child to whom this regulation applies shall be entitled to a child's special allowance and regulations 42, 44, 45, 46 and 48 of the principal regulations shall apply as if the parent had been a regular policeman at the time that he received the injury.

Child's special gratuity

8.—(1) This regulation shall apply to a child of a police cadet who dies as a result of a qualifying injury where one of the conditions set out in regulation 6(1) is satisfied and—

(a) in the case of a man, does not leave a widow entitled to a gratuity under regulation 6(3), or

(b) in the case of a woman, was the child's only surviving parent.

(2) Subject to the provisions of these regulations, a child to whom this regulation applies shall be entitled to a gratuity in addition to a special allowance and regulations 43 and 46 of the principal regulations shall apply as if the parent had been serving as a regular policeman at the time that he received the injury and as if any reference in the said regulation 43 to regulation 32 of the principal regulations were a reference to that regulation as applied by regulation 6 of these regulations.

Prevention of duplication

9.—(1) This regulation shall apply to a police cadet who becomes a member of a police force.

(2) Where a person to whom this regulation applies is permanently disabled or dies as a result of a qualifying injury and in consequence thereof an award is payable under the principal regulations to him, his widow or child, then, he or, as the case may be, his widow or child shall not be entitled to an award under these regulations.

Pensionable service and average pensionable pay

10. For the purpose of calculating an award under these regulations to or in respect of a police cadet—

(a) his period of pensionable service shall be his period of service as a police cadet on and after the date on which these regulations have effect in relation to him;

(b) his average pensionable pay shall be the aggregate of the pay to which he has been entitled in respect of his period of pensionable service divided by the number of years and fraction of a year comprised in that period, and

(c) his average pensionable pay for a period of a week shall be taken to be his average pensionable pay divided by $52\frac{1}{6}$.

Application of certain provisions of the principal regulations

11. Regulations 69, 70, 71, 72, 73, 77 and 78 of the principal regulations shall apply for the purposes of these regulations as if a police cadet were a member of a police force.

Application of certain provisions of the Police Pensions Act 1948

12.—(1) Section 4 of the Police Pensions Act 1948**(a)** (which relates to the forfeiture of pensions) shall apply to an award under these regulations as though it were a pension mentioned in subsection (1) of that section.

(2) Section 5 of the said Act of 1948 (which relates to appeals against forfeiture or refusal of a pension) shall apply to an award under these regulations as though it were a pension mentioned in subsections (1)(a) and (1)(b) of that section, and, in either case, as though a police cadet served in the police force to which he was attached.

(3) Section 7 of the said Act of 1948 (which relates to assignments of, or charges on, a pension and to unlawful conduct in obtaining a pension) shall apply to an award under these regulations as though such an award were a pension mentioned in that section.

Authority by whom payments are to be made

13. An award under these regulations shall be payable by the police authority

(a) 1948 c. 24.

maintaining the police force to which the police cadet was attached at the time when he received the injury by virtue of which the award is payable.

Gordon Campbell,
One of Her Majesty's Principal
Secretaries of State.

St. Andrew's House,
  Edinburgh.
12th February 1971.

EXPLANATORY NOTE

(This Note is not part of the Regulations.)

These Regulations (which become fully operative on 1st April 1971) have effect in relation to police cadets in Scotland who have attained the age of 18 years (Regulation 3(1)) except that such a cadet appointed before 1st April 1971 may elect that they shall not have effect in his case (Regulation 3(2)).

The Regulations give to police cadets and their dependants certain pension benefits for which members of police forces and their dependants are eligible by applying, with modifications, certain provisions of the Police Pensions Regulations 1971.

Where the Regulations have effect in relation to a police cadet, they do so to the exclusion of other statutory provisions for pension (e.g. the Local Government Superannuation (Scotland) Act 1937—c. 69) subject, however, to savings for the National Insurance Act 1965 and the National Insurance (Industrial Injuries) Act 1965 (Regulation 3(3)).

STATUTORY INSTRUMENTS

1971 No. 248 (S.39)

CHILDREN AND YOUNG PERSONS

The Approved Schools (Contributions by Education Authorities) (Scotland) Regulations 1971

Made - - - -	*8th February* 1971
Coming into Operation	*1st April* 1971

In exercise of the powers conferred upon me by section 94(1) of the Children and Young Persons (Scotland) Act 1937(**a**), and of all other powers enabling me in that behalf, I hereby make the following regulations:—

Citation, Commencement and Interpretation

1.—(1) These regulations may be cited as the Approved Schools (Contributions by Education Authorities) (Scotland) Regulations 1971, and shall come into operation on 1st April 1971.

(2) The Interpretation Act 1889(**b**) shall apply for the interpretation of these regulations as it applies for the interpretation of an Act of Parliament.

Revocation

2.—(1) The Approved Schools (Contributions by Education Authorities) (Scotland) Regulations 1969(**c**) are hereby revoked.

(2) Section 38 of the Interpretation Act 1889 shall apply as if these regulations were an Act of Parliament and as if the regulations revoked by these regulations were an Act of Parliament repealed by an Act of Parliament.

Rate of Contribution

3. The education authority named in an approved school order shall make in respect of the person to whom the order relates, throughout the time during which that person is under the care of the managers of an approved school, a contribution at the rate of £16·80 per week to the expenses of the managers of the approved school:

Provided that no contribution shall be so payable:—

(*a*) in respect of any period during which the person to whom the order relates is absent from an approved school under compulsory supervision following release, under the provisions of section 18 of the Criminal Justice (Scotland) Act 1963(**d**), or

(*b*) in respect of any period consisting of more than 14 consecutive days, during which the person to whom the order relates is, free of charge to the said managers, a patient in a hospital provided under Part II of the National Health Service (Scotland) Act 1947(**e**), or

(*c*) in respect of any period consisting of more than 14 consecutive days, during which the person to whom the order relates is under section 86(1)

(**a**) 1937 c. 37. (**b**) 1889 c. 63. (**c**) S.I. 1969/224 (1969 I, p. 611).
  (**d**) 1963 c. 39. (**e**) 1947 c. 27.

of the Children and Young Persons (Scotland) Act 1937 (which relates to escapes from approved schools, failure to return to approved schools after temporary leave of absence and other like matters) for the time being liable to be apprehended without warrant.

Gordon Campbell,
One of Her Majesty's Principal
Secretatries of State.

St. Andrew's House,
Edinburgh.
8th February 1971.

EXPLANATORY NOTE
(*This Note is not part of the Regulations.*)

These Regulations raise from £10 6s. 6d. (£10·32½) to £16·80 the weekly contributions payable to the managers of an approved school by the education authority named in an order made by a Court sending a child or young person to an approved school.

STATUTORY INSTRUMENTS

1971 No. 249 (S.40)

SOCIAL WORK, SCOTLAND

Residential Establishments (Payments by Local Authorities) (Scotland) Order 1971

Made - - -	*8th February* 1971
Coming into Operation	*15th April* 1971

In exercise of the powers conferred upon me by paragraph 2(2) of Schedule 7 to the Social Work (Scotland) Act 1968(**a**) and of all other powers enabling me in that behalf, I hereby make the following order :—

Citation and commencement

1. This order may be cited as the Residential Establishments (Payments by Local Authorities) (Scotland) Order 1971 and shall come into operation on 15th April 1971.

Interpretation

2.—(1) In this order "the Act" means the Social Work (Scotland) Act 1968.

(2) The Interpretation Act 1889(**b**) applies for the interpretation of this order as it applies for the interpretation of an Act of Parliament.

Rate of payment

3. Every local authority to whom functions in relation to establishments which immediately before the commencement of Part III of the Act were approved schools are transferred by virtue of section 1(5) of the Act, shall, in relation to those establishments, make payments to the managers thereof in respect of the expenses of carrying on the establishments at the rate of £16·80 per week in respect of every child who is required by an approved school order or by a supervision requirement to reside therein :

Provided that no such payment shall be made in respect of any such child—

(*a*) in relation to any period consisting of more than 14 consecutive days during which the child is, free of charge to the managers of the establishment wherein he is so required to reside, a patient in a hospital provided under Part II of the National Health Service (Scotland) Act 1947(**c**) ; or

---

(**a**) 1968 c. 49.
(**c**) 1947 c. 27.

(**b**) 1889 c. 63.

(*b*) in relation to any period consisting of more than 14 consecutive days during which the child was absent from the establishment wherein he is so required to reside without the approval of the managers thereof.

Gordon Campbell,
One of Her Majesty's Principal
Secretaries of State.

St. Andrew's House,
Edinburgh.
8th February 1971.

EXPLANATORY NOTE

(This Note is not part of the Order.)

This order prescribes the weekly payments of £16·80 to be made by local authorities in respect of the expenses of carrying on the establishments which were approved schools immediately before the commencement of Part III of the Social Work (Scotland) Act 1968 and in relation to which functions were transferred to local authorities under section 1(5) of that Act.

1971 No. 252

TELEGRAPHS

The Programme Distribution Systems (General Licence Charges) Regulations 1971

Made - - -	*15th February* 1971
Laid before Parliament	*24th February* 1971
Coming into Operation	*25th February* 1971

The Minister of Posts and Telecommunications, with the consent of the Treasury, in exercise of the powers conferred upon him by section 90(4) of the Post Office Act 1969(a), and of all other powers enabling him in that behalf, hereby makes the following Regulations :

Commencement, citation and interpretation

1.—(1) These Regulations shall come into operation on the 25th February 1971, and may be cited as the Programme Distribution Systems (General Licence Charges) Regulations 1971.

(2) The Interpretation Act 1889(b) shall apply for the interpretation of these Regulations as it applies for the interpretation of an Act of Parliament.

Issue Fees

2. On the issue of a licence under section 89 of the Post Office Act 1969 of a type and description specified in the Schedule hereto, the licensee shall pay an issue fee of the amount specified in relation to that type and description of licence in the said Schedule, whatever may be the duration of the licence.

Renewal Fees

3. On every occasion when, by virtue of a term or provision in the licence, a licence of a type and description specified in the Schedule hereto would cease to be in force on a particular date unless a renewal fee were paid, and the licensee desires that the licence should remain in force for a further period after that date, he shall pay on or before that date, in respect of the period following, a renewal fee of the amount specified in relation to that type and description of licence in the said Schedule.

(a) 1969 c. 48.   (b) 1889 c. 63.

Other issue and renewal fees

4. On the issue of any temporary licence or on the issue or renewal of any licence which is not of a type or description specified in the Schedule hereto, the licensee shall pay an issue or renewal fee of such amount as may in the particular case appear to the Minister of Posts and Telecommunications to be proper.

Dated 9th February 1971.

Christopher Chataway,
Minister of Posts and
Telecommunications.

We consent to these Regulations.

15th February 1971.

V. H. Goodhew,
P. L. Hawkins,
Two of the Commissioners
of Her Majesty's Treasury.

THE SCHEDULE

Type of Licence	Description of Licence	Issue Fee	Renewal Fee
1. Tourist television information service licence.	A licence to provide for customers of the Licensee a service of programmes in visual images sent by wire only with or without sound consisting of information and advertisements relating to items of interest to tourists being items of the kinds specified in the licence.	£20	£20
2. Television for public showing licence.	A licence to distribute or convey programmes in visual images sent by wire only with or without sound to a place or places in the United Kingdom to which members of the public have access (whether on payment or not) for the purpose of their being presented there to members of the public and not being a licence falling within the description of licences specified in the item numbered 1 in this Schedule.	£40 for the first place specified in the licence plus £10 in respect of each additional place specified in the licence.	£40 for the first place specified in the licence plus £10 in respect of each additional place specified in the licence.

EXPLANATORY NOTE

(This Note is not part of the Regulations.)

These Regulations provide for the issue and renewal fees payable in respect of licences for programme distribution systems.

Issue and renewal fees for standard form licences are specified in the Schedule and the Regulations also enable the Minister of Posts and Tele-communications to fix the issue fee and renewal fee payable in respect of any special licence which is not on one of the standard forms referred to in the Schedule.

STATUTORY INSTRUMENTS

1971 No. 253

INDUSTRIAL ORGANISATION AND DEVELOPMENT

The Iron Casting Industry (Scientific Research Levy) Order 1971

Laid before Parliament in draft

Made - - - *16th February* 1971

Coming into Operation *1st March* 1971

Whereas it appears to the Secretary of State that it is expedient that funds should be made available for the purpose of scientific research in connection with the iron casting industry for which there is not a Development Council :

And whereas it appears to the Secretary of State that there is an incorporated body limited by guarantee called the British Cast Iron Research Association which is capable of carrying out such scientific research satisfactorily :

And whereas the Secretary of State has consulted the organisations appearing to him to be representative of substantial numbers of persons carrying on business in the iron casting industry and the organisations representative of persons employed in that industry appearing to him to be appropriate :

And whereas a draft of this Order has been approved by a resolution of each House of Parliament :

Now, therefore, the Secretary of State, in exercise of his powers under section 9 of the Industrial Organisation and Development Act 1947(a) and all other powers in that behalf enabling him, hereby orders as follows :—

Citation, commencement, cessation of charges and revocation

1.—(1) This Order may be cited as the Iron Casting Industry (Scientific Research Levy) Order 1971 and shall come into operation on 1st March 1971.

(2) The Iron Casting Industry (Scientific Research Levy) Order 1967(b) shall not impose on any person any charge in respect of any levy period beginning after 3rd April 1971.

(3) The Iron Casting Industry (Scientific Research Levy) Order 1967 shall on 4th April 1971 by virtue of this Order be revoked.

(a) 1947 c. 40.   (b) S.I. 1967/981 (1967 II, p. 2968).

Interpretation

2.—(1) In this Order—

"emoluments" means any emoluments assessable to income tax under Schedule E of the Income and Corporation Taxes Act 1970(**a**) (other than pensions), being emoluments from which tax under that Schedule is deductible, whether or not tax in fact falls to be deducted from any particular payment thereof ;

"leviable iron castings" means iron castings as fettled, excluding pig iron and any other cast iron material re-melted or to be re-melted into other leviable iron castings.

(2) The Interpretation Act 1889(**b**) shall apply to the interpretation of this Order as it applies to the interpretation of an Act of Parliament and as if this Order and the Order hereby revoked were Acts of Parliament.

Extent of the Industry

3. For the purposes of this Order the iron casting industry (hereinafter referred to as "the industry") shall consist of the activity of casting iron (other than pig iron) by any process.

Persons to whom the Order applies

4. This Order shall apply to every person who on 4th April 1971 is carrying on, or who thereafter begins to carry on, business in the industry.

Levy periods

5. For the purposes of this Order levy periods shall be the periods of thirteen or fourteen weeks (as the case may be) ending on the Saturday nearest to the end of March, June, September and December in each year, the first levy period under this Order being the period ending on 3rd July 1971, and the relevant production quarter in relation to any levy period shall be the period of thirteen or fourteen weeks (as the case may be) immediately preceding the commencement of that period.

Payment of levies

6. Subject to the provisions of Article 8 hereof every person to whom this Order applies shall pay to the Secretary of State in respect of each levy period during the whole or any part of which he has carried on business in the industry a charge calculated in accordance with the provisions of Article 7 hereof.

Computation of levies

7.—(1) The charge to be paid by a person by virtue of the provisions of Article 6 hereof in respect of any levy period shall be the aggregate of—

    (*a*) an amount equal to 0·14 per cent. of the chargeable amount of the emoluments paid or payable by him in respect of the relevant production quarter ; and

    (*b*) an amount calculated at the rate of four new pence for every metric tonne of leviable iron castings produced by him in the relevant production quarter.

(**a**) 1970 c. 10.   (**b**) 1889 c. 63.

(2) The chargeable amount of the emoluments paid or payable by a person in respect of the relevant production quarter shall be calculated by aggregating—

    (a) the total amount of the emoluments of persons employed by him during that quarter, under a contract of service, wholly or mainly in the actual performance of any process comprised in the activity of casting iron (other than pig iron) or the purposes ancillary to such performance including persons employed as pattern makers or in the maintenance or security of premises, plant or machinery but excluding persons engaged in the supply of food or drink ; and

    (b) the total amount of the emoluments of persons employed by him during that quarter under a contract of service, including directors, managers and administrative, scientific, technical, laboratory and clerical staff, wholly or mainly in respect of—

        (i) the payment of persons specified in head (a), and

        (ii) the direction, management, control, supervision, administration or costing of the industry,

        (iii) activities carried on for the purposes of scientific research and development in connection with the industry.

Exemption from payment of levies

8. No person shall be liable to pay any charge—

    (a) in respect of the levy period in which he began to carry on business in the industry ;

    (b) if the amount of the charge calculated as aforesaid in respect of any levy period is less than £3·50.

Time for payment of levies

9.—(1) The charges imposed by this Order shall become due for payment on the expiration of four weeks after the commencement of each levy period.

(2) The amount of any such charge shall be recoverable by the Secretary of State as a debt.

(3) The Iron Casting Industry (Levy) Deposit Account, being an account opened by Her Majesty's Paymaster General on behalf of the Secretary of State, shall be the account into which all sums received by the Secretary of State in respect of any such charge shall be paid and out of which all such sums shall be issued to the British Cast Iron Research Association to meet any expenses incurred by the Association in respect of scientific research in connection with the industry.

Furnishing of information

10. The Secretary of State may by notice in writing require any person to whom this Order applies—

    (a) to furnish such returns and other information ;

    (b) to keep such records ; and

    (c) to produce for examination such books and other documents and records

as may appear to the Secretary of State to be reasonably requisite for the purpose of the recovery of any charge imposed by this Order.

Enforcement

11. Any person to whom this Order applies who is required by notice in writing by the Secretary of State under the provisions of Article 10 hereof to furnish returns or other information, to keep records or to produce for examination books or other documents or records, shall furnish such returns or other information in such form and manner and within such time, not being less than fourteen days, as may be specified in the notice or, as the case may be, keep such records or produce within such time, not being less than fourteen days, such books or other documents or records in his custody or under his control as may be so specified.

Penalties

12.—(1) If any person required under the provisions of Article 10 hereof to furnish returns or other information, to keep records or to produce for examination books or other documents or records fails to furnish, keep or produce them in accordance with the requirement he shall, unless he proves that he had reasonable excuse for the failure, be liable on summary conviction to a fine not exceeding £5 for every day during which the failure continues.

(2) If any person in purporting to fulfil any requirement imposed under the provisions of Article 10 hereof to furnish returns or other information knowingly or recklessly makes any statement which is false in a material particular he shall be liable on summary conviction to a fine not exceeding £50, or on conviction on indictment to imprisonment for a term not exceeding two years or to a fine not exceeding £100 or to both such imprisonment and such a fine.

Dated 16th February 1971.

John Davies,
Secretary of State
for Trade and Industry.

EXPLANATORY NOTE

(This Note is not part of the Order.)

This Order continues the imposition of levies on the iron casting industry to finance scientific research to be carried out in connection with the industry by the British Cast Iron Research Association. The Iron Casting Industry (Scientific Research Levy) Order 1967 ceases to have effect as respects the imposition of the levy for any period beginning after 3rd April 1971.

The principal changes are—

    (*a*) the substitution of a charge based on emoluments for the charge based on the number of persons employed ;

    (*b*) where the charge is computed on amounts of iron castings produced, the rate, at which the amount of the charge has been calculated, is expressed by reference to the new decimal currency and metric tonnes.

The general effect of these changes is to increase the yield of the levy.

STATUTORY INSTRUMENTS

1971 No. 254 (S.41)

NATIONAL HEALTH SERVICE, SCOTLAND

The National Health Service (Compensation) (Scotland) Regulations 1971

Made - - - -	*8th February* 1971
Laid before Parliament	*24th February* 1971
Coming into Operation	*1st March* 1971

ARRANGEMENT OF REGULATIONS

PART I
PRELIMINARY

PART II
ENTITLEMENT TO COMPENSATION

PART III
RESETTLEMENT COMPENSATION

PART IV
LONG-TERM COMPENSATION

In exercise of the powers conferred on me by section 35 of the Health Services and Public Health Act 1968(a) and of all other powers enabling me in that behalf, I hereby make the following regulations:—

PART I
PRELIMINARY

Citation and commencement

1. These regulations may be cited as the National Health Service (Compensation) (Scotland) Regulations 1971, and shall come into operation on 1st March 1971.

Interpretation

2.—(1) In these regulations, unless the context otherwise requires, the following expressions have the meanings hereby respectively assigned to them, that is to say:—

"accrued pension", in relation to a pensionable officer who has suffered loss of employment, means the pension to which he would have become entitled under his last relevant pension scheme in respect of his pensionable service according to the method of calculation, modified where necessary for the purpose of giving effect to these regulations, prescribed by that scheme if, at the date on which he ceased to be subject to that scheme, he had attained normal retiring age and complied with any requirement of that scheme as to a minimum period of qualifying service or contribution and completed any additional contributory payments or payments in respect of added years which he was in the course of making;

"accrued retiring allowance", in relation to a pensionable officer who has suffered loss of employment, means any lump sum payment to which he would have become entitled under his last relevant pension scheme in respect of his pensionable service according to the method of calculation, modified where necessary for the purpose of giving effect to these regulations, prescribed by that scheme if, at the date on which he ceased to be subject to that scheme, he had attained normal retiring age and complied with any requirement of that scheme as to a minimum period of qualifying service or contribution and completed any additional contributory payments or payments in respect of added years which he was in the course of making;

"accrued incapacity pension" and "accrued incapacity retiring allowance" have the same respective meanings as "accrued pension" and "accrued retiring allowance" except that the reference to a person's attaining normal retiring age shall be construed as a reference to his becoming incapable of discharging efficiently the duties of his employment by reason of permanent ill-health or infirmity of mind or body;

"the Act of 1946" means the National Health Service Act 1946(b);

"the Act of 1947" means the National Health Service (Scotland) Act 1947(c);

"additional contributory payment" has the same meaning as in the National Health Service (Superannuation) (Scotland) Regulations 1961(d);

"compensation question" means a question—

(*a*) as to a person's entitlement to compensation for loss of office or employment, or for loss or diminution of emoluments; or

(*b*) as to the manner of a person's employment or the comparability of his duties;

(a) 1968 c. 46.
(c) 1947 c. 27.
(b) 1946 c. 81.
(d) S.I. 1961/1398 (1961 II, p. 2697).

"emoluments" means all salary, wages, fees and other payments paid or made to an officer as such for his own use, and also the money value of any apartments, rations or other allowances in kind appertaining to his employment, but does not include payments for overtime, other than payments which are a usual incident of his employment, or any allowance payable to him to cover the cost of providing office accommodation or clerical or other assistance, or any travelling or subsistence allowance or other moneys to be spent, or to cover expenses incurred, by him for the purposes of his employment; and "net emoluments", in relation to any employment, means the annual rate of the emoluments of that employment less such part of those emoluments as the officer was or is liable to contribute under a pension scheme except any periodical sum payable in respect of additional contributory payments, and in relation to any employment which has been lost or the emoluments of which have been diminished, the expression means the annual rate of emoluments as aforesaid immediately before the loss or diminution as the case may be:

Provided that where fees or other variable payments were paid to an officer as part of his emoluments during any period immediately preceding the loss or diminution the amount in respect of fees or other variable payments to be included in the annual rate of emoluments shall be the annual average of the fees or other payments paid to him during the period of 3 years immediately preceding the loss or diminution, or such shorter period as the Secretary of State may deem reasonable in the circumstances;

"enactment" means any Act or any instrument made under an Act;

"local authority" means—

(a) in Scotland, any county council, town council or district council and includes any joint committee or joint board of such authorities appointed under any enactment, order or scheme; and

(b) in England and Wales, the council of a county, county borough, metropolitan borough, London borough, county district, rural parish or borough included in a rural district, the Greater London Council, the Common Council of the City of London and the council of the Isles of Scilly, any two or more of those authorities acting jointly, any joint committee, combined authority or joint board and a police authority for a county, a borough or a combined police area;

"long-term compensation" means compensation payable in accordance with the provisions of Part IV of these regulations for loss of employment or loss or diminution of emoluments;

"material date", in relation to any person who has suffered loss of employment or loss or diminution of emoluments which is attributable to any cause mentioned in regulation 4, means—

(a) in the case of loss or diminution which is attributable to an event mentioned in paragraphs (a) and (b) of section 11(10) of the Act of 1947, the date of operation of the order or scheme related to that event; and

(b) in any other case, the date of operation of the order to which the loss or diminution is attributable:

Provided that if the loss or diminution occurred before either of the said dates the expression shall mean the actual date of the loss or diminution;

"minimum pensionable age", in relation to a pensionable officer, means the earliest age at which, under his last relevant pension scheme, he could have become entitled to a pension, other than a pension payable in consequence of his redundancy or his incapacity to discharge efficiently the duties of his employment by reason of permanent ill-health or infirmity of mind or body or his retirement in the interests of the efficiency of the service;

"national service" means service which is relevant service within the meaning of the Reserve and Auxiliary Forces (Protection of Civil Interests) Act 1951(a), and includes service immediately following such service as aforesaid, being service in any of Her Majesty's naval, military or air forces pursuant to a voluntary engagement entered into with the consent of the authority or person under whom an officer held his last relevant employment;

"normal retiring age" means the age of 65 years if the officer is a male, or 60 years if the officer is a female;

"officer" includes the holder of any place, situation or employment;

"payment in respect of added years", in relation to a pensionable officer, means any payment made under regulation 33 of the National Health Service (Superannuation) (Scotland) Regulations 1961;

"pensionable officer", in relation to a person who has suffered loss of employment or loss or diminution of emoluments, means a person who immediately before such loss or diminution was subject to a pension scheme;

"pension scheme", in relation to a pensionable officer, means any form of arrangement associated with his employment for the payment of super-annuation benefits, whether subsisting by virtue of Act of Parliament, trust, contract or otherwise; and "last relevant pension scheme", in relation to a pensionable officer means the pension scheme to which he was last subject before suffering loss of employment or loss or diminution of emoluments;

"reckonable service", in relation to a person, means any period of whole-time or part-time employment in any relevant employment and includes any period of war service or national service undertaken on his ceasing to hold any such employment but does not include employment of which account has been taken, or is required to be taken, in calculating the amount of any super-annuation benefit to which he has become entitled;

"relevant employment" means employment—

(a) under the Crown or in the service of a local authority or in the service of an employing authority within the meaning of the regulations for the time being in force under section 66(1) of the Act of 1947 or section 67(1) of the Act of 1946, or

(b) preceding any of the foregoing employments which was reckonable for the purpose of any pension scheme associated with the employment which has been lost, or in which a loss or diminution of emoluments has been suffered, or

(c) in such other service as the Secretary of State may, in the case of any named officer, approve,

but, except as provided in regulations 7(1)(c) and 13(1)(c), does not include service in the armed forces of the Crown;

"resettlement compensation" means compensation payable in accordance with Part III of these regulations for loss of employment;

(a) 1951 c. 65.

"retirement compensation" means compensation payable in accordance with the provisions of regulation 20, 21, 22 or 23;

"tribunal" means a tribunal established under section 12 of the Industrial Training Act 1964(a);

"war service" means war service within the meaning of the Local Government Staffs (War Service) Act 1939(b), the Teachers Superannuation (War Service) Act 1939(c), the Education (Scotland) (War Service Superannuation) Act 1939(d), the Police and Firemen (War Service) Act 1939(e) or employment for war purposes within the meaning of the Superannuation Schemes (War Service) Act 1940(f) and includes any period of service in the first world war in the armed forces of the Crown or in the forces of the Allied or Associated Powers if such service immediately followed a period of relevant employment and was undertaken either compulsorily or with the permission of the employer in that employment.

(2) Unless the context otherwise requires, references in these regulations to the provisions of any enactment shall be construed as references to those provisions as amended, re-enacted or modified by any subsequent enactment.

(3) References in these regulations to a numbered regulation shall, unless the reference is to a regulation of specified regulations, be construed as references to the regulation bearing that number in these regulations.

(4) References in any regulation of these regulations to a numbered paragraph shall, unless the reference is to a paragraph of a specified regulation, be construed as references to the paragraph bearing that number in the first mentioned regulation.

(5) The Interpretation Act 1889(g) shall apply for the interpretation of these regulations as it applies for the interpretation of an Act of Parliament.

Part II

Entitlement to Compensation

Persons to whom the regulations apply

3. These regulations shall apply to any person who—

(a) was employed immediately before the material date for the whole or for part only of his time as an officer of—

(i) a Regional Hospital Board, or

(ii) an Executive Council or a joint committee of Executive Councils constituted for the purposes of Part IV of the Act of 1947, or

(iii) a Local Medical Committee, Local Pharmaceutical Committee, Local Dental Committee or Local Optical Committee recognised by the Secretary of State under section 33 of that Act, or

(b) would have been so employed at that date but for any national service on which he was or had been engaged.

(a) 1964 c. 16.   (b) 1939 c. 94.
(c) 1939 c. 95.   (d) 1939 c. 96.
(e) 1939 c. 103.   (f) 1940 c. 26.
(g) 1889 c. 63.

Grounds of entitlement to compensation

4. Subject to the provisions of these regulations, any person to whom these regulations apply and who suffers loss of employment or loss or diminution of emoluments which is attributable to—

(*a*) the occurrence on or after 9th September 1968 of any of the events mentioned in paragraphs (*a*) and (*b*) of section 11(10) of the Act of 1947, or

(*b*) the making on or after 9th September 1968 of an order under subsection (2), (3) or (4) of section 32 of the Act of 1947, or an order revoking an order made under any of those subsections,

shall be entitled to have his case considered for the payment of compensation under these regulations, and such compensation shall be determined in accordance with these regulations.

National Service

5.—(1) Where any person to whom these regulations apply would have been employed immediately before the material date as such an officer as is mentioned in regulation 3(*a*) but for any national service on which he was or had been engaged, then if before the expiry of 2 months after ceasing to be so engaged, or if prevented by sickness or other reasonable cause, as soon as practicable thereafter, he gives notice to the Secretary of State that he is available for employment, that person shall be entitled to have his case considered for the payment of compensation—

(*a*) if he is not given or offered re-employment in his former office or in any reasonably comparable office (whether in the same or in a different service), on the ground of loss of employment; or

(*b*) if he is so re-employed with diminished emoluments as compared with the emoluments which he would have enjoyed had he continued in his former employment, on the ground of diminution of emoluments.

(2) The loss of employment which is the cause of a claim for compensation under paragraph (1)(*a*) shall be treated as having occurred on the earlier of the 2 following dates, that is to say, the date of his being refused re-employment or a date one month after the date on which the person gave notice that he was available for employment; and the person shall be deemed to have been entitled to the emoluments which he would have enjoyed at such earlier date had he continued in his former employment.

PART III

RESETTLEMENT COMPENSATION

Resettlement compensation for loss of employment

6. The Secretary of State shall, subject to the provisions of these regulations, pay resettlement compensation to any person to whom these regulations apply and who satisfies the conditions set out in regulation 7.

Conditions for payment of resettlement compensation

7.—(1) Without prejudice to any other requirement of these regulations, the conditions for the payment of resettlement compensation to any person are that—

(*a*) he has suffered loss of employment attributable to any such event or order as is mentioned in regulation 4 not later than 10 years after the material date;

(*b*) he had not at the date of the loss attained normal retiring age;

(*c*) he had been for a period of 3 years immediately before the material date continuously engaged (disregarding breaks not exceeding in the aggregate 6 months) for the whole or part of his time in relevant employment; and for this purpose the expression "relevant employment" includes any period of national service immediately following such employment;

(*d*) he has made a claim for such compensation in accordance with the provisions of Part VII of these regulations not later than 13 weeks after the loss of employment which is the cause of his claim, or 13 weeks after the coming into operation of these regulations, whichever is the later or within such longer period as the Secretary of State may allow in any particular case where he is satisfied that the delay in making the claim was due to ill-health or other circumstances beyond the claimant's control;

(*e*) the loss of employment which is the cause of his claim has occurred for some reason other than misconduct or incapacity to perform such duties as, immediately before the loss, he was performing or might reasonably have been required to perform; and

(*f*) he has not, subject to paragraph (3), been offered any reasonably comparable employment under any body constituted under the Act of 1947.

(2) In ascertaining for the purposes of this regulation whether a person has been offered employment which is reasonably comparable with the employment which he has lost, no account shall be taken of the fact that the duties of the employment offered are in relation to a different service from that in connection with which his employment was held or are duties which involve a transfer of his employment from one place to another within Scotland.

(3) No account shall be taken for the purposes of this regulation of an offer of employment where the Secretary of State is satisfied—

(*a*) that acceptance would have involved undue hardship to the person, or

(*b*) that he was prevented from accepting the offer by reason of ill-health or other circumstances beyond his control.

Amount of resettlement compensation

8.—(1) The amount of resettlement compensation which may be paid to a person shall, for each week for which such compensation is payable, be a sum ascertained by taking two-thirds of the weekly rate of the net emoluments which that person has lost and deducting therefrom, in addition to the items mentioned in regulation 33(3) and (4), such of the following items as may be applicable—

(*a*) unemployment, sickness or injury benefit under any Act relating to National Insurance claimable by him in respect of such week (excluding any amount claimable by him in respect of a dependant); and

(*b*) two-thirds of the net emoluments received by him in respect of such week from work or employment undertaken as a result of the loss of employment.

(2) For the purposes of this regulation the weekly rate of a person's net emoluments shall be deemed to be seven three hundred and sixty-fifths of those emoluments.

Period for payment of resettlement compensation

9. Subject to the provisions of these regulations, resettlement compensation shall be payable to a person only in respect of the period of 13 weeks next succeeding the week in which he lost the employment in respect of which his claim has been made or, in the case of a person who has attained the age of 45 years, the said 13 weeks and one additional week for every year of his age after attaining the age of 45 years and before the date of the loss of employment, subject to a maximum addition of 13 such weeks.

Additional provisions relating to resettlement compensation

10.—(1) Resettlement compensation shall be payable to a person at intervals equivalent to those at which the emoluments of his employment were previously paid or at such other intervals as may be agreed between the person and the Secretary of State.

(2) Resettlement compensation shall be terminated by the Secretary of State—

(*a*) if without reasonable cause the recipient fails to comply with any of the provisions of regulation 11, or

(*b*) if on being requested to do so, he fails to satisfy the Secretary of State that, so far as he is able, he is seeking suitable employment.

Claimant for resettlement compensation to furnish particulars of employment

11. Every person claiming or in receipt of resettlement compensation shall (after as well as before the compensation begins to be paid)—

(*a*) forthwith supply the Secretary of State in writing with particulars of any employment which the person obtains or of any change in his earnings from any such employment, and

(*b*) if the Secretary of State so requires, so long as the person is out of employment and is not receiving sickness or injury benefit, register with the Department of Employment.

PART IV

LONG-TERM COMPENSATION

Long-term compensation for loss of employment or loss or diminution of emoluments

12. The Secretary of State shall, subject to the provisions of these regulations, pay long-term compensation to any person to whom these regulations apply and who satisfies the conditions set out in regulation 13.

Conditions for payment of long-term compensation

13.—(1) Without prejudice to any other requirement of these regulations, the conditions for the payment of long-term compensation to any person are that—

(*a*) he has suffered loss of employment or loss or diminution of emoluments attributable to any such event or order as is mentioned in regulation 4 not later than 10 years after the material date;

(*b*) he had not, save as is provided in regulation 29, at the date of the loss or diminution attained normal retiring age;

(*c*) he had been, for a period of not less than 8 years immediately before the material date, continuously engaged (without a break of more than 12 months at any one time) for the whole or part of his time in relevant employment; and for this purpose the expression "relevant employment" includes any period of national service immediately following such employment;

(*d*) he has made a claim for such compensation in accordance with the provisions of Part VII of these regulations not later than 2 years after the loss or diminution which is the cause of the claim or 2 years after the coming into operation of these regulations whichever is the later; and

(*e*) if the cause of the claim for compensation is loss of employment—

   (i) the loss has occurred for some reason other than misconduct or incapacity to perform such duties as, immediately before the loss, he was performing or might reasonably have been required to perform; and

   (ii) he has not been offered any reasonably comparable employment under any body constituted under the Act of 1947.

(2) Paragraphs (2) and (3) of regulation 7 (which relate to offers of employment) shall apply for the purposes of this regulation in ascertaining whether a person has been offered reasonably comparable employment.

(3) Claims for long-term compensation for loss of employment shall in all respects be treated as claims for such compensation for the loss of emoluments occasioned thereby and the provisions of these regulations shall apply to all such claims accordingly.

Factors to be considered in determining payment of long-term compensation

14.—(1) For the purpose of determining whether long-term compensation is payable to any person and, if so, the amount of the compensation (subject to the limits set out in these regulations), the Secretary of State shall have regard to such of the following factors as may be relevant, that is to say—

(*a*) the conditions upon which the person held the employment which he has lost, including in particular its security of tenure, whether by law or practice;

(*b*) the emoluments and other conditions, including security of tenure, whether by law or practice, of any work or employment undertaken by the person as a result of the loss of employment;

(*c*) the extent to which he has sought suitable employment and the emoluments which he might have acquired by accepting other suitable employment offered to him;

(*d*) all the other circumstances of his case.

(2) In ascertaining for the purposes of paragraph (1)(*c*) whether a person has been offered suitable employment, paragraphs (2) and (3) of regulation 7 shall apply in like manner as they apply for the purpose of ascertaining whether employment is reasonably comparable with employment which has been lost.

Amount of long-term compensation payable for loss of emoluments

15.—(1) Long-term compensation for loss of emoluments shall, subject to the provisions of these regulations, be payable until the normal retiring age or death of a person to whom it is payable, whichever first occurs, and shall not exceed a maximum annual sum calculated in accordance with the provisions of paragraphs (2) to (4).

(2) The said maximum annual sum shall, subject as hereinafter provided, be the aggregate of the following sums, namely—

(a) for every year of the person's reckonable service, one sixtieth of the net emoluments which he has lost; and

(b) in the case of a person who has attained the age of 40 years at the date of the loss, a sum calculated in accordance with the provisions of paragraph (3) appropriate to his age at that date:

Provided that the said maximum annual sum shall in no case exceed two-thirds of the net emoluments which the person has lost.

(3) The sum referred to in paragraph (2)(b) shall be—

(a) in the case of a person who has attained the age of 40 years but has not attained the age of 50 years at the date of the loss, the following fraction of the net emoluments which he has lost—

(i) where his reckonable service is less than 10 years, one sixtieth for each year of such service after attaining the age of 40 years; or

(ii) where his reckonable service amounts to 10 years but is less than 15 years, one sixtieth for each year of such service after attaining the age of 40 years and one additional sixtieth; or

(iii) where his reckonable service amounts to 15 years but is less than 20 years, one sixtieth for each year of such service after attaining the age of 40 years and two additional sixtieths; or

(iv) where his reckonable service amounts to 20 years or more, one sixtieth for each year of such service after attaining the age of 40 years and three additional sixtieths;

but the sum so calculated shall not in any case exceed one sixth of the said net emoluments;

(b) in the case of a person who has attained the age of 50 years but has not attained the age of 60 years at the date of the loss, one sixtieth of the said net emoluments for each year of his reckonable service after attaining the age of 40 years, up to a maximum of 15 such years; and

(c) in the case of a person who has attained the age of 60 years at the date of the loss, one sixtieth of the said net emoluments for each year of his reckonable service after attaining the age of 45 years.

(4) Where a person has become entitled (whether immediately or prospectively on attaining some greater age) to a superannuation benefit by way of annual amounts under his last relevant pension scheme, the maximum annual sum referred to in paragraph (1) shall be the maximum sum calculated under paragraphs (2) and (3) as if he had not become so entitled.

(5) Where long-term compensation is payable in respect of any period and resettlement compensation is also payable in respect of that period, the long-term compensation shall be limited to the amount (if any) by which it exceeds the resettlement compensation payable as aforesaid.

(6) Long-term compensation shall be payable to a person at intervals equivalent to those at which the emoluments of his employment were previously paid or at such other intervals as may be agreed between the person and the Secretary of State.

Long-term compensation for diminution of emoluments

16. Long-term compensation for diminution of emoluments in respect of any employment shall, subject to the provisions of these regulations, be awarded and paid in accordance with the following provisions:—

(*a*) the compensation shall consist of an annual sum which shall be payable to a person at intervals equivalent to those at which the emoluments of his employment are or were previously paid or at such other intervals as may be agreed between the person and the Secretary of State, and shall, subject to the provisions of these regulations, be payable until normal retiring age or death, whichever first occurs; and

(*b*) the said annual sum shall not exceed the maximum annual sum which could have been awarded under regulation 15 if the person had suffered loss of emoluments equivalent to the amount of the diminution:

Provided that no compensation shall be payable if the emoluments have been diminished by less than 2½ per cent.

Date from which long-term compensation is to be payable

17.—(1) Long-term compensation shall be payable with effect from the date of the claim or from any earlier date permitted by the succeeding provisions of this regulation.

(2) Where a claim for long-term compensation is duly made within 13 weeks of the occurrence of the loss or diminution which is the cause of the claim, the award shall be made retrospective to the date on which the loss or diminution occurred.

(3) Where a claim for long-term compensation is made after the expiry of the period mentioned in paragraph (2), the award may, at the discretion of the Secretary of State, be made retrospective to a date not earlier than 13 weeks prior to the date on which the claim was made:

Provided that if the Secretary of State is satisfied that the failure to make the claim within the period mentioned in paragraph (2) was due to ill-health or other circumstances beyond the claimant's control, the award may be made retrospective to a date not earlier than that on which the loss or diminution occurred.

PART V

RETIREMENT COMPENSATION AND PAYMENTS ON DEATH

Entitlement to retirement compensation and other payments

18.—(1) The Secretary of State shall, subject to the provisions of these regulations, pay retirement compensation to any person to whom this Part of these regulations applies, and shall make the other payments for which provision is made in regulations 26 to 30.

(2) Save as is provided in regulation 29, this Part of these regulations applies to a pensionable officer who satisfies the conditions set out in regulation 13.

(3) Regulation 14 shall apply in relation to retirement compensation as it applies in relation to long-term compensation.

Additional factors governing payment of retirement compensation

19.—(1) Where retirement compensation is payable under any one of regulations 20, 21, 22 and 23, such compensation shall not be payable under any other of those regulations.

(2) If a person has attained the age of 40 years at the date on which he lost his employment or suffered a diminution of his emoluments, the Secretary of State, in calculating the amount of the retirement compensation payable to that person, shall credit him with additional years of service or an additional period of contribution on the following basis, namely—

> (*a*) 2 years, whether or not he has completed any years of service after attaining the age of 40 years, and
>
> (*b*) 2 years for each of the first 4 completed years of his reckonable service between the date when he attained the age of 40 years and the date of the loss or diminution, and one year for each such year of service after the fourth,

but the additional years of service or period of contribution so credited shall not exceed the shortest of the following periods, namely—

> (i) such number of years as, when added to his pensionable service, would amount to the maximum period of such service which would have been reckonable by him had he continued in his employment until attaining normal retiring age, or
>
> (ii) the number of years of his reckonable service, or
>
> (iii) 15 years;

and in calculating the amount of any retirement compensation payable to him any period so added shall be aggregated with any years of service or period of contribution entailing reduction of the relevant pension because of a retirement pension payable under section 30 of the National Insurance Act 1965**(a)**.

(3) When retirement compensation is awarded, or when an award is reviewed under regulation 35, the additional compensation payable in consequence of any years of service or period of contribution credited to a person under paragraph (2) may be reduced or withheld to such extent as the Secretary of State may think reasonable having regard to the pension scheme (if any) associated with any further employment obtained by him.

(4) If under his last relevant pension scheme the amount of any benefit to which a person might have become entitled could have been increased or supplemented at the discretion of the authority administering the pension scheme or of any other body, the Secretary of State may increase, to an extent not exceeding that to which the person's accrued pension, accrued retiring allowance, accrued incapacity pension or accrued incapacity retiring allowance might have been increased or supplemented, the corresponding component of any retirement compensation payable to him.

(5) If under his last relevant pension scheme provision existed to enable a person to elect not to receive a lump sum payment on retirement or his widow to elect to receive a widow's pension at a higher rate, then—

> (*a*) if on becoming entitled to such a payment in respect of the employment which he has lost or the employment in which his emoluments were diminished or any subsequent employment he, or on his death his widow, so elects under the pension scheme; or

---

(a) 1965 c. 51.

(b) if at the date on which compensation becomes payable to or in respect of the person under regulation 20, 21, 22, 23, 26 or 27 he, or as the case may be his widow, has not become entitled to so elect under the pension scheme, he or she may make the like election under this regulation in relation to his accrued retiring allowance or the annual sum payable to her under regulation 26 and, if he or she does so, any retirement compensation shall be calculated by reference to the benefits that would have been payable under his last relevant pension scheme if such an election had been made and for the purpose of regulation 26 the "prescribed proportion" shall be determined accordingly.

(6) If under his last relevant pension scheme a person would have been entitled to surrender a proportion of any pension which might have become payable to him in favour of his spouse or any dependant, then, if he so desires and informs the Secretary of State by notice in writing accordingly within one month after becoming entitled to retirement compensation under these regulations, he may surrender a proportion of so much of the said compensation as is payable by way of an annual sum on the like terms and conditions and in consideration of the like payments by the Secretary of State as if the said annual sum were a pension to which he had become entitled under the said pension scheme.

(7) In calculating for the purposes of regulation 20, 21 or 22 the amount of the annual sum which is equal to a person's accrued pension, no account shall be taken of any reduction falling to be made in that pension by reason of the provisions of any Act relating to National Insurance until the person reaches the age at which under his last relevant pension scheme the pension would have been so reduced.

(8) In paragraph (2) the expression "reckonable service" includes any period of employment of which account has been taken or is required to be taken in calculating the amount of any superannuation benefit to which a person has become entitled under his last relevant pension scheme.

Retirement compensation for loss of emoluments payable to pensionable officer on attainment of normal retiring age

20.—(1) Subject to the provisions of these regulations, when a person to whom this Part of these regulations applies reaches normal retiring age, the retirement compensation payable to him for loss of emoluments shall be—

(a) an annual sum equal to the amount of his accrued pension, and

(b) a lump sum equal to the amount of his accrued retiring allowance (if any).

(2) Where an annual sum is payable under this regulation in respect of any period and resettlement compensation is also payable in respect of that period, the said annual sum shall be limited to the amount (if any) by which it exceeds the resettlement compensation payable as aforesaid.

Retirement compensation payable to pensionable officer on his becoming incapacitated or reaching minimum pensionable age

21.—(1) Where a person to whom this Part of these regulations applies and who has suffered loss of employment before attaining what would have been his normal retiring age—

(a) becomes incapacitated in circumstances in which, if he had continued in the employment which he has lost, he would have become entitled to a pension under his last relevant pension scheme; or

(b) attains the age which, had he continued to serve in the employment which he has lost, would have been his minimum pensionable age,

he shall be entitled on the happening of either event to claim, in lieu of any compensation to which he would otherwise be entitled under these regulations—

(i) in the case mentioned in head (a) of this paragraph, an annual sum equal to the amount of his accrued incapacity pension and a lump sum equal to the amount of his accrued incapacity retiring allowance (if any), and

(ii) in the case mentioned in head (b) of this paragraph, an annual sum equal to the amount of his accrued pension and a lump sum equal to the amount of his accrued retiring allowance (if any),

subject however to the conditions specified in paragraph (5).

(2) On receipt of a claim under paragraph (1) the Secretary of State shall consider whether the claimant is a person to whom that paragraph applies, and within 13 weeks after the date of the receipt of the claim—

(a) if satisfied that he is not such a person, shall notify him in writing accordingly; or

(b) if satisfied that he is such a person, shall assess the amount of compensation payable to him and notify him in writing accordingly,

and any such notification shall, for the purposes of these regulations, be deemed to be a notification by the Secretary of State of a decision on a claim for compensation.

(3) The Secretary of State may require any person who makes a claim under head (a) of paragraph (1) to submit himself to a medical examination by a registered medical practitioner selected by the Secretary of State, and in that event the Secretary of State shall also offer the person an opportunity of submitting a report from his own medical adviser as a result of an examination by him, and the Secretary of State shall take that report into consideration together with the report of the medical practitioner selected by him.

(4) If a person wishes to receive compensation under this regulation, he shall so inform the Secretary of State in writing within one month from the date of the receipt of a notification under paragraph (2) or, where the claim has been the subject of an appeal, from the date of the decision of the tribunal thereon; and the compensation shall be payable as from the date on which the Secretary of State received the claim.

(5) The calculation of compensation under this regulation shall be subject to the following conditions—

(a) where the Secretary of State, by virtue of regulation 19, has credited the person with additional years of service or an additional period of contribution, no account shall be taken of any additional years or period beyond the number of years which he could have served, had he not lost his employment, before the date on which the claim was received by the Secretary of State; and

(b) if, by reason of any provision of the relevant pension scheme for a minimum benefit, the amount of any such pension or retiring allowance is in excess of that attributable to the person's actual service, no account shall be taken of any such additional years or period except to the extent (if any) by which they exceed the number of years represented by the difference between his actual service and the period by reference to which the minimum benefit has been calculated; and

(c) if the number of years by reference to which an accrued incapacity pension or accrued incapacity retiring allowance is to be calculated is less than any minimum number of years of qualifying service prescribed by the relevant pension scheme, the amount of such pension or retiring allowance shall, notwithstanding any minimum benefit prescribed by the pension scheme, not exceed such proportion of such minimum benefit as the number of years of pensionable service bears to the minimum number of years of qualifying service.

Option to take retirement compensation prematurely

22.—(1) If a person to whom this Part of these regulations applies has suffered loss of employment after attaining the age of 50 years and so requests the Secretary of State by notice in writing, he shall be entitled, as from the date on which the Secretary of State receives such notice, to an annual sum equal to the amount of his accrued pension and a lump sum equal to the amount of his accrued retiring allowance (if any), and in that event he shall not be entitled to receive any further payment of long-term compensation after that date:

Provided that—

(i) in calculating the amount of the compensation payable to a person who has given such notice as aforesaid no account shall be taken of any additional years of service or period of contribution credited to him under regulation 19; and

(ii) where the person has claimed long-term compensation the said notice shall be given not later than 2 years after the decision on the claim has been notified or, where the decision has been reviewed under regulation 35(3), not later than 2 years after the review.

(2) Regulation 21(2) shall apply in relation to a notice given under paragraph (1) as it applies to a claim made under paragraph (1) of that regulation.

(3) Where an annual sum is payable under this regulation in respect of any period and resettlement compensation is also payable in respect of that period, the said annual sum shall be limited to the amount (if any) by which it exceeds the resettlement compensation payable as aforesaid.

Retirement compensation for diminution of emoluments

23.—(1) A person to whom this Part of these regulations applies and who has suffered a diminution of his emoluments shall be entitled to receive retirement compensation in accordance with the provisions of this regulation.

(2) The provisions of regulations 20 and 21 shall apply to any such person as if he had suffered loss of employment immediately before the diminution occurred; but the amount of the retirement compensation payable shall be the amount which would have been payable in respect of loss of employment multiplied by a fraction of which—

(a) the numerator is the amount by which his emoluments have been diminished, and

(b) the denominator is the amount of his emoluments immediately before they were diminished.

For the purposes of this calculation no account shall be taken of any reduction which might otherwise fall to be made in the accrued pension or accrued incapacity pension because of a retirement pension payable under section 30 of the National Insurance Act 1965.

(3) No compensation shall be payable under this regulation—

    (a) if the person's emoluments have been diminished by less than $2\frac{1}{2}$ per cent.; or

    (b) if the person had continued to pay superannuation contributions as if his emoluments had not been diminished.

Superannuation contributions

24.—(1) A person entitled to retirement compensation under regulation 20, 21 or 22 shall pay to the Secretary of State an amount equal to any sum which was paid to him by way of return of superannuation contributions, including any interest, after ceasing to be employed, and the Secretary of State may at the person's request repay that amount to him at any time before he becomes entitled as aforesaid, but if that amount is not paid to the Secretary of State, or is repaid by him to the person, the compensation shall be reduced by an annual amount the capital value of which is equal to the amount of the said superannuation contributions.

(2) For the purposes of this regulation the expression "superannuation contributions" shall include payments in respect of added years made by the person and any additional contributory payments made by him.

Retirement compensation of a person who obtains further pensionable employment

25.—(1) Where a person to whom this Part of these regulations applies, after suffering loss of employment or diminution of emoluments, enters employment in which he is subject to a pension scheme and thereafter becomes entitled to reckon for the purposes of that scheme any service or period of contribution which falls to be taken into account for the purpose of assessing the amount of any retirement compensation payable to him, his entitlement to retirement compensation shall be reviewed and no retirement compensation shall be payable in respect of such service or period unless the annual rate of the emoluments to which he was entitled immediately before such loss or diminution exceeds the annual rate on entry of the emoluments of the new employment by more than $2\frac{1}{2}$ per cent. of such first mentioned emoluments, and any retirement compensation so payable to him shall, in so far as it is calculated by reference to remuneration, be calculated by reference to the difference between the said annual rates:

Provided that this paragraph shall not operate to increase the amount of any retirement compensation payable in respect of diminution of emoluments beyond the amount which would have been payable if the person had attained normal retiring age immediately before he ceased to hold the employment in which he suffered the diminution of emoluments.

(2) No retirement compensation shall be payable in the circumstances mentioned in paragraph (1) if the person has continued to pay superannuation contributions as if his emoluments had not been diminished.

Compensation payable to widow or dependants of a pensionable officer

26.—(1) Payments in accordance with this regulation and regulations 27 and 28 shall be made to or for the benefit of the widow, child or other dependant or to the personal representatives of a person to whom this Part of these regulations applies.

(2) If the widow, child or other dependant of that person might have become entitled to a pension under his last relevant pension scheme, the widow, child or other dependant, as the case may be, shall be entitled to receive an annual sum equal to the prescribed proportion of any retirement compensation by way of annual amounts payable to the person under regulation 20, 21, 22 or 23 immediately before his death or, if he dies before becoming entitled to receive compensation under any of those regulations, the prescribed proportion of the compensation by way of annual amounts which he would have received under regulation 21 or 23 had he become entitled thereto in the circumstances mentioned in regulation 21(1) (*a*) immediately before his death:

Provided that—

(i) where any retirement compensation has been surrendered under regulation 19(6) or compounded under regulation 36, any sum payable under this regulation shall be calculated as if such surrender or compounding had not taken place;

(ii) where the pension scheme provides for payment of the pension to any person on behalf of a child or other dependant, any annual sum payable as aforesaid to a child or other dependant shall be paid to that person on behalf of the child or dependant in the like manner and for the like period as is provided in the pension scheme;

(iii) in calculating the sum payable as aforesaid, it shall be assumed that the retirement compensation payable, or which would have been payable, to a person under regulation 20, 21, 22 or 23 had been such sum as would have been payable if the accrued pension or accrued incapacity pension had not been reduced by reason of the provisions of any Act relating to National Insurance.

(3) Any annual sum payable to or for the benefit of a widow, child or other dependant under this regulation shall cease to be payable in any circumstances in which a corresponding pension under the pension scheme referred to in paragraph (2) would have ceased to be payable.

(4) Except where the compensation has been reduced under regulation 24, compensation payable under this regulation and regulation 27 shall in the aggregate be reduced by an amount the capital value whereof is equal to the amount of any superannuation contributions as defined in regulation 24(2) returned to the person in respect of whom the compensation is payable and either not paid to the Secretary of State or repaid by the Secretary of State to the person, the compensation under each such regulation being reduced in proportion to the capital value of each amount.

(5) In this regulation and regulation 19(5) "prescribed proportion" means the proportion which, under the last relevant pension scheme, the pension payable to the widow, child or other dependant of any person, as the case may be, bears to the person's pension.

Compensation where death gratuity would have been payable

27.—(1) If the widow or the personal representatives of a person to whom this Part of these regulations applies might have become entitled to a death gratuity under his last relevant pension scheme, she or they, as the case may be, shall be entitled to receive a sum calculated in accordance with the provisions of regulation 26(4) and paragraph (2) of this regulation.

(2) The amount of the sum referred to in paragraph (1) shall be ascertained in accordance with the method of calculation prescribed by the last relevant pension scheme for the ascertainment of death gratuity as if the person had died immediately before losing his employment, subject to the following modifications—

(a) except where the person had been in receipt of retirement compensation under regulation 22, account shall be taken of any additional years of service or period of contribution credited to him under regulation 19(2)—

(i) in the case of a person who had been in receipt of retirement compensation under regulation 21, to the extent of the period between the loss of employment and the date of the claim made under that regulation; and

(ii) in any other case, to the extent of the period between the loss of employment and the person's death;

(b) if the number of years of the person's service or period of contribution is less than the minimum number of years of qualifying service or period prescribed by the pension scheme for the receipt of a death gratuity, the said sum shall not exceed such proportion of the death gratuity calculated as aforesaid as the number of years of the person's pensionable service or period of contribution bears to the minimum number of years of qualifying service or period prescribed by the pension scheme; and

(c) there shall be deducted from such sum the amount of any retirement compensation paid to the person under regulation 20, 21 or 22, or where any part of the compensation has been surrendered under regulation 19(6), the amount which would have been so paid but for any such surrender.

(3) In calculating such death gratuity for the purposes of these regulations, an annual sum payable to or for the benefit of a widow, child or other dependant under regulation 26 shall be deemed to be a pension payable to or for the benefit of the widow, child or dependant, as the case may be.

(4) In the case of a person who has suffered diminution of emoluments, the sum payable under this regulation to his widow or personal representatives shall be the sum which would have been payable if he had suffered loss of employment, multiplied by the fraction specified in regulation 23(2); but no sum shall be payable under this paragraph in the circumstances described in regulation 23(3) (a) or (b).

Balances payable to pensionable officer's widow or personal representatives

28.—(1) If no annual sum is payable to the widow, child or other dependant of any person under regulation 26 and no sum is payable under regulation 27 and the person dies before he has received in the aggregate by way of retirement compensation a sum equivalent to the amount of any contributions paid by him under regulation 24 and not repaid to him, together with compound interest thereon up to the date of his death calculated in accordance with the method prescribed by his last relevant pension scheme for the calculation of interest, there shall be paid to his personal representatives the difference between the aggregate amount received by way of retirement compensation as aforesaid and the said equivalent sum.

(2) If any annual sum which was payable to a widow under regulation 26 has ceased to be payable on her re-marriage or death, and any sum payable to a child or other dependant under that regulation has ceased to be payable, and if the aggregate amount of the payments which were made as aforesaid to her husband by way of retirement compensation and to the widow or personal representatives under regulation 27 is less than a sum equivalent to the amount which would have been payable to the personal representatives under that regulation if no annual sum had been payable under regulation 26, there shall be paid to or among such persons as the Secretary of State may determine the difference between such aggregate amount and the said equivalent sum.

(3) For the purposes of this regulation a person who has surrendered any part of his retirement compensation under regulation 19(6) shall be deemed to have received during any period the amount of compensation for that period which he would have received but for any such surrender.

Compensation payable to non-pensionable officer on reaching retiring age

29.—(1) Where a person who is not a pensionable officer is receiving long-term compensation for loss of employment and attains normal retiring age, the Secretary of State may, if satisfied that the person would, but for the loss, have continued in the employment which he has lost for a substantial period beyond that age, continue to pay compensation to him for the remainder of his life at half its former rate.

(2) Where a person who is not a pensionable officer suffers loss of employment on or after attaining normal retiring age, the Secretary of State may, if satisfied that the person would in the normal course have continued in the employment which he has lost for a further substantial period, pay compensation to him for the remainder of his life at half the rate to which he would have been entitled under regulation 15 had he not attained normal retiring age at the date on which he lost his employment.

Persons subject to policy schemes

30.—(1) Regulations 20, 21, 22, 23 and 27 shall not apply to a person (in this regulation referred to as a "policy scheme participant") who had been participating in a scheme associated with his employment for providing super-annuation benefits by means of contracts or policies of insurance, and who, after the loss of his employment or the diminution of his emoluments, continued to participate in that scheme, or became entitled to a benefit or prospective benefit thereunder other than a return of contributions.

(2) If a policy scheme participant has lost his employment, the Secretary of State may, if the relevant scheme so permits, make such payments to or in respect of him, whether by way of the payment of premiums or otherwise, as are actuarially equivalent to the amounts by which his retirement compensation might have been increased under regulation 19(2) or (4) had he been a person to whom regulation 20, 21 or 22 applied.

(3) If a policy scheme participant has suffered a diminution of his emoluments, the Secretary of State may, if the relevant scheme so permits, make such payments to or in respect of him, whether by way of the payment of premiums or otherwise, as will secure to him the like benefits as if his emoluments had not been diminished.

(4) If a policy scheme participant becomes entitled to a benefit under such a scheme as is mentioned in paragraph (1) before reaching normal retiring age, the Secretary of State may reduce any long-term compensation payable to him by the amount of such benefit.

Intervals for payment of compensation under Part V

31. Any compensation awarded as an annual sum under this Part of these regulations to or in respect of any person shall be payable at intervals equivalent to those at which the corresponding benefit would have been payable under the person's last relevant pension scheme or at such other intervals as may be agreed between the person entitled to receive the compensation and the Secretary of State.

PART VI

ADJUSTMENT, REVIEW AND COMPOUNDING OF COMPENSATION

Adjustment of compensation where superannuation benefit is also payable

32.—(1) Where any period of service of which account was taken in calculating the amount of any compensation payable under Part IV or V of these regulations is subsequently taken into account for the purpose of calculating the amount of any superannuation benefit payable to or in respect of any person in accordance with a pension scheme associated with any employment undertaken subsequent to the loss of employment or diminution of emoluments which was the subject of the claim for compensation, the Secretary of State may in accordance with this regulation withhold or reduce the compensation payable in respect of any period for which such superannuation benefit is being received.

(2) If the part of any superannuation benefit by way of annual amounts which is attributable to a period of service mentioned in paragraph (1) equals or exceeds the part of any compensation by way of annual amounts which is attributable to the same period, that part of the compensation may be reduced or withheld, or if such part of the superannuation benefit is less than such part of the compensation, the compensation may be reduced by an amount not exceeding such part of the superannuation benefit.

(3) Where a death gratuity is payable in respect of any person, the sum payable under regulation 27 may be reduced by an amount not greater than the proportion of the death gratuity which the period of service mentioned in paragraph (1) bears to the total period of service of which account was taken in the calculation of the death gratuity.

(4) In addition to any reduction authorised by paragraph (2) or (3), if, in the circumstances mentioned in paragraph (1), compensation by way of annual amounts is attributable in part to any provision of the relevant pension scheme for a minimum benefit, the compensation may be reduced by an amount not exceeding that part.

(5) Where any additional years of service or period of contribution have been credited to a person under regulation 19(2), if the number of such years or such

period is equal to or less than the period spent in the subsequent employment mentioned in paragraph (1), the compensation by way of annual amounts may be reduced (in addition to any other reduction authorised by this regulation) by an amount not exceeding that attributable to the additional years or period so credited or, if the number of such years or such period is greater than the period spent in the subsequent employment, by such proportion of that amount as the period spent in the subsequent employment bears to the number of additional years or the period so credited.

(6) Where compensation has been calculated in accordance with regulation 25, the provisions of this regulation shall apply only in relation to such part (if any) of the superannuation benefit as is attributable to annual emoluments in excess of those to which the person was entitled on entering the new employment referred to in regulation 25.

(7) Where compensation is payable in respect of diminution of emoluments, the provisions of this regulation shall apply only in relation to such part (if any) of the superannuation benefit as is attributable to annual emoluments in excess of those to which the person was entitled immediately prior to the diminution.

Reduction of compensation in certain cases

33.—(1) If under a person's last relevant pension scheme any benefit for which the scheme provided would have been subject to reduction or suspension on his taking up other specified employment, any retirement compensation to which he is entitled shall, where such employment is taken up, be reduced or suspended in the like manner and to the like extent:

Provided that in calculating the amount of the reduction there shall be aggregated with the emoluments of the employment taken up the amount of any superannuation benefit payable to the person by way of annual amounts which is attributable to any period of service of which account was taken in calculating the retirement compensation and to so much of the emoluments as were so taken into account.

(2) There shall be deducted from the retirement compensation payable to any person any additional contributory payments remaining unpaid at the date when he suffered loss of employment; and any such payments not recovered at the date of his death shall be deducted from any compensation payable in respect of that person under regulation 26, 27 or 28(2).

(3) Where a person is entitled to compensation under these regulations and the circumstances are such that he is also entitled to—

(*a*) a redundancy payment under the Redundancy Payments Act 1965(**a**), or

(*b*) any similar payment in consequence of the loss of his employment under any contract or arrangement with the authority by whom he was employed (other than payments by way of a return of contributions under a pension scheme), or

(*c*) any payment under or by virtue of the provisions of any enactment relating to the reinstatement in civil employment of persons who have been in the service of the Crown,

the compensation which would, apart from this paragraph, become due to the person, whether by instalments or lump sum or both, shall in the aggregate be reduced by the amount of the payments referred to in this paragraph.

(**a**) 1965 c. 62.

(4) Where compensation under these regulations is payable to or in respect of any person, and that person or his widow, child or other dependant or his or her personal representatives or any other person is or are also entitled (whether immediately or on the person's attaining some greater age) to a superannuation benefit under his last relevant pension scheme—

(a) any instalment of such compensation which is payable in respect of any period shall be reduced by so much of such superannuation benefit payable in respect of the same period as is attributable to any period of service of which account was taken in calculating the compensation and to so much of the emoluments as were so taken into account; and

(b) any such compensation which is payable as a lump sum shall be reduced by the amount of any lump sum superannuation benefit which is so attributable.

(5) For the purposes of paragraph (4) no account shall be taken of any sum payable in consequence of the surrender by any person of part of his superannuation benefit by way of annual amounts under any provision in that behalf in the relevant pension scheme with a view to obtaining or increasing allowances for his widow, child or other dependant; and the person shall be deemed to have received during any period the amount of superannuation benefit which he would have received but for any such surrender.

(6) Where in any week a person is entitled to long-term compensation and is also entitled to unemployment, sickness or injury benefit under any Act relating to National Insurance, other than a benefit claimable by him in respect of a dependant, there shall be deducted from the long-term compensation payable for that week a sum equal to the amount by which the aggregate of such National Insurance benefit claimable in respect of that week and the weekly rate at which the long-term compensation would be payable but for this regulation exceeds two-thirds of the weekly rate of the net emoluments of the employment which he has lost or in which the emoluments have been diminished:

Provided that this paragraph shall not apply in relation to any such sickness or injury benefit in so far as an equivalent sum is deducted from the emoluments of his current employment and such deduction from those emoluments has not occasioned an increase in his long-term compensation.

(7) In paragraph (6) the expression "weekly rate" means seven three hundred and sixty-fifths of the relevant annual rate.

Notification of change of circumstances

34. Where—

(a) a pensionable officer after suffering loss of employment or diminution of emoluments enters any employment referred to in regulation 25 or becomes entitled to any superannuation benefit on ceasing to hold such employment, or

(b) a person entitled to long-term compensation enters employment the remuneration whereof is payable out of public funds, or ceases to hold such employment, or receives any increase in his remuneration in such employment, or

(c) a person entitled to retirement compensation enters employment in which the compensation is subject to reduction or suspension under regulation 33, or ceases to hold such employment, or receives any increase in his remuneration in such employment, or (*d*) a person entitled to long-term compensation starts to receive any benefit, any increase in benefit or any further benefit under any Act relating to National Insurance,

he shall forthwith inform the Secretary of State in writing of that fact.

Review of awards of long-term or retirement compensation

35.—(1) The Secretary of State shall, at intervals of not more than six months within a period of two years after the date on which any decision on a claim for long-term or retirement compensation for loss of employment (other than compensation payable under regulation 22) is notified to a claimant under regulation 37, or within such longer period as is specified in the subsequent provisions of this regulation, review his decision or, where the claim has been the subject of an appeal, the decision of the tribunal, and these regulations shall apply in relation to any such review as they apply in relation to the initial determination of the claim; and on such review, in the light of any material change in the circumstances of the case, compensation may be awarded, or compensation previously awarded may be increased, reduced or discontinued, subject to the limits set out in these regulations.

(2) The person to whom the decision relates may require the Secretary of State to carry out the review mentioned in paragraph (1) at any time within the period of two years mentioned in that paragraph if he considers that there has been a change in the circumstances of his case which is material for the purposes of these regulations.

(3) The Secretary of State shall carry out a review in accordance with paragraph (1), notwithstanding the expiration of the period mentioned in that paragraph, if—

(*a*) the emoluments of employment or work undertaken as a result of the loss of employment had been taken into account in determining the amount of any compensation awarded, and

(*b*) such employment or work has been lost or the emoluments thereof reduced, otherwise than by reason of misconduct or incapacity to perform such duties as the person might reasonably have been required to perform, and

(*c*) the Secretary of State is satisfied that such loss or reduction is causing the person hardship,

and where any decision is so reviewed, the decision shall be subject to further review in accordance with paragraph (1) as if the review carried out under this paragraph had been the initial determination of the claim.

(4) Paragraphs (1) and (2) shall apply in relation to any decision on a claim for long-term or retirement compensation in respect of diminution of emoluments as they apply in relation to any decision mentioned in the said paragraph (1):

Provided that—

(i) where the person to whom the decision relates ceases to hold the employment in which his emoluments were diminished, a review shall be held within three months after that date, but no further review shall be held after the expiry of that period, and

(ii) while that person continues to hold that employment, there shall be no limit to the period within which a review may take place.

(5) Notwithstanding anything contained in the foregoing provisions of this regulation, the Secretary of State shall review a decision (whether given by him or the tribunal) on a claim for long-term compensation after the expiration of any period within which a review is required to be made if at any time—

(a) the person to whom the decision relates becomes engaged in employment (hereinafter referred to as his "current employment") the remuneration whereof is payable out of public funds and which he has undertaken subsequent to the loss of employment or diminution of emoluments, and

(b) the aggregate of the net emoluments of his current employment, any superannuation benefit payable to the person by way of annual amounts which is attributable to any period of service of which account was taken in calculating the long-term compensation and to so much of the emoluments as were so taken into account and the long-term compensation payable to him exceeds the net emoluments of the employment which he has lost or, as the case may be, in which the emoluments were diminished.

(6) The Secretary of State shall further review any decision reviewed under paragraph (5) whenever the net emoluments of the person's current employment are increased.

(7) If on any review under paragraph (5) or (6) the compensation is reduced, it shall not be reduced below the amount by which the net emoluments of the person's current employment, together with any superannuation benefit payable to him by way of annual amounts which is attributable to any period of service of which account was taken in calculating the long-term compensation and to so much of the emoluments as were so taken into account, falls short of the net emoluments of the employment which he has lost or, as the case may be, in which the emoluments were diminished.

(8) The Secretary of State shall give to a person to whom a decision relates not less than 14 days' notice of any review of that decision to be carried out under this regulation unless the review is carried out at the person's request.

(9) Nothing in this regulation shall preclude the making of any adjustment of compensation required by regulation 32 or 33.

Compounding of awards

36.—(1) In a case where an annual sum which has been or might be awarded under these regulations does not exceed £26, the Secretary of State may, at his discretion, compound his liability in respect thereof by paying a lump sum equivalent to the capital value of the annual sum and, if any lump sum payment has been or might be awarded in addition to such annual sum under regulation 20, 21, 22 or 23, the Secretary of State may likewise discharge his liability in respect thereof by an immediate payment.

(2) In any other case, if the person who has been awarded long-term or retirement compensation requests him to do so, the Secretary of State may, after having regard to the state of health of that person and the other circumstances of the case, compound up to one quarter of his liability to make payments under the award (other than payments to a widow, child or other dependant under regulation 26) by the payment of an equivalent amount as a lump sum or, where any compensation has been awarded as a lump sum, by increasing that

compensation to such equivalent amount; and in calculating for this purpose the liability of the Secretary of State to make such payments, account shall be taken of the annual value of lump sum payments of compensation.

(3) The making of a composition under paragraph (2) in relation to an award of long-term or retirement compensation shall not prevent the subsequent making of a composition under paragraph (1) in relation to that award, but, subject as aforesaid, not more than one composition may be made in relation to any award.

PART VII

PROCEDURE AND MISCELLANEOUS

Procedure on making claims

37.—(1) Every claim for compensation under these regulations and every request for a review of an award of long-term or retirement compensation shall be made in accordance with this regulation.

(2) Every such claim and request shall be made to the Secretary of State in a form approved by him.

(3) Resettlement compensation shall be claimed separately from any other form of compensation claimable under these regulations.

(4) The Secretary of State shall consider any such claim or request in accordance with the relevant provisions of these regulations and shall notify the person making the claim or request in writing of his decision—

(a) in the case of a claim for resettlement compensation, not later than one month after the receipt of the claim, and

(b) in the case of a claim for, or request for the review of an award of, compensation under Part IV or V of these regulations, not later than 13 weeks after the receipt of the claim or request, and

(c) in any other case, as soon as possible after the decision;

but the decision of the Secretary of State shall not be invalidated by reason of the fact that notice of the decision is given after the expiry of the period mentioned in this paragraph.

(5) Every notification of a decision by the Secretary of State (whether granting or refusing compensation or reviewing an award, or otherwise affecting any compensation under these regulations) shall contain a statement—

(a) giving reasons for the decision;

(b) showing how any compensation has been calculated and, in particular, if the amount is less than the maximum which could have been awarded under these regulations, showing the factors taken into account in awarding that amount; and

(c) directing the attention of the claimant to his right under regulation 42, if he is aggrieved by the decision, to institute proceedings before a tribunal and giving him the address to which an application instituting such proceedings should be sent.

Claimants to furnish information

38.—(1) Any person claiming or receiving compensation or whose award of compensation is being reviewed shall furnish all such information as the Secretary of State may at any time reasonably require, and shall verify the same in such manner, including the production of books or of original documents in his possession or control, as may be reasonably so required.

(2) Any such person shall, on receipt of reasonable notice, present himself for interview at such place as the Secretary of State may reasonably require; and any person who attends for interview may, if he so desires, be represented by his adviser.

Procedure on death of claimant

39.—(1) In the event of the death of a claimant or of a person who, if he had survived, could have been a claimant, a claim for compensation under these regulations may be continued or made, as the case may be, by his personal representatives.

(2) Where any such claim is continued or made as aforesaid, the personal representatives shall, as respects any steps to be taken or things to be done by them in order to continue or make the claim, be deemed for the purposes of these regulations to be the person entitled to claim, but, save as aforesaid, the person in whose right they continue or make the claim shall be deemed for the purposes of these regulations to be such person, and the relevant provisions of these regulations shall be construed accordingly:

Provided that the Secretary of State may in any such case extend the period within which, under regulation 7 or 13, a claim is required to be made.

Calculation of service

40.—(1) For the purpose of determining the amount of any compensation payable in respect of the loss of an employment to which, or of any two or more employments to which in the aggregate, a person devoted substantially the whole of his time, any previous period of part-time employment shall be treated as though it were whole-time employment for a proportionately reduced period.

(2) For the purpose of making any calculation under these regulations in respect of a person's reckonable service, all periods of such service shall be aggregated and, except where reference is made to completed years of service, if the aggregated service includes a fraction of a year, that fraction shall, if it exceeds 6 months, be treated as a year, and shall in any other case be disregarded.

Compensation not assignable

41. Subject to any statutory provision in that behalf, any compensation to which a person becomes entitled under these regulations shall be paid by the Secretary of State and shall be payable to, or in trust for, the person who is entitled to receive it, and shall not be assignable:

Provided that, without prejudice to any other right of recovery, any compensation paid in error may be recovered by the Secretary of State by deduction from any compensation payable under these regulations.

Right of appeal from decision of the Secretary of State

42.—(1) Every person who is aggrieved by any decision of the Secretary of State with respect to a compensation question or by any failure on the part of the Secretary of State to notify him of any such decision within the appropriate time prescribed by these regulations may, within 13 weeks of the notification to him of the decision or the expiry of the prescribed time, as the case may be, institute proceedings for the determination of the question by a tribunal in accordance with the Industrial Tribunals (Employment and Compensation) (Scotland) Regulations 1967(a) and these regulations; and the tribunal shall determine the question accordingly.

(2) For the purpose of any such proceedings a person or persons may be appointed to sit with the tribunal as assessor or assessors.

(3) The Secretary of State shall give effect to the decision of a tribunal subject to any modifications that may be required in consequence of any appeal from that decision on a point of law.

Gordon Campbell,
One of Her Majesty's Principal
Secretaries of State.

St. Andrew's House,
Edinburgh.
8th February 1971.

EXPLANATORY NOTE

(This Note is not part of the Regulations.)

1. These Regulations are made under section 35 of the Health Services and Public Health Act 1968.   They provide for the payment of compensation to or in respect of persons who suffer loss of employment or loss or diminution of emoluments which is attributable to a reorganisation in the National Health Service in Scotland brought about by:—

(a) the occurrence on or after 9th September 1968 of any event mentioned in paragraphs (a) and (b) of section 11(10) of the National Health Service (Scotland) Act 1947; or

(b) the making on or after 9th September 1968 of an order under subsection (2), (3) or (4) of section 32 of the Act of 1947, or an order revoking an order made under any of those subsections.

2. Part I of the Regulations contains definitions.   Part II specifies the persons, both whole-time and part-time, to whom the Regulations apply and the grounds of entitlement to compensation.

3. The compensation is payable by the Secretary of State and is:—

(a) resettlement compensation for loss of employment (Part III of the Regulations);

(b) long-term compensation for loss of employment or loss or diminution of emoluments (Part IV);

(c) retirement compensation for loss of employment or loss or diminution of emoluments (Part V);

(d) compensation to the widow, child or other dependant or to the personal representatives of a claimant who was a pensionable officer (Part V).

(a) S.I. 1967/362 (1967 I, p. 1220).

4. Resettlement compensation is payable for a period not exceeding 26 weeks to officers with at least 3 years' service in relevant employment. The qualifying conditions and factors to be considered are set out in Regulation 7 and the method of calculating the amount of compensation is contained in Regulation 8.

5. Long-term compensation is payable to officers with at least 8 years' service in relevant employment. The qualifying and other conditions are set out in Regulations 13 and 14. The method of calculating the maximum amount of long-term compensation is laid down in Regulations 15 (loss of employment) and 16 (diminution of emoluments). It is a proportion, not exceeding two-thirds, of the net emoluments lost or of the amount by which emoluments have been diminished, as the case may be. This compensation is payable from a date determined under Regulation 17 and can be payable up to normal retiring age.

6. Retirement compensation payable to a pensionable officer for loss of employment is based upon his accrued pension rights (Regulation 20) supplemented in the case of persons aged 40 or over at the date of loss by the addition of notional years of service (Regulation 19). Retirement compensation for diminution of emoluments is an appropriate proportion of that for loss of employment (Regulation 23). In the case of a non-pensionable officer compensation not exceeding one half of the rate of long-term compensation may be paid (Regulation 29) and special provision is made for any persons whose pension arrangements are by way of policies of insurance (Regulation 30). Retirement compensation is ordinarily payable from normal retiring age but in certain circumstances may be put into payment earlier (Regulations 21 and 22). The qualifying and other conditions for the payment of retirement compensation are the same as those for long-term compensation (Regulation 18).

7. Compensation is payable to the widow, child or other dependant or to the personal representatives of a claimant who dies, where such persons would have benefited under the relevant pension scheme (Regulations 26 to 28).

8. Part VI of the Regulations provides for long-term and retirement compensation to be reviewed and for awards to be varied in the light of changes in circumstances (Regulation 35). It also contains provisions for the adjustment, suspension and compounding of compensation in certain circumstances.

9. Part VII contains provisions relating to the procedure for making claims and notifying decisions, and confers upon a claimant who is aggrieved by a decision on a compensation question or the failure of the Secretary of State to notify his decision a right to refer the question for determination by a tribunal established under section 12 of the Industrial Training Act 1964.

STATUTORY INSTRUMENTS

1971 No. 256

ROAD TRAFFIC

The Isles of Scilly (Road Traffic Regulation) Order 1971

Made - - -	16*th February* 1971
Coming into Operation	1*st March* 1971

The Secretary of State for the Environment, after consultation with the Council of the Isles of Scilly in exercise of his powers under section 108A of the Road Traffic Regulation Act 1967**(a)** as amended by Part IX of the Transport Act 1968**(b)** and of all other powers him enabling, hereby makes the following Order:—

1. The Order shall come into operation on 1st March 1971, and may be cited as the Isles of Scilly (Road Traffic Regulation) Order 1971.

2.—(1) In this Order "the Road Traffic Regulation Act 1967" means that Act as amended by the Hovercraft Act 1968**(c)**, Part IX of the Transport Act 1968 and by the Removal and Disposal of Vehicles (Alteration of Enactments) Order 1967**(d)**.

(2) The Interpretation Act 1889**(e)** shall apply for the interpretation of this Order as it applies for the interpretation of an Act of Parliament.

3. The Road Traffic Regulation Act 1967 shall apply to the Isles of Scilly, with the modifications set out in the Schedule to this Order, as if for the purposes of sections 20, 52 and 53 of that Act the Isles were a county district and as if for all other purposes the Isles were a separate county.

Signed by authority of the Secretary of State.

16th February 1971.

L. E. Dale,

An Under Secretary in the
Department of the Environment.

(a) 1967 c. 76.
(b) 1968 c. 73.
(e) 1889 c. 63.

(c) 1968 c. 59.
(d) S.I. 1967/1900 (1967 III, p. 5191).

SCHEDULE

For any definition of "local authority" for the purposes of any section, there shall be substituted " 'local authority' includes the Council of the Isles of Scilly;".

In section 104(1), for the definition of "highway authority" there shall be substituted " 'highway authority' includes the Council of the Isles of Scilly;".

EXPLANATORY NOTE

(*This Note is not part of the Order.*)

This Order applies the Road Traffic Regulation Act 1967 to the Isles of Scilly.

STATUTORY INSTRUMENTS

1971 No. 259 (L.5)

SUPREME COURT OF JUDICATURE, ENGLAND

The Supreme Court Funds (Amendment) Rules 1971

Made - - -	11*th February* 1971
Laid before Parliament	23*rd February* 1971
Coming into Operation	
for all purposes except that of rule 2(iii)	1*st March* 1971
for the purposes of rule 2(iii)	1*st April* 1971

The Lord Chancellor, in exercise of the powers conferred on him by section 7(1) of the Administration of Justice Act 1965(a), and with the concurrence of the Treasury, hereby makes the following Rules :—

1. These Rules may be cited as the Supreme Court Funds (Amendment) Rules 1971 and shall come into operation—

(i) for all purposes except that of rule 2(iii), on 1st March 1971, and

(ii) for the purpose of rule 2(iii), on 1st April 1971.

2. The following amendments shall be made to the Supreme Court Funds Rules 1927(b), as subsequently amended (c) :—

(i) in rule 3, after the definition of "brokerage", the following definition shall be inserted :—

" "Capital Fund" means the common investment fund of that name established by the Common Investment Funds Scheme 1965(d) ;" ;

(ii) the following paragraphs shall be added at the end of rule 70 :—

"(10) Subject to paragraph (11) below, no funds shall be directed to be invested, in accordance with rule 72, in the Capital Fund unless the authority giving the direction is satisfied that such funds are likely to remain so invested for at least five years.

(11) The provisions of paragraph (10) above shall not apply in any case where there is an express request by or on behalf of one or more of the persons interested or, if no such person is ascertained or traceable, by the person who pays the fund into court, for investment in the Capital Fund." ;

(**a**) 1965 c. 2. (**b**) S.R. & O. 1927/1184 (1927, p. 1638).
(**c**) The relevant amending instruments are S.R. & O. 1942/983, 1944/503, 1947/2547; S.I. 1953/264, 1965/1608, 1966/876, 1968/106, 1969/206, 1970/121 (1942 I, p. 807; 1944 I, p. 980; 1947 I, p. 2089; 1953 II, p. 2247; 1965 II, p. 4621; 1966 II, p. 2069; 1968 I, p. 302; 1969 I, p. 521; 1970 I, p. 543).
(**d**) S.I. 1965/1467 (1965 II, p. 4303).

(iii) in rule 77(1), for the words "2½ per cent.", there shall be substituted the words "3½ per cent." ;

(iv) in rule 78(1), for the words "7 per cent.", there shall be substituted the words "7½ per cent.".

Dated 8th February 1971.

Hailsham of St. Marylebone, C.

We concur,

Dated 11th February 1971.

Walter Clegg,

H. S. P. Monro,

Two of the Lords Commissioners
of Her Majesty's Treasury.

EXPLANATORY NOTE

(This Note is not part of the Rules.)

These Rules amend the Supreme Court Funds Rules by providing that no direction shall be made for the investment of money in court in the Capital Fund managed by the Public Trustee unless the money is likely to remain there for at least five years, or an express request for such investment is made by or on behalf of the person interested.

The Rules also raise from 2½ per cent. to 3½ per cent. per annum and from 7 per cent. to 7½ per cent. per annum the rates of interest allowed on money standing to the credit of a deposit and a short-term investment account respectively.

STATUTORY INSTRUMENTS

1971 No. 260 (L.6)

COUNTY COURTS

The County Court Funds (Amendment) Rules 1971

Made - - -	11*th February* 1971
Laid before Parliament	23*rd February* 1971
Coming into Operation	1*st March* 1971

The Lord Chancellor, in exercise of the powers conferred on him by section 168 of the County Courts Act 1959(a), as amended by section 9 of the Administration of Justice Act 1965(b), and with the concurrence of the Treasury, hereby makes the following Rules :—

1. These Rules may be cited as the County Court Funds (Amendment) Rules 1971 and shall come into operation on 1st March 1971.

2. The following amendments shall be made in the County Court Funds Rules 1965(c), as subsequently amended (d) :—

(i) in rule 2(1) after the definition of "the bank", the following definition shall be inserted :—

" "Capital Fund" means the common investment fund of that name established by the Common Investment Funds Scheme 1965(e) ;" ;

(ii) the following paragraphs shall be added at the end of rule 20 :—

"(5) Subject to paragraph (6) below, no funds shall be directed to be invested in the Capital Fund unless the authority giving the direction is satisfied that such funds are likely to remain so invested for at least five years.

(6) The provisions of paragraph (5) above shall not apply in any case where there is an express request by or on behalf of one or more of the persons interested or, if no such person is ascertained or traceable, by the person who pays the fund into Court, for investment in the Capital Fund." ;

(a) 1959 c. 22. (b) 1965 c. 2.
(c) S.I. 1965/1500 (1965 II, p. 4343).
(d) The relevant amending instruments are: S.I. 1966/875, 1968/107, 1969/204, 1970/228, (1966 II, p. 2068; 1968 I, p. 303; 1969 I, p. 519; 1970 I, p. 955).
(e) S.I. 1965/1467 (1965 II, p. 4303).

(iii) in rule 23(1), for the words "$2\frac{1}{2}$ per cent." there shall be substituted the words "$3\frac{1}{2}$ per cent.":

(iv) in rule 24(1), for the words "7 per cent." there shall be substituted the words "$7\frac{1}{2}$ per cent.".

Dated 8th February 1971.

Hailsham of St. Marylebone, C.

We concur,

Dated 11th February 1971.

Walter Clegg,

H. S. P. Monro,

Two of the Lords Commissioners
of Her Majesty's Treasury.

EXPLANATORY NOTE

(This Note is not part of the Rules.)

These Rules amend the County Court Funds Rules 1965 by providing that no direction shall be made for the investment of money in court in the Capital Fund managed by the Public Trustee unless the money is likely to remain there for at least five years, or unless an express request for such investment is made by or on behalf of the person interested.

The Rules also raise from $2\frac{1}{2}$ per cent. to $3\frac{1}{2}$ per cent. per annum and from 7 per cent. to $7\frac{1}{2}$ per cent, per annum the rates of interest allowed on money standing to the credit of a deposit and a short-term investment account respectively.

STATUTORY INSTRUMENTS

1971 No. 261

TRADE MARKS
The Trade Marks (Amendment) Rules 1971

Made - - -	17*th February* 1971
Laid before Parliament	26*th February* 1971
Coming into Operation –	
Rules 4 and 5	1*st April* 1971
Rule 3	1*st June* 1971

Whereas, in pursuance of the requirements of section 40(3) of the Trade Marks Act 1938(**a**), the Board of Trade have, before making the following Rules under that Act, published notice of their intention to make such Rules and of the place where copies of the draft Rules might be obtained by advertising such notice in the Trade Marks Journal and the Official Journal (Patents) on 23rd September 1970 and 30th September 1970, being the manner which the Board considered most expedient so as to enable persons affected to make representations to the Board before the Rules were finally settled :

Now, therefore, the Board of Trade, in pursuance of the powers conferred upon them by sections 40 and 41 of the Trade Marks Act 1938 and of all other powers enabling them in that behalf, and with the sanction of the Treasury, hereby make the following Rules :—

1. These Rules may be cited as the Trade Marks (Amendment) Rules 1971 and shall come into operation as respects Rules 4 and 5 on 1st April 1971 and as respects Rule 3 on 1st June 1971.

2. The Interpretation Act 1889(**b**) shall apply to the interpretation of these Rules as it applies to the interpretation of an Act of Parliament and as if these Rules and the Rules hereby revoked were Acts of Parliament.

3. The fee payable by virtue of Rule 3 of the Trade Marks Rules 1938(**c**), as amended (**d**), in respect of any of the matters specified in the Schedule hereto shall on and after 1st June 1971 be the appropriate fee so specified and, accordingly, on that date—

    (i) for Schedule 1 to the said Rules there shall be substituted the Schedule hereto ; and

    (ii) the Trade Marks (Amendment) Rules 1969(**e**) shall be revoked.

4. Where on or after 1st April 1971 but before 1st June 1971 Form TM—No. 11 is filed in respect of the renewal of registration of a trade mark or a series of trade marks the last registration of which mark or series of marks is due to expire after 31st May 1971, the fee payable in respect of such renewal shall be that which would be payable if the said form were filed on or after 1st June 1971.

(**a**) 1938 c. 22.   (**b**) 1889 c. 63.
(**c**) S.R. & O. 1938/661 (Rev. XXIII, p. 3: 1938 II, p. 3257).
(**d**) The relevant amending instruments are S.I. 1964/227, 1969/522 (1964 I, p. 408; 1969 I, p. 1450).   (**e**) S.I. 1969/522 (1969 I, p. 1450).

5. Where on or after 1st April 1971 but before 1st June 1971 Form Cotton—No. 6 is filed to secure the continued inclusion of a mark in the collection of refused marks pursuant to Rule 102 of the Trade Marks Rules 1938 in a case in which the relevant period of 14 years mentioned in that Rule is due to expire after 31st May 1971, the continuance fee payable shall be that which would be payable if the said form were filed on or after 1st June 1971.

Anthony Grant,

Parliamentary Secretary to the
Board of Trade.

17th February 1971.

We sanction the making of these Rules.

Bernard Weatherill,

Walter Clegg,

Two of the Lords Commissioners
of Her Majesty's Treasury.

17th February 1971.

SCHEDULE

LIST OF FEES PAYABLE

Matter or Proceeding	Amount	Corresponding Form
	£	
1 On application not otherwise charged to register a trade mark for a specification of goods included in one class	6·00	T.M.–No. 2 Textile–No. 2
1a On application to register a series of trade marks under section 21(2) for a specification of goods included in one class ...	6·00	T.M–No. 2 Textile–No. 2
1b On application to register a defensive trade mark for a specification of goods included in one class	9·00	T.M–No. 32
1c On application under section 37 to register a certification trade mark for a specification of goods included in one class	8·00	T.M–No. 6

1d On applications made at the same time under section 37 to register one certification trade mark for specifications of goods not all included in one class—
    In respect of every class   ...   ...
    Total fee in no case to exceed £160 for any number of classes.
	8·00	T.M–No. 6

2 On a request to the Registrar to state grounds of decision relating to an application to register a trade mark and materials used	5·00	T.M–No. 5
3 On notice of opposition before the Registrar under section 18, for each application opposed, by opponent ...	5·00	T.M–No. 7
3a On lodging a counter-statement in answer to a notice of opposition under section 18, for each application opposed, by the applicant; or in answer to an application under any of the sections 26, 27, 32 and 33, by the proprietor in respect of each trade mark; or in answer to a notice of opposition under section 35 or section 36, for each application or conversion opposed, by the proprietor...	3·00	T.M–No. 8
3b On the hearing of each opposition under section 18, by applicant and by opponent respectvely; or on the hearing of an application under any of the sections 26, 27, 32 and 33, by applicant and by proprietor respectively; or on the hearing of an opposition under section 35 or section 36, by proprietor and by opponent respectively	5·00	T.M–No. 9

Matter or Proceeding	Amount	Corresponding Form
	£	
3c On notice of opposition before the Board of Trade under paragraph 2(2) of Schedule 1 to the Act, for each application opposed, by the opponent... ...	5·00	T.M–No. 37
3d On lodging a counter-statement in answer to a notice of opposition before the Board of Trade under paragraph 2(2) of Schedule 1 to the Act, for each application opposed, by the applicant	3·00	T.M–No. 38
3e On the hearing of each opposition before the Board of Trade under paragraph 2(2) of Schedule 1 to the Act, by applicant and by opponent respectively ...	5·00	T.M–No. 39
4 For one registration of a trade mark not otherwise charged for a specification of goods included in one class	8·00	T.M–No. 10
4a For one registration of a series of trade marks under section 21(2) for a specification of goods included in one class— For the first mark ... ... And for every other mark of the series	8·00 0·50	T.M–No. 10
4b For registration under section 37 of a certification trade mark for a specification of goods included in one class ...	8·00	T.M–No. 10
4c For registration upon applications made at the same time of one certification trade mark, under section 37, for specifications of goods not all included in one class— In respect of every class ... ... Total fee in no case to exceed £160 for any number of classes.	8·00	T.M–No. 10
4d For one registration of a defensive trade mark for a specification of goods included in one class	9·00	T.M–No. 10
5 Upon each addition to the registered entry of a trade mark of a note that the mark is associated with a newly registered mark	0·50	T.M–No. 10
5a On an application to dissolve the association between registered trade marks ...	4·00	T.M–No. 19
6 On application to register a registered user of a registered trade mark in respect of goods within the specification thereof...	6·00	T.M–No. 50

Matter or Proceeding	Amount	Corresponding Form
	£	
6a On application to register the same registered user of more than one registered trade mark of the same registered proprietor in respect of goods within the respective specifications thereof and subject to the same conditions and restrictions in each case—		
For the first mark	6·00	T.M–No. 50
And for every other mark of the proprietor included in the application and statement of case	0·50	
6b On application by the proprietor of a single trade mark under section 28(8)(a) to vary the entry of a registered user thereof	6·00	T.M–No. 51
6c On application by the proprietor of more than one trade mark under section 28(8)(a) to vary the entries of a registered user thereof—		
For the first mark	6·00	T.M–No. 51
And for every other mark of the proprietor for which the same user is registered, included in the application	0·50	
6d On application by the proprietor or registered user of a single trade mark under section 28(8)(b), for cancellation of the entry of a registered user thereof ...	3·00	T.M–No. 52
6e On application by the proprietor or registered user of more than one trade mark under section 28(8)(b), for cancellation of the entries of a registered user thereof—		
For the first mark	3·00	T.M–No. 52
And for every other mark of the proprietor for which the same user is registered, included in the application	0·50	
6f On application under section 28(8)(c), to cancel the entry of a registered user of a single trade mark	3·00	T.M–No. 53
6g On application under section 28(8)(c), to cancel the entries of a registered user of more than one trade mark—		
For the first mark	3·00	T.M–No. 53
And for every other mark of the same proprietor for which the same user is registered, included in the application	0·50	

Matter or Proceeding	Amount	Corresponding Form
	£	
6h On notice under section 28(9) and Rule 112, of intention to intervene in one proceeding for the variation or cancellation of entries of a registered user of trade marks	5·00	T.M–No. 54
7 On request to enter in the register and advertise a certificate of validity, under section 47 and Rule 88—		
For the first registration certified ...	2·00	T.M–No. 49
And for every other registration certified in the same certificate ...	0·50	
7a On application under section 29(4) and Rule 76 for extension of time for registering a corporation as subsequent proprietor of trade marks on one assignment—		
Not exceeding two months	3·00	T.M–No. 14
Not exceeding four months	6·00	T.M–No. 14
Not exceeding six months	9·00	T.M–No. 14
8 On application for certificate of the Registrar, under section 22(5) and Rule 79—		
For the first mark proposed to be assigned	6·00	T.M–No. 40
And for every other mark of the same proprietor included in that assignment	0·50	
8a On application for approval of the Registrar, under section 22(6) or paragraph 2 of Schedule 3 of the Act, and Rule 79—		
For the first mark	6·00	T.M–No. 41 or 42
And for every other mark of the same proprietor included in the same transfer	0·50	
8b On application for directions by the Registrar for advertisement of assignment of trade marks in use, without goodwill—		
For one mark assigned	3·00	T.M–No. 43
And for every other mark assigned with the same devolution of title ...	0·50	
8c On application for extension of time for applying for directions for advertisement of assignment of trade marks in use, without goodwill, in respect of one devolution of title—		
Not exceeding one month	3·00	T.M–No. 44
Not exceeding two months	6·00	T.M–No. 44
Not exceeding three months	9·00	T.M–No. 44

Matter or Proceeding	Amount £	Corresponding Form
9 On application to register a subsequent proprietor in a case of assignment or transmission of a single trade mark— If made within six months from the date of acquisition of proprietorship	2·00	T.M–No. 15 or 16
If made after expiration of six months but within twelve months from the date of acquisition of proprietorship	5·00	,,
If made after expiration of twelve months from the date of acquisition of proprietorship	8·00	,,
9a On application to register a subsequent proprietor of more than one trade mark standing in the same name, the devolution of title being the same in each case— If made within six months from the date of acquisition of proprietorship For the first mark	2·00	T.M–No. 15 or 16
And for every other mark ...	0·50	
If made after expiration of six months but within twelve months from the date of acquisition of proprietorship For the first mark	5·00	,,
And for every other mark ...	0·50	
If made after expiration of twelve months from the date of acquisition of proprietorship— For the first mark	8·00	,,
And for every other mark ...	0·50	
10 On application to change the name or description of a proprietor or a registered user of one or more trade marks where there has been no change in the proprietorship or in the identity of the user— For each mark...	0·50	T.M–No. 21
11 For renewal of registration of a trade mark at expiration of last registration ...	20·00	T.M–No. 11
11a For renewal of registration of a series of trade marks under section 21(2) at expiration of last registration— For the first mark of the series ...	20·00	T.M–No. 11
And for every other mark of the series	0·50	
11b For renewal of registrations of the same certification trade mark with the same date for goods in more than one class— In respect of every class	20·00	T.M–No. 11
Total fee in no case to exceed £400 for any number of classes.		
11c Additional fee under Rule 67	3·00	T.M–No. 12

Matter or Proceeding	Amount	Corresponding Form
	£	
11d Restoration fee under Rule 68	8·00	T.M–No. 13
12 On an application to the Registrar for leave to add to or alter a single registered trade mark	6·00	T.M–No. 25
12a On an application to the Registrar for leave to add to or alter more than one registered trade mark of the same proprietor, being identical marks, the addition or alteration to be made in each case being the same—		
For the first mark	6·00	T.M–No. 25
And for every other mark	3·00	
12b On notice of opposition to application for leave to add to or alter registered trade marks, for each application opposed ...	5·00	T.M–No. 47
13 For altering one or more entries of the trade or business address of a registered proprietor or a registered user of a trade mark (unless exempted from fee under Rule 81)—		
For each entry...	0·50	T.M–No. 18
14 For every entry in the register of a rectification thereof or an alteration therein, not otherwise charged	3·00	T.M–No. 48
15 For cancelling the entry of a trade mark upon the register on the application of the registered proprietor of the trade mark	—	T.M–No. 22
15a For striking out goods from those for which a trade mark is registered on the application of the registered proprietor of the trade mark	0·75	T.M–No. 23
16 On application under any of the sections 26, 27, 32 and 33, for rectification of the register or removal of trade mark from the register	6·00	T.M–No. 26
16a On application for leave to intervene in proceedings under any of the sections 26, 27, 32 and 33, for rectification of the register or removal of trade mark from the register	5·00	T.M–No. 27
17 On request, not otherwise charged, for correction of clerical error or for permission to amend application ...	1·25	T.M–No. 20

Matter or Proceeding	Amount	Corresponding Form
	£	
18 On request by registered proprietor of a trade mark for entry of disclaimer or memorandum in the register	1·25	T.M–No. 24
19 On application to the Board of Trade under Rule 93 to expunge or vary the registration of a certification trade mark or to vary the deposited regulations of a certification trade mark or of certification trade marks of the same registered proprietor where the regulations are substantially the same	6·00	T.M–No. 36
19a On request to the Board of Trade by the registered proprietor of a certification trade mark to permit alteration of the deposited regulations thereof—		
For the regulations of one such registration	6·00	T.M–No. 35
For the same or substantially the same regulations of each other registration proposed to be altered in the same way and included in the same request	0·50	
20 On application by registered proprietor under Rule 6, for conversion of specification	1·00	T.M–No. 45
20a On notice of opposition to a conversion of the specification or specifications of a registered trade mark or registered trade marks—		
For one mark	5·00	T.M–No. 46
For every other mark of the same proprietor having the same specification	0·50	
21 On appeal from the Registrar to the Board of Trade, in respect of each decision appealed against, by Appellant... ...	5·00	T.M–No. 30
22 For a search under Rule 127 in respect of one class—		
Without application for the Registrar's advice under Rule 20	3·00	T.M–No. 28
With application for the Registrar's advice under Rule 20	4·00	T.M–No. 28
23 On request for the Registrar's preliminary advice under Rule 20, for each trade mark submitted in respect of one class...	1·00	T.M–No. 29
24 For certificate of the Registrar (other than certificate under section 19(2)) of the registration of a trade mark	0·75	T.M–No. 31

Matter or Proceeding	Amount	Corresponding Form
	£	
24a For certificate of the Registrar (other than certificate under section 19(2)) of the registration of a series of trade marks under section 21(2)	0·75	T.M–No. 31
25 For certificate of the Keeper of an entry in the Manchester Record relating to one trade mark	0·75	Textile–No. 5
25a For certificate of the Keeper of an entry in the Manchester Record relating to a series of trade marks under section 21(2)	0·75	Textile–No. 5
26 For the continuance of a Cotton Mark in the Collection of Refused Marks— For each mark in each class at the end of each period of fourteen years after date of application	8·00	Cotton–No. 6
27 For cancelling or making one or more entries of an address for service of a registered proprietor or a registered user of a trade mark, on application made after the registration in each case— For each entry...	0·50	T.M–No. 33
27a For altering one or more entries of an address for service in the register— For each entry... ... ... Total fee in no case to exceed £70 for any number of entries included in one application for alteration, where the address and the alteration in each case are the same.	0·50	T.M–No. 33
28 For inspecting register or Manchester Record, or notice of opposition, counter-statement or decision in connection with any opposition or application for rectification of the register relating to any particular trade mark, for every quarter of an hour	0·15	—
29 For permission to search amongst the classified representations of trade marks, for every quarter of an hour	0·15	—
30 For certifying office copies M.S. or photographic or printed matter	0·75	—

Matter or Proceeding	Amount	Corresponding Form
	£	
31 For extra space in the Journal advertisement, in cases where the printing block for the trade mark exceeds 2 inches in breadth or depth, or in breadth and depth—		
For every inch or part of an inch over 2 inches in breadth	0·30	—
For every inch or part of an inch over 2 inches in depth	0·30	—

The fees to be paid on any proceeding at the Manchester Branch and at the office of the Cutlers' Company shall be the same as for the similar proceeding at the Office.

For the purpose of these fees (except as specially provided above) every mark of a series under section 21, or any preceding similar enactment, shall be deemed to be a mark separately registered.

EXPLANATORY NOTE
(*This Note is not part of the Rules.*)

These Rules further amend the Trade Marks Rules 1938.

Most of the fees payable under the Rules are increased.

The new fees become payable on or after 1st June 1971, except in the case of renewal fees and continuance fees paid in advance. Such fees in respect of any period beginning on or after 1st June 1971 are increased on 1st April 1971.

STATUTORY INSTRUMENTS

1971 No. 262

DESIGNS

The Designs (Amendment) Rules 1971

Made - - - -	*17th February* 1971
Laid before Parliament	*26th February* 1971
Coming into Operation –	
Rule 4 - - -	*1st March* 1971
Rule 3 - - -	*1st June* 1971

The Secretary of State, in exercise of his powers under sections 36 and 40 of the Registered Designs Act 1949(a), as amended by the Patents and Designs (Renewals, Extensions and Fees) Act 1961(b), and of all other powers enabling him in that behalf, and with the consent of the Treasury, hereby makes the following Rules:—

1. These Rules may be cited as the Designs (Amendment) Rules 1971 and shall come into operation as respects Rule 4 on 1st March 1971 and as respects Rule 3 on 1st June 1971.

2. The Interpretation Act 1889(c) shall apply to the interpretation of these Rules as it applies to the interpretation of an Act of Parliament and as if these Rules and the Rules hereby revoked were Acts of Parliament.

3. The fee payable by virtue of Rule 3 of the Designs Rules 1949(d), as amended(e), in respect of any of the matters specified in the Schedule hereto shall on and after 1st June 1971 be the appropriate fee so specified and, accordingly, on that date—

    (i) for Schedule 1 to the said Rules there shall be substituted the Schedule hereto; and

    (ii) the Designs (Amendment) Rules 1969(f) shall be revoked.

4. Where on or after 1st March 1971 but before 1st June 1971, an application is made for an extension of the period of copyright in any registered design in respect of which the period of copyright current is due to expire after 31st May

---

(a) 1949 c. 88.   (b) 1961 c. 25.
(c) 1889 c. 63.   (d) S.I. 1949/2368 (1949 I, p. 1417).
(e) The relevant amending instruments are S.I. 1964/229, 1969/481 (1964 I, p. 428; 1969 I, p. 1370).   (f) S.I. 1969/481 (1969 I, p. 1370).

1971, the fee payable shall be that which would be payable if the application was made on or after 1st June 1971.

Nicholas Ridley,
Parliamentary Under Secretary of State,
Department of Trade and Industry.

17th February 1971.

We consent to the making of these Rules.

Bernard Weatherill,
Walter Clegg,
Two of the Lords Commissioners
of Her Majesty's Treasury.

17th February 1971.

SCHEDULE
LIST OF FEES PAYABLE

Subject or Proceeding	Amount	Corresponding Form
	£	
1. On application to register one design to be applied to a single article not being textile articles	8·00	Designs No. 2 or 3.
If made of lace	2·00	,, ,, ,,
2. On application to register one design to be applied to a set of articles not being textile articles	16·00	Designs No. 4 or 5.
If made of lace	4·00	,, ,, ,,
2A. On application to register one design to be applied to a set of textile articles:—		
Not being checks or stripes	16·00	Designs No. 4 or 5.
Checks or stripes	4·00	,, ,, ,,
3. On application to register one design to be applied to a textile article (not being checks or stripes)	8·00	Designs (Manchester) No. 1 or 3.
4. On application to register one design to be applied to a textile article (checks or stripes) ...	2·00	Designs (Manchester) No. 2 or 3.
5. On application for a copy of certificate of registration	0·75	Designs No. 6.
6. On application to Registrar to state grounds of decision and materials used under Rule 31 ...	5·00	Designs No. 7.
7. On request for extension of time within which an application for registration of a design may be completed:—		
Not exceeding one month	3·00	Designs No. 8.
,, ,, two months	6·00	,, ,,
,, ,, three months	9·00	,, ,,
8. On application for extension of copyright under section 8(2) for second period ...	20·00	Designs No. 9.
9. On application for extension of copyright under section 8(2) for third period	30·00	Designs No. 10.
10. On request for enlargement of time for payment of fee for extension of copyright:—		
Not exceeding one month	3·00	Designs No. 11.
,, ,, two months	6·00	,, ,,
,, ,, three months	9·00	,, ,,
,, ,, four months	12·00	,, ,,
,, ,, five months	15·00	,, ,,
,, ,, six months	18·00	,, ,,
11. On application to enter subsequent proprietorship, &c. under Rule 39 made within six months from date of acquisition of proprietorship, &c.:—		

Subject or Proceeding	Amount	Corresponding Form
	£	
11.—*contd.*		
In respect of one design	2·00	Designs No. 12 or 13.
Made after six but within twelve months from date of acquisition of proprietorship, &c.:—		
In respect of one design	5·00	„ „ „
Made after expiration of twelve months from the date of acquisition of proprietorship, &c.:—		
In respect of one design	8·00	Designs No. 12 or 13.
On application covering more than one design, for each additional design similarly acquired	0·50	—
12. On application for entry of notification of document in the register made within six months of date of document:—		
In respect of one design	2·00	Designs No. 14.
Made after six months but within twelve months from date of document:—		
In respect of one design	5·00	„ „
Made after expiration of twelve months from date of document:—		
In respect of one design	8·00	„ „
On application covering more than one design, for each additional design referred to in the same document as the first design ...	0·50	—
13. On application of mortgagee, licensee, or other person for entry that he no longer claims such interest:—		
In respect of each design	0·50	Designs No. 15.
14. On application to enter change of name or nationality of registered proprietor in the register:—		
In respect of each design	0·50	Designs No. 16.
15. On application for alteration of address or address for service in the register:—		
In respect of each design	0·50	Designs No. 17.
16. On request under section 21 to correct error	2·00	Designs No. 18.
17. On application by proprietor for cancellation	—	Designs No. 19.
18. On request for search under section 23 when registration number is supplied	1·00	Designs No. 20.
19. On request for search under section 23 when registration number is not supplied	4·00	Designs No. 21.
20. On application for search under Rule 48 ...	4·00	Designs No. 22.

Subject or Proceeding	Amount	Corresponding Form
	£	
21. On request for certificate of Registrar for use in obtaining registration in a foreign country or for use in legal proceedings or other special purpose	0·75	Designs No. 23.
22. On request for certificate of Registrar for use in obtaining registration in part of Her Majesty's dominions outside the United Kingdom	0·75	Designs No. 24.
23. On application for compulsory licence under section 10	8·00	Designs No. 25.
24. On application for cancellation of registration under section 11(2)	5·00	Designs No. 26.
25. On notice that hearing of an application for cancellation or compulsory licence will be attended	3·00	Designs No. 27.
26. On application for entry of Order of Court in register	—	Designs No. 28.
27. Inspection of register or design where inspection is permitted other than inspection under the second paragraph of section 22(2) ...	0·15	—
28. For certifying Office copies	0·50	—

The fees to be paid on any proceeding at the Manchester Branch shall be the same as for the similar proceeding at the Office.

EXPLANATORY NOTE

(This Note is not part of the Rules.)

These Rules further amend the Designs Rules 1949.

Most of the fees payable under the Rules are increased.

The new fees become payable on or after 1st June 1971 except in the case of fees for the extension of the copyright period in a design paid in advance. Such fees in respect of any period beginning on or after 1st June 1971 are increased on 1st March 1971.

STATUTORY INSTRUMENTS

1971 No. 263

PATENTS

The Patents (Amendment) Rules 1971

Made - - - -	*17th February* 1971
Laid before Parliament	*26th February* 1971
Coming into Operation —	
Rules 4 and 5 - -	*1st March* 1971
Rule 3 - - -	*1st June* 1971

The Secretary of State, in exercise of his powers under sections 94 and 99 of the Patents Act 1949(a), as amended by the Patents Act 1957(b), the Patents and Designs (Renewals, Extensions and Fees) Act 1961(c) and the Patents (Fees Amendment) Order 1970(d), and of all other powers enabling him in that behalf, and with the consent of the Treasury, hereby makes the following Rules:—

1. These Rules may be cited as the Patents (Amendment) Rules 1971 and shall come into operation as respects Rules 4 and 5 on 1st March 1971 and as respects Rule 3 on 1st June 1971.

2. The Interpretation Act 1889(e) shall apply to the interpretation of these Rules as it applies to the interpretation of an Act of Parliament and as if these Rules and the Rules hereby revoked were Acts of Parliament.

3. The fee payable by virtue of Rule 3 of the Patents Rules 1968(f), as amended(g), in respect of any of the items specified in the Schedule hereto shall on and after 1st June 1971 be the appropriate fee so specified and, accordingly, on that date—

(i) for Schedule 1 to the said Rules there shall be substituted the Schedule hereto; and

(ii) the Patents (Amendment) Rules 1969(h) and the Patents (Amendment No. 2) Rules 1969(i) shall be revoked.

4. Where on or after 1st March 1971 but before 1st June 1971 a request is made for the sealing of a patent in respect of which the complete specification has not been accepted before 1st March 1971, the fee payable on such a request by virtue of Rule 3 of the said Patents Rules shall be that which would be payable if the request was made on or after 1st June 1971.

(a) 1949 c. 87.   (b) 1957 c. 13.
(c) 1961 c. 25.   (d) S.I. 1970/1953 (1970 III, p. 6396).
(e) 1889 c. 63.
(f) S.I. 1968/1389 (1968 II, p. 3958).
(g) The relevant amending instruments are S.I. 1969/482, 1969/1706 (1969 I, p. 1374; 1969 III, p. 5375).   (h) S.I. 1969/482 (1969 I, p. 1374).
(i) S.I. 1969/1706 (1969 III, p. 5375).

5. Where on or after 1st March 1971 but before 1st June 1971 an application is made for a certificate of payment of a patent renewal fee in respect of any year beginning after 31st May 1971, the fee payable upon such application by virtue of Rule 3 of the said Patents Rules shall be that which would be payable if the application was made on or after 1st June 1971.

Nicholas Ridley,
Parliamentary Under Secretary of State,
Department of Trade and Industry.

17th February 1971.

We consent to the making of these Rules.

Bernard Weatherill,
Walter Clegg,
Two of the Lords Commissioners of
Her Majesty's Treasury.

17th February 1971.

SCHEDULE

LIST OF FEES PAYABLE

		Corresponding Form
	£	
1. On application for a patent	1·00	Patents Form No. 1 or Schedule 3 Form 1A.
2. On Convention application for a patent:— In respect of each application for protection in a Convention country ...	1·00	Patents Form No. 1 Con. or Schedule 3 Form 1B.
3. On filing specification:—		
Provisional	—	Patents Form No. 2.
Complete	22·00	Patents Form No. 3.
4. On application for grant of patent of addition in lieu of an independent patent	8·00	Patents Form No. 1 Add.
5. Declaration of inventorship of invention disclosed in complete specification ...	—	Patents Form No.4.
6. For extension of the period for filing complete specification	5·00	Patents Form No. 5.
7. On request for the post-dating of an application under section 6(3)	5·00	Patents Form No. 6.
8. For extension of time under Rule 30 or 33 or 50:—		
Not exceeding one month	3·00	Patents Form No. 7.
Each succeeding month	3·00	,, ,, ,,
9. On application for result of search made under sections 7 and 8	0·15	Patents Form No. 8.
10. On application under section 9(2) for deletion of reference	—	Patents Form No. 9.
11. For extension of the period for putting an application in order:—		
Up to one month after the period allowed by section 12(1)	3·00	Patents Form No. 10.
Up to two months	6·00	,, ,, ,,
Up to three months	9·00	,, ,, ,,
12. For postponement of acceptance of complete specification:—		
Up to 13 months from date of filing of complete specification	3·00	Patents Form No. 11.
From 13 months to 14 months	3·00	,, ,, ,,
From 14 months to 15 months ...	3·00	,, ,, ,,
13. On notice of opposition to grant of patent. By opponent	5·00	Patents Form No. 12.
14. On hearing by Comptroller. By each party ...	3·00	Patents Form No. 13.
15. On a request under section 16(3)	2·00	Patents Form No. 14.
16. On a claim under section 16(4)	2·00	Patents Form No. 15.
17. On an application for extension of the period under section 16(5)	3·00	Patents Form No. 16.
18. On an application for a certificate under section 16(8)	5·00	Patents Form No. 17.
19. On a claim under section 17(1) for application to proceed in name of claimants ...	5·00	Patents Form No. 18.
20. On application for directions under section 17(5)	10·00	Patents Form No. 19.

		Corresponding Form
	£	
21. On a request for sealing of a patent	8·00	Patents Form No. 20.
22. On application for extension of the period for requesting the sealing of a patent under section 19(3):—		
Not exceeding one month	3·00	Patents Form No. 21.
,, ,, two months	6·00	,, ,, ,,
,, ,, three months	9·00	,, ,, ,,
23. On application for extension of the period for requesting the sealing of a patent under section 19(4):—		
Not exceeding one month	3·00	Patents Form No. 22.
Each succeeding month	3·00	,, ,, ,,
24. On application under section 20 for amendment of a patent	6·00	Patents Form No. 23.
25. *On application for certificate of payment of renewal fee:—		
Before the expiration of the 4th year from the date of the patent and in respect of the 5th year	13·00	Patents Form No. 24.
Before the expiration of the 5th year from the date of the patent and in respect of the 6th year	14·00	,, ,, ,,
Before the expiration of the 6th year from the date of the patent and in respect of the 7th year	16·00	,, ,, ,,
Before the expiration of the 7th year from the date of the patent and in respect of the 8th year	18·00	,, ,, ,,
Before the expiration of the 8th year from the date of the patent and in respect of the 9th year	20·00	,, ,, ,,
Before the expiration of the 9th year from the date of the patent and in respect of the 10th year	24·00	,, ,, ,,
Before the expiration of the 10th year from the date of the patent and in respect of the 11th year	26·00	,, ,, ,,
Before the expiration of the 11th year from the date of the patent and in respect of the 12th year	28·00	,, ,, ,,
Before the expiration of the 12th year from the date of the patent and in respect of the 13th year	30·00	,, ,, ,,
Before the expiration of the 13th year from the date of the patent and in respect of the 14th year	34·00	,, ,, ,,
Before the expiration of the 14th year from the date of the patent and in respect of the 15th year	37·00	,, ,, ,,
Before the expiration of the 15th year from the date of the patent and in respect of the remainder of the term of the patent	40·00	,, ,, ,,

*One half only of these fees payable on patents endorsed "Licences of Right".

		Corresponding Form
	£	
26. On extension of the period for payment of renewal fees:—		
Not exceeding one month	3·00	Patents Form No. 25.
„ „ two months	6·00	„ „ „
„ „ three months	9·00	„ „ „
„ „ four months	12·00	„ „ „
„ „ five months	15·00	„ „ „
„ „ six months	18·00	„ „ „
27. Certificate of payment of renewal fee ...	—	Patents Form No. 26.
28. On application under section 24 or 25 for extension of term of patent	10·00	Patents Form No. 27.
29. On opposition to application for extension of term of patent	5·00	Patents Form No. 28.
30. On application for restoration of a patent ...	6·00	Patents Form No. 29.
31. On notice of opposition to application for restoration of patent	5·00	Patents Form No. 30.
32. Additional fee on restoration of patent ...	15·00	Patents Form No. 31.
33. On application under section 28 for sealing of patent	11·00	Patents Form No. 32.
34. On opposition to application under section 28	5·00	Patents Form No. 33.
35. Additional fee for sealing under section 28 ...	15·00	Patents Form No. 34.
36. On application to amend specification after acceptance:—		
Up to sealing. By applicant	10·00	Patents Form No. 35.
After sealing. By patentee	10·00	„ „ „
37. On notice of opposition to amendment. By opponent	5·00	Patents Form No. 36.
38. On application to amend specification not yet accepted	5·00	Patents Form No. 37.
39. On application to amend an application for a patent	5·00	Patents Form No. 38.
39a Application for the conversion of an application for a patent to a Convention application under Rule 94(2)	—	Patents Form No. 38 Con.
40. On application for revocation of a patent under section 33	5·00	Patents Form No. 39.
41. On offer to surrender a patent under section 34	—	Patents Form No. 40.
42. On notice of opposition to surrender of a patent	4·00	Patents Form No. 41.
43. On application for endorsement of patent "Licences of Right"	2·00	Patents Form No. 42.
44. On application for settlement of terms of licence under patent endorsed "Licences of Right"	8·00	Patents Form No. 43.
45. On application by patentee for cancellation of endorsement of patent "Licences of Right"...	5·00	Patents Form No. 44.
46. On application for cancellation of endorsement "Licences of Right"	5·00	Patents Form No. 45.
47. On notice of opposition to cancellation of endorsement of patent "Licences of Right"	5·00	Patents Form No. 46.
48. On application under section 37 for grant of compulsory licence or endorsement of a patent "Licences of Right"	8·00	Patents Form No. 47.

		Corresponding Form
	£	
49. On application under section 40(1) for endorsement of patent "Licences of Right" or grant of licence	8·00	Patents Form No. 48.
50. On application under section 40(3) for Order of Comptroller	8·00	Patents Form No. 49.
51. On application under section 42 for revocation	5·00	Patents Form No. 50.
52. On opposition to application under section 37, 40, 41 or 42	5·00	Patents Form No. 51.
53. On application for licence under section 41 ...	8·00	Patents Form No. 52.
54. On application under section 55(1) for directions of Comptroller	8·00	Patents Form No. 53.
55. On application under section 55(2) for directions of Comptroller	8·00	Patents Form No. 54.
56. On application under section 56(1) to determine dispute	8·00	Patents Form No. 55.
57. On reference of dispute to Comptroller under section 67(1)	8·00	Patents Form No. 56.
58. For altering name or nationality or address or address for service in register, for each patent	0·50	Patents Form No. 57.
59. On application for entry of name of subsequent proprietor in the register if made within six months from date of acquisition of proprietorship:—	2·00	Patents Form No. 58 or 60.
If made after the expiration of six months but within twelve months from the date of acquisition of proprietorship	5·00	,, ,, ,,
If made after expiration of twelve months from date of acquisition of proprietorship	8·00	,, ,, ,,
On each application covering more than one patent, the devolution of title being the same as in the first patent. For each additional patent	0·50	,, ,, ,,
60. On application for entry of notice of a mortgage or licence in the register, if made within six months from date of acquisition of interest or the sealing of the patent (whichever is the later)	2·00	Patents Form No. 59 or 61.
If made after expiration of six months but within twelve months from date of acquisition of interest or the sealing of the patent (whichever is the later) ...	5·00	,, ,, ,,
If made after expiration of twelve months from date of acquisition of interest or the sealing of the patent (whichever is the later)	8·00	,, ,, ,,
On each application covering more than one patent, the devolution of title being the same as in the first patent. For each additional patent	0·50	,, ,, ,,

	£	Corresponding Form
61. On application for entry of notification of a document in the register, if made within six months from date of document or the sealing of the patent (whichever is the later):—	2·00	Patents Form No. 62.
If made after expiration of six months but within twelve months from date of document or the sealing of the patent (whichever is the later)	5·00	,, ,, ,,
If made after expiration of twelve months from date of document or the sealing of the patent (whichever is the later) ...	8·00	,, ,, ,,
On each application covering more than one patent, for each additional patent referred to in the same document as the first patent	0·50	,, ,, ,,
62. On application for entry in the register of claim to a licence under a patent extended under section 23, 24 or 25	—	Patents Form No. 63.
63. On request to Comptroller to correct a clerical error:—		
Up to sealing	3·00	Patents Form No. 64.
After sealing	3·00	,, ,, ,,
64. On notice of opposition to the correction of a clerical error	4·00	Patents Form No. 65.
65. For certificate of Comptroller under section 77(1)	0·75	Patents Form No. 66.
66. On request for information as to a matter affecting a patent or an application therefor	1·50	Patents Form No. 67.
67. For duplicate of patent	5·00	Patents Form No. 68.
68. On notice of Order of Court	—	Patents Form No. 69.
69. On inspection of register or supply of an extract from register, or on inspection of original documents (other than provisional specifications), samples or specimens ...	0·15	
70. For office copy of patent	0·50	
71. For certifying office copies, MSS., printed or photographic ... ... each	0·50	
72. On written enquiry as to whether a patent or patents is or are in force;		
for first patent	0·50	
for each other patent in the same enquiry	0·15	

EXPLANATORY NOTE

(This Note is not part of the Rules.)

These Rules further amend the Patents Rules 1968.

Most of the fees payable under the Rules are increased.

The new fees are payable on or after 1st June 1971 except in the case of certain sealing fees and in the case of renewal fees paid in advance. Fees payable for the sealing of a patent in respect of which the complete specification was accepted on or after 1st March 1971 but before 1st June 1971 and renewal fees in respect of any year beginning on or after 1st June 1971 are increased on 1st March 1971.

STATUTORY INSTRUMENTS

1971 No. 264

NATIONAL HEALTH SERVICE, ENGLAND AND WALES

HOSPITAL AND SPECIALIST SERVICES

The National Health Service (Functions of Regional Hospital Boards, etc.) Amendment Regulations 1971

Made - - -	*17th February* 1971
Laid before Parliament	*25th February* 1971
Coming into Operation	*1st April* 1971

The Secretary of State for Social Services, in exercise of his powers under section 12 of the National Health Service Act 1946**(a)** and of all other powers enabling him in that behalf, hereby makes the following regulations:—

1.—(1) These regulations may be cited as the National Health Service (Functions of Regional Hospital Boards, etc.) Amendment Regulations 1971, and shall come into operation on 1st April 1971.

(2) The Interpretation Act 1889**(b)** applies to the interpretation of these regulations as it applies to the interpretation of an Act of Parliament.

2. The National Health Service (Functions of Regional Hospital Boards, etc.) Regulations 1969**(c)**, as amended **(d)**, shall be further amended as follows:—

In regulation 4*(b)* (3)*(c)* (which limits the cost of specified works which a Regional Hospital Board may undertake without the consent of the Secretary of State) for the amount of "£250,000" there shall be substituted the amount of "£500,000".

Keith Joseph,

Secretary of State for Social Services.

17th February 1971.

(a) 1946 c. 81.   **(b)** 1889 c. 63.   **(c)** S.I. 1969/297 (1969 I, p. 809).
(d) The amendment does not relate expressly to the subject matter of these Regulations.

EXPLANATORY NOTE

(This Note is not part of the Regulations.)

These Regulations amend the National Health Service (Functions of Regional Hospital Boards, etc.) Regulations 1969 by increasing to £500,000 the total cost of building or civil engineering works which a Regional Hospital Board may undertake without the consent of the Secretary of State.

STATUTORY INSTRUMENTS

1971 No. 265 (S.42)

COURT OF SESSION, SCOTLAND

Act of Sederunt (Rules of Court Amendment No. 4) 1971

Made - - -	16*th February* 1971
Coming into Operation	16*th March* 1971

The Lords of Council and Session, under and by virtue of the powers conferred on them by section 9(1) and (2) of the Tribunals and Inquiries Act 1958(**a**), and of all other powers competent to them in that behalf, do hereby enact and declare as follows :—

1. The Rules of Court (**b**) are hereby amended by deleting the figures "(2)" occurring after the words "section 9" in the heading of Rule 291 and in paragraph (1) of Rule 291, and by substituting in both places the figures "(1)".

2. This Act of Sederunt may be cited as the Act of Sederunt (Rules of Court Amendment No. 4) 1971, and shall come into operation on 16th March 1971.

And the Lords appoint this Act of Sederunt to be inserted in the Books of Sederunt.

Edinburgh,
16th February 1971.

J. L. Clyde,
I.P.D.

EXPLANATORY NOTE

(This Note is not part of the Act of Sederunt.)

This Act of Sederunt amends the Rules of Court by making provision for Special cases under section 9(1) of the Tribunals and Inquiries Act 1958.

(**a**) 1958 c. 66. (**b**) S.I. 1965/321 (1965 I, p. 803).

STATUTORY INSTRUMENTS

1971 No. 271

CIVIL AVIATION

The Air Navigation (General) (Third Amendment) Regulations 1971

Made - - - -	*19th February* 1971

Coming into Operation –

    (*a*) *for all purposes of Regulation* 3(1)   1*st March* 1971

    (*b*) *for all other purposes*   1*st April* 1971

The Secretary of State, in exercise of his powers under Articles 10(1A) and 26(4) of the Air Navigation Order 1970**(a)**, as amended**(b)**, and of all other powers enabling him in that behalf, hereby makes the following Regulations:

1. These Regulations may be cited as the Air Navigation (General) (Third Amendment) Regulations 1971 and shall come into operation for all purposes of Regulation 3(1) on 1st March 1971 and for all other purposes on 1st April 1971.

2. The Interpretation Act 1889**(c)** applies for the purpose of the interpretation of these Regulations as it applies for the purpose of the interpretation of an Act of Parliament.

3. The Air Navigation (General) Regulations 1970**(d)**, as amended**(e)**, shall be further amended as follows:

(1) In Regulation 4:—

    (*a*) At the beginning of paragraph (2) there shall be inserted "subject to the provisions of paragraph (4) of this Regulation" and for the proviso and Table in that paragraph there shall be substituted the following:

        "Provided that, in the case of an aircraft of which the maximum total weight authorised exceeds 12,500 lb. or which has a total seating capacity of 12 or more persons, the total weights of the passengers and crew may, subject to the provisions of paragraph (4) of this Regulation, be calculated at not less than the weights shown in Table 1 and the load sheet shall bear a notation to that effect:

(a) S.I. 1970/954 (1970 II, p. 2964).   (b) S.I. 1970/1951 (1970 III, p. 6389).
(c) 1889 c. 63.   (d) S.I. 1970/1081 (1970 II, p. 3344).
(e) There is no relevant amending instrument.

Table 1

Males over 12 years of age ... ... 75 kg.

Females over 12 years of age ... ... 65 kg.

On journeys between the United Kingdom, the Channel Islands and the Isle of Man:

Children aged 3 years or more, but not over 12 years of age ... 40 kg.

Infants under 3 years of age ... ... 10 kg.

On any other journey:

Children aged 2 years or more, but not over 12 years of age ... 39 kg.

Infants under 2 years of age ... ... 8 kg."

(*b*) For paragraph (3) there shall be substituted the following:

"(3) (*a*) Subject to the provisions of paragraph (4) of this Regulation for the purpose of calculating the total weight of the aircraft the respective total weights of the baggage and cargo entered in the load sheet shall be computed from the actual weight of each piece of baggage, cargo or cargo container and for that purpose each piece or container shall be separately weighed:

Provided that, in the case of an aeroplane of which the maximum total weight authorised exceeds 12,500 lb. or which has a total seating capacity of 12 or more persons, the total weights of the baggage may, subject to the provisions of paragraph (4) of this Regulation, be calculated at not less than the weights shown in Table 2 and the load sheet shall bear a notation to that effect:

Table 2

1	2	3	
Journey made by the aeroplane	Cabin baggage per passenger*	Hold baggage per piece	
		Scheduled Journey	Holiday Journey
Domestic	3 kg.	10 kg.	13 kg.
European	3 kg.	12 kg.	13 kg.
Intercontinental	3 kg.	14 kg.	16 kg.

*Not infants under 3 years of age on journeys between the United Kingdom, Channel Islands and Isle of Man, or under 2 years of age on any other journey.

(*b*) If Table 2 has been used, subject to the provisions of paragraph (4) for determining the weight of hold baggage, it shall also be used, subject as aforesaid, for determining the weight of the cabin baggage.

(*c*) For the purposes of this Regulation:

(i) A journey made by an aeroplane shall be treated as domestic if it is confined within an area joining successively the following points:

61°00'N 11°00'W	61°00'N 02°00'E
51°05'N 02°00'E	49°30'N 04°00'W
49°30'N 11°00'W	61°00'N 11°00'W

but excluding any journey to or from Shannon.

(ii) A journey made by an aeroplane, not being a domestic journey, shall be treated as European if it is confined within an area joining successively the following points:

66°30'N 30°00'W	66°30'N 39°00'E
30°00'N 39°00'E	30°00'N 11°00'W
24°00'N 11°00'W	24°00'N 30°00'W
66°30'N 30°00'W.	

(iii) A journey made by an aeroplane shall be treated as intercontinental if it is neither domestic nor European.

(iv) A journey made by an aeroplane shall be treated as a holiday journey and not as a scheduled journey if it is made for the carriage of passengers each of whom is carried pursuant to an agreement which provides for carriage by air to a place outside Great Britain, and back from that place or from another place to Great Britain (whether or not on the same aeroplane) and for accommodation at a place outside Great Britain."

(*c*) After paragraph (3) there shall be added the following paragraph:

"(4)(*a*) If it appears to the person supervising the loading of the aircraft that any passenger or baggage to be carried exceeds the weights set out in Table 1 or Table 2 of this Regulation he shall, if he considers it necessary in the interests of the safety of the aircraft, or if the Secretary of State has so directed in the particular case, require any such person or baggage to be actually weighed for the purpose of the entry to be made in the load sheet.

(*b*) If any person or baggage has been weighed, the weights entered in the load sheet shall take account of the actual weight of that person or baggage, or of the weight determined in accordance with the respective provisos to paragraph (2) or (3), whichever weight shall be the greater.";

(2) After Regulation 14 there shall be added the following Regulation:

"Pilot Maintenance—prescribed repairs or replacements

15. With reference to Article 10(1A) of the Order the following repairs or replacements are hereby prescribed:

(1) Replacement of landing gear tyres, landing skids or skid shoes.

(2) Replacement of elastic shock absorber cord units on landing gear where special tools are not required.

(3) Replacement of defective safety wiring or split pins excluding those in engine, transmission, flight control and rotor systems.

(4) Patch-repairs to fabric not requiring rib stitching or the removal of structural parts or control surfaces, if the repairs do not cover up structural damage and do not include repairs to rotor blades.

(5) Repairs to upholstery and decorative furnishings of the cabin or cockpit interior when the repair does not require dismantling of any structure or operating system or interfere with an operating system or affect the structure of the aircraft.

(6) Repairs, not requiring welding, to fairings, non-structural cover plates and cowlings.

(7) Replacement of side windows where that work does not interfere with the structure or with any operating system.

(8) Replacement of safety belts or safety harness.

(9) Replacement of seats or seat parts with parts approved by the Secretary of State (whether generally or in relation to a class of aircraft or the particular aircraft) not involving dismantling of any structure or of any operating system.

(10) Replacement of bulbs, reflectors, glasses, lenses or lights.

(11) Replacement of any cowling not requiring removal of the propeller, rotors or disconnection of engine or flight controls.

(12) Replacement of unserviceable sparking plugs.

(13) Replacement of batteries.

(14) Replacement of wings and tail surfaces and controls, the attachments of which are designed to provide for assembly immediately before each flight and dismantling after each flight.

(15) Replacement of main rotor blades that are designed for removal where special tools are not required.

(16) Replacement of generator and fan belts designed for removal where special tools are not required".

R. R. Goodison,
A Deputy Secretary,
Department of Trade and Industry.

19th February 1971.

EXPLANATORY NOTE

(This Note is not part of the Regulations.)

These Regulations amend the Air Navigation (General) Regulations 1970. as previously amended, as follows:

(1) For calculating the total weight of an aircraft flying for the purpose of public transport, standard weights for passengers and crew could hitherto be used instead of actual weights only if the aircraft had a total seating capacity of 12 or more persons.   Now they can also be used if the aircraft's maximum total weight authorised exceeds 12,500 lb.   A similar provision has been introduced for aeroplanes in respect of cabin and hold baggage of which the weight can now be calculated according to a table of standard weights.   This table distinguishes between domestic, European and intercontinental journeys and also between scheduled and holiday journeys.   The person supervising the loading of the aircraft, or the Secretary of State, can require any person or baggage to be actually weighed in the interests of safety and if any passenger or baggage is so weighed, then that weight or the appropriate standard weight, whichever is the greater, must be entered in the load sheet (Regulation 4).

(2) A new Regulation (Regulation 15) is introduced prescribing the repairs and replacements which can be carried out personally by the owner or operator of an aircraft of which the maximum total weight authorised does not exceed 6,000 lb. and which is flying otherwise than for the purpose of public transport. Under Article 10(1A) of the Air Navigation Order 1970, as amended, a certificate of compliance is not required in respect of the repairs and replacements now prescribed.

STATUTORY INSTRUMENTS

1971 No. 272

CUSTOMS AND EXCISE

The Import Duties (General) (No. 2) Order 1971

Made - - - -	*22nd February* 1971
Laid before the	
House of Commons	*26th February* 1971
Coming into Operation	*4th March* 1971

The Lords Commissioners of Her Majesty's Treasury, by virtue of the powers conferred on them by sections 1, 2 and 13 of the Import Duties Act 1958(a) and of all other powers enabling them in that behalf, on the recommendation of the Secretary of State hereby make the following Order:—

1.—(1) This Order may be cited as the Import Duties (General) (No. 2) Order 1971.

(2) The Interpretation Act 1889(b) shall apply for the interpretation of this Order as it applies for the interpretation of an Act of Parliament.

(3) This Order shall come into operation on 4th March 1971.

2. In Schedule 1 to the Import Duties (General) (No. 7) Order 1970(c) (which by reference to the Customs Tariff 1959 sets out the import duties chargeable under the Import Duties Act 1958), in heading 20.02 (vegetables prepared or preserved otherwise than by vinegar or acetic acid), subheading (C)(1)(*b*)(i) (tomato pulp, paste, etc. in air-tight containers) shall be amended by omitting the rate of duty specified in column 2.

V. H. Goodhew,
Bernard Weatherill,

Two of the Lords Commissioners
of Her Majesty's Treasury.

22nd February 1971.

EXPLANATORY NOTE

(This Note is not part of the Order.)

This Order removes the import duty from tomato purée, as defined in heading 20.02 (C)(1)(*b*)(i) of the Customs Tariff.

(a) 1958 c. 6.   (b) 1889 c. 63.   (c) S.I. 1970/1522 (1970 III, p. 4935).

STATUTORY   INSTRUMENTS

1971 No. 273

CUSTOMS AND EXCISE

The Import Duties (Temporary Exemptions) (No. 2) Order 1971

Made - - - -	*22nd February* 1971
Laid before the House of Commons	*26th February* 1971
Coming into Operation	*4th March* 1971

The Lords Commissioners of Her Majesty's Treasury, by virtue of the powers conferred on them by sections 3(6) and 13 of the Import Duties Act 1958(a), and of all other powers enabling them in that behalf, on the recommendation of the Secretary of State, hereby make the following Order:—

1.—(1) This Order may be cited as the Import Duties (Temporary Exemptions) (No. 2) Order 1971.

(2) The Interpretation Act 1889(b) shall apply for the interpretation of this Order as it applies for the interpretation of an Act of Parliament.

(3) This Order shall come into operation on 4th March 1971.

2.—(1) Until the beginning of 1st January 1972 or, in the case of goods in relation to which an earlier day is specified in Schedule 1 to this Order, until the beginning of that day, any import duty which is for the time being chargeable on goods of a heading of the Customs Tariff 1959 specified in that Schedule shall not be chargeable in respect of goods of any description there specified in relation to that heading.

(2) The period for which goods of the headings of the Customs Tariff 1959 and descriptions specified in Schedule 2 to this Order are exempt from import duty shall be extended until the beginning of 1st January 1972 or, in the case of goods in relation to which an earlier day is specified in that Schedule, until the beginning of that day.

(3) Any entry in column 2 in Schedule 1 or Schedule 2 to this Order is to be taken to comprise all goods which would be classified under an entry in the same terms constituting a subheading (other than the final subheading) in the relevant heading in the Customs Tariff 1959.

(4) For the purposes of classification under the Customs Tariff 1959, in so far as that depends on the rate of duty, any goods to which paragraph (1) or paragraph (2) above applies shall be treated as chargeable with the same duty as if this Order had not been made.

V. H. Goodhew,
Bernard Weatherill,
Two of the Lords Commissioners
of Her Majesty's Treasury.

22nd February 1971.

(a) 1958 c. 6.   (b) 1889 c. 63.

SCHEDULE 1

GOODS TEMPORARILY EXEMPT FROM IMPORT DUTY

Tariff Heading	Description
28.29	Aluminium fluoride Aluminium sodium fluoride
29.01	5-Ethylidenebicyclo[2,2,1]hept-2-ene
29.02	1,2,3,4-Tetrachlorobenzene
29.05	1-Phenylprop-2-yn-1-ol
29.08	Benzyl cyclohex-3-enylidenemethyl ether 5-Propenylguaethol (-OH at 1)
29.10	1,1,3,3-Tetraethoxypropane (until 4th May 1971)
29.11	n-Octanal (until 1st July 1971)
29.12	Theobromine (until 4th May 1971)
29.14	n-Butyl chloroformate Cyclohexyl chloroformate 2-Ethylhexyl chloroformate
29.15	Succinic acid
29.22	Tri-n-butylamine (until 4th May 1971)
29.23	Ketamine hydrochloride
29.25	β-Benzyl hydrogen N-benzyloxycarbonyl-L-aspartate Glycylglycine Tetramethylurea
29.31	2-n-Butoxyethyl 2-thiocyanatoethyl ether 1,2-Di-(N'-methoxycarbonylthioureido)benzene 2,2'-Thiodi-(4-tt-octylphenolato)-n-butylaminenickel(II)
29.34	3-Mercaptopropyltrimethoxysilane
29.35	2-Amino-6-methylbenzothiazole 4-Cyclododecyl-2,6-dimethylmorpholinium acetate 1,5-Decanolactone 3,4-Dihydro-2-methoxypyran 1,5-Dodecanolactone Hypoxanthine
29.38	(+)-α-Tocopherol
39.03	Hydroxybutylmethylcellulose
50.05	Singles yarns, wholly of silk, not coarser than 100 decitex (10 milligrammes per metre), and multiples thereof, not dyed and not being slub or fancy yarns Slub and fancy yarns wholly of silk, not dyed
81.02	Molybdenum flat strip in coils, containing not more than $0 \cdot 05$ per cent. by weight of iron and not more than $0 \cdot 01$ per cent. by weight of nickel as major impurities, of a thickness of not less than $0 \cdot 02$ millimetre and not more than $1 \cdot 3$ millimetres, and of a width of not less than $0 \cdot 5$ millimetre and not more than $3 \cdot 6$ millimetres
90.07	Photo-reduction cameras with upper and lower positioning beds, for the production of printed circuit masters up to 60 centimetres by 60 centimetres and integrated circuit reticules down to 5 centimetres by 5 centimetres from originals on translucent copy board not exceeding 150 centimetres by 120 centimetres, the cameras being designed to give a repeat accuracy of size of not more than 1 part in 20,000 for an image area of 25 centimetres by 20 centimetres or less and not more than 1 part in 10,000 for image areas up to 60 centimetres by 60 centimetres (until 4th May 1971)

Tariff Heading   *Description*

95.05   Coral simply shaped in the form of cabochons, marquises, boutons or the like, polished but not faceted or otherwise worked

SCHEDULE 2

Goods for which exemption from Import Duty is extended

Tariff Heading   *Description*

12.01   Castor seed (until 1st July 1971)

28.18   Magnesium oxide, dead-burned but not fused, of a purity not less than 96 per cent., containing (*a*) a total of not more than $1 \cdot 0$ per cent. by weight of aluminium compounds and iron compounds expressed as Al_2O_3 and Fe_2O_3, (*b*) a total of not more than $3 \cdot 5$ per cent. by weight of calcium compounds and silicon compounds expressed as CaO and SiO_2, the weight of silicon compounds being not less than $1 \cdot 5$ times and not more than $3 \cdot 0$ times the weight of calcium compounds; and (*c*) of which not less than 50 per cent. by weight is retained by a sieve having a nominal width of aperture of $\frac{3}{16}$ inch (until 1st July 1971)

            Magnesium oxide, dead-burned but not fused, of a purity not less than 96 per cent., which contains (*a*) not more than $0 \cdot 05$ per cent. by weight of boron compounds expressed as B_2O_3, (*b*) a total of not more than $0 \cdot 5$ per cent. by weight of aluminium compounds and iron compounds expressed as Al_2O_3 and Fe_2O_3, and (*c*) a total of not less than $1 \cdot 0$ per cent. by weight and not more than $3 \cdot 5$ per cent. by weight of calcium compounds and silicon compounds expressed as CaO and SiO_2, the weight of calcium compounds being not less than $1 \cdot 5$ times and not more than $2 \cdot 5$ times the weight of silicon compounds; and (*d*) of which not less than 35 per cent. by weight is retained by a sieve having a nominal width of aperture of $\frac{3}{16}$ inch (until 1st July 1971)

28.24   Cobaltous hydroxide (until 1st July 1971)

28.51   Deuterated potassium dihydrogen orthophosphate in the form of single crystals (until 1st July 1971)

28.52   Mixed rare earth chlorides which, when precipitated as oxalates and calcined, yield not less than 45 per cent. by weight of rare earth oxides, of which the content of cerium expressed as CeO_2 is not less than 45 per cent. by weight and the content of samarium expressed as Sm_2O_3 is not more than 3 per cent. by weight (until 1st July 1971)

29.06   Sodium biphenyl-2-yloxide (until 4th May 1971)
            3,5-Xylenol (until 4th May 1971)

29.14   Undec-10-enoic acid (until 4th May 1971)

29.15   Oxalic acid

29.16   Calcium lactate

29.25   3,4,4'-Trichloro-*NN'*-diphenylurea (until 1st July 1971)

29.31   Dithiocyanatomethane having a melting point not less than 100° centigrade (until 4th May 1971)

29.44   Rifamycin B diethylamide, *mono*sodium derivative

39.01   Nylon 6 in the forms covered by Note 3(*b*) of Chapter 39, containing not more than 2 per cent. by weight of titanium dioxide and not more than $2 \cdot 5$ per cent. by weight of carbon black, but not otherwise compounded (until 4th May 1971)

39.03   Scrap exposed X-ray film (until 4th May 1971)

Tariff Heading	*Description*

73.15   Alloy steel coils for re-rolling, which contain not less than 14 per cent. nor more than 18 per cent. by weight of chromium as the major alloying element, and not more than 0·5 per cent. by weight of nickel, and having a width exceeding 500 millimetres but not more than 1,372 millimetres, and a thickness of not less than 3 millimetres nor more than 6 millimetres (until 1st July 1971)

Hot rolled alloy steel strip in coils, containing not less than 14 per cent. by weight nor more than 18 per cent. by weight of chromium as the major alloying element, and not more than 0·5 per cent. by weight of nickel, of a width of not less than 254 millimetres nor more than 500 millimetres and of a thickness of not less than 3 millimetres nor more than 6 millimetres (until 1st July 1971)

Sheets of alloy steel, rectangular or in coils, containing not more than 3·5 per cent. by weight of silicon as the major alloying element, whether or not coated, of a width exceeding 500 millimetres but not more than 1,250 millimetres, of a thickness not exceeding 1·6 millimetres (until 4th May 1971)

81.04   Chromium, electrolytic, in the form of cathode chips, which contains not more than 0·10 per cent. by weight of total oxygen, not more than 0·015 per cent. by weight of total aluminium, and not more than 0·001 per cent. by weight of aluminium compounds insoluble in boiling 5N hydrochloric acid and in boiling fuming perchloric acid, and estimated as Al (until 4th May 1971)

EXPLANATORY NOTE

(*This Note is not part of the Order.*)

This Order provides that the goods listed in Schedule 1 shall be temporarily exempt from import duty, and those listed in Schedule 2 shall continue to be exempt from import duty, both until 1st January 1972, except for items for which an earlier day is specified.

STATUTORY   INSTRUMENTS

1971 No. 274

CUSTOMS AND EXCISE

The Import Duty Drawbacks (No. 1) Order 1971

Made - - - -	22nd February 1971
Laid before the	
House of Commons	26th February 1971
Coming into Operation	4th March 1971

The Lords Commissioners of Her Majesty's Treasury, by virtue of the powers conferred on them by sections 9 and 13 of, and Schedule 5 to, the Import Duties Act 1958(a) and section 2(5) of the Finance Act 1965(b), and of all other powers enabling them in that behalf, on the recommendation of the Secretary of State hereby make the following Order:—

1.—(1) This Order may be cited as the Import Duty Drawbacks (No. 1) Order 1971.

(2) The Interpretation Act 1889(c) shall apply for the interpretation of this Order as it applies for the interpretation of an Act of Parliament.

(3) In this Order " the principal Act " means the Import Duties Act 1958.

(4) This Order shall come into operation on 4th March 1971.

2.—(1) As respects import duty paid on any imported articles which on importation fell to be classified under any of the headings of the Customs Tariff 1959 listed in Schedule 1 to this Order, drawback shall be allowed in accordance with paragraph 2 of Schedule 5 to the principal Act on the exportation of the imported articles or goods incorporating the imported articles, but so that drawback under any entry in the said Schedule 1 shall be subject to the restrictions (if any) provided for in column 2 in that entry.

(2) Where in any entry in the said Schedule 1 the drawback is expressed in column 2 to be, or not to be, allowable for goods of a specified description, this is to be taken (unless the context otherwise requires) as restricting accordingly the description of imported articles in respect of which drawback may be allowed.

(3) Any reference in column 2 of the said Schedule 1 to a rate of duty shall, in a case where the imported articles were chargeable with duty at a preferential rate as being goods qualifying for Commonwealth preference or eligible for a Convention rate of duty within the meaning of the European Free Trade Association Act 1960(d), be construed as a reference to the full rate.

(4) No drawback of any duty shall be allowed by virtue of this Article if drawback in respect of that duty is allowable by virtue of Article 3 of this Order.

(a) 1958 c. 6.   (b) 1965 c. 25.   (c) 1889 c. 63.   (d) 1960 c. 19.

3.—(1) On the exportation of goods of a description mentioned in column 1 in any entry in Schedule 2 to this Order, being goods produced or manufactured from imported articles of any description mentioned in relation to those goods in column 2 in that entry, drawback as respects import duty paid on the imported articles shall be allowed in accordance with paragraph 3 of Schedule 5 to the principal Act and with the following provisions of this Article.

(2) Drawback under any entry in Schedule 2 to this Order shall, if a rate is shown in column 3 in that entry, be at that rate; and the quantity by reference to which any rate of drawback is stated is (according to the context) the quantity of the exported goods or the quantity actually contained in the exported goods of goods of the specified description, being either the imported articles or goods produced or manufactured from the imported articles.

(3) Where in the case of any entry in Schedule 2 to this Order no rate of drawback is specified in column 3, drawback under that entry shall be of an amount equal to the duty appearing to the Commissioners of Customs and Excise to have been paid in respect of the quantity of the imported articles which in their opinion has been used in the production or manufacture of the exported goods.

(4) Paragraph 3(2)(*a*) of Schedule 5 to the principal Act (under which, except in so far as an order provides to the contrary, rates of drawback in respect of duty on imported articles charged at a preferential rate are to be proportionately reduced) shall not apply to drawback on the exportation of goods of any description specified in Schedule 3 to this Order.

(5) The provisions of Schedule 4 to this Order shall have effect in relation to drawback under such of the entries in Schedule 2 to this Order as are specified in the said Schedule 4 (being entries relating to textiles and textile articles).

4. The Import Duty Drawbacks Orders specified in Schedule 5 to this Order are hereby revoked.

V. H. Goodhew,
Bernard Weatherill,
Two of the Lords Commissioners
of Her Majesty's Treasury.

22nd February 1971.

SCHEDULE 1

DRAWBACKS ON EXPORTATION OF IMPORTED ARTICLES OR OF GOODS INCORPORATING
IMPORTED ARTICLES

Tariff headings comprising imported articles for which drawback is allowable	*Restrictions on drawback*

Animal products

02.01 and 02.06 (meat and edible meat offals).	Allowable for beef and veal and edible offals of beef and veal; but, for boned or boneless beef or veal or edible offals of beef or veal, imported as such, allowable only on the exportation of the imported articles in the packages in which they were imported.
03.02 (fish, salted, in brine, dried or smoked).	Allowable for dried salted split fish.
04.06 (natural honey).	Allowable for honey which has been blended before exportation.

Vegetable products

07.05 (dried leguminous vegetables).	Allowable for seeds of a kind used for sowing.
08.02 (citrus fruit).	Allowable for fresh grapefruit and fresh oranges; but, for fresh oranges, allowable only on their exportation in the packages in which they were imported.
10.02 to 10.05 and 10.07 (cereals).	Allowable for seeds of a kind used for sowing.
12.01 (oil seeds and oleaginous fruit).	Allowable for groundnuts, whether decorticated or not.
12.03 (seeds, fruit and spores, of a kind used for sowing).	—
12.06 (hop cones and lupulin).	Allowable for hops, but only on their exportation in the packages in which they were imported.
14.01 (vegetable materials of a kind used primarily for plaiting).	Allowable for bamboos and rattans, whether or not washed, cut to length, sorted, split or bleached, but not further prepared.
20.07 (fruit juices).	Allowable for lemon juice not containing added sweetening matter.

Products of the chemical and allied industries

28.06 (hydrochloric acid and chlorosulphonic acid).	Allowable for hydrochloric acid of analytical reagent quality.
28.08 (sulphuric acid; oleum).	Allowable for sulphuric acid of analytical reagent quality.
28.09 (nitric acid; sulphonitric acids).	Allowable for nitric acid of analytical reagent quality.
28.10 and 28.11 (phosphorus pentoxide and phosphoric acids; arsenic trioxide and pentoxide, and acids of arsenic).	Allowable for goods for which the rate of duty under the relevant heading was an ad valorem rate of $12\frac{1}{2}$ per cent. or over.
28.12 (boric oxide and boric acid).	Allowable for boric oxide.

Tariff headings comprising imported articles for which drawback is allowable	*Restrictions on drawback*
28.13 (other inorganic acids, and oxygen compounds of non-metals).	Allowable for goods for which the rate of duty was an ad valorem rate of $12\frac{1}{2}$ per cent. or over, and for hydrofluoric acid of analytical reagent quality.
28.14 and 28.15 (halogen compounds of non-metals; sulphides of non-metals, and phosphorus trisulphide).	Allowable for goods for which the rate of duty under the relevant heading was an ad valorem rate of $12\frac{1}{2}$ per cent. or over.
28.17 (sodium hydroxide, potassium hydroxide, etc.).	Allowable for potassium hydroxide of pharmaceutical quality, for solid potassium hydroxide of a purity of not less than 88 per cent. and not more than 92 per cent., and for sodium peroxide.
28.18 (oxides, etc., of strontium, barium or magnesium).	Allowable for goods for which the rate of duty was an ad valorem rate of $12\frac{1}{2}$ per cent. or over, and for magnesium oxide of pharmaceutical quality.
28.19 (zinc oxide and peroxide).	Allowable for zinc peroxide.
28.20 (aluminium oxide and hydroxide; artificial corundum).	Allowable for aluminium oxide of analytical reagent quality.
28.21 (chromium oxides and hydroxides).	Not allowable for chromic oxide.
28.24 (cobalt oxides and hydroxides).	Allowable for cobalt hydroxides.
28.27 (lead oxides; red lead and orange lead).	Allowable for lead dioxide, and for lead monoxide of pharmaceutical quality.
28.28 (hydrazine and hydroxylamine, etc.).	Allowable for goods for which the rate of duty was an ad valorem rate of $12\frac{1}{2}$ per cent. or over, for germanium dioxide, and for cupric oxide of analytical reagent quality.
28.29 (fluorides, etc.).	Allowable for goods for which the rate of duty was an ad valorem rate of $12\frac{1}{2}$ per cent. or over.
28.30 (chlorides and oxide chlorides).	Allowable— (*a*) for goods for which the rate of duty was an ad valorem rate of $12\frac{1}{2}$ per cent. or over, but not including ammonium chloride not of pharmaceutical quality or calcium chloride not of pharmaceutical quality; (*b*) for the following chlorides if of analytical reagent quality—barium, ferric or ferrous, magnesium, manganous, and stannic or stannous.
28.32 (chlorates and perchlorates).	Not allowable— (*a*) for the following chlorates—ammonium, barium, potassium or sodium; (*b*) for the following perchlorates—ferrous, lead, lithium, magnesium, potassium or sodium.
28.33 and 28.34 (bromides, etc.; iodides, etc.).	Allowable for goods for which the rate of duty under the relevant heading was an ad valorem rate of $12\frac{1}{2}$ per cent. or over.

Tariff headings comprising imported articles for which drawback is allowable	*Restrictions on drawback*
28.35 (sulphides: polysulphides).	Allowable— (*a*) for goods for which the rate of duty was an ad valorem rate of 12½ per cent. or over, but not including antimony pentasulphide, antimony trisulphide, cadmium sulphide, mercuric sulphide (red), or zinc sulphide; (*b*) for sodium sulphide of analytical reagent quality.
28.36 (dithionites; sulphoxylates).	Allowable for goods for which the rate of duty was an ad valorem rate of 12½ per cent. or over.
28.37 (sulphites and thiosulphates).	Allowable for goods for which the rate of duty was an ad valorem rate of 12½ per cent. or over, and for sodium sulphite of analytical reagent quality.
28.38 (sulphates and persulphates).	Allowable— (*a*) for goods for which the rate of duty was an ad valorem rate of 12½ per cent. or over, but not including barium sulphate not of pharmaceutical quality, calcium sulphate or basic lead sulphate; (*b*) for the following sulphates if of pharmaceutical quality—aluminium ammonium, aluminium potassium, ferric or ferrous, magnesium, sodium and zinc; (*c*) for the following sulphates if of analytical reagent quality—aluminium, cupric or cuprous, manganic or manganous, potassium and sodium hydrogen.
28.39 (nitrites and nitrates).	Allowable— (*a*) for goods for which the rate of duty was an ad valorem rate of 12½ per cent. or over, but not including synthetic sodium nitrate; (*b*) for lead nitrate if of analytical reagent quality; (*c*) for sodium nitrite if of analytical reagent quality.
28.40 (phosphites, hypophosphites and phosphates).	Allowable for goods for which the rate of duty was an ad valorem rate of 12½ per cent. or over, for *di*ammonium hydrogen orthophosphate of analytical reagent quality, and for *di*sodium hydrogen orthophosphate of pharmaceutical quality.
28.41 (arsenites and arsenates).	Allowable for goods for which the rate of duty was an ad valorem rate of 12½ per cent. or over, and for sodium arsenate of analytical reagent quality.

Tariff headings comprising imported articles for which drawback is allowable	*Restrictions on drawback*
28.42 (carbonates and percarbonates).	Allowable— (a) for goods for which the rate of duty was an ad valorem rate of 12½ per cent. or over, but not including barium carbonate not of analytical reagent quality, basic copper carbonates or basic lead carbonate; (b) for the following carbonates if of analytical reagent quality—barium, calcium, potassium and sodium; (c) for sodium hydrogen carbonate of pharmaceutical quality.
28.43 (cyanides and complex cyanides).	Allowable— (a) for goods for which the rate of duty was an ad valorem rate of 12½ per cent. or over, but not including ferric ferrocyanide or ferrous ferricyanide; (b) for the following if of analytical reagent quality—potassium cyanide and potassium ferrocyanide.
28.44 (fulminates, cyanates and thiocyanates).	Allowable for goods for which the rate of duty was an ad valorem rate of 12½ per cent. or over.
28.45 (silicates).	Allowable for the following silicates—barium, cadmium, chromic or chromous, cobalt, cupric or cuprous, lead, magnesium, manganic or manganous, nickel, strontium and zinc.
28.46 (borates and perborates).	Allowable for goods for which the rate of duty was an ad valorem rate of 12½ per cent. or over, but not including hydrated *di*sodium tetraborate such that, if reduced to the dry anhydrous form, it would be of a purity not less than 99 per cent.
28.47 (salts of metallic acids).	Allowable— (a) for goods for which the rate of duty was an ad valorem rate of 12½ per cent. or over, but not including cobalt aluminate, cobalt zincate, lead chromate, basic lead chromate, lead titanate, zinc chromate or zinc tetroxychromate; (b) for potassium dichromate of analytical reagent quality.
28.48 (other salts, etc., of inorganic acids).	Allowable for goods for which the rate of duty was an ad valorem rate of 12½ per cent. or over, but not including ammonium cobalt phosphate.
28.49 to 28.52 (colloidal precious metals, etc.; fissile chemical elements and isotopes, etc.; compounds of thorium, uranium, etc.).	Allowable for goods for which the rate of duty under the relevant heading was an ad valorem rate of 12½ per cent. or over.
28.55 to 28.57 (phosphides; carbides; hydrides, etc.).	Allowable for goods for which the rate of duty under the relevant heading was an ad valorem rate of 12½ per cent. or over.

Tariff headings comprising imported articles for which drawback is allowable	Restrictions on drawback
28.58 (other inorganic compounds).	Allowable for goods for which the rate of duty was an ad valorem rate of 12½ per cent. or over, but not including lead cyanamide.
All headings of Chapter 29 (organic chemicals).	Allowable— (a) for goods for which the rate of duty under the relevant heading was an ad valorem rate of 12½ per cent. or over, or the greater of such an ad valorem rate and a specific rate, but not including 1,6-hexanolactam, emetine and its salts, nicotine or nicotine sulphate; (b) for amidopyrin, buta-1,2-diene and buta-1,3-diene; (c) for caffein and its salts; (d) for theobromine and its salts; (e) for the following if of analytical reagent quality—benzene, cupric or cuprous acetate and sodium acetate.
30.03 (medicaments).	Allowable for unmixed products which, if not put up in measured doses or in forms or in packings of a kind sold by retail for therapeutic or prophylactic purposes, would be classified in Chapter 28 or Chapter 29, and would be eligible for drawback.
30.04 (wadding, gauze, bandages and similar medical or surgical dressings, etc.).	Allowable for wadding containing more than 33⅓ per cent. by weight of man-made fibres.
37.02 (unexposed photographic film).	Allowable for film of a length of 12 feet or more.
37.07 (exposed and developed cinematograph film not consisting only of sound track).	—
38.03 (activated carbon and certain activated mineral products).	Allowable for activated carbon, not being of animal origin.
38.11 (disinfectants, insecticides, etc.).	Allowable for unmixed products which, if not put up as mentioned in heading 38.11, would be classified in Chapter 28 or in Chapter 29, and would be eligible for drawback.

Articles of plastic and other artificial materials, or of rubber

39.01 (condensation, poly-condensation and poly-addition products).	Allowable for polyoxymethylenes in the form of granules, being poly-addition products of not less than 90 per cent. by weight of formaldehyde and not being plasticised or otherwise compounded.
39.02 (polymerisation and co-polymerisation products).	Allowable for poly(vinyl chloride) tape nor exceeding ¾ inch in width, 15/1,000 inch in thickness or 36 feet in length, whether or not backed with adhesive.

Tariff headings comprising imported articles for which drawback is allowable	*Restrictions on drawback*
39.07 (articles of artificial resins or plastic materials, or of cellulose esters or ethers).	Allowable— (*a*) for articles of apparel (finished, unfinished, complete or incomplete) and for material cut to shape for making into apparel; (*b*) for objects of personal adornment; (*c*) for book ends; (*d*) for cigar and cigarette cases and boxes; (*e*) for clock and watch glasses; (*f*) for fancy blotters; (*g*) for inkstands; (*h*) for photograph frames; (*i*) for plastic combined bottle-stoppers and screw adaptors, but only on the exportation of lamp adaptors, of a kind suitable for the conversion of bottles into table lamps, incorporating such articles; (*j*) for powder bowls and boxes; (*k*) for receptacles imported as part of a brush, comb and mirror set; (*l*) for rosaries the beads of which are of plastic; (*m*) for smokers' ash receptacles; (*n*) for components for hand-operated appliances embodying a blade and working edge of base metal, and used for making labels or name-plates from plastic or metal strip, otherwise than by stamping the whole legend simultaneously; but not allowable, in the case of the articles referred to at (*d*) and (*j*) above, on the exportation of goods incorporating those articles as, or as part of, the packing, container or get-up of the goods.
40.06 (unvulcanised rubber in certain forms, and articles thereof).	Allowable for impregnated thread containing more than 10 per cent. by weight of silk, of man-made fibres, or of both together.
40.10 (transmission, conveyor or elevator belts or belting, of vulcanised rubber).	Allowable for goods containing man-made fibres.
40.11 (rubber tyres, tyre cases, inner tubes and tyre flaps).	—
40.13 (articles of apparel, etc., of unhardened vulcanised rubber).	—
40.14 (certain articles of unhardened vulcanised rubber).	Allowable— (*a*) for polychlorobutadiene impellers and shaft seals for self-priming flexible vane impeller pumps; (*b*) for components for hand-operated appliances embodying a blade and working edge of base metal, and used for making

Tariff headings comprising imported articles for which drawback is allowable	Restrictions on drawback

labels or nameplates from plastic or metal strip, otherwise than by stamping the whole legend simultaneously;

(c) for shock, sound and vibration damping devices consisting of bellows of synthetic rubber based on nylon fabric anchored at each end to a steel bead wire, being devices which on exportation are incorporated in machinery.

Leather and furskin, and articles of descriptions commonly made thereof

41.02 to 41.08 (leather). —

42.02 (travel goods and other cases or containers of leather or certain other materials).

Allowable—

(a) for cases, made wholly or partly of leather or material resembling leather, for musical instruments;

(b) for cigar and cigarette cases and boxes;

(c) for pocket wallets and for purses;

(d) for receptacles imported as part of a brush, comb and mirror set;

(e) for tobacco pouches;

(f) for transparent plastic pass-holders which, on exportation, are incorporated in wallets or billfolds;

(g) for women's handbags;

but not allowable, in the case of the articles referred to at (b), (c) and (e) above, on the exportation of goods incorporating those articles as, or as part of, the packing, container or get-up of the goods.

42.03 (articles of apparel, etc., of leather or of composition leather). —

42.04 (articles of leather of a kind used in machinery, etc.).

Allowable—

(a) for leather drafting bands of a kind used for textile machinery;

(b) for leather picking bands and tuggers.

42.05 (miscellaneous articles of leather or of composition leather).

Allowable for fancy blotters.

43.02 (furskins, tanned or dressed, and pieces thereof).

Allowable for furskins, tanned or dressed, not assembled.

43.03 (articles of furskin).

Allowable—

(a) for articles of apparel (finished or unfinished, complete or incomplete);

(b) for material cut to shape for making into apparel;

(c) for picking bands and tuggers.

43.04 (artificial fur and articles thereof).

Allowable for articles of apparel (finished or unfinished, complete or incomplete) and for material cut to shape for making into apparel.

Tariff headings comprising imported articles for which drawback is allowable	*Restrictions on drawback*

Wood and cork and articles thereof

44.03 to 44.08, 44.10, 44.13 and 44.14 (wood in various forms, not more than partly manufactured, wood paving blocks, railway and tramway sleepers of wood, veneer sheets and sheets for plywood).	Not allowable, in the case of heading 44.08 except for riven staves not further prepared. Not allowable, in the case of heading 44.14, except for veneer sheets and sheets for plywood, of a thickness not exceeding 5 mm.
44.15 (plywood and other laminated or inlaid wood products and the like).	Allowable for plywood, blockboard, laminboard and battenboard, containing no material other than wood and bonding material.
44.20 (wooden picture and photograph frames and the like).	Allowable for photograph frames.
44.21 (complete wooden packing cases, boxes, etc.).	Allowable for boxes of softwood boxboards not dovetailed, mortised or tenoned at the ends and not exceeding 22 inches in length, 11 inches in breadth, and 5¾ inches in depth, imported complete but unassembled; but allowable only on the exportation in the boxes of fresh or cured whole or filleted fish, other than shell-fish.
44.24 (household utensils of wood).	—
44.25 (wooden tools, tool bodies, tool handles and certain other articles of wood).	Allowable— (a) for tools; (b) for axe handles of the bent fawn foot type, not less than 24 inches in length; (c) for matchet handles; (d) for sticks of rectangular cross-section throughout, not more than 1 inch in width nor more than ¼ inch in thickness, and not more than 9 inches or less than 3 inches in length.
44.27 (certain articles of wood of a domestic, personal or ornamental kind).	Allowable— (a) for articles of personal adornment; (b) for book-ends; (c) for cigar and cigarette cases and boxes; (d) for inkstands; (e) for rosaries the beads of which are of wood; but not allowable, in the case of the articles referred to at (c) above, on the exportation of goods incorporating those articles as, or as part of, the packing, container or get-up of the goods.
44.28 (miscellaneous articles of wood).	Allowable— (a) for tops of bottle stoppers, but only on the exportation as such of bottle stoppers consisting wholly or partly of the imported top joined to a cork; (b) for curved handles pierced transversely at each end for attachment purposes, of a size and shape adapted for use in suitcases or attaché cases;

Tariff headings comprising imported articles for which drawback is allowable	Restrictions on drawback
	(c) for parts of matchet handles;
	(d) for spoons, flat, not more than 6 inches in length and not more than $\frac{1}{8}$ inch in thickness;
	(e) for sticks of circular cross-section throughout, not more than $\frac{1}{4}$ inch in diameter, and not more than 6 inches or less than 2 inches in length;
	(f) for sticks of rectangular cross-section throughout, not more than 1 inch in width nor more than $\frac{1}{4}$ inch in thickness, and not more than 9 inches or less than 3 inches in length;
	but not allowable, in the case of the articles referred to at (b) above, on the exportation of goods incorporating those articles as part of the packing, container or get-up of the goods.
45.03 and 45.04 (articles of cork and agglomerated cork).	Allowable for corks, being parts of bottle stoppers, but only on the exportation as such of bottle stoppers consisting wholly or partly of the imported cork joined to a top.

Articles of paper and paperboard

48.16 (boxes, bags and other packing containers, of paper or paperboard).	Allowable for waxed paper cartons, with inner lid and closure cap, of a capacity of not less than 12 and not more than 13 fluid oz., or not less than 25 and not more than 26 fluid oz., but only on the exportation of syrup in the cartons.
48.18 (registers, exercise books, note books, blotting-pads, etc., of paper or paperboard).	Allowable for fancy blotters.
48.21 (miscellaneous articles of paper pulp, paper, paperboard or cellulose wadding).	Allowable for rolled paper sticks of circular cross-section throughout, not more than $\frac{1}{4}$ inch in diameter, and not more than 6 inches and not less than 2 inches in length.

Textiles and textile articles

50.03 (silk waste).	Allowable for goods containing more than $33\frac{1}{3}$ per cent. by weight of man-made fibres.
50.04 to 50.10 (silk yarn, silk-worm gut and imitation catgut of silk, and woven silk fabrics).	—
51.01 to 51.04 (yarn and the like, and woven fabrics, of man-made fibres, continuous).	—
52.01 (metalised yarn).	Allowable for goods containing more than $33\frac{1}{3}$ per cent. by weight of silk, of man-made fibres, or of both together.

Tariff headings comprising imported articles for which drawback is allowable	*Restrictions on drawback*
52.02 (woven fabrics of metal thread or of metalised yarn, of a kind used in articles of apparel, as furnishing fabrics or the like).	—
53.03 (waste of sheep's or lambs' wool or of other animal hair, not pulled or garnetted).	—
53.04 (waste of sheep's or lambs' wool or of other animal hair, pulled or garnetted).	Allowable for goods containing more than 33⅓ per cent. by weight of man-made fibres.
53.06 to 53.10 (yarn of sheep's or lambs' wool or of other animal hair).	Allowable for goods containing silk or man-made fibres.
53.11 to 53.13 (woven fabrics of sheep's or lambs' wool or of other animal hair).	—
54.01 (flax, flax tow and flax waste).	Allowable for flax, flax tow or flax waste not hackled, carded or combed.
54.02 (ramie, ramie noils and ramie waste).	Allowable for ramie, ramie noils or ramie waste not carded or combed.
54.03 and 54.04 (flax or ramie yarn).	Allowable for yarn containing silk or man-made fibres.
54.05 (woven fabrics of flax or ramie).	—
55.03 (cotton waste, not carded or combed).	—
55.05 and 55.06 (cotton yarn).	Allowable for yarn containing silk or man-made fibres.
55.07 to 55.09 (woven fabrics of cotton).	—
All headings of Chapter 56 (man-made fibres, discontinuous, and yarn and fabrics thereof).	—
57.01 and 57.03 (true hemp, jute, and tow and waste thereof).	Allowable for hemp or jute, or tow or waste thereof, not carded or combed.
57.04 (miscellaneous vegetable textile fibres and waste thereof).	Allowable for goods, not carded or combed, containing more than 33⅓ per cent. by weight of man-made fibres.
57.05 to 57.07 (yarn of true hemp, jute and miscellaneous vegetable textile fibres).	Allowable for yarn containing man-made fibres.
57.09 to 57.11 (woven fabrics of true hemp, jute and miscellaneous vegetable textile fibres).	—

Tariff headings comprising imported articles for which drawback is allowable	Restrictions on drawback
57.12 (woven fabrics of paper yarn).	Allowable for woven fabric of a weight not exceeding 12 oz. to the square yard, made either entirely from paper yarn, whether treated with cellulose solution or not, or from such material with the addition of one or more strands of other material in the selvedge.
All headings of Chapter 58 (carpets, etc., and tapestries; pile and chenille fabrics; narrow fabrics; tulle and other net fabrics; lace; embroidery).	Not allowable for chenille or gimped yarns of heading 58.07 not containing silk or man-made fibres.
All headings of Chapter 59 (wadding and felt; twine, cordage, etc.; special fabrics; impregnated and coated fabrics; textile articles of industrial use.)	Not allowable for goods of heading 59.01 (wadding, flock, etc.) not containing more than 10 per cent. by weight of man-made fibres.

Not allowable for the following goods of heading 59.03—

(a) bonded fibre fabrics, impregnated or coated with rubber or in which rubber forms the bonding substance, which contain 50 per cent. or more by weight of non-textile material and 10 per cent. or less by weight of man-made fibres;

(b) articles of bonded fibre fabrics impregnated or coated with rubber or in which rubber forms the bonding substance which contain 50 per cent. or more by weight of non-textile material;

(c) rubber adhesive goods with backings of bonded fibre fabrics, being goods which contain 50 per cent. or more by weight of non-textile material.

Not allowable for goods of heading 59.04 (twine, cordage, etc.) not containing silk or man-made fibres.

Not allowable, in the case of articles of any of headings 59.01 to 59.05 (wadding, etc., felt, bonded fibre fabrics, twine, cordage, etc., and nets and netting), on the exportation of goods incorporating them as, or as part of, the packing, container or get-up of the goods.

Not allowable for the following goods of heading 59.11, namely, woven textile fabrics, impregnated, coated, covered or laminated with rubber, which contain 50 per cent. or more by weight of rubber.

Not allowable for the following goods of heading 59.17, namely, articles of woven textile fabrics, impregnated, coated, covered or laminated with rubber, which contain 50 per cent. or more by weight of rubber.

Tariff headings comprising imported articles for which drawback is allowable	*Restrictions on drawback*
All headings of Chapter 60 (knitted and crocheted goods).	—
All headings of Chapter 61 (articles of apparel, etc., of textile fabrics, other than knitted and crocheted goods).	—
62.01 and 62.02 (travelling rugs and blankets; household linen and textile furnishings).	—
62.03 and 62.04 (sacks and bags of a kind used for the packing of goods; tarpaulins, sails, awnings, sunblinds, tents and camping goods).	Allowable for articles containing more than 5 per cent. by weight of silk, of man-made fibres, or of both together; but not allowable on the exportation of goods incorporating the articles as, or as part of, the packing, container or get-up of the goods.
62.05 (miscellaneous made-up textile articles).	Allowable— (*a*) for articles containing more than 5 per cent. by weight of silk, of man-made fibres, or of both together; (*b*) for boot, shoe, corset and similar laces.
Both headings of Chapter 63 (old clothing, etc., and rags).	—

Footwear, headgear and miscellaneous articles of kinds suitable for personal use

64.01 to 64.04 (footwear).	—
64.05 (parts of footwear).	Allowable for shoe uppers incorporating woven strips of leather, whether or not containing furskin, on the exportation of shoes incorporating such shoe uppers.
All headings of Chapter 65 (headgear and parts thereof).	—
66.01 (umbrellas and sunshades).	Allowable for goods with covers or cases containing silk or man-made fibres.
67.02 (artificial flowers, foliage or fruit).	Allowable for artificial flowers, foliage or fruit, and for articles made of artificial flowers, foliage or fruit.
67.04 (wigs and other false hair, and other articles of human hair).	Allowable for hair nets.

Articles of stone, plaster, cement, asbestos, mica and similar materials; ceramic products; glass and glassware

68.04 and 68.05 (millstones, grindstones, etc. and hand polishing stones, whetstones, oil stones, etc.).	—
68.13 (fabricated asbestos and articles thereof, etc.).	Allowable for wheels of corrugated asbestos paper.
68.14 (friction material of a kind suitable for brakes, clutches or the like, with a basis of asbestos, other mineral substances or cellulose).	—

Tariff headings comprising imported articles for which drawback is allowable	Restrictions on drawback
69.03 (miscellaneous refractory goods).	Allowable for laboratory wares, but not on the exportation of goods incorporating those wares as, or as part of, the packing, container or get-up of the goods.
69.09 (laboratory, chemical or industrial wares of ceramics, and certain other articles).	Allowable for laboratory wares, but not on the exportation of goods incorporating those wares as, or as part of, the packing, container or get-up of the goods.
69.11, 69.12 and 69.13 (tableware and other articles of a kind commonly used for domestic or toilet purposes, of porcelain, china or other pottery; certain ornaments and furniture of ceramic).	Not allowable on the exportation of goods incorporating the imported articles as, or as part of, the packing, container or get-up of the goods, and not allowable in respect of any exportation on or after 1st January 1972.
70.03 (glass in balls, rods and tubes, unworked, not being optical glass).	Allowable for tubing of a kind suitable for use for scientific purposes.
70.06 (cast, rolled, drawn or blown glass in rectangles, surface ground or polished, but not further worked).	Allowable for heat-absorbing glass, surface ground and polished on both faces, and having the properties of either of the categories specified in paragraph 23 of British Standard 952:1964, being glass imported in rectangles of 10 feet or more in length and 7½ feet or more in width.
70.08 (safety glass consisting of toughened or laminated glass).	Allowable for safety glass in sizes and shapes ready for incorporation in motor vehicles.
70.09 (glass mirrors).	Allowable for hand mirrors, and for rear-view mirrors suitable for cycles or motor vehicles.
70.10 (certain containers of glass).	Allowable for syphon vases, but not on the exportation of goods incorporating the syphon vase as, or as part of, the packing, container or get-up of the goods.
70.11 (glass envelopes for electric lamps, etc.).	Allowable for glass envelopes other than those for filament lamps or for mercury arc rectifiers of the mercury pool cathode type.
70.12 (glass inners for vacuum flasks, etc.).	—
70.13 (glassware of a kind commonly used for table, kitchen, toilet or office purposes, for indoor decoration or similar uses).	Not allowable on the exportation of goods incorporating the imported articles as, or as part of, the packing, container or get-up of the goods, and not allowable in respect of any exportation on or after 1st January 1972.
70.14 (illuminating glassware, signalling glassware and optical elements of glass).	Allowable for illuminating glassware of a kind commonly used for table, kitchen, toilet or office purposes, for indoor decoration, or for similar uses, but not allowable on the exportation of goods incorporating any such articles as, or as part of, the packing, container or get-up of the goods, and not allowable in respect of any exportation on or after 1st January 1972.

Tariff headings comprising imported articles for which drawback is allowable	*Restrictions on drawback*
70.15 (clock and watch glasses and similar glasses).	Allowable for clock and watch glasses.
70.17 (laboratory, hygenic and pharmaceutical glassware, and glass ampoules).	Allowable for laboratory glassware and for glass ampoules; but not allowable on the exportation of goods incorporating the imported article as, or as part of, the packing, container or get-up of the goods.
70.18 (optical glass and elements of optical glass, other than optically worked elements; blanks for corrective spectacle lenses).	Allowable for optical glass and elements of optical glass.
70.19 (glass beads, imitation pearls, etc., and other decorative glass smallwares and articles thereof).	Allowable for articles wholly or partly of glass beads, and for objects of personal adornment.
70.21 (other articles of glass).	Allowable for face plates, cones or necks. being parts of glass envelopes for cathode ray tubes.

Jewellery, etc.

71.02 and 71.03 (unmounted precious and semi-precious stones, natural, synthetic or reconstructed).	—
71.12 (articles of jewellery and parts thereof of precious metal or rolled precious metal).	Allowable for buttons, but not on the exportation of goods (other than goods consisting only of buttons and any packing, container and get-up thereof) incorporating buttons.
71.15 (articles consisting of or incorporating pearls or precious or semi-precious stones).	Allowable— (a) for buttons, but not on the exportation of goods (other than goods consisting only of buttons and any packing, container and get-up thereof) incorporating buttons; (b) for cultured blister pearls (Mabe pearls), sorted and graded, but not on the exportation of the imported articles after they have been subjected to any process other than sorting and grading or of goods (other than goods consisting only of the imported articles and any packing, container and get-up thereof) incorporating the imported articles.
71.16 (imitation jewellery).	—

Base metals and articles of base metal

73.02 (ferro-alloys).	Allowable for ferro-molybdenum, for ferro-titanium containing not more than 2 per cent. by weight of carbon, for ferro-tungsten and for ferro-vanadium.
73.15 (alloy steel, etc.).	Allowable for stainless steel tape not exceeding $\frac{1}{2}$ inch in width, 6/1,000 inch in thickness or 21 feet in length, whether or not backed with adhesive.

Tariff headings comprising imported articles for which drawback is allowable	*Restrictions on drawback*
73.20 (tube and pipe fittings of iron or steel).	Allowable for specialised parts of aircraft, motor vehicles or machinery.
73.29 (chain and parts thereof of iron or steel).	Allowable for specialised parts of aircraft, motor vehicles or machinery.
73.32 (bolts, nuts, screws, rivets, etc. of iron or steel).	Allowable for specialised parts of aircraft, motor vehicles, clocks and watches, or machinery and for bolts, nuts and screws which are incorporated on exportation in complete hand-operated appliances embodying a blade and working edge of base metal, and used for making labels or name-plates from plastic or metal tape otherwise than by stamping the whole legend simultaneously.
73.35 (springs and leaves for springs of iron or steel).	Allowable for specialised parts of aircraft, motor vehicles or machinery and for springs which are incorporated on exportation in complete hand-operated appliances embodying a blade and working edge of base metal, and used for making labels or name-plates from plastic or metal tape otherwise than by stamping the whole legend simultaneously.
73.37 (boilers, radiators and other appliances for room heating, not electrically heated).	Not allowable except for air heaters and hot air distributors (including those which can also distribute cool or conditioned air) not designed for connection to a central heating system.
73.40 (miscellaneous articles of iron or steel).	Allowable—

    (*a*) for electrical insulator parts, being insulator caps of galvanised steel, but only on the exportation as such of electrical insulators of glass and metal incorporating the caps;

    (*b*) for ladies' handbag frames, but only on the exportation as such of ladies' handbags incorporating the frames;

    (*c*) for empty ribbon spools adapted for use in typewriters (including electric typewriters), accounting, adding, listing, book-keeping and billing machines, cash registers, weighing machines or time recorders and for parts of such spools;

    (*d*) for steel key-plates, brassed and lacquered and with a sliding bar, but without hooks or loops, being key-plates which on exportation are incorporated in key containers;

    (*e*) for spherical-headed hooks and loops which on exportation are incorporated in key containers;

Tariff headings comprising imported articles for which drawback is allowable	Restrictions on drawback
	(f) for articles which are incorporated on exportation in complete hand-operated appliances embodying a blade and working edge of base metal, and used for making labels or nameplates from plastic or metal tape otherwise than by stamping the whole legend simultaneously.
74.04 (wrought plates, sheets and strip, of copper).	Allowable for copper tape not exceeding ½ inch in width, 8/1,000 inch in thickness or 21 feet in length, whether or not backed with adhesive.
74.08 (tube and pipe fittings of copper or copper alloys).	Allowable for specialised parts of aircraft, motor vehicles or machinery.
74.11 (certain articles of copper wire or of wire of copper alloys).	Allowable for fourdrinier paper-machine wires.
74.13 (chain and parts thereof of copper or copper alloys).	Allowable for specialised parts of aircraft, motor vehicles or machinery.
74.15 (bolts, nuts, screws, rivets, etc., of copper or copper alloys).	Allowable for specialised parts of aircraft, motor vehicles, clocks and watches, or machinery.
74.16 (springs of copper or copper alloys).	Allowable for specialised parts of aircraft, motor vehicles or machinery.
74.19 (miscellaneous articles of copper or copper alloys).	Allowable— (a) for ladies' handbag frames, but only on the exportation of ladies' handbags incorporating the frames; (b) for plated drinking cups, finished bright both inside and out, of a capacity not exceeding 8 fluid oz.
75.04 and 75.06 (tube and pipe fittings and miscellaneous articles of nickel or nickel alloys).	Allowable for specialised parts of aircraft, motor vehicles or machinery.
76.04 (aluminium foil).	Allowable for aluminium tape not exceeding ½ inch in width, 6/1,000 inch in thickness or 16 feet in length, whether or not painted or backed with adhesive.
76.07 (tube and pipe fittings of aluminium or aluminium alloys).	Allowable for specialised parts of aircraft, motor vehicles or machinery.
76.15 (articles of a kind used for domestic purposes and certain other articles of aluminium or aluminium alloys).	Allowable for smokers' ash receptacles.

Tariff headings comprising imported articles for which drawback is allowable	*Restrictions on drawback*
76.16 (miscellaneous articles of aluminium or aluminium alloys).	Allowable— (a) for cigar and cigarette cases and boxes, but not on the exportation of goods incorporating those articles as, or as part of, the packing, container or get-up of the goods; (b) for rosaries the beads of which are of aluminium; (c) for specialised parts of aircraft, motor vehicles or machinery; (d) for terminal clamps for silicon carbide high temperature heating elements, but not on the exportation of goods (other than goods consisting only of the imported articles and any packing, container and get-up thereof) incorporating the imported articles; (e) for articles which are incorporated on exportation in complete hand-operated appliances embodying a blade and working edge of base metal, and used for making labels or name-plates from plastic or metal tape otherwise than by stamping the whole legend simultaneously.
77.03 (miscellaneous articles of magnesium or magnesium alloys).	Allowable for specialised parts of aircraft, motor vehicles or machinery.
78.05 and 78.06 (tube and pipe fittings and miscellaneous articles of lead or lead alloys).	Allowable for specialised parts of aircraft, motor vehicles or machinery.
79.03 (wrought plates, sheets and strip, of zinc; zinc foil; etc.).	Allowable for zinc alloy tape not exceeding ½ inch in width, 10/1,000 inch in thickness or 15 feet in length, whether or not backed with adhesive.
79.04 and 79.06 (tube and pipe fittings and miscellaneous articles of zinc or zinc alloys).	Allowable for specialised parts of aircraft, motor vehicles or machinery and for articles of zinc which are incorporated on exportation in complete hand-operated appliances embodying a blade and working edge of base metal and used for making labels or nameplates from plastic or metal tape otherwise than by stamping the whole legend simultaneously.
80.05 and 80.06 (tube and pipe fittings and miscellaneous articles of tin or tin alloys).	Allowable for specialised parts of aircraft, motor vehicles or machinery.
81.01 (tungsten and tungsten alloys, and articles thereof).	—
81.02 (molybdenum and molybdenum alloys, and articles thereof).	—

Tariff headings comprising imported articles for which drawback is allowable	*Restrictions on drawback*
81.04 (miscellaneous base metals and alloys, and articles thereof).	Allowable— (*a*) for chromium and vanadium and articles thereof; (*b*) for manganese metal (other than alloys of manganese) containing not more than 1 per cent. by weight of carbon; (*c*) for uranium depleted in U235.
82.01 (agricultural, horticultural and forestry hand tools).	Allowable for picks, for axes, bill hooks and similar hewing tools, for grass shears, and for timber wedges.
82.02 to 82.08 (tools and implements of various types, of base metal).	—
82.09 (knives).	Allowable for pocket knives.
82.11 (razors and razor blades).	Allowable— (*a*) for razors other than safety razors; (*b*) for blades and heads, and base metal parts of blades and heads, for electric shavers.
82.12 (scissors and blades therefor).	Allowable for scissors, including tailors' shears.
82.13 (miscellaneous articles of cutlery; manicure and chiropody sets and appliances).	Allowable for manicure sets, for manicure clippers and nippers, being articles not less than 4 inches in length, and for nail files.
83.01 (locks and padlocks, frames for handbags, etc., incorporating locks and keys therefor, of base metal).	Allowable— (*a*) for spring-catch locks with spring hinged hasps, of a size and shape adapted for use in suitcases or attaché cases, but not on the exportation of goods incorporating the locks as part of the packing, container, or get-up of the goods; (*b*) for ladies' handbag frames, but only on the exportation as such of ladies' handbags incorporating the frames.
83.06 (indoor ornaments of base metal).	Allowable for metal ornaments in the form of models of living creatures, flowers, foliage, fruit, or inanimate objects, being ornaments of a size and kind suitable for incorporation as decoration in clock cases, inkstands, ash trays, caskets and similar articles used for domestic or office purposes; but not allowable on the exportation of goods incorporating the ornament as part of the packing, container or get-up of the goods.
83.07 (lamps, etc., of base metal but not including electrical apparatus).	Allowable for cycle lamps.

Tariff headings comprising imported articles for which drawback is allowable	*Restrictions on drawback*
83.09 (clasps, frames with clasps for handbags, etc., buckles, buckle-clasps and certain other articles, of base metal, of kinds commonly used for clothing, travel goods etc.).	Allowable— (*a*) for ladies' handbag frames, but only on the exportation as such of ladies' handbags incorporating the frames; (*b*) for fancy buckles and clasps; (*c*) for steel key-plates, brassed and lacquered and with a sliding bar, complete with spherical-headed hooks or loops, being key-plates which on exportation are incorporated in key containers.
83.11 (bells and gongs, non-electric, of base metal).	Allowable for cycle bells.
83.12 (photograph, picture and similar frames and mirrors, of base metal).	Allowable for photograph frames and for mirrors.

Machinery and electrical equipment

All headings of Chapter 84 (boilers, machinery and mechanical appliances).	Not allowable for water closet cistern mechanisms or parts thereof, being goods of headings 84.59 or 84.61.
85.01 (electrical goods of the following descriptions: generators, motors, converters, transformers, rectifiers and rectifying apparatus, inductors).	Allowable for generators and motors (other than synchros) and rotary converters, for laboratory induction coils, for calibrated inductors, and for parts of any of those articles.
85.02 (electro-magnets; permanent magnets and articles of special materials for permanent magnets, being blanks of such magnets; electro-magnetic and permanent magnet chucks, clamps, vices and similar work holders; and certain other electro-magnetic articles).	—
85.03 (primary cells and primary batteries).	Allowable for standard cells and for parts thereof.
85.04 (electric accumulators).	Allowable for positive plates and negative plates, made of nickel plated steel, not less than $5\frac{1}{10}$ inches nor more than $5\frac{1}{5}$ inches in length, and not less than $1\frac{1}{8}$ inches nor more than $1\frac{3}{8}$ inches in width.
85.05 to 85.09 (hand tools, domestic appliances, shavers and hair clippers, with self-contained electric motors; electrical starting and ignition equipment for internal combustion engines; certain electrical equipment for cycles and motor vehicles).	—
85.11 (industrial and laboratory electric furnaces, etc.; electric welding brazing and soldering machines and apparatus and similar electric machines and apparatus for cutting).	Allowable for laboratory electric furnaces, for welding, brazing and soldering machines and apparatus and similar machines and apparatus for cutting, and for parts of any of those articles.

Tariff headings comprising imported articles for which drawback is allowable	*Restrictions on drawback*
85.12 (electric space and water heaters, electric hair dressing appliances and certain other electric appliances of a similar nature).	Allowable— (*a*) for hair driers and parts thereof and for hand and face driers and parts thereof; (*b*) for silicon carbide high temperature heating elements with a heating temperature range that exceeds 1100° centigrade, but not on the exportation of goods (other than goods consisting only of the imported articles and any packing, container and get-up thereof) incorporating the imported articles.
85.13 (electrical line telephonic and telegraphic apparatus).	Allowable for teleprinters, for morse transmitters and receivers, for morse re-perforators, and for parts of any of those articles.
85.14 (microphones, loudspeakers and amplifiers).	Allowable— (*a*) for the following, if on exportation they are incorporated in complete deaf aids, namely— (i) microphones of approximately cylindrical shape not exceeding 18 mm. in diameter and 8 mm. in thickness, exclusive of leads, or of approximately rectangular shape, with a maximum dimension not exceeding 20 mm., exclusive of leads; (ii) transistor amplifier units containing not less than two and not more than five transistors and weighing less than $1\frac{1}{2}$ oz.; (*b*) for the following, if on exportation they are incorporated in loudspeakers, namely— (i) loudspeaker cones of paper pulp; (ii) loudspeaker spiders comprising a disc, centre punched, with circular corrugation, manufactured from a plasticised fabric.
85.15 (radio etc. apparatus).	Allowable— (*a*) for electrically operated extending and retracting aerials which on exportation are incorporated in motor-cars; (*b*) for radio (including radar and television) transmitting sets, receiving sets and combined transmitting and receiving sets, complete, designed or adapted for fitting to aircraft or motor vehicles; (*c*) for radio-broadcast reception apparatus (television or sound, or both) incorporating gramophones.

Tariff headings comprising imported articles for which drawback is allowable

Restrictions on drawback

85.18 (electrical capacitors).

Allowable—

(*a*) for laboratory and standard capacitors and parts thereof;

(*b*) for tantalum capacitors, approximately cylindrical in shape, with a maximum diameter not exceeding 3 mm. and a maximum length not exceeding 7 mm., exclusive of leads, and incorporated on exportation in complete deaf aids.

85.19 (apparatus for making and breaking, protecting, connecting, regulating or controlling electrical circuits).

Allowable—

(*a*) for solenoid or motor operated switches;

(*b*) for switches, switchboards and control panels, being specialised parts of machinery, aircraft or motor vehicles;

(*c*) for precision, standard and laboratory resistors, and parts thereof;

(*d*) for carbon track volume controls incorporated on exportation in complete deaf aids, being controls of drum type with a cylindrical drum not exceeding 12 mm. in diameter and 4 mm. in thickness, or of sliding type with a length of carbon track not exceeding 7 mm.;

(*e*) for torpedo switches;

(*f*) for lampholders fitted with a plastic combined bottle-stopper and screw adaptor and suitable for use with lamps having bayonet caps $\frac{7}{8}$ inch in diameter;

(*g*) for lampholders suitable for use with lamps having Edison screw caps 1 inch in diameter;

(*h*) for two-pin plugs with flat pins;

(*i*) for two-pole 10 amp. 250 volt plugs having an earth socket and dual wiping earth contacts, and being suitable for use with socket outlets having a pin-type earthing contact or side earthing contacts, if—

(i) the diameter of the plug base is not less than 1·418 inches or more than 1·456 inches, and

(ii) the exterior length of the pins is not less than 0·688 inches or more than 0·728 inches, and

(iii) the distance between the centres of the pins is not less than 0·740 inches or more than 0·756 inches, and

(iv) the earth socket is capable of accepting pins of a diameter not less than 0·169 inches or more than 0·208 inches,

and the plugs are on exportation fitted to portable electric tools;

2ff

Tariff headings comprising imported articles for which drawback is allowable	*Restrictions on drawback*
	(*j*) for terminal straps for silicon carbide high temperature heating elements, but not on the exportation of goods (other than goods consisting only of the imported articles and any packing container and get-up thereof) incorporating the imported articles;
	but not allowable, in the case of the articles referred to at (*e*), (*f*), (*g*) and (*h*) above, except on the exportation of lamp adaptors, of a kind suitable for the conversion of bottles into table lamps, incorporating such articles.
85.20 (electric filament lamps and electric discharge lamps; arc-lamps; electrically ignited photographic flash bulbs).	Allowable for discharge lamps and for arc-lamps for cinematograph projectors, and for parts of such lamps.
85.21 (thermionic, cold cathode and photo-cathode valves and tubes; photocells; mounted transistors, etc.).	Allowable—
	(*a*) for thermionic, cold cathode and photo-cathode valves and tubes, for photocells, for mounted piezo-electric quartz crystals, and for parts of any of those articles;
	(*b*) for junction transistors, approximately cylindrical in shape, not exceeding 4 mm. in diameter and 8 mm. in length, exclusive of leads, and incorporated on exportation in complete deaf aids.
85.22 (miscellaneous electrical goods and apparatus).	Allowable for standard signal generators, radio type, for oscillators, laboratory and standard, and for parts of any of those articles.
85.24 (carbon brushes, arc-lamp carbons and other carbon articles of a kind used for electrical purposes).	Allowable for arc-lamp carbons and parts thereof, and for amorphous carbon electrodes, other than primary battery carbons.
85.26 (certain insulating fittings for electrical apparatus, being fittings wholly of insulating material apart from certain components incorporated for purposes of assembly).	—

Vehicles, aircraft and vessels

86.01 to 86.04 (rail locomotives and mechanically propelled railway and tramway rolling-stock).	—
86.06 (railway and tramway rolling-stock, the following: workshops, cranes and other service vehicles).	Allowable for cranes.
86.09 (parts of railway and tramway locomotives and rolling-stock).	Allowable for parts of rail locomotives.

Tariff headings comprising imported articles for which drawback is allowable	*Restrictions on drawback*
All headings of Chapter 87 (vehicles other than railway or tramway rolling-stock), except headings 87.10 (cycles, not motorised) and 87.13 (baby carriages and invalid carriages, not mechanically propelled).	Allowable, in the case of goods of heading 87.14 (miscellaneous vehicles, not mechanically propelled), only for trailer units of flexible or articulated motor vehicles, and for parts of such units.
88.02 (flying machines, gliders and kites; rotochutes).	Allowable for flying machines.
88.03 (parts of goods falling in heading 88.01 (balloons and airships) and 88.02).	Allowable— (i) for parts of flying machines; (ii) for wing sections, fuselage sections and under-carriage parts for gliders, but only when exported as parts of complete gliders fully assembled or in kit form.
88.04 (parachutes).	Allowable for goods of silk or man-made fibres.
88.05 (catapults and similar aircraft launching gear; ground flying trainers).	—

Optical, photographic, measuring, etc., and medical and surgical apparatus; clocks and watches; musical instruments, and sound recorders and reproducers

90.01 and 90.02 (lenses, prisms, mirrors and other optical elements, etc.).	—
90.03 (frames and mountings for spectacles, etc.).	Allowable for frames of tortoise-shell.
90.05 and 90.06 (refracting telescopes and astronomical instruments).	—
90.07 (photographic cameras; photographic flashlight apparatus, photocopying apparatus (not contact type)).	Allowable for all goods except tripods and other stands, pistol grips and photographic flashlight apparatus.
90.08 (cinematographic cameras, projectors, sound recorders and sound reproducers).	Not allowable for tripods and other stands for articles of heading 90.08, or for pistol grips for cameras of that heading.
90.09 (image projectors; photographic enlargers and reducers).	Not allowable for tripods and other stands for image projectors.
90.10 (miscellaneous photographic and cinematographic equipment and apparatus).	Allowable— (a) for cinematographic editing machines incorporating means of projection; (b) for cinematographic enlargers and reducers (optical printers); (c) for re-recorders; (d) for other optical projection apparatus; (e) for film viewing magnifiers; (f) for photo-copying machines (being non-optical) of direct contact or transfer type (other than dyeline type) with semi-dry developing system.

Tariff headings comprising imported articles for which drawback is allowable	*Restrictions on drawback*
90.11 and 90.12 (microscopes and diffraction apparatus, electron and proton, and compound optical microscopes).	—
90.13 (miscellaneous optical appliances and instruments).	Not allowable for spotlights (non-focusing) or searchlights.
90.14 (surveying, navigational, meteorological and similar instruments).	Allowable— (*a*) for instruments incorporating optical elements, but not including instruments in which the optical element is for viewing a scale or for some other subsidiary function; (*b*) for the following surveying (including photogrammetrical surveying) and hydrographic instruments—clinometers, hypsometers, co-ordinatographs, cross staff heads, and plane tables; (*c*) for the following navigational instruments—accelerometers, altimeters, and horizons (artificial), gyroscopic type; (*d*) for the following geophysical instruments—magnetometers, seismographs and variometers; (*e*) for compasses.
90.15 (balances of a sensitivity of 5 centigrams or better).	—
90.16 (drawing, marking-out and mathematical calculating instruments; measuring or checking instruments, appliances and machines; profile projectors).	Allowable— (*a*) for instruments, appliances and machines incorporating optical elements, but not including instruments, appliances or machines in which the optical element is for viewing a scale or for some other subsidiary function; (*b*) for the following other instruments, appliances and machines— (i) calculating cylinders, dials and rules, isographs, half sets, compasses (including beam compasses), dividers (including proportional dividers), bows, spring bows, ruling pens, pantographs and eidographs, and slide rules; (ii) chronographs (barrel), clinometers, coordinatographs, dividing machines and engines (linear and circular), engine indicators, harmonic analysers (planimeter type), integraphs, integrators (planimeter type), opisometers, planimeters, and spherometers; (iii) curves, drafting machines, parallel rules, protractors, precision squares, set squares, and T squares, scribing blocks of precision or surface gauges, straight edges and surface plates;

Tariff headings comprising imported articles for which drawback is allowable	*Restrictions on drawback*

(iv) gauges and measuring instruments of precision of the types used in engineering machine shops and viewing rooms;

(v) tape measures in ornamental containers with a spring-operated rewind device.

90.17 (medical, etc., instruments and appliances).

Allowable—

(a) for instruments and appliances incorporating optical elements, but not including mouth mirrors not optically worked, or instruments or appliances in which the optical element is for viewing a scale or some other subsidiary function;

(b) for cardiographs;

(c) for optometers;

(d) for myographs;

(e) for glass barrelled hypodermic syringes.

90.19 (orthopaedic appliances, etc.; artificial parts of the body; deaf aids, etc.).

Allowable—

(a) for artificial human eyes of glass;

(b) for the following articles incorporated on their exportation in complete deaf aids, that is to say—

(i) chassis with a cylindrical drum volume control not exceeding 12 mm. in diameter and 4 mm. in thickness mounted thereon.

(ii) earphones of approximately cylindrical shape, not exceeding 18 mm. in diameter and 8 mm. in thickness, or of approximately rectangular shape with a maximum dimension not exceeding 16 mm., the measurement being made (in any case) exclusive of earmould nipples and of leads.

90.20 and 90.22 to 90.27 (X-ray apparatus, etc.; miscellaneous measuring and checking instruments and apparatus, etc.).

—

90.28 (electrical measuring, checking, analysing or automatically controlling instruments and apparatus).

Not allowable for—

(a) ammeters, voltmeters, wattmeters, thermostats and thermo-regulators (other than precision types);

(b) automatic regulators of electrical quantities (other than motor driven and vibrating contact automatic voltage regulators);

(c) automatic control instruments and apparatus for controlling non-electrical quantities (other than those for automatic control of flow, depth, pressure or other variables of liquids or gases, or of temperature);

(d) telemetering instruments and apparatus.

Tariff headings comprising imported articles for which drawback is allowable	*Restrictions on drawback*
90.29 (parts or accessories of measuring and checking instruments and apparatus, etc.).	Not allowable for parts or accessories of the following— (*a*) ammeters, voltmeters, wattmeters, thermostats and thermo-regulators (except parts and accessories of precision types, and parts and accessories incorporated in refrigeration controls, being parts and accessories suitable for use solely with, or of a kind mainly used with, such controls); (*b*) automatic regulators of electrical quantities (other than motor driven and vibrating contact automatic voltage regulators); (*c*) automatic control instruments and apparatus for controlling non-electrical quantities (other than those for automatic control of flow, depth, pressure or other variables of liquids or gases, or of temperature).
All headings of Chapter 91 (clocks and watches).	—
All headings of Chapter 92 (musical instruments and sound or television image recorders and reproducers).	Not allowable for television image and sound recorders and reproducers, magnetic (classified in heading 92.11) or parts and accessories thereof (classified in heading 92.13).

Miscellaneous manufactured articles

94.03 (miscellaneous furniture).	Allowable for wooden frames for camp beds, imported without metal fittings, but only on the exportation as such of complete assembled camp beds each incorporating a wooden frame and a canvas top.
94.04 (mattress supports and articles of bedding or similar furnishing).	Not allowable for articles of expanded, foam or sponge artificial plastic material, whether or not covered.
95.01 (worked tortoise-shell and articles of tortoise-shell).	Allowable for articles of tortoise-shell.
95.02 (worked mother of pearl and articles of mother of pearl).	Allowable for articles of mother of pearl.
95.05 (worked horn, coral or other animal carving material, and articles thereof).	Allowable— (*a*) for articles of coral or shells; (*b*) for matchet handles and parts thereof of horn.
95.06 (worked vegetable carving material, and articles thereof).	Allowable for rosaries the beads of which are of coco bean.
96.02 (miscellaneous brooms and brushes, paint rollers, etc.).	Allowable— (*a*) for hair, tooth, nail, clothes, hat and shaving brushes;

Tariff headings comprising imported articles for which drawback is allowable	*Restrictions on drawback*
	(b) for brooms and brushes with filling of man-made fibres (including monofil of heading 51.01 or 51.02).
96.05 (powder-puffs and pads for applying cosmetics or toilet preparations).	Not allowable on the exportation of goods incorporating the imported article as, or as part of, the packing, container or get-up of the goods.
97.01 to 97.03 (toys).	Not allowable for parts.
97.04 (equipment for parlour, table and funfair games).	Not allowable for playing cards, or for billiard tables.
97.06 (equipment for gymnastics, athletics, sports and outdoor games).	Allowable— (a) for blade blanks for electric foils or electric épées, but only on the exportation of such foils or épées or of blades therefor; (b) for dome-shaped cork pieces, but only on the exportation of shuttlecocks incorporating them.
98.01 (buttons and button moulds, studs, cuff-links and press-fasteners).	Allowable— (a) for buttons and button moulds, and parts and blanks thereof, but not on the exportation of goods (other than goods consisting only of the imported articles and any packing, container and get-up thereof) incorporating the imported articles; (b) for cuff-links.
98.03 (fountain pens, etc., penholders, pencil-holders and the like, propelling pencils and sliding pencils).	—
98.05 (pencils, with certain exceptions, crayons, chalks and the like).	Allowable for pencils.
98.07 (hand-operated date, etc., stamps and composing sticks, and certain hand printing sets).	Allowable for hand-operated appliances embodying a blade and working edge of base metal, and used for making labels or name plates from plastic or metal tape otherwise than by stamping the whole legend simultaneously.
98.10 (mechanical lighters and similar lighters, and parts thereof).	Allowable for flint wheels for mechanical lighters and for metal gas tanks incorporated in mechanical lighters.
98.11 (smoking pipes; cigar and cigarette holders).	—
98.12 (combs, hair-slides and the like).	—
98.14 (scent and similar sprays of a kind used for toilet purposes).	—
98.15 (vacuum flasks, etc.).	Allowable for vacuum flasks and other vacuum vessels, complete with cases.

SCHEDULE 2

DRAWBACKS ON EXPORTATION OF GOODS PRODUCED OR MANUFACTURED FROM IMPORTED ARTICLES

Exported Goods	Imported Goods	Rate of Drawback (if any)
Abrasive discs.	Vulcanised fibre imported in rolls.	—
Acetylcarbromal.	2-Ethylbutyric acid.	—
Adhesive tape, of a width not exceeding 6¼ ins. consisting of paper coated on one side with adhesive.	Creped paper, manufactured entirely of semi-bleached sulphate cellulose fibre, whether wet-strengthened or not but not otherwise treated or impregnated, being paper which is imported in rolls of a width not less than 23 ins. and which is of a weight when fully extended equivalent to more than 24·5 grammes, but not more than 98 grammes, per square metre.	—
Animal black (other than ivory black and spent animal black).	Bones, de-fatted, crushed or uncrushed.	—
Animal foodstuffs, canned.	Whale meat of heading 02.04 of the Customs Tariff 1959.	—
Apricot kernel products.	Apricot kernels, shelled but not further prepared.	£1·1500 per cwt. of apricot kernels.
Beans:— 1. Canned in tomato sauce, with or without sausages, pork, kidney or bacon. 2. Canned in curry sauce.	Dried white beans, other than butter beans.	—
Biscuits (other than chocolate biscuits), cake mixes, puddings and pudding mixes.	(A) Beet sugar and cane sugar, solid, not qualifying for Commonwealth preference.	(a) Where the duty paid was at the highest rate and the sugar used in the manufacture of the exported goods was of a polarisation exceeding 98°— (i) £6·9000 per ton of sugar, (ii) £6·5750 per ton of anhydrous invert sugar. (b) Where the duty paid was at less than the highest rate and the sugar used in the manufacture of the exported goods was of a polarisation exceeding 98°— (i) £4·2780 per ton of sugar,

Exported Goods	*Imported Goods*	*Rate of Drawback (if any)*
		(ii) £4·0750 per ton of anhydrous invert sugar.
		(c) Where the duty paid was at less than the highest rate and the sugar used in the manufacture of the exported goods was of a polarisation not exceeding 98°, a rate per ton of sugar equal to the full rate of duty chargeable on the importation into the United Kingdom of sugar of the like polarisation and 100/105ths of that rate per ton of anhydrous invert sugar.
	(B) Beet sugar and cane sugar, solid, qualifying for Commonwealth preference, of a polarisation exceeding 99°.	(a) £1·0665 per ton of sugar. (b) £1·0155 per ton of anhydrous invert sugar.
Booklets, not exceeding 3½ ins. in length and 2½ ins. in width, and containing not less than 60 leaves consisting of paper coated on one side with powder.	Paper, coated on one side with powder, in sheets not less than 30 ins. in length and 18 ins. in width and of a weight when fully extended equivalent to not less than 35, and not more than 45, grammes per square metre.	—
Boots, bootees, shoes, slippers and sandals containing in the uppers (and not as linings, internal stiffening pieces, stitchings, fastenings or ornaments) leather of the following description namely, dressed leather other than patent leather, and other than glace kid being chrome tanned goatskin of smooth polished finish.	Leather of the description referred to in column 1, not imported in the form of shaped pieces for making into footwear.	—
Bromvaletone.	isoValeric acid.	—
Carbromal.	2-Ethylbutyric acid.	—
Casings for sausages and prepared meats:		
1. Casings manufactured in the form of bags of which the sealed ends are curved.	Tubing of poly (vinyl chloride) imported in reels, whether or not plasticised or pigmented.	—

Exported Goods	*Imported Goods*	*Rate of Drawback (if any)*
2. Other casings.	Tubing of any of the following materials imported in reels, whether or not plasticised or pigmented—	—
	(*a*) regenerated cellulose,	
	(*b*) poly (vinyl chloride),	
	(*c*) coated or impregnated paper of vegetable fibre.	
Castor oil and goods made therefrom:		
1. Castor oil (including dehydrated oil); fatty acids derived from castor oil (including dehydrated fatty acids).	Castor seed.	—
2. Dehydrated castor oil; fatty acids derived from castor oil (including dehydrated fatty acids).	Castor oil (other than hydrogenated castor oil).	—
3. Sebacic acid.	Castor oil.	—
Chewing gum and chewing confectionery.	Chewing gum base.	—
Chocolate:		
1. Block couverture, bakers' covering compounds, granulettes and other chocolate for further manufacturing purposes.	(A) Beet sugar and cane sugar, solid, not qualifying for Commonwealth preference.	(*a*) Where the duty paid was at the highest rate and the sugar used in the manufacture of the exported goods was of a polarisation exceeding 98°—
		(i) £6·9000 per ton of sugar,
		(ii) £6·5750 per ton of anhydrous invert sugar.
		(*b*) Where the duty paid was at less than the highest rate and the sugar used in the manufacture of the exported goods was of a polarisation exceeding 98°—
		(i) £4·2780 per ton of sugar,
		(ii) £4·0750 per ton of anhydrous invert sugar.

Exported Goods	Imported Goods	Rate of Drawback (if any)
		(c) Where the duty paid was at less than the highest rate and the sugar used in the manufacture of the exported goods was of a polarisation not exceeding 98°, a rate per ton of sugar equal to the full rate of duty chargeable on the importation into the United Kingdom of sugar of the like polarisation and 100/105ths of that rate per ton of anhydrous invert sugar.
	(B) Beet sugar and cane sugar, solid, qualifying for Commonwealth preterence, of a polarisation exceeding 99°.	(a) £1·0665 per ton of sugar. (b) £1·0155 per ton of anhydrous invert sugar.
	(C) Lecithin and other phosphoaminolipins.	
2. Chocolate confectionery, sugar confectionery containing cocoa, and chocolate biscuits.	(A) Beet sugar and cane sugar, solid, not qualifying for Commonwealth preference.	(a) Where the duty paid was at the highest rate and the sugar used in the manufacture of the exported goods was of a polarisation exceeding 98°— (i) £6·9000 per ton of sugar, (ii) £6·5750 per ton of anhydrous invert sugar. (b) Where the duty paid was at less than the highest rate and the sugar used in the manufacture of the exported goods was of a polarisation exceeding 98°— (i) £4·2780 per ton of sugar, (ii) £4·0750 per ton of anhydrous invert sugar. (c) Where the duty paid was at less than the highest rate and the sugar used in the manufacture of the exported goods was of a polarisation not exceeding 98°, a rate per ton of sugar equal to the full

Exported Goods	*Imported Goods*	*Rate of Drawback (if any)*
		rate of duty chargeable on the importation into the United Kingdom of sugar of the like polarisation and 100/105ths of that rate per ton of anhydrous invert sugar.
	(B) Beet sugar and cane sugar, solid, qualifying for Commonwealth preference, of a polarisation exceeding 99°.	(a) £1·0665 per ton of sugar. (b) £1·0155 per ton of anhydrous invert sugar.
	(C) Liquid glucose.	—
	(D) Milk powder; dried egg albumin; coconut, desiccated; pineapple, fresh; edible nuts other than coconuts, brazil, cashew, hazel, almonds and chestnuts; ginger; tartaric acid essential oils, terpeneless —orange, lemon, lime, mandarin, tangerine, peppermint, spearmint, aniseed and eucalyptus; lecithin and other phosphoaminolipins; natural gums.	—
Cigarette papers in the form of booklets.	Cigarette paper imported in bobbins or reels.	—
Cinematograph film (including sound tracks), exposed, whether positive or negative, and whether developed or not.	Unexposed film of a length of 12 feet or more.	—
Cloth oil or wool oil but neither containing less than 70 per cent. by weight of oleine fatty acids.	Animal tallow or bone grease.	—
Cocoa powder, sweetened, and drinking chocolate.	(A) Beet sugar and cane sugar, solid, not qualifying for Commonwealth preference.	(a) Where the duty paid was at the highest rate and the sugar used in the manufacture of the exported goods was of a polarisation exceeding 98°— (i) £6·9000 per ton of sugar, (ii) £6·5750 per ton of anhydrous invert sugar. (b) Where the duty paid was at less than the highest rate and the sugar used in the manufacture of the exported goods was of a polarisation exceeding 98°—

Exported Goods	Imported Goods	Rate of Drawback (if any)
		(i) £4·2780 per ton of sugar,
		(ii) £4·0750 per ton of anhydrous invert sugar.
		(c) Where the duty paid was at less than the highest rate and the sugar used in the manufacture of the exported goods was of a polarisation not exceeding 98°, a rate per ton of sugar equal to the full rate of duty chargeable on the importation into the United Kingdom of sugar of the like polarisation and 100/105ths of that rate per ton of anhydrous invert sugar,
	(B) Beet sugar and cane sugar, solid, qualifying for Commonwealth preference, of a polarisation exceeding 99°.	(a) £1·0665 per ton of sugar.
		(b) £1·0155 per ton of anhydrous invert sugar.
Cod, dried and salted.	Fresh cod, with heads and tails, from which the entrails, livers and roes have been removed.	£4·1000 per ton of dried salted cod.
Coffee: 1. Roasted coffee beans. 2. Roasted coffee in ground form, whether pure or mixed with other substances. 3. Soluble coffee powder, whether of pure coffee or a mixture of pure coffee and other substances.	Coffee beans, not being kiln dried or roasted or ground.	—
Combing oil, being a mixture of refined sperm oil, castor oil and fatty acids.	Unrefined sperm oil and castor oil.	—
Condensed milk.	(A) Beet sugar and cane sugar, solid, not qualifying for Commonwealth preference.	(a) Where the duty paid was at the highest rate and the sugar used in the manufacture of the exported goods was of a polarisation exceeding 98°— (i) £6·9000 per ton of sugar, (ii) £6·5750 per ton of anhydrous invert sugar.

Exported Goods	Imported Goods	Rate of Drawback (if any)
		(b) Where the duty paid was at less than the highest rate and the sugar used in the manufacture of the exported goods was of a polarisation exceeding 98°—
		(i) £4·2780 per ton of sugar,
		(ii) £4·0750 per ton of anhydrous invert sugar.
		(c) Where the duty paid was at less than the highest rate and the sugar used in the manufacture of the exported goods was of a polarisation not exceeding 98°, a rate per ton of sugar equal to the full rate of duty chargeable on the importation into the United Kingdom of sugar of the like polarisation and 100/105ths of that rate per ton of anhydrous invert sugar.
	(B) Beet sugar and cane sugar, solid, qualifying for Commonwealth preference, of a polarisation exceeding 99°.	(a) £1·0665 per ton of sugar.
		(b) £1·0155 per ton of anhydrous invert sugar.
Cuprammonium products, that is to say, manufactures wholly or partly of cuprammonium filament or fibres, the following:—		
1. Woven ribbons, woven labels and similar woven goods, whether in the piece or not; woven fabric.	Cuprammonium continuous filament yarn.	—
2. Warp knitted fabric, whether on a base or not.	Spun yarn of cuprammonium fibres or of cuprammonium fibres and wool.	—
3. Brushed warp knitted fabric.	Cuprammonium continuous filament yarn.	—
4. Warp knitted fabric other than brushed warp knitted fabric.	Cuprammonium continuous filament yarn.	—
Dextrins, soluble, and other modified starches, and starch adhesives (plain or compounded).	Starch, being maize starch or milo starch.	—

Exported Goods	Imported Goods	Rate of Drawback (if any)
Doors, flush, faced with fibre hardboard.	Fibre hardboard, of a weight exceeding 50 lb. per cubic foot, imported in sheets of a length exceeding 5 ft. 11⅞ ins. but not exceeding 7 ft. 0⅛ in., of a width exceeding 1 ft. 5⅜ in. but not exceeding 3 ft. 0⅛ in., and of a thickness exceeding 0·105 in. but not exceeding 0·145 in.	—
Doors, flush, faced with plywood.	Plywood containing no material other than wood and bonding material, imported in sheets, sanded or scraped on one or both sides, of a length exceeding 5 ft. 11⅞ ins. but not exceeding 7 ft. 1¼ ins., of a width exceeding 1 ft. 5⅜ ins. but not exceeding 3 ft. 1¼ ins., and of a thickness exceeding 2·85 mm. but not exceeding 4·4 mm.	—
Drafting bands of a kind used for textile machinery.	Leather of either of the following descriptions:— (a) chrome tanned calf leather imported in skins or pieces weighing less than 4 lb. each; (b) dressed vegetable tanned calf leather.	—
Dyeline natural tracing paper, sensitised but unexposed.	Natural tracing paper, coated with cellulose acetate, and weighing more than 120 but not more than 135 grammes per square metre.	—
Electrosensitive recording paper rolls of a width exceeding 8 ins.	Wet-strengthened uncalendered cellulose paper of a weight when fully extended equivalent to not less than 40 grammes and not more than 50 grammes per square metre, and containing not more than the following parts per million of the following metals:— Aluminium ... 20 Calcium ... ... 250 Iron ... ... 5 Magnesium ... 50 All other metals together (except sodium and potassium) 20	A rate for each complete 100 ft. of the exported paper calculated as follows:— where the width of the paper— does not exceed 9 ins., £0·0200. exceeds 9 ins. but does not exceed 11 ins., £0·0240. exceeds 11 ins. but does not exceed 18 ins., £0·0280. exceeds 18 ins., £0·0440.

Exported Goods	*Imported Goods*	*Rate of Drawback (if any)*
Foodstuffs, canned or bottled, the following:—	Tomato purée or paste, containing not less than 25 per cent. by weight of tomato solids.	—
1. Foodstuffs, canned in tomato sauce.		
2. Foodstuffs, other than fish, bottled in tomato sauce.		
3. Ketchups, sauces, chutneys and soups, canned or bottled.		
Fruit, fruit peel and fruit juice preserved with sugar, bottled or canned, or drained, glacé or crystallized; jams, lemon curd, fruit jelly preparations, marmalades, mincemeat, fruit purée and fruit pastes, containing added sugar.	(A) Beet sugar and cane sugar, solid, not qualifying for Commonwealth preference.	(a) Where the duty paid was at the highest rate and the sugar used in the manufacture of the exported goods was of a polarisation exceeding 98°— (i) £6·9000 per ton of sugar, (ii) £6·5750 per ton of anhydrous invert sugar. (b) Where the duty paid was at less than the highest rate and the sugar used in the manufacture of the exported goods was of a polarisation exceeding 98°— (i) £4·2780 per ton of sugar. (ii) £4·0750 per ton of anhydrous invert sugar. (c) Where the duty paid was at less than the highest rate and the sugar used in the manufacture of the exported goods was of a polarisation not exceeding 98°, a rate per ton of sugar equal to the full rate of duty chargeable on the importation into the United Kingdom of sugar of the like polarisation and 100/105ths of that rate per ton of anhydrous invert sugar.
	(B) Beet sugar and cane sugar, solid, qualifying for Commonwealth preference, of a polarisation exceeding 99°.	(a) £1·0665 per ton of sugar. (b) £1·0155 per ton of anhydrous invert sugar.

Exported Goods	Imported Goods	Rate of Drawback (if any)
Fruit cakes and other goods made with dried fruit:—		
1. Fruit cakes, fruit puddings, biscuits and sweetmeat confectionery.	Raisins, sultanas, currants, and other dried grapes and dried figs.	—
2. Mincemeat, pickles, sauces and chutneys.	Raisins, sultanas, currants and other dried grapes.	—
3. Fig jam.	Dried figs.	—
Furniture.	(A) Woven textile fabrics.	—
	(B) Plywood of birch and beech, blockboard, laminboard and battenboard, excluding veneered panels and sheets.	—
	(C) Wood in the rough, roughly squared or half squared or sawn lengthwise, sliced or peeled, of the following species, namely species of Acer, Betula, Fagus, Fraxinus, Juglans, Populus, Quercus and Ulmus; Castanea sativa; Eucalyptus diversicolor; Eucalyptus marginata.	—
Garments, the following:—		
1. Men's jackets, trousers, waistcoats and shorts, and women's trousers, shorts and skirts.	Silk fabric, being fabric— (a) woven wholly from spun yarns of mulberry silk; (b) of plain weave, showing a slub effect in both warp and weft directions; (c) free from metallic weighting; (d) weighing not less than $5\frac{1}{2}$ oz. and not more than 7 oz. per square yard.	—
2. Women's and girls': (A) Dresses (whether lined or not). (B) Jackets, unlined. (C) Skirts, unlined and not falling within paragraph 1 of this entry. (D) Two-piece ensembles consisting of a dress and jacket (whether lined or not).	Fabric, containing silk or man-made fibres or both.	—

Exported Goods	*Imported Goods*	*Rate of Drawback (if any)*
Garments, rain-proof, the following:— Raincoats; Jackets; Trousers; Over-trousers; Skirts; Headgear.	Woven fabric, whether or not proofed, being fabric of cotton or of cotton and man-made fibre and falling to be classified, on importation, under heading 55.09 of the Customs Tariff 1959.	—
Glass, laminated, in sheets, consisting of two layers of glass with a middle layer of poly(vinyl butyral).	Poly (vinyl butyral) in sheet form.	—
Glue, gelatin and other bone products, the following:—	Bones, crushed or un-crushed.	—
1. Glue and gelatin produced by a process of degelatinisation, containing not more than 16 per cent. moisture.		
2. Ossein.		
3. Gelatin produced by a process of acidulation, containing not more than 16 per cent. moisture.		
4. Calcium phosphates; mineral supplements for animal feeding containing calcium phosphates; crushed or ground degelatinised bones.		
5. Calcined bones.		
Golf clubs.	Golf club head blocks of wood or of laminated wood, being either roughly shaped by sawing or shaped by sawing and by further manufacture but not fully machined and sandpapered.	—
Heat-absorbing glass, surface ground and polished on both faces, and having the properties of either of the categories specified in paragraph 23 of British Standard 952:1964.	Glass of the description specified in column 1, imported in rectangles of 10 ft. or more in length and 7½ ft. or more in width.	—
Inked ribbons for typewriters or for other office machinery.	Woven fabric, wholly of silk, not inked, exceeding 30 cm. in width.	—
Insulated copper strip and winding wire, being, in both cases, of a high conductivity.	Polyvinyl acetal resins, polyester resins, polyurethane resins and linseed oil.	—

Exported Goods	Imported Goods	Rate of Drawback (if any)
Linseed oil, and goods made with linseed oil (other than printers' inks):		
1. Linseed oil, and mixtures consisting of linseed oil and driers.	Linseed.	£15·3500 per ton of linseed oil.
2. Linseed oil, refined or heat-treated or both; mixtures consisting of linseed oil and driers; mixtures of linseed oil and other oils, with or without the addition of driers or of rosin or of both; mixtures of linseed oil and vegetable substances, with or without the addition of water; adducts of linseed oil; putty.	Linseed oil.	—
3. Linseed oil fatty acids (being the acids obtained by the hydrolysis of linseed oil).	Linseed oil.	£16·6500 per ton of linseed oil fatty acids.
4. Linoleum, not printed, manufactured on a base of jute canvas, cotton or spun rayon cloth.	Linseed oil.	£3·4300 per ton of linoleum.
5. Linoleum, not printed, manufactured on a base of bitumenised felt.	Linseed oil.	£2·9000 per ton of linoleum.
6. Cork carpets; unpigmented linoleum composition manufactured on a base of flannelette.	Linseed oil.	£3·5400 per ton of cork carpet or linoleum composition.
7. Felt base.	Linseed oil.	£0·5000 per ton of felt base.
8. Blocks, tiles, and similar articles, of a kind used for floors, walls or staircases, consisting mainly (by weight) of cement, lime and plaster, and impregnated with linseed oil, of dimensions not greater than 10 ins. in length or width.	Linseed oil.	£1·7300 per ton of blocks, tiles or other articles.
9. Paint, enamel and varnish.	Linseed oil.	—
10. Synthetic resins.	Linseed oil.	—

Exported Goods	*Imported Goods*	*Rate of Drawback (if any)*
Lubricating oil viscosity modifiers consisting of polymerised aliphatic methacrylates dissolved in lubricating oil.	Acetone cyanohydrin, containing not more than 0·10 per cent. by weight of free hydrogen cyanide.	—
Men's shirts.	Woven fabric of spun silk.	—
Methacrylates, falling within heading 29.14 of the Customs Tariff 1959, the following—butyl methacrylate, hexyl methacrylate, lauryl methacrylate and stearyl methacrylate.	Acetone cyanohydrin, containing not more than 0·10 per cent. by weight of free hydrogen cyanide.	—
Moulding compounds in the form of granules, coloured, of polyoxymethylene, not compounded with any other substance.	Polyoxymethylenes in the form of granular powder, being polyaddition products of not less than 90 per cent. by weight of formaldehyde, and not being plasticised or otherwise compounded.	—
Neckties, bow-ties and cravats.	Woven fabric of heading 50.09, 50.10 or 51.04 of the Customs Tariff 1959.	—
Oat products.	Oats in husk.	£0·2250 per cwt. of ground, rolled or flaked oats, or oatmeal, or oat flour.
Ophthalmic lenses, single vision, other than contact lenses.	Drawn ophthalmic raw sheet glass falling within heading 70.05 of the Customs Tariff 1959.	—
Orange marmalade.	Fresh bitter oranges.	—
Oranges, bitter, prepared for use in the manufacture of marmalade.	Fresh bitter oranges.	—
Packing cases of fibreboard, corrugated or solid.	Kraft paper or kraft board, bleached or unbleached.	—
Packing cases of plywood, reinforced with steel.	Plywood which contains no material other than wood and bonding material and is of a thickness not less than 3 mm. and not more than 9 mm.	—
Panama hats.	Natural straw hoods.	—

Exported Goods	Imported Goods	Rate of Drawback (if any)
Paper bags, open-topped without flaps, or closed except for a single opening of the valve type.	Paper of any of the following descriptions, being paper of a weight when fully extended equivalent to not more than 220 grammes per square metre:— (a) paper manufactured wholly of bleached or unbleached sulphate cellulose fibre; (b) sulphite wrapping paper, machine glazed; (c) greaseproof paper, bleached; (d) greaseproof paper, unbleached; (e) glazed transparent paper.	—
Photographic film, sensitised but unexposed; photographic film base prepared for colour photography, but not sensitised.	Photographic film base (other than nitro-cellulose) imported in rolls.	—
Pigment produced or manufactured from combined cadmium.	Cadmium metal.	—
Plastic-bonded asbestos panels, that is to say, board manufactured from asbestos, lime, silica, water, and no other materials, with a single piece of laminated plastic sheeting bonded to one side or to each side, in panels— (a) of a length not less than 7 ft. 11 ins. but not exceeding 10 ft. 1 in.; (b) of a width not less than 1 ft. 11 ins. nor more than 2 ft. 1 in., or not less than 2 ft. 11 ins. nor more than 4 ft. 1 in.; (c) of a thickness not less than 0·28 in. but not exceeding 1·35 ins.	Laminated plastic sheets, consisting of resin-impregnated papers, bonded together, or of such papers bonded together and coated on one side with melamine resin, and— (a) of a length not less than 8 ft. but not exceeding 10 ft. 2 ins., (b) of a width not less than 3 ft. but not exceeding 4 ft. 2 ins., and (c) of a thickness not less than 0·024 in. but not exceeding 0·081 in.	—

Exported Goods	Imported Goods	Rate of Drawback (if any)
Poly(vinyl chloride) tape, whether or not colour-coated, and whether or not backed with adhesive, for use in hand operated appliances for making labels or name plates otherwise than by stamping the whole legend simultaneously.	Tape of the descriptions referred to in column 1 exceeding 500 ft. in length.	—
Printers' inks and printing ink base.	(A) Carbon black.	—
	(B) Linseed oil.	£15·3500 per ton of linseed oil.
Products of " improved " wood within the meaning of Chapter 44 of the Customs Tariff 1959, the following:— 1. Picking sticks, being weaving loom parts. 2. Railway fishplates. 3. Steel-rule die-blocks. 4. Rectangular panels, boards, sheets, billets, strips or blocks.	Wooden veneer sheets.	—
Quebracho extract and blends thereof: 1. Ground insoluble quebracho extract.	Solid insoluble quebracho extract.	—
2. Soluble quebracho extract, powder or liquid.	Solid insoluble quebracho extract.	—
3. Blends in powder form of quebracho extract with the following materials— (A) lignite, in which the content by weight of soluble quebracho extract is 60 per cent.; (B) mangrove extract, in which the said content is 75 per cent.; (C) mimosa extract, in which the said content is 47 per cent.; (D) myrobalan extract, in which the said content is 64½ per cent.; (E) mimosa extract and myrobalan extract, in which the said content is 33⅓ per cent.;	Solid insoluble quebracho extract.	—

Exported Goods	*Imported Goods*	*Rate of Drawback* (*if any*
(F) sulphite cellulose, in which the said content is 50, 60, 75 or 86 per cent.;		
(G) sulphite cellulose, in which the content by weight of insoluble quebracho extract is 50 per cent.		
4. Ground soluble quebracho extract.	Solid soluble quebracho extract.	—
Seasoning, liquid, produced from tabasco red pepper mash and vinegar.	Tabasco red peppers (being the fruit of capsicum frutescens, var. tabasco), mashed and provisionally preserved in brine.	—
Shuttlecocks and shuttlecock skirts.	Poly (11-aminoundecanoic acid) in the form of granules, containing fillers or plasticisers or both.	A rate of £0·1050 per kilogramme of the imported articles.
Soap (including medicated soap), and surface-active preparations and washing preparations containing soap.	Animal tallow.	—
Soft drinks, unconcentrated or concentrated; powders for such drinks; sweetened flavouring syrups and concentrates.	(A) Beet sugar and cane sugar, solid, not qualifying for Commonwealth preference.	(*a*) Where the duty paid was at the highest rate and the sugar used in the manufacture of the exported goods was of a polarisation exceeding 98°— (i) £6·9000 per ton of sugar, (ii) £6·5750 per ton of anhydrous invert sugar. (*b*) Where the duty paid was at less than the highest rate and the sugar used in the manufacture of the exported goods was of a polarisation exceeding 98°— (i) £4·2780 per ton of sugar, (ii) £4·0750 per ton of anhydrous invert sugar.

Exported Goods	Imported Goods	Rate of Drawback (if any)
		(c) Where the duty paid was at less than the highest rate and the sugar used in the manufacture of the exported goods was of a polarisation not exceeding 98°, a rate per ton of sugar equal to the full rate of duty chargeable on the importation into the United Kingdom of sugar of the like polarisation and 100/105ths of that rate per ton of anhydrous invert sugar.
	(B) Beet sugar and cane sugar, solid, qualifying for Commonwealth preference, of a polarisation exceeding 99°.	(a) £1·0665 per ton of sugar. (b) £1·0155 per ton of anhydrous invert sugar.
Sperm oil, refined, and fatty alcohol derived from sperm oil.	Unrefined sperm oil.	—
Stearine fatty acids and oleine fatty acids.	Animal tallow or bone grease.	—
Sugar, refined in the United Kingdom: (a) of a polarisation exceeding 98°.	Beet sugar and cane sugar, solid, not qualifying for Commonwealth preference.	(i) where the duty paid was at the highest rate, £6·9000 per ton of refined sugar; (ii) where the duty paid was at less than the highest rate, £4·2780 per ton of refined sugar.
(b) of a polarisation not exceeding 98°.		A rate per ton of refined sugar equal to the full rate of duty per ton chargeable on the importation into the United Kingdom of sugar of the like polarisation.
(c) in the form of fine white powder, not flavoured, containing not less than 8 per cent., and not more than 10 per cent., invert sugar.		—
Sugar confectionery, not containing cocoa.	(A) Liquid glucose.	—

Exported Goods	Imported Goods	Rate of Drawback (if any)
	(B) Beet sugar and cane sugar, solid, not qualifying for Commonwealth preference.	(a) Where the duty paid was at the highest rate and the sugar used in the manufacture of the exported goods was of a polarisation exceeding 98°— (i) £6·9000 per ton of sugar. (ii) £6·5750 per ton of anhydrous invert sugar. (b) Where the duty paid was at less than the highest rate and the sugar used in the manufacture of the exported goods was of a polarisation exceeding 98°— (i) £4·2780 per ton of sugar, (ii) £4·0750 per ton of anhydrous invert sugar. (c) Where the duty paid was at less than the highest rate and the sugar used in the manufacture of the exported goods was of a polarisation not exceeding 98°, a rate per ton of sugar equal to the full rate of duty chargeable on the importation into the United Kingdom of sugar of the like polarisation and 100/105ths of that rate per ton of anhydrous invert sugar.
	(C) Beet sugar and cane sugar, solid, qualifying for Commonwealth preference, of a polarisation exceeding 99°.	(a) £1·0665 per ton of sugar. (b) £1·0155 per ton of anhydrous invert sugar.
	(D) Milk powder; dried egg albumin; coconut, desiccated; pineapple, fresh; edible nuts other than coconut, brazil, cashew, hazel, almonds and chestnuts; ginger; tartaric acid; essential oils, terpeneless—orange, lemon, lime, mandarin, tangerine, peppermint, spearmint, aniseed and eucalyptus; lecithin and other phosphoaminolipins; natural gums.	—

Exported Goods	Imported Goods	Rate of Drawback (if any)
Suitcases, attaché cases and hat boxes; train cases, beauty cases and similar receptacles.	Board (other than vulcanised fibre board, leatherboard, imitation leatherboard and strawboard) made from paper or pulp, being board weighing more than 850 grammes per square metre of which one side only has been coloured and varnished.	—
Syrups and treacles.	Beet sugar and cane sugar, solid, not qualifying for Commonwealth preference.	—
Toilet paper in rolls or packets.	Paper of any of the following descriptions:— (a) tissue paper or machine glazed paper of a weight when fully extended equivalent to not less than 19·5 grammes and not more than 24·5 grammes per square metre; (b) crepe paper of a weight when fully extended equivalent to not less than 24·5 grammes and not more than 39 grammes per square metre.	—
Vegetables with added sugar, bottled or canned.	(A) Beet sugar and cane sugar, solid, not qualifying for Commonwealth preference.	(a) Where the duty paid was at the highest rate and the sugar used in the manufacture of the exported goods was of a polarisation exceeding 98°— (i) £6·9000 per ton of sugar, (ii) £6·5750 per ton of anhydrous invert sugar. (b) Where the duty paid was at less than the highest rate and the sugar used in the manufacture of the exported goods was of a polarisation exceeding 98°— (i) £4·2780 per ton of sugar, (ii) £4·0750 per ton of anhydrous invert sugar.

Exported Goods	Imported Goods	Rate of Drawback (if any)
		(c) Where the duty paid was at less than the highest rate and the sugar used in the manufacture of the exported goods was of a polarisation not exceeding 98°, a rate per ton of sugar equal to the full rate of duty chargeable on the importation into the United Kingdom of sugar of the like polarisation and 100/105ths of that rate per ton of anhydrous invert sugar.
	(B) Beet sugar and cane sugar, solid, qualifying for Commonwealth preference, of a polarisation exceeding 99°.	(a) £1·0665 per ton of sugar. (b) £1·0155 per ton of anhydrous invert sugar.
Veneer sheets, being sheets cut cross-section from a laminate of wooden veneer sheets.	(A) Wooden veneer sheets. (B) Timber logs of the following species, namely, species of Acer, Betula, Fagus, Fraxinus, Juglans Populus, Quercus, and Ulmus; Castanea sativa; Eucalyptus diversicolor; Eucalyptus marginata.	— —
Vinyl chloride and vinylidene chloride products, the following: 1. Tubing, lay-flat. 2. Bags. 3. Film in rolls.	Copolymers of vinyl chloride and vinylidene chloride in the form of powder.	—
Waste, textile, and yarn: 1. Textile waste which has been subjected to one or more of the following processes:— (a) pulling, (b) garnetting, (c) carding, (d) combing, (e) cutting to staple fibre lengths. 2. Yarn.	Textile fibre, in the form of waste, rags or scrap material, of man-made fibres or of man-made fibres and wool, not pulled, garnetted or further processed.	—
Weed-killer, compound, containing not less than 20 per cent. and not more than 75 per cent. by weight of sodium chlorate.	Sodium chlorate imported in the form of powder, not less than 99 per cent. pure.	—

Exported Goods	*Imported Goods*	*Rate of Drawback (if any)*
Whey powder preparations, containing lactose but no substance other than whey powder, lactose or other sugar.	Whey powder.	—
Wood tar, refined by the removal by distillation of water and volatile oils, and either unmixed or mixed only with resinous material or hydrocarbon oil or both.	Unrefined wood tar.	—
Wood-faced plastic laminates, resulting from the lamination of a single melamine-impregnated wooden veneer sheet with a backing of phenolic resin core papers.	Wooden veneer sheets.	—
Yeast products for human consumption.	Yeast and autolysed yeast, dried or liquid.	—

SCHEDULE 3

Goods Excluded from Operation of Import Duties Act 1958 Schedule 5, Para. 3 (2)(a)

1. The descriptions of goods referred to in Article 3 (4) of this Order are all descriptions of goods mentioned in column 1 of the entries specified below, except that words limiting any such entry to specified paragraphs thereof shall be taken as limiting the descriptions of goods to those mentioned in column 1 of the specified paragraphs.

2. The said entries are those in Schedule 2 to this Order beginning with or consisting of the following words:—

Electrosensitive recording paper,
Linseed oil (paragraphs 3 to 8 only),
Printers' inks.

SCHEDULE 4

Special Provisions as to Textiles and Textile Articles

1.—(1) In the entries to which this paragraph applies, any loading or dressing taken into account in determining the weight of any man-made fibres or silk for the purposes of charging duty shall be treated for the purposes of drawback under the said duty as part of those fibres or, as the case may be, that silk.

(2) This paragraph applies to the entries in Schedule 2 to this Order beginning with or consisting of the following words:—

Cuprammonium products,
Garments, the following,
Garments, rain-proof,
Inked ribbons,
Men's shirts,
Neckties.

2.—(1) In the entries to which this paragraph applies references to silk do not include noil yarn or noil yarn doubled or twisted with other yarn.

(2) This paragraph applies to the entries in Schedule 2 to this Order beginning with or consisting of the following words:—

Garments, the following,
Inked ribbons,
Men's shirts.

SCHEDULE 5

IMPORT DUTY DRAWBACKS ORDERS REVOKED

Number and Year of Order			Reference
No. 10 of 1968	...	... ...	S.I. 1968/1881 (1968 III, p. 4969).
No. 1 of 1969	...	... ...	S.I. 1969/1034 (1969 II, p. 3054).
No. 2 of 1969	...	... ...	S.I. 1969/1658 (1969 III, p. 5204).
No. 1 of 1970	...	... ...	S.I. 1970/95 (1970 I, p. 448).
No. 2 of 1970	...	... ...	S.I. 1970/270 (1970 I, p. 1021).
No. 3 of 1970	...	... ...	S.I. 1970/464 (1970 I, p. 1556).
No. 4 of 1970	...	... ...	S.I. 1970/771 (1970 II, p. 2422).
No. 5 of 1970	...	... ...	S.I. 1970/1259 (1970 II, p. 4105).
No. 6 of 1970	...	... ...	S.I. 1970/1818 (1970 III, p. 5888).

EXPLANATORY NOTE

(This Note is not part of the Order.)

This Order:—

(1) consolidates all existing provisions for the allowance of drawback of import duty under the Import Duties Act 1958 and, in addition—

(2) revokes the fixed rate of drawback of import duty in respect of exported animal black manufactured from imported bones and provides for drawback to be related to the duty paid on the quantity of imported bones actually used in its manufacture;

(3) revises the rates of drawback of import duty in respect of certain linseed oil goods manufactured from imported linseed or linseed oil; and

(4) revokes the provisions for drawback of import duty in respect of

(a) saddlery, harness, trunks and other receptacles manufactured from imported dressed leather; and

(b) tinsel cord fabric manufactured from imported tinsel cord.

STATUTORY INSTRUMENTS

1971 No. 275 (S.43)

LEGAL AID AND ADVICE, SCOTLAND

Legal Aid (Scotland) (Assessment of Resources) Amendment Regulations 1971

Made - - -	*18th February* 1971	
Laid before Parliament	*26th February* 1971	
Coming into Operation	*1st March* 1971	

In exercise of the powers conferred on me by sections 4 and 15 of the Legal Aid (Scotland) Act 1967(**a**), and of all other powers enabling me on that behalf, and with the concurrence of the Treasury, I hereby make the following regulations :—

1.—(1) These regulations may be cited as the Legal Aid (Scotland) (Assessment of Resources) Amendment Regulations 1971 and shall come into operation on 1st March 1971.

(2) The Interpretation Act 1889(**b**) shall apply for the interpretation of these regulations as it applies for the interpretation of an Act of Parliament.

(3) In these regulations a regulation referred to by a number means a regulation so numbered in the Legal Aid (Scotland) (Assessment of Resources) Regulations 1960(**c**) as amended (**d**).

(4) In these regulations a rule referred to by a number means a rule so numbered in the First Schedule to the Legal Aid (Scotland) (Assessment of Resources) Regulations 1960 as amended.

2. In the proviso to regulation 11 for the words "any increase or" there shall be substituted the words "any increase in the amount of his disposable income by an amount greater than £52 or any".

3. (*a*) for "7s. 6d." and "5s. 6d." in rule 5(1)(*f*) and (*g*) there shall be substituted "£0·38" and "£0·28" respectively ;

(*b*) for "20s." in rule 5(2) there shall be substituted "£1·00" ;

(*c*) for "40s." in rule 5(1) and (3) there shall be substituted "£2·00".

(**a**) 1967 c. 43.
(**c**) S.I. 1960/1395 (1960 II, p. 1807).
(**b**) 1889 c. 63.
(**d**) The relevant amending instruments are S.I. 1960/2194; S.I. 1966/1379 (1960 II, p. 1816; 1966 III, p. 3707).

Gordon Campbell,
One of Her Majesty's Principal
Secretaries of State.

St. Andrew's House,
Edinburgh.

16th February 1971.

We concur.

Bernard Weatherill,
V. H. Goodhew,
Two of the Lords Commissioners of
Her Majesty's Treasury.

18th February 1971.

EXPLANATORY NOTE

(This Note is not part of the Regulations.)

These regulations amend the Legal Aid (Scotland) (Assessment of Resources) Regulations 1960 so as to provide for the redetermination of an assisted person's disposable income and maximum contribution when his disposable income has increased by an amount greater than £52 (instead of £26). They also provide for the decimalisation of amounts of money in connection with the assessment of resources of applicants for legal aid.

STATUTORY INSTRUMENTS

1971 No. 287 (S.33)

LEGAL AID AND ADVICE, SCOTLAND

Act of Sederunt (Legal Aid) (Children) 1971

Made - - - -	*4th February* 1971
Coming into Operation	*1st April* 1971

The Lords of Council and Session, under and by virtue of the powers conferred upon them by section 16 of the Legal Aid (Scotland) Act 1967**(a)** and of all other powers competent to them in that behalf, do hereby enact and declare as follows:—

Citation, commencement and interpretation

1.—(1) This Act of Sederunt may be cited as the Act of Sederunt (Legal Aid) (Children) 1971 and shall come into operation on 1st April 1971.

(2) In this Act of Sederunt unless the context otherwise requires—

"the Act" means the Social Work (Scotland) Act 1967, as amended by the Act of 1968;

"Act of 1968" means the Social Work (Scotland) Act 1968**(b)**;

"assisted person" means a child or the parent of a child to whom there has been issued and in respect of whom there is in force a certificate for legal aid;

"child" means a child as defined by section 30(1) of the Act of 1968;

"legal aid" means legal aid under the Act;

"Committee" means the Supreme Court Committee or a Local Committee established by the Law Society of Scotland under the Legal Aid (Scotland) Scheme 1958;

"the Regulations" means the Legal Aid Scotland (Children) Regulations 1971**(c)**;

"the scheme" means the Legal Aid (Scotland) (Children) Scheme 1970 made by the Law Society of Scotland under section 8 of the Act.

"sheriff clerk" includes sheriff clerk depute.

(3) In this Act of Sederunt any reference to any enactment or scheme shall be construed as a reference to that enactment or scheme as amended or extended by or under any other enactment or scheme.

(4) The Interpretation Act 1889**(d)** shall apply for the interpretation of this Act of Sederunt as it applies for the interpretation of an Act of Parliament.

(a) 1967 c. 43.
(c) S.I. 1971/288 (1971 I, p. 996).
(b) 1968 c. 49.
(d) 1889 c. 63.

Proceedings for purposes of legal aid

2. For the purposes of legal aid the following shall be treated as distinct proceedings:—

   (a) an application to the sheriff for a finding under section 42 of the Act of 1968;

   (b) an appeal to the sheriff under section 49 of the Act of 1968 against a decision of a children's hearing to issue a warrant for a child's detention in a place of safety while his case awaits disposal by a children's hearing being the proceedings mentioned in section 2(5A) of the Act);

   (c) an appeal to the sheriff under section 49 of the Act of 1968 against a decision of a children's hearing other than such an appeal as is mentioned in paragraph (b) above;

   (d) an appeal by stated case to the Court of Session under section 50 of the Act of 1968.

Applications for legal aid in appeals against child's detention

3. An application for legal aid in connection with such proceedings as are mentioned in subsection (5A) of section 2 of the Act (entitlement, without enquiry as to resources, of child or parent to legal aid in appeal against child's detention) shall be made either orally or in writing to the sheriff who shall grant the application forthwith if he is satisfied that the child is entitled thereto by virtue of that subsection as read with section 1(6A) of the Act.

Applications for legal aid in proceedings before sheriff under the Act of 1968 other than appeals against child's detention

4.—(1) An application for legal aid in connection with any proceedings either in an application to the sheriff under section 42 of the Act of 1968 or in an appeal to the sheriff under section 49 of the Act of 1968, other than an appeal mentioned in section 2(5A) of the Act, shall be made by lodging an application in writing with the sheriff clerk and the application shall be brought as soon as possible before the sheriff in chambers for determination in accordance with the provisions of section 1(6A) (b) of the Act (circumstances in which sheriff may grant legal aid certificate).

(2) Where the sheriff is satisfied that an applicant for legal aid has available to him any other rights or facilities to which regulation 6(2) of the Regulations applies, the sheriff shall, except on special cause shown, refuse the application for legal aid.

(3) Where, after considering the financial circumstances of an applicant for legal aid, the sheriff is not satisfied that the applicant is unable without undue hardship to himself or his dependants to meet the expenses of the case he shall refuse the application.

(4) Where after considering the financial circumstances of the applicant the sheriff is satisfied that the applicant is unable without undue hardship to himself or his dependants, to meet the expenses of the case in question and that it is in the interests of justice that legal aid should be made available to him, the sheriff shall grant the application for legal aid.

Intimation of legal aid certificates

5. Where the sheriff grants an application for legal aid under sections 3 or 4 above, the sheriff clerk shall send to the Committee a legal aid certificate detailing the entitlement to legal aid of the applicant, and shall send a copy of the certificate to the applicant.

Provisional financial certificates

6.—(1) Where—

(*a*) a person desires to obtain legal aid in connection with an appeal under section 50 of the Act of 1968; and

(*b*) legal aid was not available, or was not sought, or was not made available to him otherwise than under section 2(5A) of the Act in the proceedings before the sheriff against whose decision the appeal is made; and

(*c*) he applies in writing to the sheriff clerk for the sheriff court of the district in which those proceedings took place for a provisional financial certificate in accordance with regulation 7 of the Regulations,

that sheriff clerk may question him and may, after such other enquiry as he thinks fit, decide whether or not to grant a provisional financial certificate.

(2) As soon as may be after the grant or the refusal of a provisional financial certificate the sheriff clerk shall report the financial and other relevant circumstances of the applicant to the sheriff in order that the sheriff may determine whether the applicant is unable without undue hardship to himself or his dependants to meet the expenses of the proposed appeal and whether he has available to him other rights or facilities to which regulation 6(2) of the Regulations applies; and the sheriff shall report his determination to the Committee and where the determination is such that legal aid cannot be made available to the applicant, the sheriff shall discharge the provisional financial certificate.

Determinations of applications for legal aid to be final

7. The determination of a sheriff on an application for legal aid under section 6(2) above shall be final:

Provided that it shall be open to a person at any time to make a further application for legal aid on the ground that there has been a material change in his financial circumstances or that he has additional facts affecting his eligibility for legal aid.

Disqualification for continuance of legal aid

8.—(1) If a sheriff or, as the case may be, the Lord Ordinary before whom there are depending any proceedings to which an assisted person is a party is satisfied that the assisted person has—

(*a*) without reasonable cause failed to comply with any proper request made to him by the solicitor acting for him to supply any information relevant to the proceedings; or

(*b*) delayed unreasonably in complying with any such request as aforesaid; or

(*c*) wilfully or deliberately given false information in connection with the proceedings to the solicitor acting for him or wilfully or deliberately concealed from him any information relevant to the proceedings; or

(*d*) without reasonable cause failed to attend at any proceedings at which he has been required to attend or at any meeting with the solicitor or counsel acting for him under the scheme at which he has reasonably and properly been required to attend; or

(e) conducted himself in connection with the proceedings in such a way as to make it appear to the sheriff or Lord Ordinary unreasonable that he should continue to receive legal aid,

the sheriff or, as the case may be, the Lord Ordinary may direct that his legal aid certificate shall be discharged.

(2) Where a sheriff or a Lord Ordinary issues a direction under the foregoing paragraph the principal clerk of session or, as the case may be, the sheriff clerk, shall send a copy of the direction to the Committee by whom the certificate was issued, and the Committee shall forthwith discharge the certificate of the assisted person concerned in relation to the proceedings before the sheriff or Lord Ordinary.

Statements on oath

9. In considering any matter in regard to the entitlement of a person to legal aid that person may be required to make a statement on oath for the purpose of ascertaining or verifying any fact material to his entitlement to legal aid.

Recovery of sums due to the Legal Aid (Scotland) Fund

10.—(1) Where an award of expenses is made in favour of a person in connection with any proceedings under the Act of 1968 in which he has received legal aid, those expenses shall be paid to the Law Society of Scotland and only that Society shall be capable of giving a good discharge therefor.

(2) Where an applicant for legal aid is entitled, through the membership of any body or through the holding of or the terms of any insurance policy, to payment of or to a contribution towards his legal expenses in connection with any proceedings under the Act of 1968 in connection with which he has received legal aid, the payment or, as the case may be, the contribution shall be made to the Law Society of Scotland by the body or insurance company concerned.

(3) Any sum paid to the Law Society of Scotland under this section shall be paid into the Legal Aid (Scotland) Fund.

And the Lords appoint this Act of Sederunt to be inserted in the Books of Sederunt.

J. L. Clyde
I.P.D.

Edinburgh .
4th February 1971.

EXPLANATORY NOTE

(This Note is not part of the Act of Sederunt.)

This Act of Sederunt provides for the granting of legal aid for certain purposes under the Social Work (Scotland) Act 1968.

STATUTORY INSTRUMENTS

1971 No. 288 (S.44)

LEGAL AID AND ADVICE, SCOTLAND

The Legal Aid (Scotland) (Children) Regulations 1971

Made - - -	18*th February* 1971
Laid before Parliament	2*nd March* 1971
Coming into Operation	15*th April* 1971

In exercise of the powers conferred on me by section 15 of the Legal Aid (Scotland) Act 1967(**a**), and of all other powers enabling me in that behalf, I hereby make the following regulations :—

Citation and commencement

1. These regulations may be cited as the Legal Aid (Scotland) (Children) Regulations 1971, and shall come into operation on 15th April 1971.

Interpretation

2.—(1) In these regulations the following expressions shall, unless the context otherwise requires, have the meanings hereby respectively assigned to them :—

"the Act" means the Legal Aid (Scotland) Act 1967, as amended by the Social Work (Scotland) Act 1968(**b**) ;

"Act of Sederunt" means the Act of Sederunt (Legal Aid) (Children) 1971(**c**) ;

"Act of 1968" means the Social Work (Scotland) Act 1968 ;

"appointed solicitor" has the meaning assigned to it by article 2(1) of the Scheme ;

"appeal certificate" means a certificate issued by the Supreme Court Committee under the Scheme ;

"assisted person" means a child or the parent of a child to whom there has been issued and in respect of whom there is in force a certificate for legal aid ;

"child" means a child as defined in section 30(1) of the Act of 1968 ;

"interim appeal certificate" means a preliminary appeal certificate issued in an appeal as a matter of urgency under these regulations ;

"interim solicitor" means a solicitor appointed as a matter of urgency under these regulations ;

"legal aid" means legal aid under the Act ;

"Legal Aid (Scotland) Fund" means the fund established under section 9 of the Act ;

(**a**) 1967 c. 43.   (**b**) 1968 c. 49.
(**c**) S.I. 1971/287 (1971 I, p. 992).

"list" means a list of counsel or of solicitors prepared and maintained under Article 12 of the Legal Aid (Scotland) Scheme 1958 or under article 5 of the Scheme ;

"parent" means a parent as defined in section 94 as read with section 30(2) of the Act of 1968 ;

"reporter" means a reporter appointed in terms of section 36 of the Act of 1968 ;

"Scheme" means the Legal Aid (Scotland) (Children) Scheme 1971, made by the Society under section 8 of the Act ;

"sheriff clerk" includes sheriff clerk depute

"Society" means the Law Society of Scotland established by the Solicitors (Scotland) Act 1949(a) ;

"the Supreme Court Committee" means the Supreme Court Committee established under article 6 of the Legal Aid (Scotland) Scheme 1958.

(2) In these regulations any reference to any enactment, regulation or scheme shall be construed as a reference to that enactment, regulation or scheme as amended or extended by or under any other enactment, regulation or scheme.

(3) The Interpretation Act 1889(b) shall apply for the interpretation of these regulations as it applies for the interpretation of an Act of Parliament.

Applications for legal aid

3.—(1) An application for legal aid in connection with proceedings to which the provisions of section 2(5A) of the Act apply may be made orally or otherwise to the sheriff.

(2) An application for legal aid in connection with proceedings before the sheriff otherwise than under the said section 2(5A) shall be made to the sheriff on such form as the Society may provide for the purpose, or in such other manner, being in writing, as the sheriff may accept as sufficient in any particular case in which exceptional circumstances obtain.

(3) An application for an appeal certificate for legal aid in connection with proceedings by way of appeal to the Court of Session, and any applications for a provisional financial certificate and for an interim appeal certificate under regulations 7 and 8 of these regulations respectively, shall be made to the Supreme Court Committee on such forms as the Society may provide for the purpose.

Information to be furnished by applicants

4. Every applicant for legal aid shall furnish such particulars as are required by any form of application provided in connection with regulation 3 of these regulations and such further particulars with respect to his case, or to his financial circumstances and those of his parent or child as the case may be, or those of the dependants of either, or to other relevant circumstances as may be required by the sheriff, or by the Society or by any committee or person acting on behalf of the Society in regard to the application.

(a) 1949 c. 63.   (b) 1889 c. 63.

Matter in part of which a person receives legal aid

5.—(1) Where a child or his parent begins to receive legal aid in respect of any proceedings after having consulted a solicitor in the ordinary way in connection with the same proceedings he shall obtain from the solicitor whom he originally consulted all documents and papers relating to the proceedings and shall produce them to the solicitor acting for him under the Scheme.

(2) When an assisted person ceases to receive legal aid while proceedings are in course, the solicitor who acted for him under the Scheme shall, if any solicitor whom that person subsequently consults so requests, forward to that solicitor all the documents and papers in his possession relating to those proceedings and shall report to him on any steps taken.

Provisions as to applicant having rights or facilities in relation to legal proceedings

6.—(1) Notwithstanding any rights or facilities that may be available to a child or his parent in relation to proceedings under Part III of the Act of 1968, legal aid shall be made available, if sought in connection with those proceedings, under the provisions, where applicable, of section 2(5A) of the Act.

(2) Where, otherwise than at any stage in proceedings to which the provisions of section 2(5A) of the Act apply, it appears to the sheriff that an applicant for legal aid, or his parent or child as the case may be, has available rights or facilities making it unnecessary for him to obtain legal aid, or has a reasonable expectation of obtaining financial or other help from a body of which he is a member the sheriff shall not, except on special cause shown, make legal aid available to him under section 2(2) of the Act and the sheriff clerk shall not, except on special cause shown, issue in his favour a provisional financial certificate under regulation 7(1) of these regulations.

(3) Where the sheriff makes legal aid available to a person, or the parent or child of a person, who is a member of a body which might reasonably have been expected to give him financial help towards the cost of the proceedings, or the sheriff clerk issues in his favour a provisional financial certificate under regulation 7(1) of these regulations the sheriff or the sheriff clerk shall require him to sign an undertaking to pay to the Society any sum received from that body on account of the expenses of the proceedings.

Issue of provisional financial certificates in respect of appeals to the Court of Session

7.—(1) Where a child or his parent seeks legal aid in connection with an appeal to the Court of Session and legal aid was not available, or was not sought by, or was not made available to him in the proceedings before the sheriff otherwise than under section 2(5A) of the Act, he shall apply in writing to the sheriff clerk for the sheriff court of the district in which the original proceedings before the sheriff took place for a provisional financial certificate that it appears that he is unable, without undue hardship to himself or to his parent or child as the case may be, or to the dependants of either, to meet the expenses of proceedings on appeal to the Court of Session and that he is not disentitled to receive legal aid by reason of regulation 6(2) of these regulations:

Provided that where, in the proceedings before the sheriff, the sheriff refused an application for legal aid under section 4(2) or section 4(3) of the Act of Sederunt a provisional financial certificate shall be granted only if the child or his parent can show, where legal aid was refused by the sheriff under section 4(2) that in relation to an appeal to the Court of Session he has available to him no rights or facilities to which regulation 6(2) of these regulations applies, or where legal aid was refused by the sheriff under section 4(3) of the Act of Sederunt that there has been a material deterioration in his financial circumstances.

(2) Where a provisional financial certificate is granted the sheriff clerk shall transmit it to the Supreme Court Committee together with the completed form of application for an interim appeal certificate referred to in regulation 8(1) of these regulations.

Issue of interim appeal certificate and appointment of interim solicitors in respect of appeals to the Court of Session

8.—(1) Where a child or his parent wishes to appeal to the Court of Session against a decision of the sheriff and—

(a) at the time of the decision by the sheriff he had the services of an appointed solicitor, such solicitor, if he is of opinion that in all the circumstances there are substantial grounds for an appeal being taken to the Court of Session by way of stated case, shall submit a statement in writing of such grounds with the application for an interim appeal certificate to the Supreme Court Committee ;

(b) at the time of the decision by the sheriff he did not have the services of a solicitor under the Act, the sheriff clerk shall assist the child or his parent to complete the form of application for an interim appeal certificate as prescribed by regulation 3 of these regulations and shall send the completed form and the provisional financial certificate to the Supreme Court Committee together with a statement in writing of the terms of his proposed appeal prepared by the child or his parent.

(2) When any statement in writing referred to in paragraph (1) of this regulation is received by the Supreme Court Committee it shall be considered forthwith by the secretary and a member, or by 2 members, of the committee, or, where circumstances so demand, by the secretary or 1 member of the committee, and unless, after such enquiry as they, or he, may deem sufficient in the circumstances, they are, or he is, reasonably satisfied that there are no prima facie grounds for an appeal in terms of section 1(6A)(c) of the Act, the committee shall issue an interim appeal certificate and otherwise the committee shall refuse to issue such a certificate :

Provided that such certificate shall not be issued unless the Supreme Court Committee has received a provisional financial certificate, where appropriate, and are satisfied in the case of an applicant who was refused legal aid under section 1(6A)(b) of the Act that it would not be unreasonable that the services of an interim solicitor should be made available to him in connection with his application for an interim appeal certificate.

(3) The Supreme Court Committee shall forthwith intimate their decision on the application for an interim appeal certificate to the applicant, and, if he be a child, to his parent, the reporter and the sheriff clerk, and that decision shall be final subject to any review that may be necessary following a determination by the sheriff, under section 6(2) of the Act of Sederunt, that an applicant who was refused a provisional financial certificate by the sheriff clerk, under regulation 7(1) of these regulations, meets the conditions for issue of such certificate.

(4) Where an interim appeal certificate is to be issued and the applicant has requested that a particular solicitor on the appropriate list should act for him

the committee shall take that request into consideration in making the appointment of an interim solicitor ; and the committee shall inform the applicant and, if he be a child, his parent, the reporter and the sheriff clerk of the appointment.

(5) The Supreme Court Committee shall discharge the interim appeal certificate if—

    (a) they receive information that the provisional financial certificate has been discharged by the sheriff ; or

    (b) they are refusing an appeal certificate ;

and such discharge of the certificate shall be intimated to the interim solicitor and his Edinburgh correspondent, the child, his parent, the reporter and the sheriff clerk.

(6) If the Supreme Court Committee are satisfied, under article 9 of the Scheme, that the applicant has substantial grounds for making the appeal and that it is reasonable that he should receive legal aid, and they have received a report, under section 6(2) of the Act of Sederunt, to the effect that otherwise there is eligibility for legal aid, they shall replace the interim appeal certificate by an appeal certificate ; and thereafter procedure in connection with legal aid for the appeal shall be in accordance with the relevant provisions of the Scheme :

Provided that the interim solicitor shall be appointed as appointed solicitor unless, on special cause shown, the Supreme Court Committee find it necessary to appoint another solicitor to act as appointed solicitor.

Duties of appointed solicitors and interim solicitors

9.—(1) Where the reporter applies for a stated case under section 50 of the Act of 1968 and the child or his parent seeks legal aid in relation thereto, the Supreme Court Committee shall, on a request by the appointed solicitor or by the child or his parent, as the case may be, issue an interim appeal certificate, provided they are satisfied, in any case in which it is appropriate, that a provisional financial certificate has been granted.

(2) (a) Where an interim appeal certificate is issued within the statutory period for application for a stated case, the appointed solicitor, or interim solicitor, shall submit it to the sheriff clerk with an application for such a case on behalf of the child or his parent.

    (b) Where an application for a stated case is made to the sheriff and an interim appeal certificate is obtained after the expiry of the said statutory period, the solicitor concerned shall lodge the interim appeal certificate with the sheriff clerk.

(3) Where an interim appeal certificate is issued, the solicitor named in the certificate shall carry out the procedure specified in the Act of Sederunt (Rules of Court Amendment No. 1) 1971(a), and he shall also send a copy of the stated case, as adjusted, to the Supreme Court Committee together with an application for an appeal certificate in the form prescribed by regulation 3 of these regulations.

(4) An interim appeal certificate issued under this regulation shall entitle the assisted person to legal aid until an adjusted stated case is lodged with the Court of Session or until such earlier date as the certificate is discharged by the Supreme Court Committee under regulation 8(5) of these regulations.

(a) S.I. 1971/66 (1971 I, p. 124).

Fees, etc., agreed by the Society to be treated as allowed on taxation

10. Where an amount is fixed by the Society, whether on account of outlays or fees, by agreement with the solicitor to whom such amount is payable in the first instance out of the Legal Aid (Scotland) Fund, that amount shall, for the purposes of Schedule 2 to the Act, be treated as if it were an amount allowed on taxation :

Provided that this regulation shall not have effect in relation to any amount if any person to or by whom such amount is payable, in whole or in part, requires it to be fixed by taxation.

Gordon Campbell,
One of Her Majesty's Principal
Secretaries of State.

St. Andrew's House,
Edinburgh.

18th February 1971.

EXPLANATORY NOTE

(This Note is not part of the Regulations.)

These Regulations make provision for the granting of Legal Aid in the proceedings specified in section 53 of the Social Work (Scotland) Act 1968.

STATUTORY INSTRUMENTS

1971 No. 289

AGRICULTURE

GUARANTEED PRICES AND ASSURED MARKETS

The Cereals (Guarantee Payments) Order 1971

Made - - -	*23rd February* 1971
Laid before Parliament	*2nd March* 1971
Coming into Operation	*1st July* 1971

The Minister of Agriculture, Fisheries and Food, the Secretaries of State respectively concerned with agriculture in Scotland and Northern Ireland and the Secretary of State for Wales, acting jointly, in exercise of the powers conferred upon them by sections 1 and 35(3) of the Agriculture Act 1957(a), as read with the Transfer of Functions (Wales) Order 1969(b), and of all other powers enabling them in that behalf, with the consent of the Treasury and after consultation with such bodies of persons as appear to the said Ministers to represent the interests of producers of cereals, hereby make the following order:—

Citation, commencement, interpretation and revocation

1. This order may be cited as the Cereals (Guarantee Payments) Order 1971, and shall come into operation on 1st July 1971.

2.—(1) In this order, except where the context otherwise requires—

"the appropriate Minister" means—

(a) in relation to England, the Minister of Agriculture, Fisheries and Food;

(b) in relation to Scotland and Northern Ireland, respectively, the Secretary of State concerned with agriculture therein; and

(c) in relation to Wales—

(i) for the purpose of the making, receipt or recovery of any payment, the Minister of Agriculture, Fisheries and Food;

(ii) for all other purposes, that Minister and the Secretary of State for Wales, acting jointly;

"cereals" means wheat, rye, oats or barley;

"determined" means determined by the Minister with the approval of the Treasury and as respects any guaranteed price to be determined in pursuance of this order means so determined by the Minister from time to time in the light of the conclusions of the Ministers from a review held under section 2 of the Agriculture Act 1947(c);

(a) 1957 c. 57.   (b) S.I. 1969/388 (1969 I, p. 1070).   (c) 1947 c. 48,

"guaranteed price", "target indicator price" and "average realised price" mean the prices determined or ascertained pursuant to article 3(1)(*a*) and (*b*) and (2) respectively of this order;

"the Minister", in relation to any part of the United Kingdom, means either the appropriate Minister in relation to that part, or that Minister and any or all of the other Ministers acting jointly;

"the Ministers" means the Minister of Agriculture, Fisheries and Food, the Secretaries of State respectively concerned with agriculture in Scotland and Northern Ireland and the Secretary of State for Wales, acting jointly;

"registered grower", in relation to any cereals, means the person for the time being registered by the Minister, in such manner and subject to such conditions as he may from time to time specify, as the grower of those cereals for the purposes of this order;

"year" means a period of twelve months commencing with the first day of July in any calendar year.

(2) The Interpretation Act 1889(a) shall apply to the interpretation of this order as it applies to the interpretation of an Act of Parliament and as if this order and the orders hereby revoked were Acts of Parliament.

(3) In this order references to Wales include, and references to England do not include, Monmouthshire.

(4) The orders specified in the Schedule hereto are hereby revoked.

Guarantee payments for wheat, barley, rye and oats

3.—(1) In respect of each year there shall be determined—

(*a*) for wheat and barley respectively—

    (i) a guaranteed price per hundredweight; and

    (ii) a target indicator price, being a price per hundredweight determined by the Minister with the approval of the Treasury having regard to the minimum import price levels prescribed for wheat and barley respectively by order under section 1(2) of the Agriculture and Horticulture Act 1964(b);

(*b*) for rye and oats respectively, a guaranteed price per hundredweight.

(2) In respect of each year the Minister shall ascertain in such manner and at such time as appears to him proper the average realised prices per hundredweight obtained by producers for wheat, barley, rye and oats respectively.

4. The guarantee payment for any year—

(*a*) for wheat and for barley respectively shall be the amount, if any, by which the guaranteed price thereof exceeds the average realised price thereof or the target indicator price thereof, whichever is the higher.

(*b*) for rye and for oats respectively shall be the amount, if any, by which the guaranteed price thereof exceeds the average realised price thereof.

5. Any guarantee payment relating to wheat, barley, rye or oats ascertained pursuant to article 4 of this order may be made by the Minister subject to such conditions as he may from time to time with the approval of the Treasury specify and may—

(a) 1889 c. 63.   (b) 1964 c. 28.

(*a*) be made in respect of any land which is shown to the satisfaction of the Minister to have been used for the purpose of growing wheat, barley, rye or oats, as the case may be, for harvesting during the year, being wheat, barley, rye or oats, harvested as grain, or available at such date as he may specify for harvesting as grain;

(*b*) be made at such a rate per acre as may be ascertained by the Minister, being a rate calculated by reference to the guarantee payment ascertained pursuant to article 4 hereof and the average yield of wheat, barley, rye or oats, as the case may be, in hundredweights per acre in the United Kingdom ascertained by the Minister during such period as may appear to him appropriate.

Guarantee payments for mixed cereals

6. Where any land has been used for the purpose of growing a crop consisting entirely of two or more cereals or consisting of a mixture of one or more cereals and other produce, the Minister may, if he thinks fit, and subject to such conditions as he may from time to time with the approval of the Treasury specify, make in respect of that land a payment—

(*a*) in the case of a crop consisting entirely of cereals, of an amount equal to, or

(*b*) in the case of a crop consisting of cereals and other produce, of an amount equal to such percentage as the Minister may from time to time with the approval of the Treasury specify of,

any payment which he might have made in respect of that land under articles 4 and 5 of this order if the crop had consisted of oats.

Reduction or withholding of payments in certain circumstances

7. The Minister may, without prejudice to his general discretion in respect of any payment under this order, in respect of any land to which article 5 or 6 hereof applies, if he is of opinion—

(*a*) that the crop of cereals obtained from the land is unduly small or has been adversely affected by the unsuitability of the land for growing the crop or by negligence in connection with the preparation of the land for, or the sowing, tending or harvesting of, the crop, or

(*b*) that any of the land has been used in the twelve months preceding the harvesting of the crop in question in a manner likely to impair its fertility, or

(*c*) in the case of a crop of cereals, or of cereals and other produce, which has been undersown with other crops, that the cereal seed sown was not sufficient to provide a proper crop of cereals or that the undersowing was done in such a manner or with seed of such a kind as to be likely to reduce the yield of the cereal, or

(*d*) that the cereals were self-sown,

reduce to such extent as he thinks fit the amount of, or withhold, any payment which he might otherwise have made under that provision in respect of that land.

Persons to whom payments may be made

8. Any payment under this order shall be made to the registered grower of the cereals in question or, if the Minister is satisfied that the interest of the registered grower in that payment has passed to some other person, to that other person.

9. Subject to such terms and conditions as the Minister, with the approval of the Treasury, may specify, the Minister may for the purposes of this order make such payments by way of advance as he may from time to time in respect of any year think fit.

In Witness whereof the Official Seal of the Minister of Agriculture, Fisheries and Food is hereunto affixed on 12th February 1971.

(L.S.) *J. M. L. Prior,*

Minister of Agriculture, Fisheries and Food.

Given under the Seal of the Secretary of State for Scotland on 15th February 1971.

(L.S.) *Gordon Campbell,*

Secretary of State for Scotland.

Given under the hand of the Secretary of State for the Home Department on 17th February 1971.

R. Maudling,

Secretary of State for the Home Department.

Given under my hand on 19th February 1971.

Peter Thomas,

Secretary of State for Wales.

We consent

23rd February 1971.

Walter Clegg,

P. L. Hawkins,

Two of the Lords Commissioners of Her Majesty's Treasury.

SCHEDULE

Article 2(4)

Orders revoked	References
The Cereals (Guarantee Payments) Order 1964.	S.I. 1964/840 (1964 II, p. 1796).
The Cereals (Guarantee Payments) (Amendment) Order 1966.	S.I. 1966/484 (1966 I, p. 995).
The Cereals (Guarantee Payments) (Amendment) Order 1968.	S.I. 1968/767 (1968 II, p. 2148).
The Cereals (Guarantee Payments) (Amendment) Order 1969.	S.I. 1969/672 (1969 II, p. 1844).

EXPLANATORY NOTE
(This note is not part of the Order.)

This order replaces the Cereals (Guarantee Payments) Order 1964 (S.I. 1964 No. 840) as amended, and provides for changes in the arrangements for guarantee payments to producers of cereals.

The changes effected by the order relate to wheat, rye and barley. For wheat and rye the previous arrangements are ended whereby grain had to be sold in order to qualify for deficiency payment. For barley the provision is removed for deductions from or additions to the basic acreage payment to take account of the timing of any sales of barley.

The deficiency payments for all cereals are placed on the same basis by this order and relate only to the acreages of the cereals which are harvested as grain or are available for harvesting as grain.

STATUTORY INSTRUMENTS

1971 No. 290

AGRICULTURE

GUARANTEED PRICES AND ASSURED MARKETS

The Cereals (Protection of Guarantees) Order 1971

Made - - -		*23rd February* 1971
Laid before Parliament		*2nd March* 1971
Coming into Operation		*1st July* 1971

The Minister of Agriculture, Fisheries and Food and the Secretaries of State respectively concerned with agriculture in Scotland and Northern Ireland and the Secretary of State for Wales, acting jointly, in exercise of the powers conferred upon them by sections 5, 9(4) and 35(3) of the Agriculture Act 1957(a) and section 70 of the Agriculture Act 1967(b), as read with the Transfer of Functions (Wales) Order 1969(c), and of all other powers enabling them in that behalf, hereby make the following order :—

Citation, commencement, interpretation and revocation

1. This order may be cited as the Cereals (Protection of Guarantees) Order 1971, and shall come into operation on 1st July 1971.

2.—(1) In this order—

"the appropriate Minister" means—

(*a*) in relation to England, the Minister of Agriculture, Fisheries and Food ;

(*b*) in relation to Scotland and Northern Ireland, respectively, the Secretary of State concerned with agriculture therein ; and

(*c*) in relation to Wales—

(i) for the purpose of the making, receipt or recovery of any payment, the Minister of Agriculture, Fisheries and Food ;

(ii) for all other purposes, that Minister and the Secretary of State for Wales, acting jointly ;

"cereal year" means a period of twelve months commencing with 1st July in any calendar year ;

"the Minister", in relation to any part of the United Kingdom, means either the appropriate Minister in relation to that part, or that Minister and any or all of the other Ministers acting jointly ;

"the Ministers" means the Minister of Agriculture, Fisheries and Food, the Secretaries of State respectively concerned with agriculture in Scotland and Northern Ireland and the Secretary of State for Wales, acting jointly ;

"registered grower" means a person registered by or on behalf of the Minister as a grower of home-grown cereals.

(a) 1957 c. 57. (b) 1967 c. 22.
(c) S.I. 1969/388 (1969 I, p. 1070).

(2) The Interpretation Act 1889(**a**) shall apply to the interpretation of this order as it applies to the interpretation of an Act of Parliament and as if this order and the orders hereby revoked were Acts of Parliament.

(3) In this order references to Wales include, and the references to England do not include, Monmouthshire.

(4) The Cereals (Protection of Guarantees) Order 1958(**b**), the Cereals (Protection of Guarantees) (Amendment) Order 1961(**c**) and the Cereals (Protection of Guarantees) (Amendment) Order 1966(**d**) are hereby revoked.

Retention of records

3. Every registered grower and every person who, for re-sale or in the course of a trade or business other than farming, buys wheat, barley or rye from a registered grower thereof shall, notwithstanding the revocation of the orders mentioned in article 2(4) above,—

(*a*) retain for two years from the end of the cereal year to which the record relates every record which immediately before such revocation he was required to keep or cause to be kept under the provisions of those orders, and shall produce any such record on demand by an authorised officer of the Minister or, in Northern Ireland, of the Ministry of Agriculture for Northern Ireland ;

(*b*) if so required by a notice in writing served on him by the Minister, furnish to such person, in such form, at such time or times and in respect of such period or periods ending on or before 30th June 1971 as may be specified in the said notice such information relating to the purchase, sale or use by him of wheat, barley or rye and additionally, in the case of a registered grower, such information relating to acreages sown by him to wheat, rye, barley, oats and mixed cereals respectively, as the Minister may require and shall produce on demand by any authorised officer of the Minister or, in Northern Ireland, of the Ministry of Agriculture for Northern Ireland such books, accounts and records in his possession or control and relating to such transactions, use or sowing as may be necessary to verify the information so furnished.

Entry on land by authorised officers

4. Any authorised officer of the Minister or, in Northern Ireland, of the Ministry of Agriculture for Northern Ireland may at all reasonable times enter upon any land used for the production of wheat, rye, barley, oats or mixed cereals and inspect and take samples of any such produce found upon land so used.

Service of notices

5.—(1) Any notice required or authorised by this order to be given to or served on any person shall be sufficiently given or served if it is delivered to him personally or left at his last known place of abode or business or sent by post addressed to him at the aforesaid place of abode or business.

(2) Any notice required or authorised by this order to be given to or served on an incorporated company or body shall be sufficiently given or served if given to or served on the secretary or clerk of the company or body. For the purposes of this order and of section 26 of the Interpretation Act 1889, the

---

(**a**) 1889 c. 63.
(**c**) S.I. 1961/1071 (1961 II, p. 2053).
(**b**) S.I. 1958/956 (1958 I, p. 78).
(**d**) S.I. 1966/485 (1966 I, p. 997).

proper address of such secretary or clerk shall be that of the registered or principal office of the company or body.

Exercise of functions in Northern Ireland

6. The functions conferred or imposed on the Minister by this order may be exercised in relation to Northern Ireland by the Minister of Agriculture for Northern Ireland.

In Witness whereof the Official Seal of the Minister of Agriculture, Fisheries and Food is hereunto affixed on 12th February 1971.

(L.S.)   *J. M. L. Prior,*
Minister of Agriculture, Fisheries and Food.

Given under the Seal of the Secretary of State for Scotland on 15th February 1971.

(L.S.)   *Gordon Campbell,*
Secretary of State for Scotland.

Given under the hand of the Secretary of State for the Home Department on 17th February 1971.

R. Maudling,
Secretary of State for the Home Department.

Given under my hand on 19th February 1971.

Peter Thomas,
Secretary of State for Wales.

We consent,
23rd February 1971.

Walter Clegg,
Bernard Weatherill,
Two of the Lords Commissioners of
Her Majesty's Treasury.

EXPLANATORY NOTE

(This Note is not part of the Order.)

This order replaces the Cereals (Protection of Guarantees) Order 1958 (S.I. 1958 No. 956), as amended, made in support of the guarantee arrangements for cereals having effect under Part I of the Agriculture Act 1957. It repeats the provision in the previous order enabling authorised officers to enter upon land used for the production of cereals and to inspect and take samples of such produce. This power of entry no longer extends to land used for the storage or sale of cereals.

The provisions in the previous order, which required registered growers and dealers in wheat, barley and rye to furnish the Minister with information and produce records, are now limited to information and production of records relating to the sowing, purchase, sale or use of cereals prior to 1st July 1971.